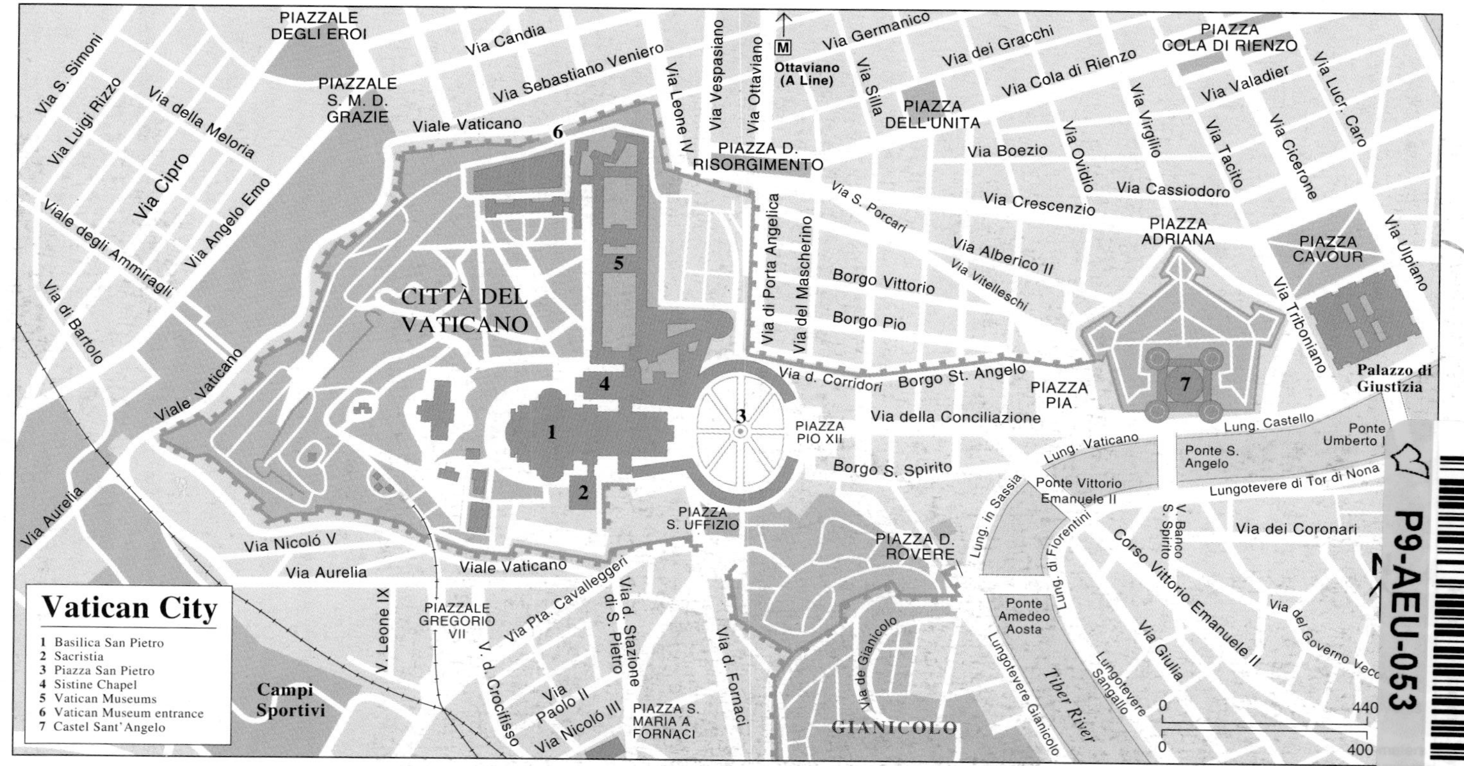

Vatican City
1 Basilica San Pietro
2 Sacristia
3 Piazza San Pietro
4 Sistine Chapel
5 Vatican Museums
6 Vatican Museum entrance
7 Castel Sant'Angelo
CITTÀ DEL VATICANO
PIAZZALE DEGLI EROI
PIAZZALE S. M. D. GRAZIE
PIAZZA D. RISORGIMENTO
PIAZZA DELL'UNITA
PIAZZA COLA DI RIENZO
PIAZZA ADRIANA
PIAZZA CAVOUR
PIAZZA PIA
PIAZZA PIO XII
PIAZZA S. UFFIZIO
PIAZZA D. ROVERE
PIAZZALE GREGORIO VII
PIAZZA S. MARIA A FORNACI
Palazzo di Giustizia
GIANICOLO
Campi Sportivi
Tiber River
Ottaviano (A Line)
M
Via S. Simoni
Via Luigi Rizzo
Via della Meloria
Via Cipro
Via Angelo Emo
Viale degli Ammiragli
Via di Bartolo
Viale Vaticano
Via Aurelia
Via Nicoló V
Via Candia
Via Sebastiano Veniero
Via Leone IV
Via Vespasiano
Via Ottaviano
Via Germanico
Via Silla
Via dei Gracchi
Via Cola di Rienzo
Via Valadier
Via Lucr. Caro
Via Boezio
Via Ovidio
Via Virgilio
Via Tacito
Via Cicerone
Via Cassiodoro
Via Crescenzio
Via S. Porcari
Via Alberico II
Via Vitelleschi
Via Ulpiano
Via Triboniano
Via di Porta Angelica
Via del Mascherino
Borgo Vittorio
Borgo Pio
Via d. Corridori
Borgo St. Angelo
Via della Conciliazione
Borgo S. Spirito
Lung. Castello
Ponte Umberto I
Ponte S. Angelo
Lung. Vaticano
Lungotevere di Tor di Nona
Ponte Vittorio Emanuele II
Lung. in Sassia
Lung. di Fiorentini
V. Banco S. Spirito
Via dei Coronari
Corso Vittorio Emanuele II
Via del Governo Vecc
Via Giulia
Lungotevere Sangallo
Ponte Amedeo Aosta
Lungotevere Gianicolo
Via de Gianicolo
Via d. Fornaci
Via d. Stazione di S. Pietro
Via Pta. Cavalleggeri
V. d. Crocifisso
Via Paolo II
Via Nicoló III
V. Leone IX
0
440
0
400

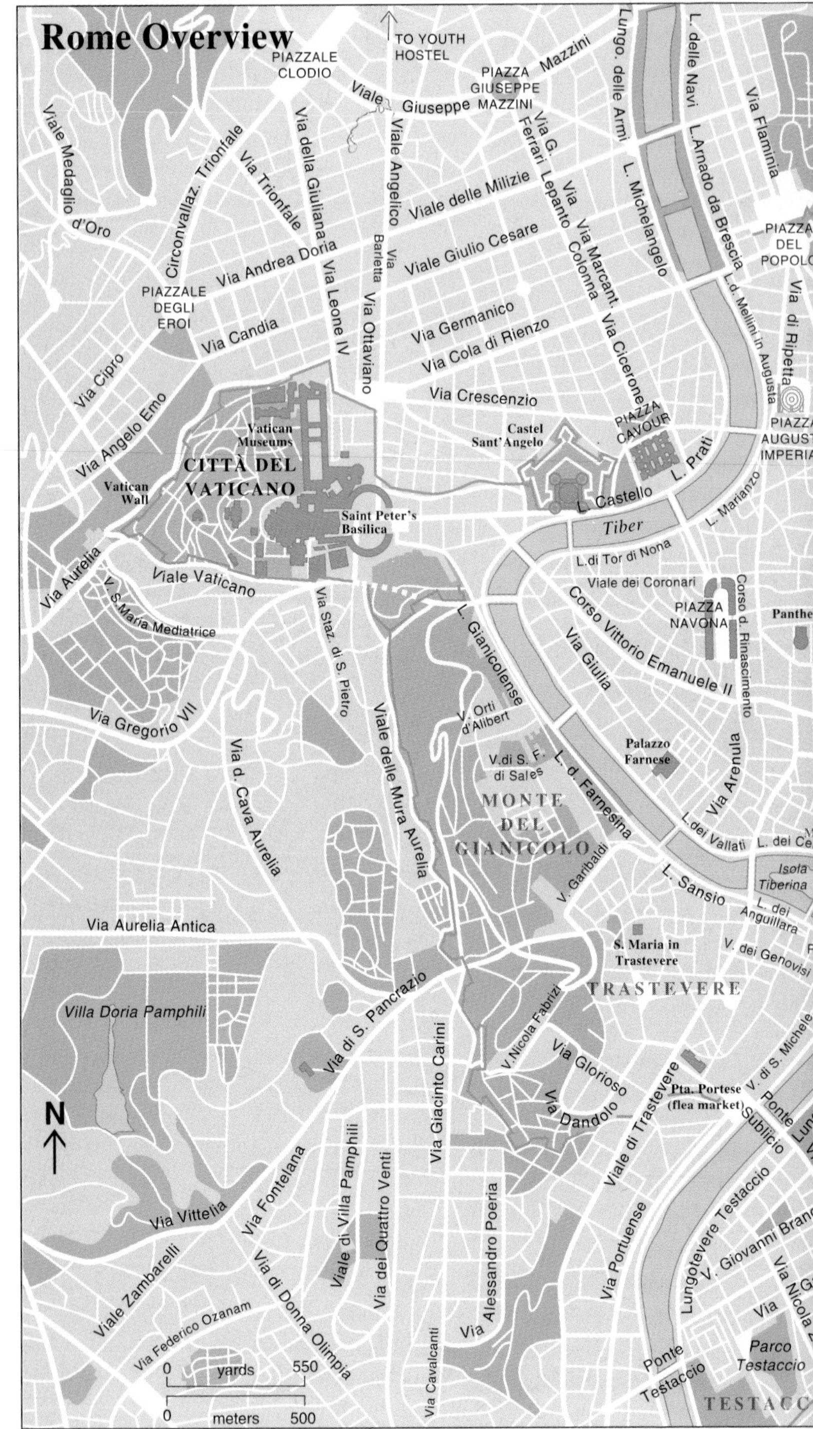
Rome Overview
TO YOUTH HOSTEL
PIAZZALE CLODIO
PIAZZA GIUSEPPE MAZZINI
Viale Giuseppe Mazzini
Viale Medaglie d'Oro
Circonvallaz. Trionfale
Via Trionfale
Via della Giuliana
Viale Angelico
Via G. Ferrari
Via Lepanto
Lungo. delle Armi
L. delle Navi
L. Michelangelo
L.Arnado da Brescia
Via Flaminia
PIAZZA DEL POPOLO
Viale delle Milizie
Via Barletta
Viale Giulio Cesare
Via Marcant. Colonna
Via Andrea Doria
PIAZZALE DEGLI EROI
Via Leone IV
Via Ottaviano
Via Candia
Via Germanico
Via Cola di Rienzo
Via Cicerone
L.d. Mellini in Augusta
Via di Ripetta
Via Cipro
Via Crescenzio
PIAZZA AUGUST IMPERIA
Via Angelo Emo
Vatican Museums
Castel Sant'Angelo
PIAZZA CAVOUR
CITTÀ DEL VATICANO
L. Prati
Vatican Wall
L. Castello
L. Marianzo
Saint Peter's Basilica
Tiber
Via Aurelia
L.di Tor di Nona
Viale Vaticano
Viale dei Coronari
V. S.Maria Mediatrice
Via Staz. di S. Pietro
L. Gianicolense
Corso Vittorio Emanuele II
Corso d. Rinascimento
PIAZZA NAVONA
Panthe
Via Giulia
Via Gregorio VII
V. Orti d'Alibert
V.di S. F. di Sales
Palazzo Farnese
Via d. Cava Aurelia
Viale delle Mura Aurelia
L. d. Farnesina
Via Arenula
MONTE DEL GIANICOLO
L.dei Vallati
L. dei Ce
V. Garibaldi
L. Sansio
Isola Tiberina
L. dei Anguillara
Via Aurelia Antica
S. Maria in Trastevere
V. dei Genovisi
TRASTEVERE
Via di S. Pancrazio
Villa Doria Pamphili
V.Nicola Fabrizi
Via Giacinto Carini
Via Glorioso
Viale di Trastevere
Pta. Portese (flea market)
V. di S. Michele
Ponte Sublicio
Via Dandolo
N
Via Fontelana
Viale di Villa Pamphili
Via dei Quattro Venti
Via Alessandro Poeria
Via Portuense
Lungotevere Testaccio
V. Giovanni Branc
Via Vittelia
Via di Donna Olimpia
Viale Zambarelli
Via Nicola
Via Federico Ozanam
Via Cavalcanti
Ponte Testaccio
Parco Testaccio
TESTACC
0 yards 550
0 meters 500

Galleria Nazionale d'Arte Moderne
Villa Borghese
Via Po
Via Salaria
Viale Regina Margherita
V. Dalmazia
V. Isonzo
Via Nizza
Via Nomentana
Corso d'Italia
Muro Torta
Via Piave
Porta Pia
Policlinico Universita
Via V. Veneto
Via Boncompagni
Spanish Steps
V. Ludovisi
XX Settembre
Biblioteca Nazionale
Viale Regina Elena
SALARIO
Museo Nazionale Romano
Via Palestro
Via dell'Università
Via del Policlinico
V. dei due Macelli
Via Sistina
Via Barberini
Via
Via del Tritone
V. d. Quattro Fontane
PIAZZA DELLA REPUBBLICA
PIAZZA DEL CINQUECENTO
Enjoy Rome
Via Castro Pretorio
Trevi Fountain
Stazione Termini
Via Marsala
Palazzo dei Quirinale
Via Nazionale
Via Tiburtina
PIAZZA SANTA MARIA MAGGIORE
Via Panisperna
Via Cavour
Via Giovanni Giolitti
Via Merulana
Via Giovanni Lanza
Via dei Fori Imperiali
PIAZZA VITTORIO EMANUELE
Viale Manzoni
Forum
PIAZZA DEL COLOSSEO
Via Emanuele Fiberto
V. S. Croce in Gerusalemme
V. Statilia
PIAZZA DI PTA. MAGGIORE
Via Labicana
Colosseum
MONTE PALATINO
Via di S. Gregorio
Via Claudia
P. DI SAN GIOVANNI IN LATERANO
Parco del Celio
Via di S. Stefano Rotondo
Palazzo Lateranense
Via dei Cerchi
(Circo Massimo) (Circus Maximus)
San Stefano Rotindo
San Giovanni in Laterano
CELIO
Via del Circo Massimo
Via d. Laterani
Via dell'Amba Aradam
Via Appia
Via della Navicella
Via delle Terme
S. Prisca
Via di
Viale Aventino
Via Druso
Via Gallia
Via Magnagrecia
P. DEI RE DI ROMA
Via Cerveteri
Nuova
Via Aventina
V. Antoniona
Terme di Caracalla
Viale Metronio
Via Etruria
Viale d. Piramide Cestia
Viale di Terme di Caracella
Via Satrico
Via Concordia
Via di Porta Latina
Via di Porta Sebastiano
Viale Giotto
Viale Guido Baccelli
Via Vetulonia
Via Siria

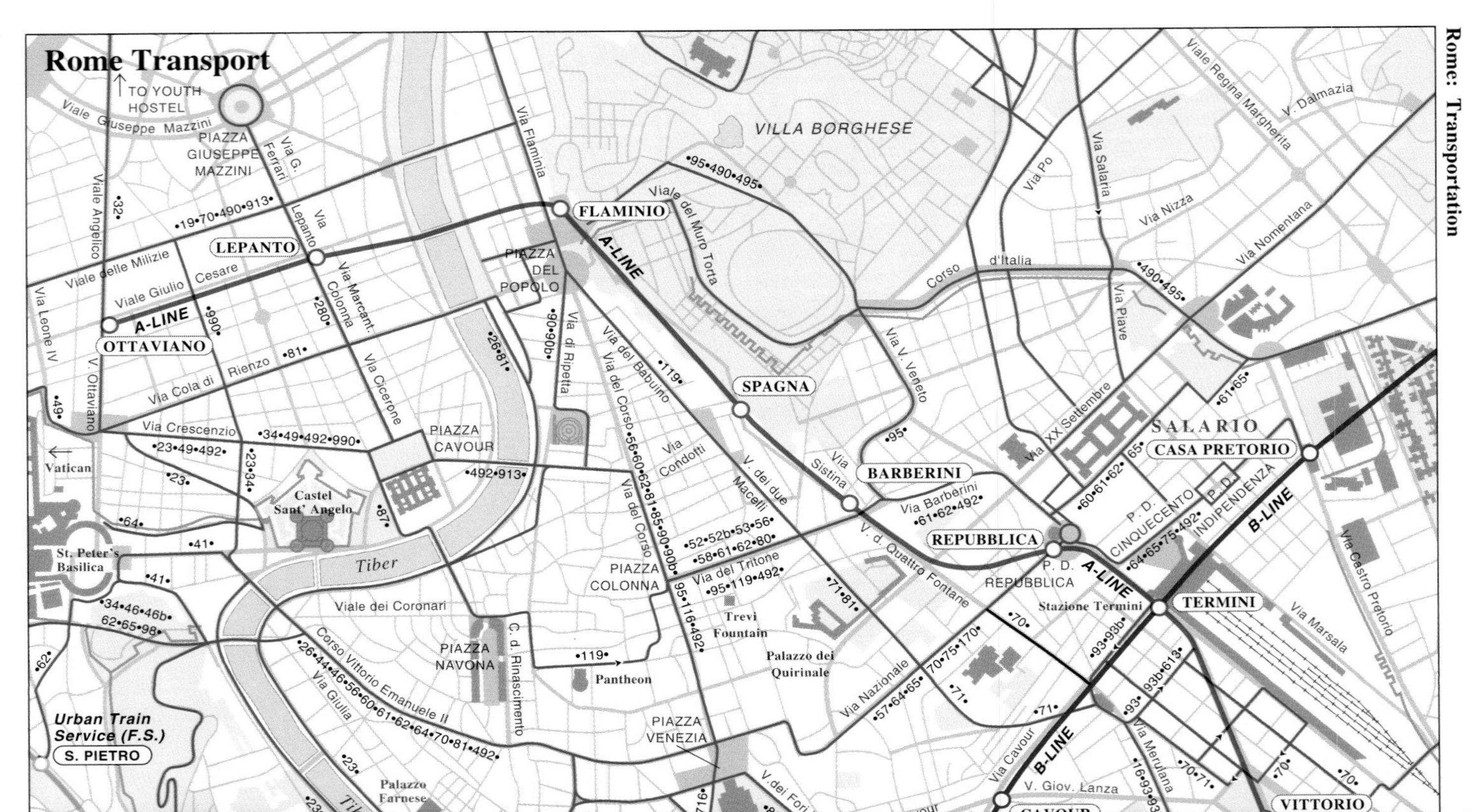
Rome Transport
TO YOUTH HOSTEL
Viale Giuseppe Mazzini
PIAZZA GIUSEPPE MAZZINI
Via G. Ferrari
VILLA BORGHESE
FLAMINIO
LEPANTO
OTTAVIANO
SPAGNA
BARBERINI
REPUBBLICA
TERMINI
CASA PRETORIO
VITTORIO
CAVOUR
A-LINE
B-LINE
SALARIO
Via Flaminia
Viale del Muro Torta
Via Po
Via Salaria
Via Nizza
Via Nomentana
Viale Regina Margherita
V. Dalmazia
Corso d'Italia
Via Piave
Via V. Veneto
Via XX Settembre
P. D. CINQUECENTO
INDIPENDENZA
Via Castro Pretorio
Via Marsala
P. D. REPUBBLICA
Stazione Termini
Via Sistina
Via Barberini
V. d. Quattro Fontane
Via Nazionale
Via Cavour
Via Merulana
V. Giov. Lanza
Viale Angelico
Viale delle Milizie
Viale Giulio Cesare
Via Lepanto
Via Marcant. Colonna
Via Leone IV
V. Ottaviano
Via Cola di Rienzo
Via Cicerone
Via Crescenzio
PIAZZA CAVOUR
PIAZZA DEL POPOLO
Via di Ripetta
Via del Babuino
Via del Corso
Via Condotti
V. dei due Macelli
Via del Tritone
Vatican
Castel Sant' Angelo
St. Peter's Basilica
Tiber
Viale dei Coronari
PIAZZA COLONNA
Trevi Fountain
Palazzo dei Quirinale
PIAZZA NAVONA
C. d. Rinascimento
Pantheon
Corso Vittorio Emanuele II
Via Giulia
PIAZZA VENEZIA
V. dei Fori
Palazzo Farnese
Urban Train Service (F.S.)
S. PIETRO

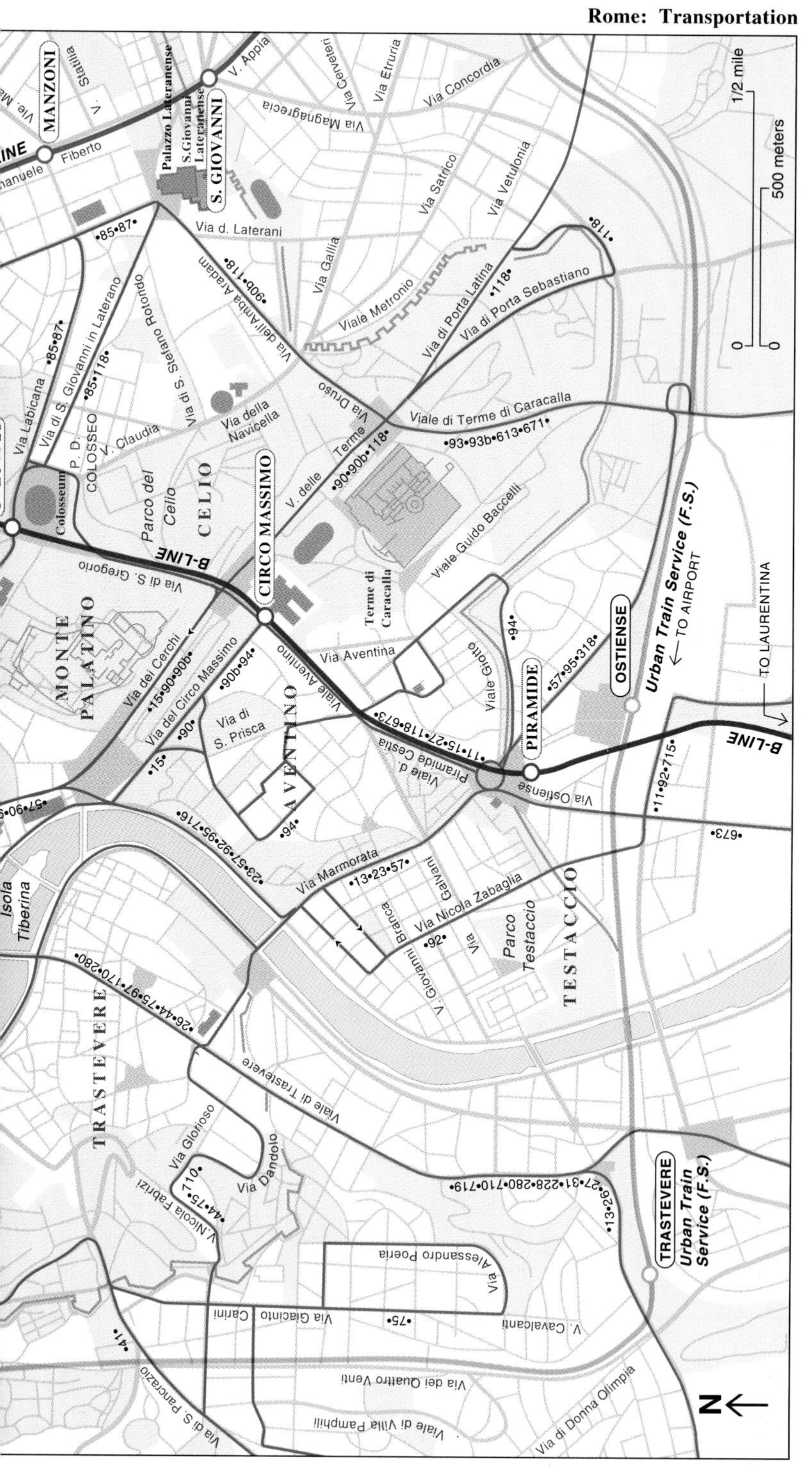
MANZONI
S. GIOVANNI
Palazzo Lateranense
S.Giovanni Laterano
V. Appia
Via Magnagrecia
Via Cerveteri
Via Etruria
Via Concordia
Via Satrico
Via Vetulonia
Via d. Laterani
Fiberto
Statilia
•85•87•
•90b•118•
Via dell'Amba Aradam
Via Gallia
Viale Metronio
Via di Porta Latina
Via di Porta Sebastiano
•118•
Via Labicana
Via di S. Giovanni in Laterano
•85•118•
Via di S. Stefano Rotondo
P. D. COLOSSEO
V. Claudia
Via della Navicella
Via Druso
Viale di Terme di Caracalla
•93•93b•613•671•
Colosseum
Parco del Celio
CELIO
CIRCO MASSIMO
V. delle Terme
•90•90b•118•
Terme di Caracalla
Viale Guido Baccelli
B-LINE
Via di S. Gregorio
MONTE PALATINO
Via dei Cerchi
•15•90•90b•
Via del Circo Massimo
•90b•94•
Via Aventina
Viale Aventino
•94•
Viale Giotto
PIRAMIDE
•57•95•318•
OSTIENSE
Urban Train Service (F.S.)
TO AIRPORT
TO LAURENTINA
Via di S. Prisca
AVENTINO
•90•
•15•
•11•15•27•118•673•
Viale d. Piramide Cestia
Via Ostiense
•11•92•715•
•673•
•23•57•92•95•716•
•94•
Via Marmorata
•13•23•57•
Via Galvani
Via Nicola Zabaglia
Via Branca
•92•
V. Giovanni
Parco Testaccio
TESTACCIO
Isola Tiberina
•26•44•75•97•170•280•
TRASTEVERE
Viale di Trastevere
Via Glorioso
Via Dandolo
•710•
•44•75•
V. Nicola Fabrizi
•27•31•228•280•710•719•
•13•26•
TRASTEVERE
Urban Train Service (F.S.)
Via Alessandro Poerio
Via Giacinto Carini
•75•
V. Cavalcanti
•41•
Via dei Quattro Venti
Viale di Villa Pamphili
Via di S. Pancrazio
Via di Donna Olimpia
N
1/2 mile
500 meters
0

Rome: "Walks"

Walks

1 Piazza del Popolo
2 Ara Pacis
3 Mausoleum of Augustus
4 Palazzo Borghese
5 Spanish Steps
6 Trevi Fountain
7 Vittorio Emanuele Monument
8 Campidoglio
9 Teatro Marcello
10 Isola Tiberina
11 Palazzo Doria Pamphili
12 Church of Santi Apostoli
13 Church of San Marcello
14 Piazza di S. Ignazio
15 Piazza di Pietra
16 Piazza Colonna/ Column of Marcus Aurelius
17 Palazzo Chigi
18 Pantheon
19 Giolitti
20 Piazza Minerva
21 Church of Santa Maria Sopra Minerva
22 Church of San Luigi dei Francesi
23 Piazza Navona
24 Church of Sant'Antonio dei Portoghesi
25 Museo Napoleonico
26 Il Gesù
27 Largo Argentina
28 Church of Sant'Andrea delle Valle
29 Palazzo del Cancelleria
30 Chiesa Nuova
31 Piazza Sforza Cesarini
32 Campo dei Fiori
33 Piazza Farnese
34 Piazza della Quercia
35 Monte di Pieta
36 Church of Santissima Trinità dei Pellegrini

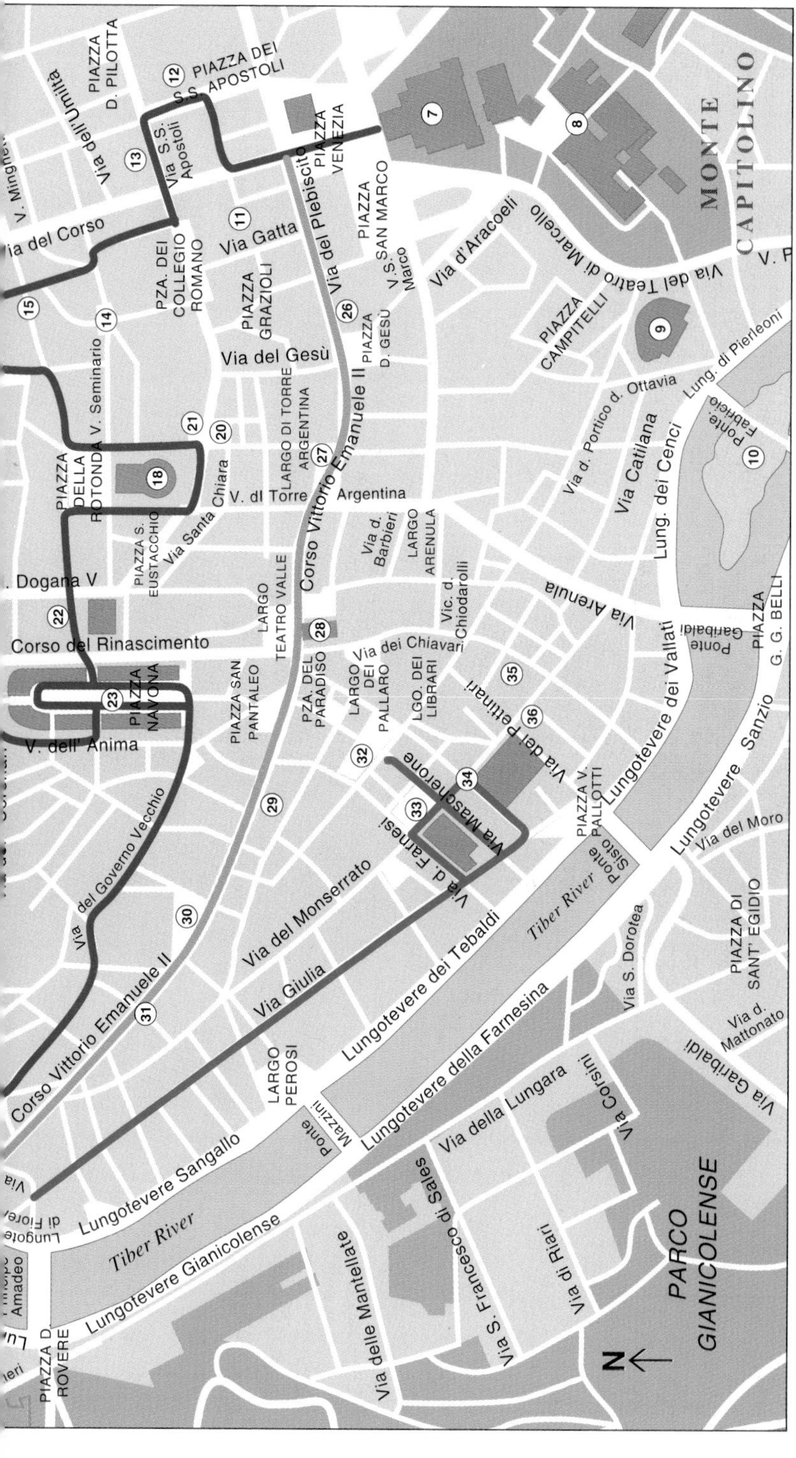

PIAZZA D. PILOTTA
PIAZZA DEI S.S. APOSTOLI
Via dell'Umiltà
V. Minghetti
Via S.S. Apostoli
PIAZZA VENEZIA
MONTE CAPITOLINO
Via del Corso
Via Gatta
PZA. DEI COLLEGIO ROMANO
Via del Plebiscito
PIAZZA SAN MARCO
V. S. Marco
Via d'Aracoeli
Via del Teatro di Marcello
V. P
V. Seminario
PIAZZA GRAZIOLI
Via del Gesù
PIAZZA D. GESÙ
PIAZZA CAMPITELLI
Lung. di Pierleoni
Via d. Portico d. Ottavia
PIAZZA DELLA ROTONDA
LARGO DI TORRE ARGENTINA
Corso Vittorio Emanuele II
Via Catilana
Lung. dei Cenci
Ponte Fabricio
V. di Torre Argentina
Via Santa Chiara
PIAZZA S. EUSTACCHIO
Via d. Barbieri
LARGO ARENULA
Via Arenula
. Dogana V
LARGO TEATRO VALLE
Vic. d. Chiodarolli
Corso del Rinascimento
Via dei Chiavari
Ponte Garibaldi
PIAZZA G. G. BELLI
PIAZZA NAVONA
PIAZZA SAN PANTALEO
PZA. DEL PARADISO
LARGO DEI PALLARO
LGO. DEI LIBRARI
Via dei Pettinari
V. dell' Anima
Via Mascherone
Via d. Farnesi
PIAZZA V. PALLOTTI
Lungotevere dei Vallati
Lungotevere Sanzio
Via del Governo Vecchio
Via d. Farnese
Ponte Sisto
Via del Moro
Via del Monserrato
Tiber River
Lungotevere dei Tebaldi
PIAZZA DI SANT' EGIDIO
Via S. Dorotea
Via Giulia
Lungotevere della Farnesina
Via d. Mattonato
LARGO PEROSI
Via Garibaldi
Ponte Mazzini
Via della Lungara
Via Corsini
Lungotevere Sangallo
Lungotevere di Fiore
Via
Lungotevere Gianicolense
Principe Amadeo
Via delle Mantellate
Via S. Francesco di Sales
Via di Riari
PARCO GIANICOLENSE
PIAZZA D. ROVERE
N

Rome: Villa Borghese

Villa Borghese

LET'S GO: Italy

"Its yearly revision by a new crop of Harvard students makes it as valuable as ever." **—*The New York Times***

"Value-packed, unbeatable, accurate, and comprehensive." **—*The Los Angeles Times***

"A world-wise traveling companion—always ready with friendly advice and helpful hints, all sprinkled with a bit of wit." **—*The Philadelphia Inquirer***

"Lighthearted and sophisticated, informative and fun to read. [Let's Go] helps the novice traveler navigate like a knowledgeable old hand." **—*Atlanta Journal-Constitution***

"All the essential information you need, from making a phone call to exchanging money to contacting your embassy. [Let's Go] provides maps to help you find your way from every train station to a full range of youth hostels and hotels." **—*Minneapolis Star Tribune***

"Unbeatable: good sight-seeing advice; up-to-date info on restaurants, hotels, and inns; a commitment to money-saving travel; and a wry style that brightens nearly every page." **—*The Washington Post***

■ Let's Go researchers have to make it on their own.

"The writers seem to have experienced every rooster-packed bus and lunar-surfaced mattress about which they write." **—*The New York Times***

"Retains the spirit of the student-written publication it is: candid, opinionated, resourceful, amusing info for the traveler of limited means but broad curiosity." **—*Mademoiselle***

■ No other guidebook is as comprehensive.

"Whether you're touring the United States, Europe, Southeast Asia, or Central America, a Let's Go guide will clue you in to the cheapest, yet safe, hotels and hostels, food and transportation. Going beyond the call of duty, the guides reveal a country's latest news, cultural hints, and off-beat information that any tourist is likely to miss." **—*Tulsa World***

■ Let's Go is completely revised each year.

"Up-to-date travel tips for touring four continents on skimpy budgets." **—*Time***

"Inimitable.... Let's Go's 24 guides are updated yearly (as opposed to the general guidebook standard of every two to three years), and in a marvelously spunky way." **—*The New York Times***

Let's Go Publications

Let's Go: Alaska & The Pacific Northwest
Let's Go: Britain & Ireland
Let's Go: California
Let's Go: Central America
Let's Go: Eastern Europe
Let's Go: Ecuador & The Galápagos Islands
Let's Go: Europe
Let's Go: France
Let's Go: Germany
Let's Go: Greece & Turkey
Let's Go: India & Nepal
Let's Go: Ireland
Let's Go: Israel & Egypt
Let's Go: Italy
Let's Go: London
Let's Go: Mexico
Let's Go: New York City
Let's Go: Paris
Let's Go: Rome
Let's Go: Southeast Asia
Let's Go: Spain & Portugal
Let's Go: Switzerland & Austria
Let's Go: USA
Let's Go: Washington, D.C.

Let's Go ***Map Guide:*** *Boston*
Let's Go ***Map Guide:*** *London*
Let's Go ***Map Guide:*** *New York City*
Let's Go ***Map Guide:*** *Paris*
Let's Go ***Map Guide:*** *San Francisco*
Let's Go ***Map Guide:*** *Washington, D.C.*

LET'S GO

The Budget Guide to
Italy
1997

Corey M. O'Hara
Editor

Amy E. Langston
Associate Editor

Lisa M. Nosal
Assistant Editor

Macmillan

HELPING LET'S GO

If you want to share your discoveries, suggestions, or corrections, please drop us a line. We read every piece of correspondence, whether a postcard, a 10-page e-mail, or a coconut. All suggestions are passed along to our researcher-writers. Please note that mail received after May 1997 may be too late for the 1998 book, but will be retained for the following edition. **Address mail to:**

Let's Go: Italy
67 Mt. Auburn Street
Cambridge, MA 02138
USA

Visit Let's Go at **http://www.letsgo.com,** or send e-mail to:

Fanmail@letsgo.com
Subject: "Let's Go: Italy"

In addition to the invaluable travel advice our readers share with us, many are kind enough to offer their services as researchers or editors. Unfortunately, the charter of Let's Go, Inc. enables us to employ only currently enrolled Harvard-Radcliffe students.

Published in Great Britain 1997 by Macmillan, an imprint of Macmillan General Books, 25 Eccleston Place, London SW1W 9NF and Basingstoke.

Map revisions pp. 2-3, 46-47, 82-83, 172-173, 294-295, 345, 381, 409, 485, 551, 579, 589 by Let's Go, Inc.

Published in the United States of America by St. Martin's Press, Inc.

ISBN: 0 333 68679 9

First edition
10 9 8 7 6 5 4 3 2 1

Let's Go: Italy is written by Let's Go Publications, 67 Mt. Auburn Street, Cambridge, MA 02138, USA.

Printed in the USA on recycled paper with biodegradable soy ink.

About Let's Go

THIRTY-SIX YEARS OF WISDOM

Back in 1960, a few students at Harvard University banded together to produce a 20-page pamphlet offering a collection of tips on budget travel in Europe. This modest, mimeographed packet, offered as an extra to passengers on student charter flights to Europe, met with instant popularity. The following year, students traveling to Europe researched the first, full-fledged edition of *Let's Go: Europe*, a pocket-sized book featuring honest, irreverent writing and a decidedly youthful outlook on the world. Throughout the 60s, our guides reflected the times; the 1969 guide to America led off by inviting travelers to "dig the scene" at San Francisco's Haight-Ashbury. During the 70s and 80s, we gradually added regional guides and expanded coverage into the Middle East and Central America. With the addition of our in-depth city guides, handy map guides, and extensive coverage of Asia, the 90s are also proving to be a time of explosive growth for Let's Go, and there's certainly no end in sight. The first editions of *Let's Go: India & Nepal* and *Let's Go: Ecuador & The Galápagos Islands* hit the shelves this year, and research for next year's series has already begun.

We've seen a lot in 37 years. *Let's Go: Europe* is now the world's bestselling international guide, translated into seven languages. And our new guides bring Let's Go's total number of titles, with their spirit of adventure and their reputation for honesty, accuracy, and editorial integrity, to 30. But some things never change: our guides are still researched, written, and produced entirely by students who know first-hand how to see the world on the cheap.

HOW WE DO IT

Each guide is completely revised and thoroughly updated every year by a well-traveled set of 200 students. Every winter, we recruit over 120 researchers and 60 editors to write the books anew. After several months of training, Researcher-Writers hit the road for seven weeks of exploration, from Anchorage to Ankara, Estonia to El Salvador, Iceland to Indonesia. Hired for their rare combination of budget travel sense, writing ability, stamina, and courage, these adventurous travelers know that train strikes, stolen luggage, food poisoning, and marriage proposals are all part of a day's work. Back at our offices, editors work from spring to fall, massaging copy written on Himalayan bus rides into witty yet informative prose. A student staff of typesetters, cartographers, publicists, and managers keeps our lively team together. In September, the collected efforts of the summer are delivered to our printer, who turns them into books in record time, so that you have the most up-to-date information available for *your* vacation. And even as you read this, work on next year's editions is well underway.

WHY WE DO IT

At Let's Go, our goal is to give you a great vacation. We don't think of budget travel as the last recourse of the destitute; we believe that it's the only way to travel. Living cheaply and simply brings you closer to the people and places you've been saving up to visit. Our books will ease your anxieties and answer your questions about the basics—so you can get off the beaten track and explore. Once you learn the ropes, we encourage you to put Let's Go away now and then to strike out on your own. As any seasoned traveler will tell you, the best discoveries are often those you make yourself. When you find something worth sharing, drop us a line. We're Let's Go Publications, 67 Mt. Auburn St., Cambridge, MA 02138, USA (e-mail: fanmail@letsgo.com).

HAPPY TRAVELS!

Contents

Maps

Acknowledgments

Team ITA Thanks: Steve, for kicking our butts; our RWs; the Map Team; Joel; Marilina and Giorgio; Michelle; Greg and his brother's wife, for gray box titles; Jen, for doing the dishes; Emily and Lisa H., for another year; Bill, for eternal Rome; Jerome, for the jaunty swish of his tail; and the Romance Room, for all their lovin'.

Corey Thanks: Amy, for pulling up that extra line; Lisa—sorry about the maps; Steve (oh, my God!); the most incredible team of researchers *ever;* Tom, for Star Wars and omelettes; Celeste, for answering the phone; Marilina, for the blueberries; Andrew and Barbara, for the dysfunctional family; the pod, for still hangin' around; Tuesday, for (where do I start?); Ian, for washing the breakfast dishes; Amnon, for the extra room; my grandparents, for encouragement; and Casey, the grinning idiot.

Amy Thanks: Corey, for being smart enough to hire me; Lisa, for her quiet way of fixing everything; Steve, for his encouragement; the Romance Room, for taunting and sassing me; Katie, for listening; and Chris, for reminding me that there's more to life than Let's Go. Thanks to those who supported me from a distance: Shannon, who makes life fun; my parents, who made it possible; and Will, who makes it all worthwhile. Special thanks to Jerome, who knows what I've been through.

Lisa Thanks: Corey, one of the best editors a girl could have; Amy, goddess of...well, let's face it, everything; Tom & Julie, the other best editors a girl could have; Steve, fabulous beyond compare; the RWs, who brightened my life; Caitlin, the *über*-babe; Miranda, wayward wanderer; Dave, fellow Dunsterite; Allison, who knows about Thomas Nast; Kath, Lynn, & Jan, for gossip and goodies; Mom, the creative genius; Dad, the passive-voice terminator; and Derek, the depth in the pool.

RWs Thank: Carol Noyes and Craig Martin; Baba; Wendy and Steph, for the letters; Hillary; RCS and HRO, for being in town; Corey, Amy, and Lisa; *la famiglia* Bordiga, *per la vostra ospitalità;* Elban beach buddies; Abacus, *per un migliaia risate;* Hotel Tina; Giuseppe *e il gatto;* and the rest of our family and friends.

Researcher-Writers

Kathleen Christian *Abruzzo, Apulia, Basilicata, Campania*
Kathleen, the art-history goddess, taught us a little lesson about the Pantheon. She trudged through southern Italy, boldly going where no woman had gone before. She clarified our info, checked out new towns, and survived the hotel-owner-crossfire in Capri. We have a sneaking suspicion that she did all this just to get back to Rome. Most importantly, Kathleen learned to find her eyedrops in the dark.

Hsiao-Yun Chu *Trentino-Alto Adige, Friuli-Venezia Giulia, Veneto, Emilia-Romagna, Le Marche*
Mei-Mei could not escape Harvard; everywhere she went, she found her fellow students. She got more mail here than we did and sent us our favorite "reader mail" of the summer. Mei-Mei's stellar prose and color-coded copybatches captivated and entertained us. She sought out the hottest nightlife throughout northern Italy, dodging potential Romeos in Verona and merchants in Venice.

Salvatore Gogliormella *Sardinia, Tuscany, Umbria*
With or without money, Sal got the job done. Nary a whitewashed wall nor a frescoed ceiling in all of Tuscany escaped Sal's observant eye. Not one to sell himself short, Sal reported each detail in fluid prose (and the world's neatest handwriting). Even flooded train tracks couldn't hold him back. An unassuming young man, he made friends from Siena to Sardinia. Our entire staff loves Sal (and Aunt Carmella).

William Kirtley *Tunisia (and Morocco, but that's another book)*
In between double-duty Morocco research, Will sent back flawless copy. Intrepid Will braved Saharan dunes and hostile hostel owners. He navigated the Tunisian telephone system with aplomb and, shooing away native guides, found his own way throughout North Africa. Will drank more tea than he can remember. He did not propose to anyone, no matter what the Tunisian prostitute says.

Jefferson Packer *Calabria, Sicily*
Braving the land of the Godfather armed only with his impeccable Italian, Jefferson rewrote the book on Sicily. He charmed the most difficult of hotel owners and wrote it up in elegant prose. He batted clean-up for Let's Go, picking up where others left off; he even researched for *Let's Go: France* on his vacation time. Always up for adventure, Jefferson and his silk bomber jacket are off to explore Greece.

Ian Pervil *Liguria, Piedmont, Lombardy, Emilia-Romagna*
Hel-lo, could Ian have been a better RW? Although he never ate donkey, Ian definitely kicked ass. Ian can tell you the location of the ugliest church in Italy. Ian climbed every mountain and forded every stream (and has blisters to prove it). He infiltrated the most stylish quarters of Italy and emerged unscathed (except for a few shopping bags). His phone calls brightened our days. Ian is *tutto quello che*.

Emily M. Tucker *Rome*
A Let's Go veteran, Emily was there for us from start to end—preparing tearsheets in the spring and proofing in the fall. In between, she finally got to research Rome.

Alejandro Sepulveda *Rome*
Alex's neverending research made us take another look at Rome. He enlivened our book with last-minute updates and details of Roman nightlife.

How to Use This Book

Let's Go: Italy 1997 is a comprehensive, useful, and entertaining guide to one of the most beautiful and culture-rich regions in the world.

Essentials. The name says it all. Granted, it is somewhat more important to know how to obtain a passport than how to import a BMW, but we try to provide for all your vacation needs. Pay particular attention to white boxes—they contain warnings and other vital information. ATMs, ziti, and everything in between is covered in the **Planning Your Trip** and **Life and Times** sections; take to heart the advice offered regarding documents and formalities, accommodations reservations, emergency telephone numbers, and health requirements listed in the former, and wile away a seemingly endless train ride thumbing through the 4000-year historical survey, food description, and literature and arts summary contained in the latter.

La bella Italia is easily divided into **six regions:** Rome, northern Italy, central Italy, southern Italy, Sardinia, and Sicily. **Tunisia** is its own chapter, with information on ferry and air connections from the Continent. The book begins with Rome and radiates out from there; this organization makes it easier for you to plan your itinerary. Italy's extensive transportation system provides inexpensive and quick links between towns and regions. You can go to sleep on the train in Palermo and wake up the next morning in Rome. Heck, you could go to sleep on the train in *Paris* and wake up the next morning in Rome.

Each city and town listing provides information on transportation to and from nearby cities or larger transportation hubs. Orient yourself with the help of **country, regional,** and **city maps.** The **Orientation and Practical Information** listings are standardized in order of their relative importance, beginning with the area's tourist office and ending with the telephone prefix.

Your Italian is rusty? The **Appendix** contains sections on **pronunciation,** helpful Italian **phrases,** and a **glossary** of the Italian, French, and Arabic terms that are sprinkled throughout the book. Some **French** and **Arabic phrases** appear in the **Tunisia Essentials.** If you get really bored, check out the **index.** Seriously.

Remember that Italy offers a little of everything, and that Tunisia is a whole different world. Visit Tuscany (with everyone else), or escape from the tourist track and venture south to towns that haven't seen a foreigner since our researcher left. Hike or ski in the Sila Massif, Abruzzo, or the Alps, and sunbathe topless in the Riviera. Sleep in Luke Skywalker's home on the edge of the Sahara. Above all, don't limit yourself to what you see in these pages; be adventurous and strike out on your own. Wherever your travels take you, *Let's Go: Italy 1997* wishes you *Buon Viaggio!*

A NOTE TO OUR READERS

The information for this book is gathered by *Let's Go*'s researchers during the late spring and summer months. Each listing is derived from the assigned researcher's opinion based upon his or her visit at a particular time. The opinions are expressed in a candid and forthright manner. Other travelers might disagree. Those traveling at a different time may have different experiences since prices, dates, hours, and conditions are always subject to change. You are urged to check beforehand to avoid inconvenience and surprises. Travel always involves a certain degree of risk, especially in low-cost areas. When traveling, especially on a budget, always take particular care to ensure your safety.

GREECE
ESPAÑA
LONDON

ESSENTIALS

GEOGRAPHY AND CLIMATE

Italy is more than just your average boot. Its landscape ranges from rocky promontories to plains, lakes, and valleys, often all in close proximity. Mountains play a particularly important role: the Alps define Italy's northern border, the Apennines run its length, and the Gargano and Sila Massifs cross the spur and foot of the boot respectively. With hill towns so prevalent, it's hardly surprising that the country has bred a form of human being capable of simultaneously negotiating three-inch heels, 13th-century cobblestone paving, and a 60° incline. Rome, Milan, and Naples, the largest Italian cities, are now surrounded by urban sprawl, but the vast majority of Italy remains a symbiotic mixture of countryside and smaller towns.

The motley landscape is broken up by substantial regions of plains. The largest area is the valley of the Po River, which stretches from Piedmont through a number of low-lying Lombard cities and across the farmlands of Emilia-Romagna. A coastal plain runs along the Tyrrhenian Sea from southern Tuscany through Lazio, culminating in Apulia, a rich farming region on the heel. In addition, many of the surrounding islands are actually mountains rising from the sea. Thus, Sicily and Sardinia have mountainous interiors, while the major cities are located along the flatter coast.

Outlining a peninsula roughly 1000km long and 150-250km across, the Italian coastline seems endless. The most noteworthy areas are the astonishingly beautiful Amalfi coast (south of Naples), the crescent of Liguria (the Italian Riviera), and the Gargano Massif (the spur jutting into the Adriatic). Other attractive mainland seashores include Calabria's Tyrrhenian coast, the wee southern coast of Lazio (near Gaeta), and the Monte Conero cliffs (just south of Ancona). Sicily and Sardinia boast beaches with Greek ruins and much more sand. For the best swimming in Sardinia, venture beyond the more touristed areas. In Sicily, try the smaller islands, such as the Aeolians, but be aware that when the currents change, they often bring refuse. Italian wilderness has been whittled away over the millennia, but is selectively preserved in the great national parks: Abruzzo National Park in the Apennines and the Alpine Gran Paradiso National Park set between Valle D'Aosta and Piedmont.

Due to the cooling waters of the ocean and the protective Alps encircling the north, Italy's climate is for the most part temperate. In the summer, the north grows fairly warm (and, in some places, very rainy), the central region wallows in stifling humidity, and the south bakes in arid heat. A breeze off the sea, however, cools both coasts. Winter in the Alps is very cold, while Milan, Turin, and Venice turn chilly, damp, and foggy. Tuscany fares similarly, with temperatures in the 30s Fahrenheit (0°Celsius), although rain is a sure bet. Southern temperatures usually remain in the 50s and 60s Fahrenheit during the winter (10-20°C). Refer to the **climate chart** in the **appendix** for more information (p. 642).

PLANNING YOUR TRIP

The best time to organize your vacation is beforehand. Creating a basic itinerary without setting it in stone enables you to call ahead for reservations without sacrificing spontaneity. A flexible game plan is required in Italy since offices, hotels, and entire towns tend to close on a whim. Despite broad stereotypes, Italy is multiregional and multifaceted, with many different accents, tastes, and cuisines. Above all, remember that small towns can be just as interesting as large cities, and are usually less congested. "Doing" Florence, Venice, and Rome may be a time-honored tradition, but it

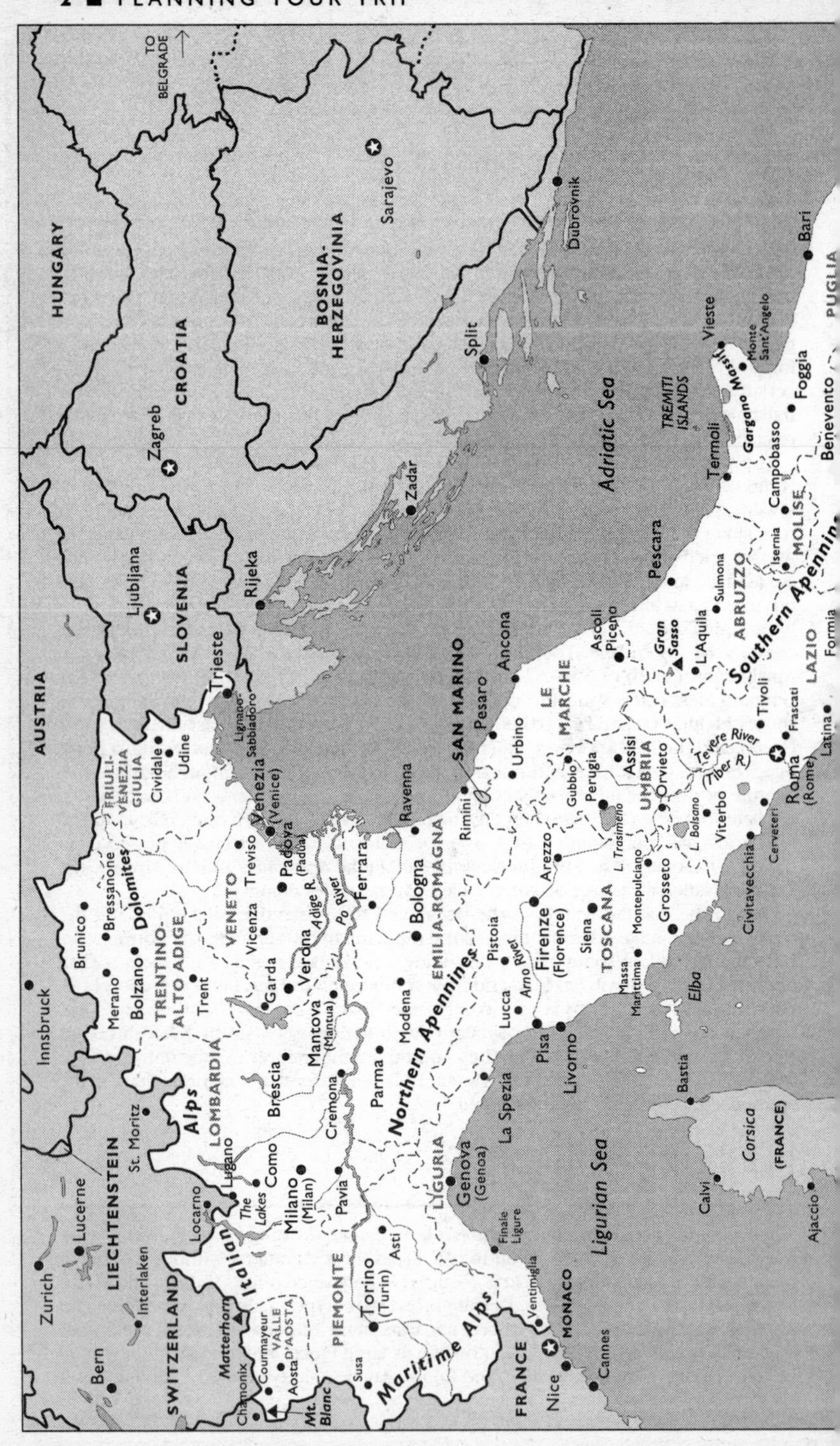

HUNGARY
CROATIA
BOSNIA-HERZEGOVINIA
TO BELGRADE
Sarajevo
Dubrovnik
Split
Zagreb
Zadar
Rijeka
SLOVENIA
Ljubljana
AUSTRIA
Trieste
Lignano-Sabbiadoro
Udine
Cividale
FRIULI-VENEZIA GIULIA
Innsbruck
Brunico
Bressanone
Dolomites
Merano
Bolzano
TRENTINO-ALTO ADIGE
Trent
VENETO
Treviso
Vicenza
Venezia (Venice)
Padova (Padua)
Garda
Verona
Adige R.
Po River
Ferrara
Mantova (Mantua)
Brescia
Cremona
LOMBARDIA
Alps
St. Moritz
LIECHTENSTEIN
Zurich
Lucerne
Interlaken
SWITZERLAND
Bern
Locarno
Lugano
Como
The Lakes
Milano (Milan)
Pavia
Italian
Matterhorn
Courmayeur
VALLE D'AOSTA
Aosta
Chamonix
Mt. Blanc
PIEMONTE
Torino (Turin)
Asti
Susa
Maritime Alps
FRANCE
Nice
MONACO
Cannes
Ventimiglia
Finale Ligure
LIGURIA
Genova (Genoa)
La Spezia
Ligurian Sea
Parma
Modena
Northern Apennines
Bologna
EMILIA-ROMAGNA
Ravenna
Rimini
SAN MARINO
Pesaro
Urbino
Ancona
LE MARCHE
Ascoli Piceno
Pistoia
Arno River
Firenze (Florence)
Lucca
Pisa
Livorno
Arezzo
Siena
TOSCANA
Massa Marittima
Montepulciano
Grosseto
Elba
Bastia
Corsica (FRANCE)
Calvi
Ajaccio
Gubbio
Perugia
L. Trasimeno
Assisi
UMBRIA
Orvieto
L. Bolsano
Viterbo
Tevere River (Tiber R.)
Civitavecchia
Cerveteri
Roma (Rome)
Frascati
Tivoli
Latina
LAZIO
Formia
Gran Sasso
L'Aquila
ABRUZZO
Sulmona
Southern Apennines
Pescara
Isernia
MOLISE
Campobasso
Termoli
TREMITI ISLANDS
Adriatic Sea
Gargano Massif
Vieste
Monte Sant'Angelo
Foggia
Benevento
Bari
PUGLIA

Italy
Porto Vecchio
S. Teresa Gallura
Costa Smeralda
Porto Torres
Olbia
Sassari
Nuoro
Alghero
Cala Gonone
Oristano
Arbatax
SARDEGNA
Cagliari
Gaeta
PONTINE ISLANDS
Ischia
Capri
Napoli (Naples)
Pompeii
Sorrento
Salerno
Paestum
CAMPANIA
Potenza
Matera
BASILICATA
Taranto
Brindisi
Lecce
Otranto
Metaponto
Gulf of Taranto
Trebisacce
Rossano
CALABRIA
Paola
Cosenza
Crotone
Sila Massif
Catanzaro
Capo Vaticano
Monasterace
Tyrrhenian Sea
Ustica
AEOLIAN (LIPARI) ISLANDS
Messina
Reggio di Calabria
Aspromonte
Capo San Vito
Palermo
Cefalú
Taormina
Trapani
EGADI ISLANDS
Marsala
SICILIA
Mt. Etna
Catania
Enna
Siracusa
Agrigento
Gela
Ragusa
Ionian Sea
Mediterranean Sea
N
0
100 miles
0
100 kilometers
Pantelleria
Tunis
Carthage
TUNISIA
Annaba
ALGERIA

is also one of the most expensive of all possible Italian vacations. Visiting one of these cities and then exploring the region around it will give you a far better sense of the area and the diversity of Italian life. You will also be able to avoid spending all of your time in a crowd of other tourists.

In order to get the most out of your experience, allow for leisure time in your itinerary. Make an effort to be polite and friendly; if you do, you'll find that most of the people you meet will respond in kind. It's even worth attempting to speak a few words of Italian—any effort, however mangled, will be enthusiastically received.

When to Go

The best time to see Italy is in either late May or early September, when you can avoid the summer crowds yet enjoy pleasant weather. Whenever you go, try to plan an itinerary based on the season, considering weather patterns, festival schedules, and tourist congestion. A winter camping plan may face endless rain, for example, and a February visit should ideally include a Venetian *Carnevale* celebration. See **Festivals and Holidays** in the **appendix** (643).

Unfortunately for most of us, summertime travel is often the only option. Consequently, tourism goes into overdrive in June, July, and August: hotels are booked solid, Michelangelo's *David* has hour-long lines, and the ocean view is perpetually obstructed by seven rows of lounge chairs. Almost without exception, hotel rates go up and trains are crowded, so reservations are vital (see box below). Although many of the best restaurants are closed for holiday in August, some youth hostels and many campgrounds open *just* for the summer, and museums and tourist offices often maintain extended hours during peak season. The best strategy is to make reservations at least a few days in advance. If you want to stay in Siena during the Palio, or spend the night on Capri, Elba, or the Amalfi Coast, however, you should make reservations months in advance.

Be aware that some areas have an *additional* high-season. The Dolomites and the Alps are popular (but expensive) skiing destinations in the winter, Rome is hectic during Easter week, and Venice livens up in the early spring for its pre-Lent festivities. In general, though, visiting Italy between September and May means enjoying the benefits of the off-season. You may be able to experience grape harvests in the fall, mild southern weather in the winter, and religious festivities in the spring.

Italy in August. A final word of warning: If you choose to travel in August, reservations are a matter of necessity. Be sure to reconfirm them shortly before you arrive, but do not send money ahead. Most Italians take their own vacations in August and close up their businesses and restaurants. Some of the industrial cities of the north become complete ghost towns, and many other cities remain alive only as tourist-infested infernos.

Useful Information

TRAVEL ORGANIZATIONS AND TOURIST BUREAUS

Council on International Educational Exchange (Council), 205 East 42nd St., New York, NY 10017-5706 (tel. (888) COUNCIL (268-6245); fax (212) 822-2699; e-mail info@ciee.org; http://www.ciee.org). A private, nonprofit organization, Council administers work, volunteer, and academic programs around the world. They also offer ID cards, including ISIC and GO25, and a range of publications, including the magazine *Student Travels* (free). Call or write for more information.

Federation of International Youth Travel Organizations (FIYTO), Bredgade 25H, DK-1260 Copenhagen K, Denmark (tel. (33) 33 96 00; fax 93 96 76; e-mail mailbox@fiyto.org), is an international organization promoting educational and social travel for young people. Member organizations include language schools, educational travel companies, national tourist boards, accommodation centers, and other suppliers of travel services to youth and students. FIYTO also sponsors the GO25 Card. See **Youth, Student, & Teacher Identification,** p. 13.

International Student Travel Confederation, Herengracht 479, 1017 BS Amsterdam, Netherlands (tel. (31) 204 212 800; fax 204 212 810; e-mail istcinfo@istc.org; http://www.istc.org). A nonprofit confederation of student travel organizations, including International Student Rail Association (ISRA), Student Air Travel Association (SATA), ISIS Travel Insurance, and the International Association for Educational and Work Exchange Programs (IAEWEP).

Italian Government Tourist Board (ENIT), 630 Fifth Ave., #1565, **New York,** NY 10111 (tel. (212) 245-4822; fax 586-9249). Write for their guide *Italia: General Information for Travelers to Italy* (containing train and ferry schedules), and for regional information as available. Branch offices: 12400 Wilshire Blvd., #550, **Los Angeles,** CA 90025 (tel. (310) 820-0098; fax 820-6357); 1 Pl. Ville Marie, #1914, **Montréal,** Québec H3B 3M9 (tel. (514) 866-7667; fax 392-1429); 1 Princes St., **London,** England WIR 8AY (tel. (0171) 408 12 54; fax 493 66 95).

Italian Cultural Institute, 686 Park Ave., New York, NY 10021 (tel. (212) 879-4242), is often more prompt and helpful than ENIT. Request the booklet entitled "Mia Italia," which is full of maps and suggestions for less touristed sites.

Animal and Plant Health Inspection Service, Attn: USDA APHIS PPQ, 4700 River Rd., Unit 60, Riverdale, MD 20737 (tel. (301) 734-8295). A division of the USDA, APHIS publishes the *Traveler's Tips* pamphlet, which provides information on which plant and animal products you can safely bring home from other countries. Consult your local Blue Pages for the number of the nearest branch.

USEFUL PUBLICATIONS

Adventurous Traveler Bookstore, P.O. Box 1468, Williston, VT 05495 (tel. (801) 860-6776; fax 860-6607; both at (800) 282-3963; e-mail books@atbook.com; http://www.gorp.com/atbook.html). Free 40 page catalogue upon request. Specializes in outdoor adventure travel books and maps for the U.S. and abroad. Their World Wide Web site offers extensive browsing opportunities.

Bon Voyage!, 2069 W. Bullard Ave., Fresno, CA 93711-1200 (tel. (800) 995-9716, from abroad (209) 447-8441; e-mail 70754.3511@compuserve.com). Annual mail order catalog offers a range of products for everyone from the luxury traveler to the diehard trekker. Books, travel accessories, luggage, electrical converters, maps, videos, and more. All merchandise may be returned for exchange or refund within 30 days of purchase, and prices are guaranteed. (Lower advertised prices from their competitors will be matched and merchandise shipped free.)

The College Connection, Inc., 1295 Prospect St., Suite A, La Jolla, CA 92037 (tel. (619) 551-9770; fax 551-9987; e-mail eurailnow@aol.com; http://www.eurailpass.com). Publishes *The Passport*, a booklet listing hints about every aspect of traveling and studying abroad. This booklet is free to *Let's Go* readers; send your request by e-mail or fax only. The College Rail Connection, a division of the College Connection, sells railpasses and flights with student discounts.

The European Festivals Association, 120B, rue de Lausanne, 1202 Geneva, Switzerland (tel. (22) 732 28 03; fax 738 40 12). Publishes the free booklet *Festivals,* which lists dates and programs of many major European festivals, including music, ballet, and theater events.

Forsyth Travel Library, P.O. Box 480800, Kansas City, MO 64148 (tel. (800) 367-7984; fax (816) 942-6969; http://www.forsyth.com). A mail-order service that stocks a wide range of city, area, and country maps, as well as guides for rail and ferry travel in Europe, including the *Thomas Cook European Timetable* for trains. See **Useful Resources,** p. 49. Also sells rail tickets and passes, and offers reservation services. Call or write for a free catalogue, or visit their web site.

Hippocrene Books, Inc., 171 Madison Ave., New York, NY 10016 (tel. (212) 685-4371; orders (718) 454-2366; fax 454-1391). Free catalog. Publishes travel reference books, travel guides, foreign language dictionaries, and language learning guides which cover over 100 languages.

Hunter Publishing, 300 Raritan Center Parkway, Edison, NJ 08818 (tel. (908) 225-1900; fax 417-0482). Has an extensive catalog of travel books, guides, language

learning tapes, and quality maps. Ask about the *Charming Small Hotel Guides* to Italy and Tuscany & Umbria, as well as other European countries (each US$13).

John Muir Publications, P.O. Box 613, Sante Fe, NM 87504 (tel. (800) 888-7504; fax (505) 988-1680). In addition to many travel guides, John Muir publishes an excellent series of books by veteran traveler Rick Steves. *Europe though the Back Door* offers great advice on the dos and don'ts of budget travel (US$19), and *Mona Winks: Self-Guided Tours of Europe's Top Museums* (US$18) will allow you to bypass a tour guide. Also available in bookstores.

Michelin Travel Publications, Michelin Tire Corporation, P.O. Box 19001, Greenville, SC 29602-9001 (tel. (800) 423-0485; fax (803) 458-5665). Publishes travel-related material, including the *Green Guides* for sight-seeing info, maps, and driving itineraries. Also offers detailed, reliable road maps and atlases, available at bookstores and distributors throughout the world.

Specialty Travel Index, 305 San Anselmo Avenue, #313, San Anselmo, CA 94960 (tel. (415) 459-4900; fax 459-4974; e-mail spectrav@ix.netcom.com; http://www.spectrav.com). Published twice yearly, this index is an extensive listing of "off the beaten track" and specialty travel opportunities. One copy US$6, one-year subscription (2 issues) US$10.

Superintendent of Documents, U.S. Government Printing Office, P.O. Box 371954, Pittsburgh, PA 15250-7954 (tel. (202) 512-1800; fax 512-2250). Publishes *Your Trip Abroad* (US$1.25), *Health Information for International Travel* (US$14), and "Background Notes" on all countries ($1 each). Postage is included in the prices.

Transitions Abroad, 18 Hulst Rd., P.O. Box 1300, Amherst, MA 01004-1300 (tel. (413) 256-3414; fax 256-0375; e-mail trabroad@aol.com). This invaluable magazine lists publications and resources for overseas study, work, and volunteering. Also publishes *The Alternative Travel Directory,* a comprehensive guide to living, learning, and working overseas (US$20; postage US$4).

Travel Books & Language Center, Inc., 4931 Cordell Ave., Bethesda, MD 20814 (tel. (800) 220-2665; fax (301) 951-8546; e-mail travelbks@aol.com). Sells over 75,000 items, including books, cassettes, atlases, dictionaries, and a wide range of specialty travel maps. Free comprehensive catalogue upon request.

Ten Speed Press, P.O. Box 7123, Berkeley, CA 94707 (tel. (800) 841-2665; orders (510) 559-1629). *The Packing Book* (US$8) provides various checklists and suggested wardrobes, addresses safety concerns, and imparts packing techniques.

U.S. Customs Service, P.O. Box 7407, Washington, D.C., 20044 (tel. (202) 927-5580). Publishes 35 books, leaflets, and flyers on various aspects of customs. *Know Before You Go* tells almost everything the international traveler needs to know about customs requirements; *Pockets Hints* is a condensed version.

Wide World Books and Maps, 1911 N. 45th St., Seattle, WA 98103 (tel. (206) 634-3453; fax 634-0558; e-mail travelbk@mail.nwlink.com; http://nwlink.com/travelbk). A good selection of travel guides, accessories, and hard-to-find maps.

INTERNET RESOURCES: GETTING IT ON-LINE

Along with everything else in the '90s, budget travel is moving rapidly into the information age. And with the growing user-friendliness of personal computers and internet technology, much of this information can be yours with the click of a mouse.

There are a number of ways to access the Internet. The most popular are the commercial internet providers, such as **America Online** (tel. (800) 827-6394) and **Compuserve** (tel. (800) 433-0389), both of which charge a user's fee. However, many employers and schools also offer gateways to the Internet, often at no cost. Learning how to navigate through cyberspace is not extraordinarily complex, but somewhat beyond the scope of this book. For more information, contact one of the commercial servers, ask a computer-using friend, or check out one of the many comprehensive guides to the Internet now available in most bookstores.

Increasingly the Internet forum of choice, the **World Wide Web** features a variety of "sites" which may interest the budget traveler. The use of search engines (services that look for web pages under specific subjects) can facilitate the search process. **Lycos** (http://a2z.lycos.com) and **Infoseek** (http://guide.infoseek.com) are two of the most popular. **Yahoo!** is a slightly more organized search engine; check out its travel links at http://www.yahoo.com/recreation/travel. However, it is often better to know a good site, and start "surfing" from there, through links from one web page to another. So *Let's Go* has compiled a list of helpful sites, from which you can begin searching for budget travel information on the Web.

Dr. Memory's Favorite Travel Pages (http://www.access.digex.net/~drmemory/cyber_travel.htm) is a great place to start surfing. Dr. Memory has links to hundreds of different web pages of interest to travelers of all kinds.

Big World Magazine (http://boss.cpcnet.com/personal/bigworld/bigworld.htm) specializes in budget travel, and its web site provides great links to travel pages.

The Student and Budget Travel Guide (http://asa.ugl.lib.umich.edu/chdocs/travel/travel-guide.html) is just what it sounds like.

Another popular source of information is a **newsgroup,** which is a forum for discussion of a specific topic. There are thousands of different newsgroups, which means that there is information available on almost any topic you can imagine. Since most newsgroups are unmoderated and unsupervised, however, the reliability of information posted within them is not always certain. Nonetheless, there are still a number of useful newsgroups for travelers.

Usenet, a family of newsgroups, can be accessed easily from most Internet gateways. In UNIX systems, a good newsreader is "tin" (just type "tin" at the prompt). There are several hierarchies of newsgroups. The "soc" groups deal primarily with issues related to society and culture; of interest to travelers to Italy are **soc.culture.italian** and **soc.culture.europe.** The "alt" (alternative) groups form a less organized hierarchy and include **alt.politics.italy** and **alt.currentevents.italy.** "Rec" groups, such as **rec.travel.air** and **rec.travel.europe,** are oriented toward recreational activities which may interest travelers. Finally, **Clari-net** posts Associated Press news wires for many different topics; travelers to Italy should take a look at **clari.world.europe.italy** and **clari.news.europe.**

Documents and Formalities

It is strongly recommended that you file applications for all necessary documents well in advance of your planned departure date. Once you have acquired the documents, it is a good idea to photocopy them all (as well as credit cards); leave a copy at home with someone you can easily contact, and carry another one with you.

When you travel, *always carry on your person two or more forms of identification, including at least one photo ID.* Never carry all identification, traveler's checks, and credit cards together. If you plan an extended stay, you might want to register your passport with the nearest embassy or consulate. Consulates also recommend that you carry an expired passport or an official copy of your birth certificate, as well as extra passport photos, in a separate part of your baggage—these items will facilitate replacement of a lost passport. If your passport has been lost or stolen, contact the local police and your embassy or consulate immediately.

ITALIAN EMBASSIES AND CONSULATES

U.S.: Embassy of Italy, 1601 Fuller St. NW, **Washington, D.C.** 20009 (tel. (202) 328-5500; fax 462-3605) and Italian Consulate, 12400 Wilshire Blvd., #300, **Los Angeles,** CA 90025 (tel. (310) 820-0622). Other consulates of Italy at 2590 Webster St., **San Francisco,** CA 94115 (tel. (415) 931-4924); 500 N. Michigan Ave., #1850, **Chicago,** IL 60611 (tel. (312) 467-1550); 630 Camp St., **New Orleans,** LA 70130 (tel. (504) 524-2271); 100 Boylston St., #900, **Boston,** MA 02116 (tel. (617) 542-0483); 535 Griswold, **Detroit,** MI 48226 (tel. (313) 963-8560); 690 Park Ave., **New York,** NY 10021 (tel. (212) 737-9100); Public Ledger Building, 100 S. Sixth St., #1026, **Philadelphia,** PA 19106 (tel. (215) 592-7329); 1300 Post Oak Blvd., #660, **Houston,** TX 77056 (tel. (713) 850-7520).

Canada: Embassy of Italy, 275 Slater St., 21st Floor, **Ottawa,** Ontario K1P 5H9 (tel. (613) 232-2401); Consulate of Italy, 3489 Drummond St., **Montréal,** Québec H3G 1X6 (tel. (514) 849-7113).

U.K.: Embassy of Italy, 14 Three Kings Yard, **London** W1Y 2EH (tel. (0171) 312 22 00; fax 312 22 30); Consulate General of Italy, 38 Eaton Place, London SW1 8AN (tel. (0171) 235 9371); Italian Consulate in Manchester, 111 Piccadilly, **Manchester** M1 2HY (tel. (0161) 236 90 24); Consulate General of Italy in Scotland and Northern Ireland, 32 Melville St., **Edinburgh** EH3 7HA (tel. (0131) 220 36 95).

Australia: Embassy of Italy, 12 Grey St., Deakin, **Canberra** City A.C.T. 2600 (tel. (06) 273 3333; fax 273 4223).

New Zealand: Embassy of Italy, P.O. Box 463, **Wellington** (tel. (644) 473 53 39; fax 472 72 55).

South Africa: Embassy of Italy, 796 George Ave., **Arcadia,** Pretoria (tel. (12) 43 55 41/2/3/4; fax 43 55 47).

PASSPORTS

Citizens of the U.S., Canada, the U.K., Ireland, Australia, New Zealand, and South Africa all need valid passports to enter both Italy and Tunisia and to re-enter their own countries. Some countries will not allow entrance if the holder's passport will expire in less than six months, and returning to the U.S. with an expired passport may result in a fine. Some countries require travelers under 16 to have passports.

Your passport is a public document that belongs to your government and may not be withheld without your consent. You may be asked to surrender it to an Italian government official; if you don't get it back in a reasonable amount of time, you should inform your nearest embassy or consulate. **In Italy and Tunisia, hotel proprietors are apt to ask you to leave your passport with them overnight as collateral. Even though this is an accepted custom, you are not *required* to leave it for any longer than it takes to write the number down.** According to Italian law, hotel owners must keep strict records of who is staying at their establishments; the police levy major fines on hotels that do not comply with this regulation.

United States Citizens may apply for a passport, valid for 10 years (five years if under 18) at any authorized federal or state courthouse or post office, or at a U.S. Passport Agency, located in Boston, Chicago, Honolulu, Houston, Los Angeles, Miami, New Orleans, New York, Philadelphia, San Francisco, Seattle, Stamford (CT), or Washington D.C. Parents must apply in person for children under age 13. You must apply in person if this is your first passport, if you're under age 18, or if your current passport is more than 12 years old or was issued before your 18th birthday. You must submit proof of U.S. citizenship (a certified birth certificate, certification of naturalization or of citizenship, or a previous passport), identification bearing your signature and either your photograph or physical description, and two identical, passport-size photographs. It will cost US$65 (under 18 US$40). You can renew your passport by mail or in person for US$55. Processing takes two to four weeks. Passport agencies offer rush service for a surcharge of US$30 if you have proof that you're departing within ten working days (e.g., an airplane ticket or itinerary). Abroad, a U.S. embassy or consulate can usually issue a new passport, given proof of citizenship. If your passport is lost or stolen in the U.S., report it in writing to Passport Services, U.S. Department of State, 111 19th St. NW, Washington D.C., 20522-1705 or to the nearest passport agency. For more info, contact the U.S. Passport Information's 24-hr. recorded message (tel. (202) 647-0518).

Canada Application forms in English and French are available at all passport offices, post offices, and most travel agencies. Citizens may apply in person at any one of 28 regional passport offices across Canada. Along with the application form, you must provide citizenship documentation and a CDN$60 fee. The application must also be signed by an eligible guarantor. Processing takes approximately five business days for in-person applications and three weeks for mailed ones. A passport is valid for five years and is not renewable. If a passport is lost abroad, you must be able to prove citizenship with another document. For additional info, call (800) 567-6868 (24hr.; from Canada only). Regional offices are located in Metro Toronto (tel. (416) 973-3251), Montréal (tel. (514) 283-2152), and Quebec (tel. (819) 994-3500). Refer to the booklet *Bon Voyage, But...* for further information and a list of Canadian embassies and consulates abroad. It is free from any passport office.

United Kingdom British citizens, British Dependent Territories citizens, British Nationals (overseas), and British Overseas citizens may apply for a full passport, valid for 10 years (five years if under 16). Apply in person or by mail to a passport office, located in London, Liverpool, Newport, Peterborough, Glasgow, or Belfast (UK£18). Processing by mail takes four to six weeks. The London office offers same-day, walk-in rush service, but you must arrive early in the morning.

Ireland Citizens can apply for a passport by mail to either the Department of Foreign Affairs, Passport Office, Setanta Centre, Molesworth St., Dublin 2 (tel. (01) 671 16 33), or the Passport Office, 1A South Mall, Cork (tel. (021) 627 25 25). Obtain an application at a local Garda station or request one from a passport office. The new Passport Express Service offers a two week turn-around and is available through post offices for an extra IR£3. Passports cost IR£45 and are valid for 10 years. Citizens under 18 or over 65 can request a three-year passport that costs IR£10.

Australia Citizens must apply for a passport in person at a post office, a passport office, or an Australian diplomatic mission overseas. An appointment may be necessary. Passport offices are located in Adelaide, Brisbane, Canberra City, Darwin, Hobart, Melbourne, Newcastle, Perth, and Sydney. A parent may file an application for a child who is under 18 and unmarried. Application fees are adjusted frequently. For more info, call toll-free (in Australia) 13 12 32.

New Zealand Application forms for passports are available in New Zealand from travel agents and Department of Internal Affairs Link Centres. Completed applications may be lodged at Link Centres and at overseas posts, or forwarded to the Passport Office, P.O. Box 10-526, Wellington, New Zealand. Processing time is 10 working days from receipt of a correctly completed application. An urgent passport service is also available. The application fee is NZ$80 in New Zealand, and NZ$130 for applications submitted from overseas under the standard service.

South Africa Citizens can apply for a passport at any Home Affairs Office. Two photos and either a birth certificate or an identity book must accompany a completed application. South African passports cost SAR80 and remain valid for 10 years. For more info, contact the nearest Department of Home Affairs Office.

VISAS

A **visa** is a stamp that permits you to visit another country; it is placed on your passport by a foreign government. Tourists from the U.S., Canada, Great Britain, Ireland, Australia, New Zealand, and South Africa do not need a visa to visit Italy for three months or less. If you intend to travel for more than three months, consider obtaining a long-term visa before departure. You may do so either by applying directly to the nearest Italian consulate or through the **Center for International Business and Travel (CIBT),** 25 West 43rd St., #1420, New York, NY 10036 (tel. (800) 925-2428 or (212) 575-2811 from NYC). The CIBT secures visas for travel to and from all countries for various fees. Travelers from countries other than those listed above should be sure to check with the Italian Government Travel Office or an Italian embassy or consulate; Italy may require visas from citizens of your country.

Entrance to Italy as a tourist does not include permission to study or work there. There are special requirements for **student and work visas,** which can be obtained from the nearest Italian consulate.

CUSTOMS: ENTERING

Make a list of any valuables you are bringing with you from home and register it with customs as you depart in order to avoid import duty charges upon your return. Do not attempt to carry firearms, explosives, ammunition, fireworks, controlled drugs, most plants and animals, or pornographic materials into Italy. To avoid problems when you transport prescription drugs, ensure that the bottles are clearly marked, and carry a copy of the prescription.

CUSTOMS: GOING HOME

Upon returning home, you must declare all articles you acquired abroad and must pay a duty on the value of those articles that exceed the allowance established by your country's customs service. Goods and gifts purchased at duty-free shops abroad are not exempt from duty or sales tax at your point of return; "duty-free" merely means that you need not pay a tax in the country of purchase.

United States Citizens returning home may bring US$400 worth of accompanying goods duty-free and must pay a 10% tax on the next US$1000. You must declare all purchases, so have sales slips ready. Goods are considered duty-free if they are for personal or household use (this includes gifts) and cannot include more than 100 cigars, 200 cigarettes (1 carton), and 1L of wine or liquor. You must be over 21 to bring liquor into the U.S. If you mail home personal goods of U.S. origin, you can avoid duty charges by marking the package "American goods returned." For more information, consult the brochure *Know Before You Go,* available from the U.S. Customs Service, Box 7407, Washington, D.C. 20044 (tel. (202) 927-6724).

Canada Citizens who remain abroad for at least one week may return with up to CDN$500 worth of goods duty-free once per calendar year. Canadian citizens or residents who travel for a period between 48 hours and six days can bring back up to CDN$200 with the exception of tobacco and alcohol. You are permitted to ship goods except tobacco and alcohol home under this exemption as long as you declare them when you arrive. Citizens of legal age (which varies by province) may import in-person up to 200 cigarettes, 50 cigars, 400g loose tobacco, 400 tobacco sticks, 1.14L wine or alcohol, and 24 355mL cans/bottles of beer; the value of these products is included in the CDN$500. For more information, write to Canadian Customs, 2265 St. Laurent Blvd., Ottawa, Ontario K1G 4K3 (tel. (613) 993 05 34).

United Kingdom Citizens or visitors arriving in the U.K. from outside the EU must declare any goods in excess of the following allowances: 200 cigarettes, 100 cigarillos, 50 cigars, or 250g tobacco; table wine (2L), strong liqueurs of over 22% alcohol content (1L), or sparkling wine and other liqueurs (2L); perfume (60 cc/mL), toilet water (250 cc/mL); and UK£145 worth of all other goods including gifts and souvenirs. You must be over 17 to import liquor or tobacco. These allowances also apply to duty-free purchases within the EU, with the exception of gifts and souvenirs, which has an allowance of UK£75. Goods obtained duty and tax paid for personal use (regulated according to set guide levels) within the EU do not require any further customs duty. For more info about U.K. customs, contact Her Majesty's Customs and Excise, Custom House, Nettleton Road, Heathrow Airport, Hounslow, Middlesex TW6 2LA (tel. (0181) 910 37 44; fax 910 37 65).

Ireland Citizens must declare everything in excess of IR£34 (IR£17 per traveler under 15 years of age) obtained outside the EU or duty- and tax-free in the EU above the following allowances: 200 cigarettes, 100 cigarillos, 50 cigars, or 250g tobacco; 1L liquor, 2L wine, or 2L still wine; 50g perfume or 250mL toilet water. Goods obtained duty and tax paid in another EU country up to a value of IR£460 (IR£115 per traveler under 15) will not be subject to additional customs duties. Travelers under 17 are not entitled to any allowance for tobacco or alcohol. For more information, contact The Revenue Commissioners, Dublin Castle (tel. (01) 679 27 77; fax 671 20 21; e-mail taxes@ior.ie; http:\\www.revenue.ie) or The Collector of Customs and Excise, The Custom House, Dublin 1.

Australia Citizens may import AUS$400 (under 18 AUS$200) of goods duty-free, in addition to the allowance of 1.125L alcohol and 250 cigarettes or 250g tobacco. You must be over 18 to import either of these substances. There is no limit to the amount of Australian and/or foreign cash that may be brought into or taken out of the country. However, amounts of AUS$5000 or more, or the equivalent in foreign currency, must be reported. All foodstuffs and animal products must be declared on arrival. For information, contact the Regional Director, Australian Customs Service, GPO Box 8, Sydney NSW 2001 (tel. (02) 213 20 00; fax 213 40 00).

New Zealand Citizens may bring home up to NZ$700 worth of goods duty-free if they are intended for personal use or are unsolicited gifts. The concession is 200 cigarettes (1 carton), 250g tobacco, 50 cigars or a combination of all three not to exceed 250g. You may also bring in 4.5L of beer or wine and 1.125L of liquor. Only travelers over 17 may bring tobacco or alcoholic beverages into the country. For more information, consult the *New Zealand Customs Guide for Travelers,* available from customs offices, or contact New Zealand Customs, 50 Anzac Ave., Box 29, Auckland (tel. (09) 377 35 20; fax 309 29 78).

South Africa Citizens may import duty-free up to 400 cigarettes, 50 cigars, 250g tobacco, 2L wine, 1L of spirits, 50mL perfume, 250mL toilet water, and other items up to a value of SAR500. Amounts exceeding this limit but not up to SAR10,000 are taxable at 20%. For more specific information contact the Commissioner for Customs and Excise, Private Bag X47, Pretoria 0001. This agency distributes the pamphlet *South African Customs Information,* for visitors and residents who travel abroad.

South Africans residing in the U.S. should contact the Embassy of South Africa, 3051 Massachusetts Ave. NW, Washington D.C. 20008 (tel. (202) 232-4400; fax 244-9417) or the South African Home Annex, 3201 New Mexico Ave. NW, #380, Washington D.C. 20016 (tel. (202) 966-1650).

YOUTH, STUDENT, & TEACHER IDENTIFICATION

The **International Student Identity Card (ISIC)** is the most widely accepted form of student identification. Flashing this card may procure you discounts for sights, theaters, museums, accommodations, train, ferry, and airplane travel, and other services throughout Europe. Make a habit of presenting it and asking about student discounts wherever you go (*c'è uno sconto studentesco?*). Don't be surprised, though, if it is not honored. Student discounts are rare and often exclusively for Italian or EU students. It never hurts to try, but don't expect much. ISIC also provides accident insurance of up to US$3000 with no daily limit. In addition, cardholders have access to a toll-free Traveler's Assistance hotline whose multilingual staff can provide help in medical, legal, and financial emergencies overseas.

ISICs are issued by many travel offices, including Council Travel, Let's Go Travel, and STA Travel in the U.S.; Travel CUTS in Canada; and any of the organizations under the auspices of the International Student Travel Confederation (ISTC) around the world (see **Budget Travel Agencies,** p. 37). When you apply for the card, request a copy of the International Student Identity Card Handbook, which lists some of the available discounts by country. The card is valid until fall semester of the following year. The fee is US$18. Applicants must be at least 12 years old and degree-seeking students of a secondary or post-secondary school. Because of the proliferation of phony ISICs, many airlines and some other services now require another proof of student identity, either a signed and stamped letter from your school's registrar attesting to your student status or your school ID card. The US$19 **International Teacher Identity Card (ITIC)** offers similar but limited discounts, as well as medical insurance coverage. For more info on these handy cards consult the organization's web site (http://www.istc.org).

Federation of International Youth Travel Organizations (FIYTO) issues a discount card to travelers who are not students but are under 26. Known as the **GO 25 Card,** this one-year card offers many of the same benefits as the ISIC, and most organizations that sell the ISIC also sell the Go 25 Card. A brochure that lists discounts is free when you purchase the card. To apply, bring proof of birthdate (a copy of your birth certificate, a passport, or a valid driver's license) and a passport-sized photo. The fee is US$16, CDN$15, or UK£5. (See **FIYTO,** p. 4.)

INTERNATIONAL DRIVER'S PERMIT

Italy honors the IDP, although it is not required for car rental in most places. It is probably a good idea to get one anyway, just in case you're in a small town where the police do not read or speak English. The IDP must be issued in your own country before you depart and must be accompanied by your regular driver's license. In Italy you may also need a "green card," or International Insurance Certificate, which can be obtained through the car rental agency.

American Automobile Association (AAA), 1000 AAA Drive (mail stop 28), Heathrow, FL 32746-5080 (tel. (407) 444-4245; fax 444-4247). The IDP is available from any AAA branch in the U.S. or by mail from the address above. The permit is valid for 1 year and costs US$10.

Canadian Automobile Association, CAA Central Ontario, 60 Commerce Valley Dr. E, Thornhill, Ontario L3T 7P9 (tel. (416) 221-4300). The IDP is available from any CAA branch in Canada or by mail from the address above (CDN$10).

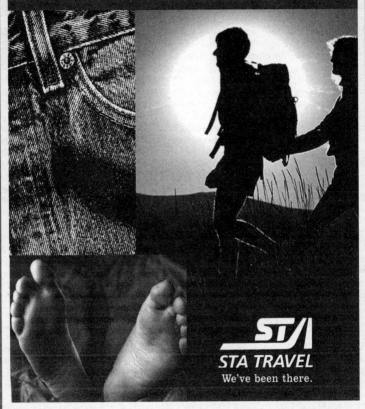

Money Matters

This book's prices and exchange rates were compiled in the summer of 1996. Since rates fluctuate considerably, be sure to confirm them before you go. **Prices may have changed as well, so do not demand that businesses honor the ones listed. Your trip will probably be easier if you are financially flexible.**

Generally speaking, you can assume that 10,000 lire equals about six bucks (at the current exchange rate, it's actually worth a little more). When estimating your budget, remember that you will probably need to keep handy a larger amount than usual. Don't sacrifice your health or safety for a cheaper tab.

CURRENCY AND EXCHANGE

US$1 = 1514lire (L)	**L1000 = US$0.66**
CDN$1 = L1102	**L1000 = CDN$0.91**
UK£1 = L2350	**L1000 = UK£0.43**
IR£1 = L2441	**L1000 = IR£0.41**
AUS$1 = L1176	**L1000 = AUS$0.85**
NZ$1 = L1031	**L1000 = NZ$0.97**
SAR1 = L337	**L1000 = SAR2.97**

The Italian currency unit is the *lira* (plural: *lire*). Coins are minted in L50, L100, L200 and L500, and the most common bills are L1000, L2000, L5000, L10,000, L50,000, and L100,000. We recommended that, before you leave home, you buy enough *lire* to last for the first 24-72 hours of your trip in order to avoid a frenzied exchange (at terrible rates) at the airport when you arrive. Otherwise, it is cheaper to buy *lire* in Italy than at home. When exchanging money in Italy, look for *"cambio"* signs, and shop around. Try to avoid exchanging at luxury hotels, train stations, and airports; the best rates are usually found at banks. Changing currency is best done in the morning; **banking hours** are usually Monday through Friday 8:30am-1:30pm, with an extra hour in the afternoon (often 3-4pm). Remember that you will have to pay a commission each time (either a percentage or a fixed fee). To minimize such losses, exchange large sums at once, but never more than you can safely carry around. It also helps to plan ahead: you don't want to get caught without *lire* at night or on a Sunday.

TRAVELER'S CHECKS

Traveler's checks are the safest way to carry large sums of money. Several agencies and many banks sell them, usually for face value plus a 1% commission. Buy them in your home currency (none of the major companies listed below sell checks in *lire*). They are refundable if lost or stolen, and many issuing agencies offer additional services to travelers. Keep in mind that traveler's checks are less readily accepted in small towns than in large cities. Be sure to bring your passport with you when you plan to use traveler's checks; some places won't accept them otherwise. Buying checks in U.S. dollars or British pounds may also facilitate the exchange process.

Refunds on lost or stolen checks can be time-consuming. To accelerate the process and avoid red tape, *keep check receipts and records in a separate place from the checks themselves.* Leave a photocopy of check serial numbers with someone at home as back-up in case you lose your copy. Never countersign checks until you're prepared to cash them. Keep careful track of your usage; record the number of each check as you cash it.

American Express (tel. (800) 221-7282 in the U.S. and Canada; (0800) 52 13 13 in the U.K.; (008) 25 19 02 in Australia; (0800) 44 10 68 in New Zealand). Elsewhere, call U.S. collect at (801) 964-6665. **In Italy, call (167) 87 20 00.** American Express traveler's checks are the most widely recognized worldwide and easiest to replace if lost or stolen—just call the information number or the American Express Travel Office nearest you. American Express offices cash their own checks commission-free (except where prohibited by law) and sell checks that can be signed by either of 2 people traveling together ("Cheque for Two"). Checks are available in 11 currencies and can be purchased at American Express Travel Service offices, banks, and American Automobile Association offices. (AAA members can buy them commission-free.) Cardmembers can also purchase checks at American Express Dispensers in Travel Service Offices of airports, or by ordering them by phone (tel. (800) ORDER-TC (673-3782)). Traveler's checks are also available over America Online. Request American Express's *Traveler's Companion,* which gives office addresses and stolen check hotlines for each European country.

Citicorp sells both Citicorp and **Citicorp Visa** traveler's checks in 7 currencies (tel. (800) 645-6556 in the U.S. and Canada, (1812) 97 47 81 in the UK; from elsewhere call the U.S. collect at (813) 623-1709). Commission is 1-2% on check purchases. Checkholders are automatically enrolled for 45 days in the Travel Assist Program (hotline (800) 250-4377, or collect (202) 296-8728), which provides access to English-speaking doctors and lawyers. Citicorp's World Courier Service guarantees hand-delivery of traveler's checks anywhere in the world.

Thomas Cook MasterCard (tel. (800) 223-9920 in the U.S. and Canada; elsewhere call the U.S. collect (609) 987-7300; in the U.K. call (0800) 62 21 01 toll-free, (1733) 50 29 95 or 31 89 50 collect). Checks available in 12 currencies. Commission ranges from 1-2% for purchases. Try buying (and cashing) the checks at a Thomas Cook office for potentially lower commissions.

Visa (tel. (800) 227-6811 in the U.S.; (0800) 89 54 92 in the U.K.; from elsewhere call the U.K. at (1733) 31 89 49, a toll call for which the charges can be reversed) provides info on where you can buy their checks locally. Any kind of Visa traveler's checks (Barclays or Citicorp) can be reported lost at the Visa number.

CREDIT CARDS

Credit cards for the budget traveler can be a blessing or a curse. On the dark side, many smaller establishments will not accept them, while those enticing, pricier, big-city establishments accept them all too willingly. Relying extensively on credit cards while abroad could be a big mistake, especially if doing so leads you to spend more than you would otherwise. However, used sparingly, credit cards can be a great boon to careful spenders and an invaluable resource in case of emergency. Perhaps the most important benefit is that holders of most major credit cards can now get cash advances around the clock from associated banks and automatic teller machines (ATMs) throughout Europe, including cities in Italy. Because you make your withdrawal in foreign currency, you benefit from the wholesale exchange rate. This service requires you to have a PIN number, available from your issuing bank. (Check with them about charges, interest rates, and ATM locations as well.) Pay your bill quickly to avoid ruinous interest rates for such advances; only withdraw what you can pay back immediately (or have someone at home take care of it while you're away). You can also reduce conversion fees by charging purchases instead of changing traveler's checks. Remember that MasterCard and Visa have different names in Europe ("EuroCard" and "Carte Bleue", respectively).

Lost or stolen cards should be reported *immediately,* or you may be held responsible for forged charges. Write down the card cancellation telephone numbers and keep them in a safe place separate from your cards. Always be sure that the carbon receipt has been torn into pieces, and watch as your card is being imprinted; an imprint onto a blank slip can be used later to charge merchandise in your name.

CASH CARDS AND ATMS

Cash cards (ATM cards) function throughout Italy at varying rates of success. You will probably want to access your own personal bank account whenever you're in need of funds, so check to see what network your bank belongs to (Cirrus and Plus are two of the most common) and how much they'll charge you for each transaction. Happily, ATMs get the same wholesale exchange rate as credit cards and often offer menus in English. It is advisable to exchange as much as you can handle safely in order to minimize fees, but there is usually a limit to the amount of money you can withdraw per day. Computer network failures are also common. Be sure to memorize your PIN code in numeral form since machines abroad often don't have letters on the keys. Also, if your PIN is longer than four digits, ask your bank whether the first four digits will work, or whether you need a shorter number. Many teller machines are on the outside walls of banks, so beware of thieves when withdrawing money. Also be sure that the ATM is actually affiliated with a bank; fake ATMs on random walls may be clever scams to steal your card.

ATM fraud is not uncommon. In the event that you should not receive the correct amount of cash, be sure to **keep your receipt.**

MONEY FROM HOME

Sending money overseas is a complicated, expensive, and often extremely frustrating adventure. Do your best to avoid it by carrying a credit card or a separate stash of emergency traveler's checks.

The easiest way to get money from home is to bring an **American Express Card.** American Express allows card holders to draw cash from their checking accounts at any of its major offices and many of its representatives' offices (up to US$1000 every 21 days; no service charge; no interest). American Express also offers Express Cash, which allows card holders to withdraw up to US$1000 in a 7-day period. There is a 2% transaction fee for each cash withdrawal (US$2.50 minimum). To enroll in Express Cash, cardmembers may call 1-800-CASH NOW/227-4669 (outside the U.S. call collect (904) 565-7875). Another approach is to wire money through the **international money transfer services** operated by **Western Union** (tel. (800) 325-6000 or (167) 01 38 39 toll-free in Italy). Rates vary with the amount of money sent and range from US$15 to US$50.

Finally, if you are an American in a life-or-death situation, you can have money sent to you via the **Overseas Citizens Service, American Citizens Services,** Consular Affairs, Public Affairs Staff, Room 4831, U.S. Dept. of State, Washington, D.C. 20520 (tel. (202) 647-5225, after hours and on holidays, 647-4000; fax 647-3000; http://travel.state.gov). For a fee of US$15, the State Department will forward money within hours to the nearest consular office, which will then pass it on according to instructions. In a dire emergency, cable the State Department through Western Union.

VALUE-ADDED TAX

The **Value-Added Tax (VAT,** in Italian, *imposto sul valore aggiunta,* or **IVA**) is a form of sales tax levied in the European Union. VAT is generally part of the price paid on goods and services. Tourists who do not reside in an EU country have a legal right to a refund of the VAT, but only for major purchases. The receipt, purchases, and purchaser's passport must be presented to and stamped by the Customs Office as you leave the EU, and the invoice must be returned to the store. Some of the more upscale stores offer "Tax-Free Shopping for Tourists," which enables you to get your VAT refund in cash when leaving from the airport or crossing borders.

BARGAINING

Bargaining is common in Italy, but use discretion. It is appropriate at outdoor markets, with street vendors, and over unmetered taxi fares (always settle your price *before* getting into the cab). Haggling over prices is out of place almost everywhere else, however, especially in large stores. Hotel haggling is more successful in uncrowded, smaller *pensioni* (*Let's Go* mentions when such activity is common). If you don't speak Italian, at least memorize the numbers. Let the merchant make the first offer and counter with one-half to two-thirds of his or her bid. The merchant will probably act extremely offended by your offer, even if the context warrants bargaining, but stand firm. Never offer anything you are unwilling to pay—you are expected to buy if the merchant accepts your price.

Safety and Security

If you are ever in a potentially dangerous situation anywhere in Italy, call the toll-free **Emergency Assistance Numbers:** 113 or 112. The nationwide telephone number for the fire department is 115, and the *Soccorso Stradale* or ACI (Italian Automobile Club) can be reached at 116.

SAFETY

Tourists are particularly vulnerable to crime for two reasons: they carry large amounts of cash and are not as savvy as locals. To avoid unwanted attention, blend in as much as possible. The gawking camera-toter is a more obvious target than the low-profile look-alike, so time spent learning local style will be well worth it. If you find yourself lost, it is better to walk purposefully into a *caffè* or shop to check your map than to check it on a street corner. Muggings are more often impromptu than planned. Try to appear confident; walking with nervous glances can be a tip that you have something valuable to protect. In addition, sunglasses can make almost everyone look self-assured (or at least cool).

When you explore a new city, extra vigilance may be wise, but don't let fear inhibit your ability to experience another culture. Ask the tourist office or the manager of your hotel for advice on areas to avoid. If you feel unsafe, stay in hotels with either a curfew or a night attendant. Daytime precautions should become nighttime mandates. In particular, stay near crowded and well-lit areas and do not attempt to traverse parks, parking lots, or any other large, deserted areas.

Exercise extreme caution when using pools or beaches without lifeguards. Hidden rocks and shallow depths may cause serious injury or even death. Heed warning signs about dangerous undertows. When renting scubadiving equipment, make sure that it is up to par before taking the plunge. If you are driving a car, learn your route before you go and familiarize yourself with local driving signals. Use seatbelts, carseats, and parking garages.

There is no sure-fire set of precautions that will protect you from all of the situations you might encounter when you travel. However, a good self-defense course will give you more concrete strategies for countering different types of aggression. Unfortunately, it might also cost you more money than your trip. **Model Mugging,** a national organization with offices in several major cities, teaches a very effective, comprehensive course on self-defense. Contact Lynn S. Auerbach on the East Coast (tel. (617) 232-7900), Alice Tibits in the Midwest (tel. (612) 645-6189), and Cori Couture on the West Coast (tel. (415) 592-7300). Course prices vary from $400-500 and are offered for women and men. Community colleges frequently offer self-defense courses at more affordable prices.

For official **United States Department of State** travel advisories, including information on crime and security, call their 24-hour hotline at (202) 647-5225. To order publications, including a pamphlet entitled *A Safe Trip Abroad,* write to the Superintendent of Documents, U.S. Government Printing Office, Washington, D.C. 20402, or call (202) 783-3238.

SECURITY

Carry all your valuables (including your passport, railpass, traveler's checks, and airline ticket) either in a **money belt** or **neckpouch** stashed securely inside your clothing. These will protect you from skilled thieves who slash backpacks and fanny packs with razors. Making **photocopies** of important documents and credit cards will help you recover them more easily; carry one copy separate from the documents and leave another at home. You may also want to keep some money separate from the rest in case of theft. Memorize your calling card number, and be discrete when using it. Never count your money in public.

If you carry a purse, buy a sturdy leather one with a secure clasp. Carry it across your body on the side away from the street with the clasp against you. Even these precautions do not always suffice; moped riders who snatch purses and backpacks often tote knives to cut the straps. For luggage, buy some small combination padlocks which slip through two zippers. Be particularly watchful of your belongings on buses or in thick crowds; if possible, carry your backpack in front of you where you can see it. Don't check baggage on trains, especially if you're switching lines, and don't trust *anyone* to "watch your bag for a second." In hostels, sleep with your wallet under your pillow as an additional precaution. Keep your valuables on you in low-budget hotels, where someone else may have a passkey, and in dormitory-style surroundings—otherwise a trip to the shower could cost you a passport or wallet. Bring a padlock to use on lockers, and try to leave valuables at home.

Among the more colorful aspects of Italian cities are the **con artists.** Hustlers often work in groups, and children, unfortunately, are among the most effective at the game. Although there is a great variety of tricks, be aware of certain classics: sob stories that require money, or saliva spit onto your shoulder, distracting you for enough time for someone to snatch your bag. Another common one, especially with small children, is to shove a newspaper or other large item directly under your face, allowing the children to clean you out while you can't see what they're doing. Be especially alert with suspicious strangers. Do not respond or make eye contact. Walk quickly and purposefully away, keeping a solid grip on your belongings. Do your best to keep threatening people away from your body; shouting or making large, attention-grabbing gestures often sends would-be pickpockets toward a quieter, more passive person. Contact the police if a hustler is particularly aggressive.

Trains are notoriously easy spots for robberies. Professionals wait for tourists to fall asleep and then carry off everything they can. When traveling in pairs, sleep in alternating shifts. When alone use good judgment in selecting a train compartment: never stay in an empty one, and try to share a compartment with older travelers or women. Keep valuables on your person, and try to sleep on top bunks with your luggage stored above you or in bed with you. Sleeping in a car is very dangerous, but if you must, park in a well-lit area as close to a police station or 24-hr. service station as possible. Sleeping outside can be even riskier; camping is recommended only in official, supervised campsites.

DRUGS AND ALCOHOL

Travelers should avoid drugs altogether. All foreigners in Italy are subject to Italian law, where drugs (including marijuana) are illegal. Your home country is essentially powerless to interfere in a foreign court. Even if you don't use drugs, beware of any person who asks you to carry a package or drive a car across the border. If you carry prescription drugs, it is vital to have a note from your doctor among your important documents. Avoid public drunkenness; it is dangerous and rude, and it may attract police attention.

Health

For **medical emergencies** in Italy, dial 113. For **police assistance**, dial 112. **First aid** (*Pronto Soccorso*) is available in airports, ports, and train stations. *Let's Go* provides the name of a **pharmacy** *(farmacia)* in each city, which in turn has a list of other pharmacies open all night and on Sundays.

BEFORE YOU GO

Though no amount of planning can guarantee an accident-free trip, preparation can help minimize the likelihood of contracting a disease and maximize the chances of receiving effective health care in the case of an emergency.

For minor health problems on the road, a compact **first-aid kit** should suffice. You can buy a ready-made kit, but it's just as easy to assemble your own. Items you might want to include are bandages, aspirin or another pain killer, antiseptic soap or antibiotic cream, a thermometer in a sturdy case, a Swiss Army knife with tweezers, a decongestant, a motion sickness remedy, medicine for diarrhea and stomach problems, sunscreen, burn ointment, and an elastic bandage.

People with asthma or allergies should be aware that larger Italian cities often have visibly high levels of air pollution, particularly during the summer, and that, as elsewhere in Europe, "non-smoking" areas are almost nonexistent. Take an **antihistamine, decongestant, inhaler,** etc. (be it prescription or over-the-counter), since there may not be an Italian equivalent with the correct dosage.

Travelers with chronic medical conditions should consult their physicians before leaving the country. Always go prepared with any **medication** you may need while away, as well as a copy of the prescription and/or a statement from your doctor, especially if you will be bringing insulin, syringes, or any narcotics into Italy (some drugs legal at home may not be legal there). Be sure to keep all medication with you in your carry-on luggage. If you wear glasses or contacts, take a copy of your prescription or bring an extra pair of glasses with you from home.

In your passport, write the names of people you wish to be contacted in case of a medical emergency, and also list any allergies or medical conditions of which you would want doctors to be aware. Take a look at your immunization records before you go. Although Europe is fairly safe, it doesn't hurt to make sure your vaccines are up to date (although the needle might). Any traveler with an important medical condition that cannot be easily recognized may want to obtain a **Medic Alert Identification Tag,** which indicates the nature of the bearer's problem, as well as the number of a 24-hr. collect-call information number (US$35 the first year, US$15 annually thereafter). Contact Medic Alert Foundation, 2323 Colorado Ave., Turlock, CA 95382 (tel. (800) 825-3785). The **American Diabetes Association,** 1660 Duke St., Alexandria, VA 22314 (tel. (800) 232-3472) provides copies of an article entitled "Travel and Diabetes" and ID cards in 18 languages explaining the condition.

Let's Go should not be your only information source on common health problems for tourists in Italy. For general health information, send for the **American Red Cross's** *First-Aid and Safety Handbook* (US$15); contact the ARC at 285 Columbus Ave., Boston, MA 02116-5114 (tel. (800) 564-1234), or look for the manual in your local bookstore. In the U.S., the ARC also offers many first-aid and CPR courses, which are well-taught and relatively inexpensive. The **United States Center for Disease Control** (based in Atlanta, Georgia) is an excellent source of general info on health for travelers around the world, and maintains an international travelers' hotline (tel. (404) 332-4559; fax 332-4565; http://www.cdc.gov). You can also write directly to the Centers for Disease Control and Prevention, Travelers' Health, 1600 Clifton Rd. NE, Atlanta, GA 30333. The CDC publishes the booklet "Health Information for International Travelers" (US$14), an annual global rundown of disease, immunization, and general health advice, including risks in particular countries.

If you are concerned about being able to access medical support while traveling, contact one of these two services: **Global Emergency Medical Services (GEMS)** provides 24-hour international medical assistance, coordinated through registered nurses. The staff has on-line access to your medical information, your primary physician, and a worldwide network of screened, credentialed English-speaking doctors and hospitals. Subscribers also receive a pocket-sized personal medical record that contains vital information in case of emergencies. For more information call (800) 860-1111; fax (770) 475-0058; or write to 2001 Westside Dr., #120, Alpharetta, GA 30201. The **International Association for Medical Assistance to Travelers (IAMAT)** offers a membership ID card, a directory of English-speaking doctors around the world who treat members for a set fee schedule, and detailed charts on immunization requirements and sanitation. Membership is free, though donations are appreciated and used for further research. Contact chapters in the **U.S.,** 417 Center St., Lewiston, NY 14092 (tel. (716) 754-4883; fax (519) 836-3412; e-mail iamat@sentex.net; http://www.sentex.net/iamat); **Canada,** 40 Regal Rd., Guelph, Ontario, N1K 1B5 (tel. (519) 836-0102) or 1287 St. Clair Ave. W, Toronto, Ontario, M6E 1B8 (tel. (416) 652-0137; fax (519) 836-3412); or **New Zealand,** P.O. Box 5049, Christchurch 5.

The **United States State Department** compiles Consular Information Sheets on health, entry requirements, and other issues for all countries of the world. Call the Overseas Citizens' Services at (202) 647-5225. If you have access to a fax, you can request these sheets by dialing 647-3000 directly from the fax machine and then following the recorded instructions. You can also obtain copies of the information from the State Department's regional passport agencies in the U.S., from the field offices of the U.S. Chamber of Commerce, and from U.S. embassies and consulates abroad. If you prefer, you can even send a self-addressed, stamped envelope to the Overseas Citizens' Services, Bureau of Consular Affairs, Room 4811, U.S. Department of State, Washington, D.C. 20520. If you are HIV-positive, call (202) 647-1488 for country-specific entry requirements or write to the Bureau of Consular Affairs, Department of State, Washington, D.C. 20520.

ON-THE-ROAD AILMENTS

Common sense is the simplest prescription for good health while you travel: eat well, drink plenty of liquids, get enough sleep, and don't overexert yourself. While traveling, pay attention to signals of pain and discomfort that your body may send you. Because of travel exhaustion and possible exposure to foreign organisms (microbes, that is), you are more susceptible to illness while you are on the road. Some of the milder symptoms that you may safely ignore at home may be signs of more serious problems overseas. The following paragraphs list some health problems commonly experienced by travelers to Europe.

Italy, especially the south, scorches in the summer. Avoid **heat exhaustion:** relax in hot weather, drink lots of non-alcoholic fluids, and lie down inside if you are getting too hot. Continuous heat stress can eventually lead to **heatstroke,** characterized by rising body temperature, severe headache, and cessation of sweating. Wear a hat, sunglasses, and a lightweight, longsleeve shirt or pants (if you can stand it) to avoid heatstroke. Victims should be cooled off with wet towels and taken to a doctor as soon as possible. These conditions are potentially fatal.

Always drink enough liquids to keep your urine clear. Alcoholic beverages are dehydrating, as are coffee, strong tea, and caffeinated sodas. If you'll be sweating a lot, be sure to eat enough salty food to prevent electrolyte depletion, characterized by severe headaches. Less debilitating, but still dangerous, is **sunburn.** If you're prone to sunburn, bring sunscreen with you. It's often more expensive and hard to find when traveling. Apply it liberally and often to avoid burns and the risk of skin cancer. If you get sunburned, drink more fluids than usual.

Extreme cold is just as dangerous as heat—overexposure to cold brings the risk of **hypothermia.** Warning signs are easy to detect as body temperature drops rapidly, rendering the body unable to produce heat. Victims may experience shivers, poor coordination, exhaustion, slurred speech, drowsiness, hallucinations, or amnesia. *Do not let hypothermia victims fall asleep.* If they are in the advanced stages, their body temperatures will drop more, and if they lose consciousness they may die. Seek medical help as soon as possible. To avoid hypothermia, keep dry and stay out of the wind. In wet weather, wool and most synthetics, such as pile, will keep you warm but most other fabrics, especially cotton, will make you colder. Dress in layers, wear a hat, and watch for **frostbite** when the temperature is below freezing. Look for skin that has turned white, waxy, and cold. If you find frostbite, do not rub the skin. Drink warm beverages, get dry, and slowly warm the area with dry fabric or steady body contact. Take serious cases to a doctor as soon as possible.

Travelers to **high altitudes** should allow their bodies a couple of days to adjust to the lower atmospheric oxygen levels before engaging in any strenuous activity. Be careful about drinking alcohol when hiking since one alcoholic beverage on a mountaintop has the same effect as three at a lower altitude.

If you're going to be doing a lot of walking, remember to treat your most valuable resource well: **lavish your feet with attention,** or at least change your socks. Wear good walking shoes, apply talcum powder to keep your feet dry, and use moleskin to pad hotspots before they become excruciating blisters. Also, take along some quick-energy foods. You will need to drink plenty of fluids (to prevent dehydration and constipation). Carry a water bottle, and drink from it even when you don't feel thirsty. Italian water is generally safe to drink unless marked *"non potabile,"* or unless it is running water on public transportation (ferries, trains, etc.). Relying on bottled mineral water for a while at the start of your trip minimizes chances of a bad reaction to the few unfamiliar microbes in Italian water.

Food poisoning can spoil any trip. Be cautious with street vendors, tap water, and perishable food carried for hours in a hot backpack. One of the most common symptoms associated with eating and drinking in another country is **diarrhea.** Many people carry over-the-counter remedies (such as Imodium AD or Pepto-Bismol), but such remedies can complicate serious infections; don't use them if you suspect you have been exposed to contaminated food or water, which may have put you at risk for cholera, typhoid fever, and other diseases. Dehydration is the most common side effect of diarrhea; the best remedy is a teaspoon of sugar or honey and a pinch of salt in eight ounces of clean water. Rest, and let the dastardly disease run its course.

Women traveling in unsanitary conditions are vulnerable to **bladder infection,** a very common and severely uncomfortable bacterial disease which causes a burning sensation and painful, difficult urination. Drink enormous amounts of vitamin C-rich juice and plenty of water, and urinate frequently. Untreated bladder infections can lead to *very* serious kidney infections. Treat an infection as best you can while on the road; if it persists, take time out to see a doctor and definitely check with one when you get home. If you often develop vaginal yeast infections, consider taking along your own over-the-counter medicine. Maggie and Gemma Moss's *Handbook for Women Travellers* (published by Piatkus Books) provides more extensive advice.

If you plan to **romp in the forest,** learn of any regional hazards. Poison ivy, poison oak, and poison sumac are plants whose surfaces cause insufferable itchiness if touched. In addition, research the indigenous snakes, spiders, and insects of the regions you are visiting. Insect repellent is a must in overgrown or forested areas. When hiking in such regions, maximize clothing coverage; long sleeves and pants tucked into boots make it harder for those biting insects to get at you and also reduce your chances of getting scratched by brambles. Watch for ticks, which may carry Lyme and other diseases. Brush them off or remove them with tweezers; do not burn them or coat them with petroleum jelly. Lyme disease is a bacterial infection which may start with a bull's-eye rash around the bite and can lead to problems in the joints, heart, and nervous system if antibiotics are not administered early.

Travelers going on to **Tunisia** should be careful to ensure that their food is well-cooked and their water pure, since traveler's diarrhea and parasitic infections are common in North Africa. You may also want to see a doctor before you leave for **hepatitis A** and **typhoid fever** vaccines, especially if you plan to travel in rural areas.

AIDS, HIV, AND STDS

On or off the road, you should be concerned about **Acquired Immune Deficiency Syndrome (AIDS),** transmitted through the exchange of body fluids with an infected individual (HIV-positive). The World Health Organization estimates that there are around 13 million people infected with the HIV virus. Over 90% of adults newly infected acquired HIV through heterosexual sex; women now represent 50% of all new diagnoses. In addition, Italy has one of the highest HIV rates in Europe.

The easiest mode of HIV transmission is through direct blood to blood contact with an HIV+ person; *never* share intravenous drug, tattooing, or other needles. The most common mode of transmission is sexual intercourse. Remember that *it is impossible to tell who may be infected* without a blood test. Health professionals recommend the use of latex condoms; follow the instructions on the packet. Casual contact (including drinking from the same glass or using the same eating utensils as an infected person) does not pose a risk.

For more information on AIDS, call the **U.S. Center for Disease Control's** 24-hour hotline at (800) 342-2437 (Spanish (800) 344-7332, daily 8am-2am). In Europe, write to the **World Health Organization,** Attn: Global Program on AIDS, 20 Avenue Appia, 1211 Geneva 27, Switzerland (tel. (22) 791 21 11), for international statistics on AIDS. You can also write to the **Bureau of Consular Affairs,** CA/P/PA, Department of State, Washington, D.C. 20520. Council's brochure, *Travel Safe: AIDS and International Travel,* is available at all Council Travel offices (see **Budget Travel Agencies,** p. 37).

Sexually transmitted diseases (STDs) such as gonorrhea, chlamydia, genital warts, syphilis, and herpes are a lot easier to catch than HIV. It's a wise idea to actually *look* at your partner's genitals before you have sex. If anything seems amiss, that should be a warning signal. When having sex, condoms may protect you from certain STDs, but oral or even tactile contact can lead to transmission.

There are no restrictions on travelers with HIV or AIDS entering Italy, nor is there any obligation to report your condition. Italians are generally very sensible about medical treatment, and the medical professionals will not pry if you get tested. **Confirm that your test is either confidential or anonymous.** AIDS education is becoming more prevalent throughout the country, and you will probably not have any problems finding condoms *(preservativi)* at any pharmacy. The **toll-free AIDS number** for Italy is (167) 86 10 61; the hotline is open Mon.-Fri. 1-6pm.

AIDS tests can be performed at any **Analisi Cliniche** (a private lab that handles all sorts of tests, from allergies to pregnancy). Look in the Yellow Pages under *Analisi* for labs, or contact one of the following *analisi cliniche* located in Rome:

Unione Sanitaria Internazionale, Via V. Orsini, 18 (tel. (06) 321 50 53), north of the Vatican, off Piazza della Libertà; or Via Machiavelli, 22 (tel. 70 45 35 44), Metro Linea A, Vittorio Emanuele stop. English spoken. Open for info 7am-7pm. Open for tests 7-11am.

Analisi Cliniche Luisa, Via Padova, 96A (tel. (06) 44 29 14 06). Take Metro Linea B to Piazza Bologna; it's just south of Viale delle Province. Pregnancy, STD, and HIV (L110,000) tests. Open Mon.-Fri. 7:30am-6pm, Sat. 8am-2pm.

GYNECOLOGY AND CONTRACEPTION

If you are heterosexual and sexually active, you will need to consider contraception. Reliable devices may be difficult to come by while traveling; bring enough to allow for possible loss or extended stays. Women on the Pill should bring a prescription, since it comes in many forms. In Italy, **condoms** *(preservativi)* can be bought over-_the-counter at pharmacies and some supermarkets.

Analisi Cliniche will perform tests for venereal disease *(malattia venerea)* and pregnancy, as well as pap smears and cryotherapy. You can also buy over-the-counter home pregnancy tests at Italian pharmacies.

Abortion is legal in Italy, although not as a means of birth control. Local health units called *consultori* advise women on rights and procedures. Contact a hospital or clinic in Italy for more information.

Insurance

Beware of buying unnecessary travel coverage. Your current policies may well extend to many travel-related accidents. **Medical insurance** (especially university policies) often covers costs incurred abroad, although **Medicare's** coverage is usually only valid for travel in Mexico and Canada. Canadians are protected by their home province's health insurance plan for up to 90 days after leaving the country; check with the provincial Ministry of Health or Health Plan Headquarters for details. Australia has a Reciprocal Health Care Agreement (RCHA) with Italy, providing tourists with basic hospital and medical coverage in case of acute illness or accident. Contact the

Commonwealth Department of Human Services and Health for more complete information. Your **homeowners' insurance** (or your family's coverage) often covers theft during travel. Homeowners are generally covered against loss of travel documents (passport, plane ticket, railpass, etc.) up to US$500.

ISIC and **ITIC** provide US$3000 worth of accident and illness insurance and US$100 per day for up to 60 days of hospitalization. They also offer up to US$1000 for accidental death or dismemberment and up to US$25,000 for injuries due to an airline or for emergency evacuation due to illness. The cards also give access to a toll-free Traveler's Assistance hotline (in the U.S. and Canada (800) 626-2427; elsewhere call collect to the U.S. (713) 267-2525). The multilingual staff can provide help in emergencies overseas. **Council** offers the inexpensive Trip-Safe plan with options covering medical treatment and hospitalization, accidents, baggage loss, and even charter flights missed due to illness; both Council and **STA** also offer a more expensive, more comprehensive plan. **American Express** cardholders receive automatic car-rental and flight insurance on purchases made with the card (tel. (800) 528-4800 for customer service).

Insurance companies usually require a copy of the police report for thefts, or evidence of having paid medical expenses (doctor's statements, receipts) before they will honor a claim. There may also be time limits on filing for reimbursement. Always carry policy numbers and proof of insurance, and try to have documents written in English. Check with the insurance carriers listed below for specific info.

The Berkeley Group/Carefree Travel Insurance, 100 Garden City Plaza, P.O. Box 9366, Garden City, NY 11530-9366 (tel. (800) 323-3149 or (516) 294-0220; fax (516) 294-1096). Offers 2 comprehensive packages, including coverage for trip cancellation/interruption/delay, accident and sickness, medical care, baggage loss/delay, accidental death and dismemberment, and travel supplier insolvency. Trip cancellation/interruption may be purchased separately at a rate of US$5.50 per US$100 of coverage. 24-hr. worldwide emergency assistance hotline.

Globalcare Travel Insurance, 220 Broadway, Lynnfield, MA 01940 (tel. (800) 821-2488; fax (617) 592-7720; e-mail global@nebc.mv,com). Complete medical, legal, emergency, and travel-related services. On-the-spot payments and special student programs.

Travel Guard International, 1145 Clark St., Stevens Point, WI 54481 (tel. (800) 826-1300 or (715) 345-0505; fax (715) 345-0525). Comprehensive insurance programs starting at US$44. Programs cover trip cancellation and interruption, bankruptcy and financial default, lost luggage, medical coverage abroad, emergency assistance, and accidental death. 24-hr. hotline.

Alternatives to Tourism

STUDY

Foreign study may be an alluring possibility, but keep in mind that programs vary tremendously in expense, academic quality, living conditions, and exposure to local students and culture. Most American undergraduates enroll in programs sponsored by domestic universities, and many colleges' advising offices provide information on study abroad. Take advantage of these resources and put in some time in their libraries. Ask for the names of recent participants, and talk to them. You may also want to check with the American Embassy in Rome for a list of all American schools in Italy.

Publications

Peterson's Guides, P.O. Box 2123, Princeton, NJ 08543-2123 (tel. (800) 338-3282; fax (609) 243-9150; http://www.petersons.com). Their comprehensive *Study Abroad* annual guide lists programs in countries all over the world and provides essential information on the study abroad experience in general. Purchase a copy at your local bookstore (US$27) or call their toll-free number.

Institute of International Education (IIE), 809 United Nations Plaza, New York, NY 10017-3580 (tel. (212) 984-5413 for recorded info; fax 984-5358). Nonprofit international exchange agency. Their library of study abroad resources is open to the public Tues.-Thurs. 11am-3:45pm. Publishes *Academic Year Abroad* (US$43 plus $4 s&h), detailing semester and year-long programs worldwide, and *Vacation Study Abroad* (US$37 plus $4 s&h), which lists over 1600 short-term, summer, and language school programs. Write for a publications list.

Organizations

Council sponsors over 40 study abroad programs throughout the world. Contact them for more information (see **Travel Organizations,** p. 4).

Centro Turistico Studentesco e Giovanile (CTS) provides information on study in Italy (see **Budget Travel Services,** p. 37).

Youth For Understanding (YFU) International Exchange, 3501 Newark St. NW, Washington, D.C. 20016 (tel. (800) TEENAGE/833-6243 or (202) 966-6800; fax 895-1104; http://www.yfu.org). One of the oldest and largest exchange programs, YFU places U.S. high school students with families worldwide for year, semester, and summer homestays.

American Field Service (AFS), 220 E. 42nd St., 3rd Floor, New York, NY 10017 (tel. (800) AFS-INFO/237-4636 or 876-2376; fax (212) 949-9379; http://www.afs.org/usa). AFS offers summer, semester, and year-long homestay exchange programs for high school students (including graduating high school seniors) and short-term service projects for adults in Italy and other countries. Financial aid available.

Italian Universities

If your Italian is fluent, consider enrolling directly in an Italian university. Universities are crowded, but you will probably have a blast and develop a real feel for the culture. For application information, write to the nearest Italian consulate. Further advice can be provided by **Ufficio Centrale Studenti Esteri in Italia (UCSEI),** Via

Lungotevere dei Vallati, 14, 00186 Rome (tel. (06) 880 40 62; fax 880 40 63), a national organization for foreign students who have already started their course of study in Italy. Remember that student visas are required for study abroad; contact an Italian consulate for an application. See **Italian Embassies and Consulates,** p. 8.

Another option is studying at an institute designed for foreigners but run by an Italian university. The following schools and organizations offer a variety of classes in Italian language, art, and culture; contact them directly for more information.

ABC Centro di Lingua e Cultura Italiana, Via Dei Rustici 7, 50122 Florence (tel. (55) 21 20 01; fax 21 21 12) and Via del Ginnasio 20, 98039 Taormina, Sicily (tel./fax (942) 234 41). Six levels of Italian language instruction offered. Small classes of less then 8 people which last 2-4 weeks.

Centro Internazionale Dante Alighieri (SienaLingue), Piazza La Lizza 10, 53100 Siena (tel. (0577) 495 33; fax 27 06 46). Offers 2- to 4-week group language and culture courses year-round, as well as extracurricular activities and accommodation services. Proof of health insurance required.

Centro Linguistico Sperimentale, Via del Corso 1, 50122 Florence (tel. (055) 21 05 92; tel./fax 28 98 17) is a "School of Italian for Foreigners." Offers intensive language courses, recreational and cultural activities, and more specific classes on contemporary Italian history and Italian cuisine.

Instituto per l'Arte e il Restauro, Borgo Santa Croce 10, 50122 Florence (tel. (055) 24 60 01; fax 24 07 09). A professional school offering 2- to 3-year degree programs in restoration of various art media, as well as introductory summer courses. Language courses are offered for foreign students.

Italiaidea, Piazza della Cancelleria, 85, 00186 Rome (tel. (06) 68 30 76 20; fax 689 29 97). Offers every level of Italian study from an intensive short-term "survival Italian course" to more advanced, semester-long courses meeting once or twice a week. Features on-site lectures and visits to historic sites. Flexible scheduling. College credit courses offered through some U.S. college and university programs in Italy. Homestays (food and lodging with Italian families) are also available.

John Cabot University, Via della Lungara 233, Rome 00165 (tel. (06) 687 88 81; fax 638 20 88; e-mail rspitzmi@nexus.it). Located in Trastevere, this American international university offers undergraduate degrees in art history, business administration, English literature, and international affairs. Foreign students can enroll for summer-, quarter-, and year-long sessions in a variety of liberal arts courses. Qualifying students may obtain academic internships in business and international organizations in Rome.

Koinè, Via de' Pandolfini 27, 50122 Florence (tel. (055) 21 38 81; fax 21 69 49) and Via Mordini 60, 55100 Lucca (tel. (0583) 49 30 40; fax 49 16 89). Offers language courses, seminars on Italian culture, and training for teachers of Italian as a foreign language. Locations in Florence, Lucca, Cortona, Orbetello, and Bologna.

Studio Fiorentino: Institute of Italian Language and Culture, Via dell'Oriuolo 43, 50122 Florence (tel./fax (055) 21 33 46). Teaches Italian language courses of various levels, including an historical and artistic language training class. Emphasis on art and literature in both coursework and extracurricular activities.

WORK AND VOLUNTEER

Legitimate employment can be difficult to find in Italy. Foreigners are most successful at securing harvest, restaurant, bar, and household work, or jobs in the tourism industry, where English-speakers are needed.

Officially, you can hold a job in European countries only with a **work permit.** Your prospective employer must apply for this document, usually by demonstrating that you have skills that locals lack. You will also need a **working visa,** obtainable from your local consulate. On the other hand, there is also the cash-based, untaxable **underground economy** *(economia sommersa or economia nera).* Many permitless agricultural workers go untroubled by local authorities, who recognize the need for seasonal labor. **European Union** citizens can work in any other EU country without working papers. Students can check with their university's foreign language department, which may have official or unofficial access to jobs abroad.

Teaching English, one of the few long-term job possibilities, can be particularly lucrative. You may be able to secure a teaching position with an American school in Italy through the **Office of Overseas Schools,** Room 245, SA-29, Dept. of State, Washington, D.C. 20522-2902 (tel. (703) 875-7800). **International Schools Services,** Educational Staffing Program, P.O. Box 5910, 15 Roszel Rd., Princeton, NJ 08543 (tel. (609) 452-0990; fax 452-2690; e-mail edustaffing%ISS@mcimail.com), recruits teachers and administrators with a bachelor's degree and two years of relevant experience. **Amicizia di Maria de Angelis,** Via XX Settembre 21/7 - 16121 Geneva GE (tel. (010) 553 10 96; fax (010) 553 11 52) is an international student organization for work and study in Italy and abroad.

Publications and Organizations

Remember that many of the organizations listed in books may have very few jobs available and usually have very specific requirements.

Vacation Work Publications, 9 Park End St., Oxford OX1 1HJ (tel. (01865) 24 19 78; fax 79 08 85). Publishes a wide variety of guides and directories with job listings and information for the working traveler. Opportunities for summer or full-time employment in countries all over the world. Write for a catalog of their publications, including those which deal specifically with Italy. Many of their books are also available in bookstores.

Addison-Wesley, Jacob Way, Reading, MA 01867 (tel. (800) 822-6339). Published *International Jobs: Where They Are, How to Get Them* in 1994 (US$16).

InterExchange Program, 161 Sixth Ave., New York, NY 10013 (tel. (212) 924-0446; fax 924-0575). Offers pamphlets on work programs and *au pair* positions.

Childcare International, Ltd., Trafalgar House, Grenville Place, London NW7 3SA (tel. (01819) 59 36 11 or 06 31 16; fax 06 34 61; e-mail office@childint.demon.co.uk; http://www.ipi.co.uk/childint), offers *au pair* positions in Italy and many other European countries. UK£60 application fee. The organization prefers a long placement but does arrange summer work.

Once in Italy, check out community bulletin boards, as well as the help-wanted columns in the English-language papers *Daily American* and the *International Daily News.* In Rome, *Wanted in Rome* (L1500) is available at newsstands, in English-language bookstores, and from the *Wanted in Rome* office at Via dei Delfini, 17 (tel. (06) 679 01 90; fax 678 37 98; e-mail 101360.2472@compuserve.com). *Metropolitan,* a bi-monthly magazine in English, is also available from bookstores in Rome. The magazine *AAM Terra Nuova* is a good source for agricultural jobs and can be obtained by contacting AAM Terra Nuova (tel./fax (055) 845 61 16).

Volunteering is another good way to immerse yourself in a foreign culture. The following organizations can place you in volunteer programs in Italy.

Council offers 2- to 4-week environmental or community service projects in over 30 countries through its Voluntary Services Department (US$250-750 placement fee). Participants must be at least 18 years old. See **Travel Organizations,** p. 4.

Volunteers for Peace, 43 Tiffany Rd., Belmont, VT 05730 (tel. (802) 259-2759; fax 259-2922; e-mail vfp@vermontel.com; http://www.vfp.org). A non-profit organization that arranges for speedy placement in one of 800 workcamps, many of which are in Europe. Most camps last for 2 to 3 weeks and are comprised of 10 to 15 people. The most complete and up-to-date listings can be found in the annual *International Workcamp Directory* (US$12). Registration fee US$175. Some workcamps are open to 16- and 17-year-olds for US$200. Free newsletter.

Service Civil International Voluntary Service (SCI-VS), 5474 Walnut Level Road, Crozet, VA 22932 (tel. (804) 823-1826; fax 823-5027; e-mail sciivsusa@apc.org). Arranges placement in workcamps in Europe (ages 18 and over), programs in which local organizations sponsor groups for physical or social work. Registration fees for the placement service range from US$50-250.

ARCHAEOLOGICAL DIGS

The **Archaeological Institute of America,** 656 Beacon St., Boston, MA 02215-2010 (tel. (617) 353-9361; fax 353-6550) puts out the *Archaeological Fieldwork Opportunities Bulletin*. This guide lists over 250 field sites throughout the world, costs US$11 for nonmembers, and is available from Kendall/Hunt Publishing, 4050 Westmark Dr., Dubuque, IA 52002 (tel. (800) 228-0810). For other questions, contact the AIA directly at the first address. For information on anthropology, archaeological digs, and art history in Italy, write to the **Centro Comune di Studi Preistorici,** 25044 Capo di Ponte, Brescia (tel. (0364) 420 91; fax 425 72). This research center is involved with the management of cultural property and the organization of congresses, research projects, and exhibitions. They offer volunteer work, grants, and research assistant positions for prehistoric art. The institute also publishes *BCSP,* the world journal of prehistoric and tribal art.

Local colleges and universities in your home country are another excellent source of information on archaeological digs in Italy and elsewhere. Check with the Departments of Classics, Archaeology, Anthropology, Fine Arts, and/or other relevant area studies; many excavations send information and applications directly to individual professors or departments rather than to the general public.

LONGER STAYS

Live and Work in Italy, written by Victoria Pybus and Rachael Robinson, provides advice on everything from residence regulations to starting a business in Italy. To order, contact **Vacation Work Publications** (see p. 29). Once in Italy, check newspapers or tourist office bulletin boards for apartment rental listings.

Specific Concerns

WOMEN TRAVELERS

Italy, along with some of its European and North African neighbors, has long been viewed as a particularly difficult area for women traveling in groups or on their own. Although women travelers do face additional safety concerns, excessive caution can take all the fun out of your trip. The best recipe for traveling safely is to inform yourself as much as possible beforehand about the conditions and customs of the area you'll be visiting. The following paragraphs are an incomplete introduction to common problems and possible means of avoiding them. When in doubt, trust your instincts and err on the side of caution.

Italian culture, friendly in general, often overwhelms foreigners. While the constant barrage (and we mean *constant*) of queries and catcalls can become annoying, most comments should not be taken as a precursor to violence. Women, whether alone or in groups, can avoid most harassment by adopting the attitude of many Italian women: walk like you know where you are going, avoid eye contact (sunglasses are indispensable), meet advances with silence and dignity, and, if still troubled, walk or stand near older women or couples until you feel safe. Many experienced travelers also recommend wearing a fake (or real, if you've got one) wedding or engagement ring. Wearing tight or suggestive clothing can attract unwanted attention, but so can attire that is perfectly modest but obviously American (sweatshirts, college t-shirts, sneakers, hiking shorts). Finally, if you're blonde and want to avoid continual outcries of "*bionda*" (or worse) as you pass, keeping your hair pulled back and covered with a hat or scarf may save you a lot of hassle.

All travelers to Italy (especially from countries like the U.S.) should be aware that the Italian conception of **personal space** is different from what you're probably used to. The guy crowded next to you on the bus or the woman gesticulating madly in your face is not necessarily threatening you or being rude; it is acceptable and normal in Italian culture to stand close to the person you're addressing, to gesture wildly, and to shout. Beyond this, if you feel at all uncomfortable, don't hesitate to seek out a police officer or a passerby. Memorize the **emergency numbers** in Italy (113 and 112). Always carry a 200-lire coin and a phone card for the phone and enough extra money for a bus or taxi. Self-defense courses suggest carrying a whistle on your key-chain—a series of short blasts can call nearby passersby to your help. If you are physically harassed on the bus or in some other crowded space, don't talk to the person directly (this often encourages him). Rather, use body language, like a well-aimed knee or elbow, to make your point. Again, if you sense real trouble ask the people around you for help. When traveling on Italian trains, avoid empty compartments, especially at night. Look for compartments with nuns or priests for maximum safety. Avoid men that shout from passing cars by walking on the sidewalk facing traffic; the car will not be able to follow you down the sidewalk, but will instead have to drive on by.

Budget **accommodations** can sometimes mean more risk than savings. Avoid small dives and city outskirts; go for university dormitories or youth hostels instead. Centrally located accommodations are easiest to return to after dark. Some religious organizations also offer rooms for women only. Inquire at the provincial tourist office for a list of these institutions, or contact the **Associazione Cattolica Internazionale al Servizio della Giovane,** Via Urbana, 158, 00184 Roma (tel. (06) 488 14 89; fax 48 90 45 23).

For additional information, see the following **publications:** *A Journey of One's Own* by Thalia Zepatos (Eighth Mountain Press, US$17) is the latest book on the market and is full of good advice. It also features a specific and manageable bibliography of books and resources. *Women Travel: Adventures, Advice & Experience* by Miranda Davies and Natania Jansz (Penguin, US$13) offers info on specific foreign countries plus a resource index. The sequel, *More Women Travel,* costs $15.

OLDER TRAVELERS

Older people in Italy are generally treated with considerable respect, and senior travelers are often entitled to travel-related discounts. Always ask about them, and be prepared to show proof of age (you probably look younger than you are). The following organizations and publications provide information on discounts, tours, and health and travel tips.

AARP (American Association of Retired Persons), 601 E St. NW, Washington, D.C. 20049 (tel. (202) 434-2277). U.S. residents over 50 receive discounts on lodging, car rental, and sight-seeing. US$8 per couple per year; US$75 lifetime.

Elderhostel, 75 Federal St., 3rd Fl., Boston, MA 02110-1941 (tel. (617) 426-7788; fax 426-8351; http://www.elderhostel.org). Those 55 and over are eligible (and may bring a spouse of any age). Programs at colleges, universities, and learning centers in over 50 countries focus on varied subjects and last one to four weeks.

Pilot Books, 103 Cooper St., Babylon, NY 11702 (tel. (516) 422-2225). Publishes *The International Health Guide for Senior Citizens* (US$5, postage US$2) and *The Senior Citizens' Guide to Budget Travel in Europe* (US$6, postage US$2).

Gateway Books, 2023 Clemens Rd., Oakland, CA 94602 (tel. (510) 530-0299; fax 530-0497; donmerwin@aol.com; http://www.hway.com/gateway). Publishes *Europe the European Way: A Traveler's Guide to Living Affordably in the World's Great Cities* (US$14), and *Adventures Abroad* (US$13), offering general hints for the budget-conscious senior considering a long stay or even retiring abroad. Call (800) 669-0773 for credit card orders.

BISEXUAL, GAY, AND LESBIAN TRAVELERS

Gay and lesbian travelers may find Italians unwelcoming, particularly in the south. Holding hands or walking arm in arm with someone of the same sex, however, is common in Italy, especially for women, and probably not an indication of homosexuality. For those fearing discrimination at hotels, consider requesting a double room as if you are two friends trying to save money; you will probably not be questioned. Sexual acts between members of the same sex are legal for those above the age of consent (16). People in large northern cities tend to be more tolerant, and gay bars are a part of the nightclub scene there. Watch for the few gay beaches *(spiagge gay)* which dot the shores.

The Italian national gay organization, **ARCI-GAY/LESBICA,** has its headquarters at P. di Porta Saragozza, 2, P.O. Box 691, 40123 Bologna (tel. (051) 644 70 54; fax 644 67 22; e-mail arcigl@iperbole.bologna.it). Roberto or Paolo will give you the info on the ARCI-GAY/LESBICA near you. *Babilonia,* a national gay magazine, is published monthly by Babilonia Edizioni, Via Ebro, 11, 20141 Milan (tel. (02) 569 64 68; 55 21 34 19).

Are You Two...Together? A Gay and Lesbian Travel Guide to Europe contains anecdotes and tips for gay and lesbian tourists in Europe. Includes overviews of regional laws and lists of organizations and gay-friendly establishments abroad. Available in bookstores. Random House, $18.

Gay's the Word, 66 Marchmont St., London WC1N 1AB (tel. (0171) 278 76 54). The largest gay and lesbian bookshop in the U.K. Staff will provide a list of titles on a given subject. Mail-order service available. Open Mon.-Wed. and Fri.-Sat. 10am-6pm, Thurs. 10am-7pm, Sun. 2-6pm.

International Gay Travel Association, Box 4974, Key West, FL 33041 (tel. (800) 448-8550; fax (305) 296-6633; e-mail IGTA@aol.com; http://www.rainbow-mall.com/igta). An organization of over 1100 companies serving gay and lesbian travelers worldwide. Call for lists of travel agents, accommodations, and events.

Giovanni's Room, 345 S. 12th St., Philadelphia, PA 19107 (tel. (215) 923-2960; fax 923-0813; e-mail gilphilp@netaxs.com). An international feminist, lesbian, and gay bookstore which carries many titles listed here. Mail-order service.

Spartacus International Gay Guides, published by Bruno Gmunder, Postfach 110729, D-10837 Berlin, Germany (tel. (30) 615 00 30; fax 615 91 34). Extensive list of gay male bars, restaurants, hotels, and bookstores, as well as laws and hot-lines, throughout the world (US$33). Available in U.S. bookstores.

Women Going Places (Inland Book Co., US$14) is an international travel and resource guide emphasizing women-owned enterprises. Geared toward lesbians, but offers advice for all women. Available in bookstores.

TRAVELERS WITH DISABILITIES

Italians are making an increased effort to meet the needs of people with disabilities. The **Italian Government Travel Office (ENIT)** will let you know which hotels and buildings are handicapped-accessible. When making arrangements with airlines or hotels, specify exactly what you need and allow time for preparation and confirmation of arrangements. Major train stations will provide aid if you make reservations by telephone 24 hours in advance. You can generally find a *portiere* to assist you for L500 to L1000 per bag. Italy's rail system is modernized, so most trains are wheelchair-accessible. For more info, call the **Italian State Railway Representative** in New York (tel. (212) 697-1482) or **Rail Europe** in the U.S. (tel. (800) 438-7245).

If you plan to bring a seeing-eye dog to Italy, contact your veterinarian and the nearest Italian consulate. You will need import documents and veterinary records certifying your dog's health.

American Foundation for the Blind, 11 Penn Plaza, New York, NY 10011 (tel. (212) 502-7600). Open Mon.-Fri. 8:30am-4:30pm. Provides info and services for the visually impaired. For a catalog of products contact **Lighthouse** at (800) 829-0500.

Graphic Language Press, P.O. Box 270, Cardiff by the Sea, CA 92007 (tel. (619) 944-9594). Publishes *Wheelchair Through Europe*. Comprehensive advice for the wheelchair-bound traveler, including specifics on wheelchair-related resources and accessible sites in various cities throughout Europe.

The Guided Tour Inc., Elkins Park House, #114B, 7900 Old York Rd., Elkins Park, PA 19027-2339 (tel. (800) 783-5841 or (215) 782-1370; fax 635-2637). Organizes travel programs for people with developmental and physical challenges as well as for persons requiring renal dialysis. Call or write for a free brochure.

Mobility International, USA (MIUSA), P.O. Box 10767, Eugene, OR 97440 (tel. (514) 343-1284 voice and TDD; fax 343-6812). International headquarters in Brussels, rue de Manchester 25, Brussels, Belgium, B-1070 (tel. (322) 410 62 97; fax 410 68 74). Info on travel programs, international workcamps, accommodations, access guides, and organized tours in 30 countries. Membership US$25 per year, newsletter US$15. Sells the periodically updated and expanded *A World of Options: A Guide to International Educational Exchange, Community Service, and Travel for Persons with Disabilities* (US$14, US$16 for nonmembers). MIUSA also teaches a series of courses on travel strategies for disabled tourists.

Moss Rehab Hospital Travel Information Service, (tel. (215) 456-9600, TDD (215) 456-9602). A telephone information resource center on international travel accessibility and other travel-related concerns for those with disabilities.

Society for the Advancement of Travel for the Handicapped (SATH), 347 Fifth Ave., #610, New York, NY 10016 (tel. (212) 447-7284; fax 725-8253). Publishes quarterly travel newsletter *SATH News* and information booklets (free for members, US$13 each for nonmembers) with advice on trip planning for people with disabilities. Annual membership US$45, students and seniors US$25.

Twin Peaks Press, P.O. Box 129, Vancouver, WA 98666-0129 (tel. (360) 694-2462, orders with MC and Visa (800) 637-2256; fax (360) 696-3210). Publishers of *Travel for the Disabled,* which provides travel tips, lists of accessible tourist attractions, and advice on other resources for disabled travelers ($20). Also publishes *Directory for Travel Agencies of the Disabled* ($20), *Wheelchair Vagabond* ($15), and *Directory of Accessible Van Rentals* ($10). Postage $3 for first book, $1.50 for each additional book.

KOSHER AND VEGETARIAN TRAVELERS

Jewish travelers who keep **kosher** should consult local tourist boards or synagogues for a list of kosher restaurants. Also useful is *The Jewish Travel Guide* (US$14, US$2.50 postage), available in the U.S. from Sepher-Hermon Press, 1265 46th St.,

Brooklyn, NY 11219 (tel. (718) 972-9010). If you are strict in your observance, consider preparing your own food on the road.

Let's Go includes **vegetarian** restaurants in its listings. You can always request a dish *senza carne* (without meat), though your request may puzzle the chef. Vegetarians can contact the **Associazione Culturale Vegetariana,** Via Treviglio, 9, 20123 Milan (tel. (02) 27 20 27 60), for information on vegetarian restaurants, foods, and stores. *The European Vegetarian Guide to Restaurants and Hotels* is available from the Vegetarian Times Bookshelf (tel. (800) 435-9610, orders only).

MINORITY TRAVELERS

We have been hard-pressed to find any resources that advise members of visible minorities on specific travel concerns. If you have knowledge of any books or organizations with this sort of information, please write and let us know. **Jewish tourists** may appreciate the *Italy Jewish Travel Guide* (US$15) from Israelowitz Publishing, P.O. Box 228, Brooklyn, NY 11229, which provides info on sites of particular religious interest.

In certain regions, particularly in the south, tourists of color or members of non-Christian religious groups may feel unwelcome. *Let's Go: Italy* does not include known discriminatory establishments in our guide. If, in your travels, you encounter discriminatory treatment, please let us know so that we can check out the establishment and, if appropriate, warn other travelers.

In terms of safety, there are no easy answers. Keep abreast of the particular cultural attitudes of the regions that you're planning to visit. Although immigrants of color do experience discrimination in Italy, tourists of color from the West, who are easily distinguishable by clothes and language, are not the usual targets of racism. Women of color may be seen as exotic, but not unwelcome. Travel in groups and take a taxi whenever you are uncomfortable. The best answer to xenophobic comments and other verbal harassment is often no answer at all. Despite all the warnings, keep in mind that your own ethnicity will not necessarily be problematic; you may well find your vacation trouble-free and your hosts open-minded.

TRAVELING WITH CHILDREN

Italians are well-known for their love of children, and you will probably encounter more cooing than complications. Most hotels will put a cot in your room for a percentage price increase, and even picky children tend to enjoy the simplest (and cheapest) of Italian foods: pizza, spaghetti, and *gelato*. There are also **discount Eurailpasses** for groups and children. Depending on the laws of your home country and the countries in which you plan to travel, children under 16 may be able to enter foreign countries on a parent's passport.

Drawing up a detailed itinerary is especially useful for those traveling with small children. Remember that you may have to slow your pace considerably. All the new sights and experiences are especially exhausting for kids—you may want to leave room for a mid-afternoon nap for everyone. Most businesses and tourist attractions in Italy are closed from around noon to 3pm anyway. For some families, it may be more convenient to travel by rental car, but train travel will often be cheaper and more interesting for children. Finally, make sure that your children have some sort of ID on their person in case they get lost and/or are faced with an emergency. If possible, teach them the emergency numbers (113 and 112).

For more information, order books from the following publishers: **Wilderness Press,** 2440 Bancroft Way, Berkeley, CA 94704 (tel. (800) 443-7227 or (510) 843-8080; fax 548-1355), distributes *Backpacking with Babies and Small Children* (US$10). **Lonely Planet Publications,** Embarcadero West, 155 Filbert St., #251, Oakland, CA 94607 (tel. (800) 275-8555 or (510) 893-8555; fax (510) 893-8563; e-mail info@lonelyplanet.com; http://www.lonelyplanet.com), or P.O. Box 617, Hawthorn, Victoria 3122, Australia, publishes *Travel With Children* (US$12, postage US$1.50). **Mason-Grant Publications,** P.O. Box 6547, Portsmouth, NH 03802 (tel. (603) 436-

1608; fax 427-0015; e-mail charriman@masongrant.com) publishes *Take Your Kids to Europe* by Cynthia W. Harriman (US$14), which is geared toward family travel.

TRAVELING ALONE

There may be personal benefits to traveling alone, among them greater independence and challenge, as well as having more opportunities to meet and interact with locals. On the other hand, you may also be a more visible target for robbery and harassment. Lone travelers need to be well-organized and look confident at all times. Try not to stand out as a tourist. *If questioned, never admit that you are traveling alone.* And try to maintain regular contact with someone at home who knows your itinerary.

Jay Ben-Lesser's **A Foxy Old Woman's Guide to Traveling Alone** encompasses practically every specific concern, offering anecdotes and tips for anyone interested in solitary adventure. It is available in bookstores and from Crossing Press in Freedom, CA (tel. (800) 777-1048) for US$11.

Packing

If you want to get away from it all, don't take it all with you.

Plan your packing according to your type of travel and the average temperatures of the region. Set out everything you think you'll need, then pack half the clothes and twice the money. Once you're on the road you'll be thankful; remember, everything you take you have to carry. If you find yourself packing "just in case," remember that almost all supplies are readily available in Italy (though not necessarily in Tunisia). See **Health,** page 20, for tips on medical and hygienic supplies you should bring from home.

LUGGAGE

Backpacks: If you intend to do a lot of hiking, you should have a **frame backpack.** Get one with an internal frame if you'll be hiking on difficult trails that require a lot of bending and maneuvering—internal-frame packs mold better to your back, keep a lower center of gravity, and can flex adequately to follow you through a variety of movements. In addition, internal frame packs are more manageable on crowded planes, trains, and automobiles, and are less likely to be mangled by rough handling. External-frame packs, however, are more comfortable for long hikes over even terrain since they keep the weight higher and distribute it more evenly. These don't travel as well, so be sure to tie down loose straps when dealing with baggage handlers. Make sure your pack has a strong, padded hip belt, which transfers much of the weight from delicate shoulders to sturdier legs. Any serious backpacking requires a pack with at least 4000 cubic inches, while longer trips require around 5000. Tack on an additional 500 cubic inches for internal-frame packs, since you'll have to pack your sleeping bag inside, rather than strap it on the outside as you do with an external-frame pack. Sturdy backpacks cost anywhere from US$125-400. This is one area where it doesn't pay to economize—cheaper packs may be less comfortable, and the straps are more likely to fray or rip quickly. Test-drive a backpack for comfort before you buy it.

Suitcase/trunk/other large or heavy luggage: Fine if you plan to live in one city and explore from there, but a bad idea if you're going to be moving around a lot. Useful features: wheels on suitcases for maneuverability, PVC frame on soft luggage, lightest possible weight, and strong linings to resist bad weather.

Daypack, rucksack, or courier bag: Bringing a smaller bag in addition to your pack or suitcase allows you to leave your big bag in the hotel while you go sightseeing. It should have secure closures for security. Use it also as an airplane carry-on; keep the absolute essentials with you to avoid the lost-luggage blues.

Moneybelt or neck pouch: Guard your money, passport, railpass, and other important articles in one of these, and keep it with you *at all times.* Moneybelts should rest *inside* the waistline of your pants or skirt, and neck pouches should be worn under at least one layer of your clothing. Avoid the ubiquitous "fanny pack," which is an invitation to thieves, even when worn in front.

CLOTHING AND FOOTWEAR

No nation outdresses Italy, so plan to admire rather than compete. Most importantly, be sure to bring clothes appropriate for visits to cathedrals and churches, since shorts, skirts above the knees, and sleeveless or cut-off shirts are usually forbidden there. In general, bring few but comfortable clothes, and keep accessories to a minimum. Climate and convenience should determine your wardrobe. Dark colors will not show the dirt they're bound to accumulate, but light colors will be cooler in hot weather. In addition, solid colors are usually easiest to mix and match. Natural fibers are also good choices since synthetics trap heat. Laundry facilities are expensive in Italy and nonexistent in Tunisia: bring non-wrinkling, quick-drying clothes that you can wash in a sink. Above all, shorts, university t-shirts, and running shoes brand you as a tourist and may be the cause of increased attention in Italy.

Women: During the summer, light cotton pants are the most appropriate travelwear and are a good option for getting by cathedral dress codes. You might also wear a long dress with a lightweight drape or shawl to cover your shoulders for church visits. Jeans may cause you problems on the road—they're hot, and hard to dry after a downpour. Shorts will definitely make you stand out and garner unwanted attention from men. Surprisingly enough, you might be just as comfortable and attract fewer stares in a knee-length skirt. Really.

Men: Again, cotton pants will probably be more comfortable than jeans. Shorts are more acceptable on men than on women and provide a break from the heat, but remember that they are considered rude if worn in cathedrals.

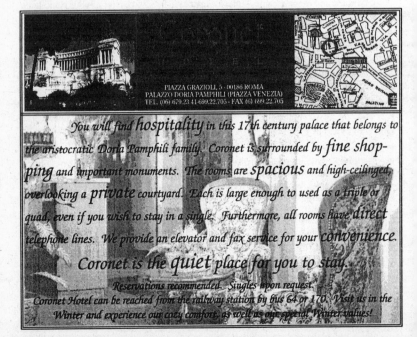

Walking shoes: Not a place to cut corners. For **city** walking, lace-up leather shoes with firm grips provide better support and are more socially acceptable than athletic shoes. If you plan to travel in the **rainy** fall or spring, you can waterproof them. For alpine forays, a good pair of **hiking boots** with adequate ankle support is essential. Wearing a double pair of socks (light silky ones underneath tough wool ones) can help prevent blisters. **Sandals** are excellent for airing out your feet after a long day or for braving the fungus in hostel showers. You could also buy a pair of Italian leather sandals once you get there. Don't forget to *break in your shoes before you leave.*

Weather protection: Raingear is absolutely essential. **Gore-Tex** fabric, which is both waterproof and breathable, is a good choice. Pack a light sweater or jacket, even in summer. **Silk bomber jackets** are warm, light, and compact. Gloves and thermal underwear are also useful for northern winters.

MISCELLANEOUS

The following is not an exhaustive list. For a **first-aid kit** see **Health,** page 20.

Washing clothes: Laundry facilities in Italy are expensive and inconvenient. Washing clothes in your hotel sink is often a better option. Bring a small bar or bottle of detergent soap, a rubber squash ball to stop up the sink, and a travel clothes line (available at camping stores) for drying.

Electric Current: Voltage is generally 220v in Italy, although some hotels offer 110v. Check before plugging in or you could fry your appliance into oblivion. Visit a hardware store for an adapter (which changes the shape of the plug) and a converter (which changes the voltage). Don't make the mistake of using only an adapter (unless appliance instructions explicitly state otherwise), or you'll melt your Clapper.

Film: Available but expensive in Italy, as it is all over Europe. Bring lots of film with you and, if you will be seriously upset if the pictures are ruined, develop it at home, too. If you're not a serious photographer, consider bringing a **disposable camera** or two rather than an expensive permanent one. They generally cost US$10-15 (not including developing). Whatever kind of camera you use, be aware that, despite disclaimers, airport security X-rays *can* fog film. To protect it, you can either buy a lead-lined pouch from a camera store or ask the security personnel to hand inspect your film. In any case, be sure to pack it in your carry-on luggage, since higher-intensity X-rays are used on checked bags.

Contact lenses: Travellers who heat-disinfect their lenses should either buy a small converter for their machine (US$20) or take chemicals to use in Italy. Note that chemicals are not safe for all lenses and are rare and expensive overseas.

Also valuable: insect repellent, travel alarm clock, plastic bags that seal shut (for damp clothes, soap, food), sun hat, sunscreen, sewing kit, clothespins, sleepsack (required in many hostels; you can make one by folding a full-size sheet in half the long way and sewing up the sides), sunglasses, Walkman, pocketknife, tweezers, plastic water bottle, small flashlight, padlock, towel, and moleskin (for blisters).

GETTING THERE

The first challenge to the budget traveler is getting there. Students and people under age 26 ("youth") qualify for reduced airfares, which are most readily available from student travel agencies. **TravelHUB** (http://www.travelhub.com) will help you search for travel services on the web.

Budget Travel Agencies

Council Travel (http://www.ciee.org/cts/ctshome.htm), the travel division of Council, is a full-service travel agency specializing in youth and budget travel. They offer railpasses, discount airfares, hosteling cards, guidebooks, budget tours, travel gear, and student (ISIC), youth (GO25), and teacher (ITIC) identity cards. U.S. offices include: Emory Village, 1561 N. Decatur Rd., **Atlanta,** GA 30307 (tel. (404) 377-9997); 2000 Guadalupe, **Austin,** TX 78705 (tel. (512) 472-4931); 273 New-

bury St., **Boston,** MA 02116 (tel. (617) 266-1926); 1138 13th St., **Boulder,** CO 80302 (tel. (303) 447-8101); 1153 N. Dearborn, **Chicago,** IL 60610 (tel. (312) 951-0585); 10904 Lindbrook Dr., **Los Angeles,** CA 90024 (tel. (310) 208-3551); 1501 University Ave. SE, **Minneapolis,** MN 55414 (tel. (612) 379-2323); 205 E. 42nd St., **New York,** NY 10017 (tel. (212) 822-2700); 953 Garnet Ave., **San Diego,** CA 92109 (tel. (619) 270-6401); 530 Bush St., **San Francisco,** CA 94108 (tel. (415) 421-3473); 4311½ University Way, **Seattle,** WA 98105 (tel. (206) 632-2448); 3300 M St. NW, **Washington, D.C.** 20007 (tel. (202) 337-6464). **For U.S. cities not listed,** call 800-2-COUNCIL (226-8624). Also 28A Poland St. (Oxford Circus), **London,** W1V 3DB (tel. (0171) 437 7767).

STA Travel, 6560 North Scottsdale Rd. #F100, Scottsdale, AZ 85253 (tel. (800) 777-0112; fax (602) 922-0793). A student and youth travel organization with over 100 offices worldwide offering discount airfares for young travelers, railpasses, accommodations, tours, insurance, and ISICs. 16 offices in the U.S. including: 297 Newbury St., **Boston,** MA 02115 (tel. (617) 266-6014); 429 S. Dearborn St., **Chicago,** IL 60605 (tel. (312) 786-9050; 7202 Melrose Ave., **Los Angeles,** CA 90046 (tel. (213) 934-8722); 10 Downing St., Ste. G, **New York,** NY 10003 (tel. (212) 627-3111); 4341 University Way NE, **Seattle,** WA 98105 (tel. (206) 633-5000); 2401 Pennsylvania Ave., **Washington, D.C.** 20037 (tel. (202) 887-0912); 51 Grant Ave., **San Francisco,** CA 94108 (tel. (415) 391-8407), **Miami,** FL 33133 (tel. (305) 461-3444). In the U.K., 6 Wrights Ln., **London** W8 6TA (tel. (0171) 938 47 11 for North American travel). In New Zealand, 10 High St., **Auckland** (tel. (09) 309 97 23). In Australia, 222 Faraday St., **Melbourne** VIC 3050 (tel. (03) 349 69 11).

Let's Go Travel, Harvard Student Agencies, 67 Mt. Auburn St., Cambridge, MA 02138 (tel. (800) 5-LETS GO(553-8746), or (617) 495-9649). Offers railpasses, HI-AYH memberships, ISICs, International Teacher ID cards, FIYTO cards, guidebooks (including every *Let's Go* book and Map Guide), maps, bargain flights, and a complete line of travel gear. All items available by mail; see enclosed catalog.

Campus Travel, 52 Grosvenor Gardens, London SW1W 0AG (http://www.campustravel.co.uk). 41 branches in the U.K. Student and youth fares on plane, train, boat, and bus travel, including flexible airline tickets. Discount and ID cards for youths and travel insurance for students and those under 35. Provides travel suggestion booklets, maps, and guides. Telephone booking service: in Europe call (0171) 730 3402; in North America call (0171) 730 2101; worldwide call (0171) 730 8111; in Manchester call (0161) 273 1721; in Scotland (0131) 668 3303.

Centro Turistico Studentesco e Giovanile (CTS), Via Genova, 16, 00184 **Rome** (tel. (06) 467 91; fax 467 92 07; e-mail ctsinfo@mbox.vol.it). With 98 offices throughout Italy, CTS provides travel, accommodation, and sight-seeing discounts, as well as currency exchange and information for students and young people. Sells *cartaverde* for discounts on train fares, the International Student Identity Card (ISIC), the International Youth Cards (FIYTO card), and the Euro Youth Card. Branch offices also in **London** and **Paris.** Open Mon.-Fri. 9am-1pm and 3:30-7pm, Sat. 9am-1pm.

CIT Tours, 342 Madison Ave. #207, **New York,** NY 10173 (tel. (212) 697-2100; fax 697-1394; e-mail alr5@ix.netcom.com); 6033 West Century Blvd. #980, **Los Angeles,** CA 90045 (tel. (310) 338-8616); 1450 City Councillors St. #1450, **Montréal,** Québec H3A 2E6 (tel./fax (800) 361-7799 or (514) 845-9137); **Toronto,** Ontario (tel. (416) 415-1060). Over 100 offices worldwide, but most are in Italy. The official representative of the Italian state railways in the US; also sells Eurail.

Educational Travel Centre (ETC), 438 North Frances St., Madison, WI 53703 (tel. (800) 747-5551; fax (608) 256-2042; e-mail edtrav@execpc.com). Flights, HI cards, Eurail and regional railpasses. Write for their free pamphlet *Taking Off*.

Rail Europe Inc., 226 Westchester Ave., White Plains, NY 10604 (tel. (800) 438-7245; fax 432-1329; http://www.raileurope.com). Sells Eurail products and passes, national railpasses, and direct tickets. Up-to-date info on rail travel.

Travel CUTS (Canadian University Travel Services, Ltd.), 187 College St., Toronto, Ontario M5T 1P7 (tel. (416) 979-2406; fax 979-8167; e-mail mail@travelcuts). Canada's national student travel bureau, with 40 offices across Canada. Also, in the **U.K.,** 295-A Regent St., London W1R 7YA (tel. (0171) 637 31 61). Discounted domestic and international flights. Issues ISIC, FIYTO, GO 25, and HI cards, as well as railpasses. Offers free *Student Traveller* magazine, and info on Student Work Abroad Program (SWAP).

Travel Management International (TMI), 3617 Dupont Ave. S, Minneapolis, MN 55409 (tel. (617) 661-8187 or (800) 245-3672). Diligent, prompt, and very helpful travel service offering student fares and discounts.

Unitravel, 117 North Warson Rd., St. Louis, MO 63132 (tel. (800) 325-2222; fax (314) 569-2503). Offers discounted airfares on major scheduled airlines from the U.S. to Europe, Africa, and Asia.

Wasteels, 7041 Grand National Dr. #207, Orlando, FL 32819 (tel. (407) 351-2537; in **London** (0171) 834 70 66). A huge chain in Europe, with 200 locations. For information in English, contact the London office. Sells the Wasteels BIJ tickets, which are discounted (30-45% off regular fare) 2nd-class international point-to-point train tickets with stopovers for those under 26; sold *only* in Europe.

By Plane

Constantly fluctuating prices make estimating airfares impossible, but a few general rules do apply. Most airlines maintain a fare structure that peaks between mid-June and early September. Midweek (Mon.-Thurs. morning) roundtrip flights run about US$40-50 cheaper than those on weekends. If you plan on traveling elsewhere in Europe, consider beginning your trip outside Italy. A flight through Brussels (on **Sabena**) or Amsterdam (on **KLM**) could cost considerably less than one to Milan or Rome. Roundtrip tickets from New York or Boston to major cities such as Florence or Rome could cost anywhere from US$400 to 800. Since inexpensive flights from Canada can cost substantially more than the lowest fares from the U.S., Canadians may want to consider leaving from the States. Also check with Travel CUTS for information on special charters (see above).

Have a knowledgable budget travel agent (or better yet, several) guide you through the options. Travel sections in Sunday newspapers often list bargain fares from the local airport. You might also be able to outfox airline reps with the *Official Airline Guide,* available at large libraries. This monthly guide lists nearly every scheduled flight in the world (including prices), along with toll-free phone numbers for all the airlines which will allow you to call in reservations directly. On the web, try the **Air Traveler's Handbook** (http://www.cis.ohio-state.edu/hypertext/faq/usenet/travel/air/handbook/top.html) for comprehensive information on air travel.

COMMERCIAL AIRLINES

The commercial airlines' lowest regular offer is the **APEX (Advance Purchase Excursion Fare).** Specials advertised in newspapers may be cheaper, but have more restrictions and fewer available seats. APEX fares provide you with confirmed reservations and allow "open-jaw" tickets (landing in and returning from different cities). Reservations must usually be made seven to 21 days in advance. There are also minimum and maximum stay limitations with hefty cancellation and change fees. For summer travel, book early. **Alitalia,** Italy's national airline, is commonly used by business travelers, but may offer off-season youth fares as well. Its main address in the U.S. is 666 Fifth Avenue, New York, NY 10103 (tel. (800) 223-5730). Look into flights to less popular destinations or on smaller carriers for lower prices. You can call **Icelandair** (tel. (800) 223-5500) for info on last-minute offers.

TICKET CONSOLIDATORS

Ticket consolidators sell unsold tickets on commercial and charter airlines at unpublished fares. The consolidator market is by and large international. Consolidator flights are the best deals if you are travelling on short notice, to an offbeat destination, or in the peak season, when published fares are jacked way up. There is rarely a maximum age or stay limit, but unlike tickets bought through an airline, you won't be able to use your tickets on another flight if you miss yours. You will also have to go back to the consolidator to get a refund, rather than the airline. Keep in mind that these tickets are often for coach seats on connecting (non-direct) flights on foreign airlines, and that frequent-flier miles may not be credited. Decide what you can and can't live with(out) before going with a consolidator.

Consolidators come in three varieties: wholesale only, who sell only to travel agencies; specialty agencies (both wholesale and retail); and **"bucket shops"** or discount retail agencies. You, as a private consumer, can deal directly only with the latter. You have access to a larger market if you use a travel agent, who can also get tickets from wholesale consolidators. Look for bucket shops' tiny ads in weekend papers (in the U.S., the *Sunday New York Times* is best). In London, the real bucket shop center, the **Air Travel Advisory Bureau** (tel. (0171) 6365000) provides a list of consolidators.

Be a smart and careful shopper. Among the many reputable and trustworthy companies are, unfortunately, some shady wheeler-dealers. Contact the local Better Business Bureau to find out how long the company has been in business and its track record. Although not necessary, it is preferable to deal with consolidators close to home so you can visit in person, if necessary. Ask to receive your tickets as quickly as possible so you have time to fix any problems. Insist on a written **receipt** that gives full details about the tickets, refunds, and restrictions, and record who you talked to and when. Beware the "bait and switch" gag, in which shady firms will advertise a super-low fare and then tell a caller that it has been sold. Although this is a viable excuse, if they can't offer you a price near the advertised fare on *any* date, it is a scam to lure in customers—report them to the Better Business Bureau. Ask also about accommodations and car rental discounts; some consolidators have access to several different types of resources.

For destinations worldwide, try **Airfare Busters,** which has offices in Washington, D.C. (tel. (800) 776-0481), Boca Raton, FL (tel. (800) 881-3273), and Houston, TX (tel. (232-8783); **Cheap Tickets,** offices in Los Angeles, CA, San Francisco, CA, Honolulu, HI, Overland Park, KS, and New York, NY, (tel. (800) 377-1000); For a processing fee, depending on the number of travelers and the itinerary, **Travel Avenue,** Chicago, IL (tel. (800) 333-3335) will search for the lowest international airfare available and even give you a rebate on fares over US$300. To Europe, try **Rebel** in Valencia, CA (tel. (800) 227-3235) and Orlando, FL (tel. (800) 732-3588); or **Discount Travel International,** New York, NY (tel. (212) 362-3636; fax 362-3236). To Italy, check with **New Frontiers** in New York, NY (tel. (800) 366-6387) and **Pino Welcome Travel,** New York, NY (tel. (800) 247-6578).

Kelly Monaghan's *Consolidators: Air Travel's Bargain Basement* (US$7 plus US$2 shipping) from the Intrepid Traveler, P.O. Box 438, New York, NY 10034 (e-mail intreptrav@aol.com), is an valuable source for more information and lists of consolidators by location and destination. Cyber-resources include **World Wide** (http://www.tmn.com/wwwanderer/www) and Edward Hasbrouck's incredibly informative **Airline Ticket Consolidators and Bucket Shops** (http://www.gnn.com/gnn/wic/wics/trav.97.html).

STAND-BY FLIGHTS

Airhitch, 2641 Broadway, 3rd floor, New York, NY 10025 (tel. (800) 326-2009 or (212) 864-2000) and Los Angeles, CA (tel. (310) 726-5000), will add a certain thrill to your itinerary, since you will be unable to control exactly when you leave and where you end up. Complete flexibility on both sides of the Atlantic is necessary. Flights cost US$169 each way when departing from the Northeast, US$269 from the West Coast or Northwest, and US$229 from the Southeast and Midwest. The snag is that instead of buying a ticket, you purchase only a promise that you will get to a destination near where you're intending to go within a window of time (usually 5 days) from a location in a region you've specified. You call in before your date-range to hear all of your flight options for the next seven days and your probability of boarding. You then decide which flights you want to try to make and present a voucher at the airport which grants you the right to board a flight on a space-available basis. This procedure must be followed again for the return trip. Be aware that you may only receive a refund if *all* available flights which departed within your date and destination-range were full. There are several offices in Europe, so you can wait to register for your return. The main one is in Paris (tel. (1) 47 00 16 30).

Air-Tech, Ltd., 584 Broadway, #1007, New York, NY 10012 (tel. (212) 219-7000, fax 219-0066) offers a very similar service. Their travel window is one to four days; rates to and from Europe are generally the following: Northeast US$169; West Coast US$249; Midwest/Southeast US$199. Upon registration and payment, Air-Tech sends you a FlightPass with a contact date when you are to call them for flight instructions. Note that the service is one way—you must go through the same procedure to return—and that *no refunds* are granted unless the company fails to get you a seat before your travel window expires. Be advised that clients' vouchers will not be honored if an airline fails to receive payment in time.

Contact the Better Business Bureau before contracting with either of these companies.

CHARTER FLIGHTS

The theory behind a **charter** is that a tour operator contracts with an airline (usually one specializing in charters) to fly extra loads of passengers to peak-season destinations. Charter flights fly less frequently than major airlines and have more restrictions, particularly on refunds. They are also almost always fully booked, and schedules and itineraries may change or be cancelled as late as 48 hours before the trip, and without a full refund. You'll be much better off purchasing a charter ticket on a regularly scheduled airline. As always, pay with a credit card if you can, and consider traveler's insurance against trip interruption. Try **Interworld** (tel. (305) 443-4929) or **Travac** (tel. (800) 872-8800). Don't be afraid to call many numbers and hunt for the best deal.

Eleventh-hour **discount clubs** and **fare brokers** offer savings on European travel, including charter flights and tour packages. Research your options carefully. **Last Minute Travel Club,** 1249 Boylston St., Boston, MA 02215 (tel. (800) 527-8646 or

(617) 267-9800), and **Discount Travel International,** New York, NY (tel. (212) 362-3636; fax 362-3236) are among the few travel clubs that don't charge a membership fee. Others (which charge US$25-50 membership fees) include **Moment's Notice,** New York, NY (tel. (718) 234-6295; fax 234-6450) and **Travelers Advantage,** Stamford, CT (tel. (800) 835-8747). Study these organizations' contracts closely; you don't want to end up with an unwanted overnight layover.

COURIER COMPANIES AND FREIGHTERS

Those who travel light should consider flying to Europe as a **courier.** The company hiring you will use your checked luggage space for freight; you're only allowed to bring carry-ons. You are responsible for the safe delivery of the baggage claim slips (given to you by a courier company representative) to the representative waiting for you when you arrive. Don't screw up or you will be blacklisted as a courier. You will probably never see the cargo you are transporting—the company handles it all—and airport officials know that couriers are not responsible for the baggage checked for them. Restrictions to watch for: you must be over 18, have a valid passport, and procure your own visa (if necessary). Most flights are roundtrip with short fixed-length stays of about a week, and only single tickets are issued (but a companion may be able to get a next-day flight). Most flights are from New York. Roundtrip fares to Western Europe from the U.S. range from US$250-400 (during the off-season) to US$400-550 (during the summer). **NOW Voyager,** 74 Varick St. #307, New York, NY 10013 (tel. (212) 431-1616), acts as an agent for many courier flights worldwide, originating primarily from New York. They offer special last-minute deals to such cities as London, Paris, Rome, and Frankfurt for as little as US$200 roundtrip plus a US$50 registration fee. Other agents to try are **Halbart Express,** 147-05 176th St., Jamaica, NY 11434 (tel. (718) 656-5000), **Courier Travel Service,** 530 Central Ave., Cedarhurst, NY 11516 (tel. (516) 763-6898), and **Discount Travel International,** (tel. (212) 362-3636).

Check your bookstore or library for handbooks such as *Air Courier Bargains* (US$15 plus US$3.50 shipping from the Intrepid Traveler, P.O. Box 438, New York, NY 10034). *The Courier Air Travel Handbook* (US$10 plus US$3.50 shipping) explains how to travel as an air courier and contains names, phone numbers, and contact points of courier companies. It can be ordered directly from Bookmasters, Inc., P.O. Box 2039, Mansfield, OH 44905 (tel. (800) 507-2665). **Travel Unlimited,** P.O. Box 1058, Allston, MA 02134-1058, publishes a comprehensive, monthly newsletter detailing all possible options for courier travel (often 50% off discount commercial fares). A one-year subscription is US$25 (outside of the U.S. US$35). If you really have travel time to spare, **Ford's Travel Guides,** 19448 Londelius St., Northridge, CA 91324 (tel. (818) 701-7414; fax 701-7415) lists **freighter companies** that will take passengers worldwide. Ask for their *Freighter Travel Guide and Waterways of the World* (US$16, plus US$2.50 postage if mailed outside the U.S.).

A final caveat for the budget conscious: don't get so caught up in the seemingly great deals. Always read the fine print; check for restrictions and hidden fees. There are amazingly cheap fares out there, but you can't get something for nothing.

By Train

Eurailpasses may be used to get to Italy from a number of European countries. They are also valid, though not as economical, for travel within Italy. They are intended for non-Europeans and must therefore be bought before arrival in Europe. All travel agents offer the same prices, which are at set by the EU. There are several varieties (including group passes); investigate the Eurail Youthpass if you are under 26 (US$418 for 15 days, US$598 for one month, US$798 for two months). Eurailpasses are not refundable once validated unless you have purchased insurance on it through the Pass Protection Plan (US$10). Contact **Rail Europe, Inc.,** 226-230 Westchester Ave., White Plains, NY 10604 (tel. (800) 438-7245, fax (800) 432-1329 in the U.S.; tel.

(800) 361-7245, fax (905) 602-4198 in Canada; http://www.raileurope.com) for the free *Europe on Track* guide to pass options and rail travel. For information on train travel within Italy, see **Getting Around by Train,** p. 45.

By Ferry

Ferry services in the port towns of Bari, Brindisi, and Otranto connect Italy to Greece. Unless you have a Eurail pass (only honored at the Brindisi port), Bari and Otranto services are cheaper, and they keep you separated from Brindisi's chaotic hordes of tourists. There are also connections from Genoa, Sardinia, and Trapani to Tunisia. See **Getting Around by Ferry,** p. 49.

For major trips it may be necessary to reserve ferry tickets at least one week ahead of time. When planning your itinerary, keep in mind that ferry schedules change unpredictably, so confirm your departure a day in advance. Some stations require that you check in two hours before your departure to avoid cancellation of your reservation. The cheapest option is *posta ponte* (deck class; preferable in the warm summer months). However, it is often only available when the *poltrone* (reclining cabin seats) are taken. Port taxes often apply. Ask for student and Eurail discounts.

ONCE THERE

Tourist Offices in Italy

The **Ente Nazionale Italiano di Turismo (ENIT)** is a national tourist office with bureaus in Rome (on Via Marghera, 2) and abroad. In provincial capitals, look for a branch of the **Ente Provinciale per il Turismo (EPT),** which provides info on the entire province. Many towns also have an **Azienda Autonoma di Soggiorno e Turismo (AAST),** the city tourist board. The Azienda tends to be the most useful and approachable. The smallest towns sometimes sport a privately run **Pro Loco** office. Recently, a new brand of tourist office, the **Azienda di Promozione Turismo (APT),** has popped up. Watch out for these, because they are allowed to present you with a list of only those hotels that have paid to be listed and some of the hotels we recommend may not be on the list. Keep an eye out for the student-oriented **Centro Turistico Studentesco e Giovanile (CTS)** and **Compagnia Italiana Turismo (CIT)** (see **Budget Travel Services,** page 39). Local offices are listed in the Practical Information section of each town.

Embassies and Consulates

Call in advance to make sure your embassy is actually open before you go. Embassies answer the phone around the clock in case of emergencies and have lists of English-speaking doctors and lawyers.

United States: Via Veneto, 121 (tel. (06) 467 41; fax 46 74 22 17). Passport and consular services open Mon.-Fri. 8:30am-noon and 2-4pm. Report stolen passports here; new passports can be issued the same day for a US$65 fee (US$40 for minors). Closed on U.S. and Italian holidays.

Canada: Consulate, Via Zara, 30 (tel. (06) 44 59 84 21; fax 44 59 89 12). Near the corner with Via Nomentana, on the 5th floor. Consular and passport services here open Mon.-Fri. 10am-noon and 2-4pm. A passport issued here costs CDN$35. English and French spoken. Embassy, Via G.B. De Rossi, 27 (tel. (06) 44 59 81).

Britain: Via XX Settembre, 80A (tel. (06) 482 54 41; fax 48 90 30 73), near the Porta Pia and the corner of Via Palestro. Consular and passport services open Mon.-Fri. 9:15am-1:30pm and 2-4pm; mid-July-Aug. open Mon.-Fri. 8am-1pm.

Australia: Via Alessandria, 215 (tel. (06) 85 27 21; fax 85 27 23 00). The office has lots of useful information for Australians (or any English-speakers) staying in Rome. Consular and passport services around the corner at Corso Trieste 25, open Mon.-Thurs. 9am-noon and 1:30-4pm, Fri. 9am-noon. A passport costs AUS$106. Australians in Italy are required to obtain a permit of stay from the police within 8 days of arrival and are not allowed to work there.

New Zealand: Via Zara, 28 (tel. (06) 440 29 28/29/30; fax 440 29 84). Consular and passport services Mon.-Fri. 8:30am-12:45pm and 1:45-5pm. Passport L137,000. If you need the passport after hours or during the weekend, a large surcharge is added.

Often there are restrictions on travel from other countries, so it is a good idea to contact your embassy before leaving to find out what these are. Some other embassies in Rome are: **Austria,** Via Pergolesi, 3 (tel. (06) 855 82 41; fax 854 32 86); **Belgium,** Via Monti Parioli, 49 (tel. (06) 360 95 11); **Czech Republic,** Via dei Gracchi, 322 (tel. (06) 32 444 59; fax 32 444 66); **Egypt,** Via Salaria, 265 (tel. (06) 855 53 61); **France,** Piazza Farnese, 67 (tel. (06) 68 60 11); **India,** Via XX Settembre, 5 (tel. (06) 48 84 642; fax 48 19 539); **Ireland,** Piazza Campitelli, 3 (tel. (06) 697 91 21); **Israel,** Via M. Mercati, 12 (tel. (06) 36 19 81); and **Spain,** Embassy: Largo Fontanella Borghese, 19 (tel. (06) 687 81 72), Consulate: Via Campo Marzio, 34 (tel. (06) 686 43 92).

Emergencies

Few legal systems are as convoluted and ambiguous as Italy's. Interpretations of the law are as varied as the dialects of the land. Your consulate will provide an attorney and advice, but after that you are on your own; you will be subject to Italian law.

If you can't avoid the police system, at least know with whom you are dealing. The **Polizia Urbana,** or **Pubblica Sicurezza** (emergency tel. 113), are the non-military police who deal with local crime. Try to contact them first if you are robbed or attacked. The **carabinieri** (emergency tel. 112) are actually a part of the Italian Army. They usually deal with the most serious crimes, such as terrorism (hence their intimidating, well-armed presence at airports). They are also a source of endless stupid Italian jokes, or *barzellette,* such as the one that claims that *i carabinieri* travel in pairs because one can read and one can write. The **Vigili Urbani** manage less violent, less serious offenses, such as traffic violations. They also give directions to lost tourists. This book provides listings of police offices and medical emergency numbers in the Practical Information section of individual cities. Consult **Safety and Security,** page 18, for further guidelines.

Getting Around

BY PLANE

Europe's train system is so efficient and airline prices are so high that it makes little sense to fly around the Continent. If you are age 25 or under, or a full-time student under 31, you may take advantage of special air passes offered by **Alitalia** or **Lufthansa.** Check with a student or budget travel agency for possible discounts, especially on high-volume routes.

BY TRAIN

The great majority of budget travelers in Europe use the economical and efficient train system. Italian trains retain the romance and convenience American railways have lost. Unfortunately, **they are not always safe.** While passengers sleep deeply, they may be robbed or attacked. Sleep wearing your money belt or neck pouch and, if you are traveling with a companion, try to sleep in shifts. Rumor has it that compartments are sometimes gassed on overnight runs to the southern departure points for Greece—be sure you open a window to thoroughly ventilate your compartment

Transportation
AUSTRIA
SLOVENIA
CROATIA
BOSNIA-HERZEGOVINIA
SWITZERLAND
LIECHTENSTEIN
FRANCE
MONACO
SAN MARINO
Adriatic Sea
Ligurian Sea
TREMITI ISLANDS
Elba
Corsica (FRANCE)
TO BASEL
TO MUNICH
TO VIENNA
TO BELGRADE
TO GENEVA
TO MARSEILLE
TO GREECE
Zurich
Lucerne
Bern
Interlaken
Innsbruck
Merano
St Moritz
Bressanone
Bolzano
Tarviso
Cividale
Udine
Ljubljana
Zagreb
Trieste
Lignano-Sabbiadoro
Rijeka
Sarajevo
Chamonix
Locarno
Lugano
Como
Aosta
Novara
Milano
Pavia
Susa
Torino
Asti
Alessandria
Piacenza
Cremona
Mantua
Brescia
Trento
Treviso
Vicenza
Mestre
Venezia
Verona
Padova
Ferrara
Parma
Reggio
Modena
Bologna
Ravenna
Zadar
Genova
La Spezia
Finale Ligure
Nice
Cannes
Pistoia
Lucca
Pisa
Livorno
Firenze
Arezzo
Siena
Rimini
Pesaro
Urbino
Ancona
Split
Dubrovnik
Gubbio
Albacina
Perugia
Assisi
Foligno
Orvieto
Terni
Viterbo
Orte
Rieti
L'Aquila
Pescara
Sulmona
Termoli
Vieste
Civitavecchia
Cerveteri
Tivoli
Frascati
Roma
Latina
Isernia
Campobasso
Benevento
Foggia
Bari
Bastia
Calvi
Ajaccio

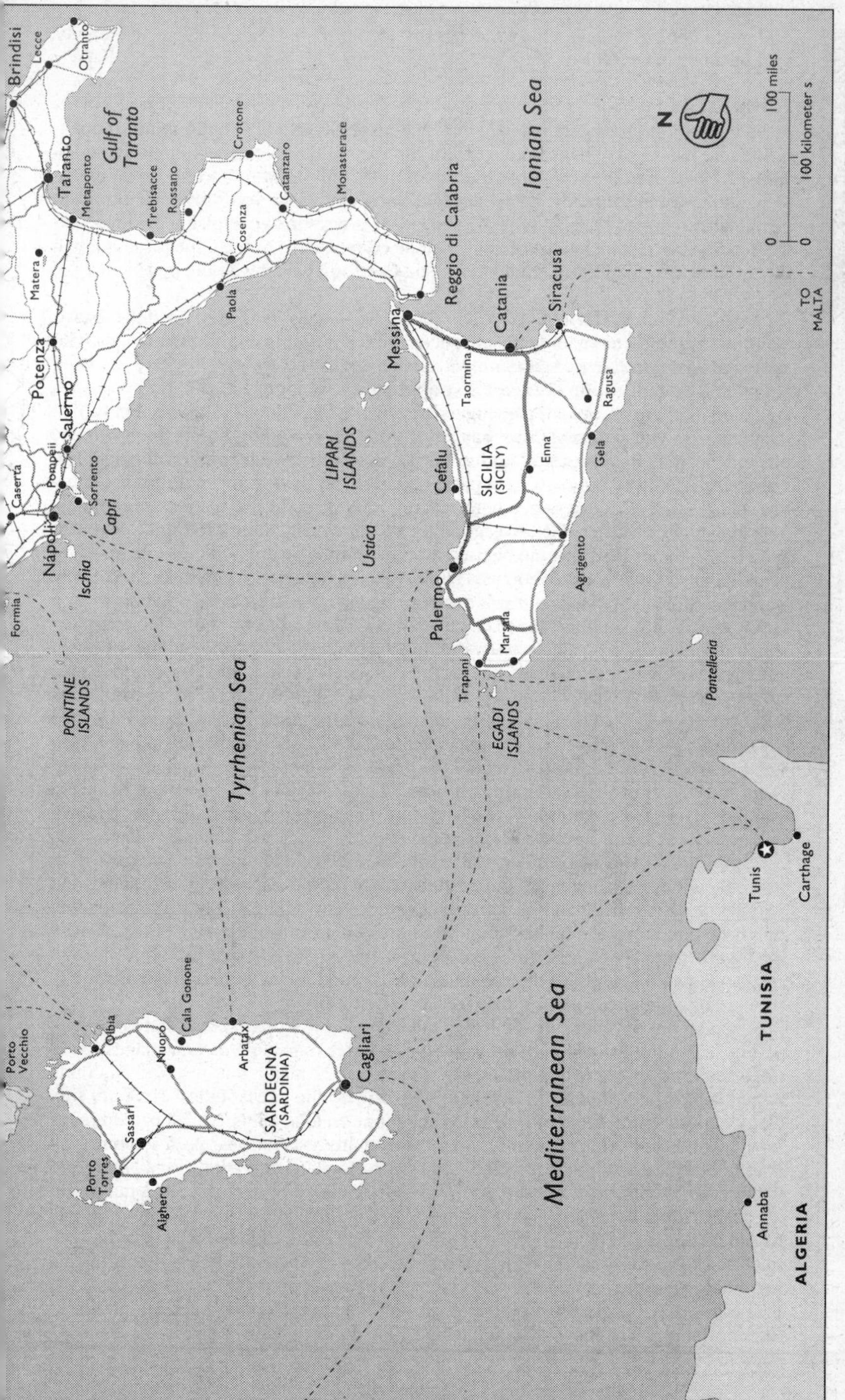

Brindisi
Lecce
Otranto
Gulf of Taranto
Taranto
Metaponto
Trebisacce
Rossano
Crotone
Catanzaro
Monasterace
Matera
Cosenza
Paola
Potenza
Salerno
Reggio di Calabria
Messina
Catania
Siracusa
Taormina
Ionian Sea
N
100 miles
100 kilometers
0
TO MALTA
Caserta
Pompeii
Sorrento
Napoli
Capri
Ischia
LIPARI ISLANDS
Ustica
Cefalu
SICILIA (SICILY)
Enna
Ragusa
Gela
Agrigento
Palermo
Marsala
Trapani
EGADI ISLANDS
Pantelleria
Formia
PONTINE ISLANDS
Tyrrhenian Sea
Tunis
Carthage
TUNISIA
Porto Vecchio
Olbia
Cala Gonone
Nuoro
Arbatax
SARDEGNA (SARDINIA)
Cagliari
Sassari
Porto Torres
Alghero
Mediterranean Sea
Annaba
ALGERIA

and avoid compartments with windows that don't open. (For more tips, see **Safety and Security,** page 18.)

Railpasses In theory, purchasing a railpass allows you to change your travel plans at will, jumping on any train to any destination at any time. Keep in mind, though, that some passes may be less convenient for use within Italy. reservations and additional fees are required for some trains, you must still stand in line for initial validation, and, most importantly, it may not save you money. Ask your travel agent for the Eurail tariff manual, then add up the second-class fares for your planned routes and deduct 5% (listed prices automatically include commission) to see if the purchase will pay off. For information on Eurailpasses, see **Getting There by Train,** p. 43.

Train Travel Within Italy The Italian State Railway, **Ferrovie dello Stato (FS),** offers inexpensive and efficient service, except during its frequent strikes. The new **national number** for train info within Italy is (147) 88 80 88. The fare between Rome and Florence, one of the more popular trips, is about L22,000 one way, second-class. Student and youth passengers are eligible for reduced rates (see below).

A railpass will probably not pay off if you are traveling solely within Italy, although it may be a practical option for travel to nearby European countries. The Italian State Railway offers its own passes, valid on all train routes within Italy. They are seldom cost-effective (since regular fares are so cheap), with a few exceptions. The **Italian Kilometric Ticket** is good for 20 trips or 3000km (1875mi.) of travel, whichever comes first, and can be used for two months by up to five people traveling together at all times. Three thousand kilometers is a long way in Italy, so it's virtually impossible for one person to break even on the Kilometric Ticket. For a couple or a family traveling widely, however, it can pay off. When used by more than one person, mileage per trip is calculated by multiplying the distance by the number of users. Children under 12 are charged half of the distance traveled, and those under four travel free. A first-class kilometric ticket costs L338,000 (US$224), second-class L200,000 (US$132). When buying the ticket, be sure the sales agent stamps the date on it. Purchase this pass from the **Italian State Railway Representative** in New York (tel. (212) 697-1482) or in Italy (where the prices are slightly lower) at major train stations and offices of the **Compagnia Italiana Turismo (CIT).** While using this pass, you must go to the ticket booth and have your mileage stamped; otherwise, you will pay hefty fines to buy another ticket on the train.

Cartaverde are available to anyone between the ages of 12 and 26. The card costs L40,000, is valid for one year, and entitles you to a 20% discount on any state train fare. If you're under 26 and plan to travel extensively in Italy, it should be your *first* purchase upon arrival. Families of four or more and groups of up to five adults traveling together qualify for discounts on Italian railways. Anyone over 60 with proof of age can get a 20% discount on train tickets with purchase of a **carta d'argento** ("silver card"), which is good for a year and costs L40,000.

Several types of trains ride the Italian rails. The *locale* stops at every station along a particular line, often taking twice as long as a faster train. The *diretto* makes fewer stops than the *locale,* while the *espresso* just stops at major stations. The air-conditioned *rapido,* an *intercity (IC)* train, travels only to the largest cities. A *rapido* supplement costs extra, but may be worth the money on long hauls. Not all *rapido* trains have second-class compartments, and a few require reservations. Be sure your train does not require a supplemental fee, even with a Eurail pass. Tickets for a *pendolino* (a direct train with first-class seats only) are well out of a budget traveler's range. On overnight trips, consider paying extra for a *cuccetta,* one of six fold-down bunks within a compartment. If you're not willing to spend the money on a *cuccetta,* consider taking an *espresso* train for overnight travel—they usually have compartments with fold-out seats.

The prices for luggage storage at train stations have recently been standardized throughout much of Italy. Plan on paying L5000 for each 12-hr. period.

Youth and Student Fares For travelers under 26, **BIJ tickets** *(Billets Internationals de Jeunesse)*, sold under the names **Wasteels, Eurotrain,** and **Route 26,** are a good alternative to railpasses. Available for international trips within Europe, interior travel within France, and some ferry routes, they knock 25-40% off regular second-class fares. Tickets are good for 60 days after purchase and allow a number of stopovers along the normal direct route of the train journey. Issued for a specific international route between two points, they must be used in the direction and order of the designated route without side- or back-tracking. You must buy BIJ tickets in Europe, at either Wasteels or Eurotrain offices (usually in or near train stations), or try directly at the ticket counter.

Useful Resources The ultimate reference for planning rail trips is the *Thomas Cook European Timetable* (US$28; US$39 includes a map of Europe highlighting all train and ferry routes; add US$4.50 for postage). In the U.S., order it from **Forsyth Travel Library** (see p. 5). The annual *Eurail Guide to Train Travel in the New Europe* (US$15) is available in most bookstores, or by writing to the Houghton Mifflin Co., 222 Berkeley St., Boston, MA 02116 (tel. (617) 351-5974; fax 351-1113).

BY BUS

Few people think of buses when planning travel within Europe, but they are available and cheap. Passes for travel between major European cities are available from **Eurobus,** 355 Palermo Ave., Coral Gables, FL 33134 (tel. (800) 517-7778 or (800) 727-2437 for students). The U.K. address is P.O. Box 5220, London W51GQ (tel. (0181) 991 55 91; fax 991 14 42). **Eurolines,** 4 Cardiff Rd., LUTON LU1 1PP (tel. (01582) 40 45 11 or (0171) 730 82 35 in London), is Europe's largest operator of coach services, offering unlimited 30- or 60-day travel between 18 major cities.

Buses in Italy serve many points in the countryside that are inaccessible by train and occasionally arrive in more convenient places in larger towns. Buses are also often crowded, so buy tickets in advance when possible. As a reward for the bumpy ride, the scenery along the way often outshines the beauty of any final destination. Bus rides in the southern Tuscan hills and along the route from Bolzano to Cortina D'Ampezzo in the Dolomites are among the most incredible.

BY FERRY

The islands of Sicily, Sardinia, and Corsica, as well as the smaller islands along the coasts, are connected to the mainland by ferries *(traghetti)* and hydrofoils *(aliscafi)*, motor boats with metal fins that lift the hull out of the water as speed is attained. Italy's largest private ferry service is **Tirrenia;** for info, contact the Rome office at Via Bissolati, 41 (tel. (06) 474 20 41). Tirrenia and other major companies (including **Moby Lines, Siremar, Caremar,** and hydrofoil services **SNAV** and **Alilauro**) make departures and arrivals in major port towns such as Ancona, Bari, Brindisi, Genoa, Livorno, La Spezia, Naples, and Trapani. Not only do ferry services allow tourists to visit the Tremiti, Pontine, and Lipari Islands, but they also give tourists a reason to spend time in a port town to which they otherwise would not have given a second thought. Use the time prior to your departure to enjoy the "Stop-Over in Bari" program or simply to indulge in the coast's fresh seafood.

BY CAR

If you're pressed for time, or touring with friends or a large family, traveling by car may prove the most enjoyable and practical way to see Italy. Keep in mind, however, that much of Italy's infrastructure was constructed before the age of the automobile. Some towns will prove virtually unnavigable; consider parking on the outskirts and walking to town centers. Reckless drivers are common in Italy, and the convoluted street system often inflames tempers.

A car can cut severely into your budget. Renting a standard economy car for one week will be at least US$300, the *Autostrade* charge substantial tolls, and gas *(ben-*

zina) computes to about L2000 per liter (about a quart). **Automobile Club d' Italia (ACI)** has border offices and branch offices nationwide. The ACI is located at Via Marsala, 8, 00185 Rome (tel. (06) 499 81; fax 49 98 22 34). If you're brave and know what you're doing, buying a used car in Europe and selling it just before you leave can provide the cheapest wheels on the Continent for longer trips. David Shore and Patty Campbell's *Europe by Van and Motorhome* (US$14, US$2 postage, US$6 overseas) guides you through the entire process of renting, leasing, buying, and selling vehicles (vans are their specialty). To order, write to Shore/Campbell Publications, 1842 Santa Margarita Dr., Fallbrook, CA 92028 (tel./fax (800) 659-5222 or (619) 723-6184). Or purchase *How to Buy and Sell a Used Car in Europe* (US$6, postage US$1; from Gil Friedman, 1735 J St., Arcata, CA 95521, tel. (707) 822-5001).

If renting a car, always check if prices quoted include tax and collision insurance. (Some credit card companies will cover this automatically.) Reserve well before leaving for Europe and pay in advance if you can. Inquire about student and other discounts and be flexible in your itinerary; it can be cheaper to pick up your car in some places than in others. Ask your airline about special packages. Minimum age restrictions vary by country, but are often between 21 and 25. If you are a student, ask about rental discounts at Council Travel or CTS. The major firms renting in Italy are **Auto Europe,** (tel. (800) 223-5555); **Avis Rent-A-Car,** (tel. (800) 331-1084); **Bon Voyage By Car,** (tel. (800) 272-3299; in Canada (800) 253-3876). **Budget Rent-A-Car,** (tel. (800) 472-3325); **Hertz Rent-A-Car,** (tel. (800) 654-3001); **The Kemwel Group,** (tel. (800) 678-0678); **Maiellano Travel Auto,** (tel. (718) 727-0044), and **Payless Car Rental,** (tel. (800) 729-5377).

For trips which are longer than 17 days, **leasing** will be cheaper than renting; it is sometimes the only option for those ages 18-20. Leases include insurance coverage and are not taxed. Expect to pay at least US$1200 for 60 days. Contact Bon Voyage by Car or Auto Europe; you must make arrangements in advance. If you have a group of six people, ask about renting a **campervan or motorhome;** these rentals can be expensive, but you'll avoid the cost and hassle of finding a hotel room.

Foreign drivers in Italy should have both an international driver's permit and an international insurance certificate (see p. 13). Maps are essential, or you may find yourself confounded by Italy's labyrinth of small roads. Contact the **Association for Safe International Road Travel (ASIRT)** at 5413 West Cedar Lane, Suite 103C, Bethesda, MD 20814 (tel. (301) 983-5252; fax 983-3663) for info on specific driving conditions in other countries. For any serious driving emergency, call the 24-hr. **nationwide roadside emergency line** at 116.

BY MOPED AND SCOOTER

Mopeds and scooters provide an enjoyable, relatively inexpensive way to tour the Italian countryside, especially in coastal areas where the view demands frequent attention. They are, however, dangerous in the rain and on rough or gravelly roads. Always wear a helmet and never ride wearing a large backpack. If you've never been on a moped before, Italy is not the place to learn. The Vespa-style motorbikes with small wheels and a center platform for your feet are particularly hazardous. Mopeds and scooters are prohibited on *autostrade*, so travel is often limited to one area. Ask about rentals at bicycle and motorcycle shops. Rates are often from L40,000 to L60,000 per day; be sure the quoted price includes taxes and insurance.

BY BICYCLE

Biking is an increasingly popular method of traveling around Europe. Remember that Italy's hills require a mountain bike with very low gears for any sustained expedition, along with an excellent set of lungs and legs. Wear visible clothing, drink plenty of water, and ride on the same side as the traffic. For info about touring routes, consult national tourist offices or any of the numerous books available. *Europe By Bike,* by Karen and Terry Whitehill (US$15), offers specific area tours (available from **The Mountaineers Books,** 1001 SW Klickitat Way #201, Seattle, WA 98134; tel. (800) 553-4453 or tel./fax (206) 223-6303). *Cycling Europe: Budget Bike Touring in the Old World* is by N. Slavinski (US$13). Michelin road maps are also clear and detailed guides. For more info, you may also want to contact the **Federazione Italiana Amici della Bicicletta (FIAB),** c/o Gianni Catania, C. Regina Margherita 152, 10152 Torino (tel./fax (011) 521 23 66; fax 88 89 81).

Be aware that touring involves pedaling both yourself and whatever you store in the panniers (bags that strap to your bike). Take some reasonably challenging day-long rides to prepare before you leave. Have your bike tuned up by a reputable shop. Learn the international signals for turns and use them. Before leaving, learn how to fix a modern derailleur-equipped mount and change a tire, and practice on your own bike before you have to do it overseas. A few simple tools and a good bike manual will be invaluable.

If you are nervous about setting out on your own, there are a number of companies which offer group bicycle tours in Italy. **CBT Bicycle Tours,** 415 W. Fullerton Pkwy., #1003, Chicago, IL 60614 (tel. (800) 736-BIKE/736-2453 or (312) 404-1710; fax (312) 404-1833), has recently added Italy to the list of European countries which it explores. In 1997, CBT will offer tours in Tuscany and the northern Lake District at prices averaging $95 per day (camping equipment, many meals, and complete van support included). **Ciclismo Classico,** 13 Marathon St., Arlington, MA 02174 (tel. (800) 866-7314; fax (617) 641-1512; e-mail info@ciclismoclassico.com), leads bike tours in Italy in April and May.

Most airlines will count your bicycle as your second free piece of luggage, but check before buying your ticket (as an extra piece, it will cost about US$50 each way). The safest way to send your bike is in a box, with the handlebars, pedals and front wheel detached. Within Europe, many ferries let you take your bike for free. You can always ship your bike on trains, though the cost varies from a small fixed fee to a substantial fraction of the ticket price. You may also be able to purchase an appropriate bike in Italy. Long- and short-term rentals are also readily available.

It is definitely worthwhile to buy proper equipment for touring; riding a bike with a frame pack strapped on it or your back is about as safe as pedaling blindfolded over ice. Bicycle accessories, such as panniers and other touring bags, are cheaper and of better quality in the U.S. **Bike Nashbar,** 4111 Simon Rd., Youngstown, OH 44512 (tel. (800) 627-4227; fax (800) 456-1223) has excellent prices and cheerfully beats advertised competitors' offers by $5. The first thing you should buy is a **bike helmet.** At about US$40, it's a lot cheaper and more pleasant than neurosurgery. To increase the odds of finding your bike where you left it, buy a U-shaped lock made by **Citadel** or **Kryptonite.** It may seem expensive (starting at US$30) until you compare it to the price of buying a new bike in Italy.

BY THUMB

***Let's Go* does not recommend hitching as a means of travel in Italy or anywhere else. Be sure to consider the risks involved before you hitch.**

Not everyone can be a brain surgeon, but most any bozo can drive a car. Hitching means entrusting your life to a random person who happens to stop beside you on the road, risking theft, assault, sexual harassment, and unsafe driving. In spite of this, there are gains: favorable hitching experiences allow you to meet local people and get where you're going cheaply. The choice remains yours.

If you're a woman traveling alone in Italy, don't hitch. It's just too dangerous. Those who choose to hitch usually do so with a companion—a man and a woman are a safer combination, two men will have a harder time finding a ride, and three will go nowhere. Bulletin boards at hostels are often cited as a good place to start looking.

Likewise, newspapers and university message boards sometimes carry ads seeking passengers to share driving and costs.

Success often depends on what you look like. Experienced hitchers stack their belongings in a compact but visible cluster, signal with an open hand rather than a thumb, and appear neat and wholesome. Hitchhiking pros usually keep the door unlocked and their belongings close at hand—in case a quick escape becomes necessary, luggage locked in the trunk will probably stay that way. They also take care never to fall asleep in cars (for obvious reasons). If a situation becomes uncomfortable for any reason, hitchers firmly ask to be let out, regardless of how unfavorable the spot seems for finding another ride. Hitching for women reportedly becomes more dangerous the farther south or off the mainland one goes, and anywhere near a large city poses a particular risk.

Accommodations

HOTELS

A note on the use of *piano*: The floor-system of hotels and other buildings in Italy can be rather confusing. *Piano terra* means ground floor, *1° piano* means 2nd floor, *2° piano* means 3rd floor, and *pianissimo* means play softly.

A provincial board classifies all hotels into a five-star system; most of the budget listings in *Let's Go* are one- and two-star options. No hotel can legally charge more than the maximum permitted by inspection, but some proprietors double their prices at the sound of a foreign voice. Remember that an official rate card must adorn the inside of the door in each room; you should ask to look at the room (and the card) before committing to anything. Keep in mind that bathrooms and breakfast often cost extra, and prices rise from year to year. In general, the most charming places are near the historic town center, while cheaper, nastier joints are located near the train and bus stations. Hotels *(alberghi)* may also be called *pensioni* (small one-to-three star hotels) or *locande* (the cheapest one-star accommodations).

Prices fluctuate regionally; expect higher prices in the north and in Rome and Florence. The cheapest hotel singles generally start at about L30,000 and doubles at L50,000. Rates tend to be lower per person in a shared room. A room with a double bed is called a *matrimoniale* (though marriage is not a prerequisite). A double with separate beds is called a *camera doppia,* and a single is a *camera singola.* Rooms with a private bath cost 30-50% more. Some places require you to pay for **full-pension,** meaning room and board (3 meals per day), or **half-pension,** meaning room, breakfast, and one other meal.

Italy has established high- and low-seasons for areas popular with tourists, especially resorts. Remember that alpine regions and seaside resort areas have different off-season months. **When there is a difference in high- and low-season prices, *Let's Go* provides this information in its listings.** You may need to write for reservations in summer tourist spots such as Florence, Venice, the Riviera, and Capri. In other areas, start looking for a room in the morning during high-season, or call a day in advance. Pick up a list of hotels and their prices from the local tourist office. (They may also quote rates over the phone.) If you plan to arrive late, call and ask a hotel to hold a room for you. Proprietors have recently become disgruntled with travelers who make reservations and don't show, however, and may not take reservations anymore. Few hotels accept phone reservations more than a day in advance.

Many small places don't have an English speaker, but this need not dissuade those who don't speak Italian from calling. Instructions on making a room reservation in Italian are included at the back of this book, and most *pensione* proprietors are used to receiving this type of call. **If you do make a reservation, keep it.** As a courtesy to hotel owners and fellow travelers (who may get turned away when a hotel is "reserved" to capacity), be sure to either keep your reservation or cancel it as soon as you know that you are not going to keep it.

An Italian law, drafted in response to 1980s terrorism, mandates that hotel owners keep a strict register of their guests. Proprietors risk immediate shutdown if they allow unregistered persons to spend the night in their rooms, so expect hotel managers to question you if you try to bring other people upstairs.

HOSTELS

Hostels are great places to meet travelers from all over the world. If you are alone, there is no better place to find a temporary traveling companion. Italian youth hostels are inexpensive and open to travelers of all ages; many are situated in historic buildings and areas of great natural beauty. They offer inexpensive meals and often provide services unavailable at hotels, including kitchen privileges, laundry facilities, and bike rental. On the other hand, you must adapt to curfews, daytime lockouts, and separate quarters for men and women (only a few hostels have doubles). You should also be advised that many hostels close in late fall and winter.

Hostel accommodations usually consist of bunk beds in dormitory-style rooms. You may be required to use a **sleep sack,** which you can either purchase or make yourself. For instructions, see **Packing: Miscellaneous** p. 37 Most hostels that require them also provide them for a small surcharge. Rates vary by hostel, but you can expect to pay around L20,000 per person including breakfast; dinners cost between L5000 and L13,000. Hostels are not as abundant in Italy as in northern Europe, and their locations are often inconvenient. Because you will be sharing a room with several strangers, security may also be less certain than in a hotel room, so keep your valuables with you.

To stay in youth hostels affiliated with **Hostelling International (HI),** you must usually be an HI member. The Italian HI affiliate organization, **Associazione Italiana Alberghi per la Gioventù (AIG),** is at Via Cavour 44, 00184 Roma (tel. (06) 487 11 52; fax 488 04 92). They offer a free fax booking service between their major hostels, as well as a variety of discounts for food and transportation throughout Italy.

Hostel Memberships

A one-year **Hostelling International (HI)** membership permits you to stay at youth hostels in Italy and Tunisia at unbeatable prices (usually US$5-20). You can save yourself potential trouble by procuring a membership card, available at most budget travel organizations (like Council Travel and STA) before you leave home. For details on the Italian hostel network, contact the HI affiliate in Rome (see above).

The Internet Guide to Hostelling (http://hostels.com) can provide additional information on these accommodations, and the HI International Booking Network (IBN) allows you to make confirmed reservations at over 300 hostels worldwide for a nominal fee. Note that not all the Italian hostels take reservations, however.

The following are national HI affiliates in English-speaking countries. In many cases, **membership must be acquired through the HI affiliate in one's own country,** not abroad. Check with your local organization before you go.

American Youth Hostels (HI-AYH), 733 15th St. NW, Suite 840, Washington, D.C. 20005 (tel. (202) 783-6161; fax 783-6171; http://www.taponline.com/tap/travel/hostels/pages/hosthp.html). HI-AYH maintains 34 local offices, but most budget travel organizations sell memberships as well. Membership cards, which are valid for twelve months from the date of issue, cost US$25, under 18 US$10, over 54 US$15, family card US$35.

Hostelling International-Canada (HI-C), 400-205 Catherine Street, Ottawa, Ontario, K2P 1C3 (tel. (613) 237-7884; fax 237-7868). The Canada-wide membership and customer service line is (800) 663-5777. One-year membership fee CDN$25, under 18 CDN$12; 2-year (over 18) CDN$35; lifetime CDN$175.

Youth Hostels Association of England and Wales (YHA), Trevelyan House, 8 St. Stephen's Hill, St. Albans, Hertfordshire AL1 2DY (tel. (01727) 855 215; fax 844 126). Enrollment costs UK£9.30, under 18 UK£3.20, lifetime membership UK£125. Various family memberships are also available.

An Óige (Irish Youth Hostel Association), 61 Mountjoy St., Dublin 7 (tel. (01) 830 45 55; fax 830 58 08; http://www.touchtel.ie). One-year membership is IR£7.50, under 18 IR£4, and family IR£7.50 per adult with children under 16 free.

Youth Hostels Association of Northern Ireland (YHANI), 22 Donegall Rd., Belfast BT12 5JN, (tel. (01232) 31 54 35; fax 43 96 99).

Scottish Youth Hostels Association (SYHA), 7 Glebe Crescent, Stirling FK8 2JA (tel. (01786) 45 11 81; fax 45 01 98). Membership UK£6, under 18 UK£2.50.

Australian Youth Hostels Association (AYHA), Level 3, 10 Mallett St., Camperdown NSW, 2050 (tel. (02) 565 16 99; fax 565 13 25; e-mail YHA@zeta.org.au). Cards cost AUS$42, under 18 AUS$12, renewal AUS$26.

Youth Hostels Association of New Zealand (YHANZ), P.O. Box 436, 173 Gloucester St., Christchurch 1 (tel. (643) 379 99 70; fax 365 44 76; e-mail hostel.operations@yha.org.nz; http://yha.org.nz/yha). Annual memberships NZ$24.

Hostel Association of South Africa, P.O. Box 4402, Cape Town 8000 (tel. (21) 419 18 53; fax 21 69 37). Membership SAR45, students SAR30, group SAR120, family SAR90, lifetime SAR225.

ALTERNATIVE ACCOMMODATIONS

Italian history comes alive when you stay in the guest house of a Roman Catholic **monastery.** Guests need not attend services but are expected to make their own beds and, often, to clean up after meals. Found in rural settings, monasteries are usually peaceful, and you shouldn't stay in one unless you want a quiet and contemplative experience. Carrying an introduction on letterhead from your own priest, pastor, or rabbi may facilitate matters, although many monasteries will accept only Catholic guests. For more info about specific regions and a list of convents, monasteries, and other religious institutions offering accommodations, write to the archdiocese *(arcivescovado)* of the nearest large town. Many regional tourist boards also maintain a list of monasteries with guest houses.

For a quiet, non-religious atmosphere, try the *agriturismo* option and stay in a **rural cottage** or **farmhouse.** Usually, you will be given a small room and asked to clean up after yourself, but you will have freedom to come and go as you please. For more info, write to the main office of **Agriturist,** Corso V. Emanuele II, 101, 00186 Rome (tel. (06) 685 23 42) or contact the tourist office in the region that you will be visiting. Also, if you plan to hike in the Alps or the Dolomites, contact the **Touring Club Italiano** (see **Camping,** p. 58), which provides detailed hiking itineraries that include stopovers in mountain refuges.

The **Associazione Cattolica Internazionale al Servizio della Giovane—Protezione della Giovane** is a religious organization that helps women find inexpensive accommodations in its own hostels, convents, and *pensioni* throughout Italy. If you don't mind the occasional 10:30pm curfew, this service is extremely convenient. (For more info, see **Women Travelers,** page 30.)

Home rentals and exchanges are a reasonable option for people traveling in groups or on extended stays. **Hometours International, Inc.,** P.O. Box 11503, Knoxville, TN 37939 (tel. (800) 367-4668; e-mail hometours@aol.com) provides lodging in apartments, houses, villas, and castles in several European countries. Write for an Italy brochure (US$8). Some private households may also rent spare rooms to tourists for the night; look for **affitta camere** notices in papers and youth travel offices. Rates vary, so be prepared to bargain. Don't expect to pay much less than what a reasonable one-star *pensione* in town would cost. **Sleeping in European train stations** is a romanticized tradition, but while often tolerated by local police, it is neither comfortable nor safe (particularly for women and solo travelers).

Student residences in Italy are inexpensive and theoretically open to foreign students during vacations and whenever there is room. In reality, these accommodations are often nearly impossible to arrange. Check with tourist offices in university towns or the **Centro Turistico Studentesco e Giovanile (CTS)** for information on accommodations in *pensioni* or dormitories.

CAMPING

Lakes, rivers, seas, and mountains are common backdrops for Italian campgrounds. In August, arrive early—well before 11am—or you may find yourself without a spot. Rates average L8000 per person (or tent) and another L7000 for a car. Many of the campgrounds are well-equipped, boasting everything from swimming pools to bars, while others may be more primitive. If several sites are available in one area, you may want to shop around. The **Touring Club Italiano (TCI),** Via Marsala, 14, Rome (tel. (06) 491 17 41), publishes books with maps and camping information, available in bookstores throughout Italy. A free map and list of sites is available from the Italian Government Travel Office or directly from **Federcampeggio,** Via V. Emanuele, 11, Casella Postale 23, 50041 Calenzano, Florence (tel./fax (055) 88 23 91).

An **International Camping Carnet** (membership card) is required by some European campgrounds, but can usually be bought there. In the U.S., it is included in a US$30 membership to **Family Campers & RVers/NCHA** (see below).

Useful Organizations and Publications

Family Campers and RVers (NCHA), 4804 Transit Rd., Bldg. 2, Depew, NY 14043 (tel./fax (716) 668-6242). Sells the International Camping Carnet, required at some European campgrounds (US$30 includes membership in the National Campers and Hikers Association, Inc., and a subscription to *Camping Today*).

Recreational Equipment, Inc. (REI), P.O. Box 1700, Sumner, WA 98352-0001 (tel. (800) 426-4840; http://www.rei.com). Publishes *Europa Camping and Caravanning* (US$20), an annually updated catalog of European campsites. REI also sells a wide range of the latest in camping gear and holds great seasonal sales. Huge selection, and many items are guaranteed for life. Merchandise available from 1700 45th St. E., Sumner, WA 98390.

The Mountaineers Books publishes *Walking the Alpine Parks in France and Northwest Italy* (US$15). See **Getting Around By Bicycle,** p. 51, for the publisher's address.

Camping Equipment

The most important things to remember when camping are: stay warm, stay dry, stay hydrated. Always pay attention to weather forecasts. Purchase the following **equipment** items before you leave. For **backpacks,** see **Luggage,** p. 35.

Sleeping bag: Choose either down (compact, lightweight, and warm, but useless when wet) or synthetic (cheaper, heavier, more durable, and warmer when wet). Bags are rated according to the lowest outdoor temperature at which they will still keep you warm. A 3-season or 20°F bag (US$135-200 for synthetic, US$150-225 for down) should usually be sufficient in Italy, except in the winter.

Pads: A cushion between your soft body and the hard ground. Closed-cell foam pads start at $13; open-cell foam pads start at $25; an air mattress cushions your back and neck for $25-50. Another good alternative is a **Therm-A-Rest**, a combined foam pad and air-mattress which inflates to full padding when unrolled.

Tents: The ideal models are free-standing, with their own frames and suspension systems. Low profile dome tents tend to be the best all-around, entailing very little unnecessary bulk. Hikers should carry a small tent weighing less than 3.5 lbs. Be sure your tent has a rain fly and that you have a **tarpaulin** or **plastic groundcloth** to put underneath it. Last year's models are often drastically reduced in price.

Camp stoves: Don't rely on campfire cooking; some regions restrict fires. Simple Coleman stoves start at $30. Or try a GAZ-powered model, which burns propane and is common in Europe. Bring a **mess kit** and a **battery-operated lantern.**

Other: Waterproof matches, calamine lotion, and water-purification pills.

Shop around locally before turning to mail-order firms; this allows you to get an idea of what the different items actually look like (and weigh), so that if you decide later to order by mail you'll have a more exact idea of what you are getting. The mail-order firms listed below offer lower prices that those you're likely to find in stores, and they can also help you determine which item you need.

Campmor, P.O. Box 700, Saddle River, NJ 07458-0700 (tel. (800) 526-4784; http://www.campmor.com). Has a wide selection of name-brand equipment at low prices. One-year guarantee for unused or defective merchandise.

Eastern Mountain Sports (EMS), One Vose Farm Rd., Peterborough, NH 03458 (tel. (603) 924-7231). Call to find the store nearest you. Though slightly higher-priced, they provide excellent service and guaranteed customer satisfaction.

L.L. Bean, Inc., Attn: Product Info, Freeport, ME 04033 (ordering: U.S. and Canada (800) 221-4221, International, (207) 865-3111; customer service: U.S. and Canada (800) 341-4341, International (207) 865-3161; fax U.S. (207) 552-3080, Canada and International (207)552-4080; TTY and TDD (800) 545-0090). Equipment and preppy clothing. Open 24hr. per day, 7 days per week, 52 weeks per year.

Wilderness and Safety Concerns

When you're out in the wilderness, the first thing to preserve is *you*—health and safety should be your primary concerns when you camp. See **Health** (page 20) for info about basic medical concerns and first-aid. *Never go camping or hiking by yourself for any significant time or distance*. If you're going into an area that is not well-traveled or well-marked, let someone know where you're hiking and how long you intend to be out. If you fail to return on schedule or if you need to be reached, searchers will at least know where to look for you.

The second thing to preserve while you are outdoors is the wilderness. The thousands of outdoor enthusiasts that pour into the parks every year threaten to trample the land to death. Don't cut vegetation, and don't clear campsites. Check ahead to see if the park prohibits campfires. Even if it is allowed, firewood is scarce in popular parks, so you may want to use a campstove for cooking. To avoid digging a rain trench for your tent, pitch it on high, dry ground. If there are no toilet facilities, bury human waste at least four inches deep and 100 feet or more from any water supplies and campsites. *Biosafe* soap or detergents may be used in streams or lakes; otherwise, don't use soaps in or near bodies of water. Always pack up your trash and carry it with you until you reach the next trash can; burning and burying pollute the environment. In more civilized camping circumstances, respect fellow campers by keeping light and noise to a minimum, especially if you arrive after dark.

Keeping in Touch

MAIL

Sending Mail to Italy

Make sure anyone sending you mail from North America allows at least two weeks for it to reach you. Mail from home can be sent to a hotel where you have reservations, or you can collect mail from most **American Express** offices if you have an American Express card or carry their traveler's checks. Have the sender write "Client Mail" on the envelope with the office's complete address. Letters addressed to the post office with the recipient's name and the phrase **fermo posta** (general delivery) will be held at the post office of any city or town. You must claim your mail in person with your passport as identification, and you may have to pay L300 per piece of mail. In major cities like Rome, the post office handling *fermo posta* is usually efficient and is open for long weekday hours. Since a city may have more than one post office, write the address of the receiving office on the envelope if possible. It's also a good idea to have the sender capitalize and underline your last name to ensure proper sorting. Before writing off a letter as lost, check under your first name, too.

Federal Express (U.S. & Canada tel. (800) 238-5355) operates in Italy, as do several Italian competitors. Express mail is available as well, but at higher rates.

Sending Mail from Italy

The postal system in Italy has justly drawn snickers from the rest of Western Europe but has recently improved its service. Aerograms and airmail letters from Italy take anywhere from one to three weeks to arrive in the U.S., while surface mail—much less expensive—takes approximately three months, if it arrives at all. Since postcards are low-priority mail, send important messages by airmail letter. Letters and small parcels rarely get lost if sent *raccomandata* (registered), *espressa* (express), or *via aerea* (air mail). Stamps *(francobolli)* are available at face value in *tabacchi* (tobacco shops), but you should mail your letters from a post office to be sure they are stamped correctly. Letters and postcards sent overseas cost L1250; within the EU L750; outside the EU (but not overseas) L900.

TELEPHONES

Directory assistance for: Italy (tel. 12; free); Europe and the Mediterranean (tel. 176; L1200), and intercontinental (tel. 17 90; L1200). For an **English-speaking operator,** dial 170. To contact the **AT&T operator,** dial 172 10 11. To contact the **MCI operator**, dial 172 10 22. A number beginning with 167 is *telefono verde,* or toll-free.

Calling Italy

Telecom recently replaced SIP and other companies as Italy's primary telephone service; although many small towns may not have made the changeover yet.

Italian phone numbers range from three to eight digits in length. *Let's Go* makes every effort to get up-to-date phone numbers, but everyone is at the mercy of the Italian phone system. Phone numbers there change with bothersome frequency. If you call an old number, you may hear a recording of the new number in Italian, possibly even in English. Phone books often list two numbers: the first is the number at the time of printing, the second (marked by the word *prenderà*) is what the number will be at some future, unspecified time.

Calls to Italy must be preceded by the international access code that enables you to call outside your country, then Italy's country code (39) *and* the city code. When calling from outside Italy, the zero should be dropped from the beginning of the city code. (See **Telephone Codes,** p. 642.) Italians usually yell into the phone when calling long-distance, but that's due more to the omnipresent loud street traffic (and the fact that Italians *always* yell when they talk) than to a bad connection. Keep in mind the time difference when you call.

Calling Home

There are four types of telephones in Italy. Those that are hold-outs from the dark ages of telecommunications take only coins. Deposit more than you think you'll need, even if your call is local. If you underestimate, you may be cut off in the middle of your conversation. At the end of your call, you can press the return button for unused coins. To place long-distance calls, initially deposit at least L2000 or a phone token *(gettone)* to activate the phone, then watch the display carefully to make sure you don't run out of money. When using these phones, be sure to dial slowly as they sometimes misdial or disconnect if you treat them roughly. Expect a couple of tries to get through to an international operator.

Scatti calls are made from a phone run by an operator (who may simply be the proprietor in a bar). Most every town has at least one bar with a *telefono a scatti,* which can be used for international calls. *Let's Go listings will most often direct you to this type of phone service, but standard payphones are also readily available in train stations and other public places.* A meter records the cost of your call, and you pay when you finish. Check with the operator before you lift the receiver, and remember that he or she may tack on a substantial service fee.

The third type of phone is most common, and accepts either coins (L100, 200 or 500) or **phone cards.** Cards can be bought for L5000, L10,000, or L15,000 from vending machines (near the phone), *tabacchi,* bars, or the post office. Pull off the tab at the corner of the card to activate it. When you insert the card into the phone, a meter subtracts lire from it as you speak and displays the remaining value. Partially used cards can be removed and re-used. If you happen to run out in the middle of a call, you must insert another card, so buy more than one if you're planning a long conversation. The fourth type of phone accepts only phone cards.

For the most part, it is not difficult to make **long-distance calls within Europe.** For person-to-person calls, tell the operator you want to to call *"con preavviso."* A collect call is *chiamata a carico del destinatario* or *chiamata collect.* **Intercontinental calls** can be made from pay phones, telephone offices, or from a *telefono a scatti.* When placing a call from a telephone office, you will be assigned to a specific booth and may have to pay a deposit. When direct-dialing is possible, you can dial two zeros and then the **country code,** followed by the city code and number. For telephone information and codes, refer to the **appendix's telephone chart** (p. 642).

A **calling card** is another, cheaper alternative; your local long-distance phone company will have a number for you to dial while traveling (either toll-free or charged as a local call) to connect instantly to an operator in your home country. The calls (plus a small surcharge) are then billed either collect or to a calling card. For more information, inquire about the **AT&T Direct** service (tel. (800) 331-1140, from abroad (412) 553-7458), **Sprint** (tel. (800) 877-4646), or **MCI WorldPhone** and **World Reach** (tel. (800) 996-7535). MCI's WorldPhone also provides access to MCI's Traveler's Assist, which gives legal and medical advice, exchange rate information, and translation services. For similar services for countries outside the U.S., contact your local phone company. In Canada, contact Bell Canada **Canada Direct** (tel. (800) 565 4708); in the U.K., British Telecom **BT Direct** (tel. (800) 34 51 44); in Ireland, Telecom Éireann **Ireland Direct** (tel. (800) 250 250); in Australia, Telstra **Australia Direct** (tel. 13 22

00); in New Zealand, **Telecom New Zealand** (tel. 123); and in South Africa, **Telkom South Africa** (tel. 09 03).

FAX MACHINES AND TELEGRAMS

Faxes may be sent from an increasing number of private enterprises (the larger the city, the greater the availability). If you're desperate, ask at the tourist office for the nearest fax service. You can use the fax at an upscale hotel for exorbitant fees. **Telegrams** can be sent from the post office.

Let's Go Picks

Although our researchers were technically at work while traveling through Italy (including Tunisia), they were also on vacation. As tourists themselves, they have chosen their own personal favorite spots in the hopes that you might find and enjoy them, too.

Best Buildings/Museums/Churches:
Museo Civico Archeologico in **Bologna** (see p. 386); the cathedral in **Trani** (see p. 459); the Botticelli galleries of the Uffizi Gallery in **Florence** (see p. 188); the *nuraghi* outdoor museum in **Barumini, Sardinia** (see p. 557); the *campanile* in **Cremona** (see p. 311); Il Vittoriale estate in **Gardone Riviera** (see p. 378); and El Bardo in **Tunis** (see p. 594).

Best Natural Sights:
The hot springs in **Ischia** (see p. 430); the mountains around **Matmata, Tunisia** (in the eerie land of the Jawas from *Star Wars;* see p. 612); the hillside at **Montepulciano** (see p. 214); the beaches of **Elba** (see p. 232) and **Tabarka, Tunisia** (see p. 625); Spiaggia di Pelosa near **Stintino, Sardinia** (see p. 572); the island of **Panarea** (see p. 501); the train ride past **Como** or anywhere in the **Italian Alps;** the **Amalfi Coast** (see p. 438); and the Blue Grotto on **Capri** (see p. 427).

Best Food:
Caffè Tubino in **Verona** (see p. 357); Café des Nattes in **Sidi Bou Said, Tunisia** (a favorite of Cervantes, Klee, and de Beauvoir; see p. 596); La Boutique del Gelato in **Venice** (see p. 333); the enormous fish at Gigino Pizza a Metro near **Sorrento** (see p. 438); Gelateria Triangolo delle Bermuda in **Florence** (see p. 185); Pasticceria Copat in **Riva del Garda** (see p. 379); Antica Focacceria S. Francesco in **Palermo** and A Giarra in **Corleone, Sicily** (see p. 515); Giolitti's gelato in **Rome** (see p. 98); best garden for picnics at Castello di Bounconsiglio in **Trent** (see p. 373); Trattoria da Sasà in **Salerno** (see p. 446); the food consortia of **Modena** (see p. 391); Gelateria di Piazza in **San Gimignano** (see p. 219); and the farmer's market in **Pozzuoli** (see p. 422).

Researcher Picks:
San Gimignano in central Italy (see p. 217); **Ascoli Piceno** in the northeast (see p. 143); **Finale Ligure** in the northwest (see p. 255); **Cuma** in the south (see p. 422); **Aeolian Islands** in Sicily (see p. 491); **Tamerza** in Tunisia (see p. 622).

Random Superlatives:
Best pick-up scene: the *duomo* steps in the university town of **Bologna** (see p. 385).
Best legal drug: *naffa* (tobacco from **Tunisia** that you tuck into your upper lip).
Longest sandwich in the world: Panetteria Ghigo Maria in **Finale Ligure** (see p. 257).
Largest astronomical clock: in **Messina, Sicily** (see p. 490).
Best place for public displays of affection: **Italy.**
Best laundromat: OndaBlu in **Rome** (see p. 86).
Most memorable Elvis sighting: Love Me Tender Gelateria in **Naples** (see p. 416).
Most memorable festival: Festa dei Porcini (mushrooms) in **Florence** (see p. 196).
Most cats: **Cosenza** (see p. 475).
Most dogs: **L'Aquila** (see p. 128).
Most rambunctious children: Foro Vittorio Emanuele in **Syracuse** (see p. 537).
Best guidebook to Italy: *Let's Go: Italy 1997.* We hope you like it too.

Life and Times

History and Politics

Kingdoms, republics, and empires have ruled the Italian peninsula, but it has been united only twice: once under the Roman Empire, and more recently by 19th-century nationalism. Italian history is a complex tapestry of events, personalities, and political parties, which *Let's Go: Italy* efficiently summarizes in about four pages.

THE PENINSULA BEFORE ROME

Excavations at Isernia, the earliest human settlement in Italy, date the first human presence on the peninsula to the beginning of the Paleolithic era (1,000,000-70,000BC). Starting around 2000BC, the so-called *Italic tribes* began to settle the area. In 900BC, however, the bad-ass **Etruscans** arrived in central Italy and subjugated many of these tribes. They also primed the land for farming by draining the swampy area that is now the center of Rome. Visit the remains of two of their largest cities at Tarquinia and Cerveteri. The Etruscan federation eventually succumbed to the invading barbarian Gauls from the north and to the increasingly powerful Romans in the south in the 5th century BC.

Beginning in the 8th century BC, the **Greeks,** who had already been trading and exploring around the boot for more than a millennium, began to settle in southern Italy. They first stopped along the Apulian coast and later founded city-states in Campania, Calabria, and Sicily, collectively known as *Magna Graecia* (Great Greece). The Greek city-states bickered amongst themselves, but effectively survived until the 3rd century BC.

ANCIENT ROME

The Monarchy: 753-510BC

According to legend, Roman history begins with Aeneas, a Trojan who led his tribe into the Tiber valley, where his fellow warriors intermarried peaceably with the locals. The city of Rome itself was founded in 753BC by two of Aeneas's descendants, the twins **Romulus and Remus.** Out of anger, greed, or duty, depending on the version of the legend, the grown-up Romulus slew his brother and became the first king of Rome, which is named after him. The new kingdom flourished under the Etruscan rulers, until the son of King Tarquinius Superbus raped the virtuous Roman matron **Lucretia.** When she committed suicide, her outraged family led the Roman populace in overthrowing the Tarquins in 510BC.

The Republic: 510-27BC

The monarchy gave way to an aristocratic **republic** with a formal beaurocratic structure (then considered a good thing) and to several centuries of warfare. In addition to waging campaigns of conquest against its neighbors, the republic suffered from inter-

> **Never Cry Wolf**
>
> Legend claims that one of Rome's Vestal Virgins (priestesses and protectors of the Eternal Flame) lost her virginity to Mars, the god of war. In a fury over the loss of her position, which in turn shamed the family name, her father killed her, and—in proper mythological form—left the twins whom she had borne to die on a mountaintop. However, a she-wolf *(La Lupa)* found and nursed the defenseless babes Romulus and Remus. Tourists can now see the trio represented in sculptures and paintings throughout Italy. Interestingly, the word *lupa* in Italian also translates into a slang word for prostitute.

nal conflict between the upper-class **patricians,** who could participate in the political decisions of the Senate, and the middle- and lower-class **plebeians,** who could not. The most important long-term contributions of the republic were the establishment of the **Roman code of law,** which would provide the underpinnings of administration for millennia and civilizations to come, and the almost completely unified control of the Italian peninsula (except for the Greek cities) by Rome.

Having conquered Italy, the republic waged its most important battles, the three **Punic Wars** (264-146BC) against the North African city of Carthage for control of the Mediterranean. During the second of these wars, the Carthaginian general **Hannibal** transported his army—elephants and all—up through Spain and over the Alps, attempting (unsuccessfully) to defeat Rome from the north. The third war resulted in the complete destruction of Carthage. The Romans sowed the land around Carthage with salt so that it would never yield crops again. It was during the Punic Wars that Rome moved toward world power, consolidating its control over the Mediterranean and establishing naval domination in order to protect supply routes.

Under the umbrella of Roman military power, trade and shipping flourished. The spoils of war and taxes enriched Rome and its upper classes, creating an environment ripe for corruption. Social upheaval quickly ensued. By 131BC, slave, farmer, and plebeian demands for land redistribution led to popular riots against the patrician class. Shortly thereafter the **Social War** erupted (91-87BC), in which tribes throughout the peninsula fought successfully for the extension of Roman citizenship and the social and economic benefits which accompanied it. **Sulla,** the general who had commanded Rome's troops during the conflict, then led the Roman army into the city (an unprecedented move), taking control in a bloody military coup.

In the wake of this latest upheaval, **Spartacus,** an escaped gladiatorial slave, led an army of 70,000 slaves and farmers in a two-year rampage down the peninsula. (See the movie of the same name starring Kirk Douglas for a re-creation.) When the dust cleared, **Pompey the Great,** a close associate of Sulla, had taken effective control of the city, but he soon found himself in conflict with his periodic co-ruler **Julius Caesar,** the charismatic conqueror of Gaul. Caesar finally emerged victorious, but a small faction, fearful of his growing power, assassinated him on the Ides (15th) of March, 44BC. Power eluded several would-be heirs (among them **Marcus Antonius,** a.k.a. Mark Antony, and **Brutus,** as in "Et tu, Brute?") before falling to Caesar's nephew, Octavian, who assumed the title of **Augustus** and instated an imperial government in 27BC.

The Empire: 27BC-AD476

Augustus, the first emperor of Rome, was also the first of the **Julio-Claudian** kings (27BC-AD68). His reign (27BC-AD14), generally considered the golden age of Rome, initiated the **Pax Romana** (200 years of peace). With the aid of a professional army and imperial bureaucracy, Augustus was able to maintain the empire, extending Roman law and civic culture out to the frontiers. Meanwhile, poets and authors crafted the Latin language into an expressive art form.

Nero, the last of the Julio-Claudian emperors, committed suicide in AD68. The following year, during which three other rulers seized and lost power in succession, is popularly known as the Year of the Four Emperors. Finally, the general **Vespasian** triumphed and initiated the **Flavian** dynasty (69-96). The empire then reached its maximum geographical expansion under the emperor **Trajan** (98-117). At his death, his adopted successor **Hadrian** fully established the **Antonine** dynasty (117-193). Antonine Emperor **Marcus Aurelius** (161-180) may be better known to posterity for his philosophical writings than for his reign, which he spent fending off barbarian invasions. The last of the Antonine emperors, **Commodius,** was assassinated in 193, and **Septimius Severus,** a general from northern Africa, took over the principate, founding the **Severan** dynasty (193-235). With the death of the last of the Severans in 235, the era of smooth dynastic succession came to an end.

Weak leadership and the southward invasions of Germanic tribes combined to create a state of anarchy in the 3rd century. **Diocletian** was one of the few major figures to secure control of the fragmented empire (284). He divided the empire into eastern and western halves and escalated the persecution of Christians. This period became known as the "age of martyrs," as Christians dressed in the hides of animals were torn to shreds by savage beasts for Roman amusement, or set on fire as street lamps. Despite this hazardous environment, approximately 30,000 Christians still remained in Rome at the end of Diocletian's violent reign.

The fortunes of the Christians took a turn for the better when **Constantine,** Diocletian's successor, converted to Christianity. Having dreamed of a huge cross in the sky and the words, *"in hoc signo vinces"* (by this sign you shall conquer), he led his troops to victory. Constantine then declared Christianity the state religion in 315 and moved the capital to Constantinople in 330. With less vigilance along the empire's Italian borders, Rome's military strength declined. In 410, **Alaric,** king of the Visigoths, deposed the last of Rome's western emperors and sacked the city. The ensuing scramble for power wasn't fully resolved until 476, when **Odoacer,** an Ostrogoth chieftain, was crowned King of Italy.

THE DARK AGES: C.500-1300

In 586, the semi-nomadic Lombards invaded Italy from the north, effectively eliminating any sense of political unity remaining from Roman times. Meanwhile, the Byzantines and Arabs fought to control Sicily and the southern peninsula. The papacy in Rome, weakened by the new power of Constantinople, was often at the mercy of these invaders. Finally, Pope Stephen II appealed to Charlemagne and his Frankish army to defend him against the vicious Lombards. This plea became an invitation to Charlemagne to add Italy to his empire. On Christmas Day 800, Pope Leo III crowned the ruler "Emperor of the Romans" in a ceremony at St. Peter's in Rome. This confusion of the powers of church and state was to become a recurring theme for centuries to come. In Florence, two rival political factions arose, defending opposing sides in these conflicts: the *Ghibellines,* who supported the Holy Roman Emperor, and the *Guelfs,* who supported the papacy.

With the declining power of Rome and other large cities, smaller Italian towns had an opportunity to assert themselves. Strengthened by trade, ambitious local leaders, and the remaining infrastructure of the Roman empire, the early years of the millennium witnessed the rise of independent and autonomous communes. These political, economic, and social units were to play a major role in Renaissance Italy.

THE RENAISSANCE

Although the papacy gradually reasserted itself, the most important figures in the 14th through 16th centuries were secular rulers from competing city-states. Ironically, such political fragmentation fostered the greatest intellectual and artistic flowering in history—the **Renaissance.** Great ruling families like the Gonzaga in Mantua, the d'Este in Ferrara, and the Medici in Florence instituted important reforms in commerce and law, and accelerated the already rapid cultural and artistic flourishing of their respective cities. Princes, bankers, and merchants channeled their increasing wealth into patronage for the artists and scholars whose work defined the era. Unfortunately for Luke Skywalker, power-hungry princes also cultivated the dark side of the Renaissance—constant warfare, usually among mercenaries. The weakened cities yielded easily to the invading Spanish army of Charles V in the 16th century. By 1556, both Naples and Milan had fallen to King Ferdinand of Aragon.

As if the frequently warring factions of the Renaissance weren't enough, Italians also had to contend with rampant disease and natural disaster. The **Black Death,** a plague which broke out in 1348 and at seven-year intervals for centuries afterward, had killed over one half of Florence's population by 1427. The other major contagion was **syphilis.** In Rome, the disease spread wildly, infecting seventeen members of the pope's family and court. To add to the city's horrors, the Tiber flooded its banks in 1495. Water gushed into the streets and surged through churches and homes. The ascetic Dominican friar **Girolamo Savonarola** of Florence proclaimed these calamities a punishment for sin and inaugurated a war on the excesses of Rome. The pope tried to silence the pesky friar, and subsequently excommunicated him, but Savonarola persevered until the Florentines themselves got sick of his persistent nagging and tortured, hanged, and burned him.

POST-RENAISSANCE: FOREIGN DOMINATION

Sixteenth-century Catholic Spaniards extended the **Inquisition** into Italy and, with invading armies, suppressed the Protestant Reformation. Spain dominated the peninsula politically for over a century, but its economy was unable to support forever the demands of controlling an empire. In 1700, Charles II, the last Spanish Habsburg, died and the war of Spanish Succession broke out. Italy was a prize disputed by the new rival European powers.

The power of **Napoleon** ushered in the nineteenth century, as the French united much of northern Italy into the Italian Republic, later called the Kingdom of Italy. France also conquered Naples in 1806. After Napoleon's fall in 1815, the **Congress of Vienna** carved up Italy anew, granting considerable political control to Austria.

THE ITALIAN NATION

Unification

In subsequent decades, strong sentiment against foreign rule prompted a movement of nationalist resurgence called the **Risorgimento,** ultimately culminating in national unification in 1870. The success of the Risorgimento is attributed primarily to three Italian heroes: **Giuseppe Mazzini,** the movement's intellectual leader, **Giuseppe Garibaldi,** the military leader whose army of 1000 defeated the Bourbons in the south, and **Camillo di Cavour,** the political and diplomatic mastermind who is ultimately credited for Italy's birth as a nation. Throughout Italy, streets and *piazze* bear the names of these heroes.

Vittorio Emanuele, the ruler of the new Kingdom of Italy, expanded the nation geographically by annexing several northern and central regions, including Tuscany. France ultimately relinquished Rome on September 20, 1870, *the* pivotal date in modern Italian history. Once the elation of unification wore off, however, age-old provincial differences reasserted themselves. Northern regions wanted to protect their money from the economic needs of the agrarian south; cities were wary of surrendering too much power to a central administration; and the pope, who had lost much of his power to the new kingdom, threatened Italian Catholics with excommunication for participating in politics. Disillusionment increased as Italy became involved in World War I, fighting to gain territory and vanquish Austria.

The chaotic aftermath of World War I paved the way for the rise of **fascism** under *"Il Duce"* **Benito Mussolini,** who promised strict order and stability for the young nation. In 1940, Italy entered World War II and joined the Axis. Success came quickly, but was short-lived. When the Allies landed in Sicily in 1943, Mussolini fell

Sleeping with the Enemy

The Italian political system is organized into potentially volatile coalitions of parties which vote as blocks. **L'Ulivo** ("The Olive Tree") is the leftist coalition currently in power, led by the **Partito Democratico della Sinistra (PDS),** a more moderate offshoot of the old **Communist Party (PCI).** The conservative right-leaning block includes the **New Christian Democrats (CCD),** Silvio Berlusconi's **Forza Italia,** and the **Alleanza Nazionale.** Recent Italian governments have had difficulty passing legislation through Parliament without creating alliances. The centrist Socialists have lost a lot of their former power and are now seeking to join forces with Berlusconi to rejuvenate the center. Even the **Rifondazione Comunista,** a more radical spinoff of the PCI, must swallow its pride and join with L'Ulivo for critical votes.

from his pinnacle of power. As a final indignity, he and his mistress, Claretta Petacci, were captured, executed, and strung up by their heels by infuriated citizens.

By the end of 1943 the new government had withdrawn its support from Germany, which promptly invaded and occupied its former ally. Italy remained divided between those supporting the king and those who favored a return to fascism.

Post-War Politics

The constitution adopted in 1948 established a new Italian Republic with a president, a prime minister, a bicameral parliament, and an independent judiciary. While the **Christian Democratic Party** quickly surfaced as the most powerful ruling party in the new republic, continual political turmoil has nonetheless resulted in more than fifty different governments since World War II.

The Italian economy sped through industrialization at an unprecedented rate, resulting in labor violence and near-anarchy in the 1970s. The *autunno caldo* ("hot autumn") of 1969, a season of strikes, demonstrations, and riots, foreshadowed the violence of the 70s. Perhaps most shocking was the 1978 kidnapping and murder of **Aldo Moro,** the president of Christian Democrats, by the leftist, terrorist *Brigate Rosse* ("Red Brigades"). Although social reform movements, especially feminism, became powerful political forces during this period of unrest, the slow and painful process of reforming electoral laws has resulted in an unprecedented political crisis in which over 2600 politicians have been implicated in scandals in the 1990s.

The **mafia** crime families have also flourished under weak national leadership, particularly in the south. Leaders of the nebulous organization command great and unseen control over Italy's society, politics, and economy. Specifically, manipulation of the black market has made the mafia a crooked pillar in the Italian economy. Today's mafia—with a heightened passion for drug-running and violence—inspires near-universal fear and resentment among Italians. The Italian Parliament passed an unprecedented anti-mafia law in 1982, followed by the Palermo *maxi processi* ("maxi-trials"), the largest series of mafia trials in history.

Divisions in Italy are not just between frightened citizens and organized criminals. Because the nation is still very young, city and regional bonds often prove stronger than nationalist sentiment. The most pronounced split exists between the highly industrialized north and the agrarian south. Despite the obstacles, Italy has nonetheless expanded at an astonishing pace, becoming the world's fifth largest economy.

Art and Architecture

It would be a travesty to approach the entire history of Italian art as a mere prelude to the Renaissance. Similarly, to visit only its most famous pieces would be to miss the pervasive presence of art in more everyday Italian settings.

Any understanding of early Italian art must begin with ancient Greece. Through trade and cultural exchange, the **Etruscans** incorporated into their art and architecture many Greek elements which later found their way into the Roman repertoire, such as the column and capital types and the temple form. The major innovation of Roman architecture, however, was the **arch,** a development in engineering which allowed for the famous Roman aqueducts, bridges, and triumphal monuments. The most famous Roman construction types are: the oval **amphitheater** (for gladiatorial and military displays, of which the Colosseum (AD80) in Rome is the most famous example), the **basilica** (a building characterized by rows of columns in which market stands and the law court were located), and the **forum** (a public square where civic structures were situated). Roman homes ranged from *insulae* (similar to apartment buildings) to large private villas.

The interiors of houses and shops were often extensively decorated, usually with **frescoes,** paintings on moist plaster that become part of the wall as the plaster dries. Sometimes a wall was painted to resemble an outdoor scene, or extra *trompe-l'oeil* doors or columns were depicted to trick the eye and make the house look bigger. In other cases, mythological or still-life scenes were executed in **mosaic,** a popular technique with the Romans.

The collapse of the Roman Empire and the rise of Christianity created a need for new aesthetic forms. The most pressing concern was the accommodation of the Catholic mass, a function for which the basilica was adapted. Art was used to edify the illiterate masses and exalt the afterlife, resulting in early Christian paintings with inexpressive human figures, minimal earthly backgrounds, and clear religious narrative and symbolism.

Two major styles emerged to dominate architecture in the Middle Ages. From AD500 to 1200, the **Romanesque** style dominated Europe, churches characterized by solid masonry masses, thick and relatively unadorned walls, and small windows. Great Italian Romanesque churches include Sant'Ambrogio in Milan, San Miniato in Florence, and the cathedrals of Pisa and Trani.

The **Gothic** style of the 12th to 14th centuries resulted from the combination of the pointed arch and the flying buttress—together, they supported the weight of the roof and allowed the heavy Romanesque wall to be replaced by the glorious Gothic window. Because the Gothic came from the European north in perceived opposition to classical Roman architecture, the style never really took root in Italy. The cathedrals of Milan and Siena are the most spectacular examples of the Lombard Gothic, using pointed arches and high ceilings but no buttresses.

In late 13th and 14th centuries, artists gradually grew more inclined to realistic representations of people and events. The most influential painter of the early **Renaissance, Giotto di Bondone** (1266?-1337) introduced the problem of how to create the illusion of three dimensions on a flat surface with his frescoes in Padua's Arena Chapel. Other painters, such as Sienese artists **Simone Martini** and **Pietro Lorenzetti,** attempted to imbue their figures with more individuality and emotion. **Masaccio** (1401-1428) is credited with the first use of the mathematical laws of perspective in his painting of *The Trinity* in S. Maria Novella in Florence. These new techniques revolutionized painting, sculpture, and architecture in Italy.

The most prominent early Renaissance sculptors were **Nicola and Giovanni Pisano,** who carved many of the elaborate pulpits in 13th-century Tuscany. Sculptures and relief carvings by **Donatello** (1386-1466), with their anatomical accuracy and realistic backgrounds, inspired later Renaissance artists. **Lorenzo Ghiberti** designed and produced several sets of bronze doors for the baptistry in Florence in the first half of the 15th century. The two most important architects of the early Renaissance are **Filippo Brunelleschi** (1377-1446) and **Leone Alberti** (1404-1472). Brunelleschi was an extraordinary engineer, who raised the great dome over Santa Maria del Fiore in Florence using his new double-shell technique. Alberti designed the Palazzo Rucellai in Florence, which became the prototype for Renaissance *palazzi.* In the high Renaissance, the great architectural mantle would be taken up by **Donato Bramante** (1444-1514), particularly in his work on St. Peter's in Rome.

The High Renaissance (1450-1520), however, was dominated by three men: **Leonardo da Vinci** (1452-1519), **Michelangelo Buonarroti** (1475-1564), and **Raphael Santi** (1483-1520). Leonardo was the original Renaissance man—artist, scientist, architect, engineer, musician, weapons designer. Although he seldom finished what he started, his designs were extraordinary. His monumental fresco *The Last Supper* (in Santa Maria delle Grazie in Milan) preserves the individuality of the depicted figures, even in a religious context. He refined the standards for human proportions and popularized the use of *sfumato,* a technique that involved the blending of dark into light tones for a smoky effect. That another genius of Leonardo's caliber existed at the same time—and in the same place—is stupefying. Michelangelo painted and sculpted with as much skill as his contemporary, but at a prolific pace. The ceiling of the Sistine Chapel, on which he created the illusion of vaults on a flat surface, remains his greatest achievement in painting. His architectural achievements are equally noteworthy, particularly in his designs for St. Peter's in Rome. But sculpture is where Michelangelo's true genius lay. Classic examples are the formal, tranquil *Pietà* in St. Peter's, its half-finished, anguished counterpart in the Castello Sforzesco in Milan, the majestic, virile *David* in Florence's Academy, and the powerful *Moses* in Rome's San Pietro in Vincoli. Raphael's short life is particularly tragic considering his tremendous artistic gifts. A proficient draftsman, his figures are technically perfect and prone to vibrant movement. His frescoes in the papal apartments of the Vatican, including the clear and balanced composition of the *School of Athens*, show his debt to classical standards and are a must for lovers of Renaissance art.

The emerging spirit of creative experimentation led to **Mannerism,** a short-lived link between the Renaissance and Baroque periods. Mannerist artists, inspired by the later works of Michelangelo, were concerned with solving abstract artistic problems, and thus their art is often self-conscious and affected. Figures produced in this style may be oddly elongated, flattened, or colored in unusual schemes.

The buildings of **Andrea Palladio** (1508-1580) are known for their classical style and centralized spaces and include works such as Villa Rotunda at Vicenza and Il Redentore in Venice. His most lasting contribution, however, may have been the *Four Books of Architecture,* which influenced countless architects, including those of the **Baroque** period that flourished in the 17th and 18th centuries. Born of the counter-Reformation and of absolute monarchy, Baroque art and architecture was intended to inspire faith in God and respect for the ruling powers, especially those of the Catholic church. It is generally grandiose, vivid, and dynamic. Painters of this era, like **Caravaggio** (1573-1610), favored naturalism—a commitment to portraying nature in all its intensity, whether ugly or beautiful. Baroque paintings are thus often melodramatic and gruesome. **Gianlorenzo Bernini** (1598-1680), the most prolific artist of the high Baroque, designed the colonnaded piazza of St. Peter's, as well as the *baldacchino* over its crossing; the façade and nave of the church are the work of **Carlo Maderno** (completed in 1614). **Francesco Borromini,** although not as popular as Bernini in his own time, was more adept than his rival at shaping the walls of his buildings into architectural masterpieces. **Tiepolo** (1696-1770), with his light-colored palate and vibrant frescoes, was a celebrated Italian allegorical painter.

Through French influence, the decorative **Rococo** style (exemplified by Tiepolo) and the formal **Neoclassical** style (a return to the strict rules of antiquity) succeeded the Italian Baroque. The Italian **Futurist** artists of the 1910s sought to transfer the aesthetics and movements of machines into art. Two of Italy's greatest artists of the 20th century were **Amadeo Modigliani** (1884-1920), whose painted and sculpted figures are most noted for their long angular faces, and **Giorgio de Chirico** (1888-1978), whose eerie painted scenes influenced the surrealists. **Marcello Piacentini's** fascist architecture, which imposes a sense of sterility on classical motifs, looms at Mussolini's EUR in Rome. To trace the current path of Italian art, you can visit modern art galleries in most major cities.

Literature

GREEK AND ROMAN MYTHOLOGY

Ovid's work is a principal source for our knowledge of Roman mythology. Usually disguised as animals or humans, the gods and goddesses often descended to earth to intervene romantically or combatively in human affairs. The 14 major deities are: **Jupiter,** king of gods; his wife **Juno,** who watches over child-bearing and marriage; **Neptune,** god of the sea; **Vulcan,** god of smiths and fire; **Venus,** goddess of love and beauty; **Mars,** god of war; **Minerva,** goddess of wisdom; **Apollo** (or Phoebus), god of light and music; **Diana,** goddess of the hunt; **Mercury,** the messenger god; **Pluto,** god of the underworld; **Ceres,** goddess of the harvest; **Bacchus**, god of wine; and **Vesta,** goddess of the hearth.

LITERATURE OF THE REPUBLIC AND EMPIRE

Roman literature exists in many forms, including plays, historical writings, philosophical treatises, and satires. **Plautus** (c.220-184BC) wrote popular comedy plays, including *Pseudolus,* which was later adapted into the Broadway musical *A Funny Thing Happened on the Way to the Forum.* The lyric poetry of **Catullus** (84-54BC), on the other hand, set a high standard for passion and provided a plethora of Latin obscenities for future high-school students. **Livy** (c.59BC-AD17) recorded the authorized history of Rome from the city's founding to his own time, while **Julius Caesar** (100-44BC) gave a first-hand account of the final shredding of the Republic in the Gallic wars. Caesar's close contemporary **Cicero** (106-43BC) penned several orations noteworthy for their carefully crafted Latin, including the speech *In Catilinam* ("O tempora, O mores!").

Despite a government prone to banishing the impolitic, Augustan Rome produced some of the greatest Latin authors of antiquity. **Virgil** (70-19BC), considered a prophet by several medieval Christian sects, wrote the *Aeneid,* an epic recounting the adventures of the Trojan hero Aeneas. **Horace's** (65-8BC) verse derives more from his personal experiences, which he worked into his prolific *Odes*, *Epodes*, *Satires*, and *Epistles.* **Ovid** (43BC-AD17) wrote poems, among them the *Amores* (perhaps more accurately titled the "lusts"), the mythological *Metamorphoses*, and the *Ars Amatoria* (a guide to scamming on Roman women).

From the post-Augustan empire, **Petronius's** (1st century AD) *Satyricon* is a bawdy, blunt look at the decadence of the age of Nero, while **Suetonius's** (c. AD69-130) *De Vita Caesarum* presents the gossipy version of imperial history. **Tacitus's** (c. AD56-116) *Histories* summarize Roman war, diplomacy, scandal, and rumor in the years after Nero's death. His *Annals* extol the upright Rome of Trajan and criticize the scandalous activities of the Julio-Claudian emperors. Finally, **Marcus Aurelius's** (AD121-180) *Meditations* bring us the musings of a philosopher-king.

EARLY RENAISSANCE

The tumult of the medieval plagues discouraged literary musings, but three Tuscan writers emerged in the late 13th century to reassert this art. Although scholars do not agree on the precise dates of the Renaissance, many argue that **Dante Alighieri** (1265-1321) marked its inception. One of the first Italian poets to write in the *volgare* (common Italian) instead of Latin, Dante is considered the father of modern Italian language and literature. In his epic poem *La Divina Commedia (The Divine Comedy)*, Dante fills the afterlife with famous historic figures, as well as his true love Beatrice. Among its chief political themes are Dante's call for social reform and his scathing indictment of those contributing to civic strife.

While Dante's work maintains a medieval flavor, **Petrarch** (1304-74) belongs more clearly to the Renaissance. A scholar of classical Latin and a founder of Humanism, he restored the popularity of ancient Roman writers and wrote love sonnets to a married woman named Laura. The third member of the medieval literary triumvirate was a close friend of Petrarch's, but **Giovanni Boccaccio's** style owes little to his friend. The *Decameron,* Boccaccio's collection of 100 stories told by ten young Florentines fleeing their plague-ridden city, ranges in tone from suggestive to downright bawdy; in one story, a gardener has his way with an entire convent!

THE RENAISSANCE AND ITS AFTERMATH

Fifteenth- and sixteenth-century Italian authors branched out from the genres of their predecessors. **Alberti** and **Palladio** wrote treatises on architecture and art theory. **Baldassare Castiglione's** *The Courtier* instructed the inquiring Renaissance man on deportment, etiquette, and other fine points of behavior. **Vasari** took time off from redecorating Florence's churches to produce a primer on art history and criticism (*The Lives of the Artists*). One of the most lasting works of the Renaissance, **Niccolò Machiavelli's** *Il Principe* (*The Prince)* is a sophisticated assessment of what it takes to gain political power. Although Machiavelli did not make many friends with his candid and brutal suggestions, he is now regarded as the father of modern political theory. Less well-known but of great literary significance is Machiavelli's comedy *La Mandragola,* a play which criticizes ecclesiastical corruption.

In attempting to live up to the title of "Renaissance man," specialists in other fields often tried their hand at writing. Among Renaissance artists, **Benvenuto Cellini** wrote about the his own art in *The Autobiography,* **Michelangelo** composed enough sonnets to fuel a fire (literally), and **Leonardo da Vinci** wrote about anything and everything in *The Notebook.* The scathing and brilliant **Pietro Aretino** created new possibilities for literature when he began accepting payment from famous people for *not* writing about them.

As Italy's political power waned, literary production also declined. However, the prolific 18th-century dramatist **Carlo Goldoni** (1707-1793) replaced the stock figures of the traditional *commedia dell'arte* with original, unpredictable characters in such works as *Il Ventaglio.* In addition, the publication of **Alessandro Manzoni's** (1785-1873) epic *I Promessi Sposi* (*The Betrothed*) in 1827 marked the birth of the modern novel in Italy.

19TH- AND 20TH-CENTURY LITERATURE

Twentieth-century exposure to communism, socialism, and fascism gave rise to revolutionary literary achievements among Italian writers. Nobel Prize-winning playwright **Luigi Pirandello** (1867-1936) contributed to modern experimental theater with his exploration of the relativity of truth; his works include *Six Characters in Search of an Author*, *Henry IV*, and *So It Is (If You Think It Is So).* **Italo Svevo,** another unconventional writer, wrote *A Life, The Confessions of Zeno*.

Italy was a center of Modernist innovation in poetry. The most flamboyant and controversial of the early poets is **Gabriele d'Annunzio,** whose cavalier heroics earned him as much fame as his eccentric verse. D'Annunzio was a true child of pleasure, or *Il Piacere,* the title of his novel published in 1889. In the mid-20th century, **Giuseppe**

Hit the Books

Italian culture has inspired numerous American and British writers. In addition, many works of Italian literature have been translated into English. One of the following books may therefore make a worthy travel companion. And don't forget Shakespeare's *Romeo and Juliet, The Merchant of Venice,* and *Julius Caesar.*

-Allanbrook, Douglas. *See Naples.* A musician's memoir.
-Casserly, Jack. *Once Upon a Time in Italy.* Reflections of an American journalist who worked in Rome from 1957 to 1964.
-Dibdin, Michael. *Dead Lagoon.* A detective novel set in Venice.
-Goethe. *Italian Journey.* The famous writer's travel diary.
-Graves, Robert. *I, Claudius* and *Claudius the God.* An hysterical work narrated by the clumsy Claudius. The BBC made an excellent TV movie of the books.
-Hoffman, Paul. *That Fine Italian Hand.* Articles and essays which provide insight into the Italian psyche.
-Hemingway, Ernest. *A Farewell to Arms.* Tale of an American ambulance driver serving in Italy during World War II.
-James, Henry. *Italian Hours.* Romantic essays of his personal journeys.
-Levi, Carlo. *Christ Stopped at Eboli.* An anti-fascist book (now also a movie).
-Lewis, Norman. *Naples '44.* Memoirs of an intelligence officer with the American Fifth Army in Naples during World War II.
-Littlewood, Ian. *A Literary Companion to Venice.* An anthology organized into seven city walks.
-Mann, Thomas. *Death in Venice.* A novel about a writer's obsession with a beautiful young boy. (It's provocative, not smutty.)
-Ruskin, John. *The Stones of Venice.* A classic of art criticism and history.
-Vidal, Gore. *Julian.* Covers just about everything, including Constantine's reign.
-Varriano, John. *A Literary Companion to Rome.* An anthology of English writings organized into 10 city walks.
-*Let's Go: Italy '97.* We couldn't put it down.

Ungaretti, and Nobel Prize-winners **Salvatore Quasimodo** and **Eugenio Montale** dominated the scene. Montale and Quasimodo founded the "hermetic movement," characterized by an intimate poetic vision and allusive imagery.

The 1930s and '40s were dominated of a group of young Italian writers greatly influenced by the works of American writers Ernest Hemingway and John Steinbeck. This school included **Cesare Pavese, Vasco Pratolini,** and **Elio Vittorini.** One of the most representative works of 1930s Italian literature is **Ignazio Silone's** *Bread and Wine,* written while the left-wing intellectual and political-activist author was in exile. The most prolific of these writers, **Alberto Moravia,** wrote the ground-breaking *Time of Indifference* which launched an attack on the fascist regime and was promptly censored. To evade the stiff government censors, Moravia employed experimental, surreal forms in his subsequent works. His later works use sex to symbolize the violence and spiritual impotence of modern Italy.

Particularly appealing prose works for travelers include **Giorgio Bassani's** *The Garden of the Finzi-Continis,* a tale of a Jewish community destroyed by the Fascists; **Cesare Pavese's** *The Moon and the Bonfires,* a narrative about a man returning to Piedmont from America; and **Elio Vittorini's** *Conversation in Sicily,* a story about a Sicilian employed in the North who travels home for self-discovery.

The works of the greatest modern Italian author, **Italo Calvino,** are (not surprisingly) those most widely available in English. Calvino's writing—full of intellectual play and magical realism—is exemplified in *Invisible Cities,* a collection of cities described by Marco Polo to Kubla Kahn. His work includes the trilogy *Our Ancestors* and the more traditional narrative *If on a Winter's Night a Traveler...,* a boisterous romp about authors, readers, and the insatiable urge to read. Perhaps most enjoyable for the traveler is *Italian Folktales,* Calvino's collection of traditional regional fairytales.

More recently, **Umberto Eco's** *The Name of the Rose,* an intricate mystery set in a 14th-century monastery (see the Sacra of S. Michele, p. 271, for more info), somehow manages to keep readers on edge while making the history of medieval Catholicism vaguely intelligible. His *Foucault's Pendulum,* with all its contrived complications, addresses the story of the Knights Templar and half-a-millennium of conspiracy theories.

Music

Musically, Italians are responsible for a number of "famous firsts:" the musical scale, the piano, and the invention of the system of musical notation still used today. **Opera** is Italy's most cherished art form—born in Florence, nurtured in Venice, and revered in Milan. Invented by the **Camerata,** an art *coterie* of Florentine writers, noblemen, and musicians, opera began as an attempt to recreate the dramas of ancient Greece by setting their lengthy poems to music. After several years of effort with only dubious success, Jacobo Peri composed *Dafne,* the world's first complete opera, in 1597. As opera spread from Florence to Venice, Milan, and Rome, the forms of the genre grew more distinct. The first successful opera composer, **Monteverdi,** drew freely from history, juxtaposing high drama, love scenes, and bawdy humor. His masterpiece *L'Orfeo* (1607) assured the survival of the genre and is still performed today.

Sacred music of the Medieval and Renaissance periods can still be heard in many of the ancient cathedrals and basilicas. The composers who wrote *musica da chiesa* (music for the church) also frequently wrote pieces for performance in the home or at court. The latter were more often than not rather naughty love songs. Early performers were generally gifted amateurs, but one can now hear the *da camera* (literally "in room") repertoire performed by professionals at the various music academies and summer festivals of Italy. *Virtuoso* instrumental music became established as a legitimate genre in 17th-century Rome. **Vivaldi** wrote over 400 concertos while teaching at a home for orphaned girls in Venice. Under Vivaldi the concerto assumed its present form, in which the soloist is accompanied by a full orchestra.

Eighteenth-century Italy exported its music. At mid-century, operatic overtures began to be performed separately, resulting in the creation of a new genre of music. The **sinfonia,** modeled after the melody of operatic overtures, was simply opera detached from its setting. Thus the symphonic art form was born, later achieving its highest expression in the hands of Italy's northern neighbors. In opera, baroque virtuosity and detail yielded to classical standards of moderation, structural balance, and elegance. To many of today's opera buffs, Italian opera is epitomized by 19th- and 20th-century composers Verdi, Puccini, Bellini, Donizetti, and Rossini. In the early 19th century, Rossini, Donizetti, and Bellini made use of the *bel canto* style of performing. *Bel canto* literally means "beautiful song" and emphasizes long, fluid lines of music.

With convoluted plots and strong, dramatic music, 19th-century Italian opera continues to dominate modern stages. Late in the 19th century came **Puccini,** the great master of *verismo* opera, which deals largely with everyday people caught in powerful and often tragic emotional dilemmas. Puccini, creator of *Madame Butterfly, La Bohème,* and *Tosca* is noted for the beauty of his music and for the strength, assurance, and compassion of his female characters. The great *bel canto* master **Rossini** boasted that he could produce music faster than copyists could reproduce it, but he proved such a procrastinator that his agents reputedly resorted to locking him in a room until he completed his now-renowned masterpieces. The transcendent musical and operatic figure of 19th-century Italy is **Giuseppe Verdi.** His operatic style developed throughout his lengthy career, virtually defining the history of 19th-century opera. From early Verdi we have *Nabucco,* a pointed and powerful *bel canto* work. The chorus *"Va pensiero"* from *Nabucco* became the hymn of Italian freedom and unity. From Verdi's middle period we have the touchingly personal dramas and memorable melodies of *Rigoletto, La Traviata,* and *Il Trovatore.* From the last third of the century, Verdi gives us the grand and heroic conflicts of *Aida,* the drama thrust of *Othello,* and the mercurial comedy of *Falstaff.* Verdi's name served as a convenient acronym for "Vittorio Emanuale, Re d'Italia," so *"Viva Verdi"* became a popular battle cry of the Risorgimento. Much of Verdi's work also promoted Italian unity—his operas include frequent allusions to political assassinations, exhortations against tyranny, and jibes at French and Austrian monarchs.

Italian music continues to grow in the 20th century. **Ottorino Respighi,** composer of the popular *Pines of Rome* and *Fountains of Rome,* experimented with rapidly shifting orchestral textures. **Giancarlo Menotti,** now a U.S. resident, has written short opera-like works such as *Amahl and the Night Visitors,* but is probably best known as creator of the Two Worlds Art Festival in Spoleto (see page 165). Known for his work with meta-languages, **Luciano Berio** defied traditional instrumentation with his *Sequence V* for solo trombone and mime. **Luigi Dallapiccola** worked with serialism, achieving success with choral works including *Songs of Prison* and *Songs of Liberation*—two pieces that protest fascist rule in Italy. And that *pagliaccio* **Luciano Pavarotti** remains universally adored.

The Media

PRINT

Throughout the larger cities in Italy, you'll be able to find some representative newspaper of your home country at one of the numerous **edicole.** These newsstands are compact stations of printed information (not to mention fire hazards) which sell newspapers, magazines, train schedules, comic books, coloring books, and sometimes even postcards. The ones you'll see the most will be the **Corriere della Sera,** a conservative publication from Milan, and **La Repubblica,** a liberal paper from Rome. Other big papers include **La Stampa** (conservative, published in Torino and owned by Fiat) and **Il Messaggero** (liberal, published in Rome). In small towns, natives are likely to purchase one of the many local papers rather than one of national import.

There are also several amazing daily sports newspapers, including **La Gazzetta dello Sport** and the **Corriere dello Sport.**

TELEVISION

If you thought American TV was sexist, then you haven't seen Italian television. Game shows, news commentary, and even children's programs are overwhelmingly populated by buxom (often topless), leggy bombshells in flashy clothes. More generally, Italian television comes in two varieties: three vaguely educational state-owned **RAI** channels and the shamelessly insipid networks owned by former Prime Minster Silvio Berlusconi. **Italia 1, Rete 4,** and **Canale 5** transmit all your favorite American trash, including "Beverly Hills 90210," "The Bold and the Beautiful," and "Saved by the Bell" (called "Bayside School"), as well as the indigenous "Non È La RAI" with its lip-synching teenagers.

Film

For Italy's major contribution to the arts in this century, go to the movies. Years before Hollywood existed, the **Cines** studios thrived in Rome. Starting in 1905-6, *Cines* created the so-called Italian "super-spectacle," extravagant re-creations of momentous historical events. One of these, Enrico Guzzani's incredible *Quo Vadis,* enjoyed international success as the first "blockbuster" hit in film history.

Shortly before World War I, the public appeal and economic success of films became increasingly dependent upon the presence of celebrities—particularly *dive* ("goddesses") like Lyda Borelli and Francesca Bertini, who epitomized the destructive yet suffering Italian *femme fatale*. With the rise of fascism, government leaders and supporters became more and more visible in the film scene. Mussolini recognized the power of popular cinema and created the *Centro Sperimentale della Cinematografia,* a national film school, and the gargantuan **Cinecittà studios**. The famous director and covert Marxist **Luigi Chiarini** attracted many students—including **Roberto Rossellini** and **Michelangelo Antonioni**—who rose to directorial fame after the war. Mussolini avoided most aesthetic aspects of the cinema but enforced a few "imperial edicts," one of which forbade laughing at the Marx Brothers.

When fascism fell, young filmmakers enjoyed a new freedom from the constraints of the regime. Mussolini's nationalized film industry had produced no great films, but it sparked the subsequent explosion of **neorealist cinema** (1943-50). *Neorealismo* rejected contrived sets and professional actors and emphasized location shooting and authentic drama. Low budget productions, partly necessitated by postwar economic circumstances, soon created a revolution in film. Neorealists first gained attention in Italy with **Luchino Visconti's** 1942 *Ossessione,* based on James Cain's pulp-novel *The Postman Always Rings Twice*. Roberto Rossellini's widely acclaimed *Roma, Città Aperta* (Open City), a 1946 movie of a Resistance leader trying to escape the Gestapo, was filmed mostly on the streets of Rome. Because of its neorealist documentary style and authentic setting, the movie appears to be actual newsreel footage. **Vittorio de Sica's** *The Bicycle Thief* (1948) was perhaps the most famous and commercially successful neorealist film.

When neorealism turned its wobbly camera to social critique, it lost its popularity and, after 1950, gave way to individual expressions of Italian genius. Post-neorealist directors **Federico Fellini** and Antonioni rejected plots and characters for a world of moments and witnesses. In Fellini's autobiographical *Roma,* a gorgeous stand-in for the director encounters an otherwise grotesque cast of characters. *La Dolce Vita* (1960), banned by the pope but widely regarded as *the* representative Italian film, scrutinizes the decadently stylish and vapid Rome of the 1950s. Antonioni's films include *L'Eclisse* (1962), *Deserto Rosso* (1964), and *Blow-Up,* a 1966 English-language hit about mime, murder, and mod London. Antonioni's *L'Avventura* chronicles the lives of bored young aristocrats, an original idea at the time.

Pier Paolo Pasolini—who spent as much time on trial for his politics as he did making films—was both a successful poet and a great, though controversial, director. An ardent Marxist, he set his first films in Italian shanty neighborhoods and in the Roman underworld of poverty and prostitution. His masterpiece, *Hawks and Sparrows,* investigates the philosophical and poetic possibilities of film.

Time, aging old-boy directors, and the lack of money for Italian films led to another era in directing. In 1974, **Lina Wertmuller's** *Swept Away*—which portrays a rich Milanese woman stranded on a desert island with a chauvinist sailor—left many feminists fuming. Those familiar with **Bernardo Bertolucci's** *Last Tango in Paris* and *Last Emperor* should see his 1970 *Il Conformista* about a man hired to assassinate his former teacher. Other major modern Italian films include Vittorio de Sica's *Il Giardino dei Finzi-Contini* (Garden of the Finzi-Continis) and **Francesco Rosi's** *Cristo Si È Fermato a Eboli* (Christ Stopped at Eboli). In the 1980s, the **Taviani** brothers catapulted to fame with *Kaos,* a film based on stories by Pirandello, and *La Notte di San Lorenzo* (Night of the Shooting Stars), which depicts an Italian village during the ludicrous and tragic final days of World War II. Recently, Oscar-winners **Giuseppe Tornatore** (*Cinema Paradiso*) and **Gabriele Salvatore** (*Mediterraneo)* have won the affection of U.S. audiences. In 1996, **Massimo Troisi's** *Il Postino* was nominated for an Academy Award for Best Picture.

Those seeking a change from "serious" films should not ignore Italy's rich comic film tradition. Actor **Totò,** the bastard son of a Neapolitan duke, was Italy's challenge to Charlie Chaplin (known as "Charlot" in Italy). Totò's genius lay in his dignified antics and clever language, which took Italian minds away from their post-WWI misery. More recent star **Roberto Benigni** is featured in many Italian comedies, as well as the American *Son of the Pink Panther* and Jim Jarmusch's *Down by Law.*

If you want to sample the Italian film scene during your trip, try one of Italy's **film festivals,** such as the International Festival of New Cinema in Pesaro in June.

Food and Wine: La Dolce Vita

Don't plan to lose weight in Italy. Although monounsaturated olive oil and complex-carbohydrate-rich pasta may be healthy, you will soon be defeated by *gelato* and pizza, coffee pit-stops, and the cholesterol haven that Italians call a dessert tray.

Italian cuisine differs radically by region. The north offers creamy sauces, exotic mushroom dishes, stuffed pasta, and flat, handmade egg noodles. **Piedmont** and its southern neighbor **Umbria** are best known for their delectable (but pricey) truffles. **Lombardy** specializes in cheeses and *biscotti* (sweet, shortcake-like biscuits). The coastal region of **Liguria** is noted for its seafood, pesto, and olive oil, while German and Austrian influences on the **Trentino-Alto Adige** and **Veneto** regions have popularized *gnocchi,* dumplings typically made of potatoes and flour and now favorites throughout Italy. Central Italy serves richer, spicier dishes. The **Emilia-Romagna** region is the world's pasta palace, its dishes loaded with meat, cream, cheese, and butter. **Tuscany** draws justifiable acclaim for its expensive olive oil and bean dishes, and **Abruzzo** is known for spicy, peppery food, grilled meats, and a wealth of game. The food of the south is often less refined, but far less expensive. Tomato sauces and tubular pasta originated in **Campania,** also the birthplace of that most renowned "Italian" food: pizza. Greek influence can be detected in **Calabria's** cuisine, with its figs, honey, strong spices, and eggplant. **Sicily** produces luscious deserts, such as *cannoli,* pastry stuffed with sweet cheeses and chocolate, and *cassata,* a rich ice cream with candied fruit.

While breakfast often goes unnoticed (coffee and *cornetto,* a croissant-shaped pastry, at most), **lunch** is the main meal of the day in Italy. If you don't have a big appetite, grab lunch at an inexpensive *tavola calda* ("hot table"), *rosticceria* (grill), or *gastronomia* (serving hot prepared dishes). A new breed of fast food joint is springing up around the country, painful to see in a place that prides itself on homemade food. **Burghy** prepares burgers, while other chains feature pasta-to-go. The ample salad bar at an Italian McDonald's may be a welcome surprise. For more authentic eats, buy picnic materials at a *salumeria* or *alimentari,* meat and grocery shops. STANDA and COOP are two large supermarket chains. Fresh fruit and vegetables are best purchased at the open markets.

Italian **dinners** begin considerably later and last much longer than their American counterparts. Generally speaking, the farther south you travel, the later dinner is served. A full supper begins with an *antipasto* (appetizer), which can be as simple as *bruschetta* (broo-SKEHT-tah), a type of garlic bread, or as fancy as *prosciutto* (cured and spiced ham) with melon. Next comes the *primo piatto* (the first course, usually pasta or soup), followed by the *secondo,* consisting of meat or fish, and accompanied by a *contorno* (small vegetable side dish). Finally comes dessert or fruit, then coffee. It is common for Italians to order at least a *primo* and *secondo,* and less-touristy restaurants may be surprised if you only want to order one of these. Many restaurants offer a fixed-price tourist **menù** that includes *primo, secondo,* bread, water, and wine. While these meals are usually a good deal, you may not have a choice as to what is served for each course.

As far as **coffee** is concerned, ordering a *caffè* will get you a small but strong Italian espresso (add a lot of sugar and down it in two sips like natives do). Ask for *caffè macchiato* (literally "spotted coffee") if you would like a drop of milk in it. Cappuccino, which the Italians drink only before noon, has frothy scalded milk (whipped cream is *not* authentic); *caffè latte* is heavier on the milk, lighter on the coffee. But the key to Italian coffee is *caffè corretto* ("corrected"): an espresso with a drop of some strong liqueur, usually *grappa.*

A **bar** is an excellent place to grab a coffee or have a quick and inexpensive bite. Take care to avoid bars on major tourist thoroughfares, where prices are often inflated. Bars offer hot and cold sandwiches *(panini)*, drinks with or without **alcohol,** and *gelato.* **Tramezzini** come with an assortment of fillings, smothered in mayonnaise and surrounded by soft, de-crusted white bread, just like Mom used to make. Try the rolls and pizza bread stuffed with *prosciutto crudo* or *cotto* (ham either cured or cooked), *formaggio* (cheese), or even *frittate* (omelettes). You can ask for them *scaldato* (heated). In smaller towns or close-knit neighborhoods, bars are both social and gastronomical centers. Children come for *gelato,* while old men come for wine and conversation. In some areas, such as Rome, it is common to pay for your food at the cashier's desk and then take the receipt to a bartender, who will take your order. In less-touristed areas it is usually customary to pay afterward.

The billing at Italian restaurants can also be a bit confusing. Many restaurants add a *pane e coperto* (cover charge) of about L2000 to the price of your meal, as well as a *servizio* (service charge) of 10-15%. In city restaurants, you may want to tip if the bill does not include service, but in family-run establishments without hired servers, tipping is less expected and may occasionally be considered offensive. In a bar, look for a sign stating either *servizio compreso* (service included) or *servizio non compreso* (not included). In the latter case, drop a few coins into the kitty on the bar. *Caffè* prices are usually lower if you don't sit down. Proprietors at all shops will force you to take a *scontrino* or *ricevuta fiscale* (receipt) when you leave. They aren't being rude—it's required by law, and you could theoretically be asked to present it with your purchases.

Italy's rocky soil, warm climate, and hilly landscape have proven themselves ideal for growing grapes, and Italy produces more **wine** than any other country in the world. Wines from the north tend to be heavy and full-bodied; most touted (and

Don't Ask, Just Drink (Italian Wines Explained)

Ever wondered just what, exactly, Italian wine names mean? Here's a quick guide: The Veneto region produces the sweet **Soave** ("delicate"), while Le Marche features a strangely colored **Verdicchio** ("greenish-yellow") with an alcohol content that is as stomach-turning as the hue. Lombardy offers the **Cortese** ("well-behaved") wine, the **Sangue di Giuda** ("blood of Judas"), and finally, the **Buttafuoco** (pronounced BOO-tah-foo-OH-koh and meaning "fire-thrower").

expensive) are Piedmont's *barolo* and *barbera,* but the equally famous and more affordable sparkling *Asti spumante* deserves a swig. (The Piedmontese also claim to have invented vermouth.) Tuscany is regarded as Italy's wine-making capital; its rich *chianti,* similar to French burgundy, is a universal favorite. Other good heavy red wines include *salerno* from Naples and *valpolicella* from the Venetian district. White wine connoisseurs should sample *soave* from Verona, *frascati* from Rome, *orvieto* from Umbria, *lacryma Cristi* (Christ's Tear) from Naples, and *tocai* and *pinot grigio* from Friuli. The hotter climate of southern Italy and the islands produces stronger, fruitier wines than the north. Try the Sicilian *marsala,* which resembles a light sherry, or *cannonau* from Sardinia.

You can usually order by the glass, carafe, or half-carafe, although bars rarely serve wine by the glass. *Secco* means "dry" and *abboccato* means "sweet." *Superiore* usually implies a higher alcohol content. When in doubt, request the local wine—it will be cheaper (typically around L3500 a liter) and best suited to the regional cuisine.

Sports and Recreation

In Italy, **il calcio** ("soccer" to Americans, "football" to Europeans) far surpasses all other sports in popularity. Some claim that Italy's victory in the 1982 World Cup did more for national unity than any political movement. More recently, their success in 1994 sparked a wave of excitement that crested with every victory and ultimately crashed with their defeat by Brazil. Every city and town has its own team, and major cities have more than one. Italian sports fans are called *tifosi*—a derivative of "typhoid-fevered." Inter-urban rivalries, such as that between Naples and Rome, can easily become overheated. The fans are raucous and energetic, and make even the noisiest of American crowds seem tame. After a major victory, Italians take to the streets in chaotic and spontaneous celebration.

Bicycling is also popular in Italy. Besides manufacturing some of the best bikes in the world, Italians host the **Giro d'Italia,** a 25-day cross-country race in May. Professional **basketball** has also become a popular sport, importing players from the United States and other countries. With the Italian Alps and the Apennines within its borders, Italy also attracts thousands of **skiers** from December to April. **Hiking** and **mountain climbing** are popular throughout the north and in the Sila Massif in Calabria. As Mediterranean pollution worsens, **swimming** has become riskier. Try the beaches in the less-populated deep south or on an Italian island. Sardinia, for example, offers crystal-blue waters with visibility to depths of up to 30m.

On evenings with nice weather in most medium-sized cities, you can participate in the long-standing Italian tradition of the **passeggiata** (the promenade). It's nothing more than what it sounds like—a walk—yet the whole town will dress up, come out, window shop, and mutually ogle. This casual interaction continues later, as people spend their evenings in the *piazze* talking, mingling, and eating *gelato.* It's a great, inexpensive way to pass the time and meet people.

Festivals and Holidays

Italy suffers no shortage of town festivals, although few holidays are celebrated uniformally nationwide. The most common excuse for a local festival is the celebration of a religious event—a patron saint's day or the commemoration of a miracle—all of which are enthusiastically celebrated. A plethora of festivals occur Easter weekend. See **Festivals and Holidays** in the **appendix** (643).

The Italian Language

One of the six Romance languages, Italian has seduced lovers for centuries. It is not only a beautiful language, but also relatively easy to learn—especially if you already have some background in Spanish or French. Since Italians usually greet even a butchered attempt at pronunciation with appreciation and good-natured humor, it's worth the effort to learn a few simple phrases before you go. Be aware that in some particularly remote areas such as in the far south, English is not spoken at all.

Modern Italian is a descendant of vulgar (spoken) Latin and was standardized in the late Middle Ages thanks to the literary triumvirate of Dante, Petrarch, and Boccaccio. All three wrote in the Tuscan dialect which, through its popularity with the educated classes, subsequently became the basis for today's *italiano standard,* although natives of every region claim that their dialect is the "true" Italian.

As a result of the country's fragmented history, variations in **dialect** are particularly strong. The throaty Neapolitan can be extremely difficult for a northerner to understand; Ligurians use a mix of Italian, Catalàn, and French; Sicilian is considered a dialect related to but separate from Italian; and Sardo, spoken in Sardinia, is more or less its own language. Some inhabitants of the northern border regions don't speak Italian at all: the population of Val d'Aosta speaks mainly French, and the people of Trentino-Alto Adige harbor a German-speaking minority. In the southern regions of Puglia, Calabria, and Sicily, entire villages speak Albanian and Greek. The differences in speech are so significant that even native Italians are often confused when traveling around the country. Today, although most Italians still converse in local dialects at home, they also communicate in *italiano standard.* This version is taught in school and pervades Italian television, although regional accents have become increasingly popular with newscasters. In order to facilitate conversation, natives usually employ standard Italian when speaking with a foreigner.

Knowing a few basic terms will make your trip much easier. In the appendix of *Let's Go: Italy,* you'll find a **glossary** of useful terms and phrases, as well as guidelines for pronunciation (page 632). Don't forget that **hand gestures** are also a large part of Italian conversation. Take a phrase book with you, and practice before you leave.

Il Cornuto

Be sure **never** to make the sign of the *cornuto* ("the horn"): pinkie and pointer fingers extended, thumb and other fingers tucked under. To point it at someone is to insult not only that person, but also the honor of his or her mother.

ROME

To the oft-asked question, *"Bella Roma, no?"* there can be only one answer. Today, in an age when we regard artistic and historical generalizations with scepticism, Rome's glory is not dimmed, its head not bowed, its ruins not—well, ruined. During the two thousand years that Rome has symbolized empire, the Caesars and the popes have been busy building up their images in the city for the benefit of prosperity. Forums, churches, temples, *palazzi,* streets, and *piazze* testify to monumental ambitions and egos. Augustus boasted that he found Rome a city of brick and left it one of marble, but his work was only the beginning. The city's myriad monuments, even those not built to commemorate someone, vividly evoke eons of history.

Today the Colosseum crumbles from pollution, and the screech of maniacal scooters precludes any semblance of tranquility. Romans live and revel in their city rather than let it stagnate as a museum: concerts animate ancient ruins, kids play soccer around the Pantheon, and august *piazze* serve as movie houses. Looking at Rome, the idea of decline and fall seems ridiculous. All its empires live on today and leave Rome undefined by any single epoch. *Bella?* No. *Bellissima.*

Orientation

In his *Early History of Rome,* Livy concluded that "the layout of Rome is more like a squatter's settlement than a properly planned city." After 2000 years of city-planning, Rome is still a splendid, unnavigable sea of one-way streets, dead-ends, clandestine *piazze,* incongruous monuments, and incurable traffic. Getting lost is inevitable, but it is also the best way to get a sense of the city.

No longer defined by the Seven Hills, modern Rome sprawls over a large area between the hills of the **Castelli Romani** and the beach at **Ostia.** The central sights lie within a much smaller compass. From Termini Station, the arrival point for most visitors to Rome, the **Città Universitaria** and the student area of **San Lorenzo** are to the east and northeast, respectively. To the south are S. Giovanni and the seedy but historic Esquiline hill, home to some of the oldest, biggest, and most beautiful churches in the city. Many of the major tourist sights slope down between the hills to the west and southwest toward the Tiber. **Via Nazionale** is the central artery connecting Termini with the city center: it runs from Piazza della Repubblica and then connects with Via IV Novembre and Via C. Battisti to the immense **Piazza Venezia,** crowned by the conspicuous white marble pile of the **Vittorio Emanuele II Monument.** From Piazza Venezia, Via dei Fori Imperiale leads southeast to the **Forum** and **Colosseum,** south of which are the ruins of the **Circus Maximus,** the **Baths of Caracalla,** and the **Appian Way. Via del Corso** stretches north from Piazza Venezia to **Piazza del Popolo** and the neighboring **Pincio.** East of the Corso, fashionable streets border the **Piazza di Spagna** and, beyond that, the lush **Villa Borghese.** South and east are the **Trevi Fountain, Piazza Barberini,** and the churches of the Quirinal Hill. From Piazza Venezia to the west, **Largo Argentina** marks the start of the Corso Vittorio Emanuele II, which leads into the *centro storico,* the medieval and Renaissance tangle of alleys, towers, churches, and fountains around the **Pantheon, Piazza Navona, Campo de' Fiori,** and **Piazza Farnese,** before crossing the Tiber to gargantuan **Castel Sant'Angelo** and the **Vatican City.** Also across the Tiber from the *centro storico* is the **Trastevere** quarter, home to countless *trattorie* and the best streets through which one can wander. Back across the Tiber from Trastevere, by way of the Tiber Island, is the old **Jewish Ghetto.** To the south of the Ghetto and the Ancient City are the peaceful **Aventine Hill,** crowned with rose gardens and churches, and the earthy, working-class **Testaccio** district.

Practical Information

TRAVEL ORGANIZATIONS

Tourist Offices:

Info-Tourism Kiosks: At Largo Carlo Goldoni (tel. 687 50 27), off Via del Corso, across from Via dei Condotti; Largo Corrado Ricci (tel. 67 80 992) near the Colosseum; and on Via Nazionale (tel. 47 45 929), near the Palazzo delle Esposizioni. Open Tues.-Sat. 10am-6pm and Sun. 10am-1pm.

Enjoy Rome: Via Varese, 39, 00185 Roma (tel. 445 18 43; fax 445 07 34; http://dbweb.agora.stm.it/markets/magenta39/enjoy.html). Exit to the right (facing away from the trains) from the main lobby in Termini, and head 3 blocks up to Via Varese. Publishes a free useful guide to the city. Helps with hotel accommodations and short-term apartment rentals. Organizes 3hr. walking tours (L30,000, under 26 or over 65 L25,000), cycling tours (call for prices), and bus tours (L46,000) throughout the city. Open Mon.-Fri. 8:30am-1:30pm and 3:30-6:30pm, Sat. 8:30am-1:30pm. Extended hours in summer.

EPT: In the **Termini Station** (tel. 482 40 70), in front of track #2. Lines can be horrendous. **Central Office,** Via Parigi, 5 (tel. 48 89 92 55 or 48 89 92 53; fax 58 82 50). Walk from the station diagonally to the left across P. Cinquecento (filled with buses) and cross P. della Repubblica. Via Parigi starts on the other side of the church, at the Grand Hotel. English spoken. Offices open Mon.-Sat. 8:15am-7pm. Pick up a map and copies of *Romamor.* Both of these offices will help you find a room; come early.

ENIT: Via Marghera, 3 (tel. 49 71 282); as you exit the tracks at Termini, head to your right and cross Via Marsala to Via Marghera. It's 2 blocks down on the left. Some information on Rome, but mostly brochures and hotel listings for the rest of Lazio, other provinces, and major cities. Open Mon.-Fri. 9am-5:30pm.

Tourist Police: Ufficio Stranieri (Foreigner's Office), Via San Vitale, 15 (tel. 46 86 27 11). English spoken. Report thefts here in person. Open 24hr.

Budget Travel:

Centro Turistico Studentesco (CTS): Via Genova, 16 (tel. 467 91), off Via Nazionale. About halfway between P. della Repubblica and P. Venezia. Open Mon.-Fri. 9am-1pm and 3-7pm, Sat. 9am-1pm. Another office at Via degli Ausoni, 5 (tel. 445 01 41) open Mon.-Fri. 9:30am-1pm and 2:30-6:30pm, Sat. 10am-1pm. Branch offices at Termini at track #22 (tel. 467 92 54; open daily 8:30am-8:30pm); at Via Appia Nuova, 434 (tel. 780 84 49; open Mon.-Fri. 9:30am-1pm and 3:30-7pm, Sat. 9:30am-1pm); at Corso Vittorio Emanuele II, 297 (tel. 687 26 72; open Mon.-Fri. 9:30am-1:30pm and 2:30-6pm, Sat. 9:30am-noon); and at Terminal Ostiense (tel. 467 92 57; open Mon.-Fri. 9:30am-1:30pm and 2:30-6pm, Sat. 9:30am-noon). ISIC and *Carta Giovane* cards L15,000 each; bring ID photo and proof of student status. A free map and currency exchange, plus discount plane, train, boat, and bus tickets and reservations. Free accommodations service, including out-of-town reservations. Bulletin boards with notices for rides, companionship, special services, etc. Lines can be aggravatingly slow; if information is all you need, it's better to phone (information tel. 467 91). The staff speaks excellent English at all locations.

Compagnia Italiana di Turismo (CIT): P. della Repubblica, 64 (tel. 47 46 555; fax 48 18 277). National travel agency that books discount train tickets and tours. Open Mon.-Fri. 9am-1pm and 2-5:30pm.

Italian Youth Hostels (Associazione Italiana Alberghi per la Gioventù), HI-AYHF: Via Cavour, 44 (tel. 487 11 52; fax 488 04 92). Plenty of advice and a list of hostels throughout Italy. HI-IYHF cards L30,000. Open Mon.-Thurs. 7:30am-5pm, Fri. 7:30am-3pm, Sat. 8am-12:30pm.

TRANSPORTATION

Flights: All roads lead to Rome, but you can fly there too.

Fiumicino (Leonardo da Vinci International): Most international, domestic, and non-charter flights touch down at Leonardo da Vinci International Airport

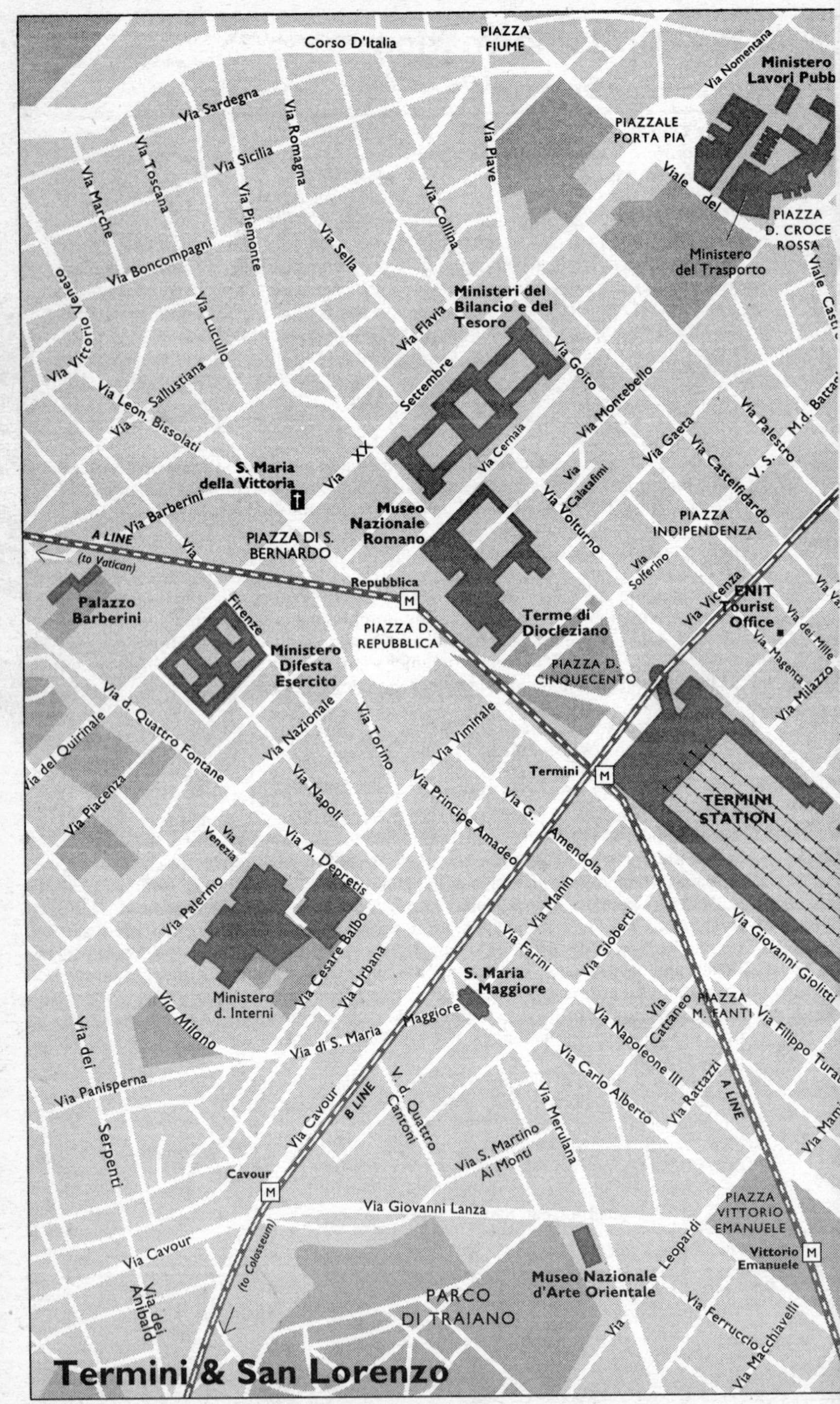

Termini & San Lorenzo
Corso D'Italia
PIAZZA FIUME
Via Nomentana
Ministero Lavori Pubb
PIAZZALE PORTA PIA
Viale del
PIAZZA D. CROCE ROSSA
Ministero del Trasporto
Viale Castr
Via Sardegna
Via Romagna
Via Piave
Via Toscana
Via Sicilia
Via Marche
Via Piemonte
Via Collina
Via Sella
Via Boncompagni
Via Lucullo
Via Vittorio Veneto
Via Flavia
Ministeri del Bilancio e del Tesoro
Via Goito
Via Sallustiana
Via Leon. Bissolati
Via XX Settembre
Via Montebello
Via Palestro
M.d. Battag
Via Cernaia
Via Gaeta
Via Castelfidardo
V. S.
S. Maria della Vittoria
Via Calatafimi
Via Volturno
Via Barberini
A LINE
(to Vatican)
PIAZZA DI S. BERNARDO
Museo Nazionale Romano
PIAZZA INDIPENDENZA
Via Solferino
Via Firenze
Repubblica
Palazzo Barberini
PIAZZA D. REPUBBLICA
Terme di Diocleziano
Via Vicenza
ENIT Tourist Office
Via dei Mille
Via. Magenta
Via Milazzo
Ministero Difesta Esercito
PIAZZA D. CINQUECENTO
Via d. Quattro Fontane
Via del Quirinale
Via Nazionale
Via Torino
Via Viminale
Termini
TERMINI STATION
Via Piacenza
Via Napoli
Via Principe Amadeo
Via G. Amendola
Via Venezia
Via A. Depretis
Via Palermo
Via Cesare Balbo
Via Manin
Via Farini
Via Gioberti
Via Giovanni Giolitti
Ministero d. Interni
Via Urbana
S. Maria Maggiore
Via Milano
Via di S. Maria Maggiore
Via Cattaneo
PIAZZA M. FANTI
Via Filippo Turat
Via dei Serpenti
Via Napoleone III
Via Carlo Alberto
Via Panisperna
Via Cavour
B LINE
V. d. Quattro Cantoni
Via Merulana
Via Rattazzi
A LINE
Via Mami
Via S. Martino Ai Monti
Cavour
PIAZZA VITTORIO EMANUELE
Via Giovanni Lanza
Vittorio Emanuele
Via Leopardi
(to Colosseum)
Museo Nazionale d'Arte Orientale
Via dei Anibald
PARCO DI TRAIANO
Via Ferruccio
Via Macchiavelli

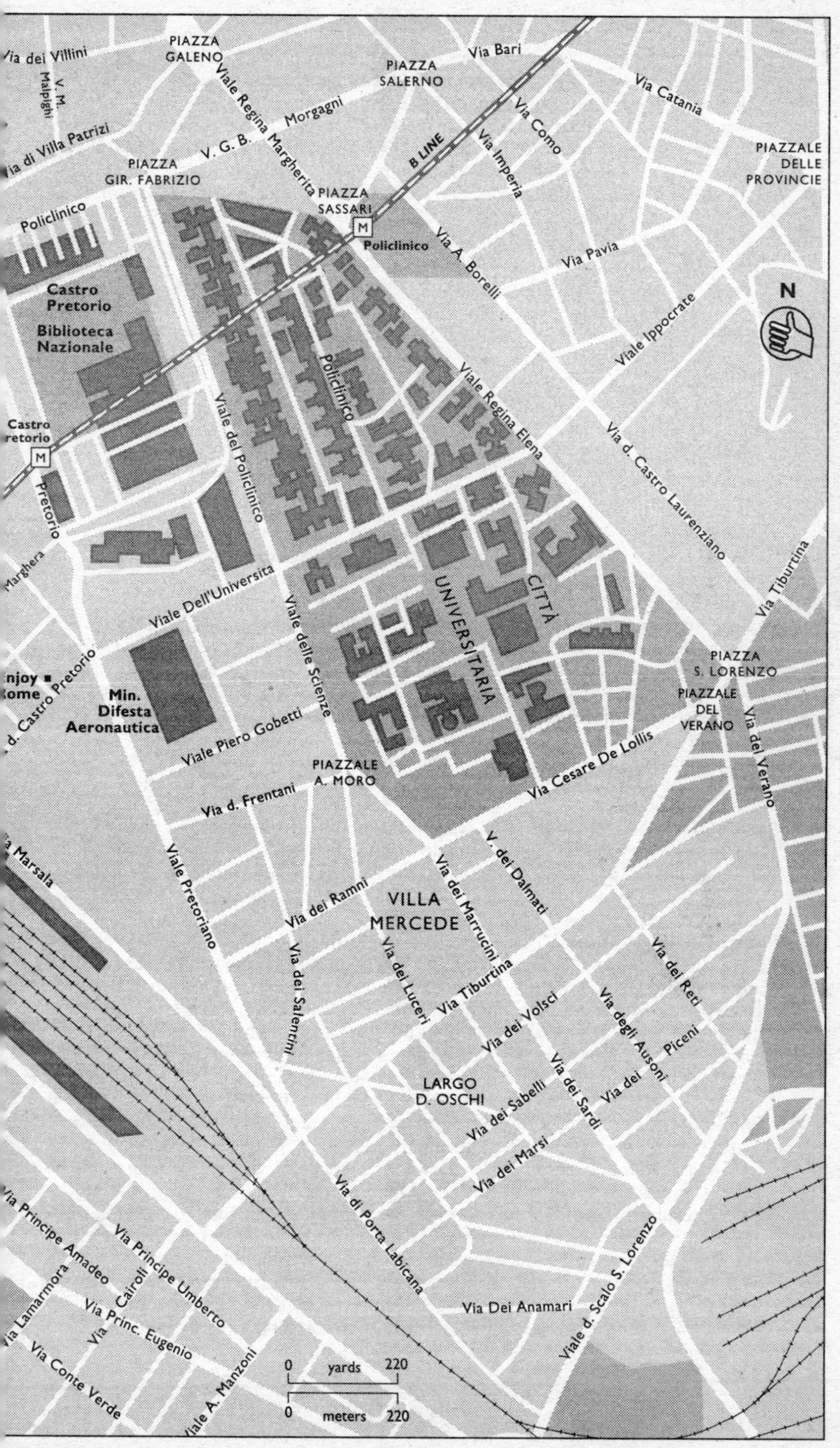

PIAZZA GALENO
Via dei Villini
V. M. Malpighi
Via di Villa Patrizi
Viale Regina Margherita
Via Bari
PIAZZA SALERNO
Morgagni
V. G. B.
PIAZZA GIR. FABRIZIO
Via Catania
Via Como
Via Imperia
B LINE
PIAZZALE DELLE PROVINCIE
Policlinico
PIAZZA SASSARI
M
Policlinico
Via A. Borelli
Via Pavia
Castro Pretorio
Biblioteca Nazionale
N
Viale Ippocrate
Policlinico
Viale Regina Elena
Viale del Policlinico
Castro Pretorio
M
Pretorio
Via d. Castro Laurenziano
Via Tiburtina
CITTÀ UNIVERSITARIA
Marghera
Viale Dell'Università
Viale delle Scienze
PIAZZA S. LORENZO
Enjoy ■ Rome
Via d. Castro Pretorio
Min. Difesta Aeronautica
Viale Piero Gobetti
PIAZZALE DEL VERANO
Via del Verano
Via Cesare De Lollis
PIAZZALE A. MORO
Via d. Frentani
Via Marsala
Viale Pretoriano
V. dei Dalmati
Via dei Marrucini
Via dei Ramni
VILLA MERCEDE
Via dei Luceri
Via dei Salentini
Via Tiburtina
Via dei Reti
Via dei Volsci
Via degli Ausoni
Via dei Piceni
Via dei Sardi
LARGO D. OSCHI
Via dei Sabelli
Via dei Marsi
Via di Porta Labicana
Via Principe Amadeo
Via Principe Umberto
Via Cairoli
Via Lamarmora
Via Princ. Eugenio
Via Conte Verde
Viale A. Manzoni
Via Dei Anamari
Viale d. Scalo S. Lorenzo
0 yards 220
0 meters 220

(switchboard tel. 659 51), referred to as **Fiumicino** for the coastal village in which it is located. Two train lines connect Fiumicino with the center of Rome: the **Termini line** and the **Tiburtina/Orte/Farasabina line.** For transfers to domestic flights from the international terminal, follow the signs for "Voli Nazionali/Domestic Flights" or take the shuttle *(navetta)* to the domestic terminal. When leaving customs, follow the signs to your left for **Stazione FS/Railway Station.** The **Termini** line goes directly to Rome's main train station and transportation hub, Termini Station. (To Termini every hour 8:08am-10:08pm, plus 7:38am, 4:38, 6:38, and 8:38pm. To Fiumicino every hour 7:22am-9:22pm and 6:52am, 3:52, 5:52, and 7:52pm. Each way 30min., L13,000.) Buy a ticket *"per termini"* at the FS ticket counter, the *tabacchi* on the right, or from one of the machines in the station. Buy tickets at the Alitalia office at track #22 at the window marked "Biglietti Per Fiumicino" or from other designated areas and machines in the station. You can also reach Fiumicino from **Tiburtina Station,** located at the Tiburtina stop on Metro Linea B (every 20-30min. 5:06am-11:05pm, 40min., L7000). Train schedules are erratic on Sundays and in August. Avoid flying into or out of Rome before 8am or after 10pm. If you must, the most reliable transportation option to or from the airport is a cab (L65,000-85,000). Request one at the kiosk in the airport or call 3570, 4994, or 6645. Otherwise, you must take the **COTRAL bus** to Tiburtina (at 1:15, 2:15, 3:30, and 5am, L7000 on the bus). From Tiburtina, bus 42N runs to Termini Station.

Ciampino: Most charter and a few domestic flights arrive at **Ciampino** airport (tel. 79 49 41). From here take the blue COTRAL bus to the Anagnina stop on Metro Linea A (L1500; departures every hr. from 6am-11pm.). Linea A takes you to Termini, the Spanish Steps, or the Vatican. At night (after 11pm or so), you may have to take a cab to and from Ciampino; airport surcharge L10,000.

Trains: Stazione Termini, the transportation hub of Rome, is the focal point of most train lines and both subway lines. The stations on the fringe of town **(Tiburtina, Trastevere, Ostiense, San Lorenzo, Roma Nord, Prenestina)** are connected by bus and/or subway to Termini. Trains that arrive in Rome after midnight and before 5am or so usually arrive at Stazione Tiburtina or Stazione Ostiense, connected to Termini during these hours by the 42N and 20N-21N respectively. To: Florence (2½hr., L24,400); Venice (5hr., L44,100); Naples (2½hr., L17,200); Milan (6hr., L47,700); Bologna (4hr., L33,400); Brindisi (7hr., L47,700); and Palermo (12hr., L68,900).

Buses: COTRAL (tel. 591 55 51), which runs between Rome and the rest of Lazio, has moved its departure points outside of the city proper to facilitate traffic; take the Metro to an outlying area and catch the bus from there: **Anagnina** for Frascati and the Colli Albani; **Rebibbia** for Tivoli and Subiaco; **Lepanto** for Cerveteri, Tarquinia, Bracciano, Lago Vico, and Civitavecchia.

Public Transportation: Tickets usable on either the bus or subway can be bought at *tabacchi*, newsstands, some bars, and machines located in stations and at major bus stops. Tickets (L1500) good for 1 Metro ride or 75min. of bus travel after the 1st validation. Once you have stamped a ticket for bus travel, you may not use it on the metro. There is a L50,000-100,000 fine for riding without a validated ticket. Daily pass L6000. *Abbonamento mensile* (monthly bus and Metro pass) L50,000, wherever tickets are sold. Student bus passes are only for students at an Italian university. Weekly bus/Metro passes are also available for L24,000.

Subway: The two lines of the **Metropolitana** intersect beneath Termini. **Linea A** runs from Ottaviano, near the Vatican, through P. di Spagna, P. Barberini, P. della Repubblica, and Termini, before heading to Anagnina and intervening stops in the southeastern suburbs of the city. **Linea B** runs from Rebibbia in the northeastern suburbs, through the university area around P. Bologna, to Termini, then on to the Colosseum, Piramide, and Magliana (change here for trains to Ostia and the beach), terminating at Laurentina in EUR. The subway is fairly safe, but watch for pickpockets. Many of Rome's sights are a trek from the nearest subway stop, but for covering large distances fast, the subway beats the bus, especially during the day, during protests, and during rush hour. The subway runs 5:30am-11:30pm.

Buses: ATAC (tel. 469 51) provides myriad booths and friendly staff for assistance in navigating Rome's efficient but dauntingly extensive system. Lozzi publishes a **Roma Metro-Bus map** (L9000), available at newsstands. Regular-service routes and numbers are marked by red shields on the yellow bus-stop signs. Some buses run only on weekdays *(feriali)* or weekends *(festivi)*. **Night routes** *(notturno)* are indicated by black shields on the newer signs or by the letter N following the number, or both. You must signal a night bus to stop for you. Don't depend too heavily on *notturno* buses, since they are often unreliable; consider a cab. After midnight, ticket salesmen ride the buses and will sell you a ticket on board.

Taxis: Stands at P. Sonnino on Viale Trastevere, P. Venezia, P. della Repubblica, Via Nazionale, P. Risorgimento, and P. del Popolo. Ride only in yellow or white taxis with meters. L4500 for the first 153.8m or 20.6sec., then L200 for each successive 153.8m/20.6sec. Night surcharge L5000; Sunday surcharge L2000; each suitcase L2000; airport surcharge L11,500-14,000 (Fiumicino) or L10,000 (Ciampino).

Car Rental: All firms will let you drop your rental car off in any other Italian city where they have an office (with an additional charge of about L50,000 north of Rome and a monumental L300,000 to the south). All locations speak English.

Maggiore: Main office (tel. 229 15 30), information only; at Termini (tel. 488 00 49), open Mon.-Fri. 7am-8pm, Sat. 8am-6pm, Sun. 8:30am-12:30pm; Fiumicino (tel. 65 01 06 78), open Mon.-Sat. 8am-11pm; toll-free national number (167) 86 70 67, open Mon.-Fri. 8:30am-6:30pm, Sat. 9am-1pm.

Hertz: At Termini (tel. 474 03 89; fax 474 67 05), open Mon.-Fri. 7am-7pm, Sat. 7am-5pm; Fiumicino (tel. 65 01 14 48 or 65 01 15 53), open Mon.-Fri. 7am-midnight, Sat. 7am-11pm.

Europcar: At Termini (tel. 488 28 54), open Mon.-Fri. 7am-8pm, Sat. 8am-6pm; Fiumicino (tel. 65 01 09 77 and 650 01 08 79), open daily 7am-11pm.

Bike or Moped Rental: Generally around L5000 per hr. or L15,000 per day. In summer, try the unmarked stands at P. di San Lorenzo at Via del Corso or Via di Pontifici at Via del Corso, both near P. di Spagna. Open 10am-1am. Look for *"noleggio bicicletta"* signs around the city, at P. di Spagna Metro stop, at P. Sonnino off Viale Trastevere, and in Villa Borghese. Mopeds and scooters run L50,000-85,000 per day. You must be 16 years old; driver's license not required. Be cautious: Rome is not the place to take your first moped or scooter ride. **Practice safe cycling and always wear a helmet.**

Rent-a-Scooter: Via F. Turati, 50 (tel. 446 92 92), steps from Termini. "Best prices in Rome": scooters from L29,000 per day. Also offers scooter tours with native Roman guides. 24-hr. roadside assistance. Open Sun.-Fri. 9am-7pm.

I Bike Rome: Via Veneto, 156 (tel. 322 52 40). Rents from the Villa Borghese's underground parking garage. The subterranean entrance is near the intersection of Via di S. Paolo del Brasile and Via della Magnolie. Bikes L5000 per hr., L13,000 per day, or L38,000 per week. Tandems, too. Mopeds L30,000 for 4hr., and L45,000 all day. Open daily 9am-8pm.

OTHER SERVICES

Currency Exchange: Large banks including **Banco d'Italia, Banca Nazionale del Lavoro,** and **Banca di Roma** operate throughout the city. **Termini** has many *cambi,* usually with low rates and/or high commissions; other booths throughout the city often offer the best exchange rates you'll find. To get a cash advance on a credit card, try Banca Nazionale del Lavoro on Via Veneto or many of the **ATMs** on Via Arenula, near the Pantheon, and on Via del Tritone.

American Express: P. di Spagna, 38, Roma 00187 (tel. 67 641; lost or stolen cards and/or checks issued in the U.S. toll-free 24hr. (167) 87 43 33; others call 72 281). Chaotic at times, but fairly efficient, and perfect English spoken. Client mail held for cardmembers. American Express Traveler's Cheques cashed at any of the small *cambi* all over the city. Excellent free maps of Rome. The ATM outside accepts AmEx cards. Open Mon.-Fri. 9am-5:30pm, Sat. 9am-3pm.

Telephones: In the main gallery in Termini. The only two metered phones in the city. Open daily 8am-9:45pm.

Lost Property: Oggetti Rinvenuti, Via Nicolo Bettoni, 1 (tel. 581 60 40), at the Trastevere train station. Open Mon. and Fri. 8:30am-1pm, Tues.-Wed. 8:30am-1pm and 2:30-6pm, Thurs. 8:30am-6pm, Sat. 8:30am-noon. **Termini,** at track #1. Open daily 7am-11pm. **ATAC,** Via Volturno, 65 (tel. 469 51). Open Mon.-Fri. 9am-noon and 2-5pm. Also check your **embassy** and the police (see above).

Laundromat: OndaBlu, Via Principe Amedeo, 70/b (tel. 47 44 66 47), off Via Cavour 2 blocks south of Termini. Open daily 8am-10pm. Also Via Milazzo, 8, off Via Marsala. Wash L6000 per 6.5kg load (40min.). Dry L6000 for 20min.

Athletic Club: Roman Sport Center, Via del Galoppatoio, 33 (tel. 36 14 358), in Villa Borghese. Take Metro Linea A to Spagna and follow the Via Veneto exit. Non-residents: aerobics, squash, pool, sauna, Turkish baths, and weight room for L25,000. Open Mon.-Sat. 9am-8pm.

Bookstores: The Lion Bookshop, Via del Babuino, 181 (tel. 322 58 37), between P. di Spagna and P. di Popolo. Well-stocked with classic and contemporary releases in English. Community bulletin board here as well (with apartment listings, etc.). Closed Aug. Open Mon. 3:30-7:30pm, Tues.-Fri. 9:30am-1:30pm and 3:30-7:30pm, Sat. 9:30am-1pm. **Economy Book and Video Center,** Via Torino, 136 (tel. 474 68 77), off Via Nazionale. Open Mon.-Fri. 9am-8pm, Sat. 9am-2pm. **Anglo-American Bookshop,** Via della Vite, 102 (tel. 679 52 52). Steps from P. di Spagna. Open Mon.-Fri. 9am-1pm and 4-8pm, Sat. 9am-1pm. **Bibli,** Via dei Fienaroli, 28 (tel./fax 588 40 97; e-mail info@bibli.it), in Trastevere. Turn right on Viale delle Fratte di Trastevere and right again onto Via dei Fienaroli. Offers books in English and provides Internet access (10hr., L50,000, valid 3 months; 25hr., L100,000, valid 6 months). Open Sept.-July Mon. 5pm-midnight, Tues.-Sun. 11am-midnight; Aug. daily 5pm-midnight.

Feminist Center: Via Lungara, 1a (tel. 686 42 01), off Via S. Francesco di Sales. Seminars, cultural events, and lesbian archives. Branch and library at Via dell'Orso, 36.

Late-Night Pharmacies: *La Repubblica* and *Il Messaggero* newspapers publish a list of pharmacies open in Aug., and all pharmacies post the names, addresses, and hours of neighboring pharmacies and all-night pharmacies. In Aug., try the following: **Farmacia Grieco,** P. della Repubblica, 67 (tel. 488 04 10 or 48 38 61), steps from Termini. Open 24hr. **Farmacia Piram,** Via Nazionale, 228 (tel. 488 07 54). Open 24hr. **Cristo dei Ferroviari,** near track #14 in Termini (tel. 488 07 76). Open until 10pm.

Police: tel. 113. **Carabinieri:** tel. 112. **Police Headquarters (Questura):** Via San Vitale, 15 (tel. 468 61). **Railway Police:** On track #1 and near track #2 in Termini.

Post Office: P. San Silvestro, 19, 00187 Roma (tel. 67 71), between P. di Spagna and the Corso. Stamps are at booths #23-25, *fermo posta* at #72. Currency exchange (*cambio;* no checks) is at booths #25-28. Open Mon.-Fri. 9am-6pm, Sat. 7am-2pm. Branch offices dot the city but most are open only in the morning. **Vatican City** is said to run a more efficient post office. The generic **postal code** for Rome is 00100; other codes are variations on the 001XX theme.

Emergency Lines: First Aid (Pronto Soccorso): 118. **Fire:** tel. 115. **Road Assistance:** tel. 116. **Anti-Violence Hotline:** tel. 683 26 90 or 683 28 20, Mon.-Fri. 10am-1pm and 4-7pm. Italian only. **Ambulance (Red Cross):** 55 10. **Hospitals: Policlinico Umberto I,** Viale di Policlinico, 255 (tel. 49 97 09 00 or 499 71), near Termini. Take Metro Linea B to the Policlinico stop. **Free first aid.** Open 24hr. **Rome-American Hospital,** Via Emilio Longoni, 69 (tel. 225 51, 225 52 90, or 225 33 33). Private emergency and laboratory services. English-speaking physician on call 24hr.

Telephone Code: 06.

TOURING TIPS

Getting lost in the streets of Rome can be either the most frustrating or enjoyable part of your stay. Rome's greatest treasures often lie hidden in the perplexing tangle of streets: the Pantheon emerges quite suddenly as you wind your way through the narrow *vie* and Bramante's Tempietto sits in the small courtyard of a lonely church.

Travel schedules and timetables are often unreliable, so it's best to call ahead whenever possible. Don't forget that much of the city will shut down during the Italian lunch "hour" from about 1pm to 3:30 or 4pm. Most shops and offices are open weekdays and Saturdays from approximately 9am-1pm and 4-8pm (in winter 3:30-

7:30pm). Most shops, businesses, and some cafés shut down on Sundays and Monday mornings, while restaurants, tourist organizations, some department stores, supermarkets, and nearly everything on Via del Corso remain open for business. In the summer, some shops may also close on Saturday afternoon. **Food stores** *(alimentari)* are usually closed Thurs. afternoons.

Numerous companies organize bus and walking tours in the city. Try **Carrani Tours** (tel. 474 25 01), **Appian Line** (tel. 488 41 51), and **American Express** (tel. 676 41) for bus tours and tour packages that include Papal encounters, dinner, and entertainment. For walking tours call **Walk Thru the Centuries** (tel. 323 17 33) or **Secret Walks in Rome** (tel. 39 72 87 28). **ATAC** also offers a no-frills, 3hr. circuit of the city, leaving from P. dei Cinquecento (Bus #110; L15,000). You can also take bus #119 for an orienting glance at some of the city's more visible monuments.

Finally, a note on **safety:** Rome is congested day and night with lost, bewildered, and distracted tourists, each loaded with cash and valuables. The thieving hordes are especially thick around the Forum and the Colosseum and on crowded buses like the #64 and 492. At night, women and men will generally feel safe walking through the center of town during all but the darkest hours. Outside the *centro storico* (historic center), however, use caution. The areas around Termini and to its south (especially near Piazza Vittorio Emanuele II and the Oppian Hill, notorious drug areas) and around Testaccio deserve special care. The area north of the city center near the Olympic Village also requires extra vigilance. Women should consult the section on women travelers in **Essentials,** page 30.

Accommodations

In July and August, Rome swells with tourists. A large quantity of rooms meets the high demand for lodging, but quality ranges significantly and hotel prices are often astronomical. Make sure the hotel charges you no more than the price posted on the back of your room's door, and be alert for additional shower and breakfast charges. The **tourist offices** in Rome will scrounge (sometimes reluctantly in peak season) to find you a room; Enjoy Rome, at Via Varese, 39, and the EPT office, at Via Parigi, 5, can be helpful. Termini swarms with officials trying to find you a place. Many of them are the real thing and have photo IDs issued by the tourist office. Some sneaky imposters, however, issue themselves fake badges and cards, and they will likely direct you to a rundown location charging significantly more than the going rate. Ask the officials for maps and directions, but exercise caution. **Associazione Cattolica Internazionale al Servizio della Giovane,** Via Urbana, 158 (tel. 488 14 19), assists women age 25 or younger in finding lodging in religious institutions.

It is illegal to "camp out" in the public places of Rome.

NORTH OF TERMINI

There are plenty of clean and reasonable *pensioni* and hotels awaiting the weary traveler within a short walk of Termini. Although once somewhat run-down, the area has recently become a trendy haven for budget travelers, cheaper than the historic center to the west and safer than the sometimes seedy Esquiline area south of Termini. With the trains behind you, exit Termini to the right, near track #1, onto Via Marsala. Small *alimentari* line Via Marghera and Via Marsala.

Pensione Papa Germano, Via Calatafimi, 14A (tel. 48 69 19). With the trains behind you, exit the station to your right and turn left on Via Marsala, which becomes Via Volturno; Via Calatafimi will be on the right. Deservedly popular with backpackers and students. Gino speaks English and will help you find a place if he's booked. Cheerful flowered walls and bedspreads. No curfew. Check-out 11am. Singles L35,000. Doubles L60,000, with bath L80,000. Triples L75,000, with bath L90,000. Quads L25,000 per person. 10% reduction Nov.-March. Reservations encouraged in summer. V, MC, AmEx.

Pensione Fawlty Towers, Via Magenta, 39 (tel. 445 03 74). Exit Termini to the right and cross Via Marsala to Via Marghera. Head up the street, turn right on Via Magenta, and look for the yellow sign. The eager English-speaking staff provides clean, comfortable accommodations and information about the city. Chat with other travelers on the terrace or in the common room. Satellite TV and communal fridge. No curfew. Singles L45,000, with shower L65,000. Doubles L70,000, with shower L85,000, with full bath L95,000. Triples with shower L90,000, with full bath L105,000. Co-ed dorm-style quads L25,000 per person.

Hotel Virginia, Via Montebello, 94 (tel. 488 17 86). Exit Termini to the east (right) onto Via Marsala, turn left and follow the street until it turns into Via Volturno. Via Montebello will be on your right. A unique and varied decor, ranging from pink sheets and lacy curtains to a portrait of Christ painted on the wall. Singles L35,000, with shower L40,000. Doubles with shower L50,000-65,000, with full bath L60,000-80,000. Triples L60,000, with shower L60,000-75,000. Quads L20,000 per person. Prices vary depending on the season. Breakfast L1400.

Pensione Tizi, Via Collina, 48 (tel. 482 01 28; fax 474 32 66). A 15-min. walk from the station. Take Via Goito from P. dell'Indipendenza, cross Via XX Settembre onto Via Piave, then take the first left onto Via Flavia, which leads to Via Collina. Pristine, new rooms with marble floors and rosy wallpaper. Check-out 11am. Singles L45,000. Doubles L65,000, with bath L80,000. Triples and quads L30,000 per person, with bath L35,000 per person. Breakfast L7000.

Hotel Matilde, Via Villafranca, 20 (tel. 445 43 65; fax 446 23 68; e-mail hmatilde@mbox.vol.it), off Via S. Martino della Battaglia (Via Solferino after crossing P. Indipendenza). Roomy quarters, outdated decor. The staff helps find restaurants, nightlife, and parking discounts. Reception open until midnight. Check-out 10am. No curfew. Singles L60,000. Doubles L90,000. Triples L120,000. Quads L140,000. V, MC, AmEx.

Pensione Piave, Via Piave, 14 (tel. 474 34 47; fax 487 33 60). Off Via XX Settembre. A step up from the garden-variety budget accommodation, and worth the extra *lire.* All rooms have private bath, telephone, and carpeted floors. English spoken. Check-in at noon. Check-out at 10:30am, but you can leave luggage all day. No curfew. Singles L45,000. Doubles with bath L80,000. Triples with bath L95,000. Quads with bath L125,000. Washer and dryer available for an extra L15,000-20,000. Personal checks accepted.

Pensione Alessandro, Via Vicenza, 42 (tel. 446 19 58). Across the street from a *pizzeria rustica,* near the corner of Via Palestro. 85 beds, 2-4 per room. A full-size Pink Panther greets you as you enter. The English-speaking owner provides tourist and nightlife information. Coffee and biscuits all day. Kitchen facilities, with microwave. No curfew. Reception open 6:30am-11pm. Check-out by 9am. Lockout noon-3pm. May-Sept. L25,000 per person. Oct.-April L20,000 per person.

Hotel Castelfidardo and **Hotel Lazzari,** Via Castelfidardo, 31 (tel. 446 46 38; fax 494 13 78). Both run by the same family. Completely new, modern rooms, clean showers, and helpful management. Singles L50,000, with bath L70,000. Doubles L65,000, with bath L80,000. Triples L85,000, with bath L110,000. Quads with bath L130,000. V, MC, AmEx.

M&J Place, Via Solferino, 9 (tel. 446 28 02). A prime location just off of Via Marsala. The young, English-speaking staff provides comfortable accommodations and ideas for evening fun. Bunk beds in large dorm-style rooms. Common TV, radio, and fridge. L20,000 per person.

Hotel Home Michele, Via Palestro, 35 (tel. 444 12 04). Cosmic forces have joined to assemble this *pensione's* unpredictable atmosphere. Michele, the cat, hangs from pink felt attached to the doors of the five rooms. Oriental furniture mixes with 70s decor. Check-out 10am. Singles L40,000. Doubles L55,000. Triples L25,000 per person. Will accommodate quads. Rates lower in winter.

Pensione Lachea, Via San Martino della Battaglia, 11 (tel. 495 72 56), off P. dell'Indipendenza. *Let's Go's* biggest fan, the warm-hearted owner will ensure every comfort. Small and colorful. 3 rooms have balconies. Check-out 11am. Singles L45,000. Doubles L60,000, with bath, L80,000. Triples L80,000, with bath L110,000. Bargaining possible if the place isn't full.

Hotel Galli, Via Milazzo, 20 (tel. 445 68 59; fax 446 85 01), off Via Marsala. Many rooms were recently renovated, with gleaming floors and bathrooms. Singles L50,000, with bath L75,000. Doubles L75,000, with bath L90,000-120,000. Triples and quads L27,000 per person. Breakfast L10,000. V, MC.

SOUTH OF TERMINI

You can reach Via Principe Amedeo, which runs parallel to the station, by taking any of the side streets off Via Giolitti outside the southwest exit of the station. The closer you get to P. Vittorio Emanuele, the less secure the area becomes at night. This neighborhood, often portrayed as busier, noisier, and seedier than other parts of central Rome, has started to clean up its act. Savvy locals and business-minded immigrants cater to budget travelers and university students who frequent the two nearby dining halls. Keep in mind that prices in this area are often negotiable and seasonal prices vary considerably.

Pensione Sandy, Via Cavour, 136 (tel. 488 45 85), near Santa Maria Maggiore. No sign; look for the Hotel Valle next door. Buzz to be let in. Run by peppy Americans and a native Roman. Plain, comfortable, dormitory rooms, generally for 3-5 people, in a great central location. L25,000 per person during the summer, L20,000 in winter (no heat, but lots of blankets). Showers included.

Pensione di Rienzo, Via Principe Amedeo, 79A (tel. 446 71 31 and 446 69 80). Tranquil, family-run retreat with grand, newly-renovated rooms overlooking a peaceful courtyard. Some rooms with balconies. Friendly, English-speaking staff. No curfew. Singles L45,000-50,000, with bath up to L80,000. Doubles L60,000-75,000, with bath L80,000-90,000. Triples L100,000-120,000. V, MC.

Hotel Kennedy, Via Filippo Turati, 64 (tel. 446 53 73; fax 446 54 17). Trendy rooms with private bath, color TV with satellite (MTV, CNN, you name it), phone, and A/C. Hearty all-you-can-eat breakfast includes cornflakes, croissant, and endless varieties of jam, cheese, and tea. Free juice and coffee all day long. English-speaking staff. 10% discount for *Let's Go* travelers under 29. Singles L60,000-99,000. Doubles L80,000-155,000. Triples L110,000-180,000. V, MC, AmEx.

Pensione Cortorillo, Via Principe Amedeo, 79A (tel. 446 69 34), at Via Gioberti. On the 5th floor. Simple, family-run establishment. Charming rooms with wooden beds. Continental breakfast included. Dinner L10,000. Singles with bath L30,000-50,000. Doubles L50,000-70,000. Triples L75,000-90,000. Try bargaining.

Hotel Orlanda, Via Principe Amedeo, 76 (tel. 488 06 37; fax 488 01 83), at Via Gioberti. Take the stairs on the right in the vestibule to the 3rd floor. Spotless, pleasant rooms, all with TV and phone. English spoken. Singles with bath L70,000-90,000. Doubles L80,000-140,000. V, MC, AmEx, DC.

WEST OF TERMINI

The area west and southwest of Termini maintains an authentic Roman atmosphere with cobblestone alleyways, traditional *trattorie*, hip wine shops, and trendy Irish pubs. This neighborhood is also home to the city's two women-only establishments.

Youth Hostel Roma Inn Keiko, Via Urbana, 96 (tel. 474 38 45). Ring "Roma Inn" buzzer. An odd mix of frat house and home sweet home. Recently renovated red-walled rooms for 1-5 people. Communal fridge and clothesline available. The youthful proprietor organizes late-night excursions. English spoken. Dorms L30,000 per person. Private singles and doubles L35,000 per person.

Hotel San Paolo, Via Panisperna, 95 (tel. 474 52 13; fax 474 52 18), follow Via S. Maria Maggiore, just off Via Cavour to your right after S. Maria Maggiore. Secure, recently renovated rooms, some with terrace and most decorated with enormous puzzles assembled by the proprietor. Hall baths are clean and private. English spoken. Singles up to L50,000. 2-bed doubles up to L85,000, *matrimoniale* with bath up to L100,000. Triple L115,000. Breakfast L8000. V, MC, AmEx.

Hotel Giugiu, Via del Viminale, 8 (tel./fax 482 77 34). Steps away from Termini. The friendly proprietors love English-speaking travelers. Large, quiet rooms with high ceilings. Breakfast L8000. Prices for *Let's Go* readers: Singles L45,000-60,000. Doubles L65,000-75,000, with bath L75,000-85,000.

YWCA (pronounced EEV-kah), Via Cesare Balbo, 4 (tel. 488 04 60 or 488 39 17; fax 487 10 28), off Via Torino. A fantastic place for women travelers who find safety in numbers. Pleasant, cheerful atmosphere; garden terrace and large TV room. Fax and photocopier available. Curfew midnight. No men. Singles L45,000. Doubles L35,000 per person. Triples and quads L30,000 per person. Showers and breakfast (7:30-8:15am) included. Lunch (1-2:15pm, reserve by 10am) L20,000.

Associazione Cattolica Internationale al Servizio della Giovane, Via Urbana, 158 (tel. 488 00 56). Can make short-term arrangements for women under 26.

PIAZZA NAVONA AND CAMPO DEI FIORI

Piazza Navona lies to the north of Corso Vittorio Emanuele II, the avenue that cuts through the historic center; Campo dei Fiori is to the south. Buses #60, 62 (by way of Via XX Settembre and Via del Tritone), 64, 75, and 170 run from Termini and stop in Largo Argentina, the transportation hub of the historic center. Rome's *centro storico* is the ideal, if increasingly expensive, base for living as the Romans do. Unfortunately, hotel proprietors charge about 10-15% more to finance the charm and the deeper sense of Roman history absent from Termini accommodations.

Hotel Mimosa, Via Santa Chiara, 61 (tel. 68 80 17 53; fax 683 35 57), off P. di Minerva behind the Pantheon. Spacious rooms in a fantastic location. A warm couple preside over this kitschy abode. English spoken. Drunkenness not tolerated. Singles L65,000. Doubles L95,000, with bath L120,000. Triples L135,000. Quads L180,000. Prices 10% lower in winter. Breakfast L5000.

Albergo della Lunetta, P. del Paradiso, 68 (tel. 686 10 80 or 687 76 30; fax 689 20 28), near the Church of Sant'Andrea della Valle. Take Corso Vittorio Emanuele II to Via Chiavari, then the first right. Tidy rooms with desks and phones. Central garden, TV lounge, and 2 lofty terraces. Singles L55,000, with bath L80,000. Doubles L100,000, with bath L180,000. Triples L130,000, with bath L180,000. Quads L160,000, with bath L210,000. Reserve ahead with a credit card. V, MC.

Albergo Pomezia, Via dei Chiavari, 12 (tel./fax 686 13 71). Telephones, matching furniture, heat in winter, and stylish bathrooms. Don't let the hall mirrors fool you—the two managers really are twins. Some rooms newly renovated. Singles L77,000, with bath L110,000. Doubles L110,000, with bath L165,000. Triples L132,000, with bath L198,000. Breakfast included (8-11am). Prices lower Nov. and Jan.-Feb. V, MC, AmEx, DC.

Pensione Navona, Via dei Sediari, 8 (tel. 686 42 03; fax 68 80 38 02, call before faxing). Take Via dei Canestrari off the southern end of P. Navona, cross Corso del Rinascimento, and continue straight. The entrance is ostensibly part of the ancient Baths of Agrippa. Quiet and clean rooms, most with bath; ask for a room facing the courtyard. If full, they can refer you to other hotels in the area. Checkout 11am. Singles L75,000, with bath L85,000. Doubles L120,000, with bath L135,000. Triples L170,000, with bath L180,000. Breakfast included.

Albergo Abruzzi, P. della Rotonda, 69 (tel. 679 20 21). In front of the Pantheon, with a gorgeous view of its façade and its noisy admirers. While cleaner than the Pantheon (and as roomy), it lacks the dome's overhead lighting. English spoken. Singles L65,000. Doubles L92,000. Rooms facing the Pantheon are L18,000 more. Triples (facing the Pantheon) L148,500. Reservations recommended in summer.

NEAR THE SPANISH STEPS

In this consumer neighborhood inexpensive accommodations are scarce, but it may be worthwhile to spend a few extra bucks to sleep in the hippest part of town.

Pensione Parlamento, Via delle Convertite, 5 (tel./fax 679 20 82, for reservations 69 94 16 97). Off Via del Corso, 1 block before the post office on the street leading up to P. San Silvestro. Glamorous roof-top terrace with flowers. Each noble room complete with safe, hairdryer, phone, and TV. Giorgio, the owner, speaks English, French, Spanish, and German. Breakfast included. Singles L80,000, with bath

L112,000. Doubles L110,000, with bath L140,000. Each additional person L35,000. Reservations recommended. V, MC, AmEx.

Pensione Panda, Via della Croce, 35 (tel. 678 01 79; fax 69 94 21 51), between P. di Spagna and Via del Corso. A light and airy refuge from the chic chaos below. Big single beds. No curfew. Singles L60,000, with bath L80,000. Doubles L95,000, with bath L130,000. Triples L120,000, with bath L160,000. Extra bed L25,000. Reservations recommended. Discount for *Let's Go* readers. V, MC, AmEx.

Pensione Fiorella, Via del Babuino, 196 (tel. 361 05 97), just off P. del Popolo. Happening location may lead to motorcycle wake-up calls. Airy, comfortable breakfast room. Curfew 1am. Singles L60,000. Doubles L95,000. Breakfast included. No reservations, so arrive early in the morning.

Pensione Jonella, Via delle Croce, 41 (tel. 679 79 66), between P. di Spagna and Via del Corso. Expansive rooms with high ceilings. Owned by friendly Carlo and his brothers, who also run Hotel Matilde. Singles L60,000. Doubles L85,000.

PRATI (NEAR THE VATICAN)

The *pensioni* on the other side of the Tiber aren't the cheapest in Rome, but they tend to be comfortable, clean, and friendly. Those in Prati are attractive for their proximity to popular sights and a safer residential area. Bus #64 from Termini ends right near St. Peter's and Metro Linea A runs to Ottaviano, the nearby metro.

Ostello del Foro Italico (HI), Viale delle Olimpiadi, 61, 00194 Roma (tel. 323 62 67; fax 324 26 13). A few km north of the Vatican. From the Ottaviano Metro stop, exit onto Via Barletta and take bus #32 (in the middle of the street) to Cadorna. Get off at the 5th stop when you see the pink Foro Italico buildings. The entrance is in the back, across the street. Inconvenient location, but they have a bus and metro ticket-vending machine. 350 beds. Red lockers big enough for 2 packs (you supply the lock). Bring earplugs. 3-day max. stay when full. Reception open noon-11pm. Lockout 9am-2pm. Sizable, mediocre lunch or dinner. Bar open 7am-10:30pm. Curfew midnight. L23,000 with HI/IYHF card (buy one at the desk for L30,000). Breakfast and curtainless showers included. Wheelchair accessible.

Pensione Ottaviano, Via Ottaviano, 6 (tel. 39 73 72 53 or 39 73 81 38), off P. Risorgimento north of P. San Pietro. Steps away from Metro Linea A and minutes from St. Peter's. The only hostel-style *pensione* in the area—3-6 beds per room. English-speaking backpackers' haven: satellite TV, individual lockers, and fridges. The energetic staff speaks English. L25,000 per person, low-season L20,000. 2 doubles available for L70,000 in summer, L45,000 in winter. No curfew.

Residence Giuggioli, Via Germanico, 198 (tel. 32 42 113). At Via Paolo Emilia, 1st floor. Beautiful antiques adorn pristine rooms. The common bath is gleaming and newly renovated. The wonderful proprietress will chat with you in Italian. Doubles L100,000, double suite with private bath L120,000.

Pensione Lady, same building as the Guiggioli, 4th floor (tel. 324 21 12). A loving couple has been running this clean, peaceful *pensione* for 30 years. Recently renovated and restored to its original charm. The rooms facing away from the street are soothingly quiet. New bathrooms. The couple takes a few weeks off each year, so call ahead. Singles L85,000. Doubles L100,000, with bath L130,000.

Pensione Nautilus, Via Germanico, 198 (tel. 324 21 18), same building as the Guiggioli, on the 2nd floor. Roomy, with clean bathrooms. Fluent English spoken. Curfew (occasionally flexible) officially 12:30am. Doubles L100,000, with bath L120,000. Triples L130,000, with bath L150,000.

TRASTEVERE

Hedonists and bohemians flock to **Trastevere,** scene of much nighttime revelry and home to many young expatriates. Bus #75 from P. Indipendenza and #170 from P. del Cinquecento run from near Termini to Trastevere. Bus #56 and 60 to Trastevere leave from Via Claudio at P. San Silvestro, south of P. di Spagna.

Pensione Manara, Via Luciano Manara, 25 (tel. 581 47 13). Take a right off Viale di Trastevere onto Via delle Fratte di Trastevere. Friendly management runs this homey establishment overlooking P. San Cosimato in the heart of Trastevere. Under renovation (to be completed by 1997; call for info). English spoken. Doubles only, L75,000. V, MC, AmEx.

Pensione Esty, Viale Trastevere, 108 (tel. 588 12 01), about 1km down Viale di Trastevere from the Ponte Garibaldi. You're almost there when you pass the towering stone municipal building on your right. Ring the buzzer on the right, labeled *"pensione."* Somewhat removed from the rowdy heart of Trastevere. Some rooms have balconies over Viale di Trastevere. Singles L50,000. Doubles L70,000.

CAMPING

In August arrive before 10am to secure yourself a spot. Rates average L11,000 per person and another L6000 per car. Camping on beaches, roads, or any flat, inconspicuous plot is not uncommon, but it is illegal. Beware mosquitoes everywhere.

Seven Hills, Via Cassia, 1216 (tel. 30 36 27 51 or 303 31 08 26; fax 303 31 00 39), 8km north of Rome. Take bus #907 from P. Risorgimento to Via Cassia, or #201 from Flaminio. Ask the driver where to stop—it's a few km past the GRA. From here, follow the country road about 1km until you see the sign. Young international campers play volleyball on the manicured grounds. Pool and a private **disco** (10pm-1am). The self-sufficient site houses a bar, market, BBQ, restaurant, convenience store, and pizzeria. The facilities use only their own currency. (Unspent money refunded when you leave.) Laundering for L15,000. Doctor on hand during the day. Daily Vatican shuttle leaves at 9:30am, returning at 1:30 and 5:30pm (L6000 roundtrip). L11,000 per person, L8000 per tent. Caravan L10,000. Camper L14,000. Bungalow L70,000-110,000. L6000 per car. Open late May-late Oct., check-in open 7am-11pm.

Flaminio, Via Flaminia Nuova, 821 (tel. 333 14 31), about 7km outside of Rome. Take bus #910 from Termini to P. Mancini, then transfer to #200. Get off on Via Flaminia Nuova when you see the "Philips" or EUCLID building (there are several stops on Via Flaminia Nuova, so keep your eyes peeled) on your right. Shady grass strewn with tents, campers, and bungalows. The landscaping is a bit rough around the edges, but they have a pool, market, restaurant, bar, and a disco that rages long into the night. Coin-operated washing machines L500. L10,000 per person, L5700 per tent. Bungalows L33,000; singles and doubles L56,000, triples L89,000, quads L120,000. Open March-Oct.

Capitol Campground, Via di Castel Fusano, 195 (tel. 565 73 44), in Ostia Antica 3km from the beach and the ruins. Swimming pool, tennis courts, markets and bar. From Magliana on Metro line B, take the Ostia Lido-Centro bus to its capolinea. Then take #05 bus to Casal Palocco. L13,000 per person, 10,000 per tent, L6000 per car. Hot showers L1000.

Food

Alimentari are your best bet for grocery staples. Food stores are open roughly Mon.-Wed. and Fri.-Sat. 8am-1pm and 3:30-7:30pm (4-8pm in summer), Thurs. 8am-1pm, but they may close Saturday afternoons in summer. There are outdoor **markets** at P. Campo dei Fiori, P. Vittorio Emanuele II, and P. San Cosimato in Trastevere that generally operate Mon.-Sat. 6am-2pm and sell a wide variety of items. The **STANDA** supermarket offers an array of food, toiletries, clothing, and other necessities. There is one on Viale Trastevere, a few blocks down from P. Sidney Sonnino, and one on Via Cola di Rienzo, several blocks down from the Ottaviano Metro stop.

For an authentic Roman culinary experience, hop on a bus to reach the university district of **San Lorenzo** or the working-class **Testaccio,** the last untouristed restaurant districts in Rome. The areas around **Piazza Navona** and **Campo dei Fiori** harbor inviting *trattorie,* and **Trastevere** has the liveliest pizzerias. Rome's restaurants offer such specialties as *carciofi alla giudia* (fried artichokes, also known as *carciofi alla romana*), *fiori di zucca* (zucchini blossoms filled with cheese, battered, and lightly fried), and *baccalà* (fried cod). You'll find *penne all'arrabbiata* (short pasta in a spicy tomato sauce) and *bucatini all'amatriciana* (long pasta in a tomato sauce with bacon) on many menus. For secondi, try *saltimbocca* (veal topped with ham in a butter sauce) or *ossobuco* (braised veal shank). Thursday in Rome is *gnocchi* day; enjoy a bowl along with the rest of the city. Most restaurants close for at least two weeks in August.

CENTRO STORICO: PIAZZA NAVONA

Authentic, inexpensive *trattorie* fill the P. Navona area, but steer clear of the main *piazza,* where restaurants entice tourists with English menus and then overcharge them shamelessly. Some of the best restaurants in the city lurk along Via del Governo Vecchio and the alleys emerging from it. Local lunch-time favorites are often unmarked; look for doorways with bead curtains or follow an Italian worker on lunch break. There is no shortage of *alimentari, tavole calde* (self-service restaurants that serve hot dishes), and *pizzerie rustiche* lining Via di Ripetta and around the Pantheon. The best *gelato* places surround the Pantheon and the main *piazza.*

Salumeria Palladini, Via del Governo Vecchio, 29 (tel. 68 61 237). An unmarked *salumeria* bustling with a Roman lunch crowd eating *panini.* Point to the fillings of your choice and eat it outside. Favorites include *prosciutto e fiche* (ham and figs) or *bresaola e rughetta* (cured beef with arugula) sprinkled with parmesan cheese and lemon juice. Great vegetable options—artichoke, peppers, mushrooms, tomatoes, and more. Hearty sandwich L2500-5000. Open in summer Mon.-Fri. 8am-2pm and 5-8pm, Sat. 8am-2pm. Closed Thurs. afternoons in winter.

Pizzeria Baffetto, Via del Governo Vecchio, 114 (tel. 686 16 17), on the corner of Via Sora. Once a meeting place for 60s radicals, Baffetto now overflows with Romans of all political persuasions. The *pizza gigante* would satisfy Pavarotti. Outdoor seating. Harried service. Pizza L5000-9000, wine L6000. Cover L1000. Open Mon.-Sat. 7:30pm-1am.

Trattoria Gino e Pietro, Via del Governo Vecchio, 106 (tel. 686 15 76), at Vicolo Savelli. Look for the reddish wood sign. The main menu is always in an exciting state of flux. Delve into the back room for a huge array of homemade *antipasti vegetali* (L7500). *Secondi* L8500-15,000. Cover L1000. Open Fri.-Wed. noon-3pm and 6:30-11pm. Closed mid-July to mid-August.

L'Insalata Ricca 2, P. Pasquino, 72, right off of the southwest corner of P. Navona. Who ever said sequels disappoint? This spin-off of the original (see page 94) is just as good. Omelettes cooked to order (L6000). The *gnocchi verdi alla gorgonzola* L9000 is outstanding. *Secondi* L8000-13,000. Cover L2000. Open daily noon-3pm and 7-11:30pm. Reservations recommended for Sat.

Piedra del Sol, Vicolo Rosini, 6 (tel. 68 73 651), off Via di Campo Marzio across from P. del Parlamente. Countless Aztec calendars and painted Mayan figures adorn the stucco walls of this little establishment. Creamy *enchiladas suizas* with chicken (L17,000). Excellent nachos as an appetizer (L9000). Happy hour upstairs midnight-1am. Margaritas L10,000. Obligatory chips and salsa L3000 per person. Open Sept.-July 7:30pm-12:30am. Closed Sun. in July. V, AmEx.

Giardino del Melograno, Vicolo dei Chiodarole, 16/18 (tel. 68 80 34 23), off Via dei Chiavari near Campo dei Fiori. The most renowned Chinese restaurant in Rome. The tourist *menù* offers a full lunch for L11,000. Shrimp, chicken, and mixed vegetables make up the delectable *pentola cinese* (L10,000). No cover or service charge. Open Sun.-Tues. and Thurs.-Sat. noon-3pm and 7-11:30pm. Reservations accepted. V, MC, AmEx.

CENTRO STORICO: CAMPO DEI FIORI

This neighborhood is the authentic, pre-commercial Rome of years gone by. Its cobblestone streets and miniature *piazze* entice those who seek spirited meals and romantic wine bars. Try Via Monserrato to the south and west of the *piazza.* Via dei Giubbonari houses cafés, bars, pastry shops, and *alimentari.*

L'Insalata Ricca, Largo di Chiavari, 85 (tel. 68 80 36 56), off Corso Vittorio Emanuele near P. Sant'Andrea della Valle. Funky modern art, innovative dishes, and an off-beat ambience with neighborly service and savory, traditional *trattoria* food. Try the *gnocchetti sardi* (L8500) or their title dish *insalata ricca,* a robust salad with everything on it (L9000). Whole wheat pasta *integrale* L9000. Cover L1500. Open 12:30-3:15pm and 6:45-11:15pm. Closed Wed. in winter.

Hostaria Grappolo d'Oro, P. della Cancelleria, 80-81 (tel. 686 41 18), on Via Cancelleria off Corso Vittorio Emanuele II. A stellar and inexpensive gastronomic ecstasy. Words are too cheap for his *antipasti* (L10,000) and *penne all'arrabbiata* (L10,000). House white wine L9000. Cover L2000. Open Mon.-Sat. noon-3pm and 7-11pm. V, MC, AmEx, DC.

Arnaldo ai Satiri, Via di Grotta Pinta, 8 (tel. 686 19 15). Take Largo dei Chiavari off Corso Vittorio Emanuele to P. dei Satiri and turn right. Unusual dishes, like spicy *fusilli con melanzane* (pasta with eggplant, L10,000), fresh *gazpacho* (L10,000), and the house speciality: pasta with cabbage cream sauce (L10,000). Outdoor dining in summer. Open Wed.-Mon. 12:30-3pm and 7:30pm-1am. V, MC, AmEx, DC.

Filetti di Baccalà, Largo dei Librari, 88 (tel. 686 40 18). Take Via dei Giubbonari off P. Campo dei Fiori; Largo dei Librari will be on your left. Don't miss this busy, unpretentious little establishment in a tiny *piazza* beneath a small church. A self-service favorite for informal *antipasti* and wine. An unforgettable *filetto di baccalà* (L5000). Wine L7000 per liter. Cover L1500. Open Sept.-July Mon.-Sat. 5:30-10:40pm, in winter 5-10:40pm.

THE JEWISH GHETTO

To the west of roaring Via Arenula, the former Jewish Ghetto has become an extremely chic dining locale. Many traditional Roman dishes originated in this neighborhood, like *carciofi alla giudia* and *fiori di zucca.*

Margarita, Via di S. Maria de' Calderari, 30. Next to the big green door to the S. Maria del Pianto church, off of P. delle Cinque Scole. Behind the green rope door (don't look for a sign), diners fight over politics in a basement filled with the smoke of frying fish. The place is tiny and almost always packed with customers awaiting delicious homemade treats. Daily specials are scrawled on the one paper menu. Homemade *gnocchi* L10,000 (on Thurs.). *Baccalà* L11,000. Cover L2000. Open Mon.-Fri. noon-3pm.

Ristorante Il Portico, Via del Portico d'Ottavio, 1E (tel. 68 30 79 37), around the corner from the Teatro di Marcello. Wonderful fresh anchovies with green beans and delicious and unusual kosher pastries in a comfortable outdoor setting. Kosher meat, wine, and marinated vegetables as well as non-kosher food. *Zuppa di ceci* (chickpea soup) L10,000. *Spaghetti cacio e pepe* (with grated cheese and pepper) L12,000. Cover L2000. Open Wed.-Mon. 12:30-3pm and 7-11:30pm.

Ristorante da Giggetto, Via del Portico Ottavio, 21-22 (tel. 686 11 05). Eat *carciofi alla giudia* (L8000) as you sit at arm's length from the ancient ruins of the Portico d'Ottavio. *Supplì* (a rice ball with mozzarella, tomato sauce, and meat) L2000. Cover L3000. Open Tues.-Sun. 12:30-3pm and 7:30-11pm.

NEAR THE SPANISH STEPS

Caveat edax (let the diner beware): the high prices in this flashy district are no guarantee of quality. Opt for a hot *panino* with mozzarella and prosciutto or a piece of *pizza rustica* at one of the area's many bars. There are *alimentari* at Via Laurina, 36 and Via di Ripetta, 233. Produce markets are on Via del Lavatore, near the Trevi Fountain, and halfway down Via Tomacelli from Trevi fountain.

La Capricciosa, Largo dei Lombardi, 8 (tel. 687 86 36 or 687 86 36), right off Via del Corso at Via della Croce. Home of the famous *capricciosa* pizza (with ham, egg, artichoke, and so on; L9000). Outdoor terrace. *Primi* (L8000-11,000) include *ravioli di ricotta e spinaci.* Desserts L6000. Cover L2000. Open Wed.-Mon. 12:30-3pm and 6:30pm-12:30am. V, MC, AmEx.

Trattoria da Settimio all'Arancio, Via dell'Arancio, 50 (tel. 687 61 19). From P. di Spagna, take Via dei Condotti and cross Via del Corso. Continue on Via della Fontanella Borghese, take the first right, then the first left. A favorite with savvy Romans. Same owners as Al Piccolo Arancio. Excellent 3-course meals L27,000-45,000. Try the *ossobuco* (braised veal shank, L15,000). Huge portions of fresh vegetables (L4000-8000) and delicious *antipasti*. Cover L2000. Fresh fish Tues. and Fri. Open Mon.-Sat. 12:30-3:30pm and 7:15pm-midnight. V, MC, AmEx, DC.

Al Piccolo Arancio, Vicolo Scanderberg, 112 (tel. 678 61 39). Near the Trevi Fountain in a little alley off of Via del Lavatore (to the right as you face the fountain). The sign says "Hostaria." Try the *carciofi alla giudia* (L5000). On Tues. and Fri. get the homemade *gnocchi al salmone* (L9000) or *linguine all'aragosta* (with lobster, L9000). Cover L2000. Arrive early. Open Tues.-Sun. noon-3pm and 7-11:30pm. Closed Aug. V, MC, AmEx, DC.

Pizzeria al Leoncino, Via del Leoncino, 28 (tel. 68 76 306). Take Via Condotti from P. di Spagna, cross Via del Corso, continue on Via della Fontana Borghese. Traditional pizzas (L8000-12,000). Wine L5000 per liter. Open Mon.-Tues. and Thurs.-Fri. 1-3pm and 7pm-midnight, Sat.-Sun. 7pm-midnight.

Ristorante e Pizzeria Er Buco, Via del Lavatore, 91 (tel. 678 11 54), steps from P. di Trevi. Possibly the oldest pizza oven in the city. It's tiny, so arrive early and avoid the crowd. Taste perfection: pizza *"Er Buco"* (tomatoes, cheese, *parmigiano,* and basil; L9000). *Bruschetta alla crema di carciofi* (with artichoke paste) L4000. Open Mon.-Sat. noon-3pm and 6:30-11:30pm.

NEAR THE COLOSSEUM AND FORUM

Despite its past glory, this area has yet to discover the noble concept of "the affordable restaurant." Head to the bars and *tavole calde* that line Via Cavour.

Taverna dei Quaranta, Via Claudia, 24 (tel. 700 05 50). Reasonable food in the shade of the mighty amphitheater. Cool and tree-shaded. Menu changes daily. Outstanding *bruschetta al pomodoro* (L3500) and such creations as *linguine alla crema di zucchini* (L9000). Beer from the tap L5000. Open noon-3pm and 8pm-midnight. V, MC, AmEx.

Hostaria da Nerone, Via delle Terme di Tito, 96 (tel. 474 52 07), just steps north of the Colosseum. Feast on *fettucine alla Nerone* (with salami, ham, beans, and mushrooms; L8000) or the more daring *fritto di cervello con zucchine o carciofi* (fried brain with zucchini or artichoke, L14,000). Wash it down with the house wine (L2000). Outdoor dining. Cover L2500. Service 10%. Open Mon.-Sat. noon-3pm and 7:30-11pm.

Trattoria di Priscilla, Via Appia Antica, 68 (tel. 513 63 79), across from the Domine Quo Vadis (near the S. Callisto catacombs). Its sign says simply "Trattoria," so look for the street number. A cozy family establishment hidden in an area rife with overpriced, tourist-oriented restaurants. *Primi* L8500. *Pollo alla romana* L13,500. Open noon-3pm and 8-11pm. AmEx, DC.

TRASTEVERE

Across the river from the *centro storico* and down the river from the Vatican, Trastevere is home to raucous beer parlors, hopping pizza joints, and a loud bohemian population. Evenings summon an eclectic atmosphere as expatriate hippies strum their guitars while elegant diners from the more costly local restaurants stroll by.

Taverna della Scala, P. della Scala, 19 (tel 581 41 00). A *trattoria* with quiet outdoor dining and an enormous selection of pizzas and pastas. Start off with a *bruschetta al pâté d'olive* (L2000-4000). *Primi* from L7000. Pizzas L5000-10,000. *Gnocchi con crema di carciofi* (in an artichoke cream sauce). Cover L2000. Open Wed.-Mon. 12:30-3pm and 7pm-midnight.

Pizzeria Ivo, Via di San Francesca a Ripa, 158 (tel. 581 70 82). Take a right on Via delle Fratte di Trastevere off Viale Trastevere and another right on Via J. Francesco a Ripa. This Trastevere legend is now a tourist favorite, but the mouth-watering pizza's still well worth the long wait and chaotic atmosphere. Pizzas L8000-16,000. Open Sept.-July Wed.-Mon. 5pm-2am.

Hostaria da Augusto, P. de' Renzi, 15 (580 37 98). Facing the church in P. S. Maria in Trastevere, take Via Fonte Olio to the right to Vicolo del Piede. A no-frills eatery popular with locals. Daily pasta specials like *gnocchi* on Thursday and *pasta e ceci* on Friday, L6000-7000. Cheap satisfying *secondi* L9000-12,000. No cover. Open Mon.-Fri. noon-3pm and 8-11pm, Sat. noon-3pm. Closed in Aug.

Pizzeria Sonnino, Viale di Trastevere, 23, 2 doors down from the big movie theater. A hectic, popular *pizza a taglio* joint. Pizza slices with potato with rosemary and *margherita* cost L1500 per *etto.* The *supplì* (vegetarian) and *crochette* are out of this world (L1000 each). Roast half-chicken L6000. *Tavola calda* pasta dishes L6000-8000. Open 8am-midnight. Occasionally closed Mon.

Alle Fratte di Trastevere, Via delle Fratte di Trastevere, 49/50 (tel. 583 57 75), just off Viale di Trastevere on the right as you walk from the river. Green gables mark this corner establishment with outside seating in the summer. The friendly Italian-American owner from New York runs his place with American efficiency and Italian culinary skill. *Bruschette* L2000-4000. *Pennette alla siciliana* L9000, and *scaloppine al limone* (tender veal in a lemon sauce) L12,000. Pizzas from L7000 Open summer daily noon-3pm and 6:30pm-1am; closed Wed. in winter.

Hostaria da Corrado, Via della Pelliccia, 39. Arrive early to sample the delectable Roman fare. Ravioli filled with mushrooms or spinach and ricotta L7000. Traditional Roman *involtine* (veal rolled around vegetables, L8000) and grilled *scamorza* cheese (L7500). Cover L1000. Open 12:30-3pm and 7:30-11pm.

Ocak Başi, Via del Moro, 24. A Turkish restaurant brimming with the smells and sounds of Istanbul (not Constantinople). Excellent fried eggplant with yogurt (L8000), *kababs* with vegetables (L8000), and baklava (L8000). Cover L1000. Open Tues.-Sun. 7:30-11:30pm. V, MC, AmEx.

Stardust, Vicolo de' Renzi, 4 (tel. 58 32 08 75). Take a right off Via dell Lungaretta onto Via del Moro right before P. S. Maria in Trastevere. Vicolo de' Renzi is the 2nd street on the left. Stardust's cuisine is a *menage à trois* of Italian desserts, American breakfast, and Middle-Eastern treats. Bagels with cream cheese L6000, chocolate-banana-hazelnut crêpes L5000, baba ghanoush L3000. Beer L4000-6000, mixed drinks L6000-12,000. Live jazz every night. No cover. Open Mon.-Fri. 1:30pm-3am, Sat.-Sun. 11:30am-2am.

ROME

THE BORGO AND PRATI (NEAR THE VATICAN)

During the day, the streets of the Prati and Borgo fill with foreigners overwhelmed and exhausted by sightseeing in Vatican City. The character of the area changes at night, as the locals head to neighborhood *trattorie* and *pizzerie* for classic Roman fare. The residential district around Via Cola di Rienzo holds some great bargains, as well as an immense indoor food market. Take Metro Linea A to Ottaviano.

Hostaria dei Bastioni, Via Leone IV, 29 (tel. 39 72 30 34), off P. Risorgimento near the Vatican Museums. A miraculous subterranean restaurant that rightly boasts its seafood specialties. *Risotto al pescatore* L10,000. Fresh fish dishes L13,000-18,000. Wine L7000 per liter. The buzz of traffic mars outdoor dining. Cover L2000. Service 10%. Open Mon.-Sat. noon-3pm and 7pm-1:30am.

L'Archetto, Via Germanico, 105 (tel. 323 11 63). The kind staff serves up Roman pizzeria grub on this quiet residential street. Pizzas (L6500-12,000), *filetti di baccalà* (fried cod, L3000), *fiori di zucca* (fried zucchini flowers, L2000), salmon *bruschetta* L4000. Open Tues.-Sun. 7pm-midnight. Closed part of Aug.

Pizzeria Il Bersagliere, Via Candia, 22A/24 (tel. 39 74 22 53), off Via Leone near Via Tolemaide. A squadron of pastel tablecloths draw the weary traveler's eye to mouth-watering pizzas (L8500-10,500); try the *fiori di zucca* pizza (L10,500). *Bruschetta al pomodoro* L2500. Cover L2000. Open Tues.-Sun. 7pm-midnight.

Armando, Via Plauto, 38-39 (tel. 68 30 70 62), off Borgo Angelico. Snazzy yet traditional. Delicious lasagna is the house specialty (L9000). *Saltimbocca alla romana* L13,000. Cover L2500. Open Thurs.-Tues. 12:30-3pm and 7-11pm.

Non Solo Pizza, Via degli Scipioni, 95 (tel. 372 58 20). Pizza comes in several varieties and is charged by weight. Round pizzas available for take-out. Try the roast chicken (L11,000), *tavola calda* pasta (3 choices per day, L7000), and *secondi* (L7500). Open Tues.-Sun. 8:30am-9:30pm.

TESTACCIO

South of the historic center and one of the oldest areas of Rome, Testaccio remains a stronghold of Roman tradition. In the Mattatoio neighborhood around the old slaughterhouses, you can eat at restaurants that serve such authentic local delicacies as *animelle alla griglia* (grilled sweetbreads) and *fegato* (liver). The hippest **nightclubs** are here as well (see **Discos and Dancing,** p. 114), particularly around Monte Testaccio, so you can boogie your oxtail-intake away. Take Metro Linea B to Piramide, bus #27 from Termini, or bus #95 from P. Venezia.

Pizzeria Ficini, Via Luca della Robbia, 23 (tel. 574 30 17). Take Via Vanvitelli off Via Marmorata, then your first left. A friendly pizzeria for those who've lost their carnivorous nerve. Pizzas L6000-8000. Wine L6000 per liter. Don't miss the *bruschetta con fagioli* (L2500). Open Sept.-July Tues.-Sun. 6-11:30pm.

Trattoria da Bucantino, Via Luca della Robbia, 84/86 (tel. 574 68 86). Take Via Vanvitelli off Via Marmorata, then take the first left. Fabulous *antipasti.* Indigenous pasta delights like *bucatini all'amatriciana* (L11,000) and *coda alla vaccinara* (stewed oxtail, L12,000). Wine L6000 per liter. Cover L2000. Open Tues.-Sun. 12:30-3:30pm and 7-11pm. Closed Aug.

Trattoria Turiddo, Via Galvani, 64 (tel. 575 04 47), in the Mattatoio district (take bus #27 from Termini or the Colosseum). Locals come here for food they grew up on, like *rigatoni con pagliata* (with tomato and lamb intestine, L10,000) and *animelle alla griglia* (L13,000). Standard Roman fare available for the weak of stomach. Vegetarians should flee in terror. Open Mon.-Tues. and Thurs.-Sat. 12:30-2:20pm and 7:30-10:20pm, Sun. 1-2:30pm; closed Sept.

SAN LORENZO

A 5-min. bus ride east of Termini on bus #71 or 492 (get off when the bus turns onto Via Tiburtina by the old city walls), San Lorenzo sits at the edge of the Città Universitaria. This trendy, tourist-free zone is home to Marxist students and cutting-edge artists. Many unpretentious *trattorie* and pizzerias offer grand cuisine for the university students and the traveler who dares to leave the historic center.

Il Pulcino Ballerino, Via degli Equi, 66/68 (tel. 494 12 55), off Via Tiburtina. Artsy atmosphere with cuisine to match. An ever-changing menu of unusual dishes like *tagliolini del pulcino* (pasta in a lemon cream sauce, L9000) or *risotto Mirò* (with arugula, radicchio, and *parmigiano,* L10,000). Cover L1000. Open Mon.-Sat. 12:30-2:30pm and 8pm-midnight. Closed Aug. 1-15. AmEx.

Pizzeria la Pappardella, Via degli Equi, 56 (tel. 446 93 49), off Via Tiburtina at Largo dei Falisci. Exquisitely inexpensive and relatively tourist-free. Try their *pappardelle* (pasta with sausage, peas, and cream sauce, L6000) or the *canneloni di carne* (L7000). Cheap pizzas, too. Open daily noon-3pm and 6pm-midnight.

Il Capellaio Matto, Via dei Marsi, 25 (tel. 49 08 41). From Via Tiburtina take Via degli Equi and take the 4th right onto Via dei Marsi. Vegetarians rejoice! *Primi* L7000-11,000. Sorceress's salad, with potato, shrimp, chicken, corn, carrot, and egg, L9000. Crêpe dishes around L6500. Spinach and ricotta ravioli L8000. Menu available in English. Cover L2000. Open Wed.-Mon. 8pm-midnight.

La Tana Sarda, Via Tiburtina, 116 (tel. 49 35 50). Personable Sardinians rush from table to table, piling plates with delicacies. Romans rave about the *gnocchetti sardi* (L8000) and the *penne alla gorgonzola* (L8000). For dessert, try the *dolcetti sardi* for L5000. Pizzas L8000-10,000. Cover L2000. Open Mon.-Sat. noon-2:30pm and 5-11pm. Closed mid-Aug. to mid-Sept.

Super Pizza Rustica a Taglio, Largo degli Oschi, 67, off Via degli Umbri. Wonderful pizza by the slice at non-tourist prices. Pizza with peppers (L1500 per *etto*) and potato with rosemary (L2000 per *etto*). Try the *fiori di zucca* (L1600 per *etto*). Open Mon.-Sat. 8am-9pm.

NEAR THE STATION

There is little reason to subject yourself to the gastronomic nightmare of the tourist-trapping restaurants around Termini; a 20-min. stroll from the station can take you to virtually any historic district this side of the Tiber—with lower prices, quieter streets, tastier viands, and a more relaxing atmosphere.

North of Termini

La Cantinola da Livio, Via Calabria, 26 (tel. 482 05 19 or 474 39 62). Take Via Piave off Via XX Settembre, then take the 4th left onto Via Calabria. This cozy, lively establishment has fresh seafood daily; live lobsters wait nervously in tanks by the door. Stellar cuisine and impeccable service. *Spaghetti alla Cantinola* L10,500. *Scampi* L19,000. *Antipasto di mare* L12,000. Cover L1500. Open Mon.-Sat. 12:30-3pm and 7:20-11:20pm. V, MC, AmEx, DC.

Da Giggetto, Via Alessandria, 43 (tel. 854 34 90), near the Porta Pia. This place claims to be "the king of pizza"—have a festive and satisfying meal and decide if it's true. The savory *bruschetta* with tomatoes and mozzarella (L4000) is just a prelude to the pizza (L7200-13,000). Open Mon.-Sat. 7pm-1am. Closed Aug.

Ristorante la Capitale, Via Goito, 50 (tel. 494 13 91), off P. Indipendenza. Perfect for those times when your *lire* just can't stretch any farther. *Primi* L7000-8000; pizzas L6000-7000. Discounts for large groups. Open Mon.-Sat. 9am-4pm and 6pm-midnight. V, MC, AmEx.

ROME

South of Termini

Da Silvio, Osteria della "Suburra," Via Urbana 67/69 (tel. 48 65 31), off Via Cavour and down the stairs on the right at the Cavour metro stop. A huge variety of traditional, authentic Roman fare at low prices. Homemade *fettucine* in a variety of styles (L8000-10,000). *Penne all'arrabbiata* L6000. Excellent *antipasto rustico* L8000. Cover L2000. Open Tues.-Sun. 1-3pm and 7-10:30pm.

Osteria da Luciano, Via Giovanni Amendola, 73/75 (tel. 488 16 40). Head south on Via Cavour from Termini and turn left after one block onto Via G. Amendola. A haven for the cheap and hungry. Hearty, generous pasta dishes L3900-5000. Huge marinated half-chicken L7000. *Menù* is a great deal at L15,000. Wine L4500. Cover L1000. Service 10%. Open Mon.-Fri. 11:30am-9pm, Sat. 11:30am-5pm.

Ristorante Due Colonne, Via dei Serpenti, 91 (tel. 488 08 52), on the left, down from P. della Repubblica on Via Nazionale after the Palazzo delle Esposizioni. By day, Romans on lunch break fill the tables. By night, American tourists struggle with the menu. Cheap, excellent pizzas L7000-13,000. *Pasta e fagioli* L6500. Open Mon.-Sat. noon-3:30pm and 7pm-midnight. V, MC, AmEx.

DOLCI (DESSERTS)

Grattachecca da Bruno, at the Ottaviano Metro stop on Viale Giulio Cesare, near Via Vespasiano. Watch Bruno go to work with his handmade ice shaver as he serves up the yummiest ice in Italy. Pick from a variety of fresh fruit. Perfect after a trip to the museums. *Grattaceccha* for L3000. Open all day until the wee hours.

Giolitti, Via degli Uffici del Vicario, 40 (tel. 699 12 43). From the Pantheon, follow Via del Pantheon (at the northern end of the *piazza*) to its end, then take Via della Maddelena to its end; Via degli Uffici del Viccario is on the right. A Roman institution revered by many as the home of Rome's greatest *gelato.* Cones L2500-4000. Open daily 7am-2am. Nov.-April closed Mon.

Palazzo del Freddo Giovanni Fassi, Via Principe Eugenio, 65/67 (tel. 446 47 40), off P. Vittorio Emanuele southeast of Termini. This century-old *gelato* factory is a confectionery altar worshiped by many. Some say the *gelato* here rivals Giolitti's. Try both and argue your calories away. Cones L2000-3000. Open Tues.-Sun. noon-midnight. In summer also open Mon. 6pm-midnight.

Jolly Pop (formerly Sweet Sweet Way), Via del Corso, 70 (tel. 36 00 18 88), near the intersection with Via Vittoria. A bright, colorful candy smorgasbord and perfect remedy for a sudden drop in blood-sugar. Gargantuan assortment of chewy, sugary morsels for L2000-3500 per 100g, chocolate morsels L4500 per 100g. Open daily 10am-8pm. V, MC, AmEx.

Tre Scalini, P. Navona, 30 (tel. 68 80 19 96). This classy, old-fashioned spot is famous for its *tartufo,* a menacing hunk of chocolate ice cream rolled in chocolate shavings. Get it at the bar for L5000 (considerably more at a table). Bar open Thurs.-Tues. 8am-1am; restaurant open Thurs.-Tues. 12:30-3:30pm and 7:30-9pm.

Gelateria Trevi di A. Cercere, Via del Lavatore, 84/85 (tel. 679 20 60), near the Trevi Fountain. A small *gelateria* of yesteryear whose famous *zabaglione* (L3000) puts the glitzy *gelaterie* down the street to shame. Open daily 10am-2am.

Pascucci, Via Torre Argentina, 20 (tel. 686 48 16), off Corso Emanuele east of P. Navona. The 6 throttling blenders on the bar have earned this place a reputation throughout the republic; they grind fresh fruit into colorful, frothy *frullati* frappes (L3300-4500). Open Mon.-Sat. 6:30am-midnight.

Yogufruit, P. G. Tavani Arquati, 118 (tel. 58 79 72), off Via della Lungaretta near P. S. Sonnino. No ancient tradition here; filled with the young and the fruitful. Tart frozen yogurt blended with just about anything: fruit, M&Ms, even Cornflakes. Cups or cones L3000-4000. Open Mon.-Sat. noon-2am.

Il Fornaio, Via dei Baullari, 5-7 (tel. 68 80 39 47), across from P. San Pantaleo, south of P. Navona. The smell of baking goodies makes it impossible to pass it by. Every cookie imaginable (*biscotti* L1800-2600 per *etto*) and luscious desserts (*mele in gabbia* L1300 per *etto*). Open daily 7:30am-8:30pm.

CAFES

In many Roman cafés, you pay one price to stand and drink at the bar and a higher price (as much as double) if you sit down at a table. There should be a menu on the wall of the bar listing the prices *al bar* (standing up) and *a tavola* (at a table). Around the historic center and the major *piazze,* the price of a cappuccino can jump from L1500 to L5000 as soon as you sit down.

Caffè Sant'Eustachio, P. Sant'Eustachio, 82 (tel. 686 13 09), in the *piazza* southwest of the Pantheon. Take Via Monterone off Corso Vittorio Emanuele II. Once a favorite haunt of Stendhal and other literary expatriates, now bursting with Romans. Cappuccino L4000, L2000 at the bar. Try their very own *gran caffè speciale* (L5000, L3000 at the bar) for a sweet, frothy, and powerful zap of climactic delight. Open Tues.-Fri. and Sun. 8:30am-1am, Sat. 8:30am-1:30am.

Bar S. Calisto, P. S. Calisto, 4, in Trastevere (tel. 583 58 69). Crowded spot across the river, where Trasteverean youth and Roman elders socialize over incredible, inexpensive cappuccino (L1200 sitting or standing) and *granita di limone* (L2000). Open Mon.-Sat. 6am-1:30am, Sun. 4pm-1:30am; closed Sun. in winter.

Caffè della Pace, Via della Pace, 3/7 (tel. 686 12 16), off P. Navona. Come prepared with a newspaper, letters to write, and clever conversations to start in order to get the most out of the *al tavolo* price. Chic and expensive, beneath vines and church façades. Cappuccino: daytime L3000 at bar, L5000 at table; nighttime L4000/L8000. Red wine L7000/L10,000 at table. Open 10am-2am.

Tazza d'Oro, Via degli Orfani, 84/86 (tel. 679 27 68), off the northeast corner of P. della Rotonda. The sign reads *"El mejor del mundo"* (the best in the world), and that may not be far from true. No place to sit down, but a great brew at fantastic prices (*caffè* L1100). Extensive tea, coffee, and coffee bean selection (L32,000-34,000 per kg.). Wonderful *granita di caffè* (L1500). Extensive coffee bean selection Chamomile tea L2000. Open Mon.-Sat. 7am-8:20pm.

Sights

Rome wasn't built in a day, and you're not going to see a substantial portion of the city in 24 hours either. The city practically explodes with monuments—ancient temples, medieval fortresses, Baroque creations of marble and rushing water—crowding next to and even on top of each other on every interwoven street. No other city in the world can lay claim to so many masterpieces of art and architecture. It's impossible to see everything the city has to offer, but you'll find that even a glimpse into this storehouse of Western civilization will be rewarding.

THE ANCIENT CITY CENTER

The Capitoline Hill (Campidoglio)

The original capitol and one of the most sacred parts of the ancient Roman city, the **Capitoline Hill** still serves as the seat of the city's government. The north side of the hill, facing P. Venezia, has completely disappeared under the gargantuan **Vittorio Emanuele II Monument** (1885). This colossal monstrosity of gleaming white marble, dubbed "the wedding cake," commemorates the House of Savoy, whose kings briefly ruled the newly unified Italy. Around the monument to the right as you face it, a staircase of 124 steep medieval steps climbs to the unadorned façade of the **Church of Santa Maria in Aracoeli,** a 7th-century church filled with a jumble of monuments from every century since. Next to the staircase rises Michelangelo's magnificent ramp, **la Cordonata,** built in 1536 so that Emperor Charles V could ride his horse ceremoniously up the hill to meet Pope Paul III. At the top of the hill is Michelangelo's **Piazza del Campidoglio.** Paul III placed the massive equestrian **statue of Marcus Aurelius** here. The original gilded bronze monument, once thought to be a portrait of Constantine, underwent restoration ten years ago and now resides in the courtyard of the Palazzo Nuovo. A copy is currently under construction and will soon fill the empty pedestal in the center of the *piazza*. Michelangelo set up the imposing statues of the twin warriors Castor and Pollux and, at the base of his ingenious split staircase, two reclining river gods and a statue of the goddess Roma.

At the far end of the *piazza* rise the turrets of the **Palazzo dei Senatori,** and on the right and left stand the twin **Palazzo dei Conservatori** and **Palazzo Nuovo,** which house the **Musei Capitolini.** The museums' collection of ancient sculpture is among the largest in the world. In the Palazzo Nuovo (on the left) look for the colossal statue of Marcus Aurelius on his horse, the morbid *Dying Gaul,* and the *Satyr* on the windowed wall nearby (the "Marble Faun" that inspired Hawthorne's book of the same title). Admission to the Palazzo dei Conservatori, across the *piazza,* is included in the ticket for the Palazzo Nuovo. The **Sale dei Conservatori** and the **Museo del Palazzo dei Conservatori** are on the first floor of the *palazzo,* and the **Pinacoteca** is on the second. In the courtyard, check out the assorted gigantic body parts of what was once a colossus of Constantine. Among the statues in the halls above are the *Capitoline Wolf* with Romulus and Remus and the *Spinario,* a sculpture of a young boy extracting a thorn from his foot. The Pinacoteca houses Bellini's *Portrait of a Young Man,* Titian's *Baptism of Christ,* Rubens's *Romulus and Remus Fed by the Wolf,* and Caravaggio's *Gypsy Fortune-Teller.* (Museums open Tues.-Sat. 9am-5pm, Sun. 9am-1:30pm. Admission L10,000, with student ID L5000, under 18 and over 60 free. Last Sun. of each month free.)

From the Campidoglio, paths lead down the other side of the hill to panoramic **views of the Forum and the Colosseum.** Stairs lead up between Palazzo Nuovo and Palazzo dei Senatori to the rear entrance of the Church of Santa Maria in Aracoeli.

The Roman Forum and the Palatine

The site of the **Forum** was originally a marshy valley vulnerable to the Tiber's flooding. The early Romans came down from the Palatine, paved the site, drained it with a covered sewer (the Cloaca Maxima), and built their first shrines to fire and water. When they founded their republic in the 6th century BC, the Romans built the Curia (the meeting place of the Senate), the Comitium Well (assembly place), and the Rostra (speaker's platform) to serve the infant democracy, along with the earliest temples (to Saturn and to Castor and Pollux) dedicated to the civic revolution. The conquest of Greece in the 2nd century BC brought to the city the new architectural form of the basilica, first used as a center for business and judicial activities. The wealthiest Roman families lined the town square in front of the Curia with basilicas, both for the good of the public and for their own reputations. (Forum and Palatine open in summer Mon.-Sat. 9am-7pm, Sun. 9am-2pm; in winter, the complex closes at least 1hr. before sunset, but as early as 3pm on weekdays and 1pm on Sun. and holidays. Admission L12,000. Last admittance 1hr. before closing.)

Before entering the Forum proper, you may want to invest in a map to help you navigate the chaotic and frequently overlapping ruins. From the gate on Via dei Fori Imperiali, follow the entrance ramp to its end and turn right; you will be on the **Via Sacra** facing the Capitoline Hill and the Arch of Septimius Severus. The main thoroughfare of the Forum and the oldest street in Rome, Via Sacra cuts through the old market square and civic center of Republican Rome. On your right, the **Basilica Aemilia,** built in 179BC, housed the guild of the *argentarii,* or money-changers. The broad space in front of the basilica is the Forum itself. Up ahead on the right, the **Curia** was one of the original buildings in the Forum, although the present structure dates from the time of Diocletian (AD303); it was used as a church from 630 until this century. Occasionally the interior is open, displaying the intricate inlaid marble pavement. The area in front of the Curia was the **Comitium Well,** where citizens came to vote. The brick platform to the left of the arch is the **Rostra.** Senators and consuls orated to the Roman plebes from here, but any citizen could mount to voice his opinion. Between the Curia and the Rostra, a flat gray stone —the **Lapis Niger** ("black stone")—marks the supposed burial place of Romulus. The hefty **Arch of Septimius Severus** at the end of Via Sacra was dedicated in AD203 to celebrate that emperor's victories in the Middle East. Halfway up the Capitoline Hill, the grey tufa walls of the **Tabularium,** once the repository of senate archives, now serve as the basement to the Renaissance Palazzo dei Senatori.

Although the three great temples of the lower Forum (dedicated to Saturn, the Emperor Vespasian, and Concord) have been closed off for excavation, the eight columns of the **Temple of Saturn** have finally shed their scaffolding. This temple was the site of the public treasury and an underground stash of sacred treasures. Across the square to the left of the Temple of Saturn, the **Basilica Julia** was used for judicial tribunals. Look for inscribed grids and circles in the steps where anxious Romans, waiting their turns to go before the judge, played an ancient version of tic-tac-toe. Near the basilica, the **Three Sacred Trees** of Rome—olive, fig, and grapevine—have been replanted. A circular tufa basin commemorates the **Lacus Curtius,** an ancient spring where a gaping chasm opened in 362BC into which Roman patrician Marcus Curtius threw himself to save the city. A relief records his sacrifice.

At the far end of the Basilica Julia, three white marble columns and a shred of architrave mark the podium of the **Temple of Castor and Pollux,** dedicated in 484BC to celebrate the Roman rebellion against the Etruscan king Tarquinius Superbus (see page 64). Across the street is the base of the **Temple of the Deified Julius,** which Augustus built in 29BC to proclaim himself the son of a god. The circular pile of rocks inside probably marks the spot where Caesar's body was cremated in 44BC (he was assassinated near Largo Argentina); pious Romans still leave flowers here on the Ides of March. To commemorate his triumphs, Augustus built the **Arch of Augustus,** marked by a marble slab next to the temple, which framed the Via Sacra. The circular building behind the temple is the restored **Temple of Vesta,** which sits on a foundation dating back to the Etruscan period. The Vestal Virgins tended the sacred fire of the city in this temple, an imitation of an archaic round Latin hut. Behind the temple stood the triangular **Regia,** the palace of the second king of Rome and later the office of the Pontifex Maximus, the city's highest priest.

The six virgins who officiated over Vesta's rites, each ordained at the age of seven, lived in spacious and celibate seclusion in the **House of the Vestal Virgins,** occupying the sprawling complex of rooms and courtyards behind the temple of Vesta. A tour through the storerooms and lower rooms of the house brings you back to Via Sacra and the **Temple of Antoninus and Faustina** (to the immediate right as you face the entrance ramp), whose columns and frieze had been incorporated into the **Church of San Lorenzo in Miranda** by the 12th century. (Its façade dates from the Baroque period.) Antoninus, one of the "good emperors" of the 2nd century AD, had the temple built in honor of his wife Faustina, who died in 141. In the shadow of the temple, the archaic **necropolis** contains graves from the Iron Age (8th century BC) that lend credence to Rome's legendary founding date of 753BC. Bodies were found in two types of tombs: hollowed-out-tree-trunk-coffins buried in ditches and cremation urns in the shape of little village huts, on display in many museums in Rome. Here the Via Sacra runs over the **Cloaca Maxima,** the ancient sewer that still drains water from the marshy valley. The street then passes the **Temple of Romulus,** a round building that probably served as the office of the urban praetor during the Empire and still retains its ancient bronze doors from the 4th century AD.

The street now leads out of the Forum proper to the gigantic **Basilica of Maxentius** (also known as the Basilica of Constantine), whose architecture Michelangelo studied before constructing St. Peter's Cathedral. The three gaping arches you see are actually only the side chapels of an enormous central hall whose coffered ceiling covered the entire gravel court, as well as another three chapels on the other side.

The Baroque façade of the **Church of S. Francesca Romana** (built over Hadrian's Temple to Venus and Rome) hides the entrance of the **Forum Antiquarium.** Most of the rooms have been closed for years, but a few on the ground floor display funerary urns and skeletons from the necropolis. (Open daily in the morning.) On the summit of the Velia at the far end of the archaeological park is the **Arch of Titus,** built by the emperor Domitian to celebrate his brother Titus's destruction of Jerusalem in AD70. The reliefs inside the arch depict the Roman sack of the great Jewish temple and the pillage of a giant menorah. The Via Sacra leads out of the Forum on the other side of the arch, an easy route to the Colosseum. To the right of the arch, a path and various stone stairways lead up to the Palatine.

The **Palatine Hill's** flowering sculpture gardens, cool breezes, and views of Rome are a refreshing change from the dusty Forum. Stairs ascend the hill through a series of terraces to the **Farnese Gardens**. Head through the avenues of roses and orange trees until you reach a look-out point with a breathtaking view of the Forum, the Imperial Fora, and the Quirinal Hill. The gardens continue along the western side of the hill, where an octagonal boxhedge maze in the center follows the layout of a real maze in the Palace of Tiberius underneath. The nearby **Casa di Livia** boasts wall paintings comparable to those in Pompeii. Swallowing up the southern part of the hill, lie the vast ruins of the solemn **Domus Augustana,** the imperial palace built by Domitian (AD81-96) and used by most of the subsequent emperors as the Imperial headquarters. The exterior walls, even in their ruined state, are so high that archaeologists are still unsure how the roof that once covered them was constructed. The easternmost wing of the palace contains the so-called **Stadium,** a sunken oval space once thought to have been a private racetrack, now believed to have been a garden.

Imperial Fora

The **Imperial Fora** lie across the street from the Roman Forum. The emperors of the first and 2nd centuries AD constructed this vast conglomeration of temples, basilicas, and public squares, partly in response to increasing congestion in the old Forum and partly for their own greater glory. With imperial aspirations of his own, Mussolini cleared the area of medieval constructions in the 1930s and built the Via dei Fori Imperiali, destroying a majority of the newly-excavated remains.

The **Forum of Trajan,** the largest and most impressive of the lot, spreads across Via dei Fori Imperiali below two Baroque churches at the eastern end of P. Venezia. The complex was built between AD107 and 113 to celebrate the emperor's victorious Dacian campaign (fought in modern-day Romania). Eight years of restoration helped reveal the almost perfectly preserved spiral of the **Column of Trajan,** one of the greatest specimens of Roman relief-sculpture ever carved. The 200-meter-long continuous frieze that wraps around the column is one of the most dense and ambitious artistic endeavors of the ancient world. The statue of the emperor that once crowned the column was replaced by a statue of St. Peter. Trajan's ashes, however, remain in the base. Up the steps on Via Magnanapoli, the **Markets of Trajan** (tel. 679 00 48) provide a glimpse of daily life in the ancient city. The semicircular complex shelters several levels of *tabernae,* or single-room stores, along cobbled streets. Almost all of the complex is open for wandering, and many rooms house sculpture found in the fora and reconstructions of the various buildings. (Open in summer Tues.-Sat. 9am-6:30pm, Sun. 9am-1:30pm; winter hours vary depending on sunset, and closing may be as early as 1pm. Admission L3750, students with ID L2500, EU members under 18 and over 60 free.) Adjacent to the Markets of Trajan, the gray tufa wall of the **Forum of Augustus** backs up against the side of the Quirinal Hill. Dedicated by the Emperor in 2BC, the huge complex commemorates Augustus's victory over Julius Caesar's murderers at the Battle of Philippi and the founding of his new imperial dynasty. Across the Via dei Fori Imperiali, in the shade of the Vittorio Emanuele II Monument, lie the paltry remains of the **Forum of Caesar.**

The Colosseum and the Arch of Constantine

The **Colosseum,** accessible from the Metro stop of the same name (Linea B), stands as the enduring symbol of the Eternal City. At its inauguration in AD80, it held as many as 50,000 spectators who watched gladiators fight both wild animals and each other. Art historians consider the triple stories of Doric, Ionic, and Corinthian columns the ideal orchestration of classical orders. Renaissance popes quarried almost all the marble stands and seats that once lined the interior for use in their own grandiose constructions. Underground lies a labyrinth of brick cells, corridors, ramps, and elevators used for transporting animals from their cages up to the arena. The upper floors provide excellent views of the city and nearby Forum. (Ground level of the Colosseum open Mon.-Tues. and Thurs.-Sat. 9am-7pm, Wed. 9am-2pm, Sun. 9am-1pm; in winter closes at least 1hr. before sunset, but as early as 3pm. Upper decks close 1hr. earlier. Ground level free, upper decks L8000.)

Between the Colosseum and the Palatine Hill stands the remarkably intact **Arch of Constantine.** After seeing a vision of a cross in the sky, Constantine triumphed over Maxentius at the Battle of the Milvian Bridge in 312 and built this arch to celebrate his conversion to Christianity. The triple arch is constructed almost entirely from sculptural fragments pillaged from older Roman monuments.

CENTRO STORICO (NORTHWEST OF THE FORUM)

Campo dei Fiori and Via Giulia

Campo dei Fiori lies across Corso Vittorio Emanuele II from P. Navona (down Via della Cancelleria). To get to this *piazza,* take bus #75, 170, or 64 from Termini and Via Nazionale to Largo Argentina, or the #56 or 60 from P. San Silvestro (south of the Spanish Steps) and Via del Tritone. From P. Venezia, take Via del Plebiscito to Corso Vittorio Emanuele II. During papal rule, Campo dei Fiori was the site of countless executions, and a statue commemorating one victim, Giordano Bruno (1548-1600), rises in the center of the square. (Bruno sizzled at the stake in 1600 for arguing that the universe had no center at all.) The only carcasses that litter the *piazza* today are those of the fish in the famous market of fruit, fish, and flowers. (Open Mon.-Sat. 7am-2pm.) The streets around the *piazza* are among the most picturesque in Rome.

Several streets lead south from Campo dei Fiori to **Piazza Farnese.** The huge, stately **Palazzo Farnese,** considered the greatest of Rome's Renaissance *palazzi,* dominates the square. Alessandro Farnese (Paul III), the first Counter-Reformation pope (1534-1549), commissioned the best architects of his day—Antonio da Sangallo, Michelangelo, and Giacomo della Porta—to design his dream abode. Since 1635, the French Embassy has rented the *palazzo* in exchange for the Grand Opera House in Paris, home of the Italian Embassy. Go around back for a glance at the gardens and the beautiful vine-covered bridge over Via Giulia.

Behind the elaborate Baroque façade of the **Palazzo Spada,** in P. della Quercia to the left of the Palazzo Farnese, you'll find the collection of the **Galleria Spada** (tel. 686 11 58). In the 17th century, Cardinal Bernardino Spada purchased a grand assortment of art, then commissioned an opulent set of great rooms to house it. The collection includes Titian's *Portrait of a Musician* and Pietro Testa's *Allegory of the*

Massacre of the Innocents. (Open Tues.-Sat. 9am-6:30pm, Sun. 9am-12:30pm. Admission L4000, under 18 and over 60 free.)

As part of his campaign in the early 1500s to clean up Rome, Pope Julius II commissioned Bramante to construct a long street leading across the Tiber to the Vatican. The eventual result was **Via Giulia,** an elegant contrast to the winding medieval streets around it. Today, the street is one of the most peaceful and exclusive in Rome, running past well-maintained *palazzi,* antique stores, and art galleries.

Piazza Navona

Emperor Domitian used the site of modern-day **Piazza Navona** as a racetrack; from its opening day in AD86, the stadium witnessed daily contests of strength and agility. As the empire fell, real-life battles with marauding Goths replaced staged contests, and the stadium fell into disuse. Large crowds returned to the *piazza* with the Renaissance, and from 1477 to 1869 the space hosted the city's market. Today, tourists fill Piazza Navona, mingling with artists and relaxing at *caffè* tables. Female travelers will have no problem finding cigarette lights or company here, as prowling Romeos vie to test their virility as well as their English.

Bernini's exuberant **Fontana dei Quattro Fiumi** (Fountain of the Four Rivers) commands the center of the *piazza*. Each of the four male river gods represents one of the world's four continents: the Ganges for Asia, the Danube for Europe, the Nile for Africa (veiled because the source of the river was unknown), and the Rio de la Plata for the Americas. Borromini's **Church of Sant'Agnese in Agone** looks down on the fountain, built by the architect's rival.

In the north end of the *piazza* stands the **Fountain of Neptune.** Giacomo della Porta designed it in the 16th century, Bernini spruced it up in the 17th, and Antonio della Bitta added the central titular Neptune in 1878.

On nearby Corso del Rinascimento, the celestial **Church of Sant'Ivo's** corkscrew cupola hovers over the **Palazzo della Sapienza,** the original home of the University of Rome, founded by Pope Sixtus IV in the 15th century. Continue down this road, turn left on Corso Vittorio Emanuele II, and walk to Piazza del Gesù to see **Il Gesù,** the mother church of the Jesuit Order. The façade of the Gesù was the prototype for numerous churches built or rebuilt during the Counter-Reformation. Look to the left of the crossing for the **Chapel of Sant'Ignazio di Loyola,** dedicated to the founder of the order who is buried under the altar. (Open daily 6am-12:30pm and 4-7pm.)

The Pantheon

The majestic **Pantheon** (tel. 36 98 31) has stood for nearly 2000 years, and its marble columns and pediment, bronze doors, and soaring domed interior are all relatively unchanged from the day they were built. The inscription across the architrave and façade reads, "Marcus Agrippa made it in his third consulship." Indeed, he did build a temple here in 27BC, but Emperor Hadrian tore it down and started from scratch in AD119, helping to design this temple dedicated to "all the gods." The classically proportioned façade, with its triangular pediment and Corinthian columns, deceives the first-time visitor into expecting an equally traditional interior.

The dome, some 43m across, consists only of poured concrete without the support of vaults, arches, or ribs. Archaeologists and architects have puzzled for centuries over how it was actually erected. The central oculus, which provides the only source of light for the building, also supports the weight of the dome, as the ring of tension

A Head Above the Rest

The Church of Saint Agnes by Borromini is dedicated to the Christian maiden who escaped the advances of the lascivious son of a low-ranking magistrate. After being stripped naked, her hair miraculously grew to cover her shameful nudity. Out of frustration and embarrassment, the powers-that-were tried to burn her at the stake, but the flames didn't even singe her. Finally, Diocletian had her head cut off. The church marks the spot where she was exposed and houses her severed skull (the *sacra testa,* or "holy head") in its sacristy.

around the hole traps all the inward forces of the sloping concrete. Romans used the sunlight falling through the hole as a sundial to indicate not only the hour but also the dates of equinoxes and solstices. Converted to the Church of Santa Maria ad Martyres, the temple weathered the Middle Ages with few losses, though it sometimes served double-duty as a fortress and even a fishmarket. Later artists and architects adored and imitated the building; it inspired countless Renaissance and Neoclassical edifices. Michelangelo, using the dome as a model for his designs of St. Peter's Basilica, is said to have made his own dome about 1½m shorter in diameter out of respect for his ancient model (see page 186). (Open June Mon.-Sat. 9am-6pm, Sun. 9am-1pm; July-Aug. Mon.-Sat. 9am-6:30pm, Sun. 9am-1pm; Oct.-May Mon.-Sat. 9am-4pm, Sun. 9am-1pm. Sun. Mass 9:45-11:15am. Free.)

Around the left side of the Pantheon, an **Egyptian obelisk** supported by Bernini's curious elephant statue marks the center of tiny **Piazza Minerva.** The unassuming **Church of Santa Maria Sopra Minerva** is Rome's only Gothic church. To the right of the entrance, six plaques mark the flood levels of the Tiber over the centuries. Inside stands a statue of *St. Sebastian* recently attributed to Michelangelo. The south transept houses the famous **Carafa Chapel** and a brilliant fresco cycle by Filippino Lippi. The altar contains the body of St. Catherine of Siena, the 14th-century ascetic and church reformer, who died in a nearby house. The painter Fra Angelico lies in a tomb under the left side of the altar. Michelangelo's *Christ Bearing the Cross* stands guard between the tombs.

NORTH AND NORTHEAST OF THE ANCIENT CITY

Via del Corso and Environs

The 15th-century popes widened **Via del Corso** (originally Via Lata during the Roman Republic), and it is now a busy shopping district. The nearby **Galleria Doria Pamphili,** P. del Collegio Romano, 1A (tel. 679 73 23), in the *palazzo* of the same name, houses treasures from the 15th through 18th centuries, including Caravaggio's *Rest on the Flight to Egypt* and *Mary Magdalene,* Bernini's *Bust of Innocent X,* and Velázquez's *Portrait of Innocent X.* The private apartments contain Filippo Lippi's *Annunciation* and Memling's *Deposition.* (Open Fri.-Tues. 10am-1pm. Admission L12,000, students L9000.)

Heading north on Via del Corso, take a left at Largo Carlo Goldoni onto Via Tomacelli and then a right onto Via di Ripetta to come to the **Piazza Augusto Imperatore** and the circular brick mound of the **Mausoleum of Augustus,** which once housed the funerary urns of the Imperial Roman family. Nearby stands the **Ara Pacis,** which commemorates the *Pax Romana*, Great Peace achieved by Emperor Augustus in the late first century BC. Covered in some of the most impressive sculpture of the Augustan age, the decorative program mixes images of Augustus with such figures from Roman mythology as Aeneas, Romulus and Remus, and the she-wolf. (Open Tues.-Sat. 9am-4pm, Sun. 9am-1pm. Admission L4000.)

Piazza del Popolo

The **Piazza del Popolo** was the first sight to greet 19th-century visitors entering the city from the north through the Porta del Popolo; indeed, the "people's square" has always been a popular gathering place. The south end of the *piazza* marks the start of three important streets: Via del Corso in the center, which runs to P. Venezia and the white Vittorio Emanuele II Monument; Via di Ripetta, built by Leo X for access to the Vatican; and Via del Babuino, cleared in 1525 by Clement VII, which leads to the Spanish Steps. Nineteenth-century architect Giuseppe Valadier spruced up the once-scruffy *piazza* in 1814, adding the two travertine fountains on the western and eastern sides. The great **obelisk of Pharaoh Ramses II** stands in the center of the *piazza.* The obelisk, some 3200 years old, was already an antique when Augustus brought it back as a souvenir from Egypt in the first century BC. On the south side of the *piazza,* Carlo Rainaldi's **Churches of Santa Maria di Montesanto** and **Santa Maria dei Miracoli** reinforce the square's symmetry. On the north side near the Porta del Popolo, behind a simple early Renaissance façade, the **Church of Santa Maria del Popolo** contains some of the most important Renaissance and Baroque art in Rome. Immediately to the right as you enter, the **della Rovere Chapel** harbors Pinturicchio's *Adoration*. The **Cerasi Chapel,** to the left of the main altar, houses two superb Caravaggio paintings, *The Conversion of St. Paul* and *The Crucifixion of St. Peter*. Bramante designed the apse behind the altar, and Raphael created the **Chigi Chapel,** second on the left, for the wealthy Sienese banker Agostino Chigi. (Open daily 7am-noon and 4-7pm.)

Villa Borghese

Climb the steps up the hill from Piazza del Popolo or take Metro Linea A to Flaminio to reach Rome's most famous patch of public green, the park around the **Villa Borghese.** Among its shady paths, overgrown gardens, and scenic terraces stand three notable art museums. Because the **Museo Borghese** has been undergoing restoration since 1984, the gallery's first-floor (and first-rate) painting collection has been shipped off for the interim to the Chiesa Grande on Via di San Michele in Trastevere (see p. 112). The ground floor and its remarkable sculpture collection remain open, though; look for some of Bernini's most famous works—*Apollo and Daphne* (Room 3), *The Rape of Persephone* (Room 4), and *David* (Room 11). (Open Tues.-Sat. 9am-2pm, Sun. and holidays 9am-1pm. Last entrance 30min. before closing. Admission L4000.)

The forbidding **Palazzo delle Belle Arti** designed by Cesare Bazzani houses the **Galleria Nazionale d'Arte Moderna,** filled with the best Italian art of the 19th and 20th centuries. The most striking works, however, are by non-Italians—Degas, Klimt, Monet, and Pollock. (Open Tues.-Sat. 9am-7pm, Sun. and holidays 9am-1pm. Admission L8000, under 18 or over 60 free.)

Along Viale delle Belle Arti stands the **Museo Etrusco di Villa Giulia,** built under Pope Julius in the 1550s. The museum houses a huge and impressive collection of Etruscan artifacts, a prodigious collection of Greek vases, and a reconstructed Etruscan tomb from the 6th century BC. (Open Tues.-Sat. 9am-7pm, Sun. 9am-1pm. Admission L8000.) The villa hosts **evening concerts** by the Santa Cecilia Music Society during the month of July; ticket prices vary. For concert information visit the Villa Giulia or call 322 65 71. (Tickets available at the museum Tues.-Sat. 10am-2pm, Sun. 10am-1pm, and on the day of the performance 6pm-intermission.)

The Spanish Steps and Piazza di Spagna

Designed by an Italian, paid for by the French, named for the Spaniards, occupied by the British, and under the sway of American ambassador-at-large Ronald McDonald, the **Spanish Steps,** in the aptly-named Piazza di Spagna, exude an international air. To reach the monument, take Metro Linea A to the Spagna stop. Built in 1725, the 137 elegant steps culminate at the rosy Neoclassical façade of the **Church of Santa Trinità dei Monti,** a worthy climax to the grand curves of the staircase. (Lower part of church open daily 9:30am-12:30pm and 4-7pm; entire church open Tues. and Thurs. 4-6pm.) Swanky **Via dei Condotti** leads from the Spanish Steps back to Via del Corso.

Trevi Fountain

From Via del Corso, take Via delle Muratte across from P. Colonna to reach the tiny Piazza di Trevi. The rocks and figures of Nicola Salvi's (1697-1751) famed **Fontana di Trevi** emerge from the back of Palazzo Poli and dominate the square. In the foreground is Neptune's winged chariot, guided by two burly tritons. Anita Ekberg and Marcello Mastroianni take a midnight dip in the fountain in Fellini's *La Dolce Vita;* the police will keep you from re-creating this scene today. Tradition claims that travelers who throw a coin into the fountain will one day return to Rome. Opposite the fountain is the Baroque **Church of Santi Vincenzo ed Anastasio,** rebuilt in 1630. The crypt preserves the hearts and lungs of popes from 1590 to 1903.

Piazza del Quirinale and Via XX Settembre

Piazza del Quirinale, at the southwest end of Via del Quirinale, occupies the summit of the tallest of Rome's seven hills. From the belvedere (reached by stairs leading from Via Scanderberg, just east of P. di Trevi), the view takes in a sea of Roman domes, including St. Peter's. The president of the republic officially resides in the **Palazzo del Quirinale,** a Baroque collaboration by Bernini, Carlo Maderno, and Domenico Fontana.

Via del Quirinale leaves the *piazza* from the north, passing the modest façade of Bernini's oval **Church of Sant'Andrea al Quirinale** (tel. 48 90 31 87) on the right. (Open Wed.-Mon. 8am-noon and 4-7pm.) Farther down the street, the undulating façade of Borromini's tiny **Church of San Carlo alle Quattro Fontane** (often called **San Carlino**) contrasts sharply with Bernini's neighboring work. This church holds the distinction of being Borromini's first and last work: though he finished the interior early in his career, he designed the façade just before his suicide. (Open Mon.-Fri. 9:30am-12:30pm and 4-6pm, Sat. 9am-12:30pm.) The intersection at **Via delle Quattro Fontane** showcases one of Pope Sixtus V's more gracious additions to the city. In the corner of each of the four surrounding buildings is a fountain with a reclining figure. From the crossroads, you can catch sight of the obelisks at P. del Quirinale, at the top of the Spanish Steps, and at Santa Maria Maggiore, as well as (in the distance) Michelangelo's Porta Pia.

At this intersection, Via del Quirinale becomes Via XX Settembre, which eventually opens into the Baroque **Piazza di San Bernardo,** site of Domenico Fontana's colossal **Moses Fountain.** The nearby **Church of Santa Maria della Vittoria** harbors Bernini's *Ecstasy of St. Theresa of Avila* (1652) in the Cornaro Chapel, the last on the left. (Open daily 6:30am-noon and 4:30-7pm.) The **Church of Santa Susanna** (1603) to the left has a distinctive Baroque façade by Carlo Maderno. Inside are Maderno's frescoes of the life of Susanna and his four statues of the prophets atop 9th-century pillars. (Mass in English Mon.-Sat. 6pm, Sun. 9 and 10:30am.)

Piazza Barberini

Down Via Barberini from Largo S. Susanna, Bernini's **Triton Fountain** spouts a stream of water high into the air over the traffic cirle of Piazza Barberini. In the north end of the *piazza* is Bernini's **Fontana delle Api** (Bee Fountain), intended for the "use of the public and their animals," its decorations alluding to the Barberini family's coat of arms. Maderno, Borromini, and Bernini all had a hand in the architecture of the sumptuous **Palazzo Barberini,** Via delle Quattro Fontane, 13. The *palazzo* houses the **Galleria Nazionale d'Arte Antica** (tel. 481 44 30), a collection of paintings dating from the 11th to 18th centuries. (The museum descriptions are in Italian, but you can purchase an informative English guide for L9000 at the entrance.) Note Filippo Lippi's *Annunciation and Donors,* Holbein's *Portrait of Henry VIII,* and the superb canvases by Titian, Tintoretto, Caravaggio, El Greco, and Poussin. Most remarkable, however, is the entrance hall ceiling, which glows with Pietro da Cortona's *Triumph of Divine Providence,* glorifying the papacy of Urban VIII and his Barberini family. The apartments on the second story merit a visit for the family's memorabilia. (Open Tues.-Sat. 9am-7pm, Sun. 9am-1pm. Admission to galleries and apartments L8000.) Twisting north from P. Barberini is the **Via Veneto,** filled by a flood of tourists, embassies, and airline offices. A short way up the street on the right, the 1626 **Church of Santa Maria della Concezione** houses the tomb of founder Antonio Barberini. The tomb's inscription reads "Here lies dust, ashes, nothing." In the **Capuchin Crypt** downstairs, the artfully arranged bones of 4000 Capuchin friars make this site one of the most bizarre and elaborately macabre in all of Rome. (Open daily 9am-noon and 3-6pm. L1000 minimum donation requested.)

Baths of Diocletian

From P. di San Bernardo, head down Via E. Orlando to **Piazza della Repubblica,** home to the ruins of the **Baths of Diocletian.** Forty thousand Christian slaves worked for nine years (AD298-306) to build these public baths, which could accommodate

3000 Romans at once. The complex also included gymnasia, art galleries, gardens, libraries, and a 30-person public toilet. In 1561, Pope Pius IV ordered Michelangelo, then 86, to transform the ruins into a church. The eventual result was the **Church of Santa Maria degli Angeli.** Despite the departure from Michelangelo's plan and years of design screw-ups, the vast interior gives a sense of the magnitude and elegance of the ancient baths. A door marked "Sacristy" leads to ruins of the frigidarium and an exhibit on the stages of the church's construction. (Open daily 7:30am-12:30pm and 4:30-6:30pm. Free.)

Around the corner on Viale Enrico de Nicola (across the street from the bus stop in front of the Termini Station), the **Museo Nazionale Romano delle Terme** (tel. 488 05 30) displays several important patrician collections along with recently excavated sculptures from Roman sites. Don't miss the *Sala dei Capolavori* (Room of Masterpieces) and the *Ludovisi Throne,* a Greek sculpture dating from the 5th century BC depicting the birth of Aphrodite. (Open Tues.-Sat. 9am-2pm, Sun. 9am-1pm. Admission L12,000, EU citizens under 18 or over 60 free.) If you can't make it to the museum, head to the special exhibit on Via Romita, next to Santa Maria degli Angeli, which features a number of rare bronze sculptures. (Open daily 10am-7pm. Free.)

EAST OF THE ANCIENT CITY

Esquiline Hill

The **Basilica of Santa Maria Maggiore,** four blocks down Via Cavour from Termini, occupies the summit of the Esquiline Hill. As one of the seven major basilicas of Rome, it is officially part of Vatican City. Although its front and rear façades are Rococo works, its interior dates from 352. The coffered ceiling was gilded with the first gold Columbus sent back from America. To the right of the altar, a simple marble slab marks the **tomb of Bernini.** (Open daily 7am-7pm. Dress code enforced.) The 14th-century mosaics in the church's *loggia* tell the story of the miraculous August snowfall that showed Pope Liberius where to build the church. (*Loggia* open 9:30am-5:40pm. Tickets L5000 at the souvenir stand just inside the entrance.)

Down Via Carlo Alberto from Piazza S. Maria Maggiore lurks the shabby **Piazza Vittorio Emanuele II,** home to Rome's biggest daily outdoor market of fresh fish, fruits, and such non-edibles as clothes, shoes, and luggage. (At night, be wary: prostitutes and drug dealers do the soliciting.) Down Via Cavour from Maria Maggiore, the steps on the left lead you up to the **Church of San Pietro in Vincoli,** home to Michelangelo's unfinished Tomb of Julius II, which features his imposing masterpiece, *Moses.* (Open daily 7am-12:30pm and 3:30-7pm.)

The Caelian Hill

The best place to ascend the **Caelian Hill,** south of the Esquiline Hill, is from the P. del Colosseo. Starting behind the Colosseum, Via di S. Giovanni in Laterano leads you to the **Church of San Clemente.** The upper church, dating from the 12th century, stands over a fourth-century basilica that in turn rests on the ruins of a first-century Roman house and the second-century **Mithraeum,** all of which cover a still-operative system of Republican drains and sewers. (Open Mon.-Sat. 9am-12:30pm and 3:30-6:30pm, Sun. and holidays 10am-12:30pm and 3:30-6:30pm.) Up the hill on Via dei Querceti (take a right off S. Giovanni in Laterano on Via SS. Quattro Coronati), the solemn **Church of Santi Quattro Coronati** stands fortified behind medieval battlements. The **Chapel of San Silvestro** on the right of the courtyard contains an extraordinary fresco cycle of the life of the Emperor Constantine. (Ring the bell and the cloistered nuns will send you a key on a lazy susan. Admission L1000.)

Via SS. Quattro Coronati leads up the hill and left onto Via S. Stefano Rotondo to the grandiose **Church of San Giovanni in Laterano,** founded by Constantine in 314. This Christian basilica, the oldest in the city, is the endpoint of the pilgrimage route from St. Peter's. The pope occasionally celebrates festival masses in the church, which is the cathedral of the diocese of Rome. The giant Gothic *baldacchino* over the altar houses two golden reliquaries with the heads of Saints Peter and Paul. A terrorist bomb badly damaged the basilica in 1993, and restoration is ongoing. (Open summer daily 7am-6:45pm; in winter daily 7am-6pm.)

As you exit the church from the side, cross the street to the right to the building housing the **Scala Santa.** Many believe that these were the marble steps outside Pontius Pilate's house in Jerusalem where Jesus stood. Pilgrims continue to ascend the steps on their knees, though they can no longer earn an indulgence. If you prefer to walk up to the chapel at the top, use the stairs on either side. (Open daily in summer 6:15am-12:15pm and 3:30-7pm; in winter 6:15am-12:15pm and 3-6:30pm.)

SOUTH OF THE ANCIENT CITY

Circus Maximus and Baths of Caracalla

Down Via S. Gregorio from the southwest side of the Colosseum is the **Circus Maximus** (600BC), a grassy shadow of its former glory. Romans once gathered here for chariot races; the turning points of the track, now marked by raised humps, were perilously sharp to ensure enough thrills and spills to entertain the crowd.

At the east end of the circus, Via delle Terme di Caracalla passes the mammoth remains of the **Baths of Caracalla,** the largest and best-preserved baths in the city. Some 1600 heat-soaked Romans could sponge themselves off here at the same time. (Open in summer Mon. 9am-2pm, Tues.-Sat. 9am-7pm, Sun. 9am-1pm; in winter closes 1hr. before sunset. Last entrance 1hr. before closing. Admission L8000, EU citizens under 18 and over 60 free.)

Via Appia and the Catacombs

Follow Via delle Terme di Caracalla, take a right on Viale di Porta Ardeatina to the beginning of the **Via Appia Antica (Appian Way).** The Appian Way was built in 312BC to connect Rome to the Adriatic port city of Brundisium, modern-day Brindisi. The road offers a glimpse of the countryside of Lazio, with avenues of cypress trees, views of the Roman countryside, and crumbling nearby tombs of both pagans and Christians. Outside the city walls lie the **catacombs,** multi-story condos for the dead, stretching tunnel after tunnel for kilometers on up to five levels. Five of the 60 around Rome are open to the public. The most notable catacombs are those of San Calisto, Santa Domitilla, and San Sebastiano, neighbors on Via Appia Antica south of the city. To get there, take bus #218 from P. di S. Giovanni in Laterano or pick it up as it hits Via Appia Antica just outside the Porta di S. Sebastiano. Get off at Domine Quo Vadis, where Via Ardeatina meets Via Appia, and walk up the tree-lined path to **San Callisto,** Via Appia Antica, 110 (tel. 513 67 25 or 513 67 27; closed Wed.). These catacombs are the largest in Rome, with almost 22km of winding subterranean paths, and they constitute the first public Christian cemetery. The four serpentine levels once held 16 popes, 7 bishops, and some 500,000 others. You can reach **Santa Domitilla,** Via delle Sette Chiese, 282 (tel. 511 03 42; closed Tues.) by getting off the #218 bus at Via delle Sette Chiese. Santa Domitilla enjoys acclaim for its paintings and inscriptions from tombstones and sarcophagi. Perhaps the most impressive, **San Sebastiano,** Via Appia Antica, 136 (tel. 788 70 35; fax 784 37 45; closed Thurs.), near the southern entrance to San Callisto, was once home to the bodies of Saints Peter and Paul. Running for seven miles on three levels and accommodating 174,000 dead, the eerie tunnels display animal mosaics, disintegrating skulls, and fantastic symbols from early Christian iconography. (All three catacombs are open 6 days a week in summer 8:30am-noon and 2:30-5:30pm; in winter until 5pm. Closing days are staggered to ensure that at least 2 catacombs are open any given day. Admission L8000. Wait for the obligatory tour in the language of your choice after purchasing a ticket.)

Testaccio

South of the Aventine Hill, the working-class district of Testaccio is known for its inexpensive *trattorie,* raucous nightclubs, and eclectic collection of monuments. In ancient times, grain, oil, wine, and marble were unloaded from river barges into giant warehouses here. Bus #27 runs from Termini down Via Cavour and across the river, entering Testaccio along Via Zabaglia. Metro Linea B also goes to Testaccio; get off at the Piramide stop. Via Zabaglia turns left onto Via Caio Cestio, which runs along the length of the peaceful **Cimitero Acattolico per gli Stranieri** (Protestant Cemetery), final resting place for many English visitors to the city, including Keats, Shelley, and Goethe's son Julius. Henry James buried his fictional heroine Daisy Miller here after she died of malaria. (Open April-Sept. Tues.-Sun. 9am-6pm; Oct.-March Tues.-Sun. 9am-5pm. Ring the bell at #6 for admission. Donation requested.) Outside the cemetery, past the well-preserved **Porta San Paolo,** stands the colossal **Pyramid of Gaius Cestius.** The emperor Aurelian fortified the city walls with the pyramid to defend against the marauding Goths in the 3rd century.

From the pyramid, take Metro Linea B or bus #673, 23, or 170 down Via Ostiense to the **Basilica di San Paolo fuori le Mura,** the largest church in the city after St. Peter's. Fire completely destroyed the original structure in 1823; the current building is a reconstruction. The body of St. Paul lies buried beneath the altar, although his head is in S. Giovanni in Laterano. (Open daily 7am-6:30pm.) The **cloister** is a peaceful vestige, lined with pairs of spiral columns enveloping a rose garden. (Open daily 9am-1pm and 3-6:30pm.)

EUR

The buildings of the **EUR** (EH-oor), an Italian acronym for the Universal Exposition of Rome, commemorates the 1942 World's Fair that Mussolini planned in order to showcase his fascist achievements. The outbreak of World War II interrupted the preparations, and the completed buildings now house Rome's museum overflow. EUR lies at the EUR-Palasport stop on Metro Linea B and on bus route #714 from Termini to P. Marconi. **Via Cristoforo Colombo,** EUR's main street, runs to P. Marconi with its 1959 modernist **obelisk,** the first of many bad takes on classical Roman architecture. To the right of the *piazza,* the **Museo Preistorico ed Etnografico Luigi Pigorini,** Viale Lincoln, 14 (tel. 54 95 22 38), features objects from various parts of the Italian peninsula from the Stone, Bronze, and Iron Ages. (Open Tues.-Fri. 9am-1:30pm, Sat. 9am-7pm, Sun. 9am-12:30pm. Admission L8000.) Nearby, Viale della Civiltà Romana leads to the **Museo della Civiltà Romana** (tel. 592 61 41; open Tues.-Sat. 9am-7pm, Sun. 9am-1:30pm; L5000) which features a plaster cast of Trajan's column and a scale model of Rome in the time of Hadrian, among other reconstructions of major Roman monuments.

To the north is **Viale della Civiltà del Lavoro** and the awkward **Palace of the Civilization of Labor,** EUR's definitive symbol. Nearby **Piazzale delle Nazioni Unite** embodies the EUR that Mussolini had intended: imposing buildings that recall Roman glory yet embody an antiseptic modern aesthetic.

WEST OF THE ANCIENT CITY TO THE TIBER

The Jewish Ghetto and the Theater of Marcellus

In **Piazza Mattei,** the graceful 16th-century **Fontana delle Tartarughe** (Tortoise Fountain) marks the center of the **Ghetto,** a lowland quarter where Jews were confined from the 16th to the 19th century. The original ghetto measured only 270m by 150m yet housed 3500 Jews. Today the area is one of Rome's most picturesque and eclectic neighborhoods, with family businesses dating back centuries and restaurants serving some of the tastiest food in Rome.

The **Sinagoga Ashkenazita** (tel. 687 50 51) at Via Catalana and Lungotevere de' Cenci defiantly proclaims its heritage in a city of Catholic iconography and classical designs. Built from 1874 to 1904, Sinagoga Ashkenazita incorporates Persian and Babylonian architectural devices, intentionally avoiding any resemblance to Christian churches, under an exuberant rainbow dome. The temple has a strictly Orthodox seating plan: women sit upstairs, apart from the men. Services, at which anyone is welcome, are performed entirely in Hebrew. Because of a 1982 attack on the synagogue, security guards must search and question all visitors. (Open only for services.) The synagogue also houses the **Jewish Museum,** which displays ceremonial objects from the 17th-century Jewish community and the original plan of the Ghetto. The collection was hidden in a Jewish ritual bath during the nine-month Nazi occupation of Rome. (Open July-Sept. daily 9am-4:30pm; Oct.-June Mon.-Thurs. 9:30am-1pm and 2-4:30pm, Fri. 9:30am-1:30pm. Hours fluctuate. Admission L8000.)

The pattern of arches and pilasters of the 11BC **Teatro di Marcello** (Theater of Marcellus) served as a model for the Colosseum; the classic arrangement of architectural orders features capitals growing more elaborate with each mounting level. A network of tunnels runs from the theater to Piazza Navona; Jews hid here in WWII. The theater is closed to the public, but the surrounding park hosts classical concerts on summer nights. (Call 481 48 00 for info.) Farther down Via di Teatro di Marcello toward the Tiber, the remains of three Roman temples dedicated to Juno, Janus, and Spes (Hope) jut out from the walls of the **Church of San Nicola in Carcere** (tel. 686 99 72). The most complete temple lies to the right of the church, its Ionic columns littering the tiny lawn and embedded in the church's wall. The left wall of the church preserves the Doric columns of the second of the temples; the third lies buried below the church. (Open Sept.-July 7am-noon and 4-7pm; Sun. mass at noon.)

The Velabrum

The Velabrum lies to the south of the Ghetto in a flat floodplain near the Capitoline and Palatine Hills, where the legendary she-wolf rescued Romulus and Remus. One block down Via Luigi Petroselli is the **Piazza della Bocca della Verità.** Both Greek and Etruscan influence are evident in the design of the rectangular **Temple of Portunus** on the right, once known as the Temple of Fortuna Virilis. The present construction dates from the late 2nd century BC, though there seems to have been a temple on the site for some years before. The **circular temple** next door, presently cloaked in scaffolding for restoration, was also built in the late 2nd century BC. Across the *piazza* is the hulking 4th-century **Arch of Janus,** a covered market for cattle traders. By the river, the exquisite **Church of Santa Maria in Cosmedin** (also called the Church of S. Maria de Scuola Greca) harbors some of Rome's most beautiful medieval decoration. The 12th-century bell tower welcomes mobs of bus-borne tourists to the famous **Bocca della Verità** (Mouth of Truth) in the portico. Originally a drain cover carved as a river god's face, the circular relief was credited with supernatural powers in the Middle Ages. Legend says that the mouth will close on a liar's hand, severing his or her fingers. (Portico open daily 9am-5pm. Church open daily 9am-noon and 3-5pm. Byzantine mass Sun. 10:30am.)

The Aventine Hill

From Piazza della Bocca della Verità, Via della Greca leads to the Clivio dei Publici, which climbs between crumbling walls to the spacious gardens and courtyards of the **Aventine Hill.** At the summit, head through the iron gate to a park where orange trees frame a sweeping view of the Tiber and southern Rome. Across the park another gate opens onto the courtyard of the **Church of Santa Sabina** with its porch of ancient columns and its towering campanile. Via di Santa Sabina continues along the crest of the hill to the **Piazza dei Cavalieri di Malta,** home of the crusading order of the Knights of Malta. Through the **keyhole** in the pale yellow gate on the right, you can see the dome of St. Peter's perfectly framed by hedges. From Santa Sabina, Via di Valle Murcia descends past a public rose garden (where a rose show blooms in May and June) to the Circus Maximus.

ACROSS THE TIBER

In the middle of the river sits the **Isola Tiberina.** Medical needs dictated the island's history. It was a dumping-ground for sick slaves until the Romans established a cult to Aesculapius, god of healing, here in the early 3rd century BC. A travertine relief of a serpent, symbol of Aesculapius, is carved on the southeast side of the boat-shaped island. The island's hospital was established in AD154. One of the bridges to the mainland, the **Ponte Fabricio** (62BC), is the oldest in Rome.

Trastevere

Trastevere, which became a part of Rome under Augustus, has a proud, independent vitality; some residents boast of never crossing the river. Trastevere's dark maze of streets and medieval quarters crisscrossed with clotheslines will give you a sense of traditional Italian life—hordes of expatriates and artists notwithstanding. Take bus #75 or 170 from Termini or #56 or 60 from Via Claudio in P. San Silvestro to Viale Trastevere. On this busy thoroughfare is the **Church of San Crisogno** with its original 5th-century foundation. To reach the **Church of Santa Cecilia in Trastevere,** dedicated to the patron saint of music, turn left at McDonald's and head down Via dei Genovesi until it ends at Via dei Vascellari. Turn right and head through the parking lot to the church's rose garden. Don't miss the famous statue of Santa Cecilia under the high altar, Stefano Maderno's marble representation of the saint when she was exhumed from her tomb in 1599.

Via di S. Cecilia merges with Via di S. Michele, which ends at Porta Portese, home to the city's largest flea market every Sunday morning. The **Chiesa Grande** at Via di S. Michele, 22 (tel. 581 67 32), temporarily houses the **Museo Borghese painting collection.** The exciting display of 16th- to 19th-century works, which includes several Caravaggio masterpieces and a Rubens, is crammed along the apse walls of a unused chapel. (Open Tues.-Sat. 9am-2pm, Sun.-Mon. 9am-1pm. Last entrance 30min. before closing. Admission L4000.) From Viale di Trastevere take Via della Lungaretta to P. di Santa Maria in Trastevere, home to the grandiose **Church of Santa Maria in Trastevere.** The church, built between 337 and 352 by Pope Julius II, has the distinction of being the first of Rome's churches to be dedicated to the Virgin. The mosaics on the exterior foreshadow the works inside. (Open daily 7am-1pm and 3:30-7pm; Sun. mass at noon and 5:30pm.)

From P. di Santa Maria in Trastevere, Via della Scala leads to the **Porta Settimania,** a gateway in the Aurelian Wall from the 3rd century. Via Lungara leads north to the magnificent Renaissance **Villa Farnesina,** home to Renaissance hotshot Agostino Chigi; Raphael, Peruzzi, and Il Sodoma frescoed his villa. Check out Raphael's *Galatea* who cavorts with dolphins as the cyclops Polyphemus lurks nearby. (Open Mon.-Sat. 9am-1pm; free.) Across the street, the **Galleria Corsini** on the first floor of the Palazzo Corsini sprawls across northern Trastevere from the Tiber to the foot of the Janiculan Hill and houses one half of the **Museo Nazionale dell'Arte Antica;** the other half hangs in the Palazzo Barberini. (Open Tues.-Fri. 9am-7pm, Sat.-Sun. 9am-1pm. Admission L8000.) Via Corsini skirts the side of the palace to meet Rome's **Botanical Gardens,** Largo Cristina di Svezia, 24. This impressive and well-maintained assemblage leads from valleys of ferns through groves of bamboo to a hilltop Japanese garden. (Entrance off Via della Lungara. Grounds open in summer Mon.-Sat. 9am-6:30pm; in winter Mon.-Sat. 9am-5:30pm. Greenhouse open 9am-12:30pm. Closed Aug. Admission L4000, under 6 free.)

Adorned with busts of obscure 19th-century Italian heroes, the **Janiculan Hill (Gianicolo)** overlooks Trastevere from the northwest. To get to the summit take Via della Scala from Santa Maria in Trastevere to Via Garibaldi. Atop the hill the **Church of San Pietro in Montorio** sits on the spot believed to be the site of St. Peter's upside-down crucifixion. The courtyard encloses Bramante's tiny, perfect **Tempietto** (1499-1502), a brilliant prototype of Renaissance order and harmony. From the front of the Tempietto you can gaze upon a magnificent view of all of Rome. (Both open daily 9am-noon and 4-6:30pm.)

Entertainment

Since the days of bread and circuses, Roman entertainment has been a public affair—concerts under the stars, street fairs with acrobats and fire-eaters, modern-day minstrels and maestros, and enchanted foreigners flooding *piazze* and cafés. At night, light floods the monuments of Rome, including the Forum, the Colosseum, St. Peter's, and the Trevi Fountain, making a walk past these sights a spectacular finish to a day of touring. Look for posters advertising local concerts, shows, and exhibits and the essential weekly cultural guides **Roma C'è** (L1500; available at newsstands) and **TrovaRoma** (included in each Thursday's edition of *La Repubblica*), which contain comprehensive lists of concerts, clubs, movies, festivals of all kinds, and special events. *Roma C'è* also includes a section in English detailing the entertainment possibilities of special interest to English speakers. The tourist office may have information or brochures on cultural activities, including *Un'Ospite a Roma.*

PUBS

The myriad pubs in Rome (many "Irish") cater to tourists and expatriates, but there's no shortage of Roman clientele. Drinks often go up in price after 9pm, so imbibe accordingly. To meet Italians (that is, the kind that don't come to foreign bars to pick up Americans), you should probably avoid the pubs and head to a nightclub or jazz bar. The *birrerie* in Trastevere offer a fair mix of foreigners and Romans.

Jonathan's Angels, Via della Fossa, 16 (tel. 689 34 26), west of P. Navona. Take Vicolo Savelli Parione Pace off Via Governo Vecchio. The atmosphere of a dark Disney ride. A hip, young crowd enjoys the live music and campy, candlelit ambience. Medium beer on tap L10,000, cocktails L15,000. Open daily 9pm-2am.

Julius Caesar, Via Castelfidardo, 49, just north of Termini near P. dell'Indipendenza. A cut above the trendy pubs throughout the city. Live music and relatively cheap drinks. The downstairs fills with blaring live music, usually vintage rock, Mon.-Sat. During happy hour (9-10pm), a beer and pizza are only L10,000. Beer on tap L5000-8000, pitchers L15,000, cocktails L10,000. Open daily 9pm-3am.

Druid's Den, Via San Martino ai Monti, 28 (tel. 488 02 58). Traveling south on Via Merulana from Via Santa Maria Maggiore, take your second right. An Irish hangout where Romans get to be tourists. Pints of Guinness and Strong Bow cider on draft L7000. Open in summer 6pm-12:30am, in winter 5pm-12:30am.

The Drunken Ship, Campo de' Fiori, 20/21 (tel. 68 30 05 35). Hipper than it was in its pre-renovation frat-house days, this slick establishment warmly welcomes backpackers with special reduced prices on drinks and jello shots (normally L2000). The DJ spins mostly American favorites and the staff speaks English. Too much happiness for just one hour—happy hour prices last 6-9pm: pint of beer L5000, pitcher L15,000, sandwiches L8000, nachos L5000. Ask about the student discount on Heineken. Open in summer 6pm-2am, in winter 5pm-2am.

MUSIC CLUBS

Rome's music clubs attract a hip Italian crowd—some have dancing and are usually much cheaper than discos. The city also has quite a few *pianobar* for more mature clientele. Most music clubs in Rome are officially private *associazioni culturali,* requiring you to pay a one-time fee for a membership card and limiting access on the weekends. Call before setting out; opening hours tend to change seasonally and/or at the manager's whim.

Alexanderplatz, Via Ostia, 9 (tel. 37 29 398), north of Vatican City. Take Metro Linea A to Ottaviano. From here, head west on Viale Giulio Cesare, take the second right onto Via Leone IV and then your first left onto Via Ostia. Night buses to P. Venezia and Termini leave from P. Clodio; to get there from the club, keep going north on Via Leone IV, which becomes Via della Giuliana. Without a doubt, *the* place to hear jazz in Rome. The dark, smoky setting of a classic underground European jazz club with sparkling walls and a funky bar. Read the messages left all over the walls by the greats who have played here, from Art Farmer and Cedar Walton to Christian McBride and Josh Redman. You must buy a *tessera,* good for 3 months, the first time you go. Open daily Sept.-June 10pm-1:15am. Shows start at 10:30pm. In the summer Alexanderplatz organizes the **Jazz & Image** festival (tel. 77 20 13 11) in the **Villa Celimontana.** Entrance generally L7000.

Yes Brasil, Via San Francesco a Ripa, 103 (tel. 581 62 67), in Trastevere, off Viale di Trastevere on the left as you come from the river. Foot-stomping live Brazilian music in crowded quarters. A favorite hang-out for young Romans. Drinks L8000-10,000. Open Mon.-Sat. 7:30pm-2am. Music 10pm-midnight.

Big Mama, Vicolo San Francesco a Ripa, 18 (tel. 581 25 51), around the corner from Yes Brasil in Trastevere. Excellent jazz and blues for the diehard fan. Weekend cover (L20,000) makes it more of a commitment; weeknights are just as fun, although less crowded. Open Oct.-June daily 9pm-1:30am (sporadically closed Sun. and Mon.).

DISCOS AND DANCING

The popular club scene changes as quickly as Roman phone numbers—check under "Dolci Notti" in *Trovaroma,* listing a day-by-day, play-by-play account of discos and happy hours. Many clubs are in the area near the notoriously unsafe Olympic Village, so think twice before going alone. The bigger clubs survive Rome's steaming summer by closing up shop and bounding beachward to **Fregene, Ostia,** or **San Felice Circeo.** Call before you head out.

The Groove, Vicolo Savelli, 10 (tel. 68 72 427). Take your 2nd left as you walk down Via del Governo Vecchio from P. Pasquino. Look for the black door and the small, probably unlit, neon sign. This cozy joint serves up some of the grooviest dance music in Rome. Sip drinks (L10,000) at the bar, then boogie down to acid jazz, funk, soul, and disco downstairs. Best of all: no cover. Open Tues.-Sun. 10pm-2am and later. Closed most of Aug.

Gilda, Via Mario de Fiori, 97 (tel. 67 84 838 or 66 56 06 49), near the Spanish Steps. Gilda becomes **Gilda on the Beach,** Lungomare di Ponte, 11, in the summer. It remains an exhilarating, hip disco in Fregene, a beach that hosts its share of hedonistic Roman commuters. Open Tues.-Sun. 11pm-4am. Admission L40,000. Step aerobics and beach volleyball classes also offered during the week.

RadioLondra, Via di Monte Testaccio, 67. Not exclusively gay, but popular with "family." The disco is small, in a cave-like bomb shelter where the music thumps; a patio provides an escape from close quarters. On weekends, the L15,000 cover includes a 1st drink. Mixed drinks L15,000. Beer from the tap L6000-8000. Upstairs is a pizzeria/pub where Italian cover bands play periodically. Pizza L7000-10,000. Club open Wed.-Mon. 11:30pm-4am. Pub/pizzeria open Wed.-Fri. and Sun.-Mon. 9pm-3am, Sat. 9pm-4am.

Gay and Lesbian Clubs

Travelers can pick up a *Pianta Gay di Roma* at any bar or disco for a detailed map with complete listings of cruising spots, bars, and baths in Rome. The gay magazine *Babilonia, La Repubblica*'s *TrovaRoma,* and *Adam* offer more information.

L'Alibi, Via Monte di Testaccio, 40-44 (tel. 574 34 48), in the Testaccio district (Piramide Metro stop). Large and elegant, the rooms spread over 3 levels, including an expansive, beautiful rooftop terrace. *The* gay club in Rome, especially in summer. Clientele mostly men and a few women. Night buses #20N and 30N pass nearby Piramide all night long, about every hr. and 30min. respectively. Open Tues.-Sun. 11pm-4am. L15,000 cover includes first drink. Thurs. free.

Hangar, Via in Selci, 69 (tel. 488 13 97; fax 68 30 90 81). Centrally located (off Via Cavour where it bends near the Colosseum; take Metro B to Cavour, or any bus down Via Cavour from Termini or up from the Colosseum). Friendly John from Philadelphia runs this small bar, once the residence of Messalina, the wife of Nero. Usually packed wall to wall with men. Cool, neon blue, and laid back. Women are certainly welcome (except on Mon., which is dirty movie night) but might feel out-of-place. Music videos, modern lighting, and a cheery crowd. Located on a well-lit street. Membership is free, and the drinks are some of the cheapest in Rome. Open Wed.-Mon. 10:30pm-2am. Closed 3 weeks in Aug.

Joli Coeur, Via Sirte, 5 (tel. 839 35 23), off Viale Eritrea. Rome's primary lesbian bar is a little out of the city center, east of Villa Ada. Kind of a seedy neighborhood; go with a friend and split the cab fare. L15,000 mandatory first drink. Open Sat.-Sun. 10:30pm-2am.

Angelo Azzuro, Via Cardinal Merry del Val, 13 (tel. 580 04 72), off Viale di Trastevere in Trastevere. Subterranean bar with a crowded dance floor and *gelato.* Black lights highlight a vast collection of bizarre statuettes, nouveau art, mirrors, and plenty of dance space. Friday is women only. The crowds arrive very late. Cover: Fri. and Sun. L10,000, Sat. L20,000. Open Fri.-Sun. 11pm-4am.

CENTRI SOCIALI

Centri Sociali, literally "social centers," are the latest entertainment craze in Rome among alternative youth. Originally squatter settlements, they're now slightly more established, featuring live music and organizing film festivals and exhibits. You pay what you can; there's usually a minimum suggested donation. They generally move from abandoned building to abandoned building, but there always seem to be some in Testaccio, especially along the river near the old slaughterhouses. *Roma C'è* usually contains a list of *centri sociali* locations and events, and you'll find advertisements for centers throughout the city.

Villagio Globale (ex Mattatoio), Lungotevere Testaccio. Take bus #27 from Termini, get off just before it crosses the river, and head left down the river. After midnight take night bus 20N/21N from Piramide back to Termini. One of the best known *centri sociali* in Rome. Closed late July to mid-September.

Ex Snia Viscosa, Via Prenestina, 173. Take bus #15 or 81 from the Colosseum or bus #14 from Termini. Theater, live music, and dance classes.

OPERA, BALLET, AND THEATER

During the regular season (Sept.-June), look for opera and the **Rome Opera Ballet** at the **Teatro dell'Opera** in P. Beniamino Gigli (tel. 481 70 03 for tickets and info). The Villa Borghese hosts summer opera and ballet performances. Look for the summer **Operafestival di Roma** (tel. 569 14 93) and occasional performances during the year at the Teatro Valle, the Teatro Manzoni, and the Loggia della Villa Medici. In the summer, there is also a festival of dance, art, and culture called **Romaeuropa** with venues throughout the city. Call 474 23 19 or 474 22 86 for information, or pick up a program at the **Museo degli Strumenti Musicali** in P. S. Croce in Gerusalemme, one of the performance locations. For **theater** listings check with the tourist office or call the information number at **Teatro Ghione,** Via delle Fornaci, 37 (tel. 637 22 94), a venue for both music and theater performances. **Teatro Sistina,** Via Sistina, 129 (tel. 482 68 41), features musicals and plays from September to May.

MUSIC

The **Accademia Nazionale di Santa Cecilia** (tel. 361 10 72) performs symphonies and chamber music in its auditorium at Via di Conciliazione, 4 (the street leading up to the Vatican). Tickets are L15,000-45,000. In summer, the company moves outdoors to the *nymphaeum* in the **Villa Giulia** (tel. 361 28 73 or 679 36 17), P. della Villa Giulia, 9. Buy tickets at Villa Giulia or from the Agenzia Tartaglia in P. di Spagna, 12 (678 45 83). The Teatro Ghione (tel. 637 22 94) hosts **Euromusica,** featuring classical concerts Oct.-April with renowned international performers (tickets L15,000-25,000). Also in winter, the **Amici di Castel Sant'Angelo** (tel. 845 61 92) liven up Hadrian's Mausoleum with concerts Saturday nights at 9pm. The **Theater of Marcellus,** on Via del Teatro di Marcello, 44, near Piazza Venezia, is home to the **Concerti del Tempietto,** a series of nightly performances from mid-June to early October. Concerts start at 9pm; tickets are L26,000. **Bramante's cloister** in the church of Santa Maria della Pace, Via Arco della Pace, 5, hosts a number of different concert series, including that of the **International Chamber Ensemble** (tel. 86 80 01 25) in July and **Mille e Una Notti** in August, organized by **L'Ippocampo** (tel. 686 84 41).

In the summer, the city's pop and rock music scene grows out of control with outdoor concerts that last all night long. The **Live Link** festival (tel. 841 90 50 or 841 91 71) at the Foro Italico hosts headliners every night from late June to late July. Head out to **Testaccio Village** on Via di Monte Testaccio, 16, for live music of all kinds from mid-June to mid-September every night starting at 9pm. **Roma Incontra il Mondo** (tel. 418 03 70), a festival of world music and *"musica etnica,"* runs from late June to early September with concerts starting at 6pm.

CINEMA

First-run cinemas in Rome tend to charge about L12,000 and, though the movies are often American, they're generally dubbed into Italian. *Cineclubs* show the best and most recent foreign films, old goodies, and an assortment of favorites in the original language. Look for posters, programs, and check out *Roma C'è*. A "v.o." or "l.o." next to any listing means *versione originale* or *lingua originale* (not dubbed).

Cinema Pasquino, Vicolo del Piede, 19A (tel. 580 36 22), off P. S. Maria in Trastevere. Rome's only exclusively English-language movie theater. Program changes daily, so call for the schedule or stop by and pick one up. L7000.

Augustus, Corso Vittorio Emanuele II, 203 (tel. 687 54 55). Films in "l.o." Tuesday.

Lead-On, Via delle Montagne Rocciose, 62 (tel. 591 55 21), in EUR. Original language movies Fridays at 5pm. Free, but make reservations.

Vatican City

Occupying 108½ independent acres within Rome, Vatican City is the center of the Catholic Church, once a mighty wheeling and dealing European power. As organized by the Lateran Treaty of 1929, the pope exercises all legislative, judicial, and executive powers over his tiny theocracy, but must remain neutral in Italian national politics and Roman municipal administration. As spiritual leader for hundreds of millions of Catholics around the world, however, the pope extends his influence far beyond the walls of his city. The nation preserves its independence, minting its own coins (in Italian *lire* but with the pope's face), running an autonomous postal system, and maintaining its army of Swiss Guards, who continue to wear the flamboyant uniforms designed by Michelangelo.

Located on the west bank of the Tiber, Vatican City can be reached from Rome's center on Metro Linea A to Ottaviano or by buses #64 or 492 from Termini, bus #62 from P. Barberini, #19 from San Lorenzo, or #23 from Testaccio. A bus connects St. Peter's to the Vatican museums (L2000; buy a ticket on the bus), but the walk is less than ten minutes. The country has a train station for official use only.

ORIENTATION AND PRACTICAL INFORMATION

Pilgrim Tourist Information Office, P. San Pietro (tel. 69 88 44 66 or 69 88 48 66; fax 69 88 51 00), to the left as you face the basilica. Ask for the sheet of "Useful Information." Excellent English spoken. Book tours of the otherwise inaccessible **Vatican Gardens.** (2hr., Mon.-Sat. at 10am, except Wed. when the Pope's in town. L18,000 per person. Gardens open Mon.-Sat. 8:30am-7pm.)

Vatican Post Offices at St. Peter's. One beside the tourist office and one on the opposite side of the *piazza*. Service from Vatican City is rumored to be more reliable than from its Italian counterpart. Open Mon.-Fri. 8:30am-7pm, Sat. 8:30am-6pm. Branch office on the 2nd floor of the Vatican Museum. No *fermo posta*. Send packages of up to 2kg and 90cm. Mail rates are the same as Italian rates.

Papal audiences are held on Wednesdays, usually at 10:30am. To attend one, write to the Prefettura della Casa Pontificia, 00120 Città del Vaticano, specifying the number of people who wish to attend, the desired date, and alternate dates. Otherwise, stop by on a Monday or Tuesday to pick up tickets for that week. The office is beyond the bronze doors to the right of the basilica, past the Swiss guards. (Open Mon.-Wed. 9am-1pm. Tickets are free.) Audiences are held in the Audience Hall behind the colonnade to the left of the basilica. During an audience, delegates from various countries give readings in their respective languages, and the Pope delivers a message in various languages, greets groups of pilgrims by name and country, and gives his blessing to the several thousand people present. Seating is limited, so arrive early. **Dress appropriately and conservatively.**

SIGHTS

The pontiff's incomparable collection of painting, sculpture, architecture, decorative arts, tapestries, books, carriages, and cultural artifacts from around the globe merits enormous amounts of your time and energy.

St. Peter's Basilica

Appropriate dress is always required and monitored in the basilica. Cover your knees and shoulders. No shorts, miniskirts, sleeveless shirts, or skimpy sundresses are allowed, but jeans and t-shirts are fine for both men and women.

As you enter the Piazza San Pietro, Bernini's colonnade draws you toward the church in a sweeping embrace. Mussolini's broad Via della Conciliazione, built in the 1930s to connect the Vatican with the rest of the city, opened up a wider view of St. Peter's than Bernini intended. The obelisk in the center is framed by two fountains; round porphyry disks set in the pavement between each fountain and the obelisk mark the spots where you should stand so that the quadruple rows of Bernini's colonnades visually resolve into one perfectly aligned row. One hundred and forty statues perch above on the colonnade; those on the basilica represent Christ (at center), John the Baptist, and the Apostles (except for Peter). The pope opens the **Porta Sancta** (Holy Door), the last door on the right side of the entrance porch, every 25 years by knocking in the bricks with a silver hammer. (The next opening will be in 2000.)

The basilica itself rests on the reputed site of St. Peter's tomb. A Christian structure of some kind has stood here since the Emperor Constantine made Christianity the state religion in the 4th century. The overwhelming interior of St. Peter's measures 186 by 137 meters along the transepts. Metal lines on the marble floor mark the puny-by-comparison lengths of other major world churches. To the right, Michelangelo's **Pietà** has been protected by bullet-proof glass since 1972, when an axe-wielding fiend attacked it, smashing Christ's nose and breaking Mary's hand.

The crossing under the dome is anchored by four niches filled with statues of saints; Bernini's **St. Longinus** is at the northeast. In the center of the crossing, Bernini's bronze **baldacchino** rises on spiral columns over the pope's marble altar. Note the many bronze bees on the canopy; the bee was the symbol of the Barberini family, of which Bernini's patron Urban VIII was a member. In the apse is Bernini's **Cathedra Petri,** a convoluted Baroque reliquary housing St. Peter's original throne in a riot of bronze and gold.

Below the statue of St. Longinus, steps lead down to the **Vatican Grottoes,** the final resting place of innumerable popes and saints. The passages are lined with tombs both ancient and modern. The exit from the grottoes is by the entrance to the cupola. You can take an elevator to the walkway around the interior of the dome or ascend 350 stairs to the outdoor top ledge of the cupola. From here there's an excellent view of the basilica's roof, the *piazza,* the Vatican Gardens, and the hazy Roman skyline. (Open April-Sept. 7am-6pm; Oct.-March 7am-7pm. Free. Dome closes 1hr. earlier and may be closed when the pope is in the basilica on Wed. morning. Admission to dome on foot L5000, by elevator (part of the way) L6000.)

On the left side of the *piazza,* through a gate protected by Swiss Guards, stairs descend to the **necropolis,** one level below the grottoes. A double row of mausolea dating from the first century AD lies here. Multilingual tours of **St. Peter's tomb** cost L10,000 per person for small groups with reservations. Apply a few days in advance to the *Ufficio Scavi* (excavation office) beneath the Arco della Campana to the left of the basilica (tel. 69 88 53 18; open Mon.-Sat. 9am-5pm). You can also request an application before your arrival in Rome from the Delegate of the Fabbrica di San Pietro, Excavations Office, 00120 Vatican City.

Vatican Museums

A 10-min. walk around the Vatican City walls brings you to the **Vatican Museums** (tel. 698 33 33). The major galleries are open Mon.-Sat. 8:45am-1pm. During Easter week and the months of April, May, September, and October, the museums are open Mon.-Fri. 8:45am-4pm, Sat. 8:45am-1pm. Last entrance is 45min. before closing. The museums are closed on major religious holidays, but on the last Sunday of each month they're open 8:45am-1pm and **free.** Otherwise admission is L15,000, students under 26 with an ISIC card L10,000, children under one meter tall free.

The Vatican Museums constitute one of the world's great collections of art, a vast storehouse of ancient, Renaissance, and modern statuary, painting, decorative arts, and sundry papal odds and ends. The galleries stretch over some four miles of the old papal palace and are stuffed with many more treasures than you could possibly see in one day. If you've only got a morning, plan your tour before you go—simply wandering will leave you more frustrated and exhausted than enlightened. The best known and most noteworthy attractions in the collection are the **Pio-Clementino Museum** with its celebrated masterpieces of ancient sculpture, the brilliantly frescoed **Borgia Apartments,** the **Raphael Stanze,** Michelangelo's incomparable **Sistine Chapel,** and the eclectic **Pinacoteca** (picture gallery). Collections off the main path include specialized galleries of Egyptian, Etruscan, Greek, and Roman art, the exhibition rooms of the **Vatican Library,** and the intermittently open **Historical Museum** with papal relics and carriages. The collections of tapestries, maps, and modern religious art are housed in long corridors leading to the Sistine Chapel.

The remaining galleries function as a conduit, taking visitors from the entrance by the Belvedere Courtyard down to the papal apartments and the Sistine Chapel and back again. The museum management has laid out four color-coded tours and tries to make visitors follow one. Tour A hits only the barest essentials, making a swift trip to the Sistine Chapel and back, while tour D hits absolutely *everything.* Tour B leads to a few more rooms, while Tour C takes clock-conscious art buffs to the magnificent Roman sculptures and Raphael rooms that A and B bypass. Once you have passed a room or gallery, it's difficult to retrace your steps.

The museum entrance at Viale Vaticano leads to a strange bronze double-helix ramp that climbs to the ticket office, where there is also a money exchange, a first aid station, and a booth selling guidebooks (L12,000) that are well worth the price. A good place to start your tour is the stellar **Pio-Clementino Museum,** the world's greatest collection of antique sculpture. Among other gems, it features the **Apollo Belvedere** and the tortured **Laocoön** group. There's also an entire room of marble animals, ranging from slobbering hounds to green porphyry crustaceans. The last room of the gallery contains the enormous red **sarcophagus of Sant'Elena,** mother of Constantine. Statues of Egyptian demigods hold up the ceiling.

From here, the Simonetti Stairway climbs to the **Etruscan Museum,** filled with artifacts from Tuscany and northern Lazio. Back on the landing of the Simonetti Staircase is the often-closed **Room of the Biga** (an ancient marble chariot) and the entrance to the **Gallery of the Candelabra.** The long trudge to the Sistine Chapel begins here, passing through the **Gallery of the Tapestries,** the **Gallery of the Maps,** the **Apartment of Pius V** (where there is a shortcut stair to the Sistine Chapel), the **Sobieski Room,** and the **Room of the Immaculate Conception.** From this room, a door leads into the first of the four **Raphael Rooms,** the sumptuous papal apartments built for Pope Julius II in the 1510s. Raphael painted the astonishing **School of Athens** as a trial piece for Julius, who was so impressed that he fired his other painters, had their frescoes destroyed, and handed the entire suite of rooms over to Raphael. The **Stanza della Segnatura** features the *School of Athens* (under restoration), considered to be Raphael's masterpiece. Depending on your itinerary, a staircase leads down to the Borgia Apartments and the horrid Museum of Modern Religious Art or more directly to the Sistine Chapel.

In Your Face

Michelangelo, for all his divine accomplishments, was all too human. In the *Last Judgement* the artist's ego manifests itself in a self-portrait, Michelangelo's own face painted on the flayed skin of St. Bartholomew (held by Galileo to the left of Christ). And when Biagio da Cesena, Master of Ceremonies to Paul III, objected to the nudity in Michelangelo's fresco, the artist was not content to tell him to go to Hell—he put him there. In immortal condemnation, Michelangelo painted Biagio's face, with an ass's ears, onto the body of the Dantean demon Minos.

The Sistine Chapel

Ever since its completion in the 16th century, the Sistine Chapel (named after its founder, Pope Sixtus IV) has served as the chamber in which the College of Cardinals meets to elect a new pope. The ceiling, which is actually flat but appears vaulted, gleams with the results of its recent restoration. The frescoes on the side walls predate Michelangelo's ceiling; on the right, scenes from the life of Moses prefigure parallel scenes of the life of Christ on the left. The cycle, frescoed between 1481 and 1483, was completed under the direction of Perugino by a team of artists that included Botticelli, Ghirlandaio, Roselli, Pinturicchio, Signorelli, and della Gatta.

The simple compositions and vibrant colors of Michelangelo's unquestioned masterpiece hover above, each section depicting a story from Genesis. The scenes are framed by the famous *ignudi*, young nude males. Monumental figures of Old Testament prophets and classical sibyls, some pondering future Christian events and others holding books of revealed wisdom, surround spandrels depicting Bible stories. The altar wall, covered by Michelangelo's *The Last Judgement,* was revealed in 1994 after a lengthy restoration. The figure of Christ as Judge hovers in the upper center, surrounded by Mary and his saintly entourage.

The Pinacoteca

Although the Sistine Chapel is a tough act to follow, the **Pinacoteca** holds one of the best painting collections in Rome, including Filippo Lippi's *Coronation of the Virgin,* Perugino's *Madonna and Child,* Titian's *Madonna of San Nicoletta dei Frari,* and Raphael's *Transfiguration.* On your way to the Pinacoteca from the Sistine Chapel, take a look at the **Room of the Aldobrandini Marriage,** which contains a series of rare and famous ancient Roman frescoes.

NEAR VATICAN CITY: CASTEL SANT'ANGELO

A short walk down Via d. Conciliazione from St. Peter's stands the hulking mass of brick and stone known as **Castel Sant'Angelo.** Built by the Emperor Hadrian (AD117-138) as a mausoleum for himself and his family, the edifice has served the popes as a fortress, prison, and palace. When the city was wracked with plague in 590, Pope Gregory the Great saw an angel sheathing his sword at the top of the complex; the plague abated soon after, and the edifice was rededicated to the angel. The intriguing fortress now contains a museum of arms and artillery and offers an incomparable view of Rome and Vatican City. Open daily 9am-7pm; in winter 9am-2pm. Closed the 2nd and 4th Tues. of each month. Admission L8000, EU citizens under 18 or over 60 free. Outside, the marble **Ponte Sant'Angelo,** lined with statues of angels designed by Bernini, leads back across the river. It is the starting point for the traditional pilgrimage route from St. Peter's to San Giovanni in Laterano on the other side of Rome.

DAYTRIPS FROM ROME (LAZIO)

When the frenzy of Rome overwhelms you, head for sanctuary in rural Lazio. The cradle of Roman civilization, this region stretches from the Tyrrhenian coastline to the foothills of the Apennines. North and south of Rome, ancient cities, some predating the Eternal City by centuries, maintain traces of the dynamic cultures of the Romans, Etruscans, Latins, and Sabines.

Tivoli

In Tivoli, water has long been the principal attraction. Ancient Romans including Horace, Catullus, and Maecenas retreated to villas lining the ravine here, where water from the River Aniene cascades down the cliffs. You can get to Tivoli by taking the Metro Linea B to its last stop at Rebibbia (L1500) and then catching a COTRAL **bus** which climbs to Tivoli (every 30min., L3000). Get off at the Largo Garibaldi, a grassy lookout with bursting fountains. In a nearby shack is the **tourist office** (tel. (0774) 31 12 99 or 33 45 22; fax 33 12 94), where the staff provides loads of historical information, maps with restaurant and hotel locations, and schedules of buses leaving Tivoli. Ask for a copy of the large yellow book entitled *Tivoli Down the Ages* to learn about countless Tiburtine sights. Open Mon.-Sat. 9:25am-3pm.

From Largo Garibaldi, walk down to Piazza Trento to find the entrance to the **Villa d'Este,** replete with spectacular terraces, gardens, and fountains. The **Viale delle Cento Fontane** runs the width of the garden. On one end of it is the **Rometta** (Little Rome), a series of fountains representing Rome and the Tiber. At the other end, the **Fontana dell'Ovato** spurts one great sheet of water 15 feet into the air. Hidden to the right of the fountain is a **papyrus museum** with a paper-making laboratory and book relics. Walk down the semicircular steps from the center of the Viale delle Cento Fontane to reach the cypress and orange groves. Nearby lurks the **Fontana della Civetta e degli Uccelli,** a waterwork said to emit bird chirps. Don't miss the **Fontana della Natura** with its colossal statue of Diana of Ephesus. Villa open May-Aug. 9am-6:45pm; Sept.-April 9am-1hr. before sunset. Admission L8000, EU citizens under 18 and over 60 free.

Follow Via di Sibilla across town to two Roman temples, the **Temple of Vesta** and the **Temple of the Sibyl,** each overlooking the waterfalls. Back down Via di Sibilla and through Piazza Rivarola, take Ponte Garibaldi to the entrance of the **Villa Gregoriana**—a park with paths descending through scattered ancient ruins to a series of lookouts over the cascades. From the opening of Gregory XVI's tunnel, the river plunges 110m down in the startling **Great Cascade.** Villa open May-Aug. 10am-7:30pm; Sept. 9:30am-6:30pm; Oct.-March 9:30am-4:30pm; April 9:30-6pm. Admission L2500, under 12 L1000.

From the Great Cascade, it's a short trip to the intriguing remains of the **Villa Adriana** (Hadrian's Villa). Either return to Largo Garibaldi and take the orange #4 bus (L1250 from the news kiosk; the #4/ bus does not go the villa), or take the COTRAL bus headed for Giudonia from Largo S. Angelo (every hr., 10min., L1500). The villa is the largest and costliest ever built in the Roman Empire. Emperor Hadrian designed its buildings in the 2nd century in the styles of monuments he had seen in his travels. The entrance gate leads to the **Pecile,** built to recall the famous *Stoa Poikile* (Painted Porch) of Athens. At the northeast corner of the Pecile, Philosopher's Hall leads to the **Maritime Theater,** Hadrian's private study and bedroom, protected by its own moat. The rest of the **Imperial Palace** sprawls nearby in well-labeled enclaves. South of the Pecile, beyond the main buildings, you'll find the **Canopus,** a murky expanse of water which replicates a canal near Alexandria, Egypt (hence the crocodile). The **Serapeum,** a semicircular dining hall, anchors the far end of the canal. Villa open May-Aug. 9am-7:30pm; Sept.-April 9am-dusk. Last entrance 1hr. before closing. Admission L8000.

Subiaco

From Tivoli you can trace the Aniene River through its stunning, untouched valley to the rocky town of **Subiaco.** As the road climbs inland, the sheer, forested crags of the Monti Simbruni rise above lush pastures and scattered vineyards. Subiaco is best

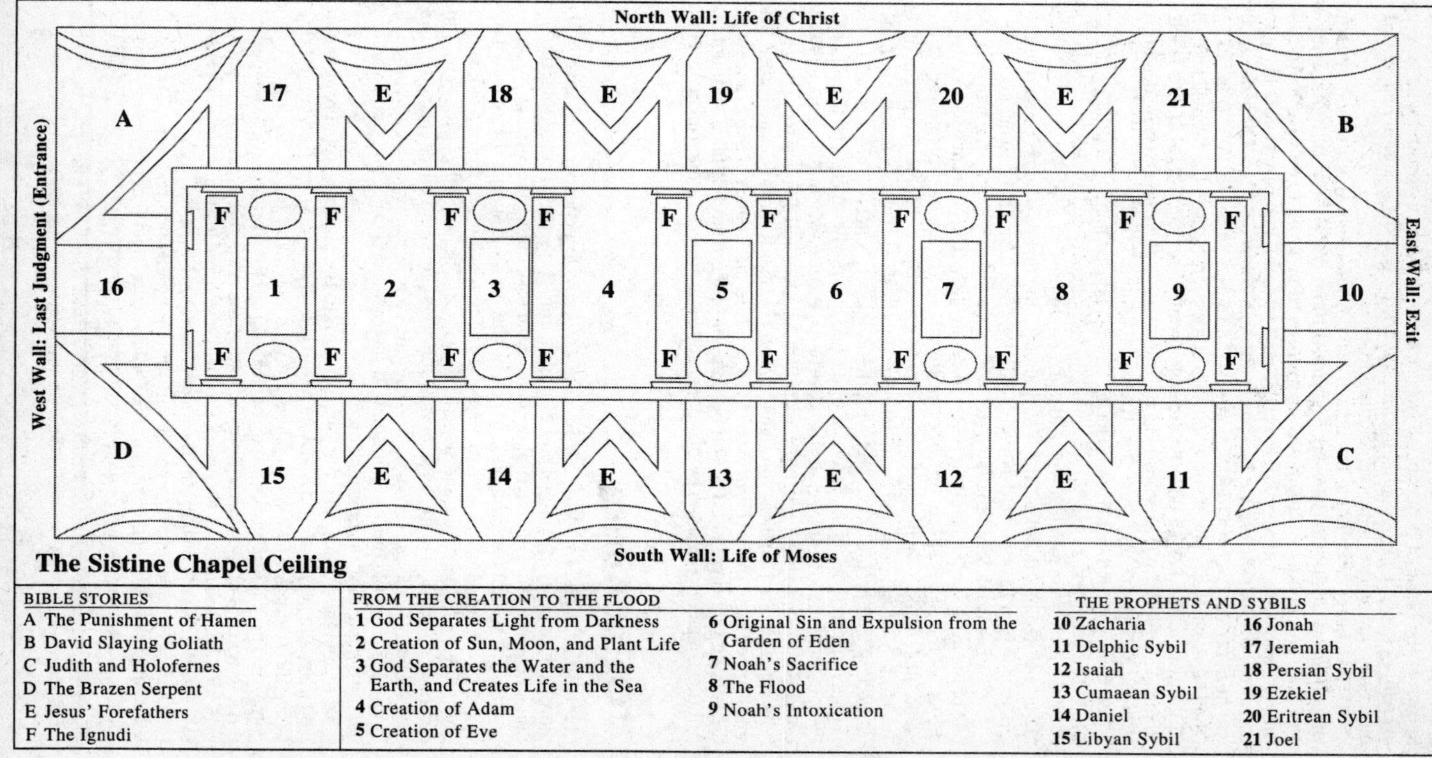

The Sistine Chapel Ceiling

BIBLE STORIES
A The Punishment of Hamen
B David Slaying Goliath
C Judith and Holofernes
D The Brazen Serpent
E Jesus' Forefathers
F The Ignudi

FROM THE CREATION TO THE FLOOD
1 God Separates Light from Darkness
2 Creation of Sun, Moon, and Plant Life
3 God Separates the Water and the Earth, and Creates Life in the Sea
4 Creation of Adam
5 Creation of Eve
6 Original Sin and Expulsion from the Garden of Eden
7 Noah's Sacrifice
8 The Flood
9 Noah's Intoxication

THE PROPHETS AND SYBILS
10 Zacharia
11 Delphic Sybil
12 Isaiah
13 Cumaean Sybil
14 Daniel
15 Libyan Sybil
16 Jonah
17 Jeremiah
18 Persian Sybil
19 Ezekiel
20 Eritrean Sybil
21 Joel

known as the home of Benedetto di Norcia, a rich 6th-century wastrel who gave up everything to live a life of contemplation. After three years of seclusion he founded a monastery, giving rise to the Benedictine Order.

COTRAL **buses** from Rome to Subiaco leave from Rebibbia at the end of Metro Linea B (every 20-50 min. Mon.-Fri. 5:50am-10:10pm, Sat. 6:20am-10:10pm; every 1-3hr. Sun. and holidays 7:10am-9:40pm). Buses from Tivoli to Subiaco leave from Largo Massimo (about every hr., except from 2:30-4pm). Purchase your ticket at the *capolinea* (L4900). Before the bus passes through Subiaco's **Arco Trionfale,** get off and head up Via Cadorna to #59, home of the **tourist office** (tel. (0774) 82 20 13). Open Mon.-Sat. 8am-2pm. If you don't stop at the tourist office, the bus will take you all the way to the **Piazza della Resistenza.** From there, catch the TRL bus labeled "Jenne/Vallepietra" which stops near the entrances to the **monasteries** (departures Mon.-Sat. 6, 10am, 2, and 7pm, Sun. 10am and 3:30pm; L1000).

The **Convento di Santa Scolastica** (tel. 855 25) housed Italy's first printing press in 1465. The complex, a huge architectural hodgepodge, encompasses three different cloisters, each built around a well and a garden. In the first, look for the words "Ave Maria" planted in artichokes. The library shelters the first two books printed in Italy. Open daily 9am-12:30pm and 4-7pm. Monks lead free tours every 30min.

The **Convento di San Benedetto** (tel. 850 39), another 500m up the hill, occupies one of the most spectacular hilltop sites in central Italy. The convent was founded on the site of the **Sacro Speco,** the rocky grotto where St. Benedict spent three years of penitential solitude. Each generation of monks carved new chapels directly out of the limestone rock and plastered them with precious frescoes. The *loggia* at the entrance to the upper church is decorated with the monastery's newest art, a series of late 15th-century frescoes of the Madonna and Child and the Evangelists by the school of Perugino. On the lowest level sits the **Grotto dei Pastori,** where Benedict taught the catechism to local shepherds. Open daily 9am-12:30pm and 3-6pm. Free.

As you leave Subiaco, head through the Arco Trionfale to Corso Cesare Battisti. The small stone **Ponte di San Francesco** (1358) leads to the **Church of San Francesco** at the summit of a small hill. The somber interior of the church is filled with notable paintings, including frescoes by Il Sodoma and an altarpiece of the nativity by Pinturicchio.

Ostia Antica

The remains of ancient Ostia (tel. 56 35 80 99) provide a cheaper alternative to the more famous ruins of Pompeii and Herculaneum. The settlement at Ostia, the first Roman colony, was a commercial port and naval base during the 3rd and 2nd centuries BC. The warehouses, shipping offices, hotels, bars, and shrines that remain testify to the port's once-thriving activity. Ostia's fortunes declined as Rome's did, and the port fell into disuse during the siege of the Goths. The silty Tiber later moved the coastline a mile or so to the west. Fortunately, though, a mud cover enabled remarkable archaeological preservation, and the brick site was stripped far less than the monumental marble precincts of Rome. Walking through Ostia, you can easily imagine the din and flow of ancient city life.

To reach Ostia Antica, take the Metro Linea B to the Magliana stop, change to the Lido train, and get off at the Ostia Antica stop (you'll need another ticket for this leg). Cross the overpass, take a left when the road ends, and follow the signs to the entrance. The **Via Ostiensis** leads through a **necropolis** of brick and marble tombs to the low remains of the **Porta Romana,** one of the city's three gates. The road then becomes the **Decumanus Maximus,** the main street, and leads into the city center. A few hundred yards inside, the **Baths of Neptune** rise on the right, paved with a mosaic of Neptune and his chariot surrounded by marine creatures. Via dei Vigili leads off to the right of the baths to the **Caserma dei Vigili** (Firemen's Barracks). Off the Decumanus on the left of the Baths of Neptune, the well-preserved **Via della Fontana** leads back to a **Fullonica,** or ancient laundry shop.

The much-restored **Theater** rises on the right. Beyond the theater lies the expansive **Piazzale delle Corporazioni** (Forum of the Corporations), which held offices of importers and shipping agents from all over the Roman world. The sidewalk is lined with mosaic inscriptions proclaiming their businesses. In the center of the *piazza* are the remains of a **Temple of Ceres,** the goddess of grain. Several dozen meters from the Piazzale delle Corporazioni, on the theater side of the Decumanus, Via dei Molini leads to the **Casa di Diana,** the best preserved Roman house at Ostia, and among the most complete in the world. Behind the House of Diana is a **museum** where a diverse collection of artifacts is displayed. Open daily 9:30am-1:30pm. Entrance to museum included in admission to site.

Back on the Decumanus, past the House of Diana, the street opens onto the **Forum of Ostia,** anchored by the imposing **Temple to Jupiter, Juno, and Minerva,** or **Capitolium.** Climb to the top for an excellent panoramic view of town. Across from the forum a street leads to a **public latrine** (on the first left), and the vast **Terme del Foro** (Forum Baths). The Via del Tempio Rotondo runs parallel to the Decumanus and passes the 3rd-century **Round Temple,** a miniature Pantheon dedicated to the cult of all emperors. At the fork in the Decumanus, the **Via della Foce** leads right to the sumptuous **House of Cupid and Psyche** (on the right), where a statue of two lovers (now in the museum) was found. The house, amazingly intact and paneled in elaborate polychrome marble, was home to one of Ostia's wealthier merchants. Farther down the street, a staircase descends to an eerie subterranean **Mithraeum,** from which a maze of sewers and cisterns spreads beneath the city.

Across the Via della Foce is the two-story **Casa di Serapide.** This house opens into the **Baths of the Seven Wise Men,** named for a fresco cycle found in one of the rooms. The circular mosaic hall was once heated by a system of hot air ducts and served as an exercise area for the bath. Take a left down Via degli Aurighi to reach the **Porta Marina.** Beyond it, on Via Severiana near the ancient river bank, the entrance to the **Synagogue** is marked by two steps leading into a vestibule.

The site is open daily in summer 9am-7pm; in winter 9am-5pm. Admission L8000. The Bureau of Archaeological Digs (tel. 565 00 22) offers free tours in Italian at the excavations (July-Oct. every Sun. morning). Look for the schedule in the Sunday edition of Rome's *Il Messaggero.*

Frascati

Frascati's lofty position on an ancient volcanic ridge, 20 minutes from Rome, has attracted fugitives from the summer heat for centuries—Frascati's sumptuous patrician villas remain one of the town's finest attractions. The rich slopes outside the town also nurture acres of vineyards where Frascati wine was born; a visit to the town is incomplete without a taste or two of the local vintage.

The **AAST tourist office,** in Piazza Marconi, 1 (tel. 442 03 31), near the **bus depot,** brims with maps and information on the area's villas. Open summer Mon.-Fri. 8am-2pm and 4-7:20pm, Sat. 8am-2pm; winter Mon.-Fri. 8am-2pm and 3:30-6:40pm. Ask the office for a free pass to the gardens of the opulent **Villa Aldobrandini,** whose striking Renaissance façade, designed by Giacomo della Porta in 1598, dominates the hill over the center of town. Behind the majestic villa, fantastical marble creatures frolic in elaborate carved niches of a garden full of gnarled oak trees. Gardens open summer Mon.-Fri. 9am-1pm and 3:30-6pm; winter, 9am-1pm only.

About 1km uphill on Guglielmo Massaia (beyond Villa Aldobrandini) is the **Chiesa dei Cappuccini** (Capuchin Church and Convent) which houses the unique **Ethiopian Museum** (tel. 942 04 00; open daily 9am-noon and 3-6pm; closed during church ceremonies; call for times), an array of weapons, handmade crafts, and personal belongings collected in Africa over 35 years by the bishop who founded the museum. The gardens of **Villa Torlonia,** adjacent to Piazza Marconi, are now a picnic-perfect community park. Frascati's other villas lie on the outskirts and are often closed, but many of the gardens host evening concerts and plays. The tourist office can equip you with info.

The 17th-century *duomo,* its rough stone façade mostly reconstructed after extensive war damage, stands in P. San Pietro. The winding streets around the *piazza* bustle with restaurants, cafés, and the all-important **wine shops.** Pick up a bottle, then forage for picnic supplies at the **market** at Piazza del Mercato, off Piazza del Duomo. For the sedentary, **Trattoria Sora Irma,** Via SS. Filippo e Giacomo, 12, serves sit-down meals with enormous vats of wine. Open Wed. through Mon., the restaurant perches above the center of Frascati. From Piazza Marconi, take a left up the steps of Via Pietro Campana; Via S.S. Filippo e Giacomo is on your left. Another place to soak up local culture (and wine), **Cantina "Il Pergolato,"** Via del Castello, 20 (tel. 942 04 64), off P. del Mercato, serves homemade wine and rustic food in a cave-like dining room. Open daily 12:30-2:30pm and 3:30-6:30pm.

If you're lucky enough to be in Frascati in October or November, you can't help but get caught up in the fevered dipsomania of the annual **vendemmia,** the celebration of the grape harvest. Vine-dressers line up their vats to receive the juicy fruits of the vineyards, to the slurred serenade of onlookers.

The Pontine Islands

A weekend playground for city-weary Romans, the Pontine Islands are among Lazio's most splendid sights. In ancient times, Nero and Agrippina were exiled to the island of Ventotene; more recently, Mussolini was imprisoned on Ponza. Italians now flock there willingly, filling the stunning archipelago in July and August.

Ponza and **Ventotene** are the only two inhabited islands, and both offer several options for staying over. Anzio, Terracina, and Formia are the main departure points for ferries to the islands. Ferry companies run *aliscafi* (hydrofoils) and slower, less expensive *traghetti* (larger ferries that also transport cars). From Rome, the best option is the train to Anzio (L5000) and then the CAREMAR ferry. **CAREMAR** has offices in Anzio (tel. (06) 983 08 04; fax 984 62 91), Formia (tel. (0771) 227 10), and Ponza (tel. (0771) 80 98 75). **Linee Vetor** only uses *aliscafi* and has offices in Anzio (tel. (06) 984 50 85; fax 984 50 97), Formia (tel. (0771) 70 07 10), Ponza (tel. (0771) 805 49), and Ventotene (tel. (0771) 851 95). **Mazzella** runs cheaper but less frequent ferries from Terracina to Ponza. Its office are in Ponza (tel. (0771) 80 160) and Terracina (tel. (0773) 723 97 98).

Anzio-Ponza: CAREMAR runs ferries daily from Anzio at 8:30am and 2pm, from Ponza at 11:15am and 5pm. Schedule varies Wed. 2½hr., L19,400-20,500. Linee Vetor has 3-5 departures per day June-Sept. 8:30am-5:30pm. 1¼hr., L35,000.

Formia-Ponza: CAREMAR *traghetti* departures at 9am and 4:30pm. Returns at 5:30am and 1:30pm. 2¼hr., L18,900. Linee Vetor runs one hydrofoil daily in each direction in the early afternoon. L35,000.

Formia-Ventotene: CAREMAR departures Fri.-Wed. 8:45am, Thurs. 1pm. Return 5:30pm. 2¼hr., L14,000 each way. If no one is at the information booth at the Ventotene port, inquire at the bar next door. Linee Vetor runs 3 *aliscafi* per day from 8:30am-5:30pm. 1hr., L26,000.

Ponza-Ventotene: Linee Vetor departure at 3pm. CAREMAR *aliscafi* departure at 6:10am. Return 7pm. 30min., L20,000.

PONZA

The Pro Loco **tourist office** (tel. (0771) 800 31) awaits at Piazza Carlo Pisacane, 5, at the far right of the port. Walk up the steps on the long yellow building with arched entrances under the "Ponza Municipio" sign. Open daily July-Aug. 9am-2pm and 4-8pm; Sept.-June 9am-2pm. Three doors to the left, at P. Pisacane, 32, is the **post office.** Open Mon.-Fri. 8:15am-1:30pm, Sat. 8:15am-noon. The **postal code** is 04027. To **exchange money,** try Banco di Napoli, also in P. Pisacane. Open Mon.-Fri. 9:05am-1:05pm. Autolinee Ponzesi **buses** (tel. 804 47) leave from Via Dante. Follow Corso Pisacane until it becomes Via Dante; the bus station will be to your left. Buses depart to Le Forna every 15min. until 1am (L3000 roundtrip). There are no official stops, so you can flag down buses anywhere. In case of **emergencies,** dial 113. The **police** (tel. 801 30) are at Molo Musco; for **first aid** and **medical care,** contact Poliambulatorio (tel. 806 87) at Via Panoramica. The **telephone code** is 0771.

Unfortunately, hotel prices have skyrocketed over the past few years due to increased tourism, and unauthorized **camping** was outlawed years ago. Hotels are spread out across the island and many are atop steep hills; consider a taxi (usually L10,000). **Pensione-Ristorante "Arcobaleno,"** Via Scotti D. Basso, 6 (tel. 803 15), is worth the haul. Go up the ramp, follow the street to the end, then veer right past the Bellavista Hotel. Turn left and follow the signs up, up, up. As you ascend the stairs, you'll curse the writer who sent you here, but when you reach the summit, you'll understand why you came: wonderful proprietors, the best views in Ponza, and excellent food. Half-pension mandatory at L80,000 per person, L90,000 in July and August. Call ahead in summer. **Casa Vitiello,** Via Madonna, 28 (tel. 801 17), is in the historic part of town. Walk up the ramp from P. Pisacane, head left at the top, then right. Follow the signs to La Torre dei Borbini; Casa Vitiello is across the street. The comfortable, tidy rooms have splendid views. L45,000-55,000 per person per night. Two agencies will help you find rooms for longer stays: **Agenzia Immobiliare "Arcipelago Pontino,"** Corso Piscane, 49 (tel. 806 78), and **Agenzia Afari "Magi,"** Via Branchina Nuova, 22 (tel. 80 98 41). They'll locate an *affitta camere* in a private home starting at L50,000-70,000 per person per night in summer, but less in winter.

The Pontine Islands are known for their *zuppa di lenticchie* (lentil soup), fish, and lobster. Several restaurants and bars line the port and spark the island's nightlife. For grocery and fruit stores, take a stroll along Corso Pisacane and Via Dante. One cheap restaurant option is **Pizzeria del Ponte,** Via Dante, 2 (tel. 803 87), next door to the bus station. With pizza at L2000-3000 per slice, you can save up for a boat tour. Open Tues.-Sat. 5am-1am. **Ristorante Lello,** Via Dante, 10 (tel. 803 95), on the other side of the bus station, specializes in regional dishes. *Secondi* L12,000. Open in summer daily 12:30-3pm and 7pm-midnight.

Ponza is full of grottoes and hidden beaches. Explore on foot or rent a boat (L80,000 and up). On Ponza the spectacular beach and surrounding white cliffs at **Chiai di Luna** are a 10-min. walk up Via Panoramica (off Via Roma). The **Piscine Naturali** (natural swimming pools) allow you to admire the whitewashed houses of **Le Forna** while bronzing in the sun. Check **Ponza Mare** on Via Banchina Nuova (tel. 80 679) for boat and scuba rentals and **Scuola Sub "Nautilus"** (tel. 80 87 01) for scuba lessons. There are numerous **scooter rental** companies near the port.

Ask at the port for a guided tour of Ponza's coastlines and the neighboring island **Palmarola** for L45,000 per person. The water is clear and turquoise; the white cliffs are tinted red by iron and yellow by sulphur. As you approach Palmarola, you will see **Dala Brigantina,** a natural amphitheater of limestone. Most trips also motor through the **Pilatus Caves,** where ancient Romans bred fish.

VENTOTENE

Tiny, tranquil Ventotene provides a refuge to rejuvenate your travel-weary bones. The tiny **tourist office** is located right on the port (follow the "i" signs) and is managed by an affable English-speaking staff. **Centro Servizio Ventotene,** Via Pozzo di S. Candida, 13 (tel. (0771) 852 73), will help you find a room in a hotel or an *affitta camere* for L35,000-45,000 per person in high-season. Open March-Nov. daily 9am-1pm and 4:30-7:30pm; only 3 days a week in winter.

The **Albergo Isolabella,** Via Calarossano, 5 (tel. 850 27), will pamper you with large, clean rooms and terrific sunset views. Mandatory half-pension costs L85,000 per person in high-season. To reach the hotel, walk up the ramps from the port to **Piazza Alcide de Gasperi** and the yellow church. Go right, pass Caffè Fredo, take another right, then a left. This road is poorly lit at night. For an elegant meal, try **Ristorante Il Giardino,** Via Olivi, 45(tel. 850 20), which serves a wonderful *zuppa di lenticchie* (lentil soup, L12,000), *fusili con zucchini* (pasta with zucchini, L8000), and a variety of seafood selections.

The somewhat dry **Museo Archeologico** is in P. Castello. Open daily in summer 9:30am-1pm, 6-8pm, and 9:30-midnight; in winter call 85 14 20 and ask Pino to open the museum. Admission L4000. Inquire here about guided tours (in Italian) of the archaeological sites **Villa Giulia** (2½hr., L6000) and **Cisterna Romana di Villa Stefania** (L5000). **Coraggio** on the Porto Romano rents **rowboats** (L10,000 per day), **motorboats** (L50,000 per day), and **scuba diving equipment** (L35,000 per day). Two splendid **beaches,** Cala Rossano and Cala Nave, flank the port.

Etruria

The Etruscans, a tribe whose origins are still shrouded in mystery, dominated northern and central Italy from the 9th through 4th centuries BC. Their tombs, housed in large earth mounds called *tumuli,* are carved out of rock in the shape of houses. Etruscan tomb paintings celebrate life, love, eating, drinking, sport, and the rough countryside. Vandalism has forced the government to close many tombs, and the artifacts that have been excavated now reside in the Villa Giulia and Vatican Museums at Rome and in the national museums in Tarquinia and Cerveteri. Still, the deserted tombs have a quiet appeal quite different from the grandeur of Rome.

CERVETERI

From Rome, take Metro Linea A or bus #70 from Santa Maria Maggiore or Largo Argentina to the Lepanto stop. Blue COTRAL **buses** run to Cerveteri from Via Lepanto (every 30-60min., L4900). The last bus returning to Rome leaves at 8:50pm. Fewer buses run on Sundays. There is a **tourist office** called "Matuna" at Via della Necropoli, 2 (tel. 995 23 04). Open Tues.-Sun. 9:30am-12:30pm and 6-7:30pm. A smaller tourist office called "Caere Viaggi", Piazza Moro, 17 (tel. 994 28 60), sits across the street from the bus stop. Open 9am-1pm, 4:30-7:30pm. From the village, it's another 2km to the necropolis along a tree-lined country road. To get there, follow the signs downhill and then to the right. Go right whenever you see a fork in the road without a sign, but don't follow the Da Paolo Vino sign at the final fork. Bring a flashlight and a picnic lunch with a bottle of Cerveteri's own wine—try the full-bodied red Cerveteri Rossi or the excellent white *nuova caere.*

The bulbous earthen tombs of the **Etruscan necropolis** (tel. 994 00 11) slumber in the carved tufa bedrock. Open May-Sept. Tues.-Sun. 9am-7pm; Oct.-April Tues.-Sat. 9am-4pm, Sun. 11am-4pm. Admission L8000. Don't miss the **Tomb of the Shields and the Chairs,** the smaller **Tomb of the Alcove** (with a carved-out matrimonial bed), and the row-houses where less well-to-do Etruscans rest in peace. Look for the colored stucco reliefs in the spectacular **Tomba dei Rilievi.** The **Museo Nazionale di Cerveteri** (tel. 994 13 54), located in **Ruspoli Castle** in P. Santa Maria Maggiore, displays Etruscan artifacts found in the Caere necropolis in the last 10 years. Open Tues.-Sun. 9am-7pm. Free. If you miss the last bus back to Rome, try the **Albergo El Paso,** Via Settevene Palo, 293 (tel. 994 30 33; fax 995 35 82), 500m from the bottom left side of the main *piazza*. Singles L65,000. Doubles L90,000. Triples L105,000. Breakfast L10,000. Shower included. V, MC, AmEx.

Navigating the Necropolis

Several features of the tombs provide clues about the bodies they contain. *Cippi* (stone markers) signify the gender of individuals inside: some are little houses and others erect rods—guess which one is which. The chambers inside are carved to resemble Etruscan houses, and grave locations are indicators of status. The small chambers in the back were reserved for the most prominent men and women, the central room housed the rest of the family, and small rooms off the antechamber held the remains of slaves and household servants. A triangular headboard on a couch marks a woman's grave; a circular one indicates a man's.

TARQUINIA

When Rome was but a village of mud huts on the Palatine hill, Tarquin kings held this fledgling metropolis under their sway. Although little remains today of the once-thriving Etruscan city, a subterranean **necropolis** of tombs bedecked with vibrant frescoes tells a stirring tale of this splendid culture.

Make Tarquinia a daytrip. The site is a local stop on the Rome-Grosseto **train** line, and buses run from the station (L1000) and beaches (L1300) to the town about every 30min. until 9:50pm. Eleven trains run from Rome-Termini daily, starting at 6:13am; the last train leaves Tarquinia at 10:55pm (1hr., L9800 each way). **Buses** also link the town with Viterbo (1hr., L4900) and Civitavecchia (30min., L3000). For info on southern Etruria (Provincia di Viterbo), try the **AAST tourist office,** P. Matteotti, 14 (tel. 84 21 64), or the tourist info office at P. Cavour, 1 (tel. 85 63 84).

Buses stop at the Barriera San Giusto outside the medieval ramparts. The **tourist office** (tel. 85 63 84) provides bus schedules and a wealth of information. Open Mon.-Sat. 8am-2pm and 4-7pm. In the adjoining P. Cavour stands the majestic **Museo Nazionale** (tel. 85 60 36), one of the most comprehensive collections of Etruscan art outside of Rome. Look for the famous **Winged Horses** upstairs. You can sun yourself and catch great views of the sea from the second-story ramparts. Open Tues.-Sun. 9am-7pm; closes at sunset in winter. A list of independent guides is posted at the entrance. Admission L8000.

The ticket from the museum also admits you to the **necropolis** (tel. 85 63 08). Take the bus marked "Cimitero" from Barriera San Giusto or walk 15min. from the museum. Head up Corso Vittorio Emanuele from P. Cavour and turn right on Via Porta. Then take Via Ripagretta to Via delle Croci, which leads to the tombs. Because of the tombs' sensitivity to air and moisture, only nine may be seen on a given day (and only from behind a metal railing in the doorway). All the tombs are adorned with wild animals, geometric designs, and banquet and sacrifice scenes.

For an inexpensive hotel within the city walls, try **Hotel San Marco,** P. Cavour, 18 (tel. 84 08 13; fax 84 23 06). All rooms in this former monastery come with bath. Singles L65,000. Doubles L100,000. Down the road from the station is **Hotel All'Oliva,** Via Palmiro Togliatti, 15 (tel. 85 73 18; fax 84 07 77), boasting bright rooms with baths, TVs, and embroidered pillows. Singles L60,000. Doubles L90,000. Breakfast included. **Hotel Aurelia,** Via A. Santi, 28 (tel./fax 85 60 62), offers rooms with rustic walls, earth-tone furnishings, and baths. Singles L60,000. Doubles L80,000.

CENTRAL ITALY

Abruzzo and Molise

Only about three hours by train from Rome, but a long stretch from the frenzy of tourism, the highlands of Abruzzo offer the traveler a tranquil retreat. The well-preserved medieval towns of L'Aquila and Sulmona are surrounded by easily accessible natural areas. To the south of Sulmona is the **Abruzzo National Park** in all its natural beauty: wild animals, hidden mountain lakes, and spectacular vistas of uninterrupted wilderness. To the north of L'Aquila looms the *Gran Sasso d'Italia* (Big Rock of Italy), the highest peak of the Apennines. In summer its ridges attract climbers and hikers, while in winter three ski resorts operate on the mountain. Unfortunately, the coastal region lacks the old-world charm and the natural beauty of the mountain cities. Pescara and the surrounding coast are a jumble of *pizzerie,* discos, and beach blankets, completely alien to the rugged interior highland. Music lovers looking for a little regional sustenance shouldn't miss *maccheroni alla chitarra* (guitar macaroni), pasta squeezed through parallel wires resembling guitar strings. *Zafferano* (saffron), the famous spice used to "gild" rice, is exported from Abruzzo.

Molise is the nation's second smallest region and has few cities of interest to tourists. Nevertheless, its mountainous areas abutting the Abruzzo National Park offer more unspoiled wilderness, where roaming bears, wolves, and boars try to avoid assimilation into the local cuisine. Also scattered through the region are medieval towns and Roman and Greek ruins. Keep in mind that much of Molise lies beyond the scope of public transportation, so a car is almost essential when traveling here.

In both regions, where train lines are painfully circuitous if they exist at all, the **ARPA** bus service proves quite useful. For information, call their office in Avezzano at (0863) 26 561. Service is sharply reduced on Sundays.

L'Aquila

L'Aquila (The Eagle) seems a fitting name for this vibrant city perched high in the Apennines. Unfortunately, hotel prices in the city center are as lofty as the town, but some reasonable accommodations lie within a short walk or bus ride from the center. Call ahead to reserve a room, or be prepared to pay for a three-star hotel.

ORIENTATION AND PRACTICAL INFORMATION

Corso Vittorio Emanuele II, the main drag, stretches between the **Castello Cinquecentesimo** to the north and the **Piazza del Duomo,** the heart of the city's historic district, to the south. Beyond the P. del Duomo, the street continues as **Corso Federico II** until it reaches the plush gardens of the **Villa Comunale** and **Via XX Settembre,** which separate the southern half of the city. Pick up a map at the tourist office; navigating the small streets can be aggravating, and street names change every few blocks.

To obtain maps and tourist information, visit the **EPT** (tel. 41 08 08 or 41 03 40) in P. Santa Maria Paganica. Turn off Corso Vittorio Emanuele onto Via Leosini; the office is just up the hill on the right. The EPT has a computer with information in English on hotels and buses, but despite the fancy technology, facts are sometimes out of date. Open Mon.-Fri. 8am-2pm and 3:30-6pm, Sat. 8am-2pm. Also stop in at the **Azienda di Turismo,** at Corso Vittorio Emanuele, 49 (tel 41 08 59). Open Mon.-Fri. 9am-1pm and 3:30-7pm, Sat. 9am-1pm. The **train station** (on the Sulmona-Termi line) is at P. delle Stazione, on the outskirts of town. Take bus #1, 3, or 3/S (L1500) to the center of town, or turn right and follow the signs to the **Fontana delle 99 Cannelle** and hike up

Central Italy
LIGURIA
Ligurian Sea
Northern Appenines
Verona
VENETO
Mantua
Vicenza
Parma
Fornova
Padova
Reggio d'Emillia
Po R.
Adige R.
Modena
Rovigo
La Spezia Marittima
EMILIA-ROMAGNA
Ferrara
Piazza al Serchio
Bologna
Viareggio
Lucca
Pisa
Livorno
Pistoia
Arno River
Faenza
Ravenna
Prato
Empoli
Firenze
Pontassieve
San Gimignano
Poggibonsi
Rimini
Castellina
SAN MARINO
Piombino
Massa Marittima
Siena
Portoferraio
Elba
TOSCANA
Arezzo
Follonica
Asciano
Urbino
Pesaro
Montalcino
Fano
Grosseto
Monte Antico
Montepulciano
Terontola
Senigallia
Gubbio
Chiusi
Lake Trasimeno
Fossato di Vico
Jesi
Giglio
Perugia
Ancona
UMBRIA
Albacina
Assisi
LE MARCHE
Orvieto
Foligno
Lago di Bolsena
Civitanove Marche-Montegranaro
Viterbo
Orte
Terni
Civitavecchia
Ascoli Piceno
Lake Bracciano
Tiber River
Adriatic Sea
N
Cerveteri
Gran Sasso
L'Aquila
Tivoli
Ostia Antica
Roma
Pescara
Frascati
Subiaco
ABRUZZO
Palestrina
Chieti
Southern Appenines
Tyrrhenian Sea
LAZIO
Sulmona
Latina
Sabaudia
Termoli
Carpinone
PONTINE ISLANDS
Formia
MOLISE
0
60 miles
Campobasso
0
60 kilometers
Bosco Redole
Ventotene

the hill. Buses arrive near the *castello,* and tickets are available in the ticket booth there. **Hiking information** can be found at **Club Alpino Italiano,** Via XX Settembre, 15 (tel. 243 42; open Mon.-Sat. 9am-1pm and 4-8pm), or **Libreria Colacchi,** Via Andrea Bafile, 17 (tel. 253 10; open Mon.-Fri. 9am-1pm and 4-8pm, Sat. 9am-1pm). The **telephone code** is 0862.

ACCOMMODATIONS AND FOOD

Although three-star hotels are plentiful, budget accommodations are scarce in L'Aquila. The **Locanda Orazi,** Via Roma, 175 (tel. 41 28 89), offers reasonable prices but is a long walk from the city center. Follow Corso Principa Umberto, which turns into Via Roma. When the place is full, the owners may not answer the door. Singles L40,000. Doubles L60,000. **Lo Shaly** (tel. 44 15 21) is another affordable alternative, located in Bazzano a block down the road from the bus stop. Catch the #6 bus (every 30min., 10min., L1500) in front of the *castello* park on Via Castello. Singles L31,000. Doubles L48,000, with bath L58,000. All prices are L3000 to L5000 higher in July and August, and half- and full-pension are available throughout the summer. Be warned that buses from L'Aquila to Bazzano stop running around 8pm, and a taxi ride will cost L15,000.

Torrone, a nougat made of honey and almonds, is to L'Aquila what chocolate is to Perugia. Manufactured in L'Aquila, this local sweet is available in stores throughout the city. Try **Tappirullan** on Corso Vittorio Emanuele. For more substantial fare, **Trattoria Da Lincosta,** at P. S. Pietro di Coppito, 19 (tel. 286 62), off Via Roma, offers a variety of regional favorites, including *agnello ai ferri* (grilled lamb, L12,000). Open Sat.-Thurs. noon-3pm and 6pm-midnight. V, AmEx. For inexpensive meals on the go, sample from L'Aquila's many *pizzerie* sprinkled throughout the city. Near the castle, the hip **Pizzeria Il Gato,** Via dal Gato, 1 (tel. 226 07), serves *antipasti, bruschetta,* and homemade pizzas (L6000-11,000). Open Wed.-Mon. noon-3pm and 6pm-midnight. The **STANDA** supermarket has everything you need for a complete picnic. Open Mon. 4-8pm, Tues.-Sat. 9am-1pm and 4-8pm.

SIGHTS AND ENTERTAINMENT

L'Aquila's **castello** dominates the pleasant park at the end of Corso Vittorio Emanuele. The Spanish built this fort in the 16th century to defend themselves against the rebelling townspeople. Its intimidating walls now house the **Museo Nazionale di Abruzzo** (tel. 63 31), which showcases art and artifacts from the whole of Abruzzo's history. Inside you'll find prehistoric elephant bones, Roman sarcophagi, Renaissance tapestries, and modern art. (Open daily 9am-2pm; holidays 9am-1pm. Admission L8000.)

From the intersection of V. XX Settembre and C. Federico II, take Viale Francesco Crispi to Viale di Collemaggio through the Villa Comunale to reach the **Basilica di Santa Maria di Collemaggio.** Construction of this church began in 1287 at the urging of local hermit Pietro da Marrone (later Pope Celestine V). The striking pink-and-white-checked façade with its elaborate carvings conceals an austere interior; the Baroque embellishments were stripped away in 1972 to restore a medieval tone.

Dating from 1292, the oldest monument in L'Aquila is the **Fontana delle 99 Cannelle** (Fountain of 99 Spouts). Take Via Sallustio from C. Vittorio Emanuele and bear left until you reach Via XX Settembre. Follow the small roads down the hill, staying to the left at the bottom. The fountain is a symbol of the city's founding, when 99 local lords came together to build a fortress that would protect the local hill towns. Each spout is unique and represents a different town. The source of the water remains unknown, despite the terrestrial upheaval of the 1703 earthquake and modern renovations of the fountain.

From November to May, the Società Aquilana dei Concerti sponsors classical concerts in the *castello* (tel. 242 62 or 41 41 61). Also of interest are the recitals at the **Festival of Classical Guitar** held in the last week in May. For ticket and schedule information, check with the Azienda di Turismo or with the **Ufficio Organizzativo**

dell'Ente Castello Cinquecentesco (tel. 242 62 or 41 41 61; fax 616 66). Monday through Saturday mornings a **market** fills the P. del Duomo with fresh food, artisan's booths, local handicrafts, and clothing from nearby stores.

■ Near L'Aquila

The craggy terrain around L'Aquila conceals isolated medieval towns, abandoned fortresses, and ancient churches and monasteries. East of L'Aquila lies the 15th-century **Rocca Calascio,** a sophisticated example of military architecture. It's surrounded by the medieval towns of **Santo Stefano di Sessanio** and **Castel del Monte,** as well as the 9th-century **Oratorio di San Pellegrino** in the town of **Bominaco.** To the west of L'Aquila are the extensive Roman ruins at **Amiternum** and the enormous **Lago di Campotosto,** the largest man-made lake in Italy, which supplies electricity to Abruzzo and the surrounding regions. ARPA buses service these sights from both L'Aquila and Sulmona (2-3 per day, 1½-2½hr., L4300-7600). North of L'Aquila, the town of **Assergi** is home to a beautiful 12th-century abbey, **Santa Maria Assunta,** which houses well-preserved frescoes. To get there, take one of the hourly #6 municipal buses (1hr., L1500) from Porta Paganica.

The **Grottoes of Stiffe** at San Demetrio ne' Vestini, 21km from L'Aquila, afford visitors glimpses of the terrain beneath Abruzzo; an underground river has carved out striking caverns and rock formations to leave hidden lakes and waterfalls. A recent cave collapse has restricted access, but what remains open is stunning nevertheless. Guided tours are available on weekends from 9am to 1pm and daily from 3pm until sunset. Daily tours are provided in July and August, and special tours are available for groups of 20 or more. Closed Dec.-Feb. For more information, contact the EPT of L'Aquila. For reservations, call or write the **Gruppo Speleologico Aquilano,** Svolte della Misericordia #2, 67100, L'Aquila (tel./fax (0862) 41 42 73).

GRAN SASSO D'ITALIA (BIG ROCK OF ITALY)

Twelve km above L'Aquila rises the snowcapped **Gran Sasso d'Italia,** the highest peak contained entirely within Italy's borders and a mountaineer's delight. Procure a map marked *carta topografica per escursionisti* or *Wanderkarte.* Make sure it includes *sentieri* (trails marked by difficulty) and a list of *rifugi* (hikers' huts charging L9000-16,000 per night). The accommodations booklet available at L'Aquila's EPT also contains a list of Abruzzo refuges. Always call these lodgings before setting out, and bring food because prices rise with the altitude. **Club Alpino Italiano** in L'Aquila (tel. 243 42) has the most up-to-date Apennine advice. To reach the peak from L'Aquila, take bus #6 (about 5 per day, 1hr., L1500; tickets at local bars and *tabacchi*) from Porta Paganico on Via Castello; make sure it's going all the way to the *funivia.* Get off at the base of the cableway. If you don't feel like hiking to the top, you can take the *funivia* halfway up (L9,000-18,000, depending on the season, the day of the week, and whether you're going up, down, or roundtrip). The *funivia* runs every hour in the summer 8:30am-5pm; June 20-Aug. 25 8:30am-6pm; and every half-hour in the winter 8:30am-1pm and 2-4:45pm. Camp and eat at **Camping Funivia del Gran Sasso** (tel. 60 61 63), an immaculate patch of grass down the hill from the cableway. L7000 per person, L6000 per tent.

The area around the *funivia* features several scenic hikes. Trail #10 (about 500m down the road) will take you up to **Monte Della Scindarella** and offers a stupendous view of the Gran Sasso and L'Aquila. The upper *funivia* station provides access to several trails. To tackle the mountain itself, take trail #3 to trail #4. For useful information on Alpine guides, inquire at the tourist office or write to **Collegio Regionale Guide Alpine,** Via Serafino, 2, 66100 Chieti (tel. (0871) 693 38). In the winter, the Gran Sasso teems with skiers. Weekly passes are available at **Camp Imperatore** (tel. 60 61 43 or 41 05 57) and **Campo Felice** (tel. 91 78 03), and lessons are available from the Gran Sasso **ski school** (tel. 40 00 12). Before you go, call (0862) 42 05 10 for a snow bulletin.

Sulmona

Sulmona's favorite son, the poet Ovid (43BC-AD17), stands immortalized in bronze in **Piazza XX Settembre,** the city's main meeting space. Although seemingly preoccupied with its ancient past, Sulmona owes much of its beauty to the prosperity of the late Middle Ages, when innumerable churches and palaces were constructed. Sulmona's intimate size and noteworthy architecture make it the perfect town in which to relax for a day or a weekend. It maintains a distinct sweetness, thanks not only to the residents' friendliness but also to the proliferation of candy stores—Sulmona has been the home of *confetti* candy since the 15th century.

ORIENTATION AND PRACTICAL INFORMATION

Sulmona is accessible by **train** on the Rome-Pescara line. There are 12 trains daily in each direction (3hr. from Rome, L3600; 1¼hr. from Pescara, L5700). To get to the town center from the station, take bus A (every 30min., L1500; buy tickets at the train station bar), or trudge two km uphill to the right upon leaving the station. Sulmona is easily reached by ARPA **bus** from L'Aquila (9 per day, 1½hr., L8100) and Pescara (5 per day, 1½hr., L8100). Buy tickets on the bus. For more bus info, call 21 04 69. The **tourist office** is at Corso Ovidio, 208 (tel. 532 76), on the third floor. Open Mon.-Sat. 8am-2pm. The **post office** on P. Brigata Maiella, 3/4, behind P. del Carmine, has telegraph and exchange offices. Open Mon.-Fri. 8:15am-5:30pm, Sat. 8:15am-1pm. **Telephone code:** 0864.

ACCOMMODATIONS AND FOOD

Albergo Stella, Via Panfila Mazara, 18/20 (tel. 526 53), is conveniently located off Corso Ovidio near the aqueduct. Rooms are clean, well-maintained, and conveniently provided with phones and TVs. Singles L35,000. Doubles L50,000, with bath L60,000. In summer, prices rise L5000 to L10,000. Breakfast L5000. The friendly and helpful proprietors of **Albergo Italia,** P. Tommasi, 3 (tel. 523 08), off P. XX Settembre, go out of their way to make guests feel welcome. Some of the elegant rooms overlook the dome of the church of the SS. Annunziata and the mountains. Singles L35,000. Doubles L65,000, with bath L75,000. **Ristorante Italia** (tel. 330 70) has an enchanting dining room and offers spectacular food with friendly service. It's located to Ovid's left in P. XX Settembre. Menu changes daily. Try the savory linguine with zucchini and cream sauce for L8000. *Primi* L8000, *secondi* L8000-11,000. Open Tues.-Sun. noon-3pm and 7-11pm. V, MC, AmEx, Eurocard. **Ristorante Stella** (downstairs from Albergo Stella) offers regional specialties at reasonable prices. Try the *maccheroni alla chitarra* (L7000). *Primi* L7000, *secondi* L7000-14,000. Cover L2000. Open daily noon-2pm and 7:15-9pm. For a light meal, try **Pizzeria Ernano,** Corso Ovidio, 263 (tel. 505 93). Inexpensive pizzas (L7500) and beer (L2500) are great for a tight budget. Open Fri.-Wed. 10am-2pm and 5-11pm. Those with a sweet tooth will not want to miss **G. Di Carlo e Figlio,** Corso Ovidio, 185, and its famous *confetti.* Open daily 9am-1pm and 3-8pm. The **STANDA** supermarket, Corso Ovidio, 15, is just past the arch at the end of the street. Open Mon.-Sat. 9am-1pm and 4-8pm.

SIGHTS

At one end of Corso Ovidio is the Romanesque-Gothic **Cathedral of San Panfilo.** Its nucleus was built a thousand years ago on the ruins of a temple to Apollo and Vesta. Take a break in the **gardens** of Sulmona, which offer shade and benches to the weary. Down Corso Ovidio from the gardens stand the **Church and Palace of SS. Annunziata.** The baroque church façade abuts the 15th-century Gothic *palazzo,* which now houses a small museum (tel. 21 02 16) featuring Renaissance Sulmonese goldwork. (Open Tues.-Sun. 9:30am-12:30pm and 4:30-7:30pm. Admission L1000.) The colossal **Piazza Garibaldi** surrounds the Renaissance **Fontana del Vecchio,** which gushes clear mountain water from the nearby medieval aqueduct (1256). A **market** takes place here daily, but expands on Wednesdays and Saturdays.

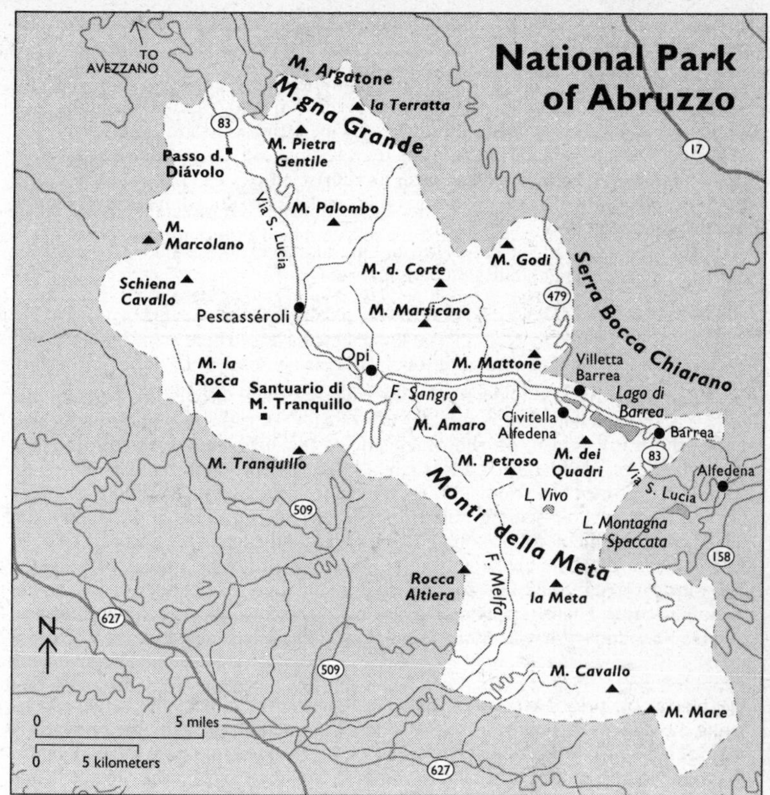

CENTRAL ITALY

Abruzzo National Park (Parco Nazionale D'Abruzzo)

Organized to protect the pristine wilderness from urban developers, the National Park occupies a huge tract of land in the mountainous wilderness of southwest Abruzzo. The mountains provide spectacular views of lush woodlands and crystal-clear lakes. Lynx have recently been reintroduced near Civitella Alfedena, joining Marsican brown bears, Apennine wolves, and Abruzzo Chamois antelopes. Pescasseroli, the park's administrative center, is the best base for exploration.

ORIENTATION AND PRACTICAL INFORMATION

Enter the park at **Avezzano** on the Rome-Pescara train line (1½hr. from Rome and 2½hr. from **Pescara**). You can also catch an ARPA bus from L'Aquila to Avezzano (40min.). ARPA buses travel from Avezzano to the park and between cities within the park. (Avezzano to Pescasseroli, Mon.-Sat. 6 per day, last return 6:15pm, Sun. at 9am only, 1½hr., L6000.) From June 12 to mid-September an ARPA bus leaves from Rome-Tiburtina for Pescasseroli daily at 7:30am and departs again for Rome at 6:30pm. (3hr.) For more information call ARPA at (0863) 265 61 or 229 21.

In Pescasseroli, check in at the **Ufficio di Zona** (tel. 919 55) by the P. Sant'Antonio bus stop for hiking information and the essential park map. At L10,000, it's expensive, but profits go toward maintaining the park. Office staff is very friendly and well-informed. Open daily 9am-noon and 3-7pm. For accommodation and restaurant info, drop by the helpful **tourist office** (tel. 91 00 97; fax 91 04 61) on Via Piave off P. Sant'Antonio. Open daily 9am-1pm and 4:30-7:30pm. In Opi, 6km to the west of town at the turn-off to Camosciara, there's an **information center** (tel. 891 70) for foreign visitors. Open July 10-Aug. Mon.-Sat. 9am-1pm and 2-5pm. A **museum** dedicated to the Abruzzo Chamois is located here. Open 9am-noon and 3-6pm.

The town of **Alfedena,** 1km from its train station and 33km from Pescasseroli, boasts picturesque archaeological sites. Its **tourist office** (tel. 873 94) in the main square stocks information on the Roman ruins and the pre-Roman **necropolis** dating from the 10th century BC.

The **telephone code** for Pescasseroli, Opi, and Avezzano is 0863; for Civitella Alfedena, Castel di Sangro, and Pescocostanzo 0864.

ACCOMMODATIONS, CAMPING, AND FOOD

Avezzano

Avezzano is notable as the juncture of the main bus route through the park and the Rome-Pescara train line (station tel. 41 35 78 or 41 37 06). The **bus station** is located behind the train station, on the other side of the *sottopassaggio* (underpass). Although decent, affordable lodging is rare, **Creati,** Via XX Settembre, 208 (tel. 41 33 47), has clean, modern rooms, all with private bath. Singles L40,000. Doubles L60,000. From the train station, walk left for 10min. and turn right at the street's end onto Via de Fiori; the hotel is another 10-min. walk to the left at the end of the street. Restaurants in Avezzano are few, but the **Pizzeria e Rosticceria Quattro Stagioni,** Via Garibaldi 60 (tel. 20 22 15), up the road from the train station, offers a convenient location, friendly, English-speaking management, and long hours. Pizza by the slice, pasta (L9000), and *caffè* will sustain you until you can leave Avezzano.

Pescasseroli

Most reasonably priced accommodations in Pescasseroli do not offer single rooms. During the off-season, however, solo travelers can often finagle a double or quad for the price of a single. **Pensione al Castello** (tel. 91 07 57), across from the park office, has large, modern rooms with private baths. In fact, they may be the nicest budget-hotel bathrooms this side of the Arno. The *pensione* is convenient to the bus stop and the trails. Singles L40,000, when available. Doubles L60,000. Full-pension offered during August for L80,000. The spectacular views are definitely worth the 2km walk uphill to **Albergo Valle del Lupo,** Via Collachi (tel. 91 05 34). Walk down Viale S. Lucia off P. S. Antonio and turn right along Viale Colle dell'Oro, following the signs. Rooms are quiet and homey, and most have a balcony overlooking the mountains. Singles with bath L35,000. Doubles with bath L60,000. Budget travelers should consider renting rooms in private houses. Obtain a list from the tourist office. Singles about L30,000-40,000. Doubles about L50,000-60,000. There are four campgrounds within 21km of town. The best is **Campeggio dell'Orso** (tel. 919 55), by the river on the Opi road. L6000 per person, L6000 per tent.

For pizza or regular restaurant fare, **Il Cerbiatto,** Via Napoli, 19 (tel. 91 04 65), offers a wide selection. A hearty bowl of *gnochetti e fagioli* (potato pasta and beans, L9000) coupled with the *maiale ai ferri* (possibly the best grilled pork chops you've ever tasted, L9000) will satisfy the hungriest of mountain-climbers. Pizzas L8000-12,000. Cover L3000. Open Thurs.-Tues. 12:30-3pm and 7-11pm. The nearby pastry shop **Pasticceria Alpina,** Traversa Sangro, 6 (tel. 91 05 61), serves a full array of award-winning goodies. Open daily 8am-10pm; in winter closed Mon. The **Delfino A&O** supermarket is on Via S. Lucia, the main highway, just past the zoo and the park office. Open daily 8:30am-1pm and 4-7pm. V, MC, AmEx.

Opi

ARPA buses follow the winding road through the park to the village of **Opi** (5km), named for the pagan goddess of abundance whose temple was located here in ancient times. Two km past the village on the bus route lies the campground **Vec-**

chio Mulino (tel. 91 22 32). L7500 per person, L8000 per tent. In August, Opi hosts the **Sagra degli Gnocchi** ("Gnocchifest"), a nationally renowned eat-along where thousands converge to consume *gnocchi,* sausages, and cheese. (*Gnocchi* are potato-flour dumplings whose consistency ranges from delicate puffs that melt in your mouth to lumps of dough that hit your stomach with a thud.)

Civitella Alfedena

Ten km past Opi, the bus reaches the village of **Villetta Barrea.** The turnoff to Civitella Alfedena, 200m farther down the road, leads to the **Pinas Nigra Campground.** The site is large and pleasant, bordered by the River Sangro. L6000 per person, L7000 per tent. In Civitella Alfedena, make yourself at home at the **Alberghetto La Torre** (tel. 89 01 21) on Via La Torre. Doubles L60,000, with bath L65,000. Extra bed L30,000. **Museo del Lupo** (tel. 89 01 41) has information on the habits and history of the Apennine wolf and the lynx. Admission L5000. Ice-cold **Barrea Lake** cuts majestically into the mountains, stretching seven km between Villetta Barrea and the neighboring village of **Barrea.**

Alfedena

Stay at **Leon D'Oro** (tel. 871 21). Singles L30,000, with bath L40,000. Doubles L60,000, with bath L75,000. A track leads 3km away from Alfedena to **Lago Montagna Spaccata,** where the intrepid (and insulated) brave the freezing waters.

EXCURSIONS

You haven't really entered the park until the bus begins the scenic ascent from Avezzano to Pescasseroli. Fields of poppies, rocky outcrops, dazzling valleys, and dizzying views will delight you. To avoid gastronomic *déjà vu,* don't eat too much before embarking on this twisting climb. If the wildlife in the park eludes you, compensate in Pescasseroli at the **museum** and **zoo** on Via S. Lucia off the main piazza. These attractions display indigenous animals, colorful gardens, and exhibits of the park's natural history. Open daily 10am-noon and 3-6pm. Admission L10,000.

You might go crazy looking for the red and orange signs that signal the trail entrances if you don't purchase the indispensable trail map (L10,000) from the Ufficio di Zona in Pescasseroli. The clear, detailed map points out where you're likely to find the animals protected in the preserve: brown bears, chamois, deer, wolves, and eagles. The trails are arranged so that all paths that begin with the same letter start from the same point. Some of the best trails are within walking distance of Pescasseroli. For a short hike, take **trail B1** up to some crumbling castle ruins (50min. roundtrip). To really stretch those legs, make the beautiful five-hour roundtrip hike to **Vicolo (Pass) di Monte Tranquillo** (1673m). Take **trail C3,** which starts at the southern end of town, up through the green Valle Mancina past the Rifugio Della Difesa. Keep climbing and you'll eventually reach the pass with its impressive view of the mountain peaks to the north.

If you can schedule your hikes to coordinate with the ARPA bus schedule, you can venture farther afield. From Civitella Alfedena (15km from Pescasseroli) take **trails I1 to K6** through the sublimely beautiful **Valle di Rose** to see the park's largest herd of chamois (more than 200). From mid-July to early September, this area can be explored only with a guide (L10,000 per person). Call Museo del Lupo (see above) to reserve a guide or to get more info about the trails. From Barrea (20km from Pescasseroli) you can take **trail K5** to the refreshing lake **Lago Vivo** (3½hr. roundtrip). Be aware that the lake dries up in late June. **Mountain bikes** are available for about L5000 per hour at **Sport House** in Pescasseroli (tel. 91 07 96). Turn left from the tourist office and cross the river, then turn right and walk along the river bank for about 5min. Several paths, including C3, are good for biking.

In winter, this area has excellent skiing, with challenging slopes and plentiful snowfall. Package deals called **settimane bianche** ("white weeks") provide room, lift tickets, and half-pension (full-pension optional). For more information, contact the tourist office in Pescasseroli. For a regional snow bulletin, call (0862) 665 10.

Termoli

Play in the sand on some of Italy's cleanest beaches, catch a ferry to wooded islands in the Adriatic, and see a number of the most cancerous suntans anywhere. Italian tourists flock to Termoli in July and August, but in early summer the town maintains a relaxed atmosphere in spite of relatively inexpensive accommodations. **Pensione Villa Ida,** Via M. Milano, 27 (tel. 26 66), located near both the beach and the train station, offers the best deal in town. Singles L50,000. Doubles L70,000. All rooms with bath, some with balconies. Breakfast included. A short distance away from the city center, the **Pensione Giorgione,** Via Rio Vivo, 40 (tel. 70 64 24), provides spacious rooms that are particularly affordable in off-season or for large groups. From the train station, walk almost to the end of Corso Umberto and take a right on Corso Vittorio Emmanuele III, which turns into Via Rio Vivo. For those who just don't want to deal with the 10-min. jaunt, bus #4 leaves from the train station every 30min. (L1000 from the driver). Singles L25,000-50,000. Doubles L75,000-90,000. Rates vary with the season. **La Sacrestia,** Via C. Ruffini, 48 (tel. 70 56 03), a pizzeria and *ristorante,* serves hearty pasta dishes (L6000-10,000), fluffy *gnocchi* (L8000), *secondi* (L9000-20,000 for their special seafood soup), and pizzas (L4000-10,000). From Corso Nazionale, take a right on Via Alfano, then a left onto Via Ruffini. You can dine outdoors, although the throngs of birds circling overhead may remind you of a Hitchcock film. V, AmEx. The **telephone code** for Termoli is 0875.

Tremiti Islands

GETTING THERE

Ferries and **hydrofoils** to the islands leave from a number of Adriatic ports, though Termoli is the most convenient departure point. **Adriatica Navigazione** runs ferries and hydrofoils from the largest number of ports and can be contacted in Termoli at **Intercontinental,** Corso Umberto I, 93 (tel. (0875) 70 53 41), or at the booth at the port. In June, a ferry leaves daily at 9am (1¾hr., L12,400 one way). Hydrofoils (45min., L21,700 one way) run on weekends in June and daily in July and August at 8:30 and 9:35am. There is also a 6pm departure on Fridays and Saturdays in June and daily in July and August. Call for departure times in other seasons. Adriatica also sends boats to Tremiti from Ortona, Vasto, Manfredonia, and Rodi (usually one departure per day). **Collegamenti Marittimi,** in Termoli, Di Brino Viaggi, P. Bega (tel. 70 39 37), also embarks to Tremiti from Termoli. A ferry departs daily at 9:15am (1½hr., L12,500). From June to Sept. 15, a faster boat leaves daily at 8:40am (55min., L21,900). Visit their booth at the port for more information.

The Marches (Le Marche)

With mountain peaks and green foothills tapering down toward the grey shores of the Adriatic, the Marches offers a graceful combination of hill and coastal landscapes. Wheat, corn, figs, and olives are harvested from the inland plains, while abundant numbers of both fish and tourists are reeled in along the coast. Summer tourism is the mainstay of the region's economy; in July and August, migrating German vacationers make the coast appear more like the North Sea than the Adriatic.

In summer the shore is warm and appealing, but a break from the sun can occasionally be a refreshing change. Luckily, local sights throughout the region provide historical diversions for exploration-minded tourists. The architectural and archaeological remains of the Gauls, Picenes, and Romans grant numerous excursion possibilities, slightly inland and easily accessible by train. Medieval Ascoli Piceno has a large, perfectly preserved historic center complete with an impressive skyline of Longobard towers. Renaissance Urbino, crowned by a fantastic elfin palace, should not be missed. History in the Marches is not exploited, but integrated into town life; medieval streets are expertly navigated by aggressive little cars, and ancient iron torch holders commonly anchor laundry lines.

Pesaro

Though Pesaro lies on the Adriatic, it is more than a mere beach town. Instead, tourism flourishes from the historic center to the shore. Museums and churches abound in the old quarter, where timeless palaces proffer a plethora of possibilities. Urban spaces from Piazza Lazzarini to Piazza della Libertà form the commercial heart of the town, while the waterfront just beyond allows visitors and locals a place to relax.

ORIENTATION AND PRACTICAL INFORMATION

Pesaro lies on the main Bologna-Lecce route along the Adriatic coast. From Rome, take a train toward Ancona (6 or 7 per day), then change at Falconara for one of the frequent local trains to Pesaro (4½hr., L26,400). The center of the old city is **Piazza del Popolo.** From the train station, walk across the small *piazza* onto Viale Risorgimento and continue on Via Branca (5min.). From P. del Popolo, the **beach** and **Piazza della Libertà** are only 5 to 10min. away, a straight walk away from P. del Popolo along **Via Rossini** (which becomes Viale della Repubblica).

Tourist Office: IAT, 3 offices. At the train station (tel. 683 78), open in summer Mon.-Sat. 9:30am-1pm and 4-6:30pm, though the hours may be erratically kept. At Via Rossini, 41 (tel. 693 41), in the town center, open daily 9am-noon and 4-6:30pm. At Piazzale della Libertà (tel. 643 02), on the beach, open in summer Mon.-Sat. 8:30am-1pm and 3-7pm. Both Via Rossini and the Piazzale offices have friendly and helpful English-speaking staff. Hours may be unreliable.

Tourist Police: V. G. Bruno, 7 (tel. 38 61 11).

Telephones: P. Matteotti, 23/24 (tel. 347 41), across the street from the bus station (AMANUP). Open Mon.-Fri. 9am-1pm and 4-7pm. Booths open 7am-11pm.

Trains: At the end of Viale Risorgimento and V. della Liberazione (tel. 330 09). To Ancona (every 30min., 1hr., L5000) and Bologna (every hr., 2hr., L9400). **Ticket counter** open daily 5:45am-9pm. **Luggage Storage:** L5000 for 12hr. Open daily 6am-11pm.

Buses: P. Matteotti, down Via S. Francesco from P. del Popolo. Buses #1, 2, 4, 5, 6, 7, 9, and 11 stop at P. Matteotti. To: Fano (frequent buses, 15min., L1400); Ancona (5 per day except Sun., 1½hr., L5000); and Urbino (8 per day, 1hr., L4100). Two express buses per day to Rome Tiburtina station (4½hr., L32,800).

Emergencies: tel 113 or 112. **First Aid:** tel. 213 44. **Nights and Holidays:** Via Nitti, 36 (tel. 45 53 79). **Emergency: Pronto Soccorso,** tel. 329 57. **Hospital:** P. Cinelli (tel. 36 11).

Police: Via Giusti, 34 (tel. 646 63)

Post Office: P. del Popolo (tel. 691 55), at the beginning of Via Rossini. *Fermo posta* at #1. Open Mon.-Sat. 8:15am-7:40pm. **Postal Code:** 61100.

Telephone Code: 0721.

ACCOMMODATIONS AND CAMPING

Ostello Ardizio (HI) (tel. 557 98), at Fosso Sejore, 6km from town. Take the **AMANUP** bus toward Fano from P. Matteotti (every 30min. 6am-9pm, L1200). From the train station, take bus #3 or walk along Via 24 Maggio (which becomes Via Manzoni). Stop when you see the "Camping Norina" sign on the beach to your left; you will be dropped off at a hotel/bar. Walk back (away from the bar) and take the road that branches off the highway to a grassy area. A yellow sign points toward the hostel. Closed for renovations; check with the tourist office for reopening date.

Pensione Ristorante Arianna, Via Mascagni, 84 (tel./fax 319 27), 100m from the beach. Spotless rooms, excellent food. All rooms with bath. Singles L40,000-

50,000. Doubles L65,000-75,000. Breakfast L8000. Full-pension (required in Aug.) L65,000, L53,000 in low-season. Reserve ahead in summer. V, MC.

Albergo Aurora, Viale Trieste, 147 (tel. 344 59 or 45 17 11; fax 41 40 47). Just a few meters from the beach. All rooms have baths and lovely tile floors. Singles L45,000, low-season L35,000. Doubles L70,000, low-season L60,000. Full-pension (required in Aug.) L70,000, L55,000 in low-season. Open April-Sept.

Camping Panorama, Via Panoramica (tel. 20 81 45), 7km north of Pesaro on the *strada panoramica* to Gabicce Mare. Take bus #3 to Capolinea. A path leads to a quiet beach. L10,000 per adult, L5500 per child, L12,000 per tent. Hot showers and use of swimming pools included. Open May-Sept.

Campo Norina (tel./fax 557 92), 5km south of the city center on the beach at Fossoseiore. Take the bus for Fano from P. Matteotti (L1400). L12,000-14,700 per person, L10,000 per tent. 4-person bungalows L90,000. Open April-mid-Oct.

FOOD

Pesaro's **public market** is at Via Branca, 5, off P. del Popolo behind the post office. Open Mon.-Sat. 7:30am-1:30pm. **Pizzerie** line the beach, while **alimentari** crowd the sidewalks on Corso XI Settembre. Veggie and macrobiotic meals are available at **Un Punto Macrobiotico,** Via Diaz, 36 (tel. 338 06).

CENTRAL ITALY

Mensa Volto della Ginevra, Via della Ginevra, 3 (tel. 343 08), near Musei Civici. Enter through the arch. A self-service cafeteria and bargain-hunter's delight. Tasty selections served in elephantine portions at surprising prices. Hearty complete meal with wine or water L10,400. Open Mon.-Fri. noon-2pm.

Harnold's, P. Lazzarini, 34 (tel. 687 86), close to Teatro Rossini. Outdoor seating in the *piazza.* Fresh, cheap, and delicious with a wide range of eccentrically named *panini* (L3500-6000). Open Thurs.-Tues. 11:30am-2am. Take-out available.

Trattoria Pinocchio, Via Venturini on P. Antaldi, 12 (tel. 347 71). Hip crowd. *Primi* L6000-9000, *secondi* L16,000-20,000. Open daily noon-2pm and 8-10pm. In summer, closed for lunch Sat.-Mon.

SIGHTS AND ENTERTAINMENT

The robust arcade and *putti*-ful window frames of the 15th-century **Ducal Palace,** home of Pesaro's ruling della Rovere clan, preside over the **Piazza del Popolo,** Pesaro's main square. The town's museums can be accessed with a **cumulative ticket,** available and valid at the Pinacoteca, Ceramics Museum, Rossini Museum, and Sea Museum. (Admission L8000, children and seniors L4000.) On **Corso XI Settembre** and its side streets, narrow alleys pass open arcades and sculptured doorways. Off the *corso* on Via Toschi Mosca, the **Musei Civici** (tel. 678 15) house a superb collection of Italian ceramics and primitives. (Open Tues.-Sat. 8:30am-1:30pm, Sun. 9am-1pm; Aug. Mon.-Sat. 9am-7pm, Sun. 9am-1pm. Admission L5000.) An extensive collection of photographs, portraits, theatrical memorabilia, letters, and scores pertinent to the composer's life awaits at the **Rossini Birthplace and Museum,** Via Rossini, 34 (tel. 38 73 57). (Open Aug.-Sept. Tues.-Sun. 10am-7pm; in winter officially open Tues.-Sun. 10am-1pm, but call ahead. Admission L3000.)

Most of Pesaro's Gothic churches hide behind lavish Baroque portals. One of these is the **Church of Sant'Agostino** on Corso XI Settembre. Enter to see its beautiful late 15th- and early 16th-century wooden choir stalls inlaid with still-lifes, landscapes, and city scenes. (Open daily 9am-12:30pm and 3:30-8pm.) Outside of town is the **Villa Imperiale** (4th- to 15th-centuries), currently owned by a duke. The lavish villa and gardens can be visited July 19 to Sept. 21 (Wed. 4pm) through the APT (tel. 636 90). Tours depart from P. della Libertà (L10,000).

The evening *passeggiata* (an intriguing mix of high fashion and casual *gelato*-eating) cruises along Viale Trieste and P. della Libertà. Older folk meander through P. del Popolo, window-shopping in ritzy stores. To watch the sunset (hey, it's free), head to **Parco Ortigiuli,** Via Belvedere, near the River Foglia. Popular nightspots are **The Bis-**

tro, Viale Trieste, 281, under Hotel Cruiser, and **Big Ben,** Via Sabbatini, 14 (tel. 674 60), between the Palazzo Ducale and the Conservatorio Rossini.

Pesaro hosts the **Mostra Internazionale del Nuovo Cinema** (International Festival of New Films) during the second and third weeks of June. Organizers make an effort to show interesting and rarely screened films. Movies new and old, commercially and independently produced, are shown in the buildings along Via Rossini and at the Teatro Comunale Sperimentale. Check at the tourist office for a schedule. Native opera composer Rossini endowed a music school, the **Conservatorio di Musica G. Rossini,** which sponsors events throughout the year. Contact the conservatory at P. Olivieri for a schedule. The annual **Rossini Opera Festival** begins in early August, but opera performances and orchestral concerts continue until September. Contact the tourist office for exact dates and prices, or reserve tickets through the information office at Via Rossini, 37 (tel. 301 61).

■ Near Pesaro: Fano

The 12km between Pesaro and Fano are home to the quietest retreats on this stretch of the Adriatic. The sandy beach on the north side of Fano is much less crowded than its Adriatic neighbors and is a good choice for those seeking a more secluded seaside vacation. The best way to reach Fano is by **train** (south of Pesaro on the Bologna-Lecce line). The blue **Bucci** buses from the Pesaro train station also stop in Fano *en route* to Urbino. Information and schedules are posted to the right of the Pesaro train station as you exit; buy tickets (L1400) on the bus. Walk right from the train station and turn right over the tracks onto Viale Battisti to reach the **tourist office** at #10 (tel. (0721) 80 35 34; fax 82 42 92). Pick up a map of the city and a list of local events here. Open Mon.-Sat. 8am-2pm and 4-7pm, holidays 8:30am-1:30pm.

Two of Fano's best budget hotels are on the quiet north-side beach. **Hotel Amelia,** Viale Cairoli, 80 (tel. 82 40 40), a 10 to 15-min. walk from the train station, offers sparkling, newly remodelled rooms only 15m from the water. Turn right out of the station, take the bridge across the train tracks, turn left after the bridge onto Via da Fabriano (the street with the tracks), and then make a right on Via Fabriano. Continue under an overpass and over a canal until you reach Viale Cairoli, and turn right. The hotel and beach are at the end of this tree-lined street. All rooms with bath. Singles L45,000-70,000. Doubles L100,000-120,000. Breakfast included. Full-pension L56,000-90,000. Open May-Sept. **Albergo Fortuna,** Viale Cairoli, 74/76 (tel. 80 35 23), next door to Amelia, offers clean, basic rooms at good prices. The one single is L40,000. Doubles with bath L65,000. Breakfast included. Full-pension L50,000. Reserve one week ahead in summer. V, MC. Several reasonable *trattorie* cluster along the beach. **Food** staples can be found at the small corner grocery store/fruit stand just inland from the hotels. Open Mon.-Sat. 8:15am-7:30pm, Sun. 8:15am-1pm. For a good, low-priced home-cooked meal, try **Trattoria Quinta** at Via le Adriatico, 42. Menu changes daily. *Primi* L5000, *secondi* L15,000, fruit or vegetable L2000. Cover L1000. Open Mon.-Sat. noon-2pm and 7-9:30pm.

Even in summer, vacationers are relatively scarce on the beaches north of Fano. To get to the quietest spots, walk left along the water until the crowds thin out.

Urbino

With humble stone dwellings huddled around the immense turreted palace on the hill, Urbino's fairytale skyline has changed little over the past 500 years. Its Renaissance monuments are linked by neatly swept winding streets, making it an appropriate home for such art treasures as Piero dell Francesca's "Ideal City." Although tourism is welcomed, the university students give the town its color.

ORIENTATION AND PRACTICAL INFORMATION

The blue **SAPUM bus** from Pesaro's P. Matteotti and train station is cheap, frequent, and direct (10 per day, 1hr., L3500). **Bucci** buses also run from Pesaro to Urbino via

Fano (8 per day, 1¼hr., L4100). After winding up steep hills, the bus will deposit you at Borgo Mercatale below the beautiful city center. A short uphill walk or a ride in the elevator takes you to **Piazza della Repubblica,** the city's hub.

Tourist Office: P. Rinascimento, 1 (tel. 26 13; fax 24 41), across from the Palazzo Ducale. Distributes a list of local hotels and a large map. Open Mon.-Sat. 9am-1pm and 3-6pm, Sun. 9am-1pm; off-season Mon.-Sat. 8:30am-2pm.

Budget Travel: CTS, V. Mazzini, 40 (tel. 20 31; fax 32 78 78.) Train and plane tickets, ISIC cards, and info on student tours. Open Mon.-Fri. 9:30am-12:30pm and 4-7pm, Sat. 9:30am-12:30pm.

Telephones: P. Rinascimento, 4, off P. Duca Federico. Open daily 8am-10pm.

Buses: Information (tel. 97 05 02). Departures from Borgo Mercatale. Timetable posted at the beginning of Corso Garibaldi, under the portico at the corner bar on P. della Repubblica. To Pesaro (10 per day, 4 on Sun., 1hr., L3500). **Bucci** (tel. (0721) 223 33) runs two daily buses from Rome. **Luggage Storage:** At the car parking office in Borgo Mercatale. L1500 for 12hr. Open 24hr.

Laundromat: Jefferson, V. C. Battisti, 12. Drop off your dirty duds and they'll be clean the next day. Wash and dry L8000 per load. Open Mon.-Fri. 9am-12:30pm and 4-7:30pm, Sat. 9am-12:30pm.

Public Toilets: Via San Domenico, off P. Duca Federico next to the APT office. L500. Open daily 7am-noon and 2-7:30pm.

Emergencies: tel. 113. **Hospital:** Via B. da Montefeltro (tel. 32 93 51 or 30 11), to the north of the city from P. Roma.

Police: P. della Repubblica, 1 (tel. 30 93 00).

Post Office: Via Bramante, 22 (tel. 25 75), right off Via Raffaello. Open Mon.-Sat. 8:30am-7:40pm. Traveler's checks available. **Postal Code:** 61029.

Telephone Code: 0722.

ACCOMMODATIONS AND CAMPING

Cheap lodging is rare in Urbino, and reservations are essential. You might want to consider staying in Pesaro and taking a daytrip to Urbino. For longer stays, contact the Director of Studies of the Università degli Studi, Via del Popolo, 11 (tel. 32 71 46 or 29 34; fax 27 99) well in advance.

Albergo Italia, Corso Garibaldi, 52 (tel. 27 01), off P. della Repubblica, near the Palazzo Ducale. A truly elegant (yet affordable) hotel with affable management. Stylish wood furniture and a patio with panoramic views out back. Singles L37,000, with bath L53,000. Doubles L64,000, with bath L80,000.

Pensione Fosca, Via Raffaello, 61 (tel. 32 96 22 or 25 42), top floor. Signora Rosina takes good care of her guests. Large, charming rooms with high ceilings. Singles L35,000-39,000. Doubles L50,000-55,000.

Hotel San Giovanni, Via Barocci, 13 (tel. 28 27). A relatively modern hotel with a helpful manager. Restaurant downstairs. Singles L35,000-53,000. Doubles L50,000-80,000. Closed July.

Camping Pineta (tel./fax 47 10), on Via San Donato in the *località* of Cesane, 2km from the city walls. Take bus #7 from Borgo Mercatale and ask the driver to let you off at the *camping.* L8500 per person, L6000 per child, L16,500 per tent. Open April-mid-Sept.

FOOD

Many *paninotecbe, gelaterie,* and burger joints are located around P. della Repubblica. Shop for supplies at supermarket **Margherita,** Via Raffaello, 37. Open Mon.-Wed. and Fri.-Sat. 7:45am-12:45pm and 5-7:45pm, Thurs. 7:45am-12:45pm. Right around the corner at Via Bramante, 20, is a **fruit and vegetable shop** that sells fresh goodies. Open Mon.-Fri. 7am-1pm and 5-8pm, Sat. 7am-1pm.

Pizza Evoé, P. S. Franceso, 3 (tel. 48 94). Very popular with a young crowd. Outdoor seating in a secluded *piazza,* around the corner from P. della Repubblica.

Pizza L4000-10,000. *Primi* L7000-10,000, *secondi* L8000-17,000. Cover L2000. Open Mon.-Sat. noon-3pm and 7pm-midnight.

Morgana, Via Nuova, 3 (tel. 25 28), across from Club 83. Traditional atmosphere, excellent food. Pizza L5000-8000. *Primi* L7000-12,000, *secondi* L6000-18,000. No cover charge. Open Sat.-Thurs. noon-3pm and 7pm-12:30am. V, MC, AmEx.

Pizzeria Le Tre Piante, Via Foro Posterula, 1 (tel. 48 63), off Via Budassi. Spectacular view from the outside tables. Delicious food and friendly service. Very popular. Pizza L5000-10,000. *Primi* L9000-10,000, *secondi* L8000-16,000. Cover L2000. Open Tues.-Sun. noon-3pm and 7pm-2am.

Un Punto Macrobiotico, V. Pozzo Nuovo, 4 (tel. 32 97 90), off V. Battisti. A delightful, healthful self-service place with selections to tempt even carnivores. Daily menu offers pasta and veggies for L4000-8000. *Menù* with fish and side dishes L12,000-14,000. Open daily noon-2pm and 7:30-9:30pm. Store at Via Battisti, 19, around the corner sells macrobiotic dry goods and staples.

Bar del Teatro, Corso Garibaldi, 88 (tel. 62 92 84), at the base of the Palazzo Ducale. Not exactly cheap, but it's got the best view in town: P. Ducale on one side and a vista overlooking the valley on the other. A cool, shady place to spend the afternoon. Cappuccino or tea outside L2500. Open Mon.-Sat. 7:30am-2am.

SIGHTS AND ENTERTAINMENT

Urbino's most remarkable monument is the Renaissance **Palazzo Ducale** (Duke's Palace). The façade, which overlooks the edge of town was designed by Ambrogio Barocchi. Two tall, slender towers enclose three stacked balconies. The interior of this palace, celebrated in Italy as "the most beautiful in the world," was designed by Luciano Laurana. Enter from P. Duca Federico. The central **courtyard** is the essence of Renaissance harmony and proportion. To the left, a monumental staircase leads to the duke's private apartments, which now house the **National Gallery of the Marches.** Its works document the transition into the age of Humanism; a fledgling attempt at perspective painting appears in Piero della Francesca's *Flagellation of Christ*. Also among the works here are Berruguete's famous portrait of Duke Federico, Raphael's *Portrait of a Lady,* and Paolo Uccello's tiny, strange *Profanation of the Host*. The most intriguing room of the palace is the duke's study on the second floor. Stunning inlaid-wood panels give the illusion of real books and shelves holding astronomical and musical instruments. Nearby, a circular stairway descends to the **Chapel of the Perdono** and the **Tempietto delle Muse,** where the Christian and the pagan are commingled. At one time, 11 wooden panels representing Apollo, Minerva, and the nine Muses covered the walls of the temple, but all have been removed (eight of them are currently in Florence's Galleria Corsini). Don't leave the palace without heading underground to see the well-documented "works" of the *palazzo,* including the duke's bath (with both hot and cold tubs), kitchen, washroom, freezer, and lavatory for the staff. An ingenious underground cistern system provided water to these rooms. (Open daily 9am-2pm. Admission L8000.)

At the end of Via Barocci lies the 14th-century **Oratorio di San Giovanni Battista,** decorated with brightly colored Gothic frescoes by L. J. Salimbeni (1416) representing events from the life of St. John. If you speak Italian, the *custode* can give you a wonderful explanation of how fresco painters used lamb's blood as ink for their sketches. (Open Mon.-Sat. 10am-noon and 3-5pm, Sun. 10am-12:30pm. Admission L3000, but you will be obliged to see S. Giuseppe next door for another L2000.) **Raphael's house,** Via Raffaello, 57, is now a vast and delightful museum with period furnishings. His earliest work, a fresco entitled *Madonna e Bambino,* hangs in the *sala.* (Open Mon.-Sat. 9am-1pm and 3-7pm, Sun. 9am-1pm. Admission L5000.) The hike up to the **Fortezza Albornoz** (turn left at the end of Via Raffaello) ends with an inspiring view of the Ducal Palace and the rest of the city: the perfect spot for a picnic. (Palace is closed for restoration. Check with the tourist office for updated info.)

Urbino's P. della Repubblica serves as a modeling runway for local youth in their chic threads. Take a walk down this fashion ramp and then stroll (or climb) the serpentine streets with the *passeggiata* at dusk. For more frenzied entertainment, dance the night away at **Club 83,** Via Nuova, 4 (tel. 25 12; opens around midnight). A cheaper alternative, and more popular with students, is the **University ACLI** on Via Santa Chiona, a bar with music and small crowds. (Night life generally picks up in August, when the Italian university summer session convenes.) In July, the **Antique Music Festival** holds concerts in various churches and theaters in town. August brings the ceremony of the **Revocation of the Duke's Court,** replete with Renaissance costumes. Check at the tourist office for the exact date.

Ancona

Ancona may have been glorious in the past but today it is a city of transit. The convenience of its port means that most people arrive by land and leave by sea or vice-versa, never stopping to explore the city itself. The route from train station to ferry is always busy, while the historic center lies quiet and dilapidated. Buildings are tall, streets dark and sooty. While the Roman Emperor Trajan might have recognized the city's value as a trade center in the 1st century AD, today's cargo consists of tired, ferry-borne tourists uninterested in the town's many historical sights. **Exercise caution at night: a number of buildings in Ancona are deserted and the town does not have many street lights.**

ORIENTATION AND PRACTICAL INFORMATION

Ferry schedules, in excruciating detail, are available at the **Stazione Marittima** on the waterfront just off P. Kennedy. Take bus #1 or #1/4 to and from the station (L1200). All ferry lines operate ticket and info booths. The **information office** (tel. 20 11 83) at the entrance of the station gives free guided tours of Ancona twice a day in summer. English spoken. Open daily 8am-2pm and 3:30-8:30pm. Make reservations if you're traveling during July or August. For ferry service, be at the station at least two hours before departure. Main ferry lines are:

Adriatica: (tel. 20 49 15 or 207 36 26; fax 20 22 96).
ANEK: (tel. 207 32 22 or 20 59 99; fax 546 08 or 207 31 54).
Jadrolinija: (tel. 20 45 16 or 20 43 05; fax 562 56).
Marlines: (tel. 20 25 66; fax 411 77 80).
Minoan/Strintzis: (tel. 20 17 08 or 207 10 68; fax 56 00 09 or 56 03 46).
SEM Maritime Co.: (tel. 552 18 or 20 14 31; fax 20 26 18 or 552 62).
Superfast: (tel. 20 20 33; fax 20 22 19).

Ancona is an important junction on the Bologna-Lecce train line and is also served by trains from Rome. The center of town, **Piazza Cavour,** is a 10-min. ride on bus #1 from the **train station** at P. Rosselli (L1000). **Corso Garibaldi** and **Corso Mazzini** connect P. Cavour to the port. The train station (tel. 439 33) also houses a **tourist office** (tel. 417 03). Open June 1-Sept.15 Mon.-Sat. 9am-12:30pm and 5-7:30pm. The main tourist office is at Via Thaon de Revel, 4 (tel. 332 49). *Fermo posta* available at the **post office,** Viale della Vittoria, 2 (tel. 20 13 20 or 517 28), off P. Cavour. Open Mon.-Fri. 8:15am-7:40pm and Sat. 8:15-1pm. For **emergencies,** tel. 288 88 (police), 113 or 116. Ancona's **postal code** is 60100, and its **telephone code** is 071.

ACCOMMODATIONS AND FOOD

In summer, people waiting for ferries often spend the night at the Stazione Marittima, but you'll find lots of reasonably priced hotels in the town center. Avoid the overpriced lodgings in the area by the train station. Make reservations or arrive early—rooms fill quickly in the summer. A 10-min. stroll from the Stazione Marittima will take you to **Pensione Centrale** at Via Marsala, 10 (tel. 543 88), one block from P. Roma, on the 4th floor. Fine rooms have high ceilings. Singles L35,000. Doubles L50,000, with bath L80,000. Or take bus #1 to Viale della Vittoria and head to **Hotel Cavour,** Viale della Vittoria, 7 (tel. 20 03 74), one block from P. Cavour. The fragile-looking elevator will take you to large rooms on the 3rd floor. Singles L38,000. Doubles L65,000-75,000. Pack a meal for your ferry ride at the old-fashioned **Mercato**

Pubblico (across from Corso Mazzini, 130). Open Mon.-Wed. and Fri. 7:30am-12:45pm and 5:15-7:30pm, Thurs. and Sat. 7:30am-12:45pm. Supermarket **SIDIS,** at Via Matteotti, 115, offers the best grocery deals around. Open Mon.-Wed. and Fri.-Sat. 8:15am-12:45pm and 5-7:30pm, Thurs. 8:15am-12:45pm. For hearty Italian fare in a cheery sky-blue-and-white decor, try **Trattoria Vittoria,** Via Calatafimi, 2/B (tel. 20 27 33), on the corner of P. Cavour and Corso Mazzini. Pizza at lunch for L6000-10,000. Fixed-price menu for L20,000 includes *primo, secondo*, vegetable, and beverage. Open Tues.-Sun. noon-3pm and 7-10:30pm. If you prefer dining *al fresco,* head to **Trattoria 13 Cannelle,** Corso Mazzini, 108 (tel. 20 60 12), off P. Roma opposite the fountain in the wall. *Primi* L9000-12,000, *secondi* L10,000-23,000. Open Tues.-Sun. 12:15-2:45pm and 8-10:30pm. Cover L2000. V, MC, AmEx.

SIGHTS AND ENTERTAINMENT

Survey the Anconan sea and sky from **Piazzale del Duomo,** atop **Monte Guasco.** Climb up Via Papa Giovanni XXIII, or take bus #11 from P. Cavour. If you decide to walk, you'll enjoy the beautiful **Scalone Nappi,** a verdant stairway street. (Follow the left-hand steps at the point where the street forks; there are 244 steps, and the view is worth every one of them.) In P. del Duomo stands the **Cathedral of San Ciriaco,** erected in the 11th century on the site of a Roman temple to Venus. Its stolid Romanesque design reflects the influences of the Apulian Romanesque from the south and the remnants of the Byzantine from the north. (Cathedral open daily 9-10:30am and 3:30-6pm.)

After decades of restoration (World War II bombings and a 1972 earthquake among its trials), the **Museo Archeologico Nazionale delle Marche** is open for business on Via Ferretti above Via Pizzecolli. The impressive collection includes the Ionian *Dinos of Amandola,* some wonderful Greek vases, and two life-size equestrian bronzes of Roman emperors. (Open Mon.-Sat. 8:30am-1:30pm, Sun. 8:30am-1pm.) Ancona's painting gallery, the **Galleria Comunale Francesco Podesti,** is housed in the 16th-century **Palazzo Bosdari** at Via Pizzecolli, 17. Carlo Crivelli's tiny, flawless *Madonna col Bambino* completely shows up Titian's *Apparition of the Virgin,* recently restored to the full glory of its original colors. (Open Tues.-Sat. 10am-7pm, Sun. 9am-1pm. Admission L5000, children, students, and seniors free. Sun. free for everyone.) Join the evening *passeggiata* on the tree-lined esplanade from Corso Garibaldi past P. Cavour to Viale della Vittoria.

Ascoli Piceno

According to legend, Ascoli was founded by Greeks who were guided westward by a woodpecker—a *picchio*—which suggested the city's surname and provided a symbol for the Marches. In another account, Ascoli was the metropolis of the Piceno people, a quiet Latin tribe that controlled much of the coastal Marches and had the woodpecker as its clan totem. Whatever its origins, Ascoli has always been fiercely independent, serving as a center of anti-Roman power during the Social Wars and successfully resisting Nazi occupation during World War II. In the late 13th century, this independent city produced its own splendid style of architecture. Ascoli is celebrated for its attractive, well-preserved historic center and romantic medieval streets that make the town seem untouched by modernity. Tucked among the mountains, it has also escaped the blight of tourism. Prices are downright reasonable and the near-empty hostel, housed in a 13th-century castle, completes the picture of Ascoli as an attractive place to stay. Stroll through the historic center and avoid the new town; in general, visit Ascoli to recollect the past.

ORIENTATION AND PRACTICAL INFORMATION

Ascoli is about one hour by bus or train from San Benedetto del Tronto, which is itself one hour from Ancona on the Bologna-Lecce train line. If you do take the train, you'll still need to hop a city bus (L1200) once you arrive. Walk straight out of the **train sta-**

tion, one block to **Viale Indipendenza,** take a right, and then walk half a block to the stop. Catch bus #2 or 3 to arrive at the historic center. Get off at the **bus station** behind the *duomo,* where the Cotravat buses stop as well. Walk between the *duomo* and the small, square baptistery to **Piazza Arringo** and its two fountains. Cross P. Arringo and continue on **Via XX Settembre** to Via del Trivio, on the right, which connects to **Corso Mazzini** and **Piazza del Popolo.**

Tourist Office: Ufficio Informazioni, P. del Popolo, 17 (tel. 25 52 50). Very helpful. Open Sun.-Fri. 8am-1:30pm and 3-7pm, Sat. 8:30am-12:30pm and 3-7pm.

Telephones: Via Dino Argelini Patriota, 145/147, off Via del Trivio. Office open Mon.-Fri. 9am-1pm and 3:30-7:30pm, Sat. 9am-1pm.

Trains: P. Le Stazione, at the end of V. Marconi. To San Benedetto (10 per day, 30min., L3400.). Ticket counter open Mon.-Sat. 6:25am-8pm.

Buses: Cotravat buses are cheaper, less crowded, and more frequent than the trains, leaving San Benedetto del Tronto for Ascoli about every 45 min. (L3100). All lines leave from Viale de' Gasperi (behind the *duomo*) except Amadio, which runs from Viale Indipendenza. Timetable outside on the wall at **Agenzia Viaggi Brunozzi,** Corso Trento e Trieste, 54/56 (tel. 25 94 60). Buy train and bus tickets here. Open Mon.-Fri. 9am-1pm and 4-7pm. **ARPA** (tel. (0861) 24 83 43) to Pescara (5 per day, 2hr., L6000). If the *agenzia* is closed, you can get tickets to S. Benedetto in *tabacchi.*

Emergencies: tel. 113.

Post Office: Via Crispi, off Corso Mazzini. Open Mon.-Sat. 8:15am-7:40pm. *Fermo posta* (at window #3) open Mon.-Sat. 8:30am-1pm and 4-7:40pm. Stamps at #4 and 5. **Postal Code:** 63100.

Telephone Code: 0736.

CENTRAL ITALY

ACCOMMODATIONS

Ostello de Longobardi, Via Soderini, 26 (tel. 25 90 07), on Palazzetto Longobardo. From P. del Popolo take Via del Trivio, which flanks the Church of San Francesco. Pass Via del Faro on the left and Via Ceci on the right. When the road forks, take Via Cairoli going left to P. San Pietro Martire and continue past the church onto Via Delle Donne. This street crosses Via Delle Torri and becomes Via Soderini. The hostel is on the street marked Via dei Longobardi to your right (there is also a yellow sign). Close to the historic center and run by an endearing owner who takes pride in the 11th-century origin of the building. He also gives free guided tours of the city. No lockout and no curfew; you get the keys. L14,000 per person. Showers L1000. Kitchen available for guests' use.

Albergo Piceno, Via Minucia, 10 (tel. 25 25 53), near the cathedral and the bus stop. Close to the center of things, and so clean you could eat off the floor. (But please don't.) Rooms without baths mean you must shower downstairs. Pleasant lounge with leather sofas. Singles L40,000, with bath L50,000. Doubles L65,000, with bath L75,000. Triples with bath L100,000.

Cantina Dell'Arte, Via della Lupa, 8 (tel. 25 57 44 or 25 56 20), behind the post office. Take the street to the left of the ugly concrete building. Gorgeous, modern rooms in the medieval heart of town. TVs and private baths included. Friendly manager. Singles L45,000. Doubles L65,000. Triples L90,000. Quads L100,000.

Hotel Pavoni, Via Navilella, 135/B (tel. 34 25 75 or 34 25 87), 3km away on the road to San Benedetto. Take bus #3 from P. Arringo (L1000). A quiet hotel on the outskirts of town. Singles L35,000, with bath L45,000. Doubles L58,000, with bath L70,000.

FOOD

Fill your tummy without emptying your pockets—an excellent meal should run about L15,000. There's also an **open-air market** in P. San Francesco behind P. del Popolo (Mon.-Sat. mornings). In P. Santa Maria Inter Vineas, you'll find the small **Tigre** supermarket. Open Mon.-Fri. 9am-1pm and 5-8pm, Sat. 9am-1:30pm.

Trattoria Lino Cavucci, P. della Viola, 13 (tel. 503 58). An excellent choice. *Primi* L4500-5000, *secondi* L7500-9000. Cover L2500. Open Sat.-Thurs. noon-3pm and 5-11pm.

Cantina dell'Arte, Via della Lupa, 5 (tel. 25 11 35), across from the hotel (no sign). Family-run restaurant with long communal tables. Delicious daily specials. *Primi* L6000-8000, *secondi* L10,000. *Menù* L15,000. Cover included in prices. Open daily noon-2:30pm and 7-9:30pm.

L'Assaggino, Via Minucia, 24 (tel. 25 55 43), at the end of Via Civo del Duca, 2 blocks from P. del Popolo. A popular self-service *pizzeria* with indoor and outdoor seating. *Primi* and *secondi* about L6000. Pizza L1500-3000 per slice. Open Mon.-Sat. 9am-9pm.

Pizzeria Italia, Corso Mazzini, 205. Near the post office. Standing only. Pizza L1500-3500 per slice. Open Mon.-Sat. 9am-9pm.

SIGHTS AND ENTERTAINMENT

Museum hours in Ascoli are constantly changing. Confirm your sightseeing plans with the tourist office in P. del Popolo.

Piazza del Popolo, the historic center of town, is a calm oasis in this busy city. The 16th-century *portici* lining two sides of the square recall the Piazza San Marco in Venice. The third side houses the 13th-century **Palazzo dei Capitani del Popolo,** whose massive portal and statue of Pope Paul III date from 1548. The history of the edifice is full of Renaissance (and later) intrigue. Originally the palace of the city's hierarch, or captain, the building was burned on Christmas Day 1535 in an inter-familial squabble; the *piazza* smoldered for two days. A decade later the palace was refurbished and dedicated to the pope, who brought peace to Ascoli. In 1938 the palace was the seat of the principal Fascist party, only to be wrested away for partisan use in early 1945. Through the entrance to the left of the main portal, an excavated area beneath the foundation of the *palazzo* is on view. Remains from the Roman era were discovered here in 1982, legitimating the view that the *piazza* was originally the forum in the Roman town known as "Asculum." Works from both the Republican and Augustan eras can be viewed here, via the serpentine wooden pathway weaving down and under the structure of the *palazzo.* The *piazza* is the forecourt for the elegant eastern end of the **Church of San Francesco** (13th-16th centuries). Its spacious three-aisled interior houses a 14th-century wooden crucifix, the only art object saved from the 1535 fire. Find the "singing columns," two sets of five low columns flanking the door on the V. del Trivio side of the church. Draw your hand quickly and firmly across the columns and hear the different tones. (Church open 8am-noon and 3-7pm.) At dusk Ascoli's youths gather near this church for a lively *passeggiata.* Abutting the church to the south, the gracious **Loggia dei Mercanti** (Merchant's Gallery, 1509-1513), now a favorite meeting place for the town elders, leads to Corso Mazzini and the austere 14th-century **Church of Sant'Agostino.** (Open 9am-noon and 3-7pm.)

Via delle Torri, off P. Sant'Agostino, runs past the stone houses of the old quarter to the 13th-century **Church of San Pietro il Martiro** and tiny **Via di Solestà.** This street, one of the oldest in the city, leads to the single-arched **Ponte di Solestà,** one of Europe's tallest Roman bridges. Cross this bridge (or the Ponte Nuovo) and walk to the edge of town (turning on Viale Marcello, right or left respectively) to find the **Church of Sant'Emidio alle Grotte,** a Baroque façade grafted onto the natural rock wall. Inside are catacombs where the first Ascoli Christians are buried.

On the other side of town, **Piazza Arringo** ("orate") derives its name from the speeches delivered here by local leaders. Try the water straight from the horses' mouths on either fountain - it's the freshest and coolest around. The massive travertine **duomo** is a blend of art and architecture from the 5th through the 20th centuries. A Roman basilica forms the transept, topped by an irregular octagonal dome from the 8th century. The two towers were built in the 11th and 12th centuries, while the lateral naves and central apse were constructed in the 1400s. In the *duomo's* **Chapel of the Sacrament,** an intricately framed polyptych of the *Virgin* *and Saints* (Carlo Crivelli, 1473) surmounts a 14th-century silver altar. (Open daily 9am-noon and 4-7pm.) Next to the cathedral stands the compact 12th-century **baptistery,** decorated with a *loggia* of blind arches. Works by Crivelli, Titian, van Dyck, and Ribera hang amidst red velvet curtains and pink walls in the **Pinacoteca Civica** (tel. 29 82 13), inside the **Palazzo Comunale** (southern flank of the *piazza*). Upstairs, you will find a collection of handsome stringed instruments and some Impressionist paintings and sculptures. (Open in summer Mon.-Fri. 9am-1pm and 3-7pm, Sat. 9am-1pm, Sun. 4-8pm; in winter Mon.-Sat. 9am-1pm, Sun. 9am-12:30pm. Admission L2500, children and seniors free.) Visit the **Museo Archeologico** (tel. 25 35 62), also on the *piazza,* for its hall of mosaics. (Open Mon.-Sat. 9am-7pm, Sun. 9:30am-1:30pm. Closed first and last Sun. of each month. Admission L4000, children and seniors free.)

On the first Sunday in August, Ascoli holds the **Tournament of Quintana,** a medieval pageant in which locals deck themselves out in colorful traditional costume. The tournament, which features armed (man-on-dummy) jousting and a torchlight procession to P. del Popolo, is the culmination of the four-day festival of Sant'Emidio, the city's patron. The **carnival** in February is one of Italy's most lively. Insanity reigns on the Tuesday, Thursday, and especially the Sunday preceding Ash Wednesday. Residents don costumes, and folk dancers perform in P. del Popolo. Happily, the event is not mobbed by tourists, but you should still make hotel reservations ahead. If you have already seen all the historical points of interest you can handle, simply relax and go with the flow in the intrinsically entertaining *passeggiate* of Ascoli. The biggest one is along Corso Trento e Trieste and P. del Popolo. Arrive between 7 and 8pm and you, too, can strut your stuff.

San Benedetto

With 5000 palm trees and as many children playing under their waving fronds, San Benedetto is a true-to-the-core beach town where rest, relaxation, and *gelato* are the only priorities. It may be called the "Riviera of the Palms," but San Benedetto has none of the chic pretensions of other Mediterranean towns; flip-flops and bathing suits are the fashion of choice here, and they won't soon go out of style.

ORIENTATION AND PRACTICAL INFORMATION

San Benedetto lies on the Bologna-Lecce train line. The train station is on **Viale Gramsci.** From the station, take bus #2 (L1200) to the *lungomare,* or walk left on Via Gramsci and turn left onto **Via Mazzocchi** toward the beach. A right on **Via delle Palme** will take you directly to **Viale delle Tamerici.**

Tourist Office: APT, Viale delle Tamerci, 5 (tel. 59 22 37 or 58 25 42; fax 58 28 93), near Via dei Tighi. Provides maps and info on hotels and campgrounds in the area. Open in summer Mon.-Sat. 8am-2pm and 4-7pm, Sun. 9am-noon; in winter Mon.-Sat. 9am-noon.

Telephones: Via Montebello, 31. Phone booths for cards and coins.

Trains: (tel. 21 31), Viale Gramisci. To: Bologna (7 per day, 2½hr., L22,600); Milan (1 night train and and 4 daily intercities, L45,000); and Ancona (10 per day, 1½hr., L7200). Ticket counter open daily 6am-9pm. **Luggage Storage:** L5000 for 12hr. Open daily 6am-9pm.

Buses: Local lines stop in front of the train station. Bus #2 travels along the waterfront. **Cotravat** buses to Ascoli Piceno leave from the station about every 45 min. (L3100). Buy tickets at Bar Massimo across from the train station.

Emergencies: tel. 113. **Hospital: Ospedale Civile** (tel. 79 31), Via Silvio Pellico.

Post Office: Via Curzi, 26 (tel. 59 21 57), near V. Crispi. **Postal Code:** 63039.

Telephone Code: 0735.

ACCOMMODATIONS AND CAMPING

Pensione Zio Emilio, Via Alessandro Volta, 24 (tel. 821 39). A quiet, friendly hotel with a pleasant downstairs dining area. All rooms clean, with sturdy furniture and bath. Run by Uncle Emilio's son. Singles L45,000, low-season L35,000. Doubles L75,000, low-season L50,000. Full-pension L82,000, low-season L50,000. Closed Oct.-May. V, MC.

Hotel Mario, Via Alessandro Volta, 24 (tel. 78 10 66). Tidy rooms with tile floors, bath, and phone. Bar and dining room downstairs serve 3 meals daily. L40,000 per person, low-season L30,000. Half-pension L57,000, low-season L45,000. Full-pension (required in Aug.) L75,000, low-season L50,000. Open year-round.

Camping Seaside, Via Sgambati (tel. 65 95 05), near the water. Small, but the only campground in town. (Cupra Marittima has more options.) L10,000 per person, low-season L4000. L20,000 per space, low-season L10,000. Open June-Sept.

FOOD

As with any beach town, sandwiches and *gelati* are always easy to find. Pack a picnic from a local *alimentari,* or try supermarket **Tigre,** with locations at Via Abruzzi, 28 and Via Ugo Bassi, 10. Open Mon.-Fri. 8:45am-12:45pm and 5-8:15pm, Sat. 5-8:30pm. On Tuesday and Friday mornings, head for the open-air **market** in Via Montebello near the station. San Benedetto's culinary claim to fame is *Benedetto alla sambenedettese,* a hodgepodge of fish, green tomatoes, peppers, and vinegar. This complicated soup requires extensive preparation; several restaurants in town can make it upon request. Try it at **Brigantino,** Via A. Doria, 9 (tel. 59 12 22).

Pub San Michele, Via Piemonte, 111 (tel. 824 29), a friendly place for fresh pizza and a cool beer. Pizzas and calzones L4500-7000. *Menù* L20,000, including *primo, secondo,* and vegetable. Cover L2000. Beer L3000 and up. Open daily noon-3pm and 7pm-2am.

Café Fuori Orario, Via C. Colombo, 7 (tel. 58 37 20), near the station. Serves up coffee, cocktails, food, and late-night snacks on a lovely terrace. They won't kick you out until dawn. *Primi* L8000. *Secondi* L9000-16,000. *Olive all'Ascolana* L5000. Desserts L5000. Open Tues.-Sun. 7:30pm-5am.

SIGHTS AND ENTERTAINMENT

Many residents of San Benedetto seem content to wander along the seaside or spend the afternoon chatting in a *caffè.* A neat local museum is the **Museo Ittico Augusto Capriotti** on Via C. Colombo, 98 (tel. 58 88 50), an old-style natural history museum of sea life. Marvel at dried fishes and huge eels floating in formaldehyde. Especially beautiful is the coral room with cases full of tree-like specimens. (Open in summer Mon.-Sat. 9am-noon and 4-7:30pm, Sun. 4-7:30pm; in winter Mon.-Sat. 9am-noon and 4-6:30pm. Free.)

Umbria

Known as the "Green Heart of Italy," Umbria has long enjoyed renown for its rivers, valleys, and wooded hills. Often shrouded in a silvery haze, this enchanting landscape proved irresistible to the ancient Umbrii who first settled the region around 1000BC. Over the centuries, ravenous barbarian hordes, aggressive neighboring Romans, and the meddlesome papacy eventually trampled the vast empire, though, sousing it in blood and looting its riches.

This foreign contact wasn't all that bad; in fact, it endowed Umbria with some of the region's most remarkable qualities. Christianity forever transformed Umbria, turning it into a breeding ground for saints and religious movements. Its great mystical tradition started with St. Benedict, who breathed life into western monasticism. Years later, tree-hugging St. Francis shamed the extravagant church with his humility, earning a reputation for pacifism that stretched all the way to the Muslim world.

The region still draws countless pilgrims each year, particularly for the artistic legacy left by Rome and the papal states. Umbria owes many of its magnificent churches and spectacular *palazzi* to the lavish lifestyles of Renaissance nobles and clergymen. Imbued with a fresh artistic spirit, the region turned out such celebrated painters as Perugino and Pinturicchio.

Today, Umbria's natural and artistic beauty continues to entice tourists by the thousands. Refreshing lakes, clear streams, and verdant ravines are enough to inspire brief jaunts into the wilderness, wresting tourists' attention away from the many ineffably charming towns. Umbria's medieval houses, picturesque cobblestone streets, and sweeping *piazze* are just what everyone scrambles to Italy to find.

Umbrian cuisine draws heavily from the region's lakes and woods. Trout, carp, and squirmy little eels are big favorites, as are all manner of grilled meats. More refined gourmands indulge in Umbria's most famous contribution to the gourmet world—truffles. To the distinguishing Italian palate, the white truffle's bouquet and flavor far surpass those of the better-known French black truffle. Both types grow in Umbria's oak forests and are commonly grated over pasta; sample for yourself. Wash down your *tartufi* with Umbria's best-known wine, the distinctive Orvieto.

Perugia

Perugians may be the most polite people you'll meet in Italy, an odd fact considering Perugia's long history as a violent and disreputable town. From its earliest days as an Etruscan *polis* through Roman domination, Perugia was a chronic troublemaker. When they grew weary of laying seige to neighboring towns, Perugians entertained themselves with the *Battaglia de' Sassi* (Battle of Stones), an annual festival during which two teams pelted each other with rocks until a sufficient number of casualties or fatalities left a winner. Even the town's most famous religious order, the Flagellants, demonstrated a penchant for violence; they wandered across Europe whipping themselves in public. Perugia's other contributions to Christianity include its imprisonment of the peace-loving St. Francis of Assisi and the poisoning of two popes. But the good times eventually ended, and Perugia found itself crushed underneath the papal heel of Paul III in 1538.

Three centuries of economic misery under the Papal States apparently taught the Perugians some manners (though not subservience—they were rebelling against the pope as late as 1859). The present-day capital of Umbria claims a delightfully civilized atmosphere seasoned by the international crowd drawn to its distinguished universities and art academies. Visitors pour in year-round to catch glimpses of the enchanting countryside and to troll through the town's medieval streets. Perugia also attracts huge crowds to its world-renowned jazz festival every July. The *palazzi* that crowd Corso Vannucci, Perugia's main street, shelter an impressive collection of medieval and Renaissance art. Interspersed are bars offering the city's contemporary masterpiece, the infamous chocolate *baci* (kisses).

ORIENTATION AND PRACTICAL INFORMATION

Perugia lies on the Foligno-Terontola line, with frequent trains to these hub stations. To get to Rome, change at Foligno for the Rome-Ancona line or at Terontola for the Florence-Rome line. Several direct trains also service Florence and Rome. From the station, local bus #36 will leave you in **Piazza Matteotti.** Buses #26 and 27 go to **Piazza Italia** (L1000). Otherwise, it's a treacherous 4-km uphill trek. From the bus station in **Piazza dei Partigiani,** follow the signs to the **escalator** (*scala mobile)* which takes you underneath the old city to P. Italia. Straight ahead, **Corso Vannucci,** the main shopping thoroughfare, leads to **Piazza IV Novembre** and the *duomo.* Behind the *duomo* lies the university area. One block to the right of Corso Vannucci you'll find P. Matteotti, the municipal center. The new **Digiplan** machines in the train station are extremely helpful (if they work), providing instant printout information on sights, museums, stores, restaurants, and more.

Tourist Office: P. IV Novembre (tel. 572 53 41 or 572 33 27). Friendly, patient, and knowledgeable staff gives info on accommodations and travel. Artistic but mislead-

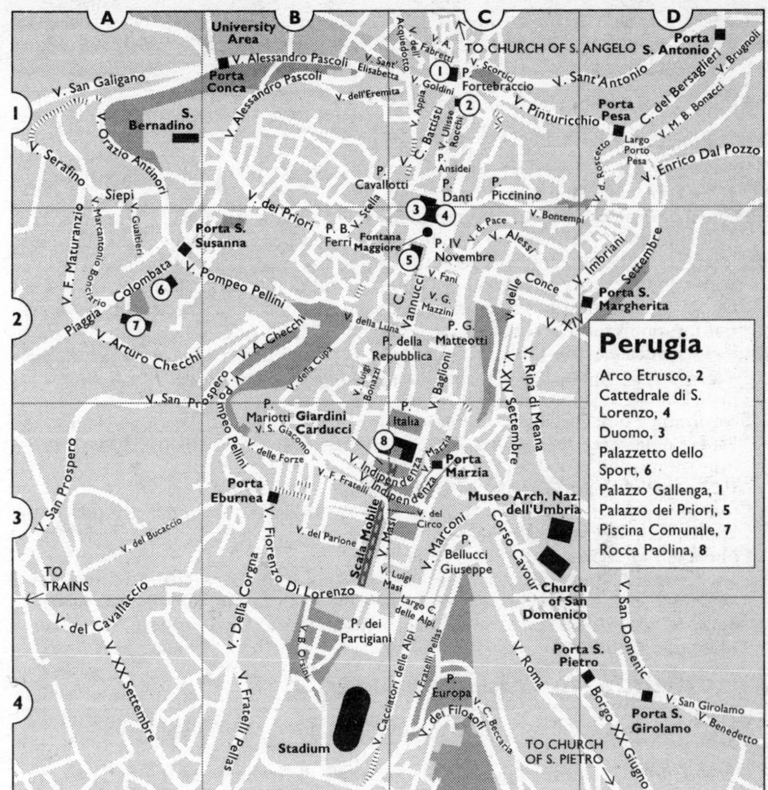

ing city map. Ask for the detailed walking guide, the *Italy Has a Green Heart* brochures, and the map of Umbria. Open Mon.-Sat. 8:30am-1:30pm and 3:30-6:30pm, Sun. 9am-1pm.

Budget Travel: CTS, Via del Roscetto, 21 (tel. 572 02 84), off Via Pinturicchio toward the bottom of the street. Student center with travel and accommodations offices. Open Mon.-Fri. 9:30am-12:30pm and 4-7pm. **CIT,** Corso Vannucci, 2 (tel. 572 60 61), by the fountain. Open Mon.-Fri. 9am-1pm and 3:30-7pm.

Currency Exchange: The best rates are found at banks; those in P. Italia have 24-hr. automatic exchange machines. At the train station, there is no commission for an exchange of less than L80,000, but the rate will be worse.

Telephones: P. Matteotti, by the post office. Open Mon.-Fri. 9am-1pm and 4-7pm.

Trains: Fontivegge, P. Veneto. **F.S.** south to: Assisi (about every hr., 25min., L3400); Foligno (about every hr., 40min., L3400); Spoleto (about every hr., 1¼hr., L5700); Orvieto (8 per day, 1¾hr., L9800); and Rome via Terontola (3hr., L25,400), via Foligno (3hr., L17,200), and direct (2½hr., L26,900). North to: Passignano sul Trasimeno (every hr., 30min., L2700); Arezzo (every hr., 1½hr., L6500); Florence (every hr., 2½hr., L20,700); and Siena (9 per day, 3hr., L21,600). **Sant'Anna** station in P. Bellucci serves Città di Castello and Sansepolcro to the north and Todi to the south. **Information: F.S.** on P. Veneto. Open 6:45am-8pm. **Ferrovia Centrale Umbra,** Largo Cacciatori delle Alpi, 8 (tel. 291 21), near the bottom of the escalator on the 1st floor. The **ticket window** in the F.S. station is open 6am-9pm. **Luggage Storage:** L5000 for 12hr. Open daily 6:20am-8:20pm.

Buses: P. dei Partigiani, down the *scala mobile* from P. Italia. City bus #28, 29, 36, 42 or CD (L1000) from the train station. **ASP buses,** P. dei Partigiani (tel. 573 17 07), to most Umbrian towns, including Gubbio (10 per day, 1¼hr., L7400); Todi (6 per day, 1¼hr., L9200); and Spoleto (one at 2pm, 1½hr., L10,400). Also service to Rome and Florence.

Taxis: tel. 500 48 88.

Public Toilets, Showers, and Baths: Viale Indipendenza, 7. Enter through the *scala mobile* under P. Italia and look for the "diurno" sign. Open daily 8am-11pm; in winter 8am-8pm. Toilet L500, shower L4000, towel and soap L1500.

Bookstore: Libreria, Via Rocchi, 1. English books L12,000-16,000. Open Mon.-Sat. 10am-1pm and 5-8pm.

Higher Education: Università per gli Stranieri, Palazzo Gallenga, P. Fortebraccio, 4 (tel. 57 46 21). The university offers courses in Italian language and culture for foreigners. The student café, replete with pinball machines, is frequented by the young and the restless. A good place to meet other travelers. Glance over the university bulletin board for cultural events and free concerts. Check with the registrar for rooms for rent (only for longer stays).

Laundromat: Lava e Lava, Via Annibale Vecchi, 5 and Via Mario Angeloni, 32. Wash L6000 per 8kg. Dry L500 for 3min. **Onda Blu,** Corso Bersaglieri, 2. Wash and dry L12,000. All open daily 8am-10pm.

Swimming Pool: Piscina Comunale (tel. 573 51 60) on Via Pompeo Pellini, near Santa Colombata. Open daily 1-7:30pm; off-season Mon.-Fri. 6:30am-8:30pm, Sat. 3-8pm. Admission L7000.

All-Night Pharmacy: Farmacia S. Martino, P. Matteoti, 26.

Emergencies: tel. 113. **First Aid:** tel. 444 44. **Hospital: Ospedali Riuniti-Policlinico** (tel. 57 81), Via Bonacci Brunamonti.

Police: tel. 112. **Questura,** P. dei Partigiani.

Post Office: P. Matteotti. Mail services available Mon.-Sat. 8:10am-7:30pm, Sun. 8:30am-5:30pm. **Currency** and **traveler's checks exchanged** Mon.-Fri. 8:10am-5:30pm, Sat. 8:10am-1pm, Sun. 8:30am-5:30pm. **Postal Code:** 06100.

Telephone Code: 075.

ACCOMMODATIONS AND CAMPING

Reservations are absolutely necessary during the Umbria Jazz Festival in July.

Ostello della Gioventù/Centro Internazionale di Accoglienza per la Gioventù, Via Bontempi, 13 (tel. 572 28 80). From P. Matteotti walk up Via de' Fari, take a right on Corso Vannucci, and go straight until you hit P. IV Novembre. Take the road to the far right out of P. Dante and pass P. Piccinino (a parking lot); follow the right fork onto Via Bontempi. The spacious kitchen and breezy terrace make up for the lack of diligent housekeeping. 3-wk. max. stay. Lockout 9:30am-4pm. Curfew midnight. L14,000 per person. Showers and kitchen use included. Sheets L2000. Open mid-Jan. to mid-Dec.

Albergo Anna, Via dei Priori, 48 (tel. 573 63 04), off Corso Vannucci. Walk up 4 floors to clean, cool 17th-century rooms; some boast ceramic fireplaces and great views. Friendly owners. Recently renovated. Singles L36,000, with bath L55,000. Doubles L55,000, with bath L74,000. Triples L75,000, with bath L110,000.

Albergo Etruria, Via della Luna, 21 (tel. 572 37 30), down the passageway by Corso Vannucci, 55, in the heart of town. Heavy wood furniture and antiques fill the rooms. Immense 12th-century sitting room presided over by parakeets. Singles L40,000. Doubles L62,000, with bath L84,000. Showers L4000.

Pensione Paola, Via della Canapina, 5 (tel. 572 38 16). From the train station, take bus #26, 27, or 42 and get off on Viale Pellini after the bus passes a large municipal parking lot on the left. Walk up the stairs; the *pensione* is on the right. Comfortable rooms with bamboo headboards and patterned tiles. Buoyant owner. Singles L40,000. Doubles L60,000. Breakfast L6000.

Camping: Paradis d'Eté (tel. 517 21 17), 5km away in Colle della Trinità. Take bus #36 from the station and ask the driver to leave you in Colle della Trinità. Bar and restaurant on the premises. L7000 per person, L6000 per tent, L3000 per car. Hot showers and pool use included. Open year-round.

FOOD

Though renowned for chocolate, Perugia also serves up a variety of delectable breads and pastries; be sure to sample the *torta di formaggio* (cheese bread) and the *mele al cartoccio* (the Italian version of apple pie). Both are available at **Ceccarani,** P. Matteotti, 16 (open Mon.-Sat. 7:30am-2pm and 4:30-8pm), or at the **Co.Fa.Pa.** bakery two doors down at #12 (open Mon.-Sat. 7:30am-1pm and 5-7:30pm). For such local confections as *torciglione* (a sweet almond bread in the shape of an eel) and *baci* (chocolate-hazelnut kisses), don't miss the old-world elegance of **Pasticerria Sandri,** Corso Vannucci, 32. This gorgeous bakery/candy shop doubles as a bar/cafe and is a great place for morning coffee. Open Mon.-Sat. 7:30am-8pm. If you prefer your chocolate cold and creamy, head to the student-infested **Gelateria 2000,** Via Luigi Bonazzi, 3, off P. della Repubblica, where the *gelato* is excellent. Cones start at L2500. Open Mon.-Sat. 8am-midnight, Sun. 3-8pm.

On Tuesday and Saturday mornings you can salivate over the **open-air market** in P. Europa. On other days, try the covered market in P. Matteotti for plenty of fruit, vegetables, and nuts; the entrance is below street level. Open Tues.-Sat. 8am-1pm. On summer nights the market becomes an outdoor café. Buy essentials at the small markets in P. Matteotti. Usually open Mon.-Wed. and Fri. 8am-1pm and 5-8pm, Thurs. and Sat. 8am-1pm. Complement your meal with a reasonably priced regional wine: *Sagrantino Secco,* a dry, full-bodied red, or *Grechetto,* a light, dry white.

Trattoria Dal Mi Cocco, Corso Garibaldi, 12 (tel. 573 25 11), up from the University for Foreigners. The menu, written in Perugian dialect, is hard to read, but your effort will be rewarded with good food. The L24,000 *menù,* with *antipasto,* two *primi,* two *secondi,* a *contorno,* dessert, and a glass of liquor, is a great value. Very busy. Open Tues.-Sun. 1-2:30pm and 8:15-10:30pm.

L'Oca Nera, Via dei Priori, 78/82 (tel. 572 18 89). Hidden in the caverns below the north-central quarter, this joint draws a crowd for its delicious food, hip atmosphere, and quick, pleasant service. Massive selection ranges from *würstel* to *gnocchi* to hamburgers (around L6500 per dish). Open Thurs.-Tues. 7:30pm-1am.

The Australian Pub, Via de Verzaro, 39 (tel. 572 02 06). A neighborhood joint for Italians, but also a great place to munch on burgers and drink a Fosters with other Anglophiles. Have a quiet dinner on the terrace, then come back for the late-night crowd. Pizzas and burgers L6000-9000. Open daily for dinner noon-2pm and 7-11pm, for drinks until 3am or whenever the last person leaves.

Tavola Calda, P. Danti, 16 (tel. 572 19 76). Wide selection of meat and vegetables served cafeteria-style with outdoor seating. A decent *rosticceria.* Pizza L2000 per slice, sandwiches from L3500. Wild late-night crowd. Open Mon.-Fri. 10am-3pm and 8-10pm, Sun. 10am-3pm.

SIGHTS

Piazza IV Novembre

The city's most interesting sights frame Piazza IV Novembre; all other monuments of distinction lie within a 20-min. walk from this spot. In the middle of the *piazza* sits the **Fontana Maggiore,** designed by native son Fra' Bevignate and decorated by Nicola and Giovanni Pisano. The bas-reliefs covering the majestic double basin depict scenes from religious and Roman history, the allegories of the months and sciences (lower basin), and the saints and other historical figures (upper basin). The beautiful fountain is now undergoing lengthy restoration.

The 13th-century **Palazzo dei Priori** presides over the *piazza,* its long rows of mullioned windows and toothlike crenelations embodying Perugian bellicosity. This building, one of the finest examples of Gothic communal architecture, shelters the impressive **Galleria Nazionale dell'Umbria,** Corso Vanucci, 19 (tel. 572 03 16). The immense collection contains fine works by Duccio, Fra Angelico, Taddeo di Bartolo, Guido da Siena, and Piero della Francesca. But after admiring these Tuscans, look for its Umbrian art. Viewing Perugian Pinturicchio's *Miracles of San Bernardino of*

Siena is the visual equivalent of eating a *bacio.* The colors and dazzling subjects by Pietro Vannucci, alias Perugino, may even be too rich for some tastes. His newly restored *Adoration of the Magi* is the gallery's premier piece. (Open Mon.-Sat. 9am-7pm, Sun. 9am-1pm. Admission L8000.)

Next door in the **Collegio del Cambio** (Banker's Guild; tel. 572 85 99), Perugino demonstrated what a talented artist could do with even a mundane commission. He suffused his frescoes with the gentle softness that he later passed on to his greatest pupil, Raphael. The latter is said to have collaborated with his teacher on the *Prophets and Sibyls.* Notice also Perugino's self-portrait *(autoritratto)* on the left wall. In the small chapel adjacent to the chamber hang paintings of scenes from the life of John the Baptist by Giannicola di Paolo (1519), including an especially grisly decapitation scene with a grinning Salomé. (Open March-Oct. Mon.-Sat. 9am-12:30pm and 2:30-5:30pm, Sun. 9am-12:30pm; Nov.-Feb. Tues.-Sat. 8am-2pm, Sun. 9am-12:30pm. Admission L5000.) Visit the **Collegio della Mercanzia** (Merchant's Guild) farther toward the *piazza* at #15 (tel. 573 03 66). This richly paneled room is the meeting room for Perugia's merchant guild; from 1390 to the present, the guild's 88 members have met here to debate tax law and local commerce. (Open March-Oct. Tues.-Fri. 9am-1pm and 2:30-5:30pm, Sat. 9am-1pm and 2:30-6:30pm, Sun. 9am-1pm; Nov.-Feb. Tues. and Thurs.-Fri. 8am-2pm, Wed. and Sat. 8am-2pm and 4-7pm, Sun. 9am-1pm. Admission L2000. Combined ticket for both the Merchants' and Exchange Guilds L6000.) You can visit the 13th-century frescoes in the **Sala dei Notari,** up the flight of steps across from the fountain, for free. (Open Tues.-Sun. 9am-1pm and 3-7pm; June-Aug. also open Mon.)

At the end of the *piazza* rises Perugia's austere Gothic **duomo.** Though it was begun in the 14th and 15th centuries, the façade was never finished. (Initially, the *perugini* were going to use some marble they stole from Arezzo during a battle, but the *aretini* made them give it back when they won the next round.) Embellishments of varying quality (15th-18th century) adorn the Gothic interior. The town is most proud of the **Virgin Mary's wedding ring,** a relic they snagged from Chiusi in the Middle Ages. The ring is kept securely under lock and key—15 sets, in fact.

Via dei Priori

Stroll down Via delle Volte della Pace from Via Bontempi, trailing along the city's old Etruscan walls; or follow Via dei Priori from behind the palace and Via San Francesco past the church of the same name to the spartan **Oratory of San Bernardino,** near the end of Via dei Priori. Agostino de Duccio built it between 1457 and 1461 in the early Renaissance style, embellishing its façade with finely carved reliefs and sculptures. Inside, a 3rd-century Roman sarcophagus forms the altar. A walk down medieval Via Ulisse Rocchi, the city's oldest street, will take you through the north city gate to the **Arco di Augusto,** a perfectly preserved Roman arch built on Etruscan pedestals and topped by a 16th-century portico. Past the newly cleaned **Palazzo Gallenga,** at the end of a little byway off medieval Corso Garibaldi, lies the jewel-like **Church of Sant'Angelo.** The 5th-century church, built upon an ancient Roman temple, is the oldest in Perugia. Its circular interior incorporates 16 sundry columns appropriated from various ancient buildings. The small park in front is an alluring picnic spot.

The East Side

At the end of town opposite the Porta Sant'Angelo, near Via Cavour, towers the imposing **Church of San Domenico,** the largest in Umbria. The church's huge Gothic rose window contrasts dramatically with the sobriety of its Renaissance interior. Don't miss the magnificently carved **Tomb of Pope Benedict XI,** finished in 1325, in the chapel to the right of the high altar. Once kept in a box tied with a red ribbon, his bones were recently placed in an encasement inside the tomb's far wall, behind a glass pane reinforced with wrought-iron. (You just never know when those necrophiliac-kleptomaniacs are going to strike next.) Near the church, in P. Bruno, the **Museo Archeologico Nazionale dell'Umbria** (tel. 572 71 41) occupies the old

Dominican convent and showcases Etruscan and Roman artifacts. (Open Mon.-Sat. 9am-1:30pm and 2:30-7pm, Sun. 9am-1pm. Admission L4000. Free for Irish, British, Australian, and New Zealand citizens under 18—the U.S. did not sign the reciprocal agreement.) Continue on Corso Cavour, past the Porta San Pietro, and you'll come to the **Church of San Pietro.** It maintains its original 10th-century basilica form, a double arcade of closely spaced columns leading to a choir. Inside, the walls (and visitors) are overwhelmed by paintings and frescoes depicting scenes of saints and soldiers; amidst the mass of paint, look for Perugino's *Pietà* along the north aisle. (Open 8am-noon and 3:30pm-sunset.)

At the far end of Corso Vannucci, the main street leading from P. IV Novembre, are the **Giardini Carducci.** These well-maintained public gardens are named after the 19th-century poet Giosuè Carducci, who wrote a stirring ode to Italy inspired by Perugia's historic zeal for independence. From the garden wall you can enjoy a panorama of the Umbrian countryside: a castle or an ancient church crowns each hill. On the corner of the street below the gardens, a semi-circular lookout point shows you in which direction you're gazing and names the monuments in view. Go around the gardens and down Via Marzia to see the **Rocca Paolina,** the 16th-century fortress built by Sangallo—long a symbol of papal oppression; its interior juxtaposes Italian antiquity and dubious modern art. Pope Paul III had Sangallo demolish this section of the city in the 1500s in order to build a prison. In 1860, when Perugia was liberated from the rule of the Papal States and became part of unified Italy, the *perugini* immediately began hacking it to pieces. (Open daily 8am-7pm. Free.) The **Porta Marzia,** an Etruscan gate in the city wall, opens onto **Via Bagliona Sotterranea.** This street within the fortress is lined with 15th-century houses that were buried when the gardens were built above them. (Gate open Tues.-Sat. 8am-2pm, Sun. 9am-1pm.) The Rocca is also accessible by the escalator.

ENTERTAINMENT

Perugia's biggest annual event is the glorious **Umbria Jazz Festival,** which draws performers of international renown for 10 days in July. (Admission L35,000-50,000. Some events free.) For more information, contact the tourist office.

Summer brings **Guarda Dove Vai,** a series of musical, cinematic, and dance performances. In September, the **Sagra Musicale Umbra** fills local churches with concerts of religious and classical music. Check Palazzo Gallenga for listings of English films and other events. If you miss the jazz festival, you can still take in some fusion of dixieland at **Il Contrappunto,** Via Scortici, 4A (tel. 573 36 37), next to the University for Foreigners. Free buses depart from P. Fortebraccio (starting at 11pm) for several nearby clubs. In town, hang with the locals at the lively **Pozzo Entrare** on Via della Volte Pace. The locals can tell you about other clubs, such as **Red Zone** (tel. 694 03 44), that can only be reached by car.

■ Near Perugia: Lake Trasimeno

This placid and somewhat marshy lake, 30km west of Perugia, is an ideal spot to find some refreshment and tranquility, a perfect refuge from Umbria's stifling heat and packed tourist centers. While pleasant and peaceful today, Lake Trasimeno witnessed some violent battles in the second Punic War. In 217BC, Hannibal's elephant-riding army, fresh from the Alps, routed the Romans on the plain north of the lake. The names of the villages, Ossaia ("place of bones") and Sanguineto ("bloody"), recall the carnage of 16,000 Roman troops.

The two main towns girding the lake, Passignano sul Trasimeno and Castiglione del Lago, are easily accessible by both bus (L9500 roundtrip from Perugia's P. Partigiani) and train. **Passignano sul Trasimeno** lies on the Foligno-Terontola line; hourly trains make the 30-min. trip from Perugia. The **Pro Loco tourist office** at Via Roma, 38 (tel. 82 76 35), overlooks the peaceful town park. Coming from the dock, turn left; coming from the station, go across the tracks away from the stationhouse and follow the road. Here you'll find maps, hotel listings, and boat schedules. Open Mon.-Sat.

9:30am-12:30pm and 3:30-6:30pm. You can **exchange currency** at Cassa di Risparmio di Città di Castello, Via Gabriotti, 2. Open Mon.-Thurs. 8:20am-1:20pm and 2:50-3:50pm, Fri. 8:20am-1:20pm and 2:35-3:35pm, Sat. 8:20-11:50am. For lodging, you'll find a great value at **Hotel Florida,** Via Due Giugno, 2 (tel. 82 72 28), right near the train station and only 100m from the water. The spotless rooms are decorated with soft hues, and some of the ceilings are graced by vibrant frescoes. Doubles with bath L60,000-75,000. Singles, triples, and quads are available upon request. Free breakfast includes a pastry, homemade fig marmalade, and a great cappuccino. Food is expensive in both towns, so bring a picnic to eat on the lakeshore. You can pick up provisions at the **Sidis Market** in P. Trento e Trieste. Open Mon.-Sat. 8:30am-12:30pm and 4:30-8pm, Sun. 8:30am-12:30pm. Grab a slice of pizza (L1100-2000) at **Pizzeria Boomerang** on Via Gabriotti, right across from the shore. Open Tues.-Sun. 9am-2pm and 4:30-9:15pm.

Castiglione del Lago, a quiet town that takes its name from the castle that towers above it, lies on the Florence-Rome train line. To get to Perugia, change at Terontola (10 per day, fewer on Sun., 1hr.). The **tourist office** at P. Mazzini, 10 (tel. 965 24 84), will help you find a hotel (singles from L60,000, doubles from L80,000), a room in a private home, or a private apartment (about L300,000 per week). You can also **change money** and get boat schedules here. Open Mon.-Fri. 8am-1:30pm and 3-7:30pm, Sat. 9am-1pm and 3:30-7:30pm, Sun. 9am-1pm. The clear choice among the hotels is the **Albergo Santa Lucia,** Via Buozzi, 84 (tel. 965 24 92), complete with a private garden and immaculate rooms, all with bath. Singles L40,000. Doubles L80,000. For food, try the shops lining Via Vittorio Emanuele, or dine at **Paprika,** Via Vittorio Emanuele, 107, whose local specialties include *spaghetti ai sapori di Trasimeno* (with eel sauce, L8000). Cover L3000. Open Fri.-Wed. noon-2:30pm and 7-10:30pm. V, MC, AmEx.

Follow in St. Francis's footsteps and spend a delightful day on **Isola Maggiore,** Lake Trasimeno's only inhabited island. It is connected to the two lakeside towns by a convenient ferry system: Passignano sul Trasimeno (every 1-1½hr., 20-35min., L4800, L8500 roundtrip) and Castiglione del Lago (every 1-2hr., 30min., L6500, L10,700 roundtrip). A **tourist information booth** sits by the dock. Open daily 10am-noon and 1-6pm. As you leave the dock, turn right and follow the path to the tip of the island (being careful not to squish the green-brown salamanders who will accompany you) to the ruined **Guglielmi castle.** A sweet old woman gives tours of the castle all day long (in Italian only). A bit farther on sits a tiny chapel enclosing the rock where St. Francis spent 40 days in 1211. From here, hike five minutes up to the **Church of San Michele Arcangelo** for a wonderful view of the island. Open Sun. 10:30am-noon and 3-6pm.

Assisi

Oh Lord, make me an instrument of your peace.

—St. Francis of Assisi

Assisi's serenity originates from the legacy of St. Francis, a 12th-century monk who generated a revolution in the Catholic church. He founded the Franciscan order, devoted to a then-unusual combination of asceticism, poverty, and chastity, while promulgating what he described as the "abundance of the divine" in the world. Today, young Franciscan nuns and monks fill the city and carry on his legacy with spiritual vigor. Assisi is still a major pilgrimage site, especially for Italian youths, who converge here for conferences, festivals, and other religious activities. You need not be particularly religious, however, to adore Assisi; St. Francis is remembered with spectacular works of art. Moreover, the town is beautifully preserved, the accommodations are terrific, and the restaurants, though somewhat expensive, are among the best in Umbria.

ORIENTATION AND PRACTICAL INFORMATION

Towering above the city to the north, the **Rocca Maggiore** can help you re-orient yourself should you become lost among Assisi's winding streets. The center of town is **Piazza del Comune.** Via Portica (which runs into Via Fortini, Via Seminario, and finally Via San Francesco) connects the *piazza* to the **Basilica of San Francesco.** Heading in the opposite direction, Corso Mazzini takes you down to the **Church of Santa Chiara,** and Via San Rufino leads up to the *piazza* and church of the same name. **Buses** from the train station run every 30min. (L1200), stopping at **Piazza Unità d'Italia** near the basilica, Largo Properzio near the Church of St. Clare, and P. Matteotti above P. del Comune.

Tourist Office: P. del Comune, 12 (tel. 81 25 34), 1 doorway to the left of the Telecom office. Information and accommodations service. Knowledgeable if unenthusiastic staff gives out a decent map and information on hotels, restaurants, events, and sights. Be sure to pick up the *Useful Information* pamphlet and ask about upcoming musical events. Open Mon.-Fri. 8am-2pm and 3:30-6:30pm, Sat. 9am-1pm and 3:30-6:30pm, Sun. 9am-1pm. Train and bus schedules outside. Note that the "tourist office" on Corso Mazzini is a travel agency.

Currency Exchange: Automatic currency-exchange machines can be found outside **Cassa di Risparmio di Perugia,** P. del Comune; **Cassa di Risparmio di Foligno,** P. Unità d'Italia; **Banca Popolare di Spoleto,** P. Santa Chiara; and **Banca Toscana,** P. San Pietro.

Telephones: P. del Comune, 11. The most beautifully frescoed phone building in the world. Open daily 8am-10pm; off-season 8am-7pm. Also at the bar in the train station.

Trains: Assisi lies on the Foligno-Terontola train line. Thirteen trains run each day from Perugia (20min., L2700). Change at Terontola for Florence (L15,500); change at Foligno for Rome (L15,500) or Ancona (L11,700). **Luggage Storage:** L5000 for 12hr. Open daily 7am-8:15pm.

Buses: ASP buses leave from P. Matteoti for Perugia (10 per day, no late-morning service, L4700), Foligno (10 per day, L2500), and other surrounding hamlets. To get to the stop from P. del Comune, walk up Via San Rufino; when you reach P. San Rufino, take Via del Torrione (to the left of the church) up to P. Matteotti. Buses run from the station, located below the town near the Basilica of Santa Maria degli Angeli, to the town (every 30min., L1200).

Car Rental: Agenzia Assisiorganizza, Borgo Aretino, 11/a (tel. 81 52 80). Prices begin at L90,000 per day, L500,000 per week. Min. age 21.

Taxis: P. del Comune (tel. 81 31 93), P. San Chiara (tel. 81 26 00), P. Unità d'Italia (tel. 81 23 78), and the train station (tel. 804 02 75).

Swimming Pool: Centro Turistico Sportivo (tel. 81 29 91) on Via San Benedetto. Take the bus marked "Linea A" from P. del Comune. Open late July-Aug. daily 9:30am-7pm. Admission L7500.

Emergencies: tel. 113. **First Aid:** tel. 81 28 24. **Hospital:** (tel. 813 91), on the outskirts. Take the "Linea A" bus from P. del Comune.

Police: Carabinieri, P. Matteotti, 3 (tel. 81 22 39).

Post Office: P. del Comune. **Exchanges currency** (L1000 commission) and **traveler's checks** (L2000 for sums up to L100,000, L5000 for any greater sum). Open Mon.-Fri. 8:10am-6:25pm, Sat. 8:10am-1pm. **Postal Code:** 06081.

Telephone Code: 075.

ACCOMMODATIONS AND CAMPING

Reservations are crucial around Easter and strongly recommended for the *Festa Calendimaggio* (early May) and in August. If you don't mind turning in early, ask the tourist office for a list of **religious institutions;** these are peaceful and cheap, but shut down around 11pm. The tourist office also has a long list of *affitta camere.*

Ostello della Pace (HI) (tel./fax 81 67 67), on Via San Pietro Campagna. Turn right as you exit the train station and then left at the intersection onto Via San Pietro

(30min.). Or take the bus to P. San Pietro and then walk down the main road 50m to the small path marked by the hostel sign. A pleasant hostel with grand rooms and spotless bathrooms. Impressive views of the town from 3 sides. Open daily 7-9:15am and 3:30-11:30pm. L20,000 per person, L25,000 in rooms with bath. Breakfast and hot shower included. L6500 for use of washer. Generous home-cooked dinner L14,000; reserve ahead.

Ostello Fontemaggio (tel. 81 36 36), on Via per l'Eremo delle Carceri. Via Eremo begins at the top of P. Matteotti and leads out the Porta Cappuccini—follow it 1km up the road, then veer right at the sign. Rooms are a bit crowded (10 beds each) but well-maintained, opening onto a sunny terrace. No curfew. Check-out 10am. **Campground** and market next door. Hostel L17,000 per person, breakfast L5000; campground L7000 per person, L6000 per tent, L3000 per car.

Albergo Italia, Vicolo della Fortezza, 2 (tel. 81 26 25), just off P. del Comune. A small but well-kept hotel in the center of town. Friendly staff speaks some English and welcomes younger guests. Rooms are comfortable and spotless; angels over the headboards ensure sweet dreams. Singles L28,000, with shower L36,500, with full bath L45,000. Doubles L47,000, with shower L54,000, with full bath L69,000. Triples L61,000, with bath L90,000. Quad with bath L100,000. Breakfast on request L5000.

Albergo La Rocca, Via di Porta Perlici, 27 (tel. 81 64 67). From P. del Comune, follow Via S. Rufino up the hill, cross the *piazza*, and go straight up Via Porta Perlicia until you hit the old arches—La Rocca is on the left. A great choice away from the crowds. Commodious, attractive rooms, some with views. Singles L31,000, with bath L44,000. Doubles L48,000, with bath L64,000. Full-pension L57,000 per person, L64,000 with bath. Breakfast L7500.

Albergo Anfiteatro Romano, Via Anfiteatro Romano, 4 (tel. 81 30 25; fax 81 51 10), off P. Matteotti. Built into the Roman amphitheater. Welcoming, clean rooms filled with antique furniture; some provide views of the Rocca. Singles L30,000. Doubles L45,000, with bath L65,000. Restaurant downstairs. V, MC, AmEx.

St. Anthony's Guesthouse of the Franciscan Sisters of the Atonement, Via Alessi, 10 (tel. 81 25 42; fax 81 37 23), located—coincidentally?—right between the Churches of Santa Chiara (take Via Sermei) and San Rufino (take Via Dono Doni). The American sisters treat you like family. No room for asceticism here—the rooms are far too comfy. Gorgeous views, a library full of English-language books, a garden, an orchard, and a relaxing terrace. Two-night min. stay. Curfew 11pm. Singles with bath L40,000. Doubles with bath L70,000. Breakfast included, served in a delightful stone-walled dining room. Open mid-March-mid-Nov. L20,000 dinner includes *primo, secondo,* two *contorni,* and dessert.

CENTRAL ITALY

FOOD

Assisi will tempt you with a sinful array of nut breads and pastries; *bricciata umbria,* a strudel-like pastry with a hint of cherries, and *brustengolo,* packed with raisins, apples, and walnuts, are particularly divine. **Pasticceria Santa Monica,** at Via Portica, 4, right off P. del Comune, boasts a good quality/price ratio. Open daily 9am-8pm. On Saturday mornings there's a **market** in P. Matteotti; on weekdays, head over to Via San Gabriele for fresh fruits and vegetables. For well-made *panini* and picnic staples, try **Micromarket A.MI.CA.,** Via Fortabella, 61, near P. Unità and San Francesco. Open Mon.-Sat. 7:30am-2pm and 3:30-8pm, Sun. 7:30am-2pm.

Pizzeria Otello, Via Sant'Antonio, 1 (tel. 81 24 15). No-nonsense *pizzeria* on a side street off P. del Comune. *Primi* L7000-10,000, *secondi* L7500-9800. Pizza L5000-10,000. Also serves *focaccia* sandwiches and big salads (L6500-9800). Cover L2000. Open for *pizza* by the slice 7:30am-noon and 4-7pm, *pizza al piatto* and lunch noon-4pm, and dinner 7-11pm. V, MC, AmEx.

Trattoria Erminio, Via Monte Cavallo, off Via Porta Perlici. Enjoy macaroni and arugula flavored with oil and garlic (L6000) or grilled chicken (L10,000) under an immense dome. *Menù* L20,000. Open Fri.-Wed. noon-2:30pm and 7-9pm.

Trattoria Spadini, Via S. Agnese, 8C (tel. 81 30 05), near P. Santa Chiara. Dine under low, white arches in a medieval atmosphere. *Menù* L19,500. Open Tues.-Sat. noon-3pm and 7-10pm.

Pallotta, Via San Rufino, 4 (tel. 81 23 07), near P. del Comune. A medieval setting overseen by a graceful proprietor. Try their specialty, *strangozzi alla pallotta* (pasta with mushrooms and olives, L10,000) and the flavorful *salsicce alla griglia* (grilled sausage, 12,000). *Menù,* including wine and fresh fruit, L23,000. Open Wed.-Mon. noon-2:30pm and 7-9:30pm. V, MC, AmEx.

SIGHTS

St. Francis, born in 1182, abandoned military ambitions at age 19 and rejected his father's wealth to embrace asceticism. His repudiation of the worldliness of the church, his love of nature, and his devoted humility earned him a huge following throughout Europe, posing an unprecedented challenge to the decadent papacy and corrupt monastic orders. He continued to preach chastity and poverty until his death in 1226, whereupon the order he founded was gradually subsumed into the Catholic hierarchy. The result was the paradoxical glorification of the modest saint through the countless churches constructed in his honor.

The enormous and lavishly frescoed **Basilica of San Francesco** bears witness to this conflict of integrity and bureaucracy. When construction began in the mid-13th century, the Franciscan order protested: the elaborate church seemed an impious monument to the wealth that Francis had scorned. As a solution, Brother Elia, then vicar of the order, insisted that a double church be erected—the lower level built around the saint's crypt, the upper level a church for services. The subdued art in the lower church commemorates Francis's modest life, while the upper church pays tribute to his sainthood and consecration. This two-fold structure subsequently inspired a new type of Franciscan architecture.

The walls of the church are almost completely covered with Giotto's *Life of St. Francis* fresco cycle, dramatically lit from the windows above. Giotto's early genius is evident in his illustration of Francis's turbulent path to sainthood. It starts on the right wall near the altar and runs clockwise, beginning with a teenage Francis in courtly dress surprised by a prophecy of his future greatness. The cycle closes with an image of the saint passing through the mystical agony of the "Dark Night." The final stage of his approach to God occurs in the 19th frame, where St. Francis receives the stigmata. Sadly, Cimabue's frescoes in the transepts and apse have so deteriorated that they look like photographic negatives. Most frescoes and sculptures have "History Tell" machines; it costs L1000 to learn the history of each work.

Pietro Lorenzetti adorned the left transept with his outstanding *Crucifixion, Last Supper,* and *Madonna and Saints.* The four sumptuous allegorical frescoes above the altar were formerly attributed to Giotto but are now thought to be the work of a painter called "Maestro delle Vele." Cimabue's magnificent *Madonna and Child, Angels,* and *St. Francis* grace the right transept. Best of all are Simone Martini's frescoes in the first chapel off the left wall, which are based on the life of St. Martin. Descend through a door in the right side of the apse to a room that houses some of St. Francis's possessions: his tunic, sandals, and sundry flesh-mortifying instruments.

The precious piece that inspired the entire edifice, St. Francis's tomb, lies below the lower church (the steps to it are marked by a sign in the middle of the right aisle). St. Francis's coffin was hidden in the 15th century for fear that the war-mongering Perugians would desecrate it; it was only rediscovered in 1818. The stone coffin sits above the altar in the crypt, surrounded by the sarcophagi of four of the saint's friends. (Mass in English in the upper church Sun. 8:30am. Tours in English of the whole structure Mon.-Sat. 10am and 3pm; meet in front of the lower church. Both churches open daily from sunrise to sunset—in summer, about 6:30am-7pm, closed on Holy Days. **Dress codes** here are very strictly enforced. No miniskirts, no short shorts, and no revealing shirts allowed. Fashion police screen visitors at the door and circulate through the basilica. No photography.)

While here, don't bypass the modern, well-lit **Museo Tesoro della Basilica,** with its graceful 13th-century French ivory *Madonna and Child,* 17th-century Murano glass work, and a fragment of the Holy Cross. (Open Mon.-Sat. 9:30am-noon and 2-6pm. Admission L3000.)

Via San Francesco leads away from the front of the upper church between medieval buildings and their 16th-century additions—note especially the **Sala del Pelegrino** (Pilgrim Oratory), frescoed inside and out. A 13th-century building at the corner of Via Fortebella and Via San Francesco was home to a **hospital for pilgrims.** At the end of the street P. del Comune sits upon the old **Foro Romano.** Enter from the **crypt of St. Nicholas** on Via Portica and stroll through the historic corridors of the Roman forum. The **Pinacoteca,** occupying the nearby **Palazzo del Comune,** houses a collection of Renaissance frescoes lifted from city gates and various shrines, as well as works by important Umbrian artists. (Both the forum and the *pinacoteca* are open daily 10am-1pm and 3-7pm. Admission L4000 for each sight. The *biglietto cumulativo* allows entry into the forum, Rocca Maggiore, and the Pinacoteca for L10,000, students L7000.)

Via San Rufino climbs steeply up from P. del Comune between closely packed old houses, opening onto P. San Rufino to reveal the squat **duomo** with its massive bell tower. The restored interior may be a disappointment after the decorative façade. (Open daily 9:30am-noon and 2:30-6pm.) Continue uphill on the cobblestone street to the left of the *duomo* as you face it and take the steps that branch off to the left. At the top is the towering, dramatic **Rocca Maggiore,** an essential sight for any visitor to Assisi. The keep has been recently restored, and views from the top are unparalleled. You can walk (or grope) around the old corridors; most of the fortress is poorly lit, if at all. (Open daily 10am-dusk; in winter 10am-4pm. Closed in very windy or rainy weather. Admission L5000. Cumulative ticket L10,000, students L7000.) In one of the courtyards of the Rocca Maggiore sits the **Museum of Martyrs and Torture.** Come visit wax figures of martyrs and models of various instruments of torture. (Same hours as the Rocca. Admission L5000.)

The pink-and-white **Basilica of Santa Chiara** stands at the other end of Assisi, on the site of the ancient basilica where St. Francis attended school. The church shelters not only the tomb (and hair) of St. Clare, the founder of the Poor Clares, but also a tunic and shoes worn by St. Francis and the crucifix that spoke to him revealing God's message. The nuns in this church are sworn to seclusion. (Open Mon.-Sat. 6:30am-noon and 2-7pm; in winter closes at 6pm.)

ENTERTAINMENT

All of Assisi's religious festivals involve feasts and processions. An especially long dramatic performance marks **Easter Week.** On Holy Thursday, a mystery play depicts the Deposition from the Cross, and traditional processions trail through town on Good Friday and Easter Sunday. Assisi welcomes spring with the **Festa di Calendimaggio** on the first Thursday, Friday, and Saturday of May. A queen is chosen and dubbed *Primavera* (Spring), and the lower and upper quarters of the city compete in a clamorous musical tournament. Classical concerts and organ recitals occur once or twice per week from April to October in the various churches. October 4 is the **Festival of St. Francis,** in which one region of Italy (a different one each year) offers oil for the cathedral's votive lamp; that region's traditional dances and songs are performed in local costumes. For one week during July, the **Gran Premio Italiano Mongolfieristico** paints the sky above nearby Santa Maria degli Angeli with racing hot-air balloons. Held during July and the beginning of August, the **Festa Pro Musica** features internationally known musicians and opera singers. For details, look for posters or ask at the tourist office. On any given evening you can join the many youth groups who flood P. del Comune and sing every folk song you can think of, including "Blowing in the Wind" and "Kumbaya," often to the accompaniment of guitar-strumming monks.

■ Near Assisi

Several churches associated with St. Francis and St. Clare stand in the immediate vicinity of town. If you travel to Assisi by train, you'll pass the huge **Basilica di Santa Maria degli Angeli,** which is actually a church inside a church. The impressive basilica shelters the tiny **Porziuncola,** the first center of the Franciscan order. The Benedictines own the building, and the Franciscans pay them a basket of carp every year for rent. In order to overcome temptation, St. Francis supposedly flung himself on thorny rosebushes in the garden just outside the basilica, thus staining the leaves forever red. Now, in deference to the saint, the bushes grow no thorns. The site grew popular when St. Francis instituted the annual **Festa del Perdono** (Aug. 2), during which an indulgence was awarded to all who came to the church. When he died in the adjacent infirmary, now **Chapel of the Transito,** the chapel began to attract throngs of pilgrims, and a whole ring of supporting chapels sprang up. Live doves nest on a statue of the saint in the courtyard. Open daily 7am-noon and 2:30-7pm.

A pleasant but steep hour-long hike through the forest above the town leads to the most memorable and inspiring sight near Assisi, the **Eremo delle Carceri** (Hermitage of Cells). Pass through the Porta San Francesco below the basilica and follow Via Marconi. At the crossroads take the left road, which passes by the Seminario Regionale Umbro. The site of St. Francis's retreats, this placid area conveys the spirit of St. Francis better than the opulent basilica. Inside the hermitage you can see the small cell where he slept, and back outside is the stone altar where he preached. Open daily from 8am to dusk.

A 15-min. stroll down the steep road outside Porta Nuova takes you to the **Convent of San Damiano,** where St. Francis received his calling and later wrote the *Canticle of the Sun.* The chapel contains fine 14th-century frescoes as well as a riveting woodcarving of Christ. Open daily 10am-noon and 3-6pm.

Gubbio

Gubbio was founded in the 3rd century BC by the ancient Umbrians, but the thriving settlement later deteriorated under a wave of invasions. Its long, tumultuous history has left a rich legacy, architecturally, culturally, and socially: graceful portals and a well-preserved theater attest to the stronghold Roman emperors once had on the city; splendid *palazzi* recall the years of subjugation under the powerful Dukes of Urbino; and the warm hospitality of the Gubbian people stretches back to the time when the city provided asylum for ailing lepers. Even without an intriguing past, Gubbio could draw tourists with its enchanting cobblestone streets and gorgeous views of the countryside. Gubbio even boasts its own school of painting, a distinct ceramic tradition, and Italy's first novelist, Bosone Novello Raffaelli.

ORIENTATION AND PRACTICAL INFORMATION

Gubbio is a tangle of twisting streets and medieval alleyways that lead to sweeping *piazze.* Of these, **Piazza della Signoria** remains the civic headquarters, set on a ledge of the hill. Buses will leave you in **Piazza Quaranta Martiri.** A short uphill walk on **Via della Repubblica,** the street directly ahead as you get off the bus, will connect you with **Corso Garibaldi,** where you can find the tourist office.

Tourist Office: Piazza Oderisi, 6 (tel. 922 06 93), off Corso Garibaldi next door to the local Communist Party headquarters. Extremely helpful. English spoken. Ask for the indexed street map. Open Mon.-Fri. 8am-1:45pm and 3:30-6:30pm, Sat. 9am-1pm and 3:30-6:30pm, Sun. 9:30am-12:30pm; in off-season Mon.-Sat. afternoon hours are 3-6pm. Also try **Easy Gubbio,** Via della Repubblica, 13 (tel. 922 00 66), on your way up the hill. The friendly English-speaking staff sells bus tickets, rents cars, has telephones and changes money—one-stop shopping for all your tourism needs. Open daily in summer 8am-midnight; in winter 8am-10pm.

Trains: There are no trains to Gubbio itself; the nearest station is at Fossato di Vico, 19km away on the Rome-Ancona line (L7200 from Ancona, L17,200 from Rome, L5700 from Spoleto). Buses connect Gubbio and the station (Mon.-Sat. 9 per day, 6 on Sun., L3800). For tickets, go to **Clipper Viaggi,** in P. San Giovanni, 15 (tel. 37 17 48), the *piazza* up the hill from P. Quaranta Martiri. Open Sun.-Fri. 9:30am-1pm and 3:30-7pm, Sat. 9:30am-1pm.

Buses: A.S.P. runs buses to and from Perugia (10 per day, 1¼hr., L7400).

Taxis: (tel. 927 38 00) in P. Quaranta Martiri.

Pharmacy: Corso Garibaldi, 12. Open daily in summer 9am-1pm and 4:30-8pm; in winter 9am-1pm and 4-7:30pm.

Emergencies: tel. 113. **First Aid:** tel. 923 91. **Hospital:** P. Quaranta Martiri, 14 (tel. 923 91).

Police: Carabinieri (tel. 927 37 31), Via Matteotti.

Post Office: Via Cairoli, 11 (tel. 927 39 25). Open Mon.-Sat. 8:10am-1:25pm. **Postal Code:** 06024.

Telephone Code: 075.

ACCOMMODATIONS

Albergo dei Consoli, Via dei Consoli, 59 (tel. 927 33 35), 100m from P. della Signoria toward P. Bruno. Stone-walled dining room downstairs. Curving wood staircase leads up to simple, neat rooms, all with bath. Doubles L75,000. Triples L100,000. Breakfast L5000. Closed Jan. V, MC, AmEx.

Albergo Galletti, Via Piccardi, 3 (tel. 927 42 47), off P. Quaranta Martiri. Small rooms on the edge of medieval Gubbio. Hospitable proprietor. Singles L35,000. Doubles L58,000, with bath from L70,000.

Pensione Grotta dell'Angelo, Via Gioia, 47 (tel. 927 34 38), off Via Cairoli. Paisley bedspreads, TVs, and wicker chairs distinguish this *pensione* from run-of-the-mill budget accommodations. Singles with bath L52,000. Doubles with bath L75,000. Half- and full-pension available. Closed Jan.

Hotel Gattapone, Via Ansidei, 6 (tel. 927 24 89), off Via della Repubblica. Carpeted, handsomely furnished rooms, all with gleaming baths. Ask for a room on the top floor—the ceilings are beamed and the views stupendous. Singles L65,000. Doubles L90,000. One family room—4 beds and a crib—L137,000. Quints L163,000. Closed Jan. V, MC, AmEx.

FOOD

Guard against expensive meals. Go to the *salumeria* at P. Quaranta Martiri, 36, across from the bus station, which makes great sandwiches for around L2500. Open daily 7:15am-1:15pm and 3:15-8pm. On Tuesday mornings there's a **market** under the *loggie* of P. Quaranta Martiri. Local delicacies await you at **Prodotti Tipici e Tartufati Eugubini,** Via Piccardi, 17. Here you can sample *salumi di cinghiale o cervo* (boar or deer sausage) and *pecorino* cheese, or pick up some truffle oil (so your truffles don't get sunburned). Open daily 8:30am-1pm and 3:30-8pm.

Taverna del Buchetto, Via Dante, 30 (tel. 927 70 34), near the Porta Romana. *Primi* L5000-8000. Tasty pizzas run L6000-9000, unless your refined palate demands one with truffles (L15,000). Enjoy the spicy *pollo alla diavola* (L10,000) in a comfortable, air-conditioned room. Open Tues.-Sun. noon-2:30pm and 7:30-10pm. V, MC, AmEx.

Ristorante Il Bargello, Via dei Consoli, 37 (tel. 927 37 24), in a little *piazza* down the road from P. della Signoria. Wine bottles line the walls. Pleasant management. Outstanding pizza L4000-9000. Full meals from L25,000. Cover L2500. Open Tues.-Sun. noon-2:30pm and 7-10:30pm. V, MC, AmEx.

San Francesco e il Lupo (tel. 927 23 44), at the corner of Via Cairoli and Corso Garibaldi, near the Azienda. A homey place in spite of the neon. *Primi* L7000-12,000, *secondi* L10,000-22,000. The L19,000 *menù* includes *primo, secondo, contorno,* and fresh fruit; the L23,000 *menù* offers better choices and a dessert as well. Open mid-July-mid-June daily noon-2:30pm and 7-9:30pm. V, MC.

SIGHTS

As you descend from the bus, the **Giardino dei Quaranta Martiri** (Garden of the 40 Martyrs) lies to your left, a memorial to those shot in reprisal for the assassination of two officials during WWII. The impressive **Church of San Francesco** stands to the right, on the site of the house of the Spadalonga family, where St. Francis is said to have experienced his powerful conversion. The central apse holds the splendid *Vita della Madonna* (Life of the Madonna), a partially destroyed 15th-century fresco series by Ottaviano Nelli, Gubbio's most famous painter. Via Matteotti behind the church will take you to the monumental **Roman theater;** well-preserved, it is still used for classical productions. Across the *piazza* from the church is the **Loggia dei Tiratoi,** where 14th-century weavers stretched their cloth so it would shrink evenly. Today it shades a handful of outdoor *caffè* and a fruit and vegetable market.

In **Piazza della Signoria** stands the **Palazzo dei Consoli,** one of Italy's most graceful public buildings. The white stone palace (1332) was built for the high magistrate of Gubbio by local boy Matteo di Giovanello (also known as Gattapone) who went on to knock 'em dead in Bologna and Perugia. Enter to examine the **Museo Civico's** idiosyncratic mix of stone sculpture and ancient coins, including the puzzling **Tavole Eugubine.** Discovered in 1444 near the Roman theater outside the city walls, these seven bronze tablets (300-100BC) provide the main source of our knowledge of the ancient Umbrian language. Their ritual text spells out the social and political organization of early Umbrian society and provide the novice with advice on how to take auguries from animal livers. Upstairs visit the stately rooms of the **Pinacoteca Comunale,** an eclectic collection of paintings, wooden crucifixes, and 14th-century furniture. (Open daily mid-March-Sept. 9am-12:30pm and 3:30-6pm; Oct.-mid-March 9am-1pm and 3-5pm. Admission for both museums L4000, students, under 18, and over 60 L2000.) Across the *piazza* stands the **Palazzo Pretorio,** also designed by Gattapone. Now a municipal building, it once served as the seat of the *podestà,* a foreign official charged with the duty of impartially overseeing public affairs.

Via dei Consoli will take you to the **Bargello** and its fountain. This 13th-century edifice is one of many medieval buildings still in use; others nearby include the 13th-century **Palazzo del Capitano del Popolo** on the street of the same name, and the 15th-century **Palazzo Beni** on Via Cavour. Apart from wool, Gubbio's main industry in the Middle Ages was ceramics. Some particularly fine examples lie in the Palazzo dei Consoli Museum. To get your own, try the **Antica Fabbrica Artigiana,** Via San Giuliano, 3 (near the Bargello), a cavernous old palace. Walk down the narrow streets that run parallel to the Camignano stream.

Climb to the top of the town where the 15th-century **Palazzo Ducale** and the 13th-century **duomo** face off. Federico da Montefeltro commissioned Luciano Laurana, designer of his larger palace in Urbino, to build a smaller but equally elegant version here. (*Palazzo* open Mon.-Sat. 9am-1pm and 3-6:30pm, Sun. 9am-1pm. Admission L4000, under 18 and over 60 free.) The *duomo,* an unassuming, pink Gothic building, boasts fine stained-glass windows (late 12th century), the decaying corpses of several of Gubbio's prominent medieval bishops, and Pinturicchio's *Adoration of the Shepherds*, temporarily closed for restoration. Check at the tourist office for details.

When the museums close for lunch, take the 7-min. birdcage chairlift *(funivia)* to the peak of **Monte Ingino** for a splendid view and prime picnicking. (Roundtrip L6000. Open July-Aug. Mon.-Sat. 8:30am-7:30pm, Sun. 8:30am-8pm; Sept. Mon.-Sat. 9:30am-7pm, Sun. 9am-7:30pm; Oct. daily 10am-1:15pm and 2:30-5:30pm; Nov-Feb.

Let's Go Crazy

The Fontana del Bargello (Bargello Fountain) has the unique power of bestowing honorary Gubbian citizenship upon anyone who runs around it three times (either direction works). Gubbians are generally considered *matti* (crazy) by other Italians for their frenzied behavior during the annual Candle Race, so this means that you too can become certifiably insane. After your run, just pick up a tacky certificate from any of the nearby souvenir shops.

daily 10am-1:15pm and 2:30-5pm; June Mon.-Sat. 9:30am-1:15pm and 2:30-7pm, Sun. 9am-7:30pm.) While you're there, visit the **basilica and monastery of Sant'Ubaldo,** Gubbio's patron saint. The basilica houses the three *ceri,* large wooden candles carried in the Corsa dei Ceri procession each May (see below), as well as Saint Ubaldo's pickled body in a glass case. On your way back to the town center, stop at the **Church of Santa Maria Nuova,** near the funicular station, which contains the lyrical *Madonna del Belvedere* by Ottaviano Nelli. Ask the custodian at Via Dante, 66, to let you in. Avoid going at midday.

ENTERTAINMENT

The **Corsa dei Ceri** (May 15), a 900-year-old tradition and one of Italy's most noted processions, focuses on the three *ceri.* Intended to represent candles, the *ceri* are huge wooden blocks carved like hourglasses and topped with little saints. Each one represents a distinct faction of the populace: the masons, the artisans and merchants, and the farmers. After 12 hours of furious flag-twirling and elaborate preparations, squads of husky runners *(ceraioli)* clad in Renaissance-style tights heave the heavy objects onto their shoulders and race up Monte Ingino. Making occasional pit stops for alcoholic encouragement, they eventually reach the Basilica of Sant'Ubaldo and plop down the *ceri* for safe keeping until the following May.

During the **Palio della Balestra,** held on the last Sunday in May, archers from Gubbio and nearby Sansepolcro gather in P. della Signoria for the latest re-match of a fierce crossbow contest dating back to 1461. If Gubbio wins, an animated parade ensues. (Gubbio's major industry these days is the production of toy crossbows—*balestre*—for tourists.) The **Bulldog Pub,** Via Ansidei, 3, is a good place for a beer year-round. (Open Tues.-Sun. 9:30pm-2:30am.)

CENTRAL ITALY

Spoleto

Like many of its peers in Umbria and southern Tuscany, Spoleto offers a beautiful hill-top setting and almost unbearably charming medieval streets. The town's biggest draw is its summer arts festival, the *Festival dei Due Mondi* (of the Two Worlds). The composer Gian Carlo Menotti selected Spoleto in 1958 to be the test site for his claim that art could be a community's bread and butter. His efforts were not misguided: Spoleto's transformation into an internationally renowned center for the arts has brought prosperity to the town. Unfortunately, prices run as high as the pretension that has spawned expressionist pizza parlors and chi-chi boutiques. Art of all sorts explodes around the town in late June and usually lingers through the summer. If you wish to rub shoulders with the artistically inclined, remember to reserve tickets and rooms far in advance. But even if you miss the festival, precious little shops and a magnificent gorge make Spoleto an inviting year-round destination.

ORIENTATION AND PRACTICAL INFORMATION

Spoleto's typically Umbrian narrow cobblestone streets make the town difficult to navigate. **Piazza del Mercato** is the social center of the city, and many shop-lined streets radiate from it. Via Brignone connects P. Mercato with **Piazza della Libertà,** home of the tourist office and city bus stop. Via del Municipio runs to **Piazza del Municipio** and Via Saffi to **Piazza del Duomo;** these two squares contain most of the city sights. To get to the center of town from the train station, walk straight up Viale Trento e Trieste, take a right through **Piazza Garibaldi** and continue along **Corso Garibaldi,** which eventually ends at **Corso Mazzini,** terminating in P. della Libertà (30min.). Or, take an ATAF bus marked *"centro"* from the station (L1200).

Tourist Office: P. della Libertà, 7 (tel. 22 03 11). A warm and savvy staff with an excellent if unwieldy map. Be prepared to wait. English spoken. Open daily during the festival 9am-1pm and 3-9pm; off-season 10am-1pm and 4:30-7:30pm.

Currency Exchange: 24-hr. automatic exchange machine at **Cassa di Risparmio di Spoleto,** Via Minervio, 14, down a flight of steps from Corso Mazzini.

Trains: (tel. 485 16) in P. Polvani. From: Rome (every 1-2hr., 1½hr., L11,700); Ancona (2hr., L13,600); Perugia (10 per day, 1hr., L5700); and Assisi (16 per day, 30min., L4200). From the station, take any *"centro"* bus to P. della Libertà and the tourist office (L1200); otherwise it's a 30-min. uphill trek. Ask for a free city map at the station's newsstand. **Luggage Storage:** L5000 for 12hr. Open 6am-11pm.

Buses: S.S.I.T. (tel. 21 22 05) connects the town to Perugia (at 6:25 and 7:10am every weekday, 1½hr., L10,400) and Foligno (5 every weekday, 40min., L5000). Buses depart from P. della Vittoria, adjacent to P. Garibaldi. **Bucci** (tel. (0721) 324 01) runs buses weekdays during Aug. to Urbino and Rimini at 9:45am and to Rome at 6:45pm; buses leave from Via Flaminia (near the API gas station). Check at the tourist office for the most recent schedules.

Taxis: (tel. 445 48) in P. della Libertà.

Box Office: Buy advance tickets at Teatro Nuovo (tel. 440 97). Open Tues.-Sun. 10am-1pm and 4-7pm.

Late-Night Pharmacy: Farmacia Scoccianti, Via Marconi, 11.

Emergencies: tel. 113. **Hospital:** Via Loreto, 3 (tel. 21 01), outside Porta Loreto.

Police: Carabinieri, Via dei Filosofi, 57 (tel. 490 44). English speaker available.

Post Office: P. della Libertà, 12 (tel. 403 73). Open Mon.-Sat. 8:10am-7:30pm. **Postal Code:** 06049.

Telephone Code: 0743.

ACCOMMODATIONS AND CAMPING

Finding accommodations is almost impossible during the summer music festival (late June to mid-July); make reservations as early as possible. The tourist office keeps a list of *affitta camere* and *agriturismo* options. Performances take place during the day, so getting back shouldn't infringe on your festival experience.

Hotel Panciolle, Via del Duomo, 3/5 (tel. 455 98), near the *duomo*. Bright, airy rooms with nondescript, modern furnishings. **Restaurant** downstairs. Singles with bath L55,000. Doubles with bath L80,000.

Albergo Anfiteatro, Via Anfiteatro, 14 (tel. 498 53). Don't let the spooky staircase put you off. Whitewashed rooms with modern furnishings. Singles L50,000, with bath L70,000. Doubles L70,000, with bath L90,000.

Camping: Monteluco (tel. 22 03 58), behind the church of San Pietro, a 15-min. walk from P. della Libertà. Take Viale Matteotti out to the tennis courts, say hi to Buffy, cross the highway, take Via San Pietro left to the church, and go up the hill. Beyond the church a dirt path branches to the right and leads directly to the campground. Pleasant and shaded, with a restaurant and a *bocce* court. L7000 per person, L6000 per tent, L3000 per car. Open April-Sept. **Il Girasole** (tel. 513 35), next to a vast sunflower field 10km from Spoleto, near the small town of Petragnano. Hourly buses connect it with the train station. Quiet, with plenty of shade, hot showers, and a small swimming pool. L9000 per person, L8000 per tent, L4000 per car. Prices lower for longer stays. Open March 25-Sept.

FOOD

An open-air market enlivens **Piazza del Mercato** Monday through Saturday from 8:30am to 1pm. At other times, try the **Lo Sfizioso** market at P. Mercato, 26 (open Fri.-Wed. 7:30am-1:30pm and 4:30-7:30pm) or the **STANDA** supermarket at Corso Garibaldi, 11 (open Mon.-Sat. 9am-1pm and 4:30-8pm). During the festival, you'll need reservations to get into most restaurants.

Trattoria Del Panciolle, Via del Duomo, 3/4 (tel. 455 98), right below the hotel of the same name. Simple country fare skillfully prepared. *Strangozzi* (a local string-like pasta) with mushroom truffles L8000. Most *secondi* L10,000. Also has outdoor tables on a shaded porch. Open Thurs.-Tues. noon-2:30pm and 7:30-10pm.

Ristorante Pentagramma, Via Tommaso Martini, 4 (tel. 372 33), off P. della Libertà. Despite the name and the decor, this is a fine traditional restaurant which cooks up Umbrian specialties. Try the tempting *degustazione* (your choice of 3 pasta dishes, L20,000) or the *zuppa di ceci* (chickpea soup, L13,000). *Secondi* L15,000. Open Tues.-Sun. noon-2:30pm and 7-10pm. V, MC.

Osteria dell'Enoteca, Via Saffi, 9. A cozy place to sample local wines and snack on light dishes like *bruschetta al tartufo* (L4500) and asparagus *frittata* (L8000). Open Tues.-Sun. 10am-midnight. V, MC.

Casa del Frulatto, Via Mazzini, 75. Whips up all manner of fresh fruit shakes right before your eyes. Try the exotic mango-papaya mix (L4500). *Gelato* and sandwiches (L3000) too. Open Tues.-Sun. 8am-1am.

SIGHTS

Tucked on a ledge midway between the great papal fortress above and the Roman Anfiteatro below rests Spoleto's monumental Romanesque **duomo.** It was built in the 12th century and then augmented by a portico (1491) and 17th-century interior redecoration. An amalgam of styles and materials, its soaring bell tower was cobbled together from fragments of Roman structures and is held up by incongruous flying buttresses. Eight rose windows animate the façade, the largest one bearing the symbols of the four evangelists. Inside, brilliantly colored scenes of the life of the Virgin by Fra Filippo Lippi fill the domed apse. Lippi died here while working on these frescoes. Lorenzo the Magnificent asked the *spoletini* to send his body back, but with tourism waning from a lack of noble corpses, Spoleto insisted on keeping it. Lorenzo could only commission Lippi's tomb, which lies in the right transept and was decorated by the artist's son, Filippino. Don't miss the gilding and frescoes of the beautiful Renaissance reliquary to the left of the altar; inside you'll find a consoling letter written by St. Francis to a fellow brother. (*Duomo* open daily March-Oct. 8am-1pm and 3-6:30pm; Nov.-Feb. 8am-1pm and 3-5:30pm.)

Sant'Eufemia, across the *piazza* to the side of the *duomo,* lacks both the stature and the frescoes of the cathedral; poor Eufemia never amounted to much in the eyes of the Vatican. Though it may not be as grand as the cathedral, the attractive Romanesque church features Umbria's first *matronei,* or "women's balconies." (Open daily in summer 10am-12:30pm and 3:30-7pm; in winter 10am-12:30pm and 2:30-6pm. Admission L3000.)

Spoleto's many classical ruins testify to its prominence in Roman times. The **theater** stands just outside the Roman walls, visible from P. della Libertà. Walk through the theater to the adjacent *loggia* and then to the **Museo Archeologico,** which has ceramic and statuary finds from the area. (Open Mon.-Sat. 9am-1:30pm and 2:30-7pm, Sun. 9am-1pm. Admission L4000.) The **Arco Romano** at the top of Via Bronzino marked the entrance to the town, and farther along, the **Arco di Druso** marked the entrance to the forum (now P. del Mercato). On nearby Via de Visiale you can enter a restored **Roman house** dedicated to the Emperor Caligula. (Open April-Sept. Tues.-Sun. 10am-1pm and 3-6pm. Admission L5000, students L3000; includes admission to the Museum of Modern Art. Same hours for both museums.)

The **papal fortress,** or Rocca, sits on the hillside above Spoleto. This fortress, formerly a prison, was used during the war to confine Slavic and Italian political prisoners. In 1943 the prisoners staged a dramatic escape to join the partisans in the Umbrian hills. Unfortunately, the Rocca is closed for renovations, though it opens to host some events of the festival. Follow the walk that curves around the fortress for panoramic views of Spoleto and the countryside. Farther on, you'll reach one of the region's most stunning architectural achievements, the 14th-century **Ponte delle Torri.** The 80-m bridge and aqueduct span the channel of the river Tessino. On the far bank rise the craggy medieval towers for which the bridge was named.

On the far side of the bridge, take the left fork past elegant villas and ancient churches to **Monteluco,** Spoleto's "mountain of the sacred grove." An invigorating 1½-hr. climb through a forest brings you to the tiny Franciscan **Sanctuary of Monteluco,** once the refuge of St. Francis and San Bernadino of Siena. (Open May-Sept. Mon.-Sat. 8:45am-12:15pm, 3-6pm, and 7-8pm, Sun. 3-6pm and 7-8pm. Buses leave P. della Libertà for Monteluco approximately every 1½hr. when it's open. Ask at the newsstand for tickets, L2600.) A 5-min. stroll down the right fork brings you to the Romanesque **Church of San Pietro,** on whose tan façade appears a menagerie of bas-relief beasties, cavorting among scenes from popular fables and the gospel. Note the wolf to the right of the door wearing a monk's cowl and holding a book.

The **Museum of Modern Art** hosts art exhibits during the summer arts festival. From Corso Mazzini, turn left on Via Sant'Agata, then right on Via delle Terme. The museum lies ahead on your right. (Open April-Sept. Tues.-Sun. 10am-1pm and 3-6pm. Admission, with cumulative ticket from the Roman house, L5000.)

ENTERTAINMENT

The **Festival dei Due Mondi,** held from late June through mid-July, has become one of Italy's most important cultural events. The festival features numerous concerts, operas, and ballets with performances by well-known Italian and international artists. Film screenings, modern art shows, and local craft displays abound. (Tickets L15,000-200,000; a few events are free. Purchase well in advance from travel agents in most large cities or send a bank check made out to the Associazione Festival dei Due Mondi Biglietteria, Festival dei Due Mondi, c/o Teatro Nuovo, 06049, Spoleto, covering the cost of the tickets plus 15% commission.) The renowned **Stagione del Teatro Lirico Sperimentale di Spoleto** (experimental opera season) runs from late-August to September. Information can be obtained from the Istituzione Teatro Lirico Sperimentale di Spoleto "A. Belli," P. G. Bovio, 1, 06049 Spoleto (tel. 22 16 45). For cultural entertainment of a different sort, check out **Pub La Fenice,** Via Porta Fuga, 43 (tel. 22 23 98; open Mon.-Sat. 7pm-2am) or **The American Bar,** P. del Duomo (open until 2am). Those in the mood to dance can head over to **La Tartaruga,** Via Filitteria, 12 (tel. 22 32 82).

■ Near Spoleto: Trevi

Trevi, perched atop a hill shrouded with olive trees, is a delightful place to spend an afternoon. The town is a spectacular sight—ancient pastel buildings line an almost completely vertical hillside. The **Piazza del Comune,** the heart of the town, features an impressive cobblestone belltower; though the 12th-century tower stopped ringing years back, it remains a powerful symbol of Trevian independence and communal might. The graceful *loggia* of the **Palazzo del Comune** once resounded with the cries of San Bernardino of Siena who preached tirelessly about the ills of usury; today it is filled only with the discourse and laughter of loitering Trevians. The *palazzo* is also home to the **Pinacoteca Comunale.** The collection includes a replica by Pinturicchio of his *Madonna e Bambino,* now in London's National Gallery, as well as archaeological finds from the area. (Museum temporarily closed, but expected to reopen in June of 1997.) Trevi's finest art collection is not in the museum, but inside the **Church of the Madonna delle Lacrime.** The church is on the site of a house on whose wall a *Madonna and Child with St. Francis* was painted in 1483. Two years later blood-colored tears were seen on the image, inspiring the construction of a chapel, then a temple, and finally a church on the site. Beautiful Renaissance frescoes grace the interior: Lo Spagna's stirring *Deposition* and Perugino's *Adoration of the Magi, Saints Peter and Paul,* and dazzling *Annunciation.* To get to the church from the town center, take Via delle Fonti; after the road curves, walk down the narrow stairs and turn left. Ask for the keys from the sprightly nuns in the orphanage next door.

The **Illumination Procession,** the oldest public spectacle in Umbria, is a candle-lit parade through town on January 27, held in honor of St. Emiliano, an intrepid bishop martyred under Diocletian. **Trevi in Piazza** fills the P. del Comune with musical and theatrical performances during the first three weeks in August.

Trevi is easily reached by train from Foligno (L1500) or Spoleto (L1700). From the station it's 4km uphill to town. Six city buses per day run to town (L1200), the last at 5:20pm; nine buses per day run to the station, the last at 4:30pm. Buy tickets at the *tabacchi* (50m uphill from the stop). The bus leaves you at P. Garibaldi. From there, take Via Roma to get to the **Ufficio di Turismo.** This outfit seems much more adept at peddling bottles of olive oil than providing tourist information. From under the pile of "Olio Trevi" order forms, the staff will fish out a sketchy map of the city and a list of producers that allow visitors to watch as the exceptional olive oil is being made. Office open daily 9:30am-1pm and 4-8pm. At #16 in the adjacent P. del Comune sits the **Pro Trevi,** a legitimate information office. Open daily 10:30am-1pm. Unless you've got plenty of dough, there aren't many places to stay in Trevi itself. **La Casarecchia,** P. Garibaldi, 19, fixes up pizza and rents a few rooms (about L50,000 for doubles and L60,000 for triples, all with bath). Pizzeria open Tues.-Sun. 5pm-1am. **Il Terziere,** Via Coste, 1 (tel./fax (0742) 783 59), just off P. Garibaldi, is both an elegant hotel and a great restaurant. Find immaculate rooms upstairs (singles L55,000, doubles L80,000) and fresh homemade pasta (*strangozzi al tartufo,* a stringy pasta with truffles, L11,000) downstairs. V, MC, AmEx.

Todi

According to legend, an eagle absconded with a tablecloth and led the founders of Todi to this rocky site. For a long time, this isolated town remained untouched by historical change; it still retains visible traces of its Etruscan, Roman, and medieval past. But modernity has rediscovered Todi—the town figures prominently in a recent TV commercial for Visa.

ORIENTATION AND PRACTICAL INFORMATION

In the Todi of today there's barely room for cars, let alone eagles with flowing tablecloths. All areas of the city that don't house an important sight (and some that do) seem to have been transformed into parking lots. **Piazza del Popolo,** the center of town, showcases the *duomo* and sundry *palazzi.* **Piazza Jacopone** and **Piazza Umberto** lie around the corner. **Corso Cavour, Via Roma, Via Matteotti,** and **Viale Cortesi** form one steep street leading downtown and out the city wall to the hotels.

Tourist Office: Todipromotion, Via A. Ciuffeli, 8 (tel. 894 38 67), just down the street from P. Umberto. Ask for a copy of the helpful *Informa Todi* brochure. Open Mon.-Fri. 9am-1pm and 3-7pm; in summer also Sat. 11am-1pm and 4-6pm.

Trains: The private **Ferrovia Centrale Umbria** provides infrequent service to Todi from Perugia via Spoleto and Terni. City bus B runs to the station 15min. before every train; it will also carry you the 4km up to the town center (L1200 at the coin machine in the station, L2000 on the bus).

Buses: ASP (tel. 894 29 39) runs 6 buses per day to and from Perugia (1¼hr., L9200); the last bus for Perugia departs at 5pm. The bus stop is at P. Consolazione, a short ride on city bus A or a pleasant 1km walk from the town's center.

Emergencies: tel. 113. **Hospital: Ospedale degli Infermi** (tel. 885 81), on Via Matteotti.

Police: Carabinieri (tel. 894 23 23), on Via Angelo Cortese.

Post Office: (tel. 894 22 02), at P. Garibaldi. Open Mon.-Sat. 8:10am-7pm. **Postal Code:** 06059.

Telephone Code: 075.

ACCOMMODATIONS AND FOOD

Unless you've got gold versions of major credit cards, hotels in Todi are pretty much out of reach, not to mention out of the way. **Hotel Tuder,** Via Maestà dei Lombardi, 13 (tel. 894 21 84; fax 894 39 52), off Via Cortesi, has luxurious singles with bath for L85,000, and doubles with bath for L110,000. The hotel lies along a busy thoroughfare, so be careful walking there at night.

Pick up provisions at the **alimentari** at Via Cavour, 150. Open Mon.-Sat. 7:45am-1:30pm and 5:30-8pm, closed Wed. afternoon. Fresh fruit and veggies are at the **Frutta e Verdura market** on the corner of P. Jacopone. Open Thurs. 7am-1:30pm, Fri.-Mon. 7am-1:30pm and 4-8pm; closed Sun. March-Sept.

Ristorante Cavour, Via Cavour, 21/23 (tel. 894 24 91). Excellent, filling meals for L22,000. Pizza around L7500. Their specialty is *tortellini al tartufo nero* (with black truffles, L13,000). Try to get a seat in the cool medieval dungeon. Open Thurs.-Tues. noon-3pm and 7:30-2am. V, MC, AmEx.

Enoteca San Lorenzo, Via San Lorenzo, 1 (tel. 894 44 00). Facing the *duomo* in P. del Popolo, take the small street to the right under the portico. Enjoy good food in a charming atmosphere—colorful dried flowers, vaulted brick ceilings, and a candle on every table. Specialties include *risotto San Lorenzo* (with mushrooms, asparagus, and bleu cheese) and *cinghiale* (wild boar), both L15,000. The L20,000 *menù* includes *primo, secondo,* and *caffè*. Cover L3000. Open Tues.-Sun. 10:30am-4:30pm and 6:30pm-midnight. V, MC. AmEx.

Bar 'l Capestio, Via G. Matteotti, 120 (tel. 894 39 57). Perfect for those who wish to avoid the exorbitant expense of full-fledged restaurant dining. It's a trip downhill from P. Jacopone to a *tavola calda* with delicious pizza, lasagna, *bruschette,* and fried vegetables. L12,000 for a healthy portion of 2 items.

SIGHTS

Piazza del Popolo is a stately ensemble of glowering *palazzi* and a somber *duomo;* the square's air of authority is only slightly diminished by the cars whizzing around its edge. This *piazza* has been Todi's focal point since Roman times and remains as the town's high point in altitude and architectural achievement. The **Palazzo del Capitano** (1290) stretches its cavernous portico across the east end of the *piazza,* its peaked Gothic windows lending relief to its imposing façade. (Open daily 10am-12:30pm and 4-8pm.) The **Pinacoteca Civica** occupies the fourth floor; keep climbing to reach the fascinating frescoes in the **Sala del Capitano del Popolo** at the top of the exterior marble staircase. Huge wooden arches soar across the immense hall. The adjoining **Palazzo del Popolo** with its distinctive crenelated profile was begun in 1213. Across from the *duomo,* the tower and façade of the **Palazzo dei Priori** (1297-1337) retain vestiges of medieval gloom, despite the rows of Renaissance windows that were carved out in the early 16th century.

Directly across the *piazza* the stout **duomo** rests solidly atop a flight of broad stone steps. It almost seems to be brooding over having been denied even a single spire or dome. The central rose window and arched doorway command attention with their intricate decoration. Inside, Romanesque columns with Corinthian capitals support a plain wall punctuated by slender windows. The delicate Gothic side arcade, added in the 1300s, shelters an unusual altarpiece: the Madonna's head emerges in high relief from the flat surface of a painting. A strangely subdued 16th-century scene of the Last Judgment occupies the church's back wall. The 8th-century crypt hides some intricate inlaid wooden stalls of the chancel. (*Duomo* open daily 8:30am-12:30pm and 2:30-6pm.)

Neighboring **Piazza Garibaldi** has been reduced to little more than a municipal parking lot, but it still opens onto a superb vista. From the *piazza,* follow the signs leading off Corso Cavour to the remaining walls of the **Foro Romano** and the nearby 12th-century **Church of San Ilario.** From here it's a brief jaunt to the **Fonti Scarnabecco,** whose 13th-century porticoes still house one working tap. Return to P. del Popolo and take Via Mazzini to the majestically angular **Church of San Fortunato.** Built by the Franciscans between the 13th and 15th centuries, the church features Romanesque portals and a Gothic interior. The story of the sacrifice of Isaac decorates the space between the first and second columns to the right of the door. Note Masolino's fresco *Madonna and Angels.* To the right of San Fortunato, a path bends uphill toward **La Rocca,** a ruined 14th-century castle. Next to the castle, follow a sinuous path, appropriately named **Viale della Serpentina,** to a breathtaking *belvedere* constructed on the remains of an old Roman wall. Farther down, the Renaissance **Church of Santa Maria della Consolazione** stands by the entrance to the town. Its mullioned windows and elegant domes welcome every visitor to Todi.

The **Mostra Nazionale dell'Artigianato** (National Exhibit of Crafts) fills the *palazzi* of P. del Popolo throughout the summer. Home to some of the finest woodcarvers in Italy, Todi displays its prized **woodwork,** both antique and modern. **Arte Europa,** a series of cultural events and theatrical performances with international themes, takes place for one weekend in mid-June. (Tickets go for about L20,000-60,000.) The city's most colorful festival is the **Mongolfieristico,** a ten-day hot-air-balloon show which occurs in mid-July. In late-August and early-September, Todi hosts its own arts festival with classical and jazz concerts, ballet performances, and film screenings. For info and tickets (about L15,000-50,000), contact the tourist office.

Orvieto

The town of Orvieto sits atop a volcanic plateau rising up from the rolling farmlands of southern Umbria. Although it originated as one of the cities of the Etruscan *Dodecapolis,* it is the city's medieval legacy that colors it most strongly today. Thomas Aquinas lectured in the local academies in the 13th century, and crusades were planned within the city walls. A well-preserved medieval center provides the backdrop for the stunning 13th-century *duomo*, which has rewarded the town's piety with fame and wealth. Orvieto is a popular tourist stop, and its residents are proud to share their rich history, their justifiably famous white *Orvieto Classico* wine, and their fine handcrafted ceramics.

ORIENTATION AND PRACTICAL INFORMATION

Orvieto lies midway along the Rome-Florence train line. From the train station, cross the street and take the funicular up the hill. When you reach **Piazza Cahen** at the top, you can walk up **Corso Cavour** to the city center (10min.) or take a **shuttle** to Piazza del Duomo. (Funicular departs every 15min., L1100, with shuttle L1400.) Corso Cavour is the town's backbone, site of most of the city's restaurants, hotels, and shops. **Via Duomo** branches to the left off C. Cavour and ends at **P. del Duomo.**

Tourist Office: P. del Duomo, 24 (tel. 34 17 22). The shuttle drops you at the door. Friendly and patient staff, but the office is often crowded. Get the incredibly complete pamphlet on hotels, restaurants, sights, and practical information. Up-to-date info on trains and buses; **city bus tickets** for sale. Open Mon.-Fri. 8am-2pm and 4-7pm, Sat.-Sun. 10am-1pm and 3:30-6:30pm. The **Tourist Information Point** on Via Duomo is actually a money-making outfit but performs some useful services: the staff will help you find a place to stay (L1000 charge) and **exchange currency** (5% commission).

Tours: Escursioni da Orvieto, Corso Cavour, 139 (tel. 34 46 78). Three fascinating itineraries take you through the underground caves, into the *duomo,* and around the city. Tours last 2-3hr. and cost L20,000-25,000.

Trains: To Florence (2hr., L15,500) and Rome (1½hr., L11,700). **Luggage Storage:** L5000 for 12hr.

Buses: COTRAL runs one daily bus from the train station to P. Cahen. Seven per day to Viterbo (L5400). **ATC,** P. Cahen, 10 (tel. 419 21) journeys to Perugia at 5:55am (L10,700) and Todi at 1:40pm (L7700). Buy tickets in the tourist office, at the *tabacchi* up Corso Cavour, or on the bus.

Emergencies: tel. 113. **Hospital:** (tel. 30 91) in P. del Duomo.

Police: (tel. 400 88) in P. della Repubblica.

Post Office: On Via Cesare Nebbia, which begins after the Teatro Mancinelli, next to Corso Cavour, 114 (tel. 412 43). Stamps are available at *tabacchi,* and mail drops dot the town. Open Mon.-Sat. 8:15am-6:40pm. **Postal Code:** 05018.

Telephone Code: 0763.

ACCOMMODATIONS AND CAMPING

Da Fiora, Via Magalotti, 22 (tel. 410 83 or 411 19), off P. della Repubblica through P. dell'Erba (take minibus B from P. Duomo or P. Cahen to P. Erba). The proprietress rents private rooms in her home. Spotless antique furniture and cozy beds covered with lace. L20,000 per person, less in winter.

Hotel Duomo, Vicolo di Maurizio, 7 (tel. 418 87), off Via Duomo, the first right as you leave the *piazza*. New owners rent out light and well-ventilated rooms, just steps away from the towering cathedral. Singles L38,000. Doubles L51,000, with bath L79,000. Triples L66,000, with bath L103,000. Breakfast L8000.

Camping: Orvieto (tel. 95 02 40), on Lake Corbara 14km from the center of town. From the station, take the local Orvieto-Baschi bus and ask to be dropped off at the site (the stop is 200m from the entrance). L9000 per person, L7500 per tent, L3500 per car. Swimming pool and hot showers included. Open Easter-Sept.

FOOD

Although the food here is expensive, you'll probably find yourself saying, "At least the wine's (*hic*) cheap." An excellent *alimentari* sits below P. della Repubblica at Via Filippeschi, 39. Open Mon.-Tues. and Thurs.-Sat. 7:30am-1:30pm and 5-8pm, Wed. 7:30am-1:30pm.

Cooperativa al San Francesco (tel. 433 02) on Via Bonaventura Cerretti. Walk down Via Lorenzo Maitani from the front of P. del Duomo, but be careful not to trip over kneeling tourists trying to fit the massive cathedral into one picture. Follow the signs, your nose, or the crowd. Extremely popular. A huge restaurant, self-service cafeteria, and pizzeria all rolled into one. Pizza (only at night) and wine L11,000. Pasta L6500-11,000. Open daily 12:30-3pm and 7-10:30pm. V, MC.

Da Fiora, Via Magalotti, 24 (tel. 411 19). Just below her rent-a-room residence, Signora Fiora has established a bustling restaurant enterprise with the best deals in town. The all-inclusive *menù* (L14,000) will fill you up as you take in a spaghetti western on TV.

SIGHTS AND ENTERTAINMENT

A quick glance at the **duomo** (1209), Orvieto's pride and joy, is almost overwhelming: its fanciful façade, intricately designed by Lorenzo Maitani, dazzles the admirer with intertwining spires, mosaics, and sculptures. The bottom level features exquisitely carved bas-reliefs of the Creation and Old Testament prophecies, and a final panel of Maitani's realistic *Last Judgment*. Bronze and marble sculptures, set in niches surrounding the rose window by Andrea Orcagna (1325-1964), emphasize the Christian canon. Thirty-three architects, 90 mosaic artisans, 152 sculptors, and 68 painters worked over six centuries to bring the *duomo* this far, and the work continues; the bronze doors were only installed in 1970. The **Chapel of the Madonna di San Brizio** (sometimes called the **Cappella Nuova**) is off the right transept; although it is undergoing lengthy restoration, the tourist office offers free tours (in Italian) of the parts being restored. Inside are Luca Signorelli's dramatic **Apocalypse frescoes,** considered to be his finest works. Begun by Fra Angelico in 1447, they were supposed to be completed by Perugino, but the city grew tired of waiting and enlisted Signorelli to finish the project. His vigorous draftsmanship, mastery of human anatomy, and dramatic compositions paved the way for the genius of Michelangelo. On the left wall hangs the *Preaching of the Anti-Christ*. On the opposite wall, skeletons and muscular humans pull themselves out of the earth in the unsettling *Resurrection of the Dead.* Beside it is the *Inferno*, with Signorelli (a blue devil) and his mistress embracing beneath the fiery display. Rumor has it that the Whore of Babylon, being carried on the back of a devil above the masses, was modeled after a woman from Orvieto who rejected Signorelli's advances. In the **Chapel of the Corporale** off the left transept, Lippo Memmi's *Madonna dei Raccomandati* hangs proudly. This chapel also holds the gold-encrusted **Reliquary of the Corporale** (chalice-cloth), to which the entire structure is dedicated. The cloth inside the box caught Christ's blood, which dripped from a consecrated host in Bolsena in 1263, thereby substantiating the doctrine of transubstantiation. (The *duomo* is open year-round 7am-1pm; afternoon hours vary monthly—2:30-5:30pm is a safe bet. Free.)

The austere 13th-century **Palazzo dei Papi** (Palace of the Popes) sits to the right of the *duomo.* Here, in 1527, Pope Clement VII rejected King Henry VIII's petition to annul his marriage with Catherine of Aragon, condemning both Catherine and English Catholicism to a bleak fate. Set back in the *palazzo* is the **Museo Archeologico Nazionale,** where you can examine Etruscan artifacts from the area and even walk into a full-sized tomb. (Open Mon.-Sat. 9am-1:30pm and 3-7pm, Sun. 9am-1pm. Admission L4000, under 18 and over 60 free.)

Return to Corso Cavour and continue to P. della Repubblica, where the **Church of Sant'Andrea** marks the beginning of Orvieto's **medieval quarter.** The church, built upon the ruins of an Etruscan temple, served as a meeting place or *comune* in the medieval republic of Orvieto. Inside, the crypt, at the beginning of the right aisle, contains recently excavated remains from the Etruscan temple.

From P. della Repubblica, take Viale dei Mercanti down into the medieval quarter and turn right onto Via Ripa di Serancia. The **Church of San Giovanni** at the end of the road sits just inside the ancient city walls and offers a truly stunning view of the countryside below. The soils of the verdant slope below P. San Giovanni are filled with the graves of thousands who perished in the Black Death of 1348.

On the east edge of town, down Via Sangallo off P. Cahen (to the left of the train station; you can take the shuttle back), descend into the **Pozzo di San Patrizio** (St. Patrick's Well). Having fled freshly sacked Rome, Pope Clement VII wanted to ensure that the town did not run out of water during a siege, and in 1527 commissioned Antonio da Sangallo the Younger to design the well. (Open daily in summer 9:30am-7pm; in winter 10am-6pm. Admission L6000, L10,000 includes the Museo Greco.) After cooling off in the clammy well shaft, enter the **Fortezza,** where a fragrant sculpture garden and tall trees crown battlements overlooking the Umbrian landscape. (Open daily April-Sept. 7am-8pm; Oct.-March 9am-7pm.)

For the most complete tour of Etruscan Orvieto, consider the **Underground City Excursions,** which depart from the tourist office. Guides lead groups on a labyrinthine path through tunnels, quarries, cellars, wells and cisterns that were dug from the *tufa* 3000 years ago. (Tour lasts about 1hr. L10,000, L6000 for students.)

On Pentecost (42 days after Easter), Orvieto celebrates the **Festa della Palombella.** Small wooden boxes filled with fireworks and connected by a metal wire are set up in front of the *duomo* and the Church of San Francesco. At the stroke of noon, the San Francesco fireworks are set off, and a white metal dove shoots across the wire to ignite the explosives. **Concerts** are held in the *duomo* on August evenings. In June, the historic **Procession of Corpus Domini,** marked by pomp and pageantry, celebrates the Miracle of Bolsena. From late-December through early-January, **Umbria Jazz Winter** rocks Orvieto's theaters, churches, and *palazzi.*

Tuscany (Toscana)

Tuscany is the stuff Italian dreams (and more than one romantic Brits-in-Italy movie) are made of. With rolling hills covered in olives and grapevines, bright yellow fields of sunflowers, and inviting cobblestone streets, it's hard not to wax poetic. Tuscany's Renaissance culture became Italy's heritage, while its regional dialect, the language of Dante, Petrarch, and Machiavelli, developed into today's textbook Italian.

Despite the appearance of eternal eminence, everything of importance in this region occurred within one outstanding half-millennium. Toward the end of the 10th century, increasingly powerful local aristocrats and their *comuni,* independent city-states, propagated intense rivalries that subsumed all local culture. Even when not engaged in all-out warfare, these *comuni* struggled to erect splendid cathedrals and august towers merely to shame neighboring towns. In the midst of this chaos, the Renaissance emerged, an unprecedented explosion of art, architecture, and humanist scholarship. The region's splendor began to decay in the early 16th century. Under the rule of the Medici family, the rich, leisured Tuscans reveled in the grandeur of the High Renaissance and then saw their region decline into to a cultural and political non-entity. Protected by a few centuries of relative serenity, the cities and towns of Tuscany remain virtually unchanged.

An extensive and convenient transportation system makes it easy to tour Tuscany's countryside. The state railroad serves all major towns and many smaller ones, though in the hill-towns the incredible vistas that bus travel affords more than compensate for the infrequent service and changeovers. With so much to see, plan your itinerary wisely; Florence and Pisa should not be missed. Once you've seen them, though, consider devoting a little time to four of the most hospitable and beautiful Tuscan cities: Siena, Montepulciano, Cortona, and Lucca. The only area to avoid is the unattractive coast. Exploring Tuscany on your own will lead you to innumerable worthwhile towns crowning hills and filling valleys. Youth hostels abound in Tuscany, a fortunate circumstance since hotels are generally on the expensive side. Reservations are advisable all summer, especially in Florence, Siena, and Pisa. Tourist office staff and most restaurant workers can tell you who lets rooms. Camping is possible at the many lakes, mountains, and coastal resorts.

It may not surprise you that this culturally rich region also boasts a famed culinary tradition. Neither southern pasta and tomatoes nor northern *risotto* and *polenta* are staples of the Tuscan table. White beans *(fagioli)* are a regional obsession, so join locals and enjoy them in everything. Other local specialties include *ribollita* (bean and cabbage stew) and *fiori di zucca fritti* (fried zucchini flowers). Meat dishes include *coniglio* (rabbit), *trippa* (tripe), *cinghiale* (wild boar), and the famous and costly *bistecca alla fiorentina* (beef steak). Tuscany's gastronomic triumph is its wine, both the red *chianti,* from the area around Florence and Siena, and the premier red, the expensive *brunello di Montalcino.* A unique Tuscan indulgence is *vin santo,* a sweet dessert wine made from grapes dried in lofts for several months before being crushed. Drink it as Tuscans do—with a plateful of *cantuccini di Prato* (crispy almond cookies) for dipping.

Florence (Firenze)

Although Florence's Dante Alighieri bitterly bemoaned his hometown's greed and viciousness in the 13th century, nearly every visitor to walk the city's cobblestone streets since then has fallen in love with it. Henry James, Albert Camus, and even cranky Mark Twain were all won over by Florence's immense beauty. The city drapes itself languidly along the Arno River, with picturesque bridges connecting the older *centro* to the Oltrarno district. Streets weave past churches, medieval fortresses, and *palazzi.* While Florence carefully maintains its Renaissance architecture and culture, it is not locked in time; the city still pulses with life, from the students scurrying through the university quarter to the businessmen whizzing by on Vespas.

Stimulated by an innovative banking system, the city evolved from a busy 13th-century wool- and silk-trading town to a center of political experimentation and artistic rebirth. Periodic civil wars disrupted Florentine civic life until the Medici clan rose to power and Lorenzo the Magnificent established peace in the 15th century. Under his rule, Renaissance culture peaked in a flurry of splendid productivity. At the height of its glory in the mid-15th century, Florence was the unchallenged European capital of art, architecture, commerce, and political thought.

Since the Renaissance, Florentines have taken great care to preserve the cultural heritage of their city. When the Arno flooded in 1966, swamping Santa Croce and the Uffizi Museum, Florentines braved the waters to rescue paintings, sculptures, and books. Although tourists flood the city today, the locals don't seem to mind. They, of all people, understand Florence's allure.

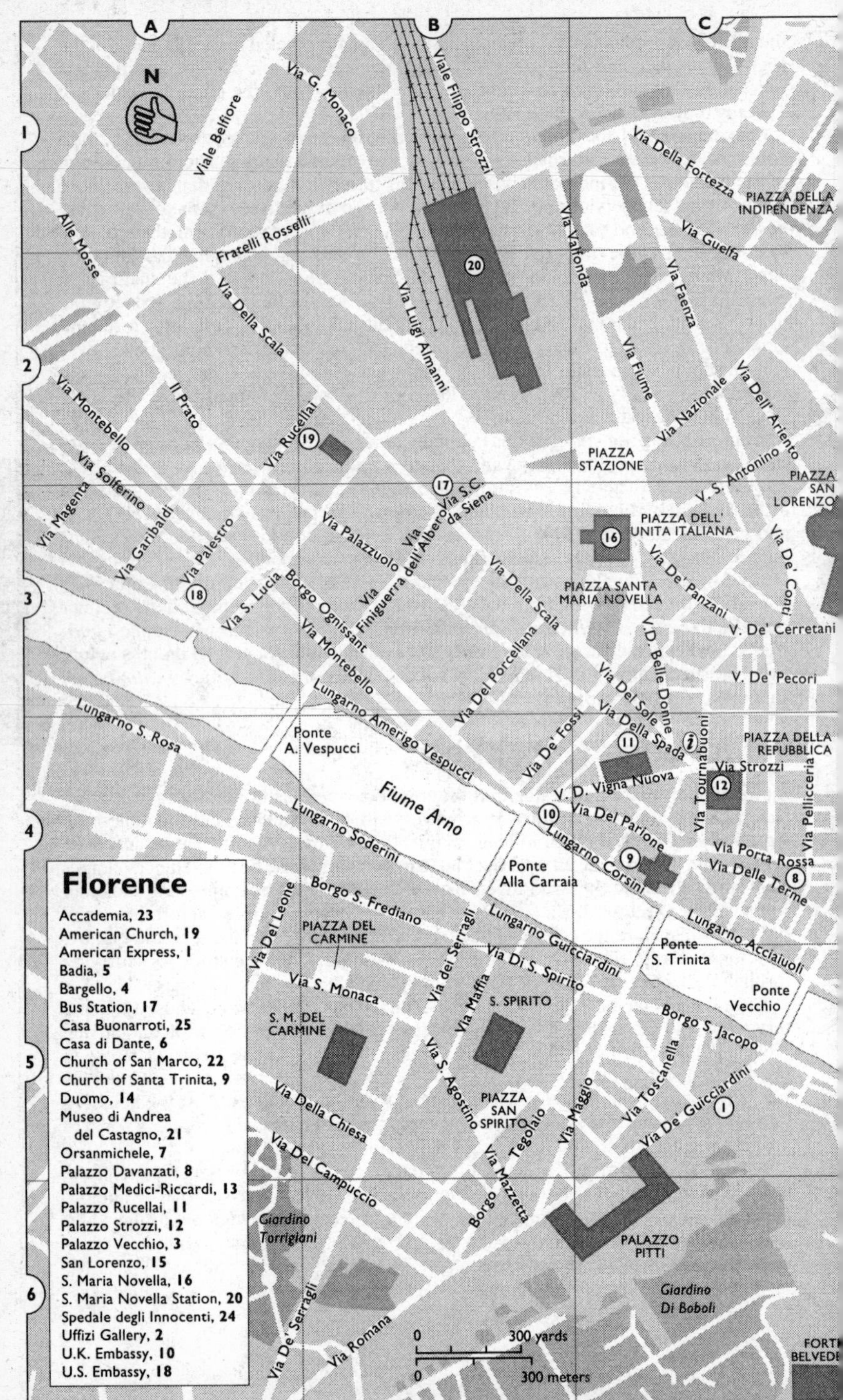

Florence

Accademia, **23**
American Church, **19**
American Express, **1**
Badia, **5**
Bargello, **4**
Bus Station, **17**
Casa Buonarroti, **25**
Casa di Dante, **6**
Church of San Marco, **22**
Church of Santa Trinita, **9**
Duomo, **14**
Museo di Andrea del Castagno, **21**
Orsanmichele, **7**
Palazzo Davanzati, **8**
Palazzo Medici-Riccardi, **13**
Palazzo Rucellai, **11**
Palazzo Strozzi, **12**
Palazzo Vecchio, **3**
San Lorenzo, **15**
S. Maria Novella, **16**
S. Maria Novella Station, **20**
Spedale degli Innocenti, **24**
Uffizi Gallery, **2**
U.K. Embassy, **10**
U.S. Embassy, **18**

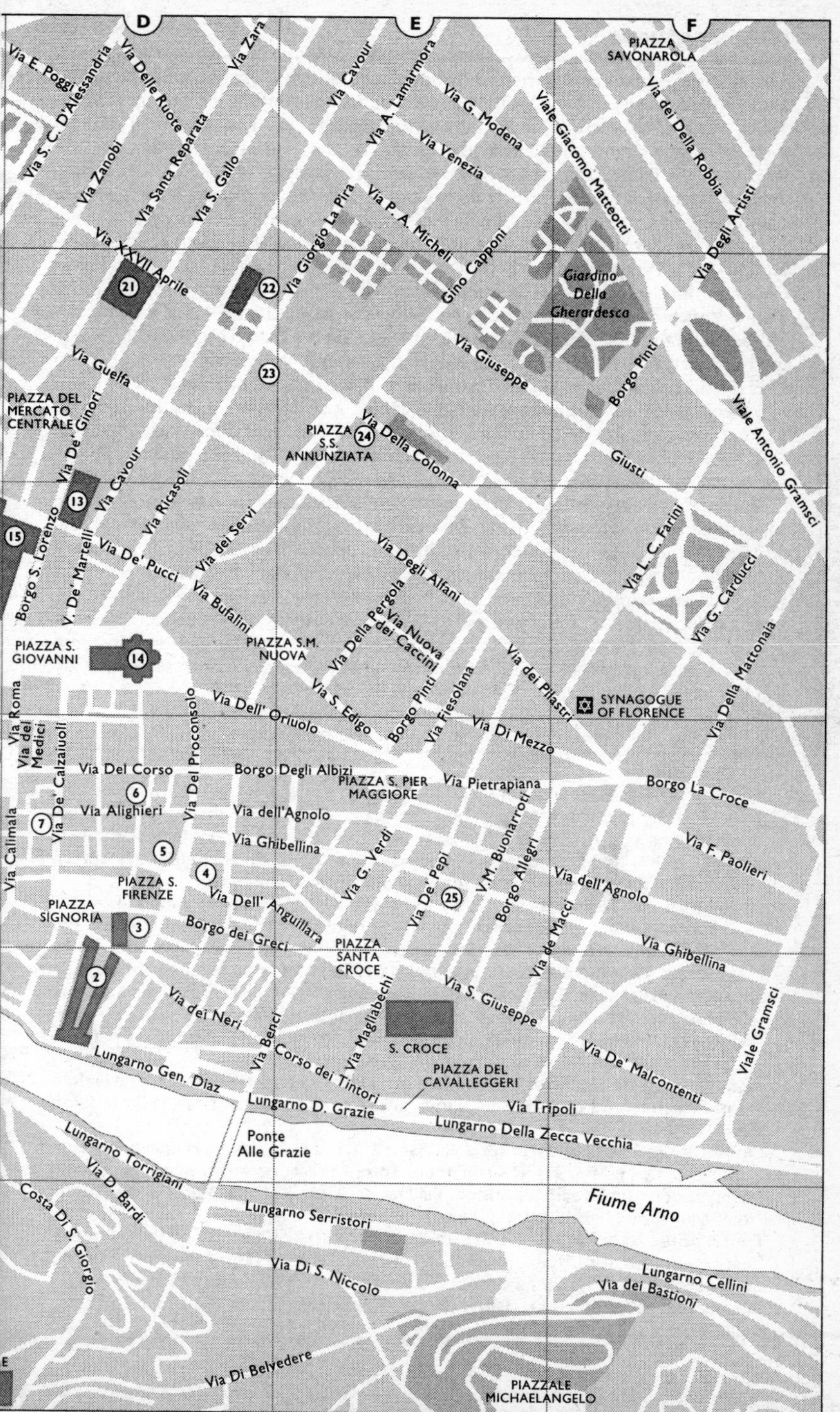
D
E
F
PIAZZA SAVONAROLA
Via E. Poggi
Via S. C. D'Alessandria
Via Delle Ruote
Via Zara
Via Cavour
Via A. Lamarmora
Via G. Modena
Viale Giacomo Matteotti
Via dei Della Robbia
Via Zanobi
Via Santa Reparata
Via S. Gallo
Via Venezia
Via Giorgio La Pira
Via P. A. Micheli
Gino Capponi
Via Degli Artisti
Via XXVII Aprile
Giardino Della Gherardesca
Via Guelfa
Via Giuseppe
Borgo Pinti
PIAZZA DEL MERCATO CENTRALE
Via Ginori
Via De' Ginori
PIAZZA S.S. ANNUNZIATA
Via Della Colonna
Giusti
Viale Antonio Gramsci
Via Cavour
Via Ricasoli
Via dei Servi
Borgo S. Lorenzo
V. De' Martelli
Via De' Pucci
Via Degli Alfani
Via L. C. Farini
Via G. Carducci
Via Bufalini
PIAZZA S. GIOVANNI
PIAZZA S.M. NUOVA
Via Della Pergola
Via Nuova dei Caccini
Via dei Pilastri
Via Della Mattonaia
Via Roma
Via Dell' Oriuolo
Via S. Edigo
Borgo Pinti
Via Fiesolana
SYNAGOGUE OF FLORENCE
Via Di Mezzo
Via del Medici
Via De' Calzaiuoli
Via Del Corso
Via Del Proconsolo
Borgo Degli Albizi
PIAZZA S. PIER MAGGIORE
Via Pietrapiana
Borgo La Croce
Via Calimala
Via Alighieri
Via dell'Agnolo
Via Ghibellina
Via G. Verdi
V.M. Buonarroti
Borgo Allegri
Via F. Paolieri
PIAZZA S. FIRENZE
Via Dell' Anguillara
Via De' Pepi
Via dell'Agnolo
PIAZZA SIGNORIA
Borgo dei Greci
PIAZZA SANTA CROCE
Via de Macci
Via Ghibellina
Via dei Neri
Via Magliabechi
Via S. Giuseppe
Viale Gramsci
Via Benci
Corso dei Tintori
S. CROCE
Via De' Malcontenti
Lungarno Gen. Diaz
PIAZZA DEL CAVALLEGGERI
Lungarno D. Grazie
Via Tripoli
Lungarno Della Zecca Vecchia
Ponte Alle Grazie
Lungarno Torrigiani
Via D. Bardi
Costa Di S. Giorgio
Lungarno Serristori
Fiume Arno
Via Di S. Niccolo
Lungarno Cellini
Via dei Bastioni
Via Di Belvedere
PIAZZALE MICHAELANGELO
21
22
23
24
13
15
14
6
7
5
4
25
3
2

ORIENTATION

Florence is easily accessible by train from Milan, Bologna, Venice, Rome, and just about any other city in Italy. From Stazione Santa Maria Novella, it's a short walk on Via de' Panzani and then left on Via de' Cerrentari to the center of Florence. This area, the heart of the city, is bounded by the *duomo* on the north, the Arno River on the south, and the Bargello and Palazzo Strozzi on the east and west.

Major arteries radiate from the *duomo* and its two *piazze:* **Piazza San Giovanni** encircling the baptistery and **Piazza del Duomo** around the cathedral. A lively pedestrian walkway, **Via dei Calzaiuoli,** runs from the *duomo* to **Piazza Signoria** and the Arno. Parallel to Via dei Calzaiuoli on the west, **Via Roma** leads from P. San Giovanni through **Piazza della Repubblica** (the city's largest open space) to the **Ponte Vecchio,** which spans the Arno to the **Oltrarno** district. Parallel to Via dei Calzaiuoli on the east, **Via del Proconsolo** runs to the **Badia** and the **Bargello.** Heading north (away from the river) from P. San Giovanni, Borgo San Lorenzo runs to **Piazza San Lorenzo** and Via dei Servi leads to **Piazza SS. Annunziata.**

For guidance through Florence's tangled center, grab a **free map** (ask for one with a street index) from one of the tourist offices (see **Practical Information** below). Sights lie scattered throughout Florence, but few are out of walking distance. Weary sightseers can take orange ATAF city buses almost anywhere.

Florence's streets are numbered in red and black sequences. Red numbers are for commercial establishments and black (or blue) numbers denote residential addresses (including most sights and hotels). Black addresses appear here as a numeral only, while red addresses are indicated by a number followed by an "r." If you get to an address and it's not what you're looking for, you've probably got the wrong color; just take a step back and look around for the other sequence.

As in the rest of Italy, most establishments close for two to four hours every afternoon. On major holidays, including the festival of Florence's patron saint San Giovanni (June 24), everything but the occasional bar closes.

PRACTICAL INFORMATION

Tourist Offices:

Consorzio I.T.A. (tel. 28 28 93 and 21 95 37), in the train station by track #16, next to the pharmacy. If you show up in person and give them a price range, they'll find you a room, but probably near the station and perhaps not the best value. L3000-10,000 commission. They also have a bulletin board for travelers trying to find each other. No train info. Open daily 8:30am-9pm.

Informazione Turistica (tel. 21 22 45 or 238 12 26), inside the round glass-and-concrete building outside the train station (exit by track #16). No booking service, but plenty of up-to-date info on entertainment and cultural events. Open April-Oct. daily 8:15am-7:15pm; Nov.-March 8:15am-2pm. **Branch office,** Chiasso dei Baroncelli, 17r (tel. 230 21 24 or 230 20 33), just off P. della Signoria. Open April-Oct. daily 8:15am-7:15pm; Nov.-March 1:45-7:15pm.

APT, Via Cavour, 1r (tel. 29 08 32). Open Mon.-Sat. 8:15am-7:15pm, Sun. 8:15am-1:45pm; Nov.-Feb. Mon.-Sat. 8:15am-7:15pm.

Consortium Italian Tourist Association, Viale Gramsci, 9a (tel. 247 82 31). Info on Florence and its environs. Finds available accommodations (commission around L4000-7000).

Tourist Police: Ufficio Stranieri, Via Zara, 2 (tel. 497 71), for visa or work-permit problems. Open Mon.-Fri. 8:30am-noon. To report lost or stolen items, go around the corner to the **Ufficio Denunce,** Via Duca D'Aosta, 3. Open Mon.-Sat. 8am-8pm, Sun. 8am-2pm. English-speaking personnel usually available.

Tours: I Bike Italy (tel. 234 23 71). Take a leisurely bike tour through the surrounding countryside for L90,000, including lunch and a wine tasting. **Country Walks in Tuscany** (same tel. number) offers a 5-mile tour through nearby Fiesole (with a picnic lunch) for L70,000. **Ufficio Guide Turistiche,** at Via Roma, 5, Via Ghibellina, 110, and Via dei Corsi, 25, offers a 3-hr. tour (no shipwreck with Gilligan, though). L160,000 for any group of up to 30 people. For info, call 230 22 83 or 28 84 48.

Budget Travel: S.T.S.-Student Travel Service, Via Zanetti, 18r (tel. 28 41 83). Student-discounted train, plane, and bus tickets. Open Mon.-Fri. 9:30am-1pm and 1:30-7pm, Sat. 9:30am-12:30pm. **CTS,** Via Ginori, 25r (tel. 28 95 70). No Eurail passes, but just about everything else, including Transalpino tickets, discount airfares, car rentals, organized trips, and ISICs. Get there *early* or expect to wait...and wait. Grab a number from the orange reel on your left as you enter. Open Mon.-Fri. 9am-1pm and 2:30-6pm, Sat. 9am-noon.

Consulates: U.S., Lungarno Vespucci, 38 (tel. 239 82 76), at Via Palestro near the station. Open Mon.-Fri. 8:30am-noon and 2-4pm. **U.K.,** Lungarno Corsini, 2 (tel. 28 41 33). Open Mon.-Fri. 9:30am-12:30pm and 2:30-4:30pm. Answering machines at both locations give after-hours instructions. Canadians, Australians, and New Zealanders should contact their consulates in Rome or Milan.

Currency Exchange: Local **banks** have the best exchange rates. Most open Mon.-Fri. 8:20am-1:20pm and 2:45-3:45pm, some open Sat. morning. **Cassa di Risparmio di Firenze** now has 24-hr. ATMs that exchange money at: Via de' Bardi, 73r; Via Nazionale, 93; Via de' Tornabuoni, 23r; Via degli Speziali, 16r; and Via dei Servi, 40r. **Banca Nazionale del Lavoro** has similar machines at Via degli Strozzi, 5, just off P. della Republica; and at Via Verdi, 18. **Banca di Roma** has ATMs at P. Gaetano Salvemini and on the corner of Via de Serragli and Lungarno Guicciardini.

American Express: Via Dante Alighieri, 20-22r (tel. 509 81). From the *duomo*, walk down Via dei Calzaiuoli and turn left onto Via dei Tavolini. The office is on the little *piazza* at its end. Cashes personal checks for cardholders. Also holds mail (free for card- and checkholders, otherwise L3000 per inquiry, whether you have mail or not). L3000 to leave messages. L10,000 to forward mail. Open Mon.-Fri. 9am-5:30pm, Sat. 9am-12:30pm.

Telephones: Via Cavour, 21r. Open daily 8am-9:45pm.

Flights: Amerigo Vespucci Airport (tel. 33 34 90), in the Florentine suburb of **Peretola.** Mostly domestic and charter flights. The orange ATAF bus #62 connects the train station to the airport (L1400). SITA (tel. 48 36 51) also runs regular buses (L6000) to the airport from their station at Via S. Caterina da Siena, 157. **Galileo Galilei Airport** (tel. (050) 50 07 07), in **Pisa.** Take the airport express from the Florence train station (7:51, 11:05am, and every hr. 1:05-5:05pm, 1hr., L7200). In Florence, ask for info at the "air terminal" (tel. 21 60 73) at platform #5 in the train station, where you can also check in, get an embarkation card, and register baggage for L2000. Open daily 7am-5:30pm. Direct train service to Rome's Fiumicino airport departs from track #16.

Trains: Santa Maria Novella Station (tel. 27 87 85 for info), near the center of town. Info office open daily 7am-9pm; after hours go to ticket window #20. Take a number from the machine on the left as you enter; the wait can be long. You can also use the bright-yellow computers to plan your trip (English option). Every hr. to: Bologna (1hr., L13,200); Siena (1½hr, L8000); Venice (3hr., L31,600); Milan (3½hr., L36,200); and Rome (2½hr., L36,200 for IC trains). **Luggage Storage:** By track #16. L5000 for 12hr. Open daily 4:15am-1:30am. **Lost Property:** For objects left on a train, go to the **Ufficio Oggetti Rinvenuti** (tel. 235 21 90), next to the baggage deposit.

Buses: SITA, Via S. Caterina da Siena, 15r (tel. 48 36 51). Frequent buses to: Siena (2hr., express bus 1¼hr., L10,500); San Gimignano (13 per day, 1½hr., L9400); Poggibonsi (13 per day, 50min., L7000); Arezzo (6 per day, 1½hr., L7500); Volterra (6 per day, 2hr., L11,300). **CAP,** Largo Alinari, 9 (tel. 21 46 37 or 21 86 03), to Prato (L3500). **LAZZI,** P. Adua, 1-4r (tel. 21 51 55), to: Pisa (L10,600); Prato (L3500); Lucca (L8600); Pistoia (L4700); and Rome (L24,000).

Public Transportation: Orange ATAF city buses traverse all of Florence, generally 6am-1am, although schedules vary by line. Tickets: L1400 for 1hr. of unlimited use, L5400 for 4 such tickets, L1900 for 2hr., and L5000 for 24hr. You must buy tickets *before boarding* and validate them with the punch-machine on board; if you're caught without one, it's a L70,000 fine, no excuses. Many bus stops are equipped with ticket-vending machines, but these take coins only. **ATAF information and ticket office** is outside the train station (tel. 565 06 22). Open daily 7am-8pm. You can also buy tickets at most *tabacchi*. Ask at the office for a **bus map.** City bus #7 goes to Fiesole, #10 to Settignano.

Taxis: (tel. 43 90, 47 98, or 42 42). Taxi stands are outside the train station.

Car Rental: Hertz, Via Finiguerra, 17 (tel. 239 82 05). Min. age 25. Open Mon.-Sat. 8am-7pm, Sun. 8am-1pm. **Avis** (tel. 31 55 88) and **Maggiore** (tel. 31 12 56) are both at the airport. In town, the Avis office is at Borgo Ognissanti, 128r (tel. 21 36 29). Open Mon.-Fri. 8am-7pm, Sat. 8am-1pm and 3-6pm. **Budget,** Via Finiguerra, 31r (tel. 21 02 38). Min. age 21. Open Mon.-Sat. 8am-12:45pm and 2:30-7pm. **Program,** Borgo Ognissanti, 135r (tel. 28 29 16). Rates start at L100,000 per day.

Parking: Most hotels in the city center do not offer parking, and leaving your car in the street is a sure way to get it towed. Many small garages dot the city but keep sporadic hours (look for a blue sign with a "P"). The underground lot at the train station and the one beneath P. della Libertà are open 24hr.

Towed-Car Retrieval: Depositeria Comunale, Via dell'Arcovata, 6 (tel. 30 82 49). ATAF buses #23 and 33 both stop nearby.

Bike and Moped Rental: MotoRent, Via S. Zanobi, 9r (tel. 49 01 13). Mountain bikes run about L3000 per hr. and L20,000 per day. Mopeds begin at L9000 per hr., L40,000 per day, L200,000 per week. No license necessary, but bring ID indicating that you are at least 18.

Hitchhiking: Hitchers take the A-1 north to Bologna and Milan or the A-11 northwest to the Riviera and Genoa. Buses #29, 30, or 35 run from the station to the feeder near Peretola. For the A-1 south to Rome and the extension to Siena, they take bus #31 or 32 from the station to exit #23, Firenze Sud. As always, **hitchhiking is extremely risky.** The **International Lift Center,** Borgo dei Greci, 40r (tel. 28 06 21), matches passengers with drivers for a fee. Open daily 10am-7pm. You must call 1 week in advance.

Lost Property: Via Circondaria, 17b (tel. 36 79 43). Open Mon.-Sat. 9am-noon.

Bookstores: After Dark, Via de' Ginori, 47r (tel. 29 42 03). New English books and magazines. Open Mon.-Fri. 10am-1:30pm and 3-7pm, Sat. 10am-1:30pm. **BM Bookstore,** Borgo Ognissanti, 4r (tel. 29 45 75). Great selection. Stocks textbooks for American study-abroad programs. Open Mon.-Sat. 9am-1pm and 3:30-7:30pm, Sun. 9am-1pm; Nov.-Feb. closed Sun. **Paperback Exchange,** Via Fiesolana, 31r (tel. 247 81 54). Swaps books. Special *Italianistica* section features novels about Brits and Americans in Italy. Open Mon.-Sat. 9am-1pm and 3:30-7:30pm; July closed Sat. afternoons; mid-Nov. to mid-March closed Mon; closed 2-3 weeks in Aug. V, MC, AmEx.

Libraries: Biblioteca Marucelliana, Via Cavour, 43 (tel. 21 06 02), 2min. from the *duomo.* Open Mon.-Fri. 9am-6:45pm, Sat. 9am-1pm. **Biblioteca Nazionale,** P. D. Cavalleggeri (tel. 24 44 41), the largest library in Florence, requires a time-consuming bureaucratic process, but the reading room is an architectural masterpiece and the collection is extensive. Open Mon.-Fri. 9am-7pm and Sat. 9am-1pm. **Biblioteca Storia dell'Arte,** Via della Pergola, 56 (tel. 275 78 37), is a beautiful art history library. Open Mon.-Fri. 8:30am-7pm, Sat. 8:30am-1:30pm.

Religious Services:

- **Anglican: St. Mark's Church of England,** Via Maggio, 16 (tel. 29 47 64). Sun. 9 and 10:30am.
- **Catholic:** In English at the *duomo.* Sat. 5pm.
- **Episcopal: The American Church,** Via Bernardo Rucellai, 9 (tel. 29 44 17). Services Sun. 9 and 11am.
- **Jewish: Tempio Israelito,** Via Farini, 4 (tel. 24 52 52). Sabbath services Fri. at sunset, Sat. 8:45am.
- **Muslim: Centro Culturale Islamico,** P. degli Scarlatti, 1 (tel. 238 14 11).

Bulletin Boards: Lists of people seeking roommates, English teachers, baby-sitters, and religious, musical, and theatrical activities conducted in English: **The American Church,** Via Rucellai, 16 (tel. 29 44 17), near the train station off Via della Scala. Open Mon., Wed., and Fri. 9am-noon. **The British Institute,** Via Tornabuoni, 2 (tel. 239 88 66), between P. Santa Novella and P. della Repubblica. **Car-Lie's American Bakery,** Via Brache, 12r (tel. 12 51 37), near Via dei Neri. Open Sept.-July 15 Mon.-Sat. 8am-noon and 4-7pm. **La Raccolta,** Via Leopardi 10 (tel. 247 90 68). A center for alternative activities with listings for roommates, apartments, activities, and classes as well. See also **Paperback Exchange** under **Bookstores** above.

Ticket Agency: The Box Office at Via Faenza, 139r (tel. 21 08 04; fax 21 31 12), sells tickets for all of Florence's theatrical performances. Advance booking service. Open Mon.-Sat. 10am-8pm.

Laundromat: Launderette, Via Guelfa, 55r. Self-service wash and dry L10,000. Open daily 8am-10pm. **Wash and Dry Lavarapido,** Via dei Servi, 105r, 2 blocks from the *duomo.* Other locations at Via della Scala, 52-54r, Via dei Serragli, 87r, Viale Morgagni, 21r, and Via Nazionale, 129r. Self-service wash and dry L12,000. Open daily 8am-10pm, last wash 9pm.

Public Toilets: Palazzo Vecchio, Palazzo Pitti, and the train stations. L500 includes a lovely paper towel. The toilets upstairs in the Mercato Centrale are free but often messy.

Public Baths: Bagno S. Agostino, Via S. Agostino, 8 (tel. 28 44 82), off P. Santo Spirito. Bath L3000. Soap and towel L2000. Open Tues. and Thurs. 3-6pm, Fri.-Sat. 8am-noon.

Swimming Pools: Bellariva, Lungarno Colombo, 6 (tel. 67 75 21). Bus #14 from the station or a 15-min. walk upstream along the Arno. Open June-Sept. daily 10am-6pm and 8-11pm. L9000 daytime, L10,000 nighttime. **Costoli,** Viale Paoli (tel. 67 57 44), in a huge sports complex at Campo di Marte. Take bus #17 from P. Unità or #10 from the train station toward the *duomo.* Arrive early. Open June-Sept. daily 10am-6pm. Admission L9000, children L55000, over 60 free.

Gym: Gymnasium, Via Palazzuolo, 49r (tel. 29 33 08). Workout equipment and daily step aerobics. L20,000 per day, L160,000 per month.

Legal Assistance: SOS Turista, Via Cavour, 1r (tel. 276 03 82). Settles disputes between tourists and hotel managers, restaurant owners, tour guides, travel agents, and transportation workers. Open April-Oct. 10am-1pm and 3-6pm.

Late-Night Pharmacies: Farmacia Comunale (tel. 28 94 35), at the train station by track #16. **Molteni,** Via dei Calzaiuoli, 7r (tel. 28 94 90). **Farmacia all'Insegna del Moro,** P. San Giovanni, 20r (tel. 21 13 43). All open 24hr.

Emergency: tel. 113. **First Aid:** tel. 47 48 91. **Medical Emergency: Misericordia,** P. del Duomo, 20 (tel. 21 22 22 or 21 95 55). Call for ambulance. **Tourist Medical Service,** Via Lorenzo il Magnifico, 59 (tel. 47 54 11). A group of general practitioners and specialists with someone on call 24hr. Office visits about L50,000, housecalls about L80,000. **Drug Addiction Service:** Borgo Pinti, 68 (tel. 275 82 72/3). A list of French- and English-speaking doctors is available from the U.S. consulate.

Police: Questura, Via Zara, 2 (tel. 497 71). Also at P. del Duomo, 5. Open Mon.-Fri. 8am-8pm, Sat. 8am-2pm.

Post Office: (tel. 21 61 22) on Via Pellicceria off P. della Repubblica. Stamps at windows #21, 22, and 23 or from the vending machines as you enter; *fermo posta* at window #24. To send packages, go behind the building to Via dei Sassetti, 4. Open Mon.-Fri. 8:15am-7pm, Sat. 8:15am-12:30pm. **Telegram** office in front open 24hr. **Postal Code:** 50100 (post office).

Telephone Code: 055.

ACCOMMODATIONS

Florence abounds with one-star *pensioni* and private *affitta camere.* If you arrive late in the day, check with the train station's accommodations service for available rooms and going rates. Sleeping in train stations, streets, or parks is a poor idea—police strongly discourage it. Make reservations *(prenotazioni)* far in advance, at least 10 days if you plan to visit at Easter or in summer. The vast majority of *pensioni* prefer written reservations with at least one night's deposit in the form of a money order; others simply ask that you call to confirm a few days before you arrive.

Some warnings about hotels in Florence: If you do make a reservation, keep it. Hotel owners have become disgruntled with travelers who make reservations and don't show, and many no longer accept reservations for this reason. As a courtesy to hotel owners and fellow travelers (who get turned away when a hotel is "reserved" to capacity), either keep the reservation or cancel it as soon as you know you don't need it. Because hotel prices change regularly, **expect higher rates than those listed**

here. Don't embarrass hotel owners or yourself by insisting on the infallibility of *Let's Go* or any other guide.

If you have any complaints, talk first to the proprietor and then, if necessary, to the **Ufficio Controllo Alberghi,** Via Cavour, 37 (tel. 276 01). The municipal government strictly regulates hotel prices; proprietors can charge neither more nor less than the approved range for their category. Rates uniformly increase by 5% or so every year; the new rates take effect in March or April.

The city's best budget lodgings are at the **Ostello Archi Rossi** near the train station and at **Pensionato Pio X** and **Istituto Gould** in the Oltrarno, but other clean and inexpensive lodgings exist throughout the city. You can easily secure **long-term housing** in Florence. If you plan on staying a month or more, check the classified ads in *Le Pulce,* a tri-weekly paper (L3500) with apartment, sublet, and roommate listings, or **Grillo Fiorentino,** a free monthly local paper (call 48 77 10 for more info). Prices range from L350,000 to L800,000 per month. If you only want to stay a month, try to strike a bargain with someone who's looking for a long-term roommate; he or she might be willing to take you short-term while seeking someone else. Also check the **bulletin boards** (see **Practical Information** above, p. 174).

Hostels

Ostello Archi Rossi, Via Faenza, 94r (tel. 29 08 04; fax 230 26 01), 2 blocks from the train station. Exit left from the station onto Via Nazionale and turn left at Via Faenza. Look for the blue neon *"ostello"* sign. A new hostel with whitewashed walls, ceramic tiles, and brick archways. Large TV room and courtyard patio. Entertaining floor-to-ceiling graffiti brightens the lobby. Room lockout 9:30am, hostel lockout 11am. Curfew 12:30am. L21,000 per person in a room with 3-9 beds; L23,000 in a room with bath. Breakfast from L2500. Dinner L12,000. Very popular, and justifiably so. Management doesn't accept phone reservations, so arrive by 11am in summer. Wheelchair accessible.

Istituto Gould, Via dei Serragli, 49 (tel. 21 25 76), in the Oltrarno. Leave the station by track #16, turn right and walk to P. della Stazione. Go straight down Via degli Avelli, with the Church of Santa Maria Novella on your immediate right. Cross P. Santa Maria Novella and continue straight down Via dei Fossi, over the Ponte alla Carraia, and down Via dei Serragli (15min.). Or take bus #36 or 37 from the station to the 1st stop across the river. One of the best lodgings in Florence: staff is happy to answer questions, and the sunny rooms are attractive and spotless. The *palazzo* itself is cool and cavernous, with a large courtyard. All the profits fund social services for local children. There are only two drawbacks: it's impossible to check in or out on Sat. afternoons and Sun., when the office is closed, and the rooms overlooking the street are often noisy. No curfew, no lock-out, and no charge for showers. Office open Mon.-Fri. 9am-1pm and 3-7pm, Sat. 9am-1pm. **Prices are charged per person.** Singles L41,000, with bath L46,000. Doubles L32,000, with bath L35,000. Triples with bath L30,000. Quads with bath L28,000. Quints with bath L24,000.

Pensionato Pio X, Via dei Serragli, 106 (tel. 22 50 44). Follow the directions to the Istituto Gould (above), then walk a few blocks farther down the street. Quiet, no daytime lockout, gregarious management, and only 3-5 beds per room. Clean rooms and bathrooms. Four comfortable lounges. 2-day min. stay, 5-day max. stay. Check-out 9am. Curfew midnight. L20,000 per person, showers included; L3000 more for a room with bath. No reservations. Usually full in summer, but turnover is high. Arrive before 9am.

Ostello della Gioventù Europa Villa Camerata (HI), Viale Augusto Righi, 2-4 (tel. 60 14 51; fax 61 03 00), northeast of town.Take bus #17 from P. dell'Unità across from the train station or from P. del Duomo (20-30min.). Tidy and popular, though far away. In a gorgeous villa with *loggia* and gardens. Manager screens a movie (in English) every night at 9pm. Reception open daily 1-11pm. Check-out 7-9:30am. Curfew midnight. L23,000 per person. If they're full, you can sleep on a bed in an outdoor tent for L16,000; breakfast is an extra L2000. L5000 extra per night for anyone without a hostel card. Sheets and breakfast included. Cheap self-service laundry facilities. Dinner L12,000. Reserve by letter or fax only.

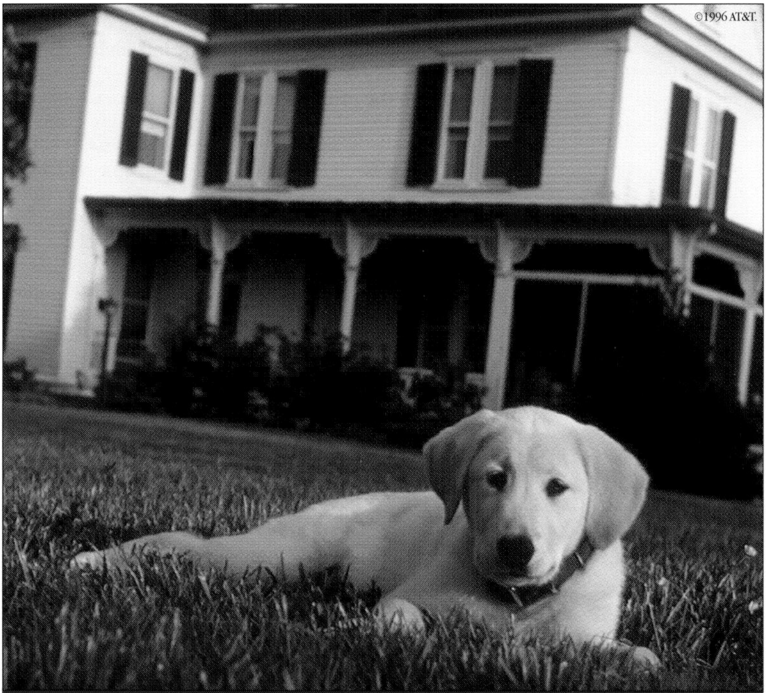

Photo: R. Olken

Greetings from LET'S GO

With pen and notebook in hand, a change of clothes in our backpack, and the tightest of budgets, we've spent our summer roaming the globe in search of travel bargains.

We've put the best of our research into the book that you're now holding. Our intrepid researcher-writers went on the road for months of exploration, from Anchorage to Angkor, Estonia to Ecuador, Iceland to India. Editors worked from spring to fall, massaging copy into witty and informative prose. A brand-new edition of each guide hits the shelves every fall, just months after it is researched, so you know you're getting the most reliable, up-to-date, and comprehensive information available.

We try to make this book an indispensable companion, but sometimes the best discoveries are the ones you make on your own. If you've got something to share, please drop us a line. We're Let's Go Publications, 67 Mount Auburn Street, Cambridge, MA 02138 USA (e-mail: fanmail@letsgo.com). Good luck and happy travels!

Suore Oblate dello Spirito Santo, Via Nazionale, 8 (tel. 239 82 02), across from the Apollo Theater. Exit left from the station onto Via Nazionale and walk 100m. The nuns take in women, married couples, and families; the atmosphere is almost oppressively peaceful. Frescoed lobby, cozy TV lounge, and breezy brick terrace. Huge rooms with modern bathrooms. Curfew 11pm sharp. Doubles with bath L75,000. Triples and quads L28,000 per person, with bath L30,000. Phone reservations accepted; written are preferred. Open July-Oct. 15.

Ostello Santa Monaca, Via S. Monaca, 6 (tel. 26 83 38; fax 28 01 85), off Via dei Serragli in the Oltrarno. This hostel often crowds many beds (about 10) into high-ceilinged rooms. Kitchen facilities, but no utensils. No meals in-house, but they sell inexpensive tickets to a nearby restaurant. Self-service laundry L12,000 per 5kg. Curfew 12:30am. L20,000 per person. Shower and sheets included. 7-day max. stay. Open 6-9:30am and 2pm-12:30am. Check-in 9:30am-1pm and after 2pm. Written reservations must arrive at least 3 days in advance.

Piazza Santa Maria Novella and Environs

Standing in front of the station, you'll be facing the back of the Basilica of S. Maria Novella. Beyond the church are budget accommodations galore. You'll be close to the *duomo,* the *centro,* and the station. Ask for a room overlooking the *piazza.*

Locanda La Romagnola and **Soggiorno Gigliola,** Via della Scala, 40 (tel. 21 15 97 or 28 79 81). Leave the station by track #5, walk across the street to Via S. Caterina da Siena, and turn right onto Via della Scala a block later. Simple rooms with plenty of space; some have frescoed ceilings or ornately carved beds. Curfew midnight. Singles L39,000, with bath L48,000. Doubles L66,000, with bath L80,000. Triples L90,000, with bath L99,000. May be closed Jan.-Feb.

Albergo Montreal, Via della Scala, 43 (tel. 238 23 31). Cozy hotel with friendly staff. Ample rooms get plenty of light and noise. Little TV lounge. Curfew 1:30am. Singles L50,000. Doubles with private shower L75,000, with full bath L82,000. Triples with bath L120,000. Quads with bath L140,000.

Hotel Visconti, P. Ottaviani, 1 (tel./fax 21 38 77), on the corner diagonally across the *piazza* from the church. Attempted neoclassical decor with huge Grecian nudes. Bar, TV lounge, and rooms with carefully planned color schemes. Friendly management serves breakfast (L12,000) on the roof garden. Open 24hr. Singles L43,000. Doubles L61,000, with bath L81,000. Triples L79,000, with bath L104,000. Quads L92,000, with bath L112,000.

Soggiorno Abaco, Via dei Banchi, 1 (tel./fax 238 19 19). With S. Maria Novella behind you, walk to the end of the *piazza* onto Via dei Banchi. Seven well-kept rooms with a medieval feel and polished wood-beamed ceilings. All rooms have fans and TVs. No curfew. Singles L65,000. Doubles L90,000, with bath L120,000. Triples L120,000, with bath L140,000. Quads available upon request. Laundry washed and dried for L5000 per load. Kitchen facilities L6000. V, MC, AmEx.

Pensione La Mia Casa, P. S. Maria Novella, 23 (tel. 21 30 61). A 17th-century *palazzo* with stunning frescoes on some of its ceilings. 300 years and innumerable American backpackers have worn it down a bit. Cleanliness varies. Every night, the proprietor screens a free documentary on Florence in English (8pm) and a relatively recent American film (9pm). Curfew midnight. Singles L40,000. Doubles L60,000, with bath L70,000. Triples L80,000, with bath L94,000. Quads L100,000, with bath L120,000. Breakfast L6000. Reservations taken 1 or 2 days in advance, but you must arrive before 1pm.

Hotel Elite, Via della Scala, 12 (tel. 21 53 95 or 21 38 32). Brass accents enhance this 2-star hotel's carefully maintained rooms. Welcoming management speaks some English. Singles with shower L80,000, with full bath L95,000. Doubles with shower L100,000, with full bath L125,000. Breakfast included.

Hotel Universo, P. S. Maria Novella, 20 (tel. 28 19 51). A fluffy black cat greets you in the peach-colored lobby. Spotless rooms with TVs. Michelangelo prints and funky armoires add flair. Singles L70,000, with bath L110,000. Doubles L110,000, with bath L130,000. Triples with bath L148,000. Quads L187,000, with bath L221,000. Breakfast included. V, MC, AmEx.

Old City (Near the Duomo)

Though tourists flood this area, budget accommodations are usually available. Many rooms provide great views of Florence's monuments, while others lie hidden in Renaissance *palazzi.*

Locanda Orchidea, Borgo degli Albizi, 11 (tel. 248 03 46). Take a left off Via Proconsolo, which begins behind the *duomo.* Dante's wife was born in this 12th-century *palazzo* built around a still-intact tower. Seven cozy, nicely decorated rooms, 4 of which open onto garden views. Singles L45,000. Doubles L68,000. Triples L105,000. Closed 2 weeks in Aug.; reservations *strongly* recommended for the rest of the summer.

Hotel Il Perseo, Via Cerretani, 1 (tel. 21 25 04), one block from the *duomo* as you head toward P. S. Maria Novella. Enthusiastic Australian owners welcome travelers to their bright, immaculate rooms, all with fans and many with absolutely breathtaking views. Cozy bar and TV lounge. Park your car for L27,000 per day. If they're full, they'll call around to find you a place to stay. Singles L60,000, with bath L70,000. Doubles L95,000, with bath L110,000. Triples L125,000, with bath L140,000. Quads L140,000, with bath L175,000. Ample breakfast included. V, MC, AmEx with 3% surcharge.

Soggiorno Bavaria, Borgo Albizi, 26 (tel./fax 234 03 13). Newly renovated rooms, some with balconies and frescoed ceilings, in a cool, quiet 15th-century *palazzo.* Huge lounge on the second floor. Singles L50,000. Doubles L80,000, with bath L90,000. Triples L90,000, with bath L100,000. Breakfast L5000.

Soggiorno Panerai, Via dei Servi, 36 (tel./fax 26 41 03). Via dei Servi radiates out from the side of the cathedral opposite the *campanile.* Serene rooms, each with a few antiques. Every 2 rooms share a bath. Coffee machine (L600 a cup) and refrigerator available to guests. Doubles L55,000. Triples L70,000. Quads L85,000.

Soggiorno Brunori, Via del Proconsolo, 5 (tel. 28 96 48), off P. del Duomo. Simple rooms with parquet floors and art posters, some with balconies. Friendly management speaks English and will help you plan excursions. Curfew 12:30am. Singles L36,000 (available in winter only). Doubles with bath L84,000. Triples L90,000, with bath L115,000. Quads L112,000, with bath L144,000.

Albergo Firenze, P. Donati, 4 (tel. 21 42 03 or 26 83 01; fax 21 23 70), off Via del Corso. Modern rooms with glossy tile floors and TVs in a beautiful *palazzo.* Central but tranquil. Singles L55,000, with bath L65,000. Doubles L79,000, with bath L91,000. Triples L105,000, with bath L120,000. Breakfast included.

Albergo Costantini, Via dei Calzaiuoli, 13 (tel./fax 21 51 28), a stone's throw from the *duomo.* A 14th-century *palazzo* with elegant frescoes and large rooms filled with cream-colored antique furniture. Singles L56,000, with bath L75,000. Doubles L75,000, with bath L100,000. Triples with bath L135,000. Quads with bath L170,000. Breakfast L15,000.

Hotel Maxim, Via dei Medici, 4 (tel. 21 74 74; fax 28 37 29). Another entrance (with elevator) at Via dei Calzaiuoli, 11. Cheerful proprietor offers clean, sunny rooms with old-fashioned furniture. Quiet rooms in the interior. Singles L55,000, with bath L75,000. Doubles L95,000, with bath L118,000. Triples L120,000, with bath L135,000. Quads L140,000, with bath L160,000. Laundry washed and dried for L18,000 per 4½kg. Some English spoken. Reservations accepted. Good breakfast included. V, MC, AmEx.

Via Nazionale and Environs

As you leave the station, take a left onto Via Nazionale to find budget hotels and hordes of tourists. If you can't avoid this quarter, at least walk away from its heart for a semblance of tranquility. Cheap establishments abound along **Via Nazionale, Via Faenza, Via Fiume,** and **Via Guelfa**—there are often several to a building.

Via Faenza, 56 houses 6 separate *pensioni,* among the best budget lodgings in the city. From the station, Via Faenza is the 2nd intersection on Via Nazionale.

Pensione Azzi (tel. 21 38 06) styles itself as the *locanda degli artisti* (the artists' inn), but anyone will enjoy the friendly management, large, immaculate rooms, and elegant dining room and terrace. No curfew. Singles L45,000. Doubles

L75,000, with bath L85,000. Triples L90,000, with bath L100,000. Quads L115,000, with bath L125,000. Breakfast L5000. V, MC, AmEx.

Albergo Merlini (tel. 21 28 48; fax 28 39 39). Large murals and red geraniums adorn the lounge/solarium. Some rooms have partial views of the *duomo.* Curfew 1:30am. Singles L45,000. Doubles L70,000, with bath L85,000. Triples L90,000, with shower L105,000. Quads L100,000, with shower L120,000. Breakfast L10,000.

Albergo Marini (tel. 28 48 24). Polished wood hallway leads to spotless rooms. Curfew 1am. Singles L50,000, with bath L70,000. Doubles L70,000, with bath L90,000. Triples L100,000, with bath L130,000. Quads L120,000, with bath L140,000. Breakfast L7000. Coffee vending machine (L1300 per cup).

Albergo Anna (tel. 239 83 22). Lovely rooms—some ceilings with frescoes, others with fans. Management and prices the same as the Pensione Azzi.

Albergo Armonia (tel. 21 11 46). Posters of American films bedeck these clean rooms. Singles L55,000. Doubles L85,000. Triples L110,000. Quads L140,000.

Locanda Paola (tel. 21 36 82). Standard rooms, some with views of Fiesole and the surrounding hills. Curfew 2am. Doubles L80,000, with shower L90,000. Triples L90,000, with shower L100,000.

Hotel Nazionale, Via Nazionale, 22 (tel. 238 22 03), near P. Indipendenza. Sunny rooms with blue carpets and comfy beds. Breakfast included. Door locks at midnight, so ask the proprietess for the key. Singles L55,000, with bath L67,000. Doubles L79,000, with bath L98,000. Triples L104,000, with bath L139,000.

Pensione Daniel, Via Nazionale, 22 (tel. 21 12 93), above the Hotel Nazionale. Basic, whitewashed rooms and recently renovated bathrooms. No curfew. Doubles L60,000. Triples L85,000. Breakfast L6000.

Via Faenza, 69:

Hotel Soggiorno d'Erico, 4th floor (tel./fax 21 55 31). Colorful mural of the Ponte Vecchio graces the hallway. Small rooms with nice views of the hills around Florence. Free kitchen use. Laundry washed for L6000 per load (no dryer). Singles L48,000. Doubles L70,000. Triples L90,000. Quads L100,000.

Locanda Giovanna. Seven basic, well-kept rooms, some with garden views. Singles L50,000. Doubles L75,000.

Locanda Pina and **Albergo Nella** (tel. 21 22 31), on the 1st and 2nd floors. Twin establishments offering basic rooms at a good price. Singles L40,000. Doubles L70,000. Quads L100,000. Free kitchen use. Laundry L5000 per load; no dryer.

Ausonia e Rimini, Via Nazionale, 24 (tel. 49 65 47). The spotless rooms are nicely decorated and well-lit. Welcoming owners. 5kg of laundry washed and dried for L12,000; ironed for L2000 per item. No curfew. Singles L70,000. Doubles L84,000, with bath L102,000. Triples L108,000, with bath L138,000. Enjoy your free breakfast on one of the marble tables. V, MC, AmEx.

Kursaal, Via Nazionale, 24 (tel. 49 63 24), downstairs from the Ausonia—same charming owners. Take advantage of its lovingly decorated 2-star rooms while they're still affordable. Satellite TV available in every room. Floral designs and Impressionist prints everywhere. Rooms toward the back are quieter. Singles L70,000, with bath L85,000. Doubles 102,000, with bath L146,000. Triples L132,000, with bath L186,000. Quads L160,000, with bath L210,000. Breakfast included. Wheelchair accessible. V, MC, AmEx.

Albergo Etrusca, Via Nazionale, 35 (tel./fax 21 31 00). Behind wallpapered doors hide rooms with tile floors and eccentric chandeliers. Free use of washer and kitchen facilities. Singles L44,000. Doubles L70,000. V, AmEx.

Near Piazza San Marco and the University Quarter

This area is considerably calmer and less tourist-ridden than its proximity to the center might suggest. Follow Via Nazionale from the station and take a right on Via Guelfa, which intersects with Via San Gallo and Via Cavour.

Hotel Tina, Via San Gallo, 31 (tel. 48 35 19 or 48 35 93). Small *pensione* with high ceilings, new furniture, and bright bedspreads. Amicable owners will find you another place if they're full. Singles L50,000-L55,000. Doubles L75,000, with bath L85,000-L90,000. Triples with bath L105,000. Quads with bath L125,000.

La Colomba, Via Cavour, 21 (tel. 28 43 23). Friendly Italo-Austrian proprietor rents out immaculate rooms. Bedspreads embroidered with flowers, some ceilings decorated to match. Windows peer across the Florentine roofscape. Negotiable curfew 1:30am. Singles L65,000. Doubles L100,000, with bath L120,000. Plentiful continental breakfast included. V, MC.

Albergo Sampaoli, Via San Gallo, 14 (tel. 28 48 34). A peaceful hotel with a proprietress who strives to make her *pensione* an American backpacker's "home away from home." A little faded, but expected renovations should brighten things up. Refrigerators on each floor. Singles L50,000. Doubles L70,000, with bath L90,000. Triples L105,000. Quads L120,000, with bath L140,000. No written reservations; call the night before you arrive.

Hotel Sofia, Via Cavour, 21 (tel. 28 39 30), just upstairs from La Colomba. Rooms with floral borders, tiny art prints, and new furniture. Curfew 1am. Singles L50,000. Doubles L80,000. Triples L120,000. Quads L140,000. Large American breakfast included.

Hotel Globus, Via Sant'Antonio, 24 (tel. 21 10 62; fax 239 62 55). Sun-drenched rooms with bright bedspreads and wicker furniture. Reception open 24hr. Singles L64,000, with bath L75,000. Doubles L95,000, with bath, L115,000. Triples L120,000, with bath L150,000. Rates much lower in the off season. Breakfast included. Reservations by phone or fax. V, MC, AmEx.

Hotel San Marco, Via Cavour, 50 (tel. 28 42 35). Three floors of modern, bright, airy rooms, highlighted by lively bedspreads. Curfew 1:30am, but you can ask for the key. Singles L60,000, with bath L70,000. Doubles L80,000, with bath L100,000. Triples with bath L135,000. Breakfast included. V, MC.

Hotel Enza, Via S. Zanobi, 45 (tel. 49 09 90). From Via Nazionale, turn right on Via Guelfa—Via Zanobi is the first cross-street. Neat rooms with wacky wallpaper and blue bathrooms, all tended by a friendly owner and her tiny dog. Curfew 1am. Singles L55,000, with bath L70,000. Doubles L75,000, with bath L95,000.

In the Oltrarno

Only a 10-min. walk across the Arno from the *duomo,* this area and its *pensione* are a respite from the bustle of Florence's hub.

Pensione Sorelle Bandini, P. S. Spirito, 9 (tel. 21 53 08). Old-world elegance on the top floor of a large *palazzo.* Handsome dark-wood ceilings and furniture. Beautiful views of the Boboli gardens and the *duomo* from the sunny *loggia.* Doubles L125,000, with bath L155,000. Triples L173,000, with bath L214,000. Quads L221,000, with bath L273,000. Some singles available in the off season. Small breakfast included. Often books to groups for L55,000 per person.

Hotel La Scaletta, Via Guicciardini, 13 (tel. 28 30 28), across the Ponte Vecchio toward the Pitti Palace. Leafy wallpaper and paisley bedspreads. Rooftop terraces with spectacular views of the Boboli gardens. Singles L70,000, with bath L85,000. Doubles L110,000, with bath L140,000. Breakfast included. V, MC.

Camping

Michelangelo, Viale Michelangelo, 80 (tel. 681 19 77), near P. Michelangelo. Take bus #13 from the station (15min., last bus 11:25pm). Extremely crowded, but offers a spectacular panorama of Florence. Fantastic facilities, including a well-stocked food store and bar. They may post a *completo* sign, but if you show up without a vehicle they will often let you in. L10,000 per person, L8000 per tent, L6000 per car, L4000 per motorcycle. Open April-Nov. 6am-midnight.

Villa Camerata, Viale A. Righi, 2-4 (tel. 60 03 15), outside the HI youth hostel on the #17 bus route. Catch the bus at P. dell'Unità or P. del Duomo. L7000 per person, L8000 per small tent. Open 1pm-midnight; if the office is closed, stake your site and come back later (before midnight) to register and pay. Check-out 7-10am.

Camping Panoramico, Via Peramonda, 1 (tel. 59 90 69), outside the city near Fiesole. Take bus #7 from the station (last buses 11:25pm and 12:30am, L1400). L11,000 per person, L9500 per tent.

Villa Favard, Via Rocca Tedalda. Take bus #14. **Free** campsite. A fenced-in area with a security guard, though you should keep an eye on your valuables anyway. No hot water, but running cold water and toilets. Open in summer only.

FOOD

Florence's hearty cuisine originated in the peasant fare of the surrounding countryside. Typified by fresh ingredients and simple preparations, Tuscan food ranks among the world's best. White beans and olive oil are the two main staples, and most regional dishes come loaded with one or the other, if not both. Specialties include such *antipasti* as *bruschetta* (grilled bread doused with olive oil and garlic, sometimes topped with tomatoes and basil). For *primi* Florentines have espoused the Tuscan classics *minestra di fagioli* (a delicious white bean and garlic soup) and *ribollita* (a hearty bean, bread, and black cabbage stew). Florence's classic *secondo* is *bistecca alla Fiorentina,* thick sirloin steak, each inch more succulent and expensive than the last. Florentines order it *al sangue* (very rare—literally "bloody"). The best local cheese is *pecorino,* made from sheep's milk. Wine is another Florentine favorite, and genuine *chianti classico* commands a premium price. (If you need a menu suggestion, Hannibal Lechter recommends *chianti* with a meal of liver and fava beans.) A liter of house wine typically costs L6000-7000 in Florence's *trattorie,* while stores sell bottles of delicious wine for as little as L4000. The local dessert is *cantuccini di prato* (almond cookies made with many egg yolks) dipped in *vinsanto* (a rich dessert wine made from raisins).

For lunch, visit one of the many *rosticcerie gastronomie,* peruse the city's push-carts, or stop by the **students' mensa** at Via dei Servi, 52, where a filling meal costs only L11,000. Open Mon.-Sat. noon-12:15pm and 6:45-8:45pm; closed mid-July-Aug. Buy your own fresh produce and meat (or stock up on that tripe you've been craving) at the **Mercato Centrale,** between Via Nazionale and the back of San Lorenzo. Open Mon.-Sat. 7am-2pm; Oct.-May Sat. 7am-2pm and 4-8pm. For staples, head over to the **STANDA** supermarket, Via Pietrapiana, 1r (tel. 24 08 09; open Tues.-Sat. 8:30am-8pm, Sun. 8:30am-1:30pm), or to any of the small markets around the city.

Vegetarian travelers will find several health-food markets operating in the city. The two best stores are named after the American book **Sugar Blues.** One is a 5-min. walk from the *duomo* at Via XXVII Aprile, 46r (tel. 48 36 66). Open Mon.-Fri. 9am-1:30pm and 4-7:30pm, Sat. 9am-1pm. The other is in the Oltrarno, next to the Institute Gould at Via dei Serragli, 57r (tel. 26 83 78). Open Mon.-Sat. 9am-1:30pm and 4:30-8pm; closed Sat. mornings and Wed. afternoons. Both stock vitamins, algae, homemade take-out vegetable tarts, and organic vegetables, all with an Italian touch. Or try **La Raccolta,** downstairs at Via Leopardi, 10 (tel. 247 90 68)—a health food center and a meeting place for Florence's alternative community. Open Mon. 4-7:30pm, Tues.-Fri. 10am-2pm and 4-7:30pm, Sat. 10am-1:30pm.

Il Cuscussú, Via Farini, 2, on the second floor of the building to the right of the synagogue, serves **kosher** meals Sun.-Thurs. 12:30-2:30pm and 7:30-9:30pm; Oct.-March no Sun. dinner; March 16-Sept. 30 no Sat. dinner. Friday dinner and Saturday lunch by reservation only. For information on **halal** vendors, ring the Centro Culturale Islamico. (See **Religious Services,** page 176.)

Santa Maria Novella and Environs

Trattoria Contadino, Via Palazzuolo, 71r (tel. 238 26 73). Filling, home-style meals perfect for the weary traveler. Lunch and dinner *menù* (L14,000 and L15,000). Feast on the *pollo cacciatore* or the *vitello con vino.* Open Mon.-Sat. noon-2:30pm and 6-9:45pm.

Trattoria da Giorgio, Via Palazzuolo, 100r. Same deal as Contadino (L15,000 *menù,* same fixins). Short on atmosphere, long on quantity. Menu changes daily, but try the homemade *fettucine alfredo* if it's available. Expect to wait. Open Mon.-Sat. 11am-3pm and 7pm-midnight.

Il Giardino, Via della Scala, 61r (tel. 21 31 41). Enjoy a hearty portion of *penne* with eggplant (L6500) or homemade *gnocchi* (L7000) under the vines of the garden.

CENTRAL ITALY

The roast veal is enough to coax anyone on to a *secondo* (L8000). *Menù* L20,000. Cover L2000. Open Wed.-Mon. noon-3pm and 7-10pm. V, MC, AmEx.

Amon, Via Palazzuolo, 26-28r (tel. 29 31 46). Cheerful, English-speaking Egyptian owner serves up scrumptious Middle Eastern food. Try the mousaka, a homemade pita filled with baked eggplant, or the *foul,* which, despite its name, is a delicious dish of beans and spices. English menu. Falafel L4000, *shish kabab* L5000. Stand-up or take-out only. Open Mon.-Sat. noon-3pm and 6:30-11pm.

La Scogliera, Via Palazzuolo, 80r (tel. 21 02 57). Try the house specialty *spaghetti alla scogliera* (topped with mussels, L15,000), or choose from a wide selection of pizzas baked in a wood-burning oven (L6000-L15,000). Dine amid green vines on the small outdoor patio. *Menù* L18,000. Cover L2000. Open Sat.-Thurs. noon-3pm and 6pm-midnight. V, MC, AmEx.

The Station and University Quarter

Trattoria da Garibaldi, P. del Mercato Centrale, 38r (tel. 21 22 67). Locals from the nearby market crowd this place, and with good reason. The food is fresh, tasty, and cheap. Menu changes daily, but the *penne ai quattro formaggi* and the *pesto alla genovese* are delicious. The huge, crisp salads are a marked improvement over the wilted lettuce served elsewhere. *Menù* L15,000. Don't worry, vegetarians; they have meatless *secondi.* Cover L2000 for meals outside the *menù.* Open Mon.-Sat. noon-3:30pm and 7pm-midnight; closes at 10pm in winter.

Trattoria Mario, Via Rosina, 2r (tel. 21 85 50), right around the corner from P. Mercato Centrale. Share huge wooden tables with the crowds of locals that flock here for lunch. Menu changes daily. Try the pasta with *ragù* (meat sauce, L5500). *Primi* L4500-L6000, *secondi* L5500-L14,000. Open Mon.-Sat. noon-3:30pm.

Trattoria da Zà-Zà, P. Mercato Centrale, 26r (tel. 21 54 11). Soups are a specialty in this hopping *trattoria;* try the *tris* ("mix of 3") bean, tomato, and vegetable soup (L9000), the *tagliatelle al pesto* made fresh every morning (L8000), or an *insalate giganti* (niçoise, greek, etc., L10,000). Cover L2000. Open Mon.-Sat. noon-3pm and 7-11pm. Reservations suggested. V, MC, AmEx.

Ristorante Il Vegetariano, Via delle Ruote, 30 (tel. 47 50 30), off Via San Gallo. Pretty landscape scenes surround you as you dine on fresh, meat-free cuisine. *Primi* L6000-7000, *secondi* L9000-12,000. Salads L5000-L7000. Cover L2000. Open Tues.-Fri. 12:30am-3pm and 7:30pm-midnight, Sat.-Sun. 8pm-midnight.

Ristorante Mirò, Via San Gallo, 57/59. Dine under a beautiful frescoed ceiling. Wide selection of creative dishes including *crema di fave e asparagi* (L8000), *penne radicchio e rucola* (L6000), and *straccetti alle erbe* (veal cutlet flavored with rosemary and garlic, L11,000). Lunch *primi* L6000, *secondi* L9000-11,000, cover L1500. Dinner *primi* L8000-14,000, *secondi* with *contorno* L8000-12,000, cover L2500. Open Mon.-Sat. 11am-3pm and 7pm-midnight.

Old City (The Center)

I Latini, Via Palchetti, 6r. From the Ponte alla Carraia, walk up Via del Moro; Via Palchetti is on the right. Be prepared to wait. Patrons dine on such delicious Tuscan classics as *ribollita* (L8000) and *stracotto alla fiorentina* (L15,000) beneath dangling hams. *Primi* L8000-12,000, *secondi* L15,000-20,000. Cover L2500. Open Tues.-Sun. 12:30-2:30pm and 7:30-10:30pm.

Trattoria da Benvenuto, Via dei Neri, 47r (tel. 21 48 33). Skillfully made *gnocchi* (L7000) and grilled *braciola* (veal chop, L9000). Cover L2000. Complete meals only. Open Mon.-Tues. and Thurs.-Sat. 11am-3pm and 7pm-midnight.

Osteria l'Toscanaccio, Via Fiesolana, 13r (tel. 24 03 05). Enjoy traditional Tuscan cuisine in a peaceful, untouristed setting. Start with the classic *ribollita* (L6000) and move on to a delicious *salsicce con fragioli. Menù* L15,000. *Primi* L6000-10,000, *secondi* L7000-12,000. Open daily noon-3:30pm and 7pm-midnight; Oct.-March closed Thurs.

Acqua al Due, Via Vegna Vecchia, 40r (tel. 28 41 70), behind the Bargello. Florentine specialties in a cozy place popular with young Italians. The *assaggio,* with 5 types of pasta, demands a taste (L11,900); getting a table, however, usually demands a reservation. A/C. *Primi* L8000-10,000, *secondi* L10,000-20,000. Cover L2000. Open daily 7:30pm-1am; Oct.-May closed Mon. V, MC, AmEx.

Aquerello, Via Ghibbelina, 156r (tel. 234 05 54). Pseudo-Memphis decor and superb, offbeat food. Duck when your *spaghetti flambé all' Aquerello* (L9500) arrives, or have your duck *à l'orange* (*anitra all'arancia*, L18,000). Cover L3000. *Menù* L26,000. Open Fri.-Wed. 11am-3pm and 7pm-1am. AmEx.

La Maremmana, Via dei Macci, 77r (tel. 24 12 26), near the Mercato Sant'Ambrogio. A rare combination: simple, well-prepared, generous, and affordable food. *Menù* starting at L20,000. Savor the *crêpes della fiorentina* (with ricotta and spinach, L8000). Justifiably busy. A/C. Open Sept.-July Mon.-Sat. 12:30-3pm and 7:30-10:30pm. V, MC, AmEx.

Trattoria I'che c'è c'è, Via de Mangalotti, 11r (tel. 21 65 89). Great food that draws a huge crowd. Try the *topini (gnocchi) al gorgonzola* (L9000) or the spicy *carrettiera* (L8000). *Menù* L19,000. *Primi* L6000-L14,000, *secondi* L13,000-L20,000. Cover L2000. Open in summer 11am-3pm and 7pm-midnight; in winter Tues.-Sun. 12:30-2:30pm and 7-10:30pm.

Acquacotta, Via dei Pilastri, 51r (tel. 24 29 07), between Borgo Pinti and P. Sant'Ambrogio. Florentines enjoy the crispy fried *coniglio* (rabbit, L15,000). Bunny-lovers can munch on a delicious *risotto alla fiorentina* (L9000) instead. Cover L2000. Open Tues. 12:30-2pm, Thurs.-Mon. 12:30-2pm and 7:30-10pm.

The Oltrarno

Oltrarno Trattoria Casalinga, Via Michelozzi, 9r (tel. 21 86 24), near P. Santo Spirito. Delicious Tuscan specialties in a pleasant, family atmosphere. Ravioli with spinach and ricotta, L6300. *Primi* L4500-L6300, *secondi* L7500-L14,500. Menu changes daily. Cover L1500. Open Mon.-Sat. noon-3pm and 7pm-midnight.

Il Borgo Antico, P. Santa Spirito, 61 (tel. 21 04 37). A jammin' restaurant with an impressive array of slightly offbeat but tasty dishes. Enormous portions. Try the *ravioli alla crema di salvia* in a sweet cream and sage sauce (L10,000). *Primi* L10,000, *secondi* L15,000-L25,000. Good pizzas and flamboyant salads for L10,000. Cover L3000. Reservations recommended. Open Mon.-Sat. 1-2:30pm and 8-11pm; *pizzeria* open until 12:30am.

Gelaterie and Bakeries

Gelato, as we know and love it today, is said to have been invented centuries ago by Florence's own Buontalenti family. As a tourist, it's your duty to sample this bit of the city's culture. Before plopping down L3000 to L4000 for a cone, however, assess the quality of any establishment by checking out the banana *gelato.* If it's bright yellow, it's been made from a mix—keep on walking. You know you've found a true Florentine *gelateria* when the banana is slightly gray, indicating that only real bananas were used. Vegans can find soy-milk *gelato* at many *gelaterie.*

Gelateria Dei Neri, Via dei Neri, 20-22r (tel. 21 00 34). A popular upstart with scrumptious *gelato,* including a mythical *"mitica"* (chocolate ice cream with just about everything mixed into it). Soy-milk *gelato* in several flavors. For a rich and creamy experience (like American ice cream), try the *semi-freddo;* grab a napkin to clean up after yourself. Cones L3000-L7000. Open daily 10:30am-midnight.

Il Granduca, Via dei Calzaiuoli, 57r (tel. 239 81 12). They do one thing, but oh, do they do it well. Delicious *gelato* with fresh fruit like papaya and mango (L2000-10,000; L15,000 for the mother of all cones). Open daily 10am-12:30am.

Vivoli, Via della Stinche, 7 (tel. 29 23 34), behind the Bargello. The most renowned of Florentine *gelaterie.* Huge selection. No cones, only cups (from L2000). Open Tues.-Sun. Feb.-July 8am-1am; Aug.-Jan. 8am-midnight.

Perché No?, Via Tavolini, 19r (tel. 239 89 69), off Via dei Calzaiuoli. Though the decor doesn't show it, this place is the oldest *gelateria* in Florence. It opened in 1939 and still serves heavenly pistacchio and chunky *nocciolosa.* Cones L2000-L12,000. Open in summer daily 9am-8:30pm; in winter Wed.-Mon. 9am-1pm.

Gelateria Triangolo delle Bermuda, Via Nazionale, 61r (tel. 28 74 90). With *gelato* this good, you may never leave. The blissful *crema venusiana* blends hazelnut, caramel, and meringue, and the *baci* oozes with hazelnuts. The owner travels to the U.S. every year to get Oreos for his *gelato.* Cones L3000-L8000.

CarLie's Bakery, Via Brache, 12r (tel. 29 26 64). Behind Via de' Benci near the river. From P. Signoria, walk between the Palazzo Vecchio and the Uffizi. Head along Via dei Neri and turn left onto Via Brache. Enjoy their fudge brownies and gooey chocolate-chip cookies. Open in summer Mon. 1-7:30pm, Tues.-Fri. 11am-7:30pm, Sat. 11am-1pm and 3-7pm; in winter daily 11am-7:30pm.

SIGHTS

> *Florence! One of the only places in Europe where I understood that underneath my revolt, a consent was lying dormant.*
>
> —Albert Camus

All Florentine, and most Italian, museums recently doubled their admission prices, making art-viewing an extremely costly endeavor—L6000-12,000 at most major venues. Many of Florence's museums are certainly worth the money, but carefully choose what you want to see and plan to spend a healthy chunk of your day at each museum. Before writing off the Uffizi (L12,000) or the Bargello (L8000), remember that they house the best collections of Renaissance art in the world. On the other hand, you can save money by exploring Florence's churches, most of which are also treasuries of great works of art. In summer, watch for *sere al Museo,* evenings when certain museums are open for free (8:30-11pm). Note that most museums stop selling tickets 30min. or 1 hour before closing.

Piazza del Duomo

In 1296 the city fathers commissioned Arnolfo di Cambio to erect a cathedral "with the most high and sumptuous magnificence so that it is impossible to make it either better or more beautiful with the industry and power of man." Filippo Brunelleschi designed the *duomo's* magnificent **dome,** the world's largest at the time. To accomplish this feat, the architect came up with the revolutionary idea of a double-shelled construction, with interlocking bricks supporting the dome during construction. He supervised every step of the building process, personally designing the system of pulleys that carried the supplies and constructing kitchens between the two walls of the *cupola* so that the masons would not have to descend for lunch. Alberti described the dome as "large enough to shelter all of Tuscany within its shadow...and of a construction that perhaps not even the ancients knew or understood"—the ultimate compliment in a period awed by the genius of Greece and Rome. The *cupola* was finished in 1436, but a 16th-century Medici rebuilding campaign removed the half-completed Gothic-Renaissance façade, not replaced until 1871, when Emilio de Fabris, a Florentine architect inspired by the colorful façades of other Tuscan structures, received the commission to put it back.

Size Isn't Everything

Architects have repeatedly outdone themselves with feats of engineering achievement in the eternal quest for bigger and better houses of worship. Back when it was built around AD125, Rome's Pantheon was the height of engineering prowess, a 43m concrete dome with a 9m hole in the roof and no keystone to distribute the weight. Thirteen centuries later, the size of Florence's *duomo* seemed an insurmountable problem until Brunelleschi designed the final double-shelled dome, rising 52m, to cap the cathedral's 46m drum. St. Peter's in Rome, begun in 1506, was first modeled on the Pantheon with a projected dome of equal proportions; when Michelangelo took over in 1546, his revised plans pictured a marvel surpassing even that of Brunelleschi. In spite of his ambition, the dome's completion in 1590 saw it rise only 44m, spanning a mere 42m—not even the width of the Pantheon. Michelangelo shouldn't be ashamed, though; even modern engineers were unable to reproduce a concrete dome of that size until well into this century.

The church claims the **world's third-longest nave,** behind St. Peter's in Rome and St. Paul's in London. Its sheer immensity makes it difficult to appreciate the art that graces its walls. A fresco in the left aisle, painted by a student of Fra Angelico, illustrates the *Divine Comedy.* The **orologio** hangs on the cathedral's back wall, but it won't give you the time of day; this 24-hour clock designed by Paolo Uccello runs backwards. (*Duomo* open Mon.-Fri. 10am-5pm, Sat. 10am-4:45pm, Sun. 1-5pm; first Sat. of every month 10am-3:30pm. Masses 7-10am and 5-7pm.)

Climb the 463 steps within the dome to the **lantern** (tel. 230 28 85), where you'll have a fantastic view of the city from the external gallery (110m high). (Lantern open Mon.-Sat. 8:30am-7pm. Admission L8000.) In the **crypt** lurk the tomb of Brunelleschi, some 13th-century tombs, and bits of mosaic. (Open Mon.-Sat. 9:30am-5:30pm. Admission L3000.)

Most of the *duomo*'s art resides in the **Museo dell'Opera di S. Maria del Fiore** (tel. 230 28 85), behind the *duomo* at P. del Duomo, 9. Up the first flight of stairs is a late *Pietà* by Michelangelo. According to legend, in a fit of frustration he took a hammer to it and severed Christ's left arm. Soon thereafter a pupil touched up the work, leaving parts of Mary Magdalene's head with visible "scars." There are other masterpieces here as well: Donatello and Luca della Robbia's wonderful *cantorie* (choir balconies with bas-reliefs of cavorting children and *putti*), Donatello's wooden *St. Mary Magdalene* (1555), and a silver altar by Michelozzo, Pollaiuolo, and Verrocchio. The sculpture that once covered the *campanile's* exterior includes Donatello's prophets and Andrea Pisano's *Progress of Man* cycle of small reliefs. The museum also houses four of the frames from the baptistery's *Gates of Paradise* (see below), and after seemingly interminable restoration will house the entire collection. (Open Mon.-Sat. 9am-7:30pm; in winter Mon.-Sat. 9am-6pm. Admission L8000. Look for the English tours in the summer Wed.-Thurs. 4pm.)

Though it was built sometime between the 7th and 9th centuries, by Dante's time the Florentines thought their **baptistery** had originally been a Roman temple. The interior contains magnificent Byzantine-style mosaics created by Florentine and Venetian masters between the 13th and 15th centuries. On the wall the elegant early Renaissance *Tomb of the Anti-Pope John XXIII,* by Donatello and Michelozzo, rests in peace, appropriately positioned so that the sculpted figure lies directly in the line of Christ's blessing. Be sure to examine the mosaics here; the scenes from hell are accurate portrayals of Dante's *Inferno.* Incidentally, the author was christened in this very baptistery. (Open Mon.-Sat. 1:30-6pm, Sun. 9am-12:30pm.)

Florentine artists competed fiercely for the commissions to execute the baptistery's famous **bronze doors.** In 1330 Andrea Pisano left Pisa (and foundry-workers traveled from Venice) to cast the first set of doors, which now guard the south entrance (toward the river). In 1401 the cloth guild announced a competition to choose an artist for the remaining doors. The original field of eight contestants narrowed to two, Brunelleschi (then 23 years old) and Ghiberti (then 20). Each received one year to complete a panel of the Sacrifice of Isaac, and Ghiberti was the victor. (The competition panels are now on display in the Bargello.)

Ghiberti's doors, now on the north side, use Pisano's quatrefoil frames, but he endowed his figures with more detail and movement. When Ghiberti finished it in 1425, his work was so admired that he immediately received the commission to forge the last set of doors. The **"Gates of Paradise,"** as Michelangelo reportedly called them, are nothing like the two earlier portals; they abandon the 28-panel design for 10 large, gilded squares, each incorporating mathematical perspective to create the illusion of deep space. Originally intended for the north side, they so impressed the Florentines that they placed them in their current honored position facing the cathedral. Ghiberti finished The Gates of Paradise in 1452 after 24 years of labor. (The doors have been under restoration since the 1966 flood and will eventually reside in the Museo del Duomo.)

Next to the *duomo* rises the 82m-high **campanile,** the "lily of Florence blossoming in stone." Giotto, then the official city architect, drew up the design and laid the foundation but died soon after construction began. Andrea Pisano added two stories to the tower, and Francesco Talenti completed it in 1359 after doubling the thickness of the walls to support the weight. The original exterior decoration now resides in the Museo del Duomo. The 414-step endurance test to the top is worth the effort—the views are magnificent. (Open daily 9am-6:50pm; Nov.-March 9am-5:30pm. Admission L8000.)

Palazzo Vecchio and Piazza della Signoria

From P. del Duomo **Via dei Calzaiuoli,** one of the city's oldest streets, leads to P. Signoria. Originally a Roman road, Via dei Calzaiuoli now bustles with crowds, chic stores, *gelaterie,* and vendors. At the far end, the area around the **Palazzo Vecchio** (tel. 276 84 65) forms the civic center of Florence. Arnolfo di Cambio designed this fortress-like *palazzo* (1299-1304) as the seat of the *comune's* government. Its interior apartments served as living quarters for the seven members of the *signoria* (council) during their one-month terms. The building later served as the home of the Medici family, transforming this symbol of communal government into the seat of autocratic rule in Florence. In 1470 Michelozzo gave the **courtyard** a new Renaissance look. It was Vasari, however, who adorned the columns with gold stucco and the walls with paintings of Austrian cities, hoping to win the favor of Francis I de Medici's Austrian wife. The courtyard contains a copy of Verrocchio's charming 15th-century *putto* fountain and several stone lions (the heraldic symbol of the city). The city commissioned Michelangelo and Leonardo da Vinci to paint opposite walls of the **Salone dei Cinquecento,** the meeting room of the Grand Council of the Republic. Although they never completed the frescoes, their preliminary cartoons, the *Battle of Cascina* and the *Battle of Anghiari,* were studies for all young Florentine artists and models for mass production by engravers. The tiny, windowless **Studio of Francesco I,** built by Vasari, is a treasure trove of Mannerist art, with paintings by Bronzino, Allori, and Vasari and bronze statuettes by Giambologna and Ammannati. The best art waits in the **Mezzanino,** however. Look for Bronzino's portrait of the poet Laura Battiferi and Giambologna's *Hercules and the Hydra.* (Open Mon.-Wed. and Fri.-Sat. 9am-7pm, Sun. 8am-1pm. Admission L15,000.)

A vast space by medieval standards, **Piazza della Signoria** came into being in the 13th century with the destruction of the homes of the powerful Ghibelline families and soon became Florence's civic center. In 1497, the religious leader and social critic Savonarola convinced Florentines to light the **Bonfire of the Vanities** in the square, a grand roast that consumed some of Florence's best art. A year later, disillusioned citizens sent Savonarola up in smoke on the same spot, marked today by a commemorative granite disc. Massive sculptures cluster in front of the *palazzo:* Donatello's *Judith and Holofernes,* Michelangelo's *David* (a copy now stands in place of the original), Giambologna's equestrian *Cosimo I,* and Bandinelli's *Hercules.* The awkward *Neptune* to the left of the Palazzo Vecchio so revolted Michelangelo that he insulted the artist: "Oh Ammannato, Ammannato, what lovely marble you have ruined!" The graceful 14th-century **Loggia dei Lanzi,** built as a stage for civic orators, became a misogynistic sculpture gallery under the Medici dukes. Here you can see Benvenuto Cellini's *Perseus Slaying Medusa,* Giambologna's *Rape of the Sabines,* whose spiral composition invites viewing from any angle, and the dynamic and violent *Rape of Polyxena* by Pio Fedi.

The Uffizi

In May of 1993, terrorists detonated a bomb in the Uffizi, killing five people in nearby buildings and destroying priceless works of art. The bombing terribly shocked Florentines and other Italians, who cherish the Uffizi as a symbol of their precious Renaissance heritage. The political disruptions equaled the cultural losses: many rooms in the Uffizi are closed to the public and will remain that way for the next few years while reconstruction progresses. You can obtain a list of the several destroyed works and the almost 40 seriously damaged works from the tourist office. Rooms 8, 29-33, and 41-45 are closed, but three important works, Michelangelo's *Doni Tondo,* Caravaggio's *Bacchus,* and Titian's *Flora* have relocated to a room near the entrance so that visitors can still see them. Other rooms may also be closed for regular restoration work; check the list at the head of the line near the ticket window. Do not skip the Uffizi because of the closed rooms; it continues to display an unparalleled collection of Renaissance works. (Open Tues.-Sat. 9am-7pm, Sun. 9am-2pm. Admission L12,000.)

Vasari designed the **Uffizi** palace (office tel. 21 83 41) in 1554 for Duke Cosimo, who needed a seat for the consolidated administration of his Duchy of Tuscany. Its elegant arcade extends from P. della Signoria to the Arno River. At the end, a bridge over the Arno features Giambologna's bust of Cosimo. Vasari included a **secret corridor** between Palazzo Vecchio and the Medici's Palazzo Pitti in the design; it runs through the Uffizi and over the Ponte Vecchio and houses more art, including a special collection of artists' self-portraits. The last Medici, Anna Maria Ludovica (1667-1743), bequeathed this art collection to the people of Tuscany, provided that it never be moved from Florence.

Before heading up to the main gallery on the second floor, stop to see the exhibits of the Cabinet of Drawings and Prints on the first floor. The few drawings displayed here only hint at the much larger collection squirreled away for scholars. Upstairs, a long corridor wraps around the building and holds an impressive collection of Hellenistic and Roman marbles that inspired many Renaissance works. The collection is arranged chronologically and promises its visitors a thorough education on Florentine Renaissance painting, as well as a choice sampling of German and Venetian art.

Room 2 starts you off in the late 13th and early 14th centuries with three great *Madonnas* by three great artists: Cimabue, Duccio di Buoninsegna, and Giotto, whose naturalistic figures foreshadow the High Renaissance (still 100 years away). **Room 3** features works from 14th-century Siena (including paintings by the Lorenzetti brothers and Simone Martini's dazzling *Annunciation*), while **Room 4** displays the less-riveting Florentine art of the same period. **Rooms 5 and 6** contain examples of International Gothic art, once popular in the royal courts of Europe.

Perhaps the most awesome room in the museum, **Room 7** houses two Fra Angelico paintings and a *Madonna and Child* by Masaccio. Domenico Veneziano's innovative *Madonna with Child and Saints (Sacra Conversazione)* is one of the first paintings to incorporate Mary and the saints into a unified space. Piero della Francesca's double portrait of Duke Federico and his wife Battista Sforza stands out for its translucent color and intricate detail. Finally, the rounded warhorses distinguish Paolo Uccello's *Rout of San Romano* (this piece is the central panel of a triptych—the Louvre and London's National Gallery each have a side). **Room 8** contains Filippo Lippi's endearing *Madonna and Child with Two Angels.* Works by the Pollaiuolo brothers and a (probably) forged Filippino Lippi occupy **Room 9.**

Rooms 10-14 are a vast Botticelli shrine: *Primavera, Birth of Venus, Madonna della Melagrana,* and *Pallas and the Centaur* practically glow after their recent restoration. **Room 15** moves into High Renaissance gear with Leonardo da Vinci's brilliant *Annunciation* and the more remarkable unfinished *Adoration of the Magi.* **Room 18,** designed by Buontalenti to hold the Medici treasures, boasts a mother-of-pearl dome and a collection of portraits, most notably Bronzino's *Bia de'Medici.* **Room 19** features works by Piero della Francesca's students Perugino and Signorelli. **Rooms 20** and **22** detour into German art history. Note the contrast between Albrecht Dürer's realistic *Adam and Eve* and Luke Cranach's somewhat haunting treatment of the same subject. **Room 21** contains major Venetian art from the 15th century. Ponder Bellini's famous and moving *Sacred Allegory* before examining Mantegna's little *Triptych* in **Room 24.**

As you cross to the gallery's other side, glance out the windows of the south corridor—the Medici commissioned an impressive view of Florence. The second half of the Uffizi showcases Florentines in **Rooms 25-27** with Michelangelo's only oil painting (the *Doni Tondo*), a string of Raphaels, Andrea del Sarto's *Madonna of the Harpies,* and Pontormo's *Supper at Emmaus.* **Room 28** displays Titian's beautiful *Venus of Urbino.* Parmigianino's preposterous *Madonna of the Long Neck,* essentially a cross between Mary and a giraffe, is in **Room 29.** Works by Sebastiano del Pionbo and

Lorenzo Lotto share **Rooms 31 and 32.** The staircase vestibule **(Rooms 35-40)** houses a Roman marble boar, the inspiration for the brass *Porcellino* that sits in Florence's New Market. Self-portraits by Rubens and Rembrandt watch over **Rooms 41 and 44** respectively, and a clutch of Caravaggios, including both his *Sacrifice of Isaac* and a *Bacchus,* hang in **Room 43.**

The Ponte Vecchio

From the Uffizi, turn left onto Via Georgofili, then right when you reach the river. The nearby **Ponte Vecchio** has spanned the Arno's narrowest point since Roman times. In fact, it was Florence's only bridge over the Arno until 1218. The Medici, in an effort to "improve" the area, kicked out the butchers and tanners, whose shops lined the bridge in the 1500s. In their place, the ruling family installed the goldsmiths and diamond-carvers whose descendants have since filled the bridge with ritzy boutiques. A German commander who led his retreating army across the river in 1944 could not bear to blow it up and instead destroyed the medieval towers and nearby buildings to make the bridge impassable. Today, peddlers and artisans line the bridge by day but make way for tourists at sunset and street musicians at night.

Around the Bargello

The heart of medieval Florence lies between the *duomo* and P. della Signoria at the 13th-century **Bargello** in P. San Firenze. This fortress was once the residence of the chief magistrate, but later became a brutal prison with torture and execution chambers. Restored in the 19th century to its former elegance, it now houses the **Museo Nazionale** (tel. 21 08 01), a treasury of Florentine sculpture. Upstairs in the Salone del Consiglio Generale, Donatello's bronze *David,* the first free-standing nude since antiquity, exemplifies early Renaissance sculpture. Compare it with the artist's marble *David* by the wall to the left. Completed about thirty years earlier (1408), this sculpture resembles a Roman patrician instead of a shy young boy. Along the wall to the right hang two beautiful bronze panels of the *Sacrifice of Isaac,* submitted by Ghiberti and Brunelleschi for the baptistery door competition (see **Piazza del Duomo,** page 186). Several della Robbia terra-cotta Madonnas reside at the other end of the room. In the *loggia* on the first floor, you'll find a menagerie of bronze animals created by Giambologna for a Medici garden grotto. Downstairs on the ground floor, Michelangelo's early works dominate the first room, including a debauched *Bacchus,* a handsome bust of *Brutus,* an early unfinished *Apollo* or *David,* and a *tondo* of the *Madonna and Child.* Devote your attention to Cellini's works on the other side of the room, especially the models for Perseus and the *Bust of Cosimo I.* Giambologna's *Oceanus* reigns in the Gothic *cortile* outside, while his *Mercury* poses in the Michelangelo room. (Open daily 9am-2pm; closed on the 1st, 3rd, and 5th Sun. and the 2nd and 4th Mon. of every month. Admission L8000.)

The **Badia,** across Via del Proconsolo from the Bargello, was the site of medieval Florence's richest monastery. Filippino Lippi's *Apparition of the Virgin to St. Bernard,* one of the most famous paintings of the late 15th century, greets you on the left as you enter. (Open Mon.-Sat. 5-7pm, Sun. 7:30-11:30am.) Around the corner in Via S. Margherita you can visit the **Casa di Dante** (tel. 28 33 43), the reconstructed house of the great poet. (Open Mon.-Wed. and Sat. 10am-6pm, Sun. 10am-2pm. Admission L5000, groups over 15 L3000 per person.) A small museum outlines Dante's life. A better example of a typical 14th-century dwelling is **Palazzo Salviati,** a few blocks down Via della Vigna Vecchia at Via dell'Isola delle Stinche.

Equidistant from the *duomo* and the Signoria is the intriguing **Orsanmichele** (tel. 28 47 15) on Via dei Calzaiuoli, built in 1337 as a granary, but later partially converted into a church. Secular and spiritual concerns also mingle in the statues along the façade: they represent the patron saints of the major craft guilds who commissioned them. These niched figures compose their own gallery of Florentine art. Look for Ghiberti's *St. John the Baptist* and *St. Stephen,* Donatello's *St. Peter* and *St. Mark,* and Giambologna's *St. Luke.* Inside, a Gothic tabernacle designed by Andrea Orcagna encases Bernardo Daddi's miraculous *Virgin.* The top floor occasionally shows temporary exhibits, but it's worth the climb just for the view of the city. (Open daily 8am-noon and 3-6:30pm. Free.)

Markets, Palazzi, and Santa Maria Novella

After hours of contemplating great Florentine art, visit the area that financed it all. In the early 1420s, 72 banks operated in Florence, most in the area around the **Mercato Nuovo** and **Via Tornabuoni.** Trade here generated profits that merchants then reinvested in land and the manufacture of wool and silk. The 1547 Mercato Nuovo (New Market) arcades housed the gold and silk trades. Pietro Tacca's ferocious statue, *Il Porcellino* (The Little Pig), actually a wild boar, appeared some 50 years later. Its snout remains brightly polished by tourists—rubbing it supposedly brings good luck. The starkly Neoclassical **Piazza della Repubblica** replaced the Mercato Vecchio as the site of the town market in 1890. The inscription *"Antico centro della città, da secolare squalore, a vita nuova restituito"* ("The ancient center of the city, squalid for centuries, restored to new life"), epitomizes that determinedly progressive age. The statue in the center, on the corner near the Upim store, is a copy of Donatello's statue of *Abundance,* which once presided over the square. In this area, you'll find several of the city's most popular *caffè;* the **Gilli,** perhaps Florence's most famous coffeehouse, was established in 1733.

As Florence's 15th-century economy expanded, its bankers and merchants showed off their new wealth by erecting palaces grander than any seen before. The great Quattrocento boom began with the construction of the **Palazzo Davanzati,** Via Porta Rossa, 13. Today the *palazzo* finds new life as the **Museo della Casa Fiorentina Antica** (tel. 21 65 18), which illustrates the wealth of the 15th-century merchants in the form of furniture, tapestries, utensils, and paintings. Watch a 40-min. video on the history of the building at 10, 11am, and noon on the fourth floor, shown either in Italian or English depending on the crowd. (Temporarily closed for renovations, projected to reopen in 1998.)

The relative modesty of the early Palazzo Davanzati gave way to more elegant and extravagant *palazzi.* The **Palazzo Strozzi** (tel. 21 59 90), on Via Tornabuoni at Via Strozzi, may be the grandest of its kind. Begun in 1489, its regal proportions and carefully rusticated façade exemplify the Florentine *palazzo* type, which has spawned endless permutations the world over. Palazzo Strozzi shelters several cultural institutes and occasionally exhibits art collections. Alberti's architectural triumph, the **Palazzo Rucellai** at Via della Vigna Nuova, 16, is renowned for its classical façade. Its newly renovated interior now houses the fascinating **Alinari Museum of Photographic History** (tel. 21 02 02), with a permanent collection of early cameras and temporary exhibits from the Alinari photo archives. (Open Sun.-Tues. and Thurs. 10am-7:30pm, Fri.-Sat. 10am-11:30pm. Admission L8000.)

Many *palazzi* owners also commissioned family chapels in the **Church of Santa Trinità** (tel. 21 69 12) on Via Tornabuoni so as to spend eternity in the best possible company. Restoration teams have placed scaffolding on the façade, but you can still see the splendid interior. The fourth chapel on the right houses the remains of a fresco cycle of the life of the Virgin and, on the altar, a magnificent *Annunciation* by Lorenzo Monaco. Scenes from Ghirlandaio's *Life of St. Francis* decorate the Sassetti chapel in the right arm of the transept. The famous altarpiece of the *Adoration of the Shepherds,* also by Ghirlandaio, resides in the Uffizi; the one you see here is a copy. (Open Mon.-Sat. 7:30am-noon and 4-6pm.)

The wealthiest merchants built their chapels in the **Church of Santa Maria Novella** (tel. 21 01 13) near the train station. The nave is undergoing restoration, but this disruption in no way detracts from the altar's beauty. Built from 1246 to 1360, the church boasts a green-and-white Romanesque-Gothic lower façade. Giovanni Rucellai commissioned Alberti to design the top half then had a chapel built inside. Frescoes covered the interior until the Medici commissioned Vasari to paint new ones in their honor, ordering most of the other walls whitewashed so their rivals would not be remembered. Fortunately, Vasari respected Masaccio's powerful *Trinity,* the first painting to use geometric perspective. This fresco creates the illusion of a tabernacle in the wall on the left side of the nave; its use of perspective pulls the viewer into its scene. The **Chapel of Filippo Strozzi,** just to the right of the high altar, contains frescoes by Filippo Lippi, including a rather green Adam, a woolly Abraham, and an excruciatingly accurate *Torture of St. John the Evangelist.* Benedetto da Mareno's Tomb of Filippo Strozzi lies behind the altar. After making a bet with Donatello over who could create a better crucifix, Brunelleschi produced the realistic wooden crucifix in the **Gondi Chapel** to the left of the high altar. Acycle of Ghirlandaio frescoes covers the **sanctuary.** (Open Mon.-Sat. 7am-12:15pm and 3-6:30pm, Sun. 3-5pm.) Visit the cloister next door to see Paolo Uccello's *The Flood* and *The Sacrifice of Noah.* Even more fascinating, the adjoining **Spanish Chapel** (tel. 28 21 87) harbors 14th-century frescoes by Andrea di Bonaiuto. (Open Mon.-Thurs. and Sat. 9am-2pm, Sun. 8am-1pm. Admission L5000.)

Around San Lorenzo

The Medici used an entire portion of the city north of the *duomo* for their own church, the spacious **Basilica of San Lorenzo** (tel. 234 27 31), and the **Palazzo Medici.** Brunelleschi designed San Lorenzo in 1419. Because the Medici had loaned the city the necessary funds to build the church, they retained artistic control over its construction. Their coat of arms, featuring six red balls, appears all over the nave, and their tombs fill the two sacristies and the Chapel of the Principi behind the altar. The family cunningly placed Cosimo's grave in front of the high altar, making the entire church his personal mausoleum. Michelangelo designed the church's exterior, but the profligate Medici ran out of money to build it so it stands unadorned. (The façade thus complements the rusticated Palazzo Medici, officially called Palazzo Medici Riccardi, diagonally across the *piazza.*) Inside the basilica, two massive bronze pulpits, Donatello's last works, command the nave. (Open daily 8am-noon and 5:30-6pm.) The **Laurentian Library** (tel. 21 07 60) next door contains one of the largest and most valuable manuscript collections in the world. Michelangelo's famous entrance portico demonstrates his architectural virtuosity; note how he reinterpreted classical forms in a Mannerist mode. (Open Mon.-Sat. 9am-1pm. Free.)

To reach the **Chapels of the Medici** (tel. 238 86 02), walk around to the back entrance on P. Madonna degli Aldobrandini. Intended as a grand mausoleum, Matteo Nigetti's **Chapel of the Principi** (Princes' Chapel) emulates the baptistery in P. del Duomo. Except for the gilded portraits of the Medici dukes, the decor is a rare moment of the Baroque in Florence. Michelangelo based the **New Sacristy** (1524) on a starkly simple architectural design that reflects the master's study of Brunelleschi. Michelangelo sculpted two impressive tombs for Lorenzo and Guiliano de' Medici embodying the four stages of the day, symbols of life and death. Guiliano's tomb features Night (the sleeping woman) and Day (the alert man). In contrast, Lorenzo's tomb supports Dawn (the woman who refuses to wake up) and Dusk (the man tired from a hard day's work). Night's unnatural physique may derive from the Renaissance refusal to work from female models. (Open daily 9am-2pm; closed the 2nd and 4th Sun. and the 1st, 3rd, and 5th Mon. of every month. Admission L10,000.) In the basement of the New Sacristy, some Michelangelo sketches are on view (ask for a free ticket at the window).

According to art historians, Brunelleschi proposed a sumptuous design for the **Palazzo Medici** (tel. 276 01) but was rejected. The palace's innovative façade, with its three levels of rustication, is instead the work of Michelozzo. The private chapel inside features Benozzo Gozzoli's beautiful fresco of the three Magi and Medici family portraits. The *palazzo* hosts exhibits ranging from Renaissance architectural sketches to Fellini memorabilia. Check with the tourist office. (Open Mon.-Tues. and Thurs.-Sat. 9am-12:45pm and 3-6:45pm, Sun. 9am-12:45pm. Admission L6000.)

Around Piazza Santissima Annunziata

The complex of religious buildings encircling P. Santissima Annunziata emanates serenity. Brunelleschi designed the right-hand *loggia* of the **Spedale degli Innocenti** (tel. 24 36 70) in the 1420s, and Antonio da Sangallo copied it on the other side a century later. The visual unity so pleased contemporary tastes that the *loggia* was continued across the façade of the church in 1601. An equestrian statue of Ferdinando de' Medici presides over the *piazza* just as the Marcus Aurelius does in Rome's Campidoglio. The **Galleria dello Spedale degli Innocenti** contains Botticelli's *Madonna e Angelo* and Ghirlandaio's *Epiphany.* (Open Mon.-Tues. and Thurs.-Sat. 8:30am-2pm, Sun. 8:30am-1pm. Admission L3000.)

Remarkable works by Fra Angelico adorn the **Museum of the Church of San Marco** (tel. 220 86 08), one of the most peaceful and deeply spiritual spots in Florence. A large room to the right contains some of the painter's major works, including the church's altarpiece. Climb the stairs to see Angelico's famous *Annunciation,* an especially vivid and colorful portrayal. Every cell in the dormitory contains its own Fra Angelico fresco, each painted in flat colors and with sparse detail to facilitate the monks' somber meditation. Michelozzo's library is another fine example of purity and vigor. After visiting, you might feel like following in the footsteps of Cosimo I, the patron of the convent, who retired here. His cell, not surprisingly, is the largest. Look for Savonarola's cell here as well. (Open daily 9am-2pm; closed the 1st, 3rd, and 5th Sun. and the 2nd and 4th Mon. of each month. Admission L8000.)

The **Accademia** (tel. 21 43 75) lies between the two churches at Via Ricasoli, 60. Michelangelo's triumphant *David* stands in self-assured perfection under the rotunda designed just for him. He moved here from P. della Signoria in 1873 after a stone hurled during a riot broke his left wrist in two places. Note the opaque finish—a cleaning inadvertently removed the original polish. In the hallway leading up to *David* are Michelangelo's four *Prisoners.* The master left these statues intentionally unfinished; envisioning a masterpiece was held prisoner inside each stone, he chipped away only enough to "liberate" them. Don't miss the impressive collection of Gothic triptychs on the second floor or the back room filled with an astounding collection of Russian icons. (Most areas of the museum are wheelchair accessible. Open Tues.-Sat. 8:30am-6:15pm, Sun. 8:30am-2pm. Admission L12,000.)

From P. S.S. Annunziata, take bus #6 to Via Andrea del Sarto, where Sarto's **Cenacolo di San Salvi** is at Via di San Salvi, 16 (tel. 67 75 70). The abbey refectory houses Sarto's stupendous *Last Supper* (1519) alongside other 16th-century Florentine paintings. (Open daily 9am-2pm; closed the 1st, 3rd, and 5th Sun. and 2nd and 4th Mon. of each month. Admission L5000.) Del Castagno's masterpiece, the **Cenacolo di Sant'Apollonia,** in the **Museo di Andrea del Castagno,** Via 27 Aprile, 1 (tel. 28 70 74), is just as impressive. This mid-15th-century fresco of the Last Supper takes up an entire wall. (Open daily 9am-2pm; closed 1st, 3rd, and 5th Sun. and 2nd and 4th Mon. of each month. Admission L2200.)

Piazza Santa Croce

The Franciscans built the **Church of Santa Croce** (tel. 24 46 19) as far away as possible from Santa Maria Novella and their Dominican rivals. Despite the ascetic ideals of the Franciscans, it is quite possibly the most splendid church in the city. Construction began in 1294 based on a design by di Cambio, but the façade and Gothic bell tower did not appear until the 19th century. A fresco cycle by Andrea Orcagna originally adorned the nave. Never heard of Orcagna? Maybe that's because Vasari not only destroyed the entire cycle, but also left Orcagna out of his famous *Lives of the Artists.* To the right of the altar, the frescoes of the **Peruzzi Chapel** vie with those of the **Bardi Chapel;** Giotto and his school painted both. Among the famous Florentines buried in this church are Michelangelo, who rests at the front of the right aisle in a tomb designed by Vasari, and humanist Leonardo Bruni, shown holding his precious *History of Florence* on a tomb designed by Bernardo Rossellino. Between the two sits Donatello's gilded *Annunciation.* The Florentines, who banished the living Dante, eventually prepared a tomb for him here. Dante died in Ravenna, however, and the literary necrophiliacs there have never sent him back. Florence did manage to retain the bodies of Machiavelli and Galileo, though, and both are buried here. (Open daily 8am-6:30pm.)

Cool *pietra serena* pilasters, Luca della Robbia *tondos* of the apostles, and rondels of the evangelists by Donatello grace Brunelleschi's small **Pazzi Chapel,** at the end of the cloister next to the church. The second cloister, also by Brunelleschi, is a perfect place to relax. The **Museo dell'Opera di Santa Croce** (tel. 24 46 19) is still recovering from the disastrous 1966 flood that left many works, including the great Cimabue *Crucifixion,* in a tragic state. The former refectory contains Taddeo Gaddi's imaginative fresco of *The Tree of the Cross,* and beneath it, the *Last Supper.* Enter the museum through the *loggia* in front of the Pazzi Chapel. (Open Thurs.-Tues. 10am-12:30pm and 2:30-6:30pm; in winter 10am-12:30pm and 3-5pm.)

From P. Santa Croce, follow Via de' Pepi and make a right onto Via Ghibellina to reach the **Casa Buonarroti,** Via Ghibellina, 70 (tel. 24 17 52). This little museum houses Michelangelo memorabilia and two of his most important early works, *The Madonna of the Steps* and *The Battle of the Centaurs.* Both pieces are in the first rooms to the left of the landing on the second floor. He completed these panels when he was about 16 years old, and they show his transition from bas-relief to full sculpture. (Open Wed.-Mon. 9:30am-1:30pm. Admission L8000, students L6000.)

A few streets north of Via Ghibellina stands the **Synagogue of Florence,** also known as the **Museo del Tempio Israelitico,** Via Farini, 4 (tel. 24 52 52/53), at Via Pilastri. When David Levi donated his fortune for the construction of "a monumental temple worthy of Florence," architects Micheli and Treves created one of Europe's most beautiful synagogues. Elaborate geometrical designs enhance the modified Moorish style of this Sephardic temple. (Open Sun.-Thurs. 11am-1pm and 2-5pm, Fri. 10am-1pm. Admission L5000, students L4000. Frequent informative tours.)

In the Oltrarno

Historically disdained by downtown Florentines, the far side of the Arno remains a lively, unpretentious quarter, even in high-season. Start your tour a few blocks west of P. Santa Spirito at the **Church of Santa Maria del Carmine.** Inside, the **Brancacci Chapel** is home to a group of influential 15th-century frescoes that were declared masterpieces even in their own time. In 1424 Felice Brancacci commissioned Masolino and Masaccio to decorate his chapel with scenes from the life of St. Peter. Masolino probably designed the series using perspective techniques not fully grasped by previous artists, but it was Masaccio who painted them, imbuing his figures with solidity and dignity. Fifty years later a respectful Filippino Lippi completed the cycle. Note especially the *Expulsion from Paradise* and *The Tribute Money.* (Open Mon. and Wed.-Sat. 10am-4:30pm, Sun. 1-4:30pm. Admission L5000.)

As Brunelleschi designed it, the **Church of Santo Spirito** (tel. 21 00 30) would have been one of the most exciting architectural works ever. He envisioned a four-aisled nave surrounded by round chapels, which the exterior would reveal as soft undulations. Brunelleschi died when the project was only partially completed, however, and the plans were altered to make the building more conventional. Nonetheless, the church remains a masterpiece of Renaissance harmony. (Open daily 8:30am-noon and 4-6pm.)

Luca Pitti, a *nouveau-riche* banker of the 15th century, built his *palazzo* east of Santo Spirito against the Boboli hill. The Medici acquired the *palazzo* and the hill in 1550 and enlarged everything possible. Ammannato redesigned the courtyard; the columns in rough blocks reflect the 16th-century preoccupation with the theme of nature versus art. During Italy's brief experiment with monarchy, the structure also served as a royal residence. Today, the **Pitti Palace** (tel. 21 34 40) houses no fewer than seven museums. The **Museo degli Argenti** (tel. 21 25 57) on the ground floor exhibits the Medici family treasures. Browse among cases of precious gems, ivories, and silver pieces, then peruse Lorenzo the Magnificent's famous collection of vases. (Open daily 9am-2pm; closed on the 1st, 3rd, and 5th Mon. and the 2nd and 4th Sun. of each month. L8000 admission gets you into the costume museum as well.) The **Museum of Costumes** (tel. 29 42 79) and the **Porcelain Museum** (tel. 21 25 57) host more items from the Medici fortune. (Porcelain Museum L4000. Museum of Costumes shares a L8000 ticket with the Museo degli Argenti, and both museums share its hours.) The **Royal Apartments** and the **Carriage Museum** (tel. 238 86 11) boast lavish reminders of the time when the *palazzo* served as the living quarters of the royal House of Savoy. (Both open Tues.-Sat. 8:30am-7pm, Sun. 8:30am-2pm. Admission L12,000.) The **Galleria Palatina** (tel. 21 03 23) was one of only a few public galleries when it opened in 1833. Today its collection includes a number of works by Raphael (most behind glass), Titian, Andrea del Sarto, Rosso, Caravaggio, and Rubens. Note the neoclassical Music Room and the Putti Room, dominated by Flemish works. (Same hours as the Royal Apartments. Admission L12,000.) The last museum, the **Galleria d'Arte Moderna** (tel. 28 70 96), houses one of the big surprises of Italian art history: the early 19th-century proto-impressionist works of the Macchiaioli school. The collection also includes Neoclassical and Romantic works. Look for Giovanni Dupré's sculptural group *Cain and Abel.* (Same hours as the Museo degli Argenti. Admission L4000.)

The elaborately landscaped **Boboli Gardens** (tel. 21 87 41) behind the palace stretch to the hilltop **Forte Belvedere** (tel. 234 24 25), once the Medici fortress and treasury. Ascend Via di Costa San Giorgio from P. Santa Felicità, to the left after crossing Ponte Vecchio, to reach the villa, an unusual construction with a central *loggia* designed by Ammannati. Buontalenti built this star-shaped bastion for Grand Duke Ferdinand I. The fortress now hosts summer exhibitions and sun-tanning exhibitionism. (Gardens open daily June-July 9am-7:30pm; April-May and Sept.-Oct. 9am-6:30pm; March 9am-5:30pm; Nov.-Feb. 9am-4:30pm. Closed the first and last Mon. of each month. Admission L4000. Fort open 9am-10pm; in winter 9am-5pm.)

The splendid view of Florence from the fort equals only the picture-perfect panorama from **Piazzale Michelangelo.** Go at sunset for the most spectacular lighting of the city. Above the *piazzale* is **San Miniato al Monte,** one of Florence's oldest churches and one of the best examples of the Romanesque style. (Take bus #13 from the station or climb the stairs from P. Michelangelo.) The inlaid marble façade with its 13th-century mosaics preludes the incredible pavement inside, which is patterned with lions, doves, and astrological signs. Inside the Chapel of the Cardinal of Portugal, you'll find a collection of superlative della Robbia terra-cottas. (Ask the sacristan to let you into the chapel. Church open daily 7:30am-7pm.)

CENTRAL ITALY

ENTERTAINMENT

For reliable information on what's hot and what's not, consult the city's entertainment monthly, *Firenze Spettacolo* (L3800). The nightly **passeggiata** promenades along Via dei Calzaiuoli; afterward Florentines frequent the ritzy cafés in P. della Repubblica and look on with amusement (or perhaps pity) as the hired singers prance about the stage in front of Bar Concerto. Street performers draw crowds to the steps of the *duomo,* the arcades of the Mercato Nuovo, and P. Michelangelo. **Caffè La Dolce Vita** in P. del Carmine draws a respectable evening crowd and is convenient to the budget lodgings in the Oltrarno. Just two blocks away, P. Santo Spirito hops with a good selection of bars and restaurants.

Lo Sfizzio, Lungarno Cellini, 1. Frequented by a boisterous crowd of beautiful people, carousing over colossal drinks on the outdoor terrace. Open daily 8pm-1am.

Fuori Porta, Monte alle Croce, 10r. For those who prefer a quieter evening of sipping wine; offers an impressive selection of *vino* by the glass from L4000. Open Mon.-Sat. 10am-midnight.

The Red Garter, Via dei Benci, 33r. A raucous mix of American students, Italian youth, flying peanut shells, and classic American rock. If you have what it takes, they might even let you on stage. Open nightly, happy hour 8:30pm.

The Fiddler's Elbow, P. Santa Maria Novella, 74. An authentic Irish pub serving cider, Guinness, and other draught beers (L6000 a pint). It's crowded and convivial but plagued by foreigners. Open daily noon-12:15am.

Robin Hood, Via dell'Oriuolo, 58r (also called the English Pub; tel. 24 45 79). Serves half-pints of beer and cider for L4000. Open 5pm-1am. Happy hour 8pm.

Angie's Pub, Via dei Neri, 35r (tel. 29 82 45). Very Italian (despite the name) and caters mostly to students, remaining generally uncrowded in the summer months. Their selection of imported beer and cider on tap starts at L4000 per glass, and they serve hamburgers on their own special rolls (L5000-L6000). Open Tues.-Sat. 12:30-3pm and 7pm-1am.

BeBop, Via dei Servi, 76r (tel. 28 91 12). A live jazz club that mixes in a bit of blues. Open daily 9pm-1am.

Dancing

Many of the discos listed below cater almost exclusively to tourists and to those Italians who have designs on foreigners.

Space Electronic, Via Palazzuolo, 37 (tel. 29 30 82), near S. Maria Novella. A young American crowd multiplied by its many mirrors. Undeniably cheesy. Beer L8000, mixed drinks L10,000. Cover and 1st drink L25,000. Free karaoke. Open Sun.-Fri. 10pm-2am, Sat. 10pm-3am; Sept.-Feb. closed Mon.

Meccanò, Viale degli Olmi, 1 (tel. 33 13 71), near Parco delle Cascinè. Popular among locals and tourists alike. Take bus #17C from the *duomo* or train station. L30,000 cover includes 1 drink; each subsequent drink L10,000. Open Tues.-Sun. 11pm-4am.

Tabasco Gay Club, P. Santa Cecilia, 3r (tel. 21 30 00), in a tiny alleyway across P. della Signoria from the Palazzo Vecchio. Florence's popular gay disco. Min. age 18. Cover L15,000-25,000. Open Tues.-Sun. 10pm-3am.

Festivals

Florence disagrees with England over who invented modern soccer, and every June the various *quartieri* of the city turn out in costume to play their own medieval version of the sport, known as **Calcio Storico.** Two teams of 27 players face off over a wooden ball in one of the city's *piazze.* These games often blur the line between athletic contest and riot. Check newspapers or the tourist office for the dates and locations of either historic or modern *calcio.* Tickets (starting at about L30,000) are sold at the Chiosco degli Sportivi (tel. 29 23 63) on Via dei Anselmi. Real games occur at the **stadio,** north of the city center. You can buy tickets (starting at L20,000) from the bar across the street from the stadium.

The most important of Florence's more traditional festivals, that of **St. John the Baptist** on June 24, features a tremendous fireworks display from P. Michelangelo (easily visible from the Arno, starting about 10pm). The summer also swings with music festivals, starting in May with the classical **Maggio Musicale.** The **Estate Fiesolana** (June-Aug.) fills the Roman theater in nearby Fiesole with concerts, opera, theater, ballet, and film. For info on tickets, contact the Biglietteria Centrale in the Teatro Comunale, Corso Italia, 16 (tel. 21 62 53 or 277 92 36), or Universalturismo, Via degli Speziali, 7r (tel. 21 72 41), off P. della Repubblica. In September, Florence hosts the **Festa dell'Unità,** an organized music and concert series at Campi Bisenzia (take bus #30). The **Florence Film Festival** is generally held in December. For more info contact the film festival office (tel. 24 07 20) at Via Martiri del Popolo. The **Festa dei Porcini** is an annual mushroom festival which lasts for three days in August. Contact the local tourist office for up-to-date information.

SHOPPING

The Florentine flair for design comes through as clearly in the window displays of its shops as in the wares themselves. Via Tornabuoni's **swanky boutiques** and the somewhat **tacky and overpriced goldsmiths** on the Ponte Vecchio proudly serve a sophisticated clientele. Florence makes its contribution to *alta moda* with the bi-annual **Pitti Uomo show** (in Jan. and July), Europe's most important exhibition of menswear, and other Pitti fashion shows. If you're looking for high-quality used and antique clothing, try **La Belle Epoque,** Volta di S. Piero, 8r (tel. 21 61 69), off P. S. Pier Maggiore, or **Lord Brummel Store,** Via della Vigna Nuova, 79r (tel. 238 23 28), off Via Tornabuoni.

The city's artisan traditions thrive at the open markets. **San Lorenzo,** the largest, cheapest, and most touristed, sprawls for several blocks around P. San Lorenzo, trafficking in anything made of leather, wool, cloth, or gold. (Open Mon.-Sat.) High prices are rare, as are quality and honesty. For everything from potholders to parakeets, visit **Parco delle Cascinè,** which begins west of the city center at P. Vittorio Veneto and stretches along the Arno River. (At night commodities of a different sort go up for sale as transvestite prostitutes solicit customers from an endless stream of cars, driven mostly by curious onlookers.) The market at the Cascinè sells clothing and shoes; many come for the used clothing vendors. For a flea market specializing in old furniture, postcards, and bric-a-brac, visit **Piazza Ciompi,** off Via Pietrapiana from Borgo degli Albizi. (Open Tues.-Sat.) Where prices are marked, Florentines will rarely haggle, so bargaining usually won't get you far; try it only if you feel the price is truly outrageous.

Books and art reproductions are some of the best souvenirs you can carry away from Florence. Famed **Alinari**, Via della Vigna Nuova, 46-48r (tel. 21 89 75), stocks the world's largest selection of art prints and high-quality photographs. (L5000-8000. Open Tues.-Sat. 9:30am-1pm and 3:30-7:30pm.) **Rizzoli's** *Maestri del Colore* series of color reproductions is also a bargain. **Feltrinelli,** Via Cerretoni, 34 (tel. 29 63 20), has an unbeatable selection of art books. (Open Mon.-Fri. 9am-7:30pm, Sat. 9am-1pm.) For a wide range of cinematic books, posters, and postcards, head over to **Libreria del Cinema dello Spettacolo,** Via Guelfa, 14r (tel. 21 64 16). **Abacus,** a tiny shop at Via de'Ginori, 30r (tel. 21 97 19), is one of many stationary stores that sell beautiful photo albums, journals, and address books, all made of fine leather and **carta fiorentina,** paper covered in an intricate floral design. You're even welcome to go and peek in at the artists. (Be sure to check for such opportunities in other stores as well, especially in the smaller leather shops and jewelry stores. Many of them only sell goods made on the premises.) Florentine **leatherwork** is generally of high quality and frequently affordable. Leather shops fill the city, but P. Santa Croce and Via Porta Santa Maria are particularly good places to look. One of the best leather deals in the city hides in one of its most beautiful churches. The **Santa Croce Leather School** (tel. 24 45 33/34 and 247 99 13), in the back of the church to the right, offers some of the best-quality artisan products in the city but has prices to match. (Open 9:30am-6:30pm, Sat. 9:30am-6pm, Sun. 10:30am-12:30pm and 3-6pm. Enter through Via San Giuseppe, 5r, on Sun. afternoons.)

Near Florence: Fiesole

Atop majestic hills just 8km to the northeast of Florence, Fiesole has long been a welcome escape from the sweltering summer heat of the Arno Valley and a source of inspiration for numerous famous figures—among them Alexandre Dumas, Anatole France, Marcel Proust, Gertrude Stein, Frank Lloyd Wright, and Paul Klee. Leonardo da Vinci even used the town as a testing ground for his famed flying machine. Fiesole's location provides **incomparable views** of both Florence and the rolling countryside to the north—it's a perfect place for a picnic or a day-long *passeggiata*. No trains run to Fiesole, but the town is easily accessible from Florence by bus. ATAF city bus #7 leaves from the train station, from P. del Duomo, and from P. San Marco during the day (less frequently at night) and drops passengers at P. Mino da Fiesole in the center of town. Fiesole features a number of churches and museums, but the town's greatest attractions are definitely its breathtaking views. Take Via San Francesco up the steep hill from the main *piazza* for a view of Florence and the valley chiseled by the Arno into the surrounding hills.

Cortona

The ancient town of Cortona (it's older than Troy) arrogantly surveys both Tuscany and Umbria from its mountaintop. This now-quiet city once rivaled Perugia, Arezzo, and even Florence in power and belligerence. But the 15th-century Florentine take-over was, artistically speaking, in Cortona's best interest; artist Fra Angelico sojourned here for a decade and painted an *Annunciation* that rivals the one in Florence's San Marco. Not much in the town has changed since it succumbed to Florentine rule; Cortona's high roost leaves little room for expansion. Serpentine cobblestone streets traverse the city, leading to marvelous medieval *palazzi* and breathtaking views of the Tuscan hills.

ORIENTATION AND PRACTICAL INFORMATION

The easiest way to reach Cortona is by **bus** from Arezzo (every hr., 30min., L4500). If you must take the train from Rome (L16,000) or Florence (L10,500), get off at either Terontola-Cortona or Camucia-Cortona. From here catch the LFI bus to P. Garibaldi in Cortona (every 30min.-1hr., L1500 and L1200 respectively). Buses leave you at **Piazza Garibaldi** just outside the main gate of the city wall. Enter through this gate and follow **Via Nazionale,** passing the tourist office almost immediately on your left, to the town's center at **Piazza della Repubblica.** From there, cross the *piazza* diagonally to the left to reach the other main square, **Piazza Signorelli.**

Tourist Office: Via Nazionale, 42 (tel. 63 03 52). Friendly and helpful, with lots of maps and brochures. Open Mon.-Fri. 8am-1pm and 3-6pm; June-Sept. also open Sat. 3-6pm, Sun. 9am-1pm.

Currency Exchange: Banca Populare, Via Guelfa, 4. Open Mon.-Fri. 8:20am-1:20pm.

Telephones: At **Bar Sport,** P. Signorelli, 16 (open daily in summer 6am-1am; in winter 6am-midnight) or **Bar Banchelli,** Via Nazionale, 64 (open daily 7am-1pm and 2:30pm-midnight).

Taxis: tel. 60 42 45.

Bike Rental: Rent a Bike, P. della Repubblica, 12A (tel. (0368) 45 01 91). Rents out mountain bikes for L20,000 per day. Delivery service. Offers guided tours of Cortona and environs.

Swimming Pool: (tel. 60 13 74), 7km away at Sodo. Take the bus for Arezzo and ask the driver to let you off at the *piscina.* Water slides! Open daily 9:30am-7pm. Admission L12,000.

Pharmacy: Farmacia Centrale, Via Nazionale, 38 (tel. 60 32 06). Open Mon.-Sat. 9am-1pm and 4-7:30pm.

Emergency: tel. 113. **First Aid: Servizio Guardia Medica Turistica,** Via Roma, 3 (tel. 60 18 17). Open 8am-8pm. **Ambulance:** tel. 63 03 75. **Misericordia:** tel. 60 30 83. **Hospital:** Via Maffei (tel. 63 91).

Police: Caribinieri, Via Dardano, 9 (tel. 60 30 06).

Post Office: Via Santucci, 1, 15m uphill from P. della Repubblica. Open Mon.-Fri. 8:15am-7pm, Sat. 8:15am-noon. **Postal Code:** 52044.

Telephone Code: 0575.

ACCOMMODATIONS

Cheap hotels are scarce in Cortona, but institutional arrangements take up the slack. The hostel, one of Italy's best, is a converted 13th-century house with exceptionally friendly management, and the nuns down the hill welcome any weary traveler.

Ostello San Marco (HI), Via Maffei, 57 (tel. 60 13 92). From the bus stop, walk up steep Via S. Margarita and follow the signs to the hostel (about 5min.). Clean and cozy with a cavernous, stone-walled dining room. 8-10 bunks per room; 1 double. Laundry facilities available. Open 7-10am and 3:30pm-midnight. L16,000 per person. Breakfast, sheets, and showers included, but no hot water late at night. Dinner L12,000; reserve ahead. Open mid-March to mid-Oct.; year-round for groups.

Istituto Santa Margherita, Viale Cesare Battisti, 15 (tel. 63 03 36). Walk down Via Severini from P. Garibaldi; the *istituto* is at the corner of Via Battisti, on the left. Echoing marble hallways take you to spacious rooms, all with bath. Curfew midnight. Singles L30,000. Doubles (no unmarried, mixed-sex couples) L50,000. Dormitory-style rooms L18,000 per person.

Albergo Italia, Via Ghibellina, 5 (tel. 63 02 54; fax 63 05 64), off P. Repubblica. This 16th-century *palazzo* offers great rooms: high, beamed ceilings, firm beds, and TVs (upon request). Pristine bathrooms, downstairs bar, and a wonderful upstairs terrace for breathtaking views. Singles L40,000, with bath L70,000. Doubles L65,000, with bath L90,000.

Albergo Athens, Via San Antonio, 12 (tel. 63 05 08). Head up Via Dardano and take a right. Usually filled with University of Georgia students, who use it as (and make it feel like) a college dorm, but if there's room, they'll fit you in. It's cheap, and you get what you pay for. Singles L30,000. Doubles L53,000.

FOOD

With several *trattorie* that serve up immense pasta dishes and an abundance of grocery stores and fruit stands, Cortona will amply feed even the budget traveler. A fine local wine is the smooth *bianco vergine di Valdichiana.* Penny pinchers can pick up a bottle (L3000) at the **Despar Market,** in Piazza della Repubblica, 23 (tel. 63 06 66), which also makes *panini* (L3000-5000) to order. Open Mon.-Tues. and Thurs.-Sat. 7:30am-1:30pm and 4:30-8pm, Wed. 7:30am-1:30pm; April-Sept. daily 7:30am-1:30pm and 4:30-8pm. V, MC, AmEx. On Saturday the same *piazza* metamorphoses into a great **open-air market.**

Trattoria La Grotta, P. Baldelli, 3 (tel. 63 02 71), off P. della Repubblica. Truly delectable fare at outdoor tables in a secluded courtyard. Sample the homemade *gnocchi alla ricotta e spinaci* (ricotta and spinach balls in tomato and meat sauce, L8000). *Primi* L6000-L8500, *secondi* from L10,000. *Menù* L22,000. Cover L2000. Open Wed.-Mon. 12:15-2:30pm and 7:15-10pm. V, MC, AmEx.

Trattoria Etrusca, Via Dardano, 35. Specializes in *primi,* serving marvelously unique (and huge!) pasta creations inside or outside along the old city walls. Try the house specialty, *tagliatelle colle zucchine* (pasta with zucchini, L8000). Open daily 12:30-2:30pm and 7:30-11pm; Oct.-May closed Thurs. V, MC.

Trattoria dell'Amico, Via Dardano, 12. This small, family-run place serves up *gnocchi al pesto* for L7000 and *pollo alla cacciatore* (chicken in a tomato sauce) for L8000. *Menù* L20,000. Open daily noon-3pm and 7-10:30pm.

SIGHTS

The most stunning sights in Cortona are the incredible views of the surrounding valleys and hills. From the ancient **Fortezza** on the summit of Cortona's rugged hill (Monte S. Egidio), you can gaze out over the Tuscan countryside. The walk to the *Fortezza* passes several small meadows with beautiful views and no people. On the other side of town at P. Garibaldi, tourists lean over the iron fence to peer down the jagged cliff to the valley floor below; you can see Umbria and Hannibal's beloved Lake Trasimeno in the distance.

In P. della Repubblica stands the 13th-century **Palazzo del Comune,** with a clock tower and monumental staircase. **Palazzo Casali,** to the right and behind the Palazzo del Comune, dominates P. Signorelli. Only the courtyard walls with their coats of arms and the outside right wall remain from the original 13th-century structure—the façade and interlocking staircase are from the 17th century. Inside the courtyard, steps lead to the **Museo dell'Accademia Etrusca,** which harbors many treasures and artifacts from the Etruscan period, as well as an overflow of carvings, coins, paintings, and furniture from the first through 18th centuries. In the first gallery is a circular bronze chandelier from the 5th century BC, mounted in a glass case suspended from the ceiling. With 16 voluminous oil reservoirs, it weighs 58kg when empty. A local farmer discovered a rare example of intricate Etruscan metalwork, the *lampadario,* while plowing his field. The same room contains a two-faced *Janus,* depicted as a full figure rather than the usual bust. In the third gallery you'll find 12th- and 13th-century Tuscan art, including works by Taddeo Gaddi, Cenni di Francesco, and Bici di Lorenzo. The museum wraps up with the 20th-century work of local boy Gino Severini, including lithographs, collages, and an intriguing *Maternità.* (Open Tues.-Sun.

April-Sept. 10am-1pm and 4-7pm; Oct.-March 9am-1pm and 3-5pm. Admission L5000.)

To the right and downhill from the Palazzo Casali is **Piazza del Duomo.** Note the brick entry of the original Church of S. Maria on the façade of the *duomo*, poking out like a sore thumb from the stone fronting. During renovations enter the church from the side door near the Palazzo Vescovile. Inside rests an impressive Baroque-canopied high altar, completed in 1664 by Francesco Mattioli. The two-floored **Museo Diocesano** across from the *duomo* houses the stunning *Annunciation* by Fra Angelico in the upstairs gallery on the right. Across the hall on the left, Christ's pain-wrenched face looks down on you from Pietro Lorenzetti's fresco of *The Way to Calvary.* Vasari's staircase leads to a frescoed oratory on the lower level containing a painted cross by Lorenzetti. Don't miss Luca Signorelli's masterpiece, *The Deposition,* a vivid portrayal of Christ's death and resurrection. (Open April-Sept. Tues.-Sun. 9am-1pm and 4-7pm; Oct.-March 9am-1pm and 3-5pm. Admission L5000.)

When afternoon sedates Cortona, head up to the **Fortezza Medicea** for a splendid view and a refreshing breeze. Take Via San Cristoforo, which winds up the hill between tall cypresses from the small church of the same name. At the top enter the tree-filled fortress, built on the remains of an Etruscan fortification. (Open mid-July to Aug. Tues.-Sun. 10am-1pm and 4-7pm.) On the way down, take **Via Crucis,** which leads away from the church of Santa Margherita. The futurist Severini designed the mosaic stations of the cross that line the path as a war memorial in 1947. Speaking of war monuments, don't miss the beautiful, heart-breaking memorial to World War I dead that guards the entrance to the **Giardino Pubblico.**

The Renaissance **Church of Santa Maria delle Grazie al Calcinaio,** designed by Francesco di Giorgio Martini, awaits visitors about 2km down the road near Camucia. The soft gray *pietra serena* stone, beautifully carved in the interior, creates a cool tonality along with the white walls. Paintings of the Signorelli school hang near the altar, and a Marcillat stained-glass window energizes the opposite wall. (Open daily 8:30am-noon and 4-7pm.) Archaeology-buffs and necrophiliacs should visit the **Meloni,** Etruscan tombs from the 7th century BC recently discovered in nearby Sodo. An elaborate stone altar lies within the massive walls of the second tomb.

ENTERTAINMENT

Of the numerous gastronomic festivals throughout the year, the most important is the **Sagra della Bistecca** of August 14-15, when the whole town pours in to feast upon bloody strips of the superb local steak. Various musical and theatrical events take place throughout the year, clustering in the summer months when Cortona absorbs the spillover from the Perugia Jazz Festival. The Azienda's informative *Cortona '97* will give you the lowdown. On nice days, relax in the **public gardens** or join in the evening *passeggiata* in the park, where they screen Italian movies in summer (L6000). If you like your entertainment a bit more lively, check out **Tuchulcha** (tel. 627 27), in P. Garibaldi. It's a popular place with American students who come to drink and dance away their homesickness. (Open Tues.-Sat. 9pm-2am.)

Arezzo

Pause in Arezzo before continuing to other Tuscan destinations and muse about the others who found inspiration here. Your illustrious predecessors include the poet Petrarch, the humanist Leonardo Bruni, the artist and historian Giorgio Vasari, and the inventor of the musical scale, Guido d'Arezzo. Michelangelo, born in the surrounding countryside, attributed his genius to the inspiration he found in Arezzo's surrounding hills and valleys. Today's Arezzo proves a curious blend of modernity and antiquity. The remains of ancient ramparts rest languidly beside busy shopping arcades and august medieval churches look down upon newly built condominiums.

ORIENTATION AND PRACTICAL INFORMATION

Arezzo lies on the Florence-Rome train line. Arezzo's train station and modern quarter lie at the bottom of a hill that ascends through the historic center and peaks at the *duomo.* Follow **Via Guido Monaco,** which begins directly across from the station in P. della Repubblica, to the park and traffic circle at P. Guido Monaco. Turn right on Via Roma and then left onto the pedestrian walkway, **Corso Italia.** The Corso leads up to the old city; **P. Grande,** its center, will be off to the right.

Tourist Office: Inform Arezzo, P. della Repubblica, 22 (tel. 37 76 78), to the right as you leave the station. The English-speaking staff is more than happy to give out free maps and other information. Open April-Sept. Mon.-Sat. 9am-1pm and 3-7pm, Sun. 9am-1pm; Oct.-March Mon.-Sat. 9am-1pm and 3-6pm; during antique fairs Sun. 9am-1pm. The main **EPT office,** P. Risorgimento, 116 (tel. 239 52) is less adept at welcoming incoming tourists but is very well-stocked with information about the entire region.

Budget Travel: CTS, P. Risorgimento, 116 (tel. 35 27 16; fax 35 06 70). Sells Eurail passes and plane tickets. Open Mon.-Fri. 9am-1pm and 4-7:30pm.

Currency Exchange: Banca Nazionale del Lavoro, Via G. Monaco, 74. Open Mon.-Fri. 8:20am-1:35pm and 2:40-4:05pm.

Telephones: On Via Margaritone, off Via Niccolò Aretino near the Archaeological Museum. Open Mon.-Sat. 8:30am-12:30pm and 3:30-6:30pm.

Trains: Information open Mon.-Fri. 8am-noon and 3-6pm, Sat. 9am-noon. From Florence (about every 30min., 1hr., L7200) and Rome (about every 2hr., 2hr., L19,000). **Luggage Storage:** To the left as you exit the tracks. L5000 for 12hr. Open daily 5:30am-9:30pm.

Buses: (tel. 38 26 44), **TRA-IN, SITA,** and **LFI** buses stop at P. della Repubblica, to the left as you exit the train station. Service to Siena (5 per day, 1½hr., L7500) and nearby hill-towns, including Cortona (LFI, about every hr., 1½hr., L4500) and Sansepolcro (SITA, about every hr., 1hr., L5500). Buy tickets at the ATAM *biglietteria,* across the street from the bus stop. Open daily 6:20am-7:40pm.

Taxis: In front of the train station. **Radio Taxi:** tel. 38 26 26. Open 24hr.

Car Rental: Autonoleggi Ermini, Via Perrenio, 21 (tel. 35 35 70). Small Fiats start at L90,000 per day. Min. age 21. Open Mon.-Sat. 8:30am-12:30pm and 3:30-7:30pm. **Avis,** P. della Repubblica (tel. 35 42 32). The cheapest car is an Opel Corsa for L165,000 per day. Min. age 23. Open Mon.-Fri. 8:30am-1pm and 3-7pm, Sat. 8:30am-1pm.

Late-Night Pharmacy: Farmacia Comunale, Campo di Marte, 7. Open 24hr.

Emergencies: tel. 113. **Guardia Medica:** tel. 30 04 44. **Hospital:** on Via Fonte Veneziana (tel. 35 67 57; at night and Sun. 35 18 00).

Police: (tel. 37 75 77) off Via Fra' Guittone near the train station.

Post Office: Via Monaco, 34, to the left of P. Monaco when facing uphill. Open Mon.-Fri. 8:15am-7pm, Sat. 8am-12:30pm. **Exchanges currency** (L1000 commission) and **traveler's checks** (L2000 commission for sums up to L100,000; L5000 for anything greater). Open Mon.-Fri. 8:15am-6pm, Sat. 8:15am-12:30pm. **Postal Code:** 52100.

Telephone Code: 0575.

ACCOMMODATIONS

The hotels of Arezzo fill to capacity during the Fiera Antiquaria (Antique Fair) on the first weekend of every month. Reservations are also necessary in the last four days of August during the Concorso Polifonico Guido d'Arezzo, a vocal competition. Otherwise, you should have little trouble finding a room.

Ostello Villa Severi, Via Redi, 13 (tel. 290 47). Take bus #4 (L1200) from the right-hand-side of Via Guido Monaco (100m up Via G. Monaco from the train station), and get off two stops after the Ospedale Civile (about 7min.). A beautiful 16th-century villa in the countryside overlooking hills and vineyards, but it's a bit of a hike from town. 4-8 bunks per room. Plenty of hot water. Open 9am-2:30pm and 6-

11:30pm. L20,000 per person. Breakfast L2000. Lunch and dinner each L14,000. Reserve ahead for meals.

Hotel Astoria, Via Guido Monaco, 54 (tel. 24 361). From the station, walk straight up Via G. Monaco, through the *piazza*, and to the hotel on the left. Most rooms are quiet, with towering ceilings and formerly mod furniture. Singles L45,000, with bath L55,000. Doubles L70,000, with bath L90,000. Triples L94,000, with bath L121,000. V, MC.

Albergo Cecco, Corso Italia, 215 (tel. 209 86). Follow Via G. Monaco from the station; take a right on Via Roma, then another 2 blocks down on the Corso (5min. from the train station). Big, clean rooms trapped in the Age of Formica. Singles L45,000, with bath L60,000. Doubles L70,000, with bath L90,000. Decent restaurant downstairs.

FOOD

Arezzo has some wonderful, inexpensive restaurants, but if you'd rather do it your way, check out the supermarket **Santa Prisca** at Via Monaco, 84. Open in summer Mon.-Fri. 8am-8pm, Sat. 8am-1pm; in winter Mon.-Tues. and Thurs.-Sat. 8am-8pm, Wed. 8am-1pm. Or try the **open-air market** in P. Sant'Agostino on weekdays and on Via Niccolò Aretino on Saturday. For excellent cheese, head over to **La Mozzarella,** Via Spinello, 25. Open Mon.-Sat. 8am-1pm and 4:30-7:30pm. Eat in the park behind the *duomo,* with an impressive view of the Tuscan countryside.

Vecchia Suizzera, Corso Italia, 57 (tel. 21 26 70). When you can't face another plate of pasta, come here to revive your faith in Italian cooking. Wonderful, innovative delights like zucchini crepes (L9000) and ravioli in an herb-specked saffron sauce (L11,000). Open Mon.-Sat. noon-2:30pm and 7:30-10:30pm. V, AmEx.

Antica Osteria L'Agania, Via Guiseppe Mazzini, 10 (tel. 253 81), off Corso Italia. Float in on the smell of burning wood. Locals pack the place to feast on homemade *gnocchi, ribollita,* and a heavenly *coniglio in porchetta* (roasted rabbit stuffed with wild fennel). All dishes L10,000. Open Tues.-Sun. noon-2pm and 7:30-10:30pm. V, MC, AmEx.

SIGHTS AND ENTERTAINMENT

The **Church of San Francesco** at P. S. Francesco forms the spiritual and physical center of Arezzo. This 14th-century structure guards Piero della Francesca's famous fresco cycle *Legend of the Cross,* the story of the wood used for Christ's cross from seed to crucifix. The city planned to complete the restoration for 1992, the 500th anniversary of Piero's birth. It's now 1997, and it's still anybody's guess as to when it will wrap up. In the meantime, the frescoes to the right of the altar, including the wonderful *Constantine's Dream,* are visible, and there's an interesting exhibit documenting the restoration process. (Open daily in summer 8am-noon and 1:30-6pm.)

As has so often been the case, the Dominicans built their church on the opposite end of town. The **Church of San Domenico** contains a superb Cimabue crucifix (1265), Spinello Aretino's *Annunciation* in the chapel to the right of the altar, and the Marcillat rose window over the door. (Open daily 7am-noon and 3-7pm.) Beyond the church at Via XX Settembre, 55, is **Vasari's house,** filled with heroic frescoes. (Open daily 9am-7pm.)

The massive **duomo,** on Via Ricasoli, encloses Piero della Francesca's *Mary Magdalene* just to the right of Bishop Guido Tarlati's tomb. Light filters into the cathedral through a series of 20-ft. stained-glass windows by Marcillat onto the altar, a wildly complex assemblage of local 14th-century carvings. The Lady Chapel (to the left near the entrance), covered by an ornate wrought-iron screen, houses a terracotta *Assumption* by Andrea della Robbia. (Open 7am-noon and 3-6:30pm.) Between the *duomo* and the fortress, a leafy park gives magnificent views of the countryside beyond its edge.

Back down Corso Italia on the left stands the Pisan-Romanesque **Church of Santa Maria della Pieve,** Arezzo's most important architectural monument and something of a city emblem. Its tower is nicknamed "the tower of a hundred holes" for the Romanesque windows that pierce the structure on all sides. A brilliantly restored polyptych by Pietro Lorenzetti, sits on the elevated presbytery, depicting the Annunciation and the Madonna and Child. (Open Mon.-Sat. 8am-noon and 3-7pm, Sun. 8:30am-noon and 4-7pm.) A chronological succession of Arezzo's best architecture surrounds **Piazza Grande,** behind the Pieve. Next to the arches of the Pieve's rear elevation, the **Palazzo della Fraternità dei Laici** mixes Renaissance and Gothic styles. A reconstruction of the **Petrone,** a column where city leaders exhibited criminals and read proclamations, rises at the *piazza*'s high point.

Arezzo's famous **antique fair** takes place on the first weekend of every month in P. Grande, but if you miss it, you can entertain yourself by browsing through the innumerable antique shops that dot the old town. The **Giostra del Saraceno** is a medieval joust performed on the third Sunday of June and the first Sunday in September. In a ritual recalling the Crusades, "knights" representing the four quarters of the town charge with lowered lances at a wooden effigy of a Turk. Feasting and processions accompany the event, and the winning region carries off a golden lance.

■ Near Arezzo: Sansepolcro

Lost in a valley among Tuscany's densely forested hills, medieval Sansepolcro is the birthplace of Piero della Francesca and is still home to some of his finest works. The town is most easily accessible by the hourly SITA bus from Arezzo (1hr., L5500), with the last bus returning to Arezzo at 7:30pm (weekend service is less frequent). Incredible views compensate for the nauseating twists in the road along the way. The bus drops you off on **Via Vittorio Veneto.**

The **Museo Civico,** Via Aggiunti, 65 (tel. 73 22 18), houses some of Piero della Francesca's most famous works. To get to the museum, take a left from the bus station, then turn left again at the next street, Via Firenzuola, and walk three minutes until you come to the street light; the museum will be on your right. The *Resurrection,* della Francesca's masterpiece, features a triumphant Jesus wearing a red and white banner. Also by della Francesca is the *Madonna della Misericordia,* a polyptych with a huge Madonna protecting a confraternity under her cloak. Don't miss Antonio and Remigio Cantagallina's *Last Supper,* with Judas in the foreground holding his money bag and looking nonplussed while a devil on the floor spits blood on him. Open daily Oct.-May 9:30am-1pm and 2:30-6pm; June-Sept. 9:30am-1pm and 2:30-7:30pm. Admission L10,000.

The **Palio della Balestra** takes place the second Sunday in September. Stay overnight and join in the revelry generated by this competition between archers of Gubbio and Sansepolcro. For maps of the region, go to Sansepolcro's **tourist office,** P. Garibaldi, 2 (tel. 74 05 36). From the museum, turn right on Via Firenzuola and then take the first left on P. Garibaldi. The tourist office is one block ahead on the left. Open daily 9:30am-12:30pm and 4-6:30pm. Maps of the region are available. Should night fall, try the comfortable **Albergo Fiorentino,** Via Luca Pacioli, 60 (tel. 74 03 50; fax 74 03 70), two blocks from the Museo Civico. Singles L40,000, with bath and TV L55,000. Doubles L60,000, with bath and TV L85,000, Triples with bath and TV L120,000. Breakfast L10,000. The **Ristorante Da Ventura,** Via Aggiunti, 30 (tel. 74 25 60), serves outstanding homemade pasta dishes. The house specialties include ravioli with spinach and ricotta filling (L9000), and *tagliatelle* with *porcini* mushrooms (L12,000), and they carve whole roasts right at the table. *Primi* from L7000, *secondi* from L10,000. Cover L2000. Open Sun.-Fri. 12:30-2:30pm and 7:30-9:30pm. Sansepolcro's **telephone code** is 0575.

Another important stop on any Piero della Francesca odyssey is the tiny chapel halfway between Arezzo and Sansepolcro, outside the town of **Monterchi.** Outside Arezzo on Highway 73 (24km), there is a fork in the road; take the right branch (Highway 221) to the chapel. Within, marvel at the unusual *Madonna del Parto,* Piero's rendition of a proud, earthy Madonna immaculately pregnant. Open Tues.-Sun. 9am-1pm and 2-7pm. Admission L5000, students L2500. The Arezzo-Sansepolcro bus stops nearby in Le Ville, where you can follow the signs to the chapel (about a 20-min. walk).

Siena

Most tourists stampede directly from Rome to Florence, bypassing Siena. Thank goodness—due to their oversight, Siena remains a gorgeous medieval city that has fewer tourists than its larger cousins to the north and south. During the 13th century, Siena's flourishing wool trade, crafty bankers, and sophisticated civil administration made it one of the principal cities of Europe—easily Florence's equal. In 1230, the belligerent (and jealous?) Florentines catapulted excrement over Siena's walls, attempting to trigger a rampant plague. The ploy failed, and in 1260 Siena routed the Florentines at the Battle of Montaperti. The century of grandiose construction that followed endowed the city with its flamboyant Gothic cathedral, the Piazza del Campo, and a multitude of *palazzi.* In 1348, however, a plague claimed half of Siena's population, and the weakened city said *adieu* to its glory days.

Today, the Sienese struggle to maintain their identity as more than just a Florentine satellite. They boast their own painting tradition, led by Duccio di Buoninsegna, Simone Martini, and the Lorenzetti brothers, who expanded upon decorative elements of Gothic art. Siena also claims the mystic tradition that produced the 15th-century Saint Catherine, an ecstatic illiterate who brought the papacy back from Avignon, and Saint Bernadino, who roamed the Italian peninsula reviving the teachings of St. Francis. Twice each summer, the Sienese offer a lavish exhibition of their city's character. The ritual **Palio,** a wild horse race with competitors from the city's 17 *contrade* (neighborhoods), is an intoxicating display of pageantry. While the *Palio* is the main attraction of Siena's tourist industry, the event is no mere show. Modern-day Sienese still identify strongly with their local *contrada* and throw a year's worth of pent-up excitement and rivalry into the races.

ORIENTATION AND PRACTICAL INFORMATION

Siena once lay on the main road between Rome and Paris; modernity finds it on a secondary train line connecting it to Florence. Change at Chiusi from Rome and the south, at Florence from points north. To reach the town proper from the train station, take any bus from the stop across the street (buy tickets from the vending machines by the station entrance or at the *biglietteria* window for bus tickets, L1400). **Buses are the easiest and most convenient way to get to Siena.** Frequent buses link Siena to Florence and the rest of Tuscany, making this town an ideal base for exploring the smaller Tuscan hill-towns. Buses climb the city's hills and stop just outside its historic center at P. San Domenico. Follow the signs to **Piazza del Campo** (also called *Il Campo*). Walking to the center from the train station can be a pleasant, if tiring, way to orient yourself with the city, but be prepared to walk at least 45min. Pick up a decent map at the information office before you set off.

Tourist Office: APT, Il Campo, 56 (tel. 28 05 51), provides info on local sights and accommodations, restaurants, and transportation to other Tuscan towns. **Currency exchange** at poor rates. Open in summer Mon.-Sat. 8:30am-7:30pm, Sun. 8am-2pm; in winter Mon.-Sat. 8:30am-1:30pm and 3:30-7pm. The **Prenotazioni Alberghiere** counter (tel. 28 80 84) in P. San Domenico will find you lodging for a L3000 fee. Open in summer Mon.-Sat. 9am-8pm, in winter 9am-7pm.

Budget Travel: CTS, Via Sallustio Bandini, 21 (tel. 28 14 58). Student travel services. Open Mon.-Thurs. 9:30am-12:30pm and 4-7pm, Fri. 9am-6pm.

Currency Exchange: 24-hr. exchange machines outside **Banca Toscana,** P. Tolomei, 9, and **Monte dei Paschi di Siena,** Via Montanini, 2, off P. Salimberi.

Telephones: Via dei Termini, 40. Available Mon.-Fri. 9am-1pm and 4-7pm. Self-service pay phones accessible daily in summer 7am-midnight; in winter 7am-9pm.

Trains: P. Rosselli. Hourly departures to Florence (L8000) and Rome (via Chiusi, L20,800). Ticket office open daily 6am-9:30pm. **Train information booth** (tel. 28

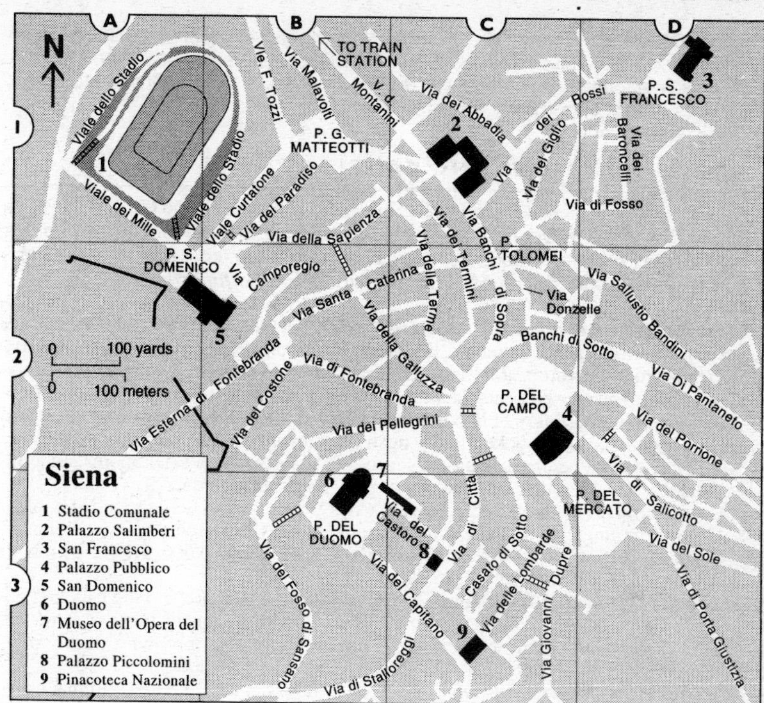

01 15) open Tues.-Sat. in summer 8:30am-7pm; in winter 8:30am-1:30pm and 2:30-4:40pm. **Luggage Storage:** L5000 for 12hr. Open 24hr.

Buses: TRA-IN/SITA, P. San Domenico, 1 (tel. 20 42 45). Service to all of Tuscany, including Florence (express bus, every hr., L10,500), San Gimignano (every hr., change at Poggibonsi, L7900), Volterra (4 per day, L7300), Montepulciano (3 per day, L8000), Pienza (7 per day, L5400), Arezzo (5 per day, L7500), and Montalcino (6 per day, L5300). Open daily 5:50am-8:15pm.

Car Rental: Hertz and **Intercar,** Via S. Marco, 96 (tel. 411 48). You must have a driver's license. Fiat Panda L150,000 per day; L400 extra for every km over 200. Vespas L80,000 per day. Min. age 21. Open daily 8:30am-1pm and 3-7:30pm.

Taxis: Stands in P. Matteotti (tel. 28 93 50) and P. Stazione (tel. 445 04). **Radio-Taxi:** tel. 492 22.

Lost and Found: Office in **Comune di Siena,** Casato di Sotto, 23. Open Mon.-Sat. 9am-12:30pm.

Bookstore: Messagerie Bassi, Via di Città, 6/8 (tel. 28 92 31). Excellent selection of books in English at reasonable prices. Open Mon.-Fri. 9am-8pm, Sat. 9am-1pm and 4-8pm. **Libreria Senese,** Via di Città, 62/66 (tel. 28 08 45). Open Mon.-Sat. 9am-8pm. Both take V, MC, AmEx.

Laundromat: Onda Blu, Casato di Sotto, 17 (toll-free tel. (167) 86 13 46). Wash and dry L12,000 per 6.5kg. Open daily 8am-10pm. Last wash 9pm.

Public Toilets: Via Beccharia (L1000; open daily 9am-7:30pm). P. San Domenico (L1000; open 7:30am-7pm). Via del Sole (L1000; open 10am-6pm). Inside the *duomo* (L500).

Pharmacy: Farmacia del Campo, P. del Campo, 26. Open daily in summer 9am-1pm and 4-8pm; in winter 9am-1pm and 3:30-7:30pm. Bulletin board outside lists the pharmacy open nights during that week.

Emergencies: tel. 113. **Ambulance: Misericordia,** Via del Porrione, 49 (tel. 28 00 28). **Hospital:** P. del Duomo, 1 (tel. 29 01 11).

Police: Questura (tel. 112), Via del Castoro near the *duomo.*

Post Office: P. Matteotti, 36. *Fermo posta* at window #12 (L300). **Exchanges currency** (L1000) and **traveler's checks** (L2000 for sums up to L100,000, L5000 for greater amounts). Open Mon.-Fri. 8:15am-7pm, Sat. 8:15am-12:30pm. Money services close at 6pm. **Postal Code:** 53100.

Telephone Code: 0577.

ACCOMMODATIONS AND CAMPING

Finding a room in Siena is usually easy, but rooms become scarce late June through August. Try to call as far ahead as possible; book months ahead for either *Palio*. For stays of a week or more, rooms in private homes are an attractive option, with singles for L40,000-L70,000. The tourist office has a list of these *affitta camere*.

Ostello della Gioventù "Guidoriccio" (HI), Via Fiorentina, 89 (tel. 522 12; fax 561 72), in Località Lo Stellino, a 20-min. bus ride from the *centro*. Take bus #15 across from the station at P. Gramsci. If coming from Florence by bus, get off at the stop after you see the large black-and-white sign announcing entry into Siena. Considering the availability of inexpensive rooms in the *centro* and the extra cost and inconvenience of bus tickets to the hostel, you might try searching for a spot inside the city's walls before making the journey. 110 beds. Some small rooms are available. Curfew 11:30pm. L20,000 per person. Breakfast included.

Alma Domus, Via Camporegio, 37 (tel. 441 77; fax 476 01), behind San Domenico. Enjoy stunning views of the *duomo* from spotless and secure rooms. Opens at 7:30am. Curfew 11:30pm. Doubles L60,000, with bath L80,000. Triples with bath L100,000. Quads with bath L125,000.

Locanda Garibaldi, Via Giovanni Dupré, 18 (tel. 28 42 04), behind the Palazzo Pubblico and P. del Campo. A homey establishment with an equally home-style restaurant downstairs. Whitewashed walls and ceilings are ribbed with dark wood. Doubles L75,000. Triples L90,000. Curfew midnight. Fills early.

Piccolo Hotel Etruria, Via Donzelle, 3 (tel. 28 80 88; fax 28 84 61). Immaculate, modern rooms, all with bright floral bedspreads, TVs, and phones. Curfew 12:30am. Singles L52,000, with bath L62,000. Doubles with bath L95,000. Triples with bath L129,000. Quads L162,000. Good breakfast L6000. Outdoor parking L10,000, indoor parking L15,000. V, MC, AmEx.

Albergo Tre Donzelle, Via Donzelle, 5 (tel. 28 03 58). Just 1 door up from the Etruria. Airy rooms with speckled tiles. English spoken. Curfew 12:30am. Singles L38,000. Doubles L62,000, with bath L78,000. Triples L84,000, with bath L105,000. Quad with bath L132,000.

Albergo La Perla, Via delle Terme, 25 (tel. 471 44), on P. dell'Indipendenza off Via Banchi di Sopra. Two floors of nondescript rooms, all with tiny bathrooms. The walls are scuffed, but pictures of the *Palio* help distract the eye. Singles L55,000. Doubles L85,000. Triples L115,000.

Albergo Cannon d'Oro, Via Montanini, 28 (tel. 443 21), near P. Matteotti. A 2-star place with tastefully decorated rooms and lovely views of gardens and hills. Singles L80,000. Doubles L100,000. Triples L135,000. Quads L160,000. Breakfast L7000-L8000. Wheelchair accessible.

Camping: Colleverde, Strada di Scacciapensieri, 47 (tel. 28 00 44). Take bus #8 or 12 from P. Gramsci. L13,000 per adult (car and tent or camper included), L5500 per child. Pool L3000, children L1500. Open mid-March to mid-Nov.

FOOD

Siena specializes in rich pastries. The most famous is *panforte,* a dense concoction of honey, almonds, and citron. For a lighter snack try *ricciarelli,* soft almond cookies with powdered vanilla on top. Both are technically Christmas sweets, but you can sample either one year-round at the **Bar/Pasticceria Nannini,** the oldest *pasticceria* in Siena, with branches at Via Banchi di Sopra, 22-24, and throughout town. **Enoteca Italiana,** in the Fortezza Medicea near the entrance off Via Cesare Maccari, sells the finest of the regional wines in Italy, from Brunello to Barolo, Asti Spumante to Vernaccia, at the lowest prices around. You can sample for only L2800 per glass. Open daily noon-1am. Siena's **open-air market** fills P. La Lizza each Wednesday (8am-1pm). Shoestringers can pick up supplies at the **Consortio Agrario** supermarket, Via Pianigiani, 5, off P. Salimberi. Open Mon.-Fri. 7:45am-1pm and 4:30-8pm, Sat. 7:45am-1pm. **COOP** is close to the train station (take bus #1). Open Mon.-Tues. and Thurs.-Fri. 8:30am-1pm and 4-7pm, Wed. and Sat. 8:30am-1pm. Alternatively, on the way to the *duomo* stop by the **Simpatica/Crai** supermarket at Via di Città. Open Mon.-Sat. 7:30am-1:30pm and 5-8pm.

Ristorante Guidoriccio, Via Dupré, 2 (tel. 443 50), right off Il Campo. A pleasant atmosphere, with vaulted ceilings and intimate lighting. Try the *tagliatelle* with asparagus cream sauce (L8000), and, for seconds, the *coniglio ai pignoli* (rabbit with pinenuts, L12,000). A/C. *Menù* L21,000. Cover L3000. Open Mon.-Sat. noon-2:30pm and 7:30-10pm. V, MC, AmEx.

Osteria San Martino, Via Porrione, 31. Delicious Tuscan dishes served on outside tables or in a 2nd-floor dining room. Sample the *spaghetti crudo* (topped with fresh tomato, basil, mozzarella, and olive oil) for L9000. *Antipasti* L4000. *Primi* L7000-9000, *secondi* L10,000. Cover L2000. Service 10%. Open Mon.-Sat. noon-3:30pm and 7-10:30pm.

Osteria Le Logge, Via Porrione, 33 (tel. 480 13), off P. del Campo. Reputedly one of Siena's very best, this charming wood- and marble-filled restaurant serves up such specialties as *malfatti all'osteria* (spinach and ricotta in egg pasta, coated with meat sauce and baked, L10,000) and *farraona farcita* (stuffed pheasant, L20,000). *Primi* L10,000-L15,000, *secondi* from L19,000. Cover L2000. Service 10%. Open Mon.-Sat. noon-3pm and 7-10:30pm. Very popular. V, MC.

Bibo, Via Banchi di Sotto, 61-63. Come for generous sandwiches (L3500) and beer (L2500). Homemade *gelato* from L2000. Open Tues.-Sun. 7:30pm-1am.

SIGHTS

Siena offers a *biglietto cumulativo,* a combined ticket that allows entry into four of its most important monuments and museums—the baptistery, the Piccolomini library, the Museo de l'Opera del Duomo, and the Oratory of St. Bernadino (L8500).

Il Campo

Where other Italian towns center on their respective *duomi,* Siena radiates from the **Piazza del Campo,** the shell-shaped brick square designed expressly for civic events. The paving stones of the *piazza* are allegedly divided into nine sections representing the city's medieval "Government of Nine" (though many observers count 11). The *campo* has always been the town's center stage. Dante described the real-life drama of Provenzan Salvani, the heroic Sienese *condottiere* who panhandled around Il Campo in order to ransom a friend. Later, Sienese mystics like San Bernadino used the *piazza* as a natural auditorium. These days the *piazza* has the dubious honor of entertaining local teenagers, wide-eyed tourists, and souvenir carts. Twice each summer, however, *Palio* reduces Il Campo to splendid mayhem as horses race around its outer edge.

At the highest point in Il Campo's central axis, you'll find the **Fonte Gaia,** a pool surrounded by reproductions of native son Jacopo della Quercia's famous carvings (1408-1419; the originals are in the Museo Civico). The water here courses through the same 25km aqueduct that has refreshed Siena since the 14th century. Closing the bottom of the shell is the **Palazzo Pubblico,** a graceful Gothic palace. (Open March-Oct. Mon.-Sat. 9am-6:15pm, Sun. 9am-12:45pm; Nov.-Feb. daily 9am-12:45pm. Admission L6000, students with school ID L5000.) A gluttonous bell-ringer nicknamed "Mangiaguadagni" (literally, "eat the profits") bestowed his moniker on the **Torre del Mangia,** the clock tower that rises like a scepter to the left. Siena's Council of Nine commissioned a tower whose prominence would overshadow any other skyscraper the nobility or clergy could erect; a pair of Perugian architects gave them the second-tallest (102m; Cremona has the tallest) structure raised in medieval Italy with, surprisingly, no subterranean foundations. (Open daily March and Nov.-Dec. 10am-4pm; April and Oct. 10am-5pm; May and Sept. 10am-6pm; July-Aug. 9:30am-7:30pm.

Admission L5000.) In front of the *palazzo* is the **Cappella di Piazza,** built in 1348 at the end of a Black Death epidemic that decimated the population. Siena took 100 years to complete the Cappella; you can trace the transition from Gothic to Renaissance architecture as pointed arches give way to gracefully rounded ones halfway up the walls.

The Museo Civico

The Palazzo Pubblico holds masterpieces of Sienese art in its **Museo Civico.** While the museum's collection ranges from medieval triptychs to 18th-century landscapes and tributes to 19th-century generals, its treasure is its extensive collection of Sienese art. The **Sala del Mappamondo** and the **Sala della Pace,** in particular, contain stellar pieces of Sienese artwork. In the first, named for a lost series of astronomical frescoes, lies Simone Martini's *Maestà* (Enthroned Virgin) and *Guidoriccio da Fogliano.* These two frescoes, facing each other across the vast room, illustrate the contradictions of Siena's medieval government. On the one hand, Siena looked to the Virgin, the town's patron saint, for guidance and legitimacy; on the other hand, it hired mercenary soldiers (*condottieri*) like Guidoriccio to wreak havoc on its enemies. In the next room, the Sala della Pace, lie Pietro and Ambrogio Lorenzetti's famous frescoes of the **Allegories of Good and Bad Government and their Effects on Town and Country.** On the right side, Good Government creates utopia: people dance in the streets, artisans toil happily, and contented farmers labor on vast stretches of fertile land that unfold to the horizon. On the left side, the Pride, Wrath, and Avarice of Bad Government wield their evil power: a gloomy, desolate landscape nurtures only thieves, sinners, devils, and sundry lost souls. The frescoes, in what was once the deliberating chamber of the Council of Nine, might well have shamed the Sienese government into civic decency, but that rule came to an end shortly after the Lorenzettis completed the frescoes. The Allegory of Good Government is remarkably well-preserved, while the Allegory of Bad Government is flaking its way into oblivion—read into this fact what you will. Upstairs on the **Loggia dei Nove,** you'll find the original della Quercia sculptures from the Fonte Gaia, now sadly decrepit. Step into the next room to witness Matteo di Giovanni's particularly ghastly rendition of the *Slaughter of the Innocents.* Head back downstairs to the entrance, cross the courtyard, and climb the tower's 300-odd narrow steps to find a spectacular view of the *duomo* and the entire city. (Museum open March-Oct. Mon.-Sat. 9am-6:15pm, Sun. 9am-12:45pm; Nov.-Feb. daily 9am-12:45pm. Admission L6000, students with school ID L5000.)

Il Duomo

The city's zebra-striped **duomo** perches atop one of its three hills. Its construction spanned two architectural eras, evidenced by the juxtaposition of Gothic pinnacles and Romanesque arches. Civic pride demanded both enormous scale and prominent position, but the limited size of the hill posed a design problem. The apse would have hung in mid-air over the edge of the hill had the Sienese not built the **baptistery** below for support. Although the baptistery is obscurely located and poorly lit, rewards await those who visit. First, the delicate and intricate frescoes that decorate all the walls of the baptistery are fine examples of Sienese artistry. Second, the elegant **baptismal font** (1417-30) boasts artwork by some of the Renaissance's greatest masters. Compare the bronze panels that decorate the lower part of the font, Ghiberti's *Baptism of Christ* to the adjacent *Herod's Feast* by his contemporary, Donatello. Ghiberti's Gothic panel is a supremely crafted celebration of tactile pleasures, while Donatello's Renaissance work is a more reserved, intellectual study of perspective and movement. Other panels are by della Quercia (*Birth of John the Baptist*), and the six bronze angels are by Donatello. (Open mid-March to Sept. 9am-7:30pm; Oct. to mid-March 9am-1pm. Admission L3000.)

Climb the stairs to the left of the baptistery to reach the P. del Duomo. On the way you'll pass through a huge arch that's part of a striped wall, the sole remnant of Siena's early 14th-century plan to construct the largest cathedral in the world.

Though pesky epidemics and its wimpy hill soon humbled the city's lofty ambitions, the existing cathedral is still one of Italy's finest. The genius of its design and the intricacy of its detail are remarkable. Elegant statues of philosophers, sibyls, and prophets, all by Giovanni Pisano, give way to impressive spires that pierce the sky.

If you're overwhelmed upon entering and not quite sure where to direct your attention, simply look down; the floor, whose inlaid **pavement** is mostly covered in a rotating cycle to help preserve the marble masterpieces, depicts a variety of intriguing themes like "Alchemy" and "The Massacre of the Innocents." The ideal time to visit is August 15 through September 15, when the best works, by the Marchese d'Adamo, are visible. To the right of the altar, pause at the Chapel of Madonna del Voto, which holds an icon of the Madonna and child resting on a gilded altarpiece. The Sienese sometimes move the well-loved icon into the cathedral for better viewing. Halfway up the left aisle you'll find the **Piccolomini altar,** a complete architectural structure designed by Andrea Bregno in 1503. At the bottom on either side are statues of St. Peter and St. Paul, two oft-forgotten works executed by Michelangelo during the same years as his *David.* A bit farther down this aisle is the lavish **Libreria Piccolomini,** commissioned by Pope Pius III to house the elaborately illustrated books of his uncle Pius II, whose collection still lines the walls. The library also contains the Roman statue *The Three Graces,* some 15th-century illuminated lyrical scores, and a vibrant 360° fresco. (Library open mid-March to Oct. 9am-7:30pm, Nov. to mid-March 10am-1pm and 2:30-5pm. Admission L2000.) The cathedral's **pulpit** is one of Andrea Pisano's best, with allegorical and Biblical reliefs wrapping around the barrel. (*Duomo* open mid-March to Oct. 7:30am-7:30pm, Nov. to mid-March 7:30am-1:30pm and 2:30-5pm. No tank tops, shorts, or mini-skirts.)

The **Museo dell'Opera Metropolitana** (cathedral museum), located beneath the arches of P. Jacopo della Quercia, which adjoins P. del Duomo, houses all the extra art that formerly graced the cathedral. The first floor contains some of the foremost Gothic statuary in Italy, all by Giovanni Pisano. Upstairs is the *Maestà,* by Duccio di Buoninsegna, originally the screen of the cathedral's altar. To enjoy the museum's greatest find, drag yourself away from the brilliant paintings and statues. At the top of the second flight of stairs, cross the room to the right, and take a flight of stairs leading down to another set of steps. There you can climb the tower for a stunning **view of Siena and Tuscany.** Climb an even smaller staircase at the end of the terrace for an even better view. (Open mid-March to early Nov. 9am-7:30pm, Nov. to mid-March 9am-1:30pm. Admission L5000.)

Around the City

Siena's **Pinacoteca Nazionale,** in the Palazzo Buonsignori down the street from the cathedral museum at Via San Pietro, 29, features works by every major artist of the highly stylized Sienese school: the seven magnificent followers of Onccio, Simone Martini, the Lorenzetti brothers, Bartolo di Fredi, Sano di Pietro, Il Sodoma, and many others. (Open Tues.-Sat. 8:30am-1:30pm. Admission L8000.)

The **Sanctuary of Santa Caterina** on Via del Tiratoio honors the most renowned daughter of Siena, a simple girl who had a vision in which she became the bride of Christ. She went on to influence popes, found a religious order, and become patron saint of Italy under Pope Pius XII in 1939. The building offers a pleasant sojourn among roses and geraniums. (Open daily 9am-12:30pm and 3:30-6pm.)

As in other Italian towns, the Franciscans and the Dominicans have set up rival *basiliche* at opposite ends of town. The **Church of San Domenico** contains Andrea Vanni's portrait of St. Catherine and dramatic frescoes by Il Sodoma (1477-1549). The *cappella* also contains the requisite relic, this one the preserved head of Catherine herself. (Church open daily 8:30am-1pm and 4-7pm.) The **Church of San Francesco** houses two mournful frescoes by Pietro and Ambrogio Lorenzetti. The huge, stark space offers a sharp contrast to the *duomo.* (Open daily 9am-1pm and 4-7pm.) The adjacent **Oratory of San Bernardino** contains several more works by Il Sodoma. (Open in summer only, the same hours as the church. Admission L2000.)

The *Palio*-obsessed may enjoy Siena's *contrade* museums. Each neighborhood organization maintains its own collection of costumes, artifacts, banners, and icons. Most require an appointment—check at the tourist office for information.

ENTERTAINMENT

The Accademia Chigiana (tel. 461 52) sponsors an excellent music festival, the **Settimana Musicale Senese,** Siena's Musical Week (late July). Siena also hosts a **jazz festival** in July, which features internationally known bopsters. For information, call 27 14 01. During the summer evenings, everyone congregates in the *campo* after a long *passeggiata* along Via Banchi de Sopra; look out for the festivals sponsored by individual *contrade* or the wide range of concerts in P. del Campo. Check the posters or the tourist office for details.

Palio di Siena

Siena's Palio takes place on July 2 and August 16. As the bare-backed horse race approaches, Siena's emotional temperature steadily rises. Ten of the 17 *contrade* (chosen by lot—there's limited space in Il Campo) make elaborate traditional preparations. Young partisans sporting the colors of their *contrada* chant in packs on the street; each *contrada* has its own (often obscene) lyrics to the same melody. Five trial races take place over the three days leading up to the race, and a final trial runs the same morning. On the eve of the race everyone revels until 3am or so, strutting and chanting around the city, pausing only to eat and drink. Just before the race, each horse walks into the church of its respective *contrada* for baptism. A two-hour parade of heralds and flag-bearers prefaces anarchy with regal pomp—the last piece in the procession is the *palio* itself, a banner depicting the Madonna and Child, drawn in a cart by white oxen. The race begins at 7pm, and it takes the jockeys about 70 seconds to tear three times around Il Campo. Officials pad the buildings of the *piazza* with mattresses, for many a rider has careened off the track. During the race, jockeys have free rein in every sense. According to the age-old, almost barbaric set of rules that guides the event, they are allowed (and even encouraged) to whip their opponents. And the straps they use are no ordinary pieces of leather; they are made

CENTRAL ITALY

And the Contestants Are...

The Contrada	The Mascot	The Colors
Aquila	two-headed eagle	yellow, black, lt. blue
Bruco	silkworm	yellow, green, navy
Chiocciola	snail	red, yellow, lt. blue
Civetta	owl	burgundy, black, white
Drago	dragon	lt. green, yellow, magenta
Giraffa	giraffe	red, white
Istrice	porcupine	white, red, black, navy
Leocorno	unicorn	lt. blue, orange, white
Lupa	she-wolf	black, orange, white
Montone	ram	yellow, red, white
Nicchio	shell	navy, yellow, red
Oca	goose	green, white, red
Onda (Wave)	dolphin	white, lt. blue
Pantera	panther	red, navy, white
Selva (Forest)	rhinoceros	green, orange, white
Tartuca	turtle	blue, yellow
Torre (Tower)	elephant	burgundy, blue, yellow

The winner in August of 1996 was Bruco, the *nonna* (the *contrada* to have won least recently), breaking their 40-year dry spell. The new *nonna* is *Torre.*

from the skin of a bull penis, especially durable and said to leave deeper welts. So bring the family and come on out.

To stay in Siena during the *Palio,* book rooms at least four months in advance—especially for budget accommodations. Write the APT in March or April for a list of individuals and companies that rent rooms or to reserve a seat in the stands. You can stand in the "infield" of the *piazza* for free, but stake out a spot early in the day. For the full scoop on *Il Palio,* ask at the tourist office and pick up their excellent program (available in English). The less-touristed *La Tratta* (the choosing of the horses) takes place on June 29 and August 13 at 10am.

■ Near Siena

SAN GALGANO

Only slightly removed from a winding country pass between Siena and Massa Marittima, the ruined 13th-century **Cistercian abbey** of San Galgano was once one of the richest and most powerful in Tuscany. Its monks served as treasurers and judges for the communes of Siena and Volterra, helped construct the duomo in Siena, and went on to become bishops and even saints. Their vast fortune permitted the monks to construct an abbey of noble proportions, but by the mid-16th century, widespread corruption had spelled the church's decline. Its very dilapidation makes San Galgano an unforgettable sight. Nature has been kind to the massive old building, the foremost specimen of Cistercian Gothic architecture in Italy: it has removed the roof completely without harming the majestic columns within. Gothic windows and rosettes frame Tuscan landscapes, and tiny birds chirp from its corners. To reach San Galgano, take the TRA-IN **bus** that runs between Siena and Massa Marittima, and get off at the San Galgano stop. One bus leaves daily from Siena at 3:50pm and returns from Massa Marittima at 6pm (L8000).

MONTALCINO

Montalcino has changed little since medieval times when it was a Sienese stronghold. With few historic monuments, Montalcino has concentrated on looking quaint and making the heavenly *brunello di Montalcino,* a smooth, full-bodied wine widely acknowledged as Italy's finest red. Take one of the **TRA-IN** buses that make the trip daily from Siena to Montalcino (1hr., L5300). If coming from Pienza (1hr., L5200) or Montepulciano (1¼hr., L6600), change buses at Torrenieri. Four buses per day meet departing buses in Torrenieri.

With its nearly impregnable walls, Montalcino sheltered a band of republicans escaping from the Florentine siege of Siena in 1555. These city walls still stand, along with the remains of the town's original 19 fortified towers. Montalcino's **fortezza** (fortress) watches over the southeast corner of town. Two courtyards beckon inside the fortress, one sunny and cheered by tiger lilies, the other sylvan and shaded by foliage. You can explore the 14th-century walls, chambers, and turrets, which offer a stunning view of the exquisite landscape. Open July 15-Sept. 15 daily 9am-1pm and 2:30-8pm; Sept. 16-July 14 Tues.-Sat. 9am-1pm and 2-6pm. Admission to ramparts L3500, inside fortress free. On the way down, stop at the small *enoteca* in the *fortezza's* cavernous main room; try the tasty sandwiches (L2500-L5000) as you sample the local wines and liquors (L2500-L4000 per glass; a glass of the famed *brunello* will cost you L6000).

Contact the **tourist office,** Costa del Municipio, 8 (tel./fax 84 93 21), for information about guided tours of the local vineyards. Office open Tues.-Sun. 10am-1pm and 3-7pm. Rooms are expensive and scarce in Montalcino; try to find a bed in a private home. The tourist office can help find lodging and **exchange currency** so you can pay for it. You might also try **Affitacamere Casali,** Via Spagni, 3 (tel. 84 82 29 or 84 71 50), which rents adequate doubles (L60,000) and triples (L81,000), all with bath. More refined, the **Albergo Il Giardino,** Via Cavour, 4 (tel. 84 82 57) has modern, tasteful doubles for L70,000, with bath L85,000. The cozy lounge has leather couches, a stone fireplace, and the friendly proprietor's collection of the finest Italian wines bottled since 1950. You'll find the best deals on *brunello* at the **COOP** supermarket on Via Sant'Agostino, off P. del Popolo. Open Mon.-Sat. 8am-1pm and 5-8pm; closed Wed. evenings. The **telephone code** for Montalcino is 0577.

To fully appreciate the local vineyards, head 5km down the road to the **Fattoria dei Barbi** in Sant'Antimo (tel. 84 82 77). You can also visit the **Azienda Agricola Greppo,** which produced the first *brunello* in 1888 and lies 3km away from Montalcino on the road to Sant'Antimo. Call before heading out to arrange a tour of the cellars (tel. 84 80 87). To sample some of the exotic **honey products** made in Montalcino, buzz over to **Apicoltura Ciacci** on Via Ricasoli, 26, up the street from the Church of S. Agostino, where you'll discover every honey product imaginable: honey soap, honey biscuits, honey milk, honey candies, and even honey *grappa*. Open daily; just ring the bell if the shop is closed, honey. The superb *trattoria* **Il Moro,** Via Mazzini, 46 (tel. 84 93 84), is itself reason enough to visit Montalcino. Sample the local catch of *cinghiale* (wild boar) with *pappardelle* (broad, homemade ribbons of pasta) for L14,000, or the mixed grill for L10,000. Open Fri.-Wed. noon-2:30pm and 7:30-10:30pm. There's a **market** brimming with picnic fare every Friday 7:30am-1pm, on Viale della Libertà.

In June, the old town comes alive for a *teatro* festival. Contact the **Ufficio di Teatro** (tel. 84 92 23 or 84 93 17) for information and tickets (about L15,000). The museum-starved might trek out 18km to the Castello di Poggio alle Mura to enjoy the **Museo del Vetro (Museum of Glass).** Luminescent works of antique glass accompany displays detailing the production process. Open daily 10am-1pm and 2-6pm. Admission L3000. If you don't have a car and aren't particularly intrigued by masochism, you might want to **rent a bike** or **moped** (L20,000 and L40,000 per day, respectively) on Viale Pietro Strozzi (tel. 84 82 82). Montalcino's most inspiring sight lies 9km away down a serpentine country road. Built in the 12th century on the remains of an 8th-century church allegedly founded by Charlemagne, the well-touristed **Abbazia di Sant'Antimo** (tel. 83 56 69) rates as one of Tuscany's most beautiful Romanesque churches, with a rounded apse and individually carved alabaster capitals. Inside, monks still give mass in Gregorian chant. Open Mon.-Sat. 10am-12:30pm and 3-6pm, Sun. 9-10:30am and 3-6pm. Buses leave Mon.-Sat. at 6, 7am, 1:40, and 4:35pm. Returning buses leave the abbey at 7:45am, 2:25, and 6:45pm. No Sun. bus service. Tickets L1800.

Montepulciano

This small medieval town, stretched along the crest of a hill, is one of the finest locations in Italy for enjoying the beautiful countryside and exquisite wine. Its smooth, garnet-colored *vino nobile* has earned the town notoriety, but the landscape and museums alone make Montepulciano an excellent daytrip from Siena.

ORIENTATION AND PRACTICAL INFORMATION

Buses drop you at the bottom of the hill outside the town. From there it's a short, steep climb to reach the **Corso,** the town's main street. Orange ATAF **buses** make the trip easier (L1100). Divided nominally into four parts (Via di Gracciano nel Corso, Via di Voltaia nel Corso, Via dell'Opio nel Corso, and Via del Poliziano), the Corso winds languorously up a precipitous hill. When you reach the end, and the street starts to level off, you'll see another calf-killing incline on your right. Climb that and rest your legs in **Piazza Grande,** the main square.

Tourist Office: Via Ricci, 9 (tel. 75 86 87), off P. Grande. Pick up the helpful booklet *Montepulciano—Perla del Cinquecento,* in English and French, which includes a list of *affitta camere*. Check before you trek, however, as such information is subject to change. Open Tues.-Sun. 9am-noon and 3-6pm.

Currency Exchange: Banca Toscana, P. Michelozzo, 2. Open Mon.-Fri. 8:20am-1:20pm and 2:45-3:45pm.

Trains: Hourly trains to Chiusi make Montepulciano a convenient stopover on the Florence-Rome line; take the bus from there (45min., L4200).

Buses: TRA-IN buses run to Montepulciano from Siena, Florence, Pienza, and Chiusi. Montepulciano is an easy trip from Siena (Mon.-Sat. 3 per day, 2hr., L8000; change at Buonconvento). Service is very limited on Sundays, so plan accordingly.

Taxis: tel. (0330) 73 27 23.

Bike Rental: A. S. Cicloposse, Via dell'Opio nel Corso, 16 (tel. 71 63 92). L7000 per hr., L30,000 per day. Free delivery.

Pharmacy: Farmacia Franceschi, Via di Voltaia nel Corso, 47 (tel. 75 73 24). Open Mon.-Sat. Oct.-May 9am-1pm and 4-7pm; April-Sept. 9am-1pm and 4:30-7:30pm. **Farmacia Sorbini,** Viale Calamandrei (tel. 75 73 52), has someone available at night to fill urgent prescriptions.

Emergencies: tel. 113.

Police: P. Savonarola, 16 (tel. 112).

Post Office: Via dell'Erbe, 12, off the Corso. You can **exchange currency** (L1000 commission) and **traveler's checks** (L2000 for sums up to L100,000, L5000 for more). Open Mon.-Fri. 8:15am-7pm, Sat. 8:15am-12:30pm. **Postal Code:** 53045.

Telephone Code: 0578.

ACCOMMODATIONS

Affitta Camere Bella Vista, Via Ricci, 25 (tel. 75 73 48), down the hill from the tourist office, rents small but adequate rooms; some have fantastic views of the countryside. Doubles with bath L55,000-L65,000. Call before you head up there.

Albergo La Terazza, Via Piè al Sasso, 16 (tel./fax 75 74 40), off the Corso. Antique-filled rooms marshalled by a friendly, gregarious proprietor who serves breakfast in a garden downstairs. Watch the Montepulcian sunset from the flower-bedecked terrace. Doubles L70,000, with bath L85,000. Mini-apartments with fully equipped kitchens: doubles L90,000, quads L160,000.

Ristorante Cittino, Vicolo della via Nuova, 2 (tel. 75 73 35), off Via di Voltaia nel Corso. Clean and homey with the smell of Mom's cooking wafting up from the kitchen downstairs. Each of their 3 doubles (L55,000) may also serve as a triple. The popular restaurant serves superb home-cooked food. Full meals around L25,000. Open July to mid-June. Restaurant and hotel closed Wed., but you can check in Wed. night if you call ahead.

FOOD

Montepulciano offers a smorgasbord of excellent, affordable restaurants. Ristorante Cittino is one of the best deals (see above). There are minimarkets all along the Corso (try **Eurospar** at #46; open Thurs.-Tues. 7:30am-1pm and 5-8pm) and a larger **Conad** supermarket in P. Savonarola at the bottom of the Corso. Open Mon.-Sat. 8:30am-8pm; closed Wed. afternoon. Thursdays bring an **open-air market** to P. Sant'Agnese, 8am-1pm.

Osteria dell'Acquaccheta, Via del Teatro, 24 (tel. 75 84 43), off the Corso as you head further up the hill. Run by a group of friends. Simple, tasty dishes and great wine. Generous serving of *bruschetta,* made with the greenest olive oil you've ever seen, L4000. Salads L4500-L7000. *Primi* L6000-L8000. Open Tues.-Sun. 12:30-3pm and 9:30pm-1am.

Trattoria Diva e Maceo, Via Gracciano nel Corso, 92 (tel. 71 69 51). Where locals go to socialize over *cannelloni* stuffed with ricotta and spinach or a divine *ossobuco.* Open Wed.-Mon. noon-4pm and 7-11pm. Closed 1st 2 weeks in July.

Caffè Poliziano, Via del Voltaio nel Corso, 27 (tel. 75 86 15). This elegant café serves up elaborate 6-course meals for about L45,000; a different local wine complements each course. Offered Thurs.-Sat. evenings only.

SIGHTS AND ENTERTAINMENT

Montepulciano boasts an impressive assemblage of Renaissance and Baroque *palazzi* dating to the 16th and 17th centuries. Noteworthy are the *palazzi* lining the lowest

CENTRAL ITALY

quarter of the Corso, Via di Gracciano. On your right at #91 is **Palazzo Avignonesi** (1507-1575), attributed to Vignola. The elegant windows of the second floor contrast sharply with the bold protruding windows of the ground floor, marking different stages of construction. The lions' heads on either side of the door belong to the same pride as the lion on top of the **Marzocco Column,** in front of the *palazzo.* The lion, the heraldic symbol of Florence, replaced the she-wolf of Siena in this spot when Florence took the city in 1511. The original statue now rests in the Museo Civico. Farther up the street at #70 rises the asymmetrical façade of **Palazzo Cocconi,** attributed to Antonio da Sangallo the Elder (1455-1534). Cross the street to #73, **Palazzo Bucelli,** whose base showcases Roman and Etruscan reliefs, urn slabs, and inscriptions collected by the 18th-century proprietor, Pietro Bucelli.

The **Church of Sant'Agostino** dominates P. Michelozzo, farther up the street. The lower part of the façade demonstrates Michelozzo's masterful classicism, while the second level emulates the Gothic style. Just in front of the Church of Madonna di Fatima looms the **Torre di Pucinella,** constructed in 1524 of wood and metal plating. The punctual Pucinella gongs the bell on the hour, keeping time for the surrounding neighborhood. Back on the Corso, which becomes Via di Voltaia nel Corso at #21, stop at the U-shaped **Palazzo Cervini.** This *palazzo's* external courtyard is typical of country villas but rare in urban residences.

To reach **Piazza Grande** and the **duomo** at the top of the hill you can either meander around and up Il Corso or scale the steep alleys to the right. The unfinished *duomo,* the Palazzo Tarugi, the Palazzo Contucci, and the 14th-century Palazzo Comunale ring the *piazza.* The construction of the *duomo* began in the 16th century when the town council deemed the existing cathedral unworthy. Under the supervision of Spinello Benci, laborers and artisans toiled arduously to build a more grandiose house of worship. After several years, the finicky council became dissatisfied once again and entreated Ippolito Scalza, an architect from Orvieto, to assume control. The product of this painstaking process is an unaccountably stark *duomo* whose rustic, unfinished façade complements its sparse interior. However unpretentious, the *duomo* does house a poignant *Assumption of the Virgin* by Taddeo di Bartolo in a triptych above the altar; some people (the citizens of Montepulciano, surprisingly enough) consider this work the artist's masterpiece. (Open 9am-1pm and 3:30-7:30pm.) The elegant white façade of **Palazzo de' Nobili-Tarugi** faces the *duomo;* two arches on the bottom left access a deep-vaulted *loggia* that cuts through the entire corner of the building. The **Palazzo Contucci,** is a graceful, if eccentric, hybrid of architectural styles. The Contucci family has made fine wine within its walls for well over a century and today runs a charming *enoteca* on the ground floor. In the mid-1400s Michelozzo completed the austere **Palazzo Comunale,** a structure that took nearly a century to build. The *palazzo's* tower offers a view that ranges from Siena's towers in the north to the snow-capped Gran Sasso massif to the south. (Open Mon.-Sat. 8am-1pm. Admission to tower L2000.)

The Palazzo Neri-Orselli, Via Ricci, 10, houses the **Museo Civico,** one of Montepulciano's foremost attractions. The museum contains a collection of enameled terracotta by della Robbia, Etruscan cinerary urns, and over 200 paintings. (Open Wed.-Sat. 9:30am-1pm and 3-6pm; Sun. 9:30am-1pm. Admission L5000.) The **Church of San Biagio,** outside the town walls, is Sangallo's masterpiece. The steep 500m walk down the hill is well worth the effort. The church is a wonder of Renaissance architecture—well-balanced, adorned with graceful detail, and gleaming on an emerald green plot of grass overlooking the hills. (Open daily 9am-6pm.) The **Caffè Poliziano** (see above), offers some of the most stunning views in Montepulciano from its marble tables. This thoroughly art nouveau café hosts concerts and art exhibits in July and August and is always a wonderful place for a drink. Otherwise, the main form of entertainment for tourists in this town consists of traipsing from one **wine store** to the next. All of them offer free samples of the wines they sell, and many don't seem overly concerned with whether you're buying or not. Try the one at Porta di Bacco, on the left immediately after you enter the city gates. (Open daily 9am-8pm.)

Around August 15, the **Bruscello** (a series of amateur concerts and theatrical productions) takes place on the steps of the *duomo.* To buy tickets (around L20,000), contact the tourist office. Visit Montepulciano the last Sunday in August to see the raucous **Bravio** (Barrel Race), held to commemorate the eight neighborhood militias who fended off the Florentines and Sienese. Pairs of youths, dressed in costumes bearing their team markings, roll barrels up the steep incline of the Corso, exchanging insults and blows as they battle their way to the Piazza Grande.

Volterra

When you finally find Volterra, you'll think you've reached the edge of the world. Perched atop a huge bluff, the town broods over the surrounding checkerboard of green and yellow fields. Drawn by the cliffs' impregnability, the Etruscans established Velathri, which by the 4th century BC had become one of the most powerful cities of the Dodecapolis. Medieval Volterra shrank to one-third the size of its ancestor, leaving a still-palpable sense of decline and desolation. Its many alabaster workshops and its impressive Etruscan museum draw tourists, but it is the melancholy air that gives Volterra its ineffable appeal.

ORIENTATION AND PRACTICAL INFORMATION

Although geographically closer to San Gimignano and Siena, Volterra has an administrative link to Pisa, from which **APT** bus service is most frequent (3 per day, 2hr., change at Pontederra, L9400). There is a small train station 9km west of town at Saline di Volterra, with trains from Pisa (L7100) and the coastal line. APT buses are timed to meet departing trains from Saline to Volterra (5 per day, L2600). All buses arrive and depart from **Piazza della Libertà,** where you can buy tickets from the vending machine or in the bars down the street. From P. della Libertà, take the only street leading out of the *piazza;* turn left onto Via Ricciarelli and walk 40m to **Piazza dei Priori,** the town's historic and administrative center.

Tourist Office: Via Turazza, 2 (tel. 861 50), just before P. dei Priori. Provides tickets for and info on buses, trains, and accommodations. Some pamphlets about the city and environs. Open daily 9am-1pm and 2-7pm; in winter Sun. 10am-1pm.
Currency Exchange: Cassa di Risparmio di Firenze, Via Ricciarelli, 5, has a 24-hr. exchange machine outside.
Telephones: At the tourist office.
Train Information: tel. 441 16.
Buses: One **SITA** bus runs every weekday to and from Florence (2½hr., L11,300). Four daily **TRA-IN** buses connect the town to Florence (2hr., L11,300), Siena (2hr., L7300), and San Gimignano (2hr., L6500); all three routes require a change at Colle Val d'Elsa; San Gimignanoa requires a second change at Poggibonsi.
Public Baths and Toilets: Via delle Prigioni, 3, off P. dei Priori. Toilets L300. Showers L2000. Open Fri.-Wed. 8am-7pm.
Pharmacy: Farmacia Amidei, Via Ricciardelli, 2 (tel. 860 60). Open 9am-1pm and 4-8pm.
Emergencies: tel. 113. **Ambulance:** tel. 861 64. **Hospital:** P. San Giovanni (tel. 919 11).
Police: tel. 860 50.
Post Office: P. dei Priori, 14 (tel. 869 69). Open Mon.-Fri. 8:15am-7pm, Sat. 8:15am-12:30pm. **Postal Code:** 56048.
Telephone Code: 0588.

ACCOMMODATIONS AND CAMPING

Ask at the tourist office for a list of *affitta camere* (rooms in private houses); doubles generally start at around L60,000.

Youth Hostel (tel. 855 77), on Via Firenzuola. Exiting either P. della Libertà or P. dei Priori, turn onto Via Matteotti and right at Via Gramsci. Walk through P. XX Settembre and down Via Manzoni; Via Firenzuola is a small street on your left. A squeaky clean hostel whose small rooms offer terrific views of the valley. Reception open 24hr. Curfew 11:30pm. L18,000; no membership required. Sheets and showers included. Breakfast L4000. Lunch and dinner each L18,000.

Seminario Sant'Andrea (tel. 860 28), P. S. Andrea. Next door to the church, about a 5-min. walk after you exit the city from Porta A Marcoli. Quiet, private rooms off frescoed hallways, some with gorgeous views. L22,000 per person, L30,000 per person in rooms with bath.

Albergo Etruria, Via Matteotti, 32 (tel. 873 77). As you exit P. Libertà, take a right before P. dei Priori; the Etruria is a few blocks down. The best prices in town for a "real" hotel. Rooms are big and nicely decorated, and there's a garden lounge. Singles L55,000, with bath L80,000. Doubles L80,000, with bath L100,000. V.

Camping: Le Balze, Via Mandringa, 15 (tel. 878 80). Exit through the Porta San Francesco and bear right on Strada Provincial Pisana; Via Mandringa will veer off to the left. This attractive campground has a pool, bar, and small market, as well as a view over Le Balze. L8000 per person, L7000 per tent, L3000 per car. Showers included. Pool use L1000. Open March-late Oct. Reservations accepted.

FOOD

An excellent selection of Volterra's game dishes and local cheeses is available at any of the *alimentari* along Via Guarnacci or Via Gramsci. Sample *salsiccia di cinghiale* (wild boar sausage) and *pecorino* (sheep's milk) cheese. For a sweet snack, try *ossi di morto* (Bones of Death), a rock-hard local confection made of egg whites, sugar, hazelnuts, and a hint of lemon. Pick up groceries at the **Despar** market, Via Gramsci, 12. Open Mon.-Fri. 7:30am-1pm and 5-8pm, Sat. 7:30am-1pm. Do your bulk shopping at the **COOP** supermarket on Via delle Casine, near P. delle Colombaie outside the city walls. Open Mon.-Tues. and Thurs.-Sat. 8am-7:30pm, Wed. 8am-1pm.

L'Ombra della Sera, Via Gramsci, 70 (tel. 866 63), off P. XX Settembre. Wild boars' heads on the wall jealously watch diners as they feast on copious portions of homemade pasta. *Primi* L8500-L12,000, *secondi* L12,000-L25,000. Munch on the *coniglio alla contadina* (rabbit with tomatoes and vegetables). L20,000 *menù* includes *primo, secondo,* and *contorno.* Cover L2700. Service 10%. Open Tues.-Sun. noon-3pm and 7-10pm. V, MC, AmEx.

Pizzeria/Birreria Ombra della Sera, Via Guarnacci, 16. Same fixed-price *menù* as the restaurant above. Also serves up great pizza (L7000-L10,000). Open Tues.-Sun. noon-3pm and 7pm-midnight.

Il Pozzo degli Etruschi, Via dei Prigioni, 30. Hearty Tuscan fare served in a private garden. Try the *risotto e porcini* (with mushrooms, L9000) and the *cinghiale alla maremmane* (L14,000). *Primi* L3000-L18,000, *secondi* L6500-L20,000. Cover L2500. Service 10%. Open Sat.-Thurs. noon-3pm and 7-10pm. V, MC, AmEx.

SIGHTS AND ENTERTAINMENT

Volterra's **Fortezza Medicea,** an elegant remnant from the Florentine domination, is the first structure you'll see as you approach the town. Volterra revolves around **Piazza dei Priori,** a medieval center surrounded by sober, dignified *palazzi.* The **Palazzo dei Priori,** the oldest governmental palace in Tuscany (1208-1254), presides over the square. (Open Mon.-Sat. 9am-1pm and 3-6pm.) Across the *piazza* sits the **Palazzo Pretorio,** a series of 13th-century buildings and towers that today house the town's most important municipal offices.

Walk behind the Palazzo dei Priori and admire the **duomo's** haphazard construction. Initiated in Pisan-Romanesque style in the 1200s, desultory work continued for three centuries without reaching completion. Inside, on the left, the **oratory** houses a series of wooden statues depicting the life of Jesus from nativity to crucifixion. The chapel off the transept holds frescoes by Rosselli, including the brilliant *Mission per Damasco.* Over the main altar stands the huge, 12th-century polychrome-wood sculpture group *Deposition from the Cross,* above which is an intricate alabaster tabernacle by Mino da Fiesole. (*Duomo* open daily in summer 7am-7pm; in winter 7am-12:30pm and 2-6pm.)

Across the *piazza* down Via dell'Arco is the massive 3rd-century BC **Etruscan arch,** one of the city's oldest gates. The black lumps of stone on the outside were once sculpted human heads that symbolized either Etruscan gods or beheaded enemy prisoners. (Choose your favorite interpretation.) On the other side of P. dei Priori, on Via dei Sarti, the **Pinacoteca Comunale** occupies the **Palazzo Minucci-Solaini** (tel. 875 80), a graceful building with an arcaded courtyard. Inside, Taddeo di Bartolo's elegant *Madonna and Saints* altarpiece will shock anyone who has seen his gruesome *Last Judgement* in San Gimignano. Another surprise awaits in the last room on the first floor. In his frenetic *Deposition* (1520), Rosso Fiorentino appears to abandon High Renaissance conventions of order and restraint, but the green body of Christ is more likely a result of aging and poor restoration. Volterra's other major attraction is the **Museo Etrusco Guarnacci,** at Via Minzoni, 15 (tel. 863 47). It displays over 600 finely carved Etruscan funerary urns from the 8th and 7th centuries BC. A stylized figure representing the deceased tops each urn; below are dramatic bas-reliefs recreating various episodes from classical mythology. (Thankfully, the museum staff has grouped together scenes from a single story and provided English interpretations.) On the first floor, you can find the museum's most famous piece, the oddly elongated bronze figure dubbed *L'Ombra della Sera* (Shadow of the Evening). Unearthed by a farmer in the 19th century, the figure served as a fireplace poker until someone realized it was actually a masterpiece of Etruscan art. (Gallery and museum open daily 9am-7pm. Admission—includes *pinacoteca, museo,* and the sacred art museum near the *duomo*—L7000, students L5000.)

Take a left on Via Lunga le Mura del Mandorlo (before Porta Marcoli) for a spectacular view of the surprisingly intact **Teatro Romano** (free). Continue past the *teatro* to the **Church of San Francesco** on the edge of town. Inside, the **Cappella della Croce,** off the right aisle, encloses frescoes by Cenno Cenni that relate the story of the True Cross. (Open daily 7:30am-12:30pm and 2-7pm.)

Exit the city through the Porta San Francesco and walk for about 30min. to **Le Balze,** where you'll find Volterra's most spectacular natural sight. The elements have carved cliffs that tower majestically over the valley floor. These gullies have been growing over the millennia, swallowing churches in the Middle Ages and uncovering an Etruscan necropolis in the 18th century.

During the last two weeks of July, the city comes alive with **Volterra Teatro,** a series of concerts and theatrical productions. For information and tickets, call the Logge dei Priori (tel. 871 08). Tickets go for about L15,000.

San Gimignano

From the road approaching San Gimignano, the hilltop village looks like a collection of skyscrapers in some great, distant city. Only upon arrival do you see that the "skyscrapers" are actually the ancient crenelated towers of a tiny but perfectly preserved medieval town. The 14 towers, survivors of the original 72, recall a tumultuous period when warring families fought battles within the city walls, using their towers for grain storage during sieges. (The towers were also convenient for dumping boiling oil on passing enemies.) Exhausted by war, San Gimignano stagnated in poverty for six centuries. But its towered horizon lured postwar tourists, whose tastes and wallets resuscitated production of the golden *vernaccia* wine. With its hordes of daytrippers, an infestation of souvenir shops, and innumerable restaurants, San Gimignano today feels a bit like some Disneyland executive's idea of MedievalLand. An overnight stay, however, promises blissful tranquility.

ORIENTATION AND PRACTICAL INFORMATION

TRA-IN buses run every 1-2 hours to Florence and Siena and less frequently to Volterra. Change buses at Poggibonsi, also the nearest train station (20min., L2400). Buses arrive at Porta San Giovanni outside town. To get to the center, enter through the *porta* and go up the hill to **Piazza della Cisterna** and the adjoining **Piazza del Duomo.** The tourist office is in P. del Duomo, to the left of the church.

Tourist Office: Pro Loco, P. del Duomo, 1 (tel. 94 00 08). No accommodations service, but lists of hotels and rooms in private homes. Organizes tours in English, Fri. at 11am. (L15,000, children free; reserve a spot before 5pm Thurs.) Also **exchanges currency** and **traveler's checks** (at poor rates). English spoken. Open daily 9am-1pm and 3-7pm. **Siena Hotels Promotion,** Via S. Giovanni, 125 (tel./fax 94 08 09), on your right as you enter the city gates, reserves hotel rooms (L3000 commission). Open Mon.-Sat. 9:30am-1pm and 3:30-7pm.

Telephones: At the Pro Loco tourist office.

Buses: TRA-IN buses leave from P. Martiri outside Porta San Giovanni. Schedules and tickets available at **Caffè Combattente,** Via S. Giovanni, 124, to your left as you enter the city gates. Open Wed.-Mon. 8am-1am. You can also purchase tickets at any *tabacchi* in town. Change at Poggibonsi for Florence (1½hr., L9400); Siena (1hr., L7900); and Volterra (1½hr., L6500).

Pharmacy: Via San Matteo, 13 (tel. 94 20 29). All-night availability to fill urgent prescriptions. Open Mon.-Sat. 9am-1pm and 4:30-8pm.

Emergencies: tel. 112. **Ambulance: Misericordia,** tel. 94 02 63. **Hospital:** Via Folgore da San Gimignano (tel. 94 03 12).

Police: Carabinieri, P. Martiri (tel. 94 03 13).

Post Office: P. delle Erbe, 8, behind the *duomo.* Open Mon.-Fri. 8:15am-7pm, Sat. 8:15am-12:30pm. **Currency** and **traveler's check exchange** available Mon.-Fri. 8:15am-1:30pm, Sat. 8:15am-12:30pm. **Postal Code:** 53037.

Telephone Code: 0577.

ACCOMMODATIONS AND CAMPING

San Gimignano caters to wealthy tourists, pushing most accommodations well beyond budget range. The new **youth hostel,** however, has made overnight stays pleasantly affordable. **Affitta camere** provide another alternative to overpriced hotels, with singles for around L60,000, with bath L80,000. Get a list from either the tourist office or the **Associazione Strutture Extralberghiere,** P. della Cisterna, 6 (tel. 94 31 90; fax 94 12 64), which finds rooms for free. Open daily 9am-8pm.

Ostello di San Gimignano, P. Repubblica, 1 (tel. 94 19 91). Turn off Via San Matteo onto Via XX Settembre and follow the signs (5min. from P. del Duomo). Cross the wasteland that is its front yard to enter this refreshingly peaceful hostel. Ceramic tile floors and amazing views of the Tuscan countryside. Curfew 11:30pm. L19,000 per bed in one of the large rooms (8-10 bunks). L21,000 for a bed in a room of 2-4 beds. Sheets and breakfast included. Reception open 7-9am and 5-11:30pm.

Albergo/Ristorante Il Pino, Via S. Matteo, 102 (tel./fax 94 04 15). Rustic simplicity in a quiet quarter of town. Beamed ceilings and red plastic bed frames. Singles with bath L50,000; you may be able to get a single without bath for L40,000. Doubles L70,000, with bath L80,000. Breakfast L8000. Reservations recommended.

Camping: Il Boschetto, at Santa Lucia (tel. 94 03 52), 2½km downhill from Porta San Giovanni. Buses run from town (L1400), but it's not a bad hike. Bar and market on the premises. Office open 8am-1pm, 3-8pm, and 9-11pm. L7500 per person, L7000 per small tent. Hot showers included. Open April-Oct. 15.

FOOD

San Gimignano's specializes in boar and other wild game, but the town caters to less-daring palates with mainstream Tuscan fare at fairly high prices. Whether you're looking to save or simply to savor, try the **open-air market** in P. del Duomo Thursday morning. A small **market** sells cheap, filling sandwiches and take-out pasta, salads, and drinks at Via S. Matteo, 19. Open Mon.-Sat. 8am-1:30pm and 4-8pm. Purchase the famous *Vernaccia di San Gimignano,* a light white wine with a hint of sweetness from **La Buca,** Via San Giovanni, 16 (tel. 94 04 07)—look for the two stuffed boars. This cooperative also specializes in terrific sausages and meats, all made at its own farm. The boar sausage *al pignoli* is especially delicious (L3000 per *etto*), and the store plays a highly educational video that depicts all the stages of its production, from little piglet to luncheon meat. A new section allows you to watch as tiny grapes metamorphose into golden wine and mushy olives into virgin oil; try to contain yourself, please. Open in summer Mon.-Sat. 9am-9pm; in winter Mon.-Sat. 9:30am-1pm and 3-7:30pm; year-round Sun. 2-7:30pm.

La Stella, Via Matteo, 75 (tel. 94 04 44). Tasty and reasonably priced. *Gnocchi all'etrusca* (with tomatoes, cream, and cheese) L7000. *Menù* includes a *primo,* your choice of a hearty *bistecca di maiale* or a light *pollo arrosto,* potatoes, and dessert for L24,000. Open Thurs.-Tues. noon-2:30pm and 7-10pm. V, MC, AmEx.

Pizzeria Perucà, Via Capassi, 16 (tel. 94 31 36). Cozy, with vaulted ceilings and great food, hidden in an alley behind Via Matteo. You can sometimes find a *menù* for L22,000. Pizza L6500-L15,000. *Primi* L6000-L15,000, *secondi* L9000-L18,000. Cover L3000. Open Fri.-Wed. noon-2:30pm and 7-10:30pm. V, MC, AmEx.

Gelateria di "Piazza," P. della Cisterna, 4 (tel. 94 22 44). Probably the best gelato you'll lick in Italy. Their award-winning recipes call for only the freshest ingredients. A *vernaccia* sorbet rivals the wine itself in both taste and freshness. The rich *cioccolato* and creamy *dolce amaro* are simply orgasmic.

SIGHTS AND ENTERTAINMENT

Famous as the *Città delle Belle Torri* (City of the Beautiful Towers), San Gimignano has always appealed to artists. During the Renaissance, they came in droves, and the resulting collection of 14th- and 15th-century works pleasantly (or perhaps ironically) complements San Gimignano's asymmetric cityscape.

Tickets for the town's museums are available at several different rates. *Biglietto intero* refers to a full-priced adult ticket. *Biglietti ridotti* are discounted tickets, available to students under 18 and families with children between the ages of 6 and 18. Children under 7 are allowed *ingresso gratuito* (free entrance) to almost all the sights. The city rightly treats itself as a unified work of art—one ticket (*biglietto intero* L16,000, *biglietto ridotto* L12,000; available at any museum or tourist sight) allows entry to nearly all of San Gimignano's sights.

Via San Giovanni, the principal street, runs from the city gate to **Piazza della Cisterna.** The triangular *piazza,* surrounded by towers and *palazzi,* adjoins **Piazza del Duomo,** site of the impressive tower of the **Palazzo del Podestà.** To its left is the **Palazzo del Popolo,** riddled with tunnels and intricate *loggie.* (Open Tues.-Sun. 9am-7:30pm.) To the right of the *palazzo* rises its **Torre Grossa,** the highest tower in town and the only one you can ascend; it's well worth the climb. Beware—the huge bell rings every day at noon. (Open March-Oct. daily 9:30am-7:30pm; Nov.-Feb. Tues.-Sun. 9:30am-1:30pm and 2:30-4:30pm. *Biglietto intero* L8000, *biglietto ridotto* L6000.) On the left stand the twin towers of the Ardinghelli, truncated due to a zoning ordinance that prohibited structures higher than the Torre Grossa.

Within the Palazzo del Popolo, the frescoed medieval courtyard leads to the **Sala di Dante.** The poet spoke here in 1299 as the ambassador from Florence, hoping to convince the city to join the Guelph league. On the walls, Lippo Memmi's sparkling *Maestà* blesses the accompanying 14th-century scenes of hunting and tournament pageantry. In the **Museo Civico** Taddeo di Bartolo's altarpiece, *The Story of San Gimignano,* teaches proper respect for this bishop of Modena. Saint Gimignano calmed oceans, exorcised demons, saved the city from the Goths, and even fought the devil himself with his trusty cross. The museum maintains an excellent collection of other Sienese and Florentine works, most notably Filippino Lippi's *Annunciation,* crafted in two circular panels, and Pinturicchio's serene *Madonna in Glory.* The room of wedding frescoes off the stairs is a unique series of 14th-century scenes that take a couple from initial courtship to a shared bath and their wedding bed. (Same hours as the tower. *Biglietto intero* L7000, *biglietto ridotto* L5000. Combined tickets with the tower are available April-Sept. 12:30-3pm and 6-7:30pm; Oct. and March 12:30-2:30pm; *biglietto intero* L12,000, *biglietto ridotto* L9000.)

The **Piazza del Duomo** houses the **Collegiata,** a church whose bare façade seems unfit to shelter a Romanesque interior covered with exceptional Renaissance frescoes. Start with the **Chapel of Santa Fina** off the right aisle, a marvel of Renaissance harmony designed by Giuliano and Benedetto Maiano and adorned with Ghirlandaio's splendid frescoes. (*Biglietto intero* L3000, *biglietto ridotto* L2000.) In the main church, Bartolo di Fredi painted beautiful frescoes of Old Testament scenes along the north aisle, while Barna da Siena provided the appropriate, if less impressive, New Testament counterparts along the south aisle. Taddeo di Bartolo's *Last Judgement* frescoes over the entrance are unfortunately chipping their way to non-existence. At the back wall, laugh and cry at the sight of St. Bartholomew, decked out in his BVDs and legions of piercing arrows. (Church and chapel open daily April-Sept. 9:30am-12:30pm and 3-6pm; Oct.-March 9:30am-12:30pm and 3-5:30pm.)

Next to the *duomo,* in P. delle Erbe, sits the **Museo d'Arte Sacra e Museo Etrusco** (Museum of Sacred Art and Etruscan Museum). Here you'll find a variety of local objects, including artifacts found in the area, Etruscan religious art from the *duomo,* and other paintings. (Open April-Sept. daily 9:30am-7:30pm; Oct. and March Tues.-Sun. 9:30am-12:30pm and 2:30-4:30pm; Nov.-Feb. Tues.-Sun. 9:30am-1:30pm and 2:30-4:30pm. *Biglietto intero* L7000, *biglietto ridotto* L5000.) One cheery addition to the San Gimignano museum scene is the **Museo di Criminologia Medioevale,** Via del Castello (tel. 94 22 43), home to an inventive collection of antique instruments of torture. (Open daily 10am-1pm and 2-7pm; in winter only on weekends and holidays. Admission L8000, students L5000.)

Dinner finishes early in the hills, and the *passeggiata* along Via San Giovanni and Via San Matteo (passing by the towers of the Salvucci clan) provides the principal entertainment. Should you find yourself at Via San Matteo at sunset, the view from the lookout point outside the city gates affords an almost mystical experience. During the summer, pass the evening under the stars at the **rocca** (fortress), where you can enjoy movies at San Gimignano's outdoor theater (L7000; weekly showings July-Aug.; check with the tourist office for info).

Pistoia

Pistoia came into its own in 1177 when it joined a handful of other Italian city-states and declared itself a free commune. Despite this bold debut, Pistoia's neighbors soon surpassed it in military, political, and economic sophistication. While Pistoia's claim to fame (or infamy) is the pistol, which it perfected in the 16th century, today the city is home to one of the world's leading train manufacturers. Pistoia isn't all steel, however; it sits amid verdant pastures and lush hills dotted with bright flowers. A handful of interesting monuments make Pistoia a good daytrip from Florence (35min.), but if you're on a tight schedule, head to the other towns of Tuscany first.

ORIENTATION AND PRACTICAL INFORMATION

From the train station, the *centro* is easily reached by walking up **Via XX Settembre** and straight on to **Via Vanucci, Via Cino,** and **Via Buozzi,** at the end of which you turn right for the *duomo* (10min.). Local **COPIT buses** (#10 and 12) make the same trip; you can buy tickets at the office across from the station (L1300). This office also sells tickets for the **Lazzi** buses which run from the train station in Pistoia to Florence (45 min., L4700; last bus leaves at 9pm in summer and 6pm during the off-season). The **tourist office** in Palazzo dei Vescovi, P. del Duomo (tel. 216 22), has elaborate, frescoed ceilings that make it a sight in itself. The friendly, English-speaking staff is highly knowledgeable and has worked with *Let's Go* readers for years. Open Mon.-Sat. 9am-1pm and 3-6pm; also open Sun. during the summer, same hours. In case of

emergencies, dial 113; the **police** *(carabinieri)* can be reached at tel. 212 12. The **post office** is just down the street at Via Roma, 5 (tel. 227 56); it **exchanges currency** and **American Express Traveler's Cheques.** Open Mon.-Fri. 8:15am-6pm, Sat. 8:15am-12:30pm. The **postal code** is 51100, and the **telephone code** is 0573.

ACCOMMODATIONS AND FOOD

A reasonable room at a reasonable price is a rare find in Pistoia, so try to visit the town on a daytrip from Florence. If you need to spend the night, your best bet is **Albergo Firenze,** Via Curtatone e Montanara, 42 (tel. 216 60; fax 231 41). The American owner is friendly, offers advice, and keeps the place perfectly clean. Bright rooms have TVs, floral bedspreads, and tile floors. Show your *Let's Go* in 1997 and you'll get the prices listed below, regardless of the hotel's price increases. Singles L42,000, with bath L60,000. Doubles L75,000, with bath L85,000. Triples L97,000. Quads L120,000. Breakfast L6000. V, MC.

Cruise side streets for grocery stores and inexpensive specialty shops. Market junkies should browse the slightly touristy **open-air market** held in P. della Sala every Wednesday and Saturday 7:30am-2pm. A daily fruit and vegetable **market** is also held on weekdays in P. della Sala, near the *duomo,* 8am-2pm and 5-7pm. A wonderful meal awaits at **Trattoria Lo Storno,** Via Lastrone, 8. Pen-and-ink portraits line this long hall of a restaurant, which serves up simple and delicious fare. *Menù* L20,000. Open daily noon-2pm, Wed. and Fri.-Sat. 7:30-9:30pm. Another sit-down option is **Pizzeria Tonino,** Corso Gramsci, 159b (tel. 333 30), near P. San Francesco. Try the wonderfully tasty and filling *gnocchi* or the zesty *spaghetti puttaniera* (both L8000); for a *secondo,* enjoy a Tuscan favorite like the grilled *salsicce* (sausage, L8000). Open Tues.-Sun. 10am-4pm and 6:30pm-midnight. V, MC, AmEx.

SIGHTS AND ENTERTAINMENT

Geographically and socially, Pistoia converges at the **Piazza del Duomo,** with the **Cathedral of San Zeno** to the right. Originally erected in the 5th century, the church has been rebuilt three times. Inside the *duomo* you'll find an impressive store of early Renaissance art; look for the della Robbia lunette over the central door and several sculptures by Verrocchio. San Zeno's greatest treasure is the *Dossale di San Jacopo,* a tremendously ornate altarpiece that dominates a plain chapel along the right. Nearly every important Tuscan silversmith alive between 1287 and 1456 worked on the piece, including the young Brunelleschi. The L1500 entrance fee is probably still being used to pay off the labor. (Cathedral open daily 8am-noon and 4-7pm.) Designed by Andrea Pisano, the octagonal 14th-century **baptistery** across from the *duomo* presents a modest interior enlivened by Nino and Tommaso Pisano's *Virgin and Child* in the tympanum. (Open Tues.-Sat. 9:30am-12:30pm and 3-6pm, Sun.-Mon. 9:30am-12:30pm.)

To the left of the *duomo* stands the **Palazzo Comunale.** Built in the 13th and 14th centuries, the *palazzo* has a curious detail on its façade: left of the central balcony an arm reaches out of the wall, brandishing a club above the black marble head below—a tribute to the 1115 Pistoian victory over the Moorish king Musetto.

One of Italy's most renowned 20th-century artists, native son Marino Marini, is celebrated at the center bearing his name in the **Palazzo del Tau,** Corso Silvano Fedi, 72. Most of the collection consists of studies and paintings, but it also includes some of the sensuous sculptures for which Marini is most famous. (Open Tues.-Sat. 9am-1pm and 3-7pm, Sun. 9am-12:30pm. Free.)

Exit P. del Duomo by Via del Duca and continue up Via dei Rossi; you will see the typically Pisan-Romanesque façade of the **Church of Sant'Andrea** on your left. Here Giovanni Pisano carved a pulpit that almost tops his efforts in Pisa. The sculptor saved the most impressive scene, the *Massacre of the Innocents,* for the panel most clearly visible from the nave. (Open daily 8am-1pm and 3-7pm.)

At the southern end of the city, on Via Cavour at Via Crispi, don't miss the 12th-century **Church of San Giovanni Fuorcivitas.** The single-naved interior is a vast, box-like space. The church contains Luca della Robbia's vibrant *Visitation* and a font by Giovanni Pisano. (Open daily 7:30am-1pm and 3-6:30pm.)

If you missed out on Woodstock '94, don't despair; the thousand or so remaining flower children of western Europe converge annually on Pistoia for the **Pistoia Blues** concert series, held during the first weekend of July. In recent years the festival has drawn the likes of B.B. King and Bob Dylan. For information and tickets, inquire at the tourist office. The city allows free camping in specially designated sites near the stadium during the festival, which culminates with the **Giostra dell'Orso** (Joust of the Bear), held in P. del Duomo on July 25, the feast day of St. James (the city's patron saint). The *Giostra* began in the 14th century as a showdown between 12 mounted knights and a dressed-up bear.

Lucca

Encircled by tree-topped ramparts, peaceful Lucca lacks the two defining characteristics of many Tuscan towns: the tourists and the hills. There are no hordes fighting for entrance to Lucca's many interesting monuments. The absence of hills translates into happier hamstrings and a unique mood in the city; the vast majority of residents ride bicycles, creating a recreational, friendly atmosphere. Exquisite churches and yellow-toned medieval houses built around the Roman amphitheater provide lasting reminders of the city's heritage.

ORIENTATION AND PRACTICAL INFORMATION

Trains provide the most convenient form of transportation to Lucca, while **Lazzi** buses also run to Pisa and Florence, stopping in many other towns on the way. The station lies just outside the city walls; from there, walk left on **Viale Cavour** and enter the first city gate on the right. Inside the walls, head left on **Via Carrara; Via Vittorio Veneto** on your right will lead you to **Piazza Napoleone** (also known as P. Grande), the hub of the city. To get to the tourist office, head to the far end of P. Napoleone (one big parking lot), turn left on **Via Vittorio Emanuele II,** and follow it until it reaches the **city wall.** The white building to your right is the tourist office.

Tourist Office: Centro Accoglienza Turistica, P. Verdi (tel. 41 96 89). Located within an old city gate. Enthusiastic staff speaks some English. The *cambio* in the building **exchanges currency** and **traveler's checks** at reasonable rates (3% service charge). Office open April-Oct. daily 9am-7pm; Nov.-March 9am-1:30pm.

Currency Exchange: Go to any of the banks in Piazza San Michele. **Credito Italiano** at #47 (tel. 475 46) is open Mon.-Fri. 8:20am-1:20pm and 2:45-4:15pm.

Telephones: Via Cenami, 19 (tel. 553 66), off P. San Giusto. Open Mon.-Fri. 9am-1pm and 4-7pm.

Trains: P. Ricasoli (tel. 470 13). To Florence (Florence-Viareggio line, 1½hr., L6500) or Pisa (30min., L2700). Information open daily 8am-noon and 3-8:30pm. **Luggage Storage:** L5000 for 12hr. Open daily 8am-8pm.

Buses: Lazzi, Piazzale Verdi (tel. 58 78 97), next to the tourist office. To Pisa (L3000) and Florence (L7700). Opens before bus departures—ask for a schedule at the tourist office.

Taxis: tel. 49 49 89 or 49 26 91.

Bike Rental: All the private places in town charge L4000 per hour and L20,000 per day. The state-run **Nolo Cicli,** under the brick archway near the tourist office, rents out cherry-red bikes (L2500 for the 1st hr., L1500 each additional hr., and L12,000 for the entire day).

Bookstore: Libreria Baroni, V. San Paolino, 47. Good selection of on-the-road standards in English. Open Tues.-Sat. 9am-1pm and 4-8pm.

Pharmacy: Standing in Piazza San Michele, you'll see at least two green crosses in every direction. **Farmacia Comunale,** Via San Girolamo, 16, off Piazza Napoleone, is open 24hr.

Emergencies: tel. 113. **First Aid: Misericordia,** tel. 49 23 33. **Hospital:** Campo di Marte (tel. 97 01).

Police: Carabinieri, tel. 112. **Questura,** tel. 45 51.
Post Office: (tel. 456 90) on Via Vallisneri, off P. del Duomo. Open Mon.-Fri. 8:15am-6pm, Sat. 8:15am-12:30pm. **Postal Code:** 55100.
Telephone Code: 0583.

ACCOMMODATIONS

Ostello della Gioventù Il Serchio, Via Brennero, 673 (tel. 34 18 11). Take bus #6 from P. Giglio (last bus 8pm), or walk out Porta S. Maria. Turn right onto Via Batoni and then left onto Viale M. Civitali, following the signs for the *ostello* (20min.). Somewhat cramped, but perfectly clean. Check-out 9am. Office open 4:30-11pm. Curfew midnight. L14,000 for bunk bed, shower, and breakfast. There is also a bar which serves food (dinner L14,000). **HI** card required.

Albergo Diana, Via del Molinetto, 11 (tel. 49 22 02), off P. San Martino. Large and appealing, with a central garden, cool tile floors, and a TV in every room. Singles L48,000. Doubles L78,000, with bath L95,000. (Those in rooms without bath will be charged L2500 extra for a shower.)

Albergo Bernardino, Via di Tiglio, 109 (tel. 95 33 56; fax 49 17 65), outside the city walls. Walk out P. Elisa, down Viale Cadorna, and make the first left. All rooms with TVs and blonde-wood furniture. Singles L50,000, with bath L60,000. Doubles with bath L90,000.

FOOD

You may have to search out Lucca's cheaper restaurants, but, once you find them, you'll be assured of good Tuscan food. The **central market** occupies the large building at the west side of P. del Carmine. Open Mon.-Sat. 7am-1pm and 4-7:30pm. An **open-air market** overruns Via dei Bacchettoni every Wednesday and Saturday 8am-1pm. Supermarkets can be found outside the city walls. The closest is **Superal,** Via Diaz, 24 (tel. 49 05 96); turn right as you walk out of P. Elisa and make the first left. Open daily 8am-8pm; closed Wed. afternoons.

Trattoria da Leo, Via Tegrimi, 1 (tel. 49 22 36), off P. del Salvatore; ask for the restaurant by name. A bustling, peach-colored hangout for locals, who come for the *minestra di farro* (L6000). *Primi* L6000-7000, *secondi* L10,000-14,000. Open Mon.-Sat. noon-2:30pm and 7:30-10:30pm.

Ristorante Da Guido, Via Battisti, 28 (tel. 472 19), at Via degli Angeli. Filled with the sounds of the latest soccer match or cycling race on the television. Warm proprietor welcomes tourists with cheap and filling meals. *Menù* L17,000. *Penne all'arrabbiata* (spicy) L4500. Most *secondi* L7000, including roasted veal or rabbit. Open Mon.-Sat. noon-2:30pm and 8-10pm. AmEx.

Pizzeria Rusticanella 2, Via San Paolino, 30, between P. Verdi and P. San Michele. Float in on the aroma of their mouth-watering pizzas. Slices from L1200. For pasta, try the *tagliatelle alla custicanello* (topped with sausage, mushrooms, tomatoes, and cheese, L6000) or *salsicce* (sausage, L6000). Lunchtime *menù turistico* L12,000. Open Mon.-Sat. noon-3pm and 6-10:30pm. V, MC, AmEx.

SIGHTS AND ENTERTAINMENT

Piazza Napoleone, in the heart of Lucca, is the town's busy administrative center. The 16th-century **Palazzo Ducale** now houses government offices. Head down Via del Duomo to the noble **Piazza San Martino,** where the ornate, asymmetrical **Duomo di San Martino** leans against its bell tower on one side and the post office on the other (the architects designed the façade around the pre-existing bell tower, which had been constructed two centuries earlier). Thirteenth-century reliefs decorate the exterior, including Nicola Pisano's *Journey of the Magi* and *Deposition*. Matteo Civitali, Lucca's famous sculptor, designed the floor, contributed the statue of St. Martin to the right of the door, and carved two beautiful sculptures of angels for the altar. His prize piece is the **Tempietto,** halfway up the left aisle, which houses the *Volto Santo.* Reputedly carved by Nicodemus at Calvary, this wooden crucifix is said to be the true image of Christ. Later, the statue passed into the hands of the bishop of

Lucca. Somewhat ignorant of navigational technique, the bishop set off in a boat without a crew or sails, but, miraculously, the boat landed safely at Luni. To settle the ownership dispute that arose between Lucca and Luni, the statue was placed on an ox-cart and the oxen were left to choose the rightful site; they turned immediately toward Lucca. (The *Volto* is taken for a ride through the town every Sept. 13 to commemorate the wise choice.) The sacristy contains the beautiful and well-preserved *Madonna and Saints* by Ghirlandaio (unfortunately, the art is undergoing extensive restoration), and Tintoretto's *Last Supper* is located in the third chapel on the right. (Open daily 9:30am-6pm; in winter 9:30am-5pm.)

From the cathedral, return to P. Napoleone past the 12th-century **Church of San Giovanni,** turn right on Via Beccheria, and continue to **Piazza San Michele,** the old Roman forum, which is surrounded by impressive brick *palazzi* from medieval Lucca. The annual **Palio della Balestra,** a crossbow competition dating back to 1443, takes place here. The participants appear in traditional costume on July 12 and Sept. 14 for the competition, which was revived for tourists in the early 1970s. The **Church of San Michele in Foro,** again with multi-patterned columns, epitomizes Pisan-Luccese architecture and has a Filippo Lippi painting of *Saints Helena, Jerome, Sebastian, and Roch.* (Open 8:30am-12:30pm and 3:30-7:30pm.)

From the *piazza,* stroll along nearby **Via Fillungo,** Lucca's best-preserved medieval street. Off P. Scalpellini rises the **Church of San Frediano,** an imposing Romanesque structure graced by a huge polychrome mosaic—*The Ascension* by Berlinghieri—on its façade. Within, the second chapel to the right holds the **mummy of Santa Zita,** the beloved Virgin of Lucca; it's in a state of decay, despite the myth that it lies untouched by time. Frescoes of the *Legend of the Volto Santo* by Amico Aspertini grace the chapel on the left. (Open 8:30am-noon and 3-7pm.) From the church, head back across Via Fillungo to **Piazza Anfiteatro.** A perfect oval of medieval houses rings the site of a former Roman amphitheater. Cut across the *piazza* to Via A. Mordini. A right on Via Guinigi brings you to the **Palazzo Guinigi,** a splendidly preserved complex of medieval palaces, alternating red brick with white marble columns. Climb the 230 steps to reach the **Torre Guinigi,** crowned by flowers and oak trees. From here you can see the Apuan Alps. (Open March-Sept. Mon.-Sat. 9am-7:30pm; Oct. Mon.-Sat. 10am-6pm; Nov.-Feb. Mon.-Sat. 10am-4:30pm. Admission L4500.)

Music lovers should not miss the **birthplace of Giacomo Puccini,** the composer of *La Bohème* and *Madama Butterfly,* on Corso San Covenzo, 9 (tel. 58 40 28). The exhibits include the piano on which he composed several of his scores, as well as letters and manuscripts, all of which you can admire while the strains of his operas filter through the apartment. (Open April-Sept. Tues.-Sun. 10am-1pm and 3-6pm, Oct.-March Tues.-Sun. 11am-1pm and 3-5pm. Free.)

Conclude your tour of Lucca with a walk or bike ride around the perfectly intact city walls. The shaded 4-km path (closed to cars) passes grassy parks and cool fountains as it progresses along the *baluardi* (battlements). From here, you can appreciate both the layout of the city and the beautiful countryside high above the moat. The **Caffè di Simo,** V. Fillungo, 58, is an elegant place to refresh yourself, complete with chandeliers, marble tables, and a zinc bar. In the 19th century, artists, writers, and Risorgimento-plotters gathered here, but they probably didn't have to pay L4000 (L1800 at the bar) for their coffee.

Lucca's calendar bulges with dance and classical music events. The musical delights of the **Estate Musicale Lucchese** linger from July to September. The **Teatro Comunale del Giglio's** opera season is also in September. During the summer, you can take in an Italian **film** under the stars in Piazza Guidiccioni. (June-Aug. nightly at 9pm; L7000, students, children, and those over 60, L4000.) The **Settembre Lucchese** is a lively jumble of artistic, athletic, and folkloric presentations. Pick up a calendar of events from the tourist office.

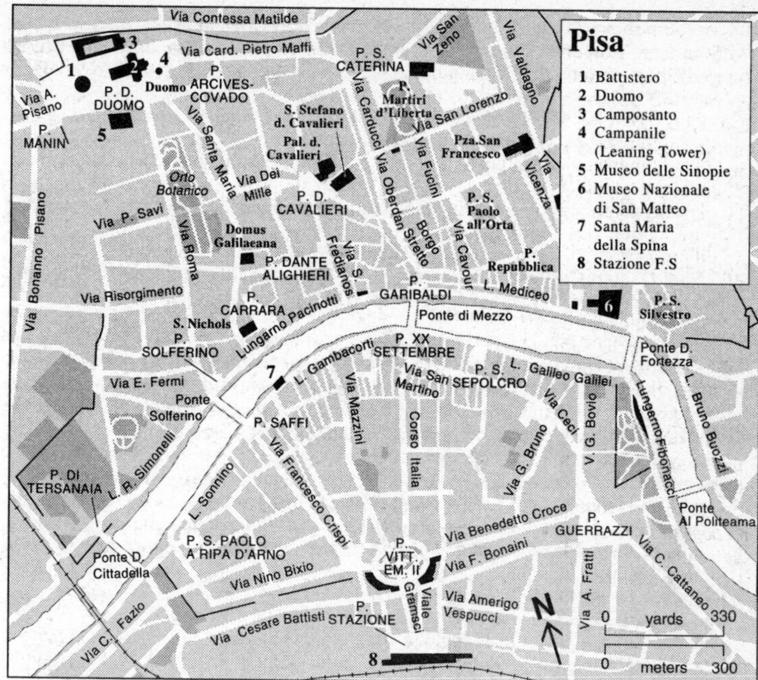

Pisa

It's hard to believe that a wobbly tower could attract so much attention. Yet every year millions of tourists descend on Pisa, turning its famed Campo dei Miracoli into a t-shirt-buying, ice-cream-licking, photo-taking madhouse. Not that the Leaning Tower isn't worth seeing; it's a prime example of the innovative architecture of the Pisan Romanesque period, whose instantly recognizable stripes and blind arcades are featured on churches from Sardinia to Apulia.

In the Middle Ages, when the unclogged Arno still flowed to the sea, Pisa was a major port city whose Mediterranean empire extended to Corsica, Sardinia, and the Balearics. These international contacts led to a cultural revival at home. Unfortunately, when the Arno silted up, Pisa's fortunes dried up, too. Pisans now thrive on tourism. Be a typical tourist and take that photo of yourself holding up the tower, but also try to branch out into the city. Its quieter squares, renowned university, and lovely riverwalks are what truly make it a beautiful Italian city.

ORIENTATION AND PRACTICAL INFORMATION

Pisa lies on the Tyrrhenian coast of Italy at the mouth of the Arno, directly west of Florence. **APT** runs both city and regional buses, connecting Pisa with other towns along the coast. Most of Pisa's important sights lie to the north of the Arno; the main train station inexplicably rests far to the south. To get to the **Campo dei Miracoli** (also known as the **Piazza del Duomo**) from the station, take bus #1 (buy tickets to the left outside the station, L1200), or walk straight up Viale Gramsci, turn left at P. Vittorio Emanuele onto P. Sant'Antonio, and take Via Crispi across the river. On the other side it turns into Via Roma, which leads to P. del Duomo (1.5km).

Tourist Office: P. della Stazione (tel. 422 91), to your left as you exit the station. Friendly, English-speaking staff hands out detailed maps. No accommodations service, but they will call around to see who has space. Open Mon.-Sat. 8am-8pm, Sun. 9am-1pm. A **branch** office is at P. del Duomo (tel. 56 04 64), inside the Museo dell'Opera, behind that leaning thing. Open daily April-Oct. 8am-8pm; Nov.-March 9am-5:30pm.

Budget Travel: CTS, Via Santa Maria, 45/B (tel. 483 00 or 292 21; fax 454 31). Day-trips, international tickets, and boats to nearby islands. Be prepared to wait at least 30min. English spoken. Open Mon.-Fri. 9:30am-12:30pm and 4-7pm, Sat. 9:30am-12:30pm.

Currency Exchange: Your best bet is a **bank** near the center of town, but the train station offers reasonable rates and is open 24hr.

Telephones: In the train station or at **Bac Bosi,** Via Mediceo, 66.

Flights: Galileo Galilei (information tel. 50 07 07). Charter, domestic, and international flights. Trains make the 4-min. trip (L1500) from the station, timed to coincide with departures.

Trains: P. della Stazione (tel. 413 85), in the southern end of town. Ticket and information office open 7am-8:30pm. Trains run between Pisa and Florence every hr. (1hr., L7200). The main coastal line links Pisa to Livorno (L2000), Genoa (L15,500), and Rome (L26,200). Local or regional trains, like those headed for Lucca (20min., L2700), often stop at Pisa's other station, **S. Rossore,** which is much closer to the *duomo* and youth hostel.

Buses: Lazzi, P. Emanuele, 11 (tel. 462 88). Frequent service to Lucca, Pistoia, Prato, and Florence. **APT** (also called **CPT**), P. Sant'Antonio (tel. 233 84), near the station. Frequent service to Livorno (L3700 or L4000, depending on the route). Seven buses each day travel to Volterra (6:45am-9:30pm, no service in early afternoon, L9400).

Taxis: tel. 54 16 00.

Car Rental: Avis (tel. 420 28), **Budget** (tel. 454 90), **Eurodollar** (tel. 462 09), **Hertz** (tel. 491 87), and **Maggiore** (tel. 425 74) all have offices at Pisa's airport. Prices start around L180,000 per day. Min. age 23. In town, **Autonoleggio Toscano** (tel. 461 27) on Viale Bonaini rents out cars starting at L80,000 per day. Open daily 9:30am-12:30pm and 3:30-7:30pm.

Bike Rental: Oue Ruote Per La Citta, Via Gobetti, 55, rents bikes for L4000 per hour or L20,000 per entire day.

Bookstore: Maxi-Livres, Corso Italia, 97. The central island is stocked with classics and lots of trashy novels in English. Great prices. Open Mon.-Fri. 9am-8pm.

Laundry: Lavanderia, Via Corridoni, 100. Turn right as you exit the train station. L5000 to wash 9kg of laundry. L5000 to dry. Open daily 8am-10pm.

Late-Night Pharmacy: Farmacia, P. del Duomo. Open all night.

Emergencies: tel. 113. **First Aid:** tel. 55 44 33 or 59 23 00. **Hospital:** (tel. 59 21 11) on Via Bonanno near P. del Duomo.

Police: tel. 58 35 11.

Post Office: P. Emanuele, 8 (tel. 50 18 69), near the station. Go to the windows on your left. **American Express Traveler's Cheques exchanged.** Open Mon.-Fri. 8:30am-5pm, Sat. 8:30am-noon. **Postal Code:** 56100.

Telephone Code: 050.

ACCOMMODATIONS AND CAMPING

Pisa has plenty of cheap *pensioni* and *locande,* but demand is always high. Call ahead and make reservations, or pick up the hotel map at the tourist office, take the bus to the *duomo,* and start looking. The youth hostel is a bit of a hike.

Centro Turistico Madonna dell'Acqua, Via Pietrasantina, 15 (tel. 89 06 22). Take bus #3 from the station and ask the driver to let you off at the *ostello.* A clean, relatively new hostel beneath an old sanctuary. Its rural setting might mean that you'll be sung to sleep by crickets and nibbled on by mosquitoes. Check-out 9am. Office open 6-11pm. Singles L30,000. L20,000 per person for beds in double or triple rooms. Sells cold drinks and bottled water.

Casa della Giovane (ACISJF), Via F. Corridoni, 29 (tel. 430 61), 10min. from the station (turn right as you leave). This women's hostel is a great place to stay if you're the right sex. Bright, clean rooms include bath. Reception open 7am-10pm. Curfew 10pm. L20,000 per person in doubles or triples. Breakfast L2500.

Albergo Gronchi, P. Archivescovado, 1 (tel. 56 18 23), adjacent to P. del Duomo. Pisa's top pick has a cool, welcoming entryway replete with stained glass and a fluffy white cat. Garden in back puts you just beyond the range of the Tower, should it topple. Curfew midnight. Singles L32,000. Doubles L50,000. Triples L68,000. Come early or reserve ahead of time; rooms fill quickly.

Hotel Galileo, Via Santa Maria, 12 (tel. 406 21). Spacious rooms with tiled floors and frescoed ceilings converge on a lounge with a soft sofa and an ebullient proprietress. Don't be put off by the dark entryway. Singles L38,000. Doubles L50,000. Triples L60,000. Quads L80,000.

Albergo Serena, Via D. Cavalca, 45 (tel. 244 91), near P. Dante. A new coat of paint has brightened this small *pensione* in the heart of the *centro.* Hot water valves may be unreliable. Singles L35,000. Doubles L50,000. Triples L68,000. Breakfast L4500.

Albergo Helvetia, Via Don G. Boschi, 31 (tel. 55 30 84), off P. Archivescovado, 2min. from the *duomo.* Large, clean rooms contain beds covered with wild spreads and walls hung with brightly painted Indonesian tribal masks. Go figure. Singles L40,000. Doubles L50,000, with bath L78,000.

Camping: The 3 campgrounds near Pisa can be dreadfully hot and crowded in summer. **Campeggio Torre Pendente,** Viale delle Cascine, 86 (tel. 56 06 65), 1km away, is the closest to town. Follow the signs from P. Manin. L9000 per person, L3500 per small tent, L6000 per large tent. Open Easter-Oct. 15. **Camping Internazionale** (tel. 365 53), on Via Litoranea in Marina di Pisa, is 10km away, on a private beach with a bar and restaurant. Take an APT bus to San Marina di Pisa (L2600). L8000-9000 per person, L10,000-11,000 per small tent, L12,000-13,000 per large tent. Open May-Sept. and sometimes during winter. **Camping Mare e Sole** (tel. 327 57), on Viale del Tirreno, in nearby Calambrone. Bungalows on the beach. L8000-9000 per person, L12,000-13,000 per large tent. Open April-Sept.

FOOD

For a more authentic ambience than that manufactured by the touristy *trattorie* near the *duomo,* head toward the river. Cheap restaurants are plentiful around the university area. In P. Vettovaglie, you'll find an **open-air market** where the vociferous haggling and colorful cornucopia of produce are reminiscent of the outdoor markets of ancient Baghdad. Bakeries and *salumerie* also abound in the heart of Pisa's residential quarter. For conveniently pre-packaged goods, head over to **Superal,** Via Pascoli, 6, just off Corso Italia. Open Mon.-Tues. and Thurs.-Sat. 8am-8pm, Wed. 8am-1:30pm. The local specialty is *torta di ceci* (or *cecina*), a delicious pizza made with chick peas, available at most *bar-pizzerie* for L2000 per slice.

Trattoria da Matteo, Via l'Aroncio, 46 (tel. 410 57), off Via S. Maria near Hotel Galileo. Friendly proprietor and a wide range of culinary treats. Start with the homemade *ravioli* (L7000) or the *gnocchi al pesto* (L6000) and continue with *scaloppina con i funghi* (veal with mushrooms, L9000). Or choose from among their 40 different kinds of pizza (L6500-9500). *Menù* L17,000. Cover L1000. Beer and a slice at the bar L6000. Open Sun.-Fri. noon-3pm and 7-10:30pm.

Il Paiolo, Via Curtatone e Montanara, 9 (tel. 425 28), near the university. This pub draws a lively crowd and offers 2 *menù:* pasta and *panino* (L11,000), *primo* and *secondo* (L13,000). For a hearty dish, order their *bistecca* (a steak covered with mushrooms, rucola, nuts, and parmesan cheese, L20,000). If your appetite is smaller, try an Italian-style grilled cheese (L7000) or a salad loaded with cheese and veggies (L6000). Open Mon.-Fri. noon-3pm and 7pm-1am, Sat. 7pm-1am.

Ristoro al Vecchio Teatro, V. Collegio Ricci, 2 (tel. 202 10), off P. Dante. Delicious, innovative combinations with an emphasis on fresh vegetables, served in a cool, garden-like room. Menu changes daily; if they have it, try the *risotto d'ortolana* (rice with vegetables) or the buttery *sfogliata di zucchine* (zucchini tart). *Primi* L9000, *secondi* L10,000, desserts L4000. Open Mon.-Fri. noon-3pm and 8-midnight, Sat. 8pm-midnight. V, MC, AmEx.

Pizzeria Il Montino, Via del Monte, 1 (tel. 59 86 95). Take Via Dini from P. dei Cavalieri. Piping hot pizzas (L5000-7000) fed to a crowd of hungry locals. Try their legendary *cecina* (L1600 per *etto*). *Primi* from L5000, *secondi* from L6000. L1000 cover and 10% service charge if you sit down. Open daily 10am-3pm and 5-10pm.

SIGHTS AND ENTERTAINMENT

Piazza del Duomo, also known as the **Campo dei Miracoli** (Field of Miracles), contains the **cathedral, baptistery, Camposanto,** and **Leaning Tower,** all rising from a plush blanket of green grass. The city offers an all-inclusive ticket to the *duomo,* the baptistery, Camposanto, the Museo delle Sinopie, and the Museo del Duomo for L17,000; to the *duomo* and another monument for L10,000; to the *duomo* and two other monuments for L12,000; *or* the *duomo* and what's behind Door #2 for just $9.99! Admission to the cathedral is L2000 (unless you're there to attend mass, but you have to look extremely pious to get past the guards).

The black-and-white façade of the **duomo** is the archetype of the Pisan Romanesque period, and the interior definitely warrants the L2000 admission. Begun in 1063 by Boschetto (who had himself entombed in the wall), the cathedral was the first structure in the Campo. Enter the five-aisled nave through Bonanno Pisano's bronze doors (1180). Though most of the interior was destroyed by fire in 1595, paintings by Ghirlandaio along the right wall, Cimabue's mosaic *Christ Pantocrator* in the apse, and bits of the Cosmati pavement remain in good condition. The cathedral's elaborate chandelier is rumored (falsely) to have inspired Galileo's gravity theories. Giovanni Pisano's last and greatest **pulpit,** perhaps designed to outdo his father's in the baptistery, sits majestically at the heart of the cathedral. Relief panels depict classical and biblical subjects; the *Nativity,* the *Last Judgment,* and the *Massacre of the Innocents* are among the most striking. Never one to resist a good allegory, Pisano carved the pulpit's supports into figures symbolizing the arts and virtues. (Open Mon.-Sat. 10am-7:45pm and Sun. 1-7:45pm.)

The **baptistery,** an enormous barrel of a building begun in 1152, measures 107m in girth and reaches 55m into the Pisan sky. The building's architecture is a blend of styles—the lower half in typical Tuscan-Romanesque stripes and the upper half in a stunning Gothic ensemble of gables, pinnacles, and statuary set in lacy tracery. Nicola Pisano's **pulpit** (1260), to the left of the baptismal font, recaptures the sobriety and dignity of classical antiquity; it is considered one of the harbingers of Renaissance art in Italy. The dome's acoustics are astounding—an unamplified choir singing in the baptistery can be heard 20km away. (Open daily in summer 8am-7:30pm; in winter 9am-4:40pm.)

The **Camposanto,** a long, cloistered cemetery covered with earth which the Crusaders brought back from Mt. Calvary, holds, among other things, the Roman sarcophagi whose reliefs inspired Nicola Pisano's pulpit. Fragments of frescoes shattered by Allied bombs during World War II line the galleries. Enter the **Chapel Ammannati** for a reprieve from the hordes of tourists and for the haunting frescoes by an unidentified 14th-century artist known for these works as the "Master of the Triumph of Death." (Open daily 9am-5:40pm; off-season 9am-4:40pm.)

Because the ground below is none too firm, all the structures in the *campo* tilt, but none so dramatically as the famous **Leaning Tower.** Intended as the *campanile del duomo,* it was begun by Bonanno Pisano in 1173 and had reached the height of 10m when the soil beneath it unexpectedly subsided. The tilt intensified as post-World War II tourists ascended in ever-increasing numbers, and the tower continues to slip 1-2mm every year. The Tower has been **closed** indefinitely, much to the dismay of the thousands of visitors who journey from around the globe to behold one of the Seven Wonders of the World. More drastic measures are being taken to halt its slow collapse—for instance, steel cables have been wrapped around the bottom story, the walls of which were thought to be in danger of fracturing. The possible construction of an aqueduct to Pisa might solve the problem for good; if all wells in the area are closed, groundwater depletion by thirsty Pisans and shower-mad tourists, which is thought to cause the Tower's settling, may be alleviated.

Cross the square from the Camposanto to the **Museo delle Sinopie,** which displays preliminary fresco sketches by Traini, Veneziano, and Gaddi, as well as other sketches discovered during restoration after World War II. (Open daily 8am-7:30pm; off-season 9am-12:40pm and 3-4:40pm.) The **Museo dell'Opera del Duomo,** behind the Leaning Tower, displays artwork from the three buildings of P. del Duomo, including the ivory *Madonna and Crucifix* and *Madonna and Child* by Giovanni Pisano. (Open daily 8am-7:30pm; off-season 9am-12:30pm and 3-4:30pm.)

Beyond P. del Duomo, museums, Romanesque churches, and *piazze* dot the city. The **Museo Nazionale di San Matteo,** on the Arno not far from P. Mazzini, includes panels by Masaccio, Fra Angelico, and Pietro Lorenzetti, and sculpture by the Pisano clan. (Open Tues.-Sat. 9am-7pm, Sun. 9am-1pm. Admission L8000.)

Piazza dei Cavalieri, designed by Vasari during Medici rule on the site of the Roman forum, held Pisa's town hall during the Middle Ages. Today it is the seat of the **Scuola Normale Superiore,** one of Italy's premier universities, thanks to the Medici who transferred Florence's university here in the 16th century. The administrative offices of the Scuola occupy the beautiful **Palazzo dei Cavalieri,** its façade decorated with busts of the Grand Dukes of Tuscany and with *graffiti* (etched, not the spray-painted kind). The black wrought-iron baskets on either end of the clock building once served as receptacles for the heads of deliquent Pisans.

Of Pisa's numerous churches, three merit special attention. Don't miss the **Church of Santa Maria della Spina,** a spectacle of Gothic art, which faces Lungarno Gambacorti against the river. From the Campo, walk down Via Santa Maria and over the bridge. Originally an oratory, the church was enlarged in 1323 and renamed Church of the Spina (Thorn) because it claims to house one of the thorns from Christ's crown. Sadly, visitors can only view the church's interior during Italy's annual Culture Week. From this church, walk with the river to your left, cross the first bridge, and go straight one block to the **Church of San Michele in Borgo.** To the right stands a statue of St. Michael the Archangel casually slaying Satan. The characteristic Pisan-Romanesque façade of the church is notable for its Latin scribblings about a 14th-century electoral campaign for University Rector. Another worthy sidetrack from P. del Duomo is the **Church of San Nicola,** between Via S. Maria and P. Carrara. Check out the famous altarpiece in the fourth chapel on the right, showing St. Nicola deflecting the arrows that a wrathful God aims at Pisa. The bell tower of the church inclines slightly, not unlike its more famous cousin. (Open daily 8-11:30am and 5-7pm.)

Occasional **concerts** are given in the *duomo,* where the acoustics are phenomenal. A former church on **San Paolo all'Orto** now holds performances of experimental music. Every June, Pisa comes alive with festivals and exhibits; on the last Sunday of the month, the annual tug-of-war, the **Gioco del Ponto,** revives the city's medieval color and pageantry. On the second weekend of every month, an antique fair fills the Ponte di Mezzo.

Livorno

Overwhelmed by the monstrous oceanliners awaiting departure for Sardinia, Corsica, Greece, and Spain, Livorno is something of a rough-and-ready port town that slumbers under a blanket of industrial soot. Famous for its port, Livorno draws tourists with its convenient ferry system. If you happen to be here with time on your hands, enjoy the few interesting monuments and excellent seafood.

ORIENTATION AND PRACTICAL INFORMATION

From the train station, take bus #1 to reach **Piazza Grande,** the center of town; buses #2 and #8 also stop at P. Grande, but only after traipsing along the periphery. Buy tickets at the booth right outside the station or at one of the orange vending machines (L1200). If you prefer to walk, cross the park in front of the station and head straight down Viale Carducci, which becomes Via dei Larderel, to **Piazza Repubblica.** Cross the *piazza* and take Via delle Galere to P. Grande.

Tourist Office: P. Cavour, 6 (tel. 89 81 11), up Via Cairoli from P. Grande, on the 3rd floor. Friendly and helpful. Open Mon., Wed., and Fri.-Sat. 9am-1pm, Tues. and Thurs. 9am-1pm and 3-5pm. **Branch office** at Calata Carrara, near the Corsica departure site (tel. 21 03 31). Open July-Sept. Mon.-Sat. 7:30-10am and 3:30-7pm.

Currency Exchange: At the train station. Fair rates. Open daily 8-11:45am and 3-5:45pm. Also at Stazione Marittima or one of the many banks on Via Cairoli.

Telephones: Piazza Grande, 5. Open Mon.-Sat. 7:30am-1pm and 3-8pm. International calls can be made *a scatti* at P. Grande, 14. Open daily 8am-9:45pm.

Trains: Frequent service connects Livorno to: Pisa (15min., L2000); Florence (1hr., L9800); Rome (3hr., L24,400); and Piombino (1hr., L7200). **Luggage Storage:** L5000 for 12hr. Open daily 5am-9:45pm.

Buses: ATL (tel. 847 111) buses to Pisa (frequent, L3700) and Piombino (about every 1½hr. 6:10am-6pm, L10,000) leave from P. Grande. **Lazzi** makes trips to Siena, Pisa, Bari, and Empoli, and is located at P. Manin, along Scali Manzoni. Office open Mon.-Fri. 9am-1pm.

Ferries: At the Stazione Marittima. From P. Grande, walk down Via Logorano, across P. Municipio to Via Porticciolo, which becomes Via Venezia and leads to the port and the Stazione Marittima. Reserve tickets about 2 weeks in advance in July and Aug., especially if you're traveling with a bicycle, motorcycle, or car. Be sure to check where and when your boat leaves; schedules change unpredictably. Prices are higher in summer and on weekends. At the Stazione Marittima, there is **currency exchange, luggage storage,** a **restaurant,** and a **nursery.** All are open before and after arrivals and departures, but generally closed at midday.

Corsica Marittima (tel. 21 05 07), sails to **Bastia (Corsica):** April through mid-Sept. Sat. afternoons and occasional other days—ask for the current schedule (3¼hr., L36,000-60,000). To **Porto Vecchio (Corsica):** July through mid-Aug. Sat. 9:30pm; mid-Aug. through mid-Sept. Sun. 9am (10½hr., L48,000-50,000).

Moby Lines (tel. 89 03 25) sails to **Bastia:** April Wed.-Fri. 8:30am, Sun. 2pm; May Wed. and Fri. 8:30am, Thurs. 2pm; June and Sept. daily, except for certain Thurs. and Sun., 8:30am; July-Aug. daily 8:30am and 8pm (4hr., L36,000-48,000). To **Olbia:** late March through April Mon.-Sat. usually 10pm; May daily 10pm; June through mid-Sept. daily 10am and 10pm; mid-Sept. through mid-Oct. daily 10am; mid-Oct. Mon., Wed., and Fri. 10pm (10hr., L42,000-85,000).

Corsica and Sardinia Ferries (tel. 88 13 80 or 89 89 79). Run to and from **Golfo Aranci (Sardinia):** mid-March through May most days 9:30pm; June daily, except for certain Wed., 9:30am and 9:30pm; July through mid-Sept. daily 9:30am and 9:30pm; mid-Sept. through early Oct. daily 9:30am (9-10hr., L42,000-85,000, day ferries cheaper).

Taxis: tel. 21 00 00.

All-Night Pharmacy: Farmacia Comunale, V. Fiume, 1, up from P. Grande.

Emergencies: tel. 113. **Hospital: Pronto Soccorso,** tel. 40 33 51 or 42 13 98.

Post Office: Via Cairoli, 12/16 (tel. 89 76 02). Most services open Mon.-Fri. 8:15am-7pm, Sat. 8:15am-12:30pm; **currency exchange booth** closes at 6pm on weekdays. **Postal Code:** 57100.

Telephone Code: 0586.

ACCOMMODATIONS

Finding a room is easy, even in summer, since few stay here longer than one night.

Pensione Dante, Scali D'Azeglio, 28 (tel. 89 34 61). Take a right as you leave the port and walk straight along the waterfront until you come to a canal on the left. The *pensione* is a few blocks ahead. Amicable family speaks English. The paisley bedspreads and orange formica furnishings are not exactly fashionable, but rooms are clean and ample; many have views of the canal. Singles L40,000. Doubles L55,000-58,000.

Hotel Cremona, Corso Mazzini, 24 (tel. 88 91 57). Take Via Rossi 1 block out of P. Cavour. Head down Via Enrico Mayer and turn right onto Corso Mazzini. Completely renovated rooms boast mosaic ceilings, wool-blend furniture, and soft pastel linens. Modern amenities include remote-control TV and alarm clock. Singles

L40,000-70,000. Doubles L70,000-110,000. Triples—one of which is wheelchair accessible—L100,000-130,000. All rooms with private bath.

Hotel Goldoni, Via Enrico Mayer, 42 (tel. 89 87 05). Take Via Rossi 1 block out of P. Cavour. Abstract art graces the entryway. The oddly shaped rooms are clean and modern. Ask for a view of the garden. Singles L40,000, with bath L50,000. Doubles L60,000, with bath L78,000. Triples L80,000, with bath L95,000.

FOOD

Livorno owes its culinary specialties, like its livelihood, to the sea. The city has its own interpretation of the classic bouillabaise—a fiery, tomato-based seafood stew called *cacciucco*. An **open-air market** sprawls along Via Buontalenti, behind the APT station. Open Mon.-Sat. 8am-1pm. Fill your brown bag at the **STANDA** supermarket off P. Grande at Via Grande, 174. Open daily 8:30am-12:30pm and 4-8pm; in winter Mon.-Sat. 8:30am-12:30pm and 3:30-7:30pm.

Hostaria dell'Eremo, Scala Ciadini, 39 (tel. 88 14 87). Just plain pretty, with pink walls, pink tile floors, and little potted plants on all the tables. Choose from their selection of fresh fish. Try the *cacciucco* (L15,000), or *Cosimo Terzo* (a house specialty with shrimp and *prosciutto*). Open Sun.-Tues. noon-2:30pm and 7:30-10:30pm. V, MC, DC.

La Cantonata, Corso Mazzini, 222 (tel. 894 04 81). Smiling owner dishes out huge plates of *spaghetti ai frutti di mare* (with seafood, L8000), the freshest fish, and brimming glasses of *chianti.* Other-worldly *riso nero* (rice turned black from squid ink) only L8000. *Secondi* L7000-18,000. *Menù turistico* L20,000. Cover L2000. Service 10%. Open Tues.-Sun. noon-3pm and 7-10:30pm.

Made In Italy, Scali Manzoni 7/9 (tel. 21 02 88), just off P. Cavour. *Menù turistico* L14,000. Try their *spaghetti alle vongole* (L6000) or a *panino,* loaded with *prosciutto,* cheese, and fresh vegetables, and toasted to perfection (L6000).

Trattoria Il Sottomarino, Via dei Terrazzini, 48 (tel. 237 71), off P. della Repubblica at the end of Via Pina d'Oro. Not cheap, but people come from all over to taste the *cacciucco*. Open Aug.-June Fri.-Wed. 12:30-2:30pm and 7:30-10pm.

SIGHTS AND ENTERTAINMENT

Located in the heart of the quarter known as **Piccola Venezia** for the canals that course through it, the **Fortezza Nuova** is protected by a complete moat. The fortress was completed in the early 1600s by the Medici family and now houses a well-maintained public garden and park; compare this fortress to the massive, sprawling **Fortezza Vecchia** (from the new fortress, walk to P. Municipio, then down Via S. Giovanni). Built by the powerful Marquises of Tuscany in the 9th century, the portly tower in the middle was the first fortification on the site. When Pisans conquered Livorno, they built a fort around the tower (out of fear it would lean over and put them out of business). In the 16th century the Medici surrounded the ensemble with robust brick walls to consolidate their hold on Livorno, by then the chief Tuscan port. Piazza Micheli, across from the port, is home to the **Monumento del Quattro Mori.** This marble figure of Duke Ferdinand I was carved by Bandini in 1595, but the four manacled bronze slaves were added by Pietro Tacca in 1626.

Livorno inspired two important contributions to painting. Foremost is the group of 19th-century painters "I Macchiaioli" (literally, "the blotters"), led by Giovanni Fattori. In the **Museo Civico Giovanni Fattori** (tel. 80 80 01) in Villa Mimbelli, located at the intersection of Via San Iacopo and Via Acquaviva, you can see their proto-Impressionist work. (Open daily 10am-1pm and 4-7pm. Admission L5000.) Livorno's second gift to art history was 20th-century portraitist Amadeo Modigliani.

Livorno's chief festival, the **Palio Marinaro,** takes place just off this stretch of coast. In mid-July rowers from the various neighborhoods of the city race traditional crafts toward the old port, spurred on by the spectators who line the banks.

Viareggio

Tucked between the colorful umbrellas that line the private beaches of the Versilian coast and the olive trees and chestnut groves that cloak the rolling foothills of the Apuan Mountains, the resort town of Viareggio sits quietly at the foot of the Riviera. Each night wealthy European tourists stroll along the shore on the wide promenade, distinguished by its grandiose 20's architecture. Yelling into their cellular phones and peering into the windows of glitzy boutiques, they seem largely unaware of the lapping waves and gentle sea breeze that make Viareggio's beaches so inviting.

ORIENTATION AND PRACTICAL INFORMATION

Lazzi buses (tel. 462 33) connect Viareggio to the neighboring towns as well as to the major cities: Pisa (20 per day, L3900); La Spezia (about every hr., L6200); Lucca (4 per day, L3900); and Florence (4 per day, L12,600, reservations recommended). All buses stop at **Piazza Mazzini,** the town's main square. Perhaps the easiest way to reach Viareggio, however, is by **train;** it lies conveniently on the Livorno-La Spezia line. **Luggage storage** is available at the train station, L5000 for 12hr. Open 7am-noon and 2-8pm. From the train station walk straight down Via XX Settembre to Piazza Mazzini. Turn right onto Viale Carducci, and walk 2½ blocks to the **tourist office** at #10 (tel. 96 22 33). The personable, English-speaking staff will give you a decent map and bombard you with brochures describing the region of Versilia. Open Mon.-Sat. 9am-1pm and 4-7pm, Sun. 9am-1pm. **Currency exchange** is available at the post office or at any of the banks along Via Garibaldi. An **all-night pharmacy** can be found at Via Mazzini, 14. In case of **emergency,** dial 113; for **first aid,** call 96 09 60. The **post office** (tel. 303 45) sits at the corner of Via Garibaldi and Via Puccini. Viareggio's **postal code** is 55049, and the **telephone code** is 0584.

ACCOMMODATIONS AND FOOD

Amidst the splendor and pretense of four-stardom hides a bevy of budget accommodations; the tourist office has a list. For clean, simple rooms right in the center of town, try **Pensione Roswitha,** Via Zanardelli, 81 (tel. 445 41). Singles L30,000-35,000, with bath L37,000-45,000. Doubles L47,000-55,000, with bath L56,000-65,000. Used to catering to a wealthy clientele, the restaurants in Viareggio are none too cheap. To avoid the ubiquitous L3000 cover and 15% service charge, head over to **Pizza al 2000,** Via Battista, 185. Great pizzas topped with everything from *prosciutto* to nutella sells for L6000-8000. Since none of the *caffè* along the promenade are reasonably priced, you might as well spend the L5000 to enjoy coffee on the roof of the elegant **Gran Caffè Margherita** overlooking the sea.

SIGHTS AND ENTERTAINMENT

Most of the shoreline has been roped off by the owners of Viareggio's private beaches. A short walk to your left as you face the water leads to the free patches of sandy beach. Both amateur hikers and ardent rock-climbers can find worthwhile trails winding through the lush hills and craggy Apuan Alps—ask at the tourist office for a list of suggested itineraries. Hard-core people-watchers will want to go instead to the ultra-posh town of **Forte dei Marmi.** Stake out a table at one of the expensive outdoor *caffè* and look on as the Armani-clad locals emerge from their secluded villas to squander their fortunes at the multitude of ritzy boutiques. When night falls, stroll along the promenade, or head over to **Club La Canniccia,** Viale Carducci, 32, and choose one of its four dance floors.

Elba

According to ancient folklore, the enchanting island of Elba grew from a precious stone that slipped from Venus's neck into the azure waters of the Tyrrhenian Sea. Throughout history, this celestial paradise has drawn the likes of Jason and his Argonauts, Etruscan miners, and Roman patricians. Of course, Elba derives its greatest fame from its association with Napoleon; the Little Emperor was sent into his first exile here in 1814, creating both a temporarily war-free Europe and a famous palindrome ("Able was I, ere I saw Elba," spake the Emperor upon his arrival). Hardly a prison, Elba lures hordes of vacationing Germans and Italians every summer with its deep turquoise waters, dramatically poised mountains, and velvety beaches. Fortunately, the best parts of the island lie off the beaten track and away from tourists, and if you come in the off-season you will have virtually the whole place to yourself.

Tourists flock to Elba in July and August, making it impossible to find lodging without a reservation several months ahead. There are alternatives. In June and September the weather is perfect and the beds plentiful. Camping is a cheap option, but beware—camping space often requires a reservation. The island also offers about 100 *affitta camere* and 30 *agriturismo* locations. Some spendthrifty backpackers secure a quiet, sandy beach and spend the night sprawled out on the breezy shore atop a pile of blankets. **Be advised: although it is relatively common, sleeping on the beach is of questionable safety.** Those who do should sleep in groups and be sure to secure their packs.

GETTING THERE

Elba does have an **airport** (tel. 97 60 11) in Marina di Campo, with flights to Florence, Pisa, Milan, Verona, and Siena. But the best way to reach Elba is by **ferry** from Piombino Marittima (also called Piombino Porto) to Portoferraio, Elba's largest city. **Trains** on the Genoa-Rome line stop at Campiglia Marittima, from which a tiny commuter train leaves for the ferries in Piombino Marittima (wait for the *porto* stop). From Florence change at Pisa to arrive at Campiglia Marittima. Both **Toremar** (1hr., L9000; **hydrofoil** 30min., L18,000) and **Navarma** (1hr., L10,000-15,000) run frequent boats to Elba, a total of about 16 per day during the summer months. Talk directly to Toremar (tel. 91 80 80) or Navarma (tel. 22 12 12) at Piazzale Premuda, 13, in Piombino. You can also buy tickets for the next departing ferry at the **FS** booth in the train station. Should you get stuck in Piombino, take a train from the port to the city (every 30min., 5min., L1500). In town, **Albergo Il Piave** sits right across from the train station at Piazza F. Niccolini, 2 (tel. 22 60 50) and has standard rooms with baths. Singles L50,000-60,000. Doubles L80,000-90,000. There is also a **tourist office,** open in summer only, at the port.

TRANSPORTATION

On Elba, **ATL** buses constitute the only form of public transportation between the major cities of Portoferraio, Marina di Campo, Marciana Marina, and Porto Azzurro (day passes L9000). Popular **boat excursions** cover various parts of the coast; contact **Etruria** in Portoferraio (tel. 90 42 73) for details. Renting a **moped** (L25,000-50,000 per day) allows you to see the more isolated parts of the island.

ORIENTATION

Elba's varied terrain and diverse attractions can accommodate almost any interest. The rugged mountains of the interior are framed by sandy beaches to the east and a stone-slab waterfront on the west. Each zone of the island attracts a distinct variety of visitor, from families in **Marina di Campo** and **Marciana Marina,** to party-hard beach fanatics in **Capo Civeri,** to the private-yacht set in **Porto Azzurro.** Wherever you decide to go, bypass Portoferraio, a chaotic port-city with the most overcrowded beach on the island. Head over to the **tourist office** as soon as you land to pick up a decent map and the essential *Notizie Utili per il Turista,* which gives information on beaches, hotels, restaurants, and entertainment for the entire island.

PORTOFERRAIO

Practical Information

Tourist Offices: APT, Calata Italia, 26 (tel. 91 46 71), on the 1st floor, across from the Toremar boat landing. Info galore: accommodations, maps, bus schedules, and brochures. They also have listings of *agriturismo* and *affitta camere* in the cities and countryside of Elba. Open in summer daily 8am-8pm; in winter Mon.-Sat. 8am-1pm and 3-6pm. There's also a **tourist info booth** at the bus station, Viale Elba, 20, which provides brochures, reserves rooms, holds luggage (L2500), and sells bus tickets. Open June 15-Sept. 15 Mon.-Sat. 8am-8pm. **Associazione Albergatori,** Calata Italia, 21 (tel. 91 47 54), offers free room-finding. Open Mon.-Fri. 9am-7:30pm, Sat. 9am-12:30pm and 3:30-7pm.

Currency Exchange: There are a zillion places in the port willing to rip you off, but instead walk up to Via Manganaro, where there are several banks, including **Banca di Roma** (tel. 91 84 59). Open Mon.-Fri. 8:30am-1:30pm and 3:10-4pm.

Telephones: In the port at the **Bar del Porto**. Open daily 6:30am-11pm. In Marina di Campo, try **Pietre Bigiotteria,** Via Roma, 41. Open Mon.-Sat. 8am-10pm, Sun. 10am-noon.

Buses: ATL, Viale Elba, 20 (tel. 91 43 92). Pick up a schedule and buy tickets at the office. Open June-Sept. daily 8am-8pm; Oct.-May Mon.-Sat. 8am-1:20pm and 4-6:10pm, Sun. 9:30am-12:30pm and 2-6:10pm. **Luggage Storage:** L2500 per item.

Ferries: Toremar, Calata Italia, 22 (tel. 91 80 80). Hydrofoil tickets available at the **Toremar Aliscafi booth** on the waterfront in front of the main Toremar office. **Navarma,** Viale Elba, 4 (tel. 91 81 01). **Elba Ferries** (tel. 93 06 76), Calata Italia, 30 (tel. 71 82 70).

Car Rental: Rent Chiappi, Calata Italia, 30 (tel. 71 82 70). Rents small Fiats, Renaults, and Mokes, L65,000-70,000 per day. Friendly staff helps you get gas and get around. Also rents **mountain bikes** (L18,000-20,000) and **mopeds** (L25,000-50,000). Insurance included. If you're planning to rent for a few days, try **Rent Mondo,** Via Fucini, 6 (tel. 91 72 76). Fiats start at L90,000 for one day, L60,000 for each additional day.

Bike/Moped Rental: TWN, Viale Elba, 32 (tel. 91 46 66; fax 91 58 99). Easily the best place to rent mopeds (L25,000 for 9am-7pm, L35,000 for 24hr.), bikes (L10,000 for 9am-7pm, L15,000 for 24hr.), and kayaks (L28,000 per day) on the island. Add 20% in July and Aug. They have branches around the island (in Marciana Marina, Porto Azzurro, Lacona, or Marina di Campo; L10,000 fee for returning to a different branch). Groups can even have luggage transported for another L10,000. 20% discount on mention of *Let's Go.* Auto driver's license required. Open 9am-1pm and 3:30-7:30pm. V, MC. Also see **Rent Chiappi,** above.

Emergencies: tel. 113. **Ambulance:** P. Repubblica, 37 (tel. 91 40 09). **Hospital:** (tel. 93 85 11), off Via Carducci. **Fire:** tel. 115.

Post Office: P. Hutre, off P. della Repubblica. Open Mon.-Fri. 8:15am-7pm, Sat. 8:15am-12:30pm. There is another **branch,** closer to the port, on Via Carducci. Open Mon.-Fri. 8:15am-1:30pm, Sat. 8:15am-12:30pm. **Postal code:** 57037.

Telephone Code: 0565 (for almost all numbers on the island).

Accommodations and Food

Overlooking the *piazza* of the *centro storico* lies the **Ape Elbana,** Salita Cosimo de' Medici (tel./fax 91 42 45). Personable, English-speaking staff shows you to your cheery, cavernous room. Singles L50,000-60,000. Doubles L60,000-80,000. Half-pension L70,000-75,000, required in August. Full-pension L85,000-90,000. If you can't do without a view of the sea, check into **Albergo Le Ghiaie** (tel. 91 51 78) on the pleasant beach of the same name. A labyrinth of white stucco walls, cloaked in flowers, connects the hotel's light and breezy rooms. Singles L50,000, in high-season L100,000. Doubles L80,000. All rooms have private bath and many have balconies.

Infested with overpriced tourist restaurants, Portoferraio is not the best place to indulge the appetite. If you select carefully at the **Osteria del Ponticello,** Via Carducci, 33, though, you probably won't blow your budget. Try their creamy *penne strascicate* (L8000). *Primi* L8000-12,000, *secondi* L12,000-15,000. Cover L1500.

Open Wed.-Mon. 7-11pm. Sustain yourself in style at the **Enoteca al Solito Posto,** a charming wine bar that also dishes out some delicious meals. Try their fresh homemade pasta (L8000-12,000). **Trattoria da Zucchetta,** P. della Repubblica, 40 (tel. 91 53 31), in the heart of the historic center, offers delectable Neapolitan dishes at moderate prices. *Primi* L6000-15,000; try the rich *gnocchi ai quattro formaggi* for L8000. *Secondi* L10,000-18,000. Pizzas L5000-14,000. Across from the port, basic picnic fare can be found at the **Margherita** supermarket, Calata Italia, 6. Open Thurs.-Tues. 7:30am-1pm and 4:30-8pm. Whichever establishment you decide to grace, be sure to taste some of Elba's *aleatico,* a sweet, full-bodied wine liquor.

Sights

If you are caught in Portoferraio with some time to spare, you won't want to miss the **Napoleon museum,** located at his one-time residence, the Villa dei Mulini (tel. 91 58 46). Inside, you'll find his personal library, furniture graced by the imperial derrière, and a good many of his letters from exile. (Open Mon.-Sat. 9am-7pm, Sun. 9am-1pm. Admission L8000.) Also consider visiting the **Museo Archaeologico** (tel. 91 73 98) on Fortezza dell Lingrella, which guides you through the history of Elba from prehistoric times to the present. (Open daily Sept.-June 9:30am-12:30pm and 4-7pm; July-Aug. 9:30am-12:30pm and 6-12pm. Admission L4000, children L2000.)

MARINA DI CAMPO

Marina di Campo's fine sandy beaches, winding their way for miles along the coast, attract masses of vacationing families. The numerous campgrounds around Marina di Campo are popular with young people. You can either bake in the sun or rent sporting equipment like **sailboards** (starting at L15,000 per hr.) or **paddleboats** (L12,000 per hr.) along the beach. **Biko's Bikes** in P. Torino rents cycles and mopeds (L25,000-40,000 per day). **Hotel Lido,** Via Mascagni, 29 (tel. 97 60 40), near the center of town (turn left from P. Torino), is only a minute from the beach. Clean and comfortable rooms, some with balconies. Doubles L55,000-65,000, with bath L70,000-99,000. Limited parking is available for guests. You must reserve by Easter for July and August. For camping, try **La Foce** (tel. 97 64 56), a well-equipped place right on the beach, or the nearby **Del Mare** (tel. 97 62 37). Open April 1-Oct. 30. Both lie to the left of Marina di Campo's waterfront. The **Minimarket** in P. Torino, half a block up from the bus stop, stocks all the essentials. Open daily in summer 7:30am-8pm; in winter 7:30am-4:30pm. Satisfy your munchies at the **Canabis Restaurant,** Via Roma, 41/43 (tel. 97 75 55), which bakes the best food around, including killer crêpes stuffed with cheese and *prosciutto* for around L6000. Nonna Tonina rises at the crack of dawn every day to whip up a heavenly *montenegrina* cake (L4000 for this taste of paradise). No brownies, though. Open daily 6am-1am. Via Roma, along the waterfront, is also chock full of *alimentari,* where you can stock up for next to nothing. In summer, the party moves to **Marina 2000** at night for dancing and carousing.

PORTO AZZURRO

If you intend to stay in Porto Azzurro, brace yourself for a major financial outlay. Sunspot of the too-thin and too-rich, Porto Azzurro shelters some of the finest beaches on the island, but the beauty doesn't come cheap. Cozy, eccentrically decorated doubles (L50,000-90,000, with bath) are available at **Da Berta** (tel. 95 361 or 85 026), an *affitta camere* off P. Palestro. Even cheaper, although decidedly more crowded and dusty, are the many campgrounds at Loc. Barbarossa, all in close proximity to the beach; the largest is **Camping Roclan's** (tel. 95 78 03). For food, **The Grill,** Via Marconi, 26, near the Blumarine Hotel, offers copious portions of *penne* with either tomatoes or clams for L8000. Open daily 8:30am-2:30pm and 6pm-1am.

MARCIANA MARINA

The strip of pebble beach that borders Marciana Marina's waterfront is just one of the countless beaches that hide in isolated coves along this part of the island. **Casa Lupi,**

Via Amedeo (tel. 99 143), is your best bet for a room here. It's a bit of a hike (10min. uphill from the beach), but it sports clean rooms behind green shutters and a terrace that looks out over a vineyard to the sea below. Singles L50,000, low-season L45,000. Doubles L75,000, low-season L70,000. All rooms with bath. Half-pension L65,000-85,000. **Albergo Imperia,** Via Amedeo, 12 (tel. 99 082; fax 90 42 59), offers comfortable rooms, decorated with paintings and sketches of the island, at reasonable prices. The personable proprietor will get you discounts at local restaurants or offer you a table in the garden if you prefer to eat in. Singles L45,000-65,000. Doubles L80,000-110,000. All have bath, TV, and refrigerator; some have balconies. **Bar L'Onda,** Via Amedeo, 4, sells great crêpes (L4000-6000) and *panini* (L3000-6000) for take-out.

Marciana Marina is the perfect base from which to explore the less developed western half of Elba. You can reach the numerous beaches along the western coast by boat; rentals are available in Capo Sant'Andrea for about L100,000 per day. From Marciana Marina, partiers head to **Club 64** in nearby **Procchio** to hear live music at night. Cover L20,000. Marciana Marina's **post office** is at Viale Loyd. Open Mon.-Fri. 8:15am-1:30pm and Sat. 8:15am-12:30pm. For **first aid,** contact the Guardia Medica Turistica, Viale Regina Margherita (tel. 90 44 36).

An amusing excursion from Marciana Marina is a visit to **Monte Capanne.** From the top of this 1019-m mountain you can see the entire island and even Corsica on a clear day. The strenuous uphill trek takes two hours, but a cable car will carry you up for L12,000, roundtrip L18,000. Open 10am-12:15pm and 2:30-6pm. To get to Monte Capanne, take the bus from Marciana Marina to Marciana and get off at the Monte Capanne stop (15min.). From Marciana you can also walk to the **Romitorio di San Cerbone** and the **Santuario della Madonna del Monte,** two sanctuaries described by one Italian writer as "dense with mysticism." If you're interested in **guided hikes** to explore Elba's natural beauty, contact **Il Genio del Bosco, Centro Trekking Isola d'Elba in Antiche Saline** (tel. 93 03 35), near Portoferraio.

NORTHERN ITALY

Liguria

Genoa divides the crescent-shaped coastal strip known as Liguria into the Riviera di Levante (rising sun) to the east and the Riviera di Ponente (setting sun) to the west. This Italian Riviera stretches 350km along the Mediterranean between France and Tuscany, forming the most famous and touristed area of the Italian coastline. Protected by the Alps from the more severe weather to the north, Liguria cultivates its crops and its lively tourist trade all year long, making it one of Italy's most prosperous regions. In summer the landscape is ablaze with deep reds and purples, while lemon and almond blossoms scent the air. In winter, olive trees shade the robust flower beds and produce what may be Italy's best oil (a title contested by Tuscany).

Ligurians are known for their cultural isolation. They claim Nordic, not Roman, ancestry and have their own vocabulary and accent, generally incomprehensible to other Italians (let alone foreigners). The distinctive character of Liguria, however, does not make its residents any less Italian, nor did it prevent them from playing a leading role in the unification of the Italian peninsula. Giuseppe Mazzini, known as the father of the Risorgimento, and Giuseppe Garibaldi, its most popular hero, were both Ligurians.

The character of the Italian Riviera differs significantly from that of its French neighbor. Here you'll find neither the arrogance nor the cultural sterility of Cannes or St. Tropez. The palm-lined boulevards and clear turquoise water may similar, but above the beach areas rise *città vecchie* or *alte* (old or upper cities)—distinctly Italian mazes of narrow cobblestone streets and tiny *piazze.*

Although slightly more expensive, the eastern Levante coast is the more picturesque of the two. It's less congested than western Ponente, and the dramatic juxtaposition of Appenine mountains and Ligurian Sea creates a landscape where pine forests hover thousands of feet above the water and tiny pebble beaches are wedged between rugged escarpments. Santa Margherita Ligure and Cinque Terre offer unobstructed havens of relaxation. But if your taste runs instead toward long stretches of sand and seemingly infinite boardwalks, head for Ponente. A short hop from the French border, its towns provide pleasant sunbathing, clear waters, and Italian techno music. For an affordable base, try Finale Ligure—a re2sort town that combines Hollywood palm trees with medieval ambience.

All the coastal towns are linked by frequent trains on either the Genoa-La Spezia or Genoa-Ventimiglia line, and frequent intercity buses pass through all major towns. Boats connect most resort towns, and local buses run to inland hill-towns.

Genoa (Genova)

Genoa's name comes from the Latin word *janua,* meaning gate, appropriate for a town that is one of Italy's busiest ports. Genoa's narrow, shop-filled streets are nestled between the lofty peaks of the coast and the slightly tainted waters of the Ligurian Sea. As early as the 13th century, Genoa's leading families were able to furnish the city with parks, palaces, and art, almost all of which can be seen today. Christopher Columbus, Giuseppe Mazzini (the Risorgimento idealogue), and Nicolò Paganini (the virtuoso violinist) are only a few of Genoa's famous figures. While Genoa is still a bustling port, international business has lent it a sense of fashion.

Built on mountains that extend almost to the water itself, Genoa's tall buildings are packed tightly together. In addition to the buses which snake uphill on narrow switchbacks, Genoa's public transportation includes both public elevators and rapidly ascending funiculars, cog-rail trolleys that provide quick access to higher altitudes. For a peaceful respite from the chaotic modern city, stick to the *creuze* (narrow footpaths) and winding *vicoli* (alleys) that meander upwards among houses, overhanging gardens, and the ubiquitous street cats. These trails offer spectacular views of the bustling city below, which, from a distance, takes on an unexpected air of cheerful tranquility.

ORIENTATION AND PRACTICAL INFORMATION

Most visitors arrive at one of Genoa's two train stations: **Genova Principe,** in Piazza Acquaverde, or **Genova Brignole,** in Piazza Verdi. Buses #40 and 37 connect the two stations (25min., L1500). From Brignole take bus #40 and from Principe take #41 to the center of town. The city stretches along the coast. From Stazione Principe to the central **Piazza de Ferrari,** take **Via Balbi** to **Via Cairdi** (which becomes **Via Garibaldi**), then turn right on **Via XXV Aprile. Via XX Settembre** runs east from P. de Ferrari toward Stazione Brignole. Avoid the free tourist office map—procure a decent one at an *edicola* (newsstand) in the train station for about L6000. Genoa's tangled streets can stump even a native.

The *centro storico* contains many of Genoa's most important monuments. Unfortunately, it is also the city's most dangerous quarter, riddled with drugs and prostitution at night. The problem is complicated by the shadowy, labyrinthine streets. You'll need a sixth sense to navigate here, even with a map, and it's an extremely bad place to get lost. Don't wander the area after dark or on Sundays (when shops are closed), and be cautious in August when the natives leave. But do visit: the sights are well worth seeing.

Genoa's double sequence of **street numbers** (red for commercial establishments, black for residential or office buildings) is confusing, especially since dirty red numerals often appear black. Don't get discouraged if you come to the supposed address of a place and it's not there; chances are you've simply come to the number of the wrong color. **Red addresses are listed in Let's Go: Italy with an "r" after the number.**

Tourist Office: EPT, Via Roma, 11 (tel. 57 67 91; fax 58 14 08). From Stazione Brignole, go right on Via de Amicis to P. Brignole, then continue up Via Serra to P. Corvetto. The tourist office is on the 3rd floor of a building near the *piazza.* Friendly, patient, and generous with its small store of useful info. Some English spoken. Open Mon.-Fri. 8am-1:15pm and 2-6:30pm, Sat. 8am-1:30pm. There are **branches** at the Principe train station (tel. 246 26 33) and the C. Colombo airport (tel. 241 52 47). Both open Mon.-Fri. 8am-8pm. For a better map and more information on youth-specific events, head to **Informegiovani** in the Palazzo Ducale at P. Matteotti, 5. Open July-Aug. Mon.-Fri. 9am-12:30pm; Sept.-June 10am-1pm and 3-6pm.

Tourist Police: (tel. 536 61) Via Diaz at the *ufficio stranieri* (office for foreigners).

Budget Travel: CTS, Via San Vincenzo, 117r (tel. 56 43 66 or 53 27 48), off Via XX Settembre. Just before the road curves, walk up a flight of stairs to the right. Student fares to all destinations. Open Mon.-Fri. 9am-1pm and 2:30-6pm. The **Associazione Albergatori per la Gioventù,** Via Cairoli, 2 (tel. 29 82 84), near P. Nunziata, sells HI cards. Open Mon.-Fri. 9:30-11:30am and 3-6pm. Closed Wed. afternoons.

Consulates: U.S., Via Dante, 2 (tel. 58 44 92); in Milan (tel. (02) 29 00 18 41). Open Mon. 4:30-5:30pm. **U.K.,** Via XII Ottobre, 2 (tel. 56 48 33). Open Tues.-Thurs. 9am-noon.

Currency Exchange: Banks abound. Sat.-Sun., when banks are closed, head to either train station. Both give slightly lower rates but only take L500, if any, commission. Open daily 7:15am-1pm and 2:30-7:30pm.

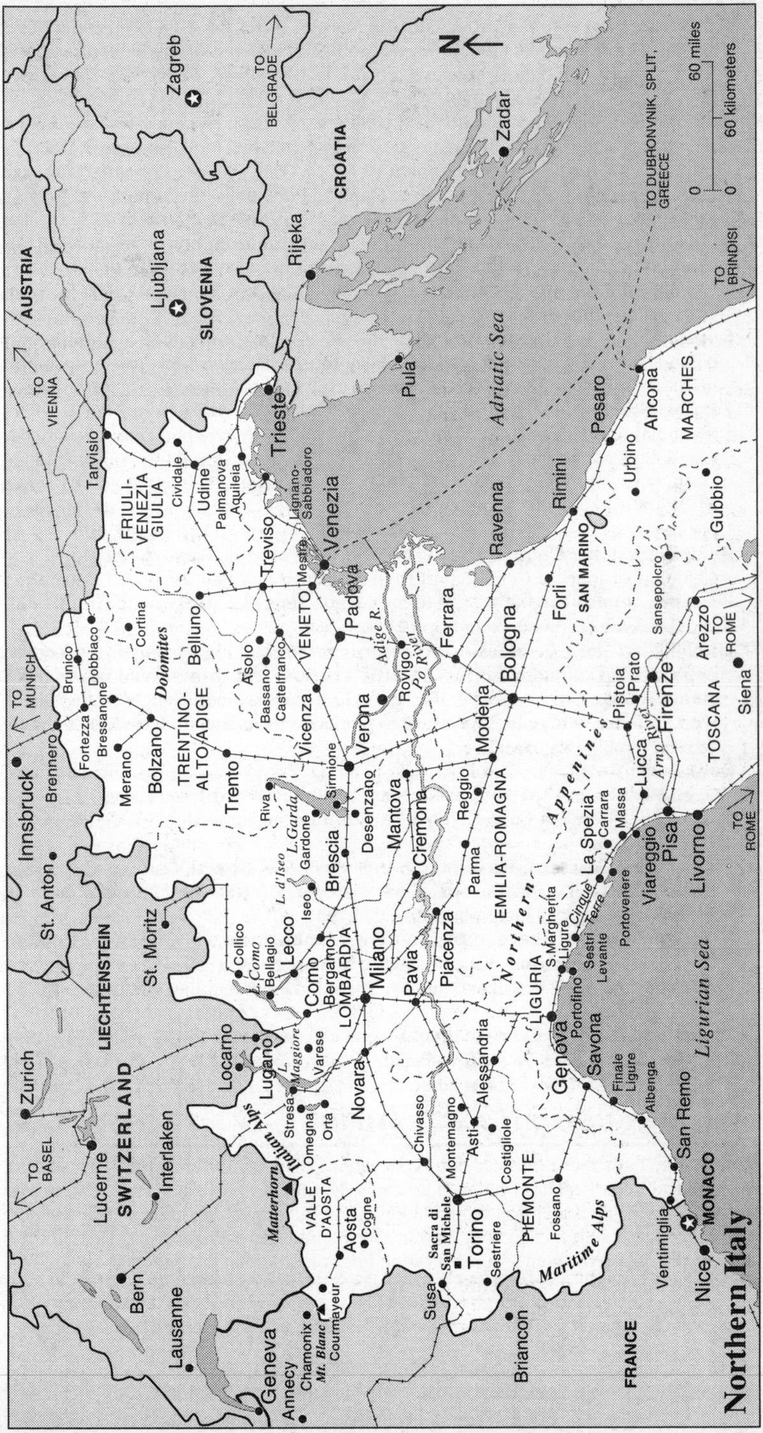

Northern Italy

American Express: Viatur, P. Fontane Marose, 3 (tel. 56 12 41), inside a travel agency. Doesn't handle money, but will authorize **check cashing** for cardmembers (they give you an authorization, which you take to a bank to get your *lire*). Open Mon.-Fri. 9am-1:30pm and 3:30-7pm.

Telephones: Stazione Brignole, to the right as you exit the station. Pay phones, directories, and real live (though curt) employees. Open Mon.-Sat. 8am-9:30pm.

Flights: C. Colombo Internazionale (tel. 24 11), in Sestiere Ponente. European destinations. You can take a bus from Stazione Principe to the airport.

Trains: Stazione Principe in P. Acquaverde, **Stazione Brignole** in P. Verdi. For train info call 28 40 81, daily 7am-11pm. Trains run from both stations to points along the Ligurian Riviera and to major Italian cities. To Turin (15 per day, 2hr., L13,600) and Rome (15 per day, 6hr., L37,000). **Luggage Storage:** L5000 for 12hr. Open 6am-10pm.

Buses: AMT, Via D'Annunzio, 8r (tel. 499 74 14). One-way tickets within the city cost L1500 and are valid for 1½hr. All-day tourist passes L4000 (foreign passport necessary). Tickets and passes can also be used for *funicolare* and elevator rides.

Ferries: Stazione Marittima (tel. 25 66 82). Major destinations are Porto Torres (Sardinia) and Palermo (each more cheaply and easily reached from elsewhere). Listed fares are one-way deck class. **Grandi Traghetti** (tel. 58 93 31) to Palermo (Mon.-Tues. and Thurs., 20hr., L142,000). **Tirrenia** (tel. 275 80 41) to Porto Torres (daily, 14hr., L70,000). **Corsica Ferries** (tel. 59 33 01 or 25 54 24) to Corsica (2 per day, 6hr., L44,000-61,000). Check with the tourist office for more info.

Boat Excursions: Cooperativa Battellieri del Porto di Genova (tel. 26 57 12). Guided boat tours of Genoa's port from the aquarium (daily at about 11:30am and 3:15pm, 40min., L10,000). Trips to the Cinque Terre (L20,000, roundtrip L33,000) and Portofino (L15,000, roundtrip L20,000).

Hitchhiking: Let's Go does not recommend hitchhiking for anyone. Women in particular should exercise extreme caution, and they should never hitch alone. Hitchers take bus #17, 18, 19, or 20 from Stazione Brignole to the Genoa West entrance, where highways lead to points north and south. It is illegal to hitchhike on the highway itself.

Bookstore: Bozzi, Via Cairoli, 4r (tel. 29 87 42; fax 29 44 21), has English books. Open Mon.-Fri. 8:30am-7pm, Sat. 8:30am-12:30pm. Closed 1 week Aug 10.

Swimming Pool: Stadio del Nuoto (Albaro), P. Dunant, 4 (tel. 362 84 09). Open daily 8am-8pm.

Pharmacies: Pescetto, Via Balbi, 185r (tel. 26 26 97); **Ghersi,** Corte Lambruschini, 16 (tel. 54 16 61); and **Europa,** Corso Europa, 576 (tel. 38 02 39) are open all night. For another all-night pharmacy, dial 192.

Emergencies: tel. 112 for medical concerns. **Ambulance:** tel. 570 59 51. **Hospital: Ospedale San Martino,** Viale Benedetto XV, 10 (tel. 353 51).

Post Office: Many offices all over the city, in both train stations, and in the airport. Try the main office at P. Dante, 4 (tel. 259 46 87), 2 blocks from P. de Ferrari, for *fermo posta* or express mail service. Another office is at Via Rela, 8 (tel. 64 67 71). Most offices are open Mon.-Sat. 8:10am-7:40pm. **Postal Code:** 16100.

Telephone Code: 010.

ACCOMMODATIONS AND CAMPING

Genoa may have more one-star hotels *per capita* than any other city in Italy, so finding cheap shelter isn't a problem. Unfortunately, finding someplace you *want* to stay *is*. Almost without exception, budget lodgings in the *centro storico* and near the port prefer to rent rooms by the hour, and no one should stay there at night. Head for the hostel, or stick to the area around Stazione Brignole; the establishments there are substantially nicer and more secure. Rooms get scarce only in October, when Genoa hosts nautical conventions.

Genoa: Centro Storico

Ostello Per La Gioventù (HI), Via Costanzi, 120 (tel./fax 242 24 57). From Stazione Principe, take bus #35 for 5 stops to Via Ambrogio Spinda, then transfer to bus #40 (which you can take directly from Brignole). Ride #40 to the end of the line, just uphill from the hostel. Everything you'd ever want: bar, cafeteria (pasta starts at L5000), elevators, free lockers, info on Genoa, laundry (L12,000 for 5kg), parking, patios, TV, wheelchair access, and panoramic views. Facilities are new and the multi-lingual staff is friendly and helpful. Bus #40 goes back to the *centro* every 10min. Open 7-9am and 3:30-midnight. Checkout 9:30am. Curfew 12:30pm. HI card required. L22,000 per person, L23,000 for family accommodations. Sheets, breakfast, and hot showers included.

Pensione Mirella, Via Gropallo, 4/4 (tel. 839 37 22). From Stazione Brignole, turn right on Via de Amicis to P. Brignole and right again onto Via Gropallo. A beautifully maintained and secure building. Large, clean, elegantly furnished rooms, complete with gold brocade wallpaper. Singles L37,000. Doubles L65,000.

Albergo Carola, Via Gropallo, 4/12 (tel. 839 13 40), 2 flights up from Mirella. Large rooms overlooking a quiet garden. Exuberant proprietor is always ready with a refreshing glass of iced tea. Singles L40,000. Doubles with shower L70,000.

Pensione Barone, Via XX Settembre, 2/23 (tel. 58 75 78), off Via Fiume near Stazione Brignole, on the 3rd floor. Delightful, family-run hotel with baroque designs on the ceilings. Immaculate facilities. Ask for towels. Singles with bath L60,000. Doubles L65,000, with bath L75,000. Large rooms sleep up to 4 people, L80,000-90,000, with bath. Self-serve coffee L1000. Desk open 9am-midnight. Call ahead, especially around Oct. 15-25. V, MC.

Camping: The area around Genoa teems with campgrounds, but many are booked solid during July and Aug. Options in the city are scarce and some unsavory; try for something on the beach. **Villa Doria,** Via al Campeggio, Villa Doria, 15 (tel. 696 96 00), is in Pegli. Take the train or bus #1, 2, or 3 from P. Caricamento to Pegli, then walk or transfer to bus #93 up Via Vespucci. The closest campground west of the city. Beautiful location, with bungalows and heated showers, as well as hospitable hosts. English spoken. L6000 per person, L9000-15,000 per tent. Also try **Genova Est,** Via Marcon-Loc Cassa (tel. 347 20 53). Take the train to Bogliasco. L7000 per person, L7000 per tent.

FOOD

The cuisine of Genoa may expand your waistline, but your wallet and taste buds will thank you. *Trattorie,* found mainly in the *centro storico,* are innumerable. The incomparable pesto, the pride and joy of Genova, is a sauce made from ground basil, pine nuts, garlic, *parmigiano* (parmesan cheese), and olive oil. Other delectables include *farinata,* ravioli stuffed with spinach and ricotta and served with a creamy walnut sauce, and *pansotti,* a fried bread made from chick-pea flour. Enhance any meal with loads of olive oil-soaked *focaccia,* a delicious flat bread topped with herbs, olives, onions, or cheese (a specialty of nearby Recco). Try a slice of world-famous Genoa salami; it's smoother and fresher than anything you'll get at home.

Trattoria Colombo, Borgo degli Incrociati, 44r (tel. 87 72 24), behind the Stazione Brignole (finding it is half the fun!). A traditional *trattoria* frequented by locals. Home-cooked meals in large quantities at great prices. *Menù* L14,000. Open Sept.-July Mon.-Sat. 12:30-2:30pm and 7:30-10pm.

Trattoria da Maria, Vico Testadoro, 14r (tel. 58 10 80), off Via XXV Aprile near P. Marose. Fresh selection changes daily. Wonderful staff helps translate the *menù* (L13,000). Open Sun.-Thurs. noon-2pm and 4:30-10pm, Fri. noon-2pm.

Brera Express, Via di Brera, 11r (tel. 54 32 80), just off Via XX Settembre near Stazione Brignole. Pizzeria and full-service restaurant. The best deal is the *menù* (L15,000), but all entrées are reasonably priced. Try the *spiedini all'Italiana* with rice and a side dish for just L8600. Open daily 11:30am-2pm and 7pm-midnight. Self-service closes at 10pm.

Sa Pesta, Via dei Giustiniani, 16r (tel. 20 86 36), south of P. Matteotti in the *centro storico.* Sa Pesta knows pesto; everyone from doctors to dockworkers converges here to wolf down incomparable Genovese specialties like *farinata* and *minestrone alla genovese* (with pesto). *Primi* L6000-8000, *secondi* L10,000. *Focaccia* and *pizzato* for takeout. Open Sept.-July Mon.-Sat. noon-2:30pm. In winter, dinner 6-10pm. Call for reservations.

Bakari, Vico del Fieno, 16r (tel. 29 19 36), to the northwest of P. San Matteo in the *centro storico.* Packs 'em in at lunch. Six different *menù,* including 3 vegetarian dinners (L18,000-25,000). Open Mon.-Tues. and Thurs. noon-2:30pm and 6-9pm, Wed. and Fri. noon-2:30pm.

Kilt 2 Self Service, Vico Doria, 1r (tel. 20 27 98), on a tiny street just off P. San Matteo in the *centro storico.* A cafeteria that dishes up otherworldly gourmet meals for L14,000. Menus change daily. Open Mon.-Sat. 1:45-2:30pm.

Self Service Rogatino, Via XII Ottobre, 29r (tel. 82 92 90). Scarf down hearty *risotto frutti di mare* as the fast-paced masses whiz by in BMWs. *Menù* L15,000. Open Mon.-Sat. 12:30-2:30 and 7-9:30pm.

Focacceria San Vincenzo, Via San Vincenzo, 185r (tel. 58 83 68), off Via XX Settembre. Bakes up a wide variety of tasty *focaccie,* plus pizza and pastries. Try the fresh *focaccia con patate* (L1600). Open Mon.-Sat. 7am-7:30pm.

Antico Forno, Via di Porta Soprana, 15 (tel. 29 99 86), on the corner of Vico dei Notari. The smell will draw you in for bread, *focaccia,* or pizza, all L1000-5000. Open Mon.-Sat. 7:30am-1:30pm and 4:30-7:30pm.

Il Fornaio, Via San Luca, 97r (tel. 28 15 80), off Via Lomellini. The place to come for the tastiest *biscotti,* bread, pastries, *focaccie,* and pizza. Open Mon.-Sat. 7:30am-1pm and 4-7:30pm. Closed Wed. afternoons.

Bananarama, Via San Vincenzo, 65 (tel. 58 11 30). Thirty different kinds of scrumptious *gelato* are sure to please anyone's palate. Or try *crema di riso* or the fresh fruit *granite* (L1500-L2500); lemon and blackberry are divine! Open daily 11am-7:30pm.

SIGHTS

From Principe to the Centro Storico

Because of its long-standing commercial strength, Genoa has managed to collect some of the finest 16th- and 17th-century works of Flemish and Italian art. The city is also well endowed with the *palazzi* and *ville* of its famous merchant families. Start your tour at the *piazza* in front of Stazione Principe, which is graced by a statue of Christopher Columbus. In the distance is the port. Nearby, just before the *palazzo*-lined **Via Balbi** on **Salita S. Giovanni,** stands one of Genoa's oldest monuments, the Romanesque church **San Giovanni di Pre'.** The stone vaulted roof and filtered light add to its Romanesque weight and cavernous feel. Next door, the 12th-century **La Commenda** housed the Knight Commanders of St. John.

Via Balbi, in the heart of Genoa's university quarter, contains some of the most lavish *palazzi* in Genoa; be prepared to see gold rivaling that at Fort Knox. At #10, the fine courtyard of the 18th-century **Palazzo Reale** (Royal Palace; tel. 247 06 40) once opened onto a beautiful seaside garden; now it looks out on a major road and the city sprawl. Upstairs, take a tour of the living quarters of past kings and queens. Everything is either gilded or velvet, complemented by the paintings of Tintoretto, van Dyck, and Bassano. (Open Wed.-Sat. 9am-7pm, Sun.-Tues. 9am-1:45pm. Admission L8000, under 18 and over 60 free.) Across the street is the **Palazzo Balbi,** home to many of the departments of the **Università di Genova.** The street runs into **Piazza della Nunziata,** formerly called *Gaustato* ("broken") for the large number of ruins in the square. Today P. della Nunziata typifies the Genovese square: small, irregular, and distinguished by formal *palazzi.* The strong neoclassical façade (1843) of the **Church of SS. Annunziata del Vestato** (1591-1620), P. Nunziata, 4 (tel. 29 76 62), conceals an incongruously Rococo interior. The gold-washed interior was almost entirely reconstructed after suffering heavy damage during World War II bombing raids. The chapels that line the aisles form an impressive gallery of 17th-century art. (Open daily 6:30-11:30am and 4-7pm. Free.)

Bookstores line Via Cairoli on its way to **Via Garibaldi,** the most impressive street in Genoa, which is bedecked with elegant *palazzi.* A glance inside their courtyards reveals fountains, frescoes, and leafy gardens. The **Palazzo Bianco** (1548, rebuilt 1712) at Via Garibaldi, 11 (tel. 29 18 03), is now home to one of the city's most important collections of Ligurian art, as well as its best Dutch and Flemish paintings. Across the street, the 17th-century **Palazzo Rosso,** Via Garibaldi, 18, houses magnificent furnishings in a lavishly frescoed interior and hosts the **Galleria di Palazzo Rosso** (tel. 28 26 41). On the second floor, you'll see several full-length van Dyck portraits and Bernardo Strozzi's masterpiece, *La Cuoca.* (Both are open Tues., Thurs.-Fri., and Sun. 9am-1pm, Wed. and Sat. 9am-7pm.) Next door to the Palazzo Bianco at Via Garibaldi, 9, **Palazzo Tursi (Palazzion Municipale),** now the city hall, showcases Nicolò Paganini's violin, the *Guarneri del Gesù.* The sound of this instrument broke the hearts of many, drove others to suicide, and convinced the rest that they were hearing angels sing. The violin is still used on rare occasions to perform Paganini's works, with less extreme consequences. (Open Mon.-Fri. 8:30am-noon and 1-4:30pm. Free.)

The *galleria* faces the vigorous Renaissance façade of the **Palazzo Municipale** (1564-70), with its beautiful roof gardens. Peer into the courtyard of the **Palazzo Podestà** (1565), Via Garibaldi, 7, to glimpse an unusual *grotto* fountain and an intriguing stucco decoration of a merman. **Palazzo Parodi** (1578), Via Garibaldi, 3, boasts an elegant doorway with noseless male figures—a freakish tribute to the owner's ancestor, Megollo Lecari, who took revenge on his enemies by chopping off their noses and ears. Via Garibaldi spills into P. Fontane Marose, from which you can take Via Interiano to P. del Portello for a public elevator (runs daily 6:50am-10:30pm; L400) that whisks you up to **P. Castelletto.** This *piazza* maintains an extraordinary vista over the entire city and port. From P. del Portello, take the *funicolare* (L1500) to reach the **Church of Sant'Anna.** A harmonious Renaissance work, Sant'Anna is also notable for its location, peeking out precariously from leafy gardens onto the steep hillside. One of Genoa's most beautiful and peaceful paths descends from the church, winding past trees and *palazzi.*

From P. Fontane Marose, Salita di Santa Caterina takes you to Piazza Corvetto. The **Villetta Di Negro** spreads out along the hill to your left, inviting you to relax amid waterfalls, grottos, and terraced gardens. Its summit houses a real treasure, the **Museo d'Arte Orientale "E. Chiossone"** (Museum of Oriental Art; tel. 54 22 85). Check out the impressive sculptures on the first floor, particularly the diminutive dog-dragon. (Open Tues. and Thurs.-Sat. 9am-1pm, every 1st and 3rd Sun. of the month 9am-1pm. Admission L6000.) From P. Corvetto, Via Roma leads to **Piazza de Ferrari,** the city's bustling center and home to a monstrous fountain resembling, naturally, a raised hubcap. Off P. de Ferrari lie P. Matteotti and the **Palazzo Ducale,** once the home of the city's rulers. Inside, visit the two beautiful courtyards, one punctuated by an elegant 17th-century fountain. On the corner opposite this imposing palace stands the ornate **Church of the Gesù,** also known as SS. Ambrogio e Andrea (1549-1606). This baroque building features *trompe l'oeil* effects, double cupolas, and two important Rubens canvases, *The Circumcision* and *St. Ignatius Healing a Woman Possessed of the Devil.*

The Centro Storico

The eerily beautiful and often dangerous historic center is a mass of confusing streets bordered by the port, Via Garibaldi, and P. de Ferrari. Due to its crime, prostitution, and drugs, the historic center is a safe spot for tourists only during weekdays when stores are open. At night, the quarter's underground activity emerges and not even the police venture in. But the *centro storico* is also home to Genoa's most memorable monuments: the *duomo,* the Church of San Luca, and the medieval Torre Embraici. As you walk, look up at the numerous sculpted and painted tabernacles, or *"Madonette,"* that adorn the corners of buildings.

Off P. Matteotti resides the **Duomo San Lorenzo.** Already in existence in the 9th century, the church was enlarged and reconstructed between the 12th and 16th centuries, resulting in a striped Gothic façade and a lopsided appearance—only one of the two planned bell towers was completed. The carved central portal decorated with lions, sirens, and vines (oh, my!) gives way to a simple interior and a checkered floor. Along the left wall, the chapel of St. John the Baptist is decorated with statues of Adam and Eve by Matteo Civitali. A vintage American bomb adorns the right wall of the church, miraculously unexploded after crashing through the roof during World War II. (Open Mon.-Sat. 8am-noon and 3-6:30pm, Sun. noon-6:30pm. Free.) Behind the *duomo,* Salita all'Arrivescovato leads to Genoa's most charming square, **Piazza San Matteo.** It contains the houses and chapel of the Doria family, the medieval oligarchy that ruled Genoa. The animal reliefs above the first floor are the trademarks of the masons who built the houses. Chiseled into the façade of the small but elaborately decorated **Church of San Matteo** (1125) are descriptions of the Dorias' great deeds, and to the left a small door protects a lovely, 14th-century cloister. If the gate is closed, you may be able to talk your way in. (Open Mon.-Sat. 7:30am-noon and

4-6:30pm, Sun. 9am-noon and 4-6:30pm.) A short walk down Via S. Matteo and Via Lampetto leads to one of Genoa's oldest churches, **Church of Santa Maria delle Vigne,** an ornate building with gold in the ceiling and large paintings on the walls. Dating from the 10th century, it retains its original Romanesque bell tower. (Open 8am-noon and 3:30-7pm. Free.)

From here head down Via Greci to **Via San Luca,** the main artery of the old quarter, where you'll find many of Genoa's most important monuments. The **Church of San Siro** was Genoa's first cathedral (rebuilt 1588-1613). A dome crowns the little yellow and gray **Church of San Luca,** a 12th-century treasure in the shape of a Greek cross. (Both open Mon.-Fri. 4-6pm. Free.) **Palazzo Spinola,** P. di Pellicceria, 1 (follow the yellow signs), demonstrates Genoa's 16th- to 18th-century mercantile wealth. Its rooms retain most of their original furnishings and are adorned by works of art donated by the Spinola family, complemented by later additions in the **Galleria Nazionale di Palazzo Spinola** (tel. 29 46 61). Don't miss the portraits of the four evangelists by van Dyck in the Sala da Pranzo. (Open Mon. 9am-1pm, Tues.-Sat. 10am-7pm, Sun. 2-7pm. Admission L8000. Under 18 and over 60 free.)

Portici di Sottoripa (medieval arcades) border the side of P. Caricamento by the port across from P. Banchi. On the other side of the piazza, the **Palazzo San Giorgio,** a part-Gothic, part-Renaissance structure, once housed the famous Genovese bank of St. George. Intense World War II bombing left much of the area in need of reconstruction, but some interesting churches remain scattered among the old tenements and medieval ruins. One is the **Church of Santa Maria di Castello,** whose foundations date back to Greek and Etruscan times. Today, it is a labyrinth of chapels, courtyards, cloisters, and crucifixes. In the chapel to the left of the high altar, you'll find the *Crocifisso Miracoloso.* According to legend, this wooden Jesus once moved its head to attest to the honesty of a young lady betrayed by her lover. (In addition, Jesus' beard grows longer every time crisis hits the city.) If you enjoy the gruesomely morbid, look for the painting of San Pietro Martire di Verona above the door in the room to the left of the sacristy. He's shown in all his glory, complete with a halo and a large cleaver in his head—the means of his martyrdom. Nearby, the medieval **Torre Embraici** (Hebrew Towers) loom over **Santa Maria di Castello,** with Guelph battlements jutting out from its rough stone surface.

The old city's newest addition, the **Museo dell'Architettura e Scultura Ligure,** occupies the former monastery of Sant'Agostino at P. di Sarzano (tel. 20 16 61). This museum surveys Genoa's history through its surviving art. Giovanni Pisano carved the most outstanding piece, a funerary monument for Margherita of Brabant, in 1312. Fragments of this monument are scattered across the continent, but the museum hopes eventually to reassemble it. (Open Tues.-Sat. 9am-7pm, Sun. 9am-12:30pm. Admission L6000.) From P. di Sarzano, Via Ravecca leads to the medieval **Porta Soprana,** which flaunts enormous twin towers and an arched entryway, the emblem of this district. Walk past the reputed boyhood home of Christopher Columbus (his father was the gatekeeper of Soprana) and the ruins of the 12th-century **Cloister of Sant'Andrea.**

ENTERTAINMENT

To explore Genoa's aquatic life, go on a luxury cruise of the harbor (see **Practical Information** above, p.238, for more details), or stare at sea lions in the well-designed **aquarium,** the largest of its kind in Europe. All of the descriptions are in English. (Open Tues.-Wed. and Fri. 9:30am-7pm, Thurs. and Sat.-Sun. 9:30am-8:30pm. L12,000.) Like any large city, Genoa usually has a number of interesting, if somewhat unpredictable, exhibitions and concerts. Ask at the tourist office for the latest information.

For nightlife, check out the bar scene around P. Matteotti and P. delle Erbe, an area inhabited by many lively little pubs and *caffè.* Try **Caffè degli Specchi,** Salita Pollaiuoli, 43r (tel. 28 12 93), one block from both *piazze.* It's a beautiful café with seats outside in the summer and upstairs in the winter. Drinks are a bit expensive (glass of wine L4000-5000) but are usually accompanied by Genovese appetizers. In the summer the action moves to **Nervi,** only minutes away by train or bus, where people can bar-hop or stroll along the *lungomare* with their cones of *gelato.*

If you're in the mood for **jazz,** try **Charlie Christian,** Via S. Donato, 20r (tel. 29 83 93), a smoky jazz and blues bar with live music, named for the father of the jazz guitar. For more active evenings, Genoa has numerous *discoteche* that open around 11pm and close around 3am. Cover charges are usually between L15,000 and L20,000. Near Via XX Settembre, off Via Fieschi, is **Nessundorma Caffè** (where "no one sleeps"), Via alla Porta degli Archi, 74r (tel. 56 17 63), a favorite with the student crowd. In the area around Stazione Brignole are **Temptatiane** at P. Tommaseo, 17r (tel. 36 86 52) and **Cézanne** at Via Cecchi, 7r (tel. 56 10 21). **Makò,** Corso Italia, 28r (tel. 36 76 52), down by the water, is slightly more elegant and expensive.

RIVIERA DI LEVANTE

Camogli

The postcard-perfect town of Camogli vibrantly displays all the colors of the rainbow. Sun-faded peach and yellow houses crowd the hilltop, vibrant red and blue-green boats bob in the water, and piles of fishing nets lie heaped over the docks along the waterfront. Camogli is a family town where everyone seems to know everyone else. The town takes its name (a contraction of "Casa Mogli", Wives' House) from the women who ran the town while their husbands manned its once-huge fishing fleet. The men are back now, and what Dickens once called a "piratical little place" has mellowed into a small, peaceful resort of 6,000, with a picturesque and friendly boardwalk scene. Those seeking a budget version of the more glamorous Portofino might find Camogli to be the right place for fun and relaxation.

ORIENTATION AND PRACTICAL INFORMATION

The town climbs uphill from the sea into pine and olive groves separated by a raised boardwalk, overlooking the pebble beach and harbor below. To get to the center of town, go right as you exit the Camogli-San Fruttuoso station. After you pass a pea soup-colored *palazzo* about 100m from the station, turn left and go down the steep stairs leading to **Via Garibaldi.** From V. Garibaldi turn right into the alley that ushers you to free beaches.

Tourist Office: Via XX Settembre, 33 (tel. 77 10 66), to your right as you leave the station. Helps with accommodations and cheerfully answers questions. English spoken. Open Mon.-Sat. 8:30am-noon and 3:30-6pm, Sun. 9:30am-12:30pm.

Currency Exchange: Banco di Chiavari della Riviera Ligure, Via XX Settembre, 19 (tel. 77 25 76 or 77 00 33). Reasonable rates.

Trains: On the Genoa-La Spezia line. To: Genoa (30 per day, 20min., L2000); La Spezia (10 per day, 1½hr., L5700); Sestri Levante (20 per day, 30min., L2700); and Santa Margherita (20 per day, 10min., L1500).

Buses: Tigullio (tel. 513 06 or 77 44 24) buses depart from P. Schiaffino to nearby towns. Buy tickets at Bar Aldo across from the tourist office or at the *tabacchi* on Via Repubblica, 25. To Santa Margherita (14 per day, L2000) and Portofino Vetta—*not* Portofino Mare, the port town.

Ferries: The cost is worth the incredible views of the peninsula's cliffs. **Golfo Paradiso,** Via Scala, 2 (tel. 77 20 91). To San Fruttuoso (May-Sept. 8-11 per day, L7000, roundtrip L12,000). They also run a nighttime trip to Portofino (Sat. leaving 9:30pm and returning 11:20pm, Sun.-Mon. leaving 3:15pm and returning 6pm, one way L12,000, roundtrip L18,000). Buy tickets on the boat.

Pharmacy: Dr. Marchi, at Via Repubblica, 4-6 (tel. 77 10 81). A sign outside lists all-night pharmacies. Open Tues.-Sat. 8:30am-12:30pm and 3:30-7:30pm.

Emergencies: tel. 113. **First Aid:** 112. **Hospital:** Corso Mazzini, 96 (tel. 741 02).

Police: At Via Cuneo, 30F (tel. 77 00 00).

Post office: Via Cuneo, 4 (tel. 77 43 32), to the left of the station under an arcade. Open Mon.-Fri. 8:10am-5:30pm, Sat. 8:10am-noon. **Postal code:** 16032.

Telephone code: 0185.

ACCOMMODATIONS

Albergo La Camogliese, Via Garibaldi, 55 (tel. 77 14 02; fax 77 40 24). Walk down the long stairway near the train station to #55, near the seafront. The large, clean rooms are a joy, and the proprietors have definitely found their calling. They refer to *Let's Go* readers as "Let's Go *amici*" and offer them a 10% discount for paying cash. When the hotel is full, they will even try to find you a room in town. Singles with bath L50,000. Doubles with bath L75,000-90,000, depending on size and view. Breakfast L7000. Phone and TV in every room. Reservations strongly recommended. V, MC, AmEx, traveler's checks.

Pensione Augusta, Via Schiaffino, 100 (tel. 77 05 92), at the other end of town. Neat and cozy rooms with TV, phone, and nearby train tracks. Singles L50,000. Doubles L65,000-100,000. All rooms with bath. V, MC, AmEx.

Albergo Selene, Via Cuneo, 16 (tel. 77 01 49; fax 77 20 38). Walk left from the station past the post office. Singles L63,000. Doubles L95,000. Triples L120,000. Breakfast included. Some rooms with balcony. V, MC, AmEx.

FOOD

For a do-it-yourself meal, go into any of the billion shops on Via Repubblica or try the **Piccaso** supermarket at Via XX Settembre, 35, near the tourist office. Open Mon.-Tues. and Thurs.-Sat. 8am-12:30pm and 4:30-7:30pm, Wed. 8am-12:30pm. An open-air **market** in the main *piazza* offers food, clothes, and bargain fishhooks. Open Wed. 6am-2pm.

Revello, Via Garibaldi, 183 (tel. 77 07 77), on the waterfront at the street's end. Offers a huge array of snacks including the Riviera's best *focaccia* and their secret treat, *camogliese al rhum,* a chocolate-covered cream puff with a rum filling (both are L2900 per *etto*). Open daily 8am-1pm and 3:30-7:30pm.

Pizzeria Il Lido, on the boardwalk at Via Garibaldi, 133 (tel. 77 50 09). Creates great pizza and provides an ocean view. Pizza from L8000-13,000, *primi* from L10,000.

Cover L2500. Don't go without a tan unless you like condescending glances. Open Wed.-Mon. 12:30-2:30pm and 7:30-10:30pm.

Slurp, Via Garibaldi, 104 (tel. 77 43 53). With a name like that, how can you go wrong? A billion innovative *gelato* flavors; their *granite* (ices) are famous. Cones L2000-3000. Open daily 10am-midnight; closed Mon. in winter.

SIGHTS AND ENTERTAINMENT

When you get tired of the beach and boardwalk you might walk the three-hour **hike** to San Fruttuoso; pick up the Camogli tourist office's useful trail map if you do, or just follow the double blue dots on the well-marked path.

To tour Camogli's limited sights in town, start with the 12th-century **Basilica of Santa Maria Assunta** on the seashore next to Piazza Colombo. From the church, stone steps lead left to the tiny but inviting **Acquario Tirrenico,** Castello della Dragonara (tel. 77 33 75). (Open summer daily 10am-11:45am and 3-6:30pm, winter Fri.-Sun. 10am-noon and 2-5:30pm. Admission L4000.) The maritime museum, **Gio Bono Ferrari,** across from the station at Via Gio Bono Ferrari, 41, honors sailors who traveled from Cape Horn to Rangoon. (Open Mon. and Thurs.-Fri. 9-11:40am, Wed. and Sat.-Sun. 9-11:40am and 3-5:40pm. Free.)

Camogli is famous for its grandiose yearly events. On the second Sunday in May, tourists descend on the town for an enormous fish fry, the **Sagra del Pesce.** The pan, constructed in 1952, measures four meters in diameter and holds over 2,000 fish. If you are not in town to grab a sardine you may still see the pan, adorning a city wall for the remainder of the year. Another spectacle is the **Festa della Stella Maris** (Festival of Our Lady of the Sea), which takes place the first Sunday of August. A procession of boats, led by the town priest, sails out to the Punta Chiappa, a point of land visible in the water a mile from the boardwalk in Camogli. About 10,000 floating candles are released from both shores. Lovers wait on the beach until the current carries all the candles together, signifying another year of unity.

Camogli offers slim pickings when it comes to nightlife, but for live music ranging from *bossa nova* to jazz, try **Porto Prego,** Piazza Colombo, 32 (tel. 77 26 66), right after Via Garibaldi ends on the boardwalk. Cover L15,000 when there's live music (includes 1st drink). Call for scheduled concerts. (Open Thurs.-Tues. 5pm-3am.) One stop away on the train is the city of Recco, which has several *discoteche.* Ask at the tourist office for more info.

■ Near Camogli

SAN FRUTTUOSO

The tiny fishing hamlet of San Fruttuoso, set in a natural amphitheater of pines, olive trees, and green oaks, is much too expensive for a prolonged stay or even a meal; nevertheless, it is worth a daytrip. The town is accessible by foot (1½hr. from Portofino Mare or Portofino Vetta) or by boat. **Golfo Paradiso** (tel. 77 20 91) runs about 12 boats per day from Camogli (L7000, roundtrip L12,000), while **Servizio Marittimo del Tigullio** (tel. 28 46 70) goes every hr. 10:30am-4:30pm from Portofino (L7000, roundtrip L12,000).

Walk to the left of the bay to reach the medieval lookout tower, the **Torre Andrea Doria** (admission L5000, children L2000), with a great view of the city and the water. Fifteen meters offshore and 18m underwater stands a bronze statue with upraised arms, the *Christ of the Depths,* which was erected in memory of casualties at sea. The statue now serves as protector of scuba divers, so if you've always been afraid to try diving, this is your chance to do it in safety. To see the statue without getting wet, visit its exact replica at the Benedictine **Abbazia di San Fruttuoso di Capo di Monte** (tel. 77 27 03), for which the town was named. Open May-Sept. Tues.-Sun. 10am-6pm; March-April and Oct. Tues.-Sun. 10am-4pm; Dec.-Feb. Sat.-Sun. and holidays 10am-4pm. Admission L5000, children L2000.

PORTOFINO

Secluded and exclusive, the tiny village of Portofino has long been a playground for the monetarily advantaged. Today, yachts the size of the Love Boat fill the harbor while chic boutiques line the streets. Only the curve of the shore and the tiny bay are enjoyed by paupers and princes alike. A nature reserve surrounds Portofino; trek through it to San Fruttuoso (90min.) or Santa Margherita (2½hr.). If you choose to hang around town, you can escape to the cool interior of the **Chiesa di San Giorgio** by following the signs uphill from the *piazza* at the bay. A few more minutes up the road to the **castle** will set you in a fairy-tale garden with a view of the sea. The castle is also home to a museum (admission L3000). To reach the *faro* (lighthouse), keep walking and climbing uphill past the castle—you will be rewarded with both a breathtaking coastline view and perhaps an orange *graista* from **Al Faro,** open April-Sept. daily 9:30am-8pm.

There's no train to Portofino, but Tigullio **buses** run along the coastline to and from Santa Margherita. (Every 20min., L1700; be sure to take the bus to Portofino Mare, not Portofino Vetta, and buy tickets at an *edicola* (newsstand) or in a *tabacchi.*) Maps and English brochures are available at the **tourist office,** Via Roma, 35 (tel. 26 90 24), on the way to the waterfront from the bus stop. Some English spoken. A large sign-board of the arrivals and departures from Santa Margherita is posted outside. Open daily 9:30am-1pm and 1:30-6:30pm in summer; 9:30am-12:30pm and 3-6pm in winter. Currency may be exchanged at the **bank** at Via Roma, 14 (tel. 26 91 64) or one of the six other banks on the street. The **post office** is at Via Roma, 32 (tel. 26 91 56). For emergencies, the **police** are at Via del Fondaco, 8 (tel. 26 90 88), and there's a **pharmacy** at P. Martiri della Libertà, 6 (tel. 26 91 01). Portofino's **telephone code** is 0185; use the **telephones** at the tourist office. To fortify yourself for the hike to San Fruttuoso, buy fruit and cool drinks at **Alimentari Repetto,** at P. Martiri dell'Olivetta, 30. Open daily 7:30am-8pm.

Santa Margherita Ligure

Santa Margherita Ligure evokes the elegance of a past era. It was once a vacation spot known for its essence of glamour and a tourist industry geared toward the wealthy. It now possesses a serenity expressed by the soft hues of blue, orange, and pink façades and by the distinguished couples who spend the summer here, found whispering in the lush garden that sits along the coast. Because Santa Margherita Ligure is less overrun by tourists than many towns in the area, come here to escape or just indulge in the fantasy of former elegance. Santa Margherita is one of the few remaining affordable Riviera towns, so stay here and explore the rest of the coast.

ORIENTATION AND PRACTICAL INFORMATION

Major inter-city trains along the Pisa-Genoa line stop at Santa Margherita. The town spreads in an arc around its small port. From the station, turn right and follow **Via Roma** down toward the waterfront. (For a shortcut, take the stairs to the right of the stop sign in front of the station and follow Via della Stazione directly to the water.) There are two main squares that cover the waterfront: the **Piazza Martiri della Libertà** and the smaller **Piazza Vittorio Veneto.** Both are lovely parks lined with palm trees. As you face the water, **Via Gramsci** winds around the port to your left, while **Via XXV Aprile** leads to the tourist office, continuing on to become **Corso Matteotti** alongside the other main square in town, the **Piazza Mazzini.**

Tourist Office: Via XXV Aprile, 2b (tel. 28 74 85). Turn right from the train station onto Via Roma, then right onto Via XXV Aprile. Information, town map, and accommodations service. An enthusiastic and helpful English-speaking bunch. Open Mon.-Sat. 9am-12:30pm and 3-7pm, Sun. 9:30am-12:30pm.

Trains: (tel. 28 66 30), in P. Federico Raoul Nobili at the summit of Via Roma. To Genoa (2 or 3 per hr., 5am-midnight, L2700) and La Spezia (2 per hr., 6am-1am, L5700). **Luggage Storage:** L5000 for 12 hr. Open daily 5:35am-7:50pm.

Buses: Tigullio buses depart from P. Vittorio Veneto at the small green kiosk on the waterfront. Ticket office open sporadically from 7:10am-7:40pm. To Camogli (every hr., 15km, L2000) and Portofino (every 20min., 5km, L1700).

Ferries: Tigullio, Via Palestro, 8/1/B (tel. 28 46 70). Boats leave from the docks at P. Martiri della Libertà. To: Portofino (6 per day, 10am-4pm, L5000, roundtrip L9000); San Fruttuoso (every hr. 10am-4pm, L10,000, roundtrip L16,000); and Cinque Terre, Monterosso, or Riomaggiore (July-Sept. daily, during winter, Sat.-Sun. 2 per day, L18,000, roundtrip L25,000).

Bike Rental: Noleggio Cicli e Motorcicli, Via Roma, 11 (tel. 28 70 45). Bikes L5000 per hr., L10,000 for 2-4hr., or L15,000 per day. Tandem or motorscooter for L15,000 per hr. or L70,000 per day. Must be over 14 and accompanied by an adult to rent a moped. Motorscooter driving license required for rental. Open sporadically off-season; March-Sept. daily 9am-noon and 2:30-6pm.

Emergency: tel. 113. For late-night and weekend medical attention, call **Guardia Medica** (tel. 603 33 or 27 33 82). **Hospital: Ospedale Civile di Rapallo,** P. Molfino, 10 (tel. 60 31), in Rapallo near the train station.

Police: On Via Vignolo (tel. 28 71 21).

Post Office: Via Roma, 36 (tel. 28 88 40), to the right of the station. Open Mon.-Fri. 8:10am-5:30pm, Sat. 8:10am-noon. **Postal Code:** 16038.

Telephone Code: 0185.

ACCOMMODATIONS

Stay away from the water. Your room won't have a view and you will have to take a short walk, but your reward will be an extra L20,000-30,000 in your pocket.

Hotel Terminus, Piazzale Nobili, 4 (tel. 28 61 21; fax 28 25 46), to the left as you exit the station. Ignore the slight rumble of trains and enjoy the grace of the Italian Riviera's famed hotel culture. Proprietor Angelo speaks perfect English and will ensure an absolutely delightful stay; enjoy his genuine compassion and scrumptious cooking. Attractive rooms with new bathrooms and windows have views of the water and hills. Singles L65,000, with bath L75,000. Doubles L90,000, with bath L110,000. All with breakfast. V, MC, AmEx.

Hotel Conte Verde, Via Zara, 1 (tel. 28 71 39; fax 28 42 11), on your right as you come down Via Roma. Was once an 18th-century *villa*. Clean, functional rooms. Prices depend on season. Singles L40,000-65,000. Doubles L70,000-120,000. Bicycles lent out free to guests. The **restaurant** downstairs gives a discount to those who stay at the hotel. English spoken, and they get CNN. Breakfast included. Reservations encouraged. V, MC, AmEx.

Albergo Annabella, Via Costasecca, 10 (tel. 28 65 31), off P. Mazzini, not far from the beach. Ample, modern rooms. Singles L50,000. Doubles L70,000. Triples L94,000. Breakfast L6000. During high season half-pension is generally required at L65,000 per person.

Hotel Nuova Riviera, Via Belvedere, 10 (tel. 28 74 03). A beautiful old villa set in a garden near P. Mazzini. Capacious, elegant rooms. Singles L70,000-75,000. Doubles L90,000-95,000, with bath L100,000. Prices negotiable. Half-pension sometimes required in summer at L63,000-85,000 per person, depending on room size. Reservations recommended.

FOOD

Markets, bakeries, fruit vendors, and butcher shops line Corso Matteotti. On Fridays from 8am to 1pm cars are ousted from the Corso and shops welcome foot-traffic with signs and occasional food samples. The **COOP** supermarket, Corso Matteotti, 9C (tel. 28 43 15) off P. Mazzini stocks basics including soy products for vegetarians. Open Mon.-Sat. 8:15am-1pm and 4-8pm. V.

Trattoria Baicin, Via Algeria, 9 (tel. 28 67 63), off P. Martiri della Libertà near the water. Papà Piero is the master chef, while Mamma Carmela rolls the pasta and simmers the sauces. Try Mamma's homemade *Trofie alla Genovese (gnocchi* mixed with potato, string beans, and pesto, L7500). *Primi* from L6000, *menù* L25,000. 10% service charge. Cover L2000. Open Tues.-Sun. noon-3pm and 7pm-midnight, but the kitchen closes at 10:30pm. V, MC, AmEx, traveler's checks.

Cutty Sark, Via Roma, 35 (tel. 28 70 09), on the right coming from the station. Furnished with dark wood and sailor's paraphernalia, this 2-story establishment has a big-screen TV and occasional live music. *Primi* (L8000-9000), 40 different types of *panini*, and a bar. Open Tues.-Sun. noon-2pm and 8pm-2am.

Rosticceria Revelant, Via Gramsci, 15 (tel. 28 65 00), east of P. Martiri della Libertà. Scrumptious meals to go. Try the lasagna (L2000 per *etto)*. Open daily during the summer 8am-noon and 4:30-8pm; in winter closed Sun. afternoon and Mon. V, MC, AmEx.

SIGHTS AND ENTERTAINMENT

Santa Margherita's main attractions are undisturbed tranquility and proximity to bustling larger ports. From 8am to 12:30pm you can ogle the day's catch at the daily local **fish market** on Lungomare Marconi, or come between 4 and 6pm to watch the fleet bring in its haul. (Market closed Wed. afternoon.) More exalted sights include the Rococo **Basilica of Santa Margherita** on P. Caprera, dripping with gold and crystal, housing fine Flemish and Italian works. To reach the **Church of the Cappuccini,** Via San Francesco d'Assisi, a favorite feline hangout, walk along the waterfront past P. Martiri della Libertà and climb the stone ramp behind the castle. For human companionship head to **Salot American Bar,** P. Martiri della Libertà, 32 (tel. 28 06 46), a gregarious place with music and drinks. Serves lunch, too. Open Wed.-Mon. 10am-2am. Pool tables and beer await at the the **Old Inn Bar,** P. Mazzini, 40 (tel. 28 60 41 or 28 66 20).

Cinque Terre

Cinque Terre ("Five Lands") consists of five connected fishing villages that cling precariously to a small stretch of cliff above the startlingly turquoise sea. The fish that once schooled in the Mediterranean have been replaced by swimming tourists, and with good reason. Cinque Terre is justly famed for impressive vistas, clear waters, and a sweet white wine called *sciacchetrà*.

The five towns in order of proximity to Genoa are Monterosso, Vernazza, Corniglia, Manarola, and Riomaggiore. Monterosso is the biggest and least charming.

ORIENTATION AND PRACTICAL INFORMATION

The listings here are for **Monterosso,** which has the most resources and is easily accessible by local train from all the villages.

Tourist Office: Pro Loco, Via Fegina, 38 (tel. 81 75 06), below the train station. Well-stocked with info on boats, hikes, and hotels. Accommodations service for Monterosso and **currency exchange** (poor rates). Open April-Oct. Mon.-Sat. 10am-noon and 5-7:30pm, Sun. 10am-noon. **IAT** (tel. 81 72 04), at the port to the south of town. Open Mon.-Sat. 10am-noon and 5:30-7:30pm, Sun. 10am-noon.

Trains: Via Fegina, on the north end of town, to the right as you face the water. To Vernazza, Corniglia, Manarola, and Riomaggiore (about every 50min., 5-20min., L1500). Pick up a schedule at the tourist office. The "Cinque Terre Tourist Ticket" is good for unlimited trips between towns in any 24hr. period and is available at any of the five train stations—ask at the ticket window (L4500).

Boats: Navigazione Golfo dei Porto (tel. 96 76 76), at the port to the right of the beach in the south end of town. To: Manarola and Riomaggiore (5 per day, L9000, roundtrip L15,000); Vernazza (5 per day, L4000, roundtrip L6000); and Portovenere (1hr., departs at 3pm and returns at 5:30pm, one way L16,000, roundtrip

L22,000). **Motobarca Vernazza** makes the trip to Vernazza about every 30min. (15min., L4000 one way, L6000 roundtrip).

Boat Rental: Pedal boats are available on the beach in front of the train station for L10,000 per hr. Wide selection of boats can be found on the beach at the south end of town: pedal boats L13,000 per hr., L65,000 per day; rowboats L10,000-13,000 per hr., L50,000-65,000 per day; kayaks L10,000 per hr., L50,000 per day; and motorboats L30,000-40,000 per hr., L150,000-200,000 per day.

Taxis: tel. 75 57 30.

Pharmacy: Via Fegina, 14, under the train station. Open Mon.-Sat. 9am-12:30pm and 4-7:45pm, Sun. 9am-12:30pm and 4-7:30pm.

Emergencies: tel. 113. **First Aid: Guardia Medica,** tel. 80 04 09. **Ambulance:** tel. 81 74 75.

Police: Carabinieri, tel. 81 75 24.

Post Office: Via Loreto, 73 (tel. 81 83 94). **Currency exchange** (L1000 fee for any sum greater than L10,000) and **American Express Traveler's Cheque exchange** (L2000 for sums less than L100,000; L5000 for sums greater than L100,000). Open Mon.-Fri. 8:10am-6pm, Sat. 8:30am-noon. **Postal Code:** 19016.

Telephone Code for all of Cinque Terre: 0187.

ACCOMMODATIONS

With the exception of Monterosso, most of the five towns' accommodations are in private homes. These *affitta camere* are plentiful, but can sometimes be difficult to locate. Ask at the tourist office in Monterosso, or just show up in one of the towns and ask around—bars are good places to start. If you're stuck in Riomaggiore, ask Ivo at **Central Bar,** Via Colombo, 144. Locate a place to sleep as early in the day as possible; accommodations often fill up by noon.

Hostel Mamma Rosa, P. Unità, 2 (tel. 92 00 50), in **Riomaggiore.** No sign, but it's across from the train station. You can also ask a local, who will send Mamma running to meet you. Known for its penchant for fun, if not for cleanliness. Co-ed dorms, outdoor showers, and cooking facilities are presided over by ebullient, lovable Mamma Rosa herself. She'll try to find room for latecomers. No curfew. Bunk beds; 4-10 per room. L25,000 per person.

Albergo Barbara, P. Marconi, 21 (tel. 81 22 01), at the port in **Vernazza.** Ask in Trattoria Capitano about the hotel upstairs. Bright, airy rooms, some with fantastic views of Vernazza's colorful port. Singles L50,000. Doubles L60,000-80,000. Triples L100,000. Quads L120,000.

Cecio (tel. 81 20 43), in **Corniglia.** On the small road that leads from Corniglia to Vernazza; follow the signs at the top of the stairs that lead to town from the train station. This wonderful restaurant (see **Food** below) also rents wonderful rooms, all with bath and a postcard-like view. Doubles L70,000 (less for longer stays).

Hotel Souvenir, Via Gioberti, 24 (tel. 81 75 95), in **Monterosso.** Quiet, family-run hotel with bright, airy rooms and friendly staff. Good breakfast included. Singles L50,000. Doubles L70,000. All rooms with tile bath.

Marina Piccola (tel. 92 01 03), near the water in **Manarola.** An upscale place with cream-colored walls, tasteful prints, and little lamps. Many rooms with mind-blowing views. All rooms with bath. Singles L80,000. Doubles L100,000.

FOOD

The uniformly overpriced seafood restaurants that crowd the five towns attest to Cinque Terre's growing tourism savvy. However, the seafood is always swimmingly fresh and the locally produced sweet wine, *sciacchetrà,* is a delicious complement. If you've got your heart set on a picnic by the beach, stock up at **Conce Superconad Margherita,** P. Matteotti, 9, in **Monterosso.** Open June-Sept. Mon.-Tues. and Thurs.-Sat. 8am-1pm and 5-7:30pm, Wed. 8am-1pm, Sun. 8am-noon.

Ristorante Cecio, in **Corniglia.** (See listing under **Accommodations** for directions.) The stone interior conveys a rustic elegance, and the outdoor patio overlooks the hills and water. Wherever you sit, you'll be served *primi* from L8000 and *secondi* from L7000. Cover L3000. Get the *spaghetti alla scogliera* (fresh shrimp, mussels, clams, and tomatoes, L10,000) for an out-of-body experience.

Focacceria Il Frontoio, Via Gioberti, 1, in **Monterosso.** The wood-burning oven fires up every kind of mouth-watering *focaccia* imaginable: with olives, onions, or herbs, or stuffed with different fillings. Slices L1500-2500. A great place to stock up before heading out on a hike. Open Fri.-Wed. 9:30am-1pm and 4-8pm.

Il Baretto, Via Roma, 31 (tel. 81 23 81), in **Vernazza.** Reasonably priced for one of Vernazza's outdoor restaurants. Have a dish of freshly caught mussels steamed in wine and herbs (L14,000) or *spaghetti al pesto* (L8000). *Primi* L8000-12,000, *secondi* from L10,000. Cover L3000. Open daily noon-2pm and 7:30-9:30pm.

SIGHTS

Nature created Cinque Terre's best sights: savage cliffs and lush tropical vegetation surround the stone sea villages. Enjoy the best views from the narrow goat paths that link the towns, winding through vineyards, streams, and dense foliage dotted with cacti and lemon trees. If you have a good pair of walking shoes, you can cover the distance between Monterosso and Riomaggiore in about five hours; or take strolls between frolics in the water. The best and most challenging hike lies between Monterosso and Vernazza (1½hr.), while the trail between Vernazza and Corniglia (2hr.) passes through some of the area's most gorgeous scenery. The road between Corniglia and Manarola (45min.) offers a similarly pleasant and rewarding hike. The final stretch, the famous "Via dell'Amore" that links Manarola and Riomaggiore (30min.) is more notable for its easy access to the water than for its view.

In Monterosso, visit the **Convento dei Cappuccini,** perched on a hill in the center of town. The convent contains an impressive *Crucifixion* by Flemish master Anthony van Dyck, who sojourned in this area during his most productive years. (Open daily 9am-noon and 4-7pm.) In Vernazza, the remains of a **castle** (up a steep staircase to your left when facing the port) offer yet another spectacular view. (Open daily 9am-8pm.)

BEACHES

There are only two public beaches in Cinque Terre, one on the south side of Monterosso (to the left as you face the harbor) and the other a long strip of pebbles between Corniglia and Manarola. You can also swim off the rocky outcroppings between Manarola and Riomaggiore, and in the inlet formed by Vernazza's harbor. Most of Monterosso's beach is reserved, with only small, unappealing patches open to the public. If good sand is what you want, it's probably worth the L2500 to reserve your own patch for the day. (Use of changing rooms, bathrooms, and showers included in the price.) Tiny trails off the road to Vernazza lead to hidden coves popular among the locals. A crowded but sandy stretch of beach lies beside the port in Vernazza. Guvano Beach is a pebbly strip frequented by nudist, fun-loving hippies. To get there, you can walk through the tunnel at the base of the steps leading up to Corniglia, but you'll have to pay L5000; you can hike down off the road between Corniglia and Vernazza for free. The rocky outcroppings between Manarola and Riomaggiore are popular among sunbathers and swimmers alike.

La Spezia

In little more than a century, the unassuming village of La Spezia has mushroomed into a thriving city, and its tiny naval dockyard has become a major commercial port. Its greatest draw for tourists is as a departure point to Corsica and as an unavoidable transfer station on the way to and from Cinque Terre. A thoroughly modern city, La Spezia boasts none of the majestic architecture, cobblestone passageways, or quiet charm that grace the neighboring villages. Instead, its disc-shaped cathedral, asphalt streets, and blaring horns may be disconcerting to travelers. Still, the swaying palm trees that line the Morin promenade, as well as the surrounding green hills, do lend the city some aesthetic value.

ORIENTATION AND PRACTICAL INFORMATION

La Spezia's main **tourist office** (tel. 77 09 00) sits beside the port at Viale Mazzini, 45. A branch office (tel. 71 89 97) is located in the train station, where the friendly, English-speaking staff is armed with pamphlets and eager to help. **Telephones** can be found near the port at Via da Passano, 30. Open Mon.-Fri. 9am-12:30pm and 3:40-7pm. **Taxis** answer at tel. 52 35 22 or 52 35 23. In an **emergency,** dial 113; **first aid** is at 53 31 11; for the **police,** call 71 81 00. The **post office** is a few blocks from the port at P. Verdi (tel. 284 76). Open Mon.-Fri. 8am-2pm and Sat. 8-11:25am. The **telephone code** is 0187.

Corsica Ferries (tel. 77 80 97) connect La Spezia to Bastia (Corsica). Purchase tickets at the round booth on the Molo Italia deck. Ferries depart at 8:15am on Tues.-Wed. and Fri. during April and daily from May-Sept. (5hr., L36,000-48,000). **Tirrenia** sends fast ferries to Olbia (Sardinia); the 5½-hr. trip costs L110,000. (Late July-early Sept., daily at 8am; ferries during the week of Aug. 11-18 leave at 10am.)

ACCOMMODATIONS AND FOOD

Albergo Terminus, Via Paleocapa, 21 (tel. 70 34 36), lies to the left as you exit the train station. The eccentric, *loggia*-style lobby leads to bright, airy rooms. Singles L32,000-37,000, with bath L45,000. Doubles L50,000-55,000, with bath L60,000-65,000. Closer to the port, **Albergo Spezia** (tel. 73 51 64), Via Cavalloti, 31 (off Via Prione), boasts ample rooms with moss-green carpets. Singles L30,000-38,000. Doubles L40,000-49,000, with bath L52,000-65,000.

While in La Spezia, try the local specialty, *mesciua,* a thick soup of beans, cornmeal, olive oil, and pepper, at any of the city's *antiche osterie.* Staples can be found at the **Coop** supermarket, Via Galileo Galilei, 31. Open Mon.-Sat. 8:15am-12:45pm and 4:30-8pm; closed Thurs. evenings. **Trattoria da Sandro,** Via del Prione, 268 (tel. 73 72 03), is adorned with cheery floral decorations and colorful brick archways. Pizzas go for L6000-12,000, but the house specialty is *trittico della casa*, a combo plate of seafood pastas (L12,000). Cover L2000. Open Mon.-Sat. noon-3pm and 6-11pm. Directly across the street, **Trattoria da Vito** draws a more down-to-earth crowd and pleases them with hearty food and a TV always tuned in to sports events. Pastas run L6000-10,000, with a tasty eggplant *parmigiana* for L6000.

SIGHTS AND ENTERTAINMENT

Most tourists opt to skip La Spezia and head over to spectacular Cinque Terre for its pretty beaches and captivating vistas. If you prefer to stay in La Spezia, however, you might want to check out its **Naval Museum** in Piazza Chiodo (tel. 77 07 50). The unique collection features tiny replicas of Egyptian, Roman, and European vessels. (Open Tues.-Thurs. and Sat. 9am-noon and 2-6pm, Mon. and Fri. 2-6pm, Sun. 8:30am-1:15pm. Admission L2000.)

■ Near La Spezia: Pontremoli

Situated on the banks of the Magra and Verde rivers, the enchanting medieval Tuscan village of **Pontremoli** rises majestically from hills of cypress and olive trees in the ancient Lunigiana Valley. Terra-cotta rooftops, 15th-century stone bridges, and labyrinthine cobblestone alleyways from the Middle Ages dot the scenery in this magnificent town. Known in Italy as the *Città del Libro* ("City of the Book"), Pontremoli hosts the international **Premio Bancarella** every July, a festival in which numerous book vendors sell their wares at *bancarelle* (open-air booths) in the central town squares, **Piazza della Repubblica** and **Piazza Duomo.** The event concludes with an awards ceremony for Italy's finest book of the year. (Umberto Eco won the prestigious award for *Foucault's Pendulum* a few years ago.)

ORIENTATION AND PRACTICAL INFORMATION

Pontremoli is located on the Parma-La Spezia train line. You can also catch the twice-daily train headed from Milan to Livorno, which stops at Pontremoli. From the **train station,** head right on **Via dei Mille** until you reach the bridge. Turn left, and cross the river onto **Via Cairoli.** The *centro storico* lies to your right as you head down Via Generale Armani to **Piazza della Repubblica,** behind the impressive 14th-century *campanile* (bell tower) known as the **Campanone.** Behind lies **Piazza Duomo.** From here, follow the signs up the twisting alleys to the **Castello del Piagnaro,** built by Cealberti and the Longobards during the 10th century, now home to the **Museo dell Statue-Stele,** housing pre-Etruscan (around 6000BC) tombstones. Although the museum is now under construction, this site still affords one of the town's most impressive views.

The **Pro Loco tourist office** (tel. 83 11 80) holds irregular hours, but can be reached off P. della Repubblica, next to the Municipio. **Taxis:** tel. 83 04 67 (train station) or 83 00 54 (P. della Repubblica). There is a **pharmacy** in P. Italia (tel. 83 01 78). The **police** can be reached at tel. 83 00 22; **ambulance:** tel. 83 00 49. The **post office** (tel. 83 00 57) lies on Via Pirandello.

ACCOMMODATIONS AND FOOD

Accommodations in Pontremoli can be costly, so the town is seen more economically as a daytrip from La Spezia. If you decide to stay, try **Hotel Napoleon** at P. Italia, 2 (tel. 83 05 44), an elegant hotel with marble floors and rooms decorated with antiques. Singles L70,000-78,000. Doubles L100,000-120,000. All rooms with TV and bath. V, MC, AmEx. At mealtime head to one of the *trattorie* in the *centro storico*. Pontremoli's claim to fame is its *testarolo:* a large, pancake-like flatbread oven-cooked in a special pot called a *testo,* then boiled quickly and topped with pesto, grated *parmigiano,* and *pignoli* (pine nuts). Try it at **Trattoria da Tonino,** known to locals as La Gravagnotti, off P. Duomo on Via Garibaldi, 16 (tel. 83 05 48). Literally a "hole in the wall," it lies at the end of a cool stone corridor. *Primi* L6000, *secondi* L10,000. Cover L2000. A seat at one of the outdoor tables will give you a great view of the peaceful countryside. A few doors down at Via Garibaldi, 22, to the right in the tiny Piazzetta di San Geminiano, is **Trattoria da Fernando** (tel. 83 06 53), where *primi* go for L6000 and *secondi* run from L10,000. Try the *risotto ai funghi* (L8000). For some delicious *gelato*, go to **Bar Moderno** on Via IV Novembre, 2.

RIVIERA DI PONENTE

Finale Ligure

A prime spot to take a vacation from your vacation, Finale Ligure is the antidote for any weary traveler suffering from train schedules and tourist attractions. Popular with the twenty-something crowd, this Riviera town is blessed with a sparkling emerald

Porn in Parliament

In 1987, the Radical Party's candidate Ilona Staller, commonly known as the ex-porn star "La Cicciolina," was elected to the house of deputies in Viareggio. The buxom blonde celebrated her win by baring her breasts to the eternally grateful city in a victory parade. In 1991, Staller married American kitsch artiste Jeff Koons, whose major works include an enormous sculpture of himself and Ilona as Adam and Eve in the Garden of Eden. She also made an innovative attempt at a peace plan during the Gulf War, offering Saddam Hussein her body if he would agree to pull out early. She has since retired from the house of deputies and has divorced Koons.

sea, a long sand beach, a boardwalk lined with palm trees and kiddie rides, and tons of *gelaterie.* Medieval turrets emerge from rocky hillsides that attract rock climbers from all over the world.

ORIENTATION AND PRACTICAL INFORMATION

The city divides into three sections: **Finalpia** to the east, **Finalmarina** in the center, and **Finalborgo,** the old city, to the west. Most of the places listed below, including the **train station,** are located in Finalmarina. The main street in town changes names several times between the station and the central *piazza,* from **Via de Raimondi** to **Via Pertica** to **Via Garibaldi,** opening into **Piazza Vittorio Emanuele II** beyond a giant stone archway. From this central *piazza* along the water are **Via della Concezione** to the west and **Via S. Pietro** to the east. The old city lies far behind the train station. To get there, take a left out of the station, go under the tracks and continue left on **Via Domenico Bruneghi.**

Tourist Office: IAT, Via San Pietro, 14 (tel. 69 25 81; fax 68 00 50), on the main street overlooking the sea (not the *lungomare,* which serves as just a promenade). Luisa has been here for over 35 years and knows her stuff. She will gladly offer both a map and maternal advice for all of your problems. Open Mon.-Sat. 8:30am-12:30pm and 3:30-7:30pm, Sun. 9am-noon. The **Associazione Alberghi e Turismo,** Via de Raimondi, 29 (tel. 69 42 52; fax 69 50 36), across from the station on the corner of Via de Raimondi and Via Saccone, helps with accommodations in the summer. Open May-Oct. Tues.-Sun. 10am-1pm and 2:30-6:30pm.

Currency Exchange: Banca Carige, Via Garibaldi, 4, at the corner of P. Vittorio Emanuelle II. Automatic machine open 24hr. Bank open Mon.-Fri. 8:20am-1:20pm and 2:30-4pm. On Sat., head to the post office.

Telephones: Via Roma, 33. Pay phones, directories, and vending machines selling tokens and phone cards. Open June-Sept. 8am-11pm, Oct.-May 8am-8pm.

Trains: P. Vittorio Veneto (tel. 69 27 77). Frequent service to: Genoa (L5700), Ventimiglia (L7200), and Santa Margherita Ligure (L8000).

Buses: SAR, Via Aurelia, 28 (tel. 69 22 75), outside and to the left of the train station. Ticket office open Mon.-Sat. 8am-12:30pm and 3-7pm. When this is closed, try **Bar Rino,** where Via Mazzini meets Via Bruneghi. To: Borgo Verezzi (L1300), Savona (L3100), Finalborgo (L1100), and other towns. No roundtrip discounts.

Bike Rental: Oddone, Via Colombo, 20 (tel. 69 42 15), on the street behind the tourist office. Bikes: L3500 per hr., L10,000 per day. Mountain bikes: L10,000 per hr., L35,000 per day. You must present a passport. Open in summer daily 9am-12:30pm and 3:30-7:30pm, in winter closed Mon. morning and Sun. V, MC.

Pharmacy: Comunale Via Ghiglieri, 6 (tel. 69 26 70), off Via Pertica. Open Mon.-Fri. 8:30am-12:30pm and 4-10pm. Closed Mon. mornings and Fri. afternoons. A posted sign shows which pharmacies are open late.

First Aid: tel. 112 or **P. A. Croce Bianca,** Via Torino, 16 (tel. 69 82 32 in Varigotti, 69 23 33 in Finalmarina, and 69 13 25 in Finalborgo). **Guardia Medica:** tel. 82 44 44 8pm-8am and Sat. 2pm until Mon. 8am. **Hospital: Ospedale Santa Corona,** Via XXV Aprile, 28 (tel. 623 01), in nearby Pietra Ligure.

Police: Via Brunanghi, 68 (tel. 113 or 69 26 66).

Post Office: Via della Concezione, 27 (tel. 69 28 38). Open Mon.-Fri. 8:10am-5:30pm, Sat. 8:10am-noon. Fax services available. **Postal code:** 17024.

Telephone code: 019.

ACCOMMODATIONS AND CAMPING

A visit to the Associazione Alberghi prior to seeking shelter could save you time and legwork. In July and August the youth hostel is always your best bet, not to mention the best view. Rooms in private homes can be arranged through the tourist office.

Castello Wuillerman (HI) (tel. 69 05 15), on Via Generale Caviglia in a red brick castle overlooking the sea. From the station, take a left onto Via Mazzini, which becomes Via Torino. Turn left onto tiny Via degli Ulivi when you hit the *Esso* gas station, and start your hellish climb up the Gradinata delle Rose. A small sign and, yes, another set of steps marks the way up to the castle on your left (320 steps altogether). Luckily, you'll never want to walk back down. This hostel has everything—regular and vegetarian meals (L14,000), newly renovated bathrooms, laundry (L5000 per 5kg), a beautiful courtyard, and a barking German Shepherd. No phone reservations. Individual rooms are hard to get here; many vacationers to Finale Ligure stay 2-3 weeks. Reception open 7-10am and 5-10pm. Check-in 5pm, but you may arrive earlier and leave your bags. Curfew 11:30pm. L18,000 per person for HI cardholders, sheets and breakfast included. Open March 15-Oct. 15.

Albergo San Marco, Via della Concezione, 22 (tel. 69 25 33), on the street facing the beach, down from the station. Enter through a restaurant with purple and lavender tablecloths. Friendly proprietors keep spotless rooms, all with bath and phone. Singles L40,000. Doubles L70,000-77,000. Hearty, full-spread breakfast included. Minimal English spoken. Full pension prices range from L60,000 to L78,000 depending on the season. Closed Oct.-Nov.

Albergo Marita, Via Saccone, 17 (tel. 69 29 04 or 69 34 15 at home), the street directly in front of the station. This small hotel is set back from the street on the left. Attractive, functional rooms, some with balconies. Prices higher in July-Aug. Singles L30,000-35,000. Doubles with bath L60,000-70,000. Breakfast L5000. Reservations required in the summer.

Camping: Del Mulino (tel. 60 16 69), on Via Piemonte. From the station take the bus for Calvisio from the stop in P. Vittorio Veneto and get off at the Boncardo Hotel, Corso Europa, 4, on the waterfront (in the Finalpia district). From here, turn left at P. Guglielmo Oberdan, then right onto Via Porra, go left under an arch onto Via Castelli, and follow it uphill. Take the stairs up to the left where an olive grove ends. You will see a yellow sign for the entrance to the campsite. About a 20-min. walk from the station, 300m from the seashore. Bar, restaurant, and mini-market on the premises, but no laundry. L9000 per person, L7000 per small tent, L12,000 per large tent; prices lower in off-season. Open April-Sept. **Camping Tahiti** (tel. 60 06 00), slightly farther away, on Via Varese. Same directions as Del Mulino, but from Via Porra turn left onto Via Orione which becomes Via Molinetti. Via Varese is on the left. L8000 per person (L9000 during July-Aug.), L7000 per tent (L8000 during July-Aug.). Hot showers L1000. Open Easter-Sept.

FOOD

Trattorie and *pizzerie* line the streets closest to the beach. Wander along the water and pick the restaurant with the best prices, or travel farther inland along Via Rossi and Via Roma.

Spaghetteria Il Posto, Via Porro, 21 (tel. 60 00 95). An elegant and creative pasta house with an unusual menu. Friendly staff forgives all foreign foibles with a smile. Try the *penne quattro stagioni* (pasta with bacon, mushrooms, tomatoes, artichokes, and mozzarella, L9500) or the *penne pirata* (with shrimp and salmon, L11,000). Plenty of options for vegetarians as well. Cover L1500. Open Tues.-Sun. 7-10:30pm. Closed for the first 2 weeks in March.

La Grotta, Vico Massaferro, 17, off Via San Pietro (along the waterfront), right across the alley from the tourist office. A restaurant originally built in the '40s to resemble a cave. A busy local hangout. Excellent, very filling pizzas from L5500. 10% service charge. No reservations. Open Wed.-Mon. 7pm-midnight.

Panetteria Ghigo Maria, Via G. Rossi, 32, off Via Garibaldi. In this bakery, a local favorite, an award hangs from the wall: *"Panino Più Lungo Del Mondo"* ("Longest Sandwich in the World"). Come here for low-priced *focaccia* slices (plain L1000, cheese L1200, and olive L1300), pizza (L1600), and authentic cookies including the popular *bombe alla crema* (L1200). Open daily 7am-1pm and 4-8pm, closed Sun. afternoons; off-season, closed Thurs. and Sun. afternoons.

Paninoteca Pilade, Via Garibaldi, 67 (tel. 69 22 20), off P. Vittorio Emanuele. If you're in withdrawal for Americana, this is the place—MTV, old Coke posters, banana splits. Right out of *Happy Days*. Fabulous *panini* ranging L3500-5000. Pizza L2500-3500 per slice. Beer on tap (L2500-7500). Open daily 10am-3am.

La Cicala delle Palme, Via San Pietro, 20 (tel. 66 22 04). Traditional, modern surroundings (red, white, and metal) give way to a traditional but extensive menu. Families of tourists fill the tables and eat well. Pizza from L7000, *primi* L7000. Open 12:15-2:30pm and 7:15pm-midnight. Closed Wednesday.

SIGHTS AND ENTERTAINMENT

Finalborgo, enclosed within solid ancient walls, is just a one-km walk up Via Bruneghi from the station. The baroque **Basilica di San Biagio,** inside the city walls through the elegant Porta Reale, features a 13th-century octagonal belfry. **Chiostro di Santa Caterina** (tel. 68 05 18), a 5-min. walk across town, has a 14th-century edifice and houses the **Civico Museo del Finale** (tel. 69 02 20), dedicated to Ligurian history. (Open June-Sept. Tues.-Sat. 10am-noon and 3-6pm, Oct.-May Tues.-Sat. 9am-noon and 2:30-4:30pm.) You can climb a tough rocky trail up to the 13th-century **Castel Govone** (closed to the public) for a spectacular view of Finale. If you're interested in more rock-climbing fun, get the lowdown on routes in Finale at **Rock Store,** Piazza Garibaldi, 14 (tel. 69 02 08), where you can obtain maps and all necessary gear. Open Tues.-Sun. 9am-12:30pm and 4-7:30pm.

If your legs still aren't tired, climb the steps at the intersection of Via Colombo and Via Torino in **Finalmarina** to the lofty 14th-century **Castelfranco.** World War II ravaged much of this structure, but it has recently been restored. The view is truly tremendous. Ask at the tourist office for hours and admission charge. Be sure to head to the Genovese baroque **Basilica of San Giovanni Battista** in the *piazza* of the same name. (Follow your nose—the entire square is decorated with gardenias.)

The towns surrounding Finale Ligure are also worth exploring. Take a SAR bus (L1300) to tiny **Borgo Verezzi.** Get off at the first stop in the town of Borgio; from here, five buses leave daily for Verezzi. From mid-July through August, performances animate **Teatro di Verrezzi,** the town's outdoor theater in the main *piazza.* The performing company is one of Italy's most renowned. (About L35,000. Call the Borgo Verezzi tourist office at (019) 61 04 12 for details.)

"Players" also frequent **Il Covo,** Capo San Donato (tel. 60 12 84). It's a small disco right next to the best free beach in Finale, right after the tunnel near the waterfront on Via Aurelia. Open Tues.-Sun. 11pm-4am; cover L20,000, Sat. L25,000. Other options include **Mirò** (tel. 60 02 19) on Via Santuario, a live disco (free on Thurs.-Fri.), and the **Scotch Club** (tel. 69 24 81) on Via San Pietro near the tourist office. Go down San Pietro and turn left past the Mironi Hotel. (Open Thurs.-Sat. 11pm-3am.)

Sanremo and Dolcedo

SANREMO

Once a glamorous retreat for Russian nobles, czars, *literati,* and artists, Sanremo is the largest resort on the Italian Riviera. Overlooking an expansive bay, the palm-lined **promenade** and the casino are the main attractions of this *very* expensive, *very* "V.I.P.," and *very* entertaining city. You can take the bus or train from Ventimiglia or Imperia. The terminally nostalgic can relive Sanremo's glory days at the city's white-washed Edwardian **Casino,** a dazzling example of Art Nouveau architecture, located at Corso Inglesi, 18 (tel. 53 40 01). The entrance fee is "only" L15,000; men must wear a coat and tie and you must be 18 to enter. Blackjack begins at 8:30pm, but early gamblers can start spinning the roulette wheel at 2:30pm. The "American Room" of one-armed bandits has neither dress code nor entrance fee (although you'll surely pay) and lures early risers with its 10am opening. Depending on how the games are going, the casino fun stops around 3am.

Also worth seeing in Sanremo are the old and splendiferous **Pigna** quarter and the Russian Orthodox **Church of Santa Caterina Martire and San Serafino,** with intricate onion-domes reminiscent of St. Basil's in Moscow. In February, Sanremo lives up to its title as *Riviera dei Fiori* with a vibrant display of floral carpets and an exciting parade of floats throughout the month. In August, the city hosts its traditional festival, **Nostra Signora della Costa,** including a procession in medieval garb complete with a "Sailors' Mass." Around the same time of year, Sanremo holds the **Humor Festival,** an international event with performances and exhibits (although Italian humor is often difficult to understand, especially if you don't speak Italian). Check with the tourist office for specifics. Sanremo's **tourist office** is located at Largo Nuvolini, 1 (tel. 57 15 71; fax 50 76 49). Open Mon.-Sat. 8am-7pm, Sun. 9am-1pm. Sanremo's **postal code** is 18038; the **telephone code** is 0184.

DOLCEDO

Take in the scene of a valley dotted with farmhouses and glistening olive groves as you approach the medieval village of **Dolcedo.** Here, tiny bridges cross the river Prino where ancient oil mills continue to press the old-fashioned way. Standing among these bridges is the 15th-century **Chapel of Santa Brigida.** A bridge on which the Knights of Malta carved "*mcclxxxxii die 3 juli hoc opus perfectum fuit*" (on July 3, 1292 this work was finished) leads to the old market square, an area that seems utterly unchanged since the Middle Ages. Make a right on Via de Amicis to the **Church of San Tommaso,** a parochial church with 17th-century arcades. Its striking half-pink-and-green, half-blue-and-gold interior seems to have exploded onto the multicolored façade.

Launch your excursion to Dolcedo from **Imperia,** on the Ventimiglia-Genoa train line, where blue Riviera Trasporti **buses** leave from in front of the Hotel Italia up to the left of the train station. Buy tickets at *tabacchi* (L2000). About 7 buses per day, labeled either Dolcedo or Lecchiore; ask the driver for specifics. Once in town, try the moderately priced **Ristorante Da Tunu,** P. Dovia, 2 (tel. 28 00 13), a full meal costs around L16,000. Wine L10,000-20,000 per liter. *Cinghiale* (wild boar) is an autumn specialty. Cover about L1500—depends on food. Open Tues.-Sun. noon-2:30pm and 7:30-9pm.

The medieval hillside village of **Cervo** is a picturesque retreat from the larger beach towns of the Riviera. Its white houses, red roofs, stone archways, and tiny *piazze* are well worth the simple excursion: take the *locale* along the Ventimiglia-Genoa line or hop a bus from Imperia. Cervo hosts an international **chamber music festival** in July and August, held in front of the baroque Church of San Giovanni Battista. Call the **tourist office** at P. Castello, 1 (tel. (0183) 40 81 97) for details.

Bordighera

Bordighera is known as the "City of Palms" because Sant'Ampelio brought the original palm seeds from Egypt and planted them in the town's fertile soil. The town's green thumb persists: it proudly supplies the Vatican with palm leaves for Holy Week. Both Queen Margaret and Claude Monet fled their gardens for relaxing winters by the sea and the lush flower-lined streets of Bordighera. Overflowing with vivid colors and perfumed air, the town provides an oasis of small-town tranquility in the overly touristed Riviera di Ponente.

ORIENTATION AND PRACTICAL INFORMATION

The bus from Ventimiglia (15min., L2000) drops you off on the main street, **Via Vittorio Emanuele II,** which runs west from the city's train station in **Piazza Eroi della Libertà.** Behind the station is the scenic **Lungomare Argentina,** a 2-km promenade along the beach. This is the **città moderna** (new town) where most offices and shops may be found. To the east, most residential neighborhoods are near the **città alta,** the historic center. Built on a hill, the picturesque 15th-century town is accessible by three gates, of which the **Porta Sottana** is the closest.

Tourist Office: Via Roberto, 1 (tel. 26 23 23; fax 26 44 55), just past the small park. From the train station, go left on Via Vittorio Emanuele and take the 1st right onto

Via Roberto. Marisa knows everything about the town; she doles out maps, hotel listings, and other info with gusto. Although she doesn't book rooms, she makes good suggestions. Open Mon.-Sat. 8am-7pm, Sun. 9am-1pm.

Currency Exchange: Floreana Viaggi e Vacanze, Via Vittorio Emanuele 165 (tel. 26 36 54). No commission on cash or traveler's checks. Open Mon.-Fri. 9am-12:30pm and 3:30-7pm. Sat. 9am-12:30pm.

Telephones: Via Roberto, 18, across from the tourist office. Pay phones only. Open 24hr.

Trains: Stazione F.S. in P. Eroi della Libertà (tel. 26 32 09). Bordighera lies on the Genova-Ventimiglia line. To Genova (every hr., 3hr., L11,700) and Ventimiglia (every hr., 8min., L1500).

Pharmacy: Farmacia Centrale, Vittorio Emanuele, 145 (tel. 26 12 46). Open Sun.-Fri. 8:30am-12:30pm and 3:30-7:30pm.

Emergencies: tel. 113. For an **ambulance (First Aid)** dial 27 51. **Medical services** can be obtained at Via Aurelia, 66 (tel. 27 51).

Post Office: 6.P. Eroi della Libertà (tel. 26 16 74 or 26 23 74), just to the left of the train station. Open Mon.-Fri. 8:10am-5:30pm, Sat. 8:10am-noon. **Postal Code:** 18012.

Telephone Code: 0184.

ACCOMMODATIONS

In summer, most hotels want clients to stay several days and require that they accept full-pension, half-pension, or at least breakfast.

Pensione Miki, Via Lagazzi, 14 (tel. 26 18 44), off Via Vittorio Emanuele II about 500m from the station as you exit to the left. Small rooms, but a serene setting, firm beds, and balconies overlooking the town and valleys. L30,000 per person. Showers and breakfast included. Full- or half-pension required during summer and Easter, L55,000-60,000 per person.

Villa Loreto, Via Giulio Cesare, 37 (tel. 29 43 32). Take Via Vittorio Emanuele left from the station for 700m, then go right on orange-tree-lined Via Rossi and left on Via Aldo Moro, which leads into Via Cesare. Though it's a bit of a hike to get there, the nuns provide just about every service in their palatial, tranquil residence graced by palm and lemon trees. Women and married couples only. Curfew 9pm; July-Aug. 10:30pm. Mandatory full-pension includes meals, L60,000-62,000 per person. Open Dec.-Sept.

Albergo Nagos, P. Eroi della Libertà, 7 (tel. 26 04 57), right next to the train station and the post office. Run by a wonderful family. Nice views, private showers, and a warm reception make up for small rooms. Singles L40,000. Doubles L60,000. Full-pension (L60,000) required July-Aug., half-pension (L50,000) required May-June and Sept.

FOOD

Bordighera is a rather trendy vacation spot, so affordable restaurants are few and far between. Some *trattorie* in the *città alta*, however, are pretty reasonable and offer the traditional flavors of Ligurian cuisine. While in Bordighera, make sure to sample the local dessert, *cubaite* (elaborately decorated wafers filled with caramel cream), and the local *Rossese* wine from Dolceaqua. The **Trattoria dei Marinai di Costa Bianca,** at Via dei Marinai, 2 (tel. 26 15 11), is an attractive place with additional outdoor seating in the tiny P. del Popolo. *Primi* from L9000, pizza from L7000. They even have an "I love you" pizza *dolce* (sweet) with chocolate, bananas, and cream. Open Thurs.-Tues. noon-3pm and 7:30-11:30pm. V, MC, AmEx. In the *città moderna,* **Crêperie-caffè Giglio,** Via Vittorio Emanuelle, 158 (tel. 26 15 30), is a popular local hangout. They have a large selection of inexpensive *panini* (from L1000) as well as delicious crêpes for meals or dessert. Don't miss the *crêpe cioccolato* made with gooey chocolate-hazelnut nutella (L5000). Open daily 11am-3am. Closed Mon. in the winter. For picnics and more affordable fare, try the **indoor market,** P. Garibaldi. Open daily 7am-1pm; in winter closed Sat. Via Libertà, 32 houses a

STANDA Supermarket. Open daily 8:30am-12:30pm and 3:45-7:45pm; in winter closed Mon. mornings.

SIGHTS AND ENTERTAINMENT

If you're up for a long but worthwhile walk, head east along Via Romana. Fork off onto Via Rossi, where cannons still guard the town above an awesome expanse of deep blue sea. Take the steps down to the **Church of Sant'Ampelio,** built around the grotto where Ampelio the hermit (and later, patron of the town) holed up. (Open Sun. at 9am, or knock on the door until someone lets you in.) The church is also open on May 14 for the **Festival of Sant'Ampelio,** complete with an impressive procession and ritual pomp and circumstance.

If you haven't seen enough flowers, the **Giardino Esotico Pallanca** (exotic garden) at Via Madonna della Ruota, 1 (tel. 26 63 47), contains over 3000 species of cacti and rare South American flora. (Open Tues.-Sun. 9am-noon and 3:30-7:30pm.) For inspiration of a more melodic nature, ask at the tourist office about concerts during May-Sept. at the **Paviliano** down on the boardwalk. If it's raining, you can always catch the latest film (dubbed in delayed Italian, of course) at **Cinema Olimpia** Via Cadorna, 3 (tel. 26 19 55), just off Via Vittorio Emanuele II. Look at the list posted outside for the movies of the month. Showings at 8:30 and 10:30pm, and they offer reduced prices for youth and students.

Ventimiglia

The quiet town of Ventimiglia lies at the mouth of the Roya river on the shores of the Mediterranean. Its numerous craggy promontories are the perfect place to sit and indulge in what Italians call *il dolce di far niente* (the joy of doing nothing). Formerly a Roman municipality, Ventimiglia retains only traces of its ancient and medieval past. A visitor may catch glimpses of this history in the colossal remains of a Roman theater to the east of town and in the winding 11th-century streets. Just minutes from the French border, Ventimiglia bustles with international energy (and plenty of duty-free shops) but maintains its small-town cleanliness and friendliness. While seen primarily as a point of departure for the French Côte d'Azur, Ventimiglia's affordability, proximity to all the famous Riviera oases, and pebble beaches make it an enjoyable as well as a functional base for exploration.

ORIENTATION AND PRACTICAL INFORMATION

As the "western door of Italy" on the French-Italian border, Ventimiglia is an important gateway in and out of the country. Frequent buses link it to the rest of the Riviera dei Fiori and parts of France, while trains run to the Italian and French Riviera. From the train station, cross the street and walk down **Via della Stazione.** The second crossroad is **Via Cavour,** and the third is **Via Roma.** Most of what you'll need can be found on these two streets. Via della Stazione eventually becomes **Corso Repubblica,** which leads to the waterfront at the **Lungo Roya G. Rossi.**

Tourist Office: Via Cavour, 61 (tel. 35 11 83). City maps and brochures about neighboring and city attractions. English spoken. Open Mon.-Sat. 8am-7pm; in summer also Sun. 9am-1pm.

Currency Exchange: Literally on every corner. Try inside the train station (tel. 35 11 54), open daily 7am-11:30pm, or right outside at Via Stazione, 3/A (tel. 35 12 15), open Mon.-Sat. 8am-12:30pm and 2:30-7pm. Neither charge commission.

Telephones: At the restaurant in the train station. Open 24hr.

Trains: P. Stazione. To: Nice (26 per day, 40min., L11,000); Genoa (23 per day, 3hr., L13,700); Cannes (25 per day, 1½hr., L17,200); and Marseilles (5 per day, L48,600).

Buses: Riviera Trasporti, Via Cavour, 61 (tel. 35 12 51), next to the tourist office. Open Mon.-Sat. 7:20am-7:30pm. On Sun., you can buy tickets on the bus. To: Sanremo (L3000), Bordighera (L2000), Imperia-Porto Maurizio (L6000, change in Sanremo), and other local towns. No roundtrip discount.

Bike Rental: Eurocicli, Via Cavour, 70/B (tel. 35 18 79). L3000 per hour, L15,000 per day. Open Mon.-Sat. 8:30am-noon and 3-7:30pm, Sun. 9am-12:30pm. MC.

Emergencies: tel. 113. **Ambulance: Croce Rossa Italiana,** Via Dante, 12 (tel. 25 07 22), or **Croce Verde Intemelia,** P. XX Settembre (tel. 35 11 75). **Hospital: Ospedale Santo Spirito,** Via Basso, 2 (tel. 27 51).

Police: P. della Libertà, 1 (tel. 34 902).

Post Office: Corso Repubblica, 8 (tel. 35 13 12), toward the water. Open Mon.-Fri. 8:10am-5:30pm, Sat. 8:10am-noon. Closes at noon on the last working day of each month. **Postal Code:** 18039.

Telephone Code: 0184.

ACCOMMODATIONS AND CAMPING

Ventimiglia is one of the Riviera's least expensive places to stay, but it fills up in July and August so reserve in advance. Consider crossing the border and staying in the **youth hostel** (tel. (033) 93 35 93 14; from Italy, dial another 0 first) in the nearby French town of **Menton** (15min. by train, L3100). **Bring your passport.**

Hotel XX Settembre, Via Roma, 16 (tel. 35 12 22). Price-wise, the best deal in town. Friendly owners and clean, slightly dark rooms decorated with jigsaw puzzle masterpieces on the walls. Singles L25,000. Doubles L40,000. Triples L55,000. Full-pension L58,000. Half-pension L43,000. Breakfast L6000. The **restaurant** serves a good meal for L20,000. Restaurant open Fri.-Wed. noon-3pm and 7:30-9:30pm. May be closed for vacation in June—call ahead.

Pensione Villa Franca, Corso Repubblica, 12 (tel. 35 18 71), next to the waterfront and the public park. Rooms are clean, if somewhat small. Friendly management and lots of exotic pet birds. They'll bring you your own pot of coffee and pitcher of hot milk for *caffè latte* in volume. Singles L46,000. Doubles around L70,000, with bath L87,000. Breakfast and showers included. V, MC.

Hotel Splendid, Via Roma, 33 (tel. 35 15 03; fax 35 81 48). Friendly proprietors offer large, stark rooms with TV and phone. Firm beds provide terrific back support while you watch the soaps. Singles L60,000, with bath L70,000. Doubles with bath L120,000. Half-pension L130,000.

Camping Roma, Via Peglia, 5 (tel. 23 90 07; fax 23 90 35), 400m from the waterfront, across the river. From the station, follow Via della Stazione and go right on Via Roma until you reach the river at Lungo Roya G. Rossi. Turn right, then turn left and cross the river after 100m. Make an immediate right on Corso Francia, and about 100m later turn right onto Via Peglia. Nice campsites with fabulous hillside panoramas. Market and bar nearby. L10,000 per person, L10,000 per tent. Free showers. Open May-Sept. 8am-midnight.

FOOD

You will pay dearly for quality, sit-down meals. The restaurant in the *pensione* above serves good meals. The covered **open-air market,** sprawling every morning along Via della Repubblica, Via Libertà, Via Aprosio, and Via Roma, is the best place to grab fresh produce. Many of the pizzerias lining the beach prepare personal-sized take-out pizzas for about L7000. The **STANDA** supermarket at the corner of Via Roma and Via Ruffini is well stocked with staples. Open Mon.-Sat. 8:30am-7:30pm, July-Aug. Sun. 8:30am-1pm. The **Buffet Stazione,** inside the train station (tel. 35 12 36) is a fastidiously clean, modern option. Slices of pizza and *focaccia* L1200, *panini* under L4600. Prices are lower if you stand. Restaurant open daily noon-3pm; bar open 5:30am-1am.

SIGHTS AND ENTERTAINMENT

Most visitors to Ventimiglia never venture beyond the beach. For those willing to sacrifice a day of tanning, however, there are a number of worthwhile sights. The Gothic **cathedral,** with an intricate portal and adjoining 11th-century baptistery, is easy to find in the old town. Take Via Banchieri after the bridge, and from there take Via Falerina. **San Michele,** a Romanesque church of the same era, is on the other side of town. Follow the signs off Via Garibaldi to P. Colleta. (Open Sun. 10:30am-noon.) The well-preserved **Roman theater** anchors the **archaeological zone** off Corso Genova to the east of the town. Turn left on Via Cavour, and continue about 1km to find it between gas stations and railroad tracks. (The zone is now "closed" to foot traffic, but it is clearly visible from Corso Genova.)

A trip to the **Balzi Rossi,** or Red Cliffs (tel. 381 13), 9km from Ventimiglia toward France, offers a glimpse of an even earlier civilization. The blue Riviera Trasporti bus from the corner of Via Cavour and Via Ruffini in Ventimiglia (3 per day, 20min., L2000) takes you to a series of **caves** where you can view the remains of Cro-Magnon cave-dwellers. The most spectacular artifacts reside in Balzi Rossi's **Prehistoric Museum** (tel. 381 13) near the seaside. (Open in summer Tues.-Sun. 9am-12:30pm and 2-6pm; in winter 9am-1pm and 2:30-6pm. Admission L4000, under 18 and over 60 free.) The **Museo Archaeologico** at Via Verdi, 41 (tel. 35 11 81 or 26 36 01) also showcases historic artifacts. (Open in summer Tues.-Fri. 9:30am-12:30pm and 5-9pm; in winter Tues.-Fri. 9:30am-12:30pm and 3-7pm; Sat.-Sun. 10am-noon. Admission L4000.) In the living world, the internationally renowned botanical **Hanbury Gardens** (tel. 22 95 07) stretch from the summit of Cape Mortola down to the sea and contain some of the world's most exotic flora, taken from three continents. Take the blue Riviera Trasporti bus (20min., L2000) from Via Cavour and Via Martiri della Libertà to La Mortola. (Open in summer daily 9am-6pm; in winter Thurs.-Tues. 10am-4pm. Admission L8500, ages 6-12 L4500, under 6 free.) You can't eat these plants, but if you want to buy and eat vegetables while shopping for the cheapest leather goods, books, and hardware imaginable, journey to the **weekly market** in Ventimiglia that takes place every Friday along the Lungo Roya G. Rossi.

■ Near Ventimiglia

Of the many beautiful and mysterious valleys and caves fanning inland from Ventimiglia, **Val di Nervia** is the most accessible. On foot, pass the Roman theater and take the road on your left. Alternatively, take the blue **Riviera Trasporti** bus from the train station in Ventimiglia (10 per day, 15min., L2000). Riviera Trasporti also runs buses to the surrounding castle-topped hills.

A medieval castle and an old city whose narrow, winding stone streets still bustle with activity crown **Dolceacqua,** 9km from Ventimiglia (L2000 by bus from the Ventimiglia train station, 10 per day). Turn right at the bottom of the new city and cross the arched Roman bridge to the orange, pink, and green Rococo **cathedral** at the bottom of the old city, then continue up the narrow streets to the wonderful **Castello dei Doria** (tel. 20 66 38; closed for renovations). Visitors and locals alike gather for the region's biggest and tastiest pizza at **Pizzeria La Rampa,** Via Barberis, 11 (tel. 20 61 98), on the left side of the new town's main *piazza* (overlooking the bridge and old city). Open Tues.-Sun. 7pm-midnight. After a big dinner, the intrepid tourist will want to catch a show. Fortunately, Dolceacqua is world-famous for its balletomania. Check with the **tourist office (IAT)** at Via Patrioti Martiri, 22 (tel. 20 66 81) or the Comune at Via Roma, 50 (tel. 20 64 44) for more info. In August, the village celebrates **Ferragosto** with swirling regional dances, traditional costumes, and mouth-watering pastries.

Piedmont (Piemonte)

The fertile Piedmont region is not only the source of the mighty Po River but has also long been a fountainhead of fine food, wine, and nobility. The area falls into three zones. The **Alpine,** with the two stellar peaks of Monviso and Gran Paradiso, contains a string of glamourous ski resorts and a huge national park that spills across the regional border into Valle d'Aosta. The **Pianura,** the beginning of the fecund Po val-

NORTHERN ITALY

ley, encompasses industrial Turin, the wineries of the Asti region, and Italy's only rice plantations. Finally, many of the region's isolated castles survey the *colline* north and south of the Po.

Piedmont has been an influential region in Italy throughout history. It was the Savoy King Vittorio Emanuele II (whose family had dominated Piedmont since the 11th century) and Minister Camillo Cavour who in 1859 ushered in the Risorgimento, creating a united Italy of which Turin was the capital from 1861 to 1865. Even after the capital moved, the region's political activity didn't end. Both the latter-day monarchists and the Red Brigades were based in Piedmont. Today, medieval towns throughout the region attempt to evoke the past as they re-create the festivals and pageantry of the Middle Ages. Piedmont's magnificent geography and rich history invite the traveler to explore this varied area.

Turin (Torino)

Turin's peaceful baroque elegance is the direct result of years of urban planning combined with the more recent influence of the locally based Fiat auto company. The Turin you're likely to encounter is cultured, courteous, and well educated. Just beyond the train station, cars circle neatly around the putting-green grass of Piazza Carlo Felice where well-rooted cosmopolitans peruse their morning *La Stampa.* Piazza Castello, the city center, pulses with university students and Armani-clad businessmen. Graceful, arcaded avenues reveal Turin's bookstores, ranging from those specializing in rare, prized volumes to the many sidewalk *bancarelle* (secondhand book stalls) lining the Via Po.

Turin, however, is also known for its counter-culture: its claim to fame as a European center of the occult, the chaos of its old-fashioned **Gran Balôn** flea market (held every second Sunday in the P. della Repubblica), and the gypsies dancing through its streets. Turin's turbulent history as the capital of Italian extremism is not always visible, but the city that sparked the Risorgimento, gave rise to the radical Red Brigades of the 1920s, and provided a forum for leftist intellectuals like Pavese and Natalia Ginzburg maintains its reputation as a cradle of revolutionary thought.

ORIENTATION AND PRACTICAL INFORMATION

Turin lies on a broad plain by the Po River, flanked by the Alps on three sides. **Stazione Porta Nuova,** in the heart of the city, is the best place to disembark. The city itself is an Italian rarity—its streets meet at right angles, making it easy to navigate either by bus or on foot. Of the four main streets, **Corso Vittorio Emanuele II** runs past the station to the river, and the elegant **Via Roma,** housing the principal sights, runs north through P. San Carlo and P. Castello. The other two main streets, **Via Po** and **Via Garibaldi,** extend from P. Castello. Via Po continues diagonally through **Piazza Vittorio Veneto** (the university center) to the Po River. Via Garibaldi stretches from **Piazza Castello** to **Piazza Statuto** and the **Stazione Porta Susa.**

Tourist Office: APT, Via Roma, 226 (tel. 53 59 01; fax 53 00 70), under the left arcade on the small, divided Piazza C.L.N. just before P. San Carlo. English spoken. Although the map of Turin lacks a street index, it can still be very useful. Open Mon.-Sat. 9am-7:30pm; in the summer, also open Sun. 9am-1pm and weeknights from 8:30-10pm. A smaller office is located at the Porta Nuova **train station** (tel. 53 13 27), next to the info office and exchange. Open Mon.-Sat. 9am-7:30pm. Both offices will help you find a room. **Informa Giovani,** Via Assarotti, 2 (tel. 442 49 76; fax 442 49 77), off Via Garibaldi between P. Castello and Porta Susa. This place is a gold mine for students: from feminist groups to fortune tellers, for info on renting bikes, getting a job, or finding an apartment, they'll have the scoop. Open Mon. and Wed.-Sat. 10:30am-6:30pm.

Currency Exchange: The exchange in the Porta Nuova Station is the easiest and offers a decent rate (open daily 7:30am-10pm). Also try the banks along Via Roma and Via Alfieri, or the automatic exchange machine by the APT office.

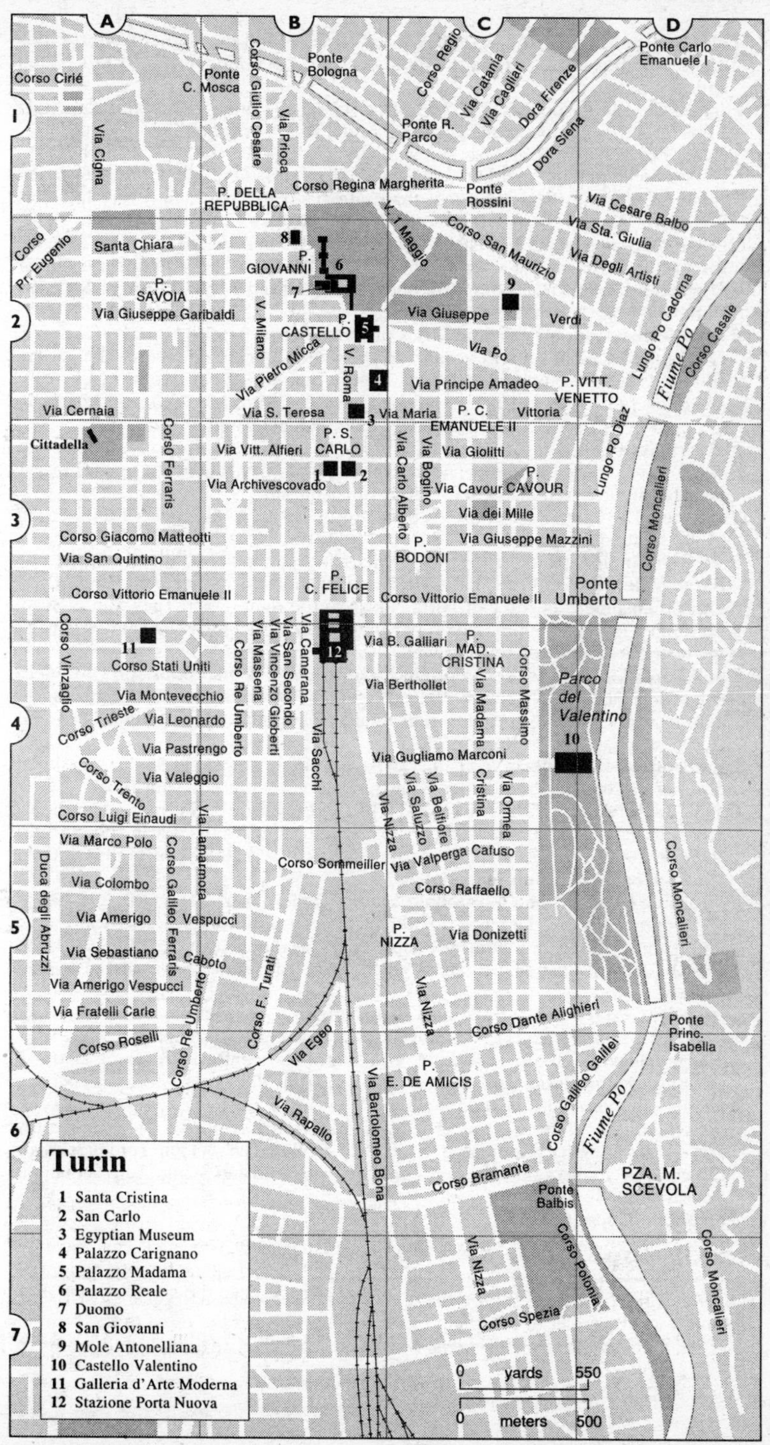
Turin
1 Santa Cristina
2 San Carlo
3 Egyptian Museum
4 Palazzo Carignano
5 Palazzo Madama
6 Palazzo Reale
7 Duomo
8 San Giovanni
9 Mole Antonelliana
10 Castello Valentino
11 Galleria d'Arte Moderna
12 Stazione Porta Nuova
Corso Cirié
Ponte C. Mosca
Corso Giulio Cesare
Ponte Bologna
Via Prioca
Corso Regio
Via Catania
Via Cagliari
Dora Firenze
Ponte Carlo Emanuele I
Via Cigna
Ponte R. Parco
Dora Siena
Corso Regina Margherita
Ponte Rossini
P. DELLA REPUBBLICA
V. 1 Maggio
Via Cesare Balbo
Corso San Maurizio
Via Sta. Giulia
Via Degli Artisti
Corso Pr. Eugenio
Santa Chiara
P. GIOVANNI
P. SAVOIA
Via Giuseppe Garibaldi
V. Milano
P. CASTELLO
Via Giuseppe Verdi
Lungo Po Cadorna
Corso Casale
Fiume Po
Via Po
Via Pietro Micca
V. Roma
Via Principe Amadeo
P. VITT. VENETTO
Via Cernaia
Via S. Teresa
Via Maria Vittoria
P. C. EMANUELE II
Lungo Po Diaz
Cittadella
Corso Ferraris
Via Vitt. Alfieri
P. S. CARLO
Via Carlo Alberto
Via Bogino
Via Giolitti
Via Archivescovado
Via Cavour
P. CAVOUR
Via dei Mille
Corso Moncalieri
Corso Giacomo Matteotti
P. BODONI
Via Giuseppe Mazzini
Via San Quintino
P. C. FELICE
Corso Vittorio Emanuele II
Ponte Umberto
Corso Vinzaglio
Via Camerana
Via San Secondo
Via Vincenzo Gioberti
Via Massena
Corso Re Umberto
Via B. Galliari
P. MAD. CRISTINA
Corso Massimo
Corso Stati Uniti
Via Berthollet
Parco del Valentino
Via Montevecchio
Via Madama Cristina
Corso Trieste
Via Leonardo
Via Sacchi
Via Pastrengo
Via Gugliamo Marconi
Via Valeggio
Corso Trento
Via Saluzzo
Via Belfiore
Via Ormea
Via Nizza
Corso Luigi Einaudi
Via Lamarmora
Via Marco Polo
Corso Sommeiller
Via Valperga Cafuso
Duca degli Abruzzi
Corso Galileo Ferraris
Via Colombo
Corso Raffaello
Via Amerigo Vespucci
P. NIZZA
Via Donizetti
Via Sebastiano Caboto
Corso F. Turati
Via Fratelli Carle
Corso Dante Alighieri
Ponte Princ. Isabella
Corso Roselli
Via Egeo
P. E. DE AMICIS
Via Bartolomeo Bona
Corso Galileo Galilei
Via Rapallo
Corso Bramante
PZA. M. SCEVOLA
Ponte Balbis
Corso Polonia
Corso Spezia
0 yards 550
0 meters 500
A B C D
1 2 3 4 5 6 7

NORTHE

Telephones: Via Arsenale, 13, off Via S. Teresa around the corner from the post office. The beautiful, space-age calling center is open Mon.-Fri. 8:30am-12:30pm and 3-7pm.

Flights: Caselle Airport (tel. 567 63 61 or 567 63 62). European destinations. Take a bus from the main **Autostazione Terminal Bus,** Corso Inghilterra, 3.

Trains: Porta Nuova (tel. 561 33 33). A city in itself. The station has anything you could ever want (supermarket, barber, post stop, etc.). One could stay forever, and some do, making the station less than safe at night. To: Milan (every hr., 2hr., L13,600); Venice (10 per day with change at Milan, 3 per day direct, 4½hr., L33,400); Genoa (every hr., 2hr., L13,600); Rome (9 per day, 9-11hr., L51,200); and Paris (4 per day, change at Lyon, 8hr., L125,000). AmEx. **Lost Property: Ufficio Oggetti Smarriti** (tel. 665 33 15), open 8am-noon and 2-5pm. **Luggage Storage:** L5000 for 12 hr. Open daily 5pm-1pm.

Buses: Autostazione Terminal Bus, Corso Inghilterra, 3 (tel. 33 25 25). Take cable car #9 or 15 west from Porta Nuova to the station. Serves ski resorts, the Riviera, and the valleys of Susa and Pinerolo. To: Courmayeur (9 per day, 4hr., L13,200); Aosta (every hr., 3hr., L10,300); Milan (15 per day, 2hr., L15,700); and Chamonix (6 per day, 3½hr., L37,000). Buy tickets daily 7am-noon and 3-7pm.

Metropolitan Transit: City buses and cable cars cost L1400. Tickets can be bought at *tabacchi* before boarding. The system is easy to navigate and a helpful map is available at most terminal offices. Buses run 5am-1am.

Taxis: tel. 57 37 or 57 30 or 33 99. Standard prices are L4500 plus L1200 per km. L4000 surcharge at night, L2000 Sun. and holidays. Baggage L1000.

Bike Rental: Most parks have rentals. Prices are standardized throughout the city. **Parco Valentino** on Viale Mattioli in Parco Valentino, a 15-min. walk down Corso Vittorio Emanuele as you exit Porta Nuova to the right. Open Tues.-Sun. 9:30am-12:30pm and 2:30-7:30pm. L2000 per hr., L4000 per half-day, L7000 per day. No age restrictions, but you must leave ID.

Bookstore: Libreria Internazionale Luxembourg, British Bookstore, Via Accademia delle Scienze, 3 (tel. 561 38 96; fax 54 03 70), across from P. Carignano. Get help from the English-speaking staff while picking up extra copies of *Let's Go.* Open Tues.-Sat. 9am-7:30pm. V, MC.

Laundromat: Lavanderia Vizzini, Via San Secondo, 30 (tel. 54 58 82). Wash and dry: 4kg L15,000. Open Mon.-Fri. 8am-1pm and 3-7:30pm, Sat. 9am-1pm.

Public Baths: Albergo Diurno (tel. 53 83 12), just outside Porta Nuova near the Via Sacchi entrance, in the train station. Go down the spiral stairs. Clean and efficient. Showers L8000. Towels included. Soap L200, shampoo L800. Toilets L1500. Open Mon.-Sat. 8am-7pm, Sun. 7am-noon.

Swimming Pool: Piscina Comunale Stadio Civile, Corso G. Ferraris, 294 (tel. 36 75 50 or 36 74 38). Take bus #41 south from Corso Vittorio Emanuele near the station. Huge and clean. Open June-Sept. Tues.-Sat. noon-7pm, L3000; Sun. 12:30-6:30pm, L5000. Changing room included. Swim caps required (available at pool, L1500).

Late-Night Pharmacies: Farmacia Boniscontro, Corso Vittorio Emanuele II, 66 (tel. 54 12 71 or 53 82 71). Centrally located. Open daily 3pm-noon.

Emergencies: tel. 113. **First Aid:** tel. 57 47. **Ambulance: Red Cross:** tel. 28 03 33. **Hospital: Mauriziano Umberto,** L. Turati, 62 (tel. 508 01).

Police: Corso Vinzaglio, 10 (tel. 558 81).

Post Office: Via Alfieri, 10 (tel. 53 58 91 or 562 81 00), off P. San Carlo. Telex, fax, and telegram service. Open Mon.-Fri. 8:15am-5:30pm, Sat. 8:15am-1pm, last day of the month 8:15am-noon. *Fermo posta* open 9am-noon and 3-7pm, Sun. 9am-noon. **Postal code:** 10100.

Telephone Code: 011.

ACCOMMODATIONS AND CAMPING

Hotels abound, but prices can be steep even for the most basic rooms. Most visitors and many locals retreat to resorts in the mountains or near the coast in the summer months and on weekends. During these times, the city is more tranquil and rooms are easier to find.

Ostello Torino (HI), Via Alby, 1 (tel. 660 29 39; fax 66 04 45). Take bus #52 from Stazione Porto Nuova (on Sun. take bus #64). Get off at the 3rd stop after crossing the Po river. Go downhill on Viale Thoveu. At the large intersection, veer to the far left onto Via Curreno. Take another left on Via Gatti, 30m away from the intersection (follow the signs for the hostel). Via Gatti branches off onto tiny Via Alby. Contemporary, clean, and comfortable with bright orange appointments. Desk open 7-9am and 3:30-11pm. Curfew 11pm. L18,000 per person, L23,000 for non-HI members. Dinner L12,000. Bring your own towel (large towels L8000). Lockers available for a L20,000 deposit. Breakfast and sheets included. Laundry (wash and dry) L10,000 per small load. **Bike rental** L8000 per day.

Albergo Magenta, Corso Emanuele, 67 (tel. 54 26 49; fax 54 47 55), to the left of the train station. Centrally located and very chic, with high ceilings, some beautiful inlaid-wood floors, and fresh flowers in the hallway. Prices are negotiable if rooms aren't full. All rooms have TV and firm beds. Singles L50,000, with bath L65,000. Doubles L60,000, with bath L70,000. Breakfast L7000. V, MC, AmEx.

Hotel Bellavista, Via B. Galliari, 15 (tel. 669 81 39; fax 668 7989), on a street slightly behind and to the right of Porta Nuova as you exit. Large, airy rooms and a sunny hallway full of plants. All rooms with TV and phone. Communal patio/balcony. Singles L70,000. Doubles L95,000, with bath L120,000. Triple with bath L140,000-145,000. Breakfast L2000-8000.

Albergo San Carlo, P. San Carlo, 197 (tel. 56 27 46 or 53 86 53), on the 4th floor. In the midst of the action, yet set back from the noisy *piazza.* Classy ski-lodge-style rooms, all with TV, fridge, and phone. Singles L60,000, with bath L80,000. Doubles L80,000, with bath L100,000.

Camping: Campeggio Villa Rey, Strada Superiore Val S. Martino, 27 (tel. 819 01 17). Take bus #61 north from the right side of the Porta Nuova across the Emanuele bridge. Get off when you see the Porta Margherita bridge on your left, then take bus #54 or walk up Corso Gabetti away from the river to the right. Quiet location in the hills above the city. L6000 per person, L3000 per small tent, L6000 per large tent. Light L2000, showers L1000. Bar, restaurant, and small supermarket on the premises. Open March 1-Oct. 30.

FOOD

Piemontese cuisine is a sophisticated blend of northern Italian peasant staples and elegant French garnishes. Butter replaces olive oil in cooking; cheese, mushrooms, and white truffles are used instead of tomatoes, peppers, and spices. *Agnolotti* (ravioli stuffed with lamb and cabbage) are the local pasta specialty, but *polenta,* a cornmeal porridge often topped with *fontina* cheese, is the more common starch. Many *secondi* involve meat simmered in wine sauces—not surprising in a region with an abundance of excellent wine. Three outstanding red wines (Barolo, Barbaresco, and Barbera) are available in Turin's markets and restaurants and are worth the extra price. The cheapest supplies are found on Via Mazzina, where fruit, cheese, and bread shops abound. There's also a supermarket **di Perdi** at Via Carlo Alberto, 15, at the corner of Via Maria Vittoria. Open Mon.-Sat. 8:30am-1:30pm and 3:30-7:30pm; closed Wed. afternoons.

Turin serves delectable local pastries, including the remarkably rich *bocca di leone,* a doughnut filled with whipped cream, fruit, or chocolate (about L3000). You can sample it at **Cossolo il Pasticciere,** Via Garibaldi, 9 (tel. 54 08 17). Their *viennesi alla crema* (L1200) are also worth a try. Open Tues.-Sun. 7am-8pm. Several trendy *gelaterie* line the near side of P. Castello coming from the station. Try the spiffy **Bar Ice Blù,** Via Antonio Gramisci, 12 (tel. 53 14 24; open Tues.-Sun. 7am-1am) or **Paradice Gelateria,** Via Roma, 307 (tel. 53 08 48; open daily 7:30am-2am), where you can sample the exotic flower flavors *rosa* and *viola.* The **open-air market** at P. della Repubblica runs Mon.-Fri. 8am-1pm. (On Sat. 8am-6pm, an assortment of non-edibles are also sold here—everything from baskets to underwear.) There is also the **Market Rossini** (cheerfully named *Simpatia* on the sign), Via Rossini, 1 (tel. 817 06 86). Open Mon.-Tues. and Thurs.-Sat. 8:30am-1pm and 4-7:30pm, Wed. and Sun. 8:30am-1pm. To mingle with the fashion nobility, try **Caffè Torino,** Via Roma, 204 (tel. 54 51 18), on

P. San Carlo, a Turin institution. If you're in an extravagant mood, sit down and savor the solicitous service provided by tuxedo-clad waiters. Cappuccino L6000 if you sit, L2500 if you stand. Open daily 7:30am-1am.

Porto di Savona, P. Vittorio Veneto, 2 (tel. 817 35 00). A Turinese institution, revered for serving the best in traditional *piemontese* fare. Frescoed walls are adorned with black and white pictures of Turin at the turn of the century. Best bets are the *gnocchi al gorgonzola* (L8000) and the *fusilli alla diavola*, a delight made with tomato, pesto, and cream sauce (L8000). Huge portions. Open Tues. 7:30-10:30pm, Wed.-Sun. 12:30-2:30pm and 7:30-10:30pm. Closed July.

Ristorante Taverna Fiorentina, Via Palazzo di Città, 6 (tel. 521 40 97), off P. Castello. A small restaurant run by the Cicerale family. If you're tired of pasta, try the *scallopine al vino bianco* (L9000). Plate of the day L7500-15,000. Cover L2500. Open Aug.-June Sun.-Fri. noon-3pm and 7-10pm. V, MC.

Ristorante da Michele, P. Vittorio Veneto, 4 (tel. 88 88 36). Friendly service in a homey atmosphere including flowered tablecloths and old Coke posters. Popular—get there early. Brick-oven pizza from L7000; *primi* L10,000-18,000. Cover L3000. Open Wed.-Mon. noon-2:30pm and 7:30-11:30pm.

Trattoria Messico, Via B. Galliari, 8 (tel. 650 87 98), 2 streets south of Corso Emanuele near Porta Nuova. No sombreros here, just a smattering of locals and tourists afraid to stray far from the station. Terrific pasta and *fettuccine messico* (L7000). On Fri. and Sat. evenings, they serve Mexican food (real enchiladas). Wine L8000 per liter. Cover L3000. Open Mon.-Sat. 11am-3pm and 7-10pm.

Trattoria Toscana, Via Vanchiglia, 2 (tel. 812 29 14), off P. Vittorio Veneto near the university. This local hit rewards those who undertake the walk. Don't miss the *bistecca di cinghiale* (boar steak, L8000), which clashes with the rose-covered tables. Open Sept.-July Sun.-Fri. noon-2pm and 7-10pm. Closed Fri. night.

Café Gran Corso, Corso Emanuele, 63 (tel. 562 93 49). A 5-min. walk to the left of Stazione Porto Nuova. The Regoni family is sure to please with fresh *panini* made to order (L3000); eat in or take out. Open Mon.-Sat. 6am-8pm.

Seven-Up, Via Andrea Doria, 4 (tel. 54 35 82). Crêpes, pizza, silky *risotto* (all around L8000) in a crisp, clean, no-caffeine atmosphere. Cover L2000. Open Aug.-June Tues.-Sun. noon-2:30pm and 6:30-11pm. V, MC, AmEx.

Brek, P. Carlo Felice, 22 (tel. 53 45 56), in the center of the action off Via Roma. Chic and delicious self-serve fare, including spectacular salads, soups, and desserts. *Primi* around L5500, *secondi* around L7000. Open Mon.-Sat.11:30am-3pm and 6:30-10:30pm. Another location at P. Solferino.

Il Punto Verde (Vegetarian), Via San Massimo, 17 (tel. 88 55 43) off Via Po near P. C. Emanuele II. Friendly pink tablecloths. A good place for lunch. *Primi* L6000-8000, *secondi* L6000-12,000, *menù* L15,000. Cover L2000. Open Tues.-Fri. noon-3pm and 7-11pm. Closed in Aug. V, MC.

SIGHTS

It's hard to say which the Turinese revere more: their successful auto industry or the (now somewhat less holy) Holy Shroud. Despite these local idols, the city has a great deal to offer those who are neither religious pilgrims nor auto buffs. Turin's museums, architectural sights, and serene gardens are on a par with some of the great capitals of Europe, and its manageable size and relative safety make it an excellent city for visitors of all interests and budgets to explore.

From P. Carlo Felice at the Porta Nuova station, **Via Roma,** flanked by arcades and the most exclusive stores, leads to the heart of the city. Just ahead, **Piazza San Carlo** displays all the formality and grandeur the 17th-century Baroque era could inspire. In the center of this perfect rectangle the statue of Duke Filiberto Emanuele on horseback stands proudly above the crowds (and cars). In addition to the elegant baroque buildings, the *piazza* features the twin churches of **Santa Cristina** and **San Carlo,** both the work of Filippo Juvarra, architect to King Vittorio Amadeo II.

Beyond P. San Carlo, Via Roma ends in **Piazza Castello,** the historic center of the city, dominated by the imposing **Madama Palace** (tel. 54 38 23), so called because the widow of Vittorio Amadeo I, "Madama Reale," Marie Christine of France, lived here. (Natives often refer to it as the Palazzo Reale, however; do not confuse it with the other royal palace in Turin.) The colossal pilasters and columns are set against Juvarra's richly decorated façade. Through history, the façade itself has incorporated ancient fragments of ancient structures into its edifice—including a Roman gate and a 13th-century castle. Inside, the **Museo Civico di Arte Antica** contains a fine collection of medieval and Renaissance objects. The **Armeria Reale** (Royal Armory; tel. 54 38 89) of the House of Savoy (tel. 54 38 89) is located just across P. Castello at #191 and contains the world's best collection of medieval and Renaissance tools of war. Upstairs in the **library** you'll find Leonardo da Vinci's self-portrait *(autoritratto)* in red ink. (Open Tues. and Thurs. 2:30-7:30pm, Wed. and Fri.-Sat. 9am-2pm. Admission L8000, under 18 and over 60 free.)

Although the city owes its glory to political rather than ecclesiastical leadership, unadulterated splendor blesses the interior of the **Church of San Lorenzo** in P. Castello. Constructed between 1668 and 1680, it is Guarini's most original creation. Follow the moldings as they weave in and out of side chapels, or count the myriad columns of every color, shape, size, and texture imaginable. The highlight is the **dome,** a multi-layered kaleidoscope of wishbones and starfish in a dynamic, swirling composition. (Open 8:30am-noon and 4-7pm.) Cross the courtyard to see the other **Palazzo Reale** (tel. 436 14 55), an apricot building that the Princes of Savoy called home from 1645 to 1865. Its red-and-gold interior houses an outstanding collection of Chinese porcelain vases. Louis le Nôtre (1697), who is more famous for his work on the *jardins* of Versailles, designed the small but sumptuous garden. (Palace open Tues.-Sat. 9am-7pm. Admission L8000, under 18 and over 60 free. Gardens open daily 9am-6pm. Free.)

The **Cathedral of San Giovanni** (tel. 436 15 40), behind the Palazzo Reale where Via XX Settembre crosses P. San Giovanni, is also a must-see. Guarini's remarkable creation, the **Cappella della Santa Sindone** (Chapel of the Holy Shroud, 1668-1694), lies within. The unrestrained black marble dome caps a somber rotunda housing one of the strangest relics of Christianity, the **Holy Shroud of Turin.** Called a hoax by some and a miracle by others, this piece of linen, now contained within a silver vessel, was thought to be worn by Christ for burial after his crucifixion. Although radiocarbon dating places the piece in the 12th century AD, no one has been able to account for the unique impressions of a crucified body on the front and back of the shroud. Before leaving the cathedral, don't miss Luigi Gagna's oil reproduction of Leonardo's *Last Supper* above the front door, considered the world's best copy of the Renaissance masterpiece. (Chapel open Tues.-Sat. 9am-noon and 3:30-5pm. *Duomo* closed for restoration; ask the tourist office for updated info.)

The **Palazzo dell'Accademia delle Scienze,** at #6 of the Via of the same name, houses two of Turin's best museums. Crammed into two floors of this Guarini masterpiece, the **Museo Egizio** (tel. 561 77 76) has a collection of Egyptian artifacts second only to the British Museum. Here you will find several copies of the Egyptian *Book of the Dead* and an intact sarcophagus of Vizier Ghemenef-Har-Bak, standing out among the large sculptures and architectural fragments on the ground floor. Upstairs is the fascinating and well-furnished tomb of 14th-century BC architect Kha and his wife, one of the few tombs spared by thieves. (Open Tues. and Thurs. 9am-7pm, Wed. and Fri.-Sun. 9am-2pm. Admission L12,000, under 18 and over 60 free.) The third and fourth floors hold the **Galleria Sabauda** (tel. 54 74 40). With masterpieces from the House of Savoy, the gallery is renowned for its paintings by Flemish and Dutch artists: van Eyck's *St. Francis Receiving the Stigmata,* Memling's *Passion,* van Dyck's *Children of Charles I of England,* and Rembrandt's *Old Man Sleeping.* The Sabauda is also home to several Mannerist and Baroque paintings, including a noteworthy Poussin, several Strozzis, and Volture's *Decapitation of John the Baptist.* (Open Tues.-Sun. 9am-2pm, Thurs. also 2-7pm. Admission L8000, under 18 and over 60 free.)

The Palazzo Carignano contains the **Museo Nazionale del Risorgimento Italiano** at Via Accademia delle Scienze, 5 (tel. 562 11 47); enter from P. Carlo Alberto on the back of the palace. One of the great Guarinis' Baroque palaces, its façade is a masterpiece of white marble relief and elegant statuary. In the 19th century, this palace housed the first Italian parliament and the cradle of Prince Vittorio Emanuele II. Today, the museum contains historic documents and other paraphernalia of national interest. On Sundays from 10:30am to noon there is a free guided tour of the exhibits. (Open Tues.-Sat. 9am-6:30pm, Sun. 9am-12:30pm. Admission L8000.)

The **Museo di Antichità** (Museum of Antiquities) at Corso Regina Margherita, 105 (tel. 521 22 51) houses several beautiful Greek and Roman busts, a collection of Greek and Cypriot ceramics, and pieces from the treasury of Marengo. There are also several artifacts from Piedmont and Valle d'Aosta. (Open Tues.-Sat. 9am-7pm, Sun. 2-7pm. Admission L8000, under 18 and over 60 free.) The **Galleria d'Arte Moderna,** Via Magenta, 31 (tel. 562 99 11), off Largo Emanuele, contains representative works of late 19th- and 20th-century masters, including Chagall, Picasso, Courbet, and Renoir. (Open Tues.-Sun. 9am-7pm. Admission L10,000.)

The **Museo Nazionale del Cinema,** P. San Giovanni, 2 (tel. 436 11 48), occupies the Palazzo Chiablese. The museum contains an excellent collection of pre-cinematic and cinema stills and maintains a library. Turin was the birthplace of Italian cinema; the seminal silent film *Cabiria* was filmed along the banks of the Po. (Closed for renovations; check with tourist office for updated info.)

Take in culture on every corner as you stroll along the streets and observe some of the most architecturally significant façades in the world. Windows lined with etched glass, portals with neo-classical columns, and doors with inlaid rosewood rival those in Venice. For a complete walking tour booklet, contact the tourist office. When you can handle no more Baroque, a *siesta* on the shady park at P. Cavour is ideal, as is an amble through the burgeoning gardens along the banks of the Po to the **Castello del Valentino** (tel. 669 93 72). A "medieval" castle built in 1884 for a world exposition, it looks like something from *Alice's Adventures in Wonderland.* The guide takes you through room after room of objects and oddities—a sink in the shape of a castle, a throne that converts to a toilet. (Unfortunately, closed for renovations.)

No Italian city would be complete without its expression of civic virility; in modern Turin, you can skip prowess-testing stairs and take a glass elevator to the top. The **Mole Antonelliana,** Via Montebello, 20 (tel. 817 04 96), a few blocks east of P. Castello, began as a synagogue in a time of political and religious instability, thus ending up as a Victorian eccentricity. The view inside the dome as you ascend to the top is dizzying. (Open Tues.-Sun. 9am-7pm. Admission L4000.)

ENTERTAINMENT

On weekends, Turin's newspaper **La Stampa** publishes an excellent section on current events, music, cinema, theater, and festivals. The arts enliven Turin from early June through July 6, when the city invites international companies to the **Sere d'Estate** festival. For info and programs, contact the **Vetrina per Truino,** P. San Carlo, 159 (tel. 442 47 40). Events L5,000-30,000. **Settembre Musica** is a month-long extravaganza of over 40 classical concerts performed all over the city. Contact the Vetrino or the tourist office for a program. **Cinemas** are prevalent in Turin, offering the latest big-budget blockbusters, obscure art films, and all-out pornography. During the academic year a number of foreign films are shown in their original languages. For a list of the titles, times, and locations all-year long, contact the Informa Giovani office. Find a listing of summer films in *Arena Metropolismi.*

During his time as a student in Turin, Erasmus said that magic pervaded the city, and Turin has since extended its reputation as a center of the occult. Get your palm read at the Porta Pila, or flirt with the world of black garb and magenta walls at **Inferno,** Via Carlo Alberto, 55 (tel. 88 95 33), and Via Po, 14 (tel. 88 91 45). Local punks come to chat more than to shop. Both open Mon.-Sat. 10am-noon and 3:30-7pm; closed Mon. morning and Sat. afternoon. If you seek more traditional attire but can't afford the chic shops lining Via Roma, try the **department store** at Via Lagrange and Via Teofilo Rossi.

As for nightlife, Turin has a number of discos. A young crowd gathers at the one in Parco Valentino (follow the loud music). **Hiroshima Mon Amour** is a centrally located club near Porta Nuova on Via Belfiore off Via Bethedet. **El Patio,** Corso Moncalieri, 346/14 (tel. 661 51 66), is nearby on the river. Make a right on Corso Moncalieri after you cross the river on C. Emanuele II, then walk past a couple of bridges. Discos and clubs are constantly changing. For an up-to-date list of performances and theme nights, pick up the weekly *News Spettacolo* at the tourist office.

■ Near Turin

When the French attacked Turin on September 6, 1706, King Vittorio Amadeo II made a pact with the Virgin Mary to build a magnificent cathedral in her honor should the city withstand the invasion. Turin went unconquered, and the result was the awe-inspiring **Basilica di Superga** (tel. 898 00 83), erected on the summit of a 672-m hill. The basilica's neoclassical portico and high drum create a spectacular dome. From the terrace you can survey the city, the Po Valley, and the Alps. Take tram #15 (L1400) from Via XX Settembre to Stazione Sassi, and then board a small cable railway for a 20-min. ride through the countryside. Open daily 8:30am-noon and 3-6pm. Free. The railway departs on the hour (L4000). The tourist office also has info about boat trips on the Po, which normally run from mid-June to mid-September (around L10,000).

Turin is just a hop, skip, and a ski-jump away from many superb hiking areas and smooth slopes. The closest resort is super-chic **Sestriere** (2035m), only an hour and a quarter away from the city. Bus service runs directly from Turin and also from the city of Oulx, which lies on the Paris-Turin train line. Sestriere has four cable ways, 20 ski lifts, excellent runs, a skating rink, and, hopefully, piles of snow. For specifics on snow conditions and lodgings, call either Turin's tourist office or **Sestriere's tourist office,** P. Agnelli, 11 (tel. (0122) 760 45 or 768 65).

Alagna Valsesia (1200km) is slightly farther away and boasts the second longest lift in the area. Still farther north, **Macugnaga** (1327m) looks in the distance with its own enormous ski lift. These resorts are also linked to Turin by bus and train. Detailed information may be obtained from the tourist office by requesting the booklets *Settimane Bianche* ("white weeks") and *Orizzonte Piemonte: Dove la Neve è "Più Neve"* for hotel information. Make sure there's snow before you go.

Sacra di San Michele

Perched on a bluff 1000m above the town of Avigliana, the massive stone monastery **Sacra di San Michele** (tel. 93 91 30) looms over the approaching traveler, seeming to grow out of the very rock on which it is built. *The Name of the Rose* was not filmed here, but that was the filmmaker's poor judgement. Umberto Eco did base the plot of his book on the monastery, and even in the summer it is not difficult to imagine monks plummeting to snowy deaths from the high windows or turning up in a vat of pig's blood stowed in some creepy corner. Although it's much easier to go by car, the 14-km hike from nearby **Avigliana** (easily reached by train from Turin—15 per day, L2700) will make you feel like a proud pilgrim. From P. del Popolo in Avigliana follow the main road, Corso Laghi, around Lago Grande and make a right on the street called Sacra di S. Michele, winding its way slowly up the mountainside. The way is clearly marked with signs, and the entire walk takes two to three hours. Public **buses** to the top no longer run, although it may be easy to hitch a ride on a private tour bus.

The Sacra, founded in AD1000, perches atop Mt. Pirchiriano and is thus notable for both its interior and the views its location offers. Upon entering the structure, the impressive Stairway of the Dead, an immense set of steps helping to buttress the building, leads outside to the beautifully carved wooden doors that depict the arms of St. Michael with the Serpent of Eden. As you enter the vast Romanesque and Gothic interior, examine the fresco to your left that depicts the *Burial of Jesus, the Death of the Virgin,* and the *Assumption*, by Secondo del Bosco (1505). Peek into **the shrine**

of St. Michael, down the small steps into the middle of the nave. There you will see three tiny chapels. In AD966 St. John Vincent built the largest one, on the left with the back wall of solid rock, and angels later consecrated the site, sanctifying the most sacred spot in the Sacra. In this crypt you'll find the tombs of medieval scions of the Savoy family. Sacra open Tues.-Fri. 11:45am-12:30pm and 5-6pm, Sat. 10:30am-12:30pm and 3-6pm, Sun. 9am-noon and 2-6pm. There are **public toilets** outside the entrance, but bring your own paper. There are **restaurants** halfway up the hill and just before the homestretch of the climb. Although restoration on the building is ongoing, it remains open to the public. For more info, contact Avigliana's **Informazione Turistico,** P. del Popolo, 6 (tel. (011) 93 86 50), where cordial workers will supply you with maps. Open Mon.-Sat. 9am-noon and 3-6pm.

Susa

Today modern and serene, Susa never lets visitors forget its noteworthy Roman origins. Surrounded by mountains and divided by a river, this tiny hamlet of 7000 was once the seat of Gaul Cottius, a prefect of the Empire. With Roman artifacts and a simple but beautiful cathedral, Susa is a grand escape from Turin's overflowing grandeur and a pleasant stopover on the way to the ski resorts of the Susa Valley.

To get to Susa from Turin, take the **train** to Bussoleno (every hr.) and change for Susa (1hr., L5000). The **SAPAV bus** line (tel. 62 20 15) serves Susa, with departures to Turin (1 per day), and Sestriere (4 per day with a change in Oulx), the most fashionable of the Piedmont ski resorts. Buses leave from the train station at Corso Stati Uniti, 33. From the station, walk up Corso Stati Uniti 50m to your right. The white stand on the park's corner is Susa's Pro Loco **tourist office,** with maps, brochures, and a money exchange. Open in summer Tues.-Sat. 9am-noon and 2-5pm, in winter Tues.-Sat. 9am-noon. **First aid/ambulance** (*pronto soccorso,* tel. 62 93 00) is across the street from the train station toward the tourist office, or try the hospital next door (tel. 62 12 12). Susa's **telephone code** is 0122.

If you plan to stay, try **Hotel Stazione,** C. Stati Uniti, 2 (tel. 62 22 26), across from the station. Marco, Loris, and Egle will fill you in on Susa's history and give you spotless rooms to boot. Singles L33,000, with shower L44,000. Doubles L68,000, with bath L78,000. Breakfast L9000. Showers included. V, MC, AmEx. On Tuesday mornings from 8am to 12:30pm, a **market** offering everything from clothes to fresh cheese fills the length of Via Palazzo di Città and Via Martiri della Libertà. Tasty, fresh *focaccia* (L1200) is available at **Piazza al Taglio,** Via Mazzini, 2, next to the bridge. Open Tues.-Sat. 10am-1pm and 4-7:30pm.

A typically Italian historical jumble, Susa's cultural wealth centers on its eclectic collection of Roman remnants and medieval structures. Medieval Susa centers on the **Cathedral of San Giusto,** a structure dating from AD1029 that houses the 14th-century *Triptych of Rocciamelone,* a Flemish depiction of the Virgin and saints in brass, as well as a fine 10th-century baptismal font carved in serpentine. Beside the cathedral, the 5th-century **Porta Romana** serves in many-windowed splendor as a symbolic centerpiece to the Roman remains scattered throughout the town. The complete Roman tour takes in the **Arch of Augustus,** the **Amphitheater,** and the **Baths** (follow the yellow signs), while the medievalist can continue on to the Romanesque church of **Santa Maria Maggiore** and its handsome *campanile.*

Asti

Located in the foothills of the Alps, Asti derives its name, not surprisingly, from the ancient Ligurian word for "high hill." Asti has bustled with activity since Roman times; BMWs and Armani suits pervade the city and attest to its success in the modern world. Asti did not fare well from the 13th to the 18th centuries, however, as the house of Savoy struggled with local princes and the city was repeatedly destroyed by war. Nevertheless, 120 13th-century towers have survived, lending the city a medieval air that is further enhanced by the winding streets. Today, Asti is known not only for the 18th-century poet Vittorio Alfieri (for whom both the central *piazza* and the main *corso* are named) and his cousin Count Benedetto (who designed much of the city) but also for its prestigious dessert wine. Enthusiastic and friendly, the people of Asti make their city an extremely pleasant place to visit.

ORIENTATION AND PRACTICAL INFORMATION

The heart of the town lies in the triangular **Piazza Vittorio Alfieri.** Most historic sights lie slightly to the west of the *piazza,* off **Corso Alfieri.**

Tourist Office: P. Alfieri, 34 (tel. 53 03 57; fax 53 82 00). Assists in finding (but not reserving) accommodations and provides information on daytrips to wineries and castles, as well as local *agriturismo* options. Pick up the *Guide to Asti and its Province* and the indispensable map of the town. English spoken. Open Mon.-Fri. 9am-12:30pm and 3-6pm, Sat. 9am-12:30pm.

Currency Exchange: Instituto Bancario di San Paolo di Torino, Corso Dante, 2 (tel. 43 42 11), at P. Alfieri and Corso Dante. Change money on the second floor. Open Mon.-Fri. 8:25am-1:25pm and 2:40-4:10pm. Also try the post office.

Telephones: P. Alfieri, 10 (tel. 39 11). Office open Mon. 3-7pm, Tues.-Fri. 9am-12:30pm and 3-7pm.

Trains: P. Marconi (tel. 53 54 00), a few blocks south of P. Alfieri. To: Turin (every 30min., 40min., L5000); Alessandria (every hr., 30min., L3400); Milan (2hr., L11,700; you will have to change trains).

Buses: P. Medaglie d'Oro, across from the train station. To: Costigliole (5 per day, Mon.-Sat., 30min., L2500); Isola d'Asti (every hr., 15min., L2000); Canelli (8 per day, 1hr., L3500); Castagnole (5 per day, 20min., L2500). Buy tickets on the bus. The tourist office can provide more schedule information.

Taxis: tel. 53 26 05 (P. Alfieri) or 59 27 22 (P. Marconi).

Emergencies: tel. 113. **Red Cross Ambulance:** tel. 41 77 41. **Hospital: Ospedale Civile,** Via Botallo, 4 (tel. 39 24 24).

Police: Corso XXV Aprile, 5 (tel. 41 81 11).

Post Office: Corso Dante, 55 (tel. 59 28 51), off P. Alfieri. Open Mon.-Fri. 8:15am-7pm, Sat. 8:15am-noon. **Postal Code:** 14100.

Telephone Code: 0141.

ACCOMMODATIONS AND CAMPING

Hotel Cavour, P. Marconi, 3 (tel. 53 02 22), across from the train station. Singles with high ceilings and wood accents L51,000, with bath L56,000. Doubles L70,000, with bath L93,000. Run by a sweet couple eager to answer questions. Desk open 6am-1am. Open Sept.-July. V, MC, AmEx.

Antico Paradiso, Corso Torino, 329 (tel. 21 43 85). A good hike from the action; take bus #3 (the one marked Canova) to the last stop on Corso XXV Aprile, at Corso Torino (L1300). Religious motifs adorn the white-washed walls. Singles L40,000, none with bath. Doubles with bath L80,000. Closed Mon. A **bar** downstairs sells super-smooth gelato for as little as L1500.

Campeggio Umberto Cagni, Via Valmanera, 152 (tel. 27 12 38). From P. Alfieri, turn onto Via Aro, which becomes Corso Volta. Take a left on Via Valmanera, and keep going (and going and going...). L5500 per person, L5000-6000 per tent. Electricity L2300. Showers free. Open April-Sept.

FOOD

Astigiano cuisine is famous for its delicious simplicity, using only a few crucial ingredients and delicious, pungent cheeses to create culinary masterpieces. Of course there's always plenty of wine, wine, wine! This region offers the celebrated *bagna calda* (hot bath), a combination of raw vegetables dipped in a sizzling pot of olive oil which is infused with garlic and anchovies. Among the most cherished cheeses produced in the surrounding area are *robiole* and *tome*. Sweet tooths will love the *bunet al cioccolato,* a hedonistic treat of peaches filled with a chocolate mixture. An opportunity to discover the fabulous flavors of the local cuisine comes every year from late September through October during the *Sette Giorni* festival. The festival occurs during the harvest of the sacred and prized *tartufo* (truffle) and is for the sole purpose of eating *really* well.

For snacking, check out the extensive **fruit and vegetable market** in the Campo del Palio. Open Wed. and Sat. 7:30am-1pm; afternoons primarily offer clothes and material goods. Another **market** is held in P. Catera, off Via Carducci in the heart of town. The **Super Gulliver Market,** Via Cavour, 81, could feed an army of Lilliputians. Open Mon.-Sat. 8am-10pm, Thurs. 8:30am-1pm. **Mercato Coperto Alimentari,** at P. della Libertà (between P. Alfieri and Campo del Palio) carries raw meats, cheeses, vegetables, and pastas—each merchant has a separate kiosk. Open Mon.-Wed. and Fri.-Sat. 8am-1pm and 3:30-7:30pm.

Leon d'Oro, Via Cavour, 95 (tel. 59 20 30). Relaxed, elegant atmosphere—pink tablecloths, mirrored walls, cherry wood, and a pink marble bar. Filling meals, including some veggie entrees and veggie pizza. Pizzas L7000-10,000, *primi* L7500. Open Thurs.-Tues. 10:30am-3pm and 6pm-1am. V, MC.

Ristorante Porta Torino, Viale Partigiani, 114 (tel. 21 68 83). Take a right on C. Alfieri at Torre Rosa. Pasta L6000. Try the *penne all'arrabbiata* if you like it hot. Salad L3000. Restaurant open Sat.-Thurs. noon-2:30pm and 7-10pm. Bar open noon-10pm.

Trattoria del Mercato, Corso Einaudi, 50 (tel. 59 21 42), at Campo del Palio. Serves typical *risotto* and *tortellini* for about L6000. *Primi* from L5000, *secondi* L8000. Cover L2000. Groups (from 8 to 50) get a discount. Open Mon.-Sat. noon-2:30pm and 7:30-9:30pm.

Gran Caffè Italia, Via Cavour, 125 (tel. 59 42 22), is on the corner of the rotary opposite the train station. Fresh *panini* (L3000) and a vast selection of drinks. Free baked snacks sometimes available. Open Oct.-Aug. Mon.-Sat. noon-2:30pm. Bar open 6:30am-8:30pm.

Pizzeria Palio, P. Alfieri, 28 (tel. 59 24 74), on the corner of P. Alfieri across from the park. Friendly staff serves pizza, pasta, and *gelato*—all in the same restaurant. Pizzas around L7000, *primi* L7000, a giant dish of gelato only L5000 (a bargain!). Cover L2000. Open Tues.-Sun. noon-2:30pm and 7pm-midnight. V, MC.

Ice Cream and Coffee, Via della Valle, 2 (tel. 35 55 73), between P. Medici and C. Alfieri. Thick frappes and a vast selection of gelato. Open Mon.-Sat. 7am-8pm.

SIGHTS

From **Piazza Vittorio Alfieri,** a short walk west on Via Garibaldi to P. San Secondo will take you to the 18th-century **Palazzo di Città** (City Hall) and the medieval **Collegiata di San Secondo.** The Romanesque tower and the magnificent Gothic decorations now stand on the very spot where San Secondo, Asti's patron saint, was decapitated. The red brick exterior conceals the medieval decor of banners and wall hangings. (Open daily 7am-noon and 3:30-7pm.) At the end of Corso Alfieri stands Asti's oldest tower, the 16-sided **Torre Rossa** (Red Tower), where the saint was imprisoned prior to his execution. The tower, with foundations dating back to the time of Augustus, adjoins the elliptical, 18th-century **Church of Santa Caterina.**

North of Corso Alfieri, several medieval streets converge at P. Cattedrale, dominated by the eclectic **Cathedral of Asti,** whose size and grandeur make it one of the most noteworthy Gothic cathedrals in Piemonte. The outside was constructed in the traditional red brick, which contrasts with the white around the doors for an intriguing checkered effect. The cathedral was begun in 1309. In the 16th and 17th centuries local artists, including native son Gandolfino d'Asti, covered every inch of the walls with frescoes; even the columns are painted to appear as though there are vines climbing up them. Deteriorating 11th-century mosaics blanket the floor around the altar. If you wander about for a few minutes, the caretaker might come out and give you an extensive private tour. (Open daily 7:30am-noon and 3-7pm.) Up Via delle Valle from Corso Alfieri, off P. Medici, is the 13th-century **Torre de Troya.** (Watch out for circling swallows. They're not aiming for you; they just want to rest in the perches of the edifice, about eight feet up.) The **Giardini Pubblici,** between P. Alfieri and Campo del Palio, provide refreshing floral settings for picnics. On the far end of the Corso is the 15th-century **Church of S. Pietro in Consavia** with a 12th-century octagonal baptistery. The church served as an army hospital in WWII; Romans, friars, and those killed in war all share the space beneath the courtyard. (Open April-Oct. Tues.-Sat. 9am-noon and 4-7pm, Sun. 10am-noon; Nov.-March Tues.-Sat. 9am-noon and 3-6pm, Sun. 10am-noon.) Exhibits by local artists shown in the baptistery often extend operating hours.

SEASONAL EVENTS

The series **Asti Teatro,** held during the last two weeks of June and the first week of July, offers theatrical productions from the medieval to the modern. The venue varies, so call the **Comune of Asti** (tel. 39 91 11) for information. Reservations are suggested. (Admission is around L25,000, students and under 12 L18,000.) On the third Sunday of September, the real theater takes place in the streets with the **Palio di Asti.** The *Palio* commemorates the town's liberation in 1200, with man and mare alike draped in medieval garb. A procession leaves from the cathedral at 2pm and passes through town to the P. Alfieri. There, the horses are relieved of their costumes for the festival's finale, one of the oldest horse races in Italy. While Siena's *Palio* may be more famous, Asti's hardly lacks color and excitement.

In June and July, the **Asti Teatro Festival** incorporates jazz, drama, and dance at the Collegio and Michelerio Palaces. The popular **donkey races and amaretto-throwing festivities** take place at the end of June in Mombaruzzo. Astian winemakers court prospective buyers with annual Bacchanalias, each dedicated to a different fruit of the vine. Throughout May you can celebrate the exposition **Vindimaggio** in the *camera del commercio,* P. Medici (tel. 53 52 11). For two or three weeks in September, agricultural Asti revels in the **Douja d'Or,** a week-long festival celebrating the splendor of the grape.

■ Near Asti

Vineyards dominate the countryside around Asti, providing both an economic base and a source of widespread renown. The sparkling *Asti Cinzano* and *Asti Spumante,* among others, come to life here. Many wineries remain under family control; a warm reception awaits visitors who take time to explore these less-touristed areas. To make an appointment, call **Valleadona** (tel. 59 20 91), which can also provide information on the nearby sites of **Cinaglio** and **Villafranca d'Asti.** Ask at Asti's tourist office for the *Carta dei Vini a D.O.C. Della Provincia di Asti,* a map of vineyards in the region offering wine tastings.

Costigliole, a brief bus ride away, is home to a medieval **castle** complete with drawbridge. Costigliole's **tourist office** can be reached at (0141) 96 60 31. Also a short distance from Asti and accessible by bus are **Isola d'Asti,** with its two medieval churches, and **Canelli,** surrounded by the muscat vineyards that produce the fruity *Asti Spumante.* Phone the **Distilleria Bocchino,** Via G. B. Giulani, 88 (tel. 81 01; fax 83 25 46) to make an appointment at the wine factory. Closed weekends. The same holds true for Castigliole's **Distelleria Beccaris,** Via Alba, 5 (tel. 96 81 27). While in Canelli, call the **Catina Sociale,** Via L. Bosca, 30 (tel. 82 33 47 or 83 18 28), for wine tasting and a gastronomical tour. While in Costigliole try the **Associazione Produttori Viticoli,** Fraz. Bionzo, 54 (tel. 96 83 59 or 96 84 58). Tours are free and open to those of all ages. Those with paleontological interests may know that the Astian period (an actual paleontologic epoch) was named after this area, where mastodon, rhinoceros, and other animal fossils have been discovered.

Acqui Terme

If it were located on the coast, Acqui Terme could pass for a very scaled-down Miami. Though tucked away in the green countryside and sporting intermittent evidence of past greatness (like its Roman aqueduct), Acqui Terme's most noted feature is the number of people seeking holistic medical care. Every year people arrive in droves to receive natural treatment for their afflictions with the help of *fanghi* (mud baths), sulphuric springs that heat up to a steamy 75°C (167°F), and treatment centers for everything from rheumatism to poor circulation. Don't despair if you're healthy and in good shape. There are still parks, museums, and sights to be seen in this peaceful little town.

ORIENTATION AND PRACTICAL INFORMATION

Acqui Terme is located about 34km from Alessandria in the province of the same name. From Milan, take any train en route to Alessandria. From Genoa, catch a train by way of Ovada (every hr., 1½hr., about L5700) to the **station** at P. V. Veneto in Acqui Terme (tel. 32 25 83). To reach the **APT tourist office,** Corso Bagni, 8 (tel. 32 21 42), from the station, take a left on Via Alessandria and another left onto Via Monteverde, which leads to Corso Bagni. The helpful English-speaking staff gives out free maps and great information about where to rent bikes, ride horses, eat, or stay. Open Mon.-Fri. 8am-2pm and 3:30-6:30pm, Sat. 9am-noon. **Currency exchange** is at Cassa di Risparmio di Torino, Corso Dante, 26 (tel. 570 01). **Telephones** are at P. Matteotti, 31. **Emergencies:** tel. 122. **Ambulance:** tel. 32 23 00 or 32 33 33. **Police:** tel. 32 22 88. The **post office** (tel. 35 64 10) is on Via Truco. **Postal code:** 15011. **Telephone code:** 0144.

ACCOMMODATIONS AND FOOD

The best hotels are located across the Bormida river. From the tourist office, take Corso Bagni over the river to Viale Einaudi, the first left (notice the huge pool on the right). **Albergo Piemonte,** Via Einaudi, 19 (tel. 32 23 82), has incredibly comfortable rooms with decades-old furniture and religious adornments. Singles L40,000, with bath L45,000. Doubles with bath L65,000. You must have a reservation. **Albergo Giaccobe,** Via Einaudi, 15 (tel. 32 25 37), has gloriously furnished rooms, some with balconies. Singles L50,000, with bath L60,000. Doubles L60,000, with bath L70,000. **Hotel Belvedere,** Via Einaudi, 8 (tel. 32 27 48), once a private villa with back and front patios, is now enclosed by a white picket fence and geraniums. Singles L35,000, with bath L63,000. Doubles L50,000, with bath L65,000. When you get hungry, head to **Vecchio Borgo,** P. della Bollente, 3 (tel. 32 26 15). Pizzas L6000-L12,000, *primi* and *antipasti* L8000- L10,000. Cover L2000. Open Tues.-Sun. 10:30am-3pm and 6:30pm-2am. V, MC. **Bue Rosso,** Corso Cavour, 62 (tel. 32 27 29), will serve up a home-cooked meal at a reasonable price. Pasta L8000, *primi* L8000, *secondi* L9000. Bar open 9am-10pm.

SIGHTS AND ENTERTAINMENT

Acqui Terme preserves more than just sagging skin. To see some well-maintained artifacts, head up the hill to the **Museo Civico Archeologico Castello dei Paleogi** (tel. 575 55). The *palazzo* was constructed in the 11th century, partially destroyed in 1646, and restored in 1815. The museum inside focuses on the Roman history of the region, and tombs, *sarcophagi,* and mosaics abound. (Open Wed.-Sat. 9am-noon and 3-6pm, Sun. 3-6pm. Admission L2000, under 18 L1000.) Multiple ceiling frescoes and painted, purple columns adorn the Romanesque **Duomo of San Guido.** Its sacristy houses the famous *Trittico* (Madonna and Child) by Rubens—ask to see it. As you cross the river, the **Acquedotto Romano** provides a beautiful backdrop to the city. Certainly don't miss feeling the steamy sulphuric water from P. Bollente. At 75°C, it's as hot as that "designer" watch you bought in P. Mattesti. Try **Bar Clipper,** Via Acquedotto Romano (tel. 32 21 65), for dancing and karaoke. (Open Tues.-Sun. 7am-2am.) Or cross the street to **Bar La Rotonda,** Via Aquedotto Romano, 98 (tel. 564 42). (Open Tues. and Thurs.-Sun. 10pm-3am.) Both clubs charge a cover of about L20,000.

Valle d'Aosta

Welcome to the land of slate roofs, overhanging eaves, and Italian Alps. Lush valleys give way to pine forests reaching up to jagged, white peaks, laced with snow even in the summer. Towns reside in the valleys, cattle and terraced wineries dot the forests, and ski chalets nestle in the mountains. While the most breathtaking entrance to the region is unquestionably the international cable car connection over the mountains from Chamonix (about L32,000), the area is also accessible by combined train/bus routes that wind their way through the Alps. Gran Paradiso National Park is truly a "big paradise"—waterfalls gush around boulders and tumble down cliffs, and the views are the stuff of dreams. Remember that it can be cool up here even in the summer months, so pack long pants and a sweater if you plan to visit.

The majestic grandeur of the mountains attracts a year-round flood of tourists. Tourism (with a capital "T") has become the primary basis for Valle d'Aosta's economy, now that the region's mining and commercial farming industries have become obsolete. Many visitors come over the mountains from France, and the French influence here is reflected in the street names and the mixture of spoken languages. A warning to the budget traveler: Valle d'Aosta's beauty is well-known, so the region enjoys a year-round bustle of tourists that keeps prices high.

HIKING

The scenic mountain trails of Valle d'Aosta are a paradise for hikers. Each area's tourist office is ready to provide assistance to all, from beginners to experienced climbers. They provide information on routes as well as lists of places to stay (mountain huts or refuges) while on the journey. July, August, and the first week of September are the best times to hike, when much of the snow has melted. In April and May, thawing snow often causes avalanches (which can be a real headache).

Let's Go offers the following tips to send you on your way: you'll need at least a sweater, a windbreaker, a pair of gloves, heavy wool socks with polypropylene liners, a compass, and a first aid kit. Because even the easiest trails have tricky stretches, you'll also need a good pair of hiking boots. Don't forget that the effects of the sun intensify with altitude—wear plenty of sunscreen, even on cloudy or chilly days. When you've gotten your gear, obtain a reliable map; *Kompass* maps (available at kiosks and hiking stores in the area) are the most accurate. On the trail, beware of poisonous snakes, which have flourished as the birds that normally prey on them have fallen victims to illegal hunting.

Despite the warnings, don't be scared! There are many people waiting to help you. The tourist offices in Aosta and in each smaller valley give out a list of campgrounds, bag-lunch *(al sacco)* vendors, and mountain huts and bivouacs (ask for the *elenco rifugi bivacchi*). Most regional offices also carry the booklet *Alte Vie* (High Roads) with maps, photographs, and helpful advice pertaining to the two serpentine mountain trails that link many of the region's most dramatic peaks. Long stretches of these trails require virtually no expertise and offer panoramic views and a taste of Alpine adventure. Both are subdivided into shorter hikes and rated with regard to difficulty, availability of food, and accommodations.

Rifugi alpini ("mountain huts") make convenient abodes for veteran mountaineers and novices alike. Some are only a cable-car ride or a half-hour walk from main roads, and many offer half-pension (around L50,000). Public refuges, or *bivacchi,* tend to be empty and free, while those run by caretakers cost about L25,000 per night. For more detailed info, contact **Societá Guide,** Via Monte Emilius, 13 (tel./fax 444 48), or the **Club Alpino Italiano,** P. Chanoux, 8 (tel. 401 94; fax 36 32 44), both in Aosta. They offer insurance and membership deals with discounts on refuges.

SKIING

Skiing the mountains of Valle d'Aosta is, in a word, fantastic; it's not, however, the bargain it used to be. **Settimane bianche,** "white-week" packages for skiers, are one source of discount rates that may keep you from spending your peak ski hours contemplating financial woes. Prices for food, hotels, and ski passes vary greatly depending on the quality of the slope. In the off-season, a one-star hotel with full-pension generally costs around L450,000 per week, half-pension L385,000, and bed and breakfast L300,000, while weekly lift passes average L80,000-100,000. In high season, prices jump by as much as 20%. Winter reservations should be made by writing directly to the hotels. For more specific information, write to the **Ufficio Informazioni Turistiche,** P. Chanoux, 8, 11100 Aosta, and request the pamphlet *White Weeks: Winter Season, Aosta Valley,* in English.

Courmayeur and **Brevil Cervinia** are the best-known ski resorts in the 11 valleys, basking in the glory and shade of Mont Blanc and the Matterhorn. **Val d'Ayas** and **Val di Gressoney** offer equally challenging terrain for lower rates. If cross-country is more to your taste, head to **Cogne,** or to **Brusson** half-way down Val d'Ayas. In Courmayeur and Brevil Cervinia, true athletes run from the swimming pools to the slopes for **summer skiing,** and in June and late September it's possible to find a room without reservations. Arrange summer package deals similar to those available in winter through the tourist office in either Brevil Cervinia or Courmayeur.

OTHER SPORTS

A plethora of activities will keep your adrenaline pumping—rock climbing, mountain biking, hang-gliding, kayaking, rafting, and swimming, to name a few. The most navigable rivers are: the **Dora Baltea,** which runs across the valley; the **Dora di Veny,** which branches south from Courmayeur; the **Dora di Ferre,** which wanders north from Courmayeur; the **Dora di Rhêmes,** which flows through the Val di Rhêmes; and the **Grand Eyvia,** which courses through the Val di Cogne. Contact the **Canoa Club Monte Bianco,** c/o Piscina Coperta Regionale di Aosta, loc. Tzambarlet (tel. (0165) 55 13 73) for info on kayaking lessons, camping, and rafting excursions. **Rafting Fenis** (tel. (0165) 71 07 60) is just minutes from Aosta and charges between L25,000 and L65,000 per person, depending on the length of the trip (1-3hr.) and the skill level. For an absolutely complete list of recreational activities, ask for *Attrezzature Sportive e Ricreative della Valle d'Aosta* from any tourist office.

Aosta

Aosta is the hub of a region whose economy is increasingly dependent upon tourism. While Aosta itself sits in the flatlands, its prices have more in common with the nearby peaks of Monte Emilius (3559m) and Becca di Nona (3142m). In exchange, Aosta offers plenty of fabulous photo opportunities—remains of bridges, triumphal arches, and theaters recall Aosta's importance as a Roman hub, and a medley of towers and churches showcases the architectural diversity of the Middle Ages. Daytrips from Aosta to the outlying alpine valleys are tricky to schedule if you want to return before night falls, so plan ahead.

ORIENTATION AND PRACTICAL INFORMATION

Aosta sits approximately in the center of the region bearing its name and is most easily reached by train from Turin (13 per day, 2-3hr., L11,700). Alps-bound visitors from the east must change trains at Chivasso. Trains stop at **Piazza Manzetti,** which lies at the end of the Avenue du Conseil des Commis opposite **Piazza Chanoux,** Aosta's central *piazza.* The main street runs east-west through the *piazza* and goes through a number of name changes. To the west of the *piazza,* it is called **Via JB de Tiller,** then **Via Aubert.** To the east it is named **Via Porta Praetoria** until it reaches the historic gate of the same name, where it becomes **Via Sant'Anselmo.** Buses to surrounding valleys stop at the bus station off Via Carrel, to your right as you exit the train station.

Tourist Office: P. Chanoux, 8 (tel. 23 66 27; fax 34 657), straight ahead and down Avenue du Conseil des Commis from the train station. Ask for *Aosta, Monument Guide,* with an excellent map of the city, a list of local hotels, and restaurant locations. Also pick up copies of the regional listings of hotels, campgrounds, and *rifugi.* The compact yearly *Orari* contains comprehensive schedules of Val d'Aosta's transportation, including cable cars. English spoken. Open Mon.-Sat. 9am-1pm and 3-8pm, Sun. 9am-1pm.

Currency Exchange: Banco Valdostano Berard, P. Chanoux, 51 (tel. 23 56 56). Efficient and friendly. Accepts Visa for cash advances. Open Mon.-Fri. 8:20am-1:20pm and 2:40-4:10pm. **Banco Commerciale Italia,** next door, has similar hours. There's also a **Banco San Paolo** two doors down in the other direction.

Telephones: Inconveniently located at Viale Pace, 9 (tel. 439 97), off Via Chanoux. Open Mon.-Fri. 8:15am-12:15pm and 2-5pm.

Trains: (tel. 26 20 57) at P. Manzetti. Frequent service to Chivasso and the intermediate stations at Chatillon, Verrès, and Pont-St-Martin, which offer access, respectively, to the valleys of Valtournenche, Ayas, and Gressoney. To: Chivasso (17 per day, 1½hr., L8000) with stops at Chatillon (L2700), Verrès (L3400), and Pont-St-Martin (L5000). To Turin (13 per day, 2hr., L11,700) and Milan (15 per day via Chivasso, 4hr., L17,200). **Luggage Storage:** L5000 for 12hr. Open 8am-noon and 2:30-5pm.

Buses: SAVDA, (tel. 26 20 27) on Via Carrel off P. Manzetti, near the train station. To: Courmayeur (12 per day, 1hr., L3600, roundtrip L6100); Great St. Bernard Pass (2 per day, 2¼hr., L7400, roundtrip L12,000); and Valtournenche (2 per day via Chatillon, 2¼ hr., L5800, roundtrip L10,500). **SVAP,** in the same station, serves closer towns. To Cogne (6 per day, 50min., L3200, roundtrip L5800) and Fenis (7 per day, 30min., L1700 each way).

Taxis: In Piazza Manzetti (tel. 26 20 10), in Piazza Narbonne (tel. 356 56), or at Viale Ginevra (tel. 318 31).

Alpine Information: Club Alpino Italiano, P. Chanoux, 8 (tel. 401 94), upstairs from the tourist office. Open Mon. and Wed.-Thurs. 5-7pm, Tues. and Fri. 8-10pm. At other times, try the **Società Guide,** Via Monte Emilius, 13 (tel./fax 444 48).

Snow Conditions: Contact the tourist office.

Pharmacy: Farmacia Chenal, Via Croix-de-Ville, 1 (tel. 26 21 33), at the corner of Via Aubert. Well-stocked with the basics, and aromatherapy herbs to boot. Open Thurs.-Tues. 9am-12:30pm and 3-7:30pm. A digital sign in the window designates the nighttime pharmacy. Closed for 3 weeks in July.

Emergencies: tel. 113. **Alpine Emergency: Mountain Rescue Service,** tel. 116. **Ambulance:** tel. 30 42 11. **Hospital: Ospedale Regionale,** Viale Ginevra, 3 (tel. 30 41).

Police: (tel. 26 21 69), on Corso Battaglione Aosta.

Post Office: P. Narbonne, 1 (tel. 441 38), the huge semi-circular building. Open Mon.-Sat. 8:15am-7pm. **Postal Code:** 11100.

Telephone Code: 0165.

ACCOMMODATIONS AND CAMPING

High season in Valle d'Aosta is generally considered late December to mid-January, all of February and March, and the two weeks around Easter Sunday. In high season, most hotels will not accept reservations for fewer than three nights. Tradition decrees that all advance reservations be done by mail with a deposit.

La Belle Epoque, Via d'Avise, 18 (tel. 26 22 76), centrally located off Via Aubert. Clean, good-sized rooms with balconies and brand-spanking-new bathrooms. The

restaurant downstairs is crowded with locals. (*Primi* L7000-9000, *secondi* L9000-13,000. Cover L2000.) Singles L35,000, with bath L45,000. Doubles L65,000, with bath L75,000. Triples L75,000, with bath L110,000. Half-pension L70,000 per person. V.

Mancuso, Via Voision, 32 (tel. 345 26). From the station, head way down Via Carducci to your left and take another left under the tracks. Rooms with flowery wallpaper, bath, some with terraces. Peaceful family atmosphere, with a **restaurant** downstairs (*menù* about L20,000). Singles L45,000. Doubles L65,000.

Monte Emilius, Via Carrel, 9 (tel. 356 92), a skip and a jump to the right from the train station, upstairs from Ristorante Le Ramoneur. Friendly management and a nightly serenade by passing traffic. Singles L50,000. Doubles L80,000. Breakfast L10,000. Reserve ahead. AmEx.

Camping: Camping Milleluci, Via Porossan, 15 (tel. 23 52 78; fax 23 52 84), in Roppoz, also 1km from Aosta. L6700 per person, L3700 per tent, L3900 per car. Open year-round. Check with the tourist office for other nearby options.

FOOD

A hearty one-dish meal is well accompanied by a sampling of local cheeses, especially *fontina,* a specialty of the region. Typical dishes are influenced by nearby Switzerland and include *fonduta,* a creamy cheese fondue ladled over meat and vegetables, and *polenta valdostana,* sizzling with melted *fontina*. Prospective picnickers should feast their eyes on the food shops spilling over with bread, cheese, and pastries that line Via de Tiller and Via Pretoriane. The most divine desserts are *tegole,* wafer-thin cookies containing ground nuts. The *brioches d'Aosta* are also worth a try and can be found at Leone Framarin, Via de Tiller, 24. Open Mon.-Sat. 7:30am-1pm and 3:30-7:30pm, closed Thurs. afternoons. The **STANDA** supermarket, Via Festaz, 10 (tel. 357 57), sells more generic merchandise. Open Mon.-Sat. 8:30am-7:30pm. The chic **Café Roma,** Via E. Aubert, 28 (tel. 26 24 22), serves cappuccino (L1800) to those who want to see and be seen, while **Gelateria Linus,** to the left of Café Roma, spoons out the best *gelato* around (about L2000). Make sure you try the native *coppa,* also known as *caffè valdostano,* and wash it down with a *caffè à la cogneintze,* a drink made with coffee, *grappa,* red wine, sugar, and the juice and peels of lemons and oranges.

Trattoria Praetoria, Via S. Anselmo, 9 (tel. 443 56), just past the Porta Praetoria. An intimate dining room where Valdostan chatter flows as freely as the wine. Try the standard Valdostan dish of *salsiccette in umido* (L10,000), locally made sausages braised in tomato sauce, with a side dish of hearty *polenta*—a bargain at L4000. *Primi* L8000-10,000, *secondi* L9000-16,000. Cover L3000. Open Fri.-Wed. 12:15-2:30pm and 7:15-9:30pm. V, MC, AmEx.

Grotta Azzurra, Via Croce di Città (Croix de Ville), 97 (tel. 26 24 74), uphill from where Via de Tillier becomes Via Aubert. Fake wood paneling and delicious fare. Locals come for the fish specialties. Try the *gnocchi alla gorgonzola* (L9000). Pizza L6000-10,000. *Primi* L7000-11,000. Cover L2000. Service 15%. Open Thurs.-Tues. noon-2:30pm and 6-10:30pm. Closed July 10-27.

SIGHTS AND ENTERTAINMENT

Ruins dating from the time of Augustus (the town's original name was "Augusta Praetoria") have given Aosta the nickname "Rome of the Alps." The virtually intact **Arco d'Augusta** marks the entrance to the ancient town. Within the Roman bounds, active

No-Bull Festivities

Only in Aosta could you witness an annual, legendairy ritual with a rousing bovine finale. A series of concerts, exhibits, and feasts throughout spring and summer culminates on the third Sunday of October with the **Bataille des Reines** (Battle of the Queens), a head-butting bash in which about 200 well trained Bessies engage in elimination rounds of brain-battering. Moo.

excavation continues to unearth a growing number of historical monuments. The sprawling remains of the **Roman Theater** are the most spectacular. Follow the signs left from Rue Porte Pretorienne. (Open Mon.-Fri. 9am-6:30pm, Sat.-Sun. 9am-noon and 2-5pm. Free.) The forum's present incarnation is a tiny, sub-ground-level park, the **Criptoportico Forense.** (Opens when visitors arrive.) Jump ahead 400 years to the 5th century AD and round off the archaeological tour with a visit to the dig sites at the **Church of San Lorenzo.** (Digs open Mon.-Fri. 9am-6:30pm, Sat.-Sun. 9am-noon and 2-5pm. Church open in summer daily 9am-8pm; in winter only during archaeological exhibitions.) The **Fiera di Sant'Orso,** the region's most famous crafts fair, is held in late January and mid-August. Aosta's weekly **outdoor market** is held every Tuesday in P. Cavalieri di Vittorio Veneto.

■ Near Aosta

Perched on the tops of almost all the mountains in the region, giant castles adorn the countryside. You can get a preview by flipping through the photo-strewn pages of *Castelli della Valle d'Aosta* at a local bookstore or by browsing the free booklets at the tourist office. **Fenis castle** (tel. (0165) 76 42 63) is dotted with turrets of all shapes and sizes. Its interior is equally noteworthy for its wooden balcony and 14th-century Gothic paintings. (Easily reached by **bus** from Aosta: 7 per day, 30min., L1700.) Farther down the valley, 1km from Verrès, rests the artistic treasure trove of the **Issogne fortress** (tel. (0125) 92 93 73), complete with a giant iron fountain. (To Verrès: 17 trains per day, 35min., L3400. Buses go directly to the castle: 2 per day, 1¼hr., L7400, roundtrip L12,000.) Both castles are open April-Sept. 9am-7pm; Oct.-March 10am-5pm. Admission L4000, under 6 free.

VALLE DEL GRAN SAN BERNARDO

A valley dotted with more medieval towers than tourists, Valle del Gran San Bernardo links Aosta to Switzerland via the Great St. Bernard Pass, including a 5854-m tunnel through the mountains. Napoleon trekked through here with 40,000 soldiers in 1800, but the pass is better known for the **Hospice of St. Bernard,** founded in 1505, home base for the patron saint of man's best friend. The legendary life-saver was stuffed for posterity and can still be seen as you drive through the pass. The hospice (just across the Swiss border—don't forget your passport) offers amazing views of international peaks and is just a tail-wag away from the dog museum.

Hotels in the area include **Mount Velan** (tel. 785 24), in the commune of Saint-Oyen, which charges L60,000 for a single and about L90,000 for a double. **Des Alpes** (tel. 78 09 16) in the commune of Saint-Rhémy-en-Bosses has singles for L45,000 and doubles for L90,000 in off-season. Camping Pineta (tel. 781 14) in Saint-Oyen has riverside spots for L6000 per person and L4500 per tent. The smaller, more serene branch of the valley leads to the communes of Ollomont and Oyace, where longer hiking trails, richer valleys, and thick forests of fir trees await exploration. For more info, contact the tourist office in Aosta or the **ski-lift office** at St. Rhémy (tel. 78 00 46) or St. Oyen (tel. 781 28). The valley's **telephone code** is 0165.

VALTOURNENCHE

The **Matterhorn** ("Cervino" in Italian) is a wonder to behold as it looms majestically over the less-wonderful town of **Brevil Cervinia**. The nondescript buildings differ only in purpose: some serve expensive food, others offer expensive accommodations, and the rest rent expensive sports equipment. In spite of the cost, many fresh-air fiends consider these man-made deterrents a small price to pay for the opportunity to climb up and glide down one of the world's most famous mountains. A cable car provides year-round service to **Plateau Rosa** (roundtrip L36,000), where summer skiers frequently tackle the slopes in lighter gear. Hikers can forgo the lift tickets and attempt the three-hour ascent to **Colle Superiore delle Cime Bianche** (2982m), with tremendous views of Val d'Ayas to the east. A 90-min. trek on the same trail leads to the emerald waters of **Lake Goillet.** For outdoor escapades complete with fearless leader, contact the **Società Guide** (tel. 94 81 69), which arranges group outings. Don't forget your passport; a number of trails go into Switzerland.

The **tourist office** at Via Carrel, 29 (tel. 94 91 36 or 94 90 86), inundates visitors with info on "white-week packages" and *settimane estive,* their summer equivalents. English spoken. Open daily 9am-noon and 3-6:30pm. If you plan to stay for a week during the summer months, look into the *Carta Estate,* a guest pass providing discounts on multitudes of post-ski activities. Six buses per day run to Cervinia-Breuil from Châtillon on the Aosta-Turin train line. Two direct buses also arrive daily from P. Castello in Milan. The **telephone code** for the valley is 0166.

Hotel Lac Bleu (tel. 94 91 03; fax 94 99 02), 2km downhill from Cervinia, offers singles at L60,000 and doubles at L110,000 (off-season L55,000 and L100,000). Relatively reasonable is **Leonardo Carrel** (tel. 94 90 77), in the locality of Avouil. Singles L49,000. Doubles L67,000. Open year-round. Camp year-round at **Glair Lago di Maen** (tel. 920 77), 39km from Aosta (L7000 per person, L7200 per tent). There are two *rifugi* in the area, and both charge about L25,000 per night or L60,000 for half-pension: **Guide del Cervino** (tel. 94 83 69) can be reached by 3½ hours of hiking or by cable car to Plateau Rosà; **Theodule** (tel. 94 94 00), a half-hour walk or 10-min. ski from Plateau Rosà, has the odd distinction of holding summer yoga classes. Restaurant prices are as steep as the Matterhorn itself, so consider stocking up at the **Despar** supermarket by the bus stop. Open daily 8am-12:30pm and 3-8pm. You can also save some dough by buying bread across the street and then heading for the nearest *Fontina* sign to purchase fillings. Try **Pizzeria Copa Pan** (tel. 94 91 40), a few doors past the tourist office—it's one of the only restaurants in the area that serves dishes in the four-digit price range. Downhill in Valtournenche, an **outdoor market** is held on Friday mornings in summer.

VAL D'AYAS

Sports enthusiasts who value economy over impressive names should consider stopping here and bypassing the more ostentatious pleasure grounds to the west. Val d'Ayas has all the same outdoor activities as its flashy neighbors—skiing, hiking, and rafting—charmingly offered without all of the hype. The pleasantly sunny towns teem with tradition, character, and history, while the towering Monte Rosa range offers numerous athletic opportunities.

Six **buses** run daily to Champoluc from the train station at Verrès (1hr., L3200, roundtrip L5500). Seventeen **trains** run to Verrès from Aosta (40min., L3400), and a comparable number cover the 90min. of track from Turin. The central **tourist office** in Brusson (tel. 30 02 40; fax 30 06 91) and branches in Champoluc (tel. 30 71 13) and Antagnod (tel. 30 63 35) provide trail maps and hotel info. English spoken. Open daily 9am-12:30pm and 3-7pm. The **telephone code** for the valley is 0125.

In Brusson, **Beau Site** (tel. 30 01 44) has the best deal on "white weeks": L360,000 for full board, even during Easter and Christmas. **Cai Casale** (tel. 30 76 68), a refuge in St. Jacques, 3km north of Champoluc, charges L25,000 per person, around L60,000 with full-pension. **Cre Fornè** (tel. 30 71 97) offers singles for L24,000 (high season L26,000) and doubles for an unbeatable L35,000 (high season L37,000). **Camping Deans** (tel. 30 02 97) also operates in Brusson. L5000 per person, L5000 per tent. Open year-round.

Mountain bikes and skis can be rented at **Agenzia Evançon,** Fraz Champoluc (tel. 30 76 48) and at many other spots in the valley. Contact the **Società Guide** (tel. 30 71 13) for hiking advice, or read through the list of itineraries on the map in Champoluc's central *piazza.* The *telecabina* lift (follow the signs) will take you up to the mountain community of **Crest,** a convenient base for excursions. (Lift operates daily 8am-5:50pm—ask the tourist office for schedule; L10,000.) If you can spare some time from outdoor pursuits, visit the **parish church** in Antagnod and its Byzantine-style dome, 17th-century wooden altar, and several prized holy relics. Before setting off, you might want to buy supplies at the *salumeria* between the Champoluc bus stop and the cable car.

VAL DI COGNE AND VALNONTEY

When Cogne's mines ran dry in the 1970s, the townspeople resorted to more genteel pursuits—delicately parting cross-country skiers from their money. The quiet village has consequently become a harmonious blend of authentic and self-conscious rusticity for the entertainment of visitors; craftsmen sculpt wood in the open air, and wildflowers abound in the surrounding meadows. In winter, the town of **Cogne** functions as the head of a 50-km entanglement of cross-country trails. A cable car transports Alpine addicts to the modest downhill facilities (roundtrip L10,000, 7-day pass L54,000). In summer, however, the pastoral community is better known as the gateway to the **Gran Paradiso National Park** (tel. 741 25). In addition to offering a seemingly endless network of hiking trails and a population of 5000 ibex, the park has the highest glacier (4061m) fully contained within Italian borders, named (aptly, albeit unoriginally) Gran Paradiso.

Cogne is an easy **bus** ride from Aosta (6 per day, 1hr., L3200, roundtrip L5800). The **tourist office,** P. Chanoux, 34 (tel. 740 40; fax 74 91 25), distributes maps of the park and hiking and transport info. English spoken. Open daily 9am-12:30pm and 3-6pm, closed Sun. afternoons. The **post office** (tel. 740 61) is on P. Chanoux. Open Mon.-Fri. 8:15am-1:40pm, Sat. 8:15-11:40am. There's a **bank** (tel. 740 20) and a **police** station (tel. 740 26) on Via Grappein. A **pharmacy,** Via Gran Paradiso, 4 (tel. 74 91 23), is open daily 9am-12:30pm and 3:30-7:30pm. In **emergencies** call: **ambulance** (tel. (0336) 23 71 35), **first aid** (tel. 74 91 07), or **alpine aid** (tel. 74 92 86, 742 04, or 740 26). For info on services call: **ski school** (tel. 743 00) or **taxi** (tel. 740 00). The **telephone code** is 0165. Cogne's **outdoor market** is held each Sunday.

For warm, flowery accommodations, try **Albergo Sylvenoire,** Via Gran Paradiso, 19 (tel. 740 37). Singles L45,000. Doubles L80,000. Prices increase 30% in July and August. **Du Soleil,** Via Cavagnet, 24 (tel. 740 33), on the main strip into town, has beautiful wood-paneled rooms and charges L40,000 per person (L49,000 in high season) with breakfast, and has an economical *settimana bianca*—L260,000. V, MC, AmEx. Campers can choose between **Camping Gran Paradiso** (tel. 74 92 02 or 741 05; L5300 per person, L9000-10,500 for car, tent, and electricity; open June-Sept.) or **Lo Stambecco** (tel. 741 52; L6000 per person, L8000-10,500 for car, tent, and electricity; open June-Sept. 20) in the *località* of Valnontey. A number of markets and bakeries are found on Cogne's three main streets. For a sit-down meal, try **Pizzeria Edelweiss,** Viale Cavagnet, 45 (tel. 74 92 44). Pizza L7000-15,000. Open daily 7pm-midnight. Takeout only 7-7:30pm.

Valnontey is a wee hamlet in the midst of the national park, notable for its convenient *alimentari,* its cluster of two-star hotels, and the **Giardino Alpino Paradisia.** The inspiration to construct a botanical garden in barren scrubland (at an altitude of 1700m) struck during the Cogne Mountain Festival in 1955, no doubt aided by several bottles of wine. Practical complications notwithstanding, the thriving gardens boast a wide array of rare alpine vegetation, including everything you ever wanted to know about lichen. Open June 10-Sept. 10 daily 9:30am-12:30pm and 2:30-6:30pm. Admission L3000, groups L2000, under 10 free. The **Mining Museum** in Cogne (tel. 74 92 64) is open June 15 to September 15 daily 10am-8pm. (Off-season Tues.-Sun. 10am-12:30pm and 2:30-6pm. Admission L4000, students L2000.) Those who find cross-country a little too staid can **brave the bungee.** Contact the tourist office in Auise (tel. 950 55) and ask about elastic fun!

Courmayeur

Italy's oldest Alpine resort remains a jet-set playground. **Monte Bianco** (Mont Blanc) is the main attraction: its jagged ridges and unmelting snowfields lure tourists with unsurpassed opportunities for hiking and skiing. Prices are astronomical, and rooms are booked solid in summer and winter (reserve 6 months ahead), but the city shuts down in June while the shopkeepers take their own vacations.

PRACTICAL INFORMATION

One omnipotent building in Piazza Monte Bianco houses everything the traveler needs. The **tourist office** (tel. 84 20 60) has maps and limited assistance. Open Mon.-Fri. 9am-12:30pm and 3-6:30pm, closes at 6pm on weekends. The **bus station and office** (tel. 84 13 97) have frequent service to larger towns. To: Aosta (11 per day, 1hr., L3600, roundtrip L6100); Turin (6 per day, 3¼hr., L13,200, roundtrip L22,800); and Chamonix (8 per day, 45min., L1500, roundtrip L2700). The same building also has a **currency exchange** (open daily 7:30am-8:30pm) and a **post office** (tel. 84 20 42) up the stairs to the right (open Mon.-Fri. 8:15am-6:30pm, Sat. 8:15-11:40am). A little wooden cabin in the parking lot houses **telephones.** Rounding out the offerings of the almighty building are the **public bathrooms** next door (L400). Courmayeur's **postal code** is 11013, and its **telephone code** is 0165.

ACCOMMODATIONS AND FOOD

Budget accommodations in Courmayeur are few and difficult to reach. At **Pensione Venezia,** Via delle Villete, 2 (tel. 84 24 61), up the hill to the left from P. Monte Bianco, get simple rooms and gruff service. Singles L45,000. Doubles L55,000. Breakfast L8000. It is strictly forbidden to walk in clogs in the rooms, as ever-present signs remind you. Alternatively, check into **Hotel Vittoria,** Via Circonvallazione, 82 (tel. 84 22 78; fax 84 23 07), in the center of town. Two-star single rooms L90,000, low-season L60,000-70,000. Doubles start at L90,000 in low-season and skyrocket from there. Includes breakfast. Pitch your tent at **CAI-Uget,** Mt. Bianco in Val Veny (tel. 86 90 97). L5100 per person, L4900 per tent. Hot showers L1000. Open June 15-Sept. and Dec.-1 week after Easter. Keep in mind that this is quite a trek, and you must walk part of the way to the refuge, 1800m in altitude. Picnicking is the best option in this town of Michelin-starred eateries. At **Pastificio Gabriella,** Passaggio del Angelo, 94 (tel. 84 33 59), toward the *strada regionale* end of Via Roma, you'll find excellent cold cuts and pâté garnished with Alpine violets. Closed for 2 weeks in July. V. **Il Fornaio,** at Via Monte Bianco, 17 (tel. 84 24 54), serves up scrumptious breads and pastries. Try the *bombolini* (L2000). Open Thurs.-Wed. morning 7:30am-12:30pm and 4-7:15pm. Closed Sunday. Wednesday is **market day** (8:30am-2pm) in nearby Dolonne (1km from Courmayeur). If you do choose to eat out, you have a few (somewhat) affordable options. **Mont Frety,** Strada Regionale, 21 (tel. 84 17 86), has an extensive pasta selection and often serves pizza in the four-digit price range. *Primi* L9000-13,000, *secondi* L9000-15,000. **Bar** open Tues.-Sat. 9am-noon. For crêpes and pizza by the slice, try **Lady-Crêpe,** Via Marconi, 7 (tel. 84 41 44), off Via Roma. Particularly yummy are the *crespelle alla valdostana,* filling crêpes wrapped with *prosciutto* and *fontina* and topped with a creamy *besciamella* sauce (L5500). Pizza and *focaccia* slices run L3000-3500. Open June-Sept. and Dec.-April daily 10am-7pm.

OUTDOOR ACTIVITIES

Even "white-week specials" are exorbitant—bed-and-breakfast deals under L40,000 per night are a dream, but locating them is a nightmare. Ski passes average L233,000 (ask tourist office for summer prices). Pick up the brochures *White Weeks, Aosta Valley* (in English) and *Courmayeur: Mont Blanc* for a complete list of prices for hotels, ski passes, ski rentals, and athletic facilities.

Nineteenth-century English gentlemen brushed off the **Giro del Monte Bianco** as a two- or three-day climbing excursion for "less adventurous travelers." Today, more level-headed guides suggest that travelers take a week or more to complete the trip. The trail leads around Monte Bianco, past Chamonix and Courmayeur, and then into Switzerland. Refuges and hotel dormitories are spaced five or six hours apart all along the route (around L25,000 per person, L35,000 bed and breakfast). You need not invest your whole vacation; one section of the larger trail makes an ideal daytrip, and two sections can amply fill a weekend. This is serious mountaineering for which you should be thoroughly equipped and trained before you head out.

For less rigorous hiking excursions, catch the bus that departs every hour from Viale M. Bianco to La Visailli, near **Combal Lake** (L3000, roundtrip L4800). A beautiful six-hour hike awaits you on the road up the valley past *Rifugio Elisabetta* to where the path (marked by a "2" in a triangle) branches off to the left and clambers up to the Chavannes Pass (2603m). The trail then runs along Mont Perce, beneath the crest, until it reaches Mont Fortin (2758m—"ooh" and "aah" at the view), where it descends once again to Lake Combal. The bus will deposit you back at Courmayeur. A map is crucial on these jaunts; arm yourself with tips at the **Ufficio delle Guide** (tel. 84 20 64) in P. Abbe-Heurl. The office faces a stone-steepled church, which also has a neat **mountaineering museum** featuring old equipment and some amazing photographs. (Open 9am-12:30pm and 3:30-7pm; in winter closes at 6:30pm. Admission L3500, under 10 L1500.)

You can see nature in its entirety while barely moving a muscle in the **Funivie Monte Bianco,** cable cars heading to the Punto Helbronner (3462m) and then Chamonix. From the top, see unparalleled views of Mont Blanc's palatial ice sheet as well as the spectacular peaks of the **Matterhorn, Monte Rosa,** and **Gran Paradiso** towering in the distance. *Funivie* depart from La Palud near the Val Ferret (a 10-min. bus ride from Courmayeur, L2500 each way). Depending on the altitude, tickets range from L15,000 to L44,000. You do not have to go all the way to Chamonix. Call 899 25 for more information. At the first stop of the *funivia,* Pavillion del M. Frety, there is a unique botanical garden, the **Giardino Alpino Saussurea** (2175m). Open daily from July 15 to September 15. Call 899 25 for details. For other nature excursions, contact Cristina Gaggini and Claudia Marcello (tel. 86 21 40), who organize trips to places like Val Ferret and Val Veny.

The Lake Country

For years, Stendhal's drippiest descriptions of lakes, flowers, and mountains have lulled even the most energetic readers to sound sleep. Alas! You, too, will be prone to ooze such florid prose upon visiting the author's place of inspiration, the Italian Lakes. Whether you intend to or not, you will assuredly bore your friends with breathless, enchanted effusions condensed into postcard form. At least you will not be alone; in August, this breezy retreat draws the entire population of northern Italy.

Diverse masses of tourists grant distinct personality to each of the lakes. Garda summons a young crowd with its limitless sailboarding opportunities by day and its assortment of nightclubs after sunset. Como hosts sophisticates from nearby Milan. Lago Maggiore retains a sleepy elegance, accentuated by the luxury hotels that line its serene shores. Swimmers prefer the cleaner waters of Garda and Orta, but any lake will do for lounging. Few spots anywhere are as perfect for a relaxing afternoon of thoughtful reflection or for the inspired composition of gooey prose.

LAKE COMO (LAGO DI COMO)

Dreamy magnificence lingers over Lake Como's northern reaches. The Mediterranean and the mountains meet at the shore: bougainvillea and lavish villas adorn the craggy backdrop, warmed by the heat of the sun and cooled by lakeside breezes. Three long lakes form the forked Lake Como, joining in the Centro Lago area with four towns: Bellaggio, Tremezzo, Menaggio, and Varenna. Villages pepper the dense green slopes—take the boat toward Colico and get off at any stop that strikes your fancy. Frequent boats and buses connect towns in all three areas of the lake.

Como

Situated on the southwest tip of the lake, at the receiving end of the Milan rail line, Como is the lake's token industrial center. The city is famous for silk manufacturing, but has luckily maintained the slow, languorous atmosphere of the smaller lake towns. While swimmers should head up the lake for cleaner waters, Como's harbor permits boats to reach the shore. After dinner, the entire city migrates to the waterfront for a *passeggiata* among the wisteria and the rows of 18th-century *ville.*

ORIENTATION AND PRACTICAL INFORMATION

Como is 40min. from Milan by train (every hr., L7700). As you leave the **Stazione San Giovanni** (tel. 26 14 94), the town is down the giant steps straight ahead. The lake is to your left. On the other side of town is another train station, the **Ferrovia Nord Milano** (tel. 30 48 00), on Via Manzoni off Lungo Lario Trieste, which serves only Milan (every 30min. in the morning, every hr. 2-5pm, L5000).

The main square, **Piazza Cavour,** opens onto the waterfront, and the **Lungo Lario Trento** winds its way around the mouth of the lake. From P. Cavour, take **Via Plinio** to **Piazza Duomo,** which becomes **Via Vittorio Emanuele II.** This area is the commercial center of Como.

Tourist Office: P. Cavour, 16 (tel. 26 20 91), in the largest lakeside *piazza* near the ferry dock. From Stazione San Giovanni, walk down the steps to Via Gallio, which becomes Via Garibaldi and leads to P. Cavour by way of P. Volta. Provides maps and extensive info in English. Also reserves rooms and exchanges currency (see below). Open Mon.-Sat. 9am-12:30pm and 2:30-6pm, Sun. 9am-12:30pm. There is another, much smaller office (tel. 26 72 14) in the train station.

Currency Exchange: Banca Nazionale del Lavoro, P. Cavour, 34 (tel. 31 31), across from the tourist office. Dependable rates and cash advances on Visa. Open Mon.-Tues. and Thurs.-Fri. 8:20am-1:20pm and 2:30-4pm, Wed. 8:20am-5:50pm. Also try the tourist office (which only cashes traveler's checks) or train station.

Telephones: On tiny Via Alertolli in little P. Goberti next to P. Cavour. Phone booths with seats!

Buses: SPT, P. Matteotti (tel. 30 47 44), at the bend in Lungo Lario Trieste. To: Menaggio (L4500); Bellaggio (L4200); Gravedona (L6700); and Bergamo (L8100). **Information** open Mon.-Fri. 8am-noon and 2-6pm, Sat. 8am-noon.

Ferries: (tel. 57 92 11). Daily to all lake towns, L2000-12,500. Departures from the piers along Lungo Lario Trieste, in front of P. Cavour. Pick up the booklet *Orari e Tariffe* for a comprehensive listing of prices and departures. Hostel guests get a special bargain: a partial lake-pass for only L15,000, full lake-pass for L21,000.

Public Transportation: Tickets available at *tabacchi* or at the hostel for patrons. L1300 for a one-use bus ticket.

Swimming Pool: Lido Villa Olmo (tel. 57 09 68). Large lawn area for sunbathing, along with a sandy stretch down below. Tops not required, but bathing caps are. L7500, L5000 if you buy tickets at the youth hostel. Open daily 10am-6pm.

Bike Rental: Along with the thousand discounts the hostel provides for its patrons, they rent bikes for L6000 per day. Do their services never end?

Pharmacy: Farmacia Centrale, Via Plinio, 1 (tel. 30 42 04), off P. Cavour. Open Tues.-Sun. 8:30am-12:30pm and 3:30-7:30pm. A listing of pharmacies offering evening services is posted outside.

Emergencies: tel. 113. **Hospital: Ospedale Valduce,** Via Dante, 11 (tel. 32 41), or **Ospedale Sant'Anna,** Via Napoleana 60 (tel. 58 51 11).

Police: Viale Roosevelt, 7 (tel. 31 71).

Post Office: Via T. Gallio, 4 (tel. 26 93 36). Open Mon.-Fri. 8:15am-5:30pm, Sat. 8:15-11am. Also at Via V. Emanuele II, 99 (tel. 26 02 10), in the center of town. Open Mon.-Fri. 8:10am-1:30pm, Sat. 8:10-11:40am. **Postal Code:** 22100.

Telephone Code: 031.

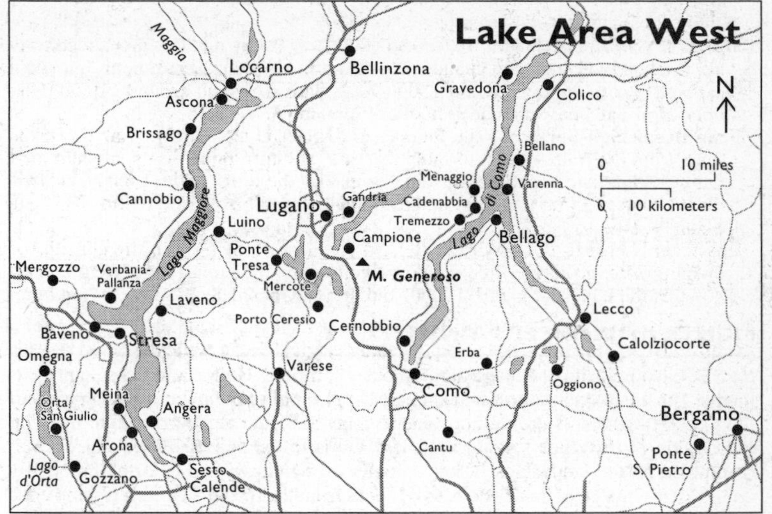

ACCOMMODATIONS

Ostello Villa Olmo (HI), Via Bellinzona, 6 (tel. 57 38 00), on the inland side of Villa Olmo. From the station, walk 20min. down Via Borgovico to your left (it becomes Via Bellinzona), or take bus #1, 6, or 11 (L1300). Lively, fun, and down-to-earth. Run by a wonderful, multilingual couple, the hostel offers bar facilities, homemade jam, incredible dinners, and discounts on assorted tickets. Crowded rooms come with your own locker and key. Self-service laundry L5000; ironing L1000. Lights out at 11:30pm. L15,000 per person, breakfast included. Full meals L14,000. Bag lunches L10,000. Open March-Nov. daily 7:30-10am and 4-11pm. Call ahead in summer. Off-season, groups by reservation only.

Protezione della Giovane (ISJGIF), Via Borgovico, 182 (tel. 57 35 40), on the way to the youth hostel. Take bus #1, 6, or 11. Run by nuns; for women only. It's not as happenin' as the hostel, but offers private rooms. Clean, with crucifixes everywhere. (It's a convent, all right.) Large, with a central courtyard and garden. Free laundry and kitchen use. Curfew 10pm. L17,000 per person.

Albergo Sociale, Via Maestri Comacini, 8 (tel. 26 40 42), on the side of the *duomo,* upstairs from a restaurant. Unadorned rooms in a central location. Singles L35,000. Doubles L60,000, with bath L80,000. Open year-round. Call ahead for reservations. V, MC, AmEx.

FOOD

Many of Como's residents eat lunch *alla Milanese,* downing a quick, satisfying meal in an inexpensive self-service joint. The food is wholesome, the atmosphere energetic, and cover charges rare. Unfortunately, finding an affordable evening meal can be a challenge. Picnickers will appreciate the **G.S.** supermarket (tel. 57 08 95) on the corner of Via Raschi and Viale Fratelli Rosselli, across from the park. Open Mon. 2-8pm, Tues.-Sat. 8am-8pm. Lakeside benches are great for free *al fresco* dining, although solo women should go prepared with *"vai via"* ("go away") in their vocabularies. You can purchase mountainous loaves of *resta* (the typical Como sweet bread, bursting with dried fruits) or the harder, cake-like *matalok* at the **Franzi Bakery** (tel. 27 20 00), at the corner of Via Vitani and Via Francesco Muratto. Open Tues.-Sun. 8:30am-12:30pm and 3:30-7:30pm. Another gem is the take-out haven **Gran Mercato,** P. Matteotti, 3 (tel. 30 47 50), near the bus station; great for breads, cheeses, and meats. Pizza L2000 per *etto.* Open Mon. 8:30am-1pm, Tues.-Fri. 8:30am-1pm and 3-7:30pm, Sat. 8am-7:30pm.

Gerad's, Via Bianchi Giovini, 10 (tel. 30 48 72), off P. Cavour. This green-tiled feeding machine will suck you in and spit you out in less than half an hour, but you'll eat well. *Primi* L6000, *secondi* L7000-9000, with *contorno* around L10,000. Bar open Mon.-Sat. 7am-8pm; meals noon-2:15pm only.

Free Break Self-Service, Viale Innocenzo XI, 19 (tel. 26 14 49). Walk down the stairs from the train station, through the park, and turn right. Spiffy, modern joint with Charlie Chaplin and Abbott and Costello on the walls. *Primi* L4000-6000, *secondi* L7000-L12,000. Open Mon.-Fri. noon-2:30pm; bistro open Mon.-Sat. 7:30-11pm. V, MC, AmEx.

Pasticceria Monti, P. Cavour, 21 (tel. 30 48 33 or 30 11 65), on the corner. For divine *gelato,* go to the little window overlooking the Lungo Lago Trento, or sit down at the tables for *primi* (L9000) and drinks. Open daily in summer 7am-2am.

SIGHTS AND ENTERTAINMENT

Near P. Cavour, Como's **duomo** harmoniously combines Gothic and Renaissance elements. The life-like sculptures that animate the exterior of the church are the work of the Rodari brothers. (Note Como residents Pliny the Elder and Pliny the Younger on either side of the door.) Against the *duomo* is the sturdy **Broletto,** the former communal palace, with thick pillars, colonnaded windows, and colorful marble balconies. The **Church of San Fedele,** two blocks from the *duomo,* bears a resemblance to Ravenna's Byzantine churches, not surprising since the Lombards built the oldest parts of the church (notably the altar and the blind arcade) during the same period. A 20th-century version of the communal palace is Giuseppe Terragni's **Casa del Fascio.** Built in 1939 to house the local fascist government, it has become an icon for modernist Italian architecture—quite the antithesis of the heavy masonry and Roman allusions of "fascist architecture."

After visiting Como's monuments, take the *funicolare* up to **Brunate** for excellent hiking and scenic views. The cars leave from the far end of Lungo Lario Trieste every 15min. in summer, every 30min. in winter. (One-way ticket L3800; roundtrip L6800, if purchased through the hostel L4500; children L2400, roundtrip L4200. Open daily. Last return in summer is Thurs.-Sat midnight and Sun.-Wed. 10:30pm; in winter daily 10:30pm.) You may chose to spend the night in one of the three rough-and-ready *baite* (guesthouses) along the trail, which provide room and board in either private or dorm-style rooms (about L30,000). Check with the tourist office in the off season to make sure they're open.

Across the lake from the *funicolare* is the **Tempio Voltiano** (tel. 57 47 05), a memorial museum dedicated to the inventor of the battery, Alessandro Volta. (Open Tues.-Sun. in summer 10am-noon and 3-6pm; in winter 10am-noon and 2-4pm. Admission L4000, groups and children under 6 L2500.) From there you can take a stroll among the villas lining the lake, including the **Villa "La Rotonda"** and the **Villa Olmo** in the park of the same name. A couple of miles away in **Cernobbio** is the world-famous **Villa d'Este,** once the luxury vacation spot of the Este family of Ferrara, now a decadent hotel with rooms starting at around L1.5 million a night.

The bustling **outdoor market** of Como is held every Tuesday and Thursday morning in and around P. Vittoria and all day long on Sunday. The fabulous Como jazz festival, **Jazz & Co.,** holds about five concerts during July in P. San Federale. Contact the tourist office for current details.

Centro Lago

Drop off your baggage, hop on a ferry, and step off whenever a villa, castle, or small town beckons you. You can explore at your leisure while staying in one of the two fantastic youth hostels, one in Menaggio (on the west shore) and the other in Domaso (on the north shore). In Menaggio, Paola and Ty run the **Ostello La Prinula (HI),** Via IV Novembre, 86 (tel./fax (0344) 323 56), one of the jolliest and friendliest hostels around. In addition to a helpful newsletter listing tons of activities (guided hikes, cooking classes, a Sri Lankan dinner...), they have great cuisine (dinner L14,000), family suites, a washing machine (washer L5000, dryer L3500), bike rental (L15,000 per day), and even an option for wine-tasting. Lockout from 10am to 5pm. Curfew 11:30pm. L15,000 per person, with breakfast L16,000. Open mid-March to mid-November. The town is home to beautiful hotels, historic streets, and unbelievable scenery. Those up to the challenge can hike to Rifugio Meniaggio, over 1000m above the lake. Once there you can rest, take photos, continue on to the difficult *ferrata*, or make less-strenuous trips to Monte Grona and the church of Sant'Amate.

The breezes in the tiny town of Domaso are perfect for windsurfing, so surfer-dudes flock to the supremely relaxing **hostel (HI)** at Via Case Sparse, 12 (tel. (0344) 960 94). It lies 16km from Como by bus and is also accessible by boat. Open all day. L14,000 per person. Open March-Oct. The northwest lakeside hosts a plethora of **campsites;** Domaso itself has 12 of them. Near the hostel are **Europa** (tel./fax 960 44; L6500 per person, L13,000 per tent) and **Italia 90** (tel. 834 46; L4000 per person, L11,500 per tent). The Como tourist office has complete camping info.

Every town on the lake has something to offer. Among the endless possibilities, **Bellagio** has picturesque steep streets and the villas of Lombard aristocrats. Explore the **gardens of Villa Melzi** (March 15-Oct. 31 9am-7pm) and partake in the extensive tour of **Villa Serbelloni.** (Tour 1½hr., L5000. Visits at 10:30am and 3pm. Closed Mon. Reservation info next to the Bellagio tourist office.) **Varenna,** on the western shore, has a perfect cluster of houses and the **Castello Vezio. Isola Comacina,** just off the coast, is the only island in the lake. First inhabited by Romans, its natural fortifications protected refugees from threatening barbarians. It was completely ravaged in 1169 during the Ten Years War, when all seven of its churches were destroyed. Only through recent excavations have the historic foundations once again seen the light of day. Other choices include the magnificent gardens of **Villa Balbianello** in **Lenno** (open April-Oct. Tues., Thurs., and Sat.-Sun. 10am-12:30pm and 3:30-5:30pm; admission L5000, ages 6-10 L3000) and the enormous azaleas and sculptures of **Villa Carlotta** in Tremezzo (tel. 404 05 or 410 11; open March-Nov; admission L9000, L5000 if you buy tickets through the hostel).

LAKE MAGGIORE (LAGO MAGGIORE)

Lacking only the frenzy of its easterly neighbors, Lake Maggiore cradles the same temperate mountain waters and picture-perfect shores. A glaze of opulence coats the air here, and a stroll past any of the grandiose shore-side hotels reveals that Maggiore is the preferred watering hole of the elite. Modest *pensioni* tucked away in the shadow of their multi-storied superiors, however, enable travelers to partake of the lake's sedate pleasures for a reasonable sum.

Stresa

Stresa retains much of the charm that lured visitors in droves during the 19th and early 20th centuries. Art nouveau hotels and villas line the waterfront, granting the city a distinguished look of refined elegance. Splendid views of the lake and mountains appear at each turn of the cobblestone streets. Italians, French, and Germans know Stresa as a paradise resort town, isolated from the daily chores of city life.

PRACTICAL INFORMATION

Only an hour from Milan on the Milan-Domodossola train line (every hr., L7200, IC supplement L4800), the town is a striking base for expeditions in the area. The **tourist office** (tel. 301 50 or 304 16) is at Via Principe Tommaso, 70/72. From the station, turn right on Via Carducci and follow the yellow signs. English spoken. Open May-Sept. Mon.-Sat. 8:30am-12:30pm and 3-6:15pm, Sun. 9am-noon; Oct.-April Mon.-Fri. 8:30am-12:30pm and 3-6:15pm, Sat. 8:30am-12:30pm. For **first aid,** tel. 318 44.

Ambulance: tel. 333 60. If you have a medical problem, find the "Hopital" sign at Via de Martini, 20 (tel. 304 28). The **post office** is at Via Roma, 5 (tel. 300 65), near P. Congressa. Open Mon.-Fri. 8:15am-6:30pm, Sat. 8:15-11:40am. Stresa's **postal code** is 28049; the **telephone code** is 0323.

ACCOMMODATIONS AND FOOD

Orsola Meublé, Via Duchessa di Genova, 45 (tel. 310 87), awaits downhill from the station. Standard rooms with terrace. Singles L40,000, with bath L50,000. Doubles L60,000, with bath L80,000. Breakfast L10,000. AmEx. Pass under the tracks and go uphill to find the beautiful, breezy rooms of **Hotel Mon Toc,** Via Duchessa di Genova, 67/69 (tel. 302 82; fax 93 38 60). Singles L60,000. Doubles L90,000. Includes breakfast. All rooms with bath. Occasional mandatory full-pension L75,000 per person. Half-pension L65,000. V, MC. Hotel Aristou, Corso Italia, 60 (tel./fax 311 95), is along the water and near the action. Go up the steps and through the ornate iron gates to splendid two-star rooms, all with bath. Desk open 7:30am-1am. Singles L65,000. Doubles L130,000, with breakfast. Stock up on necessities, as well as cheese and *prosciutto,* at the new **GS** supermarket, Via Roma, 11. Open Mon.-Sat. 8:30am-12:30pm and 3:30-7:30pm, Sun. 8:30am-12:30pm. **Taverna del Pappagallo,** Via Principessa Margherita, 46 (tel. 304 11), serves up appetizing and affordable meals in a cozy atmosphere. *Primi* L7000-11,000, *secondi* L13,000-18,000. Pizza from L7000. Cover L3000. Open Thurs.-Mon. 11:30am-2:30pm and 6:30-10:30pm; open daily during high season. Follow the diagonal continuation of Via de Amicis past Via P. Tommaso, and you'll stumble upon a number of appetizing dining possibilities. **Salumeria Bianchetti Augusto,** Via Mazzini, 1 (tel. 304 02), is great for a slice of pizza (L2000-2500) to munch on as you walk along the *lago.*

ENTERTAINMENT

From the last week in August to the third week in September, some of the finest orchestras and soloists in the world gather for the internationally acclaimed **Settimane Musicali di Stresa.** (Tickets L30,000-100,000, students L15,000 for certain concerts.) For info, contact the ticket office at Palazzo dei Congressi, Via R. Bonghi, 4, 28049 Stresa (tel. 310 95; fax 330 06). Lake Maggiore also hosts a number of randomly scheduled musical events; check with the tourist office for current details.

■ Near Stresa: Borromean Islands

The lush beauty of the **Borromean Isles (Isola Madre, Isola Bella, Isola dei Pescatori,** and the islets of **San Giovanni** and **Malghera**) has been amply touted over the past 300 years. Daily excursion tickets allow you to hop back and forth among the islands at liberty. L13,000 will buy a ticket to the nearby town of Pallanza and all of the major islands in between. The L15,000 ticket will extend your itinerary even farther to **Villa Taranto,** with sprawling botanical gardens, winding trails, and picture-perfect fountains. Open April-Oct. daily 8:30am until sunset. Ticket office closes at 6:30pm. Admission L10,000, ages 6-14 L9000. The ticket office (tel. 303 93) is located in P. Marconi and is open daily 8:30am-7pm.

The sprawling opulence of the **Palazzo e Giardini Borromeo** has made Isola Bella the most famous of the islands (for info: tel. (0323) 305 56; fax (02) 72 01 00 38). The Baroque palace, built in 1670 by Count Borromeo, overflows with priceless masterpieces: tapestries, furniture, and paintings. The 10 terraces of the gardens, liberally punctuated with statues, rise up in true wedding-cake fashion to the Borromeo family emblem, the unicorn. Neither the Borromeo family nor their verdant gardens in any way epitomizes their motto of "Humilitas." Open March 27-Oct. 24 daily 9am-noon and 1:30-5:30pm. Admission L12,000, ages 6-15 L6000.

Isola dei Pescatori is the only garden-free island. Instead, vendors have used the space to erect souvenir stands on all sides, pushing goodies from framed postcards embedded with thermometers to porcelain-esque tea sets. Still, the island has private, charming paths and a park for kids, plus a number of quick-serve restaurants.

Isola Madre (tel./fax 312 61 for info) is the longest and quietest of the three islands. The elegant 16th-century villa, started in 1502 by Lancelotto Borromeo and finished by the Count Renato 100 years later, contains the Borromeo *bambini* doll collection as well as a number of portraits. Even if you decide to skip the house, the botanical garden and its stupendous array of exotic trees, plants, and flowers are worth the entrance price. A word of warning: don't stop on the island unless you plan to see the garden, or you will be forced to wait on the single sidewalk (the only admission-free place on the island) until the next boat arrives. Open the same hours and prices as Isola Bella.

Pallanza, a coastal town near Isola Madre, offers little of artistic interest, but its lakeside dining is cheaper. You might consider having a meal here before cruising "home" to the mainland. Boats travel throughout the lake to all major towns. For info, contact the central office at Arona, Viale Barracco, 1 (tel. (0322) 466 51).

LAKE ORTA (LAGO D'ORTA)

Lake Orta remains the area's unspoiled refuge, surrounded by hills and forests and graced by several small towns. Nietzsche retreated here from 1883 to 1885 to script his final work, *Also Sprach Zarathustra.* Lake Orta lies on the Novara-Domodossola **train** line (almost every hr., 1½hr., L4200). Get off at Orta Miasino, 3km above Orta, and then either walk down to the left or catch one of the four buses that travel to the tour of **Orta San Giulio.** Connections from nearby Lago Maggiore are a twisting, stomach-turning thrill-ride over the mountain that lies between the lakes. On weekdays, **buses** leave from Stresa (L3800), traveling through Baveno on the way to Orta. Check with the tourist office for bus and train schedules. Buy train tickets out of Orta from the conductor on board.

PRACTICAL INFORMATION

Orta's **tourist office** is at Via Olina, 9/11 (tel. 91 19 37; fax 90 56 78). Open Tues.-Sat. 9am-noon and 3-5:30pm, Sun. 10am-noon and 3-5pm. In summer, if you arrive on Monday or are bound for a different town, check the office at Via Panoramica (tel. 90 56 14), across the street and down from the Villa Crespi (with the mosque-like tower). Open mid-June-mid-July Wed.-Mon. 10am-1pm and 4-7pm. The **post office** (tel. 901 57) is at P. Ragazzoni. Open Mon.-Fri. 8:30am-1:20pm, Sat. 8:30-11am, Sun. 2:30-7pm. The **postal code** is 28016; the **telephone code** is 0322.

ACCOMMODATIONS AND FOOD

Restaurant prices (and the solicitous treatment given to tourists) are a relief after those of the more commercialized lakes. Unfortunately, hotel prices have not followed suit; affordable accommodations await only the foresighted individuals who reserve early. **Ristorante Olina,** Via Olina, 40 (tel. 90 56 56), across from the tourist office, offers beautiful doubles with private baths for L80,000. Breakfast L10,000. Family rooms with kitchens are also available. V, MC, AmEx. Ornate, country-style rooms in the **Taverna Antico Angello,** Via Olina, 18 (tel. 902 59), sit above a reasonably priced restaurant. Singles L38,000. Doubles L60,000. Breakfast L5000. V, MC. For those with access to a car, the nearby lake towns of Alzo and Arola also have cheap options—contact the Orta tourist office for details. A good-sized **open-air market** sets up on Wednesday mornings in P. Motta. Good news for those lookin' for a piece of ass—Lago D'Orta is known as the home of *tapulon* (**donkey meat,** minced, well spiced, and cooked in red wine). For this and other hot meat, hop on the boat to **Ristorante San Giulio,** Via Basilica, 4 (tel. 902 34), on the tiny island of the same name, with an 18th-century dining room and lakeside terrace. *Primi* L6000-8000, *secondi*

L12,000-15,000. Cover L2500. Opens at 7:30am and provides a return boat that runs after the public ones have quit. V, MC, AmEx.

SIGHTS

Set high in the cool, verdant hills above town is the **Sacro Monte** (tel. 91 19 60), a monastic complex devoted to St. Francis of Assisi. The sanctuary was founded in 1591, and its 20 chapels boast 376 life-sized statues and 900 frescoes which together tell the life story of Italy's patron saint. (Sanctuary open daily 8am-6pm. Free.) A circular route around the **Isola di San Giulio,** across from Orta, reveals narrow streets, ivy-covered walls, and tiled roofs. The island also has a marble- and wood-adorned Romanesque **basilica** (tel. 903 58) from the 12th century, built on 4th-century foundations. (Open Mon.-Fri. 9am-12:15pm and 2-6:45pm, Sat.-Sun. 9am-12:15pm and 2-5:45pm. Free.) Small motor boats weave back and forth every 30min. during the summer (roundtrip L3000; tickets sold on board). Winter service is restricted to a couple of runs a day, but you can always hire a ride from a private boat company (complete with a driver in uniform, knee socks and all) for a very low fee. There are numerous music and sports events from May to December in the lake area. Ask at the tourist office for a schedule.

Lombardy (Lombardia)

Over the centuries Roman generals, German emperors, and French kings have vied for control of Lombardy's bounty. The agricultural riches of the region have since been augmented by industrial and business wealth, making it the cornerstone of the Italian economy. In many ways, Lombardy has more in common with countries to the north than with its own peninsula, and Lombards make periodic calls for secession in order to eliminate the forced subsidization of the Roman bureaucracy and the burdens of the economically challenged South. Since World War II, however, Lombardy's "new Italy" has attracted legions of ambitious southerners, and the province has recently become a magnet for immigrants from North Africa and the Middle East. Tension between long-time residents and recent immigrants persists, but thanks in part to this diversity, inhabitants of Lombardy are today among the least provincial of all Italians.

Cosmopolitan Milan, with its international reputation for high style and high finance, looms large in foreigners' perceptions of the region, but Lombardy is much more than a metropolis with countryside suburbs. Bergamo, Brescia, and Mantua, with their hints of Venetian influence, are culturally foreign to their western neighbor. In addition, the foothills of the Alps are not far from the southern plain, flavoring the Italian culture with hints of Swiss and Austrian influence.

Milan (Milano)

Milan lies on Roman foundations but has forged toward modernity with more force than any other major Italian city. Although it served as the capital of the western half of the Roman Empire from AD286 to 402, Milan retains few reminders of that period; the *duomo* (1386) is the city's emblem and a rare remnant of its history.

Milan's life pace is quicker than that of most Italian cities. Even the *siesta* is shorter here, translating to more precious hours for frenetic pilgrimages to glitzy boutiques. Its wide, tree-lined boulevards and graceful architecture, more reminiscent of Austria than of Italy, are elegant, but must compete with more vibrant graffiti. Although petty crime, drug dealing, and prostitution are likely to strike your eye, so should the enormous number of well-dressed Italians in designer suits. The capital of style and industry, Milan is on the cutting edge of fashion, invention, and ideas, never pausing to rest. Only in August, when the city shuts down for the entire month, do its citizens flock to quiet resort towns and breathe sighs of relief.

ORIENTATION

The layout of the city resembles a giant target, encircled by a series of concentric ancient city walls. In the outer rings lie suburbs built during the 1950s and 60s to house southern immigrants. Within the inner circle are four central squares: **Piazza Duomo,** at the end of Via Mercanti, **Piazza Cairoli,** near Castello Sforzesco, **Piazza Cordusio,** connected to Largo Cairoli by Via Dante, and **Piazza San Babila,** the business and fashion district along Corso Vittorio Emanuele. The **duomo** and **Galleria Vittorio Emanuele II** comprise the bull's-eye, roughly at the center of the downtown circle. Northeast and northwest lie two large parks, the **Giardini Pubblici** and the **Parco Sempione.** Farther northeast is the **Stazione Centrale,** Mussolini's colossal train station built in 1931. The area around the train station is a mishmash of skyscrapers dominated by the sleek **Pirelli Tower** (1959), still one of the tallest buildings in Europe. From the station, a scenic ride on bus #60 takes you to the downtown hub, as does the more efficient commute on subway line #3. **Via V. Pisani,** which leads to the mammoth **Piazza della Repubblica,** connects the station to the downtown area. It continues through the wealthy business districts as Via Turati, and finally as Via Manzoni leading to the *duomo.* To see more affordable sections of Milan, walk 5 blocks to the east of the station (left as you exit) and head straight down the less glamorous **Corso Buenos Aires.**

The **subway** (*Metropolitana Milanese,* abbreviated "MM") is the most useful branch of Milan's extensive public transportation network. **Line #1** (red line) stretches east to west from the *pensioni* district east of Stazione Centrale, through the center of town, and west to the youth hostel (Molino Dorino fork). **Line #2** (green line) links Milan's three train stations and crosses MM1 at Cadorno and Loreto. **Line #3** (yellow line) runs from just north of the Stazione Centrale to the southern sprawl of the city, intersecting with line #2 at Stazione Centrale and #1 at the *duomo.* The subway operates from approximately 6am to midnight. Among the many useful train and bus routes, **trams #29** and **30** travel the city's outer ring road, while **buses #96** and **97** service the inner road. **Tram #1,** which runs during the wee hours, departs from Centrale and runs to P. Scala and the *duomo.* Tickets for buses, trams, and subways must be purchased in advance at newsstands, ticket machines, or ticket

A Road by Any Other Name Would Smell as Street

A quick glance at the map of any Italian town raises certain inevitable questions: why is Vittorio Emanuele so important, who exactly was Garibaldi, and what the hell happened on September 20th? The multitude of streets and *piazze* with names referring to these people and events in seemingly every Italian city results not so much from a lack of creativity as from an overabundance of national pride. Many of Italy's main streets and squares are named for the heroes of Italian unification. **Giuseppe Garibaldi,** commander of the 1000 volunteer "red-shirts," provided the military muscle necessary to free Naples and Sicily from Bourbon rule in 1860, while **Giuseppe Mazzini** manned the struggle's intellectual wing. **Camillo di Cavour** was the political and diplomatic force most directly responsible for Italy's unification. He helped to establish **Vittorio Emanuele II** as the first king of the newly born Italian nation in 1861. The young monarch went on to incorporate Venice in 1866 and, on **September 20, 1870,** when France finally surrendered Rome, he was able to complete the unification of Italy.

Not to be outdone by their royalist rivals, Italian leftists have managed to enter a number of early twentieth-century heroes into the canon of *piazza* names. Among the most common names are those of the prominent socialist **Giacomo Matteotti** and the founder of the Italian Communist Party **Antonio Gramsci,** both martyrs of the early years of fascism.

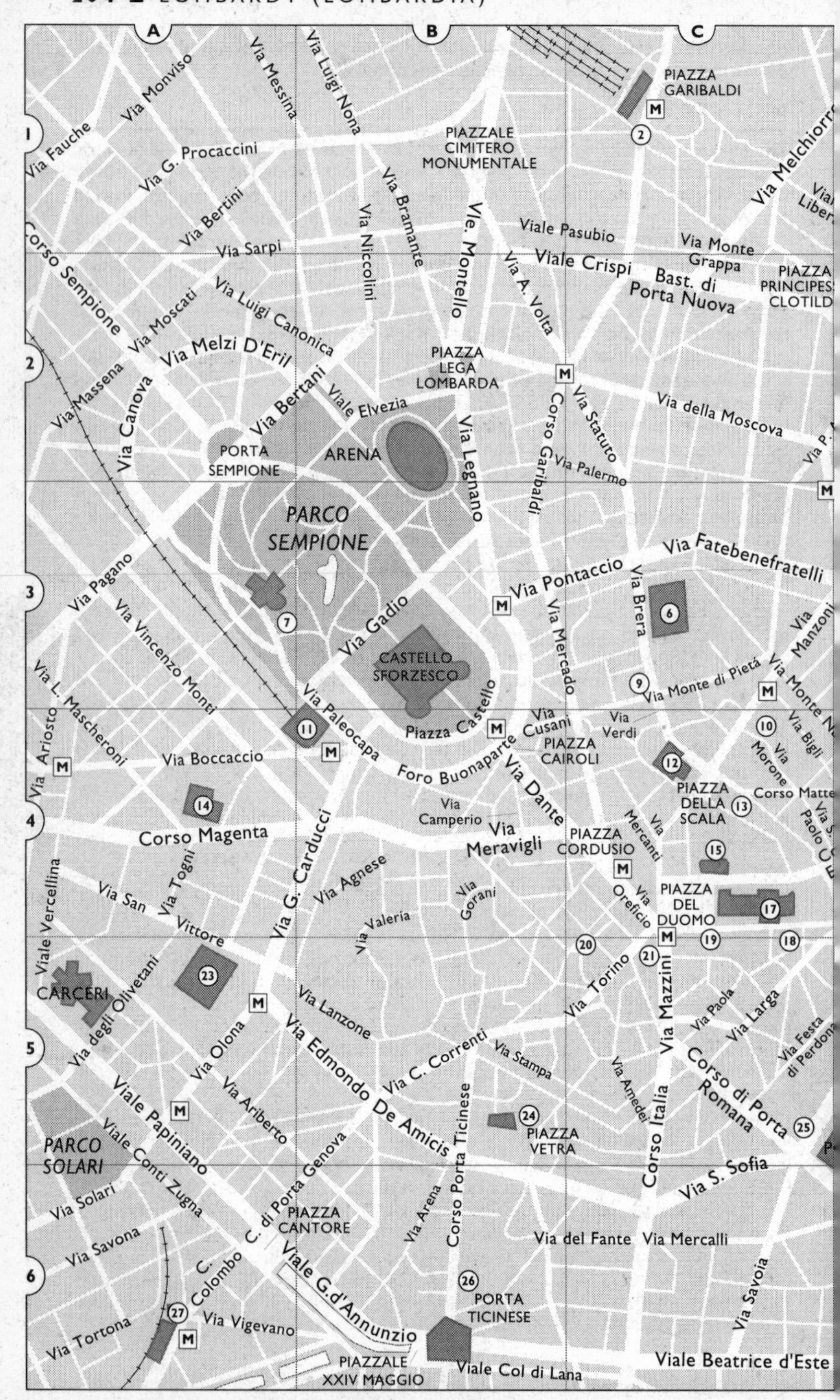
PIAZZA GARIBALDI
PIAZZALE CIMITERO MONUMENTALE
Via Monviso
Via Messina
Via Luigi Nona
Via Fauche
Via G. Procaccini
Via Bertini
Via Sarpi
Via Bramante
Via Niccolini
Vle. Montello
Via A. Volta
Viale Pasubio
Viale Crispi
Bast. di Porta Nuova
Via Monte Grappa
PIAZZA PRINCIPESSA CLOTILDE
Via Melchiorre
Corso Sempione
Via Moscati
Via Luigi Canonica
Via Melzi D'Eril
Via Massena
Via Canova
Via Bertani
Viale Elvezia
PIAZZA LEGA LOMBARDA
Corso Garibaldi
Via Statuto
Via della Moscova
PORTA SEMPIONE
ARENA
Via Legnano
Via Palermo
PARCO SEMPIONE
Via Pagano
Via Vincenzo Monti
Via Gadio
CASTELLO SFORZESCO
Via Pontaccio
Via Fatebenefratelli
Via Mercado
Via Brera
Via Manzoni
Via L. Mascheroni
Via Paleocapa
Piazza Castello
Via Cusani
PIAZZA CAIROLI
Via Verdi
Via Monte di Pietá
Via Monte Napoleone
Via Ariosto
Via Boccaccio
Foro Buonaparte
Via Dante
Via Bigli
Via Morone
Corso Matteotti
Corso Magenta
Via G. Carducci
Via Camperio
Via Meravigli
PIAZZA CORDUSIO
Via Mercanti
PIAZZA DELLA SCALA
Viale Vercellina
Via Togni
Via San Vittore
Via Agnese
Via Gorani
Via Valeria
Via Orefìcio
PIAZZA DEL DUOMO
CARCERI
Via degli Olivetani
Via Lanzone
Via Torino
Via Mazzini
Via Paola
Via Larga
Via Olona
Via Edmondo De Amicis
Via C. Correnti
Via Stampa
Via Amedei
Corso di Porta Romana
Via Festa di Perdono
Via Ariberto
Viale Papiniano
Corso Porta Ticinese
PIAZZA VETRA
Corso Italia
PARCO SOLARI
Viale Conti Zugna
C. di Porta Genova
Via S. Sofia
Via Solari
PIAZZA CANTORE
Via Arena
Via Savona
C. Colombo
Via del Fante
Via Mercalli
Viale G.d'Annunzio
PORTA TICINESE
Via Savoia
Via Tortona
Via Vigevano
PIAZZALE XXIV MAGGIO
Viale Col di Lana
Viale Beatrice d'Este
A
B
C
1
2
3
4
5
6

Milan
American Express, 9
Basilica d. Sant'Ambrogio, 22
Church of S. Eustorgio, 26
Church of S. Fidele-Palazzo Marino, 13
Church of S. Lorenzo, 24
Church of Santa Maria d. Grazie, 14
Church of S. Nazaro, 25
Church of S. Satiro, 21
Conservatorio, 16
Duomo, 17
Galleria d'Arte Moderna, 5
Galleria Vittorio Emanuele II, 15
La Scala, 12
Museo Nationale della Scienza e della Tecnica, 23
Museo Poldi-Pezzoli, 10
Museo di Storia Naturale, 4
Palazzo dell'Arte, 7
Palazzo Reale-Arcivescovada, 18
Palazzo del Senato-Ospedale Maggiore, 8
Pinacoteca Ambrosiana, 20
Pinacoteca di Brera, 6
Planetaria, 3
Stazione Centrale, 1
Stazione Nord, 11
Stazione Porta Garibaldi, 2
Stazione Porta Genova, 27
Stazione Porta Vittoria, 28
Tourist Office, 19
D
E
F
PIAZZA LORETO
Via Popora
Via Sacchini
Viale Andrea Doria
PIAZZA DUCA D'AOSTA
Via Pergolesi
Via Petrella
Viale Gran Sasso
C. Buenos Aires
Via Piccinni
Via Fabio Filzi
Via Vito Pisani
Via R. Boscovich
Via Vitruvio
Via Bened. Marcello
Via Donatello
PIAZZA PIOLA
Viale Abruzzi
Via Eustachi
Via Plinio
Via San Gregorio
Via Settala
Via Lazzaretto
Via Casati
Viale Tunisia
PIAZZA DELLA REPUBBLICA
Bast. di Porta Venezia
Viale Vittorio Veneto
Viale Regina
Via Manin
GIARDINI PUBBLICI
Via Palestro
Via Senato
Corso Venezia
Viale Piave
Luigi Maino
Via Carlo Goldoni
Viale Romagna
Via S. Andrea
Via Mozart
Via Damiano
Corso Monforte
PIAZZA S. BABILA
Corso Vitt. Emanuele II
Via Borgogna
Via Conservatorio
Viale B. Maria
Viale Premuda
PIAZZA SUSA
Viale Campania
Via Cavallotti
Corso di Vittoria
Corso XXII Marzo
N
0
400 yards
400 m
Via F. Sforza
Via San Barnaba
Via della Pace
Viale Reg. Margherita
Via Anfossi
Via Spartaco
Via Campionesi
Viale Molise
OLICLINICO
Via d. Commenda
Via Lamarmora
Monte Nero
Vle. Lazio
PIAZZALE MARTINI
PIAZZALE LIBIA
Corso di Porta Romana
Vle. Caldara
Viale Umbria
PIAZZALE INSUBRIA
Viale Filippetti

offices in a few lucky stations—bring small change. A ticket (L1500) is good for one subway ride or 75min. of surface transportation. All-day passes (L5000) are available from the **ATM** office at the Duomo and Centrale stops and are good from the first time you use them. Those planning a longer stay have several options: a two-day pass is L9000, a book of ten tickets is L14,000, and weekly and monthly passes are available (L35,000 initial payment, plus a weekly ticket pass for around L10,000; photo required). It is a good idea to have extra tickets on hand in the evening, as *tabacchi* close around 8pm and vending machines are unreliable. Riding without a ticket warrants a L30,000 fine.

PRACTICAL INFORMATION

Tourist Office: APT, Via Marconi, 1 (tel. 80 96 62/3/4; fax 72 02 29 99), in the "Palazzo di Turismo" in P. del Duomo, to the right as you face the *duomo.* Comprehensive local and regional info and an especially useful map and museum guide (in Italian). Will not reserve rooms, but will phone to check for vacancies. Some English spoken. Be sure to pick up the comprehensive *Youth in Milan* as well as *Milano Mese* for info on activities and clubs, among other things. Open Mon.-Fri. 8:30am-8pm, Sat. 9am-1pm and 2-7pm, Sun. 9am-1pm and 2-5pm. Branch office at **Stazione Centrale** (tel. 669 04 32 or 669 05 32), set back off the main hall on the 2nd floor, through the neon archway to the left. English spoken. Open Mon.-Sat. 8am-7pm.

"SOS for Tourists": Via Adige, 11 (tel. 545 65 51) for legal complaints.

Budget Travel: CIT, Galleria Vittorio Emanuele (tel. 86 37 01). Also **changes money.** Open Mon.-Fri. 9am-7pm, Sat. 9am-1pm and 2-6pm. Another office at the **Stazione Centrale** (same hours). **CTS,** Via S. Antonio, 2 (tel. 58 30 41 21). Open Mon.-Fri. 9:30am-6pm, Sat. 9:30am-noon; Sept.-May closes Mon.-Fri. 1-2pm. **Transalpino Tickets:** Next to train info office in upper atrium of Stazione Centrale (tel. 670 38 38). Open Mon.-Sat. 8am-9pm, Sun. 9am-8pm. Main office 4 blocks away at Via Locatelli, 5 (tel. 66 71 31 19). When closed, go to **Italturismo**, to the right from the station, under the grand drive-through. Open daily 7am-7:30pm.

Consulates: U.S., Via P. Amedeo, 2/10 (tel. 29 00 18 41). Open Mon.-Fri. 9-11am and 2-4pm. **Canada,** Via V. Pisani, 19 (tel. 675 81; emergencies tel. 67 58 39 94). Open Mon.-Fri. 8:45am-12:30pm and 1:30-5:15pm. **U.K.,** Via S. Paolo, 7 (tel. 72 30 01; emergencies tel. 87 24 90). Open Mon.-Fri. 9:15am-12:15pm and 2:30-4:30pm. **Australia,** Via Borgogna, 2 (tel. 77 70 41). Open daily 9am-noon and 2-4:30pm. **New Zealand,** Via d'Arezzo, 6 (tel. 48 08 25 44). Open daily 9am-noon.

Currency Exchange: All **Banca d'America e d'Italia** and **Banca Nazionale del Lavoro** branches eagerly await your Visa card. (Bank hours in Milan are generally Mon.-Fri. 8:30am-1:30pm and 2:30-4:30pm.) If you need money changed right away, try **Banca Nazionale delle Comunicazioni** at Stazione Centrale; it has pretty standard rates. L6000 fee. Open Mon.-Sat. 8:30am-12:30pm and 2-7:30pm.

American Express: Via Brera, 3 (tel. 72 00 36 93), on the corner of Via dell'Orso. Walk through the Galleria, across P. Scala, and up Via Verdi. Holds mail free for American Express members, otherwise US$5 per inquiry. Receives (but does not send) wired money; fee of L2000 on transactions over US$100. Open Mon.-Thurs. 9am-5:30pm, Fri. 9am-5pm.

Telephones: In Galleria Vittorio Emanuele. Open 8am-7:30pm. In Stazione Centrale. Open 8am-9:30pm.

Flights: Malpensa Airport, 45km from town. Intercontinental flights. **Airpullman** buses (tel. 66 98 45 09) leave every 30min. in the morning, every hr. in the afternoon from P. Luigi di Savoia, on the east side of Stazione Centrale (L12,000). **Linate Airport,** 7km from town. Domestic/European flights and intercontinental flights with European transfers; much easier logistically. The **STAM** bus to Linate (tel. 66 98 45 09) leaves Stazione Centrale every 20min. 5:40am-7pm (L4000), but it's cheaper (L1500) to take bus #73 from P. San Babila (MM1). **General Flight Info** for both airports, tel. 74 85 22 00.

Trains: Stazione Centrale, P. Duca d'Aosta (tel. 67 50 01), on MM2. The primary station. To: Genoa and Turin (every hr., 1½hr. and 2hr., L13,700); Venice (25 direct per day, 3hr., L20,800); Florence (every hr., 2½hr., L26,200); and Rome (every hr., 4½hr., L47,700). Info office open daily 7am-9:30pm. Eurailpasses and *Cartaverde* available outside the building. **Luggage Storage:** L5000 for 12hr. Open 24hr. **Lost and Found:** (tel. 63 71 26 67) at baggage deposit in Stazione Centrale. Open daily 5am-4am. **Stazione Nord** (tel. 48 06 67 71) connects Milan with Como, Erba, and Varese. **Porta Genova** has lines to the west (Vigevano, Alessandria, and Asti), and **Porta Garibaldi** (tel. 655 20 78) links Milan to Lecco and Valtellina to the northwest.

Buses: At **Stazione Centrale** (same hours). **Intercity** buses are less convenient and more expensive than the trains. **SAL, SIA, Autostradale,** and many others depart from P. Castello and the surrounding area (MM: Cairoli) for Turin, the Lake Country, Bergamo, Certosa di Pavia, and points as far away as Rimini and Trieste.

Public Transportation: ATM (tel. 669 70 32 or 89 01 07 97), in the P. del Duomo MM station. Municipal buses require pre-purchased tickets (L1500). Day passes for non-residents L5000, L9000 for 2 days. Info office open Mon.-Sat. 8am-8pm; ticket office open 7:45am-7:15pm.

Taxis: In P. Scala, P. del Duomo, P. S. Babila, and Largo Cairoli (tel. 67 67, 83 83, 85 85 or 53 53). The official Milan taxis are undergoing a city-wide campaign to change from yellow to white. They are, however, uniformly expensive, starting at L5000, with a nighttime surcharge of L5000.

Car Rental: Hertz (tel. 66 90 06). Outside the station, to the left as you exit. Open Mon.-Fri. 8am-7pm, Sat. 8am-2pm. Galleria delle Carrozze office (tel. 670 30 62). Also check with **Europcar** (tel. 66 98 15 89) and **Avis** (tel. 669 02 80) at the same place: same rates, similar hours.

Lost Property: City Council Office, Via Frioli, 30 (tel. 551 61 41). Open Mon.-Fri. 8:30am-12:45pm and 2:15-5pm.

Laundromat: Minola, Via S. Vito, 5 (tel. 58 11 12 71), on the corner with Papa Gregorio, near the *duomo*. Wash and dry 5kg L17,000, dry-clean 5kg L20,000. Open Mon.-Fri. 8:30am-6:30pm, Sat. 8am-12:30pm. **Onda Blu,** Via Scarlatti, 19 (toll-free tel. (167) 86 13 46) is self-service; 3 blocks from Stazione Centrale. Wash or dry 6.5kg for L6000, 16kg L10,000. Soap L1500. Open daily 9am-10pm.

Public Toilets, Showers, and Baths: Albergo Diurno (tel. 669 12 32), beneath P. Duca d'Aosta. Take the stairs underground from the center of the Stazione Centrale. Toilets L500. Showers L9000, with bath L10,000. Soap and towel L2500. Open Thurs.-Tues. 7am-8pm.

Swimming Pool: Cozzi, Viale Tunisia, 35 (tel. 659 97 03), off Corso Buenos Aires. Open Sept.-July Mon.-Sat. 10am-1:30pm and 5-9pm. Admission L6000, children L3000. In summer, move outdoors to **Giulia Romano,** Via Ampere, 20 (tel. 70 63 08 25). Swimcap required (available for L2500). Admission L6000, under 12 and over 60 L3000. **Lido di Milano,** P. Lotto, 15 (tel. 39 26 61 00), near the youth hostel. Open daily 10am-7pm. Admission L6000, children L3000. Small indoor kids' pool. Swimcap required (L2000).

Library: United States Information Service, Via Bigli, 11 (tel. 79 50 51), near P. S. Babila. Library with U.S. publications for perusal. Open Mon.-Thurs. 9:30am-12:30pm. **British Council Library,** Via Manzoni, 38 (tel. 77 22 21), near USIS. Open Mon. 2-6pm, Tues.-Thurs. 10am-7:30pm, Fri. 10am-6pm.

Bookstore: The American Bookstore, Via Camperio, 16 (tel. 871 89 20), at Largo Cairoli. The best selection of books in English in Milan. Open Mon. 2-7:30pm, Tues.-Fri. 10am-7:30pm, Sat. 10am-1pm and 2:30-7:30pm. Closed 2 weeks in Aug. **Hoepli Libreria Internazionale,** Via Hoepli, 5 (tel. 86 48 71), off P. Media near P. Scala. Open Mon. 2-7pm, Tues.-Sat. 9am-7pm. V, MC. **Rizzoli's,** Galleria Vittorio Emanuele (tel. 86 46 10 71) has only a small English collection, but is well-stocked with *Let's Go*. Open daily 9am-8pm.

AIDS Hotline: Centralino Informazioni AIDS, (toll-free *numero verde*: (167) 86 10 61). Also **Centri AIDS,** P. XXIV Maggio, Ex Casello (tel. 89 40 24 06), Via Fantoli, 7 (tel. 506 19 31), and Via Masaniello, 23 (tel. 453 14 25).

Handicapped/Disabled Services: Direzione Servizi Sociali, Largo Treves, 1. For general info call 62 08 69 54; wheelchair info call Dr. Guarnieri at 659 90 32.

Late-Night Pharmacy: Though nocturnal duty rotates among Milan's pharmacies, the one in Stazione Centrale never closes (tel. 669 07 35 or 669 09 35). During the day, try the **Italo-English Chemist's Shop** on P. Duomo, 21 (tel. 86 46 48 32) or at Via E. Lussu, 4 (tel. 256 72 73).

Hospital: Ospedale Maggiore Policlinico, Via Francesco Sforza, 35 (tel. 550 31), 5min. from the *duomo* on the inner ring road.

Emergencies: tel. 113. **First Aid: Pronto Soccorso,** tel. 38 83. **Ambulance:** tel. 77 33.

Police: tel. 772 71.

Post Office: Via Cordusio, 4 (tel. 869 20 69), near P. del Duomo in the direction of the castle. Stamps at #1 and 2. *Fermo posta* at the CAI-POST office to the left. Open Mon.-Fri. 8:15am-7:40pm, Sat. 8:15am-5:40pm. There are two post offices at Stazione Centrale as well. **Postal Code:** 20100.

Telephone Code: 02.

ACCOMMODATIONS AND CAMPING

There are over 50 "on-paper" bargains in Milan, but if you want a clean room in a safe and reasonably convenient location, only a few are worth your while. Every season, except August when the mosquitoes outnumber the inhabitants, is high season in Milan. A single room in a decent establishment for under L40,000 is a real find. For the best deals, try the area to the east of the train station or go to the city's southern periphery. Whenever possible, make reservations well ahead of time.

Ostello Pietra Rotta (HI), Viale Salmoiraghi, 1 (tel. 39 26 70 95; MM1: QT8). Walk to the right from the metro (so that the round church is across the street on the left) for about 10min. The hostel is on the right. "We aren't in the mountains; this is the city," say the proprietors. Thus, there is unbending enforcement of all rules (and there are many). Modern facilities and 350 beds. English spoken. HI card required, but available at the hostel for L30,000. Open 7-9am and 5pm-midnight, but no morning check-in. No exceptions to daytime lockout. Lights-out time varies between 11:20pm and midnight. Curfew 11:30pm. L23,000 per person. Breakfast, sheets, and lockers included. No individual reservations, but there is almost always room. Open Jan. 13-Dec. 20.

Due Giardini, Via Settala, 46 (tel. 29 52 10 93 or 29 51 23 09; fax 29 51 69 33; MM1: Lima). Go left on Via Vitruvio from the station and then right on Settala. "Feel-the-springs" beds, but clean and neat. The main attraction is the big, quiet garden outside. Open all night. Singles L60,000. Doubles L80,000. Triples L108,000. V, MC.

Hotel San Marco, Via Piccinni, 25 (tel. 29 51 64 14; fax 29 51 32 43; MM1-2: Loreto). From the station, head left to P. Caiazzo and turn onto Via Pergolesi, which becomes Via Piccinni. Comfy retro rooms with TVs and telephones compensate for street noise below. Friendly management speaks some English. Singles L58,000, with bath L75,000. Doubles L77,000, with bath L100,000. Triples with bath L135,000. V, MC, AmEx.

Albergo "Villa Mira," Via Sacchini, 19 (tel. 29 52 56 18; MM1-2: Loreto), off Via Porpora 2 blocks from P. Loreto. Family-run, with rooms out of a Mr. Clean commercial. Bar downstairs. Singles L40,000. Doubles with bath L60,000. Call ahead if possible.

Hotel Ca' Grande, Via Porpora, 87 (tel. 26 14 40 01; MM1-2: Loreto), about 7 blocks in from P. Loreto in a happy yellow house with a green spiked fence. Clean rooms with phones, plain beds, and a wonderful proprietor. Street below can be noisy. English spoken. Singles L48,000, with bath L68,000. Doubles L73,000, with bath L93,000. Desk closed 2-6am.

Viale Tunisia, 6 (MM1: Porta Venezia). This building houses two separate budget hotels equidistant from the station and the city center. (Both deny having a curfew, but ask to be sure.)

Hotel Kennedy (tel. 29 40 09 34), 6th floor. Pristine rooms with light blue dreamscape decor imported from the 60s. Some English spoken. Check-out 11am. Singles L50,000-65,000. Doubles L75,000-85,000, with bath L100,000-130,000. Breakfast L6000. Reservations recommended.

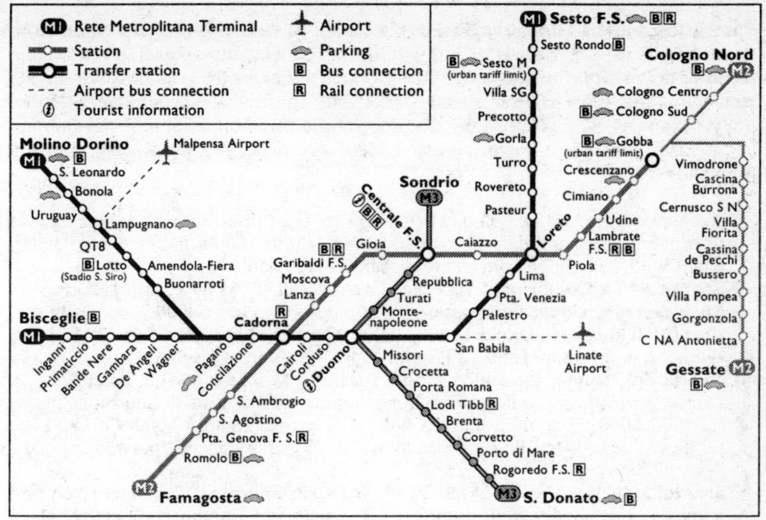

Hotel San Tommaso (tel. 29 51 47 47), on the 3rd floor. Orderly rooms with hardwood floors, some overlooking a courtyard. English spoken. Singles L45,000. Doubles L70,000. Prices may be higher Sept.-Oct., lower Dec.-Jan.

Hotel Aurora, Corso Buenos Aires, 18 (tel. 204 79 60; fax 204 92 85; MM1: Lima). Behind a grungy façade lies a spotless labyrinth of modern rooms with TVs. The courtyard and soundproof windows mute street noise. English spoken by the enthusiastic owner. Open 24hr. Singles L70,000-75,000 with bath L75,000-80,000. Doubles with bath L110,000-120,000. V, MC.

Hotel Nettuno, Via Tadino, 27 (tel. 29 40 44 81; MM1: Lima), one block over from Corso Buenos Aires. Very peaceful and quiet (albeit dark). Rooms with marble floors and 70s decor. Singles L44,000, with bath L53,000. Doubles with bath L84,000. Closes at 1am. Cash only.

Pensione Cantore, Corso di Porta Genova, 25 (tel. 835 75 65; MM2: Genova), a 15-min. walk southwest of the *duomo* down Via Corso Correnti. A bit out of the way. Contrast the exposed pipes with the grand, immaculate rooms. Friendly atmosphere. Closes 2am on weekdays, 3:30am on weekends. Singles L40,000. Doubles L65,000. Triples 90,000. Reserve at least 1 week ahead.

Camping di Monza (tel. (039) 38 77 71), in the park of the Villa Reale in Monza. Take a train or bus from Stazione Centrale to Monza, then a city bus to the campground. L4500 per person and per tent, L2000 per child under 6. Hot showers L500. Restaurant/bar nearby. Phone ahead. Open April-Sept.

FOOD

Like its fine *couture,* Milanese cuisine is sophisticated and overpriced. Specialties include *risotto giallo* (rice with saffron), *cotoletta alla milanese* (breaded veal cutlet with lemon), and *cazzouela* (a mixture of pork and cabbage). *Pasticcerie* and *gelaterie* crowd every block. Stop in a bakery for the Milanese sweet bread *panettone,* an Italian fruitcake. The newspaper *Il Giornale Nuovo* lists all the restaurants and shops open in the city, and the brochure *Youths in Milan,* available at the tourist office, has a detailed list of foreign restaurants. The largest **markets** are around Via Fauché and Viale Papiniano on Saturday, Viale Papiniano on Tuesday, and P. Mirabello on Thursday. On Saturday, the **Fiera di Sinigallia**—a 400-year-old extravaganza of the commercial and the bizarre—occurs on Viale G. d'Annunzio.

Splurge on local pastries at **Sant'Ambroeus** (tel. 76 00 05 40), a Milanese culinary shrine, under the arcades at Corso Matteotti, 7. Open 8am-8pm. For supermarkets, try **Pam,** off Corso Buenos Aires at Via Piccinni, 2 (tel. 29 51 27 15). Open daily 9am-

7pm. There's also a **Simpatia CRAI** at Via Casati, 21 (tel. 29 40 58 21). Open Mon. 8am-1pm, Tues.-Sun. 8am-1pm and 4-7:30pm. For a balanced meal at reasonable rates, sit down with the Milanese office workers at one of the countless self-service restaurants that cater to professionals under time constraints. The strategically positioned **Ciao** (tel. 86 42 67), on the 2nd floor of the Duomo Center in P. del Duomo, is especially convenient. *Primi* average L4500, *secondi* L7500. Open daily 11:30am-3pm and 6-11pm.

Pizzeria da Sasa, Via Pergolesi, 21 (tel. 669 26 74). Family-run with bouncing kids to prove it. Pizza and calzones L8000-12,000. *Primi* L8000-14,000. Cover L2500. Open Wed.-Mon. noon-3pm and 6pm-2am. V, MC, AmEx.

Ristorante "La Colubrina," Via Felice Casati, 5 (tel. 29 51 84 27; MM1: Porta Venezia). Red tablecloths and mosaic-style stone floors. Pizza L6000-9000. Daily specials L10,000-18,000. Drinks L1000-10,000. Cover L2000. Open Tues. 7-11:30pm, Wed.-Sat. noon-2:30pm and 1-11:30pm, Sun. 7-11:30pm. Closed Aug.

Pizzeria del Nonno, Via Andrea Costa, 1 (tel. 26 14 52 62; MM1-2: Loreto), off P. Loreto. Surprisingly genteel decor for a hungry, rowdy crowd. Enormous pizzas (L7000-12,000) keep their mouths full. Daily special L8000-17,000. Cover L1500 for lunch, L25,000 for dinner. Open Mon.-Fri. noon-2:30pm and 7pm-midnight, Sat. 7pm-midnight.

Tarantella, Viale Abruzzi, 35 (tel. 29 40 02 18), just north of Via Plinio. Lively and leafy place with sidewalk dining. Great *antipasti.* Immense specialty salads L13,000-15,000. Pizzas L8000-20,000 (try the *gorgonzola*). *Primi* from L8000, *secondi* from L15,000. Open Sept.-July Mon.-Fri. noon-2:30pm and 7-11:30pm, Sun. 7-11:30pm. V, MC, AmEx.

Isola del Panino, Via Felice Casati, 2 (tel. 29 51 49 25; MM1 Lima), but enter from Corso Buenos Aires. Art deco atmosphere. Try a few of their 47 different kinds of fresh *panini* for L4500-5500. Open Tues.-Sun. 8am-midnight.

Brek, Via Lepetit, 20 (tel. 67 05 149), by the Stazione Centrale. Elegant self-service restaurant, becoming increasingly popular. A/C, a non-smoking room, and English-speaking staff. *Primi* average L5000, *secondi* L7500. Open Mon.-Sat. 11:30am-3pm and 6:30-10:30pm. Another location in P. Cavour swarms with suits at lunch.

La Piccola Napoli, Viale Monza, 13 (tel 26 14 33 97; MM1-2: Loreto). A haunt for local night owls. A/C upstairs. Pizza L7000-12,000. 10% service, cover. Open late-Aug. to mid-July Tues.-Sun. 7pm-3am. V, MC.

Duomo Center, P. Duomo, 6, under the arcade on your right as you face the *duomo.* This food court houses a variety of fast-food and self-service establishments, including the rather good **Spizzico,** which sells pizza by the slice or by the pie (regular slice L3300, huge slice L4200). Open daily 7am-2am.

Peck, Via Cantu, 3 (tel. 869 30 17), off Via Orefici, 2 blocks from P. Duomo. Milan's premier *rosticceria.* Pizza and pastries by the kilo—L3000 will buy a large slice of either. You can't leave without trying the chocolate mousse (about L6000). Open Tues.-Fri. 8:45am-2:30pm and 4-7:30pm, Sat. 8am-1:15pm and 3:45-7:30pm, Sun. 8am-1pm. V, MC, AmEx.

Le Briciole, Via Camperio, 17 (tel. 87 71 85), 1 street over from Via Dante. Lively and popular with young people. Pizza L9000-15,000. Spectacular *antipasto* buffet L12,000, *secondi* L10,000-18,000. Cover L3000. Open Tues.-Fri. and Sun. 12:15-2:30pm and 7:15-11:30pm. V, MC, AmEx.

Be Bop Caffè/Ristorante/Pizzeria, Viale Col di Lana, 4 (tel. 837 69 72; MM2: Sant'Agostino or Genova), off the far side of P. XXIV Maggio. Majorly hip decor with background jazz, except after hours when the young staff pumps up the volume. Food is occasionally even health conscious. Salads are generously proportioned (L16,000-18,000). Pizza L8000-16,000. There's even *soy* pizza! Open Sept.-July Tues.-Fri. noon-2:30pm and 7:30pm-1am, Sat. noon-2pm and 7:30-1am, Sun. 7pm-midnight. V, MC, AmEx.

La Crêperie, Via Corso Correnti, 24 (tel. 837 57 08; MM1 San Ambrogio), the continuation of Via Torino. Fruit crêpes L6000, liqueur dessert crêpes L4000, and the "real food" variety L5000-7000. Lunch special of 2 crêpes and a drink L9000. Sip lemon-and-celery juice to the beat of non-stop music. Open daily 11am-1am.

Portnoy, Via de Amicis, 1 (tel. 58 11 34 29), at Corso di Porta Ticinese. No complaints here. Young, socially conscious management displays new paintings and photographs every month. *Panini* L5000. Open Mon.-Sat. 7am-2am; shorter hours in winter. Poetry readings at 8pm the last Thurs. of every month.

Pizzeria Grand'Italia, Via Palermo, 5 (tel. 87 77 59). Pizza L6000-10,000, plus a multitude of other selections. Open Wed.-Mon. 12:15-2:45pm and 7pm-1:15am; in August also open Tues. Very busy, but worth the wait.

Gelaterie

After World War II the Viel family began selling tutti-frutti *gelato* from a cart outside the *duomo.* The enterprise quickly took off and today the name Viel is synonymous with exotic, fresh fruit *gelati* (L2500-5000) and *frullati* (whipped fruit drinks, L4000-8000) all over Milan. At **Viel,** Via Marconi, 3E, next to the tourist office, you can buy a cone packed with four scoops and eat it at an outside table, one of the cheapest places to sit near the *duomo* (L2500-5000 for a large cup). For more elegant and pricey fare, take your taste buds to the jolly **Viel Frutti Esotici Gelati,** on Via Luca Beltrami, to the left as you face the Castello from Largo Cairoli (MM1: Cairoli). *Esotici frullati* from L8000 and *gelato* L7000-10,000. **Jack Frost Gelateria,** Via Felice Casati, 25 (tel. 669 11 34; MM1: Porta Venezia), off Corso Buenos Aires at Via Lazzaretto, serves enormous helpings of creamy *gelato* in a fairy-tale decor packed to capacity. Try the *bacio* (chocolate and hazelnut). Open Thurs.-Tues. 9:30am-1am. Formerly Gelateria Pozzi, **Gelateria Milano Doc,** at P. Cantore, 4 (tel. 89 40 98 30), has been renovated and offers an expanded menu, outside seating, and crazy-good *gelato* (cones L2500-3500). It's a household name in Milan. Open Mon. 4pm-1am, Tues.-Sun. 8am-1am.

SIGHTS

Around the Duomo

The **Piazza del Duomo** marks the geographical and conceptual focus of Milan, and makes a good starting point for a walking view of the city. The looming Gothic **duomo** presides over the *piazza.* Gian Galeazzo Visconti founded the cathedral in 1386, hoping to flatter the Virgin into granting him a male heir. Construction proceeded sporadically over the next four centuries and was finally completed at Napoleon's command in 1809. In the meantime, more than 3400 statues, 135 spires, 96 gargoyles, and several kilometers of tracery accumulated. Today, the *duomo* is the third largest church in the world, after St. Peter's at the Vatican and the Seville Cathedral. The façade juxtaposes Italian Gothic and Baroque elements under a filigree crown. Inside, the 52 columns rise to canopied niches with statues as capitals. The church is a five-aisled cruciform seating 40,000 worshipers. Narrow side aisles extend to the grand stained-glass windows, among the largest in the world. The imposing 16th-century **marble tomb of Giacomo de Medici** in the south transept was inspired by the work of Michelangelo. From outside the north transept, you can climb (or ride) to the top of the cathedral, where you will find yourself surrounded by a magical field of turrets, spires, and statues. (Admission L6000, with elevator L8000.) A statue of the Madonna painted in gold leaf crowns this rooftop kingdom. (Church open daily June-Sept. 7am-5pm; Oct.-May 9am-4pm. No shorts, miniskirts, or sleeveless tops. Roof open daily in summer 9am-5:30pm; in winter 9am-4:30pm.)

The **Museo del Duomo,** P. del Duomo, 14 (tel. 86 03 58), is across the *piazza* in the Palazzo Reale. This newly renovated museum displays treasures from the cathedral. (Open Tues.-Sun. 9:30am-12:30pm and 3-6pm. Admission L7000.) It also houses the **Museo d'Arte Contemporanea,** which includes a fine permanent collection of Italian Futurist art interspersed with a few Picassos. (Open Tues.-Sun. 9:30am-5:30pm. Free. Wheelchair accessible.)

On the north side of the *piazza* is the monumental entrance to the **Galleria Vittorio Emanuele II.** This four-story arcade of *caffè,* shops, and offices is covered by a glass barrel vault, a beautiful glass cupola (48m), and some restoration scaffolding.

The gallery extends from the *duomo* to the **Piazza della Scala,** where you'll find the **Teatro alla Scala** (also known as **La Scala**), the world's premier opera house. Maria Callas became a legend in this simple Neoclassical building of 1778. La Scala rests on the site of the Church of Santa Maria alla Scala, from which it took its name. To see the lavish, multi-tiered hall, enter through the **Museo Teatrale alla Scala** (tel. 805 34 18). Here a succession of petite rooms are packed with opera memorabilia, including Verdi's top hat and plaster casts of the hands of famous conductors. (Open Mon.-Sat. 9am-noon and 2-6pm, Sun. 9:30am-12:30pm and 2:30-6pm; Oct.-April closed Sun. Admission L5000.)

Pass the 16th-century Palazzo Marino opposite La Scala (now the mayor's office) and the side of the **Church of San Fedele** (1569); you will arrive at the curious **Casa degli Omenoni** (1565), embellished with eight giant statues of weary, worldly Atlas. The street ends at **Piazza Belgioioso,** a pleasant square with old Milan character dominated by the 18th-century Belgioioso *palazzo* and the house of 19th-century novelist Alessandro Manzoni. The **Museo Manzoniano** at Via Morone, 1 (tel. 86 46 04 03), showcases his life and works. Among the portraits of his friends is an autographed likeness of Goethe. (Open Tues.-Fri. 9:30am-noon and 2-4pm. Free.) Farther along down Via Morone you'll come to the entrance to Via Manzoni, the medieval **Porta Nuova**—a Roman tomb sculpture and later a Gothic niche, adorned with statues of saints. The **Museo Poldi Pezzoli,** Via Manzoni, 12 (tel. 79 48 89), contains an outstanding private collection of art that Poldi Pezzoli bequeathed to the city in 1879. The museum's masterpieces hang in the Golden Room, which overlooks a flowery garden. Famous paintings include a *Virgin and Child* by Andrea Mantegna, Bellini's *Ecce Homo, St. Nicholas* by Piero della Francesca, the magical *Gray Lagoon* by Guardi, and the museum's signature piece, Antonio Pollaiolo's *Portrait of a Young Woman.* (Open Tues.-Fri. 9am-1:20pm and 2:30-6pm, Sat. 9:30am-1:20pm and 2:30-7:30pm, Sun. 9:30am-1:20pm; Oct.-March also Sun. 2:30-6pm. Admission L10,000.)

Near Castello Sforzesco

The enormous 15th-century **Castello Sforzesco** (tel. 62 36 39 47; MM1: Cairoli), restored after heavy bomb damage in 1943, is one of Milan's best-known monuments. The first interior court is so vast that architectural details seem to disappear, while the more enclosed, smaller courtyards are dominated by Renaissance arcades. On the ground floor is a sculpture collection renowned for Michelangelo's unfinished *Pietà Rondanini,* his last work. The picture gallery features paintings by Mantegna, Bellini, and other Renaissance masters, as well as *Madonna with Angels* by Fra Filippo Lippi. (Open Tues.-Sun. 9:30am-5:30pm. Free.)

The **Church of Santa Maria delle Grazie,** on P. di Sta. Maria delle Grazie and Corso Magenta off Via Carducci (MM1: Cairoli, or bus #21 or 24), enjoys praise for the splendid tribune Bramante added in 1492. Inside, the Gothic nave with barrel vaults contrasts with the airiness of the Bramante addition. To the left a door leads to an elegant square cloister, the artist's other contribution to the church. Next to the church entrance, in what was the monastery's refectory, is the **Cenacolo Vinciano** (tel. 498 75 88), **Leonardo da Vinci's Last Supper.** The consummately famous fresco captures the apostles' reaction to Jesus' prophecy: "One of you will betray me." Scaffolding for an eternal restoration project covers only the bottom of the fresco, leaving the rest in full view. (Open Tues.-Sun. 8:15am-1:45pm. Admission to Cenacolo L12,000, under 18 and over 60 free. Wheelchair accessible.) To further your study of da Vinci, explore the **Museo Nazionale della Scienza e della Tecnica "Leonardo da Vinci,"** Via San Vittore, 21 (tel. 48 55 51, MM1: San Ambrogio or bus #50 or 54), off Via Carducci. Applied physics dominates one section, and wooden models of Leonardo's most ingenious and visionary inventions fill another huge room. (Open Tues.-Fri. 9:30am-5pm, Sat.-Sun. 9:30am-6:30pm. Admission L10,000, children and seniors over 60 L6000.)

Via Verdi, running alongside La Scala, leads to **Via Brera,** another charming street lined with small, brightly colored palaces and art galleries, just a few steps from the *duomo* (MM1: Cordusio; for doorstep service, catch bus #61 from MM1: Moscova).

The **Pinacoteca di Brera** (Brera Art Gallery), Via Brera, 28 (tel. 72 26 31), presents an impressive collection of paintings in a 17th-century *palazzo.* Works include Bellini's *Pietà* (1460), Andrea Mantegna's brilliantly foreshortened *Dead Christ* (1480), Raphael's *Marriage of the Virgin* (1504), Caravaggio's *Supper at Emmaus* (1606), and Piero della Francesca's 15th-century *Madonna and Child with Saints* and *Duke Federico di Montefeltro.* The vibrant, animated frescoes by Bramante from the *Casa dei Panigarola* provide comic relief from the dramatic intensity of the other works. A limited but well-chosen collection of works by modern masters including Modigliani and Carlo Carrà adds further contrast. (Open Tues.-Sat. 9am-5:30pm, Sun. 9am-12:30pm. Wheelchair accessible. Admission L8000.)

The **Church of Sant'Ambrogio** (MM1: Sant'Ambrogio), which served as a prototype for Lombard-Romanesque churches throughout Italy, is the most influential medieval building in Milan. Ninth-century reliefs in brilliant silver and gold decorate the high altar. The crypt contains the gruesome skeletal remains of Sant'Ambrogio and two early Christian martyrs. The tiny 4th-century **Chapel of San Vittore,** with exquisite 5th-century mosaics adorning its cupola, is through the seventh chapel on the right. As you leave the church and walk to the left, you will pass under the peculiar **Portico della Canonica** (1492) by Bramante, the end columns of which have notches resembling those of tree trunks. There's also a small museum housing a collection of works from the 4th century AD (tel. 86 45 08 95). (Open Mon. and Wed.-Fri. 10am-noon and 3-5pm, Tues. 10am-noon, Sat.-Sun. 3-5pm. Admission L3000.)

Continue your spiritual pilgrimage to the land of the dead. The vast grounds of the **Cimitero Monumentale,** several blocks east of Stazione Porta Garibaldi, are a labyrinthine network of three-story mausoleums in architectural styles ranging from Egyptian pyramids to Art Deco jukeboxes.

From Corso di Porta Romana to the Navigli

The distances between sights are greater here, so consider public transportation.

At the **Church of San Nazaro Maggiore,** on Corso di Porta Romana (MM3: Crocieta), a medieval Lombard-Romanesque edifice conceals the remnants of a 4th-century basilica. The Renaissance funerary chapel of the Trivulzio in front is the work of Bramante's pupil Bramantino (1512-1547). The tomb bears the famous epigraph: *Qui numquam quivit quiescit: Tasc* ("He who never knew quiet now rests: Silence"). (Open daily 8:30am-noon and 3-6:30pm.)

The **Church of San Lorenzo Maggiore,** on Corso Ticinese (MM2: Porta Genova, then tram #3 from Via Torino), is the oldest church in Milan and testifies to the greatness of the city during the 4th century. The building began as an early Christian church, and although rebuilt later (with a 12th-century *campanile* and 16th-century dome), it retains its original octagonal plan. To the right of the church sits the 14th-century chapel of Sant'Aquilino. Inside is a 5th-century mosaic of a young, beardless Christ among his apostles. A staircase behind the altar leads to the remains of an early Roman amphitheater. (Church open Mon.-Sat. 8am-noon and 3-6pm, Sun. 10:30-11:15am and 3-5:30pm.) Near the front of the church is the 12th-century **Porta Ticinese.**

Farther down Corso Ticinese (bus #15) stands the **Church of Sant'Eustorgio** (tel. 835 15 83), founded in the 4th century to house the bones of the Magi, spirited off to Cologne in 1164. The present building (erected in 1278) has a typical Lombard-Gothic interior of low vaults and brick ribs supported by heavy columns. The real triumph of this church, and one of the great masterpieces of early Renaissance art, is the **Portinari Chapel** (1468), attributed to the Florentine Michelozzo. (Chapel closed for restoration.) A *Dance of Angels* is carved around the base of the multicolored dome, and frescoes depict the life and death of Peter the Martyr. In the center of the chapel is the magnificent Gothic tomb of St. Eustorgius (1339) by Giovanni di Balduccio of Pisa. (Church open daily 8am-noon and 3-7pm.)

Through the Neoclassical Arco di Porta Ticinese (1801-1814), or outside the Porta Genova station (MM2), you will find the **navigli district,** the Venice of Lombardy: canals, small footbridges, open-air markets, *caffè,* alleys, and trolleys. This area is part of a medieval canal system (whose original locks were designed by Leonardo da Vinci) that transported thousands of tons of marble to build the *duomo* and linked Milan to various northern cities and lakes.

South and East of the Duomo

The long, arched 1456 **Ospedale Maggiore,** on Via Festa del Perdono near P. Santo Stefano, is one of the largest constructions of the early Renaissance. The "General Hospital"—now the University of Milan—contains nine courtyards. Inside is a grand 17th-century court and a smaller one credited to Bramante. In 1479, Bramante designed the mystical **Church of San Satiro** on Via Torino, a few blocks from the *duomo* (bus #15). Despite its modest proportions, the interior creates the illusion of wide spaces. Compare the imaginary and the real by standing at the back of the church and then behind the high altar. (Open daily 9am-noon and 2:30-6pm.)

Following Via Spadari off Via Torino and then making a right onto Via Cantù will deposit you at the tiny but lovely **Pinacoteca Ambrosiana,** P. Pio XI, 2 (tel. 86 45 14 36). The 14 rooms of the Ambrosiana display exquisite works from the 15th through 17th centuries, including Botticelli's *Madonna of the Canopy,* Leonardo's *Portrait of a Musician,* Raphael's cartoon for the *School of Athens,* Caravaggio's *Basket of Fruit*—the first example of still-life painting in Italy—and the two paintings of *Earth* and *Air* by Breughel. (Re-opens Jan. 1997. Call for the latest info.)

East of the *duomo* between P. del Duomo and P. San Babila is **Corso Vittorio Emanuele,** Milan's major shopping street, entirely rebuilt the street after World War II. Off P. San Babila, early 19th-century *palazzi* and late 20th-century Armanis and Versaces line **Via Monte Napoleon,** the most elegant street in Milan. Don't miss a stroll through the English-style **Giardini Pubblici** on a sunny afternoon. (Open roughly 7am-10pm.) A small **zoo** lies within the grounds. (Open 9:30am-5pm.) The part of **Corso Venezia** bordering the public gardens is a broad boulevard lined with sumptuous palaces.

The **Galleria d'Arte Moderna,** Via Palestro, 16 (tel. 76 00 28 19), is next to the Giardini Pubblici in the Neoclassical Villa Comunale (MM2: Porta Venezia). Napoleon lived here with Josephine when Milan was capital of the Napoleonic Kingdom of Italy (1805-1814). Important modern Lombard art hangs here, as do works by Picasso, Matisse, Renoir, Gauguin, and Cézanne. (Open Tues.-Sun. 9:30am-5:30pm. Free.) The **Museo di Milano,** Via Sant'Andrea, 6 (tel. 78 37 97), exhibits Italian art and shares an 18th-century mansion with the petite **Museo di Storia Contemporanea** (Museum of Contemporary History; tel. 76 00 62 45; MM2: San Babila). Both museums currently closed for maintenance. Call for the latest info. Also check out the **Museo Civico di Storia Naturale** (Museum of Natural History) on Corso Venezia, 55 (tel. 62 08 54 05), in the Giardino Pubblico. It holds extensive geology and paleontology collections, including a room of complete dinosaur skeletons. (Open Tues.-Fri. 9:30am-5:30pm, Sat.-Sun. 9:30am-6:30pm.)

ENTERTAINMENT

Music, Theater, and Film

Emblematic of the blend of plebeian and patrician lifestyles that characterizes the arts scene in Milan is the **Musica in Metro** program, a series of summer concerts in subway stations performed by local music students dressed in their black-tie best. Those who turn professional await the chance to perform at **La Scala,** which traditionally opens its opera season on December 7 (though there are other productions year-round). Good tickets are usually sold out long in advance, but gallery seats (notorious for inducing altitude sickness) go for as little as L30,000. (Box office tel. 72 00 37 44, open daily noon-7pm.) Two hundred gallery standing-room tickets go on sale 30min. before the show at the entrance of the *museo.* The **Conservatorio,** Via del Conservatorio, 22 (tel. 76 00 17 55), near P. Tricolore, offers classical music, while the **Teatro Lirico,** Via Larga, 14 (tel. 72 33 32 22), south of the *duomo,* is Milan's leading stage, offering everything from ballet to avant-garde plays. (Ticket office open Mon.-Fri.

10am-7pm. Admission around L50,000.) Summer brings special programs of music and culture: **Milano d'Estate** (Milan in Summer) in July and **Vacanze a Milano** (Vacation in Milan) in August. Tickets for all performances are sold at the sponsoring venue but can also be purchased through **La Biglietteria,** Corso Garibaldi, 81 (tel. 659 01 88) or other outlets (contact the tourist office).

The **Piccolo Teatro,** Via Rovello, 2 (tel. 86 27 71), near Via Dante, was founded in the post-World War II years as a socialist theater and is now owned by the city. It specializes in small, off-beat theatrical productions. (Performances Tues.-Sun. 8:30pm.) **Ciak,** Via Sangallo, 33 (tel. 76 11 00 93), near P. Argonne east of the *duomo,* is a favorite haunt of young *Milanese* for theater, films, and the occasional cabaret. Take train #5 from Stazione Centrale to Viale Argonne.

The **Teatro di Porta Romana,** Corso di Porta Romana, 124 (tel. 58 31 58 96; bus #13 from Via Marconi off P. del Duomo), is building a reputation for experimental productions and first-run mainstream plays. (Admission about L25,000.) **Teatri d'Italia** (tel. 58 31 58 96) sponsors **Milan Oltre** in June and July, a festival of drama, dance, music and much more. (Call the City Council for Culture, tel. 86 46 40 94, for more info.) For a different brand of street theater, the **Carnevale** in Milan is increasingly popular. As the crowds in Venice sport fewer costumes and more cameras each year, many come to Milan instead for the friendlier atmosphere.

Milan's cinematic scene thrives. Check any Milanese paper (especially the Thursday edition) for showings and general info. Shows on Wednesdays are L7000 (regularly L8000-L10,000). You can see films in English at a number of cinemas: Mondays at **Anteo,** Via Milazzo, 9 (tel. 659 77 32), Tuesdays at **Arcobaleno,** Viale Tunisia, 11 (tel. 29 40 60 54), and Thursdays at **Mexico,** Via Savona, 57 (tel. 48 95 18 02). Admission at all the theaters is L8000, under 18 L6000. Anteo also hosts an open-air theater in the summer called Cinema under the Stars. Old movies screen at the **Cineteca Italiana/Museo del Cinema,** Via Manin, 2/B (tel. 655 49 77; open Tues.-Fri. 3-6pm. Admission L4000.)

Clubs

Once again, check any Milanese paper on Wednesday or Thursday for info on clubs and weekend events. *Corriere Della Sera* publishes an insert called *22 Milano* on Wednesday; *La Repubblica* produces *Tutto Milano* on Thursday. *Milano Magazine* comes out every two weeks with info on bars, films, and seasonal events. Although listings are in Italian, names and addresses of clubs will be helpful even for the *italiano*-impaired. The APT tourist office also has helpful handouts. In general, Milan parties Thursday-Sunday nights and rests up during the beginning of the week. Many of the clubs listed below have different "theme nights," and cover charges vary accordingly. **Remember that everything shuts down in August, and clubs are often reincarnated in a totally different form in September.**

When night falls, Milano's youth migrates to the areas around **Porta Ticinese** and **Piazza Vetra.** Hang out on the grass in the parks, where soccer games and guitar players will entertain you, or grab a beer at one of the many *birrerie* (pubs). A safe, attractive, and chic district lies by **Via Brera;** here you'll find art galleries, small clubs, restaurants, and a thirtysomething crowd. If you decide to head for the *discoteche,* expect a cover charge around L20,000 or a mandatory first drink.

Rock: Hollywood, Corso Como, 15 (tel. 659 89 96). A small, trendy disco with scads of models. Open Tues.-Sun. 10:30pm-4am. Cover L25,000-30,000 with drink. **Plastic,** Viale Umbria, 120 (tel. 73 39 96). Milan's premier disco-pub. Underground music, fashionable New York crowd. Cover L15,000, Sat. L18,000. Open Tues.-Sun. until 3am. **Spirit,** Via Maiocchi, 12 (tel. 29 51 49 81). A pub with a wide variety of styles and sounds. Too-cool furniture and loud rock music. Open daily 9:30pm-2am.

Jazz and Folk: Capolinea, Via Ludovico il Moro, 119 (tel. 89 12 20 24). Walk out Corso Italia toward the Navigli and Porta Ticinese, south of the *duomo.* A student crowd. Cover L15,000 (includes first drink). Open Tues.-Sun. until 2am. **Le Scim-**

mie, Via Ascanio Sforza, 49 (tel. 89 40 28 74), beyond the Capolinea. Milan's premier jazz spot. Open Wed.-Mon. 8pm-2am.

Discos: City Square, Via Castelbarco, 11 (tel. 58 31 06 82). Some of the biggest dance floors in Milan, occasionally with live music. Open daily till 4am. **Open House,** Via Carducci, 25 (tel. 869 26 25). Popular with the university crowd. Theme nights. Cover L25,000, Sat. L30,000. Closed Sun.

Gay Bars and Clubs: Cicip e Ciciap, Via Gorani, 9 (tel. 87 75 55). Bar, also a restaurant in the evenings. Women only. Open Tues.-Sun. **Nuova Idea,** Via de Castilla, 30 (MM2: Gioia). Usually men only; women welcome Sat. and holidays. Open evenings Thurs.-Sun. **One Way,** Via Cavallotti Sesto San Giovanni, 204, in inner Milan. Disco and leather. Open Tues. and Fri.-Sun. **Sottomarino Giallo,** Via Donatello, 2, (tel. 29 40 10 47). A women-only club. Open Tues.-Sun. **Towanda!,** Via Imonate, 3 (tel. 69 00 88 68). A women-only bar with disco and a 2nd floor bar. Open evenings Thurs.-Sun. **Uitibar,** Via Monvisa, 14 (tel. 331 59 96). Mixed. Open Tues.-Sun. 8:30pm-2am.

Other Clubs: Ipotesi Latino Americana, P. XXIV Maggio, 8 (tel. 832 21 60). Very popular, with—yes—Latin American music. Cover L15,000. Open Wed.-Sun. **Leoncavallo,** Via Watteau, 7 (tel. 26 14 02 87). Dress as badly as you want. Cover rarely exceeds L5000. **New Zimba** ("lion" in Swahili), Via Natale Battaglia, 12 (tel. 26 14 42 65). Congo, rhythm and blues, and Caribbean music. Open Tues.-Sun. 10:30pm-3am. **New Magazine,** Viale Piceno, 3 (tel. 73 09 41). An ex-disco with phones and maps on every table. Eat, make friends, and find love. Open Tues.-Sun. 9pm-2am.

No Cover Charge: Ebony Note, Via Bocconi (tel. 58 90 16 51). Everything from Reggae to world music. Open Tues.-Fri. **Bataclan,** Piazzale Biancamano, 2 (tel. 657 28 12). Different music every night. Drinks L8000. Open Tues.-Sun.

SHOPPING

Milan's most elegant boutiques are between the *duomo* and P. Babila, especially on the excessively glamorous **Via Monte Napoleone** and off P. Babila at **Via Spiga.** Wander like a pauper among the marble and brass racks of designer merchandise in the five-floor Versace boutique. If you can tolerate the stigma of being an entire season behind the trends, purchase your famous designer duds from *blochisti* (wholesale clothing outlets). Try **Monitor** on Viale Monte Nero (MM2: Porta Genova, then bus #9), or **Il Salvagente,** Via Bronzetti, 16 (tel. 76 11 03 28), off Corso XXII Marzo (take bus #60 from MM1 Lima or MM3 Central Station). The clothing sold along **Corso Buenos Aires, Via Torino,** near the *duomo,* and **Via Sarpi,** near Porta Garibaldi, is more affordable, yet well-designed. Many of the boutiques cater to a younger crowd. Shop around the area of Corso di Porta Ticinese for *chic ma non snob* attire (MM2: Porta Genova, then bus #59). **Eliogabalo,** P. Sant'Eustorgio, 2 (tel. 837 82 93), named after a Roman emperor renowned for his preoccupation with aesthetics, offers the latest in *haute couture.* Reasonable prices for everything from clothes to groceries can be found at the **STANDA** department store at Via Torino, 45 (tel. 86 67 06), five blocks from the *duomo.* Photo booth, photocopy machine, and shoe repair are on the third floor. Open daily 9am-7:30pm. True *milanese* bargain hunters attack the giant street markets on Saturday and Tuesday to buy their threads. These bazaars are on **Via Fauché** (MM2: Garibaldi), **Viale Papinian** (MM2: Sant'Agostino) and the 400-year-old **Fiera di Sinigallia** on Via Calatafimi (Sat. only). For used clothing, try the Navigli district or Corso Garibaldi. Shop at the end of July for the end of summer sales (20-50% off) and a glimpse at the new fall lines. Clothing stores are generally open Mon. 10am-noon, Tues.-Sat. 10am-noon and 2-7:30pm. Another fabulous option is the classy Italian department store **La Rinascente,** to the left of the *duomo* (as you face it). Keep in mind that many (non-clothing) shops in Milan are closed on Monday mornings.

Pavia

Once an important Roman outpost, Pavia weathered Attila the Hun in 452 before gaining importance as the Lombard capital during the 7th and 8th centuries. Spanish, Austrian, and French forces governed Pavia in rapid succession from the 16th century until 1859, when Italy's independence movement liberated the city. With the help of agricultural and industrial development, today's Pavia has maintained a state of prosperity. Romanesque churches dating from Pavia's tranquil years as a Milanese satellite are scattered throughout the historic sector, and the 14th-century university continues to flourish. Though the center of town bustles with daily student activity, the city manages to retain the tranquility of a small town. Impress the locals by pronouncing "Pavia" correctly (hint: emphasize the second syllable).

ORIENTATION AND PRACTICAL INFORMATION

Pavia is a mere 35km south of Milan, on the train line to Genoa (30min.). The city sits on the banks of the Ticino river not far from its intersection with the Po. The train station overlooks **Piazzale Stazionale** in the modern west end of town, linked to the historic center by a walk down **Viale Vittorio Emanuele II.** Follow this street to **Piazzale Minerva,** then to Pavia's main drag, **Corso Cavour.** This leads to the city's narrow central square, **Piazza della Vittoria,** which is a block away from **Piazza Duomo.** Past P. Vittoria, the main street changes it name to **Corso Mazzini.**

Tourist Office: Via F. Filzi, 2 (tel. 221 56; fax 322 21), away from the action in a characterless section of town. From the train station, take a left on Via Trieste and then a right on Via Filzi, past the bus station. Friendly staff speaks English and hands out a good map. Ask for the booklet *Pavia and its Province.* Open Mon.-Sat. 8:30am-12:30pm and 2-6pm.

Telephones: Via Galliano, 8 (tel. 38 21), across the street and around the corner from the post office. Open Mon.-Fri. 9am-12:30pm and 2:30-6pm.

Trains: (tel. 230 00) at the head of Viale V. Emanuele II on the west end of town. To: Genoa (every 30-60min., L9800); Milan (every 30min., L3400); Cremona (4 per day, L6500); and Mantua (4 per day, L11,700). Change at Codogno for Cremona and Mantua. **Luggage Storage:** L5000 for 12hr. Open 7am-7pm.

Buses: SGEA (tel. 30 20 20), departing from the space-age station on Via Trieste (far to the left of the train station). To Milan (every hr., 5am-10pm, 1hr., L4400) via the *certosa* (charterhouse, 15min., L2000).

Taxi: tel. 274 39.

Bookstore: Libreria Ticinum, Corso Mazzini 2/C (tel. 30 39 16), off P. Vittoria. A small selection of classics and bestsellers in English. Open Mon.-Sat. 9am-12:30pm and 3-7:30pm. V, MC.

Pharmacy: Vilani, Via Bossolaro, 31 (tel. 223 15), at the corner of P. Duomo. Well stocked with homeopathic supplies. List of pharmacies with night service. In emergencies, they will provide night service for a surcharge. Open Mon.-Fri. 8:30am-12:30pm and 3:30-7:30pm.

Emergencies: tel. 113. **First Aid/Ambulance:** tel. 52 77 77, nights and holidays tel. 52 76 00. **Hospital: Ospedale S. Matteo,** P. Golgi, 2 (tel. 50 11).

Police: P. Italia, 5 (tel. 112).

Post Office: P. della Posta, 2 (tel. 212 51), off Via Mentana, 1 block over from Corso Mazzini. Stamps and *fermo posta* at #5. Open Mon.-Sat. 8:30am-5:30pm. **Postal Code:** 27100.

Telephone Code: 0382.

ACCOMMODATIONS AND CAMPING

A dearth of reasonable places to stay makes Pavia unappealing for anything but a daytrip. Consider staying at the hostel in Milan, or take advantage of the well-organized *agriturismo* program; ask the tourist office for a complete pamphlet. The **Hotel Aurora,** Viale Vittorio Emanuele II, 25 (tel. 236 64; fax 212 48), is right next to the train station. The modern rooms are decked out with modern art and snappy patterned sheets. The hotel resembles a trendy New York art gallery. All rooms have TVs. Singles L50,000, with bath L68,000. Doubles L95,000. V, MC. For **camping,** consider **Ticino,** Via Mascherpa, 10 (tel. 52 70 94). From the station, take bus #4 (toward Mascherpa) for about 10min., then get off at the Chiozzo stop. L6000 per person. L5000 for a small tent, L7000 for a large tent. Hot shower L500. Restaurant next door. Pool nearby about L7000, L10,000 on the weekends. Open March-Oct.

FOOD

Coniglio (rabbit) and *rana* (frog) are the local specialties, but if you don't eat things that hop and jump, skip right over to the *tavole calde* along Corso Cavour and Corso Mazzini. A well-loved dish is *zuppa alla pavese,* piping hot chicken or beef broth with a poached egg floating on top and sprinkled with grated *grana* cheese. **Esselunga** (tel. 262 10) is a monolithic supermarket at the far end of the mall complex between Via Trieste and Viale Battisti. Open Mon. 1-9pm, Tues.-Sat. 8am-9pm.

Ristorante-Pizzeria Marechiaro, P. Vittoria, 9 (tel. 237 39). Delicious pizzas with yummy crusts, prepared before your eyes (L5000-15,000). Reasonably priced *primi* and *secondi.* Crowded, cozy atmosphere. Summertime diners spill into the *piazza.* Cover L3000. Open Tues.-Sun. 11am-3pm and 6pm-3am. V, MC, AmEx.

Ristorante-Pizzeria Regisole, P. Duomo, 4 (tel. 247 39), under the arcade facing the *duomo.* A/C and outdoor seating available. Reasonably priced pizzas, including a *margherita* for L6000. *Primi* from L6000, *secondi* from L10,000. Open Wed.-Mon. noon-3pm and 7pm-midnight. V, MC, AmEx.

Bar Pampanin, P. Vittoria 20/B (tel. 291 67). Ask anyone in Pavia where to get *gelato* and they'll pipe "Pampanin!" Interesting flavors, including the tart, thirst-quenching *pompelmo* (grapefruit) and a spaghetti sundae made with vanilla *gelato,* whipped cream, and strawberry sauce. Regular cones L2500-3500. Do you dare to eat an entire maxi-cone for L5000? Open Thurs.-Tues. 10am-2am.

SIGHTS AND ENTERTAINMENT

For centuries the **Church of San Michele** (tel. 260 63) has witnessed the coronations of myriad luminaries, including Charlemagne in 774, Frederick Barbarossa in 1155, and a long succession of northern Italian dukes. Though it was rebuilt in the Romanesque style, this 7th-century church retains a medieval feel. Decorating the chancel are a 1491 fresco of the *Coronation of the Virgin* and bas-reliefs from the 14th century. An 8th-century silver crucifix of Theodote graces the chapel to the right of the presbytery. To get to San Michele, go down Corso Garibaldi and turn right after Via della Rochetta. (Open daily 8am-noon and 3-6pm.)

From San Michele it's a short walk to what's left of Pavia's layered-brick **duomo,** officially named the **Cattedrale Monumentale di Santo Stefano Martiro.** The **Torre Civica,** adjoining the *duomo,* collapsed in the spring of 1989, killing several people and taking with it a good portion of the *duomo's* left-hand chapel as well as some nearby houses and shops. Disputes over what ought to be done with the rubble have led to a lackadaisical restoration: barricades and scaffolding still garnish the *piazza.* The shaky brick exterior of the *duomo,* recently reinforced with concrete columns, conceals an impressive interior. Begun in 1488 and influenced by the designs of Bramante, Macaluso, and Leonardo, the *duomo* was one of the most ambitious undertakings of the Renaissance in Lombardy—typically, much of it was left incomplete until this century. The brick exterior still awaits a marble façade, and there are no plans for it in the near future. (*Duomo* under restoration.).

The prestigious **University of Pavia** (tel. 50 41), founded in 1361, sprawls along Strada Nuova. It claims such famous alumni as Petrarch, Columbus, and the Venetian playwright Goldoni. The university's most electrifying graduate, however, was the physicist Alessandro Volta, whose experiments are now on display at the university. The patron of the university, Galeazzo II of the Visconti family, earned notoriety for his research on human torture. The three towers rising from the university's property on P. Leonardo da Vinci are the remnants of more than 100 medieval towers that once punctuated the city's skyline.

Strada Nuova ends at the **Castello Visconteo** (tel. 338 53), a colossal medieval castle (1360) set in a park that once extended to the Certosa di Pavia, the Visconti's private hunting ground 8km away. Richly colored windows and elegant terra-cotta decorations border three sides of the castle's vast courtyard. The fourth wall was destroyed in 1527 during the Franco-Spanish Wars. Pavia's **Museo Civico** (tel. 30 48 16), located here, houses a picture gallery and an extensive Lombard-Romanesque sculpture collection. (Open June-Nov. Tues.-Sat. 9am-1pm, Sun. 9am-12:30pm. Admission L5000, under 18 L2500.)

From the front grounds of the castle, you can see the low, rounded forms of the Lombard-Romanesque **Church of San Pietro in Ciel d'Oro** of 1132 (tel. 30 30 36). Inside on the high altar is a marble reliquary containing the remains of St. Augustine in an ornate Gothic ark. (Open daily 8am-noon and 3-6pm.)

■ Near Pavia

Eight kilometers north of Pavia stands the **Certosa di Pavia** (Charterhouse of Pavia; tel. 92 56 13; ask to speak with Padre Tebreab). This Carthusian monastery and mausoleum was built for the Visconti family, which ruled the area from the 12th to 15th centuries. It contains four centuries of Italian art, from early Gothic to Baroque. The exuberant façade (late 1400s-1560) overflows with sculpture and inlaid marble, representing the apex of the Lombard Renaissance. The Old Sacristy houses a Florentine triptych carved in ivory, with 99 sculptures and 66 bas-reliefs depicting the lives of Mary and Jesus. The monks lead delightful tours of the complex whenever a large enough group has gathered (usually every 45min.), leaving from inside the church. Open May-Aug. Tues.-Sun. 9-11:30am and 2:30-6pm; March-April and Sept.-Oct. Tues.-Sun. 9-11:30am and 2:30-5:30pm; Nov.-Feb. Tues.-Sun. 9-11:30am and 2:30-4:30pm. Free.

Both buses and trains can deposit you near the charterhouse. **Buses** leave Pavia from the Via Trieste station (L2000) and Milan from P. Castello (L3300). From the bus stop, the *certosa* awaits you at the end of a long, tree-lined road. From the **train station,** go left around the outside wall of the monastic complex and turn inside to the right at the first opening.

Cremona

Cremona's history, like its music, is rich and vibrant. Here, Andrea Amanti created the first modern violin in 1530 and established the Cremonese violin-making dynasty. After learning the fundamentals as apprentices in the Amati workshop, Antonio Stradivarius (1644-1737) and Giuseppe Guarneri (1687-1745) raised violin-making to a new art form. Students still come to Cremona to learn the legendary craft at the International School for Violin-Making, ever hopeful of replicating the sound created by Stradivarius's secret varnish. Though the city's earth-toned buildings create a somewhat drab atmosphere, the busy concert schedule at the Ponchielli Theater and some of the most remarkable architecture in all of Lombardy lend the city a more than compensatory dose of color and life.

ORIENTATION AND PRACTICAL INFORMATION

As you leave the train station, bear to the left of the park. Walk straight ahead, crossing Via Dante and Viale Trento e Trieste, which run along the border of the city. Take **Via Palestro,** which becomes first **Via Campi** and then **Via Verdi,** until you reach **Piazza Cavour.** A left at P. Cavour leads to the **Piazza del Comune** and the adjoining **Piazza del Duomo,** where the *duomo, torrazzo,* and tourist office are located. If you get lost, just head toward the towering campanile.

Tourist Office: P. del Duomo, 5 (tel. 232 33). Friendly staff. English spoken. Ask for the *Carnet Dell'Ospite* brochure for information on hotels, museums, and restaurants. Open Mon.-Sat. 9:30am-12:30pm and 3-6pm, Sun. 10am-noon.

Budget Travel: Centro Turistico Studentesco, Via Ingegneri, 7 (tel. 41 28 78). Open Mon.-Fri. 10am-noon and 3-5:30pm, Sat. 10am-noon.

Telephones: Via Cadorini, 3 (tel. 239 11). Open Mon.-Fri. 9am-12:30pm and 2:30-6pm.

Trains: Via Dante, 68 (tel. 222 37). Get off at P. Stazione. To: Milan (10 per day, 1¼hr., L7200); Pavia (2 per day, 2hr., L6500); Mantua (16 per day, 1hr., L5700); and Brescia (every hr., 45min., L5000).

Buses: Autostazione di Via Dante (tel. 292 12), a block to the left of the train station. To: Milan (1 per day, 2hr., L9300); Bergamo (4 per day, L8400); and Brescia (every hr., L7400). Tickets at the station (open 7:20am-1pm and 2:15-6:30pm) or across the street at **La Pasticceria Mezzadri,** Via Dante, 105 (tel. 257 08; open daily 6am-8pm).

Taxi: tel. 213 00 or 267 40.

Emergencies: tel. 113. **First Aid and Ambulance:** tel. 118. **Hospital: Ospedale** (tel. 40 51 11), in Largo Priori, past P. IV Novembre to the east.

Police: Questura, Via Tribunali, 6 (tel. 48 81).

Post Office: Via Verdi, 21 (tel. 282 39). Open Mon.-Fri. 8am-7pm, Sat. 8am-1pm. **Postal Code:** 26100.

Telephone Code: 0372.

ACCOMMODATIONS

Albergo Brescia, Via Brescia, 7 (tel. 43 46 15). A 20-min. walk to the left down Via Dante and a left at P. Libertà, or take bus #1, 3, 4, or 6 from the station. Nice management, clean bathrooms, and functional rooms that are booked solid during the week. Singles L50,000. Doubles L60,000. V, MC.

Albergo Bologna, P. Risorgimento, 8 (tel. 242 58), above a pizzeria; just ring the bell. Very small singles only L30,000. Reservations recommended. **Restaurant** open Sat.-Thurs. noon-2:30pm and 7pm-midnight. Pizzas around L8000, *primi* L8000-10,000, and *secondi* L10,000-15,000. Cover L2000. V, MC.

Albergo Ideale, Viale T. Trieste, 2, near both the station and P. Risorgimento. Standard, clean rooms. Singles L40,000, Doubles L55,000.

Camping: Parco al Po (tel. 212 68), on Via Lungo Po Europa southwest of town. From P. Cavour, walk 20min. down C. Vittorio Emanuele. L6000 per person. Car and tent L10,000, camper L12,000. Showers and electricity. Open April-Sept.

FOOD

First concocted in the 16th century, the city's *mostarda di Cremona* consists of a hodgepodge of fruits—cherries, figs, apricots, melons—preserved in a sweet mustard syrup and served on boiled meats. Bars of *torrone* (nougat with an egg, honey, and nut base) are less adventurous but equally steeped in Cremonese confectionery lore. *Mostarda* can be found in most local *trattorie,* while *torrone* can be purchased in the sweet shops on Via Solferino. **Spelari,** at #25 (tel. 223 46), has been keeping dentists in business since 1836. *Torrone* L9800. Open Mon. 8:30am-12:30pm, Tues.-Sat. 8:30am-12:30pm and 3:30-7:30pm. For something a little less sweet, try the Grana Padono or the Provolone cheeses in the local *salumerie*. On Wednesday and Saturday from 8am-1pm, there is an **open-air market** in P. Marconi, past P. Cavour on Corso Verdi. For **supermarkets,** try either **GS** at Via San Tommaso, 9 (tel. 336 33; open Mon. 1-8pm, Tues.-Sat. 8am-8pm) or **CRAI** at P. Risorgimento, 30 (open Mon. 8am-12:30pm, Tues.-Sat. 8am-12:30pm and 4:30-7:30pm).

Ristorante Pizzeria Marechiano, Corso Campi, 41 (tel. 262 89). An attractive little place on the main window-shopping street. Pizzas from L9000. Cover L2500, L2000 for pizza. Open Wed.-Mon. noon-3pm and 6pm-1am. V, MC.

Ristorante Tonino, Via Antico Rodano, 9 (tel 286 87), a side street off the intersection between Via Palermo and C. Garibaldi. *Primi* from L7000, *secondi* from L8000, pizzas from L5000. Open Thurs.-Tues. noon-2:30pm and 7pm-1am.

La Bersagliera, P. Risorgimento, 12 (tel. 213 97), on the corner of Via Ghinaglia. Locals lavish praise on this family-owned establishment serving Neapolitan cuisine. Pizzas L6000-14,000. Try the *pizza Cremonese* (L11,000), with tomatoes, gorgonzola, and spinach. *Primi* L5000-10,000, *secondi* L7000-18,000. Cover L2500. Open Thurs.-Tues. 11:45am-3pm and 6:30-10:30pm. V, MC, AmEx.

SIGHTS AND ENTERTAINMENT

Violins and their production are the primary attraction in Cremona. Closest to the train station, the small **Museo Stradivariano,** at Via Palestro, 17 (tel. 46 18 86), provides a fascinating introduction to the art of Stradivarius and his contemporaries. (Open Tues.-Sun. 8:30am-6pm. Admission L5000, groups L3000 per person.) Continuing down Via Palestro, just left of P. Cavour stands the **Palazzo del Comune.** The second floor, decorated with 16th-century Renaissance terra-cottas, frames the **Saletta dei Violini (Violin Room),** showcasing five masterpieces attributed to Andrea Amati, Nicolò Amati, Stradivarius, and Guarneri. (Open June-mid-Aug. Tues.-Sat. 8:30am-6pm, Sun. 9:15am-12:15pm and 3-6pm. Admission L6000.)

Directly facing the *palazzo* in P. del Comune is the 12th-century pink marble **duomo** (officially known as **Santa Mari'Assunta**), a fine example of the Lombard-Romanesque style. The interior houses a cycle of 16th-century frescoes and, unfortunately, is forever undergoing restoration, though it is still open. (Open Mon.-Sat. 7am-noon and 3-7pm, Sun. 7am-1pm and 3:30-7pm.) To the left of the cathedral stands the late 13th-century **Torrazzo,** the tallest *campanile* in Italy at 108m. (Scale the nearly 500 steps in good weather, Easter-Nov. 1. Mon.-Sat. 10:30am-noon and 3-6pm, Sun. 10:30am-12:30pm and 3-7pm. Admission L5000.) The dome of the **baptistery** (1167) rises in a perfect, unadorned octagonal pattern, but the building is closed for renovations. (Contact the tourist office for updated information.) The Gothic **Loggia dei Militi,** across from the baptistery, completes the square. Erected in 1292, it functioned as a meeting place for the captains of the citizens' militia. The Gothic **Church of Sant'Agostino** (1345), near Via Plasio, contains Bonifacio Bembo frescoes and a *Madonna with Saints* by Perugino (1494).

Cremona is also endowed with fine Renaissance buildings, including the **Palazzo Fodri** (1499) at Corso Matteotti, 17. The columns in the courtyard bear French royal insignias in homage to Louis XII of France, who occupied the duchy of Milan in 1499. The **Palazzo Affaitati** (1561), Via Ugolani Dati, 4, flaunts an impressive marble staircase that leads to the **Museo Civico** (tel. 46 18 85). See Caravaggio's *St. Francis,* as well as 15th-century texts of Renaissance politics. (Open Tues.-Sun. 8:30am-6pm. Admission L6000.)

Cremona is alive with the sound of music all year long. **Cremona Jazz** in March and April eases the way into the summer season with a series of concerts throughout the city. (Tickets begin at L15,000.) They'll be dancing in the streets with **Estate in Musica** on evenings in July and August, when P. del Comune becomes an outdoor piano bar. Free concerts of sacred works are held in the Church of San Sigismondo during July. The May and June **Festival di Cremona** kicks off the Teatro Ponchielli season with a classical series heavy on the strings. (Tickets L20,000-25,000.) It all reaches a *crescendo* with the **opera season,** running from mid-October through early December. (Tickets begin at L25,000.) For ticket information on the Festival contact the Teatro Ponchielli ticket booth at Corso Vittorio Emanuele, 52 (tel. 40 72 73; open daily 4-7pm).

Mantua (Mantova)

Although Mantua first gained fame as Virgil's hometown, the monuments in the *centro storico* owe their existence to later rulers. Perhaps the most powerful were the members of the Gonzaga family who, after ascending to power in 1328, zealously sought to change Mantua's small-town image by importing well-known artists as well as cultivating local talent. Evidence of the Gonzagas' successful efforts includes the impressive churches of San Sebastiano and Sant'Andrea and the carefully crafted frescoes by Mantegna and Pisanelli. While prosperous commercial agriculture and bustling industry attest to modern Mantua's place in this hectic world, the historic center preserves much of the unhurried rustic flavor that its former rulers sought so fiercely to overcome.

ORIENTATION AND PRACTICAL INFORMATION

A few kilometers north of the Po, the calm waters of the Minro lagoons border the stubby, peninsular projection of Mantua, with its interlocking network of grand and tiny *piazze* that compose the historic center. The unrestricted land on the remaining side has given way to modern expansion. Most buses take you only to the edge of the historic center, but you can easily walk the rest of the way. From the train station in **Piazza Don E. Leoni,** head left on Via Solferino, then right onto Via Bonomi until you reach the main street, **Corso Vittorio Emanuele II,** on your left. Follow the *corso* and you will arrive at **P. Cavallotti,** connected by **Corso della Libertà** to **P. Martiri della Libertà.** From here, **Via Roma** leads to the *centro storico,* beginning at **P. Concordia,** with central **P. Marconi, P. Mantegna,** and **P. delle Erbe** clustered close by.

Tourist Office: P. Mantegna, 6 (tel. 32 82 53; fax 36 32 92), adjacent to the church of Sant'Andrea. From the train station, take a left on Via Solferino through P. S. Francesco d'Assisi to Via Fratelli Bandiera, and turn right on Via Verdi. Ask for *Mantova e la Festa Padana* (a calendar of events in the province) and the invaluable *Mantova: Directions for Use,* which comes with a fabulous map. Open Mon.-Sat. 9am-noon and 3-6pm, Sun. 9:30am-12:30pm.

Currency Exchange: Banks are a dime a dozen. **Banca Nazionale del Lavoro,** P. Cavallotti, 3, where Corso Vittorio Emanuele II becomes Corso Umberto, has dependable rates and cash advances on Visa. (Don't be disturbed by the *Star Trek*-esque beaming stations in the front—the natives are friendly.) Open Mon.-Wed. and Fri. 8:20am-1:20pm and 3-4:30pm, Thurs. 8:20am-5:50pm.

Telephones: Via XX Settembre, 29a (tel. 187 or 33 21). Open Mon.-Fri. 9am-12:30pm and 2:30-6pm.

Trains: P. Don Leoni (tel. 32 16 47), at the end of Via Solferino e S. Martino, southwest of town. To: Cremona (every hr., 1hr., L5700); Verona (every hr., 40min., L3400); and Milan (9 per day, 2hr., L30,600). **Luggage Storage:** L5000 for 12hr. Open 6:15am-8:15pm.

Buses: APAM, P. Mondadori (tel. 32 72 37), across and to the right as you leave the train station. Cross Corso Vittorio Emanuele II to Via Caduti. Buses to Brescia (17 per day, 1½hr., L9000). Tickets sold Mon.-Fri. 7am-1:15pm and 3-6:30pm, Sat. 7am-1:15pm. (L1300 for a ticket within the city.)

Taxis: Train station (tel. 32 53 51), P. Cavallotti (tel. 32 44 07), P. Marconi (tel. 32 44 08), or Via Albertoni (tel. 36 24 91), near the hospital.

Bike Rental: Bici a Noleggio (tel. 33 36 77), an outdoor establishment next to the lake, on the Lungolago dei Gonzaga where it intersects with Largo Vigili del Fuoco. (L4000 per hour; all day L10,000; Sun. all day L15,000.) Open Tues.-Sun. 9:30am-12:30pm and 3:30-7:30pm (additional summer hours 8:30pm-midnight).

Pharmacy: Dr. Silvestri, Via Roma, 24. Open Sun.-Fri. 8:30am-12:30am and 4:35-7:30pm. List of pharmacies offering night service posted outside.

Emergencies: tel. 113. **Ambulance:** tel. 20 12 01 or 20 12 20. **Hospital: Ospedale Civile Poma,** Viale Albertoni, 1-3 (tel. 20 11).

Police: P. Sordello, 46 (tel. 20 51).

Post Office: P. Martiri Belfiore, 15 (tel. 32 64 03 for secretary), up Via Roma from the tourist office. Open Mon.-Fri. 8am-7pm, Sat. 8:20am-1:20pm. **Postal Code:** 46100.

Telephone Code: 0376.

ACCOMMODATIONS

For a large city, Mantua has few hotel options. For the prices you'll pay, you'd expect a deluxe room in the *Palazzo Ducale;* those willing to stay in smaller nearby towns will be able to find less expensive accommodations. Ask at the tourist office for an up-to-date *agriturismo* packet listing possibilities for lodging and/or dining in a more rural setting (around L20,000 per person per night).

Ostello AIG, located near the water on Via Legnano, east of Mantua. Still undergoing major renovations, the hostel should open any day now (really), with rooms polished to a luster for your comfort.

Albergo Bianchi Stazione, P. Don Leoni, 24 (tel. 32 64 65; fax 32 15 04), across from the train station. Chic, comfortable hotel with A/C; some rooms overlook a peaceful private garden. Singles L55,000, with bath L95,000. Doubles L95,000, with bath L130,000. Open 24hr. V, MC, AmEx.

Hotel ABC Moderno, P. Don Leoni, 25 (tel./fax 32 50 02), across from the station. Staying at this hotel is like living in a museum—fragments of frescoes peer through the now-plaster walls, proof that the structure was once a convent. Rooms in the renovated section are pricey (singles L75,000; doubles with bath L105,000), while less expensive rooms are being phased out. Breakfast included. Extra bed L12,000. Desk open 6am-1am.

Albergo Maragò, Via Villanova De Bellis, 2, Loc. Virgiliana. Take bus 2M, which runs from P. Cavallotti into Virgiliana (every 30min. 6:30am-8pm, 10min.). The hotel is on the left, just past P. San Isidro. If you're looking for a bargain and you don't mind a 2km journey from the city center, try this hotel/restaurant; it has quiet, clean rooms. Singles L28,000. Doubles L40,000, with bath L60,000.

FOOD

4 Stagioni, Via Verdi, 5 (tel. 32 21 53), off P. Mantegna. Gorge on pizza, deli food, and seafood, all in one sitting at rock-bottom prices. *Primi* from L5000 cost less than a museum ticket, while *secondi* start at L9000.

Antica Osteria ai Ranari, Via Trieste, 11 (tel. 32 84 31), on the continuation of Via Pomponazzo, near Porto Catena. A slightly upscale place specializing in regional dishes. *Primi* L8000, *secondi* L9000-14,000. Don't leave without trying the Mantuan delight *tortelli di zucca* (ravioli with pumpkin, L10,000). Cover L2000. Open Tues.-Sun. noon-3pm and 7pm-midnight. Closed for about 3 weeks July-Aug. Call ahead for reservations. V, MC, AmEx.

Pizzeria Capri, Via Bettinelli, 8 (tel. 36 32 38), immediately on your right as you exit the train station. Specializes in Neapolitan cuisine—that means *real* pizza—and seafood. You can get a simple *margherita* (mozzarella) pizza for just L7000, or you can spring for one topped with fancy *porcini* mushrooms (L11,500). Open Fri.-Wed. noon-3:30pm and 6:30pm-midnight. V, MC, AmEx.

Self-Service Virgiliano, P. Virgiliana, 57 (tel. 32 23 77). From P. Sordello, take Via Fratelli Cairoli to P. Virgiliana; the restaurant is on the left corner. Clean and inexpensive. Full meals around L12,500. Cover L1600. Open Mon.-Fri. 11:45am-2pm.

SIGHTS AND ENTERTAINMENT

Cobblestoned **Piazza Sordello** forms the center of a vast complex built by the Gonzaga family. The **Palazzo Ducale** (tel. 32 02 83) towers over the *piazza,* a monument to Gonzagan "modesty." The 500 rooms and 15 courtyards, constructed over a period of 300 years (14th-17th centuries), now house an impressive collection of antique and Renaissance art. During its history, the palace spread tentacles out in all directions, acquiring the buildings that lay in its path, including the **Magna Domus** (*duomo*) and the **Palazzo del Capitano,** two 14th-century Gothic structures. Look beyond the *duomo*'s 18th-century façade to its Romanesque *campanile* and the Gothic elements on its side. Its interior hails from the late Renaissance, but the baptistery below the *campanile* was frescoed in the 13th century.

Near the entrance to the palace is the Hall of Dukes, where you'll find Antonio Pisanelli's frescoes (1439-44), discovered in 1969 under thick layers of plaster. The Gonzagas' Summer Room looks out onto a hanging garden (1579) bordered on three sides by a splendid portico. Stop for a short visit at the Dwarves' Apartments, tiny low rooms built as much to amuse the court as to house its substantial dwarf contingent. Formerly a fortress, the **Castello di San Giorgio** (1390-1406) is the most formidable structure in the complex, later converted into a wing of the palace. Andrea Mantegna's famed frescoes of the Gonzaga family (1474) adorn the walls of the **Camera degli Sposi** (Marriage Chamber). (The entire *palazzo* can be seen for L12,000. Open Tues.-Sat. 9am-1pm and 2:30-6pm, Sun.-Mon. 9am-1pm.)

Piazza delle Erbe, just south of P. Sordello, opens onto the **Rotonda di San Lorenzo.** The circular, 11th-century Romanesque rotunda (renovated early this century) is also known as "La Matildica" for the powerful noblewoman who bequeathed the rotunda to the pope. Opposite the rotunda rises Mantua's most important Renaissance creation, Leon Battista Alberti's **Church of Sant'Andrea** (1471-1594). The façade combines the classical triumphal arch motif—barrel-vaulted portal and flanking pilasters—with an antique, pedimented temple front. The gargantuan interior was the first monumental space constructed in the classical style since imperial Rome. The plan—a vaulted church with a single aisle, flanking side chapels, and a domed crossing—served as a prototype for ecclesiastical architecture for the next 200 years. The church's holy relic, a piece of earth believed to be soaked in Christ's blood, travels through the streets in a religious procession on Good Friday.

The **Palazzo d'Arco** (tel. 32 22 42), off Viale Ritentino, is highlighted by Falconetto's extraordinary zodiac chamber, a room with ornate frescoes of the astrological signs. From P. Mantegna, follow Via Verdi to the *palazzo.* (Palace open March-Oct. Tues.-Wed. and Fri. 9am-noon, Thurs. and Sun. 9am-noon and 3-5pm; Nov.-Feb. Sat.-Sun. 9am-noon and 2:30-4pm. Admission L5000.)

The spartan home of **Andrea Mantegna** on Via Acerbi, 47 (tel. 36 05 06) provides a contrast to the luxurious palaces and academies. Built in 1476, it frequently hosts traveling art exhibits. (The gallery is open for exhibitions daily 10am-12:30pm and 3-6pm; when there's no exhibition, open Mon.-Sat. 10am-12:30pm and Mon. and Thurs. 2-5pm. Free.) Opposite the house stands Alberti's **Church of San Sebastiano** (1460), whose Greek cross plan stimulated the Renaissance propensity for centrally planned churches.

A trek through P. Veneto and down Largo Parri leads to the opulent **Palazzo del Te** (tel. 32 32 66 or 36 58 86). Built by Giulio Romano in 1534 as a suburban retreat for Francesco II Gonzaga, the *palazzo* is widely considered the finest building of the Mannerist period. Its rooms demonstrate the late Renaissance fascination with the Roman villa type and a willingness to bend the rules of proportion. Idyllic murals of Psyche, remarkable for their vividness and eroticism, line Francesco's banquet hall. Another wing of the palace features regular shows of modern Italian artists alongside a collection of Egyptian art. (Open Tues.-Sun. 9am-6pm. Admission L12,000, under 18 and over 60 L10,000, students L5000.)

The **Teatro Sociale di Mantova,** P. Cavallotti (tel. 32 38 60), off Corso Vittorio Emanuele, stages operas in October and plays from November through May. (Seats from L20,000.) The **Spazio Aperto** series brings dance, music, and cinema events to

Holy Relic, Batman!

Little did you know that every Catholic church must be consecrated by a holy relic. In fact, Italy features a gut-wrenching assortment of saints' remains and ghastly holy bits—here is just a small sample of the wonders that await you. In addition to the **blood of Christ** here in Mantua are: the **tooth** of San Matteo in Salerno; San Geminiano's **arm, encased in silver** in Modena; the **head** of Saint Catherine in Siena; the **tongue and jawbone** of St. Antonio in Padua; the **head and blood** of San Gennaro in Naples; and the **body, (minus half a head)** of St. Andrew in Amalfi—the other half is in Greece.

various *piazze* and *palazzi* around town. Mantua also hosts a chamber music series in April and May. The **Mantua Jazz Festival** occurs at the end of July, complete with a street parade and concerts. On August 15, the **Concorso di Madonnari** in nearby Grazie di Curtatone brings out the *madonnari,* street artists whose chalky madonnas wash away with the first rains.

■ Near Mantua: Sabbioneta

Sabbioneta, 33km southwest of Mantua, is well worth a visit. Founded by Vespasiano Gonzaga (1532-91) as the home for his feudal court, Sabbioneta earned the title "Little Athens of the Gonzagas" because of its importance as an artistic center in the late Renaissance. Inside the well-preserved 16th-century city walls lie the fascinating, Renaissance **Palazzo Ducale, Teatro Olimpico,** and **Palazzo del Giardino.** Only the guided walk enables you to visit their otherwise inaccessible interiors. This 45min. tour in Italian (L10,000) leaves roughly every 20min. from the **tourist office,** Via Vespasiano Gonzaga, 31 (tel. (0375) 520 39). Open Tues.-Sat. 9:30am-12:30pm and 2:30-5:30pm, Sun. 9:30am-12:30pm and 2:30-6:30pm. In summer Sabbioneta stages a **Festival di Musica e Danza,** and from mid-March to mid-April, antique aficionados come for the exhaustive **Mercato dell'Antiquariato.**

Bergamo

Every city should have a castle in the clouds. Glimmering in the distance, an entire medieval city is nestled in the hills over Bergamo, complete with palaces, churches, and a huge stone fortification. The appropriately named *città alta* ("high city") recalls the town's origins with its narrow, cobblestone streets shaded by solemn, ecclesiastical façades. Below, the rapid-paced *città bassa* ("low city") is a modern metropolis. In one glance, visitors observe hundreds of years of heritage in this bustling commercial, artistic, and industrial center.

ORIENTATION AND PRACTICAL INFORMATION

Poised at the juncture of the Brembana and Seriana valleys, Bergamo is a short train ride from Milan, Brescia, and Cremona. The train station, the bus station, and numerous budget hotels are in the **città bassa.** To get to the more attractive **città alta,** take bus #1 or 3 (L1300) to the funicular, a cable-style lift, that ascends from **Viale Vittorio Emanuele II** to the **Mercato delle Scarpe** (every 15min., L1300). You can purchase a bus ticket and continue on the funicular without paying twice. Alternatively, you can rise to the challenge of the old footpath starting behind the funicular station on Viale Vittorio Emanuele II (10-20min.).

Tourist Office: In the *città bassa:* **APT** (tel. 24 29 94), straight ahead through P. Marconi from the train station, on the left. The friendly staff can provide you with a useful map. Open daily 9am-12:30pm and 2:50-7:30pm. In the *città alta:* **APT,** Vicolo Aquila Nera, 2 (tel. 23 27 30), off P. Vecchia. Open daily 9am-12:30pm and 2:50-7:30pm.

Currency Exchange: Banca Nazionale del Lavoro, Via Petrarca, 12 (tel. 39 81 11), off Viale Vittorio Emanuele II near P. della Libertà. Good rates. Open Mon.-Tues. and Thurs.-Fri. 8:20am-1:20pm and 3-4:30pm, Wed. 8:20am-5:50pm. Also in the office on the second floor of the **post office.** Open Mon.-Fri. 8:15am-5:30pm, Sat. 8:15am-1pm.

Telephones: Largo Porta Nuova, 1 (tel. 21 92 95), where Viale Papa Giovanni XXIII becomes Viale Vittorio Emanuele II. Open Mon.-Fri. 9am-12:30pm and 2:30-6pm.

Telegrams: Via Masone 2A (tel. 21 22 70), upstairs at the post office.

Trains: P. Marconi (tel. 24 76 24). To: Milan (every hr., 1hr., L5000); Brescia (19 per day, 1hr., L4200); Cremona (5 per day, 1½hr., L7200). Roundtrips are double the price. Reservation office open daily 5:50am-8:45pm. Information open daily 9:30am-noon and 2:30-4:30pm. **Luggage Storage:** L5000 for 12hr. Open 7am-9pm.

Buses: (tel. 24 81 50), across from the train station. To: Milan (every 30min. 5:40am-10:30pm, L7000); Cremona (every 30min. 5:05am-7:30pm, L8400); Como (9 per day 6:55am-6:20pm, L7500); Brescia (8 per day 6:50am-6:45pm, L6500).

Emergencies: tel. 118. **First Aid:** daytime tel. 26 91 11, at night or on Sun. tel. 25 02 46. **Ambulance: Croce Bianca Città di Bergamo,** tel. 118 or 31 68 88. **Hospital: Ospedale Riuniti,** Largo Barozzi, 1 (tel. 26 91 11).

Police: Via T. Tasso, 1 (tel. 24 91 49).

Post Office: Via Masone, 2A (tel. 21 22 70), at Via Locatelli. Take Via Zelasco from Viale Vittorio Emanuele II. Open Mon.-Sat. 8:15am-8pm. Packages are handled at Via Pascoli, 6 (tel. 23 86 98). Same hours as main office. **Postal Code:** 24122

Telephone Code: 035.

ACCOMMODATIONS

In general, the higher the altitude, the higher the price. The most affordable *alberghi* are in the *città bassa.* Ask at the tourist office about *agriturismo* and other alternatives.

Ostello Città di Bergamo (HI), Via G. Ferraris, 1 (tel./fax 36 17 24). Take bus #14 from Porta Nuova to Leonardo da Vinci. Yes, that's it, way in the distance. Although far from the action of the city, the hostel has everything imaginable—TV with satellite, gardens, and a full-service kitchen. Renovated last year, the rooms are still in mint condition and are antiseptically clean. English spoken. L22,000 per person, breakfast included. Private singles L30,000. Doubles L50,000. All private rooms with bath.

Albergo S. Giorgio, Via S. Giorgio, 10 (tel. 21 20 43; fax 31 00 72), about a 15-min. walk from the train station. Go left on Via Pietro Paleocopa, which becomes Via S. Giorgio after a few blocks. It's a short walk, but take bus #7 if you must. Although near train tracks and a construction site, the hotel is relatively quiet inside. Neat, modern rooms with TV, telephone, and sink. 37 rooms, 2 are wheelchair accessible. English spoken. Singles L30,000, with bath L46,000. Doubles L58,000, with bath L75,000. Reservations helpful but not required. V, MC.

Locanda Caironi, Via Torretta, 6 (tel. 24 30 83), off Via Borgo Palazzo. A 20-min. walk, or take bus #5, 7, or 8 from Via Angelo Maj. A family-run affair in a quiet residential neighborhood. The *trattoria* downstairs is considered one of Bergamo's best-kept culinary secrets. Singles L20,000. Doubles L35,000.

FOOD

Casonsei, a meat-filled ravioli dish, is a *bergamasco* gastronomic delight, as are the *branzi* and *taleggio* cheeses. Try them with the local *Valcalepio* red and white wines. The typical meal is accompanied by *polenta,* a staple food made from corn meal and water. Streets in the *città alta* are lined with *pasticcerie* selling yellow *polentina* confections topped with chocolate blobs intended to resemble birds. But beware of these sweet (and pricey) tourist treats: many natives have never even tried them. For necessities, shop at **Roll Market,** on the right side of Viale Vittorio Emanuele II just at the bottom of the hill heading to the *città alta.* Open Mon. 8:30am-1:15pm, Tues.-Sat. 8:30am-1:15pm and 3:30-8pm.

Keep in mind that most of Bergamo's shops are closed Monday mornings.

Città Bassa

Capolinea, Via Giacomo Quarenghi, 29 (tel. 32 09 81), off Via Zambonate. Follow Via Tiraboschi from Porta Nuova. A favorite among Bergamo's young people, this modern establishment has an energetic bar in the front and quieter restaurant in the back. Full meal from L15,000 and sandwiches from L3500. Salads large enough for a meal from L4500. Open Tues.-Sun. 11am-3pm and 6pm-2am.

Trattoria Casa Mia, Via S. Bernardino, 20 (tel. 22 06 76), off Via Zambonate. Follow Via Tiraboschi from Porta Nuova. Get a full meal "home style" (*primo, secondo,* side dish, and drink) for L15,000. Nothing fancy, just solidly good food so fresh you can hear the chef pounding the veal with a hammer in the kitchen. The trattoria draws a largely male crowd. Open Sept.-July, Mon.-Sat. 8am-3pm and 5:30-10:30pm.

Ristorante Self-Service Pastimbaldo, Via Taramelli, 23/B (tel. 22 07 55). From the station, walk down Viale Papa Giovanni XXIII, turn right on Via San Francesco d'Assisi, then turn left onto V. Taramelli. Low prices and satisfying dishes draw both students and business types. *Primi* from L4000, *secondi* from L6500. Pizza around L6000. Open Mon.-Fri. 11:45am-3pm, Sun. 11:45am-3pm and 6:30-11pm. V, MC.

Città Alta

Though you may withstand the temptations of the first bakery you pass on Via Colleoni or Via Gombito, be prepared to undergo the same trial at 20m intervals. Scattered among the many *pasticcerie,* however, are a number of reasonably priced restaurants offering more substantial food.

Papageno Pub, Via Colleoni, 1b (tel. 23 66 24). The light but filling sandwiches and *bruschetta* (L5000) are the ideal complement to this bar's main attraction: drinks. Eat a small lunch, grab some energy-enhancing tea (L6000), and hit every museum in town before dusk.

Trattoria Bernabò, Via Colleoni, 31 (tel. 23 76 92), past P. Vecchia. Every fast-food Italian restaurant outside of Italy seems modeled after this quintessential trattoria. Savor the red-checked tablecloths, wood-burning ovens, and painted landscapes. An extensive menu (starting at L15,000) provides almost every Italian delicacy you could imagine—and some you couldn't. Try the *brasato di asino* (donkey in vegetable sauce). Open Sept.-June Fri.-Wed. noon-2:30pm and 7-11:30pm. V, MC.

Trattoria 3 Torri, P. Mercato del Fieno, 7/A (tel. 24 43 66), a left off Via Gombito when heading away from P. Vecchia. This corner establishment entertains with elegance and is always full. (There are only seven tables, but outside seating is also available May-Sept.) Try the *polenta* (L15,000). *Menù* around L30,000, but *primi* begin at L8000. Cover L2000. Open Thurs.-Tues. noon-4pm and 7:30pm-midnight. Reservations recommended. V, MC.

Circolino Cooperativa Città Alta, Via S. Agata, 19 (tel. 21 57 41 or 22 58 76). This former prison is now a favorite of old and young alike. Offers sandwiches, pizzas, and salads for under L7000. Play cards, pinball, and *bocce,* an Italian game similar to bowling (but taken much more seriously). Thurs.-Tues. L4000 during the day; L5000 at night. Wed. free. Tennis shoes required. Restaurant open Thurs.-Tues. 9am-2am.

SIGHTS

Città Bassa

Begin a tour of the city at **P. Matteotti** in the heart of the *città bassa,* a favorite meeting place for tourists and native *passeggiatori* alike. In the **Church of San Bartolomeo,** at the far right of the *piazza,* you will find a superb altarpiece of the *Madonna and Child* by Lorenzo Lotto. To the right of San Bartolomeo, Via Tasso leads to the **Church of Santo Spirito,** marked by its strangely-sculpted façade. Its fine Renaissance interior (1521) houses paintings by famous dead Italians.

Via Pignolo connects the lower city with the upper, winding past a succession of handsome, 16th- to 18th-century palaces. Along the way is the tiny **Church of San Bernardino,** whose colorful interior pales behind a splendid painting by Lotto. Turning right on Via San Tommaso brings you to the astounding **Galleria dell'Accademia Carrara** (tel. 39 94 50), one of the most important art galleries in Italy. Housed in a glorious neoclassical palace, the 15 rooms of the second floor display works by virtually all the Italian notables as well as the canvases of Breughel, van Dyck, and El Greco. (Open Wed.-Mon. 9:30am-12:30pm and 2:30-5:30pm. Admission L3000, students with ID L2000, under 18 and over 65 free; free for everyone on Sun.)

Città Alta

In contrast to the modern city below, the *città alta* is a wonderfully preserved medieval town with a photo opportunity at every corner. The town is accessible by both funicular and foot. From the Carrara gallery, the terraced Via Noca ascends from the lower city to **Porta Sant'Agostino,** a 16th-century gate built by the Venetians as fortification. After going through the gate, follow Via Porta Dipinta to the heart of the *città alta,* passing two notable churches: the Romanesque **Church of San Michele al Pozzo Bianco** (12th-13th centuries), decorated inside with colorful frescoes by Lotto (open daily 8:30am-4pm), and the neoclassical **Church of Sant'Andrea,** adorned with an altarpiece by Moretto. The street continues as Via Gombito when it passes a massive 12th-century tower of the same name. The centrally located **Porta San Giacomo** provides convenient access to the *città bassa* below.

Via Gambito ends in **Piazza Vecchia,** a majestic ensemble of medieval and Renaissance buildings flanked by restaurants and *caffè*—and a prime location for people-watching. Rest your legs as you sit on the steps of the white marble **Biblioteca Civica** (1594), repository of Bergamo's rich collection of manuscripts, modeled after Venice's Sansovino Library. Across the *piazza* is the massive **Palazzo della Ragione** (Courts of Justice, 1199) and a 300-year-old sundial still in working order. To the right, and connected to the *palazzo* by a 16th-century covered stairway, stands the 12th-century **Torre Civica** (Civic Tower). (Open April-Oct. daily 10am-noon and 2-8pm.) The view from the top is well worth the climb, but protect your eardrums: in addition to the traditional curfew sounded by the 15th-century clock at 10pm, the bells ring on the hour.

A passage between the two buildings leads to **Piazza del Duomo.** Ahead is the awe-inspiring, multicolored marble façade of the masterful **Colleoni Chapel** (1476). It was designed by G. A. Amadeo (also responsible for the Charterhouse of Pavia) as a tomb and chapel for the celebrated Venetian mercenary Bartolomeo Colleoni. (Open April-Oct. daily 9am-noon and 2-6:30pm; Nov.-March 9am-noon and 2:30-4:30pm.) To the right of the chapel is the octagonal **baptistery,** featuring a red marble gallery. It is actually a reconstruction of a 14th-century baptistery that once stood as part of the **Basilica of Santa Maria Maggiore.** This basilica, adjoining the Colleoni Chapel to the left and constructed in the second half of the 12th century, is distinguished by its stark Romanesque exterior that sharply contrasts with its ornate Baroque interior. Other points of interest include the Victorian tomb of the 19th-century composer Gaetano Donizetti. (Basilica open Mon.-Sat. 8:30am-noon and 3-6pm, Sun. 10am-noon and 3-6pm.)

For a romantic conclusion to the tour, return to P. Mercato delle Scarpe and proceed left on Via alla Rocca. Situated on a site fortified since Roman times, the present Rocca is home to the **Museo del Risorgimento,** currently under restoration. The surrounding trees, flowers, and shady paths have been dubbed the **Parco delle Rimembranze** in honor of soldiers who have died in battle.

Throughout the year, Bergamo is a thriving center for the arts. The opera season lasts from September to November and is followed from November through April by the drama season, featuring Italy's most prestigious companies at the **Donizetti Theater.** In May and June, the spotlight falls on the highly acclaimed **Festivale Pianistico Internazionale,** co-hosted with Brescia. In September, Bergamo unabashedly celebrates its premier native-born composer with a festival of Gaetano Donizetti's lesser-known works. For further information, contact the tourist office or the theater itself at P. Cavour, 14 (tel. 24 96 31). In summer, the city council offers *Viva La Tua Città,* a program of free events. Ask at the tourist office for a pamphlet.

Brescia

Grab your Armani suit and head straight to Brescia. Although styles and tastes have changed over the years, relative prosperity has been the city's constant. Today, Brescia owes its place in the prosperous Lombard economy to the production of weapons and sink fixtures, endowing Brescia with the frenetic pace of a modern industrial center (or a public bathroom). At the center of the city, an avenue of ultra-elite shops and *caffè* links to smaller streets with even more elegant (and affordable) churches, *piazze,* and museums. These tiny streets make Brescia a walker's paradise where all of the sites are easily absorbed, digested, and flushed out of your system in time for more (much like a public bathroom).

ORIENTATION AND PRACTICAL INFORMATION

Brescia is between Milan (1hr.) and Verona (45min.) on the direct train line from Torino to Trieste and is the main point of departure for buses to the western shores of Lake Garda. Most of the city's architectural gems are concentrated in the thoroughly rectangular, *piazza*-packed *centro storico.* You can reach **P. della Repubblica** at the southwest corner of the *centro* by taking **Corso Martiri della Libertà** to **Corso Palestro.** Continuing diagonally through the *piazze,* you will eventually come to two aptly named streets: **Via del Castello** and **Via dei Musei.** The first leads uphill to the castle; the latter slopes down to "museum row" and the Roman archaeological site.

Tourist Office: APT, Corso Zanardelli, 34 (tel. 434 18; fax 29 32 84), across from the intersection where C. Palestro becomes C. Zanardelli en route to the city center. Set off slightly from the street, on the right. Helpful map and walking guides to the city available. Open Mon.-Fri. 9am-12:30pm and 3-6pm, Sat. 9am-12:30pm.

Currency Exchange: There are many banks in the area, including **Banco San Paolo de Brescia,** Corso Martiri della Libertà, 13 (tel. 299 21). Open Mon.-Fri. 8:25am-1:25pm and 2:40-4pm, Sat. 8:40am-12:30 pm. The *cambio* is inside to the right. The exchange window at the **post office** is inside to the right at #3.

Telephones: Via Moretto, 46 (tel. 375 12 74). Open Mon.-Fri. 9am-12:30pm and 2:30-6pm.

Trains: The short street called Viale Stazione connects the station to **P. della Repubblica.** To: Milan (every hr., 1hr., L7200); Verona (every hr., 45min., L5700); Venice (every hr., 2¼hr., L15,500); Bergamo (15 per day, 1hr., L4200); Padua (every hr., 1¾hr., L11,700); Vicenza (every hr., 1¼hr., L9800); Cremona (every 2 hr., 1¾hr., L5000). No roundtrip discount. Information open daily 8am-noon and 3-6pm. **Luggage Storage:** L5000 for 12hr. Open 7am-8pm.

Buses: (tel. 375 10 00 or 240 04 08), on Via Stazione. East-bound buses are opposite the train station in a bright orange building. West-bound buses leave from the **SIA** station just to the left of the train station. To: Milan (7am, 9am, and 5:50pm, 1¾hr., L11,100); Verona (every hr. starting at 7:15am, 2¼hr., L9500); Mantua (every 2hr., 1½hr., L8700); and Cremona (every hr., 1¼hr., L7100). Ticket office open Mon.-Sat. 6:30am-7pm.

Emergencies: tel. 113. **First Aid:** tel. 242 45 55. **Ambulance: Croce Bianca,** tel. 442 44. **Hospital: Ospedale Civile,** tel. 399 51.

Police: (tel. 425 61), on Via Botticelli.

Post Office: P. Vittoria, 1 (tel. 375 40 70). Stamps and *fermo posta* at #6 (in the room to the left). Open Mon.-Fri. 8:15am-5:30pm, Sat. 8:15am-1pm. **Postal Code:** 12001.

Telephone Code: 030.

ACCOMMODATIONS

Accommodations are reasonably priced in Brescia, but weekend rooms often fill during the week. Call a week ahead for reservations. You'll be fortunate to find any sort of bargain in the historic center. Inquire at the tourist office about *agriturismo*.

Servizio della Giovane (ACISJF), Via Bronzetti, 17 (office in the train station; tel. 375 50 40). From the station, take Viale Stazione to P. della Repubblica and pick up Via dei Mille on the far side. Via Bronzetti is on the right after a couple of blocks. Women only. Run by wholesome nuns. The spotless bathrooms connect to triples so newly furnished they look like promotional photos. Kitchen facilities. Curfew 10pm. L12,000 per person, sheets included. Call ahead for reservations.

Albergo Rigamonti, Via Mansione, 8 (tel. 481 52). From the station, follow Viale Stazione to P. della Repubblica. Take Corso G. Matteotti on the far side and turn right on Via Mansione. Also houses Albergo Mansione. Modern, tidy, and respectable. TV room, bar, and car park. Singles L32,000, with bath L47,000. Doubles L55,000, with bath L65,000. Towels provided. Open 6:15am-midnight.

Albergo San Marco, Via Spalto S. Marco, 15 (tel. 455 41). From the station take Via Foppa and turn right on Via XX Settembre. Make the next left, and turn right onto Via Vittorio Emanuele, which continues to the hotel. Rooms are clean, but stuffy in the summer. Lots of noise from the traffic below. Towels provided. Singles L30,000. Doubles L51,000. Breakfast may be purchased at the bar for L3000.

FOOD

Open-air vendors vend in the open air in P. Rovetta and P. Vittoria (normally in P. Mercato, but it is under construction) Tuesday through Friday roughly 8:30am-6pm. For grocery items, **SuperScontro** at Corso Martiri della Libertà, 26 should suffice. Open Mon. 8:30am-1:30pm, Tues.-Sun. 8:30am-1:30pm and 2:30-8pm. Whatever and wherever you choose to eat, or even if you're not eating at all, be sure to sample some of the local wines. *Tocai di San Martino della Battaglia,* a dry white wine, *groppello,* a medium red, and *botticino,* a dry red of medium age, are all favorites in Brescia and beyond.

Ristorante/Pizzeria Cavour, Corso Cavour, 56 (tel. 240 09 00), off Corso Magenta. Great pizza and pasta dishes at reasonable prices. *Pizza margherita* L6500; *primi* L7500-13,000. Try the *gnocchi alla gorgonzola* (L8000), or, for macaroni-and-cheese-lovers, the *penne 4 formaggio* (L8000), which beats Kraft any day. Cover L3000. Open Wed.-Mon. 10:30am-3pm and 6pm-midnight.

Ristorante San Marco, Via Spalto S. Marco, 15 (tel. 455 41), on a continuation of Via Vittorio Emanuele II. The wooden ceiling-beams and whitewashed walls create a cheerful atmosphere. *Primi* (from L9000) are large enough for a meal. *Secondi* from L14,000. Cover L3000. Open daily noon-2:30pm and 7:30-10pm.

Trattoria Al Frate, Via Musei, 25 (tel. 375 14 69), by the base of the hill to the castle. Satisfying portions. The ever-present drinkers who rise only for a refill are a living testament to the fine wines. *Primi* L10,000. *Secondi* are pricier. Wine from L10,000 per liter. Cover L3500. Open Tues.-Sun. 12:30-2:30pm and 7:30pm-12:30am.

Vittoria Mix, Via IV Novembre, 2, at the intersection of Via delle X Giornati, under the arcade. Italy's version of a mall food court, Vittoria Mix houses the national chains **Burghy** (burgers for about L3000), **Spizzico** (pizza for about L4000), and **Ciao** (*primi* from L4400 and *secondi* from L6200). At least one of the restaurants will be open Tues.-Sun. 10am-11pm.

SIGHTS AND ENTERTAINMENT

Some of the museums of Brescia got together and settled on a standard museum admission (L5000; under 16, over 65, and organized student groups free), as well as a standard set of hours (June-Sept. Tues.-Fri. 10am-12:30pm and 3-6pm, Sat.-Sun. 10am-12:30pm and 3-7pm; Oct.-May Tues.-Fri. 9am-12:30pm and 3-5pm, Sat.-Sun. 9am-12:30pm and 3-6pm). They've also implemented a **museum "hotline,"** the *Centro Museale Bresciano* (tel. 443 27). All groups are *required* to call in advance. In this section, museums belonging to the *centro* will be marked with an asterisk.

Beginning on Corso Palestro, buy yourself a pair of leather shoes and walk to the gigantic **Piazza della Vittoria.** Continue past the post office to the more important **Piazza della Loggia,** built when Venice ruled the city. On one side of the square stands the **Torre dell'Orologio,** modeled after the clock tower in Venice's Piazza San Marco, complete with an astronomic clock boasting suns and stars. Across from the tower, the Renaissance **loggia** (arcade), currently under renovation, houses special exhibitions and lesser-known paintings from the 16th century.

Next, go through the archways and follow the intimate paths from the clocktower to the **Piazza Paolo IV** or **Piazza Duomo.** (The people of Brescia were not content with only one *duomo,* so they built two—hence two names for the square.) Contrast the new and the old, the grandiose and the simple, in the façades of the **Duomo Nuovo** (1604-1825), an intricate structure dominated by overwhelming marble statues, and the **Rotunda** (the old *duomo*), a refreshingly simple Romanesque building with uneven windows scattered about the brick walls.

Exit the *piazza* on the same street you entered it, but turn right on Via dei Musei. Fragments of Brescia's classical roots as the Roman colony of Brixia lie buried beneath the overgrown plant life. Between the large, dark buildings stand the remaining pieces of Emperor Vespasian's vast **Tempio Capitolino.*** Upstairs is a small museum with mosaics, a medieval road map, and excellent bronzes. A few paces farther down the Via dei Musei, you'll find the **Monastery of San Salvatore and Santa Giulia,*** the final retreat of Charlemagnes's ex-wife Esmengarda. Its greatest treasure is the 8th-century Cross of Desiderius, encased in silver and encrusted with hundreds of jewels and cameos. From the Tempio Capitolino, walk through Piazza Foro to Via Gallo, which becomes Via Crispi and leads to Brescia's principal attraction, the **Pinacoteca Tosio-Martinengo.*** This unadorned, 22-room palazzo displays a fine collection of works by Brescian masters (notably Moretto), but better still is Raphael's *Cristo benedicente.* There are also first-rate works by Veneziano, Tintoretto, Clouet, Vincenzo Foppa, and Lorenzo Lotto.

Brescia has various attractions within short walking distance of the *centro storico.* Rather than fret, strummers should check out the **Museo della Chitarra** (Guitar Museum), Via Trieste, 34. (Open Mon.-Fri. 2:30-7:30pm. Free.) If you have more time and sequoia-like legs, visit the **castello** hovering on the high ground behind the Via dei Musei. If you *still* have energy after the 350+ step climb, walk to the **Museo del Risorgimento,** the **Luigi Marzoli Museo di Armi** (Museum of Arms), and the **osservatorio,** complete with camera-ready views of Brescia and its tiny surrounding communities.

The bulk of Brescia's high-brow cultural events takes place in the splendor of the **Teatro Grande.** The annual **Stagione di Prosa,** a long-running series of dramatic performances, takes place from December to April. From April to June, the focus shifts to the **Festivale Pianistico Internazionale,** co-hosted by nearby Bergamo. **Estate Aperta** includes an impressive series of concerts, theatrical performances, and films held June through September in churches, courtyards, and *piazze.* Pick up a schedule at the tourist office, or call the coordinating forces at the **Centro Teatrale Bresciano** (tel. 377 11 11).

Veneto

It is the variation, more than any overarching similarity, that best defines the character of the cities and towns of the Veneto. The region encompasses a wide range of geographical terrains, from the rocky foothills of the Dolomites and the Alps to the fertile valleys of the Po River. Although these territories were loosely linked under the Venetian Empire, the effect on local cultures was negligible. Northern cities, especially, fell under the influence of nearby Austria. Regional dialects flourish in the Veneto, yet another sign of the relative isolation in which the towns developed.

Today, the cities of the Veneto belong to the most touristed region in Italy, thanks in great part to the belle of the north, Venice. Otherwise, a sense of local culture and custom remains quite strong in each town of the region; visitors to the Veneto may well be shocked by the wealth of distinct personalities.

Venice (Venezia)

She is the Shakespeare of cities—unchallenged, incomparable, and beyond envy.

—John Addington Symonds

With glass windows open like eyes under delicately arched brows, the buildings of Venice watch over the waters in utter calmness. Venetians have good reason to call their city *La Serenissima*—the most serene. Venice awakes each morning with a refreshing absence of the speeding cars and roaring mopeds that infest other Italian cities. Her citizens make their way on foot or by boat through an ancient maze of narrow streets and winding canals. Unfortunately, the serenity is now broken by swarms of tourists that collect in the *campi* (squares) and thoroughfares of the city, searching out its wealth of museums and landmarks. These visitors often overlook the real Venice, which lies hidden in the romantic back streets and residential quarters of the city.

Driven first by Attila's hordes, then by conquering Lombards, Roman refugees joined fishermen on the low barrier islands of the swampy lagoon. An unsuccessful attack by Charlemagne in 810 led to the settlement of the inner islands that constitute the modern city. In 828, two Venetian merchants stole St. Mark's remains from Alexandria and established the city's eminence under a new patron saint. By the 11th century, ties to Constantinople and marine prowess had established Venice as the dominant middleman for trade with the Middle East. In 1204, Venice sent the penniless armies of the Fourth Crusade to raid Constantinople; the spoils of this campaign filled Venetian squares and treasuries with new prosperity. After consolidating its oligarchic government in the 14th century, the Venetian Republic defeated its rival Genoa in 1380 and expanded onto the Italian mainland. Over the next three centuries, jealous European powers to the west and unstoppable Ottoman Turks to the east whittled away *La Serenissima's* empire, while the discovery of ocean routes to the Far East robbed it of its monopoly on Asian trade. By the time Napoleon conquered it in 1797, idle Venice was little more than a decadent playground. French and Austrian rule capped off the glory days as the development of industry at Mestre drew away the archipelago's working population.

Today Venice consists of two worlds, hosting tourists and cameras from around the globe in Piazza San Marco and housing locals in the sparsely populated back streets of Cannaregio and the Ghetto. Uniting them are the architectural gems of a glorious past and the intertwining canals, the true arteries of the city.

ORIENTATION

Venice comprises 117 bodies of land distributed throughout the Venetian lagoon and is protected from the Adriatic by the Lido, an island which lies 2km farther out to sea. A 4km causeway links the urban center to the mainland. The **Santa Lucia train station** lies on the northwestern edge of the city, while the garages, car rentals, and bus terminals are across the Grand Canal in nearby **Piazzale Roma**—the last stop for all land-bound transportation. If you're in a rush to get to **Piazza San Marco** (and the central tourist office) from the station or P. Roma, take *vaporetto* #82. For a splendid introduction to the *palazzi* along the Grand Canal, take #1. If you prefer to hoof it, the 40-min. walk to San Marco starts left of the station on Lista di Spagna and follows the signs (and the crowds).

Yellow signs placed around Venice guide you to the Rialto (the bridge connecting San Marco and San Polo), the Accademia (Dorsoduro), San Marco (at the border of San Marco and Castello), P. Roma (Santa Croce), and the *ferrovia* (train station in Cannaregio). They can help you navigate the labyrinth of Venice from one end to the other, yet in doing so they can actually take you on a longer route. Moreover, these signs are the leading cause of the "pedestrian freeway" phenomenon. Liberate yourself with a real map. **Do not rely on the freebies at the tourist office, the oversimplified maps from the AmEx office, or even the one in this book.** The detailed, color-coded *Storti Edizioni* map-guide of Venice (L5000, available at newsstands and *tabacchi*) shows all the major streets and has an invaluable street index. You *will* get lost in Venice, but with a good map in hand you may not feel so helpless. Don't despair: wandering from the main pathways will reward you with cheaper prices, local hangouts, quiet *campi*, beautiful vistas, and friendly Venetians. It is true that many of the sights cluster around the Grand Canal, but it is easy enough to choose a route, find the site, and then return back to the tranquil waterways. When in doubt, check the sun and just wander in the direction you need to go.

Orientation begins with a fundamental comprehension of the **sestieri,** the sections of the city. Within each area, there are no individual street numbers but merely one long and haphazard sequence of numbers (roughly 6000 per *sestiere*). Every building, however, is also located on some type of a "street"—*fondamente, calli, campi, salizzade, canali, rii, ponti,* and *rii terrà,* (foundations, narrow streets, squares, paved roads, channels, small channels, bridges, and old channels that are now streets, respectively). To add to the confusion, it is often unclear which *sestiere* you are in at any given moment, as the boundaries are not clearly indicated. *Let's Go* supplies the *sestiere,* the number, the street name when possible, and supplements this information with some basic directions—beyond that, try asking locals.

The **Grand Canal,** the central artery of Venice, can be crossed on foot only at the **ponti** (bridges) of **Scalzi, Rialto,** and **Accademia.** *Traghetti* (gondola-like ferry boats) may seem too picturesque for practical use, but in fact they are used fairly frequently for canal crossings where there is no bridge. North of the Canal, from the station to about the Rio dei Santi Apostoli, lies the *sestiere* of **Cannaregio.** Continuing clockwise around the Canal, **Castello** is just south of the Rio di S. Giovanni Crisostomo, and **San Marco** extends from the Mercerie and P. San Marco to the Ponte Accademia. The easternmost extension of Venice is the *sestiere* of **Santa Elena.** Cross the Rialto bridge from P. San Bartolomeo, and you will find yourself in the **San Polo** district. West of San Polo and encompassing Piazzale Roma is the *sestiere* of **Santa Croce.** Now trace an imaginary line from Cà Rezzonico on the Grand Canal to the church of Santa Maria Maggiore on the *rio* of the same name: the land south of this line and hooking around to the Punta della Dogana is **Dorsoduro.**

High tides (usually November-April) cause *acque alte,* periodic floodings that swamp parts of the city (notably San Marco) under as much as three feet of water. If you don't like wet feet, check ahead with the tourist office and consult the signs posted at all ACTV landing stages. *Acque alte* usually last two to three hours, during which time planks or platforms are laid out across most major thoroughfares.

If you plan to drive to Venice, take the "Ponte della Libertà" causeway, which ends in P. Roma. Parking facilities can be found in P. Roma in the garages *comunale* and San Marco, with additional parking on the adjacent island of Tronchetto (follow the road signs). Parking on the Tronchetto "car park island" could cost you as much as L37,000 per day, while parking in the garages at the P. Roma runs up to L45,000 for 24hr. Motorists should consider leaving their cars in the parking lot at the Mestre train station on the mainland and taking a train into Venice. (All trains into and out of Venice stop at Mestre.)

Vaporetti

The alternative to walking is taking the **vaporetti,** motorboat buses that cruise the Venetian waterways. (They are also inexpensive, yet less romantic, substitutes for the *gondole*.) Most principal boats run 24 hours, with less frequent service after 11pm. A single-ride ticket costs L4000. If you plan to move around the city a lot, or if you are staying on one of the islands, you might consider purchasing an extended pass. A 24-hour *biglietto turistico,* available at any ticket office, allows you unlimited travel on all boats (L15,000). You can also purchase a three-day ticket for L30,000. The ACTV office offers a special three-day ticket for holders of the **Rolling Venice Card** for L20,000 (see **Practical Information: Tourist Offices** below).

Not all stations sell tickets all the time—buy extras, and be sure to get the type that can be machine-validated upon boarding. You can buy tickets at the booths in front

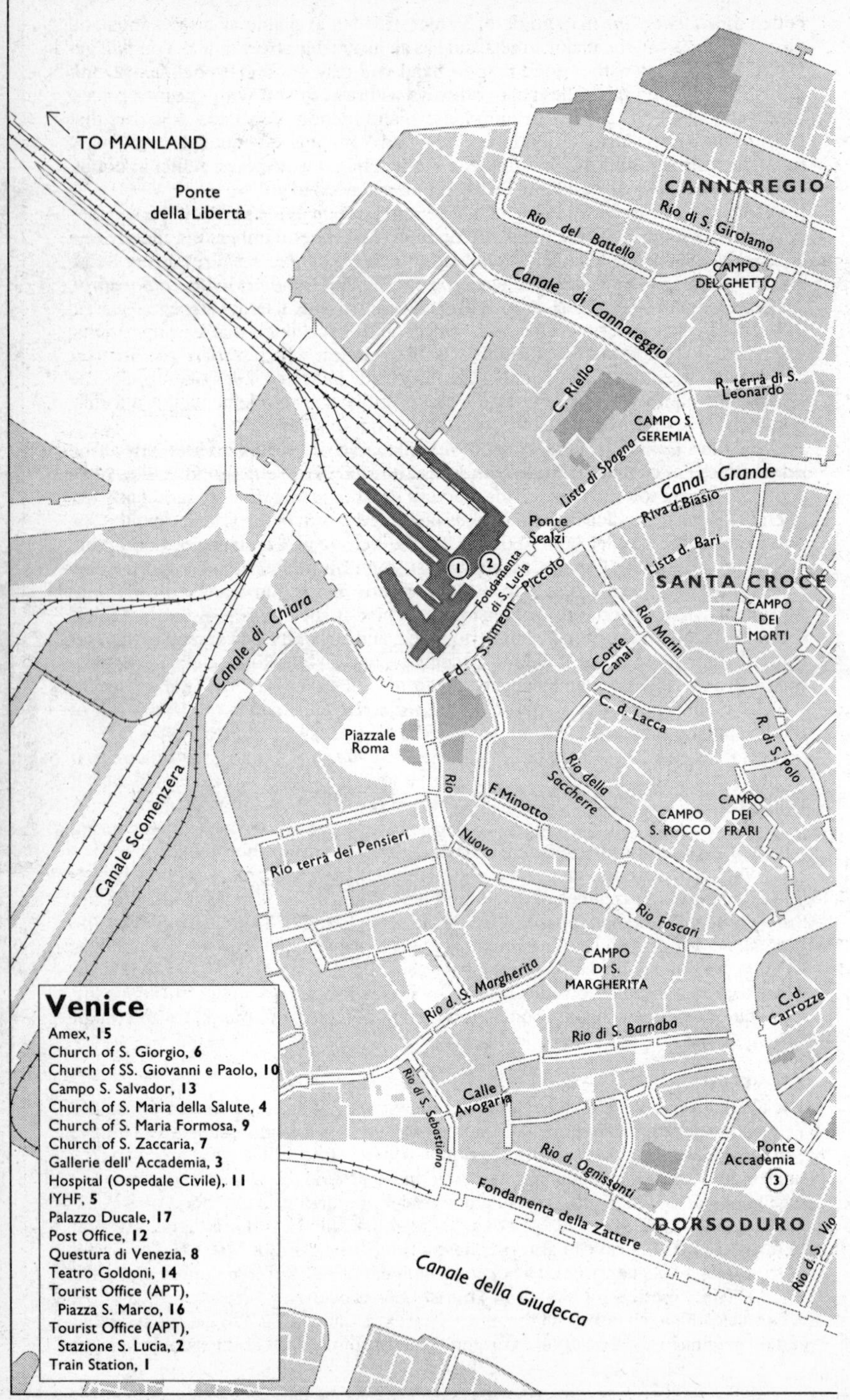

Venice

Amex, **15**
Church of S. Giorgio, **6**
Church of SS. Giovanni e Paolo, **10**
Campo S. Salvador, **13**
Church of S. Maria della Salute, **4**
Church of S. Maria Formosa, **9**
Church of S. Zaccaria, **7**
Gallerie dell' Accademia, **3**
Hospital (Ospedale Civile), **11**
IYHF, **5**
Palazzo Ducale, **17**
Post Office, **12**
Questura di Venezia, **8**
Teatro Goldoni, **14**
Tourist Office (APT), Piazza S. Marco, **16**
Tourist Office (APT), Stazione S. Lucia, **2**
Train Station, **1**

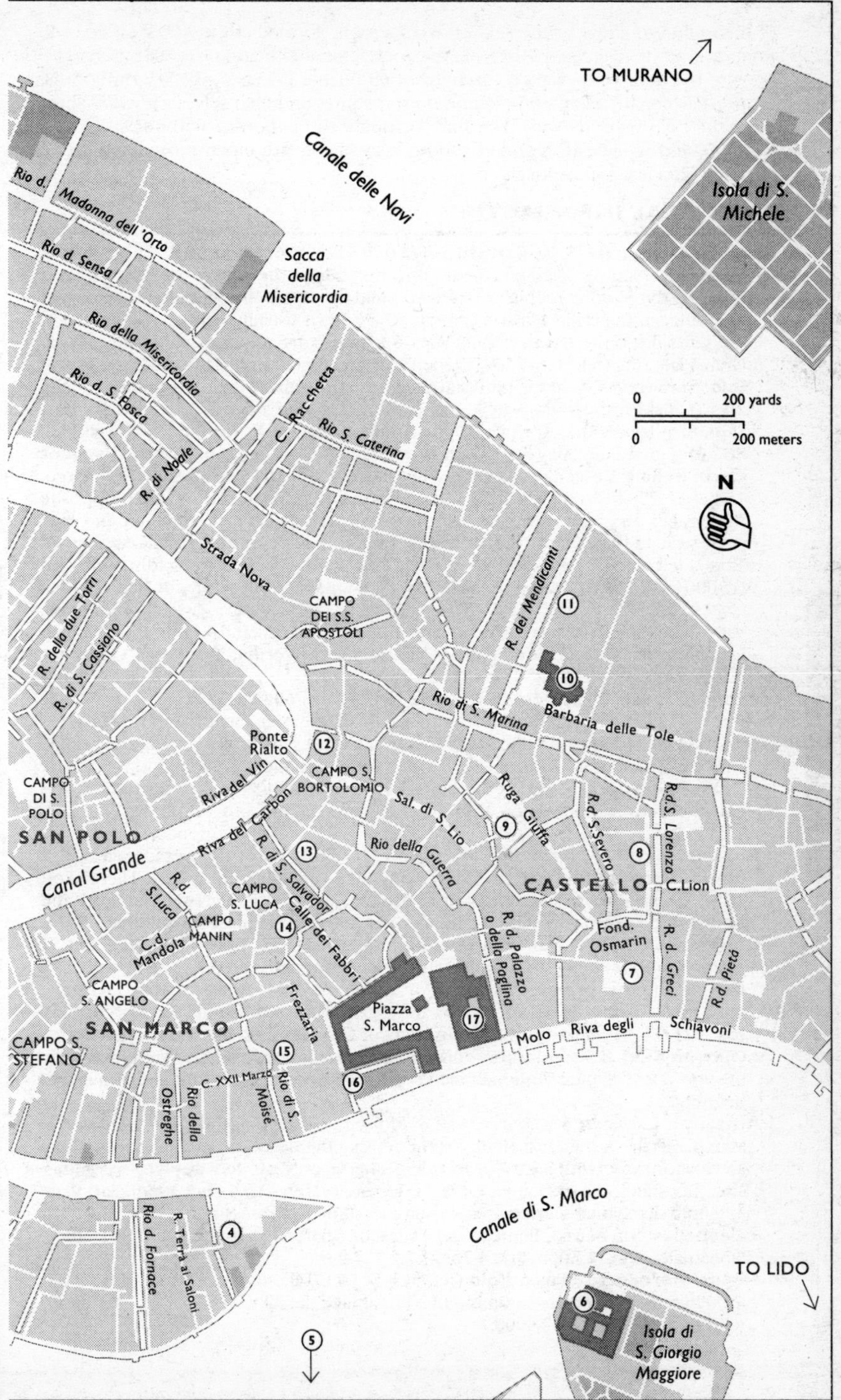
TO MURANO
Canale delle Navi
Isola di S. Michele
Rio d. Madonna dell 'Orto
Rio d. Sensa
Sacca della Misericordia
Rio della Misericordia
Rio d. S. Fosca
C. Racchetta
Rio S. Caterina
R. di Noale
0 200 yards
0 200 meters
N
Strada Nova
CAMPO DEI S.S. APOSTOLI
R. dei Mendicanti
R. della due Torri
R. di S. Cassiano
Rio di S. Marina
Barbaria delle Tole
Ponte Rialto
CAMPO S. BORTOLOMIO
Riva del Vin
CAMPO DI S. POLO
Sal. di S. Lio
Ruga Giuffa
R.d. S.Severo
R.d.S. Lorenzo
SAN POLO
Riva del Carbon
R. di S. Salvador
Rio della Guerra
Canal Grande
R.d. S.Luca
CAMPO S. LUCA
Calle dei Fabbri
CASTELLO
C.Lion
CAMPO MANIN
C.d. Mandola
R. d. Palazzo o della Paglina
Fond. Osmarin
R. d. Greci
R.d. Pietà
CAMPO S. ANGELO
Frezzaria
Piazza S. Marco
SAN MARCO
Molo
Riva degli Schiavoni
CAMPO S. STEFANO
C. XXII Marzo
Rio di S. Moisé
Rio della Ostreghe
Rio d. Fornace
R. Terrà ai Saloni
Canale di S. Marco
TO LIDO
Isola di S. Giorgio Maggiore
4
5
6
7
8
9
10
11
12
13
14
15
16
17

of the *vaporetti* stops, at the self-serve dispensers (located at the ACTV office in P. Roma and at the Rialto stop), or from the conductor after boarding (L800 surcharge). Be sure to count your change carefully when buying tickets at the station booths; tourists dashing for a departing *vaporetto* sometimes find themselves a few *lire* short once the boat is on its way. The fine for riding the *vaporetti* without a ticket is L30,000, and while enforcement can be lax, tourists are much more likely to be checked (and fined) than locals.

PRACTICAL INFORMATION

Tourist Offices: APT, Palazzetto Selva (tel. 522 63 56; fax 52 98 87 30). Exit P. S. Marco between the 2 columns, and turn right along the waterfront. The office is just past the park in a white, columned building. Open Mon.-Sat. 9:30am-3:30pm. The office at the **train station** (tel./fax 71 90 78) is usually mobbed. Get in line at the left side of the booth. Open Tues.-Sun. 8:15am-6:45pm. Also in the **Lido** at Gran Viale 6/A (tel. 526 57 21). Open in high season Mon.-Sat. 9am-2pm. **Hotel Information: AVA,** in the train station, just to the right of the tourist office (tel. 71 50 16). Makes reservations in 1- and 2-star hotels with a deposit. Open daily May-Sept. 8am-10pm; Oct.-April 9am-9pm. Another office at **P. Roma,** 540/D (tel. 522 86 40). Open daily May-Sept. 9am-10pm; Oct.-April 9am-9pm. **Youth Discount Card: Rolling Venice,** Comune di Venezia, Assessorato alla Gioventù, San Marco, 1529 (tel. 270 76 50; fax 270 76 42), on Corte Contarina. Exit P. S. Marco opposite the basilica and turn right, passing the post office. Follow the road left and continue straight through the building (look for the yellow *Comune di Venezia* signs). Take a left, then a right, and go into the courtyard. For ages 14-29, discount card (L5000) valid at many hotels, restaurants, shops, and museums in Venice. Also gives a discounted price (L20,000, normally L30,000) for the 3-day *vaporetto* pass, valid on all lines. (Pass available at any *vaporetto* ticket stand.) Comes with a map listing the locations of participating establishments. Worth it if you're in Venice for more than a couple of days.

Budget Travel: CTS, Dorsoduro, 3252 (tel. 520 56 60; fax 523 69 46) on Fondamenta Tagliapietra. Off the Dorsoduro-to-San Marco route, near Campo S. Margherita. Take Calle Piove to Calle Larga Foscari and turn right after crossing the bridge. Office on the bank of Rio Foscari. Open Mon.-Fri. 9am-12:30pm and 3:30-7pm. **Transalpino** (tel./fax 71 66 00), for international train tickets, is to the right as you exit the train station. Open Mon.-Fri. 8:30am-12:30pm and 3-7pm, Sat. 8:30am-12:30pm.

Consulates: U.K., Dorsoduro, 1051 (tel. 522 72 07). Cross the Accademia bridge from S. Marco and turn right. Open Mon.-Fri. 10am-noon and 2-3pm. The closest **U.S., Canadian,** and **Australian** consulates are in Milan; **New Zealand** and **South African** citizens should contact their respective embassies in Rome.

Currency Exchange: Banco Ambrosiano Veneto, San Marco, 4481 (tel. 290 31 11) on Calle Goldoni off Campo S. Luca. Open Mon.-Fri. 8:20am-1:20pm and 2:35-4:05pm. Another **branch** in San Marco, 2378/A on Calle Larga XXII Marzo with the same hours. Some of the best rates in the region. **Banco di Sicilia,** San Marco, 5051 (tel. 521 97 30), near the C. S. Bartolomeo. Changes cash and traveler's checks. Open Mon.-Fri. 8:30am-1:30pm and 2:50-3:50pm. Beware agencies with high commission rates; change money in banks whenever possible, and inquire about fees beforehand.

American Express: San Marco, Sal. S. Moise, 1471 (tel. 520 08 44), between S. Marco and the Accademia (look for the AmEx directional mosaic underfoot). Mail service for those with a card or traveler's checks only. No fees apply. No commission, but mediocre exchange rates. Office open Mon.-Fri. 9am-5:30pm, Sat. 9am-12:30pm. Exchange service open in summer Mon.-Sat. 8am-8pm.

Telephones: San Marco, Fontego dei Tedeschi, 5550, next to the main post office. Open daily 8am-12:30pm and 4-7pm.

Flights: Aeroporto Marco Polo (tel. 541 54 91). Take the ACTV (tel. 528 78 86) local bus #5 (every 1½hr., 30min., L1200), or take the ATVO coach (tel. 520 55 30) with luggage space for L5000.

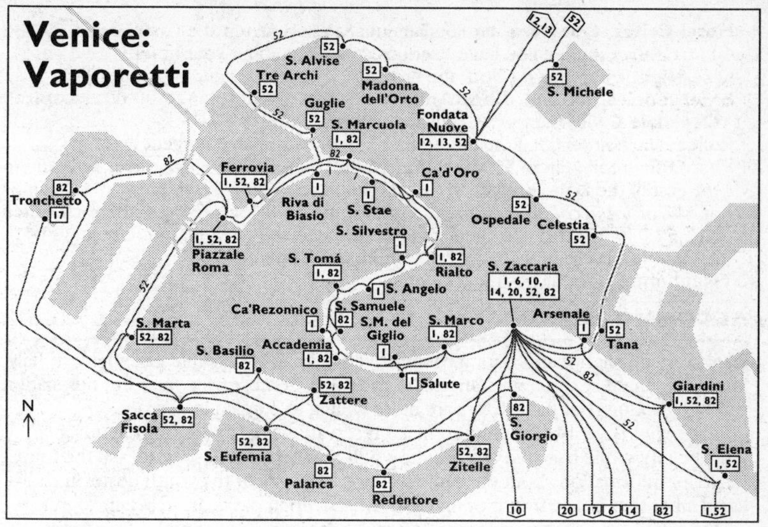

Trains: Stazione di Santa Lucia (tel. 71 55 55, lost and found 71 61 22). Info office in station across from tourist office. Open daily 7:15am-9:20pm. To: Padua (every 15min., 30min., L3400); Bologna (20 per day, 1½hr., L13,600); Milan (18 per day, 3hr., L21,000); Florence (6 per day, 3hr., L21,000); and Rome (6 per day, 5hr., L45,000). **Luggage Storage:** L5000 for 12hr. Open 3:45am-1:20am.

Buses: ACTV, local line for buses and boats (tel. 528 78 86), P. Roma. Open Mon.-Sat. 8am-2:30pm. Closed last 2 weeks in Aug. **ATP,** long-distance carrier. Buses approx. every 30min. To: the Riviera del Brenta (Villa Malcontenta L1200, Palazzo Foscari L3500, and Villa Strà L4000), Padua (L5000), and Treviso (L3800). Ticket office open daily 6:40am-10pm. Info office open Mon.-Sat. 7am-8pm.

Car Rental: Avis, P. Roma, 496/G (tel. 522 58 25). Open Mon.-Fri. 8am-7pm, Sat. 8am-1pm. **Budget,** P. Roma (tel. 520 00 00; fax 522 30 00), just down from Avis. Open Mon.-Fri. 8:30am-noon and 3:30-6pm, Sat. 8:30am-noon. Rates for both places approx. L180,000 per day, L850,000 per week, unlimited mileage. Min. age 21. Credit card required.

Bookstore: Libreria Editrice Cafoscarina, Dorsoduro, 3259 (tel. 523 89 69; fax 522 81 86), on Cà Foscari near the university. The largest selection of books in English in Venice, including *Let's Go*. Rolling Venice: 10% discount. Open Mon.-Fri. 9am-7pm, Sat. 9am-12:30pm. Also try **Libreria Turcato,** Dorsoduro, 3214 (tel. 523 18 64), on the corner at Calle del Cappeller, 2min. from the store listed above along the same route. Smaller selection in English, but more contemporary books. Rolling Venice: 10% discount. Open Mon.-Fri. 9am-12:30pm and 3-7:30pm, Sat. 9am-12:30pm and 4-7pm. V, MC.

Laundromat: Lavaget, Cannaregio, 1269 (tel. 71 59 76), on Fondamenta Pescaria. Take a left from the station, cross 1 bridge, and turn left along the canal. 3 kilos L15,000, soap included. Open Mon.-Fri. 8:30am-12:30pm and 4-6:30pm.

Public Baths: Albergo Diurno (Day Hotel), San Marco, 1266, in the *ramo secondo* ("2°" floor), off the west end of P. San Marco. Toilets L500. Open daily 7am-8pm. Also in the **station**—next to track #1. Showers L4000. Soap and towel each L500. Open daily 7am-8pm. **Toilets** are scattered throughout town; look for "WC" signs where street signs are located. *Gabinetti* (also *toilette*) can be found on either side of the Rialto, on the waterfront near P. San Marco, under the Dorsoduro side of the Accademia bridge (L500), in P. Roma near Treponte, and in Castello on Calle Morosina, 4052/A, to name but a few. Toilet L500, shower L3000, with towels L4000. Open daily 8am-7pm.

Hotel Crises: Questura, on Fondamenta San Lorenzo in the Castello (tel. 270 36 11). Contact them if you have a serious complaint about your hotel.

Late-Night Pharmacy: Check the brochure *A Guest in Venice,* or call 192.

Emergencies: tel. 113. **Boat Ambulance/First Aid:** tel. 523 00 00. **Hospital: Ospedale Civili,** Campo SS. Giovanni e Paolo (tel. 529 45 17).

Police: Carabinieri, P. Roma (tel. 523 53 33 or 112 in an emergency).

Post Office: San Marco, 5554 (tel. 522 06 06), on Salizzada Fontego dei Tedeschi to the east of the Rialto bridge, off Campo San Bartolomeo. *Fermo posta* at #4, stamps at #12 or *tabacchi* all over town. Open Mon.-Sat. 8:15am-6:45pm. **Branch office** (tel. 528 59 49) through the arcades at the end of P. San Marco. Open Mon.-Fri. 8:15am-1:30pm, Sat. 8:15am-12:10pm. **Postal Code:** 30124.

Telephone Code: 041.

ACCOMMODATIONS

Plan to spend slightly more for a room in Venice than you would elsewhere in Italy. The **APT** office at the train station and the **AVA** hotel service near the bus station will book rooms, but proprietors are more willing to bargain in person.

Single rooms vanish in summer. Make reservations up to a month in advance, or visit the city while based in a nearby town. If you become desperate, ask the tourist office for information about the campgrounds at Mestre or the youth hostel in Padua. Remember that police frown upon those who sleep in parks or on beaches.

Dormitory-style arrangements are often available in Venice without reservations, even during August and September. These accommodations often have irregular operating seasons, so check with the tourist offices to see which are open. In *pensioni,* watch out for L12,000 breakfasts and other rip-offs. Always agree on what you'll pay for before you take a room. **Remember that prices are likely to have risen since this book's publication.** The price quoted at the hotel is what you'll have to pay.

Institutional Accommodations

Ostello Venezia (HI), Fondamenta di Zitelle, 86 (tel. 523 82 11; fax 523 56 89), on Giudecca. Take *vaporetto* #82 from the station (25min., L4000) or take #82 or 52 from San Zaccaria near San Marco (5min., L4000). Get off at Zitelle and walk right along the waterfront. The hostel is in a recently renovated warehouse on the canal, but you'll feel like you're in a *caffè.* 273 beds with flimsy mattresses. English spoken. Check-in 7-9:30am and 1-10:30pm. Lockout 9:30am-1pm. Curfew 11:30pm. L23,000 per person. Small breakfast included, full meals L14,000. Membership required, but HI cards available. No phone reservations.

Foresteria Valdese, Castello, 5170 (tel. 528 67 97). Take the *vaporetto* to San Zaccharia, then walk toward San Marco over the first bridge to your left. Make a right and pass through Campo S. Zaccharia. Come up Fond. Osmarin and cross a bridge, continue on Ruga Giuffa until you reach Campo Santa Maria Formosa (5min.). From the *campo,* take Calle Longa S. M. Formosa, just over the first bridge. This building was once the 18th-century guesthouse of Venice's biggest Protestant church. Amiable management, pleasant breakfast hall, and frescoed ceilings in many rooms. Check-in 9am-1pm and 6-8pm. Lockout 10am-1pm. Bunk bed in dorm room L26,000, each additional night L25,000. Breakfast included. Reserve 1 month ahead for their 2 beautiful doubles (L70,000). Also rents 2 apartments with bath and kitchen; one L140,000 per day (4 beds), the other L155,000 per day (5 beds), breakfast not included. Phone reservations suggested, but not always accepted. Closed 15 days in Nov.

Domus Civica, ACISJF, San Polo, 3082 (tel. 72 11 03 or 52 40 46), on the corner of Calle Chiovere, Calle Campazzo, and S. Rocco, between the Frari Church and P. Roma. Along the road, follow the yellow arrows between P. Roma and the Rialto. Across the street from a bar on both sides. Men and women welcome. Church-affiliated hostel organization. Everything your heart could desire: ping-pong tables, TV room, piano. Curfew 11:30pm. Singles L35,000. Doubles L58,000. Rolling Venice or ISIC card: 20% discount. Open June to mid-Oct.

Suore Cannosiano, Fondamenta del Ponte Piccolo, 428 (tel. 522 21 57). Take boat #82 to Giudecca stop and walk left just over the bridge. Women only. Managed by nuns. Arrive any time of day to leave your bags. Check-out 7:30-8:30am. Lockout 9am-3pm. Curfew 10:30pm. Large dorm-style rooms L18,000 per person.

Cannaregio (From the Station to the Rialto)

The area around the station on Lista di Spagna offers good budget accommodations.

Hotel Calderan, Cannaregio, 283 (tel. 71 55 62), in P. San Geremia at the end of Lista di Spagna, a short walk from the station. Large rooms with matching furniture. No private baths. Some rooms overlook the square or the park behind. Friendly, family-run hotel. No English spoken. No curfew; you are given your own set of keys. Singles L40,000. Doubles L60,000. Triples L84,000. Breakfast L6000. Reserve ahead Aug.-Oct. V, MC.

Hotel Bernardi, Cannaregio, 4366, (tel. 522 72 57; fax 522 24 24). Take *vaporetto* #1 to Cà d'Oro. Walk down Strada Nuova, turn left onto Calle dell'Oca. The hotel is in a small alleyway. Gorgeous, newly renovated rooms. Owner is multi-lingual. Check-out 10:30am. Singles L45,000. Doubles with bath L105,000. Breakfast included. Rolling Venice card: 15% discount on larger rooms. V, MC.

Locanda Antica Casa Carettoni, Cannaregio, 130 (tel. 71 62 31), along the Lista di Spagna. From the station, facing the bridge, head left on the main street. Rooms steeped in antiquity described by the proud proprietor as "truly Venetian." Curfew midnight. Singles L35,000-45,000. Doubles L58,000-68,000. Triples L90,000. Closed either Aug. or Oct.

Hotel Minerva and Nettuno, Cannaregio, 230 (tel. 71 59 68; fax 524 21 39), on Lista di Spagna. From the station, face the bridge and turn left on the main street. Large, remodeled rooms and convenient locale make this a prime choice. Singles L59,000, with bath L77,000. Doubles L85,000, with bath L125,000. Triples L110,000, with bath L165,000. Quads L130,000, with bath L197,000. Breakfast included. Rolling Venice card: 10% discount. V, MC, AmEx.

Albergo Adua, Cannaregio, 233/A (tel. 71 61 84), on Lista di Spagna. Tidy rooms with flowered wallpaper, most with wall-to-wall carpeting. Small, family-run, and quiet for the neighborhood. Singles L50,000. Doubles L90,000, with bath L120,000. Triples L108,000, with bath L162,000. Quads L136,000, with bath L200,000. Breakfast L7500. V, MC.

Hotel Biasin and Hotel Marte, Ponte delle Guglie, 338-1252 (tel. 71 63 51 or 71 72 31), just beyond Campo S. Geremia toward the Rialto. Modest, clean rooms with varying sizes and prices. Singles from L35,000, with bath L60,000. Doubles from L70,000, with bath L140,000-160,000.

Hotel Rossi, Cannaregio, 262 (tel. 71 51 64), right off the Lista di Spagna. Continue from the train station, and make a left under the arch onto Calle de la Procuratie. Pleasant hotel with friendly management. Singles L60,000, with bath L70,000. Doubles L90,000, with bath L120,000. Triples with bath L150,000. Quads with bath L180,000. Breakfast included. V, MC, AmEx.

Dorsoduro and Santa Croce

Cà Foscari, Dorsoduro, 3887/B (tel./fax 71 08 17), on Calle della Frescada. Take *vaporetto* #1 or 82 to San Tomà. Get off the boat, turn left over the bridge, and follow the road right, then left. Family-run with pride. Quiet location. You'll want to take the elaborate furniture home with you. Singles 70,000. Doubles L88,000, with toilet or shower L120,000. Triples L115,000. Breakfast included. Closes at 1am. Rooms held until 2pm. Open Feb.-Nov.

Locanda Montin, Dorsoduro, 1147 (tel. 522 71 51), near Accademia. Take boat #1 to Cà Rezzonico, walk straight ahead to Campo San Barnaba, and go south through the *sottoportego* Casin dei Nobili. Cross the bridge, turn right on the Fondamenta Lombardo, and walk around the corner onto Fondamenta di Borgo. Modern paintings, restored antiques, and enthusiastic owners. Singles L55,000. Doubles L75,000, with bath L85,000. Reserve with 1 night's deposit. Closed 20 days in Jan. and 10 days in Aug. V, MC, AmEx.

San Marco (From the Basilica west to the Grand Canal)

Locande San Samuele, San Marco, 3358 (tel./fax 522 80 45). Follow Calle delle Botteghe from Campo S. Stefano (near the Accademia) and turn left on Salizzada S. Samuele. Large, attractive rooms, stone floors, and a great location. Singles L45,000. Doubles L70,000, with bath L95,000. Triples L98,000, with bath L130,000. Breakfast available. Reserve ahead with 1 night's deposit.

Alloggi Alla Scala, San Marco, 4306 (tel. 521 06 29). From Campo Manin take Calle della Vida o delle Locande, then a left and a quick right on Corte Contarini dal Bovolo. Located in a quiet and historic courtyard. Gorgeous, colorful rooms *alla carnevale.* Doubles L85,000-100,000. Extra bed L30,000. Breakfast L8000. Reserve with 1 night's deposit. Closed Aug.

Locanda Casa Petrarca, San Marco, 4386 (tel. 520 04 30). Take *vaporetto* #1 or 82 to the Rialto, walk inland and to the right until you reach Campo San Luca, then go south on Calle dei Fuseri. Take the 2nd left and then turn right onto Calle Schiavone. English spoken. Singles L70,000. Doubles L88,000, with bath L110,000. Extra bed 35% more. Phone ahead; rooms held until 3pm.

Hotel Riva, San Marco, 5310 (tel. 522 70 34), on Ponte dell'Angelo. From P. S. Marco, walk under the clock tower and take a right on Calle Larga S. Marco. Turn left on Calle Angelo and go over the bridge. A brand-new hotel packed with Venetian antiques. All rooms overlook a canal. Prime location. Singles with bath L90,000. Doubles L100,000, with bath L130,000. Triples with bath L180,000. Breakfast included. Closes at 1am. Reserve 2 weeks ahead with 1 night's deposit. Closed Nov.-Jan.

Castello (From San Marco to the Island of Sant'Elena)

Hotel Caneva, Castello, 5515 (tel. 522 81 18; fax 520 86 76), 2min. from the Rialto. Take Calle Stagneri from P. S. Bartolomeo, cross the bridge, and turn right after Campo della Fava. Most rooms overlook a canal and about half are carpeted. All include TV. Singles L60,000. Doubles L85,000, with bath L130,000. Triples L114,000, with bath L175,000. Breakfast included. Closed Nov. and Jan. V.

Locanda Sant'Anna, Castello, 269 (tel. 528 64 66). Take Via Garibaldi, which becomes Fondamenta Santa Anna, turn left on Ponte Santa Anna, then right at Corte del Bianco. *Vaporetto*: #1 or 4 to Giardini. Worth the hike for the rooms and the neighborhood. Friendly family proprietors and a refreshing absence of tourists. TV downstairs. Curfew midnight. Singles L75,000. Doubles L90,000, with shower L96,000, with toilet L120,000. Quads L180,000-200,000. Breakfast included. Reserve with 1 night's deposit. V, MC.

Pensione Casa Verardo, Castello, 4765 (tel. 528 61 27). Take Rimpetto la Sacrestia out of Campo SS. Filippo e Giacomo and across the bridge. Large rooms with eclectic furnishings. No surface spared from decoration. Singles with bath L70,000. Doubles with shower L100,000, with bathroom L120,000. Triples with shower L140,000, with bathroom L150,000. Quads with shower L160,000, with bathroom L170,000. Breakfast L10,000. Reserve with 1 night's deposit. V.

Locanda Corona, Castello, 4464 (tel. 522 91 74). *Vaporetto*: San Zaccharia. Head north on Sacrestia from Campo SS. Filippo e Giacomo, take the first right and then the first left onto Calle Corona. Fine rooms, limited hot water supply. Drop by the Fucina degli Angeli (Angel's Forge) next door for a look at the glass-blowing workshop. Singles L56,000. Doubles L84,000. Triples L118,000. Breakfast included. Showers L3000. Closed late Jan.-early Feb.

Locanda Silva, Castello, 4423 (tel. 522 76 43; fax 528 68 17). From S. Marco, walk under the clock tower and take a right on C. Larga S. Marco, then a left on Calle d'Angelo. Turn right at Calle e Ramo Drio La Fara and cross the bridge. Walk down the street to the canal and turn left. Large and fastidiously kept. Singles L55,000. Doubles L85,000, with shower L100,000, with bath L125,000. Triples L113,000, with bath L165,000. Quads L140,000, with bath L190,000. Breakfast included. Curfew 2am. Open Feb.-Nov.

Locanda Canal, Castello, 4422/C (tel. 523 45 38). Follow directions for Locanda Silva, listed above. A tidy, pleasant hotel in a calm location. Only 7 rooms. Doubles L85,000, with shower L95,000, with bath L130,000. Triples L110,000, with shower L130,000, with bath L160,000. Breakfast included.

Camping

The **Litorale del Cavallino,** on the Adriatic side of the Lido island, is an endless row of beach campgrounds. From S. Marco, take *vaporetto* #14 to Punta Sabbioni (40min.). You'll find **Camping Miramare,** Punta Sabbioni (tel. 96 61 50; fax 530 11 50), about 700m along the beach to your right from the Punta Sabbioni *vaporetto* stop. L7500 per person and L16,600 per tent in high season. Four-person bungalow L47,000, 5-person L68,000. Open Feb.-Nov. Take bus #5 to the Cà Pasquali stop. The bus passes Via Poerio (on your left). **Cà Pasquali,** Via Poerio, 33 (tel. 96 61 10; fax 530 07 97). In high season, L8800 per person, L10,000 per car. 4-person bungalow L85,500, 5-person, L124,000. Showers included. Open March-Sept. V, MC, AmEx. Another option is **Campeggio Fusina,** Via Moranzani, in the locality of Malcontenta (tel. 547 00 55). L9500 per person, L7000 per tent, and L18,000 per tent and car. English spoken. Call ahead. From P. Roma, take bus #1 (L1100) to the Fusino stop of San Marta (1hr., last bus 9pm).

FOOD

It is becoming difficult to sit down to a good meal in Venice without emptying your wallet. To avoid paying a fortune, visit any *bar* or *osteria* in town and make a meal from the vast display of meat- and cheese-filled pastries, tidbits of seafood, rice, and meat, and *tramezzini,* triangular slices of soft white bread with any imaginable filling. Venetians have long cultivated the tradition of this between-meal repast, known as the *cicchetto,* always washed down by *un'ombra,* a glass of local wine. Good deals on tourist *menù* abound on the broad **Via Garibaldi,** a lovely 15-min. walk along the waterfront from P. San Marco. Don't be afraid to walk the small alleyways, home to less touristed eateries. If you're going to splurge, try one of the local seafood dishes. *Seppie in nero* is a tasty, soft squid-like creature coated with its own ink and usually served with *polenta,* Veneto's cornmeal staple. A plate of *pesce fritta mista* (mixed fried seafood, at least L12,000) usually includes *calamari* (squid), *polpo* (small octopus), shrimp, and the catch of the day. *Fegato alla veneziana* is the familiar yet yummy liver and onions.

The Veneto and Friuli regions produce an abundance of excellent and inexpensive **wines.** Good, local white wines include the sparkling, dry *prosecco della Marca* and the dry *collio*. For reds, try a *merlot* or *marzemino. Osterie* or *baccari,* simple and usually authentic wine-and-snack bars, can be found in alleys and streets throughout the city, and they are some of the few places where locals outnumber tourists. Venetians typically drop by in the late afternoon, before dinner.

Kosher food is served in Europe's oldest Jewish quarter, the **Ghetto Vecchio** (as well as in the Ghetto Nuovo). Call or write ahead to reserve a space at the **Casa Israelitica di Reposo,** Cannaregio 2874 (tel. 71 60 02), located across the Campo del Ghetto Nuovo from the Museo Ebraico. Take a left from the station, turn left after the first bridge, and follow the yellow Hebrew signs to the *campo*. L35,000 per person. Lunch is served daily at 1pm, dinner at 7:30pm.

There are a few **street markets** in town. Located in the area surrounding the **Rialto** (San Polo side), the most famous market was once the center of trade and merchandise for the Venetian Republic. Fruit stands line the Ruga degli Orefici, and on the right are the *erberia* (vegetable) and *pescheria* (fish) markets. Another morning market appears in Cannaregio on Rio Terra S. Leonardo, just past Ponte Guglie.

Locals shop on the side streets near **Campo Beccarie** in San Polo near the Rialto. Less entertaining but more convenient are the *alimentari* food stores. In Cannaregio, **STANDA,** on Strada Nuova, 3660 (D3), near Campo S. Felice, has groceries in the back. Open daily 9am-7:20pm. In Castello near San Marco is **Su. Ve.,** on Calle del Mondo Novo, 5816, off Campo Santa Maria Formosa. Open Mon.-Tues. and Thurs.-Sat. 8:30am-1pm and 4-7:30pm, Wed. 8:30am-1pm. In Dorsoduro, go to **Mega I** at Campo Santa Margherita, 3019/B, an unmarked entrance between a phone booth and a *caffè*. Open Sun.-Fri. 9am-12:50pm and 5-7:45pm, Sat. 9am-8pm. In Giudecca, try the **Vivo** supermarket, on Fondamenta delle Zitelle, 203A (E7), to the left of the *Redentore* church. Closed Wed. afternoon and Sun.

One word of caution: don't make the mistake of trying to rinse off your sticky *gelato*-smeared hands in the canal—those stairs leading into the water have been gathering slippery moss since Michelangelo was a boy.

Cannaregio

Caffè Poggi, Campo della Maddalena, 2103 (tel. 524 07 58). Take a left from the station toward the Rialto and cross two bridges. A popular student hangout with loud music. Convenient location for a drink and light snack. *Panini* L3000-5000, wine L1000-3000 per glass. Open Mon.-Sat. 8am-1am.

Ristorante al Ponte, Cannaregio, 2352 (tel. 72 07 44), literally *on* Ponte dell'Ancoretta. Turn left at the station; walk to the 2nd bridge, past P. San Geremia. The L16,000 *menù* includes everything but beverage and features regional specialties. *Primi* L5000-10,000, *secondi* and fish L9000-22,000. Cover L3000. Service 12%. Open Wed.-Mon. 12:30-2:30pm and 6:30-9:30pm. V, MC, AmEx.

Ai Promessi Sposi, Cannaregio, 4367 (tel. 522 86 09). From Strada Nuova, take a left on Calle del Duca just before Campo SS. Apostoli, then the first left. Mellow music and lots of locals. Some outdoor seating. *Primi* L7000-10,000, *secondi* L14,000-18,000. Cover L1500. Open Thurs.-Tues. 10am-3pm and 6-10pm.

Trattoria Casa Mia, Cannaregio, 4430 (tel. 528 55 90), in the same alley as Promessi Sposi. *Primi* L9000-12,000, *secondi* and fish L18,000-24,000. Pizza L8500-12,000. Cover L2000. Service 12%. Open Wed.-Mon. noon-2:30pm and 7-10pm. Closed Aug. V, MC.

San Polo and Santa Croce

Mensa Universitaria di Cà Foscari, S. Polo, 2480 (tel. 71 80 69), on Calle del Magazen. From the main entrance of the Church of the Frari, go over the bridge, turn left, cross the next bridge, make a left and then a quick right onto Calle del Magazen. Without a doubt the best meal deal in Venice. Full meals including drink L10,500 with student ID (ISIC) or L7100 with Rolling Venice card. Open Mon.-Sat. noon-2:30pm and 6:30-8:30pm, Sun. noon-2pm.

Trattoria/Pizzeria All'Anfora, Santa Croce, 1223 (tel. 524 03 25), on Lista dei Bari. From the station, cross the Grand Canal, go straight, and then over the first bridge on your left. Walk around the Church of S. Simeon onto Lista dei Bari. A hearty eatery populated by local folk. Vine-covered patio dining out back. *Primi* L7000-16,000, *secondi* L9000-23,000, pizzas L7000-13,000. Cover L3000. Service 12%. Open Wed.-Mon. 9am-11pm. V, MC, AmEx.

Pizzeria alle Oche, Santa Croce, 1552 a/b (tel. 524 11 61). Near Campo San Giacomo. Exit Campo San Polo on Calle Bernardo and follow the yellow *Ferrovia* signs over the Parucheta bridge. According to the Venetian student population, it's the best pizzeria in town. 75 combinations of toppings. *Primi* L7000-9000, *secondi* L8500-17,000, pizzas L5000-13,500. Cover L2000. Service 12%. Open June-Sept. daily noon-3pm and 7-11pm; Oct.-May Tues.-Sun. same hours.

Trattoria alle Burchielle, Santa Croce, 393 (tel. 71 03 42), on the Fondamenta Burchielle, off the corner of P. Roma over the bridge at Campazzo Tre Ponti, the 3-bridge intersection. *Trattoria* on the bank of the small canal since 1503. Homemade *gnocchi* and pasta. *Primi* from L7000, *secondi* L10,000-15,000. Cover L1700. Service 10%. Open Tues.-Sun. noon-3pm and 7-10:30pm. V, MC, AmEx.

Osteria do Mori, San Polo, 429 (tel. 522 54 01). From the Rialto, turn left at the end of the market on Ruga Orefici, then take the first right. Venetians have frequented this snack-and-wine bar since 1571. Standing room only. Wine L1500-7000 per glass. *Tramezzini* L1500. Open late Aug.-July Mon.-Tues. and Thurs.-Sat. 8:30am-1:30pm and 5-9pm, Wed. 8:30am-1:30pm.

Aliani Gastronomia, San Polo, 655 (tel. 522 49 13), on Ruga Vecchia San Giovanni, after a left off Ruga Orefici, the street that leads to the Rialto bridge on the San Polo side. The best and most central take-out deli. Cheeses and cold cuts, lavish lasagna, roasted half-chickens, and lots of vegetables. Open mid-Aug. to July Mon.-Sat. 8am-1pm and 5-7:30pm.

Dorsoduro

Ai Pugni, Dorsoduro, 2839 (tel. 523 98 31), along the Rio di S. Barnaba and Fond. Gherardini off Campo S. Barnaba. Take *vaporetto* #1 to Cà Rezzonico. Huge, delicious pizzas as well as sandwiches and salads. *Primi* L7000-8000, *secondi* L13,000, pizzas L5500-8000. No cover charge. Open for drinks Wed.-Mon. 10am-1am, for food 1:10-3:30pm and 7pm-1am.

Crepizza, Dorsoduro, 3760 (tel. 522 62 80), on Calle San Pantalon. From Campo S. Margherita, walk across Rio di Cà Foscari and around the right side of Chiesa di S. Pantalon. Pizzas (L4000-10,000), *primi* (L6000-12,000) and *secondi* (L9000-17,000). Cover L1500. Service 10%. *Menù* (L14,500) includes *primo, secondo,* and vegetable. Open Wed.-Mon. noon-2:30pm and 7-10:30pm. V, MC.

San Marco

Rosticceria San Bartolomeo, San Marco, 5424/A (tel. 522 35 69), in Calle de la Bissa, off Campo San Bartolomeo near the Rialto Bridge. Look for the *Rosticceria* sign. Top-notch self-service. Venetian specialties such as *seppie con polenta* (squid with polenta) for L13,000. *Primi* L5500-7000, *secondi* L10,000-20,000. Cover L2000. Open Feb.-Dec. Tues.-Sun. 9:30am-2:30pm and 5-9pm.

Vino, Vino, San Marco, 2007/A (tel. 523 70 27), on Calle del Sartor da Veste, off Calle Larga XXII Marzo, which runs along the S. Marco to Accademia route. Good food, but you have to choose from what they have available. A river of wines (L1500-6000 per glass) and a sea of tourists. *Primi* L8000, *secondi* L15,000. Cover L1000. Rolling Venice card: 10% discount on food. Open for drinks Wed.-Mon. 10:30am-midnight; for food noon-2:30pm and 7-11pm.

Leon Bianco, San Marco, 4153 (tel. 522 11 80), on Sal. San Luca, which runs between Campo San Luca and Campo Manin northwest of P. San Marco. Highbrow interior and low prices make this a popular spot for the business crowd. *Tramezzini* L1600, *primi* L5000, *secondi* L6000. Open Mon.-Sat. 8am-8pm.

Castello

Trattoria Alla Rivetta, Castello, 4625 (tel. 528 73 02), off Campo SS. Filippo e Giacomo. Walk along the left side of the Basilica from P. S. Marco—the restaurant is squeezed in right before the Ponte San Provolo. One of the only authentic and reasonable places in the area. Try the fried calamari—*delizioso! Primi* L7000-9000, *secondi* L8000-17,000, excellent fish dishes L6000-17,000. Cover L2000. Service 12%. Open Tues.-Sun. 11am-10pm. Closed July 15-Aug. 15.

Cip Ciap, Ponte del Mondo Novo, 5799/A (tel. 523 66 21), off Fondamenta Santa Maria Formosa southwest of the *campo.* Deserves highest praise for its pizza (L3000-10,000, slices L1600 per *etto*). The *disco volante* (literally "flying saucer," stuffed with mushrooms, eggplant, ham, and salami, L11,500) is out of this world. Mainly take-out. Open Wed.-Mon. 6am-9pm.

Gelaterie and Pasticcerie

La Boutique del Gelato, Castello 5727, (tel. 522 32 83) on Sal. S. Lio, off Campo S. Lio. THE *gelateria* of Venice—you'll know by the tons of locals taking some home for the family. Big scoops for just a few *lire.* You'll want seconds. Open daily 10am-8:30pm.

Gelateria Mille Voglie, San Polo, 3033 (tel. 524 46 67), on Sal. S. Rocco. In the shadow of the Church of the Frari on the way to the Church of S. Rocco. One of the best and cheapest places in Venice. Cones L1000-3500. Pizza and snacks sold on the right, but the *gelato* is better. Open daily 9am-midnight.

Gelateria Santo Stefano (Paolin), San Marco, 2962/A (tel. 522 55 76), in the far corner of Campo Morosini San Stefano on the S. Marco side of the Accademia bridge. Said to have the best *nocciola* (hazelnut) and *panna* (whipped cream) in the world. Cones L1500-3000. Open April-Sept. Tues.-Sun. 9am-midnight; Oct.-Nov. and Feb.-March Tues.-Sun. 9:30am-9pm. Closed Dec.-Jan.

Gelati Nico, Dorsoduro, 922 (tel. 522 52 93), near the Zaltere *vaporetto* stop, is the pride of Venice. *Gianduiotto,* a slice of dense chocolate hazelnut ice cream dunked in whipped cream, is their specialty (L3800). Cones L2000-4000. Open in summer Fri.-Wed. 7am-11pm; mid-Jan.-mid-Dec. 7am-9pm.

Panificio F. Paronuzzi, Cannaregio, 3843, on Strada Nuova, the central street. Buy the dense *pane dei dogi* (L2800 per *etto*), and repent at your leisure. Open Mon.-Sat. 7am-8pm, Sun. 9:30-2pm.

A. Rosa Salva, San Marco, 5020 (tel. 522 53 85), on Marzaria San Salvador, 5021, near the Rialto bridge. Locals claim that it is Venice's premier bakery, and the famous *budino di semolino* (rich pudding cake, L1200) affirms this assertion. Open Mon.-Sat. 8am-8pm. Closed 2 weeks in Aug.

SIGHTS

A strict dress code applies in many Venetian churches. No shorts, tank tops, or miniskirts allowed. On a lighter note, many of the sights in Venice have student, senior, and group discounts—the "reduced" price listed here generally applies to visitors under 18 or over 60. Children under 12 are often admitted for free.

The Grand Canal

The Grand Canal bisects the main islands that constitute the city of Venice, and most important activities in the city happen on or near these shores. The splendid façades of the *palazzi* that crowd its banks testify to a history of immense wealth. From *vaporetto* #1 or 82 you can enjoy a tour of some of the greatest works of Renaissance architecture. Although their external decorations vary, the palaces share the same basic structure. Central halls running front to back provided air circulation and light, replacing the traditional central courtyards that cramped Venetian life didn't permit. A *palazzo's* ground floor (*androne*) served as an entrance hall from the canal, while the living quarters occupied the *piano nobile* (second floor). In contrast to the heaviness of the massive urban *palazzi* of the Florentine Renaissance, the overall effect is one of delicate, lacy openness.

The oldest surviving *palazzi*, some of which date from the 13th century, were influenced by Byzantine and early Christian tastes. Look for the rounded arches in low relief on the **Cà da Mosto,** a palace on the S. Marco side of the Grand Canal, just past the Rialto bridge toward the train station. Further on in the same direction is the

The Scoop on *Gelato*

It may be translated as "ice cream," but *gelato* is in a league of its own. Some tips to guide you through your quest for frozen, flavored perfection:

Look for stores that carry *gelato artigianale* or *propria produzione*—it means they make it themselves.

Singola (single) and *doppia* (double) portions are the most common. Some locales serve *gelato* in a *brioche* (sweet pastry bun), a special treat. Saying *"con panna"* will add a mound of fresh whipped cream to your serving. Some *gelaterie* require you to pay before you eat, so head first for the *cassa* (cashier) and then present your receipt to the scooper when you order.

Some flavorful vocabulary: *mela* (apple), *ananas* (pineapple), *mirtillo* (blueberry), *stracciatella* (chocolate chip), *cannella* (cinnamon), *noce/cocco* (coconut), *nocciola* (hazelnut), *miele* (honey), *latte/panna* (milk/cream), *liquirizia* (black licorice), *frutti di bosco* (forest fruits, like blackberries), *arancia* (orange), *pesca* (PES-kah, peach—DON'T say *pesce* (PESH-ay); it means "fish"), *lampone* (raspberry), and *fragola* (strawberry). There are also some flavors that don't exist in America, like *baci* (chocolate and hazelnut, like the candy), *cassata* (fruity ice cream with nuts and candied fruits), *riso* (rice), and *tiramisù* (espresso, sweet cheese, and chocolate—like the dessert).

If you can't find the fresh kind, try the prepackaged *gelati.* Some *gelaterie* also carry soy-based *gelato* for the vegan and lactose-intolerant among us; another option is a flavored ice treat called *granita.* Biting into *cornetti* is a national pastime, sure to cheer any weary wanderer.

Do not pig out. Let's Go does not recommend eating too much *gelato*.

Cà d'Oro, or "house of gold," whose name derives from the gold leaf that once adorned the tracery of its renowned façade. (*Cà* is an archaic dialect form of *casa,* or "house.") Built between 1424 and 1430, the Cà d'Oro represents the pinnacle of the Venetian Gothic (see **Cannaregio** below).

Many of Venice's Renaissance edifices are the works of three major Venetian architects: Mauro Codussi, Jacopo Sansovino, and Michele Sanmicheli. Gracing the east bank, Codussi's early **Palazzo Corner-Spinelli** (1510) is directly to the right of the S. Angelo stop between the Rialto and the Accademia Bridges, and his **Palazzo Vendramin Calergi** is directly to the right of the S. Marcuola stop, near the station. These structures represent a departure from the early Venetian style, infusing classical and Byzantine elements. Codussi's leadership inspired Sansovino's stately **Palazzo Corner** (called **Cà Granda**), located on the San Marco side of the canal directly left of the S. Maria del Giglio stop, past the Accademia, and Sanmicheli's **Palazzo Grimani di San Luca,** situated on the east bank between the S. Angelo and Rialto stops on the R. di San Luca.

San Marco and Castello

Piazza San Marco and Environs

In contrast to the narrow, maze-like streets that cover most of Venice, **Piazza San Marco** is a magnificent expanse of light and space. Gathering point for thousands of tourists and pigeons, it is undoubtedly the city's nucleus. It also functions as a crossroads for transportation, since water- and land-traffic merge at the wide Riva degli Schiavoni. Opposite the basilica, the piazza is enclosed on three sides by the **Procuratie Vecchie** (designed by Codussi, Sansovini, and others in the 15th and 16th centuries) to the south, the **Ala Napoleonica** (built in the 19th century as the French emperor's ballroom) to the west, and the **Procuratie Nuova** (begun in 1582 under the direction of Vincenzo Scamozzi) to the north. Today, these buildings house the Museo Correr, Museo Archaeologico, and Museo del Risorgimento. Attached to the Procuratie Vecchie is the fabulous, celestial **Torre dell'Orologio,** constructed between 1496 and 1499 according to Codussi's design. On top of the tower, two bronze Moors strike the hour. The fourth level features the lion of St. Mark, and the clock below indicates the hour, lunar phase, and visible constellations. The archway marks the beginning of the **Mercerie,** Venice's main commercial street leading to the Rialto. The solid brick **campanile** (96m high) originally served as a watchtower and lighthouse for the city. The current tower is an exact replica of the 16th-century campanile, which collapsed during the earthquake of 1902. (Open daily 9am-7:30pm. Admission L5000; tel. 522 40 64). The campanile is a fine photo spot, although cheaper admission, shorter lines, and better views are available at the **Campanile di San Giorgio** (tel. 528 99 00) across from P. San Marco on the small island of San Giorgio. Take the *vaporetto* to the stop of the same name (L2000 from S. Marco). (Open daily 9:30am-12:30pm and 2:30-6pm).

Construction of the **Basilica di San Marco** (tel. 522 52 05) began in the 9th century, when two Venetian merchants stole St. Mark's remains from Alexandria and packed them in pork to sneak past Arab officials. The caper is commemorated in a mosaic to the left of the three entrance arches. The basilica's cruciform plan and five bulbous domes, a direct architectural reference to the Church of the Holy Apostles in Constantinople, suggest an ambition to rival both the church in Byzantium and St. Peter's in Rome. Rebuilt after a fire in the 10th century and continually enlarged over the next half-millennium, San Marco is now a unique synthesis of Byzantine, western European, and Islamic influences. (Open daily 9:45am-7:30pm. Free.) The church sparkles with mosaics of all ages—perhaps the best are those on the atrium's ceiling. Underfoot, 12th-century combinations of marble, glass, and porphyry confuse the eyes with endless geometric intricacies. (Notice how the floor is buckled—these stones have had nine centuries to sink into the mushy ground.) The basilica's main treasure is the **Pala d'Oro** (tel. 522 56 97), a Venetian-Byzantine gold relief encrusted with precious gems. In the area behind the screen are Sansovino's bronze reliefs and his sacristy door. (Open daily 9am-4:30pm. Admission L3000.) Through a door in the atrium is the **Galleria della Basilica** (tel. 522 52 05), which provides a better view of the mosaics on the walls and floors. The recently restored *Horses of St. Mark* are on display here. (Open daily 10am-6:30pm. Admission L3000.) To the right of the altar is the **treasury,** a horde of gold and relics left over from the spoils of the Fourth Crusade. A small walkie-talkie narrates your visit to the collection. Guided tours of the basilica are given April-June and Sept.-Oct. Mon.-Sat. at 11am. Call the **Curia Patriarcale** for further information (tel. 520 03 33; English spoken).

The **Palazzo Ducale,** or Doge's Palace (tel. 522 49 51), stands between San Marco and the lagoon. Rebuilt in the 14th century after the original was destroyed by a fire, the palace epitomizes the Venetian Gothic. The exterior design combines graceful arcades and light-colored stone cladding to create an airy, delicate appearance, even on a massive structure. This same clever design was again employed in the extension of the palace one century later. The sculpted Virtues of Temperance, Fortitude, Prudence, and Charity that adorn the **Porta della Carta** are attributed to the 15th-century team of Giovanni and Bartolomeo Bon. At the side of San Marco stand the *Quattro Mori,* statues of four Roman emperors, which crusaders "borrowed" from Constantinople in 1204. Rizzo's **Scala dei Giganti** ("Giants' Stairs") rise to the second floor in the left end of the courtyard and are crowned with Sansovino's *Mars and Neptune.* Up his famous **Golden Staircase** are the Senate Chamber and the meeting room of the Council of Ten, the much-feared secret police of the Republic. Returning to the second floor, walk past some enormous globes to reach the echoing **Grand Council Chamber.** This room contains the huge, resplendent *Paradiso* by Tintoretto and Veronese's *Apotheosis of Venus.* It also houses portraits of all the doges of Venice except Marin Falier. An empty frame commemorates this over-ambitious doge, executed for treason after his unsuccessful coup attempt in 1355. Throughout the building are slits in the walls through which secret denunciations were passed to be investigated by the Ten. (Open daily 9am-7pm. Admission L14,000, includes admission to Museo Correr. Reduced price L8000.) For a **Secret Itineraries Tour** through the palace and over the Bridge of Sighs through the prison, call 522 49 51. You must call ahead for reservations, since there is no tour info at the Palazzo Ducale. (Tours Thurs.-Tues. 10am and noon, 1hr. In Italian only.)

From the Council Chamber, a series of secret passages leads across the **Ponte dei Sospiri** (Bridge of Sighs) from the back of the palace to the prisons. Casanova was among those condemned by the Ten to walk across into the hands of sadistic Inquisitors. The bridge's name alludes to the bitter groans of prisoners pondering the slim prospects of ever regaining their freedom. (Casanova did survive, however, and went on to become a librarian.)

Facing the Palazzo Ducale across P. San Marco are Sansovino's greatest hits, the elegant **Libreria** (1536) and the **Zecca** (coin mint, 1547). The main reading room of the **Biblioteca Marciana** (tel. 520 87 88), on the second floor, is adorned with frescoes by Veronese and Tintoretto. (Entrance at #12. Open Mon.-Fri. 9am-7pm, Sat. 9am-1:30pm. Prior permission required.) Venetian artists received their classical education from the sculptures in the **Museo Archeologico,** P. San Marco, 52 (tel. 522 59 78), next door. (Open daily 9am-2pm. Admission L4000.) Under the portico at the opposite end of the *piazza* from the church is the entrance to the **Museo Civico Correr** (tel. 522 56 25). It houses several of Bellini's and Carpaccio's *Courtesans,* not to mention such sundry curiosities of daily Venetian life as the foot-high platform shoes once worn by sequestered noblewomen. (Open Wed.-Mon. 10am-5pm. Ticket office closes at 3:15pm. Admission L14,000, includes admission to Palazzo Ducale. Reduced price L8000.)

The Mercerie

Starting under the arch of the Torre dell'Orologio in San Marco, the shop-filled and tourist-clogged Mercerie leads up to the **Church of San Giuliano,** commissioned by the Venetian doctor Tommaso Ragone as a monument to himself. His portrait by Sansovino glowers over the door, framed by inscriptions and allegories. The Mercerie then passes by **Campo San Salvatore,** a church consisting of three compiled square crosses. The church was originally designed and built in the early 16th century, but the façade was not completed until 1633. The church houses Giovanni Bellini's *Supper in Emmaus* and Titian's *Annunciation* (1566). (Open daily 9:30am-noon and 4:30-7pm. Free.)

Around San Marco

North of P. San Marco stands the **Church of Santa Maria Formosa.** At the bottom of the *campanile* leers a hideous carved head, which to Ruskin "embodied the type of evil spirit to which Venice was abandoned, the pestilence that came and breathed upon her beauty." Codussi's Greek-cross plan, the reconstruction of an ancient church, houses Palma il Vecchio's painting of St. Barbara, the exemplar of female beauty in Renaissance Venice. Across the bridge, a twisted alleyway leads to the haunting **Palazzo Querini-Stampalia** (tel. 241 14 11), whose intriguing, aristocratic rooms contain paintings dating from the 14th through 18th centuries. (Open Tues.-Sun. 10am-1pm and 3-6pm. Off-season closed in the afternoon. Admission L10,000, reduced price L5000.)

North of Campo Santa Maria Formosa, Calle Lunga and Calle Cicogna lead to Campo **SS. Giovanni e Paolo** and to the church of the same name (*San Zanipolo* in the Venetian dialect). This grandiose Gothic structure, built by the Dominican order over the course of two centuries (mid-13th to mid-15th), has an unusually sparse interior lined by monuments to various doges. A wonderful polyptych by Giovanni Bellini hangs over the second altar of the right-hand nave. From the left transept, enter the **Chapel of the Rosary.** Although damaged by a fire in 1867, the chapel still preserves four marvelous paintings by Veronese. If you cross the Ponte Rosso and go straight, you'll come to the Lombardos' architectural masterpiece, the **Church of Santa Maria dei Miracoli.**

To the east of San Marco, off Riva degli Schiavoni, stands the beautiful 15th-century **Church of San Zaccaria** (tel. 522 12 57). Codussi designed this striking façade, an enlarged version of his San Michele. Inside, the second altar on the left houses Bellini's masterpiece *The Madonna and Saints.* (Open daily 10am-noon and 4-6pm.) Around the corner on the waterfront is Massari's **Church of the Pietà** (building constructed in 1475, façade added in 1906), containing celebrated Tiepolo frescoes. Vivaldi was concertmaster here at the beginning of the 18th century, and concerts of his music are held in the church throughout the summer. (Open in summer daily 9:30am-12:30pm and 3-6pm; off-season only for masses and concerts.)

For a real treat, make your way through the *calli* to the **Scuola di San Giorgio degli Schiavoni,** Ponte dei Greci, 3259 (tel. 522 88 28). Here, between 1502 and 1511, Carpaccio decorated the ground floor with some of his finest paintings, depicting episodes from the lives of St. George, St. Jerome, and St. Trifone. (Open Tues.-Sun. 10am-12:30pm and 3-6pm. Admission L5000.) The nearby **Museo dei Dipinti Sacri Bizantini,** Ponte dei Greci, 3412 (tel. 522 65 81), displays religious paintings from the Byzantine and post-Byzantine periods. (Open Mon.-Sat. 9am-1pm and 2-4:30pm. Admission L6000, reduced price L3000.) Along the waterfront lie the **Giardini** (gardens), which every two years plays host to the biennial International Exhibition of Modern Art, known as the **Biennale** (go figure).

Cannaregio from the Rialto to the Ghetto

Heading north from the Rialto bridge on Salizzada San Giovanni, you will arrive at the last of Codussi's churches, **San Giovanni Crisostomo,** a refined Greek cross. The interior contains works by Giovanni Bellini and an altarpiece by Sebastiano del Piombo. Marco Polo supposedly lived under the arch in Corte Seconda del Milione.

From the Crisostomo church, head left toward the *rio* of the same name. Cross two bridges and two small squares to find the **Church of SS. Apostoli,** with an unassuming Tiepolo painting of Santa Lucia's first communion. Nearby is the **Cà d'Oro** (whose inaccessible front door taunts you from the Grand Canal), where the **Galleria Giorgio Franchetti** (tel. 523 87 90) opened in 1984. This formerly private collection displays works of minor Flemish painters and a few major pieces, including Titian's *Venus,* Mantegna's *St. Sebastian,* and Durer's *Deposition.* (Open daily 9am-1:30pm. Admission L4000.) North of here, the **Church of the Gesuiti** (tel. 523 06 25) boasts a florid green-and-white marble interior (rebuilt by Giorgio Massari in 1724), Titian's *Martyrdom of St. Lawrence*, and Tiepolo's altarpiece and ceiling fresco. In the northern corner of Cannaregio, the **Church of Madonna dell'Orto** patiently awaits the venturesome. Take scenic *vaporetto* #52 *(destra)* to the Madonna dell'Orto stop (L4000). Several works by Tintoretto, notably the *Sacrifice of the Golden Calf,* the *Last Judgement,* and the *Presentation of the Virgin*, reside within. (Open daily 9:30am-noon and 3:30-5:30pm.)

Between the church and the train station lies the **Jewish Ghetto,** the first in Europe. The term *ghetto* itself originated in Venice: the quarter was named after the knife-grinders who once worked here. Established by ducal decree in 1516, the Ghetto Nuovo remained the enforced enclave of the Jews in Venice until Napoleon's victory over the Venetian Republic in 1797. Upon entering the ghetto through the underpass off Fondamenta di Cannaregio, you can see the grooves in the marble where the gate formerly stood, trapping Jews inside at night. The area contains the tallest tenement buildings in Venice as well as five synagogues, three of which are open to the public. The **Sinagoga Grande Tedesca** is less opulent but more intriguing than the **Sinagoghe Spagnola** and **Levantina.** Tedesca is also the oldest, dating back to 1528. Drop by the **Museo Ebraico** (tel. 71 53 59) in the Campo del Ghetto Nuovo for a fascinating exhibit documenting five centuries of Jewish presence in Venice. Inquire here about guided tours of the Old Ghetto (every 30min. starting at 9:30am, L10,000). (Museum open Sun.-Fri. 9am-7pm. Closed Sat. and Jewish holidays. Admission L4000, students L3000.)

San Polo and Santa Croce

The **Ponte Rialto,** spanning the Grand Canal, is the entrance to this commercial district and an architectural gem in its own right. In the center of the **Erberia,** the grocery section of the open market, is the **Church of San Giacomo di Rialto,** the oldest in Venice. A stubby column with a staircase to the top stands in front of it, supported by a bent stone figure. The column served as a podium from which state proclamations were issued. The statue, called *il Gobbo* (the hunchback), has served as a bulletin board for public responses since Roman times.

From the **Rialto** bridge, drift with the crowd down the Ruga degli Orefici, then turn left and follow Ruga Vecchia San Giovanni to the **Church of San Polo** (*San Apponal* in the local dialect). The young Giandomenico Tiepolo completed the 14 dramatic Stations of the Cross in the chancel. Nearby, in the great Gothic Franciscan **Basilica dei Frari** of 1340 to 1443 (tel. 522 26 37), Donatello's wooden *St. John the Baptist* keeps company with a later Florentine statue of the saint by Sansovino and three purely Venetian paintings: Giovanni Bellini's triptych of the *Madonna and Saints* over the sacristy, Titian's famous *Assumption of the Virgin,* and his *Madonna of Case Pesaro.* (Open daily 9am-noon and 2:30-6pm. Admission L2000, holidays free.)

A *scuola* in Venice was a mixture of guild and religious fraternity. Members paid annual dues for the support of their needy fellow members and for the decoration of the *scuola's* premises. Among the richest and most illustrious was the **Scuola Grande di San Rocco** (tel. 523 48 64), across the *campo* at the end of the Frari. Tintoretto, who set out to combine, in his words, "the color of Titian with the drawing of Michelangelo," covered the inside with 56 paintings. To see the paintings in chronological order, start on the second floor in the Sala dell'Albergo and follow the cycle downstairs. (Open daily 9am-5:30pm; off-season Mon.-Fri. 10am-1pm, Sat.-Sun. 10am-4pm. Admission L8000, reduced price or Rolling Venice L6000.)

Dorsoduro

The Ponte dell'Accademia crosses the Grand Canal at the **Gallerie dell'Accademia** (tel. 522 22 47). This temple of Venetian-school art should top your list of things to see. Among the galleries, Room II stands out for Giovanni Bellini's *Madonna in Trono,* a sublime marriage of perspectival sense and Venetian sensibility. Room IV contains more Bellinis (from both Giovanni and his father Jacopo), as well as an early Piero della Francesca. Room V displays two amazing Giorgione canvases, *La Tempesta* and *La Vecchia.* Rooms VI-IX contain various Renaissance canvases and portraits, including Lorenzo Lotto's fine *Portrait of a Young Man*. Veronese's huge rendition of the Last Supper, displayed in Room X, enraged the leaders of the Inquisition with its indulgent improvisation—a Protestant German and a monkey figure were originally among the guests. Veronese was forced to change the name to *Supper in the House of Levi* to avoid having to make changes at his own expense. (Notice Judas the Betrayer dressed in yellow on the stairs to the left, his napkin stained with with blood to indicate that a fight has just taken place.) This room also houses several brilliant Tintorettos and Titian's last work, a brooding *Pietà.* Rounding off the collection are a number of works by Tiepolo, Canaletto, and Longhi, whose refined cityscapes are considered the height of early urban art. The wonderful cycle of *The Legend of St. Ursula* by Carpaccio (1490-95) in Room XXI boasts a scene of Ursula, 11,000 virgins in tow, trooping off to Cologne to meet martyrdom at the hands of the Huns. (Open Mon.-Sat. 9am-7pm, Sun. 9am-2pm; off-season Mon.-Sat. 9am-1pm. Admission L12,000. Students should try an ID just in case.)

The **Cà Rezzonico** (*vaporetto* stop of the same name) is on the Fondamenta Rezzonico, across the bridge from Campo San Barnabà. Designed by Longhena, it's one of the great 18th-century Venetian palaces. Inside, learn about notorious intrigues and love affairs in the **Museo del Settecento Veneziano** (Museum of the 18th Century; tel. 241 85 06). The small bedrooms and boudoirs on the second floor house delightful works by Tiepolo, Guardi, and Longhi. (Open Sat.-Thurs. 10am-5pm. Admission L8000. Seniors and children under 12 L5000. Closed for restoration; check with the tourist office for current info.)

The **Collezione Peggy Guggenheim,** Dorsoduro, 701 (tel. 520 62 88), housed in the late Ms. Guggenheim's Palazzo Venier dei Leoni near the tip of Dorsoduro, is a small and eclectic collection of modern art. It has rapidly become one of Venice's most popular museums, and rightfully so. Tasteful presentation complements the diversity of the collection itself, which includes works by Brancusi, Marino Marini, Kandinsky, Picasso, Magritte, Rothko, Max Ernst, and Jackson Pollock. The grounds feature a sculpture garden in which the late Ms. Guggenheim and her treasures (14 much-loved Lhasa Apso dogs) are buried. Incidentally, the Marini sculpture *Angel in the City* in the front of the *palazzo* was made with a detachable. . . well, you know. The late Ms. Guggenheim occasionally modified this sculpture so as not to offend certain visitors to her abode. Don't try to see for yourself. (Open Wed.-Mon. 11am-6pm. Admission L10,000, students with ISIC or Rolling Venice card L5000.) Just down the street from the Guggenheim Collection is a **Cenedesa Glass Blowing Factory** in Campo San Gregorio, 174. Witness the artistic technique here instead of traveling to outer islands. (Open Mon. and Wed.-Sat. 10am-1pm and 2-5pm. Free.)

The **Church of Santa Maria della Salute** (tel. 522 55 58), standing at the tip of Dorsoduro, is the most theatrical piece of architecture in Venice. It was designed by Longhena as the site of the dramatic *Festa della Salute* (Nov. 21), which celebrates the deal that the church struck with God, purportedly saving Venice from the plague of 1630. In the sacristy are several works by Titian and one by Tintoretto. (Open daily 8:30am-noon and 3-6pm. Admission to sacristy with donation.)

A bit north of Fondamenta Zattere, toward the western end of town, lies the 16th-century **Church of San Sebastiano** (tel. 528 24 87). It was here that Paolo Veronese took refuge in 1555 when he fled Verona, reputedly after killing a man. By 1565 he had filled the church with some of his finest paintings and frescoes. You'll marvel at his breathtaking *Stories of Queen Esther* on the ceiling. To get a closer look at the panels, climb to the nuns' choir. Here you'll also see Veronese's fresco *St. Sebastian in Front of Diocletian.* A mechanism for the illumination of the works (L500) is near the entrance. To get to the church by sea, take *vaporetto* #82 to the San Basilio stop.

Tourists are requested to limit visits to between 3:30 and 5:30pm, but the church is open in the morning as well.

Outlying Sights

Many of Venice's most beautiful churches are a short boat ride away from San Marco. Two of Palladio's most famous churches are visible from the *piazza.* The **Church of San Giorgio Maggiore,** across the lagoon (take boat #52 or 82, L2500), graces the island of the same name. The church houses Tintoretto's famous *Last Supper.* Ascend the **campanile** (tel. 528 99 00) for a superb view of the main islands. (Open daily 9:30am-12:30pm and 2-6pm. Admission L2000.)

A bit farther out on the next island, Giudecca, is Palladio's famous **Church of Il Redentore** (the Redeemer; tel. 523 14 15). During the pestilence of 1576, the Venetian Senate swore that they would build a devotional church and make a yearly pilgrimage there if the plague would leave the city. Palladio accommodated the pilgrims by enlarging the church's tribune. (Open 8am-noon and 3-7pm. Take *vaporetto* #82 from S. Marco.)

The tiny **Church of San Michele in Isola,** on its own island on the far side of the lagoon, is a Venetian masterpiece and the final resting place of sometime madman, Fascist sympathizer, and poet Ezra Pound. Begun by Codussi in 1469, the pristine marble façade was Venice's first Renaissance structure. The small hexagonal chapel to the left is a later addition. Take *vaporetto* #52 from S. Marco to the *Cimitero* (cemetery) stop.

The Islands of the Lagoon

Accessible by *vaporetto* #1, 6, 14, or 52, the **Lido** is the setting for Thomas Mann's unforgettable *Death in Venice* and Visconti's forgettable film version, both of which give a vivid impression of the sensuality and mystery for which Venice is famous. Lovers of the *belle époque* will enjoy a visit to the fabled Grand Hôtel des Bains, though it's not as exciting nowadays. From the *vaporetto* stop, follow the crowd that troops daily down Gran Viale Santa Maria Elisabetta. At the end of this road, yank off your sneakers and head for the **public beach.** Its sand, shells, and temperate summer waters make the Lido beach a perfect spot to relax.

Boat #12 departs from Fondamente Nuove near Campo dei Gesuiti for the islands of Murano, Burano, and Torcello. (Murano is also serviced by the #52.) **Murano** has been famous for its glass since 1292, when Venice's artisans decided to transfer their operations there. Today, serious glass-making coexists with tourist displays, affording visitors the opportunity to witness the glass-blowing process. The **Museo Vetrario** (tel. 73 95 86) on Fondamenta Giustiniani along the main canal has a splendid glass collection dating from Roman times onward. (Open Thurs.-Tues. 10am-5pm. Admission L8000, reduced price L5000.) Also located on Murano is the exceptional 7th-century **Basilica SS. Maria e Donato** which owes its exterior to a 12th-century renovation. **Burano,** a half-hour out of Venice by boat #12, also caters to tourists. It is famous for its lace, hawked all over Venice. The small **Scuola di Merletti di Burano** (tel. 73 00 34) on P. Galuppi documents the craft. (Open Tues.-Sat. 9am-6pm, Sun. 10am-4pm. Admission L5000, reduced price L3000.)

Today **Torcello,** the final island, is the most rural of the group. Of the first-time visitor to Venice, John Ruskin wrote, "let him not...look upon the pageantry of her palaces...but let him ascend the highest tier of the stern ledges that sweep round the altar of Torcello." The **cathedral** (tel. 73 00 84), founded in the 7th century and rebuilt in the 11th, has Byzantine mosaics inside so incredible that a 19th-century restorer took a few back to Wales with him. (Open daily 10am-12:30pm and 2-5pm. Admission L1500.) A **museum** (tel. 73 07 61) in Palazzo del Consiglio adjoins the cathedral. (Open Tues.-Sun. 10am-12:30pm and 2-4:30pm. Admission L3000.)

Never too far from water, prosperous Venetians built their farming villas along the Brenta River connecting Venice and Padua. **Palazzo Foscari** (also called "Villa Mira"; tel. 42 35 52), one of the most attractive villas on the Brenta, is now open for tours. (Open Tues.-Sun. 9am-6pm. Admission including guided tour L7000, seniors L5000.)

Villa Malcontenta (also called "Villa Foscari"; tel. 547 00 12), built by Palladio on a temple-like plan, is one of the most admired in the western world. (Open May-Oct. Tues., Sat., and the first Sun. of the month 9am-noon. Admission L10,000.) **Villa Strà** (also called "Villa Pisani"; tel. (049) 50 20 74) is renowned for its grand design by Figimelica and Preti and its interior decoration by Urbani and Tiepolo. (Open Tues.-Sun. 9am-6pm. Admission L8000.) To get to Villa Malcontenta, take bus #16 from P. Roma (L1200). To reach the other two villas, check the listings in **Practical Information: Buses,** p.327.

ENTERTAINMENT

The weekly booklet *A Guest in Venice* (free at hotels) lists current festivals, concerts, and gallery shows. Also ask for *Venice, 1997 Events.* There are concerts once or twice a week in the larger churches, particularly San Marco and Frari. Unfortunately, the grand **Teatro La Fenice,** whose florid interior can still be seen on postcards, burned down in January of 1996. Needless to say, the 1997 season was canceled. The **Festival Vivaldi** takes place in early September. In summer, Vivaldi's music is also featured in a concert series in the church of **Santa Maria della Pietà,** where he was choirmaster.

For a historical introduction to the city, a group called *Progetto Venezia* offers a slide show narrated in English on Venetian history, held at Campo S. M. Formosa, 5254. Proceeds benefit the S. Maria Formosa Church. (Call 526 23 79 or 526 92 61 for more info; fax 526 28 79. May-June and Sept.-Oct. Wed.-Fri. 7-8pm. Admission L10,000, students L8000.)

Mark Twain may have called the **gondola** "an inky, rusty canoe," but it's a canoe that only the gentry can really afford to ride. The authorized rate, which increases after sunset, starts at L80,000 for 50min., though mercenary gondoliers will frequently quote prices in the six-digit range. Rides are most romantic if procured about 50min. before sunset, and almost affordable if shared with 5 people. Venice was built to be traveled by gondola, and you will never truly get a feel for the city and its architecture until you slide quietly down the canals, pass by the front doors of the houses and *palazzi*, and experience its original pathways. There is, however, a sneaky way to get a cheap ride just for the experience. There are several bridgeless points along the Grand Canal where many Venetians need to cross. To solve the problem, *gondole* operate a short, cross-canal service. Each trip lasts only a minute or so, but this stand-up style of transportation averages a mere L2000.

For theatrical entertainment, **Commedia in Campo,** classical Venetian theater, operates outdoors in various *campi* throughout the city. Performance locations change every night. Tickets are L30,000, or you can try to sneak a peek through the curtains. Call Teatro Goldoni (tel. 520 54 22; fax 520 52 41) for more information.

The famed **Venice Biennale** (tel. 521 87 11; fax 521 00 38), centered in the Giardini di Castello, takes place every odd-numbered year, with a gala exhibit of international modern art. (Admission to all exhibits L16,000, less to see individual shows.) The **Mostra Internazionale del Cinema** (Venice International Film Festival; tel. 520 03 11) is held annually from late August to early September. Tickets (starting at 30,000) are sold at the Cinema Palace on the Lido (where the main films are screened) and at other locations—some late-night outdoor showings are free. Contact the tourist office with questions about the cinema. Other movie theaters in Venice include **Accademia,** Calle Contarina Corfù (tel. 528 77 06), just behind the Accademia Gallery (L10,000, seniors L5000) and **Olimpia,** Calle del Cavaletto, just north of P. S. Marco, which screens English language films on Wednesdays and Thursdays during the summer (L10,000, seniors L5000, Tues. L7000).

After an absence of several centuries, Venice's famous **Carnevale** was successfully (in a monetary if not entirely festive sense) revived as an annual celebration in 1979. During the ten days preceding Ash Wednesday, masked Venetians and camera-happy tourists jam the streets. Write to the tourist office in December for dates and details, and be sure to make lodging arrangements well in advance. Venice's second most colorful festival is the **Festa del Redentore,** originally held to celebrate the end of the plague (third Sun. in July). The Church of Il Redentore is connected with Zattere by a boat-bridge for the day, and a magnificent round of fireworks shoots off between 11pm and midnight on the Saturday night before. On the first Sunday in September, Venice stages its classic **regata storica,** a gondola race down the Grand Canal, preceded by a procession of decorated gondolas. The religious **Festa della Salute** takes place on November 21 at Santa Maria della Salute, with another pontoon bridge constructed, this time over the Grand Canal. Again, the festival originated as a celebration of the end of the plague.

If **shopping** is your bag, a few caveats are in order. Be careful about making purchases in P. San Marco or around the Rialto bridge. Shops that lie outside these heavily touristed areas very often boast products of better quality and selection at about half the price. (The vegetable market on the western side of the Rialto, however, is the real thing—prices for fruit and vegetables rival any supermarket's.) Venetian glass is displayed in the area near the Accademia bridge by San Marco or between the Rialto and the station in Cannaregio, though for fun you may want to look in the showroom at the glass-blowers' factory behind the Basilica of San Marco. The map accompanying the Rolling Venice card lists many shops offering reductions to cardholders. For the most concentrated and varied selections of Venetian glass and lace, trips to the nearby islands of Murano and Burano, respectively, are in order. *Vaporetto* #52 (L3000) serves Murano while #12 (L4000) travels to both Murano and Burano. Both boats leave from the Fondamenta Nuove stop.

Nightlife

Although many places shut down around midnight, there are quite a few good spots to go after the witching hour. The principal after-midnight strip is Fondamenta della Misericordia in Cannaregio, just past the Ghetto. From Lista di Spagna, cross the first main bridge, turn left on Fondamenta di Cannaregio, and look for the underpass to your right and signs pointing to the main square of the Ghetto Nuovo. Go to the square, walk straight on the bridge over the large canal, and take a right down the Fondamenta. Continue walking parallel to the canal for a few blocks, and you should be in the center of the action. (In general, you will have to keep your eyes open for clubs, especially in the S. Marco area.) Sadly, Venice's selection of nightclubs is paltry, and those that do exist tend to be meat-markets. Respectable Venetians go to Mestre and the mainland when they want to party, and most people seem to prefer mingling and dancing in the city's streets. Try **El Souk** (tel. 520 03 71), a swanky place in Calle Contarini Corfù, 1056/A, near the Accademia. Open Fri.-Wed. 6pm-4am. Cover of L15,000 includes your first drink. For a taste of history, swagger over to **Harry's Bar,** favored hangout of "Ernesto" Hemingway and real men ever since. It is located on Calle Vallaresso, in front of the San Marco *vaporetto* stop and across the bridge from the tourist office. Drinks L8000. Service 20%. Open Tues.-Sun. 10:30am-11pm. Beyond these offerings, the Lido is your best choice—hit **Nuova Acropoli** (tel. 526 04 66), at Lungomare Guglielmo Marconi (go right after you hit the beach). Open in the off-season only, Fri. and Sat. nights. Cover L12,000-20,000. Also check out **Ai Pugni** (see **Food: Dorsoduro,** page 333).

Paradiso Perduto, Fondamenta della Misericordia, 2540 (tel. 72 05 81). Bar, jazz club, and restaurant. Well-known among locals, this place is young and hip. Dark setting with *caffè*-type paintings adorning the walls and long wooden tables lit by candlelight. Outdoor seating by the canal. Live jazz and salsa on Sun. Typical Venetian fish dishes. Open Thurs.-Tues. 7:30am-late (depending on the night and the crowd). Closed Jan. 6-20 and August 1-5.

Iguana, Fondamenta della Misericordia, 2515 (tel. 71 67 22) Cannaregio. Also at Fondamenta delle Zitelle, 68 (tel. 523 00 04), just down from the hostel on Giudecca. Yes, there is Mexican food in Italy, and it's not bad. A favorite hangout for Venetian students. Entrees L7000-15,000. Open Wed.-Mon. 10:30am-3pm and 7pm-1am. Rolling Venice: 10% lunch discount plus free *aperitif.*

Devil's Forest, San Marco, 5185 (tel 520 06 23). On Calle Stagneri off Campo S. Bartolomeo and near the Rialto bridge. Upscale English pub atmosphere with stout, ale, and lager on tap, afternoon teas, cold snacks, and a diverse crowd. Drinks about L5500. Open Tues.-Sun. 8am-1am.

Haig's Bar, San Marco, 2477 (tel. 523 23 68) in Campo S. Maria del Giglio, not too far from P. San Marco. Exit on the far end of the *piazza* across from the basilica. Travel straight on Sal. S. Moisè past the AmEx office, cross 2 bridges and look for the bar next to a restaurant of the same name. A small, elegant indoor bar with patio seating outside in the *campo.* Frequented by locals, visitors, gondoliers, and business-types. Drinks L4000-10,000. Open Thurs.-Tues. 10:30am-2am.

Osteria del Sacro e Profano, S. Polo, 502 (tel. 520 19 31), on the right of the Rialto Bridge as you face S. Marco. An inviting spot for a drink and snack with friends. Mellow, jazzy music, indoor and outdoor seating. Wines from L3000. Open Tues.-Sun. 7pm-midnight.

Osteria al Mascoron, Calle Longa S. Maria Formosa, 5225 (tel. 522 59 95), off C. S. Maria Formosa. An authentic *osteria* that offers drinks, snacks, and meals. Wines from L3000 per glass. Food is more expensive (*primi* L12,000-L38,000, *secondi* L10,000-38,000). Cover L2000. Open Mon.-Sat. noon-3pm and 7pm-midnight.

Padua (Padova)

It took the prosperous Roman city of Padua over five centuries to recover from the Lombardic invasion of AD602. When its rulers finally declared independence from Byzantine and Lombard control, Padua wasted no time becoming one of the intellectual hubs of Europe. The "Bo" was founded in 1222 and is second in seniority only to Bologna among Italy's universities. Luminaries such as Dante, Petrarch, Galileo, and Copernicus all contributed to the collective genius, while native Mantegna and Florentines Giotto and Donatello beautified the town with art. Today, the university continues its intellectual traditions, and Padua bubbles with commercial activity. Although neighboring Venice steals some of its tourists, Padua is a lively and friendly city worthy of visitors.

ORIENTATION AND PRACTICAL INFORMATION

Padua's location on the Venice-Milan and Venice-Bologna train lines, as well as the availability of intercity buses, makes the city a convenient stop on almost any northern Italian itinerary. The train station is at the northern edge of town, just outside the 16th-century walls. A 10-min. walk down the Corso del Popolo—which becomes **Corso Garibaldi**—will take you into the commercial heart of town. Another 10min. down **Via Zabarella** and **Via del Santo** will bring you to the **Basilica del Santo,** the cathedral of Padua's patron saint, St. Anthony. **ACAP** city buses #3, 8, and 12 (L1300) will take you downtown directly from the station. For L5000, you can purchase a 24-hr. ticket valid for all urban lines.

Tourist Office: Two branches: one in the **Museo Civico** (tel. 875 11 53), open Tues.-Sun. 9am-7pm; the second in the **train station** (tel. 875 20 77), open Mon.-Sat. 9am-7:30pm, Sun. 8:30am-12:30pm. Pick up a map and a copy of the monthly entertainment brochure, *Padova Welcome,* for free.

Tourist Police: Ufficio Stranieri (Foreigners' Office), Riviera Ruzante, 13 (tel. 66 16 00). English interpreters available Mon.-Tues. and Thurs.-Fri. 8:30am-11:30pm.

Budget Travel: CTS, Riviera dei Mugnai, 22 (tel. 876 16 39), near the post office. Student IDs, travel information, and train tickets. Open Mon.-Fri. 9am-12:30pm and 4-7:30pm, Sat. 9am-12:30pm.

Currency Exchange: Banca Antoniana, Via VIII Febbraio, 5 (tel. 83 91 11). The best rates and no commission. **Central branch** located behind Caffè Pedrocchi, in the center of town. Open Mon.-Fri. 8:20am-1:20pm and 2:35-3:35pm. Also at P. Stazione, 7 (tel. 875 10 50).

American Express: Tiare Viaggi, Via Risorgimento, 20 (tel. 66 61 33), near P. Insurrezione. No currency exchange. Open Mon.-Fri. 9am-1pm and 3-7pm, Sat. 10am-noon.

Telephones: Corso Garibaldi, 33 (tel. 820 85 11), next to the post office. Open Mon.-Fri. 8:30am-12:30pm and 4-7pm, Sat. 8:30am-12:20pm.

Trains: P. Stazione (tel. 875 18 00), in the northern part of town at the end of Corso del Popolo, the continuation of Corso Garibaldi. To: Venice (every 15min., 30min., L3400); Verona (every hr., 1½hr., L7200); Milan (every hr., 2½hr., L19,000); and Bologna (every 30min., 1½hr., L9800). Open daily 7:20am-7pm. **Luggage Storage:** L5000 for 12hr. Open daily 4:40am-1:30am.

Buses: ATP and **SITA,** Via Trieste, 42 (tel. 820 68 44; fax 820 68 14), near P. Boschetti, 5min. from the train station. To: Bassano del Grappa (every 30min., 1¼hr., L5100); Vicenza (every 30min., 30min., L4800); and Venice (every 30min., 45min., L4800). Buses operate roughly between 6am and 9pm. Office open Mon.-Thurs. 8:30am-1pm and 2-5:30pm, Fri. 8:30am-1pm.

Car Rental: Europcar, P. Stazione, 6 (tel. 875 85 90). Offers *Treno più Auto,* a slight discount upon presentation of a train ticket to Padua. Min. age 21. About L150,000 per day, L620,000 per week. **Hertz,** P. Stazione, 1/VI (tel. 875 22 02). Min. age 25. L150,000 per day, L680,000 per week. **Maggiore,** P. Stazione, 15/bis (tel. 875 28 52). Min. age 21. L150,000 per day, L500,000 per week.

Bookstore: Draghi Libreria Internazionale, Via Cavour, 17-19 (tel. 876 03 05). A large selection of classics in English (including the *Let's Go* series). Open Mon.-Sat. 9am-12:30pm and 3:30-7:30pm.

Laundromat: Fastclean, Via Ognissanti, 6 (tel. 77 57 59), near the *Porta Portello.* Take bus #7, 9, or 15. Self-service. 1-4kg L13,000. Open Mon.-Fri. 9:30am-12:30pm and 3:30-7:30pm, Sat. 9:30am-12:30pm.

Emergencies: tel. 112 or 113. **First Aid:** tel. 821 65 70. **Hospital: Ospedale Civile,** Via Giustiniani, 1 (tel. 821 11 11), off Via San Francesco.

Police: (tel. 83 31 11), Riviera Ruzante, near V. Santa Chiara.

Post Office: Corso Garibaldi, 25 (tel. 820 85 17). Fax service and *fermo posta.* Open Mon.-Fri. 8:15am-7:30pm, Sat. 8:15am-12:30pm. Another branch at the **train station.** Open Mon.-Fri. 8:15am-1pm. **Postal Code:** 35100.

Telephone Code: 049.

ACCOMMODATIONS AND CAMPING

Cheap lodgings abound in Padua, but they tend to fill up quickly. If you can't get into the places listed below, try any of the hotels near **Piazza del Santo.** For private rooms in local homes call the **APT local tourist board** (tel. 875 20 77) or the **provincial tourist board** (tel. 820 15 54). For summer housing options at the university, call or write to **Centro Universitario,** Via Zabarella, 82 (tel. 65 42 99), or **Cattolici Popolari,** c/o Palazzo del Bó (tel. 828 31 11, ext. 399). In the summer, start your search as early as 7am.

Ostello Città di Padova (HI), Via Aleardi, 30 (tel. 875 22 19; fax 65 42 10), near Prato della Valle. Take bus #3, 8, 12, or 18 from the station. From bus #3 or 8, get off when you first glimpse the white statues on the Prato della Valle, a large, circular park on the left. Walk back toward the bridge and turn left on Via Memmo. Pass the church; Via Aleardi is on the right. From bus #12 or 18, get off at Via Cavaletto, past Prato della Valle, and walk up along Via Marin toward the church. Quiet location with large, sterile, crowded rooms. English spoken. Flexible 5-day max. stay. Open daily 8-9:30am and 6-11pm. Register and drop off your stuff anytime Mon.-Fri. Lockout 9am-5pm. Curfew 11pm. L19,000 per person, L16,000 if you stay more than 3 nights. Hot showers and breakfast included. If out-of-the-way castles suit you, consider the hostel in **Montagnana** (see page 348).

Albergo Verdi, Via Dondi dall'Orologio, 7 (tel. 875 57 44). Walk under the clock tower at the end of P. dei Signori and turn right at the end of the row of trees. Large, comfortable rooms in the center of town. Singles L39,000. Doubles L52,000. Reserve 2-3 days ahead in summer.

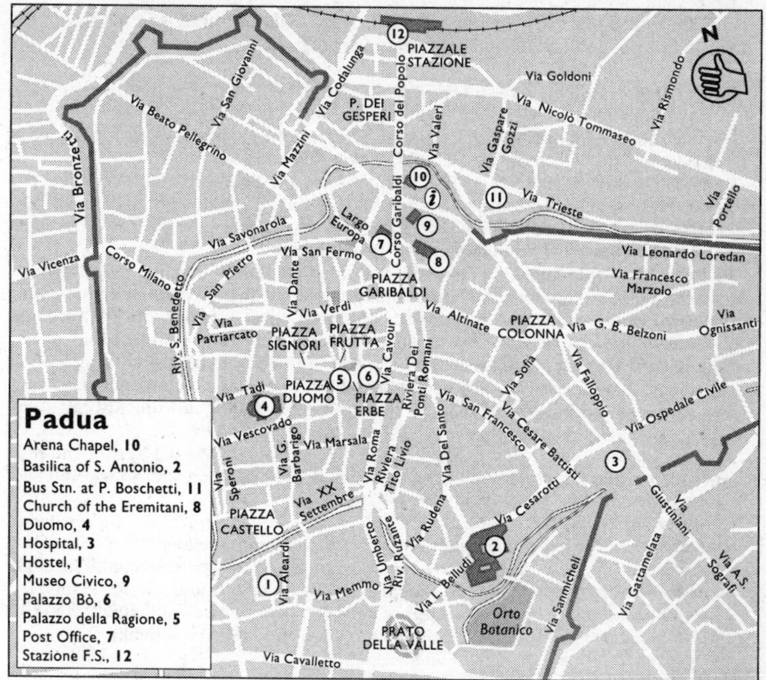

Casa della Famiglia (ACISJF), Via Nino Bixio, 4 (tel. 875 15 54), off P. Stazione. Leave the station, cross the street, and walk toward Hotel Monaco; the hostel is on a small street to your left. Women under 29 only. The good sisters reserve the right to turn away "undesirables." Curfew 10:30pm. Modern and tidy doubles, triples, and quads about L20,000 per bed. Study and kitchen open for use at night.

Albergo Pavia, Via dei Papafava, 11 (tel. 66 15 58). Take Via Roma from P. delle Erbe, turn right on Via Marsala, and left on Via dei Papafava. Rooms in front of the garden have wood floors, and rooms in back have been renovated. Rooftop clotheslines, kitchen facilities, and eating areas available. Singles L39,000. Doubles L52,000. Triples L66,000.

Camping: Montegrotto Terme, Via Roma, 123/125 (tel. 79 34 00 or 79 33 32). A 15-km bus ride from Padua. Take the ACAP bus M. Stop at the Hotel Cristallo and turn left; Via Roma is the street at the first stoplight. Walk 1km up Via Roma, following the signs to Padua. Friendly, accommodating staff. English and German spoken. Tennis, disco, and restaurants in the vicinity. Prices depend on the season, ranging up to L10,500 per adult. Open March-early Nov.

FOOD

Markets are held in P. delle Erba and P. della Frutta. Sidewalk vendors sell fresh produce, and covered booths in the archways offer meat and dairy products. During the academic year, student *mense* pop up all over town, so ask around. There's a convenient supermarket downtown, across from Caffè Pedrocchi: **PAM,** on Via Cavour in P. della Garzeria (open Mon.-Tues. and Thurs.-Sat. 8:30am-7:30pm, Wed. 8:30am-noon). Wine-lovers may sample a glass from the nearby Colli Euganei wine district or try the sparkling *lambruschi* of Emilia-Romagna. Two of the most distinctive whites are produced by **Trattoria da Nane della Giulia,** Via Santa Sofia, 1, off Via San Francesco (open Tues.-Sun. 9am-4pm and 6pm-1am); and **Spaccio Vini Carpanese,** Via del Santo, 44 (tel. 305 81; open Mon.-Sat. 9-11:30am and 4-6pm). Delicious wines run L2000-4500 per glass. Visitors to the basilica of St. Anthony can nibble on the *dolce del santo,* a sweet pastry available in nearby *pasticcerie.*

Mensa Universitaria, Via San Francesco, 122 (tel. 66 09 03). The most pleasant and convenient *mensa*. *Menù* L13,000. Open Mon.-Sat. 11:45am-2:30pm and 6:45-9pm, Sun. 11:45am-2:30pm. Check here for info on other *mense.* If this one is closed, try the *mensa* on Via Marzolo, 4, near Via Morgagni.

Brek, P. Cavour, 20 (tel. 875 37 88), across from Caffè Pedrocchi. Self-service restaurant. Interior lacks personality, but food is fast and reasonably good. *Primi* L4000-6000, *secondi* L6100-7200. Watch for these restaurants in other towns as well. Open Sat.-Thurs. 11:30am-3pm and 6:30-10:30pm.

Al Pero, Via Santa Lucia, 72 (tel. 365 61), near Via Dante. Bustling neighborhood eatery with fantastic food and entertaining waiters. To visit Veneto without tasting *polenta* would be a crime, so consider ordering some. *Primi* L4000-7000, *secondi* L6500-9000. Cover L2500. Open Mon.-Sat. noon-2:30pm and 7:30-10:15pm.

Pizzeria Al Borgo, Via Luca Belludi, 56 (tel. 875 88 57), near the Basilica of St. Anthony. A wide variety of large, yummy pizzas. Indoor and outdoor seating. Traditional pizzas L5500-10,500. More creative pizzas 10,000 and up. Cover L2000. Open Wed.-Mon. noon-3pm and 7pm-1am. AmEx.

Alexander Bar, Via San Francesco, 38 (tel. 65 28 84), off Via del Santo. One hundred beers and about 60 types of *panini* (L3000-5500). Open late, so you can take your time deciding. Open Mon.-Sat. 8:30am-2am.

Lunanuova, Via G. Barbarigo, 12 (tel. 875 89 07), in the *zona duomo*. Vegetarian restaurant in a comfortable, quiet setting, complete with mellow jazz, political bulletin boards, and an array of books and pamphlets on veggie restaurants throughout Italy. Serves brown bread—a rarity in Italy. Lunch and dinner selections L15,000-20,000. For beverages, choose between beer, wine, fruit juice, and herbal tea. Cover L2000. Open Tues.-Sat. 12:30-2:15pm and 7:30pm-midnight.

SIGHTS

You can buy a **ticket** good at most of the museums in Padua for L15,000 (L10,000 for students and groups), valid for one year and available at any of the following sights: Cappella degli Scrovegni, Museo Civico, Orto Botanico, Palazzo della Ragione, Battistero del Duomo, and the Oratorio di San Giorgio. A great deal if you plan on visiting two or more of the sites.

Despite four centuries of Venetian dominance, Padua has preserved a distinct civic identity, taking pride in its renowned artwork and revered university. The **Cappella degli Scrovegni** (better known as the **Arena Chapel**) alone merits a pilgrimage to Padua. The chapel contains Giotto's breathtaking floor-to-ceiling fresco cycle, with fantastic colors and a splendid azure sky. Executed between 1303 and 1305, these 36 perfectly preserved panels illustrate the lives of Mary and Jesus and comprise one of the most influential works of art from this period. The chapel is joined with the **Museo Civico,** an art museum that contains, among other treasures, Giorgione's *Leda and the Swan* and a recently restored Giotto crucifix. You can buy tickets for the chapel and museum at the Museo Civico. (Open Feb.-Oct. daily 9am-7pm; Nov.-Jan. 9am-6pm. Admission L10,000, students L7000, school groups L5000 per person. The museum is closed on Mon., but the chapel remains open.)

Next door, the **Church of the Eremitani** (1276-1306) boasts an imposing exterior and a beautifully carved wooden ceiling that was successfully restored after a devastating 1944 bombing. Unfortunately, Andrea Mantegna's cycle of frescoes —which once rivaled Giotto's masterpiece—was almost entirely lost. Several photos of the World War II destruction are displayed in the front left corner of the church. The restoration is miraculous, considering the extensive damage. (Open April-Sept. Mon.-Sat. 8:15am-noon, Sun. 9am-noon and 3:30-6:30pm; Oct.-March Mon.-Sat. 8:15am-noon, Sun. 9am-noon and 3:30-5:30pm. Free.)

A building complex on P. del Santo pays homage to Padua's patron St. Anthony. The 13th-century **Basilica di Sant'Antonio** (tel. 66 39 44), where the saint is entombed, is a medieval conglomeration of eight domes, a pair of octagonal campaniles, and some supporting minarets. The saint's jawbone and well preserved tongue can be seen in the central arch of a chapel at the back of the church, directly opposite the main entrance. The jawbone is kept behind glass inside the saint's gold bust, and the tongue rests quietly in a fancy gold case beneath the jawbone. Seven bronze sculptures by Donatello grace the high altar, watched over by the artist's *Crucifixion*. The **Tomb of Saint Anthony** is to your left when you stand in front of the altar and is the final destination for the thousands of pilgrims who visit the basilica each year. A permanent, free exhibition in the attached courtyard details the life of the saint. Special headsets from the front desk provide simultaneous English translation of this audio-visual display. The show lasts about 20min. and is open in summer only, 9am-12:30pm and 3-7pm. From inside the church, follow the green and orange "Mostre Antoniane" signs through the courtyard to the entrance. (Basilica open daily 7:30am-7pm.)

The adjoining **Oratorio di San Giorgio** houses examples of Giotto-school frescoes, as does the **Scuola del Santo** (tel. 875 52 35), which includes three by the young Titian. (Both open daily April-Sept. 9am-12:30pm and 2:30-7pm; Oct.-Jan. 9am-12:30pm; Feb.-March 9am-12:30pm and 2:30-4:30pm. L3000 for both museums. Closed for restoration—check with the tourist office for the latest info.)

In the center of P. del Santo stands Donatello's influential bronze equestrian statue of **Gattamelata** ("Calico Cat"), a general remembered for his agility and ferocity. Donatello modeled the statue after the Roman equestrian statue of Marcus Aurelius at the Campidoglio in Rome. Only a block away lies the peaceful **Orto Botanico** (tel. 65 66 14), the oldest university botanical garden (est. 1545). A palm tree planted in 1585 still offers shade. (Open April-Oct. Mon.-Sat. 9am-1pm and 3-6pm, Sun. 9am-1pm; Nov.-March Mon.-Sat. 9am-1pm. Admission L6000, students L3000.)

The **Palazzo della Ragione** (Hall of Justice) was built in 1218 and marks the city center. Its external *loggias* and keel-shaped roof were added in 1306. (Open Tues.-Sun. 9am-7pm; off-season 9am-1pm and 3-6pm. General admission L7000; special exhibits L10,000, students L3000.)

The **Duomo** in P. Duomo (tel. 66 28 14) was erected between the 16th and 18th centuries. Michelangelo reportedly participated in the design. The **Battistero** next door was built in the 12th century and retouched in the 13th. Inside you will find another significant cycle of 14th-century frescoes by Menabuoi. (Open Tues.-Sun. 9:30am-12:30pm and 2:30-6pm; in winter open only until 5:30pm. Admission to *Battistero* L3000, students L2000.)

The **university** campus is scattered throughout the city, but its center is in Palazzo Bò (tel. 828 31 11). In Venetian dialect *bò* means steer or castrated bull; the name derives from the sign of the inn that formerly occupied the *palazzo's* site. The scientific **teatro anatomico** (1594) was the first of its kind in Europe and hosted the likes of Vesalius and Englishman William Harvey, who discovered the circulation of blood. Almost all Venetian noblemen received their mandatory instruction in law and public policy in the **Great Hall,** and the "chair of Galileo" is preserved in the **Sala dei Quaranta,** where the physicist used to lecture. Across the street, **Caffè Pedrocchi** (tel. 876 25 76) served as the headquarters for 19th-century liberals who supported Giuseppe Mazzini. When it was first built, the *caffè's* famous neoclassical façade had no doors and was open around the clock. Every university student was entitled to a free newspaper and a glass of water. The battle between students and Austrian police here in February 1848 was a turning point in the Risorgimento. Capture the spirit for the price of a cappuccino. (Closed for renovation—check with the tourist office for the latest info.)

ENTERTAINMENT

Padua's nightlife is elusive. To get the inside scoop on the goings-on of the collegiate crowd, keep your eyes peeled for posters around the university. The evening *passeggiata* takes place in P. Garibaldi and up Via Cavour, so the *caffè* here and in nearby P. delle Frutta come to life at night. You may also want to check out **Lucifer Young,** Via Altinate, 89 (tel. 875 22 51), near the Church of Santa Sofia and the university. A hip bar in 3-D whose decorator took lessons from the lowest circle in the Divine Comedy. Drinks L6000 and up, with some food available. (Open Sun.-Tues. and Thurs.-Fri. at 7pm, Sat.-Sun. at 6pm.)

Check the posters around Palazzo Bò, or pick up a copy of the newspaper *Il Mattino,* for concert and film listings. In July the city organizes the **Cinema Città Estate,** a film series presented in the Arena Romana. Call the tourist office or the Assessorato di Turismo (tel. 820 15 30) for further information. February 8 brings the **Festa della Matricola,** during which students and professors take the day off from classes, wear ancient academic costumes, and play practical jokes on each other. An **antique market** assembles in the Prato della Valle on the third Sunday of each month. Pilgrims pack the city on the thirteenth of June, as Padua remembers the death of its patron St. Anthony (who died in 1231) with a procession of the Saint's statue and jawbone through the city, beginning at the basilica.

■ Near Padua

The **Colli Euganei** (Eugan Hills), southwest of Padua, offer a feast for the senses. Padua's tourist office has pamphlets suggesting various itineraries. The volcanic hills are rich not only in soil and hot mineral springs, but in extraordinary accommodations as well. If you've always dreamed of life in a castle, realize your aspirations with a night at the **Youth Hostel (HI)** in **Montagnana.** The town lies just outside of the *colli,* an hour by bus from either Vicenza or Padua (roundtrip L10,500). The hostel (tel. (0429) 81 07 62) offers 70 beds within the Rocca degli Alberi. For L15,000, enjoy a soft bed and hot showers run by English-speaking management. The Montagnana **tourist office** is located in P. Maggiore (tel. (0429) 813 20). Open irregularly Mon. and Wed.-Sat. 10am-noon and 4-6pm.

■ Treviso

Treviso means "three faces," and, while the name may be without historical significance, it seems particularly well-suited to this provincial capital. The tourism industry promotes the first two faces, *città d'acqua* (city of water) and *città dipinta* (painted city). Its aqueous character derives from rivulets from the Sile River that flow through town, disappearing only to resurface where least expected. As for the paint, the frescoed façades of the buildings that line the streets only hint at their former splendor. The third face of Treviso needs no glossy brochures to catch the eye: Treviso is rolling in dough (and we ain't talking bakeries). There are only four official stores in town, but be assured that Benetton was indeed born here. Without your manicure, pedicure, and personal trainer you may feel out of place in this glitzy haven for the rich; bring your Mercedes and wear your Rolex. Since Treviso's affluence keeps bargains at bay, the town is best seen as a daytrip from Venice or Padua.

ORIENTATION AND PRACTICAL INFORMATION

Treviso lies half an hour inland from Venice. The historic center is contained within the old city walls, which are bordered alternately on the inside and outside—sometimes both—by flowing water. **Via Roma** is the entrance to town; it becomes **Corso del Popolo** and leads to **Piazza della Borsa**. From here, a short walk up Via XX Settembre leads to **Piazza dei Signori,** the center of Treviso. Pedestrian-dominated **Via Calmaggiore** leads to the *duomo.*

Tourist Office: Via Toniolo, 41 (tel. 54 76 32; fax 54 13 97). Via Roma becomes Corso del Popolo as you cross the Sile River; take this to P. della Borsa, easily identified by the face-off of rival banks. Via Toniolo is to the right. Ask for a map of walking tours and bike routes. English spoken. Open Mon.-Fri. 8:30am-12:30pm and 3-6pm, Sat. 8:30am-noon.

Telephones: Via Calmaggiore, 34, off P. dei Signori. Also has public fax. Open Mon.-Fri. 9am-12:30pm and 4-7:30 pm.

Trains: P. Duca d'Aosta (tel. 54 13 52), at the southern end of town. Treviso lies on the Venice-Udine line. Ticket counter open 6am-9pm. To: Venice (every 30min., 30min., L2700); Udine (every 30min., 1½hr., L9800); and Milan (every hr., 3½hr., L33,000).

Buses: Lungosile Mattei, 21 (tel. 41 22 22), to the left just before Corso del Popolo crosses the river. Comprehensive service throughout Veneto and to the villas. To: Padua (every 30min., L5000); Vicenza (every hr., 1 hr., L6500); Bassano (9 per day, L5700); and Asolo (every hr., L4400).

Emergencies: tel. 113. **Ambulance:** 118. **Hospital: Unit Sanitaria Locale,** tel. 32 21. Take bus #1.

Police: Questura, Via Carlo Alberto, 37 (tel. 59 91).

Post Office: P. Vittoria, 1 (tel. 59 72 07 or 59 71). Stamps and *fermo posta* at #1. Open daily 8:15am-7:30pm. **Postal Code:** 31050.

Telephone Code: 0422.

ACCOMMODATIONS AND FOOD

Unfortunately for the budget traveler, Treviso's wealthy climate has spawned a number of hotels (singles run L75,000 and up) but few inexpensive budget accommodations; consider Treviso as a daytrip. Treviso is famous for its *ciliegie* (cherries), *radicchio* (red chicory lettuce), and *tiramisù,* a heavenly creation of espresso-and-liquor-soaked cake layered with sweet cream cheese. Cherries ripen in June, *radicchio* peaks in December, and *tiramisù* is always in season. If *primi* and *secondi* seem to be merely an inconvenient delay, begin with dessert at **Nascimben,** Via XX Settembre, 3 (tel. 512 91), the local espresso-and–pastry pit stop (open Tues.-Sun. 7am-2am; *tiramisù* L2500 per 100g). For your basics, shop at the **Pam** supermarket, P. Borso, 18 (tel. 539 13) in the corner of the piazza behind Banca Nazionale del Lavoro. Open Mon.-Tues. and Thurs.-Sat. 8:30am-1pm and 3-7:30pm, Wed. 8:30am-1pm. Treviso's local market, including food and clothing, takes places on Tuesday and Saturday mornings in the Via Pescheria. **All'Oca Bianca,** Vicolo della Torre, 7 (tel. 54 18 50), on a side street off central Via Calmaggiore, is a casual *trattoria* in the thick of things. Try any of the fish dishes. *Primi* L8000, *secondi* and fish L8000-14,000. Cover L2500. Open Thurs.-Mon. 9am-3pm and 6pm-midnight, Tues. 9am-3pm. V, MC, AmEx. **Brek,** Corso del Popolo, 25 (tel. 500 12), near P. Borsa, has self-service fare, including pasta and salads. The main attraction is the pleasant seating on the patio and second floor. *Primi* L4000-6000, *secondi* L5000-9000. Open Tues.-Sun. 11:30am-3pm and 6:30-10:30pm.

SIGHTS

The **Palazzo dei Trecento** (tel. 54 17 16), dominating P. dei Signori, proudly asserts Treviso's successful reemergence from a 1944 air raid (on Good Friday) that demolished half the town. Climb the stairs on the outer wall and look for the clearly marked signs underfoot that mark the position of the walls after the bomb. The building was successfully reconstructed using the original bricks, and the interior restoration blends perfectly with the original frescoes. (Open Mon-Sat. 8:30am-12:30pm. Free.)

Back in P. dei Signori, you can join in Via Calmaggiore's endless *passeggiata* and walk beneath the arcades to the seven-domed, patchwork-style **duomo,** which displays an unusual classical façade. The **Cappella Malchiostro** dates from 1519 and contains Titian's *Annunciation.* and frescoes by Pordenone. It's a strange combination, considering that the two artists were sworn enemies. (Open weekdays 7:30am-noon and 3:30-7pm; Sun. 7:30am-1pm and 3:30-8pm.) From P. del Duomo, Via

Risorgimento leads to the large Dominican church of **San Nicolò** on Via San Nicola. The mammoth, 14th-century brick structure sports a triple apse, along with some frescoed saints by Tommaso da Modena. (Open in summer Mon.-Fri. 8am-noon and 3:30-7pm; in winter Mon.-Fri. 9am-noon and 3-5:30pm. Free.)

The **Museo Civico,** also called the Bailo Museum, at Borgo Cavour, 24 (tel. 513 37 or 65 84 42) houses Titian's *Sperone Speroni* and Lorenzo Lotto's *Portrait of a Dominican* in the same room. The ground floor protects Treviso's archaeological finds, among them 5th-century BC bronze discs from Montebelluna. (Museum open Tues.-Fri. 9am-12:30pm and 2:30-5pm, Sat. 9am-12:30pm, Sun. 9am-noon and 3-6pm. Admission L3000, school groups L1000 per person.)

Bassano del Grappa

At the foot of Monte Grappa, Bassano del Grappa is a hideaway for many Italian and Austrian tourists. Visit Bassano for *grappa* liquor, mushrooms, pottery, and the emblematic wooden bridge over Ponte degli Alpini. Oh, and the *grappa.* Locals claim that Bassano's greatest asset is its proximity to the mountains, but the panoramic views from its bridges are also spectacular. Did we mention the *grappa?*

ORIENTATION AND PRACTICAL INFORMATION

Bassano's principal *piazze* lie between the train station and the **Fiume Brenta.** From the station take **Via Chilesotti** toward **Piazzale Trento** and bear right on **Via Museo** to reach the heart of town. The center is split between **Piazza Garibaldi** and **Piazza Libertà,** only one-half block apart. Walk across the **Ponte degli Alpini** (also known as the **Ponte Vecchio**) to the other side of Bassano, which has many small shops, restaurants, and charming *vicoli.*

Tourist Office: Largo Corona d'Italia, 35 (tel. 52 43 51; fax 52 53 01). From the station, walk down Via Chilesotti, across the larger Viale delle Fosse, and through the gap in the stone wall. The tourist office is the older, detached building to the right. The monthly, trilingual *Bassano News* features hotel listings, restaurants, practical information, and a town map. Open Mon.-Fri. 9am-12:30pm and 2-5pm, Sat. 9am-12:30pm.

Telephones: Caffè Danieli, P. Garibaldi. Open Tues. 7am-noon and Thurs.-Mon. 7am-9pm.

Trains: At the end of Via Chilesotti (tel. 52 50 34), a few blocks from the historic center. Ticket counter open Mon.-Fri. 6:30am-8:45pm, Sat.-Sun. 6:05am-7:45pm. To: Padua (14 per day, 1hr., L4200); Venice (16 per day, 1hr., L5700); Trent (9 per day, 2hr., L8000); and Vicenza via Cittadella (9 per day, 2hr., L3400). **Luggage Storage:** L5000 for 12hr. Same hours as ticket counter.

Buses: In P. Trento (tel. 25 025). As you head away from the train station on Via Chilesotti, turn left on Viale delle Fosse. A few different bus companies service the surrounding towns: **CO.APT** (tel. 820 68 11) to Padua (every 30min.); **A.C.T.M.** (tel. (0423) 49 75 85) to Maser (2 per day) and Possagno (every hr.); **F.T.V.** (tel. 30 850) to Vicenza (every 30min., L4800), Asiago (5 per day, L5600), Maróstica (every hr., L1900), and Thiene (every hr., L3800); **La Marca Line** (tel. in Treviso (0422) 41 22 22) to Treviso (L5500), Masèr (L3300), and Asolo. Buy tickets at Bar Trevisani in P. Trento or Bar al Termine, Viale Venezia, 45.

Hiking: Club Alpino Italiano (tel. 22 79 96), on Via Schiavonetti. Hiking and mountain information. Open Tues. and Fri. 9-11pm, Thurs. 5-7pm.

Late-Night Pharmacy: Consult *Bassano News* for the most current list.

Emergencies: tel. 113 or 112. **First Aid:** tel. 88 82 57. **Ambulance:** tel. 52 31 94. **Hospital: Ospedale Civile,** Viale delle Fosse, 43 (tel. 88 81 11).

Police: (tel. 22 84 91), Via Cá Rezzonico.

Post Office: Viale XI Febbraio, 2 (tel. 52 21 11), south of the center at P. Cadorna. Open Mon.-Fri. 8:15am-7:45pm, Sat. 8:15am-6:30pm. **Postal Code:** 36061.

Telephone Code: 0424.

ACCOMMODATIONS AND FOOD

Budget hotels are a rare breed in Bassano, so reserve ahead or consider accommodations elsewhere. Alternatively, make Bassano a daytrip on your itinerary. **Istituto Cremona,** Via Chini, 6 (tel. 52 20 32), past the main post office on Via Emiliani, is a school-turned-hostel that offers bargain-basement rates. 5-day max. stay. Check-in 7-9:30am and 6-10pm. No daytime lockout. Curfew 11pm. L15,000 per night, L18,000 with breakfast. Open late June-early Sept.

The town's most spirited claim to fame is *grappa,* a steamroller of a liquor distilled from the seeds and skins of grapes and sold in bottles of every shape imaginable. For authenticity, buy a bottle from the **Nardini** distillery by the Ponte degli Alpini. Open 8am-8pm. Numerous shops near the bridge will sell you more *grappa* and *porcini* mushrooms than your stomach can hold. On the tamer side, Bassano is also famous for its white asparagus. Depending on the season, produce can be purchased at the **open-air market** on Thurs. and Sat. 8am-1pm in P. Garibaldi.

Ottone Birraria, Via Matteotti, 50 (tel. 222 06). Pictures of everything from track runners to autumn in Vermont line the walls of this beautifully decorated eatery. The food is sumptuous, and the staff is welcoming. Don't miss it! From Hungarian goulash (L15,000) to hot sandwiches (L6000-8000). Pasta L9000-10,000. Cover L2500. Open Wed.-Mon. 10:30am-3:30pm and 7:30pm-12:30am. Closed Mon. evening. V, MC.

Al Saraceno, Via Museo, 60 (tel. 225 13). A favorite local hangout with seafood specialties and an impressive pizza repertoire. *Primi* L7000-8000, *secondi* L6000-16,000. Pizza L5000-9000. *Menù* L18,000. Cover L1000. Open Tues.-Sun. 10am-3pm and 5:30pm-1am. V, MC, AmEx.

SIGHTS AND ENTERTAINMENT

The belle of Bassano is the lovely **Ponte degli Alpini,** a covered wooden bridge dating from 1209 and redesigned by Palladio (1568-70) to resemble a fleet of ships; whether it does or not is another question. The bridge is named for the Alpine soldiers who died fighting the Austrians and Germans during World War I. Coming from the center, cross the bridge and bear left for a panoramic river view. The **Museo Civico** in P. Garibaldi (tel. 52 22 35) houses masterpieces by Jacopo da Bassano (1517-1592), including the *Flight into Egypt* and *St. Valentine Baptizing St. Lucilla.* (Open Tues.-Sat. 9am-12:30pm and 3:30-6:30pm, Sun. 3:30-6:30pm. Admission L5000, groups over 20 L2500 per person.) Next door stands the Romanesque-Gothic **Church of San Francesco,** completed in the early 14th century. The spacious interior shows few traces of the original frescoes, but the *Madonna and Child* by Lorenzo Martinelli beneath the arches of the entrance has just been restored. The recently opened **Museo della Ceramica,** housed in the splendid **Palazzo Sturm** (tel. 52 22 35) on Via Schiavonetti, displays four centuries of finely painted porcelains typical of the region. (Open Mon.-Thurs. 9am-noon and 3:30-6:30pm, Fri. 9am-noon, Sat.-Sun. 3:30-6:30pm. Admission L2000, under 18 L1000.)

Vicenza

Though dwarfed by neighboring Venice and Padua, Vicenza gains all the grandeur of a larger city from the monumental *piazze* designed by Andrea Palladio. The success of the light-industry zone on the outskirts of town allows residents to maintain a somewhat "Palladian" lifestyle—Vicenza has one of the highest average incomes in Italy. Luckily, the majesty of their surroundings has not affected the inhabitants' attitudes, and visitors to Vicenza will enjoy genuine, small-town hospitality.

ORIENTATION AND PRACTICAL INFORMATION

Vicenza lies in the heart of Veneto. The train station is in the southern part of town. **AIM** city buses #1 and 7 (L1300) run to the center of town and **P. Matteotti.** The intercity **FTV** bus station is next to the train station. To walk into town, orient yourself with a glance at the map outside the station, and set out on Viale Roma. Take a right on **Corso Palladio** (the axis of the town). P. Matteotti is at the other end, 10min. away.

Tourist Office: P. Matteotti, 12 (tel./fax 32 08 54), next to Teatro Olimpico. Offers helpful brochures and a city map. Ask for info on wheelchair-accessible facilities. English spoken. Open Mon.-Sat. 9am-12:30pm and 2:30-6pm, Sun. 9am-1pm.

Budget Travel: AVIT, Viale Roma, 17 (tel. 54 56 77), before you reach the supermarket PAM. BIJ and Transalpino tickets. Avis and Hertz rental cars. Open Mon.-Fri. 9am-1pm and 3-7pm, Sat. 9:30am-12:30pm. English spoken. **CTS,** Coutra Ponta Nova, 43 (tel. 32 38 64), near the Chiesa dei Carmini. Discount flights, tours, and ISIC cards. Open Mon.-Fri. 9am-12:30pm and 3-7pm. English spoken.

Telephones: P. Giuseppe Giustu, 8 (tel. 99 01 11), off Corso SS. Felice e Fortunato. Open daily 9am-12:30pm and 3:30-7pm. From 7pm-1am, go to Ristorante La Taverna, P. dei Signori, 47 (tel. 54 73 26). No *telefoni a scatti.*

Trains: P. Stazione (tel. 32 50 45), at the end of Viale Roma. To: Venice (every 30min., 1hr., L5700); Padua (every 30min., 30min., L3400); Milan (every 30min., 2-3hr., L15,500); Verona (every 30min., 30min., L5000). **Luggage Storage:** L5000 for 12hr. Open daily 7am-9pm.

Buses: FTV, Viale Milano, 7 (tel. 54 43 33), to the left as you exit the train station. To: Bassano (every hr., L4800); Asiago (every hr., L6500); Padua (every 30min., L4800); Thiene (every 30min., L4800); Schio (every 30min., L3800); Montagnana (3 per day, L5600). All buses run approx. 6am-9:30pm. Office open 7am-8pm.

Emergencies: tel. 113. **First Aid/Ambulance:** tel. 118 or 51 42 22 (for Croce Rossa). **Hospital: Ospedale Civile,** Viale Rodolfi, 8 (tel. 99 31 11). **Night and weekend doctor:** tel. 99 34 70.

Police: Via Muggia, 3 (tel. 50 77 00).

Post Office: Contrà Garibaldi, 1 (tel. 32 24 88), between the *duomo* and P. Signori. Open Mon.-Fri. 8am-7:30pm, Sat. 8am-1pm. **Postal Code:** 36100.

Telephone Code: 0444.

ACCOMMODATIONS AND CAMPING

Albergo Due Mori, Contrà Do Rode, 26 (tel. 32 18 86; fax 32 61 27), around the corner from Hotel Vicenza. Sparkling rooms with new furniture. Singles L50,000, with bath L60,000. Doubles L65,000, with bath L75,000. Breakfast L9000. V, MC, AmEx.

Hotel Vicenza, Stradella dei Nodari, 9 (tel. 32 15 12), off P. Signori in the alley across from Ristorante Garibaldi. Meticulously scrubbed and centrally located. Friendly management who may agree to store your luggage after check-out. Singles L50,000, with bath L65,000. Doubles L70,000, with bath L90,000.

Camping: Campeggio Vicenza, Strada Pelosa, 239 (tel. 58 23 11). Take Corso Padova out of town; Strada Pelosa is on the right. Tennis, mini-golf, and washing machines. Impossible to reach without a car. L8500 per person, L8500 per tent, L17,300 with car. Showers included.

FOOD

An outdoor produce market is held in P. delle Erbe behind the basilica every day. On Tuesday and Thursday mornings, you can hunt for food among the bizarre clothes sold in the central piazza. Thursday's market is the biggie, winding through the town. Cheese, chicken, and fish proliferate in P. del Duomo. For more mundane shopping, turn to supermarket **PAM,** Viale Roma, 1. Open Mon.-Tues. and Thurs.-Fri. 8:30am-7:30pm, Wed. 8:30am-1pm, Sat.-Sun. 8:30am-1pm and 3-7:30pm. With another entrance at Contrà Fontana, 6, **Righetti,** P. del Duomo, 3 (tel. 54 31 35), offers adequate self-service fare and great ambience, including outdoor seating. *Primi* from L5000, *secondi* from L7000. Cover L500. Open Sept.-late July Mon.-Fri. noon-2:30pm and 7-10pm; bar open 9pm-midnight. **Al Bersagliere,** Contrà Pescaria, 11 (tel. 32 35 07), off P. Erbe is small but provides great low-priced food. *Primi* L6000-7000, *sec-*

ondi L8000-12,000, bread L500. Cover L1000. Open Mon.-Tues. and Thurs.-Sat. 8am-3pm and 7-10pm.

SIGHTS AND ENTERTAINMENT

The town center, **Piazza dei Signori,** served as the forum when Vicenza was Roman and the town's showpiece when it was Venetian. Andrea Palladio's treatment of the **basilica** (tel. 32 36 81) brought the young architect his first fame. In 1546, Palladio's patron, the wealthy Giovan Giorgio Trissino, agreed to fund his proposal to shore up the collapsing **Palazzo della Ragione,** a project that had frustrated some of the foremost architects of the day. The ingeniously applied pilasters on the twin *loggie* mask the Gothic structure beneath. Look at the **Torre di Piazza** next door to get an idea of the basilica's former appearance. (Basilica open Tues.-Sat. 9:30am-noon and 2:30-5pm, Sun. 9:30am-noon. Free.) Across the piazza, the **Loggia del Capitano** illustrates Palladio's later style. The architect died with the façade unfinished, having completed only three bays and four sets of gigantic columns. Two columns symbolizing Venice complete the *piazza.* Behind the Loggia del Capitano, the **Palazzo del Comune** faces **Corso Palladio,** Vicenza's main street. Vincenzo Scamozzi's palace demonstrates a much sharper interpretation of classical architecture than the structures of Palladio, his mentor. Contrà Vescovado leads out of the piazza abutting Palazzo Porto-Breganze to the **duomo,** a large, brick, Gothic structure with a graceful apse and a Palladian *cupola.* The **Casa Pigafetta** on nearby Via Pigafetta is a unique, early Renaissance house that successfully fuses Gothic, Spanish, and classical styles.

At the far end of Corso Palladio stands Palladio's **Palazzo Chiericati,** which now houses the well-stocked **Museo Civico** (tel. 32 37 81). The collection in the first-floor *pinacoteca* includes some of Bassano's masterpieces: Bartolomeo Montagna's *Madonna Enthroned,* a Memling *Crucifixion,* Tintoretto's *Miracle of St. Augustine,* and Cima da Conegliano's refined *Madonna.* (Open Mon.-Sat. 9am-12:30pm and 2:15-5pm, Sun. 9:30am-12:30pm and 2-7pm. Closed Sun. afternoons Oct.-March. Admission L5000, students with teachers L3000. All-day ticket L9000, good for the Museo Civico, the Teatro Olimpico, and several other local museums.) The nearby **Teatro Olimpico** (tel. 32 37 81) is the last building planned by Palladio, although he died before it was completed. The city hosts productions here every year June through September, showcasing both local and imported talent. (Open Mon.-Sat. 9am-12:30pm and 2:15-5pm, Sun. 9:30am-12:30pm and 2-7pm. Closed Sun. afternoons Oct.-March. Admission L5000, groups L3000 per person, or buy the all-day ticket—see above.)

Along with performances in the **Teatro Olimpico** (admission L20,000-45,000, students L15,000-25,000), summer brings the **Concerti in Villa** concert series to Vicenza. Check with the tourist office for information about the foreign film series.

■ Near Vicenza

Venetian expansion to the mainland began in the early 15th century and provided infinite opportunity for Palladio's talents. As Venice's wealth accumulated and its maritime supremacy faded, its nobles began to turn their attention to the acquisition of real estate on the mainland. The Venetian Senate stipulated that they build villas rather than castles to preclude any possibility that they might become independent warlords. The architectural consequences are stunning, and Veneto is now home to hundreds of the most splendid villas in Europe.

Most of the Palladian villas scattered throughout Veneto are difficult to reach, but there are a few great ones close to town. The **Villa Rotonda** (tel. 32 17 93) can be reached on bus #8 or 13 and is considered one of history's most magnificent architectural achievements. This villa was a model for buildings in France, England, and the U.S., most notably Jefferson's Monticello. Open March 15-Nov. 4. Exterior open Tues.-Thurs. 10am-noon and 3-6pm, Fri.-Sun. hours vary depending on staff. Interior open Wed. 10am-noon and 3-6pm. Admission L5000 exterior, L10,000 on Wed. Discounts available for groups of 25 or more. Palladio's unfinished **Villa Thiene** on Via

IV Novembre (tel. 35 70 09) is stately but a bit forlorn, threatened by the encroaching suburbs of Quinto Vicentino. Open Mon., Wed., and Fri. 10am-12:30pm, Tues. and Thurs. 10am-12:30pm and 6-7pm. Free.

One of Palladio's most famous buildings is the **Villa Barbaro** at Masèr, which was constructed in 1560 and is an easy bus trip from Bassano. A train ride from Castelfranco to Fanzolo (on the Padua-Belluno line) also brings you to **Villa Emo,** considered one of the most characteristic Palladian villas. Its interior frescoes are renowned as well. Keep in mind that most villas in the Veneto have unpredictable schedules and allow tours of their exteriors only. Large groups, however, may be able to book a complete tour. Contact the tourist office for more information.

Verona

Traversing the old Roman Ponte Pietra on a summer's evening, with the gentle rush of the Adige River below and the illuminated towers of churches and castles glowing in the distance, you'll hardly wonder why Shakespeare set his *Romeo and Juliet* in Verona. Though many a modern-day Juliet may find her balcony hopelessly cluttered with pots of geraniums, Verona happily offers many alternative venues for lovers and tourists alike.

Verona's incorporation as a Roman town in 49BC is memorialized by the monumental city gates and the Arena amphitheater. The Scaligeri family, which dominated Verona from 1277 to 1387, also left its mark on the city, most notably with the Scaligeri bridge and tombs. Today, the city celebrates its rich cultural heritage with a summer opera festival held in the ancient Roman amphitheater.

ORIENTATION AND PRACTICAL INFORMATION

The heart of Verona lies on the south side of the **Adige River,** between **Piazza delle Erbe** and the **Arena** at **Piazza Brà.** This loop of the river contains the most scenic portions of town. From the town center, **Corso Porta Nuova** leads south to the bus and train stations. Piazza Brà is a 20-min. walk up Corso Porto Nuova from the train station or a short ride aboard **AMT** bus #11, 12, 13, or 72. Bus tickets (L1400) are available at the station and most *tabacchi.* Day passes (L4000) are also available.

Tourist Office: Via Leoncino, 61 (tel. 59 28 28), in P. Brà on the left side of the large yellow building with columns. They speak English and will help you find a room. Open Mon.-Sat. 9am-7pm; July 15-Aug. 31 Mon.-Sat. 8am-8pm, Sun. 8:30am-1pm. Additional branch in the **train station** (tel. 800 08 61). Open Mon.-Sat. 8:30am-7:30pm. **Youth Info Center:** Corso Porto Borsari, 17 (tel. 801 07 95 or 59 07 56). Open Mon. 3-6pm, Tues. 10am-1pm, Wed. and Fri. 10am-1pm and 3-6pm. Friendly, helpful staff. English spoken. **Hotel Booking Office:** Via Patuzzi, 5 (tel. 800 98 44; fax 800 93 72). Open Mon.-Fri. 9am-7pm.

Ufficio Stranieri: Lungoadige Porta Vittoria (tel. 809 05 05). Interpreter available. Open Mon.-Fri. 8:30am-12:30pm.

Budget Travel: CIT, P. Brà, 2 (tel. 59 06 49). Open Mon.-Fri. 9am-1pm and 3-7pm, Sat. 9am-1pm. English spoken. **Centro Turistico Giovanile,** Via Seminario, 10, 3rd floor (tel. 800 45 92), off Via Carducci, the first left after Via Interrato dell'Acqua Morta. Open Mon.-Fri. 9am-1pm and 3-6pm. **CTS,** Largo Pescheria Vecchia, 9/A (tel. 803 09 51), near the Scaligeri tombs. Open Mon.-Fri. 9am-noon and 5-9pm.

Currency Exchange: Cassa di Risparmio, P. Brà, centrally located on the corner of Via Roma and P. Brà. Open Mon.-Fri. 8:20am-1:20pm and 2:35-4:05pm. **Thomas Cook,** P. Brà, 2. Open Mon.-Fri. 9am-1pm and 2-7pm. Also at the **train station.** Open 7am-9pm. Numerous banks in the center of town also exchange money.

American Express: Fabretto Viaggi, Corso Porta Nuova, 11 (tel. 800 90 40), two blocks from P. Brà, across from McDonald's. Sells traveler's checks (US$) and changes them without charging commission. Holds client mail (postal code: 37122). Open Mon.-Fri. 8:30am-7:30pm, Sat. 9am-noon.

Telephones: In the post office at Piazza Viviani and in the train station.

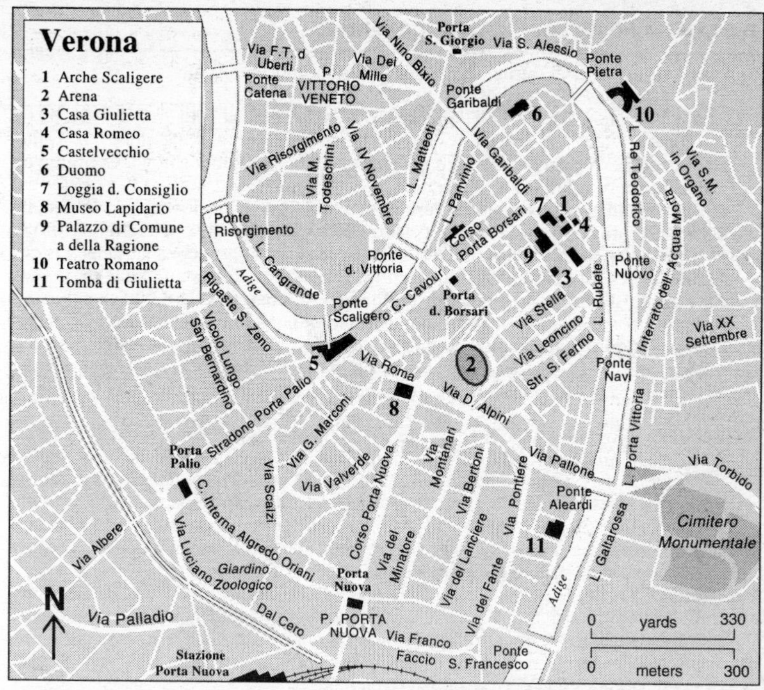

Trains: P. XXV Aprile (tel. 59 06 88 or (1478) 880 88), linked with P. Brà by Corso Porta Nuova. To: Venice (every hr., 2hr., L9800); Milan (every hr., 2hr., L11,700); Bologna (every hr., 2hr., L9800); Trent (every hr., 1hr., L8000); and Rome (6 per day, 6hr., L40,500). **Luggage Storage:** L5000 for 12hr. Open 24hr.

Buses: APT, P. XXV Aprile (tel. 800 41 29). To: Riva del Garda (every hr., 7:45am-6:45pm, L9000); Sirmione (every hr., L4600); Brescia (every hr., L9500); Montagnana (3 per day, L7000). Ticket window open daily 6am-8:30pm.

Taxis: Elitaxi (tel. 860 01 99). **Radiotaxi** (tel. 53 26 66). 6am-midnight.

Car Rental: Hertz (tel. 800 08 32), at the train station. Starting at L149,000 per day. Open Mon.-Fri. 8am-noon and 3-7pm, Sat. 8am-noon.

Bike Rental: Rent a Bike (tel. 50 49 01), on the sidewalk of Via degli Alpini, off P. Brà. L7000 per hr., L20,000 per day. Open daily 9am-7pm, off-season 10am-7pm, subject to weather conditions.

Bookstore: The Bookshop, Via Interatto dell'Acqua Morta, 3A (tel. 800 76 14), near Ponte Navi. Many classics in English (including *Let's Go*) and a small selection of German books. Open Mon. 3:30-7:30pm, Tues.-Fri. 9:15am-12:30pm and 3:30-7:30pm, Sat. 9:15am-12:30pm.

Self-Service Laundromat: Via XX Settembre, 62/A (tel. (0336) 52 28 58).

Public Toilets: P. Erbe; Cortile Mercato Vecchio; Corso Cavour (Giardini Castelvecchio); P. Brà; P. S. Zeno.

Pharmacy: tel. 192. Call for the hours and locations of nearby pharmacies.

Emergencies: tel. 113. **First Aid:** tel. 118. **Ambulance:** tel. 58 22 22. **Hospital: Ospedale Civile Maggiore,** Borgo Trento, P. Stefani (tel. 807 11 11).

Police: Questura, tel. 809 06 11.

Post Office: P. Viviani, 7 (tel. 800 39 98), also known as P. Poste. Follow Via Cairoli off P. delle Erbe. Stamps and *fermo posta* at windows #13, 14, and 16. Open Mon.-Sat. 8:15am-7:30pm. Additional branch at Via C. Cattaneo, 23 (tel. 803 41 00). **Postal Code:** 37100.

Telephone Code: 045.

ACCOMMODATIONS AND CAMPING

Reservations are crucial during the opera season of July and August.

Ostello Verona (HI), "Villa Francescatti," Salita Fontana del Ferro, 15 (tel. 59 03 60; fax 800 91 27). A 15-min. walk from behind the Arena. Walk along Via Anfiteatro (becomes Via Stella and then Via Nizza), and cross Ponte Nuovo. Continue on V. Carducci, turn left on V. Interrato dell'Acqua Morta, and walk to P. Isolo (at the end of the old gray bus station). Turn right and follow the yellow signs for "Ostello della Gioventù." From the station (platform "F"), take bus #72 or night bus #90 to P. Isolo. Located in a renovated 16th-century villa with gorgeous gardens, Ostella Verona is beautiful and well run. Friendly, English-speaking staff. 5-day max. stay. Curfew 11:30pm, with special provisions for opera-goers. L18,000 per person, including hot showers, breakfast, and sheets. Ample dinners (L12,000); vegetarian options if notified in advance. Rooms open at 5pm, but you may register and drop off bags as early as 7am. You can also **camp** in the villa's garden (L8000 per person, all inclusive; L6000 without tent). 220 beds. Reservations accepted only for groups and families.

Casa della Giovane (ACISJF), Via Pigna, 7 (tel. 59 68 80). From P. delle Erbe, walk up Corso S. Anastasia and turn onto Vicolo Due Mori (3rd left). Walk to the end of the *vicolo,* then continue straight on Via Augusto Verità. The arched double door at the end of the street is the entrance. Women only. Beautiful, spacious rooms in the historic center of town. Curfew 11pm. Those with opera tickets can be let back in after the show for an extra L3000. Single rooms L32,000. Bed in a double or triple L22,000. 45 beds. Call ahead to make sure space is available.

Locanda Catullo, Vicolo Catullo, 1 (tel. 800 27 86). Walk along Via Mazzini until you reach #40. Turn onto Via Catullo (a left if you're walking north from the Arena) and then left onto Vicolo Catullo. The hotel is on the 3rd floor. These recently renovated rooms can be very hard to get in July and August. 2-day min. stay. Singles L43,000. Doubles L65,000, with bath L85,000.

Campeggio Giulietta e Romeo, Strada Bresciana, 54 (tel. 851 02 43), on the road to Peschiera de Garda. Take the blue APT bus to Brescia from the train station (L9500). Alert the bus driver that you're going to the campground (last bus from Verona 8pm). Hot showers, large sites, pool, and store, but no romantic balconies. Check-in 8am-11pm. L12,300 for one person, with car L22,100. L5600 per additional person. Closed Dec.-Feb.

Hotel Armando, Via Dietro Pallone, 1 (tel. 800 02 06; fax 803 60 15), off Via Pallone. Small rooms, some with TV. Singles with bath L60,000. Doubles L80,000, with bath L100,000. Breakfast L8000. Open June-Sept.

FOOD

Verona is famous for its wines: the dry white *soave,* the red *valpolicella* and *bardolino.* The vendors in P. Isolo offer better prices than those in P. delle Erbe. For a large sampling, try **Oreste dal Zovo,** Via S. Marco in Foro, 7/5 (tel. 803 43 69), off Corso Porta Borsari. The congenial owner has shelves of every wine imaginable, including *grappa* from a mini-barrel. You can also crunch on microscopic snacks (L500-1000) or small *panini* (L2000). Open Tues.-Sun. 8:30am-1:30pm and 2:30-10pm. For eating essentials at reasonable prices, go to **METÁ** supermarket, Via XX Settembre, 81 (tel. 800 67 80). Open Thurs.-Tues. 8:30-midnight. For fruits and vegetables, try **Vera Frutta,** Via Interrato dell'Acqua Morta, 40a (tel. 800 48 02). Open Mon.-Sat. 8:30am-7:30pm; closed Wed. afternoons. Alternatively, try one of Verona's open-air markets. Check with the tourist office for locations and times. Most markets take place on weekday mornings.

In The Center

Trattoria Fontanina, Piazzetta Chiavica, 5 (tel. 803 11 33), near the Arche Scaligeri. Streetside terrace and pleasant atmosphere. *Primi* L8000, *secondi* L10,000-15,000. Cover L2000. Service 12%. Open Mon. noon-2pm, Wed.-Sun. noon-2pm and 7:30-10pm.

Trattoria Al Pompiere, Vicolo Regina d'Ungheria, 5 (tel. 803 05 37), the first right off Via Cappello from P. delle Erbe. Quiet, but tends to attract afternoon tourists. *Primi* L8000-9000, *secondi* L10,000-16,000. Cover L3000. *Menù* L25,000, includes *primo, secondo,* cover, and one vegetable. Kitchen open Thurs.-Tues. 11am-3pm and 6-10pm; bar open 10am-midnight. V, MC, AmEx.

Osteria Dal Duca, Via Arche Scaligere, 2 (tel. 59 44 74), next door to the Casa di Romeo. Rustic decor and central location. Fixed-price *menù* L19,000, includes *primo* and *secondo.* Drinks and desserts extra. Open Mon.-Sat. 9am-3pm and 6-10pm. V, MC.

Trattoria Alla Colonna, Via Pescheria Vecchia, 4 (tel. 59 67 18), near the main post office. Simple, clean interior. *Primi* L8000-12,000, *secondi* L10,000-18,000. *Menù* L19,000, includes *primo, secondo,* and vegetable. V, MC.

Caffè Tubino, Corso Porta Borsari, 15D (tel. 803 22 96), near the large arch of the Porta Borsari at the intersection of Via Fama. A tiny, unique café specializing in coffee and tea concoctions. A huge selection of teas, coffee, teapots, and accessories cover every available square inch of wall space. Caffiends, treat yourselves right. Open daily 7am-11pm.

Across the River

Trattoria Al Cacciatore, Via Seminario, 4 (tel. 59 42 91), left off Via Carducci just past Via Interrato dell'Acqua Morta. A genuine neighborhood joint with delicious food at low prices. *Primi* L6000-7000, *secondi* L10,000-14,000. *Menù* L16,000. Cover L2500. Open Mon.-Sat. 10am-3:30pm and 6:30-11pm. V, MC.

Nuovo Grottina, Via Interrato dell'Acqua Morta, 38 (tel. 803 01 52), off Via Carducci by Ponte Nuovo. Popular with students during the school year, and priced to stay that way. Pizza L6000-10,000. *Primi* L6000-9000, *secondi* L10,000-18,000. Cover L1500. Open Fri.-Wed. 9:30am-2:30pm and 6pm-1am.

Trattoria dal Ropeton, Via San Giovanni in Valle, 46 (tel. 803 00 40), below the youth hostel. Authentic cuisine and popular courtyard tables. Lots o' delicious food for low prices. If you're lucky, one of the waiters will entertain you with his singing. *Primi* L10,000, *secondi* L14,000. Cover indoors L1500, courtyard L2500. Open Wed.-Mon. 12:30-3pm and 7:30-11pm.

SIGHTS

A Roman amphitheater surpassed in size only by the ones in Capua and Rome, the majestic pink **Arena** (tel. 800 32 04) in P. Brà dates to AD100. The Arena's superb condition testifies to Verona's municipal pride. (Open Tues.-Sun. 8am-6:30pm, in opera season 8am-1:30pm; admission L6000, students L1500, everyone free on the first Sunday of the month.)

From P. Brà, Via Mazzini takes you into **Piazza delle Erbe,** the former Roman Forum. The center of the piazza contains the Madonna Verona fountain, installed by Cansignorio della Scala in 1368. At the far end rises the 1523 column of St. Mark (topped by a winged lion), a symbol of four centuries of Venetian domination. The **Gardello Tower,** built in 1370, stands between the imposing Baroque **Palazzo Maffei** and the two buildings that Verona's first families, the Scaligeri (della Scala) and the Mazzanti, once called home. Note the frescoed façades and spacious terraces. In the center of the piazza, almost hidden by fruit vendors' awnings, stands the **Berlina.** During medieval times, convicts were tied to this marble structure to be pelted with rotten fruit.

The **Arco della Costa,** called the "Arch of the Rib" for the whale rib that hangs from it, separates P. delle Erbe from **Piazza dei Signori.** Local legend says that the rib will fall on the first person to pass under the arch who has never told a lie. (Some incentive to be honest!) Surprisingly—or not—the rib has hung securely in place for 1000 years, witnessing the visits of popes and kings. The delicate **Loggia del Consiglio** (1493), built in the Venetian Renaissance style, stands adjacent to the *prefettura.* The grey **Palazzo della Ragione** stands on the corner. This densely knit brick and marble ensemble was the seat of the della Scala dynasty during the 14th century. Their names suggest the violent and dogged nature of the family: Cangrande (Big

Dog) was succeeded by Mastino II (The Mastiff), and then Cansignorio (Head Dog). Yet, like many of their brutish peers, the della Scala were also sensitive patrons of the arts. Dante passed many months here as the guest of Cangrande and eventually dedicated his *Paradiso* to the powerful warlord. A monument to Dante stands in the P. dei Signori, near the the Scaligeri tomb.

Through the arch at the far end of P. dei Signori lie the peculiar outdoor **Tombs of the Scaligeri** and the beautiful **Arche Scaligeri.** The **Casa di Romeo,** long the home of the Montecchi family (model for the Montagues), is around the corner from P. dei Signori at Via Arche Scaligeri, 2. At Casa Capuletti, Via Cappello, 23, more commonly known as **Casa di Giulietta** (tel. 803 43 03), you will find a tall, ivy-covered wall next to a balcony where you can wait your turn to call to your Romeo among the trinket stands. Thousands of tourists have rubbed the Juliet statue's right breast to a shine. If you're wondering, the feuding dal Capello (Capulet) family never lived here. (Open Tues.-Sun. 8am-6:30pm; admission L5000, students L1500.)

At the other end of P. delle Erbe, Corso Sant'Anastasia leads to the Gothic **Basilica of Sant'Anastasia.** Most notable among the basilica's magnificent works of art are Pisanello's *St. George Freeing the Princess* (in the Giusti Chapel in the left transept), considered one of his best paintings, and the frescoes by Altichiero and Turone. Walk down Via Duomo from the basilica to the **duomo,** decorated with medieval sculpture by local stone carvers. The first chapel on the left features Titian's ethereal *Assumption of the Virgin* (1535). The **Biblioteca Capitolare** (tel. 59 65 16), the oldest library in Europe, maintains a priceless medieval manuscript collection that scholars won't want to miss. (Cathedral open daily 7am-noon and 3-7pm. Library open Mon., Wed., and Sat. 9:30am-12:30pm, Tues. and Fri. 9:30am-12:30pm and 4-6pm. Free.)

Cross the Adige on the lovely Roman **Ponte Pietra** to reach the recently uncovered **Teatro Romano** (tel. 800 03 60), a venue for Shakespearean plays and an archaeological museum. (See **Entertainment** for more info.) The theater was built during the early Roman Empire at the foot of what is today called St. Peter's Hill. It affords a wonderful view of Verona, especially in the evening. (Open Tues.-Sun. 8am-1:30pm; admission L5000, students L1500.)

At the bottom of the hill, between the Ponte Pietra and the Ponte Nuovo, Via Interrato dell'Acqua Morta leads to the 15th-century **Church of Santa Maria in Organo.** Although Sanmicheli made a significant contribution to the façade, Giovanni da Verona completed the most delicate inlay work. The **Giardino Giusti** (tel. 803 40 29), a delightful 16th-century garden, beckons from behind the church. The garden has beautiful cypress trees as well as a small clipped-hedge labyrinth. (Open daily 9am-8pm; admission L5000, students L2000.)

The della Scala fortress, the **Castelvecchio** (tel. 59 47 34), at the end of Via Roma from P. Brà, was carefully reconstructed after its devastation during World War II. The many-leveled interior has been made into a museum with walkways, parapets, and an extensive collection of sculptures and paintings including Pisanello's *Madonna and Child,* Luca di Leyda's *Crucifixion,* and works by Andrea Mantegna, Francesco Morone, Tintoretto, and Tiepolo. (Open Tues.-Sun. 8am-6pm; admission L5000, students L1500, free on the first Sunday of each month.)

The church of **San Zeno Maggiore,** upstream from the Castelvecchio, is one of the finest examples of Italian Romanesque architecture in Verona. Built from the 10th to the 12th century, the massive brick church is dedicated to Verona's patron saint and surpasses its counterparts in artistic wealth. The 17th-century sculpted bronze doors sparked a craze throughout Italy, and the interior structure is notable for its wooden "ship's keel" ceiling and the spacious crypt area. The two-story apse contains a Renaissance altarpiece by Mantegna. (Open daily 8am-noon and 3-7pm.)

If you're staying at Ostello Verona, don't miss the **Museo Africano,** Vicolo Pozzo, 1 (tel. 800 24 18). The religious monastery started by Fr. Camboni that sends missionary workers throughout Africa runs the museum, which celebrates the ancient traditions, arts, and relics of African peoples. The staff is extremely welcoming, and a detailed guide of all the works is available in English. The museum is free and wheelchair accessible. (Open Mon.-Thurs. 9am-noon and 3-6pm, holidays 3-6pm.)

ENTERTAINMENT

Verona has used its magnificent Roman Arena to great advantage as the stage for its premier cultural event, an **opera and ballet extravaganza** in July and August. Prices start at L25,000 for unreserved gallery seats. Call 800 51 51 for tickets. Reserve tickets and hotel rooms well in advance of this busy season. *Jazz Italia* and *Praga Sinfonietta* prices start at L10,000. For more information, call 59 01 09 or 59 07 26, or go directly to arch #8 or 9 to make a reservation or a purchase. If you opt for general admission seating, be prepared to encounter crowds of operaholics who camp out up to two hours before the gates open.

The Teatro Romano stages Shakespeare productions (in Italian) every summer. Tickets start at L72,000. Reserve ahead at arch #18. Open in season Mon.-Sat. 10:30am-1pm and 4-7pm. For information call 59 28 28, for reservations 59 00 89. *Verona for You* (available at the tourist office) lists current exhibits and events.

Friuli-Venezia Giulia

Overshadowed by the touristed cities of the Veneto and the mountains of Trentino-Alto Adige, Friuli-Venezia Giulia has traditionally received less than its fair share of recognition. Trieste has been a long-standing exception to this rule, and today increasing numbers of beach-goers flock there for the least expensive resorts on the Adriatic. The area's towns owe their charm to their small size, offering an untainted slice of local life and culture that is missed in Italy's larger cities.

Friuli-Venezia Giulia was once a number of distinct provinces, as its name suggests. From the 6th to 15th centuries, the local clergy unified and maintained autonomy from the church and other states. The entire region was then appropriated by the Venetian Republic, only to be reabsorbed, Venetians and all, into Austria-Hungary. The present region is the product of a postwar union between Udine, Pordenone, Gorizia, and Trieste. The historical differences between these provinces, and the area's vulnerability to eastern forces (given its marginal geographic location in the north of Italy) combine to give Friuli-Venezia Giulia a hybrid character. The splash of political intrigue and coffee-culture elegance brought by the Austro-Hungarian Empire attracted various intellectuals to turn-of-the-century Friuli: James Joyce lived in Trieste for 12 years, during which time he wrote the bulk of *Ulysses;* Ernest Hemingway's *A Farewell to Arms* draws part of its plot from the region's role in World War I; Freud and Rilke both worked and wrote here. The mixture of Slovenian, Friulian, and Italian peoples has produced an indigenous literary tradition, which includes Italo Svevo and the poet Umberto Saba.

The Tagliamento and Natisone River Valleys shelter fertile farmlands, and the commonly spoken local dialect and hearty culinary traditions hearken to this area's peasant culture. The Carnian Alps to the north and the Julian Alps to the east present plentiful opportunities for hiking, rock-climbing, and skiing, and provide an alternative climate to the beaches of the southern coast.

Trieste

The unofficial capital of Friuli-Venezia Giulia lies at the end of a narrow strip of land sandwiched between Slovenia and the Adriatic. Given its strategically placed harbor and proximity to Austrian and former Yugoslavian borders, Trieste has been a bone of contention over the centuries. As Venice's main rival in the Adriatic until Venice finally surpassed it in power, wealth, and independence during the 9th through 15th centuries, Trieste was always coveted by the Austrians. Austria finally obtained this

Adriatic port in the post-Napoleonic real estate market and proceeded to rip the medieval heart from Trieste, replacing it with Neoclassical bombast. The Habsburgs' equally heavy-handed style of government succeeded in turning the mostly Italian population into fervent *irredentisti* clamoring for a return to the Italian nation. They emerged victorious in 1918 when Italian troops occupied the Friuli, but unification only brought more confusion: Mussolini's policies of cultural chauvinism offended anyone not already alienated by the Habsburg rulers.

Today, evidence of Trieste's multinational history lingers in the numerous buildings and monuments of Habsburg origin and in the Slavic nuances in the local cuisine. The city's Italian identity, on the other hand, is vehemently asserted by the persistence of fascist and anti-Slav parties, and more tangibly in the formidable Piazza Unità d'Italia, the largest *piazza* in Italy. The cumulative product of these conflicting forces is a cosmopolitan hub of transportation, a logical departure point for travelers to Eastern Europe.

ORIENTATION AND PRACTICAL INFORMATION

Trieste is a direct train ride from both Venice and Udine, and several trains and buses cross daily to neighboring Slovenia and Croatia. Less-frequent ferry service runs the length of the Istrian Peninsula. The gray, industrialized quays serving ferries and fishermen taper off into Trieste's equivalent of a beach—a stretch of tiered concrete populated with bronzed bodies that runs 7km from the edge of town out to the castle at Miramare. Moving inland, one encounters **Piazza Oberdan,** which opens onto the ever-busy **Via Carducci.** Shoppers pack the fashion-oriented streets that intersect with this central artery near P. Goldoni. The artistically inclined can head to the pride and glory of Trieste, **Piazza Unità d'Italia,** which looks out to the harbor. Public transportation runs throughout the city, and most buses stop in the immediate vicinity of the train station.

Tourist Office: In the train station (tel. 42 01 82; fax 41 68 06), to the right near the exit. Copious information on Trieste such as a list of *manifestazioni* (cultural events), occasionally including those in nearby cities. English spoken. Open Mon.-Sat. 9am-7pm, Sun. 10am-1pm and 4-7pm. Another office at Via S. Nicolò, 20 (tel. 63 66 77) has similar services but shorter hours. Open Mon., Wed., and Fri. 9am-noon.

Budget Travel: CTS, P. Dalmazia, 3 (tel. 36 18 79; fax 36 24 03). Agency for air and train tickets plus a variety of other vacation information. Open Mon.-Fri. 9am-1pm and 1:30-7pm. **Aurora Viaggia,** Via Milano, 20 (tel. 63 02 61; fax 36 55 87), 1 block from Via Carducci. Information on transportation and lodging in former Yugoslavia. Open Mon.-Fri. 9am-12:30pm and 4-7pm, Sat. 9am-noon.

Consulates: The **U.S.** no longer has a consulate here, but it does have an honorary representative at Via Roma, 15 (tel. 66 01 77). Ask for Sig. Bearz. Otherwise try the consulate in Milan. **U.K.,** Vicolo delle Ville, 16 (tel. 30 28 84), available Tues. and Fri. 9am-12:30pm. The closest **Canadian** and **Australian** consulates are in Milan. **New Zealand** citizens should contact their embassy in Rome. To check on the current state of visa requirements for travel eastward, contact the consulate of **Slovenia,** Via S. Giorgio, 1 (tel. 30 78 55), or of **Croatia** in Rome, Via Santi Cosma e Damiano, 26 (tel. 33 25 02 42).

Currency Exchange: Banca d'America e d'Italia, Via Roma, 7 (tel. 63 19 25). Cash advances on Visa cards. Open Mon.-Fri. 8:20am-1:20pm and 2:35-3:50pm. Also try **Assomar Cambio** in the bus station in P. della Libertà (tel. 42 53 07). Open daily 7:30am-8pm. No commission.

Telephones: Via Pascoli, 9. Open Mon.-Fri. 8:30am-12:30pm and 4-7pm. Phone booths throughout town open 24hr.

Trains: P. della Libertà (tel. 41 82 07), down Via Cavour from the quays. Ticket counter open daily 5:40am-10:20pm. Info office open daily 9am-7pm. To: Udine (15 per day, 1½hr., L7200); Venice (16 per day, 2hr., L13,600); Milan (1 per day, 5½-7½hr., L33,400); Ljubljana (4 per day, 3½hr., L16,000); and Budapest (1 or more per day, L75,000). **Luggage Storage:** L5000 for 12hr. Open daily 5am-midnight.

Buses: Corso Cavour (tel. 336 03 00), in the fringe of P. della Libertà near the train station. To Udine (8 per day, L6200) and Rijeka/Fiume (2 per day, L13,600). There are also several smaller lines that run throughout the region. Check at the station. **Luggage Storage:** L1500 for 12hr. Open daily 6:20am-8pm.

Ferries: Agemar Viaggi, P. Duca degli Abruzzi, 1/A (tel. 36 37 37; fax 77 723), by the waterfront next to the canal. Arranges trips with **Adriatica di Navigazione** and provides the latest visa requirements for entering former Yugoslavia. To: Grado (1hr., L10,000); Lignano (1¼hr., L11,500); Rovigno (3hr., L30,000); and Pirano (1½hr., L15,000). Office open Mon.-Fri. 8:30am-1pm and 3-6:30pm.

Public Transportation: ACT, Via d'Alviano, 15 (tel. 779 51). Open Mon.-Fri. 9am-1pm. Ticket for travel within the city L1200 from any *tabacchi.*

Taxis: tel. 545 33 or 30 77 30.

Rental Cars: Hertz, (tel. 42 21 22; fax 41 89 46) in the bus station, P. della Libertà. Open Mon.-Fri. 8:30am-12:30pm and 3-6:30pm, Sat. 8:30am-12:30pm. Another **Hertz** office at the airport (tel. 77 70 25). **Avis,** also in the bus station (tel. 42 15 21). Open Mon.-Fri. 8am-12:30pm and 3:30-7pm, Sat. 8am-noon. Another branch at the airport (tel. 77 70 85). Rates at both chains around L150,000 per day.

Bookstore: Libreria Cappelli, Corso Italia, 12B (tel. 63 04 14). English books (in the back right corner) and travel guides. Open Tues.-Sat. 8:30am-12:30pm and 3:30-7:30pm. V, AmEx.

Laundromat: Via Ginnastica, 36 (tel. 36 74 14). Roughly L15,000 per load. Open Tues.-Fri. 8am-1pm and 3:30-7pm, Sat. 8am-1pm.

Swimming Pool: Piscina Comunale "Bruno Bianchi," Riva Gulli, 3 (tel. 30 60 24), along the waterfront. Indoor facilities. Open Oct.-July Mon.-Sat. noon-3pm, Sun. 9am-1pm. Admission L6000.

Late-Night Pharmacies: tel. 192. Insert 3 telephone tokens for a listing.

Emergencies: tel. 113. **Ambulance:** tel. 118. **Hospital: Ospedale Maggiore,** P. dell'Ospedale (tel. 77 61), up Via S. Maurizio from Via Carducci.

Police: (tel. 379 01), on Via del Teatro Romano off Corso Italia.

Post Office: P. Vittorio Veneto, 1 (tel. 36 82 24 or 36 80 32), along Via Roma, the 2nd right off Via Ghega coming from the train station. *Fermo posta* at counter #21. Fax downstairs. Open Mon.-Sat. 8am-7:30pm. **Postal Code:** 34100.

Telephone Code: 040.

ACCOMMODATIONS AND CAMPING

Watch out for weekdays, when local companies often fill up the smaller *pensioni* with their workers. Consult the tourist office, which leaves a helpful list of Trieste's hotels and *pensioni* taped to the door for those who arrive after hours.

Ostello Tegeste (HI), Viale Miramare, 331 (tel. 22 41 02). The hostel is on the seaside, just down from the castle Miramare, about 6km from the city center. From the station take bus #36 (L1200), departing from across Viale Miramare, the street on the left of the station as you exit. After about 7min. the bus will pass California Inn and Ristorante Marinella on the right. Get off at the fork in the road and walk along the waterfront toward the hostel (look for the yellow signs). Modern hostel with uninteresting rooms but gorgeous views of the sea. Live bands play here occasionally; other times loud American music fills the air. Average of 4 bunks per room. HI members only. Registration noon-11:30pm. Checkout 9:30am. Lockout 9:30am-noon. Curfew 11:30pm. L18,000 per person. Hot showers and breakfast included. Also serves lunch and dinner (*menù* L14,000, though you can eat 1 or 2 courses for less). Reserve ahead.

Centrale, Via Ponchielli, 1 (tel. 63 94 82). Centrally located, as the name suggests, right off the canal. Ample, clean rooms. Singles L38,000, with shower L45,000, with toilet L60,000. Doubles L65,000, with bath L90,000. Triples L80,000. Showers L3000.

Hotel Alabarda, Via Valdirivo, 22 (tel. 63 02 69), on the 3rd floor. Small *pensione* with clean, well-kept doubles and triples. Only one single—call ahead to reserve. Bathrooms down the hall. Single L30,000. Doubles L60,000. Triples L90,000.

Valeria, Via Nazionale, 156 (tel. 21 12 04). From P. Oberdan take the tram to Opicina (every 20min., 6am-midnight). This hotel offers clean rooms in a peaceful suburb of Trieste. Singles L30,000. Doubles L50,000.

Camping Obelisco, Strada Nuova Opicina, 37 (tel. 21 16 55 or 21 27 44). Take the tram from P. Oberdan (L1400), and get off at the "Obelisco" stop; follow the yellow signs to the camp. In Opicina, 7km from Trieste. A beautiful, tranquil place to camp for those not umbilically attached to the beach. Nice facilities with bar. L6000 per person, L4500 per tent, L4000 per car. Light L2000.

FOOD

Many dishes in Trieste's restaurants have Eastern European overtones (usually Hungarian) and are often loaded with paprika. The city is renowned for its fish; try *sardoni in savor* (large sardines marinated in oil and garlic). Most shops and restaurants in Trieste close on Mondays. To fend for yourself, visit one of the several **alimentari** on Via Carducci, or try **Supercoop** on Via Palestrina, 3, at Via Francesco. Open Mon. and Wed. 8am-1pm, Tues. and Thurs.-Sat. 8am-1pm and 5-7:30pm. If you're near the waterfront, go to the **Despar** supermarket across from the public pool. Open Mon. and Wed. 8:30am-1:30pm, Tues. and Thurs.-Fri. 8:30am-1:30pm and 4:30-7:30pm, Sat. 8:30am-7:30pm. Trieste has a **covered market** with fruit, vegetable, meat, and cheese vendors on Via Carducci, 36D, at the intersection with Via della Majolica. Produce is fresh and inexpensive. Open Mon. and Wed. 8am-1:30pm, Tues. and Thurs.-Sat. 8am-7pm. While in town, try a bottle of *Terrano del Carso,* a dry red wine with low alcohol content that's been valued for its therapeutic properties since the days of ancient Rome. For unadulterated grapes, stroll through the open-air **market** in P. Ponterosso by the canal. Open Tues.-Sat. 8am-5:30pm.

Brek, Via San Francesco, 10 (tel. 73 26 51). Self-service restaurant. Economical, efficient, and tasty. Everything is *alla carta,* so pick and choose from fresh fruit, wine, pasta, and more. *Primi* L3500-4100, *secondi* from L7200. IYHF card: 10% discount. Open Sat.-Thurs. 11:30am-2:30pm and 6:30-10pm; May 1-Sept. 30. daily.

Paninoteca Da Livio, Via della Ginnastica, 3/B (tel. 63 64 46), inland off Via Carducci. Small, smoky shop boasts monster *panini* (L3000-7000) and dozens of brands of beer. Usually crowded. Open Mon.-Sat. 9am-3pm and 5:30-11pm. Closed last week of June and first week of July.

Pizzeria Barattolo, P. Sant'Antonio, 2 (tel. 64 14 80), along the canal. Amazing pizza (L6000-13,000). Also bar and *tavola calda* offerings. Open daily 8am-1am. ISIC: 30% discount. V, MC, AmEx.

SIGHTS

In honor of the Habsburg empress, 19th-century Viennese urban planners carved out a large chunk of Trieste to create Borgo Teresiano, a district of straight avenues bordering the waterfront and the canal. Facing the canal from the south is the district's one beautiful church, the Serbian Orthodox **San Spiridione.** (Open daily 9-11:30am. Free.) The **Municipio** at the head of **Piazza dell'Unità d'Italia** is a monument whose ornate design complements the largest *piazza* in Italy. The *piazza* itself contains beautifully designed buildings on all sides and an allegorical fountain with statues representing four continents. Enjoy a waterfront view from any of the *caffè* in the area—Caffè degli Specchi is particularly famous.

The 15th-century Venetian **Castle of San Giusto** presides over **Capitoline Hill,** the city's historic center. You can take bus #24 (L1200) from the station to the last stop at the fortress. Otherwise, you may want to begin in P. Goldoni and ascend the hill by way of the daunting **Scala dei Giganti** (Steps of the Giants)—all 265 of them. Take a right on Via Capitalina, which will take you to **Piazza della Cattedrale.** This hilltop area offers a great view of the sea and downtown Trieste and is a prime sunset-watching spot if the *bora* winds don't blow you away. Within the walls of the castle is a huge outdoor theater where film festivals are held in July and August. (Pick up a copy of *Trieste '97, Eventi Luglio-Agosto* at the tourist office.) Walk around the ramparts of the castle (open daily 8am-7pm) or peek into the museum (tel. 31 36 36), which has temporary exhibits in addition to a permanent collection of weaponry. (Open Tues.-Sun. 9am-1pm. Admission L2000.) Directly below are the remains of the old Roman city center, and across the street is the restored **Cathedral of San Giusto.** The church originally comprised two separate basilicas, one dedicated to San Giusto, the other to Santa Maria Assunta. They were joined together in the 14th century, spawning the cathedral's irregular plan. Inside are two splendid mosaics in the chapels directly to the left and right of the altar.

Down the other side of the hill past the *duomo* lies the eclectic **Museo di Storia de Arte** and the **Orto Lapidario** (Museum of Art History and the Rock Garden) at Via Cattedrale, 15 (tel. 37 05 00 or 30 86 86), in P. Cattedrale. The museum provides archaeological documentation of the history of Trieste during and preceding its Roman years and boasts a growing collection of Egyptian art and artifacts from southern Italy. (Open Tues.-Sun. 9am-1pm. Admission L2000, students L1000.) Descending the hill toward the ruins of the **Teatro Romano,** you end up only a few short blocks from P. Unità d'Italia. The *Teatro Romano* on Via del Teatro Romano off Corso Italia was built under the auspices of Trajan in the 1st century AD. Originally, gladiatorial contests were held here; later spectators enjoyed passion and blood in the slightly tamer form of Greek tragedies.

An excellent collection of drawings and a less impressive selection of paintings by Tiepolo, Veneziano, and others has been moved from the Capitoline Hill to an elegant 18th-century villa at Largo Papa Giovanni XXIII, 1, which is now the **Museo Sartorio** (tel. 30 14 79). The museum is easily reached by walking a short distance from the center along the quays. (Open Tues.-Sun. 9am-1pm. Admission L2000, reduced price L1000.)

ENTERTAINMENT

The regular opera season of the **Teatro Verdi** runs November to May, but a six-week operetta season is held in June and July. Purchase tickets or make reservations at P. Verdi, 1 (tel. 36 78 16). The theater recently closed for renovations, but performances are being scheduled for alternate locations. Contact the tourist office for current info. Inquire at travel agency **UTAT-Galleria Protti** for dates, times, and prices of all performances (tel. 63 00 63).

Caffè Tommaseo, Riva III Novembre, 5 (tel. 36 67 65 or 36 72 36), in P. Tommaseo along the canal (closed June-Aug. Sun.-Mon.), and **Caffè San Marco,** Via Battisti, 18 (tel. 37 13 73), preserve the city's turn-of-the-century coffee culture. Caffè San Marco frequently offers live musical performances, too. (Open Thurs.-Tues. 7am-2am.) Coffee in Trieste is an art form, thanks to the influence of the Viennese. It comes to you on a silver platter, with a glass of water and, if you're lucky, a few sweet pastries (typically L4000-6000). The liveliest *passeggiata* takes place along Viale XX Settembre, a largely traffic-free and *caffè*-lined avenue—a good place to relax in the shade.

■ Near Trieste

West of Trieste you can sunbathe along the rocky coast and visit the **Castello Miramare** (tel. 22 41 43), the gorgeous castle of Archduke Maximilian of Austria, who ordered its construction in the middle of the 19th century. It was rumored that anyone spending the night here would come to a bad end, a belief helped along by the decision of Archduke Ferdinand to spend the night here on the way to his assassination at Sarajevo. Poised on a high promontory over the gulf, Miramare's white turrets are easily visible from the Capitoline Hill in Trieste or from the train on the journey through the *corso;* its extensive parks are open to the public at no cost. To reach Miramare, take bus #36 (20min., L1200), get off at the stop for the hostel (see

Accommodations and Camping above, p. 361) and walk along the water. Castle museum open daily 9am-6pm. Admission L8000, with a tour in Italian. English tours L22,000. Fortunately, each room has a description and history provided in English. In July and August, a series of **sound and light shows** transform Miramare into a high-tech playground. Shows Tues., Thurs., and Sat. at 9:30 and 10:45pm. Admission L9000. The show is in English. Call the tourist office for more info.

Near the castle, a **marine park** (tel. 22 41 47) sponsored by the World Wildlife Fund, conducts several programs throughout the year, including guided introductions to the coast's marine life. The park itself is the area marked by buoys off shore surrounding Castle Miramare. Swimming is not allowed here without a guide. Guided water tours (both snorkeling and scuba) are offered. Open Tues. and Thurs. Admission L25,000, children L15,000. In Italian or English. Call the office to make reservations, which are required. Office open Mon.-Fri. 9am-7pm, Sat. 9am-5pm. You can also rent snorkel, fins, and mask for L25,000.

About 15km from Trieste in Opicina, you'll find the **Grotta Gigante** (tel. 32 73 12), the world's largest accessible cave. Staircases wind in and around the 90m-high interior, which the brochure claims could hold the whole of St. Peter's. Open March-Oct. Tues.-Sat. 9am-noon and 2-7pm; Nov.-Feb. 10am-noon and 2:30-4:30pm. Admission L10,000. Transportation is available from P. Oberdan, but you can also take bus #45 (5 per day, L1600).

The more alcohol-savvy can walk the famous and beautiful **Terrano wine-routes.** (*Terrano* is a local wine of the region.) The route begins in Opicina and goes to Vispogliano. Restaurants with regional specialties line the route and welcome tourists to dine. For more information on the wine-route, contact the tourist office.

As a more disturbing legacy of World War II, Italy's only concentration camp occupies an abandoned rice factory in a suburb of Trieste. The **Risiera de San Sabba,** Ratto della Pileria, 43 (tel. (040) 82 62 02), is accessible from Trieste by bus #8. Open Tues.-Sun. 9am-1pm. Free.

Aquileia and Palmanova

AQUILEIA

Aquileia was founded in 181BC on the banks of the now-dry Natisone-Torre River. Between AD200 and 452 it flourished as the Roman capital of the region, serving as the gateway to the Eastern Empire and as the principal trading port of the Adriatic. The Patriarchate of Aquileia was established in 313, but when the Huns and Lombards sacked the city in the 5th and 6th centuries, the Patriarch fled to Grado and then moved on to Cividale del Friuli. Aquileia finally regained control in 1019 and in celebration rebuilt its great basilica. From this point on, the Patriarchate successfully defied the popes until the port silted up and malaria set in. The disgruntled Patriarch moved on to Udine and dwindled into an archbishop, leaving behind an amazing open-air museum of Roman and early Christian art, the most important archaeological remains in northern Italy.

Aquileia can be reached by bus from Udine (16 per day, 1hr., L4100), and local buses travel to Cervignano, a train station on the Trieste-Venice line (every 30min., L1500). The **tourist office** (tel. 910 87 or 91 94 91) is a block from the bus stop in P. Capitolo. Open only April-Oct. Fri.-Wed. 9am-1pm and 4-6pm. The **telephone code** for Aquileia is 0431.

Across the *piazza* from the tourist office stands Aquileia's **basilica.** The basilica is a tribute to the town's artistic heritage, a unique conglomeration of artwork from across the centuries. The floor, a remnant of the original church, is a fantastic mosaic, animating over 700 square meters with geometric designs and realistic bestial depictions. The 9th-century crypt beneath the altar holds several 12th-century frescoes illustrating the trials of Aquileia's early Christians and scenes from the life of Christ. In the *Cripta degli Scavi,* to the left upon entering, excavation has uncovered three distinct layers of flooring, including floor mosaics from a 1st-century Roman house, which vividly illustrate the building's varied history. Basilica open daily 8:30am-7pm. Crypt open Mon.-Sat. 8:30am-7pm, Sun. 8:30am-7:30pm; in winter 8:30am-12:30pm and 2:30-5:30pm. Admission L3000.

Yellow signs and clearly delineated tourist maps make it easy to find the various ruins, but the cypress-lined alley behind the basilica runs parallel to the once-glorious **Roman harbor** and is a pleasant alternative to Via Augusta as a path to the **forum.** From there, continue to the **Museo Paleocristiano** (tel. 91 11 30), where displays explain the transition from classical paganism to Christianity, and moss covers the ubiquitous mosaics. Open daily 9am-2pm. Free.

The fruits of many excavations in Aquileia reside in the **Museo Archaeologico** at the corner of Via Augusta and Via Roma. The ground floor contains Roman statues and portrait busts; upstairs are objects in terra cotta, glass, and gold. Open Sun.-Wed. 9am-2pm, Thurs.-Sat. 9am-7pm. Admission L8000. Aquileia's one budget accommodation is the **Albergo Aquila Nera,** P. Garibaldi, 5 (tel. 910 45). Pleasant and fresh rooms, some with wood floors. Singles L40,000. Doubles L70,000. Sparkling bathrooms down the hall. Breakfast L5000. V. The **restaurant** downstairs serves lunch and dinner at reasonable prices. *Primi* L9000-10,000, *secondi* L10,000-13,000. Cover L2000. Open Fri.-Wed. noon-2:30pm and 7-10pm. For camping, try **Camping Aquileia,** Via Gemina, 10 (tel. 910 42; in winter 910 37), up the street from the forum, a shady spot with a swimming pool. Adults L7600, under 12 L4700. Tent sites L9600-12,800, 2-person bungalows L50,000-70,000. Car space L5000. Open May 15-Sept. 15. The **Desparo** supermarket on the Udine end of Via Augusta is a penny-pincher's salvation. Open Tues.-Sat. 8am-1pm and 3:30-7:30pm, Sun. 8am-1pm. The **Ristorante al Pescatore** upstairs (tel. 91 95 70) serves pizza and fish specialties. Pizza L6000-12,000, *primi* L7000-20,000, *secondi* L7000-20,000. Open Tues.-Sun. 10am-2:30pm and 6:15pm-midnight.

PALMANOVA

Palmanova, a town girded by a nine-sided Venetian fortress, lies between Udine and Aquileia on the bus route to Grado (16 per day, 20min., L2500). With a hexagonal central *piazza* and six main streets radiating out to the ramparts, Palmanova is literally a stellar example of Renaissance military planning. Its small *trattorie* and shops allow visitors to witness local Italian life far away from the hordes. The town is a nice daytrip from Trieste or Udine. The **tourist office,** Borgo Udine, 4/C (tel. (0432) 92 91 06), is on the ground floor of the **Museo Civico,** which displays manuscripts and artifacts documenting Palmanova's military history. Tourist office open Mon.-Fri. 8am-1:30pm. Museum open Thurs.-Tues. 10am-noon and 4-6pm.

Udine

Come to Udine and congratulate yourself on your unorthodox itinerary. Though not riddled with tourists, Udine is an unexpectedly captivating town. Its *piazze* are beautifully designed, and the town itself is filled with interesting historical sites. In addition to Italian, natives speak some German, some Serbo-Croatian, and the old *Friulàn* dialect, an obscure relative of equally obscure Swiss Romansch. The linguistic intermingling of Central European, Balkan, and Italian influences makes Udinese life an exotic composite. Given its turbulent history—conquered by Venice in 1420, appropriated by Austria in the late 18th century, and heavily bombed during WWII—Udine is fortunate to have escaped with its landmarks intact.

The present town is notable primarily for its graceful Gothic and Renaissance architecture and for works by the Rococo pioneer Giambattista Tiepolo. Shoppers stream through the small, attractive streets. The local sites are humble compared to those of Rome or Venice, but the city serves as a comfortable base for those who want to explore Friuli-Venezia Giulia.

ORIENTATION AND PRACTICAL INFORMATION

Udine's train and bus stations are both on Viale Europa Unita in the southern part of town. All bus lines pass the train station, but only buses #1, 3, and 8 run from Viale Europa Unita to the center of town by the **P. della Libertà** and **Castle Hill.** You can also make the 15-min. walk: from the station, go right to Piazzale D'Annunzio, then turn left under the arches to Via Aquileia. Continue up Via Veneto to P. della Libertà.

Tourist Office: P. 1° Maggio, 7 (tel. 29 59 72; fax 50 47 43). From P. della Libertà, turn right onto Via Manin and left onto P. 1° Maggio, looking for the pink-arched façade. Or take bus #2, 7, or 10 to P. 1° Maggio. Wonderful maps, copious information. Itineraries for visiting the town are on the town map and in *Udine and its Environs*. English spoken. Open Mon.-Sat. 9am-1pm and 3-6pm.

Currency Exchange: Banco Ambrosiana Veneto, Via Vittorio Veneto, 21 (tel. 51 74 11), off P. della Libertà. Has the best rates in town. Open Mon.-Fri. 8:20am-1:20pm and 2:35-4:05pm. Also in the post office, on the left as you enter. Open Mon.-Fri. 8:15am-5:30pm, Sat. 8:15am-1pm.

Telephones: Via Savorgnana, 13 (tel. 27 81), off P. Duomo. Open Mon.-Fri. 9am-12:30pm and 4-7:30pm. Also in the train station.

Trains: On Viale Europa Unita (tel. 50 36 56). **Information** office open 7am-9pm. To: Venice (22 per day, 2hr., L11,700); Trieste (19 per day, 1½hr., L7200); Milan (4 per day, 5hr., L29,800); and Vienna (6 per day, 7hr., L86,000). **Luggage Storage:** L5000 for 12hr. Open daily 7:30am-10:30pm.

Buses: On Viale Europa Unita (tel. 20 39 41), 1 block to the right of the train station as you exit. Walk through the lifeless station and turn left when you see the bus parking garage. There you'll find **Autolinea Ferrari** (tel. 50 40 12). Service to: Trieste (9 per day, 1hr., L6900); Lignano (17 per day, 1hr., L6900); Venice (1 per day, 2hr., L11,000); Grado (16 per day, 1hr., L4600); Cividale (24 per day, 30min., L2700); Palmanova (23 per day, 40min., L2700); and Aquileia (18 per day, 1½hr., L4600). Bus line offices housed in the "Pullman Bar" next door (tel. 50 24 63).

Mountain Information: The bulletin board of the **Club Alpino Italiano** is at city hall, Via B. Odorico, 3 (tel. 50 42 90). Info on skiing and upcoming trips. For hikes within Friuli-Venezia Giulia, contact **Gruppo Attività ed Informazione Ambientali,** Via Monterotondo, 22 (tel. 60 18 92) or **Società Alpina Friulana,** Via Odorico, 3. Open Mon.-Sat. 5-7:15pm, Thurs. 9-11pm. Alpine info and excursions.

Swimming Pool: Piscina Comunale, Via Ampezzo, 4 (tel. 269 67 or 269 29), near P. Diacono. Indoor pool open Sept.-May; outdoor June-Aug. Open Mon.-Fri. 10am-8pm, Sat.-Sun. noon-7pm. Shorter hours Sept.-May. L7000. Bathing cap required.

Late Night Pharmacy: tel. 192.

Emergencies: tel. 113. **First Aid:** tel. 118. **Hospital: Ospedale Civile** (tel. 55 21), in P. Santa Maria della Misericordia. Take bus #1 north to the last stop.

Police: Via Prefettura, 16 (tel. 50 28 41).

Post Office: Via Veneto, 42 (tel. 50 19 93). *Fermo posta* and stamps through the right door at desk #6. Fax at window #3. Open Mon.-Sat. 8:15am-7:40pm. Also a smaller **branch** at Via Roma, 25, straight ahead from the train station. Open Mon.-Fri. 8:10am-1:15pm, Sat. 8:05am-1pm. **Postal Code:** 33100.

Telephone Code: 0432.

ACCOMMODATIONS

The good news is that the large map outside the train station is clearly marked with the locations of Udine's hotels, some of which are real bargains. The bad news is that local workers probably snagged the best spots long ago. Many single rooms are booked by the month. In June and July students taking exams also vie for vacancies.

Suite Inn, Via di Toppo, 25 (tel. 50 16 83). Take bus #1 or #3 from the station, get off at P. Osoppo, and walk up Via di Toppo. Friendly proprietor is eager to please. Cozy sitting room with TV and piano. Beautiful, grand rooms. Doubles L65,000, with bath L80,000. Triples L110,000. Breakfast L8000. V.

Locanda Piccolo Friuli, Via Magrini, 11 (tel./fax 50 78 17). From P. Garibaldi take Via Brenari to Via Poscolle, and continue on Vicolo Gorgo. Pricey but worth it: an attractive old building with antique fixtures. Creaky wood floor, big sitting room, and frescoes complete the atmosphere. Singles with bath L55,000. Doubles with bath L80,000. Extra bed L20,000. Breakfast L8000.

Al Vecchio Tram, Via Brenari, 32 (tel. 50 25 16). Just off P. Garibaldi. Elegant staircase and large rooms. Bar downstairs. Singles L30,000-32,000. Doubles L55,000.

Locanda Da Arturo, Via Pracchiuso, 75 (tel. 29 90 70). Take bus #4 from the station, get off at P. Oberdan, and walk down Via Pracchiuso on the far side of the *piazza.* Quiet, but few rooms. Restaurant downstairs serves lunch and dinner. Singles L25,000. Doubles L45,000. Reserve ahead. Closed either July or Aug.

FOOD

A combination of Italian, Austrian, and Slovene fare, Udinese cuisine tends more toward the hearty than the *haute.* A typical regional specialty is *brovada e museto,* a stew made of marinated turnips and boiled sausage. Shop for produce weekday mornings in the **open-air market** at P. Matteotti near P. della Libertà, or head for Via Redipuglia or P. 1° Maggio on Saturdays between 8am and 1pm. Buy staples at the **Despar** supermarket at Viale Volontari della Libertà, 6, off P. Osoppo. Open Mon. and Wed. 8:30am-1pm, Tues. and Thurs.-Fri. 8:30am-1pm and 4-7pm, Sat. 8:30am-7pm. Also try the **Lavoratore** supermarket, Via Stringher, 10, down from the *duomo.* Open Mon. and Wed. 9am-1:30pm, Tues. and Thurs.-Sat. 9am-1:30pm and 4-7:30pm. Cheap pizzerias and *trattorie* cluster around Via Pracchiuso, including **Pizzamania** at #63. Slices for takeout only start at L3000. Open Tues.-Sat. 10am-1:30pm and 4-9pm, Sun. 4-9pm.

Zenit, Via Prefettura, 15/B (tel. 50 29 80). A cross between a '50s diner and a high-school cafeteria, but reasonable as a self-service place. Offers pasta, hot entrees, and salad. Popular with local businesspeople. *Primi* L4300-6500, *secondi* L6500-7500. Cover L500. Open Mon.-Sat. 11:45am-2:30pm.

Ristorante-Pizzeria Ai Portici, Via Veneto, 8 (tel. 50 89 75), under the arcade before P. della Libertà. Pizza for L6000-12,000 is reasonable, given the chic ambience. *Primi* L6000-9000, *secondi* L7000-25,000. *Menù* L16,000. Cover L1500. Open Wed.-Mon. 9am-midnight or 1am.

Osteria Ai Provinciali, Via V. Veneto, 14, under the archway. Self-service lunch place with friendly atmosphere and good, hot, inexpensive food. Menu changes daily—usually several choices of pasta and entrees. *Primi* L4500, *secondi* L6500. Open Mon.-Fri. noon-2:30pm.

SIGHTS AND ENTERTAINMENT

The heart of Udine is **Piazza della Libertà,** an elegantly elevated square. Along its higher side runs the Renaissance **Arcade of San Giovanni.** The two columns symbolizing Venice commemorate the conquest of Udine by the Venetian Republic. Across the *piazza* stands the delicate, candy-striped **Loggia del Lionello,** another architectural reminder of the conquerors' presence in Udine. Originally built in 1448, the beloved *loggia* was severely damaged by a fire in 1876, but was reconstructed shortly thereafter by popular demand.

Palladio designed the rugged **Arco Bollani** (tel. 50 18 24) in 1556. It stands in the corner near the clock tower and allows you to pass through the walls to the **Church of Santa Maria** and the **castello** of the Venetian governors. The *castello* is home to the **Museo Civico,** which exhibits a myriad of notable paintings including a frieze and several *putti* by Giambattista Tiepolo. (Open Tues.-Sat. 9:30am-12:30pm and 3-6pm, Sun.-Mon. 9:30am-12:30pm. Admission L4000, students L2000.)

In P. del Duomo, 50m from the more hectic P. della Libertà, stands the Roman-Gothic **duomo,** with several Tiepolos on display in the Baroque interior (the first, second, and fourth altars on the right side). There is a small **museum** (tel. 50 68 30) in the squat brick *campanile,* comprising two chapels with 14th-century frescoes by

Vitale da Bologna. (Museum closed for renovation. Call the tourist office for current info.) Udine has been called the city of Tiepolo, and some of this Baroque painter's finest works adorn the **Oratorio della Purità** (tel. 50 68 30), across from the *duomo.* The *Assumption* fresco on the ceiling (1759) and the *Immaculate Conception* of the altarpiece represent Tiepolo's fantastic world of light and air. (Ask the cathedral sacristan to let you in. Tip expected.)

A sizeable sampling of earlier Tiepolo frescoes is housed in the **Palazzo Patriarcale,** P. Patriarcato, 1 (tel. 250 03), at the head of Via Ungheria. Here, from 1726 through 1730, Tiepolo executed an extensive series of Old Testament scenes. The museum also displays wooden sculptures from the Friuli region from Romanesque to Baroque times. (Open Wed.-Sun. 10am-noon and 3:30-6:30pm. Admission L4000.) Several blocks south from P. della Libertà along Via Stringher, off P. XX Settembre, stands the **Church of San Francesco.** This architectural gem of the early Renaissance is considered Udine's most beautiful church. Unfortunately, it opens only for exhibitions.

There are also a number of interesting museums, including an excellent **Gallery of Modern Art** at P. P. Diacono, 21 (tel. 29 58 91), on the ring road that circles the old city. The museum transports you to the idiosyncratic worlds of de Kooning, Lichtenstein, Chagall, Picasso, and major 20th-century Italian artists. (Open Tues.-Sat. 9:30am-12:30pm and 3-6pm, Sun. 9:30am-12:30pm. Admission L4000, students L2000.) The **Friulian Museum of Popular Arts and Traditions,** Via Viola, 3 (tel. 50 78 61), northeast of the P. XXVI Luglio, exhibits a collection of regional costumes and folk art. (Closed for renovation. Check with the tourist office for info.)

From July-September, the town celebrates summer with **Udine d'Estate,** a series of concerts, performances, and guided tours of the city. Check with the tourist office for a list of events.

Cividale del Friuli

At the far edge of Italy, unknown to most tourists, sleepy Cividale saw its glory days come and go during the darkest of the Dark Ages in the 6th century. In 568, land-hungry Lombards seized what was then *Forum Iulii* and made the vanquished Roman trading center the capital of the first Lombard duchy. By the 8th century, the Patriarch of Aquileia had grabbed a piece of the action, setting off a building frenzy. Since then things have been generally quiet, despite devastating earthquakes that have twice toppled the city's monuments. Cividale thus remains the only place in Italy to see magnificent medieval art from the least-known century of Italian history.

You can easily see this tiny town in an afternoon. No need for a map—just wander through the ancient portal and follow the yellow-metal or natural-wood signs past the restaurants, shops, and *caffè* to the historical points of interest.

ORIENTATION AND PRACTICAL INFORMATION

Cividale can be reached by train from Udine (every hr., 20min., roundtrip L4000). The **train** and Rosina **bus** stations (tel. 63 10 46) open onto Viale Libertà and are a brief walk from the **center.** (Bus to Udine L2400.) Open Mon.-Fri. 8:30am-12:30pm, Sat. 8:30am-1pm. From the train station head directly onto Via Marconi, turning left through the **Porta Arsenale Veneto** when the street ends. Bear right in P. Dante, then left onto Largo Boiano. The **tourist office** at Corso Paolino (tel. 73 13 98) has an extremely helpful staff. Open Mon.-Fri. 9am-1pm and 3-6pm. In case of **emergency,** seek out the **police** on P. A. Diaz (tel. 73 14 29), or call 113. The **hospital (Ospedale Civile)** is in P. dell'Ospedale (tel. 70 81). You'll find the **post office** at Aquileia, 10 (tel. 73 11 57), toward the Ponte del Diavolo. They also have an exchange service that accepts traveler's checks. Open Mon.-Fri. 8:30am-5:30pm, Sat. 8:30am-1pm. Exchange open Mon.-Fri. 8:30am-4:30pm. The **postal code** is 33043. The **telephone code** is 0432.

ACCOMMODATIONS AND FOOD

Accommodations are not Cividale's forte. The two-star **Al Pomo d'Oro,** P. S. Giovanni (tel. 73 14 89), is a lovely old building in the medieval quarter with a restaurant downstairs. Singles with bath L55,000. Doubles with bath L85,000. Breakfast included. V, MC, AmEx. Area specialties are *gubana* (a fig and prune-filled pastry laced with *grappa*) and *Picolit,* a pricey dessert wine rarely sold outside of the Natisone Valley. Most bars stock pre-packaged *gubana,* but for fresh mouth-watering sweets, look for the "Gubana Cividalese" sign on your right as you near the **Ponte del Diavolo,** located at Corso D'Aquileia, 16. P. Diacono hosts Cividale's **open-air market** every Saturday from 8am to 1pm. The management of **Antica Trattoria Dominissini,** Stretta Stellini, 18 (tel. 73 37 63), serves up *cucina friulana* in the shadow of **Church of S. Francesco.** Ask to sit outside in the vine-roofed area with a view of the church's tower. *Primi* L8000, *secondi* L8000-12,000. Cover L2000. Open Sun.-Fri. 9am-3pm and 6-11pm. **Bar Al Campanile,** Via G. B. Candotti, 4 (tel. 73 24 67), right off the *duomo,* is a favorite with the locals, known for its local cuisine. Specialties include *prosciutto al salto.* Open Tues.-Sun. 7:30am-11:30pm.

SIGHTS AND ENTERTAINMENT

Built and expanded over the centuries, Cividale's *duomo* (tel. 73 11 44), directly on your left as you leave the tourist office, is an odd melange of architectural styles. Pietro Lombardo, who completed the bulk of the construction in 1528, deserves most of the credit. (Open 9:30am-noon and 3-7pm; in winter 9:30-noon and 3-6pm.) Walk to the far end of the *duomo* to view the 12th-century silver **altarpiece of Pellegrino II,** with its 25 saints and pair of archangels. Move on to the Renaissance **sarcophagus of Patriarch Nicolò Donato,** located to the left of the entrance. Annexed to the *duomo* is the **Museo Cristiano.** This free display includes the marvelously sculpted **Baptistery of Callisto** commissioned by the first Aquileian patriarch to move to Cividale. More significantly, the museum houses the **Altar of Ratchis,** a delicately carved work from AD749, one of the few surviving masterpieces of the Middle Ages. (*Duomo* and museum open Mon.-Sat. 9:30am-noon and 3-7pm, Sun. 3-7pm. Both free.)

The greatest Italian work of the 8th century can be found downhill at the **Tempietto Longobardo** (tel. 70 08 67), built on the remains of Roman homes (follow the signs). Although the "little temple" suffered greatly from the earthquakes of 1222 and 1976, efforts have restored a famous sextet of 8th-century stucco figures to their original form. The beautiful 14th-century wooden stalls almost compensate for the loss of the original frescoes. Another bonus is the spectacular view of river and mountains obtained from the entrance overlooking the rocky riverbed. (Temple open daily in summer 10am-1pm and 3:30-6:30pm; in winter 10am-1pm and 3:30-5:30pm. Admission L2000, students L1000.) The lush countryside rolls into the distance, and on a high vista sits the picturesque **Castelmonte Stara Gora.** For a similarly stunning view, try the **Ponte del Diavolo,** an impressive stone bridge of indeterminate age. For a better look at the bridge itself, descend the stairs to the water on the far side. Local legend has it that the devil himself threw down the great stone in the center of the river that the bridge crosses.

Trentino-Alto Adige

Austria and Italy battle for control of Trentino-Alto Adige, and in much of the region, the Austrian influences dominate. While Trentino in the south is predominantly Italian-speaking, Südtirol (South Tirol) in the north, encompassing most of the mountain region known as the Dolomite, speaks mainly German. Napoleon conquered this integral part of the Holy Roman Empire, only to relinquish it to the Austro-Hungarian

Empire. At the end of World War I, Trentino and the Südtirol fell under Italian rule. Germany curtailed Mussolini's brutal efforts to Italianize the Südtirol during the 1920s, but not before Mussolini had given every German name in the region an Italian equivalent.

Everything from street signs to cuisine to architecture intermingles Austrian and Italian traditions. As you negotiate these interwoven cultures, remember that north of Bolzano, you may get better service by trying to speak German but in Trent Italian is the ticket.

Dolomites (Dolomiti, Dolomiten)

Stunning limestone spires shoot skyward from green fields and pine forests. These amazing peaks—fantastic for hiking, skiing, and rock-climbing—start west of Trent and extend north and east to the Austrian frontier. Finding accommodations in the Dolomites is easy: there are hundreds of alpine huts and many rooms available in private homes, generally advertised by the *Zimmer/camere* signs. Pick up the complete *Südtirol Hotel Guide,* free at the provincial office in Bolzano and in local tourist offices. These offices also provide listings of all campgrounds in the region, but travelers camp almost anywhere. The **SAD** (Società Automobilistica Dolomiti) deploys a team of **buses** that covers virtually every paved road in the area with surprising frequency.

HIKING

Even the least bold can become avid Dolomitists. The terrain varies from wide, gentle trails to vertical cliffs. **Alpine huts** (*rifugi*) abound, easing journeys into the mountains. The *Kompass Wanderkarte,* the best map of the region, clearly marks all huts and is available at most newsstands and bookstores. Huts generally operate from late June through early October, but at higher altitudes the season is often shorter. The provincial tourist offices in Trent and Bolzano supply information in English on their respective provinces. Dr. Hannsjörg Hager, a noted Alpinist who speaks English and can help you pick a suitable route, runs the Alpine desk of the Bolzano office. He'll make sure the cabins are open before you get into the mountains. Bring your own food if possible, and pick up information about winter walking paths from the tourist office. Also, look for books by author and veteran hiker Gillian Price, among them *Walking in the Dolomites*, *Classic Climbs in the Dolomites*, and *Walking in the Central Italian Alps: Vinschgau, Ortler, Adamello and their Parks*. All are published by Cicerone Press. For further information about Trentino huts, contact the SAT at Via Manci, 57 (tel. 98 18 71 or 98 64 62), in Trent. Open Mon.-Fri. 8am-noon and 3-7pm.

NORTHERN ITALY

SKIING

The Dolomites offer immensely popular downhill skiing with usually sunny skies and light powdery snow. The **regional tourist office** in **Bolzano** (tel. (0471) 99 38 09) is a good source of information. For more specific information concerning prices, deals, and snow conditions contact **Club Alpino** (See **Essentials: Camping**). Major ski centers include: near Bolzano, **Alta Venosta** (around Lake Resia) and **Colle Isarco;** near Trent, **Folgaria, Brentonico, Madonna di Campiglio,** and **Monte Bondone** (especially close to the city); near Bressanone, **Val d'Isarco,** the **Zona dello Sciliar,** and **Val Gardena;** and near Corvara, **Alta Badia.**

One of the cheapest and most convenient ways to enjoy a skiing holiday in the Dolomites is to get a **settimana bianca** (white week) package deal, available from any CTS or CIT office. Prices start around L500,000 and include a week's room and board and ski passes. If you want to travel the region by bus or car, or if you're planning to stay in the region of interlocking trails around the Gruppo Sella, consider purchasing the **Superski Dolomiti** pass, good on all 464 cablecars and lifts in the

Dolomite area (around L50,000 per day, L250,000 per week, with discounts for senior citizens and children under 14.)

Trent (Trento, Trient)

When you arrive in Trent, find a cozy *pasticceria* in the center of town and order yourself a piece of *Apfel Strudel* and a cappuccino. You will have before you an edible metaphor of the city itself: a rather harmonious combination of Germanic and Mediterranean flavors. Located inside the Alpine threshold yet connected back to the Veneto by a long, deep valley, Trent became the Romans' strategic gateway to the north with their construction of two imperial roads. For centuries to follow, castle fortresses such as the Castello del Buonconsiglio proliferated in the region. The Renaissance saw the construction, mainly near the Piazza del Duomo, of numerous *palazzi* with elegantly decorated façades. Cultural and physical ownership of the city itself was contested in the 19th century but was settled once and for all at the end of World War I, when Trent became an Italian city.

ORIENTATION AND PRACTICAL INFORMATION

The bus and train stations are located between the **Adige River** and the **public gardens.** The center of town is to the east of the Adige. To get there from the station, turn right on Via Pozzo, which leads you to a helpful sign at the intersection of Via Torre Vanga. Continue on V. Pozzo, which becomes Via Orfane and then **Via Cavour,** to reach the **Piazza del Duomo** in the heart of town. Notice the frescoed façades of the surrounding *palazzi*. Most of Trent's piazze are within close walking distance of each other, making navigation quite easy. Reach the **Castello del Buonconsiglio** by following Via Roma east, away from the river. The street becomes Via Manci and then Via S. Marco as it leads straight to the city's castle.

Tourist Office: Azienda Autonoma (City Tourist Office), Via Alfieri, 4 (tel. 98 38 80; fax 98 45 08). From the station walk through the park and follow Via Alfieri to the right. Friendly, English-speaking staff. Open Mon.-Fri. 9am-noon and 3-6pm, Sat. 9am-noon. The **APT del Trentino (Regional Tourist Office),** Corso III Novembre, 132 (tel. 91 44 44; fax 39 00 05), is a 15-min. walk on the continuation of Via S. Vigilio from the rear of the *duomo*. Open Mon.-Fri. 8:30am-12:30pm and 2:30-6pm, Sat. 9am-noon.

Budget Travel: CTS, Via Cavour, 21 (tel./fax 98 15 33), near P. del Duomo. Student IDs, plane and train tickets, Transalpino tickets, and occasional organized outings. English spoken. Open Mon.-Fri. 10am-12:30pm and 3-7pm.

Telephones: Via Torre Verde, 11 (tel. 23 40 40). Open Mon. 3-7pm, Tues.- Sat. 8:30am-12:30pm and 3-7pm.

Trains: tel. 23 45 45. To: Verona (every hr., 1hr., L8000); Bolzano (every hr., 45min., L5000); Bologna (11 per day, 3hr., L17,200); and Venice (7 per day, 3hr., L17,200). **Luggage Storage:** L5000 for 12hr. Open 24hr.

Buses: Atesina, Via G. Marconi, 3 (tel. 82 10 00), next to the train station. To Riva del Garda (every hr., 1hr., L4800). Extensive local service. Ask for schedules at the information booth in the station.

Cableways: Funivia Trento-Sardagna, Via Lung'Adige Monte Grappa (tel. 23 21 1). Walk up and over the tracks, past the bus terminal. Take a right on busy Cavalcavia San Lorenzo, and you'll find the Funivia on the other side. This lift transports you to Sardagna on Mt. Bondone (every 30min., daily 7am-10pm, L1300).

Hiking Equipment: Rigoni Sport, P. Battisti, 30/31 (tel. 98 12 39). Open Mon. 3-7pm, Tues.-Sun. 9:10am-noon and 3-7pm.

Bookstore: Libreria Disertori, Via M. Diaz, 11 (tel. 98 14 55), near P. Battisti has English books. Open Tues.-Sat. 9am-noon and 3:30-7pm, Mon. 3:30-7pm. V, MC.

Emergency: tel. 113. **Alpine Emergency: CAI-SAT hotline,** tel. 23 31 66. The **fire station,** tel. 115, can also reach alpine help. **First Aid:** tel. 118. **Hospital: Ospedale Santa Chiara,** Largo Medaglie d'Oro (tel. 90 31 11), past the swimming pool and up Via Orsi.

Police: tel. 112. **Questura,** P. Mostra (tel. 98 61 13).
Post Office: Via Calepina, 16 (tel. 98 72 70), at P. Vittoria. Open Mon.-Fri. 8:10am-7:30pm, Sat. 8:10am-1pm. Another office next to the train station on Via Dogana has the same hours. **Postal Code:** 38100.
Telephone Code: 0461.

ACCOMMODATIONS

Ostello Giovane Europa (HI), Via Manzoni, 17 (tel. 23 45 67), a continuation of Via Torre Verde near P. Raffaele Sanzio. Hotel turned hostel, with sparkling rooms and hospitable staff, near the center of town. A few bikes available for use—check with the office. One- to six-person rooms. Bar and TV. Check-in from 7:15am. Lock-out 9am-5:30pm. Curfew 11:30pm. L20,000 per person. Breakfast included. Lunch and dinner L14,000.

Hotel Venezia, P. Duomo, 45 (tel. 23 41 14). Clean, spacious rooms, some with a view of the *duomo.* Great location, high quality, and fair prices. Singles L42,000, with bath L57,000. Doubles L62,000, with bath L82,000. V, MC.

Al Cavallino Bianco, Via Cavour, 29 (tel. 23 15 42), down the street from the *duomo.* Clean, airy rooms. The main draw is the life-like paint job in the living room—you'll feel like you're sitting in a sunny field. Singles L37,000, with bath L55,000. Doubles L60,000, with bath L80,000. Triples with bath L105,000. Closed in Dec. and June 16-26. V, MC, AmEx.

FOOD

Trent has a large open-air market on Thursdays with a limited selection of fruits, vegetables, and cheeses. (See **Sights** for more info.) Another option is the **Trentini** supermarket, P. Londron, 28 (tel. 22 01 96), just across P. Pasi from the *duomo.* Open Mon. 8:30am-12:30pm, Tues.-Sat. 8:30am-12:30pm and 2:30-7:30pm. The **Poli** supermarket (tel. 98 50 63) is near the station at the corner of Via Roma and Via delle Orfane. Open Mon. and Sat. 8:30am-12:30pm, Tues.-Fri. 8:30am-12:30pm and 3:15-7:15pm.

Pizzeria Duomo, P. Duomo, 22 (tel. 98 42 86). Choose from a variety of large, delicious pizzas. This local joint is popular with university students. Pizzas and calzones start at L5500. Pasta L6000-9000. Cover L1500. Open Sun.-Fri. 11:30am-2:30pm and 5-11:30pm.

La Cantinota, Via S. Marco, 24 (tel. 23 85 27 or 23 85 61), at the other end of Via Manci from Via Roma. They literally roll out the red carpet for you here. Enjoy the delicious cuisine, then drop by the piano bar after dessert. *Risotto* for at least 2 people L12,000. Pasta L8000-15,000. Cover L2000. Open Fri.-Wed. noon-3pm and 7pm-2:30am. Piano bar open 11:30pm-2:30am. Closed July.

Ristorante/Pizzeria Chistè, Via delle Orne, 4 (tel. 98 18 46), off Via Belenzani near the *duomo*. Serves huge portions that are popular with the locals. *Primi* L11,000-17,000, *secondi* L11,000-20,000. Cover L1500. Open Tues.-Sun. noon-2pm and 6:30-11pm. Closed Aug.

Ristorante Pizzeria Forst, V. Mazzurana, 38 (tel. 355 90), a few steps from P. Duomo. The rustic interior, complete with tin lamps over the bar, gives this *birreria/ristorante* a Bavarian feel. *Primi* L6800-8000, *secondi* L7000-16,000. *Menù* L21,000, includes *primo, secondo,* and one vegetable. Cover L1500. Open Tues.-Sun. 11am-3pm and 5:30-11:30pm. Closed July 3-24. V, MC, AmEx.

Ai Tre Garofani, Via Mazzini, 33 (tel. 23 75 43). Follow V. San Vigilio behind the *duomo* to Via Mazzini. Pizza L7000-9500. *Primi* L8000-9000, *secondi* L10,000-15,000. Cover L2000. Open Mon.-Sat. 11:30am-2:30pm and 6:30-8:30pm.

Gelateria Zanella, Via Suffragio, 6 (tel. 23 20 39), next to the Torre Verde. Delicious, homemade *gelato* and *semifreddo* specialties. Plenty of outdoor seating under a vine-covered bower. Open Mon.-Tues. and Thurs.-Sat. 11am-midnight.

SIGHTS AND ENTERTAINMENT

The pointed dome of Trent's Gothic-Romanesque *duomo,* the **Cathedral of Saint Vigilio,** rises in modest emulation of the looming Alps. The famed Council of Trent's decrees were delivered in front of the huge cross in the Chapel of the Holy Crucifix. (Open daily 6:40am-12:15pm and 2:30-8pm.) The remains of a 6th-century Christian basilica were recently uncovered beneath the *duomo.* Admission to this underground church is included with admission to the **Museo Diocesano,** P. Duomo, 18 (tel. 23 44 19). (Open Mon.-Sat. 9:30am-12:30pm and 2:30-6pm. Admission L5000, students L1000.) For an introduction to Trent's history, as well as an excellent view of the city from the castle's towers, take a right at the end of Via Belenzani onto Via Roma to get to the **Castello del Buonconsiglio** (tel. 23 37 70). The oldest part of the castle was built from 1239 to 1255, but much of the present structure was added in the 15th century by Giovanni Hinderbach, the governing bishop-prince. Today, the castle houses the **Museo Provinciale d'Arte**—one ticket lets you see the castle, gardens, and artwork. Check out the "Locus Reflections," the room in which the Austrians captured and condemned Cesare Battisti to death during World War I. (Open April-Sept. Tues.-Sun. 9am-noon and 2-5:30pm; Oct.-March 9am-noon and 2-5pm. Admission L7000, under 18 and over 60 L3000.) An **open-air market** occurs every Thursday from 8am to 1pm behind P. del Duomo, offering great deals on clothing and food. If you arrive in the summer, try to catch a play or performance at one of the private castles. Admission varies from *gratis* to L10,000.

■ Mountains Near Trent

Monte Bondone rises majestically over Trent and begs for pleasant daytrips and overnight excursions. Check with the tourist office (tel. 94 71 28; fax 94 71 88) in **Vaneze,** halfway up the mountain, about accommodations, ski lifts, and maps. Pick up a map at the tourist office in Trent, and then catch the cable car from Ponte di San Lorenzo, between the train tracks and the river, to **Sardagna,** a great picnic spot (every 30min., daily 7am-6:30pm, L1500; in Trent tel. 91 03 32 or 38 10 00). From there, a 10- to 12-km hike takes you to the **Mezavia Campground** (tel. 94 81 78). L5000 per person, L7000 per tent; open June to mid-Sept.

■ Bolzano (Bozen)

Although the initial schizophrenia caused by bilingual street signs may be startling, visitors value Bolzano as a culturally unique pocket of Italy. The survival of an ancient dialect in some areas of the South Tyrol reveals the relative isolation in which this region developed. While both Mediterranean and Bavarian elements are identifiable, Bolzano's culture evades generalization. Ownership of the South Tyrol has been contested in the past, but since World War I the territory has been a part of Italy. Bolzano encourages peaceful relations among its youth with mandatory instruction in both Italian and German, but the disproportionately large number of fair, rosy-cheeked bilinguals reveals definite Austrian tendencies.

ORIENTATION AND PRACTICAL INFORMATION

Bolzano's historic center rests in the hollow created by the converging Isarco and Talvera rivers and is linked by bridge to the more modern, industrial sector in the west. The main *piazze/plätze* are within close walking distance of one another, and street names are given in Italian and German. A brief walk up **Via Stazione** from the train station, or **Via Alto Adige** if you've arrived by bus, leads to **Piazza Walther.**

Tourist Office: For Bolzano only, P. Walther, 8 (tel. 97 56 56 or 97 06 60; fax 98 01 28). Provides lists of various accommodations, including hotels, campgrounds, and *agriturismo. Walks and Hikes* suggests nearby hikes of varying lengths and difficulty. *Manifestazioni* includes several pages of useful phone numbers. English spoken. Open Mon.-Fri. 8:30am-6pm, Sat. 9am-12:30pm. **Provincial Tourist Office for South Tyrol,** P. Parrocchia, 11 (tel. 99 38 08), near P. Walther across from the *duomo.* A must for those setting out for the mountains. Friendly staff speaks English. Open Mon.-Fri. 9am-noon and 2-5pm.

Budget Travel: CIT, P. Walther, 11 (tel. 97 85 16). Transalpino tickets and skiing packages. English spoken. Open Mon.-Fri. 9am-12:30pm and 3-6:30pm.

Currency Exchange: In the post office or at **Banca Nazionale del Lavoro,** in P. Walther at the end of Via Stazione, right next door to the Bolzano tourist office. Good rates, Visa services. Open Mon. 8:20am-1:20pm, Tues.-Fri. 8:20am-1:20pm and 3-4:30pm.

Telephones: P. Parrocchia, 17, near the *duomo.* Office open Mon.-Sat. 8:30am-12:30pm and 3-7pm. Booths open daily 7:30am-10pm. Also at Via Roma, 36/M, across the river near P. Adriano. Open Mon.-Sat. 8am-8pm.

Trains: P. Stazione (tel. 97 42 92). To: Trent (14 per day, 45min., L5000); Verona (27 per day, 1¼hr., L11,700); Merano (every 45min., 45min., L2400); and Milan (2 per day, 4hr., L22,600). More frequent service to Milan if you change at Trent. Information open Mon.-Sat. 7am-8pm, Sun. 9am-12:55pm and 2:30-5:25pm. **Luggage Storage:** L3000. Closed 2:12-5:24am (seriously).

Buses: SAD, Via Perathoner, 4 (tel. 45 01 11; fax 97 00 42), between the train station and P. Walther. To: Alpe di Siusi (13 per day, 1½hr., L4000); Collalbo (5 per day, 50min., L2600); Cortina d'Ampezzo (4 per day, 3½hr., L14,500); and Merano (13 per day, 1hr., L4000). Less frequent service on weekends. For information, call 460 47. **Local buses: ACT,** Via Conciapelli, 60 (tel. 45 01 11). Bus service throughout the city. All lines stop in P. Walther.

Cableways: Three cableways, located at the edges of Bolzano, will whisk you 1000m or more up and over the city to the nearest trailhead. To Colle (Kohlern), take the world's oldest cableway, the Funivia del Colle (or as the locals call it, the Kohlerer Seilbahn; tel. 97 85 45) from Via Campiglio (Kampillerstraße). Every 30min. Tickets L5000, bikes L4000. Open daily 7am-8pm. To Renon (Ritten), take the Funivia del Renon from Via Renon (5-min. walk from train station). Roundtrip L7500. To Salto's high plateaus, take Funivia S. Genesio (Jeneseiner Seilbahn; tel. 97 84 36) on Via Sarentino, across the Talvera River near Ponte S. Antonio. Tickets around L4500, roundtrip L6500. Bike (L5000) and pet (L1000) transport also possible.

Car Rental: Avis, P. Verdi, 18 (tel. 97 14 67). Open Mon.-Fri. 8am-noon and 3-7pm, Sat. 8am-noon.

Public Bikes: Via Stazione, near P. Walther. Borrow a bike for 4hr. by leaving a L10,000 deposit and ID information. Intercity cruisers, not mountain-worthy. **Bike Rental: Sportler Velo,** Via Grappoli (Weintraubengasse), 56 (tel. 97 77 19), near P. Municipale. Mountain bikes L30,000 per day. Also carries an extensive selection of retail bikes and equipment.

Camping Equipment: Sportler, Via dei Portici/Laubengasse, 37/A (tel. 97 40 33). Expensive, extensive selection. Open Mon.-Fri. 9am-12:15pm and 3-7pm, Sat. 9am-12:30pm. V, MC. You may get a better deal down the street at **Sport Reinstaller,** Via Portici, 2 (tel. 97 71 90). Open Mon.-Fri. 8:30am-noon and 3-7pm, Sat. 8:30am-12:30pm.

Swimming Pool: Piscina Coperta, Viale Trieste, 21 (tel. 91 10 00). Indoor pool. Admission L5300. Bathing cap required. Open Oct.-June Tues. and Thurs. 7-7:45am, Wed. and Fri. 12:30-2:30pm and 7-9pm, Sat. 4-7pm, Sun. 3-7pm.

Emergency: tel. 113. **First Aid:** tel. 118. **White Cross,** tel. 24 44 44. **Hospital: Ospedale Regionale San Maurizio,** Via Lorenz Böhler (tel. 90 81 11).

Police: tel. 94 76 11.

Post Office: Via della Posta, 1 (tel. 97 94 52), by the *duomo.* Open Mon.-Fri. 8:15am-5:15pm, Sat. 8:15am-12:45pm. **Postal Code:** 39100.

Telephone Code: 0471.

ACCOMMODATIONS AND CAMPING

Though Bolzano has many budget deals in the spring and fall, you'll be hard-pressed to find anything affordable in summer and winter. The romantic and luxurious possibilities on the mountainside often run cheaper than their city counterparts. (It helps to have a car or motorbike to access some of these lodgings.) Try the mountain options or ask about the *agriturismo* program at the tourist office.

Pensione Reiseggerhof, Sta. Maddalena di Sotto, 24 (tel. 97 86 94), uphill from Weinstube. Live like they do on *Lifestyles of the Rich and Famous,* in rooms overlooking the vineyards. If you're coming from the *centro,* take a car or taxi up the hill. Doubles L32,000-35,000 per person. Breakfast included.

Schwarze Katz, Sta. Maddalena di Sotto, 2 (tel. 97 54 17). Near Via Brennero, not too far from the *centro.* Hotel "Black Cat" is a family-run, friendly place with a garden restaurant popular with locals. L30,000 per person, L35,000 with bath.

Croce Bianca, P. del Grano (Kornplatz), 3 (tel. 97 75 52). Spacious, old-style rooms. Its central location renders rooms scarce in the summer and winter. Make reservations. Singles L38,000. Doubles L58,000, with bath L75,000.

Camping: Moosbauer, Via San Maurizio, 83 (tel. 91 84 92). Take bus #10A or 10B from the station (last bus at 8:30pm). Get off at the hospital stop, then walk 1km down San Maurizio toward Merano. L7500 per person, L7000 for tent, L6000 for car space. Showers included.

FOOD

Rindsgulasch is a delicious beef stew, *Speck* is tasty smoked bacon (a favorite for sandwiches), and *Knödel* dumplings come in dozens of rib-sticking varieties. The week-long *Südtiroler Törgelen* tasting spree in the fall celebrates the local vineyards. P. delle Erbe (Obstplatz) has an all-day produce **market,** with delicious goods from local farms, on every day but Sunday. Two **Despar supermarkets** (tel. 97 45 37) are situated at Via della Rena, 40 (open Mon.-Fri. 8:30am-12:30pm and 3-7:30pm, Sat. 8am-1pm), and Via dei Bottai, 29 (open summers Mon.-Fri. 8:30am-7:30pm). For baked goods, **Panificio/Backerei Lemayr,** Via Goethe, 17 (tel. 97 84 37), has a large selection, although many other shops also sell tasty pastries and breads. Open Mon.-Fri. 6:30am-12:30pm and 3:30-7:15pm, Sat. 6:30am-1pm.

Restaurant Weisses Rössl, Via dei Bottai/Bindergasse, 6 (tel. 97 32 67), the continuation of Via Laurin and Via dei Grappoli, at the end of Via dei Portici. A budget place with Austrian atmosphere. *Primi* L7000-8000, *secondi* L9000-12,000. Open Aug.-June Mon.-Fri. 7am-1am, Sat. 4pm-1am.

Spaghetti Express, Via Goethe, 20 (tel. 97 53 35). A noisy place with a young crowd. Try any of the umpteen kinds of pasta (L9500-12,500), including a dish with shrimp and champagne. Cover L1500. Open Mon.-Sat. noon-2:15pm and 6-10pm.

SIGHTS AND ENTERTAINMENT

While the Gothic **duomo** and its high filigree tower dominate P. Walther, the pastel façades surrounding the square cheerfully contrast with the stoniness of the cathedral and surrounding mountains. (*Duomo* open Mon.-Fri. 6:30am-noon and 2-6pm, Sat. 9:30am-noon.) The **Church of the Francescani** rests in a peaceful garden off P. Erbe. (Open daily 6am-noon and 2:30-6pm.) The fire towers of the **Castel Mareccio** (tel. 97 66 15) on Via C. de'Medici are later additions. (Open Mon.-Sat. 10am-noon and 3-6pm.)

The bike-borrowing option is the best way to visit the castles clustered in the nearby valleys. **Castel Mareccio,** in the center, has a core structure that dates back to the 13th century. A 15-min. bike ride up Via Weggerstein to Via S. Antonio will take you past **Castel Roncolo** (Runkelstein Castle), the most impressive of the lot (tel. 98 02 00). Guided tours of the frescoed rooms are available for groups, preferably by reservation. (Open March-Nov. Tues.-Sat. 10am-5pm. Admission L1000.) For breezy mountain views and a pleasant *passeggiata,* stroll along the far side of the Talvera River (just across Ponte Talvera).

For nightlife, check out **Club Mirò,** Piazza Domenicani, 3b (tel. 97 64 64). This large piano bar and *discoteca* is right in the center of town and hosts live concerts. (Open Fri.-Sat. 10:30pm–3am, for concerts 10:30pm-2:30am.)

Lake Garda (Lago di Garda)

Garda is the grandest and most popular of the Italian lakes, thanks to its breezy summer and mild winter. Of the lake's major towns, three in particular are worth a visit: Riva for its seclusion, reasonable prices, and splendid swimming; Gardone Riviera for its morbidly fascinating villa of Gabriele D'Annunzio; and Sirmione for its extensive Roman ruins and beautifully situated medieval castle. If you're coming from Verona, consider a daytrip to the tiny but stunning bay at **Punta San Vigilio** (just past Garda) for swimming, sunning, and picnicking.

Desenzano lies on the Milan-Venice train line, two hours from Venice, 30min. from Verona and Brescia, and one hour from Milan. Once there, you can easily get to the lake towns by buses, hydrofoils, and ferries. Check the schedules carefully and plan ahead, as buses and ferries stop running around 8-10pm. For shorter trips, take the ferry—it's cheaper than the hydrofoil and you can sit on deck. **Campgrounds** surround the lake but are concentrated between Desenzano and **Salò.** Unofficial camping is discouraged. Many private residences rent rooms (mostly doubles) in Lake Garda's larger towns. The tourist offices can provide you with a list of these accommodations.

SIRMIONE

Alas, shrewd developers realized the potential of what Catullus once lauded as the "jewel of peninsulae and islands." Today Sirmione looks like a pavilion at Disney World—the tiny, flower-lined streets, scenic archways, and manicured gardens reveal hidden cypress and olive groves inaccessible to most cars. Families run straight to the enormous medieval castle, surrounded by a moat teeming with fish, ducks, and swans (but no talking mice).

Orientation and Practical Information

Buses run to Sirmione every hour from Brescia and Verona (1hr., L5400 and L4600 respectively), and every half hour from Desenzano, the closest train station (30min., L2100). The ride down the peninsula's central artery concludes in Sirmione on Viale Guglielmo Marconi, next to the **tourist office** in the disc-shaped building at #2 (tel. 91 61 14), where you can arm yourself with maps and accommodations information. Open April-Oct. daily 9am-12:30pm and 3-6pm; Nov.-March closed Sat. evening and all of Sun. Continuing down Viale Marconi leads to Via Vittorio Emanuele, historic Sirmione's main thoroughfare, marked by the castle. The **bank** is in Piazza Castello, across from the castle (tel. 91 60 00). **Bikes** can be rented at Garda Noleggia, Via Verona, 47 (tel. 990 59 73) for L5000 per hr., L25,000 per day (proper ID required; no age restriction, but small children should be accompanied by an adult). For **medical emergencies or ambulance,** call toll-free (167) 82 10 49. In **emergencies,** dial 113. **Postal code:** 25019. The **telephone code** for Sirmione and Desenzano is 030.

Accommodations and Food

Sirmione is least damaging to one's wallet when visited as a daytrip. If you arrive in July or August without a reservation, plan on sleeping in the lake. **Albergo Meridicena,** at Via Catullo, 3 (tel. 91 61 62) is surrounded by the serene Grotte de Catullo but is steps away from the action of the city. The rooms are calming and clean, all with bath. Singles L55,000. Doubles L75,000. There are cheaper options available if you don't mind walking several kilometers from the center. Ask at the tourist office. **Sirmioncino,** Via Sirmioncino, 9 (tel. 91 90 45), behind Hotel Benaco, usually has camping space. L19,000 per person, L9000 per tent or site. Open April 15-Oct. 15. Lugana boasts two campgrounds: **Il Tiglio** (tel. 990 40 09) and **Lugana Marina** (tel. 91 91 73), both open April-Oct.

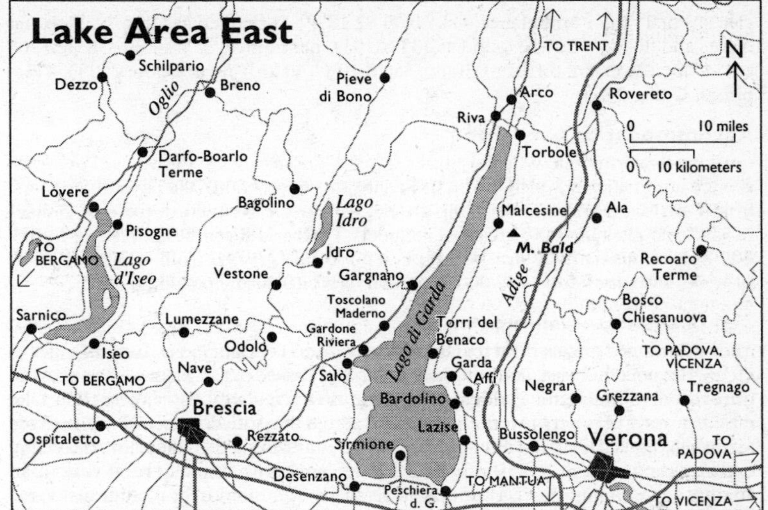

Food prices drop marginally outside the castle's immediate vicinity. Everyone in town seems to eat at **Ristorante Valentino** in Piazza Valentino off Via Vittorio Emanuele (tel. 91 61 12). Pizza from L7000, *primi* around L11,000, and *secondi* around L12,000. Sirmione's outdoor **market** in P. Montebaldo operates on Fridays from 8am-1pm.

Sights and Entertainment

Marking the central *piazza* is the conspicuous **Castello Scaligero,** built in the 13th century. You can roam around the interior and climb the lofty towers for the equally lofty sum of L8000. (Open daily April-Oct. 9am-6pm; Nov.-March 9am-1pm.) At the far end of the peninsula, the **Grotto di Catullo** contains the ruins of a Roman villa and bath complex. (Open April-Oct. Tues.-Sun. 9am-6pm; Nov.-March 9am-4pm. Admission L8000.) Between the ramparts and the ruins lie two clean and quiet public beaches and the **Church of San Pietro in Mavino.** The hilltop house of worship was originally constructed in the 9th century and now displays handsome, interior frescoes dating from the 13th century.

GARDONE RIVIERA

Formerly the playground of the rich and famous, Gardone Riviera is now home to Lake Garda's most famous sight, Gabriele D'Annunzio's villa **Il Vittoriale.** In summer the town experiences a mad rush of German tourists in search of the perfect tan. You can avoid the crowds, however, in the hills behind Gardone, an area threaded with walking paths and scented by aging lemon groves.

Orientation and Practical Information

The **APT tourist office** is at Corso Repubblica, 37 (tel. 203 47), in the center of Gardone Sotto, a small street running nearly parallel to the main thoroughfare of Corso Zanardelli. (The two streets intersect near the bus stop.) When you get off the boat, turn left onto the *corso.* Pamphlets are few, but the amiable staff fills in the gaps. Ask for the map of nearby walks. Information on accommodations, but no reservations. Open Mon.-Sat. 9am-12:30pm and 4-7pm; Nov.-March Mon.-Fri. 9am-12:30pm and 3-6pm, closed Thurs. evening. The **bank** (tel. 200 81), next door to the post office, is open Mon.-Fri. 8:25am-1:25pm and 2:40-4:10pm. **Buses** (tel. 210 61) run to and from Brescia (every 30min., 1hr., L4800), Desenzano (6 per day, 30min., L3800), Milan (2 per day, 3hr., L14,600), and Riva (3 per day, 1¼hr., L4600). In case of **emergency,** call 113 or 112; for **ambulance,** call (167) 82 10 49. For **police** call 201 79. **First aid** nights and holidays can be found at 403 61. The **post office,** at Via Roma, 8 (tel. 208 62), is open Mon.-Fri. 8:10am-1:30pm, Sat. 8:10-11:40am. **Postal Code:** 25083. **Telephone Code:** 0365.

Accommodations and Food

Gardone is worthwhile when seen as a daytrip. Rooms are expensive, and breakfast is often automatically added. If you must stay, the views of the lake beyond the forest from **Pensione Hohl,** Via dei Colli, 4 (tel. 201 60), are well worth the cost. Singles L45,000, doubles L80,000; breakfast included. **Trattoria Ristoro,** Via Trieste, 16 (tel. 209 86), about halfway up the hill, is a good deal. *Primi* from L8500, *secondi* L13,500, and *menù* from L22,000. Open Fri.-Wed. 10:30am-3pm and 6-11pm.

Sights and Entertainment

Above Gardone sprawls **Il Vittoriale,** the playground of Gabriele D'Annunzio (1863-1938), the poet, novelist, and latter-day Casanova. Parked in the garden is the prow of the battleship *Puglia,* the emblem of D'Annunzio's popularity. After World War I, he raised an army of poetry-lovers and steamed across the Adriatic to retake Fiume from infant Yugoslavia. But even Mussolini found D'Annunzio's ultra-nationalist squawking embarrassing, and in 1925 he presented the poet with a lovely rural villa in an attempt to keep him quiet. D'Annunzio regularly went into debt to stuff his house with the most expensive and useless bric-a-brac available. The fascist rummage-sale effect is most pronounced in his bathroom, which is strewn with 2000 bizarre fragments and fixtures. The *Sala del Mappamondo* contains a huge globe that aided his fantasies of global conquest, while the *Sala del Lebbroso* houses the cradle/coffin in which D'Annunzio contemplated both the concept of death and the colors of the nearby leopard skins.

Il Vittoriale is up the hill from Gardone and is best reached along Via Roma and Via dei Colli. Visit the house early in the day before the crowds arrive. Taped tours of the house are available in German, English, French, and Italian. (Open Tues.-Sun. 9am-12:30pm and 2-6pm; Nov.-March 9am-12:30pm and 2:30-5:30pm. Admission L8000 to grounds, L16,000 to both grounds and house.) To recover from the perversity, visit the **botanical gardens** laid around a stately villa halfway up the hill to Il Vittoriale (open March-Oct. daily 8:30am-7pm; admission L7000).

The **Fondazione "al Vittoriale"** (tel. 201 30 for general info, 215 51 for ticket info) puts on a summer program of plays, concerts, and dance performances in the outdoor **Teatro del Vittoriale,** located—surprise!—in the Vittoriale itself (mid-July to early Aug., cheapest seats about L20,000).

RIVA DEL GARDA

Its glorious meeting of alpine cliffs and Mediterranean climate makes Riva a worthy crown to Lake Garda. It offers sunbathing, hiking, biking, and windsurfing—a refreshing change from the normal tourist grind of churches, palaces, and castles.

Practical Information

Riva is easily reached by **bus** from Trent (8 per day, 1hr., L5200) and Verona (14 per day, 2hr., L9000). Tickets available at the bus stations or by calling the APT bus information service (tel. (045) 800 41 29). Buses run frequently to and from the closest train station at Rovereto (20min., L3200), and the Rovereto Sud exit of the Brennero Autobahn is only 15km away. The **tourist office** at Giardini di Porta Orientale, 8 (tel. 55 44 44) is near the water's edge behind a small playground on Via della Liberazione. An electric board lists hotel vacancies. Ask inside for a city map, hiking routes, and other goodies. Open Mon.-Sat. 9am-noon and 3:15-7pm, Sun. 10am-noon and 4-7pm. **Bike rental** is available at **Girelli Mountain Bike,** Viale Damiano Chiesa, 15/17 (tel. 55 66 02 or 55 32 46; L18,000 per day), and **Carpentari,** Viale Trento, 52 (tel. 55 47 19; L20,000 per day). Prices are for mountain bikes—ordinary bicycles may be available for less. For **first aid,** call 58 22 22, or 58 26 29 on nights and holidays. The

alpine rescue and fire brigade is at Via Rovereto, 19/21 (tel. 52 03 33). A **post office** is located at Viale S. Francesco, 26 (tel. 55 23 46). Besides providing mail services, they also issue traveler's checks and change money. Open Mon.-Sat. 8:15am-7:45pm; last Sat. of the month open 8:15am-noon. The **postal code** is 38066; the **telephone code** is 0464.

Accommodations and Camping

Riva is one of Lake Garda's few affordable destinations. An off-season visit may require little planning, but July and August trips demand reservations months ahead of time. The **Ostello Benacus (HI),** P. Cavour, 9 (tel. 55 49 11; fax 55 65 54), is conveniently located next to the church in the center of town. Reception is open daily 8-10am and 4pm-midnight. Friendly proprietor and clean rooms; an unusually pleasant hostel. HI members may be given precedence over nonmembers. L19,000 per person. Hot showers and breakfast included. (Bring a sleepsack, if possible.) Advance reservations are recommended in summer. Open March to mid-Nov. Or try **Garni Carla,** Via Negrelli, 2 (tel. 55 21 40; fax 55 52 96). From the Church of the Inviolata walk up Viale dei Tigli, turn left on Via Rosmini, then right onto Via Negrelli. Singles with bath L42,000. Doubles with bath L74,000. **Locanda La Montanara,** Via Montanara, 20 (tel. 55 48 57). Centrally located. Singles L26,000. Doubles with bath L56,000. Breakfast L6000. Half- and full-pension provided in the cozy downstairs *trattoria.* Reserve at least a month ahead for summer. Open mid-March to Dec. Check with the tourist office for complete **camping** listings. **Bavaria,** Viale Rovereto, 100 (tel. 55 25 24), on the road toward Torbole, has an excellent location right on the water and a *pizzeria* on the premises. Filled with die-hard windsurfing families. L9000 per person, L10,000 for parking. Hot showers L1500. Open April to Oct. **Monte Brione,** Via Brione, 32 (tel. 52 08 85), about 200m from the lake, has a swimming pool, hot showers, washing machine, and bar. L17,000 for a space, L11,000 per person, L8000 each additional person.

Food

A large **open-air market** comes to Riva every second and fourth Wednesday of the month on Vie Dante, Prati, and Pilati, while the **Orveo** supermarket inland from the tourist office holds more regular hours. Open Mon.-Sat. 8:30am-8:30pm, Sun. 8:30am-12:30pm. Slightly shorter hours Oct.-May. **Alimar SRL,** P. Cavour, 6 (tel. 55 49 11), is next to the hostel and provides the usual *mensa* combo of institutional appearances and good prices. *Primi* L5500, *secondi* with side dish L9500, *menù* L14,000. Cover L1000. Open Mon.-Fri. noon-2pm and 7:30-8pm, Sat. 11am-3pm. A more interesting choice is the **Birreria Spaten,** Via Maffei, 7 (tel. 55 36 70), which serves wonderful, large portions. The Bavarian furniture and German-speaking waitresses will make you feel as though you were in *The Sound of Music.* Pizza from L6500, *primi* from L7000, *secondi* L6000-17,000. Cover included. Open daily 10:30am-3pm and 5:30pm-11:30pm, off-season Wed.-Mon. only. AmEx. **Pasticceria Copat di Fabio Marzari,** Viale Dante, 37 (tel. 55 18 85) serves coffee, tea, pastries, and candies. Open Tues.-Sat. 7am-12:30pm and 2:30-7pm.

Sights and Entertainment

For swimming in fresh water, sunbathing on a pebble beach, and taking in stunning lake views, head to the beachfront path stretching left from the tourist office as you face the lake. Beyond the beach are attractive gardens where you can stroll among fragrant roses in the summertime.

Riva's pleasant breezes attract many windsurfers. Three windsurfing schools offer lessons and rent out equipment: **Professional Windsurfing School** (c/o Camping Bavaria; tel. 55 60 77), **Nautic Club Riva** (Viale Rovereto, 132; tel. 55 24 53), and **Windsurfing Center** (c/o Hotel Pier; tel. 55 42 30 or 55 17 30). Expect to pay L40,000 or more for a one-day rental. Ask about hourly or half-day rental, as well as one-week packages which include lessons and equipment.

Near the water, behind P. Garibaldi, is Riva's castle, **La Rocca.** Built in 1124, the original structure was remodeled several times. Its most recent renovation transformed it into a **municipal museum** displaying relics and documents from the town and its environs. Also worth a visit is the Austrian-influenced **Church of the Inviolata** (1603), up Viale Roma and across the street from the hospital. For an excursion outside of Riva, visit **Cascata Varone** (3km away), a 100-m waterfall surrounded by a breathtaking natural gorge. Buses to Varone from Riva are few and oddly timed, but you can always hike or rent a bike. **Musica Riva** (held in the last two weeks of July) is an internationally known festival featuring popular young musicians. Ask at the tourist office for a program. Admission varies from *gratis* to L15,000. Watch for the **Rustico Medioevo,** a gala festival of medieval dance and folklore that runs the week before August 15.

Emilia-Romagna

Go to Florence, Venice, and Rome to sight-see. Come to Emilia-Romagna to eat. Italy's wealthiest wheat- and dairy-producing region covers the fertile plains of the Po river valley and fosters the finest culinary traditions on the Italian Peninsula. Plan to go over budget in Emilia-Romagna, then gorge yourself on Parmesan cheese and *prosciutto,* Bolognese fresh pasta and *mortadella,* and Ferrarese *salama* and *grana* cheese. Complement these dishes with the respectable selection of such regional wines as the sparkling red *lambrusco* from Parma and *sangiovese* from Romagna.

Though the Romans originally settled this region, most of the ruins you see are remnants of medieval structures. Developed as autonomous *communi* during this time, the towns later fell under the rule of great Renaissance families whose names still adorn every *palazzo* and *piazza* in the region. In the 19th century the Italian Socialist movement was born here, and the area remains a stronghold of the left.

Emilia-Romagna looks different from the rest of Italy. Muted yellows and browns predominate, and the farm buildings are low, square, and flat-roofed. The uninterrupted plains seem to stretch on forever, and the illusion of distance is magnified by the cold gray fog of winter—replaced in summer by silver haze and stifling heat that make distant towns shimmer. A naturalistic spirit runs through the local architecture; cathedrals' arches seem to have grown into their places, and carved columns resemble ivy-clad trees.

Bologna

Blessed with Europe's oldest university and the modern-day prosperity of northern Italy, Bologna has had the luxury of developing a particularly open-minded character. Minority groups have found a voice in Bologna; several student alliances and the national gay organization make their homes here. Social tolerance and student energy have fanned local nightlife, and political activism is strong and respected.

Bologna extends this welcoming acceptance to the traditional as well. The university graduated the likes of Dante, Petrarch, Copernicus, and Tasso, while the city prides itself on its great culinary heritage. The *bolognese* taste for and generosity with rich food has even earned the city the nickname *"La Grassa,"* or "The Fat One." The magic key to the city is to find the amusements that fit your personality. Be finicky; Bologna's tremendous variety is there for your enjoyment.

ORIENTATION AND PRACTICAL INFORMATION

At the heart of north Italy, Bologna is a hub for rail lines to all major Italian cities and to the Tyrrhenian and Adriatic coasts. Buses #25 and 30 run between the train station and the historical center at P. Maggiore (tickets L1500 at most *tabacchi* and newsstands). On the north edge of P. Maggiore is P. del Nettuno. From here, **Via Ugo Bassi**

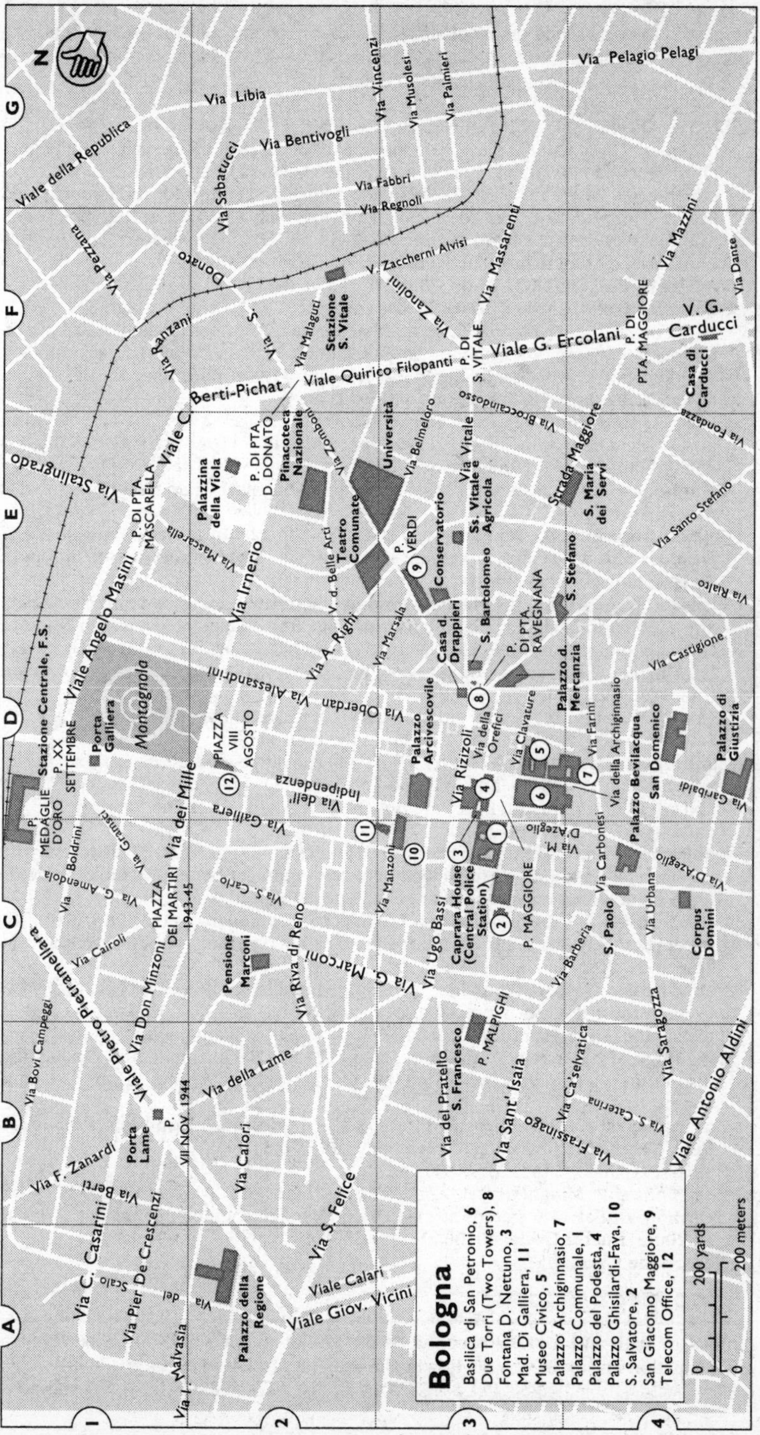

Bologna

Basilica di San Petronio, **6**
Due Torri (Two Towers), **8**
Fontana D. Nettuno, **3**
Mad. Di Galliera, **11**
Museo Civico, **5**
Palazzo Archiginnasio, **7**
Palazzo Communale, **1**
Palazzo del Podestà, **4**
Palazzo Ghisilardi-Fava, **10**
S. Salvatore, **2**
San Giacomo Maggiore, **9**
Telecom Office, **12**

0 200 yards
0 200 meters

runs west, **Via dell'Indipendenza** runs north back toward the train station, and **Via Rizzoli** runs west to **Piazza Porta Ravegnana,** site of the two towers. After dark, take the bus instead of walking to the town center.

Tourist Office: Main office in Palazzo Comunale, P. Maggiore, 6 (tel. 23 96 60), on the right side of the *piazza* as you face the basilica. Modern, genial, and efficient. Open Mon.-Sat. 9am-7pm, Sun. 9am-12:30pm. A less helpful branch is in the **train station** (tel. 24 65 41), near the main exit to the street. Stop for the free map and free accommodations service. Open Mon.-Sat. 9am-12:30pm and 2:30-6:30pm. Another well-stocked **branch office** (tel. 38 17 22) at the airport, near international arrivals. Open Mon.-Sat. 9am-1pm.

Tourist Police: tel. 33 74 73 or 33 74 75.

Budget Travel: Centro Turistico Studentesco (CTS), Largo Respighi 2/F (tel. 26 18 02 or 23 73 07), off Via Zamboni. Open Mon.-Fri. 9am-noon and 2:30-5:30pm. **University Viaggi,** Via Zamboni, 16/E (tel. 23 62 55; fax 22 85 84). Open Mon.-Fri. 9am-1pm and 2:30-6:30pm; closed 2 weeks in mid-Aug. Both issue BIJ tickets and HI cards. Big discounts on sea and air travel.

Currency Exchange: Banca di Napoli, Via Farini, 12 (tel. 23 99 71), near the main post office. Open Mon.-Fri. 8:20am-1:20pm and 2:45-3:45pm. **Banca di Sicilia,** Via dell'Indipendenza, 7. Same hours.

Telephones: P. VIII Agosto, 24, off Via dell'Indipendenza. Open 8am-10pm. Also at the train station.

Flights: Aeroporto G. Marconi (tel. 31 15 78 or 31 22 59), at Borgo Panigale northwest of the town center. Take blue suburban bus #91 from the station. European flights. Many charters available.

Trains: (tel. 24 64 90). Information window open 8am-8pm. Pick up free copies of any national train schedule at the tourist office in P. Maggiore. Trains to: Florence (every 30min., 1½hr., L13,200); Venice (every hr., 2½hr., L13,600); Milan (every hr., 3hr., L17,200); and Rome (every hr., 3½hr., L48,000). **Luggage Storage:** L5000 for 12hr. Open 24hr.

Buses: ATC buses for nearby cities depart from the terminal on the far side of P. XX Settembre (tel. 24 83 74). Walk left from the train station.

Public Transportation: ATC (tel. 35 01 11) runs Bologna's efficient urban buses, which get crowded in early afternoon and evening. Inner-city tickets cost L1500 and are valid for 1hr. after they are punched on board. Strict fine for evaders.

Taxis: tel. 37 27 27, 37 37 50, or 37 47 18.

Bookstore: Feltrinelli International, Via Zamboni, 7 (tel. 26 80 70). Browse with the university students. Large selection of contemporary books and travel guides in English, including our personal favorite. Open Mon.-Sat. 9am-7:30pm.

Laundromat: Self-Service Acqua Lavasecco, Via Todaro, 4 (tel. 24 07 40), the street parallel to Via Irnerio. Coin-operated. L13,000 per load. Open Mon.-Fri. 8am-1pm and 2-7pm, Sat. 8am-noon.

Public Baths: Diurno, P. Re Enzo, 1/B, in the building in the center of P. Maggiore, to Neptune's left. Showers, shampoo, and towels L10,000. Bathrooms L1000. Open Mon.-Fri. 8:30am-12:30pm and 3:30-7pm, Sat. 8:30am-noon.

Late-Night Pharmacy: P. Maggiore, 6 (tel. 23 85 09), in the center. Open 24hr. Also in the train station (tel. 24 66 03). Open Mon.-Sat. 7:30am-11pm, Sun. 8am-10pm.

Emergencies: tel. 113. **First Aid:** tel. 33 33 33. **Hospital: Ospedale Policlinico Sant'Orsola-Malpighi,** Via Massarenti, 9 (tel. 636 31 11).

Police: P. Galileo, 7 (tel. 23 33 33).

Post Office: P. Minghetti (tel. 22 35 98), southeast of P. Maggiore, off Via Farini. *Fermo posta* at #18, stamps at #16. Open Mon.-Fri. 8:15am-6:30pm, Sat. 8:15am-12:20pm. **Postal Code:** 40100.

Telephone Code: 051.

ACCOMMODATIONS

Prices are high and rooms scarce due to the glut of students and business travelers. The situation improves very slightly in January, July, and August.

Ostello di San Sisto (HI), Via Viadagola, 5 and 14 (tel./fax 50 18 10); English spoken. In the Località di San Sisto 6km northeast of the center of town, off Via San Donato. Ask at the tourist office for a map with directions. Catch bus #93 (away from P. dei Martiri) from Via Irnerio/Via dei Mille which cuts across Via dell'Indipendenza 3 blocks from the train station. (Mon.-Sat. every 30min., last bus at 8:15pm. After 8:15pm, you must catch bus #14C from P. Maggiore up Via dell'Indipendenza.) Pass the bridge, go around the traffic circle, and get off at the first stop after the Q8 on your left. Cross the street and walk up Via Viadagola to the hostel. On Sun. you must take bus #20, which heads from the town center toward the station. Get off at the 1st stop after the bus leaves Via San Donato, and walk the 2km to the hostel. New, clean, and well-designed. The hostel's only drawback is its distance from the city center, although San Sisto's solitude makes the town peaceful. Reception open 7-9am and 3:30-11:30pm. Lockout 9am-5pm. L20,000 per person, nonmembers L22,000. Breakfast and hot showers included. Dinner is at 8pm (L14,000).

Albergo Panorama, Via Livraghi, 1 (tel. 22 18 02 or 22 72 05). The 3rd left off V. Ugo Bassi from P. Maggiore; take the elevator to the 4th floor. True to its name, this hotel has large rooms with views of the hills behind Bologna. Friendly management. Singles L55,000. Doubles L80,000, with bath L110,000. Triples L105,000, with bath L130,000.

Albergo Minerva, Via de' Monari, 3 (tel. 23 96 52), the 5th left off Via dell'Indipendenza from P. Maggiore. Nice, breezy rooms in a central location. Singles L45,000. Doubles L80,000. Extra bed L35,000.

Albergo Apollo, Via Drapperie, 5 (tel. 22 39 55; fax 23 79 04). Take the 2nd right off Via Orefici from P. Maggiore. Couldn't be closer to the center of town. Clean white rooms with plenty of space. Hallways covered with mirrors. Singles L49,000. Doubles L81,000, with bath L106,000. Triples L110,000, with bath L144,000. Closed in Aug. V, MC.

Pensione Marconi, Via Marconi, 22 (tel. 26 28 32). Bear right from the station onto Via Amendola, which becomes Via Marconi. Spotless rooms. Desk monitored all night. Singles L45,000. Doubles L70,000, with bath L88,000.

Protezione della Giovane, Via Santo Stefano, 45 (tel. 22 55 73), just past Via Rialto from the two towers, up the grand staircase in the back. Women only. Beautiful, clean rooms, but they're often filled with students in the winter. Curfew 10:30pm. L25,000 per person. Breakfast included.

Albergo Il Guercino, Via L. Serra, 7 (tel./fax 36 98 93). Turn left out of the station and go left over the tracks on Via Matteotti. Turn left on Via Tiarini and then immediately right on Via Serra. A recently renovated hotel, a 15-min. walk from the center, 5min. from the train station. Expensive, but rooms are comfy and attractive. Midnight curfew. Singles L70,000, with bath L90,000. Doubles L100,000, with bath L120,000. Breakfast included. V, MC, AmEx.

Hotel Atlantic, Via Gallieria, 46 (tel. 24 84 88; fax 23 45 91), near the station. Friendly management, reasonable rooms, small patio, and downstairs bar. Singles L55,000, with bath L70,000. Doubles L80,000, with bath L100,000. Breakfast L10,000. V, MC.

FOOD

Bologna's cuisine centers on fresh, hand-made egg pasta in all shapes and sizes. The best of the stuffed pastas are *tortellini,* bursting with ground meat, and *tortelloni,* made with ricotta and spinach. Bologna's namesake dish, *spaghetti alla bolognese,* is pasta with a hefty meat and tomato sauce. Bologna is also renowned for salami and ham of all kinds, including (surprise!) "bologna," known locally as *mortadella,* which is nothing like the American processed product.

Restaurants cluster on side streets only minutes away from the town center; the areas around Via Augusto Righi, Via Piella, and Via Saragozza are especially good for traditional *trattorie.* **Mercato Ugo Bassi,** Via Ugo Bassi, 27, a vast indoor market, sells produce, cheeses, and meats. Open Mon.-Wed. 7am-1:15pm and 5-7pm, Fri. 7am-1:15pm and 4:30-7:30pm, Thurs. and Sat. 7am-1:15pm. Or shop Bologna's **outdoor**

market in Via Pescherie Vecchie, off P. Maggiore. Same hours. You'll find the large, American-style supermarket **Coop** off Via dei Mille at P. Martiri. Open Mon. 2:30-8pm, Tues.-Sat. 8am-7:30pm. The **PAM** supermarket at Via Marconi, 26, by the intersection of V. Riva di Reno, is also good. Open Mon.-Sat. 7:45am-7:30pm. Closed Thurs. afternoons. Near the university is the **Superconad** supermarket, Via della Bella Arti, 31/C. Open Fri.-Wed. 8:30am-7:30pm, Thurs. 8:30am-1pm. V, MC.

Mensa Universitaria Irnerio, Via Zamboni, 47, where Via Zamboni meets Via delle Belle Arti. Pick out what you want and show the cashier your ID—amazingly inexpensive for students. Full meal L6000. You can chat with local students while you eat. Open Tues.-Fri. 11:45am-3pm and 7-10pm, Sat.-Sun. 11:45am-3pm.

Lazzarini, Via Clavature, 1 (tel. 23 63 29), off P. Maggiore. Snack bar with an exquisite self-service restaurant upstairs. The menu changes daily, but look for the *tortellini alla panna* (L7000). Other pasta dishes L5000-8000. *Secondi* L5000-8000. Restaurant open Mon.-Sat. 11:45am-3pm. Snack bar open Mon.-Sat. 7:30am-8pm. V, MC, AmEx.

Ristorante Clorofilla, Strada Maggiore, 64 (tel. 23 53 43). The name sounds like throat medicine, but the food is innovative, healthy, and almost exclusively vegetarian. Bulletin board is the communication center for local environmental and social action groups. Try one of the imaginative salads (L6000-12,000) or hot dishes (L8000-10,000). Cover L1500. Also sells soy milk and a handful of other veggie products. Open Sept.-July Mon.-Sat. 12:15-3pm and 7-11pm. In winter, tea served 4-7pm.

Antica Trattoria Roberto Spiga, Via Broccaindosso, 21/A (tel. 23 00 63). One room, a couple of servers, and hearty food. *Primi* L8000, *secondi* L12,000-18,000. Cover L2000. Open Sept.-July Mon.-Sat. noon-3pm.

Trattoria Da Maro, Via Broccaindosso, 71/D (tel. 22 73 04), off Strada Maggiore. Students and locals gather here to lunch on satisfying plates of *tagliatelle* or *tortellini* (L8000) and any of the standard *secondi* (L9000-12,000). *Menù* L19,000. Cover L1500. Open Mon.-Fri. noon-3pm and 8-10:15pm, Sat. noon-3pm.

Oggi Si Vola, Via Urbana, 7/E (tel. 58 53 08). Student-chic macro-heaven. Serves macrobiotic foods and fish dishes. Cheerful and homey interior with an open kitchen. Miso soup and grilled vegetables, L10,000. Open Mon.-Fri. 12:30-2:30pm and 8-10:30pm, Sat. 8-11pm. Closed Sat. in summer.

Pizzeria La Mamma "Self Service," Via Zamboni, 16 (tel. 22 08 18). A hangout frequented by boisterous university and military students (10% discount with student ID). Table service also available. Delicious pizzas L5000-9000. *Primi* L7000-9000, *secondi* L9000-15,000. *Menù* L13,000. Cover L3000. Wine starts at L2500 per glass. Open daily noon-2:30pm and 7-10pm. Karaoke on Sun. 8pm-2:30am.

Trattoria Da Danio, Via S. Felice, 50 (tel. 55 52 02). A short walk up V. San Felice off V. Ugo Bassi rewards you with a large, appetizing menu at this humble, authentic *trattoria*. *Primi* L7000-12,000, *secondi* L6000-18,000. *Menù* L13,500. Cover L3000. Open Mon.-Sat. noon-2:30pm and 7:30-10pm. V, MC, AmEx.

Eat Your Heart Out, Chef Boyardee

Selecting the right pasta and cooking it correctly (*al dente*—firm, literally "to the teeth") is as close to Italian hearts as Mamma herself. *Lasagne* come in at least two forms: flat or *ricce* (one edge crimped). The familiar *spaghetti* has larger, hollow cousins: *bucatini* and *maccheroni* (not the Yankee Doodle kind); as well as smaller, more delicate relatives like *capellini*. Flat pastas include the familiar *linguine* and *fettuccine*, with *taglierini* and *tagliatelle* filling in the size gaps. Short, roughly two-inch pasta tubes include *penne* (cut diagonally and occasionally *rigate* or ribbed), *sedani* (curved), *rigatoni* (bigger), and *cannelloni* (biggest and usually stuffed). Funny-shaped *fusilli* (corkscrews), *farfalle* (butterflies or bow-ties), and *ruote* (wheels) are fun as well as functional. Don't be alarmed if you see pastry displays with the label "pasta"; the Italian word refers to anything made of dough and vaguely edible. What we refer to as pasta is actually *pasta asciutta* or "dry" pasta. *Buon appetito!*

G and G Pizzeria, Via San Vitale, 45A (tel. 22 34 29). Tasty, hot pizzas include the G and G special with olives, peppers, mushrooms, and mozzarella. Pizzas L5500-10,000. *Primi* L7500, *secondi* L9000-12,000. Open Sat.-Thurs. noon-2:30pm and 6pm-12:30am.

SIGHTS

The endless series of porticoed buildings lining the streets forms Bologna's most characteristic sight. During the 14th century, porticoes offered a solution to the housing crisis of a growing city; buildings expanded into the street while leaving room for mounted riders to pass underneath. The building frenzy lasted several centuries, resulting in a mixture of Gothic, Renaissance, and Baroque styles.

The tranquil expanse of **Piazza Maggiore** shows off both Bologna's historical wealth, exhibited in its collection of tidy monuments, and its modern-day prosperity. The **Basilica di San Petronio,** designed by Antonio da Vincenzo (1390), was built to impress. The Bolognese originally plotted to make their basilica larger than St. Peter's in Rome, but the jealous Church ordered that the funds be used instead to build the nearby Palazzo Archiginnasio. The marble façade of the *duomo,* displaying the town's heraldic red and white, extends to the magnificent central portal. Jacopo della Quercia (1367-1438) carved the now-eroded marble *Virgin and Child* and the Old and New Testament reliefs. The cavernous Gothic interior played host to both the Council of Trent (when not meeting in Trent) and the 1530 ceremony in which Pope Clement VII gave Italy to German king Charles V. According to legend, the pomp and pageantry of the exercises drove a disgusted Martin Luther to reform religion in Germany. The zodiacal sundial on the floor of the north aisle is the largest in Italy—it measures hours, days, and months when the sun shines through the ceiling opening onto the floor. (Open daily 7:15am-12:55pm and 2-6:45pm.)

Behind San Petronio, visit the **Palazzo Archiginnasio** (tel. 23 64 88), formerly a university building, covered with memorials to and crests of notable scholars. It now houses the town library. There's an old anatomical theater upstairs; ask the *portiere* to open it. Shattered during the bombing of 1944, the theater was reconstructed from thousands of rubbly bits. (Open Mon.-Sat. 9am-1pm. Free.)

Next to P. Maggiore, **Piazza del Nettuno** contains Giambologna's famous 16th-century bronze *Neptune and Attendants* statue and fountain. Affectionately called "The Giant" by town citizens, Neptune reigns over the seas and a collection of water-babies and rather erotic sirens. To the right, a clock tower, a beautiful terra-cotta *Madonna* by Nicolò dell'Arca, and a Menganti bronze statue of Pope Gregory XIV punctuate the large brick block of the **Palazzo Comunale.** (Open Tues.-Sat. 9am-2pm, Sun. 9am-12:30pm. Free.) Fioravanti's son Aristotle, who later designed Moscow's Kremlin, remodeled the Romanesque **Palazzo del Podestà,** across the *piazza* (facing San Petronio).

Via Rizzoli leads from P. Nettuno to **Piazza Porta Ravegnana,** where seven streets converge in Bologna's medieval quarter. The two towers here are the emblem of the city. Of the 200 towers built in the 12th and 13th centuries by aristocratic Bolognese families, only a dozen or so remain. The romanticized legend states that the two principal families of Bologna, the Asinelli and the Garisendi, competed to build the tallest and best-looking tower. The Garisendi plunged into the construction of their tower without suitably reinforcing the foundation. It sank on one side and the upper portion fell off; all that remains is the leaning section. The Asinelli were more cautious and built their tower to a sleek 97m (number four on the list of tallest Italian towers—after Cremona, Siena, and Venice, just to keep score). Reality, as usual, tells a simpler story: land movement botched an attempt to build an observation tower for the civic defense system (the lower, tilting tower), so the city started again and found greater success nearby. Climb the **Torre degli Asinelli** for an amazing view of the city; the arches of Lorraine ogli Estara are particularly breathtaking. (Open daily 9am-6pm; in winter 9am-5pm. Admission L3000.)

Going down Via Zamboni to P. Verdi, you enter the **Zona Universitaria.** Europe's oldest university campus was founded 900 years ago. Keep your eyes peeled, though, or you might miss it. The buildings at first don't appear to be affiliated with a university—only the signs over the doors let you know that these are the ancient halls of the learned. The political posters plastered everywhere reflect the idealistic bent of Bologna's college crowd and the town's position as the seat of the Italian Communist Party. If you're in town in June, look for the vulgar posters lampooning the lives of graduating students, a comic tradition.

From the the two towers, the Strada Maggiore leads east past the **Basilica of San Bartolomeo.** Stop and see the exquisite *Madonna* by Guido Reni in the left transept before proceeding to the **Church of Santa Maria dei Servi** (tel. 22 68 07), a remarkably intact Gothic church. Inside, columns support a unique combination of ogival arches and ribbed vaulting. In a left-hand chapel behind the altar hangs Cimabue's *Maestà.* Giovanni Antonio Montorsoli, a pupil of Michelangelo, executed the exquisite altar. (Open daily 6:30-11:45am and 3:30-7:45pm.)

Via Santo Stefano leads from the two towers past the pointed arches of the portico of the **Palazzo di Mercanzia,** opening onto the **Piazza Santo Stefano.** Only four of the original seven interlocking churches of the Romanesque **basilica** remain. Bologna's patron saint, San Petronio, lies buried under the pulpit of the **Church of San Sepolcro** in the center of the group. In the courtyard in the rear is the **Basin of Pilate**—the governor supposedly absolved himself of responsibility for Christ's death in this bath-size tub. One of Bologna's oldest churches is the **Church of SS. Vitale e Agricola** on Via San Vitale, whose façade incorporates bits of Roman temples, capitals, and columns. Downstairs is an 11th-century **crypt,** over which the present church was built. (Open Mon.-Sat. 8am-7pm, Sun. 10am-7pm.)

From P. Maggiore, follow Via dell'Archiginnasio to Via Farini and then Via Garibaldi to the **Church of San Domenico,** where the founder of the Dominican order is buried. Nicolò dell'Arca earned his nickname for his work on the saint's tomb, or "ark." To identify the works, consult the schema near the entrance. Look for Filippo Lippi's *Visit of St. Catherine* at the end of the right aisle.

The **Church of San Giacomo Maggiore** in P. Rossini is a true melange of Romanesque and Gothic styles. The edifice was designed in the late 13th-century, when the aristocratic clergy, who favored the older Romanesque style, began to come under the influence of the Dominicans and Franciscans, who favored the Gothic. The adjoining **Oratorio di Santa Cecilia** presents a cycle of Renaissance frescoes by Amico Aspertini. Ask the sacristan to let you in through the back of the church. Behind, in the ambulatory, is the **Bentivoglio Chapel,** commissioned by 15th-century tyrants of Bologna.

The **Museo Civico Archeologico,** Via Archiginnasio, 2 (tel. 23 38 49), has a fascinating collection of ancient objects and a tranquil central courtyard. On the first floor are Greek vases, Bronze and Stone Age tools, statues, and Roman inscriptions. Beware of mummified crocodiles in the Egyptian section downstairs. (Open Tues.-Fri. 9am-2pm, Sat.-Sun. 9am-1pm and 3:30-7pm. Admission L5000, students L2500.)

The **Pinacoteca Nazionale,** Via delle Belle Arti, 56 (tel. 22 32 32), follows the progress of Bolognese artists from primitivism to Mannerism and beyond. The first section contains a Giotto altarpiece, and the Renaissance wing houses Raphael's *Ecstasy of Santa Cecilia,* Perugino's *Madonna in Glory,* Guido Reni's *Madonna,* and Parmigianino's *Madonna di Santa Margherita.* One room holds great works by the Carraccis, three Bologna natives who helped spark the Baroque revolution. (Open Tues.-Sat. 9am-2pm, Sun. 9am-1pm. Admission L8000.)

The **Museo Civico Medioevale** (tel. 22 89 12), in the 15th-century Palazzo Ghisilardi Fava at Via Manzoni, 4, contains a superb collection of sculpted tombs of medieval *bolognese* professors. While the professors read, the students are shown dozing, daydreaming, and gossiping. The "Stone of Peace" depicts the Virgin and Child flanked by kneeling students who came to terms with the *comune* in 1321 after protesting the execution of a fellow student. The museum also contains armor, reliquary objects, and various curiosities of medieval life. (Open Mon.-Fri. 9am-2pm, Sat.-Sun. 9am-1pm and 3:30-7pm. Admission L5000, under 18 and over 60 L2500.)

The *piazzola,* a huge **open-air market** for new and used clothes and jewelry, takes place on P. VIII Agosto (Sept.-July Fri.-Sat. 8am-2pm). Literature buffs may want to investigate the **museum and house of Giosuè Carducci,** P. Carducci, 5 (tel. 34 75 92), to see the poet's works and sundry possessions. (Currently under renovation. Call the tourist office for current info.)

ENTERTAINMENT

Bologna's tremendous university population makes for an especially healthy nightlife. *Bologna Spettacolo News,* available at *caffè* and newsstands, has all the info you need about upcoming concerts and festivals, from 17th-century chamber music to 20th-century love-ins. In July and August, the city sponsors free **open-air discos.** The festival, called **Made in Bo,** is held in Parco Nord, on the outskirts of the city. Take bus #30 from Via Marconi or the train station (after 8:30pm take #25A), and ask the driver for the time of the last returning bus (usually around 12:30am). The action starts at about 10pm; no charge. A hip *discoteca* near the two towers is **Kinki,** Via Zamboni, 1. The music is alternative/progressive, and the cover ranges from L25,000 to L40,000. Saturday is lesbian and gay night. **Porto di Mare,** Vic. Sampieri, 3 (tel. 22 26 50), is a swanky disco/bar/restaurant. Music varies from hip-hop to jazz. Open Mon.-Tues. 8:30pm-1am, Wed.-Sat. 8:30pm-2am. Closed one month in summer. No cover if you buy a drink. A popular student hangout is the Irish pub **Cluricaune,** Via Zamboni, 18/B (tel. 26 34 19). With a pool table, tartan curtains, and plenty o' beer, you will be set for the evening. Open daily 11am-2am. Also check out the upscale **Cantina Bentivoglio** at Via Mascarella, 4/B, for jazz. Wines start at L8000 per bottle, pasta L8000-12,000. Open Tues.-Sun. 8pm-2am. **Cassero,** a gay bar, is located in the Porta Saragozza at the end of Via Saragozza, a popular part of town. Packed with men and the occasional women. Open daily 10pm-2am. Plenty of other bars and *osterie* are found along Via delle Belle Arti and P. Verdi.

Current **English-language films** play on Mondays at **L'Adriano,** Via S. Felice, 52 (tel. 55 51 27; L8000). **Tiffany d'Essai,** P. di Porta Saragozza, 5 (tel. 58 52 53) screens English films on Wednesdays (L8000).

Bologna's newest nighttime summer entertainment is the city-sponsored **Bologna Sogna** (Bologna Dreams) series, which features shows and concerts at *palazzi* and museums around town through July and August. Ask the tourist office for a schedule of events.

Ferrara

Ferrara earned its laurels as the home turf of the Este dynasty from 1208 to 1598. When not murdering relatives, these sensitive rulers proved themselves some of the most enlightened (albeit bloodthirsty) patrons of their age. Their court and university attracted Petrarch, Ariosto, Tasso, Mantegna, and Titian, among others. Ercole I's early 16th-century city plan broke new ground with its open, harmonious design, and the modern theater (with curtains, stage, and seated audience) was invented here. But the balding dukes eventually went heirless, and Ferrara succumbed to two and a half centuries of cruel neglect. Today, Ferrara has bounced back, her historic grand *piazze* kept lively by visitors, vendors, and street musicians.

ORIENTATION AND PRACTICAL INFORMATION

Ferrara is on the Bologna-Venice train line. When you walk out of the train station, turn left and then right on **Viale Cavour,** which leads to the Castello Estense at the center of town (1km). Buses #1, 2, and 9 also travel this route.

Tourist Office: Corso Giovecca, 21 (tel. 20 93 70; fax 21 22 66), the extension of Viale Cavour next to a church. Well-stocked. Exceptionally knowledgable folk eager to discuss everything from local politics to your dining preferences. Open

Mon.-Sat. 8:30am-7pm, Sun. 2:30-5:30pm. A **branch** office on Viale Kennedy, 2 (tel. 76 57 28), has slightly shorter hours and may be closed in off-season.

Tourist Police: Ufficio Stranieri, tel. 269 44. Assistance in English.

Telephones: Largo Castello, 30 (tel. 497 91), off Viale Cavour at the *castello.* Open Mon.-Sat. 8am-8pm. On Sun. and from midnight to 8am, try **Hotel Ripagrande,** Via Ripagrande, 21 (tel. 76 52 50).

Trains: Information, tel. 77 03 40; open Mon.-Sat. 8:30am-noon and 3-7pm. To: Bologna (33 per day, 40min., L4200); Venice (24 per day, 1½hr., L9800); Ravenna (14 per day, 1hr., L6500); Padua (hourly, 1hr., L6800). **Luggage Storage:** L5000 for 12hr. Open daily 8-10am and 11am-7pm.

Buses: ACFT (tel. 472 68) and **GGFP** (tel. 20 52 35). Main terminal on Via Rampari San Paolo. Open 9:30am-11:30pm. You can also take most buses from the train station (buy tickets at the booth next to the kiosk to your left from the trains). To Ferrara's beaches (12 per day, 1hr., L8200). Buses to Modena depart from the train station (11 per day, 1½-2hr., L8200).

Emergencies: tel. 113 or 112. **Hospital: Ospedale Sant'Anna,** Corso Giovecca, 203 (tel. 29 51 11).

Police: Corso Ercole I d'Este, 26 (tel. 29 43 11), off Largo Castello.

Post Office: Viale Cavour, 27 (tel. 20 74 86), 1 block toward the train station from the *castello.* Open Mon.-Fri. 8am-5:30pm, Sat. 8am-1pm. *Fermo posta* at window #7. **Postal Code:** 44100.

Telephone Code: 0532.

ACCOMMODATIONS AND CAMPING

Ferrara's decent budget accommodations are likely to be full. Reserve at least a day or two in advance if possible.

Albergo San Paolo, Via Baluardi, 9 (tel. 76 20 40). Walk down Corso Porta Reno from the *duomo* and turn left on Via Baluardi. Ferrara's best option. New, modern rooms in a quiet, central location. Singles L50,000, with bath L70,000. Doubles L70,000, with bath L90,000. Reservations advised.

Albergo Nazionale, Corso Porta Reno, 32 (tel. 20 96 04), on a busy street between the Chiesa di San Paolo and the *duomo.* Clean rooms with telephone. Closes at 12:30am. Singles with bath L55,000. Doubles with bath L90,000. Rooms fill quickly: reserve 4 days in advance July-Sept. V, MC, AmEx.

Camping: Estense, Via Gramicia, 5 (tel. 75 23 96). Take bus #11. L5000 per person, L4000 per child. Car space L8500. Open Easter-Oct.

FOOD

Ferrara produces an enticing array of local specialties. Don't miss the chance to gorge on *cappelletti,* delicious triangular meat *ravioli* served in a broth, or *cappellacci,* stuffed with squash and parmesan cheese and served in a light sauce of butter and sage. The gastronomic glory of the city is its robust *salama da sugo,* an aged, ball-shaped sausage of meats soaked in wine, served hot in its own juices. The traditional Ferrarese dessert is a chunk of luscious *pampepato,* a chocolate-covered almond and fruit cake. **Negozio Moccia,** Via degli Spadari, 19 (tel. 20 97 72), sells the renowned *pampepato Estenese* brand in various sizes (750g, L22,000). Open Mon.-Sat. 9am-1pm and 4:30-8pm. For picnic goodies, stop by the **Mercato Comunale,** Via Mercato, off Via Garibaldi next to the *duomo* (open Sat.-Thurs. 7am-1:30pm, Fri. 7am-1:30pm and 4-7pm), or the **Conad** supermarket, Via Garibaldi, 51/53 (open Mon.-Wed. and Fri.-Sat. 8:30am-7:30pm, Thurs. 8:30am-1pm). **All shops in Ferrara are closed Thursday afternoon.**

Trattoria da Giacomino, Via Garibaldi, 135 (tel. 20 56 44). Rumored to be among the best places in town. *Primi* L6000-8000, *secondi* L6000-15,000. Cover L2500. Open Sept.-July Sun.-Fri. noon-2pm and 5:30-10pm.

Trattoria Da Noemi, Via Ragno, 31/A (tel. 76 17 15), off Corso Porta Reno. The smells of Ferrarese cooking have wafted out of this *trattoria* for over 30 years. The *salamina* (L9000) is as succulent as ever, and a plate of the homemade *gnocchi* (L7000) makes a divine dinner. A veranda stretches out in back. *Secondi* L9000-10,000. Cover L2500. Open Wed.-Mon. noon-2:30pm and 6:30-10pm.

Osteria Al Brindisi, Via G. degli Adelardi, 9/B (tel. 20 91 42). The oldest *osteria* in Italy. Recently blessed by a full-fledged cardinal, so you can dig in without fear. Copernicus and Cellini did. No joke. Try delicious sandwiches (L5000) paired with one of the 600 varieties of wine (L1000-6500 per glass). Open Tues.-Fri. and Sun. 8:30am-8:30pm, Sat. 8:30am-midnight. V, MC.

SIGHTS

Those on an extensive tour of Ferrara's museums may wish to purchase a **biglietto cumulativo** (L20,000, good for one week) available from and valid at the Palazzo Schifanoia, the Palazzina di Marfisa d'Este, all of the Palazzo Massari museums, and several other municipal museums. Ticket for Museo Schifanoia, Palazzina di Marfisa d'Este, and Civico Lapidario L8000, students L4000. Ticket for Museo Boldini and Museo d'Arte Moderna L6000, students L4000.

Towered, turreted, and moated, the awesome **Castello Estense** (tel. 29 92 79) stands precisely in the center of town. Corso della Giovecca lies along the former route of the moat's feeder canal, separating the medieval section of town from that planned by the d'Este's architect, Biagio Rossetti. The Salone dei Giochi and the surrounding rooms retain rich frescoes on their ceilings, the best of which are in the Loggetta degli Aranci. The Lombardesque **Cappella di Renata di Francia** (Chapel of Renée of France) seems a bit out of place—as Renée herself, a Protestant married to a Catholic, must have felt. Parisina, the wife of Duke Nicolò d'Este III, was killed with her lover, the Duke's natural son Ugolino, in the damp prison underneath. This tragedy concealed beneath the castle's surface of unruffled elegance inspired Browning to pen "My Last Duchess." (Open Tues.-Sun. 9:30am-5:30pm. Admission L10,000, groups over 20 L8000, student groups L4000. Closed for renovations—check with the tourist office for updated info.)

Walk down Corso Martiri della Libertà to P. Cattedrale and the **duomo.** Alongside the church under the double arcade, little shops and vendors operate much as they did in the Middle Ages. Reshaped by every noble with designs on Ferrara, the cathedral and the castle remain the effective center of town. Rossetti designed the tall slender arches and terra-cotta that ornament the apse, and Alberti (1404-1484) executed the pink *campanile* covered with Estense seals and crests. Notice the *faux* rose windows in the left and right portions of the façade. (Church open Mon.-Sat. 7:30am-noon and 3-6:30pm, Sun. 7:30am-1pm and 4-7:30pm.) Upstairs in the **Museo della Cattedrale** (tel. 20 23 92) are Cosmè Tura's 15th-century *San Giorgio* and *Annunciation* from the Ferrarese school and Jacopo della Quercia's *Madonna della Melagrana.* (Museum open Tues.-Sun. 10am-noon and 3-5pm. Free.)

From behind the *duomo,* turn left and then right on Via Voltapaletto, which becomes Via Savonarola. At #30 is the **Casa Romei** (tel. 24 03 41), the 15th-century dwelling of a Ferrarese merchant, filled with some of the most richly decorated rooms of the period. The museum displays statues and frescoes salvaged from destroyed churches in Ferrara. (Open Mon.-Fri. 8:30am-2pm, Sat.-Sun. 8:30am-7pm. Admission 4000.) Continue on Via Savonarola, turn right at Via Madama, and take the first left. Only the carved door of the **Palazzo Schifanoia,** Via Scandiana, 23 (tel. 641 78), hints at the wealth of artwork inside. The magnificent frescoes in the Saloni dei Mesi offer particularly accurate and vivid depictions of 15th-century courtly life. (Open Mon.-Fri. 8:30am-2pm, Sat.-Sun. 8:30am-5pm. Admission L6000, over 60 L3000. Second Mon. of the month free.)

Cross the street from the *palazzo,* find Via Mellone (to your right), and continue until you reach Via XX Settembre. The **Palazzo Ludovico Il Moro,** Via XX Settembre, 124, features a courtyard designed by Rossetti. Inside, the **Museo Archeologico Nazi-**

onale (tel. 662 99) houses extensive finds from the Greco-Roman city of Spina and an outstanding collection of Athenian vases. (Closed for restoration.)

Returning to the Palazzo Schifanoia and Via Madama, continue straight until you reach Corso Giovecca, Ferrara's boring main drag. Turn right to find the recently restored **Palazzina di Marfisa d'Este,** Corso Giovecca, 170 (tel. 20 74 50), a splendid palace in miniature. (Open daily 9am-12:30pm and 3-6pm. Admission L3000, second Mon. of the month free.)

From the Castello Estense, cross the main road onto Corso Ercole I d'Este. At the corner of Corso Rossetti lies the **Palazzo dei Diamanti,** outshining all other ducal residences. Inside, the **Pinacoteca Nazionale** (tel. 20 58 44) contains the best work of the Ferrarese school. Most impressive are the *Passing of the Virgin* (1508) by Carpaccio and the incredibly detailed *Massacre of the Innocents* by Garofalo. (Open Tues.-Sun. 9am-2pm. Admission L8000, student groups free.)

Turn right onto Corso Porta Mare to find the **Palazzo Massari** museum complex at #9. The **Museo Civico d'Arte Moderna** (tel. 20 69 14) includes the *Collezione Boldini,* with paintings by the 19th-century Italian Giovanni Boldini. The museum often hosts special exhibits by well-known contemporary Italian and European artists. The *Museo Documentario della Metafisica* (tel. 20 69 14) documents the inception of metaphysical art in a collection of works by Giorgio de Chirico, Carlo Carrà, Tino Puenté, and Giorgio Morandi, Italy's greatest 20th-century painters. Other museums in Palazzo Massari include the **Museo Ferrarese dell'Ottocento,** housing a hodgepodge of 19th-century Italian paintings, and the tiny **Galleria della Fotografia** and **Galleria Civica,** both of which display local work. (All museums in the complex open daily 9:30am-1pm and 3:30-7pm. Palace admission L10,000.)

Continue on Corso Porta Mare and turn left on Via Vigne to reach the **Cimitero Ebraico** (Jewish cemetery). Here the Finzi and Contini lie buried, along with most of Ferrara's 19th- and 20th-century Jewish community. Ring the bell and the custodian will let you in. Look for the monument to Ferrarese Jews murdered at Auschwitz.

ENTERTAINMENT

Each year on the last Sunday of May, Ferrara re-creates the ancient **Palio di San Giorgio.** This event, dating from the 13th century, is a lively procession of delegates from the city's eight *contrade* (districts) followed by a series of four races in P. Ariostea: the boy race, the girl race, the donkey race, and finally the great horse race. The flag-waving ceremony of the eight *contrade* takes place two weeks earlier in P. del Municipio. In July and August, Ferrara hosts **Estate a Ferrara,** a music and theater festival that brings diverse performances to the city's *piazze.* (Contact the tourist office for a schedule.) During the third or fourth week of August, street musicians and performers from near and far come to display their talents in the annual **Busker's Festival.**

Modena

It is fitting that Modena is the hometown of Luciano Pavarotti—operatic tenor virtuoso and avid eater—and the Ferrari and Maserati factories. Like all three, Modena purrs with prosperity. Conquered by the Romans in the 3rd century BC, the city owed its early prominence to its location; the region's principal road, Via Emilia, ran through the heart of this town. Modena is easily visited as an excursion from Bologna or Parma, or as a stopover between the two.

ORIENTATION AND PRACTICAL INFORMATION

Modena lies roughly midway between Parma and Bologna. From the train station, take bus #7 or 11 (L1300) to **Piazza Grande** and the center of town. Alternatively, walk left on Via Crispi, right down **Corso Emanuele,** right around the **Palazzo Ducale,** and finally to **Via Emilia** (Modena's main street) and **Piazza Grande** by way of Via Battisti. Be advised, however, that Via Emilia changes names and street numbers from Via Emilia **Ovest** on the west side of the center, to Via Emilia **Centro** in the center, and then to Via Emilia **Est** on the east. (Makes sense, huh?)

Tourist Office: Piazza Grande, 17 (tel. 22 66 60; fax 20 66 59), across from the back of the *duomo*. The brand-new office stocks a warehouse of information. Get facts and maps from computers, volumes of books, or slightly-hurried personnel. In the same office as **Informazione Città** (tel. 20 65 80) and **Informa Giovani** (tel. 20 65 83), geared specifically to young people. The office also keeps bulletin boards with job and housing notices. Open Mon.-Tues. and Thurs.-Sat. 10:30am-12:30pm and 4-7pm.

Budget Travel: Hersa Viaggi, Via Emilia Est, 429 (tel. 37 28 63). On the outskirts of the city center; offers information and numerous student discounts. Open Mon.-Fri. 8am-12:30pm and 3-7pm, Sat. 8am-12:30pm.

Currency Exchange: Credito Italiano, Via Emilia Centro, 102 (tel. 41 21 11). On the corner across from Via Scudari and the tourist office.

Telephones: Via Università, 21, off Corso Canalgrande. Office open Mon.-Fri. 8:30am-12:30pm and 2:30-5:30pm.

Trains: P. Dante Alighieri (tel. 21 82 26). To: Bologna (every hr., 30min., L3400); Parma (every 30min., 30min., L5000); and Milan (about every hour, 2hr., L15,500). **Luggage Storage:** L5000 for 12hr. Open 6:35am-11:25pm and 1:50-8:10pm.

Buses: ATCM, Via Fabriani (tel. 30 88 01), off Viale Monte Kosica, which leads to the right from the train station. Take the center street at the circle. Bus #7 to Ferrara (every hr., L8200) and bus #2 to Maranello (every 1-2hr., L3500).

Bike Rental: At the train station. L2000 for first 2hr., L500 per hr. thereafter. Open 6:30am-12:30pm and 1:40-8pm.

Late-Night Pharmacy: Farmacia Comunale at Via Emilia Est, 416 (tel. 36 00 91), closed 12:30-3:30pm.

Emergencies: tel. 113 or 115. **Pronto Soccorso (First Aid):** tel. 36 13 71. **Ambulance: Blue Cross,** tel. 34 24 24. **Hospital: Ospedale Civile,** Piazzale San Agostino (tel. 20 51 11).

Police: Viale Amendola, 152 (tel. 34 44 48).

Post Office: Via Emilia Centro, 86 (tel. 24 35 09 or 24 21 37). Open Mon.-Sat. 8:15am-5:30pm. **Postal Code:** 41100.

Telephone Code: 059.

ACCOMMODATIONS AND CAMPING

Locanda Sole, Via Malatesta, 45 (tel. 21 42 45), off Via Emilia Centro at P. Muratori, west of P. Grande. Only 100m from the town center. Cool, airy, simple rooms that now have TVs. English spoken. Singles L35,000. Doubles L60,000. Showers included. Closed first three weeks of Aug.

Albergo Leoncino, Via Emilia Ovest, 407 (tel. 334 19). Take bus #12 or 19 west to the Via Emilia Ovest stop. Continue down the street, cross Viale Autodromo, and find the hotel on your left. Rooms and bathrooms are bare and exceedingly clean. Singles L30,000. Doubles L52,000, with bath L60,000.

Camping: International Camping Modena, Via Cave Ramo, 111 (tel. 33 22 52), in Località Bruciata. Take bus #19 (to Rubiera) west from the station for about 10min. to within ½km of the site. Buses run from 6:20am-7:50pm. L4000 per person, L1500 per tent. Open April 1-Sept.

FOOD

Thanks to the low plains area around the rich Po river basin, inhabitants of Modena and its environs till some of the most fertile soil on the Italian peninsula. Modena, like nearby gastronomic centers Bologna and Parma, produces unsurpassed *prosciutto crudo* and the sparkling *lambrusco* red wine. Modena's own claim to culinary fame derives from the curiously tame but fragrant and full-bodied balsamic vinegar that the Modenese sprinkle liberally over salads, vegetables, and even fruit. Balsamic vinegar is often aged for decades, and the finest vinegars can do damage upwards of L100,000 per bottle. Top off a meal with the local *vignola* cherries, considered some of the tastiest in Italy.

Stock your picnic basket at the **Mercato al Minuto Commestibili,** a few steps down Via Albinelli from Piazza XX Settembre. Locals come to this community food bazaar to haggle over prices for everything from bread to snails. (Open daily 6:30am-2pm; Sept.-May also Sat. afternoons 5-7pm.) To watch local Modenese society in action, grab a cup of coffee at any **Bar Molinari,** located on every corner, including Via Emilia, 153 (tel. 22 23 57). Small pastries run L1200, large ones (all you'll need for lunch) L3200. Open daily 6:30am-6pm.

Trattoria Da Omer, Via Torre, 33 (tel. 21 80 50), off Via Emilia across from P. Torre. Look for the hand-painted sign among the jewelry and fur stores; Via Torre's entrance is almost hidden. Chef Omer is the saving grace of Modena with his reasonably priced, meticulously prepared delicacies. *Tortellini fiocco di neve,* filled with fresh cheeses and seasoned with butter and sage, is pasta at its prime for L10,000. Zesty vegetable buffet from L4000 to L10,000. Cover L3000. A/C. Open Mon.-Sat. 12:30-2:30pm and 7:30-10pm. V, MC.

Mensa Il Chiostro, Via San Geminiano, 3 (tel. 23 04 30). From Via Emilia, turn right on Via San Carlo, which becomes Via Canalino. Via San Geminiano is on your left. This self-service restaurant is located in the courtyard of an antique cloister. *Primi* L3000, *secondi* L5000. Cover L1150. Open Mon.-Fri. 11:45am-2:30pm, Sat. noon-2pm.

L'Aragosta, Via Emilia Centro, 192 (tel. 22 22 75). A/C, but you can also dine outside under a big white tent. Pizzas L7000-10,000. *Primi* L9000. *Secondi* L14,000-22,000. Try the *scaloppina all'aceto balsamico* (veal in balsamic vinegar sauce, L14,000). Cover L3000. Open Tues.-Sun. 12:15-3pm and 6:30pm-1am, though it may not open on time. V, MC, AmEx.

NORTHERN ITALY

SIGHTS

One of the best-preserved Romanesque churches in Italy, Modena's **duomo,** in P. Grande, dates from the early 12th century. Its patron, the Marchioness Matilda of Canossa, held a fiefdom that backed the Holy Roman Emperor over the pope. As a result, the decorations on the religious buildings that she sponsored often bear political significance. The *duomo* also houses a somewhat gruesome relic of patron saint San Geminiano—his arm, encased in silver (1178), which takes to the streets in a religious procession on January 31. The sculptor Wiligelmo and his school decorated most of the *duomo* with stylized carvings that draw on local, Roman, Biblical, and even Celtic themes. Carvings around the doors depict scenes from the Old Testament and from San Geminiano's travels to Asia. (*Duomo* open daily 6:30am-noon and 3:30-7pm.)

The **Ghirlandina Tower,** the symbol of Modena, looms over the *duomo*. Built in the late 13th century, the 95-meter tower weaves together both Gothic and Romanesque elements. A memorial to those who died fighting the Nazis and Fascists during World War II stands at the base. (Open Mon.-Fri., Sun. and holidays 10am-1pm and 3-7pm. Admission L2000.)

The **Palazzo dei Musei,** in Largo Sant'Agostino at the western side of Via Emilia, contains both the **Biblioteca Estense** (tel. 22 22 48) and the **Galleria Estense.** The library's collection of masterpieces includes a 1501 Portuguese map of the world and a 1481 copy of Dante's *Divine Comedy*. Don't miss the **Bible of Borso d'Este,** a 1200-page tome partially illustrated by the 15th-century Emilian painter Taddeo Crivelli. (Open Mon.-Thurs. 9am-7pm, Fri.-Sat. 9am-1pm. Free.)

The **Galleria Estense** (tel. 22 21 45), the picture gallery on the floor above the library, is a well-stocked and meticulously organized collection. The long gallery on the right after you enter begins with earthy Emilian "primitives" and ends with Cosmè Tura's *St. Anthony of Padua.* Beyond, an excellent Flemish section features Joos van Cleve's *Virgin and Child with St. Anne.* The Mannerist and Baroque galleries that follow contain works by Tintoretto and El Greco, as well as Velàzquez's famous portrait of Francesco I d'Este. (Open Tues., Fri.-Sat. 9am-7pm, Wed.-Thurs. 9am-2pm, Sun. 9am-1pm. Admission L8000, under 18 and over 60 free.) On the second floor of the palace rests the newly restored **Archaeological Museum,** which focuses on topics such as Florentine paper-making, early electromagnetic experiments, and paleolithic stone tools. (Open Tues.-Sat. 9am-noon, Tues. and Sat. also 4-7pm, Sun. 10am-1pm and 4-7pm. Admission L4000, under 18 and over 60 free.)

Modena's claim to international economic fame is the **Ferrari** automobile. The factory is located southwest of Modena in **Maranello.** (See **Practical Information: Buses,**see Buses: ATCM, Via Fabriani (tel. 30 88 01), off Viale Monte Kosica, which leads to the right from the train station. Take the center street at the circle. Bus #7 to Ferrara (every hr., L8200) and bus #2 to Maranello (every 1-2hr., L3500)., p. 391. for information on buses to Maranello.) After the Maranello stop, buses head straight to the factory. Though you're not allowed to sniff around the inner workings of this top-secret complex, you can view a truly astounding display of antique and modern Ferrari cars, Formula One racers, and trophies at the nearby **Galleria Ferrari,** the company museum, Via Dino Ferrari, 43 (tel. 94 32 04). To reach the museum from the Ferrari factory bus stop, continue along the road in the same direction as the bus for about 200 yards, and then screech a right at the sign that says Galleria Ferrari; the museum is located in an oversized glass-and-steel structure on the left, about 100 yards down the street. More than twenty Ferraris are on display; fantasize about the stately antiques of yesteryear or the flashy turbos of the 90s. (Open Tues.-Sun. 9:30am-12:30pm, 3-6pm. Admission L10,000; ages 6-15 and over 60, L5000.)

If you're more of a food fan than a Ferrari freak, consider a visit to one of the many local foundations specializing in typical food products. The **Consorzio del Prosciutto di Modena** is at Viale Corassori, 72 (tel. 34 34 64). For wine-tasting possibilities, contact the **Consorzio Tutela del Lambrusco di Modena,** Via Schedoni, 41 (tel. 23 50 05). Queries regarding the native *vignola* cherries can be directed to the **Consorzio della Cigliegia Tipica di Vignola,** Via Barozzi, 2 (tel. 77 36 45), in the hamlet of Savignano sul Parano. For information on local balsamic vinegar production, call the **Consorzio Produttori di Aceto Balsamico** at the Chamber of Commerce, Via Ganaceto, 134 (tel. 20 82 98) and ask for Signor Costanzini.

You can sample some fresh Modenese cuisine at the weekly **markets** in the Parco Novi Sad (held Mon. 7:30am-1:30pm). There is also a market in Piazza XX Settembre. (Open Mon.-Sat. 6:30am-2pm and 4:30-7:30pm.)

On another note, if you're on a really hell-bent pilgrimage, you can find **Pavarotti's house.** He lives in the big villa hidden more or less at the corner of Stradello Chiesa and Via Giardini. But don't get your hopes up about hearing Luciano belt out "La donna è mobile" from his balcony—he's known to be a recluse.

ENTERTAINMENT

For one week—usually sometime around the end of June and the beginning of July—the **Settimana Estense** enlivens Modena with special exhibits, art shows, street vendors, and a costumed bonanza in which residents dress up in Renaissance garb for an authentic *corteo storico* (historic parade). During July and August, the city sponsors a music, ballet, and theater series called **Sipario In Piazza.** You might even happen on a performance by Pavarotti. Contact the Ufficio Sipario in Palazzo Comunale, Piazza Grande (tel. 20 64 60; open Mon.-Sat. 10am-12:30pm and 4-7pm) for information and tickets (L15,000-30,000). Winter brings **opera** to Modena's **Teatro Comunale,** Corso Canal Grande, 85 (tel. 22 56 63). On the fourth weekend of every month, the city puts on the **Fiera d'Antiquariato** at the Ex Ippodromo park northwest of the town center (take bus #7), a boisterous celebration of food, folks, and fun. To experience Modenese life in the fast lane, check out the list of **discos** at the tourist office or at Informa Giovani. (Unfortunately, the discos are outside the city limits and fairly hard to reach without a car.)

Parma

Parma's role in the international limelight derives from the dedication with which its citizens *(parmigiani)* craft their incomparable delicacies. Parmesan specialties include the sweet and silky-smooth *prosciutto crudo,* the sharp and crumbly *parmigiano* (Parmesan) cheese, and the sweet, sparkling white wine *Malvasia.*

Parma is also a city that has been favored by the arts. Sixteenth-century Mannerist painting came into full bloom under Parmigianino, and Giuseppe Verdi resided in Parma while composing some of his greatest works. His music, in fact, lured Napoleon's second wife Marie-Louise (and her money) to Parma. Stendhal, then an unknown French functionary, chose the city as the setting of his 1839 novel *The Charterhouse of Parma*. Today the city cultivates a mannered elegance, recalling the artistic eminence of the 16th century and the refinement of the 19th century.

ORIENTATION AND PRACTICAL INFORMATION

Parma lies about 200km northwest of Bologna, conveniently served by the Bologna-Milan train line. The historic center lies on the eastern side of the **Torrente Parma** (in summer it's no torrent, but a dry riverbed). Walk left from the station to **Via Garibaldi,** then right 1km to the town center. Turn left on Via della Repubblica to reach **Piazza Garibaldi,** people-watching site extraordinaire. The main streets branch off this piazza, with **Via Mazzini** running west, **Via della Repubblica** extending east, **Strada Cavour** heading north toward the *duomo,* and **Strada Farini** branching south in the direction of the **Cittadella,** the park that houses Parma's youth hostel and the *Luna Park* carnival in spring and summer.

Tourist Office: P. del Duomo, 5 (tel. 23 47 35). From the station, walk left and turn right down Via Garibaldi, then make a left onto Strada Pisacane. Written info on all nearby towns, but not necessarily in English. Ask for the *Informagiovani* newsletter, full of everything from daytrip advice to job listings (in Italian). Don't despair: English is spoken. Open Mon.-Sat. 9am-12:30pm and 3-5pm. Also try **Punto Informazione** in the *municipio,* the enormous fountain-adorned government building in P. Garibaldi. Open Mon.-Sat. 8:30am-12:30pm.

Currency Exchange: Credito Italiano, Via Mazzini, 8/A (tel. 28 10 74). Open Mon.-Fri. 8:20am-1:20pm and 3-4:30pm. Use the **train station** as a last resort.

Telephones: (tel. 26 51), underground in P. Garibaldi in the front of the city hall. Looks and sounds like the entrance to a subway. Stairs lead to self-service phones and loud callers. Open daily 7:30am-midnight.

Trains: P. Carlo Alberto della Chiesa (tel. 77 11 18, rarely answered). To: Milan (every hour, 1½hr., L11,700); Bologna (every 30min., 1hr., L7200); Florence (7 per day, 3hr., L15,500, but ask about alternative routes). **Luggage Storage:** L5000 for 12hr. Open 6:30am-10pm.

Buses: (tel. 21 41), on Viale P. Toschi before the Ponte Verdi. Automated self-service ticketing. More convenient than trains to provincial towns. To: Colorno (9 per day, L2500); Fontanellato (6 per day, L3600); Torrechiara (L3600); Busseto (8 per day, L5800); Bardi (4 per day, L6600).

Taxis: tel. 20 69 29 (general number).

Bookstore: Feltrinelli, Via della Repubblica, 2 (tel. 23 74 92), on the corner of P. Garibaldi, has books in English. Open Mon.-Fri. 9am-7:30pm, Sat. 9am-1pm and 3:30-7:30pm.

Pharmacy: Farmacia Guareschi, Strada Farini, 5 (tel. 28 22 40). Open Mon.-Fri. 8:30am-1:30pm, Sat. 8:30am-12:30pm and 3:30-7:30pm. For night service, there's the **Farmacia Costa,** Via Emilia Est, 67/g (tel. 426 85). Take Strada della Repubblica, which becomes Emilia Est. Open 7:30pm-8:30am.

Emergencies: tel. 113. **First Aid:** tel. 28 58 30. **Ambulance:** tel. 118. **Hospital: Ospedale Maggiore,** Via Gramsci, 14 (tel. 99 11 11 or 25 91 11), over the river past the Palazzo Ducale.

Police: Questura (tel. 21 94), Borgo della Posta.

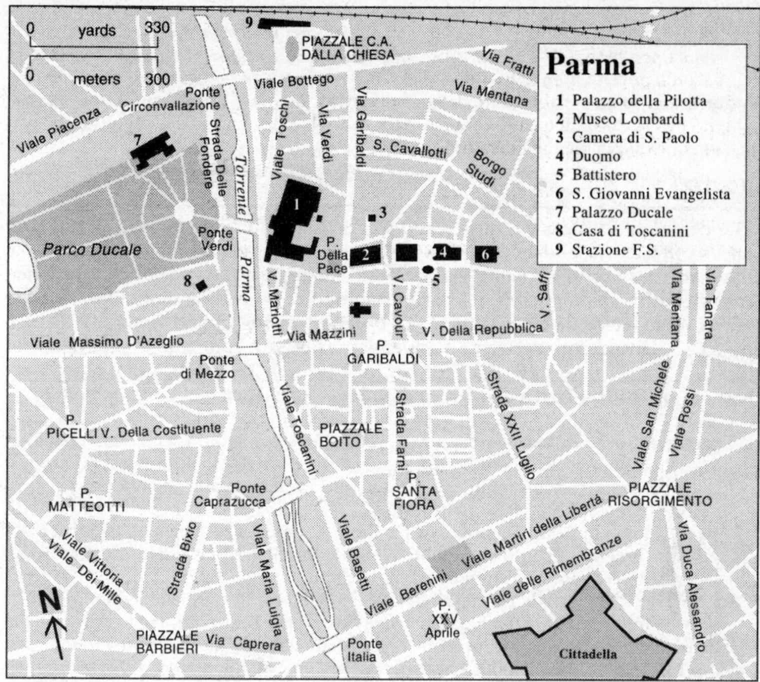

Post Office: Via Melloni, 4/C (tel. 23 75 54), between Via Garibaldi and Strada Cavour, near the *duomo.* Open Mon.-Fri. 8:20am-1:20pm and 3-4:30pm. Also a **branch** across the street from the station, at Via Verdi, 25 (tel. 20 64 39). Open Mon.-Fri. 8am-noon. **Postal Code:** 43100.

Telephone Code: 0521.

ACCOMMODATIONS AND CAMPING

Ostello Cittadella (HI), Via Passo Buole (tel. 96 14 34). From the station, take bus #9. Ask the driver if he's going toward the *ostello* (last bus 8pm; L1300). Get off after about 15min. when the bus turns left on Via Martiri della Liberazione. Follow Via Liberazione 2 blocks and turn right onto Via Passo Buole. At the end of Via Passo Buole, enter the large white portico surrounded by ancient walls and look for the hostel on your left. From P. Garibaldi, take bus #2. Hostel occupies a 15th-century fortress. Eight spacious, 5-bed rooms and luxurious hot showers. 3-day max. stay. Lockout 9:30am-5pm. Strictly enforced curfew 11pm. L15,000 per person. HI members only, but may accept student ID.

Casa della Giovane, Via del Conservatorio, 11 (tel. 28 32 29). From Via Mazzini, turn left on Via Oberdan; Via del Conservatorio winds around to your right. Women only. An upbeat, young atmosphere with beautiful rooms, sturdy furniture, and polished wood floors. Free use of washing machine. Curfew varies with season; usually 10:30pm. Half-pension L30,000 per person for women under 25, L20,000 for room only. Women over 25 (exceptional cases only) L35,000 for half-pension, L22,000 for room only. Breakfast and afternoon snack included. Dining room is open to women daily 12:30-2:30pm (full meal L10,000).

Locanda Lazzaro, Borgo XX Marzo, 14 (tel 20 89 44), off Via della Repubblica. No sign, but upstairs from the restaurant of the same name. Eight homey rooms. Singles L45,000, with bath L48,000. Doubles with bath L65,000. V, MC, AmEx.

Albergo Leon d'Oro, Viale Fratti, 4 (tel. 77 31 82), off Via Garibaldi. From the station, go 2 blocks left. Attractive rooms with a fresh coat of paint. No private baths.

Singles L45,000. Doubles L55,000. Call ahead for a reservation. **Restaurant** downstairs open Mon.-Fri. 12:15-2:15pm and 7:30-10pm with *primi* around L10,000 and a L2500 cover. Open Sept.-July.

Camping: At the Ostello Cittadella (see above), the only campground near Parma. Has electrical outlets and a public park nearby. 3-day max. stay. L10,000 per person, L8000 per tent. Open April-Oct. 30.

FOOD

The cuisine of Parma is unequaled and wonderfully affordable. Native *parmigiano* cheese, *prosciutto,* and an abundance of local sausage varieties fill the windows of the numerous *salumerie* along Via Garibaldi. *Malvasia* is the wine of choice. When exported, this sparkling white loses its natural fizz, so carbon dioxide is added—here's your chance for the real thing. An **open-air market** can be found at P. Ghiaia, off Viale Mariotti past Palazzo Pilotta. Open daily 8am-1pm and 3-7pm. Shop for basics at **Supermarket 2B,** Via XXII Luglio, 27/C (tel. 28 13 82). Open Mon.-Wed. and Fri.-Sat. 8:30am-1pm and 4:30-8pm, Thurs. 8:30am-1pm.

Trattoria Corrieri, Via Conservatorio, 3 (tel. 23 44 26). From Via Mazzini, go left on Via Oberdan; Via del Conservatorio winds to your right. Whitewashed arches, brick columns, red and white tablecloths, and hanging salami and cheeses create a colorful atmosphere. Devour traditional *tortelli di zucca* (ravioli stuffed with sweet squash in a cheese sauce) or try the *tris,* a mix of *tortelli* with *asparagi* and *erbette* (greens). Each dish L8000. Wines from L9500 per carafe. Cover L3000. Open Mon.-Sat. noon-2:30pm and 7:30-10:30pm. V, MC, AmEx.

Le Sorelle Pichi, Strada Farini, 27 (tel. 23 35 38), near P. Garibaldi. Open for lunch only. A traditional *salumeria* that hides one of the best *trattorie* in town in the back. Seems to be a well-kept local secret. Menu changes often. *Primi* L10,000, *secondi* L12,000. Cover L3000. *Trattoria* open Mon.-Sat. noon-3pm. *Salumeria* open 8:30am-1pm and 4-7pm for picnic fixings.

Mensa Universitaria di Parma, Vicolo Grossardi, 4 (tel. 21 36 32), on the 1st floor of a huge concrete building on your way to the Parco Ducale. Cross the bridge from Via Mazzini, which becomes Via Azeglio on the other side. Vicolo Grossardi hides to your right at the arcade. Full meal only L7500 for students (flashing your ISIC works), L12,000 for non-students. Open Mon.-Fri. noon-2pm and 7-9pm, Sat. noon-2pm. Closed Aug. and 2-3 weeks in Dec.

Pizzeria La Duchessa, (tel. 23 59 62) in P. Garibaldi. An excellent *trattoria* with a grand variety of pizzas. Large outdoor dining area is great for people-watching in the evening. Be prepared to wait for a seat. Pastas average L9500, pizzas L8000-12,000, and *secondi* from L10,000. Try the *risotto della casa* (rice, tomatoes, *prosciutto,* cheese, and butter) for a mild but filling lunch (L9500). Half-liter of wine L5000. Open Tues.-Sun. 10:30am-2:30pm and 7pm-1am. V, MC.

Cluny Bar, (tel. 28 41 44) at the corner of Via Cavour and P. Garibaldi. Centrally located, this is where the masses come for Parma's creamiest *gelato.* A good-sized cone will cost you L2000. Open Mon.-Sat. 7am-midnight. Say hello to the English-speaking New Yorker behind the bar.

SIGHTS AND ENTERTAINMENT

Parma's cathedral and baptistery reside in **Piazza Duomo.** Masterpieces fill the 11th-century Romanesque **duomo** (tel. 23 58 86), like the *Descent from the Cross* bas-relief by Benedetto Antelami in the south transept and the Episcopal throne supported by piers in the apse. In the dome Correggio's *Virgin* rises to a gold heaven in a spiral of white robes, pink *putti,* and blue sky. (Open daily 9am-noon and 3-7pm.)

The **baptistery** (tel. 23 58 86), in pink and white marble, was built between the Romanesque and Gothic periods. Walk through the beautifully sculpted portals by Antelami to see the stunning 13th-century frescoes. (Open daily 9am-12:30pm and 3-6pm. Admission L3000, students L500.)

Behind the *duomo* in P. San Giovanni is the **Church of San Giovanni Evangelista** (tel. 23 55 92), with a Correggio-frescoed cupola. Along the left nave over the first, second, and fourth chapels are frescoes by Parmigianino. (Open daily 6:30am-noon and 3:30-8pm. Free.)

To reach another of Correggio's works, head back toward the river on Strada al Duomo, turn right on Strada Cavour, then take a quick left-right to his fresco **Camera S. Paolo** (tel. 23 33 09). It is located in the small courtyard behind the gate that opens off Via M. Melloni, which is actually by the back door of the post office. (Open daily June-Aug. 9am-7:30pm, Sept.-May 9am-1:45pm. Free.)

Works by other artists are found at the monolithic **Palazzo della Pilotta.** From the Camera, cross Via Garibaldi and P. Marconi. Constructed in 1602, the palace expresses the authoritarian ambitions of the Farnese dukes. The Farnese built two complexes, the Pilotta Palace and the **Cittadella** (now a park on the other side of town), in an attempt to unify the city. Today the Palazzo houses several museums, the most important being the **Galleria Nazionale** (tel. 23 33 09). Enter the gallery through the **Farnese Theater** (1615), an imitation of Palladio's Teatro Olimpico in Vicenza, but much larger than the original. The theater also houses an extraordinary art collection that includes works by Correggio, Parmigianino, and Dosso Dossi. Leonardo da Vinci's *Testa di una Fanciulla* (Head of a Young Girl) is here as well. (Gallery open daily 9am-1:45pm. Admission L12,000, includes theater. Theater open daily June-Aug. 9am-1:45pm, Sept.-May 9am-7:30pm.) Also in the Palazzo della Pilotta, the sizable **Museo Archeologico Nazionale** (tel. 23 37 18) displays coins, bronzes, and sculptures of Greek, Etruscan, Roman, and Egyptian origin. (Open Tues.-Sun. 9am-1:30pm. Admission L4000.)

Outside the *duomo* district a French flavor lingers, the aftertaste of Gallic influences from the 16th to 18th centuries. The **Museo Glauco Lombardi,** in the Palazzo di Riserva at Via Garibaldi, 15 (tel. 23 37 27), has a collection of period pieces devoted to Parma from the reign of Marie-Louise. (Open April-Sept. Tues.-Sat. 9:30am-12:30pm and 4-6pm, Sun. 9:30am-1pm; Oct.-March Tues.-Sat. 9:30am-12:30pm and 3-5pm, Sun. 9:30am-1pm. Free.) Unfortunately, many of the French *palazzi* were blasted to pieces during the war, but enough of the older buildings survive to convey the surroundings depicted in Stendhal's novels.

To remedy cultural overload, retreat to the grounds of Marie-Louise's palace in the Baroque **Ducal Park,** located west of the Pilotta Palace over the Ponte Verdi bridge. (Open 7am-midnight; Dec.-Jan. 7:30am-5:30pm.) South of the park on Borgo Rodolfo Tanzi is the birthplace of **Arturo Toscanini** (1867-1957), conductor *extraordinaire* (tel. 28 54 99). It now houses a small museum with memorabilia from the *maestro's* life. (Open Tues.-Sat. 10am-1pm and 3-6pm, Sun. 10am-1pm. Free.)

Observe the production of either *Parmigiano* cheese or *prosciutto di Parma* by contacting the **Consortio di Parmigiano,** Via Gramsci, 26/A (tel. 29 27 00), or the **Consortio di Prosciutto,** Via M. Dell'Arpa, 8/B (tel. 24 39 87). They'll provide a guided tour of the facilities and a free sample at the end.

The city of Parma sponsors a summer music festival, **Concerti Nei Chiostri,** featuring classical music in the area's churches and cloisters. (Call 28 32 24 for information daily 5-7pm. Admission at the door L23,000; under 18 L18,000.) You can also contact the tourist office for info; ask for a brochure listing local summer concerts and festivals, including morning concerts in the Ducal Park and starlit performances in neighboring castles. Be sure to see one of Italy's premier opera houses, the **Teatro di Reggio** (tel. 21 89 10), next to P. della Pace. Check with the tourist office for prices of cheaper standing-room tickets from October to May. Just visiting is free.

■ Near Parma

Enthusiasts of Italian architecture and opera will be pleased by the offerings of the small towns around Parma. The city is surrounded by medieval castles nestled in the greenery of the neighboring hills. If you have a car, drive straight to Torrechiara and the 15th-century **Castello Torrechiara,** constructed by Pier Maria Rossi. Learn the true meaning of love in the **camera d'oro,** a room covered with intricate terra-cotta carvings and golden frescoes. Rossi designed the room for his lover Bianca. Open Tues.-Sat. 9am-1pm, Sun. 9am-1pm and 3-7pm. Admission L8000.

No composer knows love better than opera giant Giuseppe Verdi, whose native hamlet of **Roncole Verdi** rests on the Parma plain 3½km outside the city of **Busseto** (from Parma 15 buses daily to Roncole and Busseto, 30min.). To see where this son of a poor innkeeper received his earliest inspiration, visit the house and museum at **Verdi's birth site** (tel. (0524) 924 87 or 92 23 39) in Roncole. In Busseto proper, within the walls of the ancient **Rocca,** you'll find the famous **Teatro Verdi,** opened in 1868 (and, unfortunately, closed now for renovations). Three km away from Busseto (on the same bus line) lies the **Villa Sant'Agata** (tel. (0524) 83 02 10), Verdi's residence during sabbaticals from his work in Milan. Fed up with Busseto's infamous gossip about his affair with a premier *diva,* he decided to place his home in secluded Sant'Agata. Parts of this mansion are open to the public and remain unaltered from the time of his death in 1901. Open April-Oct. Tues.-Sun. 9-11:40am and 3-6:40pm. Admission L5000, groups L4000 per person, student groups L1000 per person. Call ahead for reservations.

Piacenza

Tucked into the distant northwest corner of Emilia-Romagna, almost bordering on Piemonte, Piacenza eschews a tourist economy to embrace home-grown prosperity. True to its name, this town oozes with pleasantness. Piacenza houses several noteworthy monuments of the Renaissance and the Middle Ages, and the city makes a convenient stopover on your way to Parma or Bologna.

ORIENTATION AND PRACTICAL INFORMATION

Piacenza lies on the main rail line between Milan (L6500) and Bologna (L11,700), as well as on a secondary line that connects to Turin (L15,500) through Alessandria. The **train station** information line is 32 06 37. From the station, located in **Piazzale Marconi,** walk along the left side of the park on Viale delle Mille, and take a right on Via Alberoni at the far side of the park. Bear right onto Via Roma and left onto Corso Cavour, which leads directly to the **Piazza dei Cavalli.** The **tourist office,** P. Mercatini, 10 (tel. 32 93 24), tucked in to the left of the Gothic palace off P. Cavalli, distributes a map full of useful information (in English) on hotels and sights. English spoken. (Open Tues.-Sat. 10am-1pm and 4-7pm, Sun. 10am-1pm.) Many banks in the center (except the Banca d'Italia) have **currency exchange** services, as does the post office. The **telephone office** (tel. 54 41 11) is at Via Vittorio Emanuele, 118, but for phone booths try P. Cavalli or Via Garibaldi. **Taxis** can be reached at 32 38 53, 32 22 36, or 75 47 22. For first aid, call the **hospital** at 30 11 11, or the **Red Cross,** tel. 32 47 87. **Ambulance:** tel. 118. Piacenza's **post office** is at Via San Antonio, 38-40 (tel. 32 06 98); the **postal code** is 29100. **Telephone code:** 0523.

ACCOMMODATIONS AND FOOD

The most convenient lodging option is the **Hotel Moderno,** Via Tibini, 29 (tel. 38 50 41 or 32 92 96; fax 38 44 38). Walk along the left side of the park onto Via Tibini. True to its name, the hotel offers newly renovated rooms with modern, sturdy furniture and well-scrubbed bathrooms. Singles L50,000, with bath L60,000. Doubles L65,000, with bath L80,000. Another option, only a few blocks away, is **Hotel Corona,** Via Roma, 141 (tel. 32 09 48), above a **pizzeria** (pizza from L7000). From the train station, follow Viale delle Mille along the left side of the park and take a right on Via Roma. Singles L40,000. Doubles L60,000. Half-pension L50,000. V, MC, AmEx. As in any Italian town, specialty shops selling meats, cheeses, bread, and fruit are omnipresent. Shop in the markets along **Via Calzolai,** near the center. The **outdoor market** is held every Wed. and Sat. in P. Duomo and P. dei Cavalli in the *centro storico.* Local specialties include *tortelli,* filled with spinach and ricotta, and *pisarei e fasö,* a hearty bean-and-pea soup. Steer clear of anything containing the word *cavallo,* unless you really are hungry enough to eat a horse. All meals are safe at **Osteria Del Trentino,** Via del Castello, 71 (tel. 32 42 60), off P. Borgo, a charming restaurant where you may choose to eat out back in the leafy garden. *Primi* average L8000, *secondi* L12,000. Cover L2500. Open Mon.-Sat. noon-3pm and 8pm-midnight. V, MC, AmEx.

SIGHTS

The entire *centro storico* is off-limits to automobile traffic, making it a haven for pedestrians. The central square, **Piazza dei Cavalli,** is named for the two massive, 17th-century equestrian statues by Francesco Mochi that are located there. Even though the statues were intended as tributes to the riders, Duke Rannucio I and his father Duke Alessandro Farnese, the horses seem to dominate their masters. The true masterpiece of the piazza, however, is the gothic **Palazzo del Comune,** now called **Il Gotico.** The building was constructed in 1280 when Piacenza was a leading member of the Lombard League, a powerful trading group of city-states in northern Italy. From P. dei Cavalli, follow **Via XX Settembre** to the **duomo,** constructed between 1122 and 1233, with its unadorned, three-aisle nave. The crypt, a maze of thin columns, is one of the spookiest in Italy—grab a friend's hand when you visit. (*Duomo* open daily 8am-noon and 3-6pm.)

The **Palazzo Farnese,** in P. Cittadella at the opposite end of Corso Cavour from P. dei Cavalli, houses the **Museo Civico,** which includes both the **Museo delle Carrozze** and the **Museo del Risorgimento** (tel. 282 70 or 269 81). The most notable work in the collection is a Botticelli fresco depicting Christ's birth. (Open Tues.-Wed. and Fri. 9am-12:30pm, Thurs. 9am-12:30pm and 3:30-5:30pm, Sat. 9am-12:30pm and 3-5pm, Sun. 9:30am-noon and 3:30-6:30pm. Admission L4500, under 18 and over 60 L3000. For only the Museo delle Carrozze or the Museo del Risorgimento, under 18 and over 60 L2500 or L1000.) The **Galleria Ricci Oddi,** Via Sirio, 13 (tel. 207 42), south of P. Sant'Antonino, exhibits a collection of contemporary and modern art, including works by Klimt and A. Bocchi.

Ravenna

Ravenna's moment of historical superstardom came and went 14 centuries ago, when Justinian and Theodora, rulers of the Byzantine Empire, made it the headquarters of their campaign to restore order to the anarchic west. Though they were ultimately unsuccessful, the city remained the seat of the Exarchs of Byzantine Italy for two centuries. This period inspired some of the most important works of Byzantine art outside Istanbul. In fact, you haven't really seen *tesserae* (mosaic bits) until you've visited Ravenna. Once known as *biblia pauperum,* or "the poor man's bible," mosaics may indeed eclipse the need for words. Literary pilgrims also come to Ravenna, the site of Dante's tomb. After a long day of dutiful sight-seeing, Ravenna offers visitors the serenity of a small town with character. Locals cruise by on peaceful evening bike rides as bats soar between church towers and poplar trees.

ORIENTATION AND PRACTICAL INFORMATION

Ravenna makes a good daytrip from Bologna or Ferrara, and if you can find accommodations it is also a quiet place to spend the night. The train station sits at the east end of town in P. Farini. **Viale Farini** leads from the station straight into **Via Diaz,** which runs to **Piazza del Popolo,** the center of town.

Tourist Office, Via Salara, 8 (tel. 354 04; fax 48 26 70). From the train station, take Viale Farini to P. del Popolo. From there, take Via Muratori to P. XX Settembre and turn right on Via Matteotti. Follow this to its end, go left on Via Cavour, and take the 1st right. Useful maps and accommodations info. Open Mon.-Sat. 9am-1pm and 3-6pm, Sun. 9am-noon; in winter closed Sun. **Video Info** around the corner on San Vitale. **Branch office** outside the train station to your left. Also rents **bikes** at L2000 per hour, L15,000 per day. Open Mon.-Sat. 6:15am-8pm.

Budget Travel: CTS, Via Mazzini, 11 (tel. 399 33). Friendly office. English spoken. ISIC and HI cards sold. Discount airfares. Open Mon.-Fri. 9:30am-12:30pm and 3:30-7:30pm, Sat. 9am-12:30pm.

Currency Exchange: Via Diaz is lined with banks. Most are open Mon.-Fri. 8:20am-1:20pm and 2:45-3:45pm, Sat. 8:20-11:20am. Also at the post office.

Telephones: Via Rasponi, 22, off P. XX Settembre. Very helpful staff. Open Mon.-Fri. 8:30am-12:30pm and 2:30-5:30pm. Self-service booths open daily 8am-11pm. **Albergo Diana,** Via Rossi, 4, also has phones. Open 8pm-8am.

Trains: In Piazza Ferini. To: Bologna (5 per day, 1¼hr., L7200); Ferrara (9 per day, 45min., L6500); Florence (3 per day, 3hr., L15,500); and Venice (via Ferrara, 3hr., L17,800). **Ticket counter** open Mon.-Sat. 6am-8:15pm, Sun. 6am-8pm. **Luggage Storage:** L5000 for 12hr. Open daily 9am-1pm and 2:30-5:45pm.

Buses: ATR (regional) and **ATM** (municipal) buses depart from outside the train station for the coastal towns of Marina di Ravenna (L1700), Lido di Classe (L3800), and others. Buy tickets at the ATM booth across the *piazza* from the station (L1200 for most towns)—get a return ticket too, as they're difficult to find in the suburbs. Office hours Mon.-Sat. 6:30am-8:30pm, Sun. 7am-8pm; in winter Mon.-Sat. 6:30am-7:30pm, Sun. 7:30am-7:30pm.

Public Toilets: Via Pasolini, 20, off Via Cavour. Super-modern and disinfected after every use. L400. Another at P. Baracca, and a third upstairs to your left as you enter the Mercato Coperto in P. Costa.

Police: tel. 112 for emergencies, or P. del Popolo, 26 (tel. 333 33).

Emergencies: tel. 113. **First Aid:** tel. 330 11. **Hospital: Santa Maria delle Croci,** Via Missiroli, 10 (tel. 40 91 11).

Post Office: P. Garibaldi, 1, off Via Diaz before P. del Popolo. Open Mon.-Fri. 8:15am-7pm, Sat. 8:15am-12:50pm. *Fermo posta* at #1. A smaller branch on V. Carducci, near the station, is open Mon.-Fri. 8:15am-6:25pm, Sat. 8:15am-1pm. **Postal Code:** 48100.

Telephone Code: 0544.

ACCOMMODATIONS

Ravenna does not abound with budget accommodations, but the beach towns nearby have plenty of campgrounds and a few hotels. Ask the tourist office for a list.

Ostello Dante (HI), Via Nicolodi, 12 (tel./fax 42 04 05). Take bus #1 from Viale Pallavicini, left of the station (last bus shortly after 9pm, L1200). A clean, simple hostel in the eastern suburbs. 6-bed rooms. Reception open 7-9:30am and 5-11:30pm. Lockout 9am-5pm. Curfew 11:30pm. L20,000 per person, L22,000 per person in family rooms. Breakfast included. Dinner L14,000.

Hotel Ravenna, Viale Marconcelli, 12 (tel. 21 22 04; fax 21 20 77), to the right as you exit the station. Neat, clean rooms with tile floors. Bar and cozy TV room downstairs. Handicapped accessible. Singles L40,000, with bath L60,000. Doubles L65,000, with bath L75,000. Prices may rise if the hotel gets the two-star classification it is hoping for. V, MC.

Albergo Al Giaciglio, Via Rocca Brancaleone, 42 (tel. 394 03). Walk along Viale Farini, then turn right across P. Mameli. All rooms carpeted and clean. Singles L35,000, with bath L45,000. Doubles L52,000, with bath L65,000. Triples L80,000, with bath L90,000. Breakfast L5000. Meals available in the restaurant downstairs. Closed 2 weeks in Dec. V, MC.

FOOD

Those looking for tasty local fare at budget prices may be disappointed in Ravenna. If you're staying at the hostel, you may want to eat the L14,000 dinner or L6000 spaghetti there. Hostelers also benefit from the adjacent bargain supermarket **Coop,** Via Aquileia, 110. Open Mon. 3:30-7:45pm, Tues. 8:15am-1:15pm and 3:30-7:45pm, Wed.-Fri. 8:15am-7:45pm, Sat. 8am-8pm. The busy **Mercato Coperto** occupies P. Andrea Costa, up Via IV Novembre from P. del Popolo. Open Mon.-Sat. 7am-2pm and Fri. 4:30-7:30pm.

Bizantino, in P. Andrea Costa, inside the Mercato Coperto. Self-service restaurant with stylish, iron-detailed interior. *Primi* L5000-6300, *secondi* L6900-7500. Full meal L14,000. Cover L1000. Open Mon.-Fri. 11:45am-3pm.

Mensa Il Duomo Self-Service, Via Oberdan, 8 (tel. 21 36 88), off P. del Duomo. Well-prepared self-service. Popular; come early. Pasta L3500. Full meal L12,100. Wine L1100 per glass. Cover L1200. Open Sept.-July Mon.-Fri. 11:40am-2:30pm.

Ristorante-Pizzeria Guidarello, Via Gessi, 7, off P. Arcivescovado beside the *duomo.* A huge place with surprisingly good food—a real *trattoria.* Try the *Fantasia della Casa,* 3 differently prepared meats with mixed veggies. *Primi* L5000-9000, *secondi* L6500-15,000. Cover L2500. Open daily noon-2:15pm and 7-9:30pm. Same fare available at the owner's other restaurant, **Galleria da Renato** (tel. 236 80), nearby at Via Mentana, 31. Same hours, but closed on Sun. V, MC.

Ristorante San Vitale, Via Salara, 20 (tel. 353 63). A bit more expensive, but includes full service. Sleek black-and-white interior. Menu includes seafood pasta and grilled fish, with meat and vegetables for fish-haters. *Primi* L8000-10,000, *secondi* L10,000-18,000. Open Wed.-Mon. noon-2:30pm and 7-10:30pm. V, AmEx.

SIGHTS AND ENTERTAINMENT

If you're staying in Ravenna or thoughtfully making the rounds on the church-mosaic-museum circuit, consider buying a comprehensive ticket to the city sights (L9000, students L7000). The ticket is available and valid at the Basilica di San Vitale, the Basilica of Sant'Appolinare, the Mausoleum of Galla Placidia, the Battistero Neoniano, the Museo Arcivescovile, and the Basilica dello Spirito Santo.

Inside and out, the 6th-century **Basilica di San Vitale,** Via San Vitale, 17 (take Via Argentario off Via Cavour), is a jewel. An open courtyard overgrown with greenery leads to the treasured interior which glows with brilliant mosaics. On the ceiling of the main apse, Christ is depicted on a field of vivid blue. No less glorious are the likenesses of Emperor Justinian and his wife Theodora, San Vitale's powerful patrons. The sparkling golden tiles consist of thin sheets of gold sandwiched between layers of glass. (Open April-Sept. daily 9am-7pm; Oct.-March daily 9am-4:30pm. Admission L5000.) The oldest and most interesting mosaics in the city cover the interior of the **Mausoleum of Galla Placidia,** behind the basilica. The mechanism for illuminating the artworks is outside. (Open April-Sept. daily 9am-7pm; Oct.-March daily 9am-4:30pm. Entrance included with admission to the basilica.)

Walk through the gate between San Vitale and the mausoleum into the cloister of the church's former convent, to reach the sprawling **Museo Nazionale** (tel. 344 24) on Via Fiandrini. The collection features works from the Roman, early Christian, Byzantine, and medieval periods. (Open Tues.-Sun. 8:30am-7:30pm. Admission L8000, EU citizens under 18 and over 60 free.)

The **duomo** (tel. 391 96), due south in P. Duomo, has a light, fancy Baroque interior. (Open daily 7:45am-noon and 3-6:30pm.) In the **Battistero Neoniano,** next door on Via Battistero (tel. 336 96), some poorly restored mosaics in Hellenistic-Roman style reside on the lower level, with three levels of 5th-century mosaics above. (Baptistery open daily 9am-7pm. Admission L4000.)

A small but precious collection of mosaics from the *duomo* is on display in the **Museo Arcivescovile,** nearby in P. Arcivescovado. While you're there, check out the mosaic chapel and the Throne of Maximilian, perhaps the best piece of ivory carving in the Christian world. (Open daily 9am-7pm. Admission L4000.) Compare the mosaics in the Battistero Neoniano with those in the **Battistero degli Ariani** (tel. 344 24) on Via degli Ariani off Via Diaz. This baptistery was used by the Arians, a sect condemned as heretical for doubting the doctrine of the Trinity. (Open 9am-7pm.) So you want more mosaics? Continue to the **Church of Sant'Apollinare in Classe** (tel. 47 30 04), a 6th-century basilica 5km south of the city (bus #4 or 44, every 30min. from the train station, L1200). The classical architecture yields to Byzantine depictions of angels and apostles on the heavily decorated triumphal arch. (Open Mon.-Fri. 9am-12:30pm and 2-7pm, Sat.-Sun. 2-5pm. Admission L4000.)

If seeing one more mosaic is your personal version of Hell, then you shouldn't miss the **tomb of Dante Alighieri** (1265-1321), located at the end of Via Dante Alighieri. (Open daily 9am-noon and 2-5pm, but sometimes left open during the lunch hour. Free.) There is also a **Dante Museum,** Via Dante Alighieri, 4 (tel. 302 52), whose Dante library is 18,000 volumes strong. (Open Tues.-Sun. 9am-noon and 3:30-6pm. Admission L3000, free on Sun. and holidays.)

On the third Saturday and Sunday of each month, a large **antique market** gathers in the center of town. In June and July, the city sponsors the creatively named **Ravenna Festival,** featuring operas, classical concerts, folk music, and drama. Contact **Teatro Alighieri,** Via Mariani, 2 (tel. 325 77), for programs and information. An annual **Dante Festival** during the second week in September brings the Afterlife to Ravenna with exhibits, readings, and performances. This festival is given under the auspices of the Church of S. Francesco (tel. 332 56).

Rimini

Rimini! Sunglasses, warm waves, string bikinis, half-naked children with buckets full of sand, tall drinks at sunset, discos and go-go music, lawn chairs, the scent of cocoa butter, and drippy *gelati* characterize this popular tanning spot of the mid-Adriatic. If you want culture, visit the inland historic center, an alluring jumble of medieval streets dominated by the Malatesta Temple and crumbling Roman arches. Otherwise, head straight to the beach.

ORIENTATION AND PRACTICAL INFORMATION

Rimini is a major stop on the Bologna-Lecce train line and its airport serves many European cities, mostly with charter flights. To walk to the beach from the station (15min.), turn right at Piazzale C. Battisti, make another right into the tunnel when you see the yellow arrow indicating *al mare,* then follow **Via Principe Amadeo.** Bus #11 can also take you there. Buy tickets (L1500, L5000 per day) at the kiosk in front of the station or at *tabacchi.* To reach the historic center of town, take **Via Dante Alighieri** from the station (a 5-min. walk).

Tourist Offices: IAT, Via Dante Alighieri, 86 (tel. 513 31 or 514 80), across the *piazza* from the train station. Friendly, English-speaking staff. Open daily 8am-8pm. **Branch office** at P. Fellini, 3 (tel. 543 19 or 540 19; fax 542 90), near the water. Open daily 8am-8pm; off-season 8am-2pm. **Hotel Reservations-Adria** in the train station (tel. 39 05 30) finds rooms for free. Open daily 8am-8pm.

Budget Travel: CTS, Grantour Viaggi, Via Matteuci, 4 (tel. 555 25; fax 559 66), off Via Principe Amadeo. Tickets, ISIC cards, and info on group tours. Open Mon.-Fri. 9am-12:30pm and 3:30-7pm, Sat. 9:30am-noon.

Telephones: P. Ferrari, 22, in the Galleria Fabbri off Via Tempio Matestiano, which intersects with Via IV Novembre. Open daily 8am-10pm. Also at Viale Carducci, 30 and Viale Trieste, 1. Both open daily 8am-11pm. Or try any of the bars along the beach or near the station.

Flights: Miramare Civil Airport (tel. 37 31 32) on Via Flaminia. Mostly charter flights. Destinations and rates vary. Check with local travel agencies.

Trains: P. C. Battisti and Via Dante (tel. 535 12). Trains to Bologna (14 per day, 1½hr., L9800) and Milan (15 per day, 3hr., L26,200). Periodic trains to Rome (L27,800). Trains every hr. to Ravenna (1hr., L4200). **Luggage Storage:** L5000 for 12hr. Open 24hr.

Buses: TRAM intercity bus station at Viale Roma on P. Clementini (tel. 39 04 44; fax 39 08 26), a few hundred meters from the station. Service to many inland towns and San Marino (11 per day, 1hr., L5000). Many buses leave from the train station, where you can buy tickets in the orange booth. **Fratelli Benedettini** (tel. 90 38 54) and **Bonelli Bus** (tel. 37 24 32) run buses every hour to San Marino center (50min., L4000).

Car Rental: Hertz, Viale Trieste, 16/A (tel. 531 10), near the beach off Viale Vespucci. L640,000 per week or L155,000 per day with unlimited mileage, including tax. Open Mon.-Sat. 8:30am-1pm and 3-8pm, Sun. 8:30am-1pm. Another office at the airport (tel. 37 51 08).

Emergencies: tel. 113. **First Aid:** On the beach at the end of Viale Gounod, beyond Viale Pascoli. Free walk-in clinic for tourists. Open in summer daily 9:30am-noon and 3:30-7pm. **Ambulance:** 24hr. service (tel. 38 70 01). **Red Cross:** Via Savonarola, 6 (tel. 530 67 or 547 80), near the canal. **Hospital: Ospedale Infermi,** Via Settembrini, 2 (tel. 70 51 11). English-speaking doctors.

Police: Corso d'Augusto, 192 (tel. 510 00).

Post Office: Corso Augusto, 8 (tel. 78 16 87), near the Arch of Augustus off P. Tre Martiri. *Fermo posta* at #10. Open Mon.-Sat. 8:10am-7:10pm. Also at the beach on Viale Mantegazza at Viale Vespucci. Open Mon.-Fri. 8:15am-1:30pm, Sat. 8:15am-noon. Also at Via Roma, 64. Open Mon.-Fri. 8:30am-7pm, Sat. 8:15am-noon. **Postal Code:** 47037.

Telephone Code: 0541.

ACCOMMODATIONS AND CAMPING

During high season (the last week of June through the end of August), your best chance of finding a room is through the tourist or accommodations offices. Reserve in advance by phone to avoid hassles. Via Pola abounds with budget hotels, and the tourist office can give you a complete list of hotels and campgrounds. Rimini's hotel seasons are divided into "high" (last week in July and the first 3 weeks in August), "shoulder" (first 3 weeks in July and the last week in August), and "low" (Sept.-June) and are listed in that order when possible.

Ostello Urland (HI), Via Flaminia, 300 (tel. 37 32 16), by the airport, a 25-min. ride on bus #9 (L1800). Get off at Via Stokholm (ask the bus driver), and follow the signs. Lockout 9am-5pm. Curfew 11pm. L15,000 per person. Non-HI members pay an additional L5000. Breakfast included. Dinners L14,000. Call ahead. Closed for renovations, but they hope to reopen by summer of '97.

Albergo Filadelphia, Via Pola, 25 (tel. 236 79). Clean rooms, soft beds, and an owner with a soft spot for Americans and *Let's Go* readers. L35,000/30,000/25,000 per person. Reduced prices for extended stays. Reservations are helpful.

Hotel Pigalle, Via Ugo Foscolo, 7 (tel. 39 10 54). Clean and classy hotel on a quiet street. Jazz posters, a peaceful terrace, and a young, snazzy staff. All rooms with bath. Singles L50,000/L42,000/L35,000. Breakfast included. Full-pension required in Aug at L70,000/L55,000/L50,000. Open mid-June to mid-Sept.

Pensione Mille Fiori, Via Pola, 42 (tel. 256 17), down the street from the currency exchange. Large rooms, all with bath. Singles and doubles (per person): with meals L58,000/45,000/37,000, without meals about L12,000 less. Make reservations for July and Aug. Full-pension required in Aug. Open Easter-Sept.

Hotel Card, Via Dante, 50 (tel. 264 12; fax 543 74), close to the train station, but very respectable. This 2-star offers 63 tidy rooms with big beds, high ceilings, and TVs at 1-star prices. Very helpful English-speaking manager. Singles L58,000, low-season L38,000; with bath L78,000, low-season L52,000. Doubles L88,000, low-season L56,000; with bath L118,000, low-season L73,000. Extra beds 35% more. Breakfast L9000. V, MC, AmEx.

Camping: Maximum (tel. 37 26 02 or 37 02 71). Take bus #9 or 11 to stop #23 ("Miramare"). July 6-Aug. 24: L10,000 per person, L7800 per child, L19,000 per tent. May 14-July 5 and Aug. 25-Sept.: L6000 per person, L5000 per child, L7000 or L12,500 per tent. Also try the campsites and bungalows at **Italia** (tel. 73 28 82), Via Toscanella, 112, in Viserba di Rimini, 1½km north of Rimini. From the train station, take bus #4 directly to the campsite. L12,000 per adult, L9000 per child, L15,000-20,000 per tent.

FOOD

Rimini's seaside swarms with sterile eateries. Fortunately, you can survive on just the resort's delicious snacks. Look in the center of town for affordable full meals. For brown-baggers, Rimini's **covered market,** between Via Castelfidardo and the Tempio, provides an array of foodstuffs. Open Mon., Wed., and Fri.-Sat. 7:15am-1pm and 5-7:30pm, Tues. and Thurs. 7:15am-1pm. The **rosticceria** in the market offers cheap seafood. Closer to the beach are the supermarkets **STANDA,** Via Vespucci, 133 (open daily 9am-11pm; V, MC), and **Margherita,** Viale Trieste, 34 (open Mon.-Wed. and Fri. 7:30am-1pm and 5-8pm, Thurs. 7:30am-1pm.)

Mensa Dopolavoro Ferroviario, Viale Roma, 70 (tel. 553 88). Near the train station, to the left off Via Dante and down a driveway. Food is fresh and service friendly. *Primi* L4300, *secondi* L6400, *menù* L14,500. Menu changes daily. Open daily 11am-3pm and 6-10pm.

Ristorante-Pizzeria Pic Nic, Via Tempio Malatestiano, 30 (tel. 219 16), off Via IV Novembre at the *tempio.* Huge buffet overflowing with gourmet specialties. *Primi* L7000-9000, *secondi* from L7500. Mozzarella blankets the homemade *lasagne al forno* (L8000). Try the *pizza bianco verde,* a fire-baked cheese and herb delight (L8000). Cover L2000. Open Wed.-Mon. noon-3pm and 7pm-1am.

Gelateria Nuovo Fiore, Viale Vespucci, 7 (tel. 236 02), with a 2nd location at Viale Vespucci, 85. Endless flavor selection. Cones L2500-5000. House *aperitivo* L4000. Open March-Oct. daily 8am-3am; Jan.-Feb. Sat.-Sun. 8am-3am.

SIGHTS

Any tour of Rimini's historic center should begin with the Renaissance **Tempio Malatestiano** on Via IV Novembre (tel. 511 30). The church was originally constructed in Franciscan Gothic style; in the 1440s, however, the ruler Sigismondo Malatesta ("Sigmund Headache") transformed the church into a classical monument to himself and his fourth wife Isotta. See his image atop the two black elephants at the foot of the niche in the first chapel on the left. Sigismondo Malatesta was the only person in history canonized to hell by the pope, who described him as a heretic guilty of "murder, violation, adultery, incest, sacrilege, perjury so dissolute that he raped his daughters and sons-in-law and as a boy often acted as the female partner in shameful loves, and later forced men to act as women." But Siggy was also a soldier and patriot who ruled Rimini at its height (1417-1468) and employed such artists as Piero della Francesca and Leon Battista Alberti, who designed the exterior of the new church. (Open daily 8am-1pm and 3:30-7pm; closes at 6pm in winter.)

Alberti modeled the front of the Tempio Malatestiano after the Roman Arch of Augustus, which still stands at the gates of Rimini (see below). Limestone now fills the two front arches, originally intended to hold the sarcophagi of Sigismondo and Isotta. The large single-aisled interior and wooden-trussed roof recall the temple's original Franciscan design. The sprightly sculptures which appear in most every chapel are the creations of Agostino di Duccio. (Open daily 7am-noon and 3-7pm.)

A short distance from the temple, **Piazza Tre Martiri,** named after three partisans hanged by the Fascists in 1944, forms the ramshackle, noisy city center on the former site of the Roman forum. The most striking vestige of Rimini's past glory is the **Arch of Augustus** at the end of Corso d'Augusto. The oldest Roman triumphal arch (27BC), it blends the architectural elements of arch, column, and medallion.

Rimini's medieval center and favorite hangout, **Piazza Cavour,** off Corso d'Augusto, contains one of the oddest ensembles of buildings in Italy. The tall Renaissance arcade of the **Palazzo Garampi** contrasts dramatically with the adjoining fortress-like **Palazzo dell'Arengo** (1207) and the smaller **Palazzo del Podestà** (1334). Between the first two buildings is an Italian version of Brussels's famous *Le Pisseur*. Perpendicular to the municipal building, the pink brick **Teatro Comunale** (1857), an auditorium destroyed by a bomb in World War II, completes the second side of the square. On the third side, a motley collection of shops, bars, and offices surrounds the Renaissance entrance to the **fish market** (1747). Four stone dolphins in the corners of the market once functioned as fountains, filling the small canals (still visible under the benches) with water used to clean the fish. Two curious sculptures pose in the center of the *piazza:* an eccentric, moss-encrusted fountain (1543) engraved with an inscription about the presence of Leonardo da Vinci, and a seated, sumptuously garbed Pope Paul V (1614) brandishing ferocious eagles.

Also worth seeing is the old fortress, **Rocca Malatestiana,** built by Sigismondo between 1437 and 1446 (behind the Communal Theater). Inside is the new **Museo Dinz Rialto** (tel. 78 57 80), a museum of ethnology with exhibits on the aboriginal cultures of Africa and Polynesia. (Open Mon., Wed., Fri. 8am-1:30pm; Tues. and Thurs. 8am-1:30pm and 3:30-6pm. Admission L4000, children and students L2000.) One noteworthy church is the **Church of Sant'Agostino;** its choir contains a great cycle of Gothic frescoes. The **Museo della Città,** Via Tonini, 1 (tel. 214 82), inside the former Jesuit college, has a collection of Roman mosaics and Renaissance and Baroque paintings. (Open Mon., Wed., and Fri. 8:30am-1:30pm, Tues., Thurs., and Sat. 8:30am-1:30pm and 3:30-6pm, Sun. 10am-1pm and 3:30-6pm. Admission L4000, children and seniors L2000.)

ENTERTAINMENT

Don't be too flattered by Rimini's roving photographers offering "modeling deals"—attractive as you may be, it's actually a ploy aimed to get tourists to buy photos. A picture may be worth a thousand words, but it's not worth your *lire.*

Rimini is notorious throughout Europe for its **sleazy pickup scene.** *Passeggiata* is a euphemism for the wild cruising you can witness (or participate in) nightly along the *lungomare* on **Viale Amerigo Vespucci** and **Viale Regina Elena.** The *discoteche* in Rimini are among the largest and most dazzling on the continent, and there are literally hundreds to choose from. One of the area's flashiest discos is **Cocorico,** in Riccione on V. Chietti, 44 (tel. 60 51 83), accessible by bus #10 or 11 from the Rimini station. With six bars and four dance floors playing underground, techno, and house music, you can boogie the night away for a mere L50,000. (Open Sat. nights.) A cheaper option near the beach in Rimini is the **Rag Club,** Via le Beccadelli, 7 (tel. 502 86). Music includes rock, hip hop, and alternative, and there's no cover if you buy a drink. (Open Fri. and Sat. nights.) Check posters around town and ads in local papers to find out about concerts in various discos and clubs. Also hang on to the discount passes that you are likely to pick up around the Marina Centro—lucky ladies may get in free. Rimini has instituted a **Blue Line** bus service (L4000 per night) that runs from mid-July to August for carless disco-goers. Various lines originate at the station and travel between the beach towns nearby (2-5:30am, every 30min.-1hr.).

San Marino

What may be the most successful tourist attraction in Italy is not even Italian. Though San Marino closely resembles the surrounding hill towns, this 26-square-kilometer patch of turf is actually its own nation. The novelty of the cute little republic's size is the basis of its wildly profitable tourist industry; cobblestone streets are bloated with trinket stands, aimed at the tourists who come here just to have their passports stamped with the mark of another country. Perhaps the most worthwhile souvenir you can take with you, however, is the memory of the stupendous view from Piazza della Libertà, where the stone castle is set like a white herald against a field of Disneyland blue.

ORIENTATION AND PRACTICAL INFORMATION

San Marino's streets wind around **Mount Titiano.** Helpful signs lead pedestrians from one attraction to the next—happily, there are few cars in the center of town. **Piazza della Libertà** is the pride of the republic and overlooks gorgeous hills below.

Tourist Office: Contra Omagnuno, 20 (tel. 88 24 00 or 88 29 98; fax 88 25 75), has maps and historical info. Open Mon. and Thurs. 8:15am-2:15pm and 3-6pm, Tues.-Wed. and Fri. 8:15am-2:15pm. A **branch office** in Contrada del Collegio (tel. 88 29

14), near P. Garibaldi, has similar services. Open daily June-Sept. 8:30am-5:30pm; in off season closed weekends and noon-2:30pm.

Currency: San Marino mints its own coins in the same denominations as Italian *lire*, and both are are used interchangeably.

Border Controls: None. But bring your passport; the tourist office can stamp it.

Telephones: Like Italian phones, they accept phone cards and coins.

Trains: The closest station is in Rimini, connected to San Marino by bus.

Buses: Fratelli Benedettini (tel. 90 38 54) and **Bonelli Bus** (tel. 37 24 32) run buses every hour from the train station in Rimini to San Marino center (50min., L4000). Buy tickets at the booth or in the bus lot outside the station in Rimini, or at the bus lot in San Marino.

Cableways: San Marino's *funivia* runs from Contra Omagnano down to Borgo Maggiore (L3000 one way, L5000 roundtrip).

Taxis: In P. Lo Stradone (tel. 99 14 41).

Emergencies: tel. 112 or 115. **Ambulance:** tel. 118.

Post Office: Viale Antonio Onofri.

Coin and Stamp Office: In P. Garibaldi (tel. 99 21 56).

Telephone Code: from Italy 0549; country code 378 (from other countries).

ACCOMMODATIONS, FOOD, AND SIGHTS

San Marino's hotels are small and expensive. Since you can see the republic in one day, make it a daytrip from Rimini or Ravenna. Food is generic tourist fare; a *menù* for about L25,000 can be found on every corner, and snack bars abound.

From the bus lot, walk up the stairs on the right and through the Porta San Francesco, following the signs to Piazza della Libertà. The **Palazzo Pubblico** (1894) is the white beacon standing against the sky. (Under restoration; check with the tourist office for info.) Gorgeous vistas and a free workout await visitors to San Marino's **three towers. Rocca Guaita** dates from the 13th century and was extensively restored in the 19th and 20th centuries. Climb around the various ramparts—the castle has two towers, a chapel, and a prison. (Open daily May 15-Sept. 15 8am-8pm; March-May 14 and Sept. 16-Oct. 31 8:30am-12:30pm and 2:30-6:30pm; Nov.-Feb. 9am-12:30pm and 2:30-5pm. Admission L4000. A L6000 cumulative ticket also covers admission to the Rocca Cesta.) Continue on the castle trail to the **Rocca Cesta** (tel. 99 12 95). Inside you'll find an arms museum with armor, chain mail, spears, rifles, and other goodies. (Same hours as Rocca Guaita. Admission L4000, included when you buy the cumulative ticket.) The third tower, **Rocca Montale,** dates from the 13th century and can only be viewed from the outside.

Nearer the center of town is the **Church of San Francesco** (tel. 99 11 57) on Via Basilicus, which dates from the 14th century. Linked with the church is San Marino's **Museo d'Arte** and **Pinacoteca** (tel. 99 11 60), a well-exhibited but rather unimpressive collection of religious art and relics. (Museum has same hours as Rocca Guaita. Admission L4000.)

SOUTHERN ITALY

Campania

In the shadow of Mount Vesuvius, the fertile crescent of Campania cradles the Bay of Naples and the larger Gulf of Salerno. Looking out from Naples, the region's capital and chief port, Charles Dickens justly observed, "The fairest country in the world is spread about us." The fiery fields of Hades to the west and the desolate ruins of Pompeii hiding beneath the smoldering crater of Vesuvius belie this idealistic image of the region, yet captivate visitors nonetheless.

In the Great Book of Tourism it is written that Everyone Must Go to Pompeii, Capri, and Amalfi; fortunately, Campania also shelters equally worthwhile but more obscure treasures. Procida and Ischia make less-touristed island adventures for those bored with the pleasure-island of Capri and its steep cliffs, lush vegetation, and luminescent grotto. The historically inclined may well prefer the intact mosaics and frescoes of Herculaneum to those missing from Pompeii. Alternatively, explore ancient Greece at the temples of Paestum or the ruins of the Phlegrean Fields. And while you Must Not Miss the Amalfi Coast, a little exploration will reward the patient traveler with out-of-the-way gems.

Naples (Napoli)

Don't believe everything you hear about Naples; it's *not* that bad. True, its mile-long markets are bombarded by hordes of crazed shoppers and shouting merchants, traffic jams follow one after the other like recurring nightmares, stoplights are regarded as optional, and mopeds race down the sidewalk almost as often as down the street. But somehow Neapolitans thrive on this chaos, and the city has a remarkable vitality. Superb museums and wonderful Renaissance and Baroque churches reward those who can endure Naples's rough edges. Local cuisine is both exquisite and inexpensive, and lodging is remarkably affordable. Even the budget traveler can afford to splurge in Naples, and those who do treat themselves will have no regrets.

GETTING IN AND OUT OF NAPLES

Naples is southern Italy's transportation hub. Frequent **trains** from the Stazione Centrale connect Naples to Italy's other major cities, including the port of Brindisi. **Ferries and hydrofoils** run from Naples's Molo Beverello to the islands of Capri, Ischia, Procida, Sardinia, and Sicily. The tourist office brochure *Qui Napoli* and the newspaper *Il Mattino* both carry up-to-date ferry schedules. Hydrofoils (Alilauro and SNAV) leave the port of Mergellina for the islands and the peninsula of Sorrento. Ferry schedules and prices change constantly, so it's best to check ahead. Hitchhiking can be risky in and around Naples; solo travelers, particularly women, should seek other forms of transport.

Ferries: Prices between companies differ minimally; those listed below apply to weekdays in high-season. Prices are often higher on weekends.

Caremar (tel. 761 36 88). Ticket office on Molo Beverello open daily 6am-11pm. Hydrofoils and ferries to: **Capri** (4 per day, 1¼hr., L8800); **Ischia** (9 per day, 1¼hr., L8800); **Procida** (6 per day, 1hr., L7500). Less frequent in off season.

Siremar Lines (tel. 761 36 88). Ticket office at Molo Angioino (next door to Molo Beverello) open daily 9am-9pm. Ferries leave from there on sporadic days at 9pm, but never on Wed. Peak fares (July-Sept.) to: **Stromboli** (8hr., L70,900); **Lipari** (12hr., L78,600); and **Vulcano** (13hr., L79,300).

Tirrenia Lines (tel. 720 11 11). Ticket office at Molo Angioino open daily 9am-9pm. To **Palermo** (daily 8pm, 11hr., L69,100, L2000 port tax) and **Cagliari** (Oct.-May Thurs. 7:15pm, June-Sept. 5:30pm, late June-mid-Sept. also Sat. 5:30pm, 16hr., L65,000, L2200 port tax).

Trains: Information (tel. (147) 88 80 88). **Information booths** and *Digiplan* machines at Stazione Centrale. Both services open daily 7am-9pm. To: Milan (8hr., L61,800, express L83,700); Rome (1-2 per hr., 2½hr., L17,200); Syracuse (9hr., L51,200, express L70,600); and Brindisi (6½hr., L29,800).

Flights: Aeroporto Capodichino (tel. 789 61 11), on Viale Umberto Maddalena northwest of the city. Take bus #14 from P. Garibaldi in the city center, or call for info on the airport shuttle (tel. 531 17 06). A taxi from P. Dante should cost L25,000 with L1500 airport surcharge. Connections to all major Italian and European cities. **Alitalia,** Via Medina, 41/42 (tel. 542 51 11), off P. Municipio. Open Mon.-Fri. 8:45am-5:30pm. **TWA,** Via Partenope, 23 (tel. 764 58 28). No flights from Naples, but services Rome and other airports. Open Mon.-Fri. 9am-5:30pm. **British Airways** (tel. 780 30 87), in the airport. Daily flights to London.

TRANSPORTATION WITHIN NAPLES

Taxis: (tel. 556 44 44), no English spoken. Be sure to take only taxis with meters. L4000 plus L100 per 100m or 20sec. Minimum L6000. Sun. and holidays L2000 extra; 10pm-7am L3000 extra. L500 per piece of luggage.

Car Rental: Avis (tel. 554 30 20), at Stazione Centrale. Open Mon.-Fri. 8am-1pm and 3-7:30pm, Sat. 8:30am-1pm and 4-6pm. A small car that barely fits 5 will cost about L160,000 per day, L700,000 per week. **Hertz,** P. Garibaldi, 69 (tel. 20 62 28), rents small cars at L130,000 per day and L635,000 per week. Open Mon.-Fri. 8am-1pm and 2-7pm, Sat. 8am-noon.

Public Transportation: The system in Naples has been standardized so that one ticket is valid for all modes of transport: bus, train, *metropolitana,* and funicular (up the Vomero hills). Tickets are available in 2 types, either for 1½hr. (L1200) or the entire day (L4000). City buses congregate in P. Garibaldi outside the train station. All stops have signs indicating their routes and destinations. To cover long distances (i.e., from Mergellina to the station), use the efficient subway (tram #4). Three high-speed **local trains** head to the outlying towns: **Circumvesuviana** (tel. 779 24 44) to Herculaneum, Pompeii, and Sorrento; **Cumana** (tel. 551 33 28) to Pozzuoli and Baia; and **Circumflegrea** (tel. 551 33 28) to Cuma. Catch the Circumvesuviana at the Stazione Centrale (one floor underground) and the other two at the Montesanto station by the subway stop.

Buses #150 and 104: From P. Garibaldi to the city center (P. Municipio), the bay (Riviera di Chiaia), and Mergellina (for the youth hostel and Pozzuoli).

Trams #1 and 4: From the station to Mergellina. Stops at the Molo Beverello port. Catch it in front of the Garibaldi statue near Stazione Centrale.

Metropolitana: The subway system is convenient for service from the train station to points west: P. Cavour (Museo Nazionale), Montesanto (*Cumana, Circumflegrea,* funicular), P. Amedeo (funicular to Vomero), Mergellina, and Pozzuoli. Go to platform #4, 1 floor underground, at Stazione Centrale.

Funiculars: Connects the lower city to the Vomero and S. Martino: **Centrale,** the most frequently used, from P. Fugo on Via Roma/Toledo; **Montesanto** from P. Montesanto; **Chiaia** from P. Amedeo. Run Mon.-Sat. every 15min. 7am-10pm, Sun. reduced service 8am-7pm.

ORIENTATION AND PRACTICAL INFORMATION

Immense **Piazza Garibaldi,** on the east side of Naples, contains the central train station and the major city bus terminal. The broad, commercial **Corso Umberto I** leads southwest from P. Garibaldi, ending at **Piazza Bovio.** From here Via Depretis branches to the left, leading to **Piazza Municipio** and nearby **Piazza del Plebiscito,** an area of stately buildings and statues. On the water at the foot of P. Municipio lie **Molo Beverello** and the **Stazione Marittima,** the point of departure for ferries. Turn right from P. del Plebiscito and go up **Via Toledo** (also called **Via Roma**). Walk through the old quarter to **Piazza Dante,** the **university district,** and **Spaccanapoli**

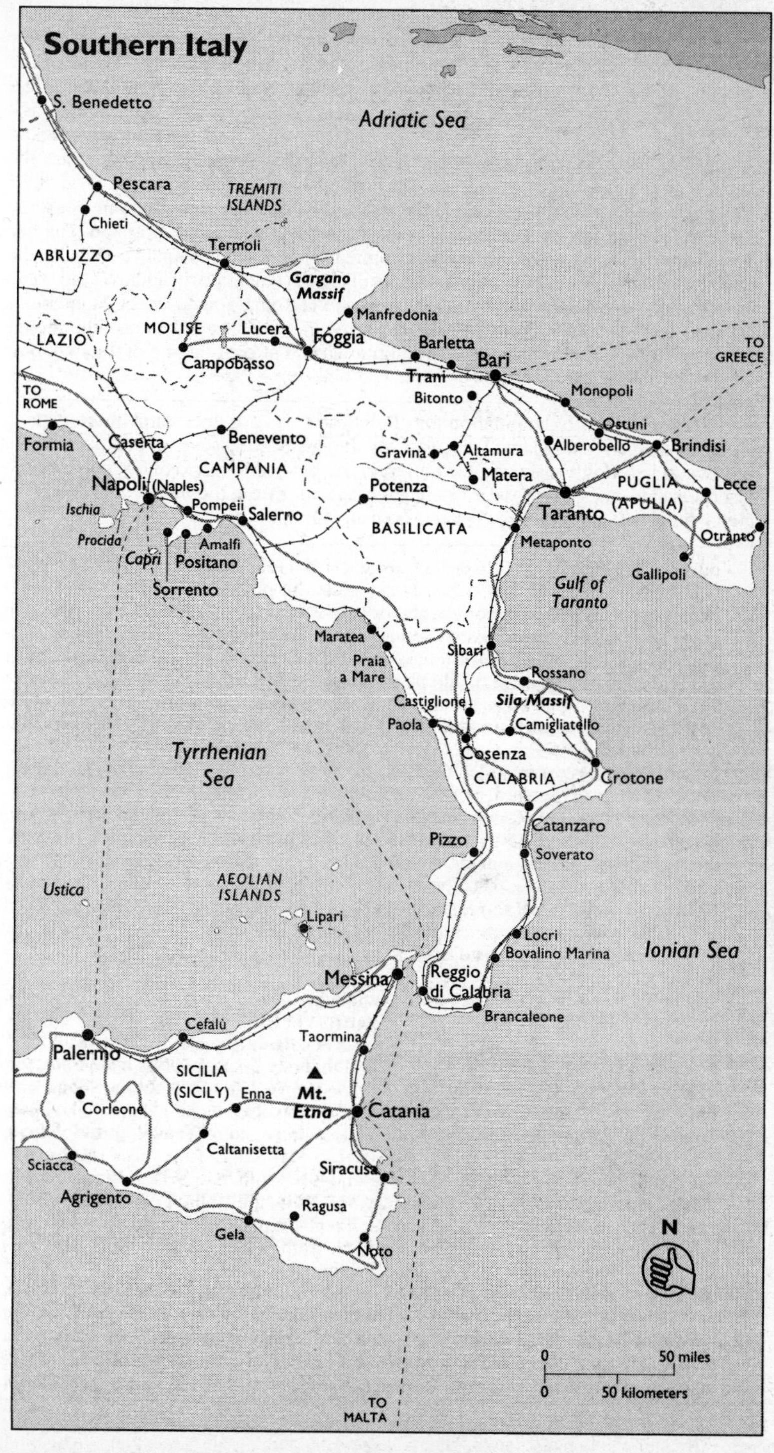
Southern Italy
S. Benedetto
Adriatic Sea
Pescara
TREMITI ISLANDS
Chieti
ABRUZZO
Termoli
Gargano Massif
Manfredonia
MOLISE
Lucera
Foggia
LAZIO
Campobasso
Barletta
Bari
TO GREECE
Trani
Bitonto
TO ROME
Monopoli
Ostuni
Formia
Caserta
Benevento
Gravina
Altamura
Alberobello
Brindisi
CAMPANIA
Matera
Napoli (Naples)
Potenza
PUGLIA (APULIA)
Lecce
Ischia
Pompeii
Salerno
Taranto
Procida
Amalfi
BASILICATA
Metaponto
Otranto
Capri
Positano
Sorrento
Gulf of Taranto
Gallipoli
Maratea
Praia a Mare
Sibari
Rossano
Castiglione
Sila Massif
Paola
Camigliatello
Cosenza
Tyrrhenian Sea
CALABRIA
Crotone
Catanzaro
Pizzo
Soverato
Ustica
AEOLIAN ISLANDS
Lipari
Locri
Bovalino Marina
Ionian Sea
Messina
Reggio di Calabria
Brancaleone
Cefalù
Palermo
Taormina
SICILIA (SICILY)
Mt. Etna
Enna
Corleone
Catania
Caltanisetta
Sciacca
Siracusa
Agrigento
Ragusa
Gela
Noto
N
0
50 miles
0
50 kilometers
TO MALTA

(literally "splitting Naples"), a straight, narrow street whose name changes every few blocks. Lined with palaces and churches, Spaccanapoli follows the course of the ancient Roman road through the middle of historic Naples. (Be careful not to get *yourself* split in two by the hordes of youngsters on mopeds who use this alley as a racecourse.) Along the coast past P. Plebiscito, you'll find the **Santa Lucia** and **Mergellina** districts and the public gardens, **Villa Comunale.** Farther west are the most scenic areas of Naples: hillside **Via Posillipo** (older than the historic quarter), **Via Petrarca** (winding up above Mergellina), and **Via Manzoni** (running along the crest of the ridge). A park crowns the cliffs of panoramic **Capo di Posillipo.** The hilltop **Vomero** district above Santa Lucia commands a view of Mount Vesuvius to the east, historic Naples below, and the Campi Flegrei (Phlegraean Fields) to the west. The Vomero can be reached by funicular from Via Roma/Toledo or the Montesanto station (northwest of P. Dante). If you plan to be in town for a few days, either invest in a detailed city map from a *tabacchi* (about L7000) or pick up one of the two tourist maps from a tourist office.

In spite of its terrible reputation for crime, Naples is not necessarily more dangerous than any other large European city. It does have its share of pickpockets, however, so don't make yourself a target for petty thievery. Follow common sense safety rules, don't wear flashy jewelry, and review the **Safety and Security** (page 18) and **Women Travelers** (page 30) info.

Tourist Offices: EPT (tel. 26 87 79), at the central train station. Helpful to a fault—you'll have to wait as they exhaustively assist the people in front of you. They'll even call hotels and ferry companies for you. Pick up a map and the indispensable guide *Qui Napoli,* featuring everything from train schedules to entertainment listings (in English and Italian). English spoken. Open Mon.-Sat. 8am-8pm. **Main office,** P. Martiri, 58, Scala B, 2nd floor (tel. 40 53 11), inside Ferragamo's *palazzo.* Take bus #150. Open Mon.-Fri. 8:30am-2:30pm. Also at **Stazione Mergellina** (tel. 761 21 02) and the **airport** (tel. 780 57 61). In theory open Mon.-Fri. 8:30am-2pm and 5-7:30pm. **AAST,** P. Gesù Nuovo (tel. 552 33 28). Take bus #185 up Via Roma toward P. Dante, get off at Via Capitelli, and follow it to the *piazza*—right in front of the Church of the Gesù Nuovo. Helpful and professional. Open Mon.-Sat. 9am-7pm, Sun. 9am-2pm. **Other offices** at Castel dell'Ovo (tel. 764 56 88) and the Palazzo Reale (tel. 41 87 44; fax 41 86 19). Both open daily 9am-2pm. For specific info on arts and entertainment, check out the *Posto Unico,* a poster/calendar covering events at theaters, restaurants, and clubs. **Qui Napoli Computer Information,** with multilingual terminals located throughout the city in public buildings and sights, conveniently offers tourist info and more.

Tourist Police: Ufficio Stranieri, at the Questura, Via Medina, 75, off Via Diaz. Assists with passport problems.

Budget Travel: CTS, Via Mezzocannone, 25 (tel. 552 79 60), off Corso Umberto. Student travel information, ISIC/FIYTO cards, and booking service. Open Mon.-Fri. 9:30am-1pm and 3-6pm, Sat. 9:30am-noon. **Eurostudy Travel,** Via Mezzocannone, 87 (tel. 552 09 47; fax 551 16 42). Open Mon.-Fri. 9:30am-1:30pm and 3-6pm, Sat. 9:30am-12:30pm. **CIT,** P. Municipio, 72 (tel. 552 54 26), and at the Stazione Marittima (tel. 552 29 60). The city's most complete travel agency. Open Mon.-Fri. 9am-1pm and 2:30-6pm. For ferry reservations to Greece, go to **Travel and Holidays,** Via Santa Lucia, 141 (tel. 764 01 29), near P. Plebiscito. Take bus #150 from P. Garibaldi. Open Mon.-Fri. 9am-1:30pm and 3-6:30pm, Sat. 9am-1:30pm. **Italian Youth Hostel Organization (Associazione Alberghi Italiani per la Gioventù),** Salita della Grotta, 23 (tel. 761 23 46). An excellent resource for info on youth hostels and special HI and Transalpino plane, train, and ferry discounts. HI cards L30,000. Open Mon.-Fri. 9am-1pm and 3-6pm.

U.S. Consulate: (tel. 583 81 11 or 761 43 03; 24hr. emergency tel. (0337) 79 32 84), on P. della Repubblica (sometimes called "P. Principe di Napoli" on maps) at the west end of the Villa Comunale. Passport and consular services. Open Mon.-Fri. 8am-noon; open 2-4pm for emergencies only. Bring proof of citizenship.

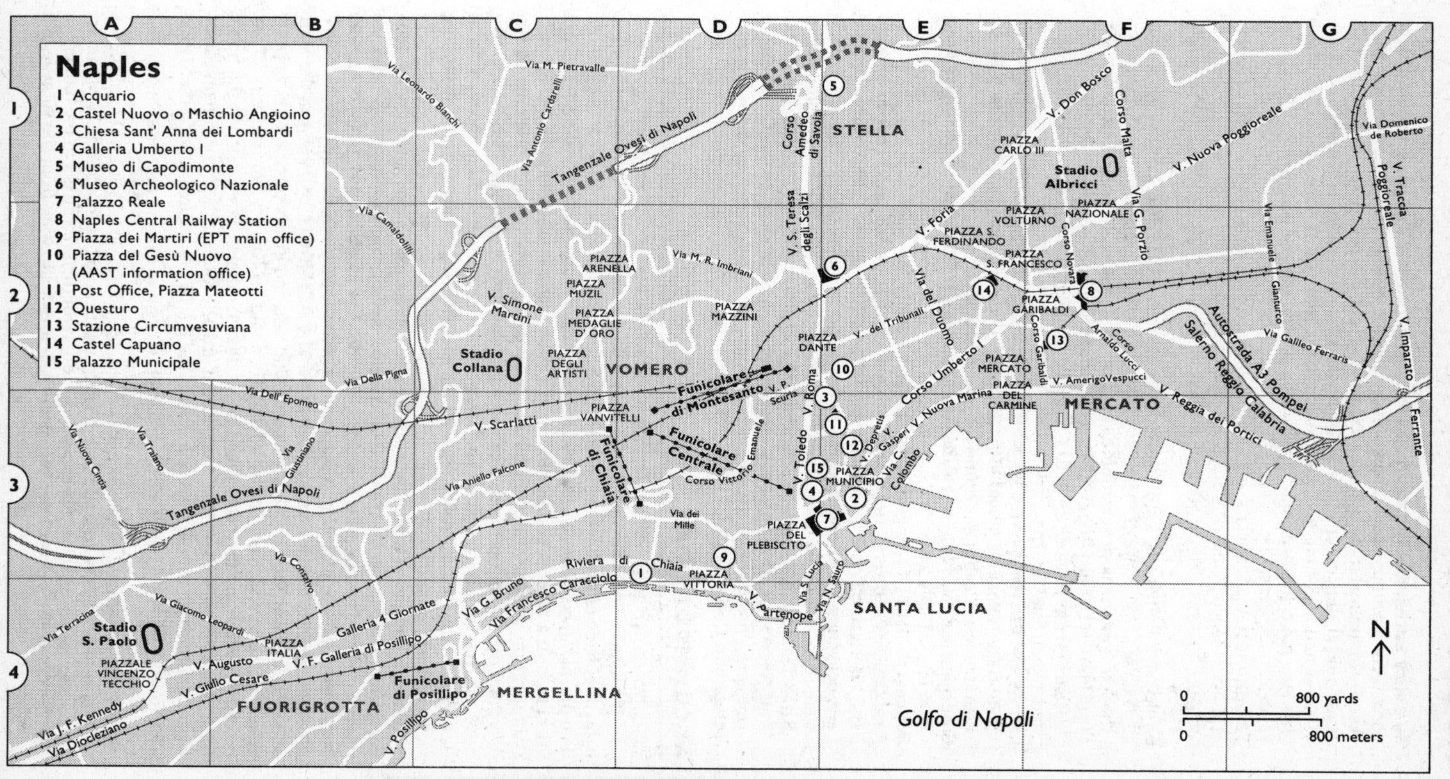
Naples
1 Acquario
2 Castel Nuovo o Maschio Angioino
3 Chiesa Sant' Anna dei Lombardi
4 Galleria Umberto I
5 Museo di Capodimonte
6 Museo Archeologico Nazionale
7 Palazzo Reale
8 Naples Central Railway Station
9 Piazza dei Martiri (EPT main office)
10 Piazza del Gesù Nuovo
(AAST information office)
11 Post Office, Piazza Mateotti
12 Questuro
13 Stazione Circumvesuviana
14 Castel Capuano
15 Palazzo Municipale
STELLA
VOMERO
MERCATO
SANTA LUCIA
MERGELLINA
FUORIGROTTA
Golfo di Napoli
Stadio Albricci
Stadio Collana
Stadio S. Paolo
Funicolare di Montesanto
Funicolare Centrale
Funicolare di Chiaia
Funicolare di Posillipo
Tangenziale Ovest di Napoli
Autostrada A3 Pompei
Salerno Reggio Calabria
PIAZZA DANTE
PIAZZA GARIBALDI
PIAZZA MUNICIPIO
PIAZZA DEL PLEBISCITO
PIAZZA VITTORIA
PIAZZA VANVITELLI
PIAZZA ITALIA
PIAZZA CARLO III
PIAZZA NAZIONALE
PIAZZA MERCATO
Corso Umberto I
V. Toledo
V. Roma
Via del Duomo
V. Foria
V. Nuova Poggioreale
Riviera di Chiaia
Via Francesco Caracciolo
V. Partenope
V. Posillipo
V. Scarlatti
0 800 yards
0 800 meters

Currency Exchange: The few banks willing to change money are slow and charge L3000 commission. Banks' main offices offer the most efficient transactions. Closest to the train station is **Banca Nazionale del Lavoro** (tel. 799 11 11) on P. Garibaldi, at the corner of Corso Umberto. Open for exchange Mon.-Fri. 8:30am-1:30pm and 2:45-4pm. You can also exchange money in Stazione Centrale, which has long hours but bad rates. Open daily 8am-1:30pm and 2:30-8pm.

American Express: The closest office is in Sorrento (tel. (081) 807 30 88).

Telephones: Via Depretis, 40, on the street off P. Bovio at the end of Corso Umberto. Open Mon.-Fri. 9:30am-1pm and 2-5:30pm.

Luggage Storage: Follow signs on ground floor of the train station. L5000 for 12hr. Open 24hr.

Bookstore: Feltrinelli, Via S. T. d'Aquino, 70 (tel. 552 14 36). Turn off Via Roma/Toledo onto Via Ponte di Tappia at the Motta restaurant. The store is 20m ahead on the left. An extensive selection in English, including yours truly. Open Mon.-Fri. 9am-8pm, Sat. 9am-1:30pm. **Universal Books,** Rione Sirignano, 1 (tel. 66 32 17), upstairs on the 1st floor, by Villa Comunale. Multilingual. Open Mon.-Fri. 9am-1pm and 4-7pm, Sat. 9am-1pm.

Late-Night Pharmacy: (tel. 26 88 81), at Stazione Centrale by the Ferrovie dello Stato ticket windows. Open Mon.-Fri. 24hr. On weekends, one pharmacy in the area stays open 24hr.; *Il Mattino* lists the schedule.

Emergencies: tel. 113. **First Aid: Ambulance,** tel. 752 06 96. **Psychiatric First Aid:** tel. 743 43 43.

Police: tel. 794 11 11. English speakers always available.

Post Office: P. Matteotti (tel. 551 14 56), on Via Diaz, which runs between P. Bovio and Via Toledo. *Fermo posta* L250 per letter. Offers special *EMS Servizi Postacelere,* delivering packages anywhere in the world in 3 days (from L46,000 for packages up to ½kg to the U.S.). Open Mon.-Fri. 8:15am-7:30pm (EMS only until 6pm), Sat. 8:15am-noon. Also at Galleria Umberto, 21 (tel. 552 34 67), and Stazione Centrale (tel. 553 41 21). Both open same hours as main branch. **Postal Code:** 80100 (for *fermo posta* at P. Matteotti).

Telephone Code: 081.

ACCOMMODATIONS

When you arrive at the central train station, hotel-hawkers will inevitably approach you. If you need to stay near the train station and all you want is a cheap bed for the night, following one of them may be the easiest route. If you're planning to stay more than one night, however, you may want seek out accommodations farther away from the station in a nicer section of town. The area around the **university,** between P. Dante and the *duomo,* offers good alternatives. Hotels here cater primarily to students and offer well furnished, clean rooms at low prices, though it's hard to find a room when school is in session. The **Mergellina** area at the far end of the waterfront (served by subway and trolley) has an inexpensive youth hostel and outstanding views of Vesuvius and Capri.

Although Naples has some fantastic lodgings at great prices, be cautious when renting a room. Don't give up your passport before seeing your room, always agree on the price *before* you unpack your bags, and be alert for shower charges, obligatory breakfasts, and the like. When selecting a place to stay, check for double-locked doors and night attendants at the main door. The **ACISJF** (tel. 28 19 93), at the Stazione Centrale near the EPT, helps women find safe and inexpensive rooms. Supposedly open Mon. and Wed.-Thurs. 3-7pm, Tues. and Fri.-Sat. 9:30am-1pm and 3-7pm, but don't depend on their scheduled hours. Phone numbers are posted at the booth (or try tel. 40 41 28). If you have a complaint, call the tourist office. For info on **camping,** check out some of the smaller towns in the Bay of Naples area, among them **Pozzuoli** (see page 421) and **Pompeii** (see page 431).

Ostello Mergellina (HI), Salita della Grotta, 23 (tel./fax 761 23 46). Take the *Metropolitana* to Mergellina and make 2 sharp rights onto Via Piedigrotta. Walk under the overpass and follow the signs up to your right (*before* you get to the tunnel), or tag behind the kid with the backpack. A 5- to 10-min. walk from the subway, not far from the waterfront and hydrofoil port. Well maintained 2-, 4-, and 6-person rooms, all with bath. Though there are 200 beds, reserve one in July and Aug. Lockout 9:30am-4pm. Check-out 9am. Curfew 12:30am. L20,000 per person. Breakfast, sheets, and shower included. Private doubles L44,000. Self-service cafeteria downstairs offers à la carte items and full meals for L12,000.

Pensione Teresita, Via Santa Lucia, 90 (tel. 764 01 05). Take bus #106, 128, or 150 from P. Garibaldi. Cozy, if a little run down. All rooms with TV, fridge, and telephone. Hall toilets and showers. Singles L35,000. Doubles L55,000.

Near Piazza Dante and Vomero

Take bus #185, CS, or CD from the train station to the bargain hotels around P. Dante. This area makes a great base for exploration of the historic quarter, although tourists should be cautious when wandering the narrow alleys alone or at night. To reach the chic Vomero, catch the *metro* to Montesanto and take the funicular up.

Soggiorno Imperia, P. Miraglia, 386 (tel. 45 93 47). From P. Dante, walk east through the arch to the left of the clock tower. Continue on Via San Pietro a Maiella, to the right of Pizzeria Bellini. Walk through P. Miraglia and look for the second set of large, bright green doors on the right side of the narrow street. Climb 4 floors to bright, clean rooms in a 16th-century *palazzo*. Young, friendly management accustomed to working with students. English spoken. Singles L30,000. Doubles L50,000. Call 1-2 days in advance during July-Aug. and at Easter.

Albergo Duomo, Via Duomo, 228 (tel. 26 59 88), near Via S. Biagio. Spacious white-and-baby-blue-trimmed rooms, all with TV and bath. Immaculate. Curfew 1-2am. Singles L60,000. Doubles L80,000. Triples L100,000. Quads L120,000.

Soggiorno Sansevero, P. San Domenica Maggiore, 9 (tel. 551 59 49), in Palazzo Sansevero. A small but charming hotel with large, attractive rooms, each named for a location or monument around Naples and decorated with a painting of that area. Singles with common bath L40,000, with private bath L70,000. Doubles L80,000, with bath L100,000. Extra beds L20,000.

Albergo Orchidea, Corso Umberto, 7 (tel. 551 07 21), Scala B, on the 5th floor (bring a L50 coin for the elevator). Take bus # 150, 152, or 104 from P. Garibaldi to P. Bovio. On this noisy but safe *piazza* (the police station is around the corner) you'll find dazzling rooms with high ceilings, small balconies, and great views. All rooms with private shower. Singles L65,000-70,000. Doubles L90,000. Triples L130,000. Quads L150,000. Prices lower Oct.-June.

Pensione Margherita, Via Cimarosa, 29 (tel. 556 70 44 or 578 28 52), on the 5th floor (bring a L50 coin for the elevator). In the Vomero outside the Centrale funicular station and downhill from the Montesanto station. The lowest prices in this posh residential district. Well kept rooms, some with terrace, in a peaceful location with kind management. Curfew midnight. Singles L46,000. Doubles L82,000. Extra bed L30,000. Breakfast and hall showers included (towel L1000).

Near Piazza Garibaldi

Although many hotels in the P. Garibaldi are worthy of your disdain, others are clean, safe, and even plush. Use caution and common sense when picking a hotel in this area, particularly if you are traveling alone or arriving at night.

Casanova Hotel, Via Venezia, 2 (tel./fax 26 82 87). Take Via Milano from P. Garibaldi and turn left at its end. Clean, airy rooms, knowledgable management, and a rooftop terrace with bar service. Some rooms with TV, fridge, and phone. Prices for *Let's Go* users: singles L25,000, with bath L35,000; doubles L51,000, with bath L60,000-69,000; triples L90,000. Breakfast L8000. V, MC, AmEx.

Hotel Ginevra, Via Genova, 116 (tel. 28 32 10). Turn right as you exit the station, walk 2 blocks up Corso Novara, and take the 2nd right onto Via Genova. Pleasant, spotless rooms. Solo women travelers may feel more comfortable elsewhere. English spoken. Singles L36,000. Doubles L60,000, with bath and TV L70,000. Triples L80,000, with bath and TV L95,000. 10% discount with *Let's Go.* Breakfast L5000. Laundry service L8000 per load. V, MC, AmEx.

Hotel Ideal, P. Garibaldi, 99 (tel./fax 26 92 37), to the left of the station. Its location steps away from the train station and its enormous, brightly lit sign make it a safe choice for travelers arriving late at night. Try to call ahead to arrange prices and arrival times. Elegant, well furnished rooms with TV and phone; modern and secure. English spoken. Prices with *Let's Go:* singles L40,000, with bath L50,000; doubles L60,000, with bath L90,000; triples with bath L100,000. Breakfast included. V, MC, AmEx.

Albergo Zara, Via Firenze, 81 (tel. 28 71 25; fax 26 82 87). From the train station, turn right onto Via Torino, then take the 1st left. Clean, old rooms, some with decorative ceilings. Cozy TV room. Singles, doubles, and triples L30,000 per person, L28,000 per person for groups of 3 or more.

FOOD

Pizza, that world-famous staple, was a Neapolitan invention. Skillful *pizzaioli* (pizza chefs) combine sweet local tomatoes, fresh mozzarella cheese, extra-light dough, and a wood-burning oven to yield an exquisite pie. Stands throughout the city sell slices of pizza fresh out of the oven for about L1000—popular late-morning snacks. Try the stands around P. Capuana and P. Mercato, to the north and south of the train station. Naples's most venerable (though not its oldest) pizzeria is **Antica Pizzeria Da Michele,** near the train station (see **Near Piazza Garibaldi** on p. 416 below).

Neapolitans love **seafood.** Fortunately, they prepare it well. Try fresh *cozze* (mussels) in soup or with lemon. Savor *vongole* (clams) of all varieties, including razor clams, and their more expensive second cousin, the *ostrica* (oyster). *Aragosta* (crayfish) is sweeter than lobster, and *polipi* (octopus) is one of the cheapest (and chewiest) sources of protein around. The city's most notable wines are *lacryma christi* ("Christ's tear"), usually accompanying seafood, and the red *gragnano.*

Spaghetti, now an Italian trademark, was first boiled in the kitchens of Naples — don't mumble any nonsense about Marco Polo and China to the Neapolitans if you want to stay on their good side. Today, the city's most famous pasta dishes are the savory *spaghetti alle vongole* (with clams) and *alle cozze* (with mussels); both creatures still reside in their shells atop the pasta when it is delivered to your table.

Naples's most beloved pastry is *sfogliatella,* filled with sweetened ricotta cheese, orange rind, and candied fruit. It comes in two forms, *riccia,* a flaky-crust variety, and *frolla,* a softer, crumblier counterpart. The city's foremost *sfogliatella* producer is **Pintauro,** Via Roma/Toledo, 275 (tel. 41 73 39), near the Centrale funicular station, a tiny bakery that has been around since 1785. It sells both varieties, piping hot, for L1800 each. Open May-July Mon.-Sat. 8:30am-7:30pm, Sept.-April Wed.-Mon. 8:30am-8pm.

Have fun at Neapolitan **markets.** On **Via Soprammuro,** off P. Garibaldi, you can create your own meal from the edible grab bag. Open Mon.-Sat. 8am-1:30pm.

Near Piazza Dante

The historic center around P. Dante, served by buses #185 and CD, shelters some of the city's most delightful *trattorie* and *pizzerie* amidst its narrow, winding streets. You'll find some of the cheapest and most authentic food on Via dei Tribunali.

Pizzeria Sorbillo, Via dei Tribunali, 35. A tiny hole-in-the-wall restaurant, but a testimony to Neapolitan pizza-making. The cheapest pizza in the area (from L3500). In

The Via to Margheritaville

Pizza Margherita will be the most common pizza variety you'll see in Italy, but it has nothing to do with tequila or Jimmy Buffet. This culinary tradition originated when the queen of Italy, Queen Margherita, visited Naples around the turn of the century. To honor her, a local *pizzaiolo* made her a pizza with tomato sauce, mozzarella, and basil—red, white, and green, the three colors of the Italian flag. *Buon appetito!*

summer, try your pizza with *filetto* (fresh tomato chunks) for L1000 extra. Beer L2000. Open Mon-Sat. noon-3pm and 7-11pm.

Papaloca/Le Bistrot dell'Università, Via Sedile di Porto, 51, off Via Mezzocannone near P. Bovio. Relaxed, informal atmosphere draws a college crowd. You'll be hard pressed to beat their L11,000 lunch *menù* (includes *primo, secondo,* and side dish). *Primi* from L4500. Cover L1000. Open for lunch Sept.-mid-Aug. Mon.-Fri. noon-4pm; Sept.-June also open Wed.-Sun. 7-11pm with Colombian fare.

Pizzeria Port'Alba, Via Port'Alba, 18 (tel. 45 97 13), inside the Port'Alba arch on the left side of the P. Dante clock tower. Established in 1830, this is the oldest *pizzeria* in Italy. Try the *Port'Alba* with *frutti di mare* (seafood, L10,000), or the pungent *pugliese* (with strong onions, L8000). Cover for *pizzeria* L2000, for restaurant L2500. Service 15%. Open Thurs.-Tues. 9am-2am.

Trattoria Fratelli Prigiobbo, Via Portacarrese, 96 (tel. 40 76 92). From P. Dante, walk 400m down Via Roma toward the port, turn right at the Motta restaurant, and walk 2 blocks. Dirt-cheap seafood *secondi,* such as roasted *calamari* (L6000). *Primi,* including *gnocchi alla mozzarella,* around L4000. Also has pizza (L4000-5000). Wine L2000 for a half-bottle. Open Sept.-early Aug. daily 8am-midnight.

Gelateria Della Scimmia, P. della Carità, 4 (tel. 552 02 72). The bronze monkey that hangs on the storefront practically symbolizes superior ice cream and desserts. Try the *formetta,* an ice-cream sandwich with thin, crispy wafers—you pick the flavors (L2000). Cones L2500-4000. Open Thurs.-Tues. 10am-midnight.

Piazza Amedeo

P. Amedeo, with its own metro stop, is a favorite hangout for Naples's youth. Along its scenic avenues, just north of the Villa Comunale, you'll find several trendy *caffè* and pubs. Restaurant prices are high, but explore the side streets for great finds.

Osteria Canterbury, Via Ascensione, 6 (tel. 41 35 84). Take Via Vittoria Colonna from P. Amedeo, make the 1st right down a flight of stairs, then turn right and immediately left. The area's best, most affordable lunchtime meals. The elegant interior, with lots of wood and fresh flowers, prepares your senses for a delicious meal. Devour the pilgrims' favorite *penne di casa Canterbury* (pasta with eggplant, cheese, and tomato sauce, afternoons L6000, L9000 at night). Cover L2000. Service 12%. Open Sept.-July Mon.-Sat. 1-3:30pm and 8:30pm-midnight. V, AmEx.

Pizzeria Trianon da Ciro, Via Parco Margherita, 27 (tel. 41 46 78), off P. Amedeo. This stylish place attracts a snobby crowd on weekends but has gained a popular weekday following for its large, tasty pizzas (L5500-10,500). *Pizza Trianon* is their trademark, with 4 sections piled with eggplant, *prosciutto,* ricotta, peppers, and mushrooms (L12,000). Service 15%. Open Mon.-Sat. 10am-3pm and 6pm-1am, Sun. 6pm-1am. Reservations may be necessary Sat. nights. V, MC, AmEx.

Mergellina

Take the subway or tram #4 to **Mergellina,** southwest of P. Amedeo on the waterfront, an excellent area for informal but hearty Neapolitan dining. **Piazza Sannazzaro,** in the center of Mergellina, is famous for its many *trattorie* which serve the beloved local *zuppa di cozze.* Via Piedigrotta and the surrounding streets also present affordable fare.

Pizzeria Da Pasqualino, P. Sannazzaro, 79 (tel. 68 15 24). Outdoor tables, amazing pizza (L5000-10,000), terrific seafood, and fried snacks. Know what's hot, Italian, mussel-bound, and will really spice up your evening? The *cozze impepata* (mussels in pepper broth, L8000) of course! Wine L3000 per bottle. Cover and service included. Open Nov.-Sept. Wed.-Mon. noon-midnight.

Vomero

A cable car transports you to Vomero, the city's favorite culinary enclave. Restaurants are generally expensive, but **Via Bernini** and **Via Kerbaker,** both off Via Scarlatti near the funicular stations, offer some reasonably priced *trattorie.*

Trattoria La Pentolaccia, Via Kerbaker, 124 (tel. 556 71 34). Enter around the corner at P. Durante, 1. A local favorite. Go for the house fish specialty, *farfalle salmone* (L7000). Small but varied menu changes daily. If you liked Thumper in *Bambi,* you'll love him *alla cacciatore* (L6500). Bunny-lovers can settle for the *pasta e fagioli* (L4500). Excellent house wines L4000 per liter. Cover L500. Open Mon.-Sat. 12:30-3pm and 8-11:30pm.

Trattoria da Sica, Via Bernini, 17 (tel. 556 75 20). Family-run. Serves traditional Neapolitan fare like *vermicelli alla puttanesca* (pasta with tomatoes, olives, and capers, L6000). A local hangout. Excellent wines from L4000 per bottle. Cover L1000. Service 12%. Open Oct.-Aug. Fri.-Wed. noon-3:30pm and 8pm-midnight.

Osteria Donna Teresa, Via Kerbaker, 58 (tel. 556 70 70). Wonderfully homey atmosphere. Try the excellent *pasta al forno* (baked pasta, L8000). The specialty is *spaghetti alle vongole* (L10,000). *Menù* L18,000. Wines L3000 per bottle. Open Sept.-July Mon.-Sat. noon-3:30pm and 8pm-midnight.

Love Me Tender Gelateria, Via Bernini, 100 (tel. 556 74 77). Elvis lives! Great *gelato* and all the Elvis paraphenalia you heart desires. Cones L2000-4000. Open daily 10am-1am.

Near Piazza Garibaldi

Tourist-ridden and expensive restaurants dominate P. Garibaldi. Fortunately, high-quality, low-cost meals can be found on the side streets just off the *piazza.* These areas become seedy at night, so eat early.

Antica Pizzeria da Michele, Via Cesare Sersale, 1/3 (tel. 553 92 04), to the right off Corso Umberto. Not far from the train station, near Pizzeria Trianon da Ciro. Only makes the two most traditional types of pizza: *marinara* (tomato, garlic, oregano, and oil, L4000) and *margherita* (tomato, mozzarella cheese, and basil, L5000). Open Sept. to mid-Aug. Mon.-Sat. 8am-11pm.

Trattoria da Maria, Via Genova, 115 (tel. 28 27 11), the 2nd right off Corso Novara. In a city where tradition, simplicity, and hospitality come first, Papà Riccio and his family have kept their small, unrefined *trattoria* true to the Neapolitan style. All pasta L5000-6000. The popular favorite is *penne "sciuè sciuè"* (pasta with mozzarella, tomato, and basil, L6000). *Secondi* from L6000. Local wines L5000-8000. Open Mon.-Sat. noon-3:30pm and 6:30-10pm. Closed Aug. 5-20.

Pizzeria Trianon da Ciro, Via Pietro Colletta, 44/46 (tel. 553 94 26), near Antica Pizzeria da Michele. From P. Garibaldi, follow Corso Umberto, take a right 200m down on Via Egizaca a Forcella, then a left at the 1st *piazza*. With marble tables and wood-burning ovens, this ancient pizzeria (the big sister of the one off P. Amedeo) is just as famous as Da Michele down the street. Many prefer its larger and more innovative selections (such as *8-gusti,* a pizza divided into 8 differently flavored sections, L12,500). Pizzas L5500-12,500. Service 15%. Open Mon.-Sat. 10am-4pm and 6pm-midnight, Sun. 6-11:30pm.

Avellinese da Peppino, Via Silvio Spaventa, 31 (tel. 26 42 83). From the train station, take the 3rd left on P. Garibaldi. In a well lit area. Locals and tourists dine at the outdoor tables, lured by tasty seafood dishes like *spaghetti alle vongole* (L7000). *Gragnano* wine L3000 per bottle. *Menù* L16,000, cover and wine included. Cover L1500. Service 12%. Open daily 11am-midnight.

La Brace, Via Silvio Spaventa, 14 (tel. 26 12 60). Across the street from da Peppino. Another great option in a ramshackle neighborhood. Hearty and inexpensive. *Primi* around L6000, *secondi* around L8000. Pizza (12" around) served all day, from L4500. Service 13%. Open Mon.-Sat. noon-midnight.

SIGHTS

Although much of Naples is beautiful, interesting, and friendly, the unpleasant region around the train station often deceives and disheartens first-time visitors to the city. **Piazza Garibaldi,** locally known as the "Zona Vasta," is a confusing conglomeration of hotels, bars, buses, and black-market dealers. Naples's main artery, **Corso Umberto,** leads away from the *piazza.* Although it is an impressive boulevard lined with beautiful cast-iron street lamps and 19th-century buildings, sections of it mutate into a transvestite strip at night. A couple of detours lead off the *corso* into the interesting alleys of old Naples.

Corso Umberto ends in **Piazza Bovio** at the 17th-century **Fountain of Neptune,** with a view over P. Municipio of the massive **Castel Nuovo.** Charles of Anjou commissioned the castle in the 13th century to replace the waterfront Castel dell'Ovo which was too susceptible to attack. Rebuilt to commemorate King Alfonso I's 1443 arrival in Naples, it is one of the earliest examples of Renaissance architecture in the city. Its doorway, the remarkable double-tiered **Laurana Arch** (1467), is topped by a finely modeled central panel depicting King Alfonso I in his chariot.

Continue away from the station past P. Municipio to **Piazza del Plebiscito,** the most regal square in the city. The enormous Neoclassical **Church of San Francesco di Paola** (1816-1831) stands opposite the **Royal Palace** (1600-1602). Rome's Pantheon served as the model for this huge church. (Open daily 7am-noon and 4-5:30pm.) On the second floor, the former royal apartments now house the **Palace Museum** (tel. 580 81 11) and the plush 18th-century **Court Theater.** Tapestries hang on many of the walls, and the palace exhibits an impressive collection of Romantic paintings. (Palace and museum open Tues.-Sun. 9am-1:30pm, Sat.-Sun. also 4-7:30pm. Admission L8000.) In summer the palace holds occasional concerts. Tickets begin at L4000.

Next to the palace stands the **Teatro San Carlo,** vying with Milan's La Scala as the most distinguished opera theater in Italy. Its gray-and-white Neoclassical façade dates from an 1816 reconstruction. Unfortunately, the theater itself is closed to the public except for shows. (Ticket office open Tues.-Sun. 10am-1pm and 4:30-6pm when there is a performance.) Opera season runs October to June. The cheapest tickets are L15,000, but this section is often sold out to season ticket holders. (Ticket office tel. 797 23 31, theater tel. 797 21 11.) Also neighboring the *palazzo* is the **Galleria Umberto,** a four-story arcade of shops and offices constructed between 1887 and 1890 in imitation of Milan's Galleria Emanuele.

Spaccanapoli (Historic Naples)

Starting at the side of P. del Plebiscito and stretching through the heart of the city's historic district is **Via Roma,** first called Via Toledo by the Spanish and still occasionally labeled that way on maps and signs. At the corner of the small, busy P. Trieste e Trento, off P. Plebiscito, rests the Jesuit **Church of San Ferdinando** (1622). Inside, a lectern, fonts, and chairs bear the emblem of the king of Spain. A Ribera painting of Sant'Antonio hides in the sacristy. (Church open daily 8am-12:30pm and 4:30-7pm.)

From the church, walk up the street and angle to your right through P. Carità to reach P. Monteoliveto, where you'll encounter the unassuming **Church of Sant'Anna dei Lombardi,** a museum of Renaissance sculpture. Its most noted work, Guido Mazzoni's *Pietà* (1492), sits in the chapel at the end of the right transept. Note the beautiful monument to Maria d'Aragona by Antonio Rossellino and Benedetto da Maiano in the Piccolomini Chapel, to the left of the entrance. (Open daily 7:15am-1pm.) Walk up Calata Trinità Maggiore from the church to reach **Piazza Gesù Nuovo.** On one side of the *piazza* stands the **Church of the Gesù Nuovo,** erected between 1584 and 1601, with a dark pyramid-grid façade taken from a 15th-century Renaissance palace. Colored marble and typically florid Neapolitan frescoes adorn the light interior. (Open daily 7am-1pm and 4-7:30pm.)

On the other side of the square rises the **Church of Santa Chiara** (1310), one of the principal monuments of medieval Naples. It was rebuilt in the Gothic style after World War II bombs damaged it. Sarcophagi and tombs from the Middle Ages litter the large, simple interior. Behind the main altar stands the impressive multi-tiered tomb of Robert I of Anjou, who died in 1343. As you exit the church, head to the right to enter the **Convent of the Clarisse,** an oasis of serenity amidst Naples's chaos. Vine-covered walkways crisscross the courtyard, bordered by columns and benches. (Church open daily 7am-noon and 4-8pm. Cloister open Mon.-Sat. 8:30am-12:30pm and 4-6pm, Sun. 8:30am-12:30pm.)

Take Via Benedetta Croce from P. Gesù Nuovo to the **Church of San Domenico Maggiore.** A 14th-century church with a 19th-century Gothic interior, San Domenico combines neo-Gothic pointed arches and windows with Neapolitan Baroque frescoes. The 13th-century painting that spoke to St. Thomas Aquinas, a resident of the church's adjoining monastery, hangs in the Chapel of the Crucifix on the right side of the altar. (Open daily 7:30am-noon and 4-7pm.)

Hidden on Via De Sanctis, a small side street off the upper corner of P. San Domenico Maggiore, is the **Chapel of San Severo.** The chapel, now a private museum, features several magnificent marble sculptures, including the 18th-century *Veiled Christ* by Sammartino. Downstairs, check out the two grisly 18th-century corpses. One legend claims that the alchemist Prince Raimondo of the San Severos, who built the chapel, murdered his wife and her lover by injecting them with a poisonous elixir that preserved their veins, arteries, and vital organs—you judge for yourself. (Open Mon. and Wed.-Sat. 10am-5pm, Tues. and Sun. 10am-1:30pm. Admission L6000, students L2000.)

Via Benedetto Croce, Via San Biagio dei Librai, and Via Vicaria Vecchia are just three of the names **Spaccanapoli** takes as it follows the course of the old Roman road Decumanus Maximus. This street in the heart of the old city is a narrow way enclosed by tall tenements and decaying *palazzi.* On Via San Biagio dei Librai lie the Renaissance **Palazzo Sant'Angelo** (#121), **Monte di Pietà** (Banco di Napoli, #114), and **Palazzo Marigliano** (#37). Via San Biagio ends at Via del Duomo, where you'll find the 18th-century **Church of San Giorgio Maggiore.** In the vestibule of its warm yellow interior stand the antique columns and walls of a 5th-century Paleo-Christian structure. Diagonally across from the church rises the beautiful Renaissance **Palazzo Cuomo** (1464-90). You can enter the foyers of most of these private palaces Monday through Friday from roughly 9am to 2pm.

One block uphill, to the left on Via Duomo, runs **Via dei Tribunali,** possibly the most representative of all Neapolitan streets. Try to avoid getting run over in the tiny alley as cars and scooters race between palaces, churches, and *pizzerie,* while black-market cigarette dealers peddle their wares from roadside fruit crates (offering discounts to local priests and *carabinieri*). Take refuge from this mayhem in the place where Petrarch once sought shelter from a terrible storm, the 13th-century **Church of San Lorenzo Maggiore** on P. San Gaetano, to the left on Via dei Tribunali from Via Duomo. Boccaccio first met Fiammetta here in 1334 as well. Inside, stop by the tombs of Catherine of Austria and Robert of Artois. (Church open 7:30am-noon and 5-7pm.) Don't miss the **Greek and Roman ruins** underneath the church that include an ancient city street lined with shops. (Excavations open Mon.-Sat. 9am-12:30pm. Free.) Grab a bite across the street at **Pizzeria Di Matteo,** Via Tribunali, 94 (tel. 45 52 62), a favorite hangout of students and presidents; as pictures lining the walls attest, Bill Clinton came here during his visit to the G7 conference in 1994. (Open Mon.-Sat. 8am-midnight.) Continue down Via Tribunali to the Neapolitan Baroque **Church of San Paolo Maggiore,** built on the ruins of a 9th-century church that had, in its turn, been built on the ruins of a Roman Dioscuri temple. You will then come to **Piazza Bellini** and the open excavations of the ancient Greek city walls, discovered underneath the *piazza.*

The shops of Naples's traditional artisans line Spaccanapoli and surrounding alleys in the historic quarter. Off the *piazza* of the church of San Domenico Maggiore, the **Calace Strumenti Musicali** workshop, Vico San Domenico Maggiore, 9, 1st floor (up the stairs on the left of the courtyard), still crafts mandolins, guitars, and other instruments by hand using techniques passed down through the generations. (Open Mon.-Sat. 8:30am-6:30pm.) **Scultura Sacra Lebro,** Via San Gregorio Armeno, 41, a family operation, is one of the last to produce hand-carved and painted religious statues. (Open Mon.-Fri. 9am-1:30pm and 4-7:30pm, Sat. 9am-1:30pm.) The most endearing shop in old Naples may be the tiny **Ospedale delle Bambole** ("doll hospital"), Via San Biagio dei Librai, 81 (tel. 20 30 67), near Via Duomo, founded in 1899. The mirthful shopkeeper is well suited to his merciful calling. (Open Mon.-Fri. 10:30am-1:30pm and 4:30-8pm, Sat. 10:30am-1pm. Closed 3 weeks in Aug.)

Unlike the cathedrals of other Italian cities, Naples's **duomo** loiters on an obscure *piazza* (on Via Duomo, to the left from Via San Biagio). The building was founded as a 4th-century Paleo-Christian basilica, to be rebuilt and consecrated in 1315. Although the façade is late-19th-century neo-Gothic, it retains its original doors. A Baroque veneer covers the Gothic arches in the interior, except in the two chapels decorated with 14th-century frescoes. Halfway down the left side, enter the **Church of Santa Restituita,** the first Christian basilica in Naples. Fragments of the original 4th-century structure remain as the nave's columns. Others are preserved in a 5th-century baptistery (the oldest in Western Europe) with a blue-and-green-frescoed dome. The entrance to the baptistery lies at the end of the right aisle. A beautiful 17th-century bronze grille protects the Baroque **Chapel of San Gennaro.** Reputedly, relics of St. Januarius located here stopped lava from Mount Vesuvius from entering the city. The high altar bears a silver reliquary containing the head of the saint and two vials of his coagulated blood. According to legend, disaster will strike the city if the blood fails to liquefy on festival days (the first Sat. of May, Sept. 19, and Dec. 16). Beneath the *duomo,* excavations have exposed remarkably intact Greek and Roman roads that run under the modern city. (Enter through S. Restituita. L5000 ticket also allows entrance into the baptistery.) Call for a special tour of the excavations (tel. 44 90 97). (Cathedral open daily 8am-12:30pm and 5-7pm. S. Restituita and excavations open Mon.-Sat. 9am-noon and 4:30-7pm, Sun. 9am-noon.)

Continue up Via Duomo and turn left at P. Cavour to visit the must-see **Museo Archeologico Nazionale** (tel. 44 01 66), a world-class museum that houses many of the astonishing treasures of Pompeii and Herculaneum. Since few pieces are adequately labeled, you should pick up an English guidebook at the souvenir shop (L10,000) or leave your passport at the information desk and borrow a copy of the museum's own guide (available in English). The tremendous sculptures of the Farnese collection are stored in the rooms upstairs to the right. The **Farnese Hercules** presents the hero at a rare moment of repose in his otherwise busy life, while the **Farnese Bull,** the largest known ancient sculpture, depicts the bull as it tramples Dirce (her punishment for mistreating Antiope, who stands by looking somewhat bemused). Upstairs on the mezzanine level, you'll find paintings and mosaics from the Vesuvian cities of Pompeii, Herculaneum, and Stabiae. Don't miss the tender *Portrait of a Woman,* the frescoes and furnishings from the Iseum at Pompeii, and the famous wall-size **Alexander Mosaic.** This mosaic, thought to be a copy of a Greek painting, depicts a young and fearless Alexander routing a terrified army of Persians led by King Darius. The top floor houses more paintings, some extraordinary statues taken from the Villa dei Papiri, and an extensive collection of ancient ceramics—vase-painting fans should definitely pay a visit. Unfortunately, many of the museum's exhibits close at inconvenient times (though groups are often admitted then anyway). Check at the info desk about tours leaving at 10:30, 11:30am, and 12:30pm. (Open Wed.-Sat. 9am-2pm, Sun. 9am-1pm; hours subject to change. Admission L12,000.)

Santa Lucia and Mergellina

The 12th-century **Castel dell'Ovo** (Egg Castle), a massive Norman structure of yellow brick and incongruously converging angles, stands on the promontory of the port of Santa Lucia, dividing the bay in two. (Open for exhibits only.) Sunbathers load the nearby seaside rocks on warm days. To the west lies the **Villa Comunale,** a waterfront park dotted with sycamores and palms and graced by sculptures, fountains, and an **aquarium** (tel. 583 31 11). The oldest in Europe, this zoological institute features a collection of 200 species of fish and marine fauna native to the Bay of Naples. (Open June-Sept. Mon.-Sat. 9am-6pm, Sun. 10am-6pm; Oct.-May Mon.-Sat. 9am-5pm, Sun. 9am-2pm. Admission L3000.) A streetcar runs along the Riviera di Chiaia, where at #200 you'll find the **Villa Pignatelli,** with one of the few verdant villa gardens left in the city. Walk along the bay in the late afternoon or early evening to see the Villa Comunale fill with locals taking their *passeggiata.* Via Sauro, in the Santa Lucia section, is the traditional place to watch the sunset. At the foot of the hills of Posillipo,

Mergellina affords the most celebrated view in Naples. Climb Via Petrarca for a post-card-perfect panorama.

Vomero and the Hills

The breezy calm of the hillside residential district of Vomero is an antidote to the frantic pace of the rest of Naples. Set aside a full morning, or perhaps two, to visit Vomero's important historical sights, the Villa Floridiana and the Monastery of St. Martin. Funiculars to this area leave from Via Roma/Toledo across from the Galleria, from P. Amedeo, and from P. Montesanto.

The **Villa Floridiana** (entrance at Via Cimarosa, 77) crowns a knoll embellished with camellias, pine trees, and a terrace overlooking the bay. The villa itself, a graceful white Neoclassical mansion (1817-19), houses the **Museo di Duca di Martina** (tel. 578 84 18), which contains porcelain, ivory, pottery, and several 17th-century Neapolitan paintings. A tranquil park surrounds the villa. (Museum open Tues.-Sat. 9am-2pm, Sun. 9am-1pm. Admission L4000, under 18 and over 60 free. Park open daily 9am-1hr. before sunset—typically 7pm in summer and 4pm in winter. Free.)

The huge Carthusian **Certosa di San Martino** (Monastery of St. Martin) rises from a spur of the Vomero hill near Castel Sant'Elmo. Erected in the 14th century, it was remodeled during the Renaissance and Baroque periods. It now houses the **Museo Nazionale di San Martino** (tel. 578 17 69), documenting the art, history, and life of Naples from the 16th century to the present. (Open Tues.-Sun. 9am-2pm. Admission L8000; under 18 and over 60 free.) The **Castel Sant'Elmo** (tel. 578 40 30), begun in 1329 under the Anjou reign, provides a remarkable view from its ramparts. (Open Tues.-Sun. 9am-2pm. Admission L4000.)

The **Museo e Gallerie di Capodimonte** (tel. 744 13 07) occupy a restored 18th-century palace in the sylvan hills north of the Museo Nazionale. Masterpieces and kitsch compete for attention along the walls; most of the former are on the second floor, the latter on the first. Among the many works are Masaccio's *Crucifixion,* Filippino Lippi's *Annunciation and Saints,* Parmigianino's *Antea,* Titian's *Portrait of Paul III,* Michelangelo's stunning drawing of *Three Soldiers,* and two Breughels—*The Allegory of the Blind* and *The Misanthrope.* The museum may be temporarily closed; call before you trek out. (Open Tues.-Sat. 10am-6pm, Sun. 9am-2pm. Admission L8000, under 18 and over 60 free.) Take bus #110 or 127 from Stazione Centrale, #22 or 23 from P. del Plebiscito, or #160 or 161 from P. Dante. (Gardens around museum open daily 7:30am-8pm; off-season 7:30am-5 or 6:30pm.)

Down Via Capodimonte from the museum is the **Church of the Madonna del Buon Consiglio,** which Neapolitans refer to as "Little St. Peter's." Inside, in the third chapel on the left (the Chapel to the Duchesses of Aosta), is a copy of Michelangelo's *Pietà,* slightly smaller than the one at the Vatican. Outside, under the portico, is a copy of his *Moses.* The 2nd-century **Catacombe di San Gennaro** (tel. 741 10 71; enter from outside the church) are noted for their frescoed early Christian chapels. (Guided tours daily at 9:30, 10:15, 11, and 11:45am. Admission L5000.)

ENTERTAINMENT

The monthly *Qui Napoli* and the weekly poster *Posto Unico,* both available at the tourist office, provide excellent info on happenings in Naples. Most of *Qui Napoli* is translated into English, including brief descriptions of the city's major sites and tour listings. *Posto Unico* publishes lists of films, *discoteche,* and clubs (in Italian).

Once occasions for famous parties, Naples's religious festivals have become times for sales and shopping sprees. The city celebrates the **Festa di San Gennaro,** patron saint of Naples, on September 19. The festivals of **Madonna del Carmine** (July 16) and the **Assunta** (Aug. 15) culminate in spectacular fireworks displays. During Christmas, hundreds of *presepi* (crèches) decorate the city, and on Easter the town hosts a large parade. In July the city hosts free concerts in P. S. Domenico Maggiore. Ask for information about the **Sole a Mezzanotte** series.

Most of Naples slumbers at night, except for the Sunday evening *passeggiata,* when the Villa Comunale along the bay fills with folks taking in the cool air. The young elite strut their stuff around **Piazza Amedeo.** Via Posillipo beckons those who savor the smell of the sea (take bus #140 from P. del Gesù Nuovo) and Via Petrarca is ideal for a romantic stroll (take bus #C21 from P. Plebiscito). Or join legions of amorous couples at the scenic park at Capo di Posillipo (take bus #140 to the end).

Naples' nighttime hotspots include **Piazza di Spagna,** Via Petrarca, 101 (tel. 575 48 82); **Chez Moi,** Parco Margherita, 13 (tel. 40 75 26; take the *metro* to P. Amedeo); and the larger **Madison Street,** Via Sgambati, 47 (tel. 546 65 66), in Vomero. A respectable crowd frequents all three. They feature dancing Friday through Sunday starting at 10pm and charge a L15,000-20,000 cover. (Madison Street puckers up during the week as well. All open Sept.-July.) Ask around to get the latest on the club scene. **Airone,** V. Petrarca, 123 (tel. 575 01 75) and its piano bar play host to a more mature clientele. Although Naples has no exclusively gay or lesbian clubs, **ARCI-Gay/Lesbica** (tel. 551 82 93) has free advice on nighttime hotspots and gay and lesbian nights at local clubs.

If you find the discos too pricey, check out **Piazza Bellini,** which closes to traffic on summer evenings. cafés and bars set out tables, and young people fill the *piazza.* You don't even need to order a costly drink (beer L5000 and up) to sit down.

SHOPPING

Throughout the city, but particularly in the **Duchesca** region (off Via Mancini near P. Garibaldi) and the **Pignasecca** region (off P. Carità), street vendors peddle belts, radios, shoes, and other inexpensive items. Never buy electronic products here—even brand-name packages have been known to contain only bricks. As in all crowded areas in Naples, hold on tight to your valuables on Pignasecca's streets. (Markets are generally open Mon.-Sat. 9am-5pm, but many close Tues. at 2pm.)

For those who prefer to window shop at fancy stores, the main shopping districts center around Corso Umberto, Via Roma/Toledo, Via Chiaia near P. Trieste e Trento, and Via dei Mille in the Santa Lucia region. The most modern and expensive shopping district is in the hills of Vomero along perpendicular **Via Scarlatti** and **Via Luca Giordano.** Two affordable clothing chains that sell contemporary Italian casual wear are **Wiscky & Coca** and **Omonimo.**

■ Near Naples: Campi Flegrei

The Bay of Naples originally served as a strategic trading port for the Greeks, who associated its westerly peninsula with the underworld. Hades didn't scare them off, however; imposing monuments from the earliest Greek colonies in Italy blanket the area. The volcanic lakes and bubbling mud baths of the Phlegrean (Burning) Fields later became posh Roman baths: spas for Roman elite. You can still visit the baths at Baia or see the area's impressive ruins at Cuma (Cumae)—though it might be more fun to swim at a local beach in Miseno. The sights of the fields are spread widely throughout the area, so allow a full day to see them.

POZZUOLI

Although somewhat shabby and neglected since an earthquake in 1980, **Pozzuoli** has several ancient ruins worth seeing. It is also the most convenient jumping-off point for the islands of Procida and Ischia and home to the nicest camping near Naples (and incidentally, the birthplace of Sophia Loren). Both the subway from Naples's Stazione Centrale (line #4, L1200) and the Ferrovia Cumana train from Montesanto in Naples (southwest of P. Dante, L2000) go to the town. The Ferrovia Cumana station is conveniently located on the port, while the *metropolitana* subway station is a 10-min. walk away. To get to the **port** from the subway, take Via Solfatara down a series of hairpin turns, then turn right on Corso della Repubblica and again on Via Cosenza. Grab a map and info on local sights at Pozzuoli's **tourist office,** P. Matteotti, 1A (tel. 526 66 39), where V. Solfatara and C. della Repubblica intersect under a bridge. (Ignore signs pointing to the administrative office.) Open Mon.-Fri. 9am-2pm; English spoken. **Traghetti Pozzuoli** (run by the parent company Linee Lauro) runs the most frequent ferry line to Ischia (18 per day in summer, 1½hr., L6500). **Procida Lines** runs (of course) to Procida (10 per day in summer, 1hr., L4000). Buy tickets at the *biglietteria marittima* on the port (tel. 526 77 36).

Pozzuoli's **camping** is the best in the area. Large and well run, **Camping Vulcano Solfatara** (tel. 526 74 13), up Via Solfatara past the *metro* stop, provides a swimming pool, restaurant, and access to the Solfatara Crater. In summer, L12,000 per person, L8000 per tent; 2-person bungalows L70,000, 4-person L100,000. Open April-Oct. For indoor lodging, stay in one of the four rooms at **Il Capitano,** V. Lungomare Colombo, 13 (tel. 526 22 83). Doubles L70,000. AmEx. Grab picnic supplies at the **fruit market** on the port, open 7am-1pm. If you like seafood, you can eat the fresh catch on a shady outdoor terrace at **La Trattoria da Gigetta,** Via Roma, 4-5 (tel. 526 15 63). Their specialty, *zuppa di pesce,* goes for L25,000, but you might try splitting it with a friend. Pasta dishes L8000-12,000, *secondi* L8000-12,000, pizzas L5000-10,000. Cover L2000. Open Thurs.-Tues. noon-3pm and 8-10pm.

Pozzuoli's **Anfiteatro Flavio,** built under the Flavian emperors in the first century AD, stands on Via Solfatara downhill from the subway station. Its unusually well preserved underground galleries held the machinery used to raise and lower animal cages. Open daily 9am-2hr. before sunset. Admission L4000. The **Tempio di Serapide,** on the port, was not a temple at all, but an ancient city market that just happened to enclose a statue of the god Serapis. An unusual form of volcanic activity, bradyseism—slow earthquakes that can raise or lower the entire region by several feet over the course of a few months—has intermittently submerged, shaken, and lifted this site. With its puddles of water and eerie, half-submerged pillars, the marketplace looks like a miniature Atlantis just risen from the sea. From Via Solfatara, to the right of the subway station, snag any of the city buses going uphill to reach the still-active **Solfatara Crater** (tel. 854 30 60). Alternatively, walk the easy route uphill from the metro station (20min.) to see the steaming fissures and bubbling mud. Open 9am-1hr. before sunset. Admission L6000.

BAIA

By way of the Ferrovia Cumana (L2000 from Naples or Pozzuoli) or from any of the **SEPSA** bus stops located throughout Pozzuoli (L1500 by bus; call 551 33 28 for SEPSA info), take the 20-min. ride to **Baia,** in ancient times considered a hotbed of hedonism. Today, this untouristed *parco archeologico* replaces the frustration of Pompeii's crowds and locked doors. See the ruins of past glory at the recently excavated **Roman baths** (tel. 868 75 92), one of the few extant ancient building complexes where you can climb stairs to the second and even third floors. Don't miss the so-called Temple of Mercury, a large, domed bath chamber whose floor lies underwater, creating an eerie echo chamber. Baths open daily 9am-2hr. before sunset (6:20pm in June, 3pm in Jan.). Admission L4000.

CUMAE (CUMA)

Take the bus from Baia (every 20min., L1000 on the Napoli-Torregaveta line) or the Circumflegrea train from Naples (L2000) to **Cumae,** one of the most impressive sites in the Campi Flegrei. Cumae was the earliest Greek colony on the Italian mainland (founded in the 8th century BC) and the mother of Pozzuoli, Naples, and many cities of the Magna Graecia. Its highlight is the **Antro della Sibilla,** a long cave-gallery that sheltered the Cumaean Sibyl, the most famous oracle west of Greece and the prophet who counseled Aeneas in Virgil's epic. In this great hallway, used as a pizza oven prior to its rediscovery in 1932, devotees awaited the Sibyl's prophecies. Ascend the acropolis to the ruined **Temple of Jove.** (Take the steep stairs that tunnel up through the rock.) Some people sneak into the huge gallery underneath the promontory; it leads past subterranean cisterns to other ruins farther inland. The whole sprawling site requires at least an hour's visit. Bring a flashlight. Open daily 9am-2hr. before sunset. Admission L4000.

A bit to the north is **Lake Averno,** a spooky haunt that Homer and Virgil described as the entrance to Hades. The castle off the point contains the **Archaeological Museum of the Campi Flegrei** (tel./fax 523 37 97), with sculpture and ruins from the area and a collection of ancient plaster casts of lost Greek sculpture. Open Mon.-Sat. 9am-1hr. before sunset, Sun. 8am-2pm. L4000.

Although you can visit both Baia and Cuma as daytrips from Naples, pleasant beachfront hotels abound in the nearby city of Misena. Take the Circumflegrea to Baia or Fusaro, then the SEPSA bus to Misena (L1000). At the last bus stop in Misena stands the **Villa Palma Hotel,** Via Misena, 30 (tel. 523 39 44), a modern and comfortable choice steps away from the beach and a short bus ride from Cuma and Baia. Singles L50,000. Doubles L65,000-70,000. Breakfast included.

Inland from Naples

CASERTA

There is little reason to visit Caserta, or rather, one very large reason: the magnificent **Palazzo Reale** (Royal Palace; tel. 32 14 00), locally called the "Reggia." Upon leaving the train station (45min. from Naples, L3400), you will see the palace smack dab in front of your face. Commissioned by the Bourbon King Charles III to imitate Versailles, the enormous building has 1200 rooms, 1790 windows, and 34 staircases. Frescoes and intricate marble floors adorn the royal apartments. Pass through the three libraries that hold original manuscripts, and you will come to the *presepe,* an immense nativity scene set in an Italian market. Open July-Oct. Mon.-Sat. 9am-1:30pm, Sun. 9am-1pm. Admission L8000. Behind the Reggia are the vast **palace gardens.** If you like to frolic barefoot in the grass, now's the time to do it (but don't let the caretakers catch you): three km of lush green lawns, fountains, sculptures, and carefully pruned trees culminate in a 75-m man-made waterfall. If you don't feel like attempting the long walk, take the bus (L1500) or a romantic horse-and-buggy ride (price varies). Pack a lunch and a bottle of water, especially if you plan to walk. Gardens open daily 9am-1hr. before sunset. Admission L4000. If you're around on July 26, catch the **Festival of Sant'Anna,** when music and fireworks light up the town. Early September brings concerts to Caserta Vecchia in a festival known as **Settembre al Borgo:** 20 nights of theater, comedy, music, and dancing.

One train stop from Casterta lies **Capua** and the remains of one of the most impressive Roman amphitheaters. Larger and more complete than Pozzuoli's amphitheater, this massive structure has a rival only in the contemporaneous Colosseum in Rome. From Caserta, take the train to the Santa Maria Capua Vetere stop (L2000). Walk straight one block, then make the first left onto Via G. Avezzana. Take your first left, then walk 150m and turn right onto Via E. Ricciardi, which becomes Via Amphiteatro. At the end, you can't miss the enormous ruins. Open daily 9am-1hr. before sunset. Admission L4000.

If you're too tired to trek elsewhere after touring the palace, gardens, or amphitheater, stay at **Hotel Baby,** Via G. Verdi, 41 (tel. 32 83 11), to the right as you exit the station. With friendly management and clean rooms, this hotel is a secure choice in the somewhat run-down train station neighborhood. Singles L70,000. Doubles L80,000. Triples L110,000. Quads L140,000. Hungry after a long stroll in the park? Try **O Masto,** Via S. Agostino, 10 (tel. 32 00 42), which has such homestyle meals as tasty *spaghetti alla carbonara* (L7000). *Primi* L6000-8000, *secondi* L8000. Open Tues.-Sun. 10am-midnight. **Tavola Calda Il Corso,** Corso Trieste, 221 (tel. 35 58 59), serves full meals with drink for about L18,000. Open Mon.-Sat. 10am-midnight. Caserta's **EPT** offices are located at Corso Trieste, 37 (tel. 32 11 37), at the corner of P. Dante; and in the Palazzo Reale (tel. 32 22 33). Pick up a brochure on the Reggia. Open Mon.-Fri. 9am-1pm. **Telephones** are at Via Roma, 53. **Avis Rent-a-Car** (tel. 44 37 56) is in the train station. Open Mon.-Fri. 9am-1pm and 2-6pm, Sat. 9am-2pm. The **post office** is on Viale Ellittico, to the left of P. Carlo III in front of the train station. Caserta's **postal code** is 81100; the **telephone code** is 0823.

BENEVENTO

According to legend, this town's original name was *Maleventum* (Bad Wind), but after the Romans defeated Pyrrhus here in 275BC, they decided it might be a "good wind" *(Benevento)* after all. Traces of the Roman Empire include **Trajan's Arch,** constructed in AD114, and the huge **Roman theater** from the 2nd century BC—one of the most complete in Italy (admission L4000). The Church of S. Sofia (762), with an attached monastery, has become the **Museo del Sannio.** Displays include a large collection of archaeological remains from the area that date as far back as the Iron Age. Open Tues.-Sun. 9am-1pm. L5000. Benevento can be reached by train from either Caserta (1hr., L5700) or Naples (2hr., L6900). From the train station, take bus #1 (L800 in *tabbachi,* L1000 on the bus) or just walk: head left on Viale Principe di Napoli, over the bridge, and left again on Corso Garibaldi (10min.). The **EPT tourist office** (tel. 254 24) hides in the far corner of P. Roma off C. Garibaldi. The office houses an amazing store of info on the town's monuments and on a few other cities as far away as Bologna. Open Mon.-Sat. 8am-2pm and 4:30-8pm. Benevento's **postal code** is 82100; the **telephone code** is 0824.

Albergo della Corte hides at P. Piano di Corte, 11 (tel. 548 19). Follow the narrow V. Bartolomeo Camerario, off C. Garibaldi, across from Banca di Roma. Newly renovated singles are L45,000, doubles L70,000, all with bath. They offer discounts for groups or extended stays. Near Trajan's Arch, **Ristorante e Pizzeria Traiano,** Via Manicotti, 48 (tel. 250 13), has scrumptious meals for about L22,000. Open Wed.-Mon. noon-11pm. Before returning to Naples, sample Benevento's *Strega* liqueur, appropriately named after the legendary powerful witches of ancient Benevento. The recipe is a centuries-old secret.

The surrounding countryside enchants with steep hills, farms, and vineyards. Visit the village of **Montesarchio** together with its 15th-century castle, or **Sant'Agata dei Goti** and its Romanesque cathedral. (The bus terminal is on Viale dei Rettori.)

BAY OF NAPLES: ISLANDS

Lingering off the shores of the Bay of Naples, the pleasure islands of **Capri, Ischia,** and **Procida** beckon the culture-weary traveler with the promise of beautiful natural sights and first-rate accommodations. Large **ferries** *(traghetti)* and **hydrofoils** *(aliscafi)* leave daily from Naples's Molo Beverello at the end of P. Municipio. (Take bus #150 or tram #1 or 4 from Naples's *stazione centrale.*) You can also head for the islands from Naples's Mergellina port or from Sorrento and Pozzuoli. The route via Pozzuoli, accessible on Naples's Ferrovia Cumana (L2000), may involve the least hassle for jaunts to Ischia and Procida: ferries are inexpensive and frequent.

■ Capri

The Roman emperor Augustus fell in love with this island's fantastic beauty in 29BC and swapped its more fertile neighbor, Ischia, for it. His successor Tiberius passed his last decade here in the island's natural splendor, leaving several villas scattered about. Today's visitors seem content to pay top *lira* for mass boat excursions to the renowned Blue Grotto and to gawk at the rich and famous in Capri's town center, Piazza Umberto I. Yet solitude lurks a short walk from the city center. You might consider renting a moped on the mainland and bringing it to Capri or Ischia on the ferry, since distances between sights, ports, and hotels are great. **Be sure to wear a helmet when riding a moped:** drivers in Capri are kamikaze, and traffic rules are enforced. The efficient buses will serve those without death wishes.

Most budget travelers avoid the high prices of Capri and find solace in **Anacapri,** literally "over Capri," which sits high on a plateau of **Monte Solaro** (589m). It is less frequented by daytrippers and qualifies as a budget version of paradise. Due to the ever-present English- and German-speaking crowds, most residents of the island are trilingual and usually prefer to speak in English than wait for your attempts at Italian.

ORIENTATION AND PRACTICAL INFORMATION

Most ferries dock at **Marina Grande** on the north side of the island. From here the **funicular** runs to **Piazza Umberto** in the town of Capri (every 15min., 6:30am-9:20pm, L1500). Buses leave from town to **Marina Piccola** (on the south shore) and **Anacapri** (every 15min., 6:30am-1:40am, L1500). Expensive clothing stores and pastry shops crowd the narrow streets that radiate off P. Umberto. **Via Roma,** to the right, leads to Anacapri after winding up the mountain. The bus to Anacapri also follows this route and drops you in **Piazza Vittoria. Via Giuseppe Orlandi,** running in both directions from P. Vittoria, leads to the cheapest and best establishments.

Tourist Office: In Capri, at the end of the dock at Marina Grande (tel. 837 06 34). Open Mon.-Sat. 8:30am-8:30pm, Sun. 8:30am-2:30pm. Also in P. Umberto, under the clock (tel. 837 06 86). Open Mon.-Sat. 8:30am-10pm, Sun. 8:30am-2:30pm in the summer. In Anacapri, the information office is at Via Orlandi, 19/A (tel. 837 15 24), off the main *piazza,* to the right as you get off the bus. Open Mon.-Sat. 8:30am-8:30pm; Nov.-May 9am-3pm.

Currency Exchange: Cambio, Via Roma, 33 (tel. 837 07 85), across from the main bus stop in Capri. Open daily 8:30am-9pm. Also at P. Vittoria, 2 (tel. 837 31 46), in the center of Anacapri. Open March-Nov. daily 8am-6pm. Worse rates than at the post office but no commission (either location).

Telephones: (tel. 837 55 50). Behind the funicular stop in Capri. Public fax. Open daily 9am-1pm and 3-11pm; Oct.-June 9am-1pm and 3-8pm. Public phones in Anacapri at P. Vittoria, 4 (tel. 837 33 77). Open daily March-Sept. 8am-7pm; Oct.-Feb. 9am-1pm and 3-7pm.

Buses: (tel. 837 04 20). In Capri, buses depart from Via Roma for Anacapri, Marina Piccola, and points in between. In Anacapri, buses depart from P. Barile off Via Orlandi for the Grotta Azzurra (Blue Grotto), the *faro* (lighthouse), and other points nearby. There's also a direct bus line between Marina Grande and P. Vittoria in Anacapri. Buses cost L1500 per ride; tickets available on the bus.

Ferries: Caremar (tel. 837 07 00) runs ferries from Naples's Beverello port to Capri (6 per day, 6:30am-7:40pm, last return 6pm, L8800) and from Sorrento (5 per day, 7:55am-7:40pm, last return 6:45pm, L5200). **Alilauro's** hydrofoil (tel. 837 75 77) runs to and from Ischia once daily (L18,000).

Luggage Storage: Caremar ticket office (tel. 837 07 00) in Marina Grande, L2000 per bag. Also at the funicular in Capri (L2000 per bag) and in P. Vittoria in Anacapri (L2000 per bag). Open daily 7am-8pm.

Public Toilets and Showers: At the funicular in Capri (L500) and at P. Vittoria, 5, in Anacapri (L500, showers L2500).

Swimming Pool: Bagni Nettuno, Via Grotta Azzurra, 46 (tel. 837 13 62), above the Blue Grotto in Anacapri. Take the bus from Anacapri center. Full use of outdoor pool, reclining chair, shower, and changing room surrounded by scenic cliffsides for a special *Let's Go* price of L10,000 per day (regularly L15,000). From their cove, you can easily swim into the Blue Grotto (see **Sights** on p.427). Open mid-March to mid-Nov. daily 9am-7pm.

Emergencies: tel. 113. **First Aid:** (tel. 837 81 49). For minor medical assistance in summer, call the **Guardia Medica Turistica** in Capri (tel. 837 10 12). **Hospital: Ospedale Capilupi,** Via Provinciale Anacapri (tel. 837 00 14 or 837 87 62), between Capri and Anacapri.

Police: Via Roma (tel. 837 72 45). They'll connect you with an English speaker.

Post Office: Central office in Capri on Via Roma (tel. 837 72 40), a couple of blocks downhill from P. Umberto. Open Mon.-Sat. 8:15am-7:20pm. **Changes money** at the best rate in town. L2000 commission, L5000 for sums over L100,000. Open Mon.-Fri. 8:15am-6pm, Sat. 8:15am-1pm. Another office in Anacapri at Viale de Tommaso, 4 (tel. 837 10 15). Open Mon.-Fri. 8:15am-1:30pm, Sat. 8:15am-noon. **Postal code:** 80073.

Telephone code: 081.

ACCOMMODATIONS

Call in advance and reconfirm reservations—it's possible to find impromptu vacancies in July but not in August. Makeshift camping is illegal, and heavy fines are strictly imposed. Note that budget accommodations in Capri town are nonexistent.

Anacapri

Villa Eva, Via La Fabbrica, 8 (tel. 837 15 49 or 837 20 40). Set high among the gardens and trees, this hotel is the perfect vacation setting. A scenic 30-min. walk from the Grotta Azzurra and a 15-min. walk from P. Vittoria. Call from the port and Mamma Eva or her husband Vincenzo will pick you up. Vincenzo built the beautiful rooms, bar, and swimming pool (admission L4000). They also provide a barbecue for your use. L25,000 per person. Private doubles L60,000, Sept.-June L50,000. Group discounts. Call a few days in advance to confirm your reservations, especially in Aug. English spoken. V, MC, AmEx.

Hotel Caesar Augustus, Via Orlandi, 4 (tel. 837 14 21), another 100m past Hotel Loreley. It's difficult to dispute their claim of the "most beautiful view in the world." Once the most expensive luxury hotel on the island, it still retains much of the luxury without the cost. All rooms with terrace and bath. Singles L40,000 and doubles L80,000 upon mention of *Let's Go*. Open Easter-Oct.

Il Girasole, Via Linciano, 47 (tel./fax 837 23 51). A great place for students and backpackers: a comfortable terrace, well kept rooms, a private pool (L5000), and inexpensive meals. Call from Marina Grande and they'll pick you up, or walk 5min. from the last bus stop in P. Caprile. L40,000 per person, Sept.-June L35,000. V, MC, AmEx.

Hotel Loreley, Via G. Orlandi, 16 (tel. 837 14 40; fax 837 13 99), 100m back toward Capri from P. Vittoria. Large, bright rooms with baths. Special *Let's Go* prices: singles L50,000, Sept.-June L45,000; doubles L100,000, Sept.-June L80,000. Breakfast L5000. Open April-Oct. V, MC, AmEx.

Capri Town

Pensione Quattro Stagioni, Via Marina Piccola, 1 (tel. 837 00 41). From P. Umberto, walk 5min. down Via Roma. Turn left at the 3-pronged fork in the road and look for the 2nd gate on the left. Though hot in summer, the cozy flower-filled rooms are spotless and have sensational views. All rooms with bath. Singles L80,000. Doubles L130,000. Breakfast included. 10-15% discounts Sun.-Fri. and during low-season. Half-pension required in Aug., L150,000. Open March 15-Oct.

FOOD

Capri's food is as glorious as its panoramas. Savor the local *mozzarella* on its own, or with tomatoes, oil, and basil in a dish known as *insalata caprese*—many consider it the best summer meal in the world. The *ravioli alla caprese* is hand-stuffed with the tastiest of local cheeses. Don't miss the *torta di mandorla* (chocolate almond cake). Accompany meals with the local red and white wines, which bear the *Tiberio* label. Restaurants often serve *Capri DOC,* a light white wine. If restaurant prices make you gasp, buy food from one of the groceries instead. Take the right prong of the fork at the end of Via Roma in Capri town to reach the **STANDA** supermarket. Open Mon.-Sat. 8:30am-1:30pm and 5-8pm, Sun. 9am-noon; July-Aug. Mon.-Sat. 8:30am-1:30pm and 5-9pm, Sun. 9am-noon. Ask at your hotel for local low-cost restaurants, but don't expect to pay less than L25,000 for a full meal.

Anacapri

Ristorante Il Cucciolo, Nuova Trav. Veterino, 50 (tel. 837 19 17). A preview of paradise, this restaurant is a wonderful stop on a walk back from the Grotta Azzurra and a must for guests at Villa Eva (only 5min. away). Follow the signs from the bus stop for Villa Damecuta. The fish is fresh, the herbs come straight from the garden, and everything is served on a terrace with expansive views of the bay. The *ravioli caprese* (L9000) and *agnolotti* (pasta stuffed with spinach and ricotta, L8500) are delicious. Cover L2750. Open March 15-Oct. 20 Wed.-Mon. noon-3pm and 7pm-midnight.

Trattoria Il Solitario, Via Orlandi, 96 (though the tile says #54; tel. 837 13 82), 5min. from P. Vittoria. An amazingly tranquil, ivy-covered hideaway. *Cannelloni alla caprese* L9000, homemade pasta L9000, salads L5000. Cover L2500. *Menù* L15,000. Open daily 12:15-3pm and 7pm-midnight; Sept. 21-June 19 closed Mon.

Le Arcate, Via T. de Tommaso, 24 (tel. 837 33 25 or 837 35 88). Located a few steps off P. Vittoria on the main road heading away from Capri. Sample generous portions of pasta (L7000-10,000), excellent seafood dishes, lighter sandwiches, and even hamburgers (L3500). Cover and service charges waived upon mention of *Let's Go.* Open daily noon-3pm and 7pm-2am; in winter closed Thurs.

Capri Town

Buca di Bacco, Via Longano, 35 (tel. 837 07 23), off P. Umberto I. Elegant yet affordable. *Pennette alla bacco* (L9000) is the specialty. Pizza at night L6000-11,000. Service 15%. Open Dec.-Oct. Thurs.-Tues. noon-2:30pm and 7-11pm. Open Wed. in Aug. V, MC, AmEx.

Moscardino, Via Roma, 28 (tel. 837 06 87). Limited but excellent selection in a maritime setting. *Primi* L8000-15,000, *secondi* L11,000-30,000. Cover L2500. Service 11%. Open Tues.-Sun. 11am-3pm and 7pm-1am. V, MC, AmEx.

SIGHTS AND ENTERTAINMENT

There is no question about it: visitors to Capri must see **Grotta Azzurra** (Blue Grotto). Light enters the cavern through a hole in the rock beneath the water, causing the whole grotto to glow a fantastic neon blue. Unfortunately, visiting is expensive if you want to stay dry: L15,000 plus tip pays for boat "tours" barely long enough to let your eyes adjust. Thousands of tourists each week find it worth the cost, but locals say the most impressive way to visit is to swim when the boats stop running (before 9am or after 6pm). Visitors who try this excursion go with friends (for safety) and only when the waters are calm, as the entrance to the grotto is small and rocky. You can get to the grotto by motorboat from Marina Grande (about L10,000) or by bus from Anacapri.

Leaving every day from Marina Grande at 9am, **boat tours** show you Capri's coast from the most impressive vantage point for L18,000. There are many rock and pebble **beaches** around the island. Take a boat from the port (L8000) or descend north between vineyards from P. Umberto to **Bagni di Tiberio,** a bathing area amid the ruins of an imperial villa. A bus or a 10-min. walk down the path (to the left where Via Roma splits in three) brings you to the gorgeous southern seaside stretch of Marina Piccola. Cavort in the clear water among immense lava rocks or rent a **kayak** or a **motor boat** (L8000 and L30,000 per hr. respectively). Call Bagni le Sirene (tel. 837 76 88) for more info.

If you prefer the **cliffs** to the sea, take Via Longano from P. Umberto in Capri center and then make the trek up to the left on Via Tiberio to the Roman emperor Tiberius's ruined but still magnificent **Villa Jovis** (1hr.). Legend has it that Tiberius tossed those who displeased him over the precipice; *Let's Go* advises walking down. (Open daily 9am-1hr. before sunset. Admission L4000.) The view of Capri from the nearby chapel **Santa Maria del Soccorso** is unrivalled. On the descent along the path, a short detour takes you to the **Arco Naturale,** a majestic stone arch, off Via Matermania on the eastern cliffs. On a clear day you can see as far as Paestum through the weathered arch. The *belvedere* (scenic overlook) from **Punta Cannone** shows off the dramatic cliffs of the southern coast. Capri's tourist office can suggest walking itineraries to see the less-touristed parts of the island.

Until the completion of the cliffhanging roadway a few decades ago, only a narrow Phoenician staircase joined **Anacapri** to the lower town. Luckily, you have the opportunity to take the bus (L1500). Upstairs from P. Vittoria and to the left (past Capri's Beauty Farm) you'll find **Villa San Michele.** The villa was the lifelong work of Swedish author and physician Axel Munthe, who built it earlier this century on the site of one of Emperor Tiberius's villas. Henry James called it "the most fantastic beauty, poetry, and inutility that I have ever seen clustered together." The villa houses remarkable classical sculptures retrieved from Capri's sea bottom. (Open in summer 9am-6pm; in winter 10am-3pm. Admission L6000.)

From P. Vittoria in Anacapri, take the 12-min. chairlift (roundtrip L7500) to the top of **Monte Solaro.** (Open daily 9:30am-1hr. before sunset.) The view is terrific: on a clear day, you can see the Apennines to the east and the mountains of Calabria to the south. A bus from the central *piazza* leads to the **faro,** Italy's second-tallest lighthouse, where you can snorkel, tan, or dive from the rocks along with countless Italians. Call the Capri Diving Club (tel. 837 14 40) for **scuba** lessons or equipment rentals. Follow the yellowish brick road of Via Orlandi off P. Vittoria in Anacapri to reach the most inexpensive (but still expensive) tourist **shopping** on Capri.

Nighttime action doesn't come cheap either. The largest club in Anacapri is **Zeus,** Via Orlandi, 21 (tel. 837 11 69). Admission is L30,000, but passes from local hotels, including the ones we list, slash L10,000. (Women often get in free.) For live music, head down the street to **Underground,** Via Orlandi, 259 (tel. 837 25 23).

Ischia

Across the bay from overrun Capri, larger, less glamorous Ischia (EES-kee-yah) displays a variety of landscapes, including beautiful beaches, natural hot springs, ruins, forests, vineyards, lemon groves, and a once-active volcano. According to Greco-Roman mythology, the island is home to the giant Typhoeus, who responded to Jupiter's scorn with the fury of volcanoes. Now he seems content simply to heat the hot springs of the area's many exclusive spas.

ORIENTATION AND PRACTICAL INFORMATION

The bus (route 1) follows the coast in a counterclockwise direction, passing most of the island's towns and points of interest. From **Ischia Porto** (an almost perfectly circular port formed by the crater of an extinct volcano) you come to **Casamicciola Terme,** with its overcrowded beach, and then to **Lacco Ameno**—the oldest Greek settlement in the western Mediterranean, now known for the island's cleanest boardwalk. The bus heads on to **Forio,** the hippest area on Ischia thanks to its tree-lined streets and popular bars.

Tourist Office: (tel. (081) 99 11 46; fax 98 19 04), at the midpoint of the main port. Open Mon.-Sat. 8am-1pm and 3-8pm. Some English spoken. Has listings of local tours and can help with accommodations.

Buses: SEPSA, in P. Trieste, the main departure point (just off Ischia Porto). Buses leave every 30min., 5am-midnight (one way L1200). Morning (L2500), afternoon (L2800), and full-day (L4000) tickets are valid to destinations all over the island. Don't neglect to purchase tickets, as employees check often.

Ferries: Caremar (tel. 99 17 81) and **Linee Lauro** (tel. 837 75 77) have main offices right by the tourist office. Caremar is generally less expensive. Ferries to Ischia from: Naples (almost every hr. 8am-7pm, L8800) and Pozzuoli (3 per day, L6100); Procida (8 per day, L3400). Linee Lauro runs from Sorrento to Ischia (L16,000) and connects the island to Capri with a hydrofoil once daily (L18,000).

ACCOMMODATIONS

The abundant hotels in Ischia run the gamut from reasonable to exorbitant. Most *pensioni* are in Forio; stay in Ischia Porto only if you want to be close to the ferries. By late July and August, rooms are hard to come by without reservations made a month in advance. Few hotels offer singles, and since rooms are in such high demand, some hotel owners may not rent rooms for just one night. There are several good camping options to make the island easier on your money belt.

Forio

Pensione di Lustro, Via Filippo di Lustro, 9 (tel. 99 71 63). Close to the Forio beaches. At first you might think you've mistakenly stumbled into botanical gardens—the central courtyard and stairs overflow with tropical plants. Large terrace provides gorgeous views. Truman Capote slept here in '68. *Let's Go* price: doubles with bath in June L85,000; July-Aug L100,000. Prices lower in off-season.

Hotel Villa Franca and **Baia Verde,** Strada Statale 270, #183 (tel. 98 74 20; fax 98 70 81). Take bus #1, 1/, or C.S. from Ischia Porto and get off at the stop for the San Francesco beach. Two hotels with the same prices and the same management. Good for families. Well kept rooms, many with terrace. A pretty patio, and 3 swimming pools: 2 cold mineral baths and 1 thermal bath. A 15-min. walk from the beach. English spoken. All rooms with bath. *Let's Go* prices: singles L45,000; doubles L80,000. Breakfast included. Half-pension L55,000 for singles, L100,000 for doubles. Open March-Oct.

Casamicciola Terme

Pensione Quisisana, P. Bagni, 34 (tel. 99 45 20). Take bus #3 from the port to the *piazza*. Comfortable, family-run establishment with luxurious rooms. A 15-min. walk from the beach. Curfew midnight. Doubles with bath L65,000-67,000. In Aug. obligatory full-pension L63,000-66,000 per person, depending on the room. Extra bed 25% more. Open May-Oct.

Ischia Porto

Il Crostolo, Via Cossa, 32 (tel. 99 10 94). From the bus station at P. Trieste, ascend the main street and take a right at the top. Charming owner. Large terrace. All rooms newly renovated, with bath. L40,000 per person, low-season L30,000. Half-pension required in July (L60,000) and Aug. (L80,000).

Albergo A. Macri, Via Iasolino, 96 (tel. 99 26 03), a small street on the right as you come into the port, near the *traghetti* dock. Modern rooms, most with balcony, on a quiet side street. *Let's Go* prices: singles L30,000, with bath L35,000; doubles L55,000, with bath L65,000. L5000 more per person mid-July to mid-Aug.

Camping

The most economical accommodations, two delightful campgrounds lie near Ischia Porto. Prices here are for August and run L2000-5000 less in June and July.

Eurocamping dei Pini, Via delle Ginestre, 28 (tel. 98 20 69), the quieter of the 2 camping sites, a 20-min. walk from the port. Take Via del Porto onto Via Alfredo de Luca, walk uphill and take a right on Via delle Terme, where you will see the arrow indicating camping. L12,000 per person, L7000 per tent. 2-person bungalows with bath and kitchen facilities L65,000 (reserve ahead). The tent site is more scenic than the bungalow site.

Camping Internazionale, Via M. Mazzella (tel. 99 14 49), a 15-min. walk from the port. Take Via Alfredo de Luca from Via del Porto and bear right onto Via M. Mazzella at P. degli Eroi. (There are 2 Via Mazzellas, Michele and Leonardo, that run parallel.) Luxuriant foliage and tranquil surroundings. L14,000 per person, L10,000 per tent. Immaculate 2-person bungalows with bath L75,000, L15,000 per additional person. Bathless bungalows slightly cheaper. Open May-Oct.15.

FOOD

Ischia has numerous outdoor eateries and *alimentari,* and plenty of fruit vendors. Walk away from the touristed boulevards for shops with better prices. Restaurants are generally exorbitant, but a few gems exist. **Emiddio,** at Via Porto, 30, is right on the docks at Ischia Porto. Their *ravioli alla panna* (L7000) reign supreme. Other *primi* go for L4000-9000. Open daily noon-3pm and 7pm-midnight. Cover L1500. V, MC, AmEx. Or try **Ristorante Zelluso,** Via Parodi, 41 (tel. 99 46 27), to the left as you enter Casamicciola; look for the white sign and walk down the alley. The outdoor section is great for families or large groups. Scrumptious pizza L6000. Cover L2000. Service 10%. AmEx.

SIGHTS

Most visitors to Ischia go to the beach at **Citara** (get off at the Hotel Imperial bus stop past Forio). For something new try **Sorceto** (on the far side of the island), which features relaxing hot springs ranging from tepid to boiling. Beautifully situated and somewhat remote, the beach is the perfect spot to lounge and soak your aching feet. (For healthy skin, try rubbing the light green porous rocks together to form a cleansing lather.) Reach the beach by boat-taxi from the Sant'Angelo port (L5000 per person; ask for a group discount and remember to arrange for your pick-up) or take the 15-min. walk down from the Panza bus stop. Those ready for more hiking should take the CD or CS bus to Fontana and head for the peak of **Mt. Epomeo** (788m); the view extends from Terracina to Capri.

For those weary of beaching, Ischia's scattered sights provide a reprieve from the sun and surf. Near Ischia Porto, the **Castello d'Ischia** (1441), built by the King of Spain on the site of a 5th-century BC Greek fortress and destroyed repeatedly over the years, stands on a little island of its own (Ischia Ponte), connected to Ischia by a 15th-century footbridge. Take bus #7 to Ischia Ponte. The **cathedral** in the castle, mostly destroyed by WWII bombing, displays a mix of Roman and Baroque styles. Below, the **crypt** houses colorful 14th-century frescoes by the school of Giotto. The **nuns' cemetery,** which belonged to the Poor Clares from the 16th through 18th centuries, is somewhat ghastly; when a nun died, the order propped the decomposing body on a stone throne as a constant (and fragrant) reminder to the other nuns of their own mortality. The castle also contains an exposition room with changing modern art exhibits. (Open daily 9am-sunset. Admission L8000.)

The church of **Santa Restituta** houses the ruins of Lacco Ameno's ancient villas dating back to the 8th century BC. In a cross-section of soil, you can see a record of the island's numerous civilizations. (Open Mon.-Fri. 9:30am-noon and 5-7pm, Sat.-Sun. 9:30am-noon.) Also check out the 14th-century church **Santa Maria di Loreto,** with red, blue, white, and gold marble pillars. For some dancing, head to the clubs **Valentino** (tel. 98 25 69; L25,000) and **Charly** (tel. 99 14 16; L20,000), out on Via Roma from Ischia Porto, or to the outdoor club **Castello** (L25,000) in the castle at Ischia Ponte.

Procida

A small island of fisherfolk and farmers, Procida prefers to remain a spectator as its neighbors transform into country clubs. The island compensates for its less dramatic scenery with colorful and chaotic local culture. **Caremar, Linee Lauro,** and **Aliscafi SNAV** run **ferries** to the island from Naples (40min., L8000), Ischia (15min., L3400), and Pozzuoli (35min., L4000). **Hydrofoils** are L5100 to Ischia and L12,600 to Naples. The **AAST tourist office** (tel. 810 19 68) is on Via Roma by the ferry ticket offices to the far right of the main port. They have a useful but old map of the island (L3000) and can help you find an apartment for L30,000-60,000 a night for two people. Open daily 9am-1pm and 4:30-8pm. Short stays are difficult to accommodate. The **ETP Residences office,** Via Principe Umberto, 1 (tel. 896 90 67; fax 896 00 66), can also help you find an apartment. In August, reservations and a minimum stay of 1-2 weeks are required. Procida's **telephone code** is 081.

Buses (tickets L1000 in *tabacchi,* L1200 on the bus) serve the island with three principal routes starting at the main port, the northernmost point of the island. The buses leave every 20min. from 7am to midnight. One route takes you to the west coast of **Ciraccio** and **Pozzo Vecchio,** the most tranquil beaches on the island. A second route covers the middle and southern regions of the island, bringing you past the hotels and campgrounds and stopping at the port of **Chiaiolella,** the site of the liveliest restaurants and the beach of the same name. You can walk or take the third bus route to the **Abbazia Arcangelo San Michele** (St. Michael's Abbey) on the easternmost and highest hilltop in Procida. Open daily 9am to noon and 4 to 7pm. On the way up you'll see the medieval walls of **Terra Murata** (the old city; tel. 896 76 12) on

Via San Michele just below the monastery. The abbey's plain pastel yellow façade, redone in 1890, belies the interior, where you'll find ornate 15th-century gold and lead frescoes and bleeding Christ figures. Open mornings and after 5:30pm. On the way down, check out the crowds to the left on **Chiaia,** the island's most popular beach. Stop to admire the Pantheon-domed **Santuario Mariano** and its 1810 façade on P. dei Martiri. From Chiaiolella you can cross the footbridge to the islet of **Vivara,** a wildlife sanctuary and breeding ground for the rabbits that *procidani* cook up in their famous stew. To see those bunnies on your plate, try **Ristorante Pizzeria Da Michele** in Chiaiolella, Via Marino Chiaiolella, 21 (tel. 896 74 22). Watch the nightlife heat up over a tasty dish of spaghetti with mussels (L8000). Open daily 8am-2am (closes at 8pm in winter). For dessert, ask at any bar for the refreshing and potent lemon liquor *(limoncello)* made from Procidan lemons.

If you dislike lemons, don't spend the night: it's hard to find a hotel here that isn't surrounded by lemon groves and private gardens. **Eldorado,** Via Vittorio Emanuele, 228 (tel. 896 80 05), is a prime example. Its four choice rooms have vaulted, decorative ceilings. Singles with bath L40,000. Doubles L60,000, with bath L65,000. Prices are L5,000 higher July-Aug. **Pensione Savoia,** Via Lavadera, 32 (tel. 896 76 16), has eight large rooms and a comfortable terrace. Behind the hotel stretches a garden of lemon trees, grapevines, flowers, and chickens. Singles L35,000, in summer L40,000. Doubles L60,000, in summer L65,000. In Aug. full-pension required, L65,000. **Hotel Riviera,** Giovanni da Procida, 36 (tel. 896 71 97; fax 896 76 11), is larger and no less friendly (and still surrounded by lemons). All rooms with bath, phone, and breakfast; some also have a view of the sea. Singles L50,000. Doubles L100,000. Full-pension required July-Aug., L100,000. L10,000-20,000 less in off season for longer stays. Open April-Sept. Pitch your tent at the well maintained and colorful **La Caravella** on Via IV Novembre (tel. 896 92 30). L9000 per person, L9000 per small tent, L10,000 per large tent. Bar on grounds. For bungalows, try **Graziella,** on Via Salette (tel. 896 77 47) on the beach. Take the bus to P. Urno and walk 500m to Spiaggia Ciraccio. Four-person bungalows L90,000, low-season L70,000.

BAY OF NAPLES: VESUVIUS

Pompeii (Pompei)

> *Stand at the bottom of the great market-place of Pompeii, and look up at the silent streets... over the broken houses with their inmost sanctuaries open to the day, away to Mount Vesuvius, bright and snowy in the peaceful distance; and lose all count of time, and heed of other things, in the strange and melancholy sensation of seeing the Destroyed and Destroyer making this quiet picture in the sun.*
>
> —Charles Dickens, *Pictures from Italy*

On August 24, AD79, life in the prosperous Roman city of Pompeii suddenly halted. Mount Vesuvius's fit of towering flames, suffocating black clouds, and seething lava buried the city—temples, villas, theaters, and all—under more than 20 feet of volcanic ash. Except for the few lucky ones who dropped everything and ran at the first tremors of catastrophe, the inhabitants of Pompeii suffered a nasty live burial. Perhaps the most ghastly—and evocative—relics of the town's untimely death are the "frozen people": plaster casts made of the victims' bodies in the hardened ash, preserving their last contortions and expressions of horror. The excavation of Pompeii is ongoing; from the first unearthings in 1748 through current digs, every decade has brought to light new finds that provide the clearest and most vivid picture of daily life in the Roman era.

PRACTICAL INFORMATION

The quickest route to Pompeii (25km south of Naples) is the **Circumvesuviana train** line from Naples's Stazione Centrale (toward Sorrento, 35min., L2700, Eurailpasses not valid). Get off at the Pompei Scavi/Villa dei Misteri stop just outside the west entry. (Ignore the inconvenient Pompeii Santuario stop). An alternative is the less frequent **state train,** leaving from the main track at the station, which stops at Pompeii en route to Salerno (7 per day, 7:10am-1:15pm, L2500). The FS train station is a 10-min. walk to the east entrance, straight on Via Sacra, then left in front of the *santuario* onto Via Roma.

To get to the **site** of Pompeii, head downhill from the Villa dei Misteri station and take your first left. The **tourist office** is at Via Sacra, 1 (tel. 850 72 55), on the way to the ruins from the FS train station. Follow the road to the right of the Circumvesuviana stop to the branch office at the bottom of the hill. Pick up a free map and the informative pamphlet *Notizario Turistico Regionale.* Both offices open Mon.-Fri. 8am-3pm and 5-7pm in summer; 8am-3pm in low-season. Via Sacra office also open Sat. 8am-noon. Pompeii's **telephone code** is 081.

ACCOMMODATIONS AND FOOD

Unless you wish to tour Pompeii extensively, there is no reason to stay overnight in the dull modern city. If you decide to do so, however, the **Motel Villa dei Misteri,** Via Villa dei Misteri, 11 (tel. 861 35 93), uphill from the Circumvesuviana station, is a wonderful option, with comfortable, clean, modern rooms and a terrific pool. A/C available. Doubles with bath L70,000; extra bed L15,000. Full-pension L80,000. **Soggiorno Pace,** Via Sacra, 29 (tel. 863 60 25), has large, quiet rooms with common bath and a peaceful garden for L20,000 per person. **Pensione Minerva,** Via Roma, 137 (tel. 863 25 87), near the east entrance to the site, rents doubles for L65,000, low-season L60,000. Triples L75,000. All rooms have showers. The cheapest accommodations are the local campgrounds, all near the ruins. Unfortunately, they tend to be somewhat ruined themselves. **Camping Zeus** (tel. 861 53 20), outside the Villa dei Misteri Circumvesuviana stop, is convenient and respectable. L7000 per person, L5000 per large tent, L3000 per small tent. Not far away, on Via Plinio, the main road that runs from the ruins, **Camping Pompeii** (tel. 862 25 82; fax 850 27 72), with the same ownership and prices as Zeus, has attractive bungalows for L50,000 for two people and L90,000 for four. If you're desperate you can sack out on the floor of its indoor lobby for L6000 per night. These places are eager for customers, so you can usually bargain them down at least 15%.

Stock up at the **GS** supermarket, Via Statale, km 24, on the main road between the east and west entrances to the archaeological site. Take advantage of the great prices and air-conditioning. Open Mon.-Sat. 8am-8:30pm, Sun. 9am-1pm; closes Thurs. 2pm. An alternative to the nearby McDonald's, **La Vinicola** at Via Roma, 29, tempts with a pleasant outdoor courtyard and abundant *gnocchi con mozzarella* (L5500). Also try the *zuppa di cozze* for L5000. Cover L1500. Service 15%. Open daily 10am-midnight. More expensive and tastier meals are found at the **Trattoria-Pizzeria dei Platani,** Via Colle San Bartolomeo, 8 (tel. 863 39 73), off the main town *piazza* in front of the church. *Cannelloni* is L9000, and the *menù* is L20,000. Cover L2000. Open daily 9:30am-10pm.

SIGHTS

A comprehensive walk through Pompeii will probably take four or five hours; pack a lunch and a water bottle, as the cafeteria is hideously expensive. **Guided tours** are expensive as well but are probably the best way to savor the details of life and death in the first century AD. Call **GATA Tours** (tel. 861 56 61; fax 536 85 77) or **Assotouring** (tel. 862 25 60) for info. The tour guides are wise to freeloaders and go beyond evil stares to actually yelling at offenders. If a tour is too rich for your blood, consider

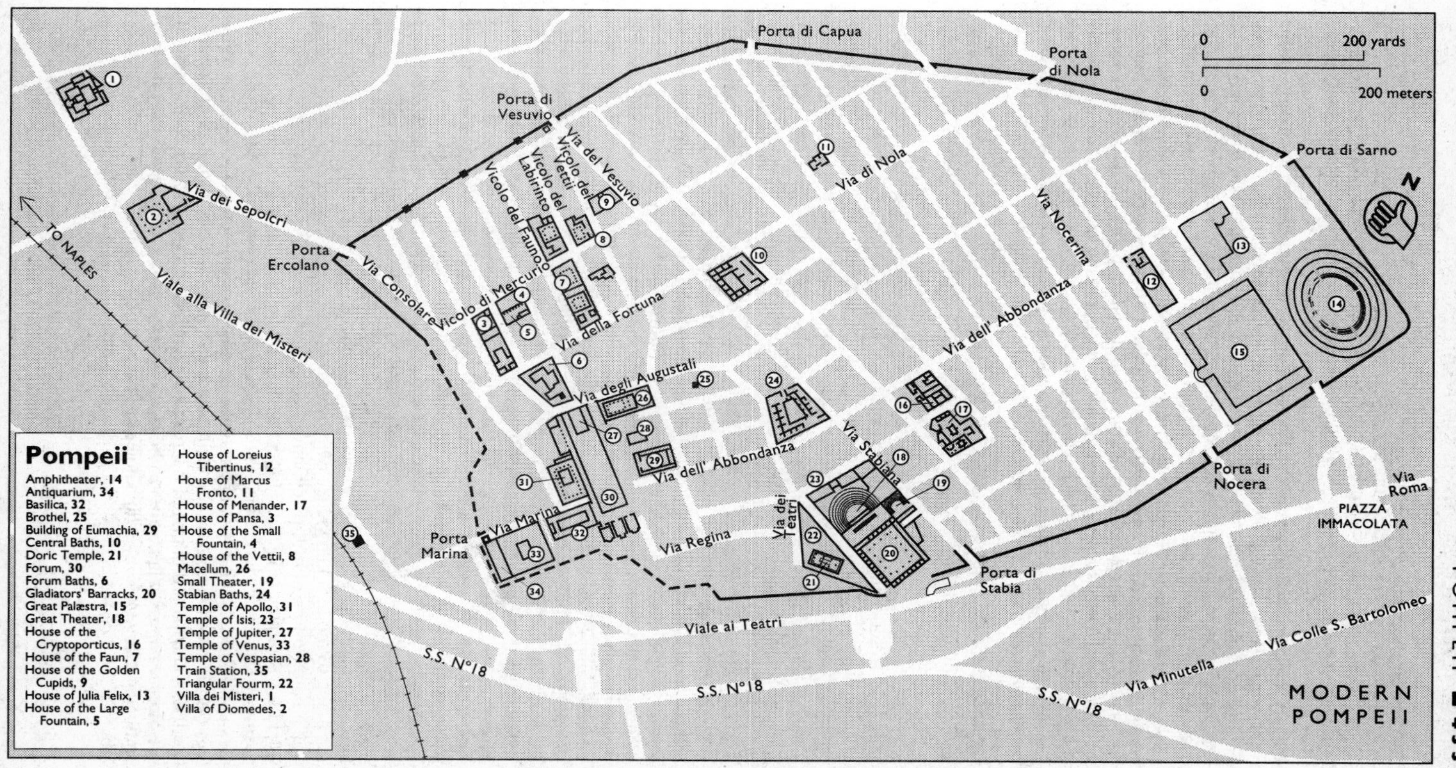
Porta di Capua
Porta di Nola
0 200 yards
0 200 meters
Porta di Vesuvio
Via del Vesuvio
Vicolo dei Vettii
Vicolo del Labirinto
Vicolo del Fauno
Porta di Sarno
Via di Nola
N
Via dei Sepolcri
TO NAPLES
Porta Ercolano
Via Consolare
Vicolo di Mercurio
Via della Fortuna
Viale alla Villa dei Misteri
Via Nocerina
Via dell' Abbondanza
Via degli Augustali
Via Stabiana
Via dell' Abbondanza
Porta di Nocera
Via Roma
PIAZZA IMMACOLATA
Porta Marina
Via Marina
Via dei Teatri
Via Regina
Porta di Stabia
Viale ai Teatri
Via Colle S. Bartolomeo
S.S. N°18
S.S. N°18
Via Minutella
S.S. N°18
MODERN POMPEII
Pompeii
Amphitheater, 14
Antiquarium, 34
Basilica, 32
Brothel, 25
Building of Eumachia, 29
Central Baths, 10
Doric Temple, 21
Forum, 30
Forum Baths, 6
Gladiators' Barracks, 20
Great Palæstra, 15
Great Theater, 18
House of the Cryptoporticus, 16
House of the Faun, 7
House of the Golden Cupids, 9
House of Julia Felix, 13
House of the Large Fountain, 5
House of Loreius Tibertinus, 12
House of Marcus Fronto, 11
House of Menander, 17
House of Pansa, 3
House of the Small Fountain, 4
House of the Vettii, 8
Macellum, 26
Small Theater, 19
Stabian Baths, 24
Temple of Apollo, 31
Temple of Isis, 23
Temple of Jupiter, 27
Temple of Venus, 33
Temple of Vespasian, 28
Train Station, 35
Triangular Fourm, 22
Villa dei Misteri, 1
Villa of Diomedes, 2

buying the informative *How to Visit Pompeii* (ed. Bonechi) for L8000 ("special price for you, pretty lady"), available outside all site entrances.

The west entrance leads past the Antiquarium (permanently closed since the 1980 earthquake) to the **Forum,** surrounded by a colonnade. Once dotted with statues of emperors and gods, this site was the commercial, civic, and religious center of the city. Showcases along the west side display some of the gruesome body-casts of the volcano's victims. To the right rises the **Temple of Jupiter,** mostly destroyed by an earthquake that struck 17 years before the city's bad luck got worse; to the left is the **Temple of Apollo,** with statues of Apollo and Diana (these statues are copies; the originals are in Naples) and a column topped by a sundial. To the left of the temple is the **basilica,** or law-court, whose walls are decorated with stucco to imitate marble. On the opposite long side of the forum, to the left of the so-called **Building of Eumachia** (note the carved doorframe of animals and insects hiding in scroll-like plants), the **Temple of Vespasian** houses a delicate frieze depicting the preparation for a sacrifice.

Follow the Forum north by the cafeteria and enter the **Forum Baths** to the left on Via di Terme. Parts of the body casts here have chipped away to reveal teeth and bones underneath. Remarkable terra-cotta figures decorate the rooms to the right. Exit to the right, and on the left find the **House of the Faun,** where a small bronze dancing faun and the spectacular Alexander Mosaic (now in Naples) were found. Before the door, a mosaic proclaims *Have* (welcome). Continue to the left on Via della Fortuna and turn left on Vico di Vetti to see the **House of the Vettii,** home to the most vivid frescoes in Pompeii. In the vestibule is a depiction of Priapus (the god of fertility) displaying his colossal member; in ancient times, phalli were believed to scare off evil spirits, but now they seem only to invite hordes of tittering tourists.

Walk back on Vico di Vetti and continue on Vico del Lupanare, where there is a small **brothel** (the Lupenon) with several bed-stalls. Above each stall a pornographic painting depicts with unabashed precision the specialty of its occupant. Continue down the street to the main avenue, Via dell'Abbondanza. The **Stabian Baths,** privately owned and therefore fancier than the Forum Baths (just think: ritzy spa vs. YMCA), lie to the left. The separate men's and women's sides each include a dressing room, cold baths *(frigidaria),* warm baths *(tepidaria),* and hot or steam baths *(caldaria).* Via dei Teatri across the street leads to a huge complex consisting of the **Great Theater,** constructed in the first half of the 2nd century BC, and the **Little Theater,** built later for music and dance concerts. North of the theaters stands the **Temple of Isis,** Pompeii's monument to the Egyptian fertility goddess. Exit the temple to the right and pass two fine houses, the **House of Secundus** and the **House of Menander** (so named because a painting of the comic poet hangs on the wall, not because he actually lived there). At the end of the street, turn left to return to the main road. The Romans believed that crossroads were particularly vulnerable to evil spirits, so they built altars (like the one here) designed to ward them off.

Turn right down Via dell'Abbondanza and note the red writing on the walls. You'll see everything from political campaign slogans to declarations of love—apparently graffiti hasn't changed much in 2000 years. At the end of the street rest the **House of Tiburtinus** and the **House of Venus,** sprawling complexes with gardens replanted according to modern knowledge of ancient horticulture. The nearby **Great Palestra** was a common gathering place, and the **amphitheater** (80BC), the oldest in the world still standing, held 12,000 spectators.

Complete your day with a visit to the **Villa of the Mysteries,** outside the main complex and 10min. uphill from the Circumvesuviana station. A renowned cycle of paintings (in the room directly to the right of the entrance) depicts an initiation into the Dionysian cult. You don't need a separate ticket, but you can't return to the central site after leaving it. (Entrances to Pompeii open 9am-1hr. before sunset (June-July 8pm, Nov.-Dec. 3:45pm). Admission L12,000.)

■ Near Pompeii

ERCOLANO (HERCULANEUM)

Neatly excavated and impressively intact, the remains of the Roman town of Herculaneum (modern Ercolano) hardly deserve the term "ruins." Once a wealthy residential enclave on the Roman coast road, Herculaneum does not evoke the tragedy of Pompeii—all but a handful of its inhabitants escaped the ravages of Vesuvius. In less-crowded tours than those offered in Pompeii, you can wind your way through the 15 or so houses and baths open to the public. Two-thousand-year-old frescoes, furniture, mosaics, small sculptures, and even wooden doors seem as vital now as they ever were, preserved by the mud from the volcano's avalanche. The **House of Deer** (so named for a statue of a deer being savagely attacked by greyhounds) is one of the more alluring villas. The owners also had a statue of a *Satyr with a Wineskin* and a statue of the town's namesake Hercules in a drunken stupor trying to relieve himself. The **baths,** with their largely intact warm and hot rooms and giant vaulted swimming pool, evoke images of past opulence. **The House of the Mosaic of Neptune and Aphrodite,** which belonged to a rich shop owner, is famous for its mosaic depicting—well, take a guess. Also notable is the Samnise House, with first-style decoration and a mock colonnade made of stucco.

To get to Ercolano, take any Circumvesuviana train toward Pompeii from Naples's central train station to the Ercolano stop (15min., L2000). Walk 500m downhill to the **ticket office.** The site is open daily 9am-1hr. before sunset (June-July 8pm, Dec. 3:45pm). Admission L12,000. Before entering, consider purchasing the little blue *Istituto Poligrafico dello Stato* guide to Herculaneum, with an excellent map, reliable text, and some beautifully clear black-and-white illustrations (L10,000). Be forewarned that the neighborhood surrounding the site can be less than savory at times; solo travelers and women should be on guard.

MT. VESUVIUS

Take a peek inside the only active volcano on the European continent. **SITA** buses run from Ercolano up to the crater of Vesuvius (6 per day, last return 5:50pm, L2000 each way). Once there, you must buy a ticket for a tour (L5000). Hikers can take the orange city bus #5 (L1800 each way) to the base of the mountain and climb from there; bring plenty of water and wear decent shoes. Experts say the trip is safe—the last eruption was March 31, 1944.

■ Sorrento

In the *Odyssey,* the men of Odysseus's crew shielded their ears from the spellbinding song of the Sirens, who inhabited Sorrento's peninsula off nearby Positano. If the Sirens still exist, chances are they chant in English and German to camera-laden foreigners, luring them into tourist traps and ritzy boutiques. Sorrento remains charming in spite of the tourists, and poised between Naples, Capri, and the Amalfi Coast, the town makes a convenient base for the daytripper and offers several inexpensive accommodations for those drawn by the bewitching song.

ORIENTATION AND PRACTICAL INFORMATION

A short throughway leads you from the train and bus station to P. Angelina Lauro and **Corso Italia,** Sorrento's main street. Fifty meters to the left lies **Piazza Tasso,** the center of town. Past the *piazza,* you come to the **old quarter** and the **cathedral.** Facing the sea in P. Tasso, Via de Maio is on your left and a stairway straight ahead leads to the **port.**

Tourist Office: Via L. de Maio, 35 (tel. 807 40 33; http://www.vol.it/sorrento). From P. Tasso, take Via de Maio through P. Sant'Antonio and continue to the right toward the port. The office is to the right within the Circolo del Forestiere, in the room on the left as you enter. English-speaking staff is helpful with maps, accommodations service, and info on cultural events. Make sure to grab a free copy of *Surrentum,* the monthly tourist magazine. Open April-Sept. Mon.-Fri. 8:45am-7:45pm, Sat. 8:45am-7:15pm; Oct.-March Mon.-Sat. 8:30am-2pm and 3:45-6:15pm.

Tourist Police: Vico 3° Rota, (tel. 807 30 88), a left off Corso Italia 1 block after Viale Nizza, to the right of the station. Ask for the English-speaking foreigners' office (*Ufficio Stranieri*).

Currency Exchange: Exchange desks can be found along Corso Italia and in the old quarter, daily 9am-9pm. Worse rates than the post office, but no commission.

American Express: Acampara Travel, P. Angelina Lauro, 12 (tel. 807 30 88). Open Mon.-Sat. 9am-1pm and 4-8:30pm. Cash advances on AmEx cards only on weekday mornings.

Telephones: P. Tasso, 37 (tel. 878 24 00). Leave the train station and turn right immediately before you come to the *piazza.* Public fax machine. Open daily 9am-1:30pm and 4-10:30pm.

Trains: Circumvesuviana (tel. 536 89 32) to Naples, passing Pompeii and Torre Annunziata (2 per hr., 4am-11pm, L4200).

Buses: SITA (tel. 878 27 08). Blue buses depart for towns on the Amalfi Coast from the Circumvesuviana station. Almost every hr. 6:30am-9:45pm to: Positano (L2000), Praiano (L2700), Amalfi (L3400), and Salerno (L6100). From Amalfi, change buses and pay an additional L1500 to go to Atrani, Ravello, or Scala. Buy all SITA tickets at bars, *tabacchi,* or the newspaper shop in the train station, and validate them when you board the bus. **CITAL** runs to Rome at 6am and 5pm (L30,000). The bus to Sorrento from Rome leaves at 7am and 3pm from the Tiburtina station. **Local orange buses** leave from P. Tasso every 20-30min. for the port, Punta del Capo, and other regions of the city (L1000 within the city, L1500 for points outside the city).

Ferries: The cheapest route to Capri. Descend the stairs at P. Tasso. **Caremar** (tel. 807 30 77; fax 807 24 79) is the least expensive and runs most frequently. Boats leave daily at 8, 10am, 2:45, 5:45, and 7:45pm (less frequently in winter), 1hr., L5300. **Alilauro hydrofoils** (tel. 807 30 24) take 15min. for the crossing (L8500), and run 7 times daily 8:40am-5:15pm. Hydrofoils also run to Ischia (L16,000) and Naples (L10,000).

Car and Moped Rental: Sorrento Rent-A-Car, Corso Italia, 210/A (tel. 878 13 86). The only moped rental place from Sorrento to Salerno. Mopeds L50,000 per day, L280,000 per week. Also rents Vespa 125s (for 2 people), L70,000 per day, L394,000 per week. Helmet and insurance included. Passport and credit card required. Driver's license required for vehicles with engines 50cc and over.

Laundromat: Terlizzi, Corso Italia, 30 (tel. 878 11 85), in the old quarter. Coin-op (L15,000 wash and dry) and dry-cleaning.

Emergencies: tel. 113. **Hospital: Ospedale Santa Maria Misericordia,** Corso Italia (tel. 533 11 11).

Post Office: Corso Italia, 210T-U (tel. 878 16 36), near P. Lauro. Open Mon.-Sat. 8:15am-7:20pm. **Exchange money** here, where you will most likely get the most favorable rates in town, 8:15am-5:30pm (commission L2000, L5000 for sums over L100,000). **Postal code:** 80067.

Telephone code: 081.

ACCOMMODATIONS AND CAMPING

Plentiful lodging options make up for Sorrento's dearth of sights; the tourist office is helpful in finding an empty room. Reservations, however, are still a good idea in July and August. Some Sorrento hotels allegedly charge more than their established prices. If you feel you're being overcharged, ask to see the official price list; you can then write a letter to the EPT and perhaps eventually get a refund. **Prices listed below are for high-season.**

Hotel Elios, Via Capo, 33 (tel. 878 18 12), halfway to the Punta del Capo. Take the "A" bus from P. Tasso (L1500). A friendly couple runs this comfortable, tranquil hotel with a view of the bay. *Let's Go* prices: singles L35,000; doubles L60,000.

Hotel Loreley et Londres, Via Califano, 2 (tel. 807 31 87), on the waterfront near P. Lauro. The Sorrento hotel you've dreamed of, with views of cliffs and sea. Doubles with bath, including breakfast on a delightful terrace, L110,000. Full-pension (L100,000) required in Aug.

Hotel Savoia, Via Fuorimura, 48 (tel. 878 25 11), on the street off the right hand of the statue in P. Tasso. The best bet if you're arriving in the summer without reservations. Friendly English-speaking management. Singles with bath L65,000. Doubles L85,000. Breakfast L8000, for 2 people L15,000.

Hotel City, Corso Italia, 221 (tel. 877 22 10), left on Corso Italia from the station. A bit noisy at night. Money exchange, tickets for ferries and excursions, and a small bar. Comfy doubles with bath (some with garden patios) L80,000. Singles (available Oct.-June) L55,000. Extra bed L20,000. Breakfast L5000.

Camping: Nube d'Argento, Via del Capo, 21 (tel. 878 13 44; fax 807 34 50). From the station, follow Corso Italia past P. Tasso until it becomes Via del Capo. It's a 25-min. walk, so you may want to take the bus from P. Tasso (L1500). An ideal location by the ocean, with a swimming pool, hot showers, market, and restaurant. Check-out noon. L13,000 per person, L6000 per tent, L13,000 per large tent. Two-person bungalows L90,000. **Villaggio Verde,** Via Cesarano, 12 (tel. 807 32 58; fax 807 30 28). From P. Tasso take bus #2 (L1500) or turn left on Via Fuorimura. Follow this road (it turns into the brick Via Atigliana) for 15 min. and turn left at the Napoli sign. L9000 per person, L8000 per tent. Two-person bungalows L110,000, 4-person bungalows L150,000.

FOOD

Sorrento is famous for its *gnocchi,* potato dumplings smothered in zesty tomato sauce and mozzarella cheese. Also popular are the local *cannelloni,* pasta tubes stuffed with cheese and herbs, and *Nocillo,* a dark liqueur made from the hefty local walnuts. Unfortunately, many of the affordable restaurants in Sorrento cater to the Germans with *Würstel* and to the British with fish and chips. With a little effort you can avoid the overpriced tourist menus and find traditional fare in and around the city center. Otherwise, the **STANDA** supermarket at Corso Italia, 221, is a less expensive option. Open Mon.-Wed. and Fri.-Sat. 8:30am-12:55pm and 5-8:55pm, Thurs. 8:30am-12:55pm. From P. Tasso, follow Via San Cesareo until it turns into Via Fuoro, where you will find fresh fruit, fish, or bargain shoes sold at a variety of **market stands.** Go in the morning for the best deals.

Ristorante e Pizzeria Giardiniello, Via Accademia, 7 (tel. 878 46 16). Take the 2nd left off Via Giuliani, which runs off Corso Italia at the cathedral. Mamma Luisa does all the cooking in this family-run establishment set in a peaceful garden. Her *gnocchi* transcend poetry (L6000). Try the *bocconcini al Giardiniello,* tiny pizza-like pastries with *prosciutto* and mushrooms (L7000 for 10). Cover L1500. Open June-Sept. daily 10:30am-3pm and 7pm-2am; Oct.-May Wed.-Mon. 10:30am-3pm and 7pm-midnight. V, MC.

Ristorante Sant'Antonino, Via Santa Maria delle Grazie, 6 (tel. 877 12 00), off P. Sant'Antonino near the tourist office. Popular with locals and tourists. *Farfalle con zucchine* (bow-tie pasta with zucchini, L8000) and famed *gnocchi alla sorrentina* (L9000). *Menù* from L20,000. Long wine list. Open Feb.-Nov. daily noon-3pm and 7pm-midnight. V, MC, AmEx.

Ristorante-Pizzeria Il Mulino, Via Fuorimura, 7 (tel. 878 12 16; fax 807 28 99), off P. Tasso. Try the heavenly *canneloni alla Mulino* (L8000), or the *impepata di cozze* (mussels; L10,000). Pizzas L5000-10,000. No cover. Open daily noon-4pm and 7:30-11pm. V, MC.

Snack Bar 2000 (tel. 878 13 51), on Largo Sedil Dominova, dominating a *piazza* on Via Cesareo in the old quarter. A pleasant, shady place to rest your feet and watch the tourists. Spaghetti with tomato sauce, L5000; watery cappuccino L2000. Open daily 9am-11pm.

Gigino Pizza a Metro (Pizza by the Meter), Via Nicotera, 11, at Vico Equense (tel. 879 84 26), a 10-min. train ride from Sorrento. Take the Circumvesuviana to the Vico Equense stop, go left as you exit the station, and follow the winding road uphill to its end at P. Umberto. Take a left on Via Roma and another left on Via Nicotera. This is unofficially the world's largest *pizzeria,* a massive 2-story facility with monstrous wood-burning ovens that cook *pizza a metro* (1m-long pizza; from L28,000). A meter will feed at least 5 starving tourists; starving Italians, however, are likely to eat elsewhere. Smaller pizzas available from L5000. Cover L1000. Service 13%. Open daily noon-1am.

SIGHTS AND ENTERTAINMENT

The westerly orientation of the beaches makes sunset swims truly memorable. For a free swim, take the bus all the way to **Punta del Capo** and walk 10min. down the footpath to the right. On the coast you will also see the remains of the ancient Roman **Villa di Pollio.** The ruins aren't really worth visiting unless you take a dip in the beautiful cove or farther out on the point. Nearby lies **Sant'Agata** (9km by SITA bus from the train station, L1500), a tiny city perched high in the hills. Known as the "city on the two gulfs," its majestic height allows for a great vantage point from which to see both the Bay of Naples and the Gulf of Salerno. The **Church of Sant'Agata** boasts a 13th-century mother-of-pearl altar.

Jazz and classical music are performed about every other night throughout July and August at the outdoor atrium of the **Chiostro di San Francesco,** near the Villa Comunale on the water. (Showtime 9pm. Admission L25,000, ages 26 and under L15,000; some tickets for L15,000 and L10,000.) Free events from July through September take place in the Villa Comunale, the Chiostro di San Francesco, and the town's two ports. Get a list at the tourist office. From November to March, the Sorrento Tourist Board organizes **Sorrento Inverno,** a free entertainment program that includes movies, concerts, local folklore exhibits, and guided tours of the town.

The area around P. Tasso heats up and gets down after dark. People swarm the streets, look out over the bay, and careen around on mopeds. The outdoor **Blue Mare Club** on Punta del Capo is as beautiful as you'd ever want your *discoteca* to be. (Open in summer only.) Even the winter stays hot at the imaginatively named **The Club,** held in the Bar Fauno in P. Tasso.

AMALFI COAST

Many people choose the Amalfi Coast as a place to relax after doing some serious European country-hopping; they usually leave more than satisfied. The bold, arresting bluffs and tiny towns nestled into steep coastal ravines merit all the superlatives of the tourist brochures. A calm sea, delicious seafood, and sumptuous fruits temper the rugged southern shore, which divides the Bay of Naples from the Gulf of Salerno. Taste the fresh peaches, yellow plums, sweet figs, and huge lemons.

The coast is accessible by SITA buses leaving Sorrento and Salerno every two hours, ferry and Circumvesuviana service (the Meta stop) from Naples on a less regular basis, and daily CITAL buses from Rome. Prone to sea-sickness? Take the ferry between towns (really); they're faster, steadier, and less harrowing than rides on the blue SITA buses, although those with a stronger stomach shouldn't miss the roller-coaster bus ride and its spectacular views. If you don't mind a little danger in your life, rent a moped or scooter and stop at any gorgeous place that strikes your fancy. (Leave extra luggage at a train station.) But be warned: the Amalfi Coast is not the place to learn how to ride a moped.

Positano

Although Positano looks as if it might slip into the sea and summer tourists flock here by the dozens, the town is still an ideal place to bask in coastal Italian culture. Stroll up the cliffside stairway for spectacular views of the sea, or explore the inescapable glamorous boutiques.

ORIENTATION AND PRACTICAL INFORMATION

Positano is 35min. from Sorrento by SITA bus. Get off at the Bar Internazionale stop and either walk down the winding stairway (affectionately known as the "Thousand Steps") to the village or take the local orange bus, which makes its rounds every 30min. on the town's only street open to traffic (L1000; buy tickets on the bus). When leaving, buy tickets in advance from the Bar Internazionale for trips to Sorrento, the Amalfi Coast, and Naples; if you're heading for Rome, buy tickets on the CITAL bus (departs 4:20pm, L26,000). The terse but well informed **tourist office** is at Via del Saraceno, 4 (tel. 87 50 67). Facing the town from the port, walk to the left up Via Giovanni and take a right immediately before the arch. Open Mon.-Fri. 8:30am-2pm, Sat. 8:30am-noon. **Telephones** are located inside the restaurant Giardino degli Aranci on Via dei Mulini and directly behind the tourist office on Via Giovanni. Numerous **ferry** companies provide extensive service; buy tickets at the *biglietteria marittima* at the port. To: Capri (morning only, L10,000); Amalfi (3 per day, L7000); and Salerno (5 per day, L7500). **Alilauro hydrofoils** run to Capri (3 per day, L15,000) and down the coast (Amalfi L7000, Salerno L14,500). There is also limited service to Sorrento and Naples. Small companies on Marina Grande will take you on a boat tour of Capri's coast and the Blue Grotto (9am, L30,000 per person), or ferry a group of four to a nearby secluded beach. Call 87 50 32 for prices and info. A **pharmacy** sells drugs at Via dei Mulini (tel. 87 58 63). The **emergency number** is 113; **police** are at Chiesa Nuova (tel. 87 52 77). Positano's **telephone code** is 089.

ACCOMMODATIONS AND FOOD

According to legend, Homer's Sirens inhabited the three Isole dei Galli off Positano's beach. If you feel the dangerous pull of the Sirens' call and want to stay in Positano, try one of the many *pensioni* in the area, reserving early in the summer. **Casa Guadagno,** Via Fornillo, 22 (tel. 87 50 42), earns praise for pampering its patrons with spotless rooms, beautifully tiled floors, sublime views, and heating in the winter. To get there, take the local bus down from Bar Internazionale and ask to be let off by the hotel. Follow the signs and take the left fork. Call ahead, as the 10 rooms with bath are often reserved early. Doubles L80,000, larger doubles with slightly better views L90,000. Next door, **Villa Maria Luisa,** Via Fornillo, 40 (tel. 87 50 23), has bright rooms and the jolliest owner in Italy. All rooms with bath. Singles L50,000. Doubles L85,000, low-season L75,000. Extra bed L30,000. Just down the street from the hotels, **Il Saraceno D'Oro,** Via Pasitea, 254 (tel. 87 53 90), serves cheap, great pizza to go from L4000. If you sit down, pizzas start at L7000; *spaghetti alla saracena,* bathed in a sauce of tomatoes, tuna, mushrooms, and peppers, is L7000. Pizza is available in the evenings only. Cover L2000. Open Thurs.-Tues. 12:30-2:30pm and 7:30-11:30pm. At the top of the hill toward Montepertuso rests **Il Ritrovo,** Via Montepertuso, 53 (tel. 87 54 53). Try the *penne al ritrovo* (L7000), with mushrooms, tomatoes, and sausage, or the *grigliata di carne* (L12,000), a sampling of fresh meats. Meals L25,000-30,000. Open daily 10am-3pm and 7pm-midnight. If you're heading to Praiano, consider stopping first at **La Taverna del Leone,** Via Laurito, 43 (tel. 87 54 74), on the main road. Enjoy frozen strawberries, pears, peaches, and even walnuts filled with sorbet (L3500 per 100g)—or get a full meal. Cover L3000. Open daily 1-4pm and 7pm-midnight. Closed Tues. Oct.-April. V, MC, AmEx. Remember to have another ticket handy so you can hop back on the bus.

SIGHTS

Spiraling upward from Marina Grande, Positano's grey but attractive beach, **Via dei Mulini,** is a study in tourism, with scads of boutiques mobbed by well dressed foreigners. For more traditional sight-seeing, the 17th-century church of **Santa Maria Assunta,** located in P. Flavio Gioia, crowns the Positano landscape with a beautiful tiled dome. Hop the bus from Piazza dei Mulini on the port (or from Bar Internazionale; about every 2hr., L1000) or hike the 45-min. trail to **Montepertuso,** a high cliff pierced by a large *pertuso* (hole). On the way, stop at the locals' favorite freshwater spring and ponder the small Madonna nearby. **L'Uomo e il Mare** (tel. 87 54 75) offers numerous boating itineraries; you can take a personalized tour of the coast or go night fishing for squid. (Tours start at L20,000. Call to arrange itineraries and prices. English spoken.) On August 15, Positano puts on a **fireworks** display over the sea in celebration of its patron saint, Santa Maria Assunta.

■ Near Positano: Praiano

Six kilometers down the coast (25min. by bus due to the winding road, L1500), Praiano provides wonderful and inexpensive accommodations, including the only camping on the coast. It also makes a great mealtime trip for those who wish to avoid the expensive restaurants of touristed towns.

On the road from Positano, next to the church with the blue and gold domes, is the restaurant **San Gennaro,** Via San Gennaro, 75 (tel. 87 42 93). Try the titillating tastes of their *spaghetti alla puttanesca* (made quickly and dished up hot for L6000), or their clam and mussel sauté (L10,000). In the evenings, pizza starts at L5500. Open daily noon-midnight. Once in Praiano, enjoy the panorama from the excellent campground-hotel **La Tranquillità,** Via Roma, 10 (tel. 87 40 84), located on the road to Amalfi (ask the bus driver to stop at the Ristorante Continental/La Tranquillità). The rooms offer the coast's most awe-inspiring views of the surrounding caves, castles, and sea, while the spotless campsite sits atop precipitous cliffs. A long stairway takes you down to a stone dock and the resplendent green water. Camping L20,000 per person. Clean, new bungalows with bath: singles L50,000, doubles L80,000. Open Easter-November. Don't leave the coast without savoring a meal at the open-air **Ristorante Continental,** above La Tranquillità. It's the place to go for fresh mountain air, endless views, and exquisite food. *Primi* are L7000-11,000, *secondi* are L9000-15,000, and local wine runs L8000 per bottle. Cover L3000. Open Easter-Nov. daily noon-3pm and 8pm-midnight. Alternative accommodations may be found at **La Perla,** Via Miglina, 2 (tel. 87 40 52), located 100m toward Amalfi from La Tranquillità on the main road. Rooms are sparse, but all have bath and terrace. Singles L58,000, low-season L48,000. Doubles L94,000, low-season L84,000. MC, AmEx.

There's a marvelous beach up the road toward Positano, but you must be willing to descend 400 steps to reach it (keep the return trip in mind). Around the bend from Praiano as you walk toward Amalfi you'll find a ramp down to **Marina di Praia,** a 400-year-old fishing village tucked in a tiny ravine. The **Grotto dello Smeraldo** lies halfway between Praiano and Amalfi; the SITA bus will drop you off at the elevator entrance to the grotto. The cave's green water isn't as stunning as Capri's azure equivalent, but the multilingual guides try to make up for it with silly tricks like spotting Lincoln's and Mussolini's profiles in the rock formations. Admission and tour L5000. Tour available in English. Open May-Sept. 9am-5pm; Oct.-April 10am-4pm.

■ Amalfi

Amalfi was the first Sea Republic of Italy and has been a bustling seaside town since Roman times. Although the port may seem inconsequentially small, the town was once home to Flavio Gioja, inventor of the compass, and the place of origin of the "Tabula de Amalpha," a code of laws that governed the sea until 1570. After the Norman conquest and the earthquake of 1343, Amalfi fell from its maritime pre-eminence. Today, however, it has the life, noise, and chaos of a city many times its size. Fortunately, the tourist crunch isn't as intense as that in Sorrento, and the milieu is far more enchanting. Known as the "pearl of the coast," Amalfi attracts the travel-weary with the promise of strolls on bayside promenades, coffee in the intimate *piazza* in front of the cathedral, and forays into the hills of the surrounding coast.

ORIENTATION AND PRACTICAL INFORMATION

Buses stop in **Piazza Flavio Gioia.** Note the statue of the *piazza's* namesake, shown looking at his newly invented compass. To reach the main square, head away from the water and pass through the white, arched portal into **Piazza del Duomo.** The city's main street is **Via Lorenzo d'Amalfi,** leading uphill from the *piazza.*

Tourist Office: Corso delle Repubbliche Marinare, 27 (tel. 87 11 07; fax 87 26 19), on the water toward Salerno from the bus stop. Friendly staff has limited info; ask for the city pamphlet, hotel list, and map. Open Mon.-Sat. 8am-2pm.

Telephones: In the courtyard by the tourist office. Open daily 8am-8pm.

Buses: P. Flavio Gioia (tel. 87 10 09), on the waterfront. Blue **SITA** buses leave regularly for Sorrento (L3400), Positano (L2000), and Salerno (L2700); local orange buses leave every hr. for Ravello and Scala (L1500). Buy tickets at the SITA bar in P. Flavio Gioia, 2 or at the **Travel Tourist** office at P. Flavio Gioia, 4.

Ferries: Several companies sail from the port to the right of P. Flavio Gioia. Get up-to-date ferry info (prices change frequently) and buy tickets at the Travel Tourist office (see Buses, above). **Gabbiano** propels April-Oct. to Capri (1 per day, L11,000) and Salerno (4 per day, L4000). **Alilauro** runs 3 hydrofoils a day from Salerno to Capri via Amalfi and Positano (L17,000 to Capri, L7000 to Positano).

Boat Rental: Raffaele Florio (tel. 87 21 47), on the beach in the port area by the restaurant Lo Smeraldino. Small boats L25,000 per hr. Farther down the street, **Lido delle Sirene,** P. dei Protontini (tel. 87 14 89), rents small boats for L60,000 per 2hr. Also offers water skiing for L60,000 per 15min.

Luggage Storage: P. Gioia, 4. L3000 per bag. This office also has many maps and pamphlets unavailable at the tourist office. Open daily 8am-8:30pm; in summer 8am-9:30pm.

Emergencies: tel. 113. **First Aid (Guardia Medica):** Piazza Municipio, 4 (tel. 87 27 85), to the right of the tourist office. Open 24hr.

Police: Carabinieri, Via Casamare, 19 (tel. 87 10 22).

Post Office: Corso delle Repubbliche Marinare, 35 (tel. 87 13 30), next to the tourist office. Open Mon.-Fri. 8:15am-6:30pm, Sat. 8:15am-1pm. **Postal Code:** 84011.

Telephone Code: 089.

ACCOMMODATIONS

Staying in Amalfi can be expensive. Accommodations fill up in August, so reserve at least one month in advance. The best bargain nearby is A' Scalinatella, a stone's throw away in the less crowded village of Atrani.

Hotel Lidomare, Via Piccolomini, 9 (tel. 87 13 32; fax 87 13 94), through the passageway across from the *duomo.* Take a left up the stairs, then cross the *piazzetta.* Terrific rooms in a 700-year-old house. All rooms with bath, TV, and telephone, some with A/C, and most with a view of the water. Antique lounge with color TV and piano. Run by a dynamic duo. Singles L60,000. Doubles L100,000. Low-season prices L10,000 less. Breakfast included.

Hotel Amalfi, Via dei Pastai, 3 (tel. 87 24 40; fax 87 22 50), to the left off Via Lorenzo as you go uphill. A 3-star establishment with immaculate rooms, attentive management, terraces, and citrus gardens. All rooms with bath. English spoken. Singles L60,000-80,000. Doubles L100,000-150,000. Breakfast included. Mention *Let's Go* and they may charge prices closer to the minimum.

Pensione Proto, Salita dei Curiali, 4 (tel. 87 10 03). Take Via Lorenzo d'Amalfi from P. Duomo, and go right into the tiny alley by the sign for the Church of Maria Addolorata. Comfy but run-down rooms. English spoken. Singles L37,000. Doubles

L55,000, with bath L65,000. For groups of 4-6 people, L25,000 per person. Breakfast L10,000. Discount at La Shahrazad for hotel guests.

FOOD

Via Lorenzo d'Amalfi is paved with gold: golden bottles of *limoncello,* that is, a lemon liqueur that has become the specialty of the Amalfi Coast. In every shape and size, on racks, on shelves, and in baskets, bottles of this tart but delicious beverage—served ice-cold—line the street. Try some along with *passolini,* a regional specialty of plump raisins wrapped in lemon leaves (but don't eat the leaves).

Trattoria La Perla, Salita Truglio, 3 (tel. 87 14 40), around the corner from the Hotel Amalfi. Elegant and moderately priced. Terrific seafood. Try the bountiful *spaghetti al profumo di mare* (with "the scent of the sea", L10,000) or the *menù* (L21,000). Open daily noon-3:30pm and 7pm-midnight; Oct.-May closed Tues.

Shahrazad Club (tel. 87 33 80), on Via dei Prefetturi, 10m to the left of the cathedral and up the stairs. Abbreviated tourist *menù,* including wine, for L10,000. Full meal L18,000. In the evenings the downstairs becomes a piano bar, and the multilingual owner tickles the ivories. Open daily 8:30am-2:30pm and 6:30pm-2am.

Bar-Gelateria Royal, Via Lorenzo d'Amalfi, 10 (tel. 87 19 82), near the *duomo.* Fancy setting, not fancy prices. The excellent hand-churned ice cream here is possibly Amalfi's best, though you may have to sample a lot to be sure. Their specialty is the *pastiera napoletana,* with bits of Neapolitan Easter fruitcake. Cones L2000-3000. Open daily 11am-2am; Oct.-May closed Mon.

SIGHTS

The 9th-century **duomo** imparts grace, elegance, and dignity to the Piazza del Duomo. Rebuilt in the 19th century according to the original medieval plan, the cathedral features a façade of varied geometric designs typical of the Arab-Norman style. The **bronze doors,** crafted in Constantinople in 1066, started a bronze-door craze that reached all the way to Rome. (Cathedral open daily 7am-1:30pm and 3-8pm. Appropriate dress required.) To the left of the church the **Chiostro Paradiso** (Cloister of Paradise), a 13th-century cemetery, has become a graveyard for miscellaneous column, statue, and sarcophagus fragments, while its museum houses mosaics, sculptures, and the church's treasury. Its Arabic arches create a romantic setting for piano and vocal concerts on Friday nights from July through September. Concert tickets are L5000. From the cloister, you can reach the crypt of the cathedral, which houses **the remains of St. Andrew** (except his face, which the Pope donated to St. Andrew's in Patras, Greece; the back half of his head is in the altar here). (Cloister open daily 9am-1:30pm and 3-8pm. Admission L3000 for cloister, museum, and crypt. Multi-lingual guides available.)

The 9th-century **arsenal,** on the waterfront by the entrance to the city center, contains relics of Amalfi's former maritime glory. To escape the tourist throngs, walk down the main street past the *duomo* to the ceramic workshop **Ceramiche Giovanna Fusco,** Via delle Cartiere, 22, where you can see pottery made before your very eyes. (Open Jan. 7-Aug. 17 and Aug. 26-Dec. 22 Mon.-Sat. 9am-1pm and 3-6pm.) Just before the workshop, several yellow signs point to a path that leads up to one of the treasures of Amalfi, the **Valle dei Mulini** (Valley of the Mills). Hike along a stream bed by the old paper mills for a pastoral view of lemon groves and rocky mountains. On the way, stop by the **Museo della Carta,** dedicated to the history and art of paper. (Open Tues.-Thurs. and Sat.-Sun. 9am-1pm. Admission L2000.) On June 26 and 27 the town celebrates its patron Sant'Andrea; among much pomp and circumstance, a horde of men runs a solid metal statue of the saint up the cathedral's numerous stairs, leaving behind a shining trail of sweat.

■ Near Amalfi

ATRANI

If you stay in Amalfi, your first excursion should be to **Atrani,** a quiet beachside village of 1200 inhabitants just around the bend. The pebble beach here is the perfect place to float in the warm water and admire the stunning mountain backdrop. Locals claim the town is the smallest in Europe, and it's not hard to believe; the one drivable road provides access, and locals hang out in the one *piazza*. From Amalfi, walk 5min. along the waterfront toward Salerno. If you're burdened with a weighty pack, take the bus toward Salerno one stop (L1500). To walk to Atrani, either pass directly through the tunnel or descend the stairs that pass through the Ristorante Zaccaria just before you arrive at the tunnel. Cross the parking lot and under the arch into the town's only *piazza,* **Piazza Umberto I.** Atrani's main street, **Via dei Dogi,** heads up through the **Valley of the Dragons,** named for the torrent of water and mist (like smoke from a dragon) that runs through the town and out to sea every winter. The investiture of some of Amalfi's doges took place in the town's **Church of San Salvatore dei Birento,** which faces you as you enter the town's main archway. Although the church has been remodeled, the 11th-century Byzantine bronze doors are still intact. Thirteenth-century **Santa Maria Maddalena,** with its tiled cupola and gorgeous view of the coast, is also worth a visit.

One of the cheapest places on the coast, **A' Scalinatella,** P. Umberto, 12 (tel. 87 19 30), is Atrani's best budget accommodation. The congenial family that manages this quasi-hostel caters to students and budget travelers, and the backpackers come in droves. L25,000 in low-season and L30,000 in July and August will buy you a bunk bed, breakfast, and a pasta course at the Ristorante La Piazzetta (see below). As you climb up Via dei Dogi from the port, clean **public toilets** are on the left, and **phones** are on the right. **Ristorante La Piazzetta** (tel. 87 14 92) on P. Umberto I offers a *menù* for L16,000, discounted to L11,000 for guests at A' Scalinatella. Try the grilled fish or spaghetti with *frutti di mare,* but don't expect consistent quality. Open daily 7-11pm. **Le Arcate** (tel. 87 13 67), on the waterfront, offers a full *menù* including a sampling of seafood *antipasti;* a full meal will cost around L30,000. Open June-Sept. daily, Oct.-May Tues.-Sun. 12:30-3:30pm and 7:30pm-12:30am. V, MC, AmEx.

MINORI

Minori was once Amalfi's arsenal and as such suffered attacks from all its enemies. In these more peaceful times, however, the city is better known for its lemons (exported all over the world), its beaches, and its family atmosphere. Those on an antiquity-kick may want to check out the delightfully cool, underground **Roman villa** with frescoes and black and white mosaics. The entrance to the villa and the small villa museum lies off Via Nazionale behind the S. Lucia Hotel. Open daily 9am-7pm. Free. The **beach,** with the closest this coast gets to real sand, is a favorite place for locals to knock around a volleyball.

The coastal SITA bus (L1500 from Amalfi or Atrani) stops on Via Nazionale, which runs to the water. The Pro Loco **tourist office** at P. Umberto I, 18 (tel. (089) 87 70 87 or 87 76 07), hands out a small pamphlet with a map of the city. Open Mon.-Sat. 9am-noon and 4-8pm. **Public toilets** can be found at the heart of the city, where Via San Pietro splits off from Corso Vittorio Emanuele III across the street from the Banco di Napoli.

For a place to stay, homey and inexpensive **Albergo Capri,** Via Lama, 19, 3rd floor (tel. 87 74 17) is a good bet. Take the road through the bell tower of the Church of San Trofimena. Doubles L44,000, with bath L49,000. June-Sept. L6000-10,000 more. Extra bed 15% more. The **Caporal Hotel** (tel. 87 74 08; fax 87 71 66) on Via Nazionale provides some of the finer amenities, like a phone and TV in each room. Singles with bath L70,000. Doubles with bath L100,000. Half-pension L90,000. Oct.-May L10,000-20,000 less. V, MC, AmEx. For a satisfying meal, try **La Botte,** Via S. Maria Vetrana, 15 (tel. 87 78 93). Savor splendid *scialetelli con frutti* (L9500) at the outdoor tables. Pizza L6000-8000. Cover L2000. Open in summer daily noon-3:30pm and 7:30pm-1am; in winter closed Tues. V, AmEx.

Ravello

Ravello is an ideal spot for an afternoon stroll, a good read, or quiet contemplation. The town has retained the medieval beauty and picturesque landscape prized by Boccaccio, who dedicated part of the *Decameron* to it, and by Wagner, who made it the setting for the second act of *Parsifal*. Whether or not you sense yourself on the brink of creative genius, it's definitely worth the trip up the mountain. The bus ride is easier, but the 4-km hike up from Amalfi has the more spectacular views.

ORIENTATION AND PRACTICAL INFORMATION

Ravello is a short bus ride from Amalfi (every hr. 7am-10pm, L1500). From the bus stop, walk through the tunnel to **Piazza Vescovado,** the town's center and nighttime hang-out. The English-speaking **tourist office,** at P. Vescovado, 13 (tel. (089) 85 70 96; fax 85 79 77), to the left of the cathedral, has helpful brochures, maps, and up-to-date accommodations information. Open Mon.-Sat. 8am-8pm; Oct.-April Mon.-Sat. 8am-7pm. To the left of the tourist office sits the **post office.** Open Mon.-Fri. 8:15am-1:30pm, Sat. 8:15am-12:10pm. The **postal code** is 84010. Next door you will find the **pharmacy.**

ACCOMMODATIONS AND FOOD

Two affordable options are available if you're planning to spend the night. The dramatically situated **Hotel Villa Amore,** Via dei Fusco, 5 (tel./fax 85 71 35), en route to Villa Cimbrone, has cute, tidy rooms and a garden overlooking cliffs and the sea. It's hard to argue with their welcome sign, which states, "A stay at Villa Amore gives peace to the soul and joy to the heart." All rooms have bath and balcony. Singles L60,000, June L50,000. Doubles L105,000, Sept.-May 95,000. Half-pension is required in July and August for L85,000. V, MC. Up the street to the left of the tourist office, **Albergo Toro,** Viale Wagner, 3 (tel./fax 85 72 11), lends pleasant, comfortable rooms on an oleander-filled side street and has a cozy covered terrace. All rooms with bath. Singles L90,000, Oct.-May L55,000. Doubles L100,000, Sept.-May L65,000. Breakfast included. Half-pension is required in July and August for L90,000. V, MC, AmEx. Several **alimentari** and assorted specialty food shops line Via Roma off P. Vescovado. For a sit-down meal try **La Colonna** at Via Roma, 20 (tel. 85 78 76). The affable young owner Alfonso speaks English and is well-known throughout the town for his delectable fish and homemade pasta. A full meal will cost around L30,000. Open daily 12:30-3pm and 7pm-midnight. Nov.-May closed Tues. At **Cumpà Cosimo,** Via Roma, 44/46 (tel. 85 71 56), you can savor a variety of local specialties with an *assaggio di primi* (L15,000), a sampler of all the available pasta dishes. Although many wines savored around the globe are decanted under a Ravello label, actual wine from the area is neither common nor commercially available; make friends in the town if you hope to try some.

SIGHTS AND ENTERTAINMENT

The beautiful churches, ivy-covered walls, and meandering gardens of **Villa Rufolo,** 360m above the sea, inspired Wagner to genius. A medieval tower with beautiful Norman-Saracen vaulting and statues representing the four seasons serves as the entry to the famous Moorish cloister. Enter through the arch toward the bus stop from P. Vescovado. (Open daily 9:30am-1pm and 3-7pm. Admission L4000, under 12 L2000.)

Outside Ravello's **duomo** on P. Vescovado you can see the Amalfi coast's third set of famous bronze doors. (Not to be outdone by the neighbors, Ravellan artisans modeled these 12th-century doors on Amalfi's set.) Inside, a simple nave arcade of antique columns sets off two pulpits decorated with elaborate mosaics. To the left of the altar stands the chapel of San Pantaleone, patron saint of the town. Walk behind the painting to see his "unleakable" blood, preserved in a cracked vessel. San Pantaleone was beheaded at Nicomedia on July 27, 290. Every year on this day the city holds a **festival** and the saint's blood reputedly liquefies. (Open daily 9am-1pm and 3-7pm, Oct.-May 9am-1pm and 2-5pm.) Inside the *duomo* is a **museum,** open the same hours as the church. (Admission L2000.)

Follow the signposts for **Villa Cimbrone** on the small road passing to the right of Villa Rufolo. Floral walkways and gardens are the prelude to some of the most magnificent views on the Amalfi coast. (Open daily 9am-7:30pm. Admission L5000.) Walking back to the town center, you'll pass the **Chiostro di San Francesco,** which exhibits **Italian modern art** throughout the summer.

Ravello's numerous **classical music festivals** (held the weeks of New Year's Day, Easter, and during parts of June, July, and September) host internationally renowned musicians. Concerts draw crowds to the cathedral and the gardens of Villa Rufolo. Tickets run from L30,000, and they may be purchased at the tourist office. Call 85 81 49 for more info.

Salerno

The capital of the Norman Empire from 1077 to 1127 and home to Europe's first medical school, Salerno was almost completely destroyed by the bombs of World War II. The big-city atmosphere and postwar buildings are a shock to the system of a traveler accustomed to the Amalfi Coast's relatively peaceful coastal villages. Nevertheless, inexpensive food and accommodations make Salerno an excellent base for exploring the area. Extensive train and bus connections facilitate transit to Calabria and allow for daytrips to Paestum, the Amalfi Coast, and Pompeii.

ORIENTATION AND PRACTICAL INFORMATION

From the train station on **P. Vittorio Veneto,** the expansive and remarkably clean **Corso Vittorio Emanuele** veers off to the right (closed to traffic). A 15-min. walk brings you to Via dei Mercanti and the **old quarter,** the most historically interesting and vivacious part of the city. Alternatively, continue straight on **Via Mauro** from the train station, cross Corso Garibaldi and come to **Piazza della Concordia** on the waterfront. **Lungomare Trieste** runs along the coast, and **Via Roma** heads off to the right from the *lungomare*.

Tourist Office: EPT, P. Veneto (tel. 23 14 32), to the right as you leave the train station. Limited info on the Amalfi Coast. Pick up a copy of the essential guide *MEMO,* complete with hotel, restaurant, club, and special events listings. English spoken. Open Mon.-Sat. 9am-2pm and 3-8pm.

Budget Travel: CTS, P. A. Santelmo, 7 (tel. 72 19 75). From Lungomare Trieste, take bus #6, 8, or 11 south about 2km to the intersection with Via Mantegna at Bar Marconi, then follow Via Mantegna to P. Santelmo. Open Mon.-Fri. 9:30am-1pm and 4:30-7:30pm, Sat. 9:30am-noon.

Telephones: Corso Garibaldi, 31/32, set in from the street to the left as you leave the train station. Open Sun.-Fri. 9:30am-1pm and 2-5:30pm.

Trains: P. Veneto (tel. 25 50 05). Trains depart every hr. 6am-9:30pm to Pompeii (40min., L2700) and Naples (1hr., L5000). 3 trains daily to Paestum on the Salerno-Paola line (45min., L4200). Information office at the first door to the right outside the station. Open daily 8am-noon and 1-6pm. **Luggage Storage:** Follow the signs in the station to the huge warehouse. Bags and bikes L5000 for 12hr.

Buses: SITA, Corso Garibaldi, 117 (tel. 79 50 21). Ticket office open daily 5am-9pm. Buses to Naples (every 15-30min. 6am-9pm, L5000) leave from Corso Garibaldi outside SITA office. Buses run on a seasonal schedule. In summer, buses for the Amalfi coast depart from P. della Concordia to: Amalfi (frequent buses 6am-10:30pm, L2700); Sorrento (14 per day, 6am-8:30pm, L6100) with stops at the coastal towns of Praiano (L3400) and Positano (L4200). Sun. buses run less frequently. **ATACS** (tel. 22 58 99) city bus #41 leaves every 20min. from outside the train station to

Pompeii (6:05am-10:10pm, 30min., L3400). Several bus lines run from P. Concordia to Paestum (1hr., direction "Agropoli," L5600).

Ferries: Departures from P. della Concordia or Molo Manfredi. (Molo is a 15-min. walk to the right while facing the port at P. della Concordia.) A good alternative if the careening bus ride along the Amalfi Coast scares you. Check the *MEMO* guide at the port for current departure times and prices. 6-9 ferries daily in the summer (fewer in winter) to **Amalfi** (L4000) and **Positano** (L7500). 3-5 daily in summer to **Capri** (L12,000). Hydrofoils take half the time but run less frequently (3 daily in summer). To: **Amalfi** (L7000), **Positano** (L13,000), and **Capri** (L17,000).

Emergencies: tel. 113. **First Aid:** tel. 33 99 99. **Hospital: S. Lenardo** (tel. 67 11 11).

Police: tel. 113.

Post Office: Corso Garibaldi, 203 (tel. 22 99 70). Open Mon.-Sat. 8:30am-5:30pm. **Branch office** at P. Veneto (tel. 22 99 98), to the right as you leave the train station. Open Mon.-Fri. 8:15am-1:30pm, Sat. 8:15am-12:10pm. **Postal Code:** 84100.

Telephone Code: 089.

ACCOMMODATIONS

Ostello della Gioventù "Irno" (HI), Via Luigi Guercia, 112 (tel. 79 02 51). Exit the train station and turn left onto Via Torrione, which runs along the tracks. After about 300m you'll come to Via Mobilio, which will take you left under the tracks. The second stairway on the right, about 300m ahead, leads up to Via Luigi Guercia. Clean rooms, hot showers, kitchen facilities, TV room, and kind management. Curfew 12:30am. Lock-out 10:30am-2pm. L15,000 per person, L2000 for sheets. Ask at desk for a list of eateries that offer discounts to hostel clientele.

Albergo Santa Rosa, Corso Vittorio Emanuele, 14 (tel. 22 53 46), off the *piazza* in front of the train station. Clean, bright, and reasonably priced. English spoken. Curfew midnight. Singles L40,000. Doubles L60,000. All rooms without bath.

Hotel Salerno, Via Vicinanza, 42 (tel. 22 42 11), the first left off Corso Emanuele. The furniture was new in the 50s and hasn't died yet. Phones in the rooms and TV lounge. Singles L35,000, with bath L55,000. Doubles L65,000, with bath L75,000.

Pensione Cinzia, C. Vittorio Emanuele, 74 (tel. 23 27 73). Large, airy rooms, all of which are doubles with common bathrooms (L50,000).

FOOD

Salerno serves up such typical Campanian culinary delights as *pasta e fagioli* (pasta and bean soup) and seafood, augmenting this menu with unusual specialties of its own, such as *milza* (spleen). Nearby Battipaglia produces the famous *mozzarella alla buffala,* fresh cheese made from water buffalo milk. Shop cheap at the **STANDA** supermarket, Corso Vittorio Emanuele, 228, near the old quarter. Open Mon.-Fri. 9am-1pm and 4:30-8:30pm, closed Mon. afternoon. Or, nearer the youth hostel, try **Di Luccio,** Via Mobilio, 62. Open Mon.-Sat. 7am-9:30pm.

Trattoria-Pizzeria Da "Sasà" La Casereccia, Via Diaz, 42 (tel. 22 03 30), to the right, 300m down Corso V. Emanuele from the train station. A lot of fun for those who *parlano* a little *italiano*. There's no menu—it all depends on what's fresh. Full meal L15,000-20,000. Open Sat.-Thurs. 12:30-3pm and 8-11:30pm.

Hosteria Il Brigante, Via F. Linguiti, 4 (tel. 22 65 92), near the cathedral. Follow C. Vittorio Emanuele to Via dei Mercanti and turn right on Via del Duomo, going through the gate to the left just past the cathedral. Try the *pasta alla Sangiovannara,* with zucchini and scampi. Full meals from L15,000. Open Tues.-Sun. 8:30pm-midnight. Lunch by reservation only. AmEx.

Pizzeria Del Vicolo della Neve, Vicolo della Neve, 24 (tel. 22 57 05). From Via dei Mercanti, take the first left after Via Duomo. In the old city, this piece of Salerno's history opened its doors 500 years ago. Full meal from L20,000. Cover L2000. Service 12%. Open Thurs.-Tues. 8pm-3am.

Ristorante Il Caminetto, Via Roma, 232 (tel. 22 96 14). Near the AAST tourist office. A family-run restaurant with low prices. Savor *risotto alla pescatore,* a delicious mix of rice and seafood, for only L8000. Pizzas L5000-9000. Cover L2000. Service 12%. Open Thurs.-Tues. noon-3:30pm and 7pm-midnight. V, MC.

SIGHTS AND ENTERTAINMENT

Meandering through Via dei Mercanti and its tiny side-streets, you can get a feel for the hustle and bustle of life in the Middle Ages in Salerno's **medieval quarter.** It was once the capital of the Norman empire (1077-1127) and home to Europe's oldest medical school (9th-century texts were already calling it ancient). From Via Mercanti, turn right on Via Duomo to see the **cathedral,** begun in 845 and rebuilt 200 years later by Norman leader Robert Guiscard. The atrium contains an ancient pool surrounded by columns taken from Paestum, while the crypt houses the **holy tooth** of the city's patron saint, San Matteo. In the attached museum you can see the fine work of medieval ivory-carvers from Amalfi. (Cathedral open daily 10am-noon and 4-6:30pm. Museums open daily 9am-1pm and 4-7pm.) In the nearby Largo Casavecchia, the **Museo della Ceramica** exhibits local ceramic art. (Open Mon.-Sat. 9am-1pm, Thurs. also 4-7pm. Free.)

Turn left off Via Mercanti and stroll along the waterfront **seawall.** Revel in the divine Amalfi coastline, and witness the sights and sounds of the nearby fishing harbor. The hamlet of **Vietri sul Mare** is home to hundreds of artisans and to the closest beach to Salerno. (Take the SITA bus toward Sorrento, 15min., L1500.) The other option—Paestum's strand—is farther away, but its stretches of white sand beat the rocky beaches of the Amalfi Coast.

Take bus #19 from Teatro Verdi (at the far end of Via Roma, every 2hr.) to the medieval **Castello di Arechi** (tel. 22 72 37), which dates from the 8th century. You can view Salerno's majestic surroundings, though there is actually little to see *inside* the castle. (Open Tues.-Sun. 9am-1pm. Free. Buy bus tickets at bars and *tabacchi;* L1500 per half day, L2500 per full day.)

Don't miss the evening *passeggiata,* when the *lungomare* overflows with people strolling and enjoying ice cream. From June through August, an **arts festival** features free concerts and theater in the atrium of the cathedral and at the city's stadium. Salerno also hosts several **international film festivals** from June through October at Cinema Capitol in the city center. (Admission up to L7000.) In July, experience both hot and cool at the international **blues festival.** (Buy tickets at the stadium. Weekly passes L35,000.)

The area around Salerno rocks with **discos,** but prices are steep without passes. Women can often get in free, but take that as its own warning. From June through September, the nighttime hotspot is **Fuenti** (tel. 26 18 00), located in Cetara, 4km west of Salerno. Situated on the coastal cliffs, it features three full floors of open-air dancing. Open Sat.-Sun. 10pm-4am. In the winter, Salerno lives it up at **Living** (tel. 79 92 01), on Via Gelsi Rossi near the hostel. (Open Oct.-May Thurs.-Fri. 8:30pm-2am, Sat. 9:30pm-3am, and Sun. 6:30pm-3am.) The cheapest way to get into these clubs is to look for free passes handed out at random. Ask at the hostel, and check the magazine *MEMO* (at the tourist office, the hostel, and some local bars) for special events and club listings, including those outside Salerno.

Paestum

Not far from the Roman ruins of Pompeii and Herculaneum, the Greek temples of Paestum are among the best-preserved in the world, rivaling even those of Sicily and Athens. Greek colonists from Sybaris founded Paestum as Poseidonia in the 7th century BC, and the city quickly became a flourishing commercial and trading center. After a period of Lucanian (native Italian) control in the 5th and 4th centuries BC, Poseidonia fell to the Romans in 273BC and was renamed. Paestum remained a Roman town until the Appian Way was extended from Rome to Brindisi and trade began to bypass the city. Plagued by malaria and pirates, Paestum's last inhabitants abandoned the city in the 9th century AD, leaving the ruins relatively untouched.

ORIENTATION AND PRACTICAL INFORMATION

Buses from Salerno (every 30min., 6am-8pm, L4200) let you off on **Via Magna Graecia,** the main modern road; ask to stop at the ruins *(gli scavi)* or at your hotel to save yourself a walk. Be sure to check return bus times in advance. If you catch one of the infrequent **trains** (5 during the day from Salerno, L4200), head straight out of the station and through Porta Sirena, the most intact of the ancient city gates. A short walk brings you to V. Magna Graecia. The last bus back to Salerno passes by at 7:30pm and the last train at 10:10pm. Another option is to take the bus to nearby Agropoli (L1800) where there are many other train connections. The **tourist office** is at P. Basilica 151/153 (tel. 81 10 16). Open Mon.-Sat. 8am-2pm. You can also call **Cointur,** which is not in Paestum but can help with reservations over the phone (tel. 72 47 47; some English spoken). Paestum's **telephone code** is 0828.

ACCOMMODATIONS AND FOOD

Paestum makes a great daytrip from Salerno, but if you want to spend the night, **Albergo delle Rose,** Via Magna Graecia, 193 (tel. 81 10 70), is a relatively inexpensive option with luxurious rooms. Singles L45,000. Doubles L80,000. Prices are L5000-10,000 lower from Oct. to April. A 10-min. walk on Via Principe di Piemonte to the right past the ruins and toward the coast will bring you to numerous **campsites. Apollo** (tel. 81 11 78) provides a soccer field, bar, and *discoteca*. L6000 per person, L11,000 per tent. 4-person bungalows L60,000. Open May to September, **Dei Pini** (tel. 81 10 30) also keeps you well fed, with a *pizzeria,* bar, and food store on-site. English is spoken. Groups of 4 or more preferred. L40,000 for 4 people in low-season; L60,000 in high-season. Open year-round. Restaurants in Paestum are scarce, so you may want to pack a picnic lunch before you go. With outdoor seating under a large tent that looks like something from the stereotypical deserts of Arabia, **Oasi** (tel. 81 19 35) on V. Magna Graecia, 100m to the left of the museum, serves full meals (about L20,000) during the day and pizzas in the evening (from L5000). Cover L1500. Service 15%. Open Jan.-Sept. daily and Oct.-Nov. Tues.-Sun. noon-3pm and 7pm-midnight.

SIGHTS

The ancient Greeks built Paestum on a north-south axis, marked by the still-paved Via Sacra. (Looking at the ruins from the modern V. Magna Graecia, which runs parallel to Via Sacra, north is to your right.) Most guided tours start from the Porta Giustizia at the southern end of Via Sacra.

Paestum's three **Doric temples** rank among the best-preserved in the world. Built without any mortar or other cement, the buildings were originally covered by roofs of terra-cotta tiles supported by wooden beams. All the stone you see now was once painted. For a more detailed discussion of the history, architecture, and archaeology of the temples and site, look for *Paestum: Guide to the Excavations and Archaeological Museum* (ed. Matonti; available in any of the roadside shops, L6000).

When excavators first uncovered the three temples, they misnamed them. Although recent scholarship has led to new guesses for the temples' dedications, the old names have stuck anyway. The southernmost temple, the so-called **basilica,** is the oldest, dating to the second half of the 6th century BC. Its unusual plan, including a main interior section (*naos*) split in two by a single row of columns down the middle, has inspired the theory that the temple was dedicated to two gods, Zeus and Hera, instead of just one. The next temple to the north, the **Temple of Poseidon** (actually dedicated to Hera), was built 100 years after the "basilica," in the middle of the 5th century BC. The Temple of Poseidon incorporates many of the same optical refinements that characterize the Parthenon in Athens. On the temple's roof are some small lions' heads; when it rained, water from the gutters came pouring out of their mouths. The third major Doric temple, the **Temple of Ceres** (whose dedication is now disputed), lies off to the north of the Forum. This temple was built around

500BC (placing its construction date between those of the other two temples). It became a church in the early Middle Ages then was abandoned in the 9th century.

Continuing north on Via Sacra, you come to the Roman **Forum,** even larger than the one at Pompeii. The Romans leveled most of the older structures at the center of the city to make room for this proto-*piazza,* the commercial and political arena of Paestum. To the right, a large, shallow pit marks the site of the pool in an ancient **gymnasium.** East of the gymnasium lies half of the Roman **amphitheater** (the modern road buries the rest).

The **museum** on the other side of V. Magna Graecia houses an extraordinary collection of ancient pottery and paintings taken primarily from the tombs discovered in the area. Those well versed in mythology can play guessing games with sculptural panels from a sanctuary dedicated to Hera discovered nine km to the north of Paestum. According to legend, Jason and the Argonauts founded the temple. Also of note are the paintings from the famous **Tomb of the Diver,** rare examples of Greek wall painting. (Archaeological site open 9am-1hr. before sunset; ticket offices close 1hr. earlier. Museum open 9am-7pm. L8000 admits you to both ruins and museum.)

After visiting the ruins, you may want to worship the sun at the **beach** 2km to the east. The golden sand stretches for miles—unfortunately, much (but not all) of it is owned by resorts that require you to rent a chair for the day. Ask around for directions to a *spiaggia pubblica,* where you can take a free dip in the Mediterranean.

In July and August, Paestum hosts an international festival of music, drama, and dance. Contact the tourist office for event and ticket info.

Apulia (Puglia)

Welcome to hard-core Italy, where the sun's scorching rays and the people's intense passions continually threaten to bring things to a boil. Conversations, complete with elaborate hand gestures, quickly progress from pleasant joking to frenzied yelling, and then back again. Some travelers interpret the southerners' mercurial passions as rudeness, but you'll have a better understanding (and a better time) if you try to see them as part of an uninhibited zest for life. Unfortunately, a legacy of *machismo* persists which women may find threatening, especially in large cities. In public, the best tactic for dissuading persistent, obnoxious behavior is to ignore it.

The heel of Italy's boot, Apulia has been prized throughout the centuries for its fertile plains and numerous natural ports. Once part of ancient Greece, the Romans later controlled the region as a vital stop on the trade route to the East. With the Middle Ages came an onslaught of invaders, whose influences have created a conglomerate culture. Modern Apulia, having served its time on "skid row," is regaining prominence as the richest and most educated region in southern Italy. In its interior, remote medieval villages and whitewashed, cone-roofed *trulli* houses dot a cave-ridden plain, while the ports along the shore have a distinctly Middle Eastern air.

Apulia is as accessible to contemporary tourists as it was to ancient invaders. Direct train lines run from Naples to Bari and from Bologna to Lecce, and rail service is supplemented within the region by the private Ferrovie Bari-Nord, Ferrovie Del Sud-Est, Ferrovie del Gargano, and Ferrovie Calabro-Lucane lines. (Eurailpass and *cartaverde* are not valid on these private lines.) The transportation hubs of Foggia, Brindisi, and Taranto are perhaps best viewed from the station as you make your connections. Base yourself in Bari or Lecce instead.

Bari

Bari, the capital of Apulia, is an enjoyable and inexpensive base for exploration of the region and a pleasant departure point for Greece. The city has been transformed into a backpacker's haven thanks to the dedicated efforts of the "Stop-Over in Bari" program. Its staff will do everything they can think of to make your stay entertaining, interesting, and cheap (see below). Because of its port and central location, Bari was once a major stronghold of Byzantine power in southern Italy and later an important point of departure for the Crusades. Today, the modern city is divided into the new city, composed of wide streets laid out on a well organized grid, and the small and increasingly poor old city. Pickpockets and petty thieves abound, particularly inside the winding streets of the old city, so hold purses and cameras tightly and wear money belts inside your clothes. But try not to let fear of thievery diminish your enjoyment of the city's great seafood and hopping nightlife.

THE "STOP-OVER IN BARI" PROGRAM

Twelve years ago, local government and grass roots organizations came up with a unique idea to make Bari a mecca for backpackers from all over. They designed the "Stop-Over in Bari" program and inaugurated a free campsite to entice those heading to Greece to stop and enjoy all Bari has to offer. Between **mid-June** and **mid-September,** Stop-Over provides immeasurable assistance to non-resident travelers under 30. Although older visitors are not eligible for Stop-Over's freebies, they should still stop by the offices for the most complete and up-to-date info on Bari.

Outside the central train station parks a raucously painted double-decker **bus** with a large "Stop-Over in Bari" sign above. Relax while the MTV-generation, multilingual staff kindly provides you with every piece of info you could possibly need about Bari, ferries, and more. At the bus stop, watch international television (daily 4pm-midnight), or use Stop-Over's free internet hours to check your e-mail (Mon. and Wed. 6:30-8pm). Another **info booth** is inside the **Stazione Marittima.** Open daily 8:30am-8:30pm. Stop-Over's **main office** at Via Nicolai, 47 (tel. 521 45 38; fax 521 18 22) has more detailed information on sights and events, and provides free luggage storage. Open Mon.-Sat. 8:30am-8:30pm and Sun. 9am-6pm.

Pick up a daily Stop-Over **newsletter** for info on discounted restaurants, supermarkets, shops, museums, nightlife, and cultural events. For free accommodations, take bus #5 (last departure 11pm, but be there no later than 10:45pm) or #3 (a longer route) to Pineta San Francesco, a **campground** with a bar, free showers, and more free luggage storage. They'll provide a tent if you don't have your own. All city buses are free as long as you are under 30 and a non-resident of Bari—just flash your passport or the special card that they'll give you at the campground. Be aware that buses to the campground are infrequent.

Stop-Over also offers various events and seminars (such as pizza-making or miniature *trulli* building) at the campground throughout the summer. All events are free. For nighttime entertainment, Stop-Over also organizes two weekly **rock concerts** and four major concerts with bands from throughout Europe. To make it even more like summer camp, they bus their guests on free excursions to sites around Apulia (such as Castel de Monte and Alberobello) on Sundays. Tour Bari for free using their **bicycles** and **skateboards** but don't leave them unattended; you don't get a lock. They also provide free copies of an English edition of Luca Conti's *Inter-Rail Man,* a funny and detailed guide to railpass travel from a personal perspective. The **summer hotline** is 577 23 49 (at the Pineta). Visit their web page at http://www.inmedia.it/StopOver, or e-mail them at StopOver@inmedia.it.

FERRIES

Getting to Greece from Bari is cheaper and more appealing than from highly industrial Brindisi (unless you have a Eurail or InterRail pass). Ferries go to **Corfu** (10hr.), **Igoumenitsa** (12hr.), and **Patras** (19hr.). There are no discounts for Eurailpass or *cartaverde* holders, but most lines offer special student rates and a 10% discount on roundtrip tickets (Poseidon discounts 20% for roundtrip). The following list of ferry companies includes the lowest prices (deck class) for each destination. The high-season varies slightly from company to company, year to year, and place to place (ah, l'Italia!), but generally runs from the first week of July to the last week of August.

Tickets and info can be obtained directly at the Stazione Marittima or at the offices listed below. **You must check in at the Stazione Marittima two hours before departure.** After check-in, police will examine your passport. **OTE,** the travel agency connected with Stop-Over (open year-round; see Budget Travel, below), also has ferry and ticket info.

Poseidon Lines, c/o Morfimare, Corso de Tullio, 36/40 (tel. 521 00 22; fax 521 12 04). Box 11-12 at the port. To **Igoumenitsa** (L41,000/L59,000; students L32,800/ L47,200). Departures Tues. and Thurs. 7pm, Sat. 5pm, and Sun. midnight. From Greece, Poseidon ferries head to **Cyprus** and **Israel.**

Ventouris Ferries, c/o Pan Travel, Via S. Francesco d'Assisi, 95, Stazione Marittima Box 9-10 (tel. 524 43 88; fax 524 67 79). To: **Patras** and **Cefalonia** (L65,000/ L85,000; students L60,000/L75,000), departing daily in the summer at 8pm; **Corfu** and **Igoumenitsa** (L45,000/L65,000; students L35,000/L60,000). To Corfu in June on scattered days, July to mid-Sept. daily. To Igoumenitsa late Jan.-June on scattered days, July-Sept. daily. Departs 7 or 8pm.

Marlines, c/o P. Lorusso & Co., Car Ferry Terminal Box 3-4 (tel. 521 76 99; fax 521 77 34). To **Corfu** and **Igoumenitsa** (L40,000/L72,000; return ticket L36,000/ L65,000). April to mid-June departures Mon. and Wed. 7pm, Fri. 6pm, and Sat. 11pm. Mid-June to Sept. departures daily 9pm.

ORIENTATION AND PRACTICAL INFORMATION

Via Sparano leads straight from the train station two blocks to **Piazza Umberto I,** the main square in town. Farther along Via Sparano, the streets are lined with fancy boutiques that provide some of the city's best window shopping. At the end of V. Sparano is **Corso Vittorio Emanuele II** and the edge of the old city. Those attempting the long walk to the **port** should skirt the old city's hopelessly winding streets by turning left on Corso Emanuele II and right at Piazza della Libertà onto Via Giuseppe Massari. Walk around the castle, head right, and follow the coast. For a more leisurely stroll, turn right off V. Sparano onto Corso Emanuele II; this takes you past **Corso Cavour** to **Piazza Eroi del Mare,** a favorite nighttime hangout for many of the city's young people. To reach the port from here, follow Lungomare Imperatore Augusto along the water, and head to the left on Corso Senatore A. de Tullio.

Tourist Office: Stop-Over should satisfy your every need, but there's also **EPT,** P. Aldo Moro, 33A (tel. 524 22 44), to the right as you leave the station. Regional and local maps of Apulia. English spoken, sort of. Open Mon.-Sat. 9am-1pm.

Budget Travel: OTE, tel. 521 45 38. From the station, walk 1 block past P. Umberto and to the left. Located in Stop-Over's main office at Via Nicolai, 47. Info on student discount travel. Open Mon.-Sat. 8:30am-8:30pm, Sun. 9am-6pm.

Currency Exchange: At the information desk in the F.S. train station (open daily 7am-8:45pm), or at the **Automobile Club Italiano** at the ferry terminal (only when boats are arriving or departing).

American Express: Morfimare, Corso de Tullio, 36/40 (tel. 521 00 22), near the port. Open Mon.-Fri. 9am-1pm and 3:30-7:30pm, Sat. 9am-noon.

Trains: F.S. train station in P. Aldo Moro (tel. 521 68 01). Bari lies on train lines from Rome (6 per day, 8hr., L37,000) and Milan (10 per day, 10hr., L65,400). Frequent trains connect Bari with Apulia's larger towns: Foggia (1½hr., L9800); Taranto (2hr., L9800); Brindisi (2hr., L9800); and Lecce (2½hr., L11,700). The station is also home to several private lines, including the **Ferrovie del Sud-Est** (tel. 558 32 22; to Castellana Grotte, Alberobello, and Martina Franca), on the last track of the central station, the **Bari-Nord** (tel. 521 47 14; to Bitonto, Barletta, Andria, and Ruvo di Puglia), and the **Ferrovie Apulo-Lucane** (tel. 572 52 22; to Matera in Basilicata), both to the left as you exit the main station. Eurailpasses and *cartaverde* are only good on F.S. trains.

Bookstore: Feltrinelli, Via Dante, 91 (tel. 521 96 77), carries a decent collection of classics in English. Open Mon.-Fri. 9am-8pm, Sat. 9am-1pm, but hours vary.

Emergencies: tel. 113.

Police: tel. 113. **Carabinieri:** tel. 112.

Post Office: (tel. 521 03 81), in P. Battisti behind the university. From P. Umberto, take a left on Via Crisanzio, then the first right on Via Cairoli. Located near Stop-Over's main office. Open Mon.-Fri. 8:20am-8pm, Sat. 8:20am-1pm. **Postal Code:** 70100.

Telephone Code: 080.

ACCOMMODATIONS

Ostello del Levante (HI), Palese Marina, Lungomare Massaro, 33 (tel. 530 02 82). Take the train to the Bari-Palese stop (L1500) or bus #1 from Corso Cavour to Palese, and then walk to the beach. The hostel resides outside the city and has clean rooms and bathrooms. Formerly (and occasionally still) a home for the mentally handicapped, so watch which column you check when you register. 3-6 beds per room. HI card required. Lockout 9am-4:30pm. Curfew 11:30pm. L16,000 per person. Breakfast included. Full dinners L14,000.

Pensione Fiorini, Via Imbriani, 69 (tel. 554 07 88). From the train station, walk straight one block past P. Umberto I, and turn right on Via Dante, which turns into Via Imbriani. Rooms have high ceilings and balconies, but few have private baths. Management loves foreign tourists. Small singles L30,000. Doubles L59,000, with bath L69,000. Showers L5000.

Pensione Giulia, Via Crisanzio, 12 (tel. 521 66 30; fax 521 82 71). From the station, turn left just before P. Umberto. Clean, spacious, and recently remodeled rooms. Singles L50,000, with bath L65,000. Doubles L70,000, with bath L90,000. Triples L110,000, with bath L120,000. Quads L140,000. Breakfast included. V, MC, AmEx.

Pensione Romeo, Via Crisanzio, 12 (tel. 521 63 52; fax 523 72 53). Downstairs from Pensione Giulia. Hmm. Small singles L39,000, with bath L50,000. Doubles with bath L80,000.

FOOD

As much as the city seems to cater to Greece-bound tourists, it is incredibly easy to find a good, authentic, Apulian meal for a reasonable price. Restaurants in the old town are very old-world, often providing neither menus nor itemized checks. If you don't have time to sample the restaurants, take advantage of the many colorful **markets,** like the daily vegetable frenzy in P. del Ferrarese. **Super CRAI,** V. de Giosa, 97 (tel. 524 74 85), three streets to the right of P. Umberto I while facing away from the station, is a great place to stock up for the ferry ride; it will undoubtedly be cheaper and tastier than food bought onboard. Open Mon.-Sat. 8am-2pm and 5-8:30pm.

Vini e Cucina Da Nicola, Strada Vallisa, 23, in the old city. Take a right off Via Sparano onto Corso Emanuele. From P. IV Novembre, enter the old city on your left; the restaurant will also be on your left. Inexpensive dining at its best. Don't let the mostly male clientele and no-frills service frighten you off. No menu—dishes change daily. The *calamari* (if available) is exquisite. *Menù* L11,000. Open Mon.-Sat. noon-3pm and 7pm-midnight.

Taverna Verde, Largo Adua, 18/19 (tel. 54 03 09), in a triangular *piazza* on the *lungomare.* From Corso Cavour (parallel to Via Sparano and two blocks to the right), turn right onto Via Cognetti. Black-tie service at black-t-shirt prices. *Orecchiette alla barese* (the regional pasta speciality) L7000. Local wine L3000 per bottle. Cover L3000. Open Mon.-Sat. noon-3pm and 8-11pm. V, MC, AmEx.

Osteria delle Travi, Largo Chiurlia, 12, at the end of Via Sparano. Turn left through the arches at the entrance to the old city. Sample true *Mezzogiorno* cuisine such as pasta with arugula or *ricotta e braciola* (stuffed horsemeat). Full meals L17,000 without drinks. Open daily 12:30-3pm and 7:30-10:30pm.

El Pedro Self-Service, Via Piccinni, 152 (tel. 521 12 94), off Via Sparano. Go left one block before Corso Emanuele. Not a Mexican restaurant, but a great cafeteria serving authentic Apulian specialties, different every day. Complete meal with drink about L16,000. Open for lunch only, Mon.-Sat. noon-3pm.

SIGHTS

A strategic port on the Italian coast, Bari has always been a primary point of attack for invading armies. To help deter and defend against encroaching troops, Bari's citizens built the old city as a labyrinth; residents could hide in the narrow, twisting passageways or use them to ambush those less familiar with the streets. Thieves have learned to use the maze of the old city to their advantage, and it can become a nightmare for the careless tourist. **Do not venture alone into the old city, especially at night.** Avoid flashy watches and jewelry; keep valuables inside front pockets; and hold purses, bags, and cameras tightly so that thieves cannot grab them. Stick to the larger streets, and use a map—don't make yourself a target for crime.

On the other hand, don't let petty criminals scare you off entirely; the old city is of immense historic interest and well worth visiting. On its outskirts, right in front of the cathedral, the **Castello Svevo** (Swabian Castle) evokes the grandeur and power of three different periods. The Norman Ruggiero II founded the structure with a castle proper and four keeps. Frederick II (1230-1240) then rearranged it into a trapezoid. The pointed door and beautiful mullioned windows in the north, toward the sea, were constructed in this period. Finally, Isabel of Aragon and Sona Sforza reorganized the internal court and added the bulwarks and angular keeps in the 16th century. Almost all of the castle is closed for the excavation of a recently discovered **Roman city** and Byzantine-period site. You can, however, admire plasters of Apulian sculpture from the 11th to 16th centuries and treasures removed from the basilica in the **Gypsoteca.** (Open daily 9am-12:30pm and 3:30-6:30pm. Admission L4000, under 18 and over 59 free.)

Enter the **old city** behind the castle and follow P. Massari to P. Federico II di Svevia. Turn right at P. Odegitria, which leads to the **cathedral.** Begun at the end of the 12th century during the peaceful years of Norman rule, the cathedral displays a typically austere Romanesque façade, somewhat modified by baroque decorations around the doors. Its interior is a fine example of Romanesque architecture, with a choir and chapel protruding from the nave. (Open daily 8am-noon and 4-7pm.)

Yes, Virginia, there is a **Santa Claus,** and he's dead. His remains were stolen from Asia Minor by 60 Baresi sailors in 1087—they don't call Bari *scippolandia* ("petty thieves' land") for nothing. The victorious sailors refused to hand over the saint to the local clergy, claiming that they had vowed to construct a special shrine for his remains. From the cathedral, follow V. Crociate north to Santa's final resting place, the **Church of San Nicola,** completed in the 12th century (by the Catholic Church, not the sailors). The church's spartan appearance is better suited to a fortress. In fact, the tower on the right survives from a Byzantine castle that originally occupied the site. Inside, an historical mish-mash awaits. An 11th-century episcopal throne hides behind the high altar, and gaudy 17th-century paintings adorn the ceiling. The crypt, with its windows of translucent marble, houses the remains of St. Nicholas. To the left as you enter is a Greek Orthodox shrine, built for pilgrims visiting from the east. On the back wall are several 17th-century paintings of the saint's life, among them a scene of the resurrection of three children who were sliced to bits and plunged into a barrel of brine by a nasty butcher. (Open daily 8am-noon and 3:30-7pm, except during mass.)

A St. Nick-Knack

In St. Nicholas's crypt at the Church of San Nicola, to the far right, is a red alabaster pillar that originally stood among those still in place in the crypt. Legend has it that St. Nicholas brought this pillar from Myna; a 17th-century painting in the back depicts angels helping him lift it. Now iron bars protect it from visitors who would chip it into souvenirs. But traditional beliefs about the pillar seem rather dubious in light of the fact that St. Nick *never once set foot in Italy.* Thus, we are left with several unresolved and intriguing questions—Who brought the pillar here? And why? How old is it? And was it carried by angels or eight tiny reindeer?

Follow Lungomare Augusto from behind the church and along the sea to the right toward the next gate, at P. Mercantile, the site of a colorful morning **market.** The *piazza* lies under the open porch and clock tower of the **Sedile,** the medieval meeting place of local councils. Continuing farther along the *lungomare,* you will come first to the innumerable fish markets at P. Eroi del Mare, then on to **Molo San Nicola** (San Nicola's Wharf). The gray-and-white towered building in the distance, the **Palazzo della Provincia** (tel. 541 24 21) on Lungomare N. Sauro, houses the **Pinacoteca Provinciale** on its top floor. This museum displays paintings by Veronese, Tintoretto, and Bellini. Ask to see the works of Francesco Netti, Bari's most acclaimed artist and possibly Italy's most impressive Impressionist painter. (Open Tues.-Sat. 9am-1pm and 4-7pm, Sun. 9am-1pm. Free.)

ENTERTAINMENT

Bari is the cultural nucleus of Apulia, and Stop-Over will help you experience cultural events or nightlife to its fullest. The Stop-Over newsletter has the latest daily information on events and the ever-changing hotspots, and Stop-Over itself sponsors everything from recycling workshops and kite festivals to comic-strip shows.

Unfortunately, one of the most renowned theaters in Italy, the **Teatro Petruzzelli,** was almost completely destroyed by a fire in October of 1991 and is closed indefinitely. **Teatro Piccinni** (tel. 521 37 17), however, still offers a concert season in the spring. In summer, occasional concerts are also held in the *castello.* Entertainment listings crowd *Ecco Bari,* the tourist office's entertainment guide, and the *Bari Sera* section of *La Gazzetta del Mezzogiorno* (the local newspaper).

Reiff, Largo Adua, serves American food and has live music. (Open Tues.-Sun. 8pm-2am.) **Kanthos,** on Via XXIV Maggio, plays live country, jazz, and blues on Tues. and Wed. (Open Mon.-Sat. 8:30pm-1:30am.) For dancing, groove to the English/American/Italian disco beat at **Arena,** Via Tridente, 15/21. (Open Tues.-Sun. 8pm-1:30am.) For coffee, sweets, and colorful caricature drawings of the owner by a local artist, head to **Caffè Tazza d'Oro,** across from El Pedro Self-Service on Via Picciuni. (Open daily 9am-10pm.) Or grab a pint at **Pellicano,** an English-type pub at Via Quarto, 10. A cool place to chill on a hot summer evening is the always-crowded P. Eroi del Mare on the waterfront, a popular hangout for the local youth.

The great commercial event of the year, the **Levante Fair,** runs for 10 days in mid-September. The largest fair in southern Italy, it displays goods from all over the world in the huge fairgrounds by the municipal stadium, off Lungomare Starita. From mid-April to the beginning of June, the **Festival of San Nicola** takes place in Bari. Every Sunday an image of the saint is carried from church to church (but don't try to sit on his lap). From July 13 to 25, 1997, Bari will proudly host the **13th Annual Mediterranean Games,** a competition of European, African, and Middle Eastern countries in sports such as soccer, fencing, gymnastics, and cycling. Ask Stop-Over for more information.

■ Near Bari

The numerous train lines that radiate from Bari make daytripping easy and affordable. The nearby towns are arranged in groups along these routes: Barletta and Trani to the northwest along the coast; Bitonto, Ruvo di Puglia, and Castel del Monte to the west; Altamura and Gravina in Puglia on the way to Matera; Castellana Grotte, Alberobello, and Martina Franca to the south on the way to Taranto; and Polignano a Mare, Egnazia, and Ostuni to the southeast on the way to Brindisi.

RUVO DI PUGLIA

Midway between Bari and Barletta on the Bari-Nord line (from Bari 40min., last return 10:20pm, L3400), Ruvo di Puglia began as a Greek colony in about the 8th century BC and reached the pinnacle of its influence four to five centuries later. Ruvo later passed into Roman hands, and in AD463 those fun-loving Goths destroyed the town in a fit of mayhem. The three-naved Apulian-Romanesque **cathedral,** begun in the 13th century and restored several times from the 16th through 19th centuries, marks the high point of the town's gradual rebuilding process. The exterior ornamentation is carved in characteristic Apulian Romanesque style; the enthroned figure at the top may represent Christ, or perhaps Federico II, prolific builder of local *castelli.* To the right of the cathedral stands the **campanile,** which originally served a military function. The **Jatta Museum,** to the right of the cathedral, contains a collection of over 2000 classical and later-era terra-cotta vases. Open Mon.-Thurs. and Sun. 9am-1pm, Fri.-Sat. 9am-1pm and 4-7:30pm. Free. To get to the *centro storico* from the station, turn right and take Corso Duca della Vittoria, following the signs that lead to the cathedral.

CASTEL DEL MONTE

Situated halfway between the Murge and the sea, Castel del Monte (c. 1240) evokes a by-gone world of fantasy and chivalry. It is easily the most impressive of Frederic II's ubiquitous castles. According to legend, the castle housed the Holy Grail; in reality, it served as a hunting lodge and later as a prison. The striking octagonal layout is aligned astronomically, leading scholars to hypothesize that the castle—not intended for military defense, despite its imposing presence—was also designed as an observatory. Castle open Mon.-Sat. 8:30am-7pm, Sun. 9:30am-2pm, but you can only reach it by bus on weekdays. Admission L4000. From Bari take the 6:50am Bari-Nord train to Andria (1hr., roundtrip L10,000) and catch the morning bus toward Spinazzola. Check with the bus company for the last return time. Food is expensive in Castel del Monte, so bring your lunch.

CASTELLANA GROTTE

Take a Sud-Est train from Bari toward Alberobello to reach Castellana Grotte, home to Italy's finest caverns (1hr. from Bari, 40min. from Alberobello, L4200 each way, last return to Bari 7pm, to Alberobello 7pm). The town was named after the caves, so the new train station by the cave entrance is redundantly named Grotte di Castellana Grotte. The town itself is a 2km hike away. The cave tours (most in slow Italian, but one per day in English at 10:30am) start at *La Grave,* an enormous pit used as a garbage dump until the rest of the caverns were discovered in 1938. The real highlight waits at the end of the tunnel—the Caverna Bianca (White Cavern), covered by a landscape of stalactites. In 1996 only partial tours of the caverns were offered, but the management expects to reopen the full tour in the spring of 1997. You must have a guide to tour the caves. In the summer, tours leave every hr. 8:30am-12:30pm and 2:30-6:30pm; additional tours begin at 1 and 7pm. In the winter, tours start hourly 8:30am-12:30pm and at 1pm, with a minimum of five people. Admission and tour L15,000. For more information, call 896 55 11 or fax 896 18 48.

EGNAZIA, POLIGNANO, AND BEACHES

Midway between Bari and Brindisi on the coast lie the ruins of Egnazia. This former Greek city was famed for its pottery, which characteristically superimposed yellow, purple, and white designs on a glossy black background. Under the name Gnathia, Egnazia served as a Greek port, and was later made into a Roman city. The ruins of the port are the most extensive Roman remains in Apulia; unfortunately, they're mostly underwater and are currently being studied by scubadiving archaeologists. What you can see along the coast are the curious rectangular pools which are in fact the remains of tombs cut into the rocky coast. Within the archaeological park you can view impressive remains of the Greek **acropolis** and the Roman city. Most of the fabulous **mosaics** were moved to the **museum** (tel. 72 90 56) and restored. Museum and archaeological zone open daily 8:30am-1:30pm and 2:30-6:30pm. Admission L4000. Museum wheelchair accessible. Across Via Traiana, which ran roughly parallel to the Appian Way but along the coast, lie two early Christian **basilicas** built between the 4th and 6th centuries AD.

If you don't have a car, a trip to the excavations requires a bit of planning and endurance. Travel first to the **Fasano** train station (50min. from Bari, every hr., L5000; 45min. from Brindisi, almost every hr., L5000). The Egnazia train station actually lies farther from the remains. At the Fasano train station, purchase four bus tickets. Take the bus from the train station to the last stop at the town center (about every 45min., L1000). Then, catch the bus to *scavi di Egnazia* (the excavations). Departures roughly every 2hr. 7:10am-7:25pm, except at 3:10pm. You can get great picnic fare two blocks uphill from the Fasano bus station at **Furleo,** Via San Francesco, 33. Open Fri.-Wed. 7:30am-5pm. Fasano's wild things come out to play at **Zoosafari,** where lions, crocodiles, and the like roam uncaged (tel. 71 30 55). Open daily 10am-5:30pm.

Several picturesque towns and beautiful beaches punctuate the stretch between Bari and Fasano. **Polignano** (30min. from Bari, L3200) graces the nearby steep cliffs with its tranquil old town. Head down **Viale dell Rimembranze** from the station (the street name changes to Via Fani and then Via Neapolis) to P. Aldo Moro. In the far corner, the Arco Marchesale leads into the old city. If you've got a hankering for hiking, follow the road over the bridge to the left of the gate and make your way down the coast past the ports. As you cross the bridge, look over on the left, where a tiny footbridge marks the path of the ancient Via Traiana. A 4km walk brings you to the 9th-century abbey **Abbazia di San Vito.** The elegant arches and domed nave here were added in the 16th century.

Work on that tan at **Cozze,** the beach closest to Bari (30min., L2900). The more frequent connections to **Monopoli** and its sandy beach (instead of Cozze's pebbles) may make the slightly longer trip worthwhile (45min. from Bari, L4900).

The Gargano Massif

The Gargano Massif once ranked among the most popular pilgrimage destinations in Europe. The Archangel Michael was said to have appeared in a cave here in the 5th century, and in ancient times the same cavern was occupied by a respected oracle. Now the peninsula is renowned for the 65km of beaches on its north and east coasts, some of the nicest in continental Italy. The inland is covered by the **Foresta Umbra,** which abruptly gives way to classic Mediterranean terrain in the south. The Gargano is succumbing to the twin blights of southern coastal areas—smokestacks and beach umbrellas—so visit the region soon, before it becomes an industrial tract interrupted by the occasional seaside town.

SIPONTO

Three km southwest of Manfredonia, the ancient city of Siponto was abandoned after a 12th-century earthquake and plague. The sole remains of the ancient city surround the remarkable **Church of Santa Maria di Siponto.** The church was built during the 11th century in Puglian-Romanesque style, though the blind arcade shows strong Pisan influence and the square plan and cupola also point to Byzantine roots. To reach Siponto, take the train toward Manfredonia via Foggia.

The High Murge

ALTAMURA

Trains on the **Ferrovia Apulo-Lucane** line from Bari to Matera cross gently rolling hills on the way to the quiet town of **Altamura** (frequent departures from Bari 6:00am-8:15pm, L3900; from Matera, L2400). Although one of the largest cities in the Murge region, the old town has managed to retain its tranquility. From the FAL train station, go right, walk through the unpleasant underpass, and continue straight up Via Regina Margherita for 1km. A portal in the old city wall leads to Corso Frederico II di Svevia. On the left, down Corso Frederico, you can see the petite **Church of San Nicolò of the Greeks,** a simple church serving the Greek Orthodox community. A bit farther down towers the *campanile* of the **cathedral.** Admire the portal depicting the Virgin Enthroned and the Last Supper; two weepy lions await you inside. Look for the treasury and women's gallery, too. The Pro Loco **tourist office** (tel. 84 39 30) is in P. della Repubblica, on C. Frederico before you come to the cathedral. Open Mon.-Sat. 9am-noon and 5-7pm.

As you go up C. Frederico, the tiled dome of the **Liceo Cagnazzi,** which houses the town archives and library, rises over the crest of the hill on the left. Just past the school is the **Hotel Svevia,** Via Matera, 2a (tel. (080) 871 17 42; fax 871 26 77), the least expensive hotel in Altamura (which isn't saying much). Large, bright rooms come with phone, TV, and bath. Singles L85,000. Doubles L115,000. The management will often give *Let's Go* readers a 20% discount on rooms and in the restaurant. **"Lo Sfizzietto" Il Rè della Griglia** (tel. 84 10 53) serves tasty calzones (L4000), pizzas (L4500), *menù* (L15,000) and other regal fare at Via La Maggiore, 2. Look for the sign off Corso Frederico, 30m from the gate. Open Tues.-Sun. 10am-2am.

GRAVINA IN PUGLIA

Gravina in Puglia seems even more rustic and tranquil than Altamura until you discover the oddities on the edge of town. To get to the town, take a Gravina train (FAL lines) from Altamura (10 per day 6am-10pm, 10min., L1600). To the right of the station as you exit stands the church of the **Madonna delle Grazie,** with an eagle sprawled across its façade. The big bird is the symbol of the Orsini clan, a powerful Roman family that spawned a number of popes. From here, take the underpass to the far side of the tracks and walk right to the train station. Go straight onto Corso Aldo Moro, continuing on Via Vittorio Veneto past the **Palazzo di Città.** About 300m up Via Veneto, at the intersection of Via del Museo, a faded blue sign points toward the **Museo Ettore Pomarci Santomasi,** Via del Museo, 20 (tel. 85 10 21), which exhibits archaeological finds from the area. Open daily 9am-1pm, Sat. afternoons also 3-6pm. Admission L5000. Hour-long tours leave on the half-hour.

From Via Veneto, turn left onto Via Cassese and walk to P. della Repubblica. Several eerie sights await at the end of Via Matteotti to the right. In P. Domenico, pray that your sins aren't too bad, because **Purgatory Church** on the right would be a creepy place to spend eternity. (Closed for renovations. In Italy, this could very well mean eternity.) The two skeletons on the portal are supported by bears, another Orsini mascot. To the left of the church and right of the **biblioteca** (1743) lies a street leading to the **basilica,** an immense four-aisled edifice. A narrow path behind and to the left of the *biblioteca* runs through a particularly decrepit section of town. At the bottom lies the entrance to **an area superstitiously avoided by all locals.** Ravines and vestiges of cave dwellings give new meaning to the name *gravina.* Some of the remnants are bones, which now rattle around in the **Grotto-Church of San Michele.** The gate to the grotto area and church stays locked, but pay a few hundred *lire* to one of the kids nearby, who will summon the caretaker. The same method will work for entrance to the **Church of San Vito Vecchio** on the right toward the top of the hill.

■ Trulli District

Hundreds of unusual, cone-shaped dwellings, known as *trulli,* cluster in the **Valley of Itria,** between Bari and Taranto. Many stories surround the origin of the *trulli.* Here's the tourist-office version: the first recorded *trulli* were built in the 1400s, but the peculiar buildings did not take their current, mortarless form until 1654. Sometime that year, the local Court heard of an impending royal inspection and ordered the *trulli*—considered substandard peasant housing—razed to the ground to avoid fines. After the inspection, the Court ordered the buildings rebuilt without mortar so that they could be dismantled easily before future royal visits to the farming community. Alternatively, the *trulli* may simply be inexpensively constructed, sturdy homes which make good use of local building materials. Today, the *trulli* have been incorporated into residences, restaurants, and tourist-infested boutiques.

ALBEROBELLO

The greatest concentration of *trulli* clusters in Alberobello, 1½hr. south of Bari on the Ferrovie del Sud-Est train line to Taranto (15 per day but fewer on Sun. and more on school days, L5700 from Bari, L1500 from Locorotondo, L2000 from Martina Franca). From the train station, bear left and take Via Mazzini, which becomes Via Garibaldi, to the P. del Popolo. A left turn from the *piazza* will take you to **Largo Martellota,** the commercial center of the small town. Continuing across the *piazza,* you will come to the **Monti region,** the thick of the *trulli* zone. With more than 1000 *trulli,* a *trullo* church, and the **Trullo Siamese** (with two domes), the area would look just like a gnome city were it not crawling with tourists. Beware the limpid-eyed locals who beg you to visit the interior of their *trullo.* Many have become gift shops, and even where signs read *Ingresso Libero* ("Free Entrance") you will be pressured to buy at least a postcard. Bring sunglasses if the day is bright, as the white *trulli* are blinding in the sun. Bear left at the church at the end of C. Vittorio Emanuele, then make a quick right. Straight ahead is the **Trullo Sovrano,** or Sovereign Trullo. This mammoth two-story structure, the only true two-story *trullo,* was built in the 19th century as headquarters for a religious confraternity and *carbonari* sect.

The city's many street-side tourist maps will help you navigate the important sites. Eating and sleeping in Alberobello can be expensive, so it's less costly to visit the *trulli* as a Bari-based daytrip. For those determined to spend the night here, though, **Hotel Airone,** Via Coldilana, 30 (tel. 932 28 04; fax 932 28 03), to the right from the station and a right just before the hospital, is a great three-star alternative to sleeping in the street. The hotel's friendly management offers new and modern facilites, a quiet lounge, a bar, and telephones in the rooms. Singles L55,000. Doubles L85,000. In a more central location right off Piazza del Popolo, the recently remodeled **Hotel Lanzillotta,** Piazza Ferdinando IV, 31 (tel. 72 15 11; fax 72 11 79), also provides comfortable and well-equipped rooms. Singles L40,000. Doubles L70,000. **Gli Ulivi**, Contrada Popoleto, 15 (tel. 932 37 96), has excellent food and quality service. Ask directions from Alberobello (it's ½km from town); follow the highway toward Putignano and cross the bridge to the left. Near the athletic fields (look for the big sign). A full, scrumptious meal can cost under L22,000. Splurge and try the *antipasto* of the house (L12,000), or save some *lire* and *mangia* pizza (L4000-7000). Open only Jan.-Aug. daily noon-2:45pm and 8pm-midnight. Alberobello's **postal code** is 70011. The **phone code** is 080.

Barletta

Barletta's claim to fame arises from a battle that occured five centuries ago. On the first or second Sunday of September, the city fills with crowds of German and Italian tourists for a reenactment of the *Disfida*—a battle in which 13 Italians battled 13 Frenchmen in defense of their chivalric honor. To commemorate the Italian victory, the city comes alive each year with medieval ceremonies and elegant costumes. The city is also home to Romanesque churches, a castle built by Frederick II, and an immense, ancient bronze statue of a Byzantine emperor.

ORIENTATION AND PRACTICAL INFORMATION

The historic quarter of Barletta and most of its interesting sights lie along **Corso G. Garibaldi** and **Corso Vittorio Emanuele.** From the train station, walk straight ahead across the piazza and down Viale Giannone to C. Garibaldi. Turn right, then left on C. Emanuele. Barletta is 15min. north of Trani on the Bologna-Lecce train line, one hour from Bari (L5000), and six hours from Bologna (L44,100). For more info, the AST **tourist office,** Via D'Aragona, 95 (tel. 33 13 31), offers maps and brochures. From C. Emanuele, turn right and walk one block on C. Garibaldi. The unmarked Via D'Aragona is to the left, on the left side of P. Caduti in Guerra. Open Mon.-Sat. 8am-2pm. Barletta's **telephone code** is 0883.

ACCOMMODATIONS AND FOOD

The only budget accommodations are at **Pensione Prezioso,** Via Teatini, 11 (tel. 52 00 46), just off P. del Plebiscito. From the train station, walk straight down Via Giannone through P. Aldo Moro and straight to Via da Cordova until you reach the gardens of P. del Plebiscito. Rooms are small but quiet. Singles L30,000. Doubles L60,000. On the same piazza, **Pizzeria Dai Saraceni,** P. del Plebiscito, 65 (tel. 51 71 00), offers complete meals for L22,000. Try their tasty *pizza ai Saraceni* (with ham, artichokes, olives, and capers, L6500). Cover L2000. Service 20%. Open Tues.-Sun. noon-3pm and 7:30pm-1am. From Corso Emanuele, walk one block past P. Caduti in Guerra and one block to the left of Via Barletta to Via G. de Nittis for the **DOK** supermarket. Open Thurs. 8:30am-1:30pm, Fri.-Wed. 8:30am-1:30pm and 5:30-9pm. What the city lacks in restaurants it makes up for in fresh seafood, sold on most corners near Via da Cordova.

SIGHTS

The 12th-century **Church of San Sepolcro** graces the center of town on C. Vittorio Emanuele at C. Garibaldi. The façade preserves remnants of the original portal. The only decorations remaining in the recently restored church interior are the large 13th-century baptismal font to the left of the entrance, the 16th-century Byzantine-style Madonna at the end of the right aisle, and 14th-century frescoe fragments adorning the walls. (Open April-Oct. Mon.-Sat. 9:30am-noon and 6:30-9pm; Nov.-Mar. 9:30am-noon and 5:30-8:30pm.) On a low podium next to the church towers the five-meter-tall **Colosso.** This 4th-century bronze statue from Constantinople represents a Byzantine emperor—possibly Valentinian I—holding the cross and orb, symbols of the spiritual and temporal realms of his power. As the Venetians were hauling home the loot from the Fourth Crusade, a shipwreck sent the Colosso overboard and eventually to Barletta's shore. It was then dismembered by friars who melted its bronze limbs to make church bells. The limbs you see today were fashioned in the 15th century. Oddly enough, he ended up looking like a tennis pro preparing to serve. Walk down C. Emanuele to see the refreshingly austere and eccentric architecture of the 11th-century **Church of San Giacomo** at #143.

Return to C. Garibaldi, turn left, and venture into the old town. About a block before the *duomo,* 10m off C. Garibaldi on Via Cialdini, is the **Cantina Della Sfida,** where the fabled confrontation of the knights took place. The *cantina* itself is simply the basement of a medieval palace. Note the huge stone cistern in the back. Via del Duomo veers off to the right and brings you to the enormous **castle** (tel. 57 86 20). The fortress, first a Saracen outpost, was subsequently enlarged by the Normans and rebuilt by Frederick II. Carl V (1532-1600) ordered the final and most substantial change. (Open May-Sept. Tues.-Sun. 9am-1pm and 4-7pm, Oct.-April 9am-1pm and 3-4pm. Admission L3500, under 14 L1000. Half-hour guided tour available in English.) The castle now houses a **Museo** and **Pinacoteca** (picture gallery) with an impressive collection of works by the local Giuseppe de Nittis. (Closed temporarily, but will reopen soon. Check with the tourist office for the most recent info.)

Trani

Situated between Bari and Barletta on the F.S. train line, Trani welcomes visitors with its peaceful gardens, clear water, and scenic old city. The town curls around a small bay, with the historic quarter stretched along the waterfront and the gardens resting on the right arm. Trani's jewel, a magnificent 11th-century Romanesque **cathedral,** stands tall on the water's edge at the tip of a small promontory on the left arm, with the imposing 13th-century **Castello Svevo** lurking nearby. Across the *piazza* from the train station at Via Cavour, 140, is the **tourist office** (tel. 58 88 25; fax 58 88 30).

Open in summer Mon.-Fri. 8:30am-12:30pm and 4-6pm, Sat. 8:30am-12:30pm; in winter Mon.-Fri. 8:30am-12:30pm and 3:30-5:30pm, Sat. 8:30am-12:30pm. Down Via Cavour, in the P. della Repubblica, you'll find an AAST **tourist booth** (tel. 432 95) that gives out great maps and recommends restaurants and hotels (same hours as the other office). From P. della Repubblica, continue straight on Via Cavour to P. Plebiscito and the lush seaside **public gardens,** or head left on Via Pagano through P. Mazzini and turn right on Via Beltrani, continuing through the old city to the cathedral. Hold on to your valuables as you walk through this section. If you go right off Via Beltrani onto Via Sinagoga you'll eventually stumble upon a 13th-century **synagogue,** one of four in what was once the Jewish Quarter. The building was later converted into the **Church of Santamaria Scolanova** and is now closed to the public. As you walk back to the town center from the cathedral, follow the coast to the right and you'll pass the 18th-century Baroque **Church of Santa Teresa** and the 12th-century **Church of Ognissanti,** built by the Knights Templar, with its beautiful front portal.

To extend your daytrip, check into **Albergo Lucy,** P. Plebiscito, 11 (tel. 410 22), a 17th-century *palazzo* with huge rooms and elegant, high ceilings. Doubles L70,000. Extra bed 35% more. All rooms come with bath; some have kitchens. For a picture-perfect morning view of the sunrise on the Adriatic, try **Hotel Regia,** P. Archivo, 2 (tel. 58 45 27; fax 55 37 98), next to the cathedral. Singles L50,000. Doubles L85,000. Breakfast L5000. Extra bed 35% more. Half-pension (L75,000) and full-pension (L100,000) available. All rooms with bath and phone. V, MC. Good, affordable food abounds in Trani. A block off the midpoint of the port at Via Zanardelli, 17, **La Vite** (tel. 412 75) serves up Greek specialties and 90 different types of tea. Enjoy generous portions to the beat of jazz music. *Menù* L20,000. Open Mon. and Wed.-Sat. noon-3pm and 5pm-3am, Sun. 5pm-1am.

Brindisi

American and British backpackers, ferry offices, and the port are what most visitors see of Brindisi, lingering here just long enough to catch a ferry for Greece. In recent years, the town has developed much of its economy around the ferry industry; it takes only a glance at the backpackers lining the streets in front of restaurants advertising "Tourist Menu" in English to realize to what extent Brindisi depends on tourists. Unfortunately, the city has little to offer travelers other than cheap Eurail passage to Greece. Although the narrow medieval alleys and flowered 19th-century streets remain from a bygone era, they are sadly obscured and overshadowed by the busy port. Come here, if anyplace, to get away from old-world charm.

FERRIES

All ferry passengers in Brindisi, including InterRail and Eurailpass holders, must pay a L10,000 port tax. June 10 to Sept. 30 there is a L19,000 supplementary fee (not including the port tax).

Brindisi is Italy's major departure point for ferries to Greece, since InterRail and Eurail discounts are only valid through the port here. Ferries leave for: **Corfu** (10hr.), **Igoumenitsa** (12hr.), **Patras** (20hr.), and **Cefalonia** (Hellenic Mediterranean Lines, 16½hr.). From Patras, bus service (4hr., L30,000; buy tickets at the *stazione marittima)* and train service (railpasses valid) will take you to **Athens.** Most ferries leave in the evening, but many tourists choose to arrive in the morning to buy tickets early. **Be warned: robberies on overnight trains are relatively common.** When possible, avoid the non-stop overnight trains from Rome that make excellent targets for petty thieves.

Numerous ferry companies large and small serve Brindisi, each with different fares and rebates. The cheapest option is always deck class, which is fine in summer—sleeping horizontally outside can often be more comfortable than spending the night in an airline-type seat in a smoky room. But nights can be chilly; be sure to bring warm clothes, and consider a sleeping bag in cooler seasons. **Adriatica,** Via Regina Margherita, 13 (tel. 59 04 71; fax 59 04 72), near the *stazione marittima,* and **Hellenic Mediterranean Lines,** Corso Garibaldi, 8 (tel. 52 85 31; fax 52 68 72), have high regular prices but offer **InterRail** and **Eurailpass** holders free deck passage on a space-available basis—you could get bumped by a paying passenger.

InterRail and Eurailpass holders should go directly to the main offices listed above to get their tickets—many travel agencies try to double-talk you into commission-based services. Those without railpasses should consider leaving from **Bari** (page 450), a larger city with many tourist facilities and inexpensive lodging and food, or **Otranto** (page 467), a beautiful small town to the south of Brindisi. From either of these ports, departures may be both cheaper and less crowded. For those intent on leaving from Brindisi, Hellenic Mediterranean Lines often offers discounted "bargain" fares: L32,000 in low-season, L75,000 in high-season on selected departures to Corfu and Igoumenitsa. **Fragline ferries,** c/o Silverling, C. Garibaldi, 95 (tel. 52 83 33), also has special reduced fares beginning at L38,000 on selected days. Call ahead to determine which fares are reduced. **Ventouris,** c/o Venmare srl, C. Garibaldi, 79 (tel. 52 16 14; fax 52 16 54), has few reduced fares but low regular fares. To Igoumenitsa (L45,000/L60,000).

With all companies, buying a **roundtrip ticket** saves 10-20%. For groups of at least 10, there are reductions of approximately 10% on one-way and 20% on roundtrip tickets. Bicycles travel free, motorcycles for about L25,000.

You pay the obligatory port tax when you buy your ticket. The office will give you a boarding card, which must be stamped at the police station one flight up at the maritime station. On the same floor you'll find **public showers** (L3000) and a waiting lounge. You lose your reservation on most lines if you don't **check in at least two hours before departure.** Allow plenty of time for late trains and the 1-km walk from the train station to the ferry station. From mid-July to mid-August, it may be worth the effort to purchase ferry reservations at line offices or from travel agents in other cities before you get to Brindisi.

ORIENTATION AND PRACTICAL INFORMATION

> Brindisi's popularity as a port has made it a haven for petty thieves. Although the city does not have the reputation of Bari's old city, travelers should beware; watch your passports and money. Be cautious about venturing out in the evening, especially women and especially alone. Lone backpackers are considered particularly easy targets; store your pack or stick to populated areas.

All that ferrygoers need to know about Brindisi is that **Corso Umberto** runs straight out from the train station and passes through **Piazza Cairoli** with its large, ugly fountain. Continue past this *piazza,* then veer left as you pass through Piazza del Popolo and Piazza della Vittoria onto **Corso Garibaldi,** which leads to **Piazza Vittorio Emanuele** and the *stazione marittima.* **Via Regina Margherita** runs to the left of P. Vittorio Emanuele and leads to more ferry offices.

Tourist Office: EPT, V. Regina Margherita, 5 (tel. 52 19 44), 1 block to the side of P. Vittorio Emanuele. Friendly staff speaks English, but the office provides few tourist itineraries or pamphlets. Open Mon.-Fri. 9am-1:30pm, and Tues. 3-6:30pm.

Currency Exchange: Banca Nazionale del Lavoro, Via Santi, 11, uphill from P. Vittoria. Open Mon.-Fri. 8:20am-1:35pm and 2:45-4pm. To avoid the poor rates at the *stazione marittima,* change money at one of the many exchanges lining Corso Umberto and Corso Garibaldi, all of which offer direct U.S.-Greek conversions. Few places in Brindisi offer good rates, and many charge commissions.

American Express: InterMed, Corso Umberto I, 145 (tel. 56 38 34). Both purchase and refund of traveler's checks available. Open daily 7am-9:30pm.

Telephones: Via XX Settembre, 6. From the train station, turn left on Via S. Lorenzo off Corso Umberto, and then take the 2nd left. *Telefoni a scatti* available. Open Mon.-Fri. 9:15am-12:50pm and 3:30-6:30pm.

Trains: P. Crispi. Both **FS** and **Ferrovie del Sud-Est.** From: Naples (6hr., L47,900); Rome (via Barletta, 4 per day, 7hr., L47,700); Milan (via Ancona and Bologna, 4 per day, 12hr., L72,400). To: Bari (frequent departures, 1½hr., L9800); Taranto (every hr., 1¼hr., L5700); Lecce (frequent departures, 30min., L3400). **Luggage Storage:** Open daily 6:40am-10:40pm. L5000 for 12hr. Also available at the port. Open daily 8:40am-10:40pm.

Buses: Ferrovie del Sud-Est, at the train station (tel. 52 59 91), handles buses throughout Apulia. **Marozzi,** c/o Agestea, V. Regina Margherita, 8 (tel. 52 16 84), wheels to Rome 3 times daily (7½hr., L50,700-55,000). Call for departure times and locations. **Miccolis,** c/o Agenzia Marittima Perrino, C. Garibaldi, 109 (tel./fax 56 06 78), roams to Naples at 6:05am, 3:05, and 6:05pm (5hr., L40,000).

Public Showers: By the waiting lounge, 1 flight up at the *stazione marittima*. Surprisingly clean. Showers L3000, toilets L500. Open daily 6am-midnight.

Emergencies: tel. 113. **Ambulance:** tel. 52 14 10 or 22 20 78. **Hospital: Ospedale di Summa,** (tel. 20 42) in P. Antonio.

Police: tel. 113.

Post Office: P. Vittoria, 10 (tel. 52 39 56). Open Mon.-Fri. 8:15am-7:30pm, Sat. 8:15am-1pm. **Postal Code:** 72100.

Telephone Code: 0831.

ACCOMMODATIONS

Not many people choose to stay the night in Brindisi. However, inexpensive hotel rooms are available, so don't end up on top of a backpack in one of the *piazze* along C. Garibaldi—a miserable and dangerous experience.

Ostello della Gioventù "Brindisi," 3km away in Casale (tel. 41 31 23). Take bus #3 or 4 from the train center (L1000), or call the hostel for a ride from the station. A youth hostel but will often accept older guests during off-season. Rooms are relatively clean, but you may want to shower at the *stazione marittima*. Open 24hr. No daytime lockout. L18,000 per person. Breakfast and sheets included. Kitchen and laundry room available.

Hotel/Pensione Altair, Via Tunisi, 4 (tel./fax 52 49 11), off Corso Garibaldi near the *stazione marittima.* Spacious, modern rooms. Singles L35,000, low-season 25,000, with bath L50,000/30,000. Doubles L50,000, low-season L40,000, with bath L70,000/50,000.

FOOD

A wonderful **open-air market,** off Corso Umberto on Via Battisti, sells fresh fruit by the ton. Open Mon.-Sat. 7am-1pm. Pizza and *focaccia* are made in huge sheets and sold by weight. The **Sidis** supermarket, Corso Garibaldi, 106, is well stocked but crowded with Greece-bound backpackers. Open Mon.-Sat. 8am-1:15pm and 4:15-8:30pm, Sun. 9am-1pm. Avoid the restaurants on the main drag; often, advertised "tourist menus" have small portions and are hardly worth the "extra-low" price. Better options lie on nearby side-streets.

Spaghetti House Osteria Cucina Casalinga, Via Mazzini, 57. From the train station take the 2nd left off Corso Umberto onto Via Bruno. Delicious fare and a proprietor who loves *Let's Go* readers. Try the *spaghetti alle Ulive* (L5000). Full meal of pasta, beverage, and bread for about L7500. Cover L500. Open daily 9am-9pm; closed Sun. in winter.

Ristorante La Forchetta, Via Mazzini, 13. Walk down the street 2 blocks from the Spaghetti House, or turn left at P. Cairoli while facing the port and then make a quick right. Pizzas (L4000-8000) and a small selection of other dishes. Full meal L10,000. Open Tues.-Sun. noon-midnight.

Trattoria L'Angoletto, Via Pergola, 3 (tel. 52 50 29), 200m up Corso Garibaldi from the port. Pleasant, elegant outdoor eating. Pizza L5000-10,000. Open Wed.-Mon. 9am-midnight.

SIGHTS AND ENTERTAINMENT

Facing the port, turn left on V. Regina Margherita. A block down, on the stairs facing the water, you will find the **column** which marked the end of the Appian way. If you look closely, you'll see a marble capital graced by the figures of Jove, Neptune, Mars, and eight tritons. The column's twin, which once stood on the adjacent base, now resides in Lecce. Via Colonne runs from behind the column to P. Duomo. Here you'll find the **cathedral** (11th-century, but rebuilt in the 18th) where emperor Frederick II wed Jerusalem's Yolande. Next door is the **Archaeological Museum** (tel. 22 14 01), which houses Greek pottery and some impressive Greek bronze sculptures recovered from the sea. (Open Mon., Wed., and Fri. 9am-1pm, Tues. 9am-1pm and 3:30-6:30pm. Free.) Continue across P. Duomo and down Via Tarantini to the **Cloister of San Benedetto,** whose peaceful courtyard is just the place to read a book while you wait for your ferry.

Across the bay from the column rises another Freudian monument in the somewhat odd form of a 52m-high rudder; the **Marinaio d'Italia** (1933) celebrates the sailors of Italy. Hop over to it on one of the red and white **Casale** ferries that leave every 15min. from Banchina Montenegro, to the left as you face the water (10min., L800). Three km inland from the Marinaio lies the church of **Santa Maria del Casale.** The pride of Brindisi, this multi-colored, elaborately adorned building is reminiscent of Byzantine design. If you're stuck overnight around the first week in July, you can party at the **Festa dell'Unità.** The **P.C.I.** (Italian Communist Party) solicits votes with nightly dancing, movies, music, and even a fashion show. (Most events are free and take place in Via Grandi.)

■ Near Brindisi: Ostuni

Rising out of a landscape of sea, dark red earth, and olive trees, the *città bianca* (white city) of Ostuni appears completely ethereal from afar. The walls of the *centro storico* are kept blindingly white, partly as protection from the elements, but also to maintain the town's traditional status as "The White Queen." From the train station (1½hr. from Bari, L6500; 30min. from Brindisi, L3400), take the shuttle bus to **Piazza della Libertà** (Mon.-Sat. every 30min., Sun. on the hr. L1000). For a divine view of the old city, climb Corso Vittorio Emanuele for 5min. and relax on the scenic terrace. Return to the *piazza* and climb Via Cattedrale up through the center of the old town. The **Convento delle Monacelle** (Convent of the Little Nuns) on Via Cattedrale sports a baroque façade and is topped by a blue-, yellow-, and white-tiled dome of Moorish inspiration. Crowning Ostuni's hill, the **cathedral** (1437) stands as the last Byzantine building erected in southern Italy. Don't forget to wander through the city's side streets. As you descend on Via Cattedrale, turn left on Via B. Continelli, where you'll find the modest **Church of San Giacomo di Compostella,** a family chapel founded in 1423. On August 26th and 27th Ostuni celebrates St. Oronzo with the **Cavalcata,** a parade of costumed horses and riders.

Ostuni's AAST **tourist office** at C. Mazzini, 6 (tel. 30 12 68), near where Via Cattedrale juts off, provides assistance and a great booklet entitled *Ostuni, the white queen of olive trees.* Open June-Aug. Mon.-Sat. 9am-12:30pm and 4:30-8pm. From September to May, go to the tourism administrative office at Via V. Continelli, 47 (tel. 30 37 75) down Via Roma to Via Pepe. Open Mon.-Sat. 8am-2pm. Ostuni's delights do not require more than a daytrip—avoid the steep prices at local hotels. For refueling and a change of color, go to the kitschy **Osteria del Tempo Perso,** Via G. Tanzarella Vitale, 47 (tel. 30 33 20), in the old city behind the cathedral. The plentiful *antipasto* smorgasbord (L12,000) will satisfy you with its sampling of local dishes. Open Tues.-Sun. 5:30pm-12:30am, holidays noon-3pm and 8pm-midnight. V, AmEx.

Lecce

A hidden pearl in the oyster of Italian tourism, Lecce is where Italians go when foreign tourists invade Florence. Lecce has an astounding collection of well preserved 15th-, 16th-, and 17th-century palaces, scads of Roman ruins, and an impressive number of Baroque and Rococo churches. A succession of conquerors—Cretans, Romans, Saracens, Swabians, and more—passed through here, but the city's modern form was defined under Habsburg Spain in the 16th and 17th centuries. Merchants, aristocrats, and the religious orders of the Counter-Reformation competed to display their wealth, creating the Leccese Baroque buildings that we see today.

The "Florence of the Mezzogiorno" provides an ideal starting point for a tour of the Salento Peninsula, Italy's high heel. While the University of Lecce's student scene ensures the presence of nighttime activities, your days will be occupied with visits to local castles, strolls through olive groves, and tours of the area's many archaeological sites and ruins dating back thousands of years.

ORIENTATION AND PRACTICAL INFORMATION

The southeastern terminus of the state railway system, Lecce lies some 35km south and inland of Brindisi. Many streets in Lecce lack signs, but it's a pleasant place to lose yourself. An enjoyable 10-min. walk takes you to **Piazza Sant'Oronzo,** the main square. From the station, take **Viale Quarta,** cross **Viale Gallipoli,** and continue on Via Cairoli which winds through the historic district and becomes **Via Paladini.** Turn right onto **Via Vittoria Emanuele,** and P. Sant'Oronzo will be straight ahead past a few churches. **Via Libertini** and the **Piazza del Duomo** will be on the left.

Tourist Office: EPT and **AAST** (tel. 24 80 92), inside Castello Carlo V. Helpful, informed, and somewhat English-speaking. Open Mon.-Fri. 9am-1pm and 5-7pm, Sat. 9am-1pm.

Budget Travel: CTS, Via Palmieri, 91 (tel. 30 18 62). From P. Sant'Oronzo, take Via Emanuele and turn right on Via Palmieri. Flight and train info and tickets. Open Mon.-Fri. 9am-1pm and 4-8pm, Sat. 9am-12:30pm.

Telephones: Telecom (SIP), Via Oberdan, 13d (tel. 31 42 99). From the post office, cross Viale Cavalloti and walk straight on Via 47° Rgt. Fanteria for 6 blocks. Open daily 7am-10pm.

Trains: P. Stazione, about 1km from the town center. Buses #1, 2, 3, 13, 14, and 15 run from the train station to the center of town (buy tickets at a newsstand, L1000). 25 trains per day run to Brindisi (30min., L3400). **F.S.** (tel. 30 10 16) travels north to Taranto (change at Brindisi, 8 per day, 2hr., L9800) and to Bari (frequent departures, L11,700). The provincial **Ferrovie del Sud-Est** (tel. 66 81 11) runs down the Salento Peninsula to Gallipoli (8 per day, 1hr., L10,000 roundtrip) and Otranto (change at Maglie, 4 or 5 per day, 1½hr., L8400 roundtrip).

Buses: Sud-Est, Via Boito (tel. 34 76 34), easily accessible by urban bus #7 (L1000) from the train station. To: Otranto (2 per day, 1½hr., L6000); Gallipoli (5 per day, 1hr., L4000); Taranto (2 per day, 1½hr., L7500); and other Apulian destinations. **STP,** Via Adua (tel. 30 28 73), heads to the smaller cities of the Salento Peninsula. From the train station, walk left on Viale Gallipoli and turn right at its end.

Emergencies: tel. 113. **Ambulance:** tel. 68 54 03 or 65 54 11. **Hospital: Ospedale Vito Fazzi,** (tel. 66 11 11) in P. Bottazzi.

Police: (tel. 31 53 42 or 113) on Viale Otranto.

Post Office: (tel. 30 30 00) in Piazzetta Libertini, behind the castle from P. Sant'Oronzo. Open Mon.-Fri. 8:15am-5:30pm, Sat. 8:15am-1pm. **Postal Code:** 73100.

Telephone Code: 0832.

ACCOMMODATIONS AND CAMPING

Grand Hotel, Viale Quarta, 28 (tel. 30 94 05; fax 30 98 91), ½-block in front of the station. Elegant and faded, with plush red carpeting and luminous woodwork. Beware the *piazza* in front of the hotel at night, when Lecce's prostitutes show their stuff. Singles L51,000, with bath L72,000; low-season L42,000 and L52,000. Doubles L81,000, with bath L125,000, low-season L67,000 and L99,000.

Hotel Cappello, Via Montegrappa, 4 (tel. 30 88 81; fax 30 15 35). From the station, take the 1st left off Viale Quarta onto Via Don Bosco and follow the signs. Nice and modern, but be prepared for a rude awakening by the morning trains. All rooms with bath, telephone, TV, and fan. Singles L50,000. Doubles L80,000. Triples L100,000. Quads L120,000.

Camping: Torre Rinalda (tel. 38 21 61), 3km from the beach. Local discounts on food and entertainment included in high-season. Take bus #18 to Litoranea. July 7-Aug. 26 L10,000 per person, L8500 per tent. Off-season L8500 per person, L7500 per tent.

FOOD

Regional specialties range from the hearty *cicerietria* (chickpeas and pasta) and *rustici* (mozzarella and tomato wrapped in a delicate pastry shell) to *confettoni* (chocolate candies made from a top-secret recipe at De Matteis Oronzo—see below). Buy picnic supplies at **Salumeria Loiacono,** Via Fazzi, 11, in P. Sant'Oronzo, a century-old cheese store. The indoor food **market** next to the post office provides a chance to haggle. Open Mon.-Fri. 5am-1pm, Sat. 5am-1pm and 4-8pm.

Ai Tre Ghiottoni, Via Dalmazio Birago, 7 (tel. 24 79 07), down Via Libertini and through Porta Rudiae. Snack on *rustico,* or feast on *risotto* with asparagus and roast squid (each L8000). *Menù* L20,000. Open daily 8am-midnight.

Gambero Rosso, Via M. Branccio, 16 (tel. 24 15 69) serves inexpensive local specialties in a relaxed setting. *Orecchiette* made slightly larger in Leccese style, L6000. Open Sat.-Thurs. noon-3pm and 7:30-11pm.

Garden Liberty, Viale Quarta, 28 (tel. 30 94 05), inside the Grand Hotel, one block up Viale Quarta from the train station. During the summer, the hotel offers dining under their orange grove. Feast on local specialties in elegance. *Primi* L8000, *secondi* L8000-10,000. Open daily noon-2:30pm and 7:45-10:30pm.

De Matteis Oronzo, Via Marconi, 51 (tel. 30 28 00), near the castle. Come to this fantastic candy store for *confettoni* or their *cotognata leccese*, dried fig candies so delicious they're specially ordered by the Pope. Look for His picture. Open Tues.-Sun. 6am-10:30pm.

SIGHTS AND ENTERTAINMENT

Unfortunately, recent restoration teams have whitewashed the naturally golden stone of several local buildings. This process has left much of the ornamentation, like many of the delicate carvings and inscriptions, difficult to see. The moral (of course): if it's Baroque, don't fix it.

For those with a one-church limit, the definite place to hit is the **Church of Santa Croce** (1548-1646)—the supreme expression of Leccese Baroque. From P. Sant'Oronzo, head down Via Templari and brace yourself for the extravagance of the church's façade. Most of the area's accomplished architects contributed their efforts to this church at some time or another; Gabriele Riccardi drafted the original design, and his disciples completed the church after his death. A wonderfully animated altar (1614) by F. A. Zimbalo adorns the chapel to the left of the apse. (Open daily 9am-7:30pm.) To the left of Santa Croce stands the **Palazzo Celestini.** Giuseppe Zimbalo—nicknamed "Lo Zingarello"—designed the lower half of the façade, while his pupil, Giuseppe Cino, finished the upper portion. Diagonally across the street sprawls the Florentine-style **Palazzo Adorni** (under restoration). View both from the street outside.

Lecce has a seemingly endless supply of superb churches. Return to P. Sant'Oronzo and take a right down Via Emanuele to the exquisite **Piazza del Duomo,** blindingly white after recent restorations. In front looms the **cathedral,** founded in 1114 but "Zingarelloed" between 1659 and 1670. The interior dates mostly from the 18th century, with the exception of two Leccese altars. (Open daily 8-11am and 4:30-7:30pm.) Attached to the right side of the cathedral, the **Palazzo Vescovile** (Bishop's Palace) has been remodeled several times since its original construction in 1632. The open porticos held shops in the days when an annual fair took place in the *piazza.* Farther to the right, you'll encounter the flamboyant **seminary** (1709), designed by Cino. The final component of the *piazza,* the **campanile** (1682), is more restrained.

A stroll down Via Libertini to the left takes you to the phantasmagorically complex **Church of San Giovanni Battista (Church of the Rosary),** Lo Zingarello's last work. Here, the artist seems to have surrendered to Baroque abandon; finely carved trees, birds, and angels almost overflow the tiny alley where the church stands. Walk back up Via Libertini and turn left on Via Palmieri (across from P. Duomo); a 5-min. walk brings you to the **Arco di Trionfo,** erected in 1548 in honor of Charles V, whose coat of arms adorns the front. Located in an ancient cemetery beyond the arch, the **Church of SS. Nicolò e Cataldo** was founded in 1180 by the Normans and modified in 1716 by Cino. Small mausolea of every conceivable style cluster around the narrow paths of the cemetery next door.

Lecce also offers an impressive array of ancient ruins. The **Column of Sant'Oronzo,** towering in front of the tourist office, is one of the two that marked the termination of the Appian Way in Brindisi. Now a statue of the saint tops the column. Also in Piazza Sant'Oronzo lies a partially excavated 2nd-century AD **amphitheater.** If you ask about its ruins at the Foreign Office of the Credito Popolare Salentino bank next door, they may take you down to their basement, where several more arches of the amphitheater still stand.

On Viale Gallipoli, 30, near the station, you'll find the **Museo Provinciale,** housing terra cotta votive statues, marble sculptures, Greek pottery, and a collection of 4th-century BC inscriptions. (Open Mon.-Sat. 9am-1:30pm and 2:30-7:30pm, Sun. and holidays 9am-1:30pm. Free. Wheelchair accessible on steep ramps.) The **pinacoteca** on Via Imperatore Adriano, 79 (Convento S. Antonio), has a collection of 17th- and 18th-century religious paintings. (Open Mon.-Fri. 9am-noon and 4:30-7pm. Free.)

This quiet city comes alive in July and August. **Estate Musicale Leccese** (July 1-Aug. 15) is a festival of music and dance. Ask at the EPT for *Calendario Manifestazioni,* which describes seasonal goings-on in the whole province. Many of the *piazze* in the old quarter fill with local youths after dark. Pop by Piazzetta del Duca d'Atena and take part in the local scope scene, or shake your booty at **Corto Maltese,** Via Giusti, 13. (Open Wed.-Mon. 9pm-2am.) For current info on nighttime hotspots and musical and theater events, pick up a copy of *Notes-Appunti dal Salento* from the tourist office or at local bars and clubs.

SALENTO PENINSULA

Foreign tourists often overlook Italy's high heel, home to beautiful sandy beaches on two seas, hidden grottoes, medieval fortresses, and some of Italy's oldest and best-preserved art and architecture. With cultural roots stretching back past the Greeks, the peninsula is worthy of exploration. Roam the enchantingly varied coastline, or venture to the inland villages to sample wine and olives.

Otranto

Though not as easily accessible from the north as Bari and Brindisi, Otranto makes a fine starting or ending point for a tour of the Adriatic Coast. The small town's few but well-preserved sights, enchanting medieval streets, and clean port are a refreshing change from the less-appealing ports farther north. When Ottoman Turks conquered the town in 1480 with the hope of further invading Italy, the town's 800 survivors opted to join their comrades in death rather than convert and side with the Turks. The bodies under glass in the towns's cathedral remain a grim reminder of the locals' loyalty.

ORIENTATION AND PRACTICAL INFORMATION

Take the **train** to Otranto from Lecce via Maglie (9 trains per day, 5am-6:20pm, 1½hr., L4200). From the train station, turn right at the circle and bear left down the hill on **Via Pantaleone.** Ignore the signs pointing right; instead, go through the stoplight. Continue on V. Pantaleone to the **tourist office** (tel. 80 28 90) at #12. Open Mon.-Sat. 9am-1pm. Farther down is the Lungomare d'Otranto with the beach and pale blue water by. Walk 3 blocks to the right to **Piazza de Donno,** and you'll see the entrance to the old town to the left down Via Vittorio Emanuele II. Turn right on **Via Basilica** to come to the cathedral and the tourist office, or continue straight on Corso Garibaldi, which leads to P. del Popolo. From there, a path takes you up to the Church of San Pietro. To get to the **post office,** turn right at the stoplight on Via Pantaleone; the office is on your left at the corner of Via Paolo and Via Eula. Otranto's **postal code** is 73028; the **telephone code** is 0836. **Ferries** from Otranto travel to three different countries. Buy tickets at the port, a 10-min. walk from P. de Donno (over the hill of Via San Francesco and left on Via del Porto at the bottom).

Turkey: Rainbow Lines (tel. 80 15 78; fax 80 27 46). To Çeşme (July Sat. 9:30pm; mid-Aug. Sat. 2:30pm; mid-Aug.-Sept. Tues. 9:30pm; deck passage L130,000; high-season L160,000; L30,000 discount on return trip).

Albania: Rainbow Lines. To Vlorë (Tues., Thurs.-Fri., and Sun. 9:30am; L60,000; L20,000 discount on return). To Durrës (Tues. and Fri. 10:30pm; L60,000; L20,000 discount on return). **Linee Lauro.** To Vlorë (Mon., Wed., and Sat. 9am; L60,000; L10,000 discount on return). To Durrës (Wed. 11pm; L70,000; L10,000 discount on return).

Greece: Linee Lauro (tel. 80 60 61; fax 80 60 62). To Corfu (July-mid-Sept. Sat. 11pm, Sun. 6:30am) and Igoumenitsa (July-mid-Sept. Sat.-Sun. 11am; July L49,000, Aug.-mid-Sept. L69,000; students L9000 discount).

ACCOMMODATIONS AND FOOD

Lodging in Otranto can be expensive and difficult to find during high-season, but check with the tourist office about renting a room in a local home. Many of Otranto's hotels have obligatory half-pension on the order of L80,000 per person in August. The **Albania Hotel,** with its large, white rooms with bath, TV, telephone, and A/C, is just off P. de Donno on Via S. Francesco (tel. 80 11 83). Singles L50,000. Doubles L80,000. Half-pension required in July (L75,000) and August (L80,000). All rooms with bath and TV. V, MC, AmEx. The **Hotel Bellavista,** Via Vittorio Emanuele, 18 (tel. 80 10 58), has the best view in town and a high-class attitude to match. Singles L50,000. Doubles L70,000. Half-pension required in July (L70,000) and August (L80,000). All rooms with bath. The **market** by P. de Donno sells fruit, vegetables, meat, and fish. Open Mon.-Sat. 7am-1pm and 5-9pm. The **Taverna del Leone Marino,** Corso Garibaldi, 14, offers quality sit-down fare at respectable prices: L20,000 will net you a feast of fresh fish and a plate of pasta. Open daily noon-3pm and 7-11pm. Closed November.

SIGHTS AND ENTERTAINMENT

If you have some time in town, don't miss Otranto's **cathedral,** paved with a phenomenal 11th-century mosaic of the Tree of Life. The mosaic—visited by Dante as he wrote the Divine Comedy—extends the entire length of the nave and depicts religious, mythological, and historical figures, from King Arthur to Alexander the Great. (And that's just the "A"s.) Cathedral open daily 8am-noon and 3-5pm. The **crypt** houses a melange of columns pilfered from Greek, Roman, and Arab sites.

Take C. Garibaldi to P. del Popolo and follow the signs to the 8th-century Byzantine **Church of San Pietro,** the town's oldest church. In contrast to the town's massive cathedral, this humble building in a tiny *piazza* seems to be hiding from the public. Red, pink, and blue mosaics of the Garden of Eden brighten the church's intimate interior. Overlooking the town, the 16th-century **Aragonese castle** looms with imposing walls and a newly excavated moat. Note the street-level line on the castle wall showing where the moat had been filled in for centuries. In August, Otranto welcomes tourists with a feast in honor of the martyrs. On September 4, the town celebrates again with the **Festa della Madonna dell' Altomare.**

A few miles north of Otranto the beach **Torre dell' Orso** sleeps cradled in pine woods at the end of a beautiful inlet. A bemused Madonna sits at the **Grotta della Poesia,** a small pool of clear water enclosed by low cliffs and a natural bridge. Another grotto rests a few meters away, covered in religious inscriptions from the Messapic through Roman eras. The coast south of Otranto, bordered by limestone cliffs and dotted with flat-roofed homes, is more rugged than the sandy beaches to the north. If you have a car, toodle down to **Porto Badisco,** legendary landing point of Aeneas and a stunningly beautiful swimming hole. Farther south, take a bath at the legendary thermal springs of **Santa Cesarea Terme.** The **tourist office** gathers dust at Via Roma, 209 (tel. (0836) 94 40 43). Six km south of here is the **Zinzulusa Grotto,** filled with stalactites and stalagmites (*zinzuli* in the local dialect). Two Ferrovie del Sud-Est buses run daily to Santa Cesarea Terme from Via Adua in Lecce.

Gallipoli

Electricity nearly killed Gallipoli (*not* the Gallipoli of World War I fame in Turkey), but fish and tourism are bringing it back. A wealthy resort town in the 1600s, Gallipoli hosted sumptuous homes for the rich. These Renaissance palaces remained in their elegant states until the advent of electric light destroyed the town's oil-based economy. To reach the old city from the train station, walk on Viale Borvio and turn right on **Corso Roma,** the main street of the modern quarter. Cross the bridge to reach the old city, perching on a tiny but beautiful island with only Corso Roma connecting it to the mainland. Train travelers heading straight to the old quarter can disembark at the Gallipoli Porto station at the foot of the old city. Near the bridge on the shore opposite the castle is the **Piazza Fontana Greca** and its odd fountain. The Greeks originally constructed the fountain, the Romans later altered it by adding the middle section, and the Renaissance saw the addition of the ornate top section.

The Pro Loco **tourist office,** C. Roma, 225, near P. Fontana Greca, has limited info on local accommodations and prices. Open July-Aug. daily 10am-noon and 5-8pm; Sept.-June Mon.-Sat. 10am-noon. The **post office** is at P. Imbriani, to the left as you cross the bridge into the old city. Open Mon.-Fri. 8:30am-5:30pm, Sat. 8:30am-1pm. **Postal code:** 73014. **Telephone code:** 0833. If you have a trip to Gallipoli planned in advance, book a room at the city's **Seminary,** V. de Pace, 51, next to the cathedral. Here you'll receive hot showers, a private room, and kitchen privileges for L25,000 a night. Open July to September. Write at least 3 months in advance to Z. Conatta, Via de Pace, 30, 73014 Gallipoli (or call 26 41 64 in the evenings). **Pensione Al Pescatore,** Riviera C. Colombo, 39 (tel./fax 26 36 56), to the right as you cross the bridge, charges L55,000 for singles and L90,000 for doubles. Large, elegant rooms with TV, phone, and bath face onto a small courtyard. Prices rise L10,000 in July. Half-pension (L100,000) is required in August. V, MC, AmEx. **Baia de Gallipoli** (tel. 26 69 06), a campsite about 3km from town, charges L10,200 per person, L8300 per tent, L4000 per car, and L95,000 per two-bed bungalow. Open June-September. Exquisite homemade sauces make the pizza at **La Tonnara,** Via Garibaldi, 7 (tel. 26 44 17), across from the cathedral, some of the best in Puglia. Open daily noon-3pm and 7:30-11pm.

Stretching along Gallipoli's northern coast are two beautiful beaches, **Santa Maria al Bagno** and **Santa Caterina.** Buses leave from P. Fontana Greca several times daily (July-Aug., L2000). To the south, take the beach road to Lido San Giovanni and its pebbly sand beach (entrance L2500), or continue down Lungomare Galileo Galilei to the free Baia Verde (a 10-min. walk from town). Agenzia de Luca, C. Roma, 217 (tel. 26 42 43; fax 26 38 41), offers **glass-bottom boat tours** and **sailing excursions** to groups of eight people or more. Open Mon.-Sat. 9am-12:30pm and 5-9pm. At night, young Gallipolitans check each other out on the Corso Roma, where bars and cafés stay open well into the night.

Taranto

Outcast Spartans supposedly founded Taranto in 706BC, naming it for Taras, son of the sea-god Neptune. Archaeological evidence, however, shows that the site was populated in the second millennium BC. For some time Taranto was one of the most important cities in Magna Graecia, and in the 3rd century BC the city managed to hold back Rome's advances with the help of King Pyrrhos of Epirus (the inspiration for the term "Pyrric victory"). Today, even those accustomed to the economically-depressed cities of the south may be stunned by Taranto's shabbiness. Tourists wishing to head straight from the train station to Taranto's world-famous museum should pause a moment to contemplate the desolate, crumbling old city. In the modern new city, endless rivers of cars and *motorini* burn through the streets, adding more pollution to the noxious clouds emitted by the port factories.

ORIENTATION AND PRACTICAL INFORMATION

Taranto is sandwiched on a peninsula between two seas, the Mare Piccolo and the Mare Grande. The **old city** rests in the center on a small island, joined by bridges to the **new city** in the southeast and the port area and train station to the north. **Be careful of pickpockets during the day, and avoid the old city altogether at night.** Grab a map of the city from the information booth in the station, and walk to **Piazza Garibaldi,** the new city's main square. **Trains** depart frequently from P. Duca d'Aosta to Brindisi (1½hr., L5700) and Bari (1½hr., around L9800). **Buses** run to: Bari (4 per day, 2hr., L8500), Matera (5 per day, 1¾hr., L7500), and Naples (3 per day, 4hr., L31,000). For local traveling, you can get a city bus full-day pass for L2500. At the EPT **tourist office,** Corso Umberto, 113 (tel. 453 43 92), in the new city, the genial, English-speaking staff provides help with accommodations. Open Mon.-Fri. 9am-1pm and 5-7pm, Sat. 9am-noon. In **emergencies,** call 113 (police, tel. 112). The **post office** is on Lungomare Vittorio Emanuele II (tel. 43 59 51). Open Mon.-Fri. 8:15am-5pm, Sat. 8:15am-12:30pm. **Postal code:** 74100. **Telephone code:** 099.

ACCOMMODATIONS AND FOOD

Unlike many other Apulian cities, Taranto abounds with inexpensive, comfortable lodgings. Most hotels line the brightly lit streets of the new city and the end of the well traveled *lungomare* in the old city, but exercise caution when walking around there. **Albergo Pisani,** Via Cavour, 43 (tel. 453 40 87), across the bridge in the new city off P. Garibaldi, is the new place in town. Singles with bath L40,000. Doubles with bath L70,000. **Albergo Sorrentino,** P. Fontana, 7 (tel. 471 83 90 or 470 74 56), has large, once-elegant rooms just over the bridge as you go from the port area or train station to the old city. Singles L30,000. Doubles L40,000, with bath L50,000.

Taranto's economic problems have left it with one great advantage over more touristy towns: seafood is good, plentiful, and inexpensive. Try *cozze* (mussels) in basil and olive oil or spaghetti with *vongole* (clams), but avoid anything raw. Grab your daily bread at the **STANDA** supermarket in P. Immacolata (open Mon. and Sat. 9am-1pm, Tues.-Fri. 9am-1pm and 4:30-8:30pm) or at the daily **market,** in the *piazza* just across the bridge into the old city (open daily 7am-1:30pm). **Trattoria Gatto Rosso da Rino,** Via Cavour, 2 (tel. 452 98 75), off P. Garibaldi, specializes in seafood. The *spaghetti mare misto* (mixed sea pasta) is a primo *primo* (L6000), as are the *tubetti alle cozze* (tubular pasta with mussels, L6000). Cover L1500. Open Tues.-Sun. noon-3pm and 7-11pm. **Ristorante Basile al Ristoro,** Via Pitagora, 76 (tel. 452 62 40), has spaghetti with pesto that may make you want to kiss the cook (L6000, kiss extra). Offerings vary with the season. *Primi* from L6000, *secondi* from L7000. *Menù* L20,000. Open Sun.-Fri. noon-3pm and 8-11pm. V, MC.

SIGHTS AND ENTERTAINMENT

The most telling testimony to Taranto's former glory resides within the excellent **Museo Nazionale** (tel. 453 21 12), in P. Garibaldi. This museum's collection of

Magna Graecian art rivals those of Reggio and Naples, and its terra-cotta figure collection is the world's largest. The displays feature ancient marble and bronze sculptures, mosaics, Greek pottery, jewelry, coins, and prehistoric artifacts. (Open daily 9am-2pm. Admission L8000.) The old city is what remains of a Byzantine village built after Saracen invaders razed the original settlement to the ground. Walk through the astoundingly desolate landscape and marvel that such decay also harbors a remarkable **cathedral.** This church was built in the 10th century on a Greek cross plan, but a Latin arm was added in 1170. Much of the present structure dates from a 1713 rebuilding, but the Byzantine exterior walls and cupola are still visible. As you approach the chancel, look for remains of the original mosaic under your feet (hint: find the camels). Take the stairs down to the **crypt** adorned with 13th-century frescoes. Before leaving the cathedral, peek into the **Chapel of San Cataldo,** whose extraordinary inlaid-marble walls attest to the wealth of 18th century Tarantine aristocrats. Locals may not admit it, but the statue inside is not solid silver—it's a ceramic reproduction made after the silver original was stolen. (Open daily 8am-noon and 4-8pm.)

Every night from about 6 to 11pm, the entire stretch of **Via d'Aquino** pulses with scoping crowds. The action centers on **Piazza Garibaldi,** where you can also hear the navy band accompany the lowering of the flag at sundown. Taranto's **Holy Week Festival** draws crowds from around the country. In a ceremony rooted in medieval Spanish ritual, men clothed in white robes parade to Taranto's various churches. The festivities begin the Sunday before Easter. Call the tourist office for more information. On May 10, the city celebrates the **Festa di San Cataldo** with a procession of boats escorting the statue of San Cataldo around the harbor, climaxing in a stirring display of fireworks.

Basilicata

Basilicata is a region with more farm animals than people. Infertile soil and few natural resources have also made the region one of the poorest areas in Italy. The tourist industry is slowly bringing the area to life, creating a more and more desirable stopover—the beaches are less crowded than those at Apulian resorts, and they remain clean and unspoiled. Even if you're just passing through the area, don't miss the breathtaking sights of Matera.

Matera

A few decades ago, Matera represented the quintessence of Italian poverty, its primary residential area consisting of houses built in caves *(sassi)*. The government forced the citizens to abandon their unsafe and unsanitary houses in 1952, but recently many of the ancient rock-hewn houses have been restored and occupied once again. Strikingly beautiful and oddly captivating, the city which calls itself "The Heritage of Humanity" has not yet become a major tourist center, but is a fine daytrip or weekend stopover for anyone seeking refuge from the summertime crowds.

ORIENTATION AND PRACTICAL INFORMATION

From the train and bus stations at **Piazza Matteotti,** head down Via Roma to **Piazza V. Veneto,** the heart of the city. Climb Via del Beccherie (off P. Veneto to the left of Banco di Napoli) to **Piazza Duomo** and the *sassi.* The small paths, steep stairs, and labyrinthine passages would give even the Minotaur a headache, so take a map. No good ones exist for the *sassi* (construction and destruction continually close and reopen paths), but try the freebie from the tourist office. **Don't ignore the warning signs: *crollo* means collapse, and many of the old buildings just might.**

Tourist Office: APT, Via de Viti de Marco, 9 (tel. 33 19 83; fax 33 34 52). From the station, walk down Via Roma and take your 2nd left. Maps, pamphlets, and conversation in English. Open Mon.-Sat. 8am-2pm. The better-marked tourist office farther up V. Roma is almost always closed. **Cooperativa Amici del Turista,** P. San Pietro Caveoso (tel. 31 01 13), in the *sassi* (slated for a new location in 1997), and **Cooperativa Amici dei Sassi,** P. Sedile (tel. 33 10 11), halfway up V. Beccherie, provide detailed L6000 maps and free advice on exploring the *sassi.* Open daily 9:30am-1pm and 3:30-6:30pm; Oct.-Feb. erratic morning hours.

Tourist Aid: Via Gattini 47b (tel. 33 67 48).

Telephones: Via del Corso, 5 (tel. 24 21), off P. Veneto. Open Mon.-Fri. 9am-12:30pm and 2:30-6pm.

Trains: There are 4 stations in Matera. Centrale is, not surprisingly, the main one. **Ferrovie Apulo-Lucane** (tel. 38 70 94) runs from Bari, through Altamura, and on to Matera. Departing from Bari every hour or so (1½hr.; L6500 to Matera Centrale).

Buses: SITA buses (tel. 33 28 62) head to Matera from P. Castello in Taranto (4 per day, 2hr., L7500) and from Metaponto (5 each morning, 1½hr., L5000). For tickets or info on SITA buses from Matera, go to the company office at the top of Via Roma. **Grassani** buses (tel. 72 14 43) run to Potenza twice per day, but more seldom on Sun. and holidays (1½hr., L9000; buy tickets on the bus).

Emergencies: tel. 113. **Ambulance:** tel. 33 35 21. **Hospital:** (tel. 33 41 81), on Via Lanera.

Police: tel. 112 or 33 42 22.

Post Office: (tel. 33 18 22), on Via del Corso off P. Veneto. Open Mon.-Sat. 8:15am-7:40pm. **Postal Code:** 75100.

Telephone Code: 0835.

ACCOMMODATIONS

Many choose to visit Matera as a daytrip from Taranto or Bari. The picturesque hillsides and extensive *sassi,* however, may convince you to stay longer. You can find a reasonably priced room if you arrive early in the day, but you're best off making reservations at the Albergo Roma a few days in advance. The youth hostel **Matera Sassi,** Via San Giovanni Vecchio, 89 (tel./fax 33 10 09), will open soon.

Albergo Roma, Via Roma, 62 (tel. 33 39 12), by the tourist office. Family-run, friendly, clean, and conveniently located, although occasionally noisy. Fills up fast during festival period (late June-early July). Singles L38,000. Doubles L55,000, with bath L60,000. Extra bed L15,000. Unofficial curfew 11:30pm.

De Nicola, Via Nazionale, 158 (tel. 38 51 11). Follow Viale A. Moro from P. Matteotti to Via Anunzia Tella on the left, which becomes Via Nazionale. A bit of a hike from the station, but your best chance for finding a room late in the day. You can also get there on an orange city bus (#1, 2, or 6; L1000). Modern rooms with bath, TV, and telephone. Singles L66,000-86,000. Doubles L105,000-134,000.

FOOD

While in Matera, try some of the local specialties: *favetta con cicore* (a soup of beans, celery, chicory, and croutons, all mixed in olive oil), or *frittata di spaghetti* (pasta with anchovies, eggs, bread crumbs, garlic, and oil). Experience true Materan grit by gnawing on *pane di grano duro;* made of extra-hard wheat, this bread's shelf-life is almost as long as a Twinkie's. **Panificio Perrone,** Via dei Sariis, 6 (tel. 33 44 11), off Via Lucana, sells this and more traditional bread and a variety of sweets, including tasty *biscotti al vino* (cookies baked with wine). Open Mon.-Sat. 6am-2pm and 4-9pm, closed Thurs. afternoon. The daily fruit **market** is between Via Lucana and Via A. Persio, near P. Veneto. Open Mon.-Sat. 7am-1pm. Down the block from the tourist office sits the **Divella** supermarket, Via Spine Bianche, 6. Open Mon.-Sat. 8:30am-1:30pm and 5-8:30pm, closed Thurs. evenings.

Ristorante Pizzeria Il Terrazzino, Vico San Giuseppe, 7 (tel 33 25 03), off P. Veneto to the left of the Banco di Napoli. Savor local delicacies in a cave dug into the cliffs or on the outdoor terrace that offers a perfect view of the *sassi.* Try handmade pasta like *cavatelli alla boscaiola,* with a sauce of tomatoes, mushrooms, and *prosciutto*. Cover L3000, L1000 for pizza. Open Mon. and Wed.-Sun. noon-4pm and 7pm-midnight, Tues. noon-4pm in summer only.

Trattoria Lucana, Via Lucana, 48 (tel. 33 61 17), off Via Roma. Begin with the *orecchiette alla materana* (ear-shaped pasta with tomatoes and fresh veggies, L7000), and continue with the *bocconcini alla lucana* (thinly sliced veal with mushrooms, L12,000), their specialty. Cover L2000. Service 10%. Open Mon.-Sat. 12:30-5pm and 8-10:30pm. Closed early Sept. V, MC.

SIGHTS

Before venturing to the *sassi,* take a quick peek in the 13th-century **Church of San Giovanni Battista** on Via San Biagio off P. Veneto. Much of the church remains in near-original condition. Moved by its harmonious interior architecture, some proclaim it one of the most beautiful churches in Italy.

Enter the heart of the *sassi* zone from P. Veneto by climbing Via delle Beccherie. From P. Sedile, Via Duomo leads to the **duomo** in P. del Duomo. The cathedral (1268-70) is a Puglian-Romanesque construction with a high nave, a rose window, and richly carved portals. Inside, the 15th-century carved choir stalls compete with the 16th-century **Chapel dell'Annunziata** for your attention. (Under partial renovation. Officially open daily 9am-noon, but often unlocked until 7 or 8pm.)

From P. Sedile, two well marked paths **(Itinerari Turistici)** head to the *sassi* in the valleys of **Sasso Caveoso** (to the right) and **Sasso Barisano** (to the left). Of obscure origin, the *sassi* come in several types. The oldest, inhabited around 7000 years ago, are crumbling structures that line Sassa Barisano along and below Via Addozio and below the *duomo* to the west. The second type includes the carved nooks around Sasso Caveoso in the valley to the east of the *duomo,* the oldest dating from around 2000BC. The more elaborately carved homes in the rock around Via Buozzi (which stems from Via Madonna delle Virtù near the *duomo*) are around 1000 years old. Most *sassi* were evacuated after the new city was erected, but young couples have recently been renovating many of the ancient homes. In addition, most of the 6th-century *chiese rupestri* (rock churches) remain unmodified. The more than 120 churches still display remnants of 12th- through 16th-century frescoes.

From the scenic balcony on Via Madonna delle Virtù, wind through Sasso Caveoso to the right and you will arrive at the **Churches of San Pietro Caveoso, Santa Maria d'Idris,** and **Santa Lucia alle Malve.** These churches preserve beautiful 11th-century Byzantine frescoes painted on the caves. (No regular hours, but if they are closed try asking the caretaker to let you in and provide a brief tour. Tip him about L2000.) A nearby *sasso* is furnished as it was when ten people and two horses shared its two small rooms. (Open daily 9am-2pm and 3-8pm; reduced hours in winter; L2000, including tour.) As you roam the Sasso Caveoso, you'll be approached by children offering "tours." You are better off going with the organized tours, which are more expensive but worth the extra cost. The **Amici del Turista**'s rates start at L45,000 for 1-4 people, while the **Amici dei Sassi** offer a L50,000 student tour. Up Via Buozzi from the Church of San Pietro, the **Museo Nazionale Domenico Ridola,** Via Ridola, 24 (tel. 31 12 39), houses an excellent prehistoric and early classical art collection in a former 17th-century monastery. (Open daily 9am-7pm. Admission L4000.)

ENTERTAINMENT

Matera lets loose during the **Festival of Santa Maria della Bruna,** held during the last week of June and first week of July and accompanied by numerous musical and sporting events. The festival reaches its climax on July 2, when a procession of shepherds leaves the *duomo* at dawn, followed at dusk by a float holding a Madonna and illuminated by thousands of small lights. The ornate cart rumbles along Via XX Settembre while warriors in medieval costume and clergy on horseback march solemnly alongside. At the end of the procession, everyone participates in the *Assalto al Carro,* in which relic-hungry spectators tear apart the cart after the Madonna and other valuables have been removed to safety.

Metaponto

Metaponto's beaches are clean, beautiful, and less crowded with foreigners than many beach resorts in southern Italy. Its tourist industry is quickly expanding, however: be prepared for high-priced hotels lining the waterfront and large umbrellas for rent everywhere. Regardless, the sparkling sea and nearby Greek ruins make Metaponto a great daytrip from Taranto or Matera.

ORIENTATION AND PRACTICAL INFORMATION

Metaponto is an important **train junction** on the Taranto-Reggio line (16 per day to Taranto, 1hr., L4200; 5 per day to Reggio, 6hr., L33,400), with a connection to Naples by way of Potenza (5hr., L20,800). **Bus** service connects the Metaponto station with Matera (8 per day, 7am-8pm; in winter 5 per day, 7am-5:30pm; L5000). The SITA bus from Matera alternates with the Chiruzzi line, resulting in almost hourly service between the three small areas that compose Metaponto (L1500): **Lido** (with beach and hotels), **Scalo** (the train station), and **Borgo** (the museum and archaeological sites). To hike from the station to the hotels in the Lido district (2km), walk straight 50m from the station to the highway, **Viale Jonio,** then turn right and follow the footpath up to the overpass, continuing straight past the campgrounds to the beach area. If you turn right on the highway from the station and continue straight across, you get to the Borgo (500m). If you turn right at the sign for the Temple of Apollo, you will arrive at the Greek ruins, while a left leads straight to the museum.

The Lido is a small area around **Piazza Nord** where the bus drops you off. Here you can rent **bikes** (L3000 per hr., tandems L8000 per hr.). Across P. Nord and a few meters straight along Viale delle Nimfe is P. Lido and the volunteer-run **tourist office.** Open June-Sept. daily 8am-8pm. The **post office,** by the Archaeological Museum, is open Mon.-Sat. 8:30am-5:30pm. Metaponto's **postal code** is 75010; the **telephone code** is 0835.

ACCOMMODATIONS AND FOOD

The least expensive hotel in town is the pleasant **Hotel Kennedy** (tel. 74 19 60), on Viale Jonio at the first intersection. Large, 70's-chic doubles with balconies and bath go for L60,000. When it's not crowded, one person may use a double for L40,000. Extra bed L20,000. Half-pension is generally required July 15-31 (L55,000) and August (L65,000). A similar 70's-style resort hotel with slightly higher prices is the **Hotel Sacco** (tel. 74 19 55; fax 74 19 75), located on P. Lido. In July and late August, singles L65,000, doubles L105,000, and extra bed L30,000. In early August, singles L75,000, doubles L120,000, and extra bed L35,000. From September to June, singles L55,000, doubles L90,000, and extra bed L25,000. **Camping** is the most economical option if you plan to hang out for a few days. **Camping Magna Grecia,** Via Lido, 1 (tel. 74 18 55), lies 500m off Via Ionio from the strand. From August 1 to 20, L10,000 per person, L10,000 per tent, L3500 for electricity, and L4000 per parking space. Prices are lower at other times. With all the comforts of home and Disneyland, Magna Grecia's tennis courts, swimming pool, game rooms, disco, and bars will keep you occupied if you don't want to take their shuttle to the beach. The pizzeria **Coop Tur,** Viale delle Sirene, 12, sits to the left of the tourist office. They bring a tasty pizza (from L4000) to your plastic beachside table. Open June-mid-Sept. daily noon-2:30pm and 7pm-1am.

SIGHTS

After enjoying the clear water and fine sand of Metaponto's **beach,** rent a bike, walk, or catch the bus to the **Archaeological Museum** (tel. 74 53 27). For directions see **Orientation and Practical Information** above. The museum displays ancient jewelry, vases, and figurines, most connected to the ruins at the nearby Parco Archeologico. (Open daily 9am-7pm. Admission L4000, under 18 and over 60 free.) At the turnoff to the museum, taking a right instead of a left will lead you 500m to the ruins of the Doric **Temple of Apollo Licius** and a **Greek Theater** (7th-6th century BC). Turn right toward Toranto after 3km, and it will be another 5km to the **Tavole Palatine,** the well-preserved ruins of a Greek temple of Hera. The famous Greek triangle-lover Pythagoras taught here until his death in 479BC.

■ Tyrrhenian Coast: Maratea

Just over the border in the Basilicata region, the area known as Maratea comprises the beach towns of **Aquafredda, Fiumicello,** and **Marina di Maratea,** as well as the hillside town of **Maratea** proper. 1960 saw the creation of the Redentore, a 22-m statue of Christ, on a cliff overlooking the four towns and the sea. This area makes a great daytrip from Praia a Mare. To get to Marina di Maratea, ride a scooter along the gorgeous winding road, or take the train (8 per day until 10:20pm, L2000).

Fiumicello and Maratea

From Marina di Maratea, catch a boat to Fiumicello from Spiaggia Maccarro (L14,000) or get off the train at Maratea station (*not* Marina di Maratea) and follow the highway from the station to the left down toward the beach. Lodging in Fiumicello is sparse and expensive, but an attractive option is **Hotel Settebello,** Località Fiumicello (tel. 87 62 77). Walk out of your L60,000 double right onto the beach. All rooms with bath, telephone, and A/C. Grab a bite to eat on a peaceful outdoor patio at **El Sol,** Via Santa Venere, 151 (tel. 87 69 28). A good selection of pizza ranges in price from L4000 to L8000. Cover L2000.

Hikers may enjoy the uphill walk to Maratea proper, "town of the 44 churches," about 300m up the side of the mountain from the train station. Though getting there is more than half the fun, the views are breathtaking and the town secluded yet friendly. A low-priced hotel is scheduled to be finished in Piazza Vittolo by summer 1997. Take a break from the hike at **Il Ghiottone,** Via Petra del Pesce, 11 (tel. 87 75 96). A great selection of sandwiches from L4000 (including the ubiquitous "*cis* burger"), *primi* from L5000, and *secondi* from L5000. Just up the street at Piazza Buraglia is the **Pizzeria le Tre Rose,** where you can get appetizer, pizza, and drink for L10,000.

Maratea Castrocucco, down the road from the Marina, is the site of **Camping Maratea** (tel. 87 75 80). The main AAST **tourist office** is on Via Santa Venere (tel. 87 69 08) and has colorful booklets on the area and its surroundings plus helpful listings of hotels and prices. Open June-Sept. Mon.-Sat. 8am-2pm and 4-7pm, Sun. 9am-1pm and 3-6pm; Oct.-May Mon.-Fri. 8am-2pm and 4-7pm, Sat. 8am-2pm. The **post office** at the port can also be of some help to tourists. Open Mon.-Sat. 8am-2pm and 3-9pm, Sun. 9am-12:30pm and 5-8pm. The **telephone code** for Maratea is 0973.

Calabria

The region of Calabria is located in the southern part of Italy, from boot-tip to arch. Calabrian history began with the ancient Greeks and the wealthy towns of **Sibari** and **Locri.** Legions of Byzantines, Saracens, Normans, and Aragonese followed, leaving behind their own marks on the region's population and cities. The coming of the World Wars also marked the formation of organized crime—the *'ndrangheta*—which caused thousands of Calabrians to leave their homes in search of a better life. Today the effects of the "crime-families" are felt less here than they are in the rest of Italy; the mob, like many individuals, seems to have given up on Calabria.

Whatever Calabria lacks in developed tourism, it makes up for in dramatic landscapes and unspoiled wilderness. The few level spots along the shore, like the towns of **Marina di Maratea** and **Praia a Mare,** are beach paradises; most of the rest of the coastline boasts steep cliffs falling into the steamy Mediterranean. The inland town of **Cosenza** lies in the heart of the Sila Massif, a huge granite plateau (1100-1700m) that offers some of Italy's best hiking. Near the southern tip of Calabria is **Reggio di Calabria,** a dynamic city whose superb archaeological museum houses the famous Bronze Warriors from Riace. On a venture north along the sandy but bleak beaches of the Ionian Coast lies **Gerace,** a little-touristed town that preserves relatively unspoiled Byzantine monuments.

Cosenza

Set on seven lush hills, Cosenza is conveniently divided into two parts. A flat urban metropolis bustles on one side of the Busento River, while on the other, an old city shares the hill with a castle built by Frederick II. Besides offering opportunities to shop in glitzy stores and walk along historic cobblestone paths, Cosenza's greatest attribute is its location, which makes it the perfect base for hiking in the Sila Massif.

ORIENTATION AND PRACTICAL INFORMATION

Getting around Cosenza is not difficult once you realize that there are two bus stations and two train stations. From the **new station (Cosenza),** trains service the western coast, Northern Italy, and Sicily; from the **old station (Cosenza Centro),** trains service the eastern coast or the arch of the boot. One block away from Cosenza Centro stretches **Corso Mazzini,** a main thoroughfare which runs parallel to the tracks of Cosenza and connects the old town with the **main bus station** at **Piazza Fera.** To reach C. Mazzini, exit the old station, follow the walkway, cross the street in front of the station, walk one block, and turn right onto C. Mazzini. Once on C. Mazzini with the old station to your right, the old town is behind you and the **central bus station** is straight ahead about eight blocks.

Tourist Office: APT, Corso Mazzini, 92 (tel./fax 278 21 or tel. 272 71). Halfway between the bus station and the old town, next to the STANDA supermarket. There is another office, more difficult to reach, but nearer to the new train station on Via Rossi opposite the rotary (tel. 39 05 95; open Mon.-Fri. 9:30am-1pm and 4-7:30pm). English speaker available in the afternoons.

Telephones: *Telefoni a scatti* on Via dell'Autostazione, above the central bus station. Open daily 8:10am-8pm.

Trains: (tel. 48 15 21/22/23/24). The **Cosenza station** is on Via Popilia at the *superstrada.* To: Paola, on the Rome-Reggio di Calabria coastal line (over 20 per day, 20min., L2600); Metaponto (5 per day, change at Sibari, 3hr., L11,700). A "shuttle" train connects the two stations (every 20min. or so, 7am-8pm, L1000), as does bus #5 (every 15min., 6am-12:30am, L1100). From **Cosenza Centro** (off P. Matteotti), trains depart for Camigliatello, San Giovanni, and other cities in the Sila. **Cosenza Monaco, Cosenza Campanella, and Cosenza Casali** are three other stations in and near the city.

Buses: At the new train station or off P. Fera, at the opposite end of C. Mazzini from the old train station. City buses L1100 one way. Get schedules at the information booths in the new train station (tel. 48 26 40). Gate #1 for Catanzaro, #15 for the Tyrrhenian coast. Snack bar open 24hr. Irregular schedule on Sun. and holidays.

Emergencies: tel. 113. **Ambulance: Croce Bianca,** Via Beato Angelo d'Acri, 29 (tel. 39 35 28). **Hospital: Ospedale Civile dell'Annunziata** (tel. 68 11), on Via Felice Migliori. On weekends, call 318 31.

Police: Questura (tel. 360 01).

Post Office: (tel. 264 35 or 268 08), on Via Vittorio Veneto at the end of Via Piave off Corso Mazzini. Open Mon.-Sat. 8:15am-7:30pm. **Postal Code:** 87100.

Telephone Code: 0984.

ACCOMMODATIONS

Affordable lodgings cluster around the old station, just a few blocks from the old city. This quarter is blessed with a good *pensione* and cursed with evil tourist traps like expensive craft stores and cafés.

Albergo Bruno, Corso Mazzini, 27 (tel. 738 89), 1 block from the train station. Offers spacious rooms, recently renovated bathrooms, and free use of the kitchen, pool table, TV room, and musical instruments (guitar, piano, drum set). Family-run. Singles L35,000, with bath L50,000. Doubles L55,000, with bath L70,000. Triples L75,000, with bath L90,000. Quads L90,000, with bath L100,000.

Hotel Grisaro, Via Monte Santo, 6 (tel. 278 38), is worth every lira for a recently refinished L50,000 single. Rear entrance on Viale Trieste, off C. Mazzini about 3 blocks. Singles with bath L60,000. Doubles with bath L90,000. Triples with bath L120,000. Quads with bath L140,000. All rooms with TV. Disabled access available. Breakfast (cappuccino and pastry) included.

Camping: The best in the area is at the Sila Massif (see p. 477) and in the seaside towns of **Scalea** and **Marina di Belvedere.** Two sites on Scalea's Tyrrhenian waterfront are **Camping il Gabbiano** (tel. (0985) 205 63), with beach bungalows and free hot showers. L8000 per person, L9000 per tent. Open mid-June-mid-Sept. **Campeggio Moby Dick** (tel. (0985) 202 78) is well organized with sporting activities (soccer, beach volleyball, tennis, and ping-pong). Free hot showers and beach bungalows. L15,900 per person or per tent, but prices can go up to L26,600 in high-season. Open June-Sept. While staying here, pay a visit to another beautiful beach up north, **S. Nicole.**

FOOD

Cosenza's best dishes are prepared *ai funghi* (with fresh mushrooms from the forests of the Sila). Pack a sack of goodies from the **STANDA** supermarket, C. Mazzini, 98 (tel. 746 32), in the basement of the department store. Open Mon.-Fri. 9am-1pm and 4:30-8:30pm, Sat. 9am-1pm. Visit a street vendor for the best produce in town.

Trattoria Tre Lanterne, Via Rivocati, 15 (tel. 728 76). Take a left out of the old train station toward Mario Martire bridge. Turn right onto Via Rivocati and head downhill just before the bridge. Look for (surprise!) 3 lanterns on the left. Complete dinner (*primo, secondo,* salad, and drink) for L15,000.

Da Quintino, Piazza Riforma, 1 (tel. 250 89), is downhill on Via Veneto from the post office and up Corso Umberto from the old train station. The chef whips up a mean *spaghetti alla carbonara* for L5000. *Primi* from L5000, *secondi* from L6000. Open Mon.-Sat. 8am-3pm and 5-10pm.

Gran Caffè Renzelli, Corso Telesio, 46 (tel. 268 14) is in "the historical location of Cosenza." Climb to the cathedral, then take a left after crossing M. Martire Bridge. Try some *torroncino,* a delectable almond nougat, with your coffee.

SIGHTS AND ENTERTAINMENT

All historic sights of interest in Cosenza lie in the old city across the shallow **Busento River** from the old train station. Follow C. Mazzini to its end (to the left with your back to Cosenza Centrale), cross the *piazza,* turn left, and then make an immediate right. Cross the Mario Martire bridge, turn left onto Corso Telesio, and climb uphill to the 12th-century Romanesque **cathedral** where Frederick II was crowned. The winding streets are lined with abandoned shops, wood-workers, fruit stands, and clotheslines. Keep your head up and your mouth closed—there's no telling what will be tossed from the medieval windows. Once in the cathedral, note the mural of the *Madonna and Child* (1863) on the right side. The city's prized possession—the tiny, ornate **Byzantine Cross** donated by Frederick II—adorns the *Arcivescovato* near the cathedral. The colorful artifact bears a Christ and mourning Madonna on the left arm, a supplicating St. John the Evangelist on the right, and the archangel Michael above. A 12th-century **Norman Castle** built by Frederick II lies at the top of the hill, the city's highest point. The castle itself is not open to the public, but the view at the top is well worth the long uphill hike on cobblestone roads. For more information call the *Teatro Comunale* (tel. 741 65) or the tourist office.

■ Tyrrhenian Coast: Praia a Mare

On the coast at the top of the boot, near Maratea in Basilicata, lies the small but lively beach town **Praia a Mare** (train station Praja; from Naples 2½hr., L17,200; from Reggio 3hr., L20,800). If you follow Via Stazione (which turns into Via Polo) from the station, you'll quickly arrive at the long stretch of sandy beach. A 15-min. walk to the left brings you to **Spiaggia di Fiuzzi,** a beautiful beach where the imposing island, **Isola di Dino,** looms in front of you, and a 13th-century Norman castle is on the left. Those who missed or loved Capri should take a tour of Dino's many caves, one of which displays the same eerie luminescence as the Blue Grotto. Boats leave from the beach in front of the island between 9 and 10am (about L12,000 per person; tel. 77 92 75 for info). Back in the town proper, you can take a break from the sun in the **Santuario Madonna della Grotta,** a peaceful chapel set in a mountain cave. From the station, take your second left on the main street, Via Giugni. After 100m, turn left on Via della Grotta and bear right at all forks.

The Pro Loco **tourist office** changes location periodically, but the friendly folks at the travel agency **Suenobi,** Via Stazione, 11 (tel. 77 70 52) will direct you to it and help you themselves the best they can. Exiting the station, you'll see it directly in front of you to the right. Clean, cozy rooms at the cheapest rates in town are at **Pensione La Piedigrotta,** Via Maiorana, 45 (tel. 721 92), on the way to the Santuario Madonna della Grotta. When you see the chapel above, the hotel will be on your right. Singles L30,000, with bath L35,000. Doubles L45,000, with bath L55,000. Ask for a room on the side away from the train tracks, since trains rumble by all night. On the waterfront to the left of Via Polo, the restaurant **Riviera,** Piazza Sturzo, 2 (tel. 732 79), is beautifully situated for sunset dinners. Pizza from L4500, *primi* from L6000, and *secondi* from L8000. Try the "Riviera" pizza (L7000), with mushrooms, eggplant, salami, prosciutto, and anything else the chef has a mind to add. The owners have another restaurant down the beach in front of the Isola di Dino, **Cooperativa Azzurro 87,** Località Matinera.

If you've been waiting for a relatively safe place to experiment with a scooter or moped, Praia is a good bet. **Noleggio Praia 90,** Via Cilea, 27 (tel. 734 55), rents 1-person scooters (L80,000 per day, L350,000 per week). For the 5-min. walk from the station, turn right on Via Longo, left on Via Verga, and then left on Via Cilea. You need to present your passport and be staying at a local hotel. Open daily 9am-1pm and 4:30pm-1am, occasionally 2am. There's also a **Scooter Martino** (tel. 743 70) on Via Stazione directly across from the travel agency as you come out of the station. Praia's **telephone code** is 0985.

The Sila Massif

Located in the heart of Calabria is the **Sila Massif,** a 2000-sq.km plateau of pristine wilderness. It consists of three main zones: La Greca to the north, La Grande in the center, and La Piccola on the coast. These areas constitute one of Italy's last mountain chains still covered with virgin forest. Although slower than bus service, train travel in this area should not be missed. From Cosenza Centrale, trains no more than 20m in length inch their way up and through the mountains, accessing incredible views. You'll be awed by the feats of engineering required to build the route.

CAMIGLIATELLO

To reach **Camigliatello** from Cosenza, you can take either a bus (10 per day, 45min., L2800) or a train (3 per day, 1½hr., L2500). Camigliatello, a small alpine town with fairytale streets, is the first major stop you'll come to on the train line from Cosenza and is the area's best base for exploration. Upon arrival you should confer with the hiking experts at Pro Loco **tourist office,** Via Roma, 5 (tel. 57 80 91), a hike up the hill from the train station to your right. Ask for their useful map of the Sila. Open daily 9am-12:30pm and 3:30-7:30pm. You can also find a map at one of the many tourist shops on Via Roma. The office at the **Parco Nazionale di Calabria** (tel. 57 97 57), at the western end of the park (10km northwest of Camigliatello), sells a detailed map with descriptions of ten suggested hikes. Most of them begin and end at **Cupone,** the site of the office. **Cooperativa "Natura Insieme,"** Via C. Alvaro, 70 (tel. 57 87 66), organizes guided hiking and biking excursions through the Sila as well as cross-country skiing and tours of historic Cosenza. Translators are available for all tours (L50,000 extra). English spoken at the office. Tours range from L50,000 to L150,000. Office hours Mon.-Sat. 9am-1pm and 3-7pm. There is a **post office** (tel. 57 80 76) at the intersection of Via del Turismo and Via Roma. Walk uphill on V. Roma, and the office is on the left, just past the sign for Hotel Tasso. Open Mon.-Fri. 8:15am-1:30pm, Sat. 8:15am-12:10pm.)The **bank,** the Cassa di Risparmio de Calabria e de Lucania, is also on Via Roma, 61 (tel. 57 80 27). Open Mon.-Fri. 8:20am-1:20pm and 2:35-3:20pm. The local **telephone code** is 0984.

Cheap meals and lodging in Camigliatello are few and far between. Try **La Baita,** Via Roma, 99 (tel. 57 81 97), to the right as you exit the station. Somber, neat rooms, all with baths. No singles. Doubles L80,000. Triples L93,000. **Hotel Mancuso,** Via del Turismo, 51 (tel. 57 80 02), is around the corner from the station. Make your first right on Via Roma and then an immediate left on Via del Turismo. Nicely decorated bedrooms with an attractive dining room downstairs. Singles L36,000. Doubles with bath L80,000. Triples with bath L100,000. Quads with bath L120,000. Half-pension L65,000. Full-pension L90,000. Group discounts available. For campers, **La Fattoria** (tel. 57 83 64) lies about 3km from Camigliatello on the road to Lago Cecita. **Lorica,** 37km from Camigliatello, is also close to several campsites, among them **Park 108,** right off Via Nazionale (tel. 53 70 77 or 99 22 27); ask for assistance at Lorica's Pro Loco **tourist office** (tel. 53 70 69) on Via Nazionale.

While in Camigliatello, picnic on the local specialties—cheeses, cured meats, and marinated mushrooms. The main drag overflows with *salumerie,* which can provide you with sandwich supplies, as well as family-owned restaurants offering regional delicacies. **Ristorante "La Stragola,"** Via Roma, 160 (tel. 57 83 16), up the hill from the train station on the left side of the street (look for the wagon wheel), offers complete meals including beverages for L25,000. V, AmEx. Or try **Ristorante Pizzeria al Buongustaio,** Via del Turismo, 34 (tel. 57 81 54). Two immediate rights off Via Roma at the sign for the Hotel Meranda. (Look for a red sign snuggled within a row of pine trees.) Share a romantic pizza—yes, in southern Italy even pizza can be romantic. *Menù* (including *primo, secondo,* and drink) L25,000.

Amazing **skiing** conditions draw downhill diehards from Christmas until mid-March. Camigliatello's **Tasso Ski Trail** (tel. 57 81 36 or 57 94 00) on Monte Curcio is about 3km from town, up Via Roma and left at Hotel Tasso. Visit in the summer just for the memorable views. (Lift runs daily every 15min., 8:30am-6:30pm. Roundtrip L5000.) Ask at the tourist office for rental information.

Reggio di Calabria

Contemporary Reggio is the end result of a devastating earthquake in 1908. From the rubble a town arose, lacking old-world charm but brimming with designer stores and turn-of-the-century ornate **palazzi**. Besides serving as a transportation hub to Sicily, it provides a taste of modern hustle-and-bustle at the tip of Italy's least modernized region. History buffs should not miss the National Museum and its famous bronze figures, tokens of Calabria's ancient glory as part of Magna Graecia.

ORIENTATION AND PRACTICAL INFORMATION

Most traffic in Reggio is along **Corso Garibaldi,** running north and south along the length of the town and connecting the town's major sights. With your back to the

Stazione Centrale, walk straight through **P. Garibaldi** to the Corso. A left turn will take you into the heart of the town. A few blocks to the left, **C. Vittorio Emanuele III** and **Lungomare Matteotti** run nearly parallel. City buses (L800) continuously trace a route along the three roads toward the **Stazione Lido** 1½km to the north.

Tourist Office: APT booth (tel. 271 20), at the central train station. Useful maps and directions. Open Mon.-Sat. 8am-2pm and 2:30-8pm. Two other booths hold similar hours at the **airport** (tel. 64 32 91 or 64 35 70) and at the **main office** on Via Roma, 3 (tel. 211 71). Another **APT office** is at Corso Garibaldi, 329 (tel. 89 20 12). English spoken. Open Mon.-Fri. 7:45am-7:45pm.

Currency exchange: Banca Nazionale del Lavoro, Corso Garibaldi 431 (tel. 85 11). Open Mon.-Fri. 8:20am-1:20pm, 2:45-4pm. Or at the **FS** info booth inside the station, 7am-9pm.

Telephones: Corso Vittorio Emanuele, 110 (tel. 89 75 79). Outside, behind the post office. Open daily 8am-10pm.

Airport: Svincolo Aeroporto, (tel. 64 22 32), 5km south of town. Catch orange bus #113, 114, 115, or 125 from P. Garibaldi outside S. Centrale (L1000). Service to all major cities in Italy.

Trains: Reggio has 2 train stations. All trains stop at the **Stazione Centrale,** P. Garibaldi (tel. 89 81 23), at the southern end of town. The less-frequented **Stazione Lido** (tel. 86 36 64) sits at the northern end of town off Via Zerbi, much nearer to the museum, port, and beaches. To Rome (15 per day, 7hr., L51,200, *rapido* L70,600) and Naples (20 per day, 5hr., L37,000, *rapido* L52,500).

Ferries: The majority of trains and ferries cross to Messina from **Villa San Giovanni** (15min. north by train, L1500). **Caronte** lines have the most frequent and fastest service. From Villa S. Giovanni, follow the signs to the private ferry services. Three companies provide service directly from **Reggio. Ferrovie dello Stato** (tel. 86 36 75), at the port 5 blocks to the left of Stazione Lido (facing inland), accepts all Inter-Rail, Eurail, and kilometric tickets for the Sicily crossing. **Tirrenia,** Via B. Buozzi, 31 (tel. 89 20 32) is across Viale D. Genoese Zerbi from Stazione Lido. Turn left at the sign for Hotel Lido and walk 1 block up Via III Settembre to Via Buozzi. Ticket office open Mon.-Fri. 8:30am-1pm and 4-7pm. **SNAV** (tel. 295 68), next to Ferrovie dello Stato, specializes in hydrofoil service.

Villa San Giovanni-Messina: Ferrovie (tel. 75 82 41 or 75 14 13) ferries 3:20am-4:45pm (14 per day, 35min., L1800).

Reggio-Messina: Ferrovie (tel. 86 36 75) ferries 7:15am-8:45pm (17 per day, 20min., L4200). **SNAV** (tel. 295 68) hydrofoils Mon.-Fri. 7:15am-8:40pm (24 per day, Sat. 18 per day, 20min., L4500 one way).

Reggio-Lipari Islands: SNAV hydrofoil (6-7 per day, L33,700 to Vulcano, L53,000 to Alicudi).

Emergencies: tel. 113. **First Aid:** tel. 34 71 06. **Hospital: Ospedale Riuniti** (tel. 34 71 17), on Via Melacrino.

Police: (tel. 471 12), on Via S. Caterina in the northern end of town near the port.

Post Office: Via Miraglia, 14 (tel. 81 21 52), near P. Italia. Open Mon.-Fri. 8:15am-7pm, Sat. 8:15am-1:30pm. **Postal Code:** 89100.

Telephone code: 0965.

ACCOMMODATIONS

Pensione S. Bernadetta, Corso Garibaldi, 585 (tel. 89 45 00), right across P. Garibaldi from the central train station all the way up on the 5th floor. It may not be fancy, but it's certainly not expensive. Singles L20,000. Doubles L40,000.

Albergo Noel, Viale Genoese Zerbi, 13 (tel. 33 00 44 or 89 09 65), a few blocks north of Stazione Lido. With the sea behind you, turn left as you exit the station. Location handy to port and museum. Restaurant will do in a pinch. All rooms with bath and TV. Singles L45,000. Doubles L60,000. Triples L75,000. V, MC. Reserve July-Sept.

Hotel Diana, Via Diego Vitrioli, 12 (tel. 89 15 22), off Corso Garibaldi, halfway between Stazione Centrale and the museum. Look for large signs. Singles with bath

L45,000. Doubles with bath and telephone L90,000. Triples L122,000. One-month advance reservation required in August.

FOOD

Reggio's chefs feel most at home making *spaghetti alla calabrese* (noodles dressed in a potent pepper sauce), *capocollo* ham (salami spiced with local hot peppers), and *pesce spada* (swordfish caught off neighboring Bagnara Calabra). At Corso Garibaldi, 107, toward the S. Lido end, supermarket **STANDA** (tel. 231 06) supplies the basics. Open Mon. and Wed.-Sat. 8:30am-1pm and 4:45-8:15pm, Tues. 8am-1pm. There is also an **A&O** supermarket (tel. 33 02 59) at Corso Garibaldi, 587, across from the train station. Open Mon.-Sat. 8am-3pm.

La Pignata, Via Demetrio Tripepi, 122 (tel. 278 41), up Via Giutecca from Corso Garibaldi near the *castello.* An elegant restaurant with carved wooden ceilings and nude panel-paintings inside. Standard pizza prices (L5000-10,000) make up for pricey *ristorante* menu (*primi* from L8000, *secondi* from L13,000). *Menù* L22,000, includes their choice of *primo, secondo,* side dish, and fruit. Try the delicious pizza *rignate* (L7000), loaded with prosciutto, anchovies, onions, and olives. Cover L3000. Open Mon.-Sat. 12:30-3pm and 7-11:30pm. V, MC, AmEx.

Cordon Bleu, Corso Garibaldi, 205 (tel. 33 24 47), close to the theater, modern, and chic. *Calamari* (L8000) and assorted pastries (L1000-2000) are especially delectable. Wine L6000 per bottle. Cover L1000. *Primi* from L6000, *secondi* from L5000. Open for "real food" Thurs.-Tues. 10:30am-midnight. Another location is at C. Emanuele III, 39 (tel. 89 11 61), where you can sit in a lush garden and listen to piano accompaniment. Same hours, no food (it's a bar and *gelateria* only).

Pizzeria Rusty, Via Crocefisso, 14 (tel. 925 30), half a block from P. Duomo and next to the *duomo* itself. The other location, on V. Romeo next to the museum, is conveniently located near the **antica gelateria.** Mouth-watering pizza L10,000-12,000 per kilo (a lot of pizza). Any combination of mushrooms, anchovies, eggplant, prosciutto, or artichokes on a square of dough. Open daily 3:30-11pm.

SIGHTS AND ENTERTAINMENT

If you're passing through Reggio, you might as well stop and spend a day by the sea. The **lungomare,** a pleasant park overlooking the water and the rugged Sicilian coast, stretches from one end of Reggio to the other. While you're at it, don't miss the **Museo Nazionale,** P. de Nava (tel. 81 22 55), on Corso Garibaldi near the Stazione Lido. The museum documents the history of Magna Graecia with material from excavations in Calabria and underwater treasure-hunts off the coast. Notable are the works in the upstairs gallery by southern Italian artist Antonello da Messina and a set of dramatic Greek tablets from the 5th and 6th centuries BC that tell the stories of Persephone, Castor and Pollux, and Achilles and Agamemnon. The masterpieces of the museum are the **Bronzi di Riace,** two beautiful, bronze Greek statues preserved for over 2000 years in the gentle waters of the Ionian and found off the coast of Riace, Calabria in 1972. After painstaking restoration, the statues were identified as Greek originals and dated to the mid-5th century BC, the Golden Age of Greek sculpture. (Open daily 9am-7pm; closed every 1st and 3rd Mon.)

The continuously rebuilt *duomo* on C. Garibladi, five blocks from Stazione Centrale, houses the 16th-century tomb of Gaspare Fosso, the Chapel of the Sacrament restored after the 1908 earthquake, and precious metalwork from the 1400s. Up the street from the *duomo,* off of Via Crocefisso on Via Aschenez, stand the ruins of the medieval *castello,* fortified in the 19th century by the Aragonese. Calabrians finish off the summer with **the celebration of the Madonna della Consolazione.** The festival lasts four days in mid-September and concludes with fireworks.

■ Near Reggio di Calabria

SCILLA

A picturesque fishing village, Scilla lies about 30km from Reggio along the Tyrrhenian coast. The stunning beach resort sits above the famous rock that, according to Homer, hid a ship-devouring female monster with six heads and twelve feet. With tall green mountains ending in soft blue waters, Scilla today offers sublime views and relaxing beaches. Scilla is accessible from Reggio by train (8 per day, 30min., L2600) or by bus (12 per day, last bus 9pm, L2500) and is well worth the trip. If you stay in Scilla, try to get a room at **Pensione Le Sirene,** Via Nazionale, 57 (tel. 75 40 19 or 75 41 21). Near the beach (1 block back from the *lungomare*), Le Sirene offers shady, communal terraces that overlook the sea and cool rooms with ceiling fans and showers. Singles L44,000. Doubles L68,000. Triples L105,000. Breakfast included. Reservations recommended June-Aug.

The cheapest meals around are at **Pizzeria San Francesco,** Via Cristoforo Colombo (tel. 75 46 91), on the beach near the central train station. Pizza runs L5000-10,000. Try the "Franceso," loaded with the works. The local wine can be hazardous to your health. Also at Via Umberto I, beneath the castle. Open Thurs.-Tues. noon-midnight. Walk 10min. uphill toward the castle from the beach to relax with a drink at **Vertigine,** P. San Rocco, 14. Outdoor seating features dizzying views of the ocean and castle. The restaurant specializes in seafood; L18,000 will net you a plateful of the day's catch. Drinks from L1500. *Primi* from L6000, *secondi* from L8000. Cover L2000, service 10%. Open daily noon-3pm and 7:30pm-midnight.

The summer night spot is the open disco created under the arch of a bridge by the *superstrada.* **Il Ponte** offers giant-screen video music as well as a superb outdoor *ristorante.* Before you dance the night away be sure to visit the **Church of Maria S.S. Immacolata,** right next to the castle. Inside, you'll enjoy 14 bronze sculptures depicting the Crucifixion, as well as an awe-inspiring altar-painting. (Open vaguely 8-11am and 3-7pm.) The **Church of San Rocco,** up the hill from the Immacolata, is currently in restoration, but worth the climb for the view of the beach.

BAGNARA CALABRA AND ASPROMONTE

Eight km north of Scilla rests this typical Tyrrhenian fishing village with crumbling buildings and swordfishing boats bobbing offshore. Catch a train from Reggio (17 trains daily, L3400) or Scilla (13 trains daily, L1500). The road north of town offers a view of Sicily and the Lipari Islands. Bring a picnic, as local prices tend to be astronomical. The **A&O** supermarket, Via Garibaldi, 127 (tel. 37 24 83), offers a cheap haven. Open Mon. and Wed.-Sat. 8am-1pm and 4:15-8:15pm. **Ristorante La Torre,** P. Cesare Battista, 11 (tel. 37 17 09), has no set menu and serves what they catch. Expect to pay about L20,000 for a delicious plate of fresh swordfish; prices fall as the season progresses. English spoken.

The **Aspromonte region,** a bump that developed after Italy kicked Sicily, presides over southern Calabria in pine-and-birch-covered glory and awaits those who can't get to the Sila for their nature break. To reach the center of the area take one of nine daily blue buses (#127 or 128) in front of Reggio's central train station to **Gambarie** (L2900). Here visitors enjoy a fabulous view of Sicily and the straits of Messina from the heights of **Puntone di Scirocco** (1660m), accessible by chairlift. Hop a train to the beach at **Melito di Porto Salvo** on the southern tip of the Italian peninsula. It's one of the area's nicest swimming locales. (15 per day, 11 on Sun., 30min., L2700.)

■ The Ionian Coast

The stupefying beaches that stretch from Reggio di Calabria around the cape toward Metaponto in Basilicata are sparsely populated with Italian and German tourists and rarely frequented by anyone else. The beaches offer both a cool dip in the Ionian Sea and a nice contrast to the mountains in the distance. If a strip of sand is all you desire, consider hopping on a train from either Reggio di Calabria or Crotone and getting off when the scenery looks inviting. **Soverato** (130km from Reggio, L13,600) offers one of the most expansive, scenic, and popular strips; the beaches at **Bovalino Marina, Palizzi,** and **Brancaleone** are closer and almost as agreeable. All travelers should be forewarned that trains along the Ionian coast often have erratic schedules and multiple connections, so give yourself ample time to get where you want to go.

CROTONE

Behind the factory façade of Calabria's most industrial city there remain a few glimpses of history. The western half (the new town) is centered along the main drag, **Via Vittorio Veneto,** which extends from the town's central square, **Piazza Pitagora,** to Crotone's western limits. At night the town shuts down except for the groups of kids that hang out in the *piazze*. The other half of Crotone (the old city) is a cluster of interconnected old buildings wrapped around a hill. Exploring this historical section without a map may leave you lost forever in a maze of narrow alleyways, so grab one before you visit the **cathedral,** one block from the main square **Piazza Pitagora,** and the 16th-century **Castle of Carlo V** on Via Risorgimento. Open Mon.-Sat. 8:30am-1:30pm and 3-7pm. Free.

Crotone has limited budget offerings. Just off Piazza Pitagora is **Albergo Italia,** Piazza Vittoria, 12 (tel. 239 10). Quiet, affordable rooms in a great location, though the dust rag may have missed a few spots. Curfew 11:30pm. Singles L30,000, with bath L35,000. Doubles L50,000, with bath L60,000. To reach the vibrant **Paninoteca Ristorante Speak Easy,** Via Firenze, 44 (tel. 96 27 98), turn right off Via Vittorio Veneto one block after Piazza della Resistenza; the restaurant is halfway down the block on your left. The wait is long, but the food is wonderful. Try the *pasta alla panna e al prosciutto* for L7000. *Primi* from L6000, *secondi* from L5000, *panini* from L4000. Cover L1000 for restaurant. Open daily 10:30am-12:30am or whenever they feel like closing.

Trains run to Crotone from Rome and Reggio. More locally, **buses** run from Camigliatello (1-2 per day, 1hr., L5800) to Piazza Pitagora. The **tourist office** is located at Via Torino, 148 (tel. 231 85), off Via Vittorio Veneto. Once you feel you have left civilization, keep going two blocks (across Corso Mazzini); the APT office is on your right on the second floor. Open daily 8am-2pm. **Telephones** are available at Bar Londra, Via M. Nicoletta, 11 (tel. 238 52). Open 8:30am-10:30pm. The **post office** (tel. 211 43) is on Via Tedeschi, one block from Piazza Pitagora. Open Mon.-Fri. 8:15am-1:30pm, Sat. 8:15am-noon. The **telephone code** is 0962.

LOCRI AND GERACE

The town of **Locri,** about 90km from Reggio and 150km from Crotone, is not where you want to spend your time, although it makes a great starting point for excursions to the shore, the mountains, or scattered archaeological sites dating from the 7th century BC. **Trains** run to Locri several times daily from Reggio (L8000) and Crotone (L11,700). Wilderness-lovers should consult the **tourist office** at Via Fiume, 1 (tel. 296 00) for maps and information. To get there, follow Via G. Matteotti past the library (#160) and the elaborate park on the right off Via Umberto; Via Fiume is a small street to the left. Open Mon.-Sat. 8am-8pm. Take the bus from the train station to **Ciminà,** and start your hike up on **Monte Petrotondo.** The **post office** is on Via Roma, one of the main roads (tel. 201 80 or 202 97). Locri's **telephone code** is 0964.

Locri is the most organized of the several towns along this coast but has only one reasonable accommodation, **Hotel Orientale,** Via Tripoli, 33 (tel. 202 61). Head straight for three blocks from the train station to Via G. Matteotti, running parallel to the tracks, and turn right. Via Tripoli is a small street to the left, across from the park. A friendly owner presides over dingy L40,000 singles and L80,000 doubles. The cleanliness level may make some uneasy. From the train station, an immediate right will bring you to the **Paolo Iervase** supermarket, Via R. Margherita, 65 (tel. 204 64). Open Mon.-Sat. 7:30am-1pm and 4-9pm. Continue down this road until you come to an intersection where you can see the beach to your right. Head toward the beach and cross the railroad tracks to reach **Bar Eros,** Via Lungomare (tel. 299 18), which offers arcade games, pool tables, and foosball, as well as a great rooftop view. Open 24hr. A variety of sandwiches, many *all'americana,* from L2500. Eat outside in a garden covered with grapevines and lined with American video games. In the summer, Locri meets at **La Playa,** Via Lungomare (tel. 214 31), for its beachside disco and L20,000 *menù*. Open daily 9am-4am or later, depending on the crowd.

Locri Epizefiri, 3.5km south of Locri, is the site of numerous ruins from the ancient days of the first Greek colonizers. A well preserved theater, an Ionic temple to Athena, and a sanctuary dedicated to Pan all await exploration an hr. along the shore from Locri proper. Consult the site plan at the nearby museum before you go. Excavations open daylight hours; free. Museum open daily 9am-7pm, closed alternate Sundays; L4000.

To reach the taciturn town of **Gerace,** 10km inland from Locri and high above the Calabrian countryside, grab a bus in front of Locri's train station (6 per day, except on Sun. and holidays, roughly L1500 each way). Gerace's pride and joy is its **cathedral,** Calabria's largest. The structure's imperial crypt is supported by 26 ancient Greek columns pilfered from Locri. From the crypt, climb the stairs into a Romanesque interior of grand proportions. Outside the main portal of the cathedral and down the street to the left is the town's historic center, **Largo delle Tre Chiese.** The **Castello di Roberto il Guiscardo** is currently being renovated, but the trek up to Gerace's pinnacle is still worth it for the best view in southern Calabria.

SICILY (SICILIA)

"Without Sicily, Italy cannot be fully understood. It is here one finds the key to all things."

—J.W. Goethe

Throughout the ages, every great nearby civilization has at one time turned its attention toward Sicily, transforming its landscape and people but never conquering its independent spirit. The Greeks, Romans, Arabs, Normans, and Aragonese have all held Sicily, the largest island in the Mediterranean—usually with the support of an invading army. While this series of hostile takeovers was a curse for the Sicilian people, it was undeniably a boon to Sicily's cultural heritage. Each wave of conquerors left its own imprint upon the island, offering the 20th-century visitor a fascinating and diverse cultural landscape. Today, Sicily is invaded only by tourists eager to take in its legacy of over three millennia. The island's inhabitants continue to hold on to their traditions, a testament to their resilience during centuries of occupation, creation, and destruction.

Sicily's turbulent recorded history began with Greek colonialism in the mid-8th century BC, when a group of Corinthian settlers founded Syracuse. In the 6th and 5th centuries BC, the Greek city-states of Sicily were among the most powerful and populous in the Mediterranean. A succession of external struggles with the Carthaginians and internal conflicts among the various cities occupied Sicilians from the late 5th century until 211 BC, when the Roman capture of Syracuse (and defeat of Carthage) brought the entire island under Roman control. In the 9th century AD, Sicily became a Muslim outpost second in importance only to Spain. It later served as the seat of the Norman court and subsequently became the pawn of Renaissance dynasties. The next phase of Sicilian history was one of harsh Aragonese rule; the Bourbons' shortsighted agricultural policies exhausted the rich volcanic soil and reduced much of the Sicilian interior to a parched wasteland. In 1860, Garibaldi and his "redshirts" defeated the Bourbon troops and declared the island "liberated," meaning that it merely became a part of the Kingdom of Italy. Even that juncture was superficial; cultural, economic, and geographical conditions ensured that the island of Sicily was a long way from assimilation into Italy.

The tempestuousness of Sicilian political life has been matched by the island's dramatic climatic extremes. To Giuseppe Lampedusa, Sicily's prince-turned-writer, it was a "landscape which knows no mean between sensuous sag and hellish drought." The Sicilian countryside is dominated by sheer, rock-strewn crags, rendering much of the land non-arable. Much of what can be cultivated has been converted to olive, citrus and almond groves. Sicily is dominated by Europe's highest volcano, Mt. Etna, which the locals simply call "the mountain." The island's position at the edge of the European geologic plate has resulted in a succession of seismic and volcanic catastrophes that have periodically snuffed out the lives of inhabitants. Those not destroyed seem to have drawn strength from survival; the fruits of Sicily's artistic and intellectual heritage range from Selinunte's stark ancient grandeur to Noto's baroque frivolity, from the irrefutable logic of Pythagoras to the wry irrationalities of Pirandello.

Modern Sicily bears the scars of its history quietly, speeding into the future. Locals install condom-vending machines in front of medieval cathedrals and raise petrochemical refineries beside Greek acropolises. New waves of immigrants arrive from North Africa each year. Most recently, Sicilians have begun to reject the "tradition" of mafia control; more and more Sicilians are expressing their frustration with continued mob activity and the perceived stagnation of a government that has had limited success in stemming the tide of violence. Recent demonstrations against the mafia have brought thousands into the streets to demand an end to corruption. Unfortu-

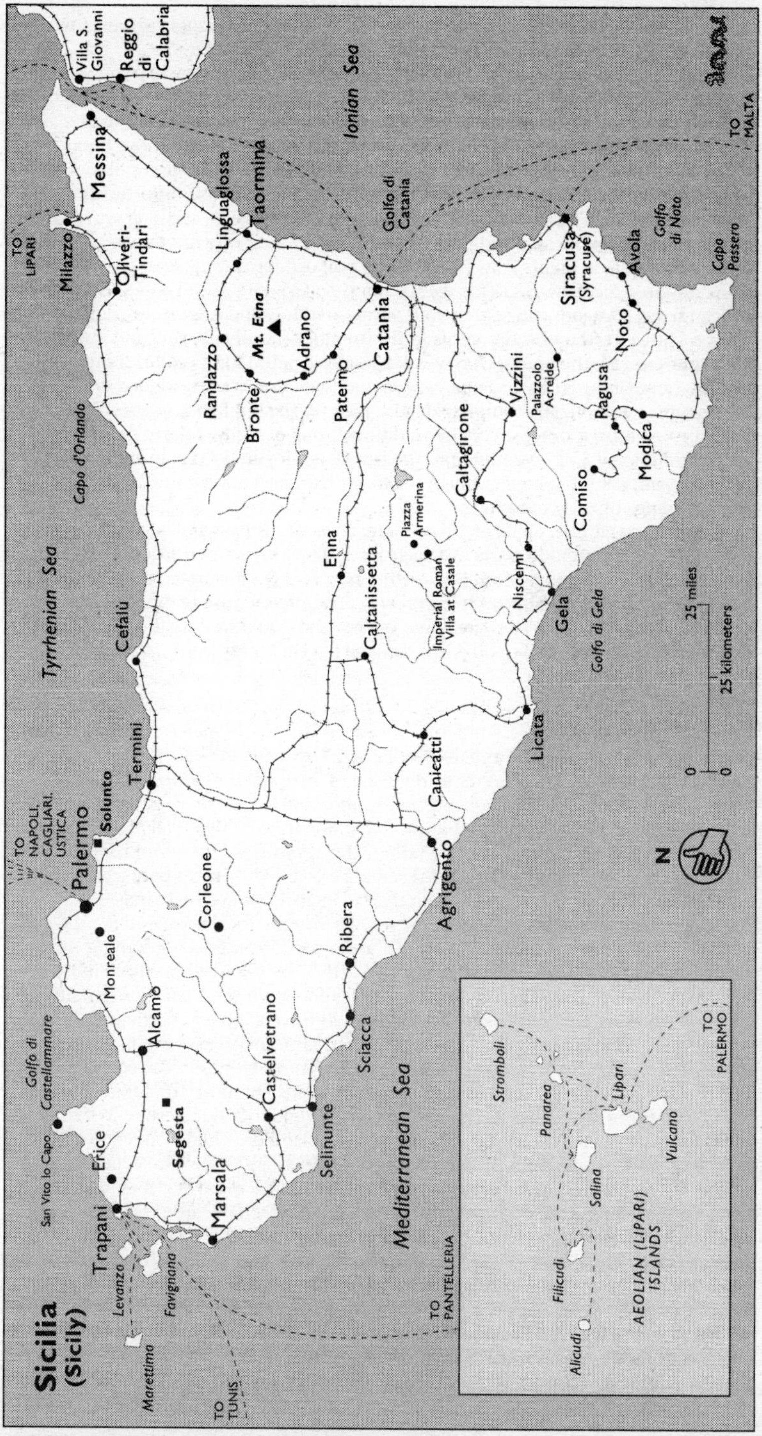

Sicilia (Sicily)

Golfo di Castellammare
San Vito lo Capo
TO NAPOLI, CAGLIARI, USTICA
Tyrrhenian Sea
Capo d'Orlando
TO LIPARI
Milazzo
Messina
Villa S. Giovanni
Reggio di Calabria
Trapani
Erice
Palermo
Solunto
Monreale
Levanzo
Marettimo
Favignana
Alcamo
Segesta
Termini
Cefalù
Oliveri-Tindari
TO TUNIS
Marsala
Corleone
Randazzo
Linguaglossa
Bronte
Mt. Etna
Taormina
Castelvetrano
Adrano
Selinunte
Enna
Paterno
Ionian Sea
Sciacca
Ribera
Caltanissetta
Catania
Golfo di Catania
Mediterranean Sea
Piazza Armerina
Imperial Roman Villa at Casale
TO PANTELLERIA
Agrigento
Canicattì
Caltagirone
Niscemi
Vizzini
Licata
Palazzolo Acreide
Gela
Siracusa (Syracuse)
Comiso
Golfo di Gela
Ragusa
Noto
Avola
Modica
Golfo di Noto
Capo Passero
TO MALTA
N
0 25 miles
0 25 kilometers

Stromboli
Panarea
Filicudi
Alicudi
Salina
Lipari
AEOLIAN (LIPARI) ISLANDS
Vulcano
TO PALERMO

SICILY

nately, change cannot happen quickly; the number of defendants currently awaiting trial will fill courtrooms for years to come. (See **The Mafia** below.)

Because of Sicilian immigration to the United States, and to some extent because of the welcomed American invasion in 1942, *Statunitensi* (particularly *Sicilo-Americani)* receive an exceptionally warm welcome. Women, however, should be aware that male attention in Sicily is often aggressive and unceasing, and those unequipped with the extensive lexicon of Sicilian cut-downs are particularly susceptible. Cases of serious physical harassment and assault are relatively few, but, unfortunately, petty crime is rampant. The larger cities (Palermo, Catania, Messina, and Trapani) are notorious for their pickpockets and purse-snatchers, and their downtown districts can be especially unsafe at night. Travel in groups if you can, or stay close to busy areas.

In summer, Sicily swelters for weeks at a time (35-45°C/100-120°F). The burning African *scirocco* winds can scorch your vacation in July and August. In addition, haze and brush fires often obscure vistas in the summer months. Spring and autumn are ideal times to visit the island. Holy Week in Sicily is noted for its colorful processions, among them Good Friday in Enna, where marchers don white, hooded costumes in the Spanish tradition. For complete details, pick up the booklet *Easter in Sicily,* available at most tourist offices. For the traditional tour of Sicily, follow the coast; for a tour of traditional Sicily, venture into the heartland. If you do visit in summer, follow local custom: eat a big lunch, take a two-hour nap, and enjoy the island in the cool early evenings or early morning.

As for the local fare, Sicilians pride themselves on using wholesome raw ingredients. Specialties include pasta with sardines, *frutta martorana* (sugar candies), swordfish, green peppers, *panellas, arancini al riso* (Sicilian riceballs with meat fillings), *cannoli,* and *cassata* (rich ice cream). The *melanzane* (eggplant) and *pomodori* (tomatoes) of the island are some of the best you'll find in all of Italy, and try eating *gelato* like the natives do—in a *brioche* (sweet pastry bun).

THE MAFIA

Non-Sicilians have a Hollywood-influenced vision of the mafia: pin-striped suits, machine guns, horse-heads, and the Godfather. The mafia in Sicily is very different in reality. For starters, *mafiosi* refer to themselves as *uomini d'onore* (men of honor). In fact, the system of mafia is a complicated and rigid structure based on hierarchical relationships, mutual respect, and territorial boundaries. At the head of a family is the person we refer to as the "don," or rather, the *rappresentante* who represents his family to the other families. The Representative is aided by anywhere from one to a cabinetful of Advisors; lower down on the chain are *capodecine* (heads of ten) who manage groups of *soldati* (soldiers). Even lower are the local youths who aren't true *mafiosi*, but work for the local don in the hopes of someday becoming *mafiosi.* Mafia families control an established area of action, be it a neighborhood in Palermo or the entire city of Catania. Women are excluded from the mafia system; mothers and wives are prized family members but seen as too talkative to participate in secret operations. Contrary to popular belief, women and non-mafia children were once immune from the blood feuds of mafia interaction; only in recent years have dons seen fit to assassinate the innocent, much to the dismay of more "traditional" *mafiosi.*

The system of *mafia* has its roots in the *latifondi* (agricultural estates) of rural Sicily. Land managers and salaried militiamen (read: landlords and bouncers) provided both land and people with protection from robbery, and out of this class grew the mafia. *Mafiosi* were powerful because people owed them favors; they were strong because they supported each other; and they were feared because they did not hesitate to kill offenders. Some *mafiosi* today claim that they descend from a group called *I Beati Paoli* (The Blessed Pauls), a Robin Hood-like secret society that protected the poor and dispensed "true" justice to the inhabitants of Palermo in the 19th century. While the mafia suffered under Fascist-era purges, Allied support toward the end of World War II helped get the organization back on its feet. Since the mid-80s, the Italian government has seriously tried to curtail mafia influence, with inconclusive results. Among Sicilians (especially the *palermitani),* one thing is certain: they've had enough. Present and increasingly vocal, opposition to the mafia continues to grow. As a result, camouflaged security guards toting machine guns are stationed outside every court building, as well as at every apartment building where a judge lives.

While you're traveling through Sicily or (southern Italy for that matter), avoid mentioning "the mafia." Whereas some Sicilians will be pleased to talk about the changing tide of opinion against the mafia, you're more likely to get one of two responses: some locals who don't want to talk about the mafia will deny that it exists, while others will immediately cease being friendly. While chowing down in Cosenza, one recent researcher mentioned the word "mafia" in conversation and was treated to the abrupt silence and direct stares of a nearby tableful of men. *Uomini d'onore* of today dislike the term "mafia" and its derivatives; they refer to their system as *Cosa Nostra* or "our thing." Unfortunately, over the course of the last half-century, mafia activities have expanded to include national politics, drug-smuggling, and, most recently, the assassination of high-profile judges. "Their thing" has expanded to become a serious problem for Italy and the world at large.

One final note: be aware that "mafia" refers only to *Sicilian* organized crime; the *Camorra* in Naples and the *'ndrangheta* of Calabria are separate, mutually disdainful networks.

TRANSPORTATION

Flights from all major Italian cities service Palermo and Catania. The easiest way to reach Sicily from Rome is a train-ferry combination to Messina (from Rome via Reggio di Calabria, L52,700). **Tirrenia,** in Palermo (tel. (091) 33 33 00), the largest private ferry service in Italy, is the most extensive and reliable, though you should still beware the summer tourist rush and strikes. Prices and schedules vary according to specific dates; approximations are given below. Listings are for Tirrenia and include low- to high-season prices for *poltrone* (reserved reclining deck chairs). Tickets can often be purchased at travel agencies, either in foreign countries or within Italy.

Reggio di Calabria-Messina: 17 per day on the state railroad ferry, *Ferrovie dello Stato (*tel. (090) 67 55 82), 6am-8:40pm (20min., L4200) or take the hydrofoil from the same terminal at the Reggio port (20 per day, L4500).

Villa San Giovanni-Messina: 32 per day (around the clock) on the state railroad ferry (L1500).

Genoa-Palermo: From Genoa, mid-July-mid-Sept. Tues., Thurs., Sat. at 5pm, Sun. at noon; mid-Sept.-mid-July Tues., Thurs., and Sat.-Sun. at 5pm. From Palermo, mid-July-mid-Sept. Wed., Fri., Sun. at 11am; mid-Sept.-mid-July Mon., Wed., Fri., Sun. at 4pm. (24hr., L50,000-70,000).

Naples-Palermo: From Napoli daily at 8:00pm. From Palermo mid-July-mid-Sept. daily at 10pm, mid-Sept.-mid-July daily at 8pm. (11hr., L53,600-69,100). There is also a hydrofoil for L96,000, 1 daily, 4hr.

Cagliari-Palermo: From Cagliari Fri. at 7pm. From Palermo Sat. at 7pm. (14hr., L42,000-60,000).

Cagliari-Trapani: From Cagliari Sun. 7pm. From Trapani Tues. 9pm. (11hr., L42,000-60,000).

Trapani-Tunis: From Trapani Mon. at 9am (9hr.). From Tunis Mon. at 8pm (10hr.). (L92,000).

Trains in Sicily only partially deserve their reputation for tardiness; even the diminutive *Elettromotrici* are reasonably reliable and convenient. Two major bus companies, the private, air-conditioned, and punctual **SAIS,** and the public, often steamy **AST,** serve many of the destinations that are inaccessible by train. Even trips that can be made by train are faster and cheaper by bus. There's no central transportation authority in Sicily, so check in every city and with every driver for the bus schedules to your next destination. Give yourself a few extra hours to get where you're going, especially if you're heading for isolated ruins, and if you hear the word *sciopero,* head home—it means that there is a strike.

Hitchhiking is difficult on long hauls; hitchers reputedly have the best luck near the turn-offs to roads for short, specific trips. **Hitchhiking in Sicily is risky, particularly for women and solo travelers—*Let's Go* does not recommend it. Driving** in Sicily isn't that safe either. You'll need an International Driver's Permit (available at AAA; see *Documents and Formalities* in the *Essentials* section, page 8), a rental car, and nerves of steel. Travelers (drivers and pedestrians alike) should be aware that most Italians drive without regard to lanes, safe driving distance, or impending doom. And Sicilians are particularly fond of their car horns, an annoying tendency that may save your life. **Pedestrians** should note that simple tasks like crossing the street can become a real challenge here. One strategy is to follow other people across, using them as a buffer between you and the speeding cars. Another alternative is to treat oncoming traffic as if it were a charging rhinoceros: make eye contact and pray to the local saint. Most Italian streets were designed to accommodate two friendly people passing each other on foot, not two maniacal *vespa* riders intent on calling the other's bluff. Make your mother happy, look both ways before crossing.

THE NORTHERN COAST

Messina

History has handed Messina (pop. 400,000) misfortune after misfortune. According to legend, the city was founded as Zancle in 730BC by the Zancleans, led by King Minos. The city was then captured and renamed Messene by Anaxilas, the tyrant of Reggio, in 493BC. A century later the Carthaginians came and razed the site. Thereafter, the city fell into the hands of everyone from the Marmertines to the Normans to Richard the Lionheart. Messina grew to prosperity under Norman rule and burgeoned as a Crusader port, remaining a proud bastion at the periphery of European civilization for 600 years.

After the 17th century it was all downhill. After rebelling against Spanish rule in the late 1600s the city was economically blacklisted and shrank to one-eighth its former size. It went on to be devastated by plague in 1743, demolished by an earthquake in 1783, bombarded from the sea in 1848, struck by cholera in 1854, slammed by more earthquakes in 1894 and 1908 (the latter killing 70,000 of a population of 170,000), and flattened by both Allied and Axis bombs during World War II. What is left is a city that has struggled time and again to rebuild itself, and now seems to have taken one too many blows to get up off the canvas. Buildings in Messina generally date back no more than a few decades, and nearly all appear to have been hastily constructed; even the cathedral, rebuilt twice in this century alone, is essentially new. A sense of impermanence hangs about, as if Messina's inhabitants know that yet another disaster will strike and they will have to rebuild it anew.

ORIENTATION AND PRACTICAL INFORMATION

Major transportation routes and tourist offices cluster around the train station at P. della Repubblica. Right in front of the train station runs **Via G. la Farina;** on the left (with your back to the station) **Via Tommaso Cannizzaro** leads to the center of town, meeting **Viale S. Martino** (the city's main drag) at **Piazza Cairoli.** Cross Via Farina from the station and to the right lies **Via Primo Settembre** which crosses **Corso Garibaldi** and ends at **Piazza del Duomo.** Corso Garibaldi runs along the harbor to both the hydrofoil dock and Corso Cavour.

> Women should not walk alone in Messina at night, and no one should roam the streets near the train station or the harbor after 10pm. Stay near the more populated streets around the *duomo* and the university. Be wary of pickpockets and purse-snatchers, and keep your money in a secure place.

Tourist Office: AAPIT (Azienda Autonoma Per l'Incremento Turistico), Via Calabria 301 (tel. 640 22), outside the Central Station to the right in P. della Repubblica, offers a deluge of maps and information on Messina and the Lipari Islands. English sometimes spoken. Open Mon.-Sat. 8:15am-7pm. **Ufficio Informazioni Comunali,** (tel. 67 29 44) next door to the APT. Replete with materials and maps on Messina, the Lipari Islands, Taormina, and other areas within the province of Messina. Open Mon.-Thurs. 8am-2pm and 2:30-5:30pm, Fri.-Sat. 8am-2pm. **AAST,** P. Cairoli, 45 (tel. 293 52 92 or 293 62 94). Open mornings only.

Telephones: Ask at the Telecom office on Corso Cavour, down the street from the post office near the *duomo.*

Currency Exchange: Cambio/Ufficio Informazioni (tel. 67 52 34 or 67 52 35), just inside the train station. Good rates plus information on trains and buses.

Trains: at P. della Repubblica (tel. 67 52 34). To: Palermo (12 per day, 5:30am-8:05pm, 3½hr., L19,000); Syracuse (11 per day, 5:45am-8:10pm, 3hr., L15,500); Rome (5 per day, 11:05am-12:15am, 9hr., L51,200); and Milazzo, the main port for the Lipari Islands (10 per day, 5:30am-8:15pm, 40min., L3400). **Luggage Storage:** L5000 for 12hr.

Buses: SAIS, at P. della Repubblica, 20 (tel. 77 19 14), to the left of the train station. To: Taormina (15 per day, 1½hr., L5100); Catania (24 per day, 1½hr., L9500); and Rome (1 per day at 9:30pm, 10hr., L65,000, under 20 or over 60 L55,000). **Giuntabus** (tel. 67 37 82 or 67 57 49), in the town center, on Via Terranova, 8. To Milazzo (14 per day, 6am-6:15pm, 40min., L5500 one way).

Ferries: Stazione Marittima, same building as train station, on the water, 300m to the right of P. della Repubblica. To Reggio (17 per day, 20min., L4200) and V. San Giovanni (every 30min., 15min., L1500). **Hydrofoils: SNAV** (tel. 36 40 44, 36 21 14 for reservations; fax 36 40 45), a blue, one-story building on Corso Vittorio Emanuele II, 1km north of train station off Corso Garibaldi. To the Lipari Islands (4-5 per day June 1-Sept. 30, 2hr., L30,000-50,000). Save L10,000 by taking the train to Milazzo and catching the ferry there.

Public Transportation: ATM buses leave from P. della Repubblica and go into town. Purchase tickets (L1200; L3500 for all-day bus pass) at any *tabacchi* or newsstand. Detailed bus info on the signs with yellow borders outside the station.

Lost Property: at the **Municipio di Messina,** where Via Vettovaglie hits the harbor (to the right from P. della Repubblica). Open Mon.-Sat. 9am-noon. Ask for **oggetti smarriti.**

Late-Night Pharmacy: tel. 192. All pharmacies are open Mon.-Fri. 8:30am-1pm and 4:30-8pm. After that, they are on a rotation with at least 2 open during the night and on weekends; check with the tourist office for a list.

Emergencies: tel. 113. **Hospital: Ospedale R. Margherita,** Via Libertà (tel. 36 51 or 36 54 54); **Policlinico Universitario,** Via Consolare Valeria (tel. 69 26 50).

Police: tel. 113. **Carabinieri:** tel. 449 30 or 112.

Post Office: at P. Antonello, off Corso Cavour near the *duomo* (tel. 77 05 45). *Fermo posta* at window #12. Open Mon.-Fri. 8:15am-6:30pm, Sat. 8:30-1pm. **Postal Code:** 98100.

Telephone Code: 090.

ACCOMMODATIONS AND CAMPING

Hotel Monza, Viale San Martino, 63 (tel./fax 67 37 55), at Via Cannizzaro. Leafy lobby welcomes you to newly renovated, classy rooms. Pricey but central and one of few options in Messina. Singles with shower L55,000, with bath L68,000. Doubles with shower L89,000, with bath L110,000. Triples with shower L120,000, with bath L148,000. V, MC.

Hotel Touring, Via Scotto, 17 (tel. 293 88 51). Exit the train station, go under the overpass, and turn right (hotel is 100m away). Hallways of mirrors and faux-marble lead into stark rooms. Convenient for travelers stranded between trains. Singles L35,000, with bath and TV L60,000. Doubles L60,000, with bath and TV L100,000. Triples L90,000, with bath and TV L140,000.

Camping: Il Peloritano (tel. 34 84 26). Take bus #81 from the station (leaves every 30min.) L5500 per person per tent. Make sure to stock up on food before you go. Showers available. L5000 per person per tent.

FOOD

Relatively inexpensive restaurants and *trattorie* can be found in the area around Via Risorgimento, reached by following Via Cannizzaro one block past P. Cairoli. In summer, try the legendary *pesce spada* (swordfish) direct from the Straits of Messina, delectable enough to earn Homer's mention in the *Odyssey.* On Via S. Cecilia, eight blocks from P. Maurolico down Via C. Battisti, there is an outdoor **market.** Open daily 6am-2pm. Otherwise, your best bet is the *rosticcerie* or *paninoteche* that line the main avenues. Messina may be big, but it still has a very small restaurant scene and even smaller nightlife. There is a good-sized **STANDA** supermarket in P. Cairoli 222, at the center of town (tel. 292 77 38). Open Mon. 4-8pm, Tues.-Sat. 9am-8pm. Fresh fruit and vegetables are cheaper on the street, like the inexpensive blood oranges in P. Carducci.

Osteria del Campanile, Via Loggia dei Mercanti, 9 (tel. 71 14 18), behind the *duomo* and right next to the post office. Look for the yellow awning. Great pizza in an elegant old dining room from L6000 (white pizza from L4000). *Menù turistico* L18,000. Cover L2000 for the restaurant, which features the daily catch at L7000 per 100g. *Primi* from L9000, *secondi* from L10,000. AmEx.

Safari Sandwich, Via G. Venezian, 83 (tel. 67 59 89), off P. Duomo. Good for a quick fix while on safari at the cathedral. Generous sandwiches from L3000. TV and music upstairs in winter. Open Thurs.-Tues. 8am-midnight.

Ritrovo Vittorio Emanuele, Corso Cavour (tel. 67 92 39), in the galleria across from the post office. Relax under a stained glass roof with delicious *gelato* (L2000 for a lavish cone) or a variety of crêpes from L6000. Open Tues.-Sun. 6am-1am.

Bar Rosé, Corso Cavour (tel. 34 41 93), at Via S. Camillo, just down the street from the post office. Filling *panini a piastra* (on a flat, broad roll) from L1500, named after characters from *The Lion King.* Outdoor tables are great for people-watching. Open daily 7am-9pm.

SIGHTS

Messina has seen many monuments built over its long history, and it has also seen most of them crumble to the ground. It is a city undergoing a constant facelift; many sights have only recently shed their scaffolding, if they are not still under restoration.

The **Piazza del Duomo's** wide open spaces and large flagstones provide some relief from the asphalt hustle and bustle of the rest of Messina. The *piazza* contains the 12th-century **duomo** (open daily 8am-12:30pm and 4-7pm; currently under restoration) and the squat **Church of SS. Annunziata dei Catalaní** from the same period. The cathedral's stark exterior features an ornate portal portraying the Archangel Gabriel and the Madonna with saints. In front of the church, lazy nudes recline on a richly embellished base in the **Fontana di Orione** (circa 1547), the work of Michelangelo's pupil Angelo Montorsol. The clock tower houses what is supposedly the world's largest astronomical clock. The Grim Reaper keeps time until the grand spectacle at noon, when a mechanical procession of animals, angels, and legendary figures reenacts the local legend of the Madonna della Lettera, patron saint of the city, and a creaky recording of Schubert's "Ave Maria" blares loud enough to reach Reggio. A **festival** in her honor takes over the town every June 3; another festival, the **Ferragosto Messinese,** takes place Aug. 14-15, featuring the 150,000-strong "Procession of the Giants." Messina is a city of hidden churches and sanctuaries and spectacular vistas from hillside verandas. One way to see the city is to follow your eyes toward any of the domes that you see off side streets. Chances are that you will end up, after a climb, rewarded with a view of the city and not-so-distant Calabria.

Just down the road from the hydrofoil port on Viale della Libertà is the **Museo Regionale** (tel. 36 12 92). Founded in 1806 with five private collections, it was adopted by the state in 1904 as a repository for the furnishings, valuables, and works of art recovered from churches and civic buildings after the 1894 earthquake. Today it includes a collection of Renaissance and Baroque masterpieces, among them *The Polyptych of the Rosary* (1473) by local hero Antonello da Messina, an Andrea della

Robbia terra-cotta of the Virgin and Child, and Caravaggio's *The Adoration of the Shepherds* (1608) and *Resurrection of Lazarus* (1609). Take bus #8 from the station or P. Duomo and get off at P. Museo (20min.). Walk part of the way back to view the harbor's sickle-shaped form, which led the original Greek settlers to name the colony "Zancle" (the Greek word for scythe). (Museum open Mon., Wed., and Fri. 9am-1:30pm; Tues., Thurs., and Sat. 4-6:30pm, Sun. 9am-12:30pm.) If all of Messina seems closed for renovation, take solace with the fish in the **Acquario Comunale** (tel. 488 97), Villa Mazzini. Open daily 9am-2pm.

The route traveled by bus #8 through nearby ramshackle fishing villages provides some great waterfront scenery (L1200, departs from the train station; L3500 for an all-day unlimited bus pass). Get off at whichever stop catches your eye, or wait until the **Lungolago** (20min. from the station at Messina), along a long lake overlooked by crumbling villas and lined with cafés and palm trees.

AEOLIAN ISLANDS (ISOLE EOLIE)

Set in the sparkling Mediterranean, the **Aeolian** (or **Lipari**) **Islands** are all places of remarkable beauty. The breezy islands are renowned for their fiery volcanoes and long rocky beaches. The archipelago comprises one of the last areas of unspoiled seashore in Italy and has only recently become a tourist spot. Food and accommodations are more expensive than elsewhere in Sicily; prices peak in the August high-season, for which you'd better make reservations on the main islands no later than May. Fortunately, Lipari has a youth hostel. Each of the seven isles has a unique character; visit Lipari for a well equipped tourist center, a castle, and easily navigable vistas; Vulcano for bubbling mud baths and a sulfurous crater; Stromboli for spectacular colors and a restless volcano; Panarea for inlets and a more elite clientele; Salina for grottoes and luxuriant vegetation; Filicudi for winding trails and coastal rock formations; and, finally, Alicudi for a rare dose of solitude.

Before traveling to any of the other islands, you may want to buy food at the **UPIM** supermarket on Corso Vittorio Emanuele in Lipari (see **Lipari: Food**) in order to avoid paying L1000 for a roll or one apricot in the poorly-stocked *alimentari* or spending L30,000 on dinner at a *pensione*. **The telephone code for the islands is 090.**

GETTING THERE

The archipelago lies off the Sicilian coast, north of **Milazzo,** the principal and least expensive embarkation point (on the Messina-Palermo train line; 18 per day 5:30am-8:13pm, 40hr. from Messina, L3460; 3hr. from Palermo, L15,500). **Giuntabus,** Via Terranova, 8 (tel. (090) 67 37 82 or 67 57 49) also services the town. (From Messina, 14 per day 6am-6:15pm, 4 on Sun., 45min., L5500. Also daily from Catania airport at 3:45pm April-Sept., L20,000.) The bus is much more convenient than the train; it takes you directly from Messina to Milazzo seaport. **Ferries** leave much less frequently from **Naples's** Molo Beverello port. Hydrofoils (about twice the ferry price) run regularly in late July and August from **Messina, Naples, Cefalù, Palermo,** and **Reggio di Calabria.**

To get to the port in Milazzo from the train station, take the orange bus in front of the station. Get your ticket at the bar (L600) and ask to get off at the ferries *(traghetti).* The train station has moved far away from the port—at least 5km. If you

Dealt an Unfortunate Blow

As described in Homer's *Odyssey,* the **Aeolian** (or **Lipari**) **Islands** are the domain of Aeolus, King of the Winds. Aeolus makes a present to Odysseus of a bag of winds to help quicken his return trip. His sailors—not the brightest of seafarers—ignore Aeolus' warning and open the bag, letting out the proverbial cat and blowing themselves right back to the islands. The moral: take a ferry.

get hungry waiting for the boat, there's a Punto Convenienza **supermarket** (tel. (090) 928 10 13) down the street on Via Colonello Magistri, which turns off to the right at the gas station on Via dei Mille along the port. Open daily 8:30am-1pm and 5-8:30pm. Ferry offices can be found on **Via dei Mille,** while *aliscafi* (hydrofoils) and their owners repose on **Via Rizzo.**

Siremar and **Navigazione Generale Italiana (NGI)** operate reliable **ferries** out of Milazzo. Siremar also services several smaller islands and Naples (tel. (081) 551 21 12 in Naples). For **hydrofoil** services to the islands, go to Siremar or **SNAV.** Pick up hydrofoil and ferry schedules in every port (ask for *un orario generale)*. Schedules and prices tend to vary from season to season, so always call ahead to check. Frequencies listed are for June through September. Unless stated, prices are the same for both lines. Connections can be made between any stops in a line.

SNAV: In Milazzo: Via L. Rizzo, 17 (tel. 928 45 09 or 928 78 21; fax 928 76 42 or 988 02 66). In Lipari: tel. 981 24 48. In Messina: Cortina del Porto (tel. 36 40 44).

Siremar: In Milazzo: tel. 928 32 42; fax 928 32 43. In Lipari: tel. 981 22 00.

Navigazione Generale Italiana: In Milazzo: Via dei Mille, 26 (tel./fax 928 34 15 or tel. 928 40 91). In Lipari: Via Ten. Mariano Amendola, 14 (tel. 981 19 55). In Vulcano: Molo di Levante (tel. 985 24 01). In Salina: P. Santa Marina (tel. 984 30 03).

Ferries: Milazzo-Vulcano-Lipari-Salina: To Vulcano (1½hr., L10,800); Lipari (2hr., L11,600); Salina (3hr., L14,700). **Siremar:** 4-6 daily at 7am-6:30pm (Salina 7am-2:30pm). **NGI:** 2-4 daily at 6:30am-10pm.

Milazzo-Panarea-Stromboli via Vulcano and Lipari: To Panarea (3¼hr., L13,900) and Stromboli (5hr., L18,500). **Siremar:** Fri-Wed. 7am, Thurs. 2:30pm. **NGI:** Thurs. 6:30am.

Milazzo-Filicudi-Alicudi via Vulcano, Salina, and Lipari: To Filicudi (4½hr., L20,100) and Alicudi (5½hr., L22,300). **Siremar:** daily 7am (2:30pm Thurs.). **NGI:** Sat. 6:30am.

The increasingly popular **hydrofoils** *(aliscafi)* run twice as often as ferries do, for twice the price and in half the time. From May 15 to October 15, SNAV runs to Lipari from Messina (4 per day 7:05am-6:30pm, L31,400) and Reggio di Calabria (5 per day, L33,700). Cabins are air-conditioned, although it's never quite as cool as one might hope. Frequencies listed below are for June through September; off-season schedules are more erratic, with as few as a third the number of trips. Connections can be made between any two points in a route unless otherwise noted.

Milazzo-Vulcano-Lipari-Salina: To: Vulcano (40min., L18,400); Lipari (55min., L19,700); and Salina (1½hr., L22,800). **Siremar:** 6-12 daily, 7:05am-7:00pm (7:05am-6:00pm for Salina). **SNAV:** 6 daily, 7:30am-7:30pm.

Milazzo-Panarea-Stromboli via Vulcano and Lipari: To Panarea (1¾hr., L23,700) and Stromboli (2½hr., L28,700). **Siremar:** 4 daily, 6:15am-3:00pm. **SNAV:** 3 daily at 6:40, 7:25am, and 2:20pm.

Milazzo-Filicudi-Alicudi via Vulcano and Lipari: To Filicudi (2hr., L31,100) and Alicudi (2½hr., L38,300). **Siremar:** 1 daily at 7am or 1:45pm. **SNAV:** 4 daily at 6:40, 7:25, 9am, and 2:20pm.

Lipari

...a floating island, a wall of bronze and splendid smooth sheer cliffs.

—Homer

Lipari is the largest and most developed of the islands off the coast of Sicily. In the town of the same name, pastel-colored houses surround the base of a medieval *castello,* the site of an ancient Greek acropolis. Although placid in appearance, Lipari bustles with summer activities from folk festivals to discos. The town's best beaches, **Spiaggia Bianca** and **Spiaggia Porticello,** are easily reached by bus. The beautiful hostel inside the *castello* makes Lipari an ideal base for daytrips to the neighboring six islands and their splendid beaches.

ORIENTATION AND PRACTICAL INFORMATION

The looming *castello* sits at the middle of town's shoreline, dividing the ferry dock to the right from the hydrofoil landing just to the left as you approach by sea. From Piazza Ugo di Sant'Onofrio in front of the hydrofoil dock, **Via Garibaldi** runs around the base of the *castello* to Piazza Mazzini, at the ferry dock. Farther inland the main street, **Corso Vittorio Emanuele II,** runs parallel to the harbor.

Tourist Office: AAST dello Esole Eolie, Corso Vittorio Emanuele, 202 (tel. 988 00 95; fax 98 11 190), up the street from the ferry dock. English spoken. Open July-Aug. Mon-Sat. 8am-2pm and 4:30-10pm, Sun. 8am-2pm, Sept.-June Mon.-Sat. 8am-2pm and 4:30-7:30pm.

Telephones: (tel. 981 12 63), in Boutique Ruggiero (with the yellow awning) on Via Maurolico, off Corso Vittorio Emanuele. Open Mon.-Sat. 8am-1pm and 3-8pm, Sun. 9am-1pm. At other times use the Hotel Augustus, Via Ausonia, the first right off Corso Vittorio Emanuele from the port. Open daily 9am-11pm.

Currency Exchange: Banca del Sud (tel. 981 13 47) and **B.A.E.** (tel. 981 21 18), both on Corso Vittorio Emanuele. AmEx cheques accepted. Open Mon.-Fri. 8:30am-3:30pm. Other exchanges will change money at poor rates, but are always available in an emergency. Compare rates with exchange available at the post office (cash only). For a cash advance on a credit card, try the friendly *bancomat* machine at Sicilcassa up the street in Piazza Monfalcone.

Public Transportation: Autobus Urso Guglielmo, Via Cappuccini (tel. 981 12 62 or 981 10 26). Ticket office open daily 9am-1pm; tickets can also be bought on the bus. To: Quattrocchi (10 per day, L1500); Aquacalda (10 per day, L2000); Quattro-pani (10 per day, L2000); and Canneto (10 per day, L1500).

Taxis: Corso Vittorio Emanuele (tel. 981 11 10) or Marina Corta (tel. 981 11 95).

Bike/Moped Rental: Foti Roberto, Via F. Crispi, 31 (tel. 981 23 52 or 981 25 87), on the beach to the right of the ferry port. Bicycles L5000 per hr., L20,000 per day. Mopeds and scooters L30,000 per 2hr., L45,000 per day. They ask for a L100,000 deposit and your passport number. Open Easter-Oct. 15 daily 9am-6pm.

Pharmacy: Farmacia Internazionale, Corso Vittorio Emanuele, 128 (tel. 981 15 83). English-speaking doctor sometimes on duty. Open Mon.-Sat. 9am-1pm and 5-9pm. V, MC.

Emergencies: tel. 113. **First Aid:** tel. 988 52 26. **Night Emergency: Guardia Medica,** tel. 981 10 10. **Hospital:** tel. 988 51.

Police: tel. 112. **Carabinieri:** tel. 981 13 33.

Post Office: Corso Vittorio Emanuele, 207 (tel. 981 13 79), one block up from the tourist office, in the building that looks like two stacked steam-pipes. *Fermo posta.* Open Mon.-Fri. 8:30am-1:30pm, Sat. 8:30am-1pm. The **postal code** for Lipari is 98055, for Canneto-Lipari 98052, and for the rest of the islands 98050.

Telephone Code for the Islands: 090.

ACCOMMODATIONS AND CAMPING

As you get off the boat or walk around, locals will ask if you are looking for *affitta camere* (private rooms and apartments). These are often the best bargains but prices vary according to demand; proprietors ask for higher prices earlier in the day, then lower the costs later if their rooms haven't filled up. Try bargaining, but expect to pay at least L20,000 per person from September to June; start at L30,000 in August. Inquiring at local shops (try the bait-and-tackle store on Via Garibaldi near the hydro-foil dock) is often a useful route for finding *affitta camere.*

Lipari is invaded by more and more tourists as the summer progresses, and reaches full capacity in August. Hotels fill almost instantaneously and owners raise their prices by as much as 25%. Make reservations as far in advance as possible, even for late June and early July.

Ostello Lipari (HI), Via Castello, 17 (tel. 981 15 40, off season 981 25 27), 120 beds, on the hill within the walls of the fortress, next to the cathedral, 300m from port ferry. Strict management sternly enforces 11:30pm curfew. Nevertheless, it's probably the best deal on the islands. Their sign warns to you keep an eye on your valuables. (You can leave cameras, jewelry, etc. with the proprietors.) Reception open daily 7:30-9am and 6pm-midnight, downstairs only noon-2pm (to check in luggage). Strict check-out policy; by 9am you, your luggage, and your passport must be out of their hair or else they charge you for an extra night. HI card required when near capacity. L12,000 per person. Hot shower L3000. Sheets and blankets free. Kitchen facilities (L500 extra for use). Breakfast L3000. Lunch and dinner each L10,000-16,000 only if enough demand (book them in the morning). Reservations recommended in July and Aug. Open March-Oct.

Locanda Salina, Via Garibaldi, 18 (tel. 981 23 32), a few steps up from the hydrofoil port. Attractive rooms overlooking the water. Communal terrace with great view. Singles L35,000. Doubles L60,000. Reserve several days in advance for June, weeks ahead for Aug.

Hotel Europeo, Via Vittorio Emanuele, 98 (tel. 981 15 89). Great location with airy rooms on the bustling *corso.* Singles L40,000, with bath L45,000. Doubles L70,000, with bath L80,000. Showers L2000. Reserve early for June-Aug.

Camping: Baia Unci, 2 Via Marina Garibaldi (tel. 981 19 09 or 981 25 27; fax 981 17 15), 2km from Lipari at the entrance to the hamlet of Canneto. This small, shady expanse has amiable management and a cheap self-service restaurant (roasted swordfish a bargain at L11,000). L12,500 per person, with tent L18,000. Open March 15-Oct. 15. Restaurant open daily noon-2pm and 7pm-midnight.

FOOD

Try any dish with the island's famous *capperi* (capers), and follow it up with the indigenous, extremely sweet *Malvasia* dessert wine. Unfortunately, eating cheaply on Lipari is something of a challenge. Anieri Bartolo's **Upim** supermarket (tel. 981 15 87), Corso Vittorio Emanuele, 212, stocks the basics. Open Mon.-Sat. 8am-3:20pm and 4-11pm. V, MC, AmEx. The *alimentari* lining Corso Vittorio Emanuele are generally open seven days a week.

Trattoria d'Oro, Via Umberto I, 32 (tel. 981 13 04 or 988 00 61). Look for the red and white sign pointing off Corso Vittorio Emanuele. Packed with locals, which means noise during soccer season. The *menù* is an especially good buy (L20,000). Try the delicious stuffed calamari (L12,000) or the grilled swordfish (L13,000). Wonderful *spaghetti all'isolana* (L8000) with a mouth-watering sauce of anchovies, capers, tomatoes, and spices. Open daily 11:30am-3:30pm and 6:30pm-2am. V, MC, AmEx.

Il Galeone, Corso Vittorio Emanuele, 220 (tel. 981 14 63 or 981 26 35). Good pizzas and a handy location, close to the ferry docking site. Tempts with 32 types of pizza (L7000-12,000). Try the *pizza Eoliana* with basil, capers, fresh tomatoes, and onions (L10,000). *Primi* from L7000, *secondi* from L10,000. Cover L3000. Open June-Sept. daily 8am-midnight, Oct.-May Thurs.-Tues. 8pm-midnight (pizza available only after 7pm). V, MC.

Moby Dick, Via T.M. Amendola (tel. 981 18 76), on the ferry port. *Menù* L17,000. Excellent pasta "Moby Dick" (with cream, mushrooms, ham, and nutmeg) for L9000. No cover. Open daily 5:30am-2am.

Trattoria A Sfiziusa, Via Roma, 29 (tel. 981 12 16), 100m from the hydrofoil dock. *Spaghetti alla sfiziusa* in a spicy vegetable seafood sauce L7000. *Primi* L6000-9000, *secondi* L11,000-25,000. *Menù* L18,000. *Menù à la carte* around L25,000, plus L2000 cover. Open daily noon-2:30pm and 7pm-midnight; closed Fri. in winter. V, AmEx.

Pasticceria Subba, Corso Vittorio Emanuele, 92 (tel. 981 13 52). If you still have room after dinner, try anything from this *pasticceria,* named one of Italy's best by a popular magazine. If you want to die and go to heaven, go for the *paradiso,* a lemon-stuffed dumpling topped with almonds. Open Thurs.-Tues. 7am-2am.

SIGHTS AND ENTERTAINMENT

Lipari Town

A medieval **castello** crowns the town; within its walls stand three churches and a **duomo** which contains an 18th-century silver statue of San Bartolomeo (above the high altar) and a 16th-century Madonna (in the right transept). The ruins opposite the cathedral in the *parco archeologico* reveal layers of civilization dating back to at least 1700BC. Many of the artifacts found here decorate the exterior of the superb **Museo Archeologico Eoliano** (tel. 988 01 74), occupying the two buildings flanking the cathedral. Open Mon.-Fri. 9am-2pm and 4-7pm; no entrance 30min. before closing time. Free. Inside the museum is the *serione geologico-vulcanologica,* an exposition of the volcanic history of the islands. The fortress holds a small archaeological park and a neoclassical amphitheater (worth a visit just for the incredible view of Lipari town and the ocean). Open Mon.-Sat. 9am-7pm. A walk around the island or town is a treat in and of itself. The twilight view of the Marina Lunga from near the *municipo* is potently romantic (right at the base of the *castello* entrance—look for the illuminated cross on the far peak). Even better—for both your eyes and your camera—plan your ferry ride to another island at sunset.

As the sun sets and breezes blow in off the water, squeeze into your spandex and bop over to the **Discoteca Turmalin,** Piazza Giuseppe Mazzini (tel. 981 15 88), right on the waterfront, outside the castle walls and to the right as you exit. Even if you don't dig your date, you can enjoy the view while you dance. (Cover L12,000. Open daily 10am-2am, Sept.-June Sat. 10am-2am.) Another alternative is **Ritrovo Eolclub,** Via Troncoa, 11 (tel. (0330) 69 52 97), an entertainment-complex fantasy with billiards (L9000 per hr.), foosball, air hockey, ping-pong tables, a card-playing room (L3000 per night), large-screen TV, more video games than you can shake a stick at, juke box, and a "kiddie park." Open daily 5pm-2am. From the ferry port, take a right off Vittorio Emanuele and go 20m. In a blowout party to celebrate the patron St. Bartholomew (and to mark the end of the summer tourist season), Lipari goes crazy with a colorful procession, fireworks, and other **festivities** on August 24.

Around the Island

Lipari is known for its beaches and hillside panoramas. Go all out—rent a moped or a bike and take a day to tour the island (but keep your wits about you—the roads are narrow and the cars zip by). Work your way counterclockwise from Lipari's marina, where you'll first stop at **Canneto,** a small town fronted by a rocky beach. To get to the **Spiaggia Bianca** (White Beach) north of Canneto, take the waterfront road to the "No Camping" sign, then walk up the stairs of Via Marina Garibaldi and bear right down the narrow, cobblestoned path along the water's edge for 300m. There's good swimming all along this area. The beach is the spot for topless (and sometimes bottomless) sunbathing. Protect your delicate flesh, though—the pebbles are sharp and the sun hot. From Canneto center, explore the secluded sandy coves flanking Spiaggia Bianca by renting one of the rafts, kayaks, or canoes that line the beach at Via M. Garibaldi (L6000-8000 per hr., L25,000-35,000 per day). Buses leave the Esso station at Lipari's ferry port for Canneto 10 times daily (16 per day July-Sept., L1500).

Just a few kilometers north of Canneto lies **Pomiciazzo,** where dozens of pumice mines line the road. On clear days, spectacular views of Salina, Panarea, and Stromboli adorn the horizon. Travel a few kilometers north and you're at **Porticello,** where you can bathe at the foot of the pumice mines while small flecks of the stone float on the sea's surface. As you dive beneath the waves for polished black obsidian, note the red and black veins of pumice and obsidian that stretch from the beach into the seabed.

After passing through Acquacalda (a nice enough beach, but nobody likes to be in "hot water"), the island's northernmost city, you'll see signs for the **Duomo de Chiesa Barca,** right on the border of **Quattropani.** Head up the slope toward the church and check out some of the homes lodged in the obsidian hills. After a series of twists, turns, and some *very* steep inclines you'll finally reach the church and be blessed with a phenomenal view.

Traveling south, across the island from Lipari town, you'll pass through **Varesana,** where the road splits: one route leads to **M.S. Angelo** (dominating the center of the island; follow signs for **Pirrera**) and the other runs to **Pianoconte,** where lava-coated battle gear has been unearthed. After this fork, the next stop on the main road is **Quattrocchi** (Four-Eyes), so called for its view of the four headlands that lie off the island's coast. If you make it to the Quattrocchi Belvedere (4km from Lipari, but a heady climb), you receive in return a noble vista of Lipari's *castello,* Vulcano, and the *Faraglione,* a series of monoliths rising from the sea between Vulcano and Lipari. South of Quattrocchi sits **Monte Guardia,** home to UNESCO's **Geophysical Observatory** (not open to the public) and a close-up view of Vulcano. There is another observatory on V. Stradale Serra, slightly north of Lipari town. Go and ask for Signor Salvatore (tel. 981 10 81), smile a lot, and ask to see Stromboli's craters via TV camera. If he's not too busy, you're in for a treat.

From July 1 to Sept. 30 only, catch a "Bus Tour of the Isle of Lipari" (daily at 9:30, 11:30am, and 5:00pm, L5000). The other alternative is to take a **boat** from the hydrofoil port in Lipari and tour around Lipari and its neighboring islands. Excursions are run by **SEN** (Società Eolie di Navigazione) Via Vittorio Emanuele, 247 (tel. 981 23 41; fax 981 12 40), next to the hydrofoil port, which conducts tours of Salina and Lipari (Mon.-Thurs. at 10am, return 6:15pm, L35,000); Alicudi and Filicudi (Fri. at 9am, return 8:30pm, L50,000); Panarea (Tue.-Wed. and Fri.-Sun. at 10am, return 1pm, L30,000); Stromboli (Tues.-Wed. and Sat.-Sun. at 3pm, return 11:15pm, L45,000); and Vulcano (Thurs. at 9am, return 1pm, L20,000). If these prices are too high, try privately contracting a fishing boat for a personalized excursion. Bargain for a decent price—about L12,000 per person per hr. is reasonable. Consult the **NGI** office, Via Ten. M. Amendola (tel. 981 19 55), near the ferry port, for other ways to experience the islands.

Vulcano

Stretch out and immerse yourself; the hand of the god Vulcan will hold you gently, transforming thoughts into bubbles of music and culture.

—a signpost in Vulcano

The psychedelic sensations promised by these words may elude you, but if you are seeking an escape from the crowds of Lipari, this island could be worth a visit. Climb up to the sulfurous crater; take a dip in the bubbling sea or sink deeply into the therapeutic mud. But beware: some geologists think the gurgling volcano may explode within the next twenty years. For now, the great crater lies dormant at the island's center. Easy access from Lipari (by hydrofoil, L4000; by ferry, L2400) and the density of sulfur in the air make Vulcano an excellent daytrip.

The island's history, not surprisingly, has always been tied to its volcano. Frequently mentioned in historical accounts (among them Aristotle's and Thucydides'), the island was believed to be the primary residence of Hephaestus (Vulcan), god of fire and blacksmiths. Medieval lore took the crater to be the entrance to Hell. Today Vulcano continues to simmer, huffing and puffing sulphur but not blowing anything down—yet. Vulcano is a summer island; if you get here before June or after September, most restaurants will be closed and it will be tough to find a place to stay. (A larger island like Lipari is more convenient in the off-season.)

ORIENTATION AND PRACTICAL INFORMATION

Ferries and hydrofoils dock at **Porto di Levante,** on the eastern side of the isthmus between **Il Cardo** (the mountain to the left as you approach the port) and the Vulcanello peninsula (to the right). **Porto di Ponente,** along with **Spiaggia Sabbie Nere** (Black Sands Beach—one of the few smooth ones on the Aeolian Islands), lies across the isthmus on the west side of the island. Vulcano has no street signs, so it will often take more than an address to find what you're looking for. Don't be afraid to ask for directions, even if you don't speak Italian (the old men who sit outside the bar at the port are especially happy to oblige). From the dock at P. di Levante, **Via Provinciale** curves to the left (toward the volcano), and **Via Porto Levante** to the right leads into the center of town. After 200m Via Porto Levante bears to the left and turns into Via Lentia; a bit farther on you'll hit **Via Porto Ponente,** which leads to the right down to the port of the same name.

Tourist Office: AAST, Via Provinciale, 41 (tel. 985 20 28; July-Aug. only). For information on **rented rooms** *(affitta camere),* call 985 22 15. Otherwise, get info from the Lipari tourist office, listed above.
Currency Exchange: Vulcan Tours, Porto di Levante (tel. 985 22 15).
Telephone: Cartolibreria Sciacchi tano, Via Mercalli (tel. 985 22 00).
Buses: Scaffidi Tindaro (tel. 985 20 94 or 985 30 17) runs 8 per day from the port to Vulcano Piano (9am-6pm, L2000).
Ferries: To Milazzo (6 per day, L9900) and Lipari (5 per day, L2400). **Hydrofoils** to Milazzo (10 per day, L18,400) and Lipari (10 per day, L4000).
Taxis: tel. 985 24 04.
Boat, Auto, Scooter, and Bicycle Rentals: Campisi Vulcano Car, Via Comunale Levante (tel. 985 25 74). **Marturano Giuseppe,** Porto Levante (tel. 985 24 19). **Truscello Rita,** Porto Levante (tel. 985 25 27).
Pharmacy: Farmacia Bonarrigo, Via Favaloro, 1 (tel. 985 22 44). Open daily 9am-1pm and 5-9pm.
First Aid: tel. 985 22 20.
Police: tel. 985 21 10.
Post Office: On the other side of the island in the hamlet of Vulcano Piano, on Via Piano (tel. 985 31 43 or 985 30 02). Open Mon.-Fri. 8am-1:30pm, Sat. 8am-11:20am.
Telephone Code for the Islands: 090.

ACCOMMODATIONS AND CAMPING

Keep in mind that all of Vulcano reeks with pervasive sulfur vapors—the island's accommodations are no exception.

Residence Lanterna Blù, Via Lentia, 58 (tel. 985 21 78). Rents cozy apartments for longer stays. Each with tiny kitchen, bath, A/C, and private terrace shaded by flowering vines. Two-person apartments May-June L60,000; July and Sept. L70,000; August L100,000. Extra bed L20,000. One-time fee of L18,000 charged for cleaning the apartment at the end of your stay. Open Jan. 16-Dec. 14.
Pensione La Giara, Via Porto Levante, 18 (tel. 985 22 29), on the way to the crater from the hydrofoil port. They use a daunting bell-curve to work out how much to charge for rooms: L29,000 (April-May); L35,000 (June); L45,000 (July); L64,000 (Aug.); L42,000 (Sept.); and L25,000 (Oct.). Breakfast included.
Camping: Campeggio Togo Togo (tel. 985 23 03), 800m from the port, on Via Porto Levante in the Vulcanello area behind the Sabbie Nere beach. Large and conveniently located. Rudimentary facilities. L10,000 per person, L10,000 per tent. Open June-Sept.
Bungalow al Togo, at the far end of Via Lentia at Piazza T. Ponente (tel. 985 21 28). Small, run-down but comfortable 4-person bungalows with stoves. Lockers for valuables. L30,000 per person, much more during peak season.

FOOD

The **Tridial Market** general store (tel. 985 22 22) is located off Via P. Levante. (Open daily 8am-1:30pm and 4-8pm.) **Panificio Alongi,** Via Provinciale 28 (tel. 985 21 87), is one of the island's best bakeries. To get there, hook a left on Via P. Levante from Via Provinciale as you're heading away from the port. You can always grab a quick munchie at the vegetable stand directly across the street from the mud bath.

Ristorante Il Castello, Vulcano Porto (tel. 985 21 17). Tall ceiling and a patio enhance the bargain dining. Self-service lunch L14,000. Dinner menu L20,000-25,000. Open daily noon-2pm and 8pm-1am.

Ristorante al Cratere, Via Provinciale, 31 (tel. 985 20 45), just past the entrance to the path to the crater. Great food that won't dissolve your budget. *Fettuccine fresche al cratere* (with eggplant, zucchini, *pesto,* and baked ricotta, L8000) and aromatic grilled swordfish (L14,000). Excellent imported beer (from L3000). Open daily 9am-4pm and 6pm-midnight.

Il Sestante-Ritrovo Remigio, Via Porto Levante (tel. 985 20 85), right on the port. Hot and cold sandwiches, *gelato,* and probably the widest selection of tasty desserts on the Lipari Isles. *Tiramisú* (L3000), *cassata* (L4000), *cannoli* (L2000), and an awesome selection of marzipan fruits. Proprietor Tony speaks perfect English. Piano bar and dancing July 1-Sept.10. Open daily 6am-3am.

Ristorante Il Palmento, Via Porto Levante (tel. 985 25 52 or 985 21 09). A volcanic luau. Pizza from L8000-14,000. Open daily noon-4pm and 6:30pm-midnight. V, MC.

Taverna del Marinaio, Via Favaloro (tel. 985 24 26), just across from Tridial Market. Pizzas from L7000. Or be a little daring and order their specialty *"spaghetti alla riccio"* (with sea urchin) for L15,000. *Menù* L25,000. Cover L1500. Open daily noon-3:30pm and 7pm-closing. V, MC, AmEx.

SIGHTS

One way to begin your visit to Vulcano is to tackle the 1hr. hike to the **Gran Cratere** (Great Crater) along the snaking footpath beside the crater's fumaroles. Be warned: between 11am and 3pm the sun transforms the side of the volcano into a furnace, so head out in the early morning or late afternoon. Make sure you have sunscreen, a hat, plenty of water, and good climbing shoes. The climb is challenging; there are some fairly steep inclines, but it's worth it. On a clear day you'll be able to see all the other islands from the top. But don't inhale: the sulfur smoke spouting from the volcano is saturated with toxins. To get to the path from the port, follow Via Piano for 200m and look for the *"cratere"* signs.

Just up Via Provinciale from the port sits the **Laghetto di Fanghi** (mud pool) to your right, a bubbling pit where hundreds of zealots come to spread the allegedly therapeutic glop all over their bodies. You can't miss the smell. If you have no dermatological crises, or simply would rather not bathe in dirt, wade in the nearby waters of the **acquacalda** just behind the *laghetto.* Here, underwater volcanic outlets make the sea percolate like a jacuzzi; don't scald your feet! For cooler pleasures, visit the crowded beach and crystal-clear waters of Sabbie Nere, just down the road from the *acquacalda* (follow the signs off Via Ponente through the black sand). Those wanting to enjoy themselves a little further out to sea can hire boats (from L90,000 per day) from **Centro Nautico Baia di Levante** (tel. 982 21 97), on the beach facing the port. (Open May-Oct. 9am-6pm.)

A **bus** runs from the pier to **Volcano Piano** on the other side of the island. There's little to do except visit the skeleton of the **Church of Sant'Angelo,** admire the vistas, and savor the aroma of sun-ripened ginger. In the opposite direction from the pier lies **Vulcanello,** with a peninsula all to itself. Like its bigger (and more interesting) sibling across the way, it comes complete with noxious fumes; on the other hand, the colors of the rocks along the way help to compensate for the odor.

Stromboli

Viewed from Lipari or Vulcano, the island of Stromboli looks like a giant iceberg jutting out of the water. Upon closer inspection you'll see that the opposite is true: Stromboli is a volcano, and an active one at that. In a different sense, Stromboli town (pop. 370) lies dormant until the bustling summer tourist season. Foreigners converge on the island from mid-June to early September, making cheap accommodations almost impossible to find—don't plan on staying in July or August unless you camp overnight. In the slow off-season, many *pensioni* are closed and owners are reluctant to rent rooms for fewer than three nights at a time. It's well worth it to call ahead since ferries are rare.

Two towns cling to the volcano's slopes. **Ginostra** (pop. 15 in winter) is a collection of idyllic sun-bleached houses that offers a view of Sicily and all the rest of the islands, as well as an unspoiled paradise of labyrinthine walkways, luxuriant vegetation, and a surprisingly diverse population of Italo-australians, year-round natives, and Germans and Northern Italians with summer houses. Ginostra also houses the smallest port in the world; from the ferry or hydrofoil you get on a rowboat that delivers you to the shore. Otherwise Ginostra is inaccessible except by hiking up the volcano from Stromboli town and climbing down the other side. On the opposite side, the adjoining villages of Piscità, Ficogrande, San Vincenzo, and Scari have fused to comprise Stromboli town on the island's northeast corner. The **Church of San Vincenzo** rises above the town and is replete with Rodinesque sculptures of the Holy Trinity. From the ferry and hydrofoil dock, Via Roma leads up the hill to the church at Piazza Vincenzo. **Corso Vittorio Emanuele,** dipping and turning from P. Vincenzo to the edge of town, is as close as Stromboli comes to having a main drag. Via Filzi and Via Nunziante branch off of the *corso* to the right; both meet up with Via Marina (which originates at the ferry dock) at **Ficogrande** (big fig), a beach with sand as black as coal. From here 2km in the distance rises **Strombolicchio,** a gigantic rock with a small lighthouse perched on its rim. The ravages of the sea have eroded the rock from 56m high to a mere 42m in the past 100 years. **Boats** for hire make their way out to the base of Strombolicchio (L12,500-20,000), from which one can climb the stairs (reinforced with concrete in the '20s).

PRACTICAL INFORMATION

Stromboli's **post office** (tel. 98 60 27) lies on Via Roma. Open Mon.-Sat. 8:10am-1:20pm. **Siremar** runs **boat** and **hydrofoil** services to: Lipari (hydrofoil only, 2-3 daily, 8:10am-4pm, L23,700); Panarea (2 daily, 8:10am-4pm, L11,900); Salina (2-3 daily, 9:45am-5:10pm); and Vulcano (3 daily, 7:25am-3pm, L27,700). The **ferry** from Lipari runs L13,900. **Change money** at Le Isole d'Italia on Via Roma (tel. 98 62 74), a travel agency. Open Mon.-Sat. in summer 10am-12:30pm and 5-8pm. The town **pharmacy** is on Via Roma (tel. 98 60 79). Open 8:30am-11pm, Sept.-June 14 9am-6pm. For **first aid** call 98 60 97 or go to the Guardia Medica on the Ficogrande side of the church; for **police** call 98 60 21. The **telephone code for the islands** is 090.

ACCOMMODATIONS

Hotels on Stromboli are booked solid for August by the previous winter. In other months, **Pensione la Nassa** (tel. 98 60 33) is a good bet (on Via Fabio Filzi just 20m before the beach at Ficogrande as you depart from the port). Open June-Sept. **Pensione Roma,** Via Roma, 15, next to Ristorante da Luciano (tel. 98 60 88) and owned by the Ristorante's proprietor, is 5min. from the ferry dock up on Via Roma, almost at the top of the hill to the right. Barter for rooms, starting around L20,000 per person. **Villa Petrusa,** Via V. Emanuele, 13 (tel. 98 60 45; fax 98 61 26), has pricey but well kept singles (L60,000) and doubles (L90,000) in high-season (July-Aug.), but the rest of the year you can talk them down since the flow of people is so erratic. There is a **Pensione Petrusa** (tel. 981 23 05) just up from the port at Ginostra, which has off-season singles for L25,000 and doubles for L50,000. Prices double in August. Call ahead to reserve expansive rooms with incredible views of the other island. Signora Petrusa also runs a restaurant for the clientele, but prices start at L10,000 for *primi.* **Affitta camere** are available for extended periods of time. Inquire at bars, stores, or the tourist office.

FOOD

The best deals can be had at the **Duval Market** (tel. 98 60 52), to the left off Via Roma right before the church. Open daily 8:30am-1pm and 5-9pm. V, MC, AmEx. On a breezy terrace overlooking the sea you'll find **La Lampara** at Via Vittorio Emanuele,

27 (tel. 98 60 09), between the church and Via Nunziante. Grilled swordfish (L12,000) and pizzas (L8000-15,000) are quite filling. *Primi* from L8000, *secondi* from L12,000. Try the heavenly *tiramisù* (L5000), possibly the best on the Aeolian Isles. Open late May-Oct. daily noon-2pm and 6pm-1am. **Ristorante da Luciano,** Via Roma, 15 (tel. 98 60 88), provides you with a tremendous view of the beach, the sea, and Strombolicchio hulking in the distance. Good pizza can be had for as little as L7000, but the rest of the menu is daunting (*primi* from L12,000, *secondi* from L15,000). Open daily noon-2pm and 5:30-11:30pm. Just 100m from the port on Via Roma (#34) is the *rosticceria* **La Trattola** (tel. 98 60 46). Pizza runs L5000-15,000. Ask for the "Stromboli pizza"—actually shaped like the volcano. Open daily in summer noon-2:30pm and 6pm-late.

SIGHTS

Società Navigazione Pippo (tel. 98 61 35) runs an evening **boat trip** from Stromboli to see the molten crimson trail of the *Sciara del Fuoco* ("Trail of Fire," a blackened slope illuminated by sporadic cascades of lava and molten rock; you can also walk from Ginostra on the other side of the island). Boats leave the port at 10pm and return at 11pm (L15,000). They also operate daily tours of the island (10:10am-1:10pm and 3:10-6:10pm, L20,000 per person). **Pino and Stefano,** another boat rental/tour service, will take you anywhere around the island you wish to go (tel./fax 98 60 03 or tel. 98 60 28).

Let's Go does not recommend, advocate, or otherwise take responsibility for anyone hiking the volcano, but hopes that if you do, you'll be smart about it. A red triangle with a black vertical bar means "danger."

An ordinance passed in 1990 made hiking the volcano without a guide officially illegal, but it hasn't seemed to stop people. If such criminality doesn't suit you, look into a trip with the **Guide Alpine Autorizzate** (tel. 98 62 11), the island's authorized guides. (The hike leaves at 6pm and returns between 11pm and midnight.) Those who choose to ignore the law (and to feign ignorance of the four languages on the warning signs) head on up. Travelers often stash their bags at the Villa Petrusa (see above). Hikers should take sturdy shoes, a flashlight, snacks, at least 2-4 liters of water, and warm clothes for the exposed summit (sleeping bag is a real bonus); otherwise, pack as light as possible. Any excess weight can make the experience very unpleasant. The hike takes about three hours up and two down. Reaching the summit around dusk—one really can't see anything but smoke during the day—allows adventurers to camp out and see the brilliant lava bursts by night.

To reach the volcano, hikers follow Corso Vittorio Emanuele (from P. Vincenzo) a good kilometer or so until a large warning sign and a fork in the road appear; bear to the right. When a secluded stretch of beach comes into view, the path turns upward and (after 400m) cuts between two white houses, the last structures hikers see except for the *ristorante-bar* L'Osservatorio a little farther on. Smart hikers take only the well-trodden shortcuts—anything else will lead to a maze of thick brambles and reeds. Halfway up the slope is the island's best view of the **Sciara del Fuoco.** Finally, the trail degenerates into a scramble of volcanic rock and ash; hikers must follow the striped red, orange, and white rock markings. Those who don't follow very carefully will end up stranded in a landslide of loose volcanic ash, sand, and soil. The warning signs at the top ridge are sincere: not long ago, a photographer fell to her death in search of a closer shot. At all costs, avoid climbing with heavy loads or in the dark, since the last part gets steep. For an overnight trip, hikers bring a sturdy food bag, plastic to place between themselves and the wet sand, warm clothing, and foul weather gear for the frigid fogs that envelop the peak.

Other Islands

The remaining three *Eolie* provide an uncrowded detour from the ordinary, whether you're in the mood for a rural fishing village or an overindulgent resort.

PANAREA

The smallest of the Aeolian Islands, Panarea has gained a reputation as an elite playground for such celebrities as Barbra Streisand and Princess Di. If you so desire to join the ranks of Panarea's clientele, you should know that it is no more daunting to your wallet than the other islands and you're likely to meet many English speakers. At the southern end of the island, Punta Milazzese offers perhaps the most spectacular rough-hewn cliffs in all of the islands, if not in all of Sicily. It also houses the ruins of a Bronze Age settlement. Up at the Northern end, the beach at Calcara is near the thermal springs at Acquacalda. The town at the port consists of one main street, Via San Pietro, that loops around the collection of whitewashed terraces parallel to the port. Follow San Pietro south out of town until you hit the path leading straight to Punta Milazzese and the beach. Hotels are pricey and booked solid in August; in other months try **Pensione Rodè Pasqualdro,** Via del Porto, for airy *affitta camere* with communal terraces for L35,000 per person (July-Aug. L40,000). There's also **Hycesia,** on Via San Pietro (tel. 98 30 41), which has comparable rooms and prices with views of beautiful gardens instead of the sea. Rooms come with TV, fan, and bathroom. Up the street on Via San Pietro is the town post office and the **Da Bruno** supermarket (tel 98 30 02). Open daily 7:30am-9:30pm. There's also a *panificio* next door with good pizza *al taglio* for L2000 a slice. Open daily 7:30am-1pm, 5-8pm. If you want a real meal, head to **Tesoriero Antonio** (tel. 98 30 33) on Via San Pietro for great pizza from L8000 on a flowery terrace. Follow signs for da Antonio (they're the same place). Or munch on a filling L5000 *panino* at **Ritrovo da Tindero,** (tel. 98 32 62), at Piazza Lauricella up the street from Pensione Rodè. Open daily 8am-midnight.

SALINA

A verdant paradise and the second-largest island, **Salina** is renowned for the rock formations at Semaforo di Pollara and Punta Lingua, and for some of the best *Malvasia* wine around. Salina is relatively uncorrupted by tourism; its beaches are uncrowded and its sleepy character intact, but there's talk going around that it is becoming the next overtouristed Capri. Hotel prices are already high, making Salina a better daytrip than destination. From Lipari, Salina is accessible by Siremar **hydrofoil** (7 per day, 1hr., L10,500) and **ferry** (3 per day, L5400). Salina's main port, where both the ferries and hydrofoils dock, is the **Porto Santa Marina.** Unless otherwise noted, the listings for food and accommodations that follow are all located in the small settlement that rises above Santa Marina's docks. From the port, Via Lunga Mare heads to the right toward **Malfa** and **Pollara,** site of the last eruption on the island some 12,000 years ago. Pollara is also a geological wonder: a verdant half-submerged crater with a town tucked in just where the land hits the water. From Malfa a road cuts through the center of the island through Valdichiesa and down the slopes of Rinella, where some of the hydrofoils dock. The town of **Lingua,** famed for its clear water, lies just south of **Santa Marina,** 3km to the left on Via L. Marel. From Lingua and Valdichiesa, paths extend to the peak of **M. Fossa delle Felci,** which towers an impressive 962m above the island. If you show up on August 15 for the **Feast of the Assumption of the Virgin,** you'll be surrounded by pilgrims en route to the **Sanctuary of the Madonna del Terzito,** nestled in Valdichiesa and dating to the early 1600s. **Buses** run frequently (10 per day) to any of these towns from the port; consult the schedule posted outside the SNAV ticket office next to the docks (approx. L1200 per town). Get a roundtrip ticket (L5500) for a great tour of the island. The patient driver might even stop for picture-taking.

Pensione Mamma Santina, Via Sanità, 40 (tel. 984 30 54), has singles for L35,000 and doubles for L55,000, with bath L60,000 March-June; July-Sept. obligatory half-pension L70,000. Mamma Santina's is a long, steep walk through narrow streets, but worth the climb. To get there from the port, walk up into town and take a right on the first cross street you see, Via Risorgimento; after about 250m, a sign for Mamma Santina's will point the way. Via Sanità is a narrow path woven into the hill. Take the bus or *aliscafo* to Rinella for Salina's only true budget accommodations: **Camping Tre Pini** (tel. 980 91 55) charges L10,000 per person, L12,000 per tent (open March-Oct.), with market, bar, restaurant, and TV; located by the sea. **Ristorante da Franco** (tel. 984 32 87) is a long haul, but there's no better view on all of Salina. Follow signs from the top of Via Risorgimento. Homegrown *antipasti* and *primi* are L8000-12,000. *Macaroni Siciliano* is yummy and filling (L8000). Open daily noon-3pm and 8pm-midnight; July-Aug. 8pm-midnight. **Mamma Santina** (tel. 984 30 54) also runs a small eatery, especially convenient if you're staying there for the night. The *menù* goes for L28,000, wine included. (Dinner only 8-11pm.) The cheapest way to eat, as usual, is the cold lunch route; try any *alimentari* or market you find on Via Risorgimento.

Posta Telegrafo is at Via Risorgimento, 130, and is open Mon.-Sat. 8am-1:20pm. There is a full-fledged **post office** on Via Marina Garibaldi (tel. 984 30 28). The **postal code** is 98050. **Police** in Salina are at 984 30 19. Find a telephone at **Rago Mario** (tel. 984 30 68). There is a **bank** (tel. 984 31 21) by the port where you can change your money. Open summer only; the only year-round bank is down the road 7km in Malfa. The **Farmacia Comunale** (tel. 984 30 98) sits at the bottom of Via Risorgimento, 111, ready to help. Open Mon. 5-8pm, Tues.-Fri. 9am-1pm and 5:30-8:30pm.

FILICUDI

West of Lipari, **Filicudi** presents an array of volcanic rock formations and the enchanting **Grotta del Bue Marino** (Grotto of the Monk Seal) on the side opposite the port (accessible only by boat, roughly L20,000 per person). The best way to Filicudi is to rent a vespa (L30,000 per day). Heading to the right up the hill of **Montepalmieri** as you arrive at the port brings you to the rocky terraces of **Fossa Felci** (774m) and one of the island's **post offices** (tel. 988 99 43). As you head further up to the town of **Valdichiesa** with its rapidly deteriorating church (note its precariously balanced bell tower), consider the paths that run around to the western edge of the Fossa and down to **Pecorini,** home to a set of ancient Greek inscriptions (and another post office). The island's one paved road carries you to the port, as the peninsula **Capo Graziano** reaches into the sea from the right. **La Canna,** an impressive rock spike (71m high, 9m wide), points up from the sea a kilometer from Filicudi's west coast. It's easily visible if you take the footpath around the Fossa; otherwise rent a boat (L15,000-20,000) or grab a ferry to **Alicudi** (Siremar L5400), which will pass right by the suggestive Rock. The **police** are at tel. 988 99 42.

For the best deal on the island, head to the vivacious **Pensione Villa Rosa,** up the hill from the port about 30min. along the highway to Pecorini (tel. 988 99 65). Spotless rooms with bath presided over by a friendly proprietress. L25,000 per person, *mezza pensione* L65,000. From July 15-Aug. 30, singles L50,000, doubles 100,000, triples 120,000, full pension L135,000. V.

ALICUDI

On the westernmost fringes of the Aeolian islands sits isolated **Alicudi,** the estranged cousin of Filicudi. At 5sq.km, it is little more than a speck in the sea. With one telephone, a hotel, 120 inhabitants, no paved roads, and recently-installed electricity (Feb. 91), Alicudi is just the place to go if you're headed nowhere in particular. Left of the port, make your way over the stones to untouristed **Tonna.** The **Albergo Ericusa** (tel. 988 99 02; fax 988 96 71) is the only place on the island and *very* expensive; half-pension runs at L85,000 and full pension at L98,000. Open June-Sept., but call before you come—it's a looong way back to civilization. Full pension is advisable; food is expensive here, too.

Cefalù

Cefalù was once a quiet fishing village, but now the fishermen have opened up shops and restaurants to accommodate the visitors drawn by its beaches, pleasant streets, and mixed-bag architecture. Unfortunately, hotels fill up during the summer, and the prospects of finding an inexpensive *pensione* are fairly dismal even in the off season. Visit Cefalù as a stopover or daytrip from Palermo, only an hour away by train. You can easily tour the town in half a day and still have time for a swim, either in the crowded waters right below town or at the beaches a short bus ride away.

ORIENTATION AND PRACTICAL INFORMATION

Via A. Moro leads to the right from the station into town. At the first big intersection, **Via Roma** runs off to the left and back into Cefalù's modern quarter. To get to the **old city,** continue on Via Moro as it turns into Via Matteotti and then (at P. Garibaldi) into Corso Ruggero. **Via Lungomare** runs the length of Cefalù's main beach before it passes into the old city as **Corso Vittorio Emanuele.**

Tourist Office: Corso Ruggero, 77 (tel. 210 50; fax 223 86), in the old city. English spoken. If you don't see anyone, check in back. Open June-Sept. Mon.-Sat. 8am-8:30pm, Sun. 8am-2pm; Oct.-May Mon.-Fri. 8am-2pm and 4-7pm, Sat. 8am-2pm.

Currency Exchange: Banca S. Angelo (tel. 239 22), near the station at the corner of Via Giglio and Via Roma. Open Mon.-Fri. 8:30am-1:30pm. For 24-hr. access, try the change machine by the **Banca di Sicilia** (tel. 211 03), in P. Garibaldi.

Telephones: Agenzia San Mauro, Via Vazzana, 7 (tel. 234 43). In front of the *lungomare.* Open Mon.-Sat. 9am-1pm and 4-7:30pm.

Trains: Stazione F.F.S.S., off Via Gramsci (tel. 211 69). To: Messina (17 daily, 2½hr., L13,600); Milazzo (6 daily, 2½hr., L11,700); and Palermo (14 per weekday, 1hr., L5700).

Buses: SPISA, Via Umberto I, 28 (tel. 243 01), up to the right from P. Garibaldi. Buses serve all local towns for under L2000 and leave from in front of the train station.

Taxis: P. Stazione (tel. 225 54) and **P. Duomo** (tel. 211 78).

Pharmacy: Cirincione, Corso Ruggero, 144 (tel. 212 09).

Emergencies: tel. 113. **Nighttime First Aid:** tel. 236 23. **Hospital:** Via A. Moro (tel. 920 11).

Police: tel. 217 29 or 211 04 or 112.

Post Office: Via Vazzana, 2 (tel. 92 17 03), off Via Roma. Open Mon.-Sat. 8:10am-6:30pm. **Postal Code:** 90015.

Telephone Code: 0921.

ACCOMMODATIONS AND CAMPING

Pensione delle Rose, Via Gibilmanna (tel. 218 85). Turn right on Via A. Moro from the station. At the first stoplight, turn right onto Via Mazzini and continue up the hill until it turns right again on Via Umberto, which becomes Via Gibilmanna, a quasi highway with no sidewalk. Make a final right at the *pensione* sign, walk past the apartment complex, and left up the flowered-vine pathway. Attractive, sparsely furnished rooms with spectacular views of the town. All rooms with bath. Breakfast included. July-Aug. doubles L80,000; Oct.-June doubles L66,000. During summer, half-pension L70,000. Full-pension L85,000. V, MC.

Locanda Cangelosi, Via Umberto I, 26 (tel. 215 91), off P. Garibaldi. *The* budget shack. Only 4 rooms, so call in advance for the cheapest cot in the old city. June-Sept. singles L35,000; doubles L70,000. Oct.-May singles L25,000; doubles L60,000. 3-min. hot showers L2000. Anyone can wander in off the street, so keep an eye (or better yet, a hand) on your valuables.

Pensione La Giara, Via Veterani, 40 (tel. 215 62; fax 225 18), off Corso Ruggero, near the beach and *duomo*. Comfortable rooms with balconies; community terrace offers a gorgeous view and peaceful outdoor dining. Half-pension required in Aug. July-Aug. singles L50,000; doubles L110,000. Restaurant downstairs. AmEx.

Camping: Costa Ponente, Località Ogliastrillo (tel. 200 85), 3km west at Contrada Ogliastrillo (a 45-min. walk or a short ride on the Cefalù-Lascari bus, L1500). Swimming pool and tennis court. L8500 per person, L7000 per small tent, L9500 per large tent; Sept.-June L6800 per person, L5500 per small tent, L8000 per large tent. Nearby **Camping Sanfilippo,** Località Ogliastrillo (tel. 201 84) charges L7800 per person, L6300 per small tent, L9000 per large tent. Both campgrounds run markets in the summer, but you're probably better off stocking up at the STANDA in the center of Cefalù (see below).

FOOD

Affordable restaurants cluster around Corso Ruggero and Via Vittorio Emanuele, and many fine pizzerias converge on Via C. O. di Bordonaro and the *lungomare*. Shop for basics at the **STANDA** supermarket, Via Vazzana (tel. 245 00) near the post office. Open daily 8:30am-1pm and 5-8:30pm. There is also a huge **SIGMA** supermarket on Via Roma, 61. Open daily 8am-1pm and 4:30pm-8pm.

Pizzeria "da NINO," Via Bagni, 11 (tel. 225 82), to the right down the *lungomare*. Low prices, outdoor dining, and a seaside view make it worth the crowd. Women receive free fans. Simple, great entrees like *pizza margherita* (L5000) or *spaghetti al pomodoro* (L5000). June-Sept. noon-3pm and 7-11pm. V, MC, AmEx.

L'Antica Corte, Cortele Pepe, 7 (tel. 232 28), off Corso Ruggero to the left, past the *duomo* as you head toward the sea. Eat outdoors in a tiny courtyard under a grapevine or indoors in the air-conditioned basement. Fabulous seafood, *primi* (L7000-10,000), and pizzas (L6000-11,000). *Menù* L20,000. Open daily noon-3pm and 7pm until they decide to close. Pizza served after 7pm. V, MC, AmEx.

Pasticceria Pietro Serio, Via G. Giglio, 29 (tel. 222 93), the first left off Via Moro from the train station. A sleek *caffè* offering a huge assortment of pastries and fantastic *gelato,* only a few paces from the station. Open Mon.-Tues. and Thurs.-Sun. 7am-1pm and 3-10pm.

SIGHTS AND ENTERTAINMENT

Throughout the old city, you can catch glimpses of history in the Arab windows, Saracen walkways, and medieval archways. In P. Duomo off Corso Ruggero, you'll find Cefalù's austere 11th-century Norman **cathedral,** supposedly erected by Roger II in gratitude for divine protection from a shipwreck. The golden stone and solidity of the square-tower echo the monumentality of the Rocca behind it. Inside, 16 Byzantine and Roman columns support superb capitals, and the elegant horseshoe arches exemplify the Saracen influence on Norman architecture in Sicily. The famous **Christ Pantocrator mosaic** (one of three in Sicily) graces the central apse; together this mosaic, the Madonna and angels below, and the Apostles date to 1148. (Open daily 8:30am-noon and 3:30-6:30pm. Proper dress required—shoulders and knees should be covered.) The interior of the church is currently undergoing renovation, so you will have to step around the mosaics lying on the floor.

Opposite the cathedral, the private **Museo Mandralisca,** Via Mandralisca, 13 (tel. 215 47), houses a small collection of paintings, Greek ceramics, Arab pottery, antique money, stuffed birds, and Antonello da Messina's *Ritratto di Ignoto* (*Portrait of an Unknown Man,* 1470-1472), the face featured on most Sicilian tourist brochures. You're not just paranoid: the eyes do follow you wherever you go, but they do that to everyone. (Hours vary according to season, generally 9:30am-12:30pm and 4-6pm. Admission L5000.)

At the end of Via XXV Novembre on Via Vittorio Emanuele (hugging the beach) is the curious semi-subterranean, 16th-century **lavatoio medievale** (medieval laundromat). Don't drink the water coming from its fountains, and try your best not to inhale the noxious fumes spewed from the ancient tubs. (Open daily 8am-8pm.)

The city derives its name from the Greek *kephaloidion* (head) because of the shape of the **Rocca** looming above the town. For a bird's-eye view, make the half-hour haul up by way of the Salita Saraceni, which begins near P. Garibaldi off Corso

Ruggero. Follow the brown signs for *"pedonale Rocca."* On the mountain, walkways lined with ancient stone walls lead to the **Tempio di Diana** (Temple of Diana), situated amid beautiful and aromatic pines and overlooking the city and the sea. Dating to the 4th century BC, the temple was first used for sea-cult worship and later as a defensive outpost.

From July to September Cefalù hosts the **Incontri d'Estate,** which features opera, classical, contemporary, and Sicilian folk music in outdoor concerts. The Sicilian Symphony Orchestra is a featured performer at these concerts. Shows are moved to the *duomo* from August 4 to 6 to accommodate the **Fiesta di San Salvatore** (in honor of Cefalù's patron saint), celebrated with a rousing display of fireworks and marching bands. Two of Cefalù's most attractive beaches, **Spiaggia Mazzaforno** and **Spiaggia Settefrati,** are located west of town on SPISA's Cefalù-Lascari bus line. In late September and early October, Cefalù also takes part in the nationwide film festival, **Le Città del Cinema,** free and open to the public. Ask at the tourist office for more info.

■ Near Cefalù: The Ruins of Tyndaris

Seventy-five km east of Cefalù and just 15km west of Milazzo lies **Tindari,** site of the ruins of **Tyndaris.** Dating from the 4th century BC, the Greek settlement was founded high on a hill as a fortification against enemy attacks. Tyndaris chose its political allies well, siding with Rome in the Punic Wars and supplying ships for the expedition that destroyed Carthage in 146BC. However, an earthquake in AD365 destroyed the city, and the Arabs mopped up the remains in 836. Unearthed only in the mid-1900s, the ruins are now home to a museum, several archaeological curiosities, olive groves, and spectacular views of the Aeolian Isles.

Bus service is erratic, so trains are your best bet to get to Tindari. Plan ahead, however, as even trains are infrequent, especially on weekends. To reach the ruins, take the train to Oliveri-Tindari and make the 40-min. hike up the hill. Follow your first right out of the station until the street ends; bear left under the highway and then right past a grove of lemon trees. When you come to a green gate, go left (following the white arrows). Finally, bear right when the path forks.

The first sight you'll see upon climbing the hill to the ancient site is the **Santuario di Tindari** (tel. 36 91 67 or 36 90 03), erected less than 30 years ago for the **Madonna Nera** (Black Madonna). Local legend has it that a statue of this eastern madonna washed up on the shores of Tindari hundreds of years ago, and the current sanctuary stands on the site where the first church in her name once stood. Open daily 7:30am-7pm. Across from the entrance to the sanctuary, a path leads to the heart of the ruins, including the **basilica,** or *ginnasio,* and **agora** (tel. 36 90 23; ruins open daily 9am-1hr. before sunset). The **theater** perches 125m farther down, cut into the hill and boasting an impressive panorama of the surrounding seascape. The **museum** adjacent to the theater has a series of knick-knacks uncovered from the site and drawings illustrating what life was like in the ancient town. Just in front of the museum proceeds the main street of the town, the **decumanus.** Follow it to the right as you exit the museum; it curves past the base of the basilica and leads to the **Casa Romana,** an old Roman house replete with intricate mosaics. All around the site stand bits and pieces of the city's walls as well as the original city gate, which stood on the main road en route to the *santuario.* The **tourist office** in nearby Patti, at P. Marconi, 11 (tel. 24 11 54; fax 24 11 36), has info on performances of **Greek drama** in the ancient theater.

■ Palermo

Though known for many things, Sicily's capital Palermo is above all a crossroads of Mediterranean cultures. First the Phoenecian city "Ziz," later held under Roman and Byzantine sway, Palermo blossomed under Saracen (831-1071) and Norman (1072-1194) rule and emerged as one of Europe's most prominent cities. Hohenstaufen, Angevin, Aragonese, and Bourbon overlords followed. In modern times, Palermo has earned notoriety of a less lofty sort: it is considered to be the cradle of Italian organized crime (for more information see **The Mafia,** page 486). Since the election of Palermo's first publicly avowed anti-mafia mayor in 1993, the city has taken significant steps toward revitalizing its historic district, much of which was destroyed by Allied bombing during World War II. Anti-mafia graffiti and newspapers proclaiming solidarity indicate that much, if not most, of Palermo stands behind these efforts. Slowly rebuilding architectural treasures from the debris, Palermo (pop. 700,000) offers the tourist many of the attractions of a modern metropolis as well as a labyrinthine tour through one of Europe's most dramatic post-war landscapes. Like any big city, Palermo also offers the tourist reason to be cautious, especially at night. Street smarts will come in handy as you explore this fascinating patchwork city.

ORIENTATION AND PRACTICAL INFORMATION

Palermo and its crescent-shaped harbor lie at the end of the fertile **Conca d'Oro** (Golden Conch) basin. To the north, Monte Pellegrino's 610-m limestone mass separates the city from **Mondello,** its beautiful, sandy beach. Palermo's center is blessed with two pairs of parallel main drags. From the station, **Via Roma** runs straight through the historic district to P. Sturzo at the western side of the city center. Parallel to Via Roma, to your left as you exit the station, **Via Maqueda** runs to the Teatro Massimo and P. Verdi, where it becomes **Via R. Settimo** and continues into Palermo's newer section as **Viale della Libertà.** Perpendicular to Via Roma and Via Maqueda, **Corso Vittorio Emanuele** runs the length of the historic district to the sea, neatly dividing the district into two equal halves. From Teatro Massimo, **Via Cavour** heads north to the area around the port.

Behind the grandiose *palazzi* lining the main avenues you'll find a maze of alleys and *piazze*. These tiny, winding streets contrast with the grid of the modern quarter to the west of Via Cavour. The historic district is characterized by open-air markets, innumerable dogs searching for leftovers, and streets that change name seemingly at whim; the newer part of town is home to many of the best restaurants and, at night, better-lit streets.

A Crash Course in Sicilian Street Smarts

Palermo, like any big city, has good neighborhoods and bad neighborhoods; unlike many big cities, it shuts down at night and illumination is at a premium. Knowing where to go and how to get there is essential, especially after 8:30 or 9pm. Whenever possible, stick to the main streets of Via Roma or Corso Vittorio Emanuele: you may feel like the only pedestrian on earth, but the stream of cars and scooters is reassuring and continues late into the night, even on weekdays. The areas around the train station and the port are particularly questionable after shops close in the evening. During the day the city is a different beast entirely, though there are still good reasons to be cautious. Don't carry cameras around your neck or wear flashy jewelry or watches; women should not carry purses. Above all, walk as if you own the town. No one is easier to single out in a sea of power-walking Palermitans than someone looking lost or disoriented.

PRACTICAL INFORMATION

Tourist Office: P. Castelnuovo, 34 (tel. 605 83 51 or 605 81 11), 2km up Via Maqueda (turn right onto V. Maqueda from the station) or take bus #101 or 107 going toward Teatro Politeama; the office is in the building opposite the theater across the park. Open Mon.-Fri. 8am-8pm and Sat. 8am-2pm. English spoken. Detailed info on Palermo (maps and brochures) and other places of interest such as Cefalù, Monreale, and Ustica. The booth at the **airport** (tel. 59 16 98) is open daily 8am-8pm. For info on cultural and civic events, the Assessorato Comunale Turismo can offer toll-free assistance in Italian at (167) 23 41 69.

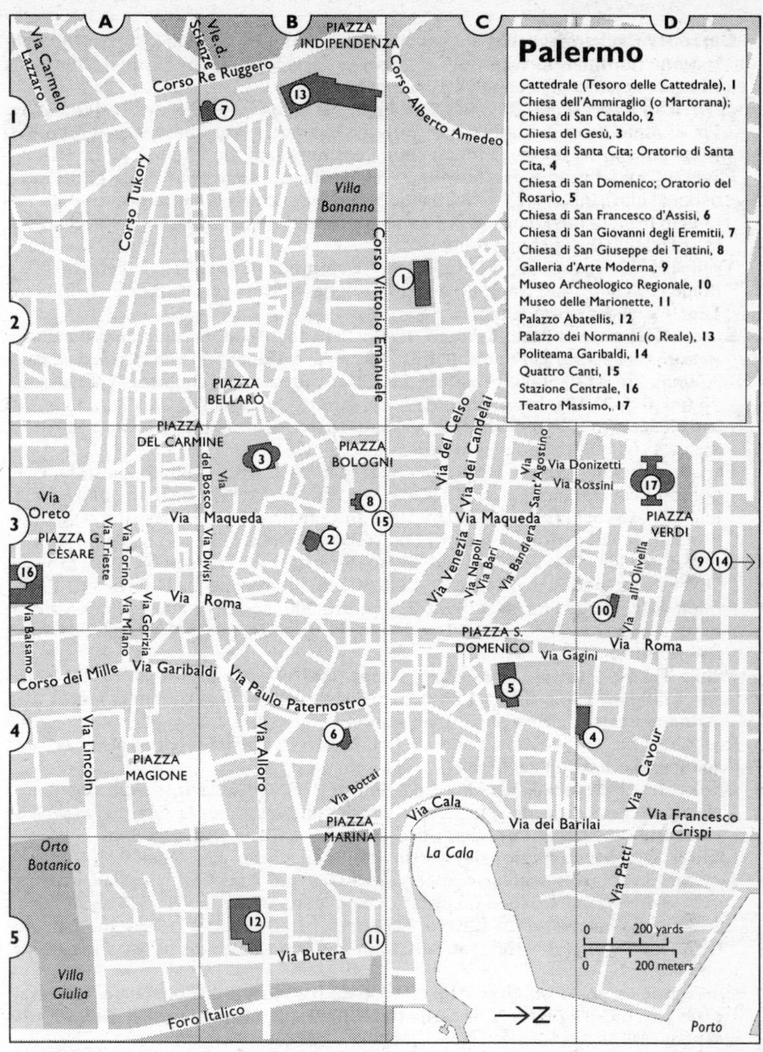

Telephones: Via Lincoln, across from the train station. Open 24hr. Also in P. Ungheria, to the left off V. R. Settimo past Teatro Massimo. Open Mon.-Fri. 8am-1pm and 4-8pm, Sat. 8:30am-noon.

Budget Travel: CTS, Via Garzilli, 28/G (tel. 32 57 52). Take Via Maqueda to P. Castelnuovo; go 1 block past P. Castelnuovo on Via Libertà and turn left on Via Carducci. 2 blocks farther you'll hit Via Garzilli; the office is on your right. Harried but efficient. Open Mon.-Fri. 9am-1pm and 4-8pm, Sat. 9am-1pm.

Consulate: U.S., Via Re Federico, 18 (tel. 611 00 20), off Viale della Libertà. Take bus #28 from V. della Libertà. Open Mon.-Fri. 8am-12:30pm and 3-5pm. Emergencies only. **U.K.,** Via C. Cavour, 117 (tel. 32 64 12); **Australian** citizens should contact their embassy in Rome (tel. (06) 83 27 21), as should **Canadians** (tel. (06) 440 30 28) and **New Zealanders** (tel. (06) 440 29 28).

Currency Exchange: Banks are generally open Mon.-Fri. 8:20am-1:20pm. The train station "information window" changes cash and American Express Traveler's Cheques at generally bad rates 8am-1pm and 2-8pm.

American Express: G. Ruggieri and Figli, Via E. Amari, 40 (tel. 58 71 44). Follow Via E. Amari from P. Castelnuovo toward the water. Very busy. Open Mon.-Fri. 9am-1pm and 4-7:30pm, Sat. 9am-1pm. Regarding card theft: tel. (06) 722 82.

Flights: Cinisi-Punta Raisi (tel. 601 93 33 for domestic info; tel. 702 01 11 for international info), 20km west of Palermo. Public buses connect the airport to P. R. Settimo in front of the Politeama 5:30am-11pm (every 30min., L4500). Taxis charge at least L60,000 for the same route.

Trains: P. Césare (tel. 616 18 06), on the eastern side of town. To: Milan (L86,000); Rome (L68,900); and Naples (L54,600). **Luggage Storage:** At track #7. L5000 for 12hr. Open daily 6am-10pm.

Buses: Cuffaro, Via Paolo Balsamo, 13 (tel. 616 15 10), to the right as you exit the station, runs to Agrigento (Mon.-Sat. 7 per day, 5:45am-8pm, Sun. 3 per day, 8am-3:30pm, 2hr., L10,5000, roundtrip L17,000). **Autoservizi Segesta,** Via Balsamo, 26 (tel. 616 79 19), has over 20 daily departures direct to Trapani (2hr., L11,700) and Milazzo (L11,500). **SAIS,** Via Balsamo, 16 (tel. 616 60 28). To Catania (20 daily, 2½hr., L16,000), continuing to Syracuse (L4000 more).

Ferries: Tirrenia (tel. 33 33 00), in Calata Marinai d'Italia within the port. Entry to port off Via Francesco Crispi. To Naples mid-July to mid-Sept. at 10pm; mid-Sept. to mid-July at 8pm (11hr., L53,600-69,100), and a hydrofoil (1 per day, 4hr., L96,000). To Cagliari Sat. at 7pm (14hr., L42,000-60,000). Open Mon.-Sat. 8:30am-1pm and 2:15-8pm, Sun. 9am-11:45pm and 3-8pm. **Siremar,** Via Francesco Crispi, 118 (tel. 58 24 03). Open 8:30am-1pm and 4-6:30pm. Siremar has daily ferries to Ustica (Mon.-Sat. at 9am, Sun. at 8:15am, 2½hr., L18,500) and hydrofoils 3 times daily in July and Aug. (at 10:30am, 3:30, and 7pm, 1¼hr., L28,700). **SNAV** (tel. 58 65 33) also runs ferries.

Public Transportation: orange **City Buses (AMAT),** Via A. Borrelli, 14 (tel. 32 13 33). L1500 for a 1-hr. ticket, L5000 for a 1-day pass. Buy tickets from *tabacchi*. The main terminal is in front of the train station.

Lost and Found: Questura centrale (tel. 21 01 11). The train station also has a lost and found office (tel. 603 32 79).

Bookstore: Feltrinelli, Via Maqueda, 395 (tel. 58 77 85), across from the Teatro Massimo. Stocks a wide selection of classics and mysteries in English, as well as yours truly and numerous other travel guides. Open Mon.-Sat. 9am-8pm.

Library: Biblioteca Regionale, Corso Vittorio Emanuele, 429. Open 9am-7pm.

Gay and Lesbian Resource Center: Arci-Gay and **Arci-Lesbica,** Via Genova, 7 (tel. 33 56 88). Information on events. Open Mon., Wed., and Fri. 5-7:30pm.

Late-Night Pharmacy: Lo Cascio, Via Roma, 1 (tel. 616 21 17), near the train station. Open Mon.-Fri. 24hr., Sat.-Sun. 8pm-9am. Consult tourist office for seasonal openings.

Emergencies: tel. 113. **First Aid:** tel. 666 22 01. **Hospital: Policlinico Universitario** (tel. 655 37 27), or **Villa Sofia** (tel. 780 81 11), near the station. **Road Assistance:** 116.

Police: tel. 112.

Post Office: Via Roma, 322 (tel. 160 or 695 91 11), by the Museo Archeologico, 2 blocks from Via Cavour. Open Mon.-Sat. 8:15am-7:30pm. *Fermo posta* at window #15 or 16. **Postal Code:** 90100.

Telephone Code: 091.

ACCOMMODATIONS AND CAMPING

Finding a decent and inexpensive place to stay is a breeze. A vast array of *alberghi* blesses **Via Roma** and **Via Maqueda** (look up for the signs). After dark, women especially should avoid the eastern part of town by the train station.

Hotel Cortese, Via Scarparelli, 16 (tel. 33 17 22). From the train station, walk 10min. down Via Maqueda to Via dell'Universita; look for the sign to the left. Turn left and go another 200m. Probably the nicest hotel in its price range despite its not-so-safe location. Impeccable, modern rooms with new furniture. Huge market right next door. Singles L25,000, with shower L35,000. Doubles L45,000, with shower L55,000. All rooms with TV. Half- or full-pension available. V, MC, AmEx.

Hotel Luigi, Salita S. Caterina, 1 (tel. 58 50 85). Incredible location on P. Praetoria (some rooms look out on the Fountain of Shame). Simple rooms are on a dark hallway, but well lit Via Maqueda and Corso Vittorio Emanuele outside make up for it. Singles L25,000, with bath L40,000. Doubles L50,000, with bath L60,000.

Albergo Castiglia, Via Gorizia, 8 (tel./fax 617 23 41), the 3rd right off Via Roma when coming from the train station. Simple, clean, and well-lit. Great location near station. A steal at L32,000 for a single and L55,000 for a double with your *Let's Go Italy 1997*.

Hotel Lampedusa (Attinasi), Via Roma, 111 (tel./fax 617 14 09 or tel. 616 68 81). Sleek, renovated rooms for great prices right on the main drag. Singles L40,000. Doubles L60,000, extra bed L82,000. All rooms with bath, TV, and phone. Communal terrace upstairs has a wonderful view of the surrounding historic district.

Petit Hotel, Via Principe di Belmonte, 84 (tel. 32 36 16), to the left off Via Roma 3 blocks after Via Cavour as you head from the station. Quiet and clean, in a relatively safe neighborhood crowded with posh *caffè*. The gracious hostess has even been known to throw a few of your whites in with her sheets. Singles L35,000, with shower L45,000. Doubles L60,000, with shower L65,000. AmEx.

Albergo Cavour, Via Manzoni, 11 (tel. 616 27 59), on the 5th floor. From P. G. Césare in front of the station, hang a right on Via Lincoln; Via Manzoni is the first street on your left. Large rooms, classic wood-paneled elevator. Singles L35,000. Doubles L45,000, with nice bathrooms L55,000. Showers L3000.

Hotel Ariston, Via M. Stabile, 139 (tel. 33 24 34), in the busy part of town far from the station. Take Via Roma 3 blocks past Via Cavour, or take bus #122 and get off before Via E. Amari. Spotless modern rooms overlook a small courtyard. Singles L32,000, with bath L42,000. Doubles (all with TV) L45,000, with bath L55,000.

Albergo Letizia, Via Bottai, 30 (tel. 58 91 10). From Via Roma head toward the water on Corso Vittorio Emanuele; Via Bottai is the 8th street on your right, just before the entrance to P. Marina. Spacious rooms with high ceilings, in a neighborhood with well populated streets near the Foro Italico along the sea. Singles L38,000, with shower L50,000. Doubles L65,000, with shower L75,000. Extra bed 35% more.

Camping: Trinacria, Via Barcarello, 25 (tel. 53 05 90), at Sferracavallo by the sea. Take bus #101 to Gasperi from Teatro Politeama, then #628 to Sferracavallo; look for the start of the Lido. The campsite is across the road. In July, L6500 per person, L6500 per tent; in August, L7000 per person, L8000 per tent. Also at Sferracavallo is **Campeggio dell'Ulivo,** Via Pegaso (tel. 53 30 21). Get off bus #628 at Via del Mandarino; the 3rd street up is Via Pegaso. L9000 per person, tent included.

FOOD

Palermo is famous for its *pasta con le sarde* (with sardines and fennel) and *rigatoni alla palermitana* (with a sauce of meat and peas). The most popular seafood is swordfish, either plain *(pesce spada),* rolled and stuffed *(involtini di pesce spada),* or rolled smaller with a toothpick stuck in *(spiedini di pesce spada).* Eggplant comes in every shade of purple, in forms from slender to stout. At certain stands in the markets you can get octopus simmered to order (snack portion about L1500). Also try *pane con panelle,* tasty fried balls of chick pea flour sliced and sandwiched. The pinnacle of local cuisine is *spaghetti al broccoli affogati alla palermitana,* spaghetti combined with spicy fried broccoli. *Arancini,* rice, pea, and meat balls, is also a Sicilian delicacy. For dessert, Sicily claims to have invented *cassata* (a sweeter-than-sugar ricotta pastry), discovered *paste con gelo di melone* (pastries with watermelon-paste filling), and perfected *gelato*. You be the judge about the last claim.

The **STANDA** supermarket has outlets at Viale della Libertà, 30 (tel. 33 16 21), in the northern end of town past P. Castelnuovo at Via R. Séttimo, 18/22 (tel. 58 60 19), and on Via Roma, 59 (tel. 616 90 43). All three open daily 9am-1pm and 4-8pm. Closed Mon. mornings and Wed. afternoons. For most provisions, you're better off at the three huge daily **open-air markets,** all open Mon.-Fri. 8am-2pm: **Ballarò,** off Via

Maqueda to your left a few blocks from the train station; **Vucciria,** a block north of Via Roma just past Corso Vittorio Emanuele; and **Capo,** near Teatro Massimo.

Hostaria al Duar, Via Ammiraglio Gravina, 31 (tel. 32 95 60), off Via Roma 3 blocks north toward the port. Award-winning Italian and North African fare. Experience Tunisia's finest with the *Completo Tunisio* (L15,000, drink and cover included). A la carte *secondi* from L3500. On the Italian side of the menu, *primi* from L6000, *secondi* from L10,000. Open Tues.-Sun. 1-3pm and 7pm-midnight.

Il Gastone, Via Mariano Stabile, 134/A (tel. 611 28 21). Take a break from Palermo's hustle and bustle inside this quiet *pizzeria/ristorante* off Via Roma, 2 blocks after Via Cavour heading away from the station. Look for the sign with the dapper gentleman. Watch through a window in the back as they make your pizza (from L6000; pizzas served only at dinner). *Primi* from L6500, *secondi* from L7000. Mouthwatering *bucatini amatriciana* (L75000) in a sauce of tomatoes, onions, and prosciutto. Open Sat.-Thurs. noon-3pm and 7pm-midnight.

Antica Focacceria S. Francesco, Via Alessandra Paternostro, 58 (tel. 32 02 64), off Corso Vittorio Emanuele across from the Church of S. Francesco. A 161-year-old pizzeria: dark wood, cast iron, and aged cacophony. Pizza about L3000 per slice, made in front of you in the antique oven. Superb *rollata,* bread rolled around spinach, prosciutto, and *cacciacavallo* cheese, L3500. *Panelle* to die for, L3000. Open Tues.-Fri. 9:30am-10pm, Sat.-Sun. 9:30am-midnight.

Osteria Lo Bianco, Via E. Amari, 104 (tel. 58 58 16), off Via Roma as you head toward the port. Local crowds wipe the sweat from their brows between each delectable bite at this 90-year-old Palermo custom. If you're lucky, they'll have some *pesce spada or zuppa di cozze*. Sample local wines from the barrels perched safely overhead (L3000 per liter). Open Mon.-Sat. noon-3pm and 7-11pm.

Trattoria da Pino, Via Spezio, 6, on P. Sturzo at the other end of Via Roma from the station. Palermo's best-kept budget secret, this is an oasis of simple, delectable Sicilian fare. Menu changes daily to accommodate the day's catch. A meal of *spaghetti con le sarde* (incredible) and *pesce spade arroste* (possibly the best on the island) comes to about L17,000 with wine. Open daily noon-3:30pm and 8-11pm.

Il Mirto e la Rosa, Via Principe di Granatelli, 30 (tel. 32 43 53). Upscale vegetarian fare amid cathedral-like arches and thirtysomething Palermitans. The one restaurant in Palermo where vegans won't have to explain twice. The *primi* (from L6000) are the best bargains—the portions are huge. Try *fettuccine gustosella,* in an aromatic sauce of tomatoes, pine nuts, peppers, garlic, and basil. *Secondi* (from L6000) are mostly veggie imitations of traditional favorites, and they also have fish. Pizza from L6000. *Menù* L20,000, wine included. Lunch *menù* L14,000 *(primo* and *secondo)*. Cover for dinner L2500. Open 12:30-3pm and 8-11pm.

Trattoria il Crudo e il Cotto, P. Marina, 45/A (tel. 616 92 61). Palermo's most affordable outdoor dining in a neighborhood close to the *Foro Italico*. Tempting specials like *papardelle con feta* (L7000) or tuna with mint (L15,000) on top of a more modestly priced permanent menu (*primi* from L6000, *secondi* from L8000). Delicious *farfalle verdissime,* spinach bowtie pasta in a potent spinach sauce, L7000. Veggie burger L8000. Open Wed.-Mon. 12:30-3pm and 8-11pm or whenever customers roll away from their tables into the sultry Palmeritan night.

So you've finished dinner and you couldn't eat another bite? Palermo's not done with you yet: *gelaterie* and *pasticcerie* are waiting in the shadows to pounce. Along the *Foro Italico,* an amusement park/seashore strip at the end of Corso Vittorio Emmanuele, **da Ilardo** dishes out L2000 cones and L2500 *brioscie* (soft buns filled with gelato) until 2am. Near the station, **da Ciccio,** Corso dei Mille, 73 (tel. 616 15 37), will do the same for you without the long walk to get there. Make a left from Via Balsamo after the bus ticket offices. More dedicated stomachs should convince their owners to hop on a bus to the Lido at **Mondello** (take bus #806 from Teatro Politeama). **L'Antico Chiosco** draws Palermitans and beach bums alike to sample its mouthwatering *gelato* (L2000 per cone or *brioscia*), *latte di mandorlo* (almond milk, L1500), *cassata* to write home about, and *gelo di melone* in various tantalizing forms (stuffed in a bun, L2000). A final *nota bene* about Palermitan food: those tempted by the candy vendors outside the Teatro Massimo may find themselves picking pieces of tenacious, sun-sealed, plastic *torrone* wrappers out of their teeth.

SIGHTS

Its ancient glory followed by seven centuries of neglect and then heavy bombing during World War II, Palermo is an incongruous mix of the splendid and the shabby. The bizarre sight of Palermo's half-crumbled, soot-blackened 16th-century *palazzi* startles visitors accustomed to the cleaner historic districts of northern Italy. In the past several years, however, efforts have slowly begun to clean, rebuild, and reopen structures like the magnificent Teatro Massimo, closed for over 20 years due to water damage and mafia-induced lethargy. Peek into random courtyards on your path to find the *cortili* for which the city is famous. For a glimpse of Palermo's ravaged splendor, climb the red marble staircase to the top floor of Via Maqueda, 26 (across from the Orfeo cinema).

From Quattro Canti to San Giovanni degli Eremiti

The intersection of Corso Vittorio Emanuele and Via Maqueda forms the **Quattro Canti,** where each corner celebrates a season, a king of Spain, and one of the city's patron saints. The Canti date from the early 17th century, when Sicily was under Spanish rule. Next to the statue of Philip III in the Quattro Canti, the dismal gray façade of the **Church of San Giuseppe dei Teatini** (1612) belies its "as much as you can put on the walls without tearing them down" Baroque interior. Don't miss such details as the upside-down angels supporting the fonts at the entrance or the frieze of children playing musical instruments on the wall of the south transept.

Farther down Via Maqueda and to the left as you approach the station, **Piazza Bellini** embraces the **Church of San Cataldo** (1154), a Norman building whose red domes and arches give it the air of a mosque. **La Martorana,** or, more properly, **Santa Maria dell'Ammiraglio** (built for an admiral of the Norman king Roger II), shares San Cataldo's leafy platform. Baroque additions partially conceal its 12th-century structure. The Byzantine mosaics inside are 12th-century equivalents of celebrity photos: here's Roger I with Jesus, there's George the Admiral with the Mother of God. (Both open Mon.-Sat. 8am-1pm and 3:30-6:30pm, Sun. 8am-1pm.)

To the right across Via Maqueda from P. Bellini, **Via Ponticello** winds through a crowded neighborhood to the **Chiesa del Gesù** (or Casa Professa, built 1363-1564). Look for its green mosaic dome. The stucco conceals a dazzling multicolored marble interior and an almost Dalí-like depiction of the Last Judgment. Standing in Il Gesù's courtyard, you can see the effects of American bombing during World War II. The **Quartiere dell'Albergheria,** the inner core of the city, never quite recovered from the war's destruction—as evinced by the numerous shattered buildings, including the one next to the church.

Farther along Via Ponticello, one of Palermo's three main open-air **markets** extends from **Piazza Ballarò** to the **Church of the Carmine.** This 17th-century *chiesa* has a mosaic dome that is all emerald fans and gold swirls—it looks like the spawn of a Ming vase and a parlor room teacup. The area around the church, replete with narrow streets and hidden gardens, warrants exploration.

Venturing from the Quattro Canti onto **Corso Vittorio Emanuele,** heading away from the harbor, you will pass the dilapidated *palazzi* of the **Piazza Bologni** to the left before confronting the striking exuberance of Palermo's **cattedrale** up on the right. Begun by the Normans in 1185, it absorbed elements of every architectural style from the 13th through 18th centuries, though the most striking exterior elements are the original Norman towers and the three-apsed eastern side. Inside, the chapels on the left contain six royal tombs (four canopied and two set in the wall) of Norman kings and Hohenstaufen emperors dating from the 12th to 14th centuries. The *tesoro* (treasury) to the right of the apse contains episcopal rings, chalices, croziers, and a dazzling array of sacerdotal vestments from the 16th and 17th centuries. (Open daily 7am-noon and 4pm-6pm. L1000 to see the treasury, crypts, and chiseled *sarcophagi* hosting various saints and city patrons.) The *cattedrale* is connected by the flying buttresses to the former Archbishop's palace (1460).

Set behind a tropical garden near the church on Corso Emanuele, the **Palazzo dei Normanni** (entrance in back) contains the **Cappella Palatina** (1132-40). Built by Roger II, it exhibits a fantastic fusion of styles—a carved wooden stalactite ceiling, a cycle of golden Byzantine mosaics rivaled only by those of Ravenna and Istanbul, and marble walls with geometric designs. In the apse, an enormous Christ looms above a 19th-century mosaic of the Virgin. Before leaving, visit the **Sala di Ruggero** (King Roger's Hall) one floor above the Palatina, a room adorned with mosaics in flora and fauna motifs. Because the *palazzo* is now the seat of the Sicilian Parliament, you must wait at the desk for an escort. (Palace open Mon. and Fri.-Sat. 9am-noon unless Parliament is in session. Chapel open Mon.-Fri. 9am-noon and 3-5pm, Sat. 9am-noon, Sun. 9-10am and noon-1pm.)

Perhaps the most romantic spot in Palermo is the garden and cloister of the **Church of San Giovanni degli Eremiti** (St. John of the Hermits), at Via dei Benedettini, 3. As you exit the Cappella Palatina, follow the castle walls to the right to P. della Pinta; V. dei Benedettini is to the right. To get there from the station, take bus #122 and get off before P. Independenza. With courtyard fountains and bougainvillea vines, this paradise is furnished with gazebos and stone archways. Built in 1132 by fanciful Arab architects, the church is topped by pink domes. Beside the church a tropical garden shades 13th-century cloisters. (Open Mon. and Wed. 3-6pm, Tues. and Thurs.-Sun. 9am-1pm.).

From the Church of San Francesco to the Villa Giulia

The churches and palaces east of Via Roma toward the old port (La Cala) lie in a maze of tiny, serpentine streets. The 13th-century **Church of San Francesco d'Assisi** on Via Paternostro (off Corso Vittorio Emanuele about five blocks from Via Roma and to the right as you head to the harbor) features an intricate rose window and a zigzag design common to many churches in the area. The restored Gothic interior was augmented by side chapels in the 14th and 15th centuries and adorned with Renaissance and Baroque accessories. (Open daily 7:30-10:45am and 4-6pm.)

Master of stucco Giacomo Serpotta (1656-1732) decorated the **Oratory of San Lorenzo,** just a few doors down Via Imacolatella (to the left as you face the church of San Francesco). This monochrome stucco has a hard finish that looks like carved stone when viewed from afar. Caravaggio's last known work, *The Nativity* (1609), was stolen from the altar in 1969—hence the seven locks on the oratory door. The inlaid mother-of-pearl benches are too impressive to sit on. (Open erratically; the oratory is maintained by an elderly neighbor in her spare time. To enter, ring at #5 and be prepared to make a L3000 *offerta.*)

The **Giardino Garibaldi,** a park several blocks further toward the sea on Corso Vittorio Emanuele, is replete with royal palms, fig trees, and giant banyans. The two fig trees are the oldest and most distinctive: they grow wildly, each with over 100 separate trunks that fuse into larger arteries. Follow signs from P. Marina to the **Museo Internazionale delle Marionette,** Via Butera, 1 (tel. 32 80 60), which showcases Sicily's proud tradition of puppetry as well as collections of puppets from India, England, and the Congo. (Open Mon.-Fri. 9am-1pm and 4-7pm, Sat. 9am-1pm. Puppet shows on request. Admission L5000, students L2000.) Signs in P. Marina also point toward the part-Gothic, part-Renaissance **Palazzo Abatellis** (1495), housing one of

The Fountain of Shame

Piazza Pretoria, (up Via Maqueda from the station) features a 16th-century fountain originally intended for a Florentine *villa.* The fountain features, among other unpublishable things, **nude men and women half-heartedly attempting to cover their genitalia** and (gasp!) eyeing one another suggestively. The *Palermitani* were so shocked when it was unveiled that they nicknamed the sculpture "the fountain of shame." Decide for yourself whether or not you can handle it.

Sicily's superb regional galleries. Upstairs, an entire room is devoted to painter Antonello da Messina (1430-1479), Sicily's number-one son. Works by Leandro Bassano (1557-1622), Vincenzo da Pavia, and Leonardo Macaluss round out the collection. (Open Mon.-Sat. 9am-1:30pm, Tues. and Thurs. 9am-1:30pm and 3-5:30pm, Sun. and holidays 9am-12:30pm. Admission L2000.)

Down Foro Italico to the east is an **amusement park** that opens every day in the late afternoon when the Sicilian sun has cooled enough. Past the park, on Foro Umberto I along the harbor, **Villa Giulia** has an eclectic garden that harbors a little something for everyone: band shells, playgrounds, menageries, sculpture, floral gardens, and cenotaphs. (Garden open Mon.-Fri. 9am-6pm, Sat.-Sun. 9am-1pm.)

From the Church of San Matteo to the Museo Archeologico

Most of Palermo's other noteworthy sights lie along **Via Roma** north of Corso Vittorio Emanuele as you walk away from the station. The Baroque **Church of San Matteo** (on Corso Vittorio Emanuele) conceals an ornate marble interior and four statues by Serpotta in the pilasters of the dome. (Open daily 8am-noon and 4-7pm.) On Via Roma to the right, just a block past its intersection with Corso Vittorio Emanuele, is the 12th-century **Church of Sant'Antonio,** revamped in the 14th and 19th centuries. You can see the original structure in the square frame and the columns of the chancel. (Open Mon.-Sat. 8am-noon and 6:30-8:15pm, Sun. 7:30am-1pm.) Just past the intersection, on Via Vucciría off Corso Vittorio Emanuele, is another **market.** Dozens of varieties of seafood, fruits, and vegetables, including six-foot zucchini, tantalize the palate and the eye. (Open Mon.-Tues. and Thurs.-Sun. 8am-8pm.)

The **Church of San Domenico** fronts the *piazza* of the same name on Via Roma (to the right with the station behind you). Rebuilt in 1640, the church is Sicily's Pantheon, containing tombs of distinguished citizens. The **Oratory of the Rosary,** behind San Domenico on Via dei Bambinai (ring at #16), houses a famous altarpiece by Van Dyck, *Madonna of the Rosary with St. Dominique and the Patroness of Palermo* (1628). (Both church and oratory open daily 7:30am-noon.)

Via Meli extends from P. San Domenico and leads—surprise!—to P. Meli. By bearing left on Via dei Bambinai, through P. Valverde and onto Via Squarcialupo, you'll find the **Church of Santa Cita** to your left on V. Valverde. The exterior was damaged during the war, but a rose window remains, lighting the interior with baroque color and texture. The marble arches on the east wall of the choir and the sarcophagus in the second chapel on the left remain from the original Renaissance structure. The **Oratory of Santa Cita,** behind the church (ring at Via Valverde, 3), encloses Serpotta's *Virtues,* reliefs of New Testament scenes, and, on the short wall near the entrance, a depiction of the Battle of Lepanto, where Cervantes lost a hand. (Both church and oratory open daily 4-5:30pm.)

The **Museo Archeologico Regionale** awaits you at P. Olivella, 4 (tel. 662 02 20; fax 611 07 40), left on Via Bara two blocks before Via Roma hits Via Cavour as you head away from the station. This museum occupies a 17th-century convent and displays a remarkable collection in two spectacular courtyards. In the bronze collection is the Greek *Ram of Syracuse* (3rd century BC), renowned for its realism. (Open Mon.-Sat. 9am-2pm, Tues. and Fri. 9am-2pm and 3-6:30pm, Sun. and holidays 9am-1pm. Admission L2000.)

Other Sights

Across Via Maqueda from the Archaeological Museum sits the **Teatro Massimo.** Constructed from 1875 to 1897 in a robust Neoclassical style, the theater is the largest indoor stage in Europe after the Paris Opera House. The Massimo has been undergoing reconstruction since 1974, but the interior is scheduled to reopen in 1997. The exiled opera and symphony perform in the **Politeama Garibaldi** (farther up Via Maqueda, which becomes Via Ruggero Settima), a huge circular theater built in 1874. The entrance is a triumphal arch crowned by a bronze chariot and four horses. The theater also houses the **Galleria d'Arte Moderna.** (Theater performances Jan.-late May and mid-July to Aug. Admission from L30,000. Gallery open Tues.-Sun. 9am-1pm,

Wed. 9am-1pm and 3:30-5:30pm. Admission L5000.) A new arrival to Palermo's cultural scene is the **Lo Spasimo theater** (tel. 616 14 86), off Via Abrano Lincoln, to your left heading toward the port, within the walls of the old city. The space was once a convent and church of the same name; it is now snazzily renovated and home to numerous plays, classical music concerts, and art shows. Ask for a list of concerts and plays at the tourist office. (Open daily 7am-midnight.)

The **Convento dei Cappuccini,** on Via Cappuccini (tel. 21 21 77), welcomes amateur paleontologists and the morbidly fascinated into its **catacombs.** 8000 bodies—some mummified and intact, all sorted by profession—inhabit lengthy subterranean corridors. The baby girl is preserved so well that she looks alive. Take bus #109 from Stazione Centrale to P. Indipendenza, and walk the rest of the way; alternatively, take bus #124 from Politeama. (Open daily 9am-noon and 3-5pm; tours offered intermittently by friars. Free, but *offerta* expected.)

Monte Pellegrino, an isolated mass of limestone rising from the sea, is Palermo's principal natural landmark, separating the city from the beach at Mondello. Near its summit, the **Santuario di Santa Rosalia** marks the site where Rosalia, a young Norman princess, sought ascetic seclusion. Her bones were discovered in 1624 and brought to Palermo, where they vanquished a raging plague. The present sanctuary stands over the cave where she performed her ablutions; its trickling waters are said to have miraculous powers. The summit of Monte Pellegrino (a 30-min. climb from the sanctuary) offers a gorgeous view of Palermo, Conca d'Oro, and, on a clear day, the Lipari Islands and Mount Etna. Take bus #812 from Politeama.

ENTERTAINMENT

Palermo shuts down at night, except in a few select places. When the weather is warm, families and couples hang out on Foro Italico along the sea, by the amusement park. Weekend nights bring crowds of young people mobbing Corso Vittorio Emanuele as they stroll from one street musician to the next. At midnight, select restaurants dish out free pasta. Many bars are hard to find in the back streets (and even harder to find your way back from), but you might give **Avenida** a try after 10:30 or 11pm. The bar is on Via Venezia, between V. Roma and V. Maqueda, near C. Emanuele, and is open until 2 or 3am. **Di Martino,** another favorite, comes alive after 10pm. It's on Via Mazzini, off Viale della Libertà one block before Teatro Politeama heading toward the station.

The major summer event in Palermo takes place at the **Teatro di Verdura Villa Castelnuovo.** From the first week of July through the first week of August, an international festival of ballet, jazz, and classical music jams in this open-air seaside theater. For tickets and information, contact the **Politeama Garibaldi** (tel. 605 33 15), P. Ruggero Séttimo, across from the tourist office. Open Tues.-Sat. 10am-1pm and 5-7pm, Sun. 10am-1pm. The **Festa di Santa Rosalia,** held July 10-15, gives the city an excuse to shed its usual sobriety and binge on music and merriment.

Palermo resorts to two other beaches along with the Lido at Mondello. **Sferracavallo** is a roomier but rockier beach (take bus #101 or 107 from Politeama to P. de Gasperri, then #628 to the beach), while **Addaura** entertains the young Palermitan jet-set crowd in summer (bus #833 from P. Sturzo).

For more in-depth information on cultural events and nightlife, pick up a copy of *Un Mese a Palermo,* a monthly brochure in Italian available at any APT office.

■ Near Palermo

MONREALE

About 10km southwest of Palermo lies the golden city of **Monreale** and its magnificent Norman-Saracen **duomo,** Santa Maria La Nuova (c. 1174). At the time of its construction this cathedral was the biggest in Europe. The church's incredible **medieval mosaics** supposedly inspired Jacques Cartier to name his Canadian city Montreal. One hundred thirty panels depict the Old and New Testaments against a brilliant gold background, over which a massive Christ Pantocrator (Ruler of All) presides. To read this brilliant Bible, start with Creation at the upper right-hand corner of the main chapel and work back to the present under Christ Pantocrator, where Virgin and Child sit with attendant angels (L500 to light up mosaics). The **tesoro** (treasury), off the transept, sits in one of the most raucously Rococo chapels in Italy (admission L2500). Outside, circle around to see the Arab-style inlay behind the apse and a spectacular view of the *Conca d'Oro* below. Then step in to see the intricate arches and multicolored inlay of the **cloister,** renowned for the capitals of its colonnade (228 paired columns in all, each one unique). Considered to be the richest collection of Sicilian sculpture anywhere, the capitals run the gamut of styles: Greco-Roman, Saracen, Norman, Romanesque, Gothic, and various combinations thereof. In the corner by the lesser colonnade and its fountain, look for the capital depicting William II offering the Cathedral of Monreale to the Virgin. Be sure to climb up to the **roof** (access from inside the cathedral; look for the sign) and look down on the central apse. Two doors down from the cloister is the entrance to a series of quiet **gardens** that look out over Palermo and its sprawling expanse. Cathedral open daily 8am-noon and 3:30-6pm. Cloister open July-Sept. Mon., Wed., and Fri. 9am-1pm and 3-6pm, Tues., Thurs., and Sat. 9am-1pm, Sun. 9am-12:30pm; Oct.-June ask at cathedral. Admission to cloister L2000, to roof L2000.

Buses #389 and 309 leave for Monreale from Palermo's P. Indipendenza (bus #109 runs from the station to P. Indipendenza), and take you directly to P. V. Emanuele. When you hop off the bus, the *duomo* is to the right; Via Roma runs uphill to the right. **Tourist information** (tel. 656 45 70) resides in the building to the left of the church. Surrounding the *duomo* in the *piazza* lies an array of pizzerias, pastry shops, and restaurants. Take your pick, then sit and observe the festivities; the locals celebrate as many as three weddings in the *duomo* per day.

USTICA

The volcanic island of **Ustica** lies within reach of Palermo, 36 miles off the coast. Settled first by the Phoenicians, then by pirates and exiled convicts, this marine reserve features prime snorkeling and grotto-hopping opportunities. Inquire at the Palermo tourist office for further details. **Siremar** runs ferries and hydrofoils out to the island (see Palermo **Orientation and Practical Information: Ferries,** p. 508).

CORLEONE

Nestled in a fertile valley surrounded by rough-hewn cliffs, the sleepy town of Corleone lies 35km south of Palermo. Though well-known to fans of *The Godfather* as the hometown of the title character, Corleone is inclined to downplay this dubious claim to fame. Aside from ads for "Don Corleone bitters," there is little to remind visitors of the mafia. Instead, Corleone features enchanting 14th-century churches and Arab-Norman mosques, beautiful views of the surrounding countryside, and an eclectic collection of artifacts at the **Civic Museum,** Via Orfanotrofio, 4 (tel. (091) 846 49 07), including the oldest set of Greek inscriptions in Sicily. Visit, if only to experience the museum's funky late 18th-century courtyard. Open Mon., Wed., and Fri.-Sun. 8am-2pm, Tues. and Thurs. 8am-2pm and 3:30-7pm. Free. Next to the museum and by **Piazza Garibaldi,** the town's **14th-century church** boasts an altarpiece by Pietro Novelli. Not far away, the **Saracen Tower** (also known as "Soprano castle") stands dramatically on a cliff overlooking the town.

Gallo and **AST buses** run from Palermo (15 per day Mon.-Sat. 6:15am-7:15pm; 1¼hr., L5400, L9100 roundtrip, last return to Palermo 5:10pm). Gallo also runs buses from Sciacca (2 per day Mon.-Sat. 5:50am and noon; 3hr., L7500, L12,700 roundtrip, last return 1:25pm). Should you feel like staying in Corleone, the sole budget hotel is the attractive **Hotel Belvedere** (tel. 846 40 00). The spotless rooms in this three-star establishment are equipped with bath, TV, and telephone. Singles L35,000. Doubles L70,000. Triples L100,000. V, MC, AmEx. The hotel's restaurant, **A Giarra** (tel. 846 49 64), is also one of a limited selection and is extremely affordable. *Primi* from

L3500, *secondi* from L7500. The *pesce spada* is a bargain at L12,000 and far better than what you'll find in many seaside towns. An endless parade of freebies comes with your meal, including *bruschetta* and a neon-blue *aperitif.* The restaurant is open Tues.-Sun. 7:30pm-midnight. To get to the hotel, ask to be let off there on your way from Palermo or Sciacca. The hotel is then about a 10-min. walk from town. You can also get to the hotel by taking the tiny orange city bus (L700) from the Gallo/AST bus stop in front of Bar Bentivegna in town. There's an awesome **map** of the city posted on the gate to the *ville comunale* across the street from the bar.

THE WESTERN COAST

Trapani

Trapani, reputed to be "Sicily's friendliest city," is not your typical Italian town. Situated on a peninsula on the northwestern tip of Sicily, it is continually bombarded on all sides by hot North African *scirocco* winds. In addition, the cultural influence of North Africa can be detected in the city's churches and cuisine. Good hotels and convenient transportation make Trapani a desirable base for expeditions to the neighboring Egadi Islands, the beaches of the western coast, the Greek ruins at Segesta, or the breathtaking mountain town of Erice.

FERRIES

Ferries and *aliscafi* (hydrofoils) leave Trapani for the Egadi Islands (Levanzo, Favignana, and Marettimo), Ustica, Pantelleria (an island 20min. off the Tunisian coast), Naples, Lampedusa, Linosa, and Tunisia. All boats leave from the docks across from P. Garibaldi by Via Ammiraglio Staiti, which runs the length of the southern side of the peninsula. Ferry tickets are available from **Siremar,** Via Ammiraglio Staiti, 61/63 (tel. 54 05 15), down the street from the port, or from **Tirrenia** (tel. 218 96) in the same building. More convenient are the ticket offices in front of the hydrofoil/ferry dock: **Siremar** (tel. 277 80), **Ustica** (tel. 271 01), and **Alilauro** (tel. 240 73) all open 30min. before departure times. You can also purchase tickets for these lines from the travel agents along Via A. Staiti. The following departure times are for mid-June through mid-September, and prices are the same on all commercial lines. Keep in mind that the schedules for inter-island ferries can be less than reliable.

Trapani-Favignana: 3 ferries per day, 7am-3:45pm (1-1½hr., L5400). 24 hydrofoils per day (6am-8pm, 25min., L9200).

Trapani-Levanzo: 2 ferries per day, 7am-9:50am (1-1½hr., L5400). 30 hydrofoils per day (7am-9:30pm, 15-30min., L9200).

Trapani-Marettimo: 1 ferry per day at 9:50am (2½hr., L12,000). 9 hydrofoils per day (8:15am-6:25pm, 1hr., L21,000).

Trapani-Pantelleria: 1 ferry per day at midnight (5¾hr., L36,800). 1 hydrofoil **(Ustica line)** Tues., Fri., and Sun. at 8:45am (2½hr., L59,000).

Trapani-Tunis (Tunisia): Ustica hydrofoil Tues., Fri., and Sun., at 8:45am to Pantelleria also goes to Kelibia, Tunisia (3hr., L89,000). **Linea Lauro (Alilauro):** 1 ferry to Tunis at 11pm on Mon. from July to mid-Sept. (9hr., L85,000).

ORIENTATION AND PRACTICAL INFORMATION

Trapani sits on a peninsula, 2hr. west of Palermo by train (L11,700). An express bus makes the trip in the same time, rolling from Via Paolo Balsamo, 26, next to the train station in Palermo, to P. Garibaldi in Trapani, by the port in the old city (L11,000). Trains also run from Agrigento, though less often (about 4 per day, 3½-4hr., L15,200). Buses are more convenient and frequent, running straight from Agrigento to P. Garibaldi and back.

The train station and main bus station are located on the edge of the old city. Crossing **Piazza Umberto** in front of the train station, take **Via Osorio** on the left to **Via XXX Gennaio,** the unofficial border between the old and new towns. Make a right onto **Corso Italia,** which runs straight into the heart of the historic district. Once in **Piazza Sant'Agostino,** with Corso Italia behind you, you will find the tourist office straight ahead and the port to your left.

Tourist Office: Ufficio Informazioni Turistiche (tel. 290 00 or 240 04), at P. Satorno, up Via Torrearsa from the port. Armfuls of handouts on cultural events, as well as train and bus schedules, info on surrounding towns, and an indispensable map of Trapani. English spoken. Open Mon.-Sat. 8am-8pm, Sun. 9am-noon and 8am-8pm in August. **APT main office,** Via S. Francesco d'Assisi (tel. 270 77 or 259 46), supplies in-depth material on the town and region to tour groups.

Currency Exchange: In the train station. Open Mon.-Sat. 7am-noon and 3:30-5:30pm. For better rates but a longer walk, try the banks lining Via Garibaldi. Open 8:10am-1pm.

Flights: V. Florio Airport (tel. 84 12 22), in Birgi en route to Marsala. 16km outside the city. 4 buses per day leave from P. Garibaldi.

Trains: P. Stazione (tel. 280 71 or 280 81). Office open Mon.-Sat. 5:40am-8:20pm and Sun. 5:45am-7:50pm. **Luggage Storage:** L5000 for 12hr. Open 8am-9:30pm.

Buses: AST, Via Virgilio, 20 (tel. 210 21). Buses leave from the main bus station at P. Malta, beside the train station. To Erice (Mon.-Sat. 11 per day, 6:30am-7:30pm, Sun. 5 per day, 9am-7pm; 45min., L2500, roundtrip L4300) and San Vito Lo Capo (Mon.-Sat. 9 per day, 7am-8pm, Sun. 3 per day, 8:30-4:30pm; 1½hr., L4400, roundtrip L7300). **Tarantola** (tel. (0924) 310 20 or 325 98) buses run from P. Garibaldi to Segesta (Mon.-Sat. 6 per day, Sun. 2 per day, L4000, roundtrip L6700).

Public Transportation: SAU, the orange city bus, has its main terminal at P. Vittorio Emanuele (tel. 203 97), near the train station. It can be taken all over the city for L1100. Tickets are available at most *tabacchi.*

Emergencies: tel. 113. **Hospital: Ospedale Sant'Antonio Abate,** Via Cosenza, very far from town (tel. 80 91 11).

Police: Via Virgilio (tel. 113). **Carabinieri:** Via Orlandini, 19 (tel. 271 22).

Post Office: P. Vittorio Veneto (tel. 291 28), at the other end of Via Garibaldi from the fish market. Open Mon.-Fri. 8am-7pm. **Postal Code:** 91100.

Telephone Code: Old town, 0923. For Erice and the new town, 0924.

ACCOMMODATIONS AND CAMPING

Cheap, tidy hotels cluster around the port, in the heart of the old city. Trapani and its neighbor Erice are also blessed with a youth hostel equidistant between the two.

Ostello per la Gioventù (HI), Strada Proviniciale, Trapani-Erice, KM 2 (tel. 55 29 64). While not the handiest or cheapest of hostels, this one offers a peaceful, wooded setting complete with cheery red bunk beds, the scent of evergreen, and kick-ass cappuccino for breakfast. To get there, take SAU bus #23. Get off at Ospedale Villa dei Gerami and follow Via Manzoni away from the city. Take the second right onto Via Trento and then start climbing the hill on Via Sant'Anna. The AST bus to Erice via Via Martogna will drop you at the front door of the hostel (L3600 roundtrip). Unfortunately, there are only 4 buses per day; all the rest of the buses to Erice pass through Valderice instead. 6-person rooms. L19,000 per person. Breakfast included. L14,000 for a second meal of your choice. Curfew midnight, "except in special cases." Breakfast 8:15-8:45am. Lunch 1-1:45pm. Dinner 8-9pm. Closed from 10am-5pm, even for check-in. Space for camping available (no tents provided). Free sheets and showers (but bring your own towel).

Pensione Messina, Corso Vittorio Emanuele, 71 (tel. 211 98), on a Renaissance courtyard just a few blocks from P. S. Agostino. Big rooms, firm beds, pink bathroom. Run by a friendly, slightly rambunctious family. Singles L20,000. Doubles 40,000. Breakfast L3500.

Albergo Moderno, Via Genovese, 20 (tel. 212 47). Head away from P. S. Agostino, turn right off C. Vittorio Emanuele onto Via Roma, and take a left on Via Genovese.

Trapani's oldest hotel. Quiet, musty rooms with a nautical theme. Sedate atmosphere. Singles L28,000, with bath L40,000, with bath and TV L45,000. Doubles L44,000, with bath L60,000. Triples L59,000, with bath L81,000.

Albergo Maccotta, Via degli Argentieri, 4 (tel. 284 18), behind the tourist office. Despite the overly soft beds, beautifully renovated rooms are a great value. Singles L30,000, with bath L40,000. Doubles L50,000, with bath L70,000. V, MC.

Albergo Nuovo Russo, Via Tintori, 4 (tel. 221 66; fax 266 23), off Corso V. Emanuele to the left. Six floors of long carpets, soft armchairs, and African art. You can live it up at a low price in this 3-star hotel, as long as you don't mind not having your own bathroom. All rooms have telephones; free TV upon request. English spoken. Singles L38,000, with bath L63,000. Doubles L70,000, with bath L100,000. A/C L5000. Breakfast L5000. Reserve 1 month ahead for Aug.

Camping: Capo San Vito and Castellamare del Golfo, on the opposite side of the cape, harbor many campgrounds (8 trains run daily to Castellamare). **Near Capo San Vito: Camping La Fata,** Via del Secco, 40 (tel. 97 21 33). Charges L8000 per person, L6500 per small tent, and L12,000 per large tent. **Camping Soleado,** Via della Secca (tel. 97 21 66). Charges L9000 per person, L8000 per small tent, and L10,000 per large tent. Both open year-round. **Near Castellamare del Golfo: Baia di Guidaloca** (tel. 54 12 62); **Nausicaa** (tel. 330 30); and the cheapest, **Ciauli** (tel. 390 49), which charges L7000 per person, L5500 per small tent, L8500 per large tent. The others charge about L1500 more. All open June-Sept.

FOOD

Unlike the hotels, food in Trapani tends not to be cheap. Take your money to the **open-air market** in P. Mercato di Pesce, at the end of Via Torrearsa, and stock up on seafood. This market is such an institution that the *piazza* was named after it. Open Mon.-Sat. 8am-1pm. Pick up essentials at the supermarket **Margherita,** Via San Domenico, 32, between the port and the train station. Open Mon.-Sat. 8am-1:30pm and 5-8pm. Trapani is known for its sardines and its *couscous di pesce*. Also try a *biscotto coi fichi,* the Italian fig-newton; all of the bakeries along Corso V. Emanuele stock them for about L400 each. The **mini-STANDA,** Via Liberta, 12, 3rd floor (tel. 211 14) is next to the open-air market. Open Mon. 4-8pm, Tues.-Sat. 9am-1pm and 4-8pm. Remember that almost everything in Trapani, except churches, closes on Sunday. The most notable exceptions are the *paninerie* and *gelaterie* near the port on P. XVII Novembre, open every night to accommodate Trapani's young and nutritionally challenged.

Pizzeria Calvino, Via Nasi, 71 (tel. 214 64), 1 block off Corso Vittorio Emanuele as you head toward the port. All of Trapani comes here for small take-out pizzas (L6000) before soccer games. Savor *lasagne al forno* (L6000). Cover for sit-down 20%. Open Tues.-Sun. 5:30pm-1am.

Pizza Sport, Via Liberta, 16 (tel. 87 37 51). Come watch the pies fly at this hyper but friendly take-out parlor. Oval and round pizzas (small from L5000, medium from L7000, large from L12,000). Wide selection; the *trapanese,* with anchovies, eggplant, and sausage, is particularly memorable. Open evenings.

Ristorante da Bettina, Via San Francesco d'Assisi, 69 (tel. 200 50), near the port at Via Serisso. A classy, Arab atmosphere with a sometimes-bubbling fountain, large ceiling fan, and soft classical music. Pricey, but worth it. Try their specialty *couscous con pesce* (L9000). *Primi* from L9000, *secondi* from L8000. Vegetarian *secondi* (including a mouthwatering roasted radicchio) from L4000. Delicious crabmeat ravioli L9000. Open Tues.-Sun. 10am-midnight. AmEx.

Trattoria da Salvatore, Via Nunzio Nasi, 19 (tel. 54 65 30), around the corner from Albergo Russo. Good food, but overeager waiters. *Couscous* L6500, *bucatino con sarde* L6000. *Spaghetti al pomodoro* (L5000) to write home about (no, really). Cover L2000. The house wine will clean your teeth, but it's only L1000 for a generous ¼liter. Open Mon.-Sat. noon-3:30pm and 7-11pm. AmEx.

SIGHTS AND ENTERTAINMENT

You can tour most of Trapani's major sights in one fun-filled afternoon. Begin one block off Corso Italia on Via S. Elisabetta, where the Gothic-Renaissance **Church of Santa Maria** displays a beautiful marble canopy sheltering a della Robbia sculpture. Farther up Corso Italia you'll hit P. S. Agostino, which runs right into P. Saturno by way of Via S. Agostino, bringing you to the older, more ornate historic district. Here you'll find the façade of the former **Church of Sant'Agostino** (14th century), with a Gothic portal and rose window. The **Fontana di Saturn,** a triple-tiered fountain supported by sirens, dates from the late 16th century.

Elaborate façades line the main street of the old city, **Corso Vittorio Emanuele II.** At one end, the 17th-century **Palazzo Seratorio** houses temporary art exhibits on its main floor; the **Collegio dei Gesuiti** (1636) contains an 18th-century carved-walnut cupboard; and the **cathedral** displays a striking green-tiled dome and pink stucco walls. Down a small street to the left on Via Giglio, the tiny Baroque **Church of Purgatorio,** Via San Francesco d'Assisi (tel. 213 21), sports free-standing sculpture and a small emerald dome outside and a group of 20 wooden statues inside. This collection, called *I Misteri* (The Mysteries), is carried in a procession around town on Good Friday. Their bearers call out, asking if anyone knows whose they are or what their function is. No one ever does, so they are returned to the church for another year. Their identities have been a mystery for over 600 years. (Church open Tues. 10am-noon, Fri. 10am-noon and 4-7pm.)

Viale Regina Elena runs along the port to **Viale Duca l'Acosta,** where fishermen dry and mend their nets. Trapani was once supported by its tuna market, and these fishermen still practice the old trade. Those willing to get up before dawn can watch the fishermen do their stuff, then continue up to the tip of the city to see the sunrise at the **Torre di Ligny,** which doubles as the **Museo di Preistoria.** (Museum of Prehistory, tel. 223 00. Open 9am-1pm and 4-8pm. Admission L2000.) From the Torre you can wind back through town to Corso Vittorio Emanuele. Take a left onto Via Libertà past the fish market at P. Mercato di Pesce to **Via Garibaldi,** whose cream-colored *palazzi* are rivalled only by those of Corso V. Emanuele.

Farther out in the new quarter lies the **Museo Nazionale Pepoli** (tel. 55 32 69; fax 53 54 44). It's a grueling walk, so instead take **SAU** bus #24, 25, or 30 from P. Vittorio Emanuele, 2 blocks to the right of the train station (L1100). The museum's magnificent baroque staircase leads to a collection of local sculptures and paintings, coral carvings, and folk-art figurines. (Open Tues. and Thurs.-Fri. 9am-1pm and 3-6pm, Wed. and Sat. 9am-1pm, Sun. 9am-12:30pm. Admission L2000, Sun. free.)

Settimana dell'Egadi, in late May, greets the new crop of tourists with music, food, and archaeological tours. Trapani also sponsors an annual festival of opera, operetta, ballet, cabaret, and dance, called the **Luglio Musicale Trapanese** (tel. 214 54; fax 229 34), which attracts well-known Italian artists as well as troupes from abroad. It takes place in an open-air theater at Villa Margherita, the city park, during July and early August. (Shows begin at 9pm. Tickets from L21,000.) Even when not serving as an opera house, Villa Margherita is home to a small **zoo** with a swan pond and various furry friends.

■ Near Trapani

SAN VITO LO CAPO

The gentle shores of San Vito lo Capo (also known as Capo San Vito) offer immense, sandy beaches and a vast selection of *gelaterie.* Although it is a major resort for northerners, the town remains inexpensive, authentic, and clean—an ideal place to relax for a day. **Rent a bicycle carriage** at the Ditta Russo Anna, Via Nino Bixio, 14 (tel. 97 29 42), and practice your Italian driving skills by careening down the sidewalks. (Tandem bikes L10,000 per hr.) For more seclusion, drive 12km to the **Riserva dello Zin-**

garo, a nature preserve with pastoral, cow-lined trails leading to crystalline coves. The bus connects to the preserve through Castellamare.

Buses to San Vito leave from the Trapani *autostazione* at P. Malta (Mon.-Fri. 9 per day, 7am-8pm, Sun. 3 per day, 8:30am-4:30pm, 1¼hr., L4400 one way, L7300 roundtrip). The last weekday bus to Trapani leaves at 9:30pm (Sun. return trips run 10am-6pm). For more info on the Zingaro nature reserve, ask (in English) at the Trapani tourist office. If you're inclined to stay, look for **Pensione Costa Gaia,** Via Savoia, 123-125 (tel. 97 22 68 or 97 23 75), on the main drag about four blocks from the beach. All rooms have A/C and bath. Low-season is from October to mid-July. Singles L40,000, low-season L35,000. Doubles L70,000, low-season L60,000. Full-pension L90,000, low-season L80,000, half-pension L80,000, low-season L70,000. There are also many camping options in the area (see **Trapani: Accommodations and Camping,** page 517).

ERICE

Erice hovers near the coast, 750m above sea level. Once the biggest town in the area with Trapani as its port, Erice's mountain slopes could only support a limited number of houses, so the town expanded to the nearby harbor. In ancient times, Erice was one of Sicily's most revered sites and the mythical home of several goddesses of fertility: first the Elymian Astarte, then the Greek Aphrodite and the Roman Venus.

Both the city and the vistas it affords are visual delights. The outer walls date back to the 16th century BC, while the town inside is virtually unchanged from medieval times. There are a number of worthwhile sights, particularly the **Norman castle,** with its medieval towers (adorned with TV broadcast aerials in typical Sicilian fashion) and the lush adjoining "Balio" **gardens.** There is also a 14th-century **duomo** and a 13th-century bell tower, which has additionally served as a watch-tower and a prison. Perhaps the greatest pleasure of visiting Erice is strolling the cool cobblestone streets while savoring the panoramic views of the coast (you can occasionally see all the way to Tunisia). The **Museo Comunale di Erice,** P. Umberto I, houses a small but interesting collection of odds and ends from all stages of Erice's long and illustrious history. Come just for the uncanny sensation of looking *down* on a crucifix. Open Mon.-Sat. 8:30am-7:30pm, Sun. 8:30am-1:30pm. Free.

The **AAST tourist office** awaits you in a tiny, easily missed stone cottage at Via C. A. Pepoli, 11 (tel. (0923) 86 93 88), on the hill near the bus stop. Open Mon., Wed., and Fri. 8am-2pm, Tues., Thurs., and Sat. 8am-2pm and 4-8pm. The **bus** from Trapani leaves from P. Malta, Montalto (Mon.-Sat. 12 per day, 6:45am-9:30pm, Sun. 5 per day, 9am-6:15pm, 45min., L2500, L4300 roundtrip. Last bus back weekdays at 10:15pm, Sun. at 7:15pm). Hotel prices are lofty, so Erice is best seen as a daytrip from Trapani. If you're stuck, the cheapest place is the **Edelweiss,** Cortile P. Vincenzo, 9 (tel. 86 91 58). Singles with bath L100,000. Doubles L130,000. Breakfast included. You can also try the private **youth hostel** between July 15 and August 30 on Viale delle Pinete or the **HI youth hostel** in Trapani (see page 517).

Food is equally costly. At **La Vettu,** Via G. Fontana, 5 (tel. 86 94 04), *primi* and *secondi* start at L10,000. Decent pizza can be had in the evenings for L6000. Open daily 9am-1:15pm and 3-8:30pm. Down the street, the **Antica Pasticceria del Convento,** Via Guarnotta, 1 (tel. 86 90 05), concocts sinfully good sweets for L12,000 per kilo. While strolling through the gardens, stop at windy **Chalet del Balio** on Villa Comunale. *Panini* and *pizza al taglio* from L3500. *Arancina* L3000. Open daily 9am-10pm, on summer nights until 3 or 4am.

SEGESTA

Segesta, with impressive ruins and the most dramatic of landscapes, is a must-see for anyone exploring western Sicily. The monumental unfinished **temple,** dating to the 5th century BC, provides a rare glimpse of an ancient work in progress, instructing archaeologists about how ancient temples were constructed. Try the optical "hat trick"—if you place a hat on one corner of the temple steps, and look at it at eye level from the long side of the temple, the hat will disappear from view: the steps bend but appear to be straight. There is also a majestic **theater,** where the ancient Elymi (native Sicilians who inhabited Segesta) went to see plays.

Segesta has been razed and rebuilt five times in its history, but is finally here to stay. From mid-July through the first week of August in odd-numbered years (including 1997), classical Greek, Indian, and Japanese plays are performed in the ancient theater. Special buses leave P. Politeama in Palermo 1¾hr. before showtime and P. Marina in Trapani 1hr. before showtime. Buy the L15,000-25,000 tickets from a travel agent in Palermo or Trapani. To avoid the 20-min. walk to the theater, an air-conditioned bus runs to the top (every 30min. 9:30am-6pm, L2000 roundtrip). **Buses** to Segesta from other towns are run by **Autoservizi Tarantola** (tel. 310 20 or 325 98; 6 per day Mon.-Sat., 2 on Sun., L4000, roundtrip L6700). Trains from Palermo or Trapani are much less frequent, more expensive, and less convenient.

Egadi Islands (Isole Egadi)

The summer sun is far kinder to the Egadi Islands than to scorched Sicily. Cats lounge on the terraces of whitewashed houses, soothed by the warm massage of the *scirocco* breezes. You may want to bypass Favignana, hackneyed tourist trap and relic of the archipelago's tuna trade, and head straight for the outlying islands of Marettimo and Levanzo, connected by sporadic ferry and hydrofoil service (see **Trapani: Ferries** page 516). These rough and barren islands—strewn with wildflowers and grazing sheep—offer archaeological wonders, sea grottoes, hiking trails, and amazing views.

LEVANZO

The prehistoric cave art in the **Grotta del Genovese,** about an hour on foot from the port, is only accessible on a guided tour in Italian. Visit Via Calvario, 27 (tel. (0923) 92 40 32), right down the street from the Siremar ticket office, and ride on a small boat (1½hr., L15,000) or a donkey (3hr., L20,000) to the cave. The Paleolithic incisions and ocher-grease paintings depict the early fishing trade and its attendant rituals. (The figures resembling bugs are actually dancing women.) The Neolithic paintings also feature animals that no longer inhabit Levanzo, illuminating the intriguing geological history of the archipelago. The island also offers a number of secluded beaches for sunbathing and grottoes for swimming. One daily ferry departs for Marettimo at 12:20pm.

Levanzo lacks a bus system and a tourist office, so pick a road and start walking. Accommodations on the Egadi Islands are cheap but few. **Albergo Paradiso** (tel. 92 40 80) has newly renovated rooms overlooking the sea. Singles L43,000, Sept.-June L30,000. Doubles L75,000, Sept.-June L60,000. Telephone reservations are crucial; call two weeks in advance. The **Albergo dei Fenici** (tel. 92 40 83), right behind the Paradiso, features a large terrace and an even better view, a common room with TV, and airy hallways. Singles L40,000. Doubles L75,000. Both hotels are booked solid for August by mid-March. Sundown draws locals and travelers to the seaside *caffès,* **Bar Romana** and **Bar Arcobaleno,** where an evening of cards and a warm North African breeze can easily stretch one cappuccino (L1500) into four. Open 'til everyone decides to go to bed.

MARETTIMO

Marettimo, the most remote of the Egadi Islands, also offers the most rustic atmosphere. Newly established hiking trails take you up and down its rocky cliffs, and on clear days the view stretches as far as Tunisia. The Pizzo Falcone (884m) is the highest point on the islands. A hike there takes about 2hr. but is worth every minute. The island is dramatic, lush, and wonderfully aromatic. A handful of *caffè, gelaterie,* and the **Trattoria Il Pirate,** off the old port, vend sandwiches and *gelato.* If you like Marettimo enough to stay overnight, ask at Il Pirate about renting a room in a private house for L20,000-30,000 per night, and be prepared to haggle. There are no official accommodations on the island. **Alilauro** offers one ferry per day at 6:45pm to Trapani (via Levanzo and Favignana) in high-season only. **Siremar** also runs to Trapani (3 per day, 6:50am-4:05pm).

Marsala

When the island-city of Mozia was destroyed at the hands of the Syracusans in 397BC, the survivors fled to the mainland of Cape Lilybeo and founded Marsala. The Arabs actually named the town: *Mars-Alí*, or "port of Alí." These days, most Italians know the city as home to the famous Marsala wine. Although it is best visited on your way to Mozia, the city's museums and archaeological sites are worth your time.

From the train station, **Via Roma** is a straight shot into Marsala's historic center, changing into **Via XI Maggio** at P. Matteotti. Following Via XI Maggio will land you in front of the 18th-century **Palazzo Comunale** and the Baroque **duomo** standing in **Piazza della Repubblica.** A variety of sculpture from the 16th-century school of Gagini decorates the church's vast interior. Behind the *duomo* at Via Garraffa, 57, the **Museo degli Arazzi** (tel. 71 29 03) contains eight elaborate 16th-century Flemish tapestries illustrating Titus's war against the Jews. Explanations are provided in English and Italian. Open Tues.-Sun. 9am-1pm and 4-6pm. Admission L1000. At the end of Via XI Maggio lies **Piazza della Vittoria,** sitting between the city and the sea. To the right is the entrance to Marsala's *zona archeologica.* To the left is the **Museo Baglio Anselmi** (tel. 95 25 35), that houses the remains of a 35m Carthaginian warship believed to have sunk during the Battle of the Egadi Islands, the battle that ended the First Punic War in 241BC. Open Mon.-Tues., Thurs.-Fri., and Sun. 9am-1:20pm, Wed. and Sat. 9am-1:20pm and 4-7pm.

The nearby **Villa Romana,** a Roman tenement, is one of the few excavated buildings in the vast archaeological zone. (Open upon request at the Museo Lilybeo.) The small 5th-century **Church of San Giovanni,** next to the museum, conceals the **Grotta della Sibilla,** a cave which housed a mythical Sibyl and her oracles. Check out the mosaic fragments speckling the floor. The tourist office can let you in. Church open only during the 3-day festival of the saint June 22-24. To witness the production of Marsala wine, take a free tour of the **Cantina Florio** facilities (tel. 78 11 11), located on Lungomare Mediterraneo past Via S. Lipari, to the left behind the train station. Open to the public Mon.-Thurs. 3-6pm, Fri. 11am-1pm. Closed in August, like the rest of Marsala.

To get to Marsala from Trapani, take a **bus** from P. Malta (3 per day, 6:50am-2pm, L3700 each way). The **Pro Loco tourist office,** Via XI Maggio, 100 (tel. 71 40 97), right next to the Palazzo Comunale, will direct you to other Marsala distillers, including **Pellegrino** (tel. 95 11 77) and **Intorcia** (tel. 99 91 33 or 99 90 36), and will help find accommodations. Open daily 8am-2pm and 3:30-7:30pm. **Trattoria da Pino,** Via San Lorenzo, 27 (tel. 71 56 52), offers a L16,000 *menù.* From P. Repubblica, head away from the station on Via XI Maggio and bear left on Via Curatolo, which eventually becomes Via San Lorenzo. Open Mon.-Sat. 12:30-2:30pm and 7pm-midnight. AmEx. For those on a shoe-string budget, make your way over to supermarket **STANDA,** Via Cammareri Scurtil, 10 (tel. 71 54 76 or 95 17 67). Open 9am-1:30pm and 4-7:30pm. The cheapest hotel in town is the **Garden,** Via Gambini, 36 (tel. 98 23 20). Follow signs from the right of the train station. It's pricey but has gorgeous marbled hallways, chandeliers, and spic 'n' span rooms. Singles L40,000, with bath L50,000. Doubles L60,000, with bath L80,000. Marsala's **telephone code** is 0923.

Near Marsala

MOZIA

Mozia (also known as San Pantaleo) witnessed a monumental naval battle in 397BC, when Dionysius of Syracuse annihilated the Carthaginian Himilco with the aid of a new weapon, the catapult. The islet lies 8km north of Marsala, across a thin strait traversed by a rickety little boat. It is now nearly deserted; a boatman will come and pick you up when he sees you waiting on the dock (Mon.-Sat. 9am-6pm, L4000, groups L3500 per person; Oct.-March boat runs in morning only). Remaining from the original child- and animal-sacrificing inhabitants are a fenced-in *tophet* (sacrificial area) and a dry dock on the other end of the tiny island. Many of the island's archaeological finds are displayed in the tiny **Museo Whitaker** (tel. 71 25 98) at the port, including a 5th-century BC Greek statue called the "Youth of Mozia." Admission L5000. A walk around the cactus-studded island will reveal the ancient fortifications, dating to 600BC. The island itself may not thrill you, but the salt flats and windmills, characteristic of the region, are worth the bus trip. **Municipilizatta** (tel. 95 11 05) runs bus #10 from P. del Popolo in Marsala to a boat bound for Mozia (8 per day, 10am-7pm, returns 10:30am-7:30pm). The boat to Mozia leaves from a pier at the end of the road where the bus lets you off.

SELINUNTE

A magnificent jumble of ruins atop a plateau overlooking the Mediterranean, Selinunte awes with its immensity and desolation. Founded in the 7th century BC by the citizens of Megara Hyblaea, the city's fortunes took a decided downturn in 409BC, when the place was sacked by Segesta and Carthage; it was finally destroyed by its own (Carthaginian) people in 241BC in anticipation of a Roman attack. Selinunte remains shrouded in an air of mystical isolation that justifies its Arabic title: "the place of the idols." Ruins open 9am-sunset. Admission L2000. Ticket office closes 1hr. before sunset. About a kilometer inland, the enormous half-quarried drums for unbuilt columns lie abandoned in a stone outcropping.

Getting to Selinunte can be a challenge. From Palermo, Trapani, or Marsala, take the bus or train to **Castelvetrano.** If you're lucky, you'll catch the 2:15pm **FS bus** that leaves straight from the train station for Selinunte (L2000 one way, L3400 roundtrip). If not, orange **city buses** leave for Selinunte from P. Matteotti (5 per day, Mon.-Sat. 7:15am-5pm, Sun. 9am-7:15pm, L2000 one way). To get there from the train station, follow Via Veneto up the hill; turn left onto Via Vittorio Emanuele, which leads straight into P. Matteotti. The city bus also passes by the AST **bus stop** at P. San Giovanni. The **Lumia bus** from **Sciacca** and **Agrigento** stops below the hospital down the hill from the AST bus stop. Selinunte's **telephone code** is 0924.

If you're stuck between buses, **Hotel Zeus,** Castelvetrano's only official hotel, is up the hill from the station at Via Veneto, 6 (tel. 90 55 66; fax 90 55 65). All rooms have bath, TV, and telephone. Singles L45,000. Doubles L80,000. Cheaper stays (and more pleasing countryside) await in Selinunte. For a wonderful hotel run by an equally wonderful family, head for **Il Pescatore** at Via S. D. 13n, 31 (tel. 463 03). The first-floor "blue bathroom," cleaned four times a day, has earned an international reputation. An immaculate single goes for L25,000. Doubles L45,000. Reserve by June for rooms in July and August. If Il Pescatore is full, beautiful doubles with bath, A/C, and free parking for L70,000 can be had right on Selinunte's romantic beachfront at **Lido Azzurro,** Via Marco Polo, 98 (tel./fax 462 56). V, MC, AmEx, DC. For a single, try **Costa d'Avorio,** across from Il Pescatore. Simple, quiet rooms go for L30,000, with bath L40,000. Doubles L50,000, with bath L60,000. The beachfront is lined with touristy, moderately over-priced eateries; the restaurant associated with Lido Azzurro, **Baffo's Ristorante-Pizzeria** (tel. 462 11), offers a good selection of pizza from L6000, *primi* from L7000 (try the fettucine with Sicilian *pesto*—tuna, garlic, tomatoes, and basil), and *secondi* (fish, meat, or omelettes) from L7000. Cover L2000. Service 10%. Open from noon to 3pm and 7pm 'til the *vacche* come home.

THE SOUTHERN COAST

Agrigento

The Greek poet Pindar once lauded Agrigento as "Man's Finest City," and in spite of some serious competition, Agrigento still holds the title. Founded by Greek colonists in the 6th century BC, the city stands on a mountain ridge, looming protectively over its famous Valley of the Temples. The *centro storico* is a cobblestone web of welcoming streets, where tourist boutiques and butcher shops sit comfortably side by side. The city has tree-lined Parisian-style avenues and squares, plus 4km of golden beach thrown in nearby for good measure. Luigi Pirandello, winner of the 1934 Nobel Prize in Literature, was born here—something no Agrigentan will let you forget. Add to all this the fact that the city boasts some of the world's best preserved classical Greek architecture, and maybe you'll side with Pindar after all.

ORIENTATION AND PRACTICAL INFORMATION

Agrigento lies midway along Sicily's southern coast. The train and bus terminals, and the street connecting them, divide the modern city from the old town. The cobblestoned main drag of the historic district, **Via Atenea,** leads away from **Piazza Moro,** between the train station at **Piazza Marconi** and the bus terminal at **Piazza Roselli.** Agrigento is built on a steep incline; the historic district and Via Atenea perch above the train station. Buses and the post office lie farther up from P. Moro.

Tourist Office: Ufficio Informazioni Assistenza Turisti (AAST), Via Atenea, 123 (tel. 204 54). Extremely helpful and good-natured staff speaks English. Ask for the indispensable map of the city. Open in summer 8:30am-1:30pm and 4:30-7:30pm. The **main AAST office** is farther from the action at Via Empedocle, 73 (tel. 203 91; fax 202 46). There is also an **AAPIT** office on Viale delle Vittoria, 255 (tel. 40 13 52 or 40 13 53; fax 251 85). Viale delle Vittoria is the arrow-straight avenue that starts at the train station and heads out of town.

Telephones: Via dei Gasperi, off Via Cicerone from P. Vittorio Emanuele.

Trains: In P. Marconi, below P. Moro. Trains run from the station to Palermo (11 per day, 8 on Sun., 1½hr., L11,700) and Catania via Caltanissetta and Enna (4 per day, 3hr., L15,500 to Catania; 2hr., L9800 to Enna). Ticket office open 6:10am-3:10pm and 4:10-8:10pm.

Buses: Up the hill past P. Vittorio Emanuele, in P. Roselli, an otherwise empty lot. (Helpful city map posted next to bus stop.) From Trapani, **Autoservizi Lumia,** Via Pindaro, 3/C, Agrigento (tel. 204 14, 40 14 94 or 59 64 90) runs four buses from Trapani daily (departures from Trapani's P. Garibaldi; 4hr., L15,200, L25,900 roundtrip). Buses to Sciacca, Marsala, and Castelvetrano. From Marsala, take the train to Castelvetrano (15 per day, 1hr., L3700), and then one of four daily buses to Agrigento (L9600) via Selinunte and Ribera. **TUA** buses (tel. 41 20 24) to Gela, where you can switch to a **Società Autolinee Licata** (SAL or Licata) bus (in Agrigento, tel. 40 13 60) to Agrigento. **Autoservizi Cuffaro** (in Agrigento tel. 59 64 90) makes 6 trips per day to and from Palermo's P. Balsamo (7am-6:30pm, 2¼hr., L10,500, L17,000 roundtrip). Finally, **SAIS** buses, V. Favara Vecchia (tel. 59 52 60 or 59 59 33; ticket office down the hill from P. Roselli at Via Ragazzi del 99) serve Catania (5 per day, 2½hr., L16,500, L28,000 roundtrip).

Ferries: Siremar, Via Molo, 1, Porto Empedocle (tel. 63 66 85). Take a bus from the train station (at least 1 per hr., L2000). To the **Pelagie Islands,** Linosa (L47,000) and Lampedusa (L59,000), one per day at midnight, arriving Linosa at 6:45am, Lampedusa at 8:15am, and Linosa at noon (leaves Lampedusa at 10am). Tickets at the Siremar office in the port. Get there at least 1hr. before departure.

Public Transportation: Most orange TUA city buses depart from the train station. L1000 buys a 1½-hr. ticket at most *tabacchi.* #2 or 2/ (*barrato,* with a slash through the number) run to San Leone (Agrigado's beautiful beach); #1, 2, and 2/

run to the Valley of Temples; #1/ runs to Pirandello's house. Or take the bus to **Porto Empedocle** (L2000 one way) and get off at *la casa di Pirandello.*

Emergencies: tel. 113. **Hospital: Ospedale Civile San Giovanni di Dio** (tel. 49 21 11; emergencies tel. 40 13 44), off P. S. Giuseppe on Via Atenea.

Police: (tel. 59 63 22) in P. Moro.

Post Office: P. Vittorio Emanuele (tel. 59 51 50), with a fascist mosaic out front. Fermo posta Mon.-Sat. 8:10am-1:20pm. Packages 8:10am-6pm. Letters 8:10am-1:30pm and 1:50-7:40pm. Telegrams up the outside stairs from the main entrance Mon.-Sat. 8:05am-7:45pm. Letters and packages Sunday 8:30am-6:45pm. **Postal Code:** 92100.

Telephone Code: 0922.

ACCOMMODATIONS AND CAMPING

Unlike the town itself, Agrigento's budget accommodations are not a pretty sight. There seems to be a sharp dichotomy between grungy and overpriced, with nothing in between. Be aware that some of the more expensive hotels are rumored to be mafia-owned. A pleasant (but less convenient) alternative is to pitch a tent at one of the two well-run beachfront campgrounds at nearby San Leone (see bus info below).

Hotel Bella Napoli, P. Lena, 6 (tel./fax 204 35 or tel. 205 92), off Via Bac Bac, which leads uphill from the high end of Via Atenea. Simple, adequately cleaned rooms are sparsely furnished. Beds as firm as soggy bread. Rooftop terrace overlooks the valley. Singles L25,000, with bath L40,000. Doubles L55,000, with bath L75,000. Triples with bath L95,000. AmEx.

Hotel Belvedere, Via San Vito, 20 (tel. 200 51), at the top of the stairs which begin by the Restaurant Kalos, opposite P. Moro. Agrigento's nicest (and priciest) 2-star, with sleek modern rooms, funky antique furniture, and a quaint sitting garden overlooking P. Moro and the valley. Singles L40,000, with bath L65,000. Doubles L60,000, with bath L85,000. All-you-can-eat breakfast L4000.

Hotel Concordia, Via San Francesco, 11 (tel. 59 62 66). Only as a last resort. Some rooms have windows—need we say more? Make sure your door locks before accepting a room. Singles L20,000-30,000, with bath L25,000-40,000. Doubles L30,000-50,000, with bath L48,000-77,000.

Camping: Two campgrounds lie right on the beach, 3km from San Leone in an area known as **Le Dune.** Bus #2/ goes there directly from the train station through San Leone proper. Bus #2 goes to San Leone, if you're in the mood for a pretty beachfront hike. **Camping Internazionale Nettuno** (tel. 41 62 68) on Via L'Acquameno, right at the bus stop, has a market, restaurant, bar, and evening pizzeria that aren't too overpriced. L7500 per person, L7000 per tent. Up the road is the **Camping Internazionale,** Via Alessandro Giuliana Alaimo, 2 (tel./fax 41 61 21). This separate campground is run by a family of extroverts. L8000 per person, L9000 in July and Aug. Small tent L7000, large tent L10,000; in July and Aug. L8000 and L11,000, respectively. Both campgrounds open year-round in 1997.

FOOD

There are a few small fruit and vegetable stands in front of the Hotel Concordia (open Mon.-Sat. mornings). Agrigento's **STANDA** doesn't stock food, so your best bet is one of the small *alimentari* lining Via Pirandello or Via Atenea. Indulge a sweet tooth at the candy stalls along Viale della Vittoria (open all day and well into the evening). The specialty is *torrone,* a nut-filled nougat. The "market" by the soccer field consists of a bunch of stalls selling cheap clothes.

Trattoria Atenea, Via Ficani, 32 (tel. 202 47), the 4th right off Via Atenea from P. Moro. Quiet courtyard. Two-course lunch L15,000; dinner *menù* L12,000. Extensive seafood offerings. *Calamari* (squid) and *gamberi* (shrimp) are L9000. The house specialty is *grigliata mista di pesce* (mixed grilled fish, L9000). All pasta L5000. Wine L4000 per liter. Open Mon.-Sat. noon-3pm and 7pm-midnight.

Paninoteca Manhattan, Salita M. Angeli, 9 (tel. 209 11), up the steps to the right off Via Atenea near P. Moro. Creative Italian sandwiches with creative American names start at L4000. The "Rockfeller" combines tuna, pepper, lettuce, *insalata russa* (mayo, shredded carrots, potatoes, and peas), tabasco, and a healthy dose of whiskey (L5000). Open Mon.-Sat. 8am-4pm and 7pm-midnight. **Another location** on Via Atenea, 227 at P. del Purgatorio (tel. 59 66 95) provides full restaurant fare. *Primi* from L8000, *secondi* from L7000 (a hamburger). Ten kinds of beer from L4000. *Menù* L18,000.

Trattoria Black Horse, Via Celauro, 8 (tel. 232 23), off Via Atenea. An interesting family-run establishment. If you're lucky, you might even get to overhear the chef singing Verdi. *Tronchetto dello chef (*a thick lasagna packed with peas, ham, and meat sauce, L6500) is the specialty. *Menù* includes cheese, fruit, salad, omelette, and *primo del giorno* for L13,000. *Primi* from L6500, *secondi* from L8000. Cover L2500. Service 10%. Open Mon.-Sat. noon-3pm and 7-11pm. V, MC, AmEx.

Ristorante Pizzeria La Corte degli Sfirzii, C. Contarini, 6 (tel. 59 55 20), in the Cortile Contarini off Via Atenea. Fine food. Go for the *pizza menù:* your choice of pizza, *insalata mista,* and wine or beer, including cover and service for L14,000. Pizza and *primo menù* L16,000. Regular *menù* L18,000. Kiddie *menù* L10,000. During summer, ask to be seated in the private garden in the back. Open Thurs.-Tues. noon-3pm and 7:30pm-2am. V, MC.

Trattoria de Paris, Piazza Lena, 7 (tel. 254 13). Conveniently located next to the Hotel Bella Napoli. The only thing French is the name—sample the tasty Italian fare. All *primi* L8000, most *secondi* L10,000, fish L13,000. Try the *rigatoni alla Pirandello* with tomatoes, prosciutto, mushrooms, and cream. *Menù* L20,000. Open Mon.-Sat. noon-3pm and 7:30-11pm. V, MC, AmEx.

SIGHTS AND ENTERTAINMENT

Valle dei Templi

Agrigento's star attraction is the **Valle dei Templi** (Valley of the Temples), a couple of kilometers down the hill from the modern city. (Open 8:30am-sunset.) Take bus #1, 2, or 2/ from the train station (L1000) and ask to be dropped off at the *quartiere ellenistico-romano.* Walk to the **Museo Nazionale Archeologico di San Nicola** to orient yourself. The museum contains a notable collection of artifacts, including Greek vases from Agrigento and the rest of central Sicily. (Open Mon.-Sat. 8am-12:30pm. Free.) The adjacent **Church of San Nicola,** a 13th-century Romanesque-Gothic church on the site of a Greek sanctuary, preserves Roman sarcophagi with reliefs depicting the death of Phaedra (second chapel on the right). Unfortunately, the church is only opened officially for weddings. Walking one km down the busy road in front of the museum will bring you to a dirt lot, a snack bar, lots of tour buses, and the Valley of the Temples.

With the exception of the Temples of Concord and of Juno, the structures here were destroyed by a combination of earthquakes and early Christian anti-paganism. In the site adjacent to the parking lot are the ruins of the **Tempio di Giove Olimpico.** Had its construction not been halted by the Carthaginian sack of the city in 406-405BC, it would have been one of the largest Greek temples ever built. Now little is left; most of the temple's stone was carted away in the 18th century to build a jetty at nearby Porto Empedocle. The temple's 38 18m columns were supported by 8m *telemones*—sculpted male figures which function as columns. A reconstructed *telamon* lies among the ruins. Farther along in the same area, four columns and an entablature represent the piecemeal effort to rebuild the 5th-century BC **Tempio di Castore e Polluce** (Castor and Pollux). Across from the parking lot are the few remaining columns of the **Tempio di Ercole** (Hercules), the oldest temple here, dating from the 6th century BC.

Uphill from the Temple of Hercules looms the **Tempio della Concordia,** one of the best-preserved Greek temples in the world, complete with 34 columns. Erected in the mid-5th century BC out of limestone (now weathered to a golden hue), it owes its remarkable state of preservation to early sanctification as a Christian church by the then-bishop of Agrigento San Gregorio delle Rape (St. Gregory of the Turnips). The niches in the interior walls, originally created for Christian worship, are still visible.

The **Tempio di Giunone** (Juno) dates from the same period as the Temple of Concord. Though not nearly as well-preserved, it offers a great view from the top of the hill. The beehive-like holes in the ground on your way down are really the remnants of a **paleochristian necropolis.**

Other Sights

The most interesting building in medieval Agrigento is the small, 11th-century Norman **Church of Santa Maria dei Greci,** which occupies the site of a 5th-century BC Doric temple. Follow the signs up the hill from the top of Via Bac Bac off Via Atenea. Part of the wooden Norman ceiling remains, as well as fragments of the 14th-century Byzantine frescoes and the Greek columns of the original temple. Look for the secret tunnel, which you can enter from the courtyard. It preserves the stylobate (the platform beneath the columns) and the six stumps of the ancient temple. (If closed, call 59 54 79.)

The **Church of Purgatory** in P. Purgatorio off Via Atenea houses eight statues representing the Virtues. To the left of the church, underneath a sleeping lion, is the entrance to a network of underground channels and reservoirs built by the Greeks in the 5th century BC. (Closed for restoration.) Wandering behind the church on Via Fodera will lead you to **Santo Spirito,** a complex containing a chapel, charterhouse, and refectory (now used as a library), founded by Cistercian nuns at the end of the 13th century. The church displays beautiful stucco work (1693-1695) by Serpotta, illustrating scenes from Christ's life. Ring the bell on the church door to enter.

For a change of pace, visit the birthplace of playwright **Luigi Pirandello** in P. Kaos (tel. 51 11 02). Take the Lumia bus to this small museum of books and notes. (Open daily 8am-1:30pm.) Pirandello's tomb is located under his favorite pine tree, a few hundred meters from the house. (Grounds open Mon.-Sat. 8:30am-1hr. before sunset. Free.) The **Settimana Pirandelliana,** a week-long outdoor festival of plays, operas, and ballets in P. Kaos, happens in late July and early August. (Tickets L10,000-20,000. Ask at the tourist office or call 235 61 for info.) The **Teatro Pirandello** recently reopened inside the town hall. Ask at the tourist office for info on performance dates and times.

The first Sunday of February brings the **Almond Blossom Festival,** an international folk event in the Valley of the Temples. In early July, townsfolk throw bread to the effigy of St. Calogero, recalling the townspeople's fear of food contamination during the plague. **San Leone,** 4km from Agrigento (take bus #2 or 2/), is draped with splendid stretches of beach. Beginning in the early evening, local youth gather in front of the beachside **Aster** game room/pizzeria (tel. 41 23 66) to strut their stuff and sing along to the music pouring out of the café. (Open daily noon-midnight.)

■ Near Agrigento: Sciacca

Sciacca (SHAHK-kah) is well-known throughout Italy as the site of thermal-mineral baths. While most of the services offered by the majestic therapeutic **Terme di Sciacca** (down the hill from the bus stop) are a bit out of the budget traveler's reach (sulfuric bath L35,000, vapor caves L23,000, massage L35,000), the town also holds other appeal for visitors. The **Church of St. Agostino,** built in 1753 on Via Padre G. Cusmano, is a squat, stone building with an impressive portal and bell tower. Walk a short way up Via Valverde to the **Church of Santa Maria delle Giummare,** with its courtyard altar sunken into an outdoor cave. Stroll up Via Conte Luna to the impressive 14th-century **Castello di Conti Luna** (tel. 99 30 44). Open Mon.-Sat. 10:30am-1:30pm and 4pm-7:30pm, Sun. 10:30am-1:30pm and 4:30-7:30pm. In the center of the old city lies Piazza G. Noceto. Look for the free-standing 14th-century **tower.**

The best of all that Sciacca has to offer can probably be seen on a daytrip. If you wish to spend the night, however, cheap lodgings can be found at the **Pensione Buenos Aires,** Via Triolo, 11 (tel. 218 37), close to the *comune* in the historic center. In addition to the ceramic dolls in the lobby, you'll find pleasantly affordable rooms. Singles L25,000. Doubles L50,000. Half-pension L40,000. Full-pension L55,000. If you're hungry, the best deal can be found at the **Ristorante Miramare,** Piazza Scandaliato, 6 (tel. 260 50). True to its name, the restaurant has a great view of the port and water. Pizza from L7000, *menù* L20,000.

Busline **Lumia,** Via Pindaro (tel. (0922) 204 14), will make the trip to Agrigento for L6800 (8 per day Mon.-Sat., L11,500 roundtrip). Purchase tickets at **Bar Lorenz** at V. della Vittoria, 7. **Linea Gallo** buses, with an office at V. della Vittoria, 22 (tel. 210 86), head from the bus stop down the street to Corleone (2 daily, 5:50am-12pm, 3hr., L7500 one way, L12,700 roundtrip) and Palermo (L11,000 one way, L17,000 roundtrip). The **AAST tourist office,** Corso Vittorio Emanuele, 84 (tel. 211 82), should be able to answer any tourist questions. Public **telephones** can be found at Via Roma, 38 (tel. 210 62). The **post office** is on Via dei Gasperi, 103 (tel. 841 22). For **emergency assistance** call 234 99; **carabinieri** can be reached at tel. 211 19 and 216 40. The **telephone code** for Sciacca is 0925.

Enna

This mountaintop city may be Sicily's best-kept secret. Rising above the poorest and only landlocked province in Sicily, Enna provides a view of life in the island's interior. Ennans are prone to modesty and self-deprecation, and coastal Sicilians view them with a condescending eye, a combination which has kept Enna out of the Sicilian tourist industry for years. However, Enna is a cool, animated city with numerous *piazze* offering panoramas of the surrounding countryside. Ennans like to point out that theirs is a city of true tranquility, as well as the only provincial capital without a mafia presence. The town has been used as a military base throughout history, passing through Greek, Roman, Arab, Norman, Lombard, and Bourbon hands. The only vestiges of this past are a huge medieval castle, a Lombard tower, and a curiously remodeled cathedral.

ORIENTATION AND PRACTICAL INFORMATION

Enna, located at the center of the island, is known as the "navel of Sicily." It is easily accessible by bus (from Catania and Palermo) and train (from Catania). To get to the center of Enna from the bus depot, head downhill on Via Vittorio Emanuele. This road runs directly into **Via Roma,** Enna's main strip, which heads off in two directions from P. Matteotti. Via Roma leads past **Piazza Vittorio Emanuele** and all the way up to the **Castello di Lombardia** on the left; to the right it winds through a residential and shopping district, eventually coming to an end in the vicinity of the **Torre di Federico II.**

Tourist Office: AAPIT, Via Roma, 411 (tel. 52 82 88). One of Sicily's best. Extremely informed and well-organized. Pick up the fine map of Enna. Open Mon. and Wed. 9am-1pm and 3:30-6:30pm, Tues. and Thurs.-Sat. 9am-1pm. **AAST,** P. Colajanni, 6 (tel. 261 19 or 50 08 75), 100m up and to the right from AAPIT. Small but efficient. Open Mon.-Sat. 9am-1pm and some afternoons.

Numero Verde Turistico: tel. (167) 22 11 88.

Telephones: Try **Albergo Sicilia,** P. Colajanni.

Currency Exchange: Banks are along Via Roma, between P. Vittorio Emanuele and P. Umberto I. You can also change money at the post office Mon.-Fri. 8:10am-5:30pm, Sat. 8:10am-1:20pm.

Trains: From: Catania (12 per day, 1hr., L7200); Palermo (7 per day, 2hr., L12,700); and Agrigento (L9800 one way). Enna's train station (tel. 50 09 10 or 50 12 28) is 5km downhill from the center of town. Fortunately there are 11 buses per day (L1500) connecting the station to the city center; the schedule is posted in the train station.

Buses: SAIS, Viale Diaz (tel. 50 09 02), a short walk uphill from P. Matteotti or the Tower. Open daily 6am until 8 or 8:30pm. To: Palermo (L12,000); Catania (8 per day, 3 on Sun., L8500); Gela (L8600); Caltanissetta (L4000); and Piazza Armerina (7 per day, 40min., L3700 one way). To Pergusa, take the orange city bus #2 from P. San Francesco (L600 one way).

Emergencies: tel. 113. **First Aid: Guardia Medica** (tel. 454 89). **Ambulance:** tel. 219 33. **Hospital: Ospedale Umberto I** (tel. 451 11).
Police: tel. 112. **Carabinieri:** (tel. 50 12 67, 50 12 91, or 50 13 21) on P. Europa.
Post Office: Via Volta, 1 (tel. 50 09 50). Take a left off Via Roma just before the AAPIT and walk to the right behind the building labeled "Provincia." Open Mon.-Sat. 8:10am-7:20pm. **Postal Code:** 94100.
Telephone Code: 0935.

ACCOMMODATIONS AND FOOD

Enna is expensive, so don't plan to sleep here. If an overnight stay is inevitable, however, the town's only hotel is the **Hotel Sicilia,** P. Colajanni, 7 (tel. 50 08 50), on Via Roma past the AAPIT office. This modern building is posh and clean, with a great view, phone, hairdryer, and TV in every room. Singles L80,000. Doubles L150,000. Triples L200,000. All-you-can-eat breakfast is included. All rooms have showers. V, MC, AmEx. If there are no vacancies at the hotel, or too many vacancies in your wallet, head down the mountain to the smaller (and cheaper) town of Pergusa (see **Near Enna,** page 530). Check at the tourist office about lodgings; Enna occasionally sponsors a youth hostel in town.

Enna's most famous food is its *piacentino* cheese: sharp, spicy, and available at **Centro Formaggi,** Via Mercato Sant'Antonio, 33 (tel. 50 07 29). Just follow your nose from Via Roma to P. Umberto. Open daily 8am-2pm and 5-9pm. There's also a **TOPS Discount Alimentare** up the steps behind the bus station. **Ristorante La Fontana** at Via Volturo, 6 (tel. 254 65), is well-known for its Sicilian cuisine. The specialty is *risotto all'Ennese* (with tomatoes, mushrooms and olives, L7000). Also good is the *cavatelli alla Siciliana* (tomato, eggplant, mushrooms, and hot peppers, L7000). *Menù* L20,000. Cover L2000. Service 15%. Open daily 9am-4pm and 7:30pm-midnight. V, MC, AmEx.

For an incredible sunset over Enna's valley (and good food to boot), head to **La Rupe,** Via Michelangelo, 14 (tel. 265 05), perched on a cliff between the *castello* and the *Rocca di Cerere.* Great pizza from L4500, including a dynamite *cappricciosa* with hard-boiled eggs, prosciutto, peas, and mushrooms. *Rigatoni a quattro formaggio* is delectable, too (L6000). *Primi* from L6000, *secondi* from L10,000. Cover L1000. Service 10%. Open Wed.-Mon. noon-3pm and 7:30pm until the last mouth has been fed.

SIGHTS AND ENTERTAINMENT

Via Roma ascends through the old city to the **cathedral.** Founded in 1307 and renovated in the 16th century, it has a slender Baroque façade. The polygonal transepts, the apses, and the south door remain from the original medieval structure. Behind the cathedral, the small **Museo Alessi** (tel. 240 72) displays the *duomo's* treasures and some Greco-Roman artifacts and medieval paintings. (Free, but closed for renovation; check the tourist office for more info.) Across P. Mazzini from the *duomo* is the **Museo Varisano** (tel. 50 04 18), which exhibits pottery shards and figurines. (Open Tues.-Sun. 9am-1:30pm and 3:30-6:30pm. Free.)

Frederick II constructed the **Castello di Lombardia** (tel. 50 09 62) on a 5000-year-old foundation at the eastern end of town in order to maintain central control of the island. Only six of the original 20 towers now stand. The castle grounds offer a thrilling view of the Sicilian landscape, but its interior is closed for renovation. The **Torre di Federico II,** an octagonal lookout with well-preserved Gothic vaulting, rises 24m at the opposite edge of the city, surrounded by the city's winding **public garden.** (Garden open daily 9am-8:30pm. Free.) A secret tunnel once connected the tower with the Castello di Lombardia. To get to the tower, walk along Via Roma past the Upim department store (away from P. Vittorio Emmanuele). Via Roma turns into Via Libertà. Turn left onto Viale 4 Novembre to reach the foot of the public gardens.

One of Enna's largest festivals is the **Festa della Madonna.** Held on July 2, it is marked by the incessant popping of firecrackers and the renowned flavor of *mastazzoli* (apple cookies). Parties also accompany the feasts of **Sant'Anna** on the last Sunday in July and **San Valverde** on the last Sunday in August. Enna's most renowned festival, however, occurs at **Easter.** Different groups and religious orders don unique costumes for the Holy Week parade, the "*Processione del Venerdì Santo,*" revealing the Spanish influence once quite strong in Sicily.

Down the hill at the **Autodromo di Pergusa,** processions are of another (faster) sort. Pergusa's racetrack hosts international Gran Prix auto races from March to October. The most important ones take place between June and October. (For info, call 258 25 or 256 60 for the *Ente Autodromo di Pergusa,* Piazza V. Emanuele, 24, Enna, or the Secretary of the Autodromo in Pergusa at 54 10 69.) There is also a **national park** on Lake Pergusa, next to the race track.

■ Near Enna

PERGUSA

Enna's lack of cheap hotels is compensated for in the nearby lakeside village of Pergusa. What this haven lacks in size (Pergusa could be called a "one-horse town" if it had even that), it makes up for with its enchanting setting. Pergusa provides the perfect nightcap to a day spent wandering the streets of Enna. It can be reached from Enna proper by **bus #4,** which makes the 7km trip from the bus station and from Via Roma just below P. Vittorio Emanuele (L600). Buses leave every 1-2hr. but can be erratic. To stay in Pergusa, search out the **Miralogo** (tel. 54 12 72) on Contrada da Staglio, right before the entrance to the town. With soft towels, cheery bedspreads, and telephones in every room, Miralogo is pristine and comfortable. All rooms come with bath. Singles L40,000. Doubles L60,000. Half-pension L65,000. Full-pension L80,000. Breakfast L3000.

Pergusa might also be the place to head for dinner from Enna. The **Proserpina,** Via Nazionale, 8 (tel. 54 10 31), is the local favorite. Although the specialty is seafood, the cheap pizzas (from L3500) are superb. *Menù* L17,000. Ask to sit in the courtyard out back. Open 12:30-3pm and 7pm-1am. AmEx. Pack a lunch at the **mini-market** at Via Nazionale, 16 (tel. 54 11 88), and picnic in the pine-forest **Parchi Attrezzati** (on the far side of the course). Market open 6:30am-2:30pm and 4-10pm. Or try **Da Carlo,** Via Nazionale, 34 (tel. 54 11 94 or 54 10 30). The restaurant downstairs is cozy, but its menu is a bit pricey. *Primi* from L7000, *secondi* from L11,000. Upstairs is a great pizzeria/gelateria/bar combo. Pizza from L4500, tortillas L3500. Cover L2500. Pizza is only available 7:30-11pm. AmEx.

The **pharmacy** of Dr. Persico (tel. 54 13 59) is on Via Nazionale. Open 9am-1pm and 5-9pm. For emergencies, contact the **Carabinieri** (tel. 217 77).

PIAZZA ARMERINA AND VILLA ROMANA DEL CASALE

The golden Baroque buildings of **Piazza Armerina** rise gracefully on three knolls overlooking the Ennese countryside. Nearby is the **Villa Romana del Casale,** an ancient Roman country house that preserves some of the ancient world's finest mosaics, a must-see for anyone within a 100-mile radius.

Orientation and Practical Information

Piazza Armerina is a 45-min. **bus** ride from Enna (7 per day, 3 on Sun. and holidays, L3700, L6100 roundtrip). Buses also run directly from Piazza Armerina to Palermo (L14,000), Catania, and Syracuse, and straight from Pergusa (L2900). Buses arrive at and leave from P. Cascino, off Via Gaeta in the new city. Most buses also continue to P. Umberto I at the base of the old city. Via Garibaldi takes you uphill to the historic district, where the friendly but somewhat clueless staff at the **tourist office,** Via Cavour, 15 (tel. 68 02 01; fax 68 45 65), will do what they can for you. Open Mon.-Sat. 8am-2pm. The **Quattrino pharmacy** is at P. Garibaldi, 31 (tel. 68 00 44), on the way to the *duomo*. Open 9am-1pm and 4-8pm. **Pronto Intervento:** tel. 113. **Hospital: Ospedale Chiello** (tel. 98 11 11). **Carabinieri:** tel. 68 20 14. **Telephone Code:** 0935.

Accommodations and Food

Piazza Armerina has no inexpensive accommodations, but if you're stuck, try the **Hotel Villa Romana,** P. Alcide de Gasperi, 18 (tel./fax 68 29 11), at the bottom of Via Roma, which begins in P. Garibaldi. They offer some budget rooms with common bathrooms and showers. Singles L40,000. Doubles L80,000. Unfortunately, there are very few, and they go fast. Ritzy singles with bath L100,000. Doubles with bath L135,000. Triples L180,000. Breakfast L10,000. Out by the road to the mosaics (4km outside the city), the **Trattoria La Ruota** (tel. 68 05 42) also runs an informal **campground.** The owners are helpful, the food yummy, and the lodging price negotiable (L2000-4000 per person; bring your own tent). Catch the bus from Piazza Armerina to Villa Romana and ask the bus driver to let you off at the *trattoria*. **Picnics** are generally the best eating option in Piazza Armerina. **Strazzanti Alimentari,** P. Garibaldi, 15 (tel. 68 00 84), is well stocked. If the urge for restaurant fare is too strong to resist, head for **Pepito** at Via Roma, 140 (tel. 827 37), right next to the Hotel Villa Romana. Pizza (in the evening only) from L4500. Cover L2000. Open noon-3:30pm and 7-11pm. V, MC, AmEx.

Sights and Entertainment

The **villa** lies 5½km southwest of town (tel. 68 00 36). Be sure to pick up a guide (along with a map) at the tourist office in Enna or Piazza Amerina. The villa was probably a hunting lodge of Maximanius Heraclius, co-emperor with Diocletian at the turn of the 4th century AD. Occupied until the Arab period, sacked in 1160, and buried by a landslide soon after, it remained undiscovered until 1916. The villa houses 40 rooms of incredibly vivid **mosaics,** the largest and most intact of their kind in the world. They range through every conceivable theme: chariot races, big-game hunts, pudgy Cupids fishing, Ulysses blinding the Cyclops, and even the Ancient Sicilian Bikini Team: the bizarre **Sala delle 10 Ragazze** (Room of the Ten Maidens) portrays a group of women in skimpy outfits playing catch, lifting weights, and crowning themselves with garlands. The so-called **Cubicolo Scena Erotica,** near the exit to the villa, is hardly a big deal—you've seen much steamier on *Melrose Place.* Don't miss the stunning **Ambulacrum of the Great Hunt,** with the gorgeous personification of Africa in the right-hand exedra, the **Diaeta of Arion,** with the hero Arion riding on a dolphin, and the **Vestibule of Polyphemus.** From May to early September, buses (L500) shuttle back and forth between the villa and Piazza Armerina. (Departures on the hr. 9-11am and 4-6pm; buses return on the ½hr. 9:30-11:30am and 4:30-6:30pm.) Orange **ATAN** buses monkey around (get it? Orange ATAN... orangutan? oh, nevermind) in front of the Hotel Villa Romana on Via Sturze at the base of Via Roma coming from the old city. (Villa open daily 9am-1:30pm and 3:30pm-sunset. Admission L2000. Bad pun free.) If you're really taken by the mosaics, ask for info about some of the other nearby ancient *ville*, such as **Morgantina, Ardone,** and **Nicosia.**

Piazze filled with pine, eucalyptus, poplar, and cedar trees punctuate Piazza Armerina's narrow medieval streets. In the center is **Piazza Garibaldi,** with several 18th-century buildings. The **duomo** (1627) at the summit of the town peers down with its imposing 17th- and 18th-century Baroque façade and a 15th-century Gothic-Sicilian belfry. Inside, the painted crucifix and the Madonna in the chapel to the left both date from the 15th century. Above the high altar, a Baroque tabernacle contains a Byzantine icon of the *Madonna della Vittoria,* a gift of Pope Nicholas II. It is carried in a procession during the **Feast of the Assumption** (August 15). The Feast of the Assumption is preceded on August 13-14 by the **Palio dei Normanni,** a costumed horse race commemorating the liberation of Sicily from the Saracens by the Norman Count Roger III.

Ragusa

The provincial capital of Ragusa has quietly avoided the frenetic pace acquired by other Sicilian cities, simultaneously managing to escape inclusion on most tourist itineraries. A steep 200-m incline separates the original city, *Ragusa Ibla,* from its modern addition, *Ragusa Superiore.* Since an earthquake destroyed the city (along with many others in southern Sicily) in 1693, Ibla's oldest architecture is from the early Baroque. Though the pace of life in Ragusa is decidedly lethargic, its views of the lush surrounding countryside, its *palazzi* with their ornate balconies, and its peaceful, contemplative atmosphere away from other tourists might just be the break from it all that you've been looking for.

ORIENTATION AND PRACTICAL INFORMATION

The train and bus stations are in P. del Popolo and neighboring P. Gramsci, respectively. To reach the city center from these adjacent *piazze,* hang a left as you exit either station onto **Viale Ten. Lena,** and follow it through P. Libertà and over the Ponte Senatore F. Pennavaria, the northernmost of three bridges crossing the Vallata Santa. The road over the bridge becomes **Via Roma,** which ends at the other side of town. **Corso Italia,** off Via Roma, leads downhill for several blocks, changes into **Via 24 Maggio,** and ends at the **Church of Santa Maria delle Scale.** From here, stairs and roads zig-zag the rest of the way down the hill to **Ragusa Ibla.** In Ibla, Via Ten. di Stefano leads straight past the AAPIT to the *piazza* of the **duomo.** At the opposite end of the *piazza,* Corso XXV Aprile leads to the end of Ibla at the Giardino Ibleo and the remains of **San Giorgio Vecchio** (the church, not the man).

Tourist Office: AAPIT, Via Capitano Bocchieri, 33 (tel. 62 14 21), in Ragusa Ibla; look for signs in P. del Duomo. Provides brochures and city maps, as well as info on nearby beaches and sights. Open Mon.-Sat. 8am-2pm.

Telephones: V. Maiorana, on the city side of Ponte Vecchio (the middle bridge). Open Mon.-Fri. 9am-12:30pm and 3:30-7pm.

Currency Exchange: Banks on Via Lena and Via Roma and in P. San Giorgio in Ragusa Ibla.

Trains: Train station is in P. del Popolo, at the southern end of the new town. From Syracuse (5 per day, 2½hr., L9800) and Gela (5 per day, 1½hr., L6500). One or two trains per day to/from Palermo (L24,400 one way). To get to Agrigento, change at Caltanissetta (L15,500 total one way).

Buses: In P. Gramsci at the southern end of the new town. **Etna** buses to Catania (12 per day Tues.-Sat., 15 on Mon. 5:30am-7pm, 2hr., L8900, L15,100 roundtrip). **AST** buses to: Syracuse (6 per day, 5:30am-7:15pm, 2½hr., L7500, L12,700 roundtrip); Gela (4 per day starting at 8:25am, L5400, L9100 roundtrip); and Palermo (3 per day, 5:30am-3:15pm, 2 on Sun. 3:15 and 5:30pm, 3½hr., L17,900, L30,500 roundtrip). Connections to Agrigento and Enna through Gela. Buy tickets for all buses at **Bar Salinitro** across the street from the bus depot.

Emergencies: tel. 113. **Ambulance: Ambulanza Croce Bianca,** Via L. da Vinci, 29 (tel. 65 26 60). 24-hr. service. **Hospital: Ospedale Civile,** right across from the train station on Via Leonardo da Vinci (tel. 62 14 10 during the day; tel. 62 39 46 for nighttime and holiday emergencies).

Police: tel. 112.

Post Office: (tel. 62 40 43) on P. Matteotti, 2 blocks down Corso Italia from Via Roma. Open Mon.-Sat. 8am-7:30pm. **Postal Code:** 97100.

Telephone Code: 0932.

SICILY

ACCOMMODATIONS AND CAMPING

One advantage of Ragusa's out-of-the-way location is that three-star hotels are priced extremely reasonably. The downside is that they are practically your only option.

Hotel San Giovanni, Via Transpontino, 3 (tel. 62 10 13), off the center bridge on the station side. A quiet, sleek hotel with great beds and marble bathrooms. TV in every room. Singles L33,000, with bath L50,000. Doubles L48,000, with bath L80,000. Breakfast included. V, MC, AmEx.

Hotel Jonio, Via Risorgimento, 49 (tel. 62 43 22). Walk down Viale Sicilia from P. del Popolo. Close to the train station. Darker than Hotel San Giovanni, but the showers are strong and hot. A TV and hardwood parquet floors in every room. Singles L34,000, with bath L58,000. Doubles L56,000, with bath L89,000. Breakfast L7000. V, MC, AmEx.

Camping: Ragusa's campgrounds are at **Marina,** 20km to the south. Tumino buses (tel. 62 31 84) run regularly from P. Gramsci in Ragusa to P. Duca degli Abruzzi in Marina (30min., L2900, L4900 roundtrip). **Baia del Sole** (tel. 23 98 44) is at Lungomare Andrea Doria. L6000 per person, L6000 per small tent, L10,000 per large tent, L14,000 per 6-person tent. **Campeggio Internazionale** (tel. 23 91 18) on Via Duilio runs L7000 per person, L7000 per small tent, L10,000 per large tent. Oct.-May prices drop by L500-1000. Buy supplies at SMA in Ragusa before heading out (see below).

FOOD

While in Ragusa, make a point to try some *panatigghie,* thin pastries filled with cocoa, cinnamon, and ground meat. Unfortunately, they aren't cheap, and neither are the *trattorie* where they're sold. If you're low on cash, visit the immense yet organized **SMA** supermarket on Viale Sicilia, downhill to the right from the train station. Open Mon.-Sat. 8:30am-2pm and 5-8pm, closed Wed. afternoon. AmEx.

Pizzeria La Grotta (tel. 22 73 70) on Via G. Cartia, the 2nd right off Via Roma at the red sign. A back-alley joint with melt-in-your-mouth pizza (L2000 per slice) and *calzoni* (L2000). Open Thurs.-Tues. 6pm-midnight.

La Valle, Via Risorgimento, 70 (tel. 22 93 41). From the station, take a right onto Viale Sicilia, then walk downhill past the gas station. *The* place young Ragusans recommend, though also on the pricey side. Picture menu shows off their wide variety of pizza L5000-11,000. *Primi* from L7000, *secondi* L7000-17,000. Cover L2500. Open Sat.-Thurs. noon-3pm and 7:30pm-midnight. V, MC, AmEx.

Caffè Trieste, Corso Italia, 76 (tel. 62 10 61), across from the post office. Superior Sicilian pastries (L1500-2000) and perfect iced *espresso* (L1700). Their specialty is *focaccia* (L2500). Fight with the locals for the one tiny table out front. Open Mon.-Sat. 6am-9pm or earlier, depending on business.

SIGHTS AND ENTERTAINMENT

The ornate Baroque façades of Ragusa's churches contrast with their often simple interiors—just as well, since many are closed to tourists due to vandalism attempts. Side streets delight with their ornamented doorways and balconies. The upper town boasts an **Museo Archaeologico** (tel. 62 29 63), one floor down and in back of the STANDA off Via Roma, with artifacts from the nearby Syracusan colony of Camarina. Go down the stairs to the ground level under the bridge, turn right, walk up the road a few steps, and take another right. If you see graffiti along the way, you're on the right path. (Open Mon.-Sat. 9am-2pm and 3-5:30pm, Sun. 9am-1pm. Free.) Via Santa Anna, your first right off Via Roma, is crossed by **Via della Frecce** and **Via dei Vespri,** two small streets lined with some of Ragusa's most charming homes.

To get to Ragusa Ibla, you can take the #3 city bus (L600, tickets in *tabacchi*), which leaves every hr. on the ½hr. from in front of the train station at P. del Popolo, and every hr., 10min. after the hr., from Corso Italia, next to the new town's *duomo.* The bus ride is fairly long; a prettier and quicker alternative is to make the steep 10-min. walk from the Church of Santa Maria delle Scale at the very bottom of Corso Italia (Via XXIV Maggio).

The stairs at Santa Maria offer a stellar view of Ragusa Ibla, crowned by a monastery and the 18th-century dome of **San Giorgio.** (Proper dress is required in the cathedral: no shorts, tank tops, or mini-skirts.) Descend under the roadway to P. Repubblica, at the bottom of 200m of tricky staircases. The road to the left circumscribes the town, passing abandoned monasteries and a lush valley of farmland. (On the way, try to spot the humorous balcony carvings.) You'll eventually come to the beautiful **Piazza del Duomo di San Giorgio,** at the top of the city. Corso XXV Aprile runs downhill from the *piazza* and ends at the **Giardino Ibleo,** home to two churches and shaded walks. There's also a small statue of Triton next to one church, but hidden by palms.

Below the entrance to the gardens is the **Portale di San Giorgio,** one of the few 14th-century structures to survive the 1693 earthquake. An **antique market** takes place the last Sunday of each month at Giardino Ibleo.

In summer, any citizen who owns a swimsuit spends the weekend at **Marina di Ragusa,** a drab resort strip. Autolinee Tumino (tel. 62 31 84) runs 14 buses per day to Marina (last departure 8:30pm, last return 10pm, L2900, L4900 roundtrip). A complete schedule is posted in the Polleria Giarrosto in Marina's P. Duca degli Abruzzi. In the same *piazza,* savor Marina's best **gelato** at Delle Rose, where the scoops are so enormous that they have to give you *two* cones. Since 1990 Ragusa has also hosted an international piano/voice/composition competition every year in late June. Organized by a Sicilian-American professor at NYU, it takes place in the theater of the Palazzo Comunale in Ragusa Ibla. For more info, visit the tourist office.

THE EASTERN COAST

Syracuse (Siracusa)

The most beautiful and noble of the Greek cities.

—Titus Livius (Livy), on Syracuse

If you were visiting Sicily in ancient times, Syracuse would have been the principal attraction. Founded by the Greeks in 734BC on the island of Ortigia, the town grew quickly, swelling across the 40m strait that separates the island from *terra firma* and expanding into a much larger and even more prosperous development (Neapolis) on the mainland. From the 6th to 3rd centuries BC, Syracuse was arguably the greatest city in the Western world, cultivating such luminaries as Theocritus, Archimedes, and the great Greek lyric poet Pindar. The city also boasts the world's largest theater and the first known cookbook. These accomplishments, however, occurred in antiquity—today's *siracusani* can only lament their city's millennia-long decline. Some say Syracuse began to slide in 211BC, when the Romans sacked the city. Others set the fatal date at AD668, when the emperor Constans was bludgeoned to death with a soap dish while bathing here. But the city's prominence was most seriously undermined in AD879, when the Arabs conquered Sicily and established Palermo as the capital of the island. Today, Syracuse is a somewhat grungy home to more history than it can handle, as modernity squeezes its way around the ruins scattered throughout the city. Nonetheless, the well-organized museums, the archaeological park, and the delightful atmosphere of Ortigia make Syracuse a worthwhile stop on your Sicilian itinerary.

ORIENTATION AND PRACTICAL INFORMATION

Syracuse lies on the eastern coast of Sicily, near the southern tip. A bridge joins the island of **Ortigia** to the mainland. This bridge becomes **Corso Umberto I** and leads past **Foro Siracusano** at the town center to the train station. From Foro Siracusano, cross the train tracks to the left of the Pantheon to reach **Corso Gelone,** which heads through the modern town to the archaeological park. Heading right from the Pantheon brings you to another set of train tracks. Go under the bridge to your left to find **Viale Cadorna,** which leads to the Sanctuary and the Museo Archeologico.

Tourist Office: APT, Via San Sebastiano, 43 (tel. 46 14 77). Take a right onto Viale Teocrito at the end of Corso Gelone; Via San Sebastiano is to your left before the Sanctuary. It's a 15-min. walk from the bus and train stations, but their maps, brochures, and advice in broken English are worth the walk. Open Mon.-Sat. 9am-1pm and 3-6:30pm. APT also has a **booth** (tel. 605 10) at the entrance to the archaeological park. Open daily 9am-1pm. In Ortigia, try the friendly **AAT** office at Via Maestranza, 33 (tel. 46 42 55), just off P. Archimede. Open Oct.-June Mon.-Sat. 8am-2pm and 4:30-7:30pm.

Telephones: On Via Teracati, at the end of Corso Gelone. Strongest A/C in Sicily. Open Mon.-Fri. 9am-12:30pm and 4-7:30pm.

Currency Exchange: The city has plenty of **banks,** especially in Ortigia, though the ticket office at the train station has rates that are just as good as the banks'. Open 7am-8:30pm. The small post office in P. delle Poste also has an exchange.

Trains: Via Francesco Crispi, midway between Oritigia and the archaeological park. Ticket office open daily 7am-8:30pm. To: Catania (10 per day, 1½hr., L7200); Taormina (6 per day, 2¼hr., L11,700); Messina (9 per day, 4hr., L15,500); Ragusa (5 per day, 2¼hr., L9800); Noto (11 per day, 35min., L3400); Rome (3 per day, L65,400); and Milan (2 per day, L83,700).

Buses: SAIS ticket office at Via Trieste, 28 (tel. 667 10). Open daily 5am-8pm. To: Catania (12 per day, 3 on Sun., 1¼hr., L6100, roundtrip L10,300); Palermo (5 per day, 1 on Sun., 4hr., L20,000, roundtrip L30,000); and Noto (11 per day, 3 on Sun., 1hr., L3700, roundtrip L6100). **AST** ticket office (tel. 46 27 11), next door to the post office. To: Catania (14 per day, 7 on Sun., L10,300); Noto (14 per day, 4 on Sun., L6100); and Piazza Armerina (7am, 3hr., L11,700, roundtrip L19,500); Ragusa (5 per day, 2 on Sun., L7500, roundtrip L12,700). Catch the buses at P. Marconi, where you can buy bus tickets (either AST or SAIS) from the newsstand located behind the *fermata* sign.

Public Transportation: Orange **ASAT** buses leave from P. delle Poste. Numbers 21, 22, and 24 head by Fontane Bianche, and #23 goes to Aranella. Tickets (L600) are available in most *tabbacchi.*

Pharmacy: La Madonnina, Corso Gelone, 1 (tel. 664 28). Open 8:30am-1pm and 4:30-8pm.

Emergencies: tel. 113. **Late-Night Emergencies: Guardia Medica** (tel. 225 55), on Via Reno a block from the station. **Hospital:** (tel. 685 55) on Via Testaferrata.

Police: (tel. 46 35 66) on Via S. Sebastiano.

Post Offices: P. delle Poste, 15 (tel. 684 16), a left after you cross the bridge to Ortigia. The larger one (tel. 669 95) holds *fermo posta*. Open Mon.-Sat. 8:15am-7:40pm. The smaller office across the street (tel. 689 73) will change money Mon.-Fri. 8:30am-5:30pm, Sat. 8:30am-1pm. **Postal Code:** 96100.

Telephone Code: 0931.

ACCOMMODATIONS AND CAMPING

The area between the train station and the bridge to Ortigia offers a wide selection of cheap stays. A room on Ortigia is nicer, but you'll pay for it. Women traveling alone should be especially wary of the area around the train station at night.

Pensione Bel Sit, Via Oglio, 5 (tel. 602 45), sign posted off Corso Gelone. Close to the train station. These 5th-floor rooms are modern and basic, with soft lighting and softer beds. Lock your windows onto the communal terrace before you head out. Singles L30,000, with bath L35,000. Doubles L40,000, with bath L50,000. Reserve one week ahead in Aug.

Albergo Aretusa, Via Francesco Crispi, 73 (tel. 242 11), just down the street from the train station. This reasonably priced 2-star hotel features spacious rooms and friendly management. English spoken. Singles L38,000, with bath L45,000. Doubles L55,000, with bath L60,000. Breakfast L5000. The restaurant downstairs whips up a "superfast lunch" for L12,000. AmEx.

Hotel Centrale, Corso Umberto, 141 (tel./fax 605 28); follow the signs from the train station. Bare-bones rooms with firm beds provide the perfect resting place if your train gets in at 1am. Ants have been known to lodge here occasionally as well, so leave food elsewhere. English spoken. Pay phone in the lobby. Singles L25,000. Doubles L40,000.

Hotel Milano, Corso Umberto I, 10 (tel. 669 81). An unpromising lobby leads to surprisingly well kept and recently renovated rooms. Prices are prominently posted downstairs as you enter to avoid arguments or misunderstandings. Singles L30,000, with bath L40,000. Doubles L50,000, with bath L65,000. Extra bed L1500. Reservations recommended in July and Aug.

Hotel Gran Bretagna, Via Savoia, 21 (tel./fax 687 65). Your only budget option on Ortigia. Luxurious carpeting on the stairs lets you know you're in for a hotel with an attitude. Singles L49,000, with bath L58,000. Doubles L82,000, with bath L93,000. Breakfast included. Half-pension (L64,000-73,000) required if you're staying more than 3 days.

Camping: Fontane Bianche, Viale dei Lidi, 476 (tel. 79 03 33), near the beach of the same name. Take bus #21 or 22 (L600) from the post office. Twenty km from Syracuse. L5000 per person, L7700 per small tent, L8000 per large tent. Open May-Oct. Buy basics at a Syracuse supermarket before you go.

FOOD

Though many restaurants in Syracuse cater to tourists well endowed with funds, you'll find budget eateries on Ortigia and scattered throughout the area between the train tracks and the archaeological park. In addition, an **open-air market** markets goods on Via Trento, near the Temple of Apollo on Ortigia. Open Mon.-Sat. 8am-early afternoon. The **Linguanti** supermarket, Corso Umberto I, 174 (tel. 46 29 24), across the street from the Hotel Centrale, is a warehouse filled to the brim with staples; produce is sold outside. Open Mon.-Tues. and Thurs.-Sat. 5:30am-8:30pm, Wed. 5:30am-1:30pm. For a surreal K-Mart-like experience, head to the **FAMILA** "hypermarket" at Viale Teracati, 34. Open Mon.-Tues. and Thurs.-Sat. 8:30am-1:45pm and 4:30-8:15pm, Wed. 8:30am-1:45pm. V, MC.

Spaghetteria do Scugghiu, Via D. Sciná, 11, off P. Archimede. An ancient Syracusan institution. Eighteen delicious types of spaghetti, most L6000. Try the *spaghetti a modo nostro* (L6000) for a special treat. Liter of wine L5000. *Secondi* L8000-15,000. Cover L1500. Open Tues.-Sun. noon-3pm and 5pm-midnight.

Trattoria Paolina, Via F. Crispi, 14 (tel. 70 23 21), on P. Marconi. The world's drabbest neighborhood, but inside await a cage full of warbling birds and good food at unbeatable prices. *Primi* L5000-6000. *Secondi* L8000-11,000. *Menù* L20,000. Cover L2000. Open Mon.-Sat. 11am-3pm and 7-10pm.

Pizzeria Trattoria Del Forestiero, Corso Timoleonte, 2 (tel. 46 12 45). Quality food without quantity price, halfway between the Sanctuary and the Foro Siracusano. Go under the train tracks at the bridge; the restaurant will be in front of you on the other side of P. Euripide. Unashamedly good *pennette al salmone* with gobs of cream (L8000). Grilled tuna or swordfish is a deal at L10,000. Wide range of pizza (from L4500) also available for takeout in the evenings. Cover 2000.

Ristorante Pizzeria? (Punto Interrogativo), Via Santa Teresa, 16 (tel. 46 31 74). A reasonably priced seafood mecca just steps from the duck pond on Ortigia. *Primi* start at L9000, but the best deals are the *secondi* (L10,000-15,000), which are unquestionably good (sorry). Open Thurs.-Tues. noon-3pm and 6:30-11pm.

SIGHTS

The major sights in Syracuse are concentrated in two main areas a few kilometers apart: the island of Ortigia and the archaeological park north of the train tracks.

Ortigia

Cross the bridge from Corso Umberto, the main approach to the island, and you'll abruptly find yourself in a small village with a life separate from that of the mainland. The ruins of two Greek temples and several Gothic and Renaissance churches and *palazzi* scatter themselves along the winding streets of the island. Just after the bridge to Ortigia are the ruins of the **Temple of Apollo,** the oldest peripteral (columns on all sides) Doric temple in Sicily (575BC). All that remain are two columns supporting a piece of entablature and parts of the *cella* wall enclosed in a fence. The lawns surrounding the ruins are in much better shape.

Up Corso Matteotti to the right is **Piazza Archimede,** the principal square of the old city. The partially moss-covered **Fountain of Diana** (undergoing restoration) spits forth a gurgling trickle of water amidst its whinnying horses and fish-riders. Original Gothic windows grace the 15th-century **Palazzo Lanzo** at #6; note the beautiful 14th-century Catalàn staircase in the courtyard. Down Via dei Montalto, a small passageway capped by a tiny portal leads to a fantastic external view of the **Palazzo Montalto** (1397), the fanciest of the Gothic palaces in town, with triple windows set in pointed arches with Arabic decoration.

The **duomo** is one of Italy's most extraordinary buildings. More than 2300 years separate the 18th-century baroque façade from the attached 5th-century BC **Temple of Athena.** The cumulative effect of the intervening centuries represents every period of Italian architecture. Once admired by Cicero, the temple was converted to a three-aisled Christian basilica in the 7th century. Of the 34 original columns, 26 remain, embedded either in the solid side walls, in the entrance, or in the Byzantine chapel at the end of the north aisle. The arches were carved directly out of the stone walls (as in Agrigento's Temple of Concord). An inscribed excerpt from a papal bull issued by Leo X in 1517 decorates the 16th-century wooden ceiling and asserts the importance of the church. (*Duomo* open daily 8am-noon and 4-7pm.) Electronic audio-visual info booths (L400) give mini-lectures on the cathedral.

Fragrant oleander trees and elegant *palazzi* line **Piazza del Duomo,** in front of the cathedral. At #24, the graceful façade of the **Palazzo Benevantano,** reconstructed in 1788, conceals a serpentine balcony. At the far end of the square, wiggly columns frame the entrance to the **Church of Santa Lucia alla Badia** (1695-1703; open only during church services). Santa Lucia, martyred at the hands of Christian-hating emperor Diocletian in the 3rd century AD, is Syracuse's patron saint.

From the *piazza,* wander down Via Picherale to the ancient **Fonte Aretusa,** a "miraculous" freshwater spring by the sea. Legend claims that it immortalizes the nymph Arethusa, who escaped from her admirer Alpheus through a tunnel. The goddess Diana transformed her into this fountain and transfigured Alpheus into a river in Greece that supposedly feeds this spring via Arethusa's getaway tunnel. Bring some bread to feed the ducks and swans that revel in the fresh water. Steps lead from here to the **Foro Vittorio Emanuele,** a tree-lined walk along the harbor.

From the fountain, walk back into the city along Via del Capodieci to reach the opulent **Galleria di Palazzo Bellomo** at #16 (tel. 696 17). This 14th- to 15th-century *palazzo* is a treasure trove of various forms of art, from ornate Sicilian carriages to Byzantine Bible scenes to wax crèches depicting the birth of Christ. Paintings of note are an *Annunciation* by Antonello da Messina and the gigantic *Burial of Santa Lucia* (1608) by Caravaggio. (Museum open Mon.-Sat. 9am-1:30pm, Sun. 9am-12:30pm. Admission L2000, under 18 and over 60 free.)

Archaeological Park

Syracuse's larger monuments are in or near the **Archaeological Park** (tel. 662 06) on the north side of town. Follow Corso Gelone to the intersection of Viale Teocrito; the entrance to the park is down Via Augusto to the left. (Open daily 9am-2hr. before sunset. Admission L2000, free for European Community residents who are under 18 or over 60.) The **Greek theater,** with its trapezoidal orchestra, was originally scooped out of solid rock around 475BC; not long afterwards, the Greek playwright Aeschylus produced his *Persians* here. The orchestra was made semi-circular in 335BC and enlarged in the 3rd century BC; at 138m in diameter, the theater is among the largest of its type and age known today. The *cavea,* or auditorium, originally had 59 rows of seats (now 42) in nine wedges, seating up to 15,000 people. You can still distinguish the three divisions of the theater—the *cavea,* the semi-circular orchestra pit, and the rectangular stage, which had a two-story permanent set consisting of niches and colonnades. Classical Greek plays are now staged in the theater every other year (see **Entertainment** below).

The **Paradise Quarry,** outside the entrance to the Greek theater, is a flowered area bordering the two large grottoes of the chalk cliffs: the **Orecchio di Dionigi** (Ear of Dionysius) and the **Grotta dei Cordari** (Cordmakers' Cave). The latter is closed to the public for safety reasons, but visitors can still see the former, an artificial grotto of cathedral proportions (65m long, 11m wide, and 23m high). Its name originally derived from its resemblance to a giant earlobe; its exceptional acoustics spawned the later legend that the tyrant Dionysius placed his prisoners here so he could eavesdrop on their conversations.

Exiting the theater/quarry area, you'll come to a fence through which you can see the **Altar of Hieron II** (241-215BC), once used for public sacrifices. At 198m by 23m, it is the world's largest known altar. Walk up the hill and enter the other gate to get to the **Roman amphitheater,** constructed in the 2nd century AD. As you exit the park, follow the perimeter from the outside (with the green fence on your left) and make a left onto Via E. Romagnoli to find the **tomb of Archimedes,** sitting behind a fence on a busy street corner. The tomb is dug entirely out of rock, even down to the triangular portico and crude columns at its entrance.

The extensive **Catacombe di San Giovanni,** a few blocks away down Viale Teocrito and across from the main APT office, are sporadically frescoed catacombs dug between AD315 and 360. One (obviously heat-exhausted) traveler once reported that a minotaur lurks in the depths of these dark and winding passages; take care not to get lost. Outside the catacombs lie the ruins of a building said to be the first Christian church in Sicily. The 4th-century **crypt of San Marziano** (the first bishop of Syracuse) lies below the ruins, where you'll find some haunting yet faded frescoes and Latin inscriptions. (Open March 15-Nov. 14 9am-6pm; Nov. 15-March 14 9am-1pm. Admission L2000, under 10 L1000.) The entire city is rumored to rest on a labyrinth of similar underground galleries, some running all the way to Catania, dug to provide refuge from invaders.

Down Viale Teocrito from the park, on the grounds of the Villa Landolina, the three-year-old **Museo Archeologico Regionale Paolo Orsi,** Viale Teocito, 66 (tel. 46 40 22), displays one of the world's best collections of Greek artifacts. Its holdings consist of clay figurines, fossils, elephant skeletons, and a collection of Greek vases that'll make your head spin. The museum's *pièce de résistance* is the headless statue of *Venus Anadiomene.* (Open Tues.-Sat. and 1st and 3rd Sun. of each month 9am-1pm. Admission L2000, under 18 and over 60 free.) Spend a few minutes at the **Museo del Papiro,** Viale Teocrito, 66 (tel. 616 16), behind the Paolo Orsi, with replicas of paper-making tools, fascinating samples of ancient papyrus art, and such papyrus products as boats and baskets. (Open Mon.-Sat. 9am-1:30pm. Free.) Down the hill toward the Sanctuary, visit the **Centro del Papiro,** where you can see artisans creating ready-to-buy (and pricey) equivalents of papyrus postcards. (Open daily 8am-7:30pm. Free, if you avoid buying anything.) Across from the Museo del Papiro is Syracuse's newest monument, the space-age **Santuario della Madonna delle Lacrime** (tel. 640 77). The French architects Michel Anrault and Pierre Parat, winners of a 1957 international competition, built the sanctuary to commemorate four days in 1953 when a statue of the Madonna cried continuously here. Tourists and pilgrims alike have flooded the spot ever since, and the stands outside selling souvenir "sacred objects" may shock the reverent and irreverent alike. You can see the sanctuary from any part of the city (it's easy to use as a marker), so even if you don't visit, it will mystify you at every turn. (Open daily 10:45am-noon and 5-6pm.)

ENTERTAINMENT

Every even-numbered year (i.e., not until '98), the city stages **Greek classical drama** in the spectacular setting of the Greek Theater. The cheapest seats cost L15,000-20,000; ask for details at the APT office. Tickets for **Instituto Nazionale del Dramma Antico (INDA)** are available at the theater box office (open 10am-1pm and 6-9:30pm) and on Ortigia at Corso Matteotti in the Palazzo Greco (open 9am-1pm). General admission is L15,000, reserved seats start at L30,000. Shows begin at 9pm. (The theater holds 15,000 people—don't worry about ticket availability.)

Beachcombers can travel 18km on bus #21, 22, or 24 (L600) from Syracuse to **Fontane Bianche,** a crescent-shaped beach frequented by a jet-set crowd. A smaller, less spectacular beach, but more popular with the locals, is **Arenella,** 8km from the city (bus #23 from P. della Poste, every 1½hr., 5 on Sun., L600).

Natives rate Ortigia nightlife a *"niente"* (nothin'), but don't give up so easily. The abundance of brightly lit monuments makes the tiny island a nightly stage for the *pas-*

seggiata. The prime place to promenade is along the port in the **Foro Vittorio Emanuele.** After 8pm, a sea of *siracusani* and their rambunctious children floods the area by the water, taking breaks in the café, admiring the trinkets for sale, or gawking at the foreign luxury yachts docked nearby. The APT tourist office organizes an evening boat tour of the port, walking tours of Ortiga by night, and a daytrip to Pantalica Necropolis (each L5000 per person).

■ Near Syracuse

PANTALICA

In a river gorge about 30km northwest of Syracuse, near Sortino, the eerie neolithic necropolis at **Pantalica** merits a visit. The gouged-out sockets of more than one thousand tombs stare out from looming cliffs. Bring a flashlight. Pantalica is most easily accessible by car, but you can take a bus from Syracuse to Sortino and walk the remaining 6km; or call **Zuccalà** (tel. 46 42 98), which runs half-day tours from Syracuse for L35,000 per person.

NOTO

After the city suffered complete destruction in a 1693 earthquake, the wealthy Landolino family rebuilt **Noto,** 32km southwest of Syracuse, in Baroque opulence. A cascade of palaces and churches, some set atop monumental staircases and others behind tropical gardens, glitters along **Corso Vittorio Emanuele.** Find this road by following Viale Marconi right above Noto's **Giardini Pubblici** (Public Gardens) through the **Porta Reale** (1838). The **APT tourist office,** P. XVI Maggio (tel. 83 67 44), on Corso Vittorio Emanuele, provides a free map of the most beautiful buildings. English spoken. Open in summer Mon. 8am-2pm, Tues.-Sat. 8am-2pm and 4-7pm, Sun. 8:30am-1:30pm. The office is located just behind the **Fontana d'Ercole** (1757). While Noto lavishes care on its 18th-century edifices, its Romanesque, Gothic, and modern structures languish in acute disrepair. The first site you reach as you approach the city center from Corso V. Emanuele is the **Church of S. Francesco all'Immacolata** (1704). Open daily 7:30am-noon and 4-8pm. The town's most noteworthy sight is the **duomo,** located a few blocks before the tourist office. Construction of the cathedral began immediately after the earthquake of 1693. Note that it bears the mark "S.P.Q.N." above the huge bronze door, Noto's version of Rome's *senatus populusque romanus*. Inside, you'll be captivated by 12 frescoes of saints glaring down at you from the *duomo's* ceiling. Open daily 8am-noon and 4-8pm. Dress appropriately.

Noto is easiest seen as a daytrip from Syracuse. If you choose to stay over, try the clean, pleasant, and distant **Albergo Stella,** Via F. Maiore, 44 (tel. 83 56 95). Singles L35,000. Doubles L60,000, with bath L70,000. Showers L2000. Payphone in lobby. **Trattoria del Carmine,** Via Ducezio, 1/A (tel. 83 87 05), the second right off Via S. La Rosa downhill from P. XVI Maggio, looks out at the Church of the Carmine. *Primi* L6000, including the *tagliatelle alla capricciosa* with a rich sauce of ground vegetables, garlic, and oil. *Secondi* L9000-13,000. Try the *antipasto rustico* for L3000 (cheese, olives, mushrooms, and dried tomatoes). Open daily noon-4pm and 7:30pm-midnight; closed Mon. in winter. V, MC, AmEx. Eggplant is a specialty at **Trattoria al Buco,** Via Zanardelli, 1 (tel. 83 81 42), the first left off Corso Vittorio Emanuele after the Porto Reale. Try the *tagliatelle alle melanzane* (egg noodles with eggplant) for L5000. *Menù* L15,000. Cover L1000. The owners also offer *affitta camere* (tel. 83 81 42 or 89 44 05) at L60,000 for a double with bath and use of kitchen. Restaurant open daily 10am-3:30pm and 7-10pm. In the same building as the magnificent Immacolata is the equally magnificent **Pasticceria La Vecchia Fontana,** Corso Vittorio Emanuele, 150 (tel. 83 94 12). Drop by for a homemade *gelato* or *latte di mandorla* (L2000), an incredible pastry (L20,000 a kilo), or a snail-shaped homemade marzipan. Upstairs is a beautiful sitting area under the Baroque arch of the original building. Open Tues.-Sun. 7am-midnight.

SAIS and **AST buses** leave from Syracuse in a steady stream from 5:45am to 7:50pm (22 per day, 5 on Sun., 40min., L3700, L6300 roundtrip); the last bus heads back at 9:15pm (7:15pm on Sun.). The ticket office is across the street from the bus stop in the Bar Efirmmedio. You can also reach Noto by train (10 per day, 30min., L3200), but it's a 20-min. walk uphill to town from the station. Fine beaches are only 7km away at **Noto Marina;** buses leave from the Giardini Pubblici (July-Aug. Mon.-Sat. 4 per day, rest of the year 2 per day, L1200; buy tickets on the bus).

Catania

Catanians claim that their city prepares them for any surprise the rest of the world could offer. The metropolis *is* intimidating, with chaotic traffic, immense, collapsing housing projects, and the unfortunate status as Italy's most crime-ridden city. Beneath the squalid veneer of its sooty *palazzi,* however, Catania reveals an intriguing urban mosaic. The city is a patchwork of modern and historic, where GAPs abut Baroque church façades and youngsters in Levis and Ramones t-shirts abut nasty, mean-tempered old men who predate the church façades. This ancient city has been repeatedly leveled (often by the nearby volcano) and rebuilt since its initial founding as a Greek colony in 729BC. Its most recent incarnation was shaped by the monstrous 1693 earthquake, after which G. B. Vaccarini embellished the city with sumptuous Baroque buildings. Walls of dark volcanic stone lend a characteristic pall to the historic quarter, matched by gray concrete elsewhere. The birthplace of the famous 19th-century opera composer Vincenzo Bellini, Catania remembers him with an active year-round cultural life. Despite rumors to the contrary, Catania offers just the sort of shabby elegance and expansive architectural proportions that you may miss after leaving Italy's northern cities.

ORIENTATION AND PRACTICAL INFORMATION

Catania lies between Messina and Syracuse on Sicily's eastern coast. The main street, **Via Etnea,** runs north from P. del Duomo out of the city center but becomes less interesting a few blocks after the public gardens at **Villa Bellini.** The bus and train stations are located east of the town center at **Piazza Giovanni XXIII,** near the water. With your back to the train station, cross the *piazza* and turn left onto **Corso Martiri della Libertà** (at points there is a sidewalk on only one side of the street). This road ends at P. della Republica; jog to your right onto bank-laden **Corso Sicilia,** which crosses Via Etnea at P. Stesicoro and the Bellini monument. Budget accommodations, the public gardens, and shi-shi boutiques await to your right; to your left lie the *duomo,* the small university, and the Teatro Bellini.

While Catania is notorious for its petty thievery, it is nevertheless conquerable by the cautious traveler. Don't let the threat of crime spoil Catania for you. Be cautious walking around the city, especially at night, and leave expensive watches or jewelry somewhere safe. Don't be afraid to make a scene if you feel threatened. Be particularly wary of staged distractions. Check the **Essentials** sections on **Safety and Security** (page 18) and **Women Travelers** (page 30) for further important information.

Tourist Office: AAPIT (tel. 730 62 33 or 730 62 22), on Via Cimarosa, off Via Etnea below the Villa Bellini. On the ground floor of what Catanians affectionately refer to as *il grattacielo* ("the skyscraper"). A snazzy city map and info on cultural events. Open Mon.-Fri. 9am-1pm and 4-7pm, Sat. 9am-1pm. **Branch offices** at the train station (tel. 730 62 55) and at the airport (tel. 730 62 66). Both open Mon.-Sat. 8:30am-1pm and 2:15-7:30pm.

Budget Travel: CTS, Via Garofalo, 3 (tel. 715 04 34), up the hill from the intersection of Via Etnea and Corso Sicilia. Student travel information. Open Mon.-Fri. 10am-1pm and 4-7pm.

Currency Exchange: At the **banks** near the intersection of Via Etnea and Corso Sicilia, or else at the **Ufficio Informazioni** near the ticket office in the train station.

English spoken. Open 7am-8pm. The **post office** will change money for you Mon.-Sat. 8:15am-1pm.

American Express: La Duca Viaggi, Via Etnea, 65 (tel. 31 61 55 or 31 67 11). Cardholders can get emergency cash, pay monthly AmEx bills, and have incoming mail held for up to one month here. This office is also a good place to inquire about ferries to Malta. Open Mon.-Fri. 9am-1pm and 4-7:30pm, Sat. 9am-noon.

Telephones: At the corner of Via Muscatello and Via Longo, just north of P. Roma past the gardens of the Villa Bellini. Open Mon.-Sat. 8am-8pm, Sun. 4-7pm.

Flights: Fontanarossa (tel. 34 53 67). Take bus #24 from the train station. Daily flights to Malta with **Air Malta,** Via Ventimiglia, 117 (tel. 53 99 83), where Corso Sicilia turns into Corso Martiri della Libertà.

Trains: P. Papa Giovanni XXIII (tel. 53 16 25). To: Syracuse (18 per day, 1¾hr., L7400); Messina (every hr., 2hr., L8000); Enna (11 per day, 1½hr., L7400); Palermo (6 per day, 4hr., L19,000); and Taormina-Giardini Naxos (every hr., 1½hr., L4200). Information window open 7am-9pm.

Buses: SAIS, Via D'Amico, 181 (tel. 53 61 68), in the right corner of the *piazza* as you exit the train station. Open 5am-8:30pm. To: Messina (8 per day, 1½hr., L9500); Taormina (15 per day, 1½hr., L2500); Syracuse (8 per day, 1½hr., L6100); Enna (7 per day, 1¼hr., L8500); Palermo (22 per day, 3hr., L17,000); and Agrigento (7 per day, 3hr., L10,500). In the same offices, **ETNA** (tel. 53 27 16) takes you from the train station to Piazza Armerina (7 per day, 2hr., L8600); Ragusa (10 per day, 2hr., L8900); and Palermo (L17,000). **AST,** Via Luigi Sturzo, 220 (tel. 28 12 80), in the left corner of the same *piazza.* Open 5am-8:30pm. In addition to local routes, AST also journeys to Syracuse (13 per day, 1½hr., L6100). All bus services are reduced considerably on Sun.

Public Transportation: AMT. From the train station, "alibus" goes to the airport and bus #27 travels to the beach. Buy tickets (valid 1½hr., L1300, L2000 roundtrip) at *tabacchi* or newsstands. If you're caught without one, your fine will be 60 times the ticket price.

Ferries: To Malta with **Marangolo Viaggi,** Via Vittorio Veneto, 57 (tel. 37 66 51). Open Mon.-Sat. 9am-1pm and 3:30-7:30pm. Student fares from L120,000.

Late-Night Pharmacy: Crocerossa, Via Etnea, 274 (tel. 31 70 53).

Emergencies: tel. 113. **First Aid: Guardia Medica** (tel. 726 26 00; nighttime and holidays). **Ambulance: Pronto Soccorso Ambulanze** tel. 49 77 77. **Hospital:** (tel. 32 65 33) on Via Vittorio Emanuele, off Via Plebiscito.

Police: tel. 112 or 31 77 33.

Post Office: Via Etnea, 215 (tel. 31 15 06), in the big building next to the Villa Bellini gardens. Open Mon.-Sat. 8:15am-7:40pm. **Postal Code:** 95100.

Telephone Code: 095.

ACCOMMODATIONS

Catania is blessed with many centrally located, cheap hotels off Via Etnea between the *duomo* and the post office. As always, reservations are a good idea in August and even September, when Sicily cools off a little and tourists come to explore.

Pensione Gresi, Via Pacini, 28 (tel. 32 27 09), off Via Etnea near Villa Bellini and the post office. Don't let the charred doors on the 1st floor discourage you; the *pensione* on the 3rd floor is very clean. Rooms have carved ceilings, gorgeous bathrooms, and antique furniture. Singles L35,000. Doubles L59,000, with bath L74,000. Breakfast L7000.

Pensione Ferrara, Via Umberto, 66 (tel. 31 60 00; fax 31 30 60), off Via Etnea across from the Bellini gardens. Snazzy, renovated rooms, many with private terraces, offer a breezy alternative to Catania's oppressive summer heat. Singles L35,000, with bath L43,000. Doubles L56,000, with bath L69,000.

Pensione Südland, Via Etnea, 270 (tel. 31 24 94 or 31 13 43), across from the post office. Large, bare rooms, some opening onto a courtyard and others facing noisy Via Etnea. Elegant and often full. Singles L35,000, with bath L47,000. Doubles L52,000, with bath L66,000. Breakfast L5000.

Pensione Rubens, Via Etnea, 196 (tel. 31 70 73). The very cheerful proprietor retired from a job at a fancy hotel, so he can usher you, in English, to your simple but attractive room. A/C optional (but a tempting option for summer afternoons) at L500 for 45min. Singles L34,000. Doubles L50,000. Triples L70,000.

FOOD

Don't leave Catania without trying their famous eggplant-and-ricotta spaghetti, named after composer Vincenzo Bellini's well-known opera *Norma.* Keep an eye out for another local favorite, the extremely small *masculini* (fresh anchovies, not men). A sprawling **market** extends from the end of Via Pacini (off Via Etnea) all the way to Corso Sicilia. Open Mon.-Sat. from early morning until 2pm. Another market, almost as big, can be found on Via Pardo off P. del Duomo; the main attraction is fish, but there is food of all kinds. The **SMA** supermarket lurks at Corso Sicilia, 50. Open Mon.-Tues. and Thurs.-Fri. 8:30am-1pm and 4-8pm, Wed. 8:30am-1pm. V, MC. Try the **Gelateria del Duomo,** across from the elephant fountain, for a variety of mysterious but delicious flavors with names like Alessandra and Giuseppe.

Trattoria la Paglia, Via Pardo, 23 (tel. 34 68 38). Come at lunch for the experience of eating in the heart of the busy market near P. Duomo. Carefully prepared seafood *primi* and *secondi* are tasty, but you have to swallow the bill for a whole meal (around L20,000-25,000 with wine and fruit) since there's no written menu. *Primi* from L6000, *secondi* about L8000-12,000. Solo women should be cautious in this area at night. Open Mon.-Sat. 8am-midnight.

Ristorante Rapido, Via F. Corridoni, 17, off Via Umberto a block from Via Etnea. An excellent deal is their *pranzo fisso* with *primo, secondo,* and wine (L13,000). Simple, filling *primi* from L5000. Open Mon.-Sat. noon-3pm and 6:30-10pm.

Nuova Trattoria del Forestiero, Via Coppola, 24/26 (tel. 31 62 83), in the neighborhood around the Teatro Bellini. Follow the candle-lit path from Via Sangiuliano to this secluded outdoor spot. Upscale *primi* L8000, *secondi* from L7000. Open for dinner Mon.-Sat.

Trattoria Calabrese, Via Penninello, 34 (tel. 32 24 61), off Via Etnea near the amphitheater. This native family whips up a delicious *pasta alla Norma* for L6000. *Primi* from L5000, *secondi* from L6000. Open Mon.-Sat. 8am-10pm, Sun. evenings.

Mythical Pub, Via Michele Rapisardi, 8, in the shadow of Teatro Bellini. (Yes, it really exists.) Watch Catania's beautiful people watch each other on weekend nights. Relax with imaginative cocktails for about L7000, or sample their legendary range of *panini* and pizza from L5000. Two warnings: the food falls short of the tastebud's expectations, and to a Catanian, a hamburger (L8000) has a chunk of ham right in the middle. Open from 9pm until everyone leaves.

SIGHTS

At the center of Catania's **Piazza del Duomo,** Vaccarini's lava **Fontana dell'Elefante** (Elephant Fountain, 1736) boasts a unique anatomical feature. Vaccarini, true to biological reality, carved his elephant (the symbol of the city) without visible testicles. When the statue was unveiled, horrified Catanian men concluded that this was a slur on their virility and demanded corrective measures; Vaccarini's acquiescence was, um, monumental. Residents pledge that visitors may attain citizenship by smooching the elephant's massive tush, but the altitude of the pachyderm's backside precludes such aspirations. Stand behind the cool fountain at the rear end of the square for a good view of the **cathedral,** introduced by an open space at its side which allows light to play fully on the Baroque regalia. The other buildings on the square (the 18th-century Palazzo del Municipio on the left, the former Seminario dei Chierici on the right) are striped black and white to mirror the side of the *duomo.*

Beware the Animal Spirits!

According to Catanian legend, each of the city's many animal fountains is inhabited by an animal spirit. Anyone who falls asleep by one of these fountains will lose their soul to the resident animal spirit and never wake up. Sweet dreams! **Let's Go does not recommend losing your soul to a resident animal spirit.**

The church interior, with a Baroque barrel-vaulted nave and domed side aisles, once looked quite different, as 1950s restoration work revealed. Stumps of old columns were found, as well as the tall pointed arches of the original three apses. The two transept chapels have exquisitely paneled Renaissance frames (1545). One of them, the Norman **Chapel of the Madonna** (right), also contains a beautiful Roman sarcophagus and a 15th-century statue of the Virgin. Twenty-five feet from the chapel, you can see the body of Catania's beloved priest, the Beato Cardinale Dusmet, his bony (quite literally) fingers sticking out of the vestments. To the right as you come through the main entrance is **Bellini's tomb,** guarded by a marble angel. The words and music inscribed above it are from *Sonnambula,* one of the composer's four principal works, and translate as "Ah, I didn't think I'd see you wilted so soon, flower." Proper dress is required for entry to the *duomo*.

Opera buffs shouldn't leave the city without a visit to the **Museo Belliniano,** off Via Vittorio Emanuele II from P. Duomo, across from the Church of San Francesco. The museum holds a modest collection of memorabilia from the composer's friends and family, as well as several original manuscripts of his works. Next door in the same courtyard stands the Museo Emilio Greco, chock full o' drawings of naked women. (Both museums open Mon.-Sat. 9am-1:30pm and Sun. 9am-12:30pm. Free.)

Up the hill from P. del Duomo at Via Vittorio Emanuele, 266, is the entrance to the **Greco-Roman Theater** (415BC). Behind the theater (entrance around back) is the similar but smaller **Odeon.** Mt. Etna's 1669 eruption coated the marble of both theaters in lava. (Open daily 9am-1hr. before sunset. Free.) In mid-July, **Catania Musica Estate** takes place on a stage set up in the Odeon; inquire at the AAPIT.

Up Via Etnea the **Bellini Gardens,** complete with serpentine walkways and a miniature duck pond, offer a lush refuge against the background of Mt. Etna. A few blocks before the gardens, at the intersection of Via Etnea and Corso Sicilia, are the ruins of a 2nd-century **Roman amphitheater,** just below street level. A later inscription reads: "For me, Christ made the city of Catania sublime."

ENTERTAINMENT

The **Teatro Bellini** (tel. 31 20 20) is the city's principal theater for opera and concerts. The symphony season begins in September (tickets from L15,000), and the opera season runs from October to June (tickets from L18,000). From July to September, the city and province host performances (mostly in the Odeon) of music, theater, and dance. All events are free, and schedules are plastered about town. Up Viale Africa from the train station, a renovated factory holds the dramatic theater of the Centro Fieristico, which also offers a summer series of dance, music, and theater. Ask at the tourist office for more info. The AAPIT puts out a free monthly bulletin *(Lapis),* available in most bars and at their office, on **nightlife** in Catania, including movies, concerts, and festivals.

La Plaja is a pleasant but crowded beach within view of a nearby power-plant (take bus #27 or D in June-Sept. only). **La Scogliera** is a better choice, farther away from Catania's port and with a clear bathing area by igneous cliffs (bus #34 from P. Duomo, 30min.).

SICILY

■ Near Catania: Mount Etna

Mt. Etna is one of the world's largest active volcanoes, and, at 3350m, is the largest and highest in Europe. The Greek poet Hesiod envisioned Etna as the home of Typhon, the last monster conceived by Earth to fight the gods before the dawn of the human race. If so, Typhon remains restless; a 1985 eruption destroyed much of the tourist station near the summit. Etna blew its top again in 1992, damaging the towns along its slopes.

Ferrovia-Circumetnea **trains** circumnavigate the volcano's circumference, stopping at the local villages of Adrano, Randazzo, and Giarre. From Catania, use **Stazione Borgo,** Via Caronda, 350 (tel. 541 24); Via Caronda is the street that forks off Via Etnea to the right just after the Bellini Gardens. At this station, you can hop on a train that runs along Etna's entire inland perimeter, finishing near the coast at Giarre-Riposto (3 per day, last one leaves Catania at 11:05am, 3½ hr., L7500). From Giarre-Riposto you can make connections onto the national railway and get back to Catania (or go on to Taormina) in less than an hour. If you'd like to do some real hands-on exploring, an AST **bus** leaves from Catania's central train station at 8:15am for **Rifugio Sapienza,** making a 10-min. rest stop at Nicolosi (where you can fill up your picnic basket), and returns at 4:15pm (roundtrip L6700). From Sapienza (1900m), you can hike up to **Torre del Filosofo** (The Philosopher's Tower, 2920m) and back in about 5hr. From here, about all you can see are the looming peaks of Etna's craters and the rising steam. The hike is difficult because the ashy, pebbly terrain slips underfoot; it's like climbing up a beach at a 35° angle. The other option is the (expensive) cable-car service that runs to 2500m and is then supplemented by 4x4s up to 2920m. (9am-4pm, last return 4:30pm. One way to 2500m L14,200, roundtrip L25,700. One way to 2920m L25,700, roundtrip L45,000. Children under 10 half-price. Closed if winds are high.)

From the Philosopher's Tower it is possible to hike another 2hr. to the **craters** themselves (roughly 1hr. to return). While the view is incredible, it may not be to die for; in fact, the trail is so difficult and the volcanic activity so unpredictable that all guided tours have been suspended. **A few years ago 11 tourists died when one of the craters erupted unexpectedly.** If you choose to brave the hike, take the necessary precautions—tell someone you are going up, make the trip with a partner, and carry sunscreen and water. However you choose to get up the volcano, you're in for thrilling sights: hardened lava, huge boulders, and unearthly craters. Bring a sweater and windbreaker; winds are ferocious, and even in mid-July pockets of snow sometimes remain. On the way down from the Tower, be sure to check out the **Valle de Bove,** Etna's original crater. If you are going up by Jeep, don't worry: the driver will stop to let you look.

Stock up on food before you leave, or explore the numerous eateries around the volcano's base. As a last resort the self-service cafeteria at the tourist station serves decent pizzas (L2000) and pasta (L7000). Contact **CIT,** Corso Umberto, 101 (tel. (0942) 233 01), and **SAT,** Corso Umberto, 73 (tel. 246 53), in Catania, to find out whether tours of Etna are available.

Taormina

The story goes that Neptune shipwrecked a boat full of Greeks off the eastern coast of Sicily in the 8th century BC, and only one sailor survived to crawl ashore. He was so inspired by the beautiful scenery that he decided to found a city, and Taormina (or, as it was called then, Tauromenium) was born. Historians, however, will tell you that the Carthaginians founded Tauromenium at the turn of the 4th century BC, only to have it wrested away almost immediately by the Greek tyrant Dionysius. Regardless of its origin, Taormina is a city of unsurpassed beauty—a clifftop covered by mansions, pine trees, and flowers, with a hazy blue coastline stretched below.

ORIENTATION AND PRACTICAL INFORMATION

The easiest way to get to Taormina is by **bus** from Messina or Catania. Although **trains** from Catania and Messina are more frequent, the train station is located far below Taormina; further access to the city depends on buses that make the run uphill every 15-75min. until 10:20pm (L1500). Taormina's main streets are closed to cars, and the town's small size means you can walk anywhere. From the bus depot, take a left up Via Pirandello to **Corso Umberto I,** the main drag, which runs the length of the town. Innumerable stepped side streets branch off this road. Via Naumachia leads downhill to **Via Bagnoli Croci,** which continues on to the public gardens. The four principal *piazze* are along Corso Umberto I.

Tourist Office: P. Santa Caterina (tel. 232 43; fax 249 41), in Palazzo Corvaia off Corso Umberto at P. Vittorio Emanuele. Helpful and well-organized, if they can slow down enough to notice you. English and French spoken, but not always Italian—this spot is a French vacation favorite. Excellent city map. Open Mon.-Sat. 8am-2pm and 4-7pm. May be open Sun. July-Aug.

Currency Exchange: Cambio Valuta, Corso Umberto, 224, right before P. S. Antonio. Open Mon.-Sat. 9am-1pm and 4-8pm. Also at hordes of other places on the *corso.* The ticket office in the bus depot will exchange cash only. Open early morning until 7pm. The train station will change money daily 5:40am-9:40pm.

American Express: La Duca Viaggi, Via Don Bosco, 39 (tel. 62 52 55), right on P. IX Aprile. Cash advances and traveler's check refunds. Holds mail for one month. Open Mon.-Fri. 9am-1pm and 4-7:30pm, Sat. 9am-noon.

Telephones: Via San Pancrazio, 6 (tel. 246 69), at the top of Via Pirandello in the Avis office. Open Mon.-Sat. 8am-1pm and 3-8pm, Sun. 9am-1pm.

Trains: (tel. 510 26 or 515 11). At the bottom of the hill, halfway between Taormina and neighboring Giardini-Naxos. To: Catania (29 per day, 45min., L4200), Messina (29 per day, 50min., L4200), Enna (L11,700), Palermo (L22,600), and Agrigento (L19,000).

Buses: SAIS (tel. 62 53 01). Ticket office open daily 6am-8:15pm. To Catania (12 per day, 4 on Sun., L5100) and Messina (16 per day, 6 on Sun., L5100) as well as local destinations. **CIT** offers "Etna Tramonto," a sunset trip up the volcano (June-Oct. Mon. and Wed., L65,000 per person).

Car Rental: Avis, Via San Pancrazio, 6 (tel. 230 41). Open Mon.-Sat. 8:30am-12:30pm and 4:30-8pm, Sun. drop-off only 9am-noon. V, MC, AmEx.

Moped Rental: Autonolo "City," P. Sant'Antonio, 5 (tel. 237 69), around the corner from the post office. Scooter L20,000 a day. Vespa L30,000 (must be at least 18 and have a license). They also rent cars for L80,000 a day, L340,000 per week. Open Mon.-Sat. 8am-noon and 4-8pm. Also try **California** (tel. 237 69) or **Sicily on Wheels** (tel. 62 56 57), both on Via Bagnoli Croci, across the street from the entrance to the public gardens, with similar hours and rates.

Pharmacy: Farmacia Ragusa, P. Duomo, 9 (tel. 280 58 or 280 22). Open daily 8:30am-1pm and 3:30-8:30pm. Your prescription must be marked "Urgent" to have it filled here.

Emergencies: tel. 113 and 537 45. **First Aid: Guardia Medica,** tel. 62 54 19. **Hospital: Ospedale San Vincenzo** (tel. 57 91), in P. San Vincenzo.

Police: tel. 112 or 232 32; fax 231 05.

Post Office: (tel. 230 10; fax 212 42), on P. S. Antonio at the top of Corso Umberto I near the hospital. Open Mon.-Sat. 8:30am-6:30pm. **Postal Code:** 98039.

Telephone Code: 0942.

ACCOMMODATIONS AND CAMPING

Reservations are a must in August; a call ahead in July will also save you much grief, but not all *pensioni* accept phone reservations. Additional accommodations are available in the nearby towns of Mazzarò, Spisone, and Giardini-Naxos; bus service to these areas stops around 9pm, but you can hike down steep trails to the first two.

Pensione Svizzera, Via Pirandello, 26 (tel. 237 90; fax 62 59 06), between the bus station and the town center. A little expensive, but worth every *lira.* The rose-colored building looks out over the magnificent coastline. Kept so neat even the Swiss would be impressed. All rooms have bath. Breakfast included. English spoken. Singles L50,000. Doubles L80,000. Triples L108,000. Open March-Nov. Usually booked in Aug. Telephone reservations recommended.

Villa Pompei, Via Bagnoli Croci, 88 (tel. 238 12), overlooking the public gardens. Run by sweet sisters who may give discounts for longer stays. Singles L35,000. Doubles L52,000, with bath L60,000. Extra bed L15,000.

Inn Piero, Via Pirandello, 20 (tel. 231 39), near the base of Corso Umberto in two buildings that look over the sea. Colorful, recently renovated rooms. Singles L40,000. Doubles L63,000. V, MC, AmEx.

Pensione Puglia, Via Dionisio, 1° (tel. 283 15), up the hill from the STANDA supermarket. Taormina's lowest-priced rooms are a fair walk from the bus, in a quiet and untouristy end of town. Breakfast included. About L25,000-35,000 per person, but don't be afraid to barter. Half-pension L60,000.

Camping: Campeggio San Leo, Via Nazionale (tel. 246 58), on the cape 200m up the hill from the train station. Take any bus from Taormina that passes the station on its route (L1500). L7000 per person, L8000 per small tent, L10,000 per large tent. Open year-round.

FOOD

Cheap eateries are few and far between; avoid everything off Corso Umberto I. Even buying bread, cheese, and fruit can be expensive unless you try the **STANDA** supermarket, Via Apollo Arcageta, 49 (tel. 237 81), at the end of Corso Umberto, one block up from the post office. Open Mon.-Sat. 8:30am-1pm and 5-9pm.

Trattoria da Nino, Via Pirandello, 37 (tel. 212 65), between the buses and the town center. The sign that says "Stop, you have found the best home-made cooking and pasta in Taormina" may very well be correct. *Primi* from L5500. *Secondi* (omelette) from L6000. Open daily noon-3:30pm and 6-11:30pm; closed Fri. in winter. V, MC, AmEx.

San Pancrazio, P. San Pancrazio, 3 (tel. 231 84), at the end of Via Pirandello. Crowded outdoor tables and a great location. Pizza L8500. *Cannelloni alla Siciliana* L7000. Cover L1500. Open Wed.-Mon. noon-3pm and 7-11pm. V, MC, AmEx.

Trattoria da Giorgio, Via Cappucini, 1 (tel. 248 93). Typical Sicilian cuisine. *Primi* and *secondi* each from L6000. "Any type of pizza you so desire," L6000-10,000. No cover or service charge. Open Mon.-Sat. 6am-midnight. V, MC, AmEx.

Gastronomia la Fontana, Via Constantino Patricio, 28 (tel. 234 78), up the hill to the right from the end of Via Pirandello. A variety of pizzas, *panini,* and savory pastries such as *cipolline* and *arancine,* each L2000-2500. Stand-up or take-out. Open Tues.-Sun. 9am-3pm and 7pm-midnight.

SIGHTS AND ENTERTAINMENT

Goethe thought the 3rd-century **Greek Theater** in Taormina commanded one of the most beautiful views in the world; see if *you* would sell your soul for the panorama. (Open daily 9am-7pm. Admission L2000, under 18 or over 60 free.) To get there, walk up Via Teatro Greco, off Corso Umberto I at P. Vittorio Emanuele. As you exit the theater, the grand Timeo Hotel, Taormina's first, is on your left. Descend Via di Giovanni and follow the signs to the **Villa Comunale,** a beautiful park complete with benches, flowered hedges, and a gorgeous view of Giardini-Naxos below. The park also houses—of all things—an old-fashioned submarine. (Open daily 8am-8pm.)

On the other side of P. Vittorio Emanuele, behind the tourist office, is the **Roman Odeon,** a small theater now partly covered by the Church of Santa Caterina next door. Farther up Corso Umberto, P. del Duomo showcases Taormina's 13th-century **duomo,** rebuilt during the Renaissance. (Open "when the Monsignor wants it to be open"; try the morning or early evening hours.) The Gothic interior shelters paintings by Messinese artists and a fine alabaster statue of the Virgin. A walk along Via Circonvallazione, which runs parallel to and above Corso Umberto, leads you to a small set of steep stairs that snakes up the mountainside to the **castello,** accessing Taormina's finest view.

In the summer, the city sometimes hosts **Taormina Arte,** an international festival of theater, music, and film (late July-Sept.). Most performances are in the Greek Theater or in the public gardens. (Admission L7000-50,000. For info call 211 42, visit the outdoor offices in P. Vittorio Emanuele, or inquire at the tourist office.) Taormina is home to a number of overpriced, uninteresting **discos.** Nightlife concentrates in nearby Giardini-Naxos (see below). One worthwhile nightspot in Taormina is **Tout Va,** Via Pirandello, 70 (tel. 238 24; fax 238 25), an open-air club with great views, although it's a tiring 30-min. trek from town. (Cover from L15,000. Open in summer daily 10pm-3:30am.) **Le Perroquet** (tel. 244 62), on Via Roma and P. S. Domenico de Guzman (walk downhill from P. IX Aprile), is a popular **gay club** with erratic hours; weekend nights are obviously your best bet. (Cover L15,000.)

Near Taormina

Taormina's closest and most popular beach is the **Lido Mazzarò** below town. Down the road to the right and 100m off the coast is the tiny **Isola Bella,** a national nature preserve. The *lido* is accessible by the cable car from Via Pirandello in Taormina (every 15min., L2000 one way, L2500 after 8:15pm). Open daily 8am-1:30am. Huge lines form for the return trip at "rush hour" from 5 to 7pm. Some of the nearby towns, **Castelmola** in particular, are scenic and just a short bus ride out of town. While in Taormina, don't miss the **Gole Alcantara,** a nearby haven of gorgeous gorges, wonderful waterfalls, and radical rapids. SAIS runs three buses there (9:15am, 12:15, and 2pm) but only one back (2:20pm, L4400, L7300 roundtrip). The water is so cold that you may want to rent a wetsuit from the Gole Alcantara office (tel. 98 50 10) for L10,000. L3000 will get you into the "water park." Remember to bring a towel, sunscreen, a change of clothes, and a pair of shoes you don't mind using to climb rapids.

Giardini-Naxos

Giardini-Naxos was the site of the first Greek colony in Sicily (734BC). In its heyday, the city (then called Naxos) had about 10,000 inhabitants. The region's beauty allowed the Naxians to live the good life—until they took the wrong side in the big Athenian-Syracusan conflicts of the late 5th century BC and were destroyed by Syracuse in 403BC. Nonetheless, the citizens of Syracuse have cause to be jealous today; with its gorgeous beach, active nightlife, and rich historical tradition, Giardini is a must-see for anyone touring eastern Sicily.

PRACTICAL INFORMATION

Only 5km away from Taormina, the township of Giardini shares a train station with its sister city. **SAIS** buses run from Giardini to the train station to Taormina in a continuous daily flow (36 buses per day) from 5:30am to 10pm (L1500 one way, L2500 roundtrip). The **AAST** tourist office, Via Tysandros, 54 (tel. (0942) 510 10; fax 528 48), is by the beach. English spoken. Open Mon.-Fri. 8:30am-2pm and 4:30-7:30pm; closed afternoons in winter. There is a **post office** at Via Erice, 1 (tel. 510 90). In an **emergency,** call the **Ospedale Civico** at 537 45; to reach the **carabinieri** call 516 66.

ACCOMMODATIONS AND FOOD

Hotels in Giardini are often filled in August—either make reservations in advance or visit at another time. The **Hotel Villa Mora,** Via Naxos, 47 (tel. 518 39), is a real Sicilian treat. The management has stocked the hotel with an outstanding medley of furnishings, including TVs. Cool off in the evenings at the attached seafront Mediterranean bar. Off-season singles from L50,000. Doubles from L75,000. Breakfast L6000. Half-pension L83,000. Full-pension L98,000. Prices rise significantly in August, when half- or full-pension is mandatory. In the **Pensione Otello,** Via Tysandros, 62 (tel. 510 09), all rooms have either bath or shower and a balcony overlooking the sea. Singles from L35,000. Doubles from L70,000. Breakfast included. Restaurant and bar on premises. For **camping,** try **Maretna** (tel. 527 94) on Via Pietralunga, a cheap alternative to the beachfront hotels. Campsites from L5000.

You can buy cheap food at the **Sigma** supermarket, Via Dalmazia, 31, down the street from the central bus stop. Open Mon.-Sat. 8am-12:30pm and 5-8pm. **Calypso,** Via IV Novembre, 267 (tel. 512 89), is right on the seafront. Pizza from L4000. Pasta from L5000. *Menù* L18,000. Open 11am-3pm and 7-11pm. V, MC, AmEx. **La Sirena,** Via Schisò, 36 (tel. 518 52), is next to the archaeological museum at the far end of town. Pizza from L5000. Cover L1000. Open daily noon-3pm and 8-11pm. V, MC, AmEx. Seafood is the house specialty at **Angelina,** Via Calcide Eubea, 2 (tel. 514 77). *Primi* from L6000. Open daily 7am-4am; closed Wed. in winter. V, MC, AmEx. For a quick, cheap bite, try the **Laboratorio Artigianale Micelli,** Via Stromboli, 9 (tel. 518

40), off Via Schiso. *Sfoglie con spinaci* (L2000) is a tasty treat. Try their pizza (L2500), *pasta al forno* (L4000), or savory pastries (L1800-2500). Open March-Oct. daily 9am-midnight.

SIGHTS AND ENTERTAINMENT

Recent excavations in the **archaeological park** have revealed the outlines of the city walls, built with huge irregular blocks of solidified lava. Unfortunately, the remains are so scant that they're unlikely to interest anyone who isn't a Ph.D. candidate in archaeology. (Open Mon.-Sat. 9am-1pm. Free.) The **archaeology museum** (tel. 510 01), on the Capo Schisò peninsula on the other side of Giardini, shows further evidence of the city's earliest inhabitants, including an inscribed ceramic cup, the earliest written document surviving from the colony. (Open daily 9am-2pm and 3-7pm; closed Mon. afternoons. Free.) At the tip of Capo Schisò is a **Nike statue** (the goddess, not the shoe), as well as a great view of Giardini's beaches with Taormina in the background.

At night, Giardini turns into a hip youth hangout. Most of the city's *gioventù* head over to **Mister Roll,** Via Jannuzzo, 31 (tel. 65 30 87). This pizzeria/sandwich joint doubles as a karaoke bar. (Open daily in summer from 8pm 'til the last person leaves. Closed Mon. in winter.) When you're done eating, consider heading over to the **Marabu** disco/restaurant/pianobar at Ctr. Scavi Naxos (tel. 540 76). Open in summer only. **Velvet** is at Via Jannuzzo, 4. Open in winter only.

SARDINIA (SARDEGNA)

Sardinia is the perfect antidote to Italy-overdose. When you're fed up with all the Botticellis and Brunelleschis, when you'd trade all the Gucci in the world for a single Gap, when the sight of one more church interior will surely send you screaming into the path of the nearest speeding Fiat, come to Sardinia to recover from all the refinement. Inspired by the island's mountainous terrain and rustic villages, D. H. Lawrence proclaimed it "not a bit like the rest of Italy." Although parts of the northern coast have sprouted the concrete condominiums of the modern tourist industry, much of Sardinia persists in its gorgeously untamed state. The mysterious ruins, the wild horses and pink flamingos, the wind-carved rock formations, and the deserted beaches all provide happy evidence that Lawrence's assessment still holds true today.

An old Sardinian legend says that when God finished making the world, He had a handful of dirt left over, which he threw into the Mediterranean and stepped on, thus creating Sardinia. One might add that the contours of that divine foot formed some of the world's most spectacular landscapes. Ancient civilizations that settled in Sardinia some 3500 years ago made a unique contribution to that topography—**nuraghi.** These cone-shaped fortified tower-houses, of which over 7000 survive today, were built of huge blocks of stone and assembled without the aid of mortar. This ancient culture also erected bird-shaped **Giants' Tombs** to house their collective dead and forged amusingly detailed figurines to bury with them.

The first recorded invaders of this constantly besieged land were the seafaring Phoenicians, followed by the Carthaginians in the sixth century BC. It was the practical Romans, however, who turned the island into an agricultural colony. After both the Vandals and the Moors weakened Rome's hold, local independent governments arose. The 13th century, however, brought a new wave of foreign invasions. The Pisans, the Aragonese, and the newly united Spanish all succeeded in conquering the island. Even Napoleon tried (but failed) to take Sardinia in 1793 in an offensive launched from Corsica. From Sardinia, Vittorio Emanuele, who became king of Italy in 1861, began his campaign to unify Italy. With the aid of its favorite son Giuseppe Garibaldi, he incorporated the island into the Italian state. Mussolini did much for Sardinia's transport networks, and many inhabitants still remember him fondly. In 1948, the island gained back some of its ancient independence when the Italian government granted it autonomous administration.

For much of this century the economy of Sardinia depended exclusively on agriculture. Only decades ago, *padroni* (landlords) still held the land, and poor farmers toiled under a system akin to serfdom. Due to the growing influence of the Italian Communist Party—both its founder, Antonio Gramsci, and its late Secretary General, Enrico Berlinguer, were Sardinians—much of the land is now owned by those who work it, although large sections of Sardinia's scenic coastline have recently fallen into the hands of foreign speculators. Despite an Italian campaign to promote the island as a vacation destination, the tourist industry is not uniformly developed. Many of the island's attractions remain virtually inaccessible without a car.

GETTING THERE

The cheapest way to go is on the ferry, *posta ponte* (deck class), from Civitavecchia to Olbia (usually around L30,000). Beware the summer tourist rush (late July through August) and the strong possibility of strikes when planning your trip to Sardinia. If you want to travel at the height of the tourism season, reserve tickets two weeks prior to departure. Prices listed below are for *poltrone* (reserved reclining deck chairs); note that prices vary greatly according to season. *Posta ponte* fares are often available only when all the *poltrone* are taken. **Tirrenia** operates the most ferries and offers the cheapest fares, but long delays occasionally mar the service. There are often extra ferries from June to September and ferry times change regularly, so check a current schedule. Tickets can often be purchased at travel agencies, either in foreign countries or within Italy.

Civitavecchia-Olbia: Both ways daily at 11pm (7hr., L33,900). There is also a **Ferrovie dello Stato** train connection from the ferry directly to Golfo Aranci, near Olbia (4 per day, 20min., L2700).

Civitavecchia-Cagliari: From Civitavecchia daily at 6:30pm and from Cagliari daily at 6pm (13hr., L35,000-64,000).

Civitavecchia-Arbatax: From Civitavecchia Wed. and Fri. at 6:30pm; late July-early Sept. additional Sat. ferries (11hr.). From Arbatax Sun. at midnight; June-Sept. Tues. at 8pm and Fri. at midnight; Oct.-May Wed. at midnight (10½hr., L29,000-52,000).

Genoa-Olbia: From Genoa, June-mid-July and Sept. daily at 6pm; mid-July-Aug. daily at 5 pm; Oct.-May Mon., Wed., and Fri. at 6pm. From Olbia, June-Sept. daily at 8:30pm; Oct.-May Tues., Thurs., and Sat. at 8:30pm (13hr., L38,000-70,000).

Genoa-Cagliari: From Genoa (mid-June-mid-Sept. only) Tues. and Thurs. at 4:45pm. From Cagliari Tues. and Sun. at 3pm (21hr., L54,000-94,000).

Genoa-Porto Torres: From both cities daily at 7:30pm (12½hr., L38,000-70,000).

Genoa-Arbatax: From Genoa Fri. at 6pm. High-season service also Wed., low-season service also Mon. Mid-July-mid-Sept. Mon. and Fri. at 7pm. From Arbatax, Sat. at 2pm, mid-July-mid-Sept. Sat. at 4pm (19hr., L38,000-72,000).

Naples-Cagliari: From Naples June-Sept. Thurs. at 5:30pm. From Cagliari Oct.-May at 7:15pm and Wed. at 6:30pm; mid-June through mid-Sept. additional Fri. ferries (16hr., L32,000-65,000).

Palermo-Cagliari: From Palermo Sat. at 7pm. From Cagliari Fri. at 7pm (14hr., L35,000-60,000).

Trapani-Cagliari: From Trapani Tues. at 9pm. From Cagliari Sun. at 7pm (11hr., L35,000-60,000).

Tunis-Cagliari: From Tunis Mon. at 8pm. From Cagliari Sun. at 7pm (22hr., L91,000-107,000).

Tirrenia offices are located in **Civitavecchia,** Stazione Marittima (tel. (0766) 288 01/2/3); **Genoa,** Stazione Marittima, Ponte Colombo (tel. (010) 275 80 41); **Palermo,** Calata Marinai d'Italia (tel. (091) 33 33 00); **Rome,** Via Bissolati, 41 (tel. (06) 474 20 41); **Naples,** Rione Sirignano, 2 (tel. (081) 720 11 11); **Trapani,** Corso Italia, 48 (tel. (0923) 218 96); and throughout Sardinia. In the **United States,** 683 South Collier Blvd., Marco Island, FL (tel. (813) 397-3384). In **England,** 40/42 Kenway Rd., London (tel. (0171) 244 84 22).

Linea dei Golfi runs ferries between Olbia and Piombino, and between Olbia and Livorno. *Posta ponte* L34,000-60,000. **Meridiana** runs ferries to cities across Europe.

Flights also link Olbia, Alghero, and Cagliari to most major Italian cities, as well as to Paris, Geneva, Zurich, Munich, and Frankfurt. Flights are faster, but the chaos of an Italian airport and the agony of paying exorbitant fares should discourage most budget travelers. Check with local travel offices for schedules, fares, and discounts.

ONCE THERE

Transportation

Public transportation in Sardinia is an inexpensive but somewhat inefficient way to see the island. Buses tend to miss many of Sardinia's treasures, including several spectacular campgrounds located next to Roman ruins or hidden sea coves. It is possible to plan a decent itinerary around the bus schedule, but watch out: if you get stuck late in the day in a town you're ready to escape, you may end up spending the night there. The three main bus companies are ARST, PANI, and FS. **ARST** links almost every village on the island to the nearest big town. Its service is oriented toward local residents; the bus stops on request at any cluster of houses as well as at the planned

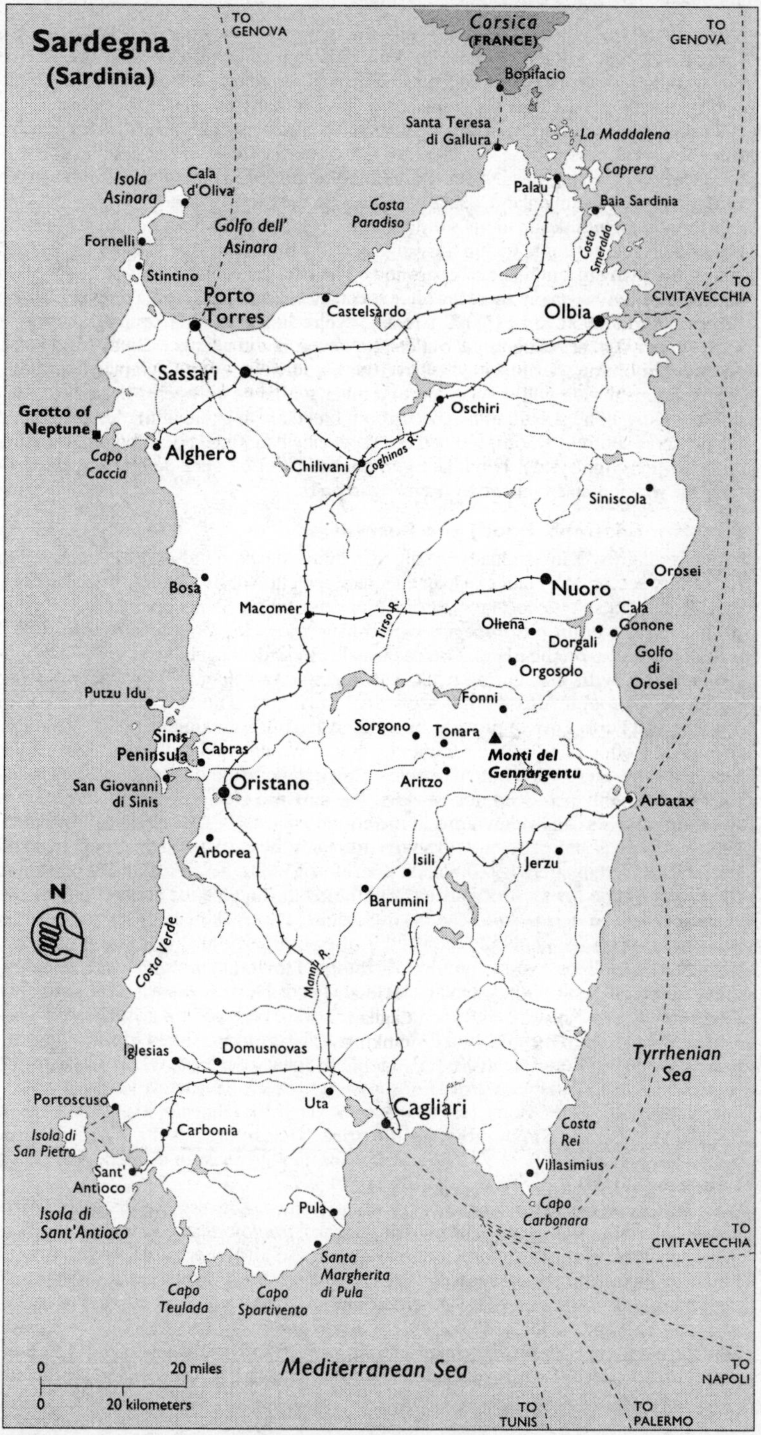

Sardegna (Sardinia)

TO GENOVA
Corsica (FRANCE)
TO GENOVA
Bonifacio
Santa Teresa di Gallura
La Maddalena
Caprera
Palau
Baia Sardinia
Costa Smeralda
Isola Asinara
Cala d'Oliva
Costa Paradiso
Golfo dell' Asinara
Fornelli
Stintino
Porto Torres
Castelsardo
Olbia
TO CIVITAVECCHIA
Sassari
Oschiri
Grotto of Neptune
Capo Caccia
Alghero
Chilivani
Coghinas R.
Siniscola
Bosa
Orosei
Nuoro
Macomer
Tirso R.
Cala Gonone
Oliena
Dorgali
Orgosolo
Golfo di Orosei
Putzu Idu
Fonni
Sorgono
Tonara
Sinis Peninsula
Cabras
Monti del Gennargentu
San Giovanni di Sinis
Oristano
Aritzo
Arbatax
Arborea
Jerzu
Isili
N
Barumini
Costa Verde
Mannu R.
Iglesias
Domusnovas
Tyrrhenian Sea
Portoscuso
Uta
Cagliari
Isola di San Pietro
Carbonia
Costa Rei
Sant' Antioco
Villasimius
Isola di Sant'Antioco
Capo Carbonara
Pula
TO CIVITAVECCHIA
Santa Margherita di Pula
Capo Teulada
Capo Spartivento
Mediterranean Sea
0 20 miles
0 20 kilometers
TO NAPOLI
TO TUNIS
TO PALERMO

SARDINIA

stops. **PANI,** in contrast, connects only the major cities—Mocomer, Porto Torres, Cagliari, Sassari, Oristano, and Nuoro—and although some buses stop at one or two intervening towns, many only stop at their final destinations. **FS** supplements its limited train service with buses to some of the most remote towns.

Train service has improved in recent years and remains significantly less expensive than bus service. For those not in a hurry, trains offer views of the countryside that are sacrificed with highway travel. Trains are often timed to meet ferries arriving from or departing to the mainland, usually stopping at the port.

The most prized destinations simply cannot be reached without a car. **Car rental** rates have recently come within the range of many budget travelers, allowing them to stay at the many magnificent campgrounds. The best car rental deals will be found in larger cities, where many agencies offer special weekend packages. Prices otherwise range from L50,000 to L175,000 per day. **Mopeds** are another option, starting at L30,000 per day. (Finding rental outlets, however, is a challenge.) **Bikes** seem to be an enticing option, but unless you have the leg muscles of an Olympian, Sardinia's mountainous terrain will reduce you to a hiker with a two-wheeled backpack. Anyone traveling alone should think twice about bicycling in some of the less-populated inland areas south of Nuoro; women are especially cautioned about biking or hiking alone in the countryside. **Hitchhiking in Sardinia can be very dangerous, particularly for women and even when traveling in pairs.**

Accommodations, Food, and Recreation

Virtually all growth in Sardinia's rapidly expanding vacation industry has occurred in the luxury sector. Most cities lack an adequate selection of moderately priced accommodations. Consult the local tourist office, and ask for the semi-dependable and comprehensive *Alberghi e Campeggi,* which lists prices for all hotels, *pensioni,* and official campsites on the island. You can usually find a decent single in town for about L30,000 per night, but during peak season single travelers will probably have to scrounge for roommates. Rooms are scarce in August. The two **youth hostels** (in Alghero and Porto Torres) provide an inexpensive but sometimes unreliable alternative, as they often fill up in the summer or shut down unexpectedly. Both lie near the beach and have crowded but airy rooms. **Camping** outside official campsites is illegal, but discreetly practiced nonetheless. **Agriturismo** is an excellent alternative to *pensioni;* tourists can live on farms in the countryside and eat dinners with host families, but a car is almost always necessary to reach these rural destinations (bed and breakfast approximately L30,000, half-pension L55,000, full-pension L70,000). Ask the tourist office for a list of participating farms in the area, or contact one of the agencies that run *agriturismo* centers in Sardinia. They will make reservations without the booking fee generally required in the summer months. If you write early enough, they will send you a complete directory of their *agriturismo* locations in Sardinia, complete with photos. Offices include: **Terra Nostra,** Associazione Sarda per l'Agriturismo, Via Sassari, 3, 09123 Cagliari (tel. (070) 66 83 67); **Agriturist,** Associazione Nazionale per l'Agriturismo, l'Ambiente, e il Territorio, Corso Vittorio Emmanuele, 101, 00186 Rome (tel. (06) 651 23 42) or Viale Trieste, 6, 09123 Cagliari (tel. (070) 66 83 30); **Turismo Verde,** Consorzio Agrituristico Sardegna Verde, Via Mariano Fortuny, 20, 00196 Rome (tel. (06) 366 99 31) or Via Libeccio, 31, 09100 Cagliari (tel. (070) 37 37 33); **Cooperativa Agrituristica "Dulcamara,"** Santa Maria La Palma, 07040 Sassari (tel. (079) 99 91 97); and **Consorzio Agriturismo di Sardegna,** Piazza Cattedrale, 17, 09170 Oristano (tel. (0783) 739 54).

Sardinia's **cuisine,** like its terrain, is rustic and rugged. A menu often includes hearty dishes like *sa fregula* (pasta in broth with saffron), *malloreddus* (dumplings with saffron), or *culurgiones* (ravioli stuffed with cheese and beet roots, covered with tomato sauce, lamb, and sausage). The most celebrated dishes are a vegetarian's nightmare: grilled pigs or goats, *cordula* (lamb entrails), and pork cooked in lamb's stomach. Fish and shellfish abound on the island and are often served in novel ways. Don't leave there without sampling such distinctive local specialties as *pane frattau,* a thin bread covered with eggs, cheese, and tomato sauce, and *seadas,* a delicious dough stuffed with sweet cheese, sugar, and honey. One infamous product of Sardinian shepherds is *formaggio con vermi* (cheese with worms living inside), considered a delicacy but, thankfully, rare. Look for daily outdoor markets in older neighborhoods, where you can get fresh bread, fruit, and goat and sheep cheese. The typical Sardinian bread, called *pane carasau* or *carta da musica,* is thin and crisp. In the summer months, apricots, peaches, and nectarines provide succulent picnic fare. The local honey spread on bread makes an excellent breakfast—Sardinian *miele* is an unusual and inexpensive delicacy you shouldn't miss. The local wines, often sweet and strong, warrant a taste or two (or more). Try *vernaccia d'Oristano* (which has a heady almond aftertaste) with fish, or the robust *cannonau di Sardegna* with meat.

For those interested in an alternative vacation amidst uncorrupted nature, Sardinia has much to offer. Over half of Italy's endangered species are found here, and various wildlife federations are petitioning the Italian government for more sanctuaries to protect these species from the constantly encroaching tourists. **Hiking and trekking** have become increasingly popular in the area, and guides from various cooperatives lead groups along shepherds' paths in the golden hills of the interior. Most local tourist agencies have info on local trekking adventures, or contact Ignazio Porcedda, an English speaker who arranges excursions in Sardinia with **Guide Ambientali Escursionistiche (GAE),** Cooperativa Turistica "Sinis," Campeggio Nurapolis, 09070 Narbolia, Oristano (tel. (0783) 522 83). **Horse-lovers** will find much to do in Sardinia, an area famous for its beautiful horses. Among other things, you can design your own riding adventures by contacting one of the local horse centers (ask at the tourist office).

Cagliari

Deservedly one of Sardinia's most popular destinations, Cagliari gracefully combines the verve and vigor of a bustling city, the rich history of a medieval town, and the panoramic splendor of gorgeous natural settings. Its wide boulevards abound with elegant boutiques, lively bars, and clamorous municipal buildings, while its narrow passages twist and turn around Roman ruins, Carthaginian fortifications, and Spanish churches—all enduring remains of Cagliari's tumultuous past. Nearby, placid lakes host pink flamingos, and beautiful beaches draw busloads of locals and tourists alike. From Cagliari, make daytrips to the *nuraghic* ruins near Barumini, the Phoenician-Roman city of Nora, and the Costa del Sud beaches.

ORIENTATION AND PRACTICAL INFORMATION

Hugging the harbor on one side and sporting outdoor *caffè* on the other, **Via Roma** will be right in front of you upon arrival by train, boat, or bus. At Via Roma's western end, **Piazza Matteotti** houses the train station, the ARST station, and the tourist office. To the east the road terminates in **Piazza Deffenu, Piazza Amendola,** and the PANI station. Across from P. Matteotti, broad **Largo Carlo Felice** climbs up the steep hill that leads to the **castello** and the historic center of town.

Tourist Office, P. Matteotti (tel. 66 92 55 or 66 49 23). Look for the oddly shaped cubicle in the park in front of the train and bus station. Sporadic hours, but when there, the sprightly, multilingual staff offers substantial information on the local sights. Open in summer Mon.-Fri. 8am-8pm, Sat. 8am-2pm; in winter Mon.-Sat. 8am-2pm. For additional help, try **ESIT** at Via Mameli, 97 (tel. toll free (167) 01 31 53). Open daily in summer 8am-8pm, in winter 9am-7pm.

Budget Travel: CTS, Via Cesare Balbo, 4 (tel. 48 82 60). Information on discounts and packages for students. Open Mon.-Fri. 9am-1pm and 4-7:30pm, Sat. 9am-1pm. **Associazione Italiana Studenti Sardi: Memo Travel,** Via Pitzolo, 1/A (tel. 40 09 07) offers general travel information. Open Mon.-Fri. 9am-1pm and 4:30-8pm, Sat. 9am-1pm.

Currency Exchange: In the train station at the information desk. Convenient, but poor rates. Open Mon.-Sat. 7:30am-7:25pm. For more *lire* for your money try any of the many banks that line Largo Carlo Felice. Open Mon.-Fri. 8am-1pm.

Telephones: Via Angioy, 4, off P. Matteotti. Open daily 8am-9:45pm. **Faxes** sent for L2000 per page.

Airport: In the village of **Elmas** (tel. 24 02 00). 24 ARST buses run between the airport and the city terminal at P. Matteotti daily.

Trains: Ferrovie dello Stato, P. Matteotti (tel. 65 62 93). Multi-lingual info. Open daily 5:15am-9pm, and 24-hr. convenient ticket machines. To: Olbia (6 per day, 4hr., L22,600); Porto Torres (1 per day, 4hr., L22,600); Sassari (6 per day, 3hr., L20,800), and Oristano (25 per day, 1½hr., L8000). **Ferrovie Complimentarie della Sardegna** (tel. 49 13 04), P. della Republica. A private railroad with supplementary services to Arbatax (L10,500). **Luggage Storage:** L5000 for 12hr. Open 5:45am-9pm.

Buses: PANI, P. Darsena, 4 (tel. 65 23 26), on the corner of Via Roma and Viale Regina Margherita; look for the red PANI sign. To: Sassari (7 per day, 3½hr., 3 non-stop L26,000, 4 requiring change at Macomer L24,400); Oristano (5 per day, 1½hr., L11,300); and Nuoro (4 per day, 3½hr., L21,600). Open Mon.-Fri. 6:30-7, 8-8:30am, 9am-2:15pm, and 5:30-7pm, Sat.-Sun. 1:30-2:15 and 5:30-7pm. **ARST,** P. Matteotti, 6 (tel. 65 72 36), serves local towns, including Pula (18 per day, L3900), Uta (12 per day, L2800); Barumini (at 2 and 5pm, L7200); and the airport (24 per day, L1300). Open daily 8am-2pm.

Ferries: Tirrenia, at the Stazione Marittima (tel. 66 60 65). Service to: Genoa (L54,000-74,000), Civitavecchia (L35,000-64,000), Palermo (L35,000-60,000), and Tunis (L91,000-107,000). Open Mon.-Fri. 9am-1pm and 4-7pm. Call toll-free for info, (167) 82 40 79. For port info in Italian, call 66 33 28.

Public Transportation: Orange ACT buses run in the city and beyond. All lines depart from P. Matteotti; buy tickets at the newsstand inside the ARST station (day pass, unlimited rides, L3100). Buses P, PQ, and PF go to the beach at Il Poetto. Ask at the tourist office about the special bus for the *castello* that departs from the end of Via Roma.

Car Rental: Ruvioli, Via dei Mille, 11 (tel. 65 89 55). Min. age 21. Major credit card (recommended) or L500,000 deposit. L106,000 per day. L167,000 per weekend. L522,000 per week. Reserve one week in advance. Another branch location at the airport (tel. 24 02 23). Open Mon.-Sat. 9am-9pm. **Avis,** at the airport or the train station (tel. 66 81 28). Min. age 23. From L180,000 per day. Open Mon.-Fri. 9am-1pm and 4-7pm, Sat. 8am-1pm. Also try **Hertz,** at the airport (tel. 24 00 37) or at the ARST station (tel. 66 81 05). Min. age 25. Walk-up price L180,000, though cheaper rates are available with reservations. Open Mon.-Fri. 9am-12:30pm and 4:30-7pm, Sat. 9am-12:30pm.

Laundry: Lavanderia Erica, Via Ospedale, 109. Up the hill toward the Roman amphitheater, across the street from the hospital. Bus #8 will take you there. Self-service L7000 for 5kg wash, 10min. of drying time L2000. Open daily 8am-10pm.

Pharmacy: Farmacia Dr. Spano, Via Roma, 99 (tel. 65 56 83). Open Mon.-Sat. 9am-1pm and 4:50-10:10pm.

Emergencies: tel. 113. **First Aid:** tel. 27 33 45. **Hospital:** military hospital on Via Ospedale, 46 (tel. 66 57 55), by the Chiesa di San Michele. Near Il Poetto lies **Ospedale Marino,** Viale Poetto, 12 (tel. 37 36 73).

Police: Via Amat, 9 (tel. 602 71).

Post Office: P. del Carmine (tel. 66 83 56). Take Via Sassari from P. Matteotti. Open Mon.-Fri. 8am-4:30pm and Sat. 8am-noon. Changes American Express Traveler's Cheques. **Postal code:** 09100.

Telephone Code: 070.

ACCOMMODATIONS

Cagliari has an ample stock of inexpensive places to stay, but with fierce competition year-round: university students from September until mid-July, tourists from July to mid-September. Ask the tourist office in P. Matteotti for help.

Allogio Firenze, Corso Vittorio Emanuele, 50 (tel. 65 36 78 or 65 52 22), off Largo Carlo Felice, on the 3rd floor. Sweet proprietress welcomes you into her very Italian home. Immense rooms with wrought-iron balconies and imposing furniture. The walls are covered with paintings and sketches by the hostess's mother, her guests, and other notables. Singles L36,800. Doubles L46,000. Pets allowed.

Pensione Vittoria, Via Roma, 75 (tel. 65 79 70), next to the movie theater. An elegant family-run *pensione*—one of the nicest in Cagliari—with cavernous, majestic rooms, mosaic floors, beautiful furnishings, and views of the sea. Singles L50,000, with bath L58,000. Doubles L80,000, with bath L95,000.

Hotel La Terrazza, Via Santa Margherita, 21 (tel. 66 86 52; fax 66 08 63), the street to the left at the top of P. Jenne (at the top of Largo Carlo Felice). A bit of a walk, but you'll be rewarded with a friendly staff and clean rooms on a quiet street. The newly remodeled rooms offer huge beds. Close to the *centro storico*. Singles L40,000, with bath L60,000. Doubles L60,000, with bath L80,000.

Alberto La Perla, Via Sardegna, 18 (tel. 65 16 79). Airy rooms, complete with balcony, recliner, and floral bedspread. Common living rooms equipped with TVs. Singles L44,000. Doubles L56,000. Enormous triples with vast terraces L73,900.

Albergo Palmas, Via Sardegna, 14 (tel. 65 16 79). Small, simply decorated rooms in an excellent location. Singles L38,000. Doubles L45,000, with bath 52,000.

FOOD

For basic foodstuffs and a cluster of cheap restaurants, head to **Via Sardegna,** where many small shops provide fruit, cheese, and bread. Try **Panetteria Mura,** Via Sardegna, 40, a small market and a heavenly bakery that offers soy milk and other hard-to-find protein products. Open Mon.-Sat. 7:40am-1:30pm and 4:30-8:30pm. On Sundays, explore the **food market** on the far side of the stadium in Borgo Sant' Elia. Fresh fruit and seafood reward the careful shopper and fearless bargainer.

Trattoria Lilicu, Via Sardegna, 78 (tel. 65 29 70). Established 80 years ago and still run by the same family, this *trattoria* serves up such traditional *sardi* dishes as *lacetti di agnelle* (L10,000) and fresh *pecorino* cheese (L5,000). A wild boar's head greets you as you enter. Open Mon.-Sat. 12:30-3pm and 8:30-11pm.

Trattoria Gennargentu, Via Sardegna, 60 (tel. 65 82 47). A *salumeria* and a restaurant. Join the locals for a delicious Sardinian feast of *spaghetti alle arselle e bottarga* (spaghetti loaded with baby clams and seasoned with ground fish eggs, L12,000) and a zesty *salsiccia arrosto* (L7000). Cover L2500. The wine list is as long as the menu. Open 12:15-2:55pm and 7-10:55pm. V, MC, AmEx.

Ristorante Stella Marina, Via Sardegna, 140 (tel. 66 66 92), near the PANI station. Boasts a colorful mural, aquamarine linens, and fresh flowers on every table. *Primi* L8,000-12,000, *secondi* L5,000-21,000. Cover L3,000.

Ristorante Pizzeria Downtown, P. Jenne, 18, at the top of Largo Carlo Felice. Fill up after an exhausting climb to the *castello* with their lunch *menù* (L15,000), including *riso nero,* shrimp, and *tiramisù*. Or try their pizza *alla* downtown, loaded with every topping imaginable (L12,000). Open daily noon-2:30pm and 8pm-12:30am.

Antica Hostaria, Via Cavour, 60, is reputedly one of Cagliari's best restaurants and is not wholly outside the budget traveler's reach. Though founded in 1852, this beautiful restaurant maintains a turn-of-the-century art nouveau decor. Elegantly serves *malloreddus* (L10,000), along with more *haute* fare like veal in a *vernaccia* sauce (L13,000). Open Mon.-Sat. noon-2:30pm and 8-11pm. V, MC, AmEx.

SIGHTS

The conspicuous pink towers of the **Bastione di San Remy** mark the division between the modern port and the cramped medieval quarter on the hill above. Climb up the double stairway at **Piazza Costituzione** for a spectacular view of the Golfo degli Angeli, flamingos, the marshes to the west, and the "Devil's Saddle," a rock formation set amid the mountains surrounding Cagliari. Narrow steps behind the *bastione* lead to medieval Cagliari, where wrought-iron balconies overflow with pink geraniums and the intimates of *cagliaritani* drying in the sun. The alarmingly narrow streets wind their way up the hill to the **duomo,** a stunning exemplar of Pisan geometry refinished in the Romanesque style of Pisa's own cathedral. Dazzling gold mosaics sit atop each entryway. The pulpits on either side of the main entrance, depicting scenes from the New Testament, are the work of Guglielmo Pisano, as are the four wrestling lions at the base of the 12th-century altar. The ornate wooden balcony to the left of the altar served as the seat of the Piedmontese king, who refused to sit among the people because he thought he saw the wild look of regicide on their scowling faces. Before leaving, glance below at the **sanctuary** carved into the island rock in 1618. The colorful marble inlays, many of which depict Sardinian saints with sharp objects protruding from their bodies, cover the 292 niches containing the relics of early Christian martyrs.

The **Torre di San Pancrazio** crowns the hill on P. Indipendenza, and its mate, the **Torre dell'Elefante,** lies below on Via Università. Erected at the beginning of the 14th century, they once guarded Cagliari's castle. Pass under the Torre di San Pancrazio to the **Arsenale,** from whose lofty towers you can admire the cityscape. Though the menacing spear above the entrance recalls the structure's original purpose, the Arsenale today houses the **Cittadella dei Musei,** a modern complex of research museums that includes the **Museo Archeologico Nazionale.** The collection holds Phoenician ceramics and Roman glass, but most impressive are the many detailed, Gumby-like figurines culled from nearby *nuraghi,* in poses of everyday *nuraghi* life. Some descriptions are in (poor) English. (Open daily in winter 9am-7pm; in summer 9am-2pm and 3-8pm. Admission L4000, under 18 and over 65 free.) The same complex also houses the **Pinacoteca Nazionale,** which holds ceramics (mostly 16th century) and religious paintings lifted from nearby churches. Except for one painting by Pietro Cavaro in which Mary Magdalene looks as if she's about to bite Christ's foot, the museum is generally uninteresting. (Open daily 8:30am-7:30pm. Admission L4,000, under 18 and over 60 free.) Both museums are wheelchair accessible.

To the right of P. Arsenale from the museums, more lovely views of the city and sea await discovery. Viale Buon Camino leads to the **Roman amphitheater,** one of the most significant Roman ruins in Sardinia. The 2nd-century BC theater follows the natural outcropping of the rock. Check out the underground store rooms where the animals were kept for the shows. (Open daily 9am-1pm and 5-8pm. Guided tours in Italian only, 9am-1pm. Free.) Continue down Via San Ignazio da Laconi to the university **botanical gardens** with over 500 species of plants—many rare, some extinct, and most unique to Sardinia. (Open daily 8am-1:30pm, April-Sept. also open 3-6:30pm. Free guided tours offered on the second and fourth Sundays of each month. Admission L1000, children L500.)

ENTERTAINMENT

Merchants converge on the terraces of the Bastione di San Remy for a **flea market** on Sunday mornings. Sift through used clothes, toys, and assorted junk. Show off your new garb at one of Cagliari's many nightclubs: **Doctor Blue,** Viale Monastir, 210 (tel. 54 25 42); **Red Fox,** Via S. Giovanni, 400 (tel. 40 16 14, closed Sundays); and **Fuori Orario,** Via Forlianini, 12 (tel. 30 39 99, closed Mondays). Clubs open at 9pm and close for the month of August (when dancing goes outdoors). AICS cards are required for admittance and can usually be purchased at the door for the one-time fee of L25,000. Such discos as the popular **Jazzino,** Viale Diaz, require no AICS. Nearby **Assemini** is home to several clubs, including **K2, Woodstock, Kilton,** and the gargantuan **Eurogarden.** All open 11pm and are closed Mon. Bus #9 from P. Matteotti goes to Assemini, but you'll need a taxi to get back. If you have a car or moped at your disposal and appreciate big pick-up scenes, you may enjoy a night at the beach with the young local crowd.

On the first of May, Sardinians flock to Cagliari for the stupendous **Festival of Sant'Efisio,** faithfully honoring a deserter from Diocletian's army who saved the island from the plague but couldn't save himself from a beheading. A costumed procession escorts his effigy from the capital down the coast to the small church that bears his name. From July to September, the city hosts an **arts festival.** The amphitheater comes alive with concerts, operas, and classic plays, while outdoor movies are shown at the Marina Piccola off Spiaggia del Poetto.

■ Near Cagliari

BEACHES

Il Poetto, Cagliari's most popular stretch of pure white sand and emerald-sapphire water, spans 10km from the massive Sella del Diavolo (Devil's Saddle) to the Margine Rosso (Red Bluff); behind it are the salt-water **Stagno di Molentargius** (Ponds of Molentargius), a popular flamingo hangout. City buses P, PQ, and PF cart natives and tourists alike to the sea (20min., L1300; tickets must be bought beforehand at the newsstand or the green bus kiosk in P. Matteotti). Once you see the beach from the bus, wait a few stops to avoid the crowded areas. For more private sunning and swimming head to **Cala Mosca,** a smaller, slightly less-crowded beach surrounded by dirt paths leading to isolated coves. To get there, take city bus #5/12 to Stadio Amsicora (ask the driver or look out the window to your left) and then city bus #11 to the beach. It takes a bit longer to reach than Il Poetto but is worth the trip.

DAYTRIPS

The ruins of **Barumini,** an agricultural village in the rolling countryside, lie 60km north of Cagliari and 1km west of the Nuraghi of Su Nuraxi. Open daily 8am-dusk. These ruins constitute the biggest and best-preserved complex of *nuraghi* in Sardinia. Set atop a hill, the village was laid out with huge rough-hewn blocks that demonstrate the defensive nature of this civilization. Ask the well informed staff for a free tour (in Italian only), or climb through the murky tunnels on your own. Horse lovers should watch for the *cavallini di Giara*—a small, sleek breed unique to Sardinia—galloping across the plateau of nearby **Gestiu** (2km away, follow the signs). The only direct service from Cagliari to Barumini is the ARST bus at 2 and 5pm (1½hr., L7200). Buses return to Cagliari only in the morning, so if you want get back in the evening, take the FS bus at 6pm (L3500) to San Luri. Once in San Luri, go to the FS train station to catch the commuter train to Cagliari at 7:03pm (L4200).

The tiny village of **Uta** (20km west of Cagliari) shelters the Church of Santa Maria, one of the island's most notable Romanesque buildings. Built around 1140, the church is a deft fusion of French and Pisan architectural styles. Twelve ARST buses per day commute from Cagliari (40min., L2800).

Ruins and beaches provide relief from Cagliari in nearby **Pula.** ARST buses will get you to Pula (about every hr., 30min., L3000), where you can see the treasures of nearby Nora displayed in the archaeological museum. In front of the *municipio*, to the right as you enter the museum, you can catch a little orange shuttle to the ruins, or you can walk 30min. along Via Nora; follow the signs. Open May-Sept. 9am-7:30pm, Oct.-April 9am-noon and 2pm-sunset. Admission L4000. The city of **Nora,** reputedly the oldest city in Sardinia, was settled by Phoenicians (circa 850BC) who coveted its strategic location at the end of a high, narrow peninsula on the Mediterranean. The prosperous town passed through the hands of the Carthaginians and the Romans, finally to be abandoned in the 8th century AD after too many pirate raids. Today Nora lazily watches over its pale-emerald waters in one of the most serene spots in southern Sardinia. Explore the remains of Punic temples, patrician homes, and a remarkably well preserved Roman theater, or take a short walk up to the watchtower for an awe-inspiring view of the site and the coastline. For those with knowledge of Italian, a free guided tour will fill in the historical gaps, but you can call ahead for tours in English (tel. 920 91 38). The guidebooks in English (L10,000) offer more pictures than explanations. All signs are in Italian. Open daily May-Sept. 9am-8pm, Sept.-April 9am-sunset. Free. Another option from Pula is the glittering beach of **Santa Margherita** (buses every hr., 30min., L1100). The hotels in S. Margherita are geared to those in their golden years with gold in their pockets, but the beaches are uncrowded and beautiful.

NUORO PROVINCE

Most guidebooks would have you believe that Nuoro is the last bastion of true Sardinian culture. If that's the case, then the traditional Sardinian dress is Benetton and the folk music is techno. Although many of the province's inland towns are quite isolated, only the older women wear the typical black dress draped with a Spanish *fazzoletto* (shawl); in a generation or so even this custom may disappear. Nuoro is a modern capital that makes an excellent base for exploring the province's rich archaeological treasures and beautiful, rugged countryside. Unfortunately, you'll need a car to reach many of the region's most intriguing locales.

Nuoro

ORIENTATION AND PRACTICAL INFORMATION

If you arrive by PANI bus, turn left and take Via B. Sassari right into **Piazza Italia.** If ARST bus was your carrier of choice, turn left off the little side street where you've been dropped and you'll be facing the train station and the ARST ticket counter. Turn right onto Via Lamarmora and follow it to **Piazza delle Grazie.** From there, if you turn left and follow Via IV Novembre up the hill, you'll come to **Piazza Italia.** Or cross P. della Grazie and keep going up **Corso Garibaldi,** a pedestrian walkway, to reach Nuoro's main square, **Piazza Vittorio Emanuele,** and beyond it, the *duomo.* Bus #4 makes the same trip from the station and saves you a 15- to 20-min. walk, while buses #5, 6, and 7 all end up at P. Vittorio Emanuele after various trajectories.

Tourist Office: P. Italia, D9 (tel. 300 83). Stocked with an array of booklets and brochures, the multi-lingual staff is eager to evoke Nuoro's past and offer hiking info. Information office generally open Mon. and Thurs. 9am-1pm and 3:30-7pm, Wed. and Fri. 9am-1pm and 3:30-7pm, Sat. 9am-1pm. The office on the 4th floor of the same building is usually open Mon.-Fri. 8am-2pm and Tues.-Wed. 4-7pm.

Telephones: At the bar next to the tourist office or one block away at Via Brigata Sassari, 6. Open Mon.-Sat. 8:30am-12:30pm and 3-7pm, Sun. 8am-1pm.

Trains and Buses: The **train** and **ARST** station is located on the corner of Via Lamarmora and Via Stazione. For bus info, call 322 01. Train to: Cagliari (1 per day, 4hr., L19,000). ARST buses to: Oliena (L1700), Orgosolo (L2800), and Cagliari (L18,400). The **PANI** station lies on Via B. Sassari, 15 (tel. 368 56), which you can reach by walking up Via Stazione and following it to the right. Buses to Sassari (6 per day, L13,100) and to Oristano and Cagliari (4 per day, L11,300 and L21,900 respectively). Municipal buses cost L1100 per ride. Buy tickets beforehand in the *tabacchi* in the station, or in the pizzeria in the southwest corner of the station. Bus #4 runs from P. Vittorio Emanuele to the station every 20min. **Luggage Storage:** At the station. Ask at the ticket counter. L1500 per day.

Car Rental: Autonoleggio Maggiore, Via Convento, 32 (tel. 304 61). From L132,000 per day. Min. age 21. Open Mon.-Sat. 8am-1pm and 3:30-7pm.

Emergencies: tel. 113. **Fire:** tel. 115. **Ambulance/Medical Emergency:** tel. 300 35 or 23 22 99.

Post Office: P. Crispi, 8 (tel. 302 78), off Via Dante. **Currency exchange** available at good rates. Open Mon.-Fri. 8:15am-5:30pm and Sat. 8:15am-12:20pm. **Postal Code:** 08100.

Telephone Code: 0784.

ACCOMMODATIONS

Inexpensive hotels are few and far between in Nuoro, and the campgrounds are quite far away in neighboring towns. Nearby *agriturismo* options include **Belloi Salvatore,** Monte Ortobene (tel. 379 15) and **Costa Tonino,** Costiolu (tel. 309 48). If you are unable to find accommodations in Nuoro, consider staying in Orgosolo or Oliena, where more rooms tend to be available.

Mini Hotel, Via Brofferio, 13 (tel. 331 59), off Via Roma. Firm beds bedecked with embroidered sheets. All rooms with bath—some cramped, some cavernous. Singles L60,000. Doubles L75,000. Triples L101,000. Family-run, so curfew is 11pm.

Hotel Grillo, Via Mons. Melas, 14 (tel. 386 78), off Via Manzoni. Follow the signs from P. delle Grazie. Dark wood furniture and ultra-soft beds. Added perks: TV and hairdryer. All rooms with bath, most with wrought-iron balconies. Breakfast in the restaurant downstairs L6000. Singles L72,000. Doubles L95,000. Half-pension: L65,000 in double, L82,000 in single. Full-pension: L78,000 in double, L95,000 in single. V, AmEx.

FOOD

Cheap restaurants are scarce. Try a bar on Corso Garibaldi or P. Vittorio Emanuele for a sandwich, or for more substantial provisions head to the **supermarket** on Via Manzoni, next to the Alitalia office. Open Mon.-Fri. 8am-2pm and 5-8pm, Sat. 8am-2pm. For fresh fruit, cheese, and meat, explore the enclosed **market** at P. Mameli, 20, off Via Manzoni. Open Mon.-Tues. and Thurs.-Sat. 8am-1pm and 4:30-7pm, Wed. 8am-1pm. Across the street and uphill from the ARST station awaits the **Ippo Mercato**; look for the smiling pink hippo. Open daily 8:30am-2pm and 5-8pm.

Il Portico, Via M. Bua, off the north end of P. Vittorio Emanuele. White arches connect rustic stone pillars. Join the locals in enjoying the L18,000 *menù,* which includes *primo, secondo, contorno,* fruit, and drink. Sample the house specialty, *ravioli di ricotta alla crema di carciofi* (L10,000). Cover L1000 for pizza, L2000 for everything else. Open Tues.-Sun. 12:30-2:30pm and 8-10:30pm. V, MC.

Canne Al Vento, Viale Repubblica, 66 (tel. 20 17 62), a 10-min. walk down Via Lamarmora from P. delle Grazie. Handsome decor, dominated by blond wood and enlivened by bright flowers. A generous serving of *pane frattau* (a classic Sardinian dish of cheese, egg, and tomato sauce on a bed of thin, crisp bread; L8500) will bring you to the height of gastronomic ecstasy. Try their *fettina* (a flavorful veal cutlet, L9000) or *porcetto,* a Sardinian staple and the house specialty. Cover L2500. Open Mon.-Sat. 12:30-3pm and 8-10:30pm.

Pizzalandia, Viale Repubblica, 2 (tel. 20 36 24); take a right as you exit the train station. Pizzas baked to perfection in a wood-burning oven (L5000-7000). Sit-down or take-out. You can call ahead and have your pizza prepared before you arrive. Open daily 7pm-midnight.

SIGHTS AND ENTERTAINMENT

Nuoro is home to a few small treasures. Ethnography buffs may enjoy the **Museo della Vita e delle Tradizioni Popolari Sarde** (Museum of Sardinian Life and Popular Traditions), Via Mereu, 56. Masks, traditional costumes, and a good deal of wool recall the days when the land, the men, and the sheep interacted more closely. On Via Grazia Deledda lies the **home of Grazia Deledda** (the winner of the 1926 Nobel Prize for Literature), now a museum celebrating her life. Both museums open April 3-Oct. 16 daily 9am-1pm and 3-7pm; June 15-Sept. 9am-7pm. (Admission for one museum L3000, combined ticket L5000.)

For a picnic, take the orange ATP bus #8 from P. Vittorio Emanuele up to **Monte Ortobene** (3 per day, L1100) or hike up the hillside (about 6 km; follow the signs, be aware of cars, and don't venture into the side paths if you're alone). At the peak lies a shady park where a bronze statue of Christ the Redeemer overlooks the neighboring hamlets. From the bus stop on Monte Ortobene, walk 20m down the road to get a good view of colossal **Monte Corrasi,** which dwarfs the neighboring town of **Oliena.** Named for a local writer, the surreal **Piazza Sebastiano Satto** lies off Via Roma and Corso Garibaldi. Imitating the Sardinian megaliths, the *piazza* sprouts huge pillars of rock with alcoves cut into them, each cradling statuettes that tell Satto's story. Nuoro still celebrates one folklore festival, the **Sagra del Redentore,** on the last two Sundays of August. Nuoro's natives claim that while in other parts of Sardinia such rites exist to placate tourists, here they are truly felt.

■ Near Nuoro

OLIENA

Oliena lies sheltered by the rocky terrain of Monte Corrasi. Catch the ARST bus from Nuoro (13 per day, L1700) to this undeveloped heartland village where black-clad women attend mass daily and old men cluster in *piazze* for hours on end to discuss whatever it is old men discuss. There are several churches in Oliena; the town's houses of worship even outnumber its *tabacchi.* Sadly, the most inspiring, **Santa Croce** on Via Grazia Deledda (which contains an ancient wooden tabernacle with an eerily realistic wooden sculpture of Christ's body in a coffin), recently closed for reconstruction. For information on the town, call the **tourist office** at 28 80 52.

Ci Kappa, on Via Martin Luther King (tel. 28 87 33) is a famous bar, restaurant, and hotel, with a view onto Corso Vittorio Emanuele II and the mountain. The rooms are modern and comfortable; all have private baths, TVs, and A/C. Ask for a room with a balcony looking over the pastel town and pale-grey cliffs. Singles L50,000. Doubles L70,000. For an inexpensive alternative accommodation, check with the Terranostra agency for available *agriturismo* rooms.

ORGOSOLO

Penetrating the area south of Oliena is difficult due to sparse public transportation; **ARST** buses run roundtrip at inconvenient hours. The trip to remote **Orgosolo** is a twisting tour (40min., L2700) through rugged green, vineyard-clad mountains. The area's bloody history of *banditismo* was made famous throughout Italy by the 1963 *The Bandits of Orgosolo;* a mural in the town immortalizes the film. The outer edges of the town are quite modern, with sand-colored apartment buildings, on-going construction, and occasional busloads of students, yet the winding streets of the *centro* still seem untouched by these developments. Welcome additions to Orgosolo's buildings include bright Picasso-esque murals depicting society's ills from commercialism to fascism to imperialism. Francesco del Casino, a local teacher, initiated the painting in the 1960s after studying art in Latin America. Schoolchildren from lands as far off as Russia have since come to make their own contribution to this outdoor museum.

If you can't tear yourself away from the murals or the mountain views, or if you decide to hike in the surrounding hills and need a place to stay in Orgosolo, follow the signs to the **Hotel Sa'e Jana,** Via E. Lussu (tel. 40 24 37), near the third ARST bus stop. This family-run hotel offers attractive, spacious rooms. Even the room numbers, true to the town's artistic leanings, are painted on colorful designs. The **restaurant** downstairs serves good, simple food. All rooms with bath. Singles L40,000. Doubles L70,000. Half-pension L70,000. Full-pension L80,000. The center of town holds the **Petit Hotel,** Via Mannu, 9 (tel. 40 20 09), off Corso Repubblica. More artwork by del Casino decorates the stairway, and bright rooms and hospitable staff welcome you to Orgosolo. Singles with private bath outside the room L40,000, with bath inside L45,000. Doubles L55,000 and L65,000, respectively.

CALA GONONE

Just over 1hr. east of Nuoro by ARST bus (4 per day via Dorgali, L5000) lies **Cala Gonone,** the gateway to several spectacular beaches and caves. Cala Gonone's own beaches are pebbly and crowded, but a walk or ride down the dirt road along the coast leads to sandier and less-populated beaches. Boats leave at 10, 11am, and 3pm daily, more frequently in July and August (L16,000), for the stunning **Grotta del Bue Marino** (Cave of the Monk Seal), one of the last haunts of this elusive creature. The seals rarely appear during the day, though, and the cave itself is the main attraction. Illuminated caverns, stalactites, and lakes stretch for nearly 1km. Unfortunately, stampeding crowds and the locked gate isolating the glowing *grotto* mar the experience. Just down the coast lies the vast beach of **Cala Luna.** Encircled by marshes and caverns, the beach is accessible only by boat (L12,000, combined ticket for cave and beach L25,000). Boats also run to the more remote and equally breathtaking beaches of **Cala Sistre** (L18,000) and **Cala Mariolu** (L25,000), both accessible only by boat. **Consorzio Marittimo Transport** has monopolized the boat transport market to beaches. Call 93 305 for reservations. **Cala Osal** is accessible only by car. Charter boats (**Boat Marine Charter,** tel. 935 46) and rentals (**Noleggio Gommone,** tel. (0337) 81 16 58) are also available at the port, though expensive (starting at L50,000 and L100,000 respectively). The **telephone code** is 0784.

Cala Gonone recognizes its allure to wealthy tourists, so budget accommodations are hard to come by. Try the newly renovated **Piccolo Hotel,** Via Colomba, 32 (tel. 93 232; fax 932 35). The gracious proprietor lends elegant, immaculate rooms with balconies overlooking a quiet garden or the nearby shore. Singles with bath L30,000-80,000. Doubles with bath L60,000-95,000. A large, well equipped, and expensive **campground** can be found on Via Collodi (tel. 931 65), across from the city park. April through mid-May and the latter half of Sept. L20,500 per adult, L11,900 under 12. Mid-May through July and the first half of Sept. L21,900 and L11,900. Aug. L23,900 and L14,900. Shower included.

The stunning mountains and scruffy hills that separate Nuoro from Cagliari hide towns of varying degrees of quaintness. One beautiful village is **Aritzo,** on the ARST bus line and near Gennargentu mountain (2000m high). The **Hotel Castello,** Corso Umberto (tel. 62 92 66) is pretty and modern. All rooms have fantastic views of the surrounding countryside. Singles with bath L45,000. Doubles with bath L60,000. Half-pension L70,000. Full-pension L80,000. Wheelchair accessible.

ORISTANO PROVINCE

The province of Oristano sustains a quiet life, cradling the glorious beaches and fascinating ancient ruins of the Sinis peninsula. The mineral wealth of the region attracted prehistoric settlers, who left stone *nuraghi* as their legacy. Many *oristanesi* still draw their sustenance from the fruits of the land. Its provincial, agricultural feel distinguishes Oristano from the more touristed regions of Sardinia.

Oristano

ORIENTATION AND PRACTICAL INFORMATION

Piazza Roma is the center of town. To get there from the train station, follow **Via Vittorio Veneto,** the street farthest to the right as you exit the station, straight to **Piazza Mariano,** and then take **Via Mazzini** to Piazza Roma (a 20-min. walk). The ARST station (with a helpful map outside) and the tourist office are located at the south end of **Via Cagliari.** To get to P. Roma from there, follow **Via Emanuele** from nearby **Piazza Mannu.** From the PANI station (located on **Via Lombardia** on the other side of town—north of P. Roma) head toward Via Tirso. Make a right and then an immediate left onto Via Cagliari. When you come to Via Tharros, turn left again; this street will take you directly into the square.

Tourist Office: Via Cagliari, 278, 6th floor (tel. 731 91 or 741 91), near P. Mannu across from the ARST station. Helpful, well-informed staff with info on the town and region. Open Mon. and Thurs.-Fri. 8am-2pm, Tues.-Wed. 8am-2pm and 4-8pm. There is a **Pro Loco** at Via Vittorio Emanuele, 8 (tel. 741 91), an independent tourist office with information on Oristano only. Open Mon.-Fri. 9am-noon and 5-8pm, Sat. 9am-noon.

Telephones: P. Eleanora d'Arborea, 40, opposite the Church of San Francesco. Open Mon.-Fri. 9am-1pm and 4:30-8pm, Sat. 9am-1pm.

Trains: P. Ungheria (tel. 722 70), about 1km from the town center. To: Sassari (6 per day, 3hr., L13,600); Olbia (6 per day, 4hr., L15,500); and Cagliari (16 per day, 1hr., L8000).

Buses: PANI, Via Lombardia, 30 (tel. 21 22 68), at a bar. Three buses leave daily to: Cagliari (8:55am, 4:10, and 9:35pm, 1½hr., L11,300); Nuoro (7am, 3:30, and 7:50pm, 2hr., L11,300); Sassari (7am, 3:30, and 7:50 pm, 2¼hr., L13,900). **ARST,** Via Cagliari (tel. 780 01), connects local routes and runs 2 slower buses to Cagliari (7:10am and 2:10pm, 1¾hr., L11,300).

Taxis: At the train station, some at P. Roma (tel. 702 80) during the day.

Emergencies: tel. 113. **First Aid:** tel. 743 33. **Ambulance:** tel. 782 22. **Main hospital,** Via Fondazione Rockefeller (tel. 742 61).

Post Office: For *fermo posta,* Via Liguria, 60 (tel. 21 17 78), near the PANI station. L300 for pick-up. Open Mon.-Sat. 8:15am-7:40pm. To change money, go to the branch in P. Ungheria near the train station. Open Mon.-Fri. 8:15am-5:30pm and Sat. 8:15am-1pm. **Postal Code:** 09170.

Telephone Code: 0783.

ACCOMMODATIONS AND CAMPING

The hotel selection here is extremely limited. Oristano caters primarily to travelers on their way to the beaches; competition is low, keeping prices high. For *agriturismo* options, check with the tourist office or the **Consorzio Agriturismo di Sardegna,** Piazza Cattedrale, 17 (tel. 739 54). This private housing will be less expensive but farther away (and often difficult to reach). More affordable lodging can be found in Cabras, but buses don't go there until July.

Piccolo Hotel, Via Martignano, 19 (tel. 715 00). From the tourist office, take a left at P. Mannu, and the first right onto Via G. Angioy. Via Martignano is the first left after the curve. The best budget option you'll find in town. Friendly owner, clean rooms, and firm beds make up for what the hotel lacks in interior design. All rooms with large bath, many with balconies. Singles L50,000-60,000. Doubles L80,000-90,000. Small breakfast (*caffè* and *cornetto*) L4000.

I.S.A., P. Mariano, 50 (tel. 36 01 01). Take Via Mazzini from P. Roma. All rooms boast immaculate baths, baby-blue decor, TV, and A/C. Singles L70,000. Doubles L100,000. Half-pension L95,000. Full-pension L115,000. Breakfast L7000.

Hotel CaMa, Via Veneto, 119 (tel. 743 74), near the train station. Modern, sterile, and very brown. All rooms with bath and A/C. Singles L76,000. Doubles L98,000.

Camping: Marina di Torregrande, Via Stella Maris (tel./fax 222 28), 100m out of Torre Grande toward Oristano (7km). Facilities galore; packed in summer. The nearby tar plant may mean an occasional waft of noxious fumes. L10,000 per tent. Open May-Sept. Bungalows house 4 for around L90,000 (off season L50,000).

FOOD

You can buy the basics as well as special *Sardi* products (like the sweet *pippias de zuccheru*) for rock-bottom prices at the **Euro-Drink** market, P. Roma, 22. Open Mon.-Fri. 8:15am-1pm and 5-8pm, Sat. 5-8pm. The **STANDA** supermarket, at the corner of Via Diaz and Via Cavour, is open 24hr.

La Torre, P. Roma, 52 (tel. 707 84). This local favorite serves traditional Sardinian fare like *gnocchi all'orgosolese* (L9000) and *gamberoni alla vernaccia* (shrimp in a wine sauce, L7000). Restaurant open daily noon-3pm and 7-11pm. *Pizzeria* open daily 6:30-11pm.

Trattoria del Teatro, Via Parpaglia, 13, off P. Roma. All the basics, done up right. Open Mon.-Sat. noon-2:30pm and 8-10:30pm. AmEx.

Mike and Maty, Via Veneto, 109, near the train station. Small hand-held pizzas wrapped up like *gyros* (L2000) and regular-sized pizzas (starting at L5000). One of the few places in town open daily (7-10pm).

Gelateria Christina, Via Mazzini, 9 (tel. 740 52). Blissful *gelato* (L1000) prepared fresh daily. Choose from a plethora of flavors.

SIGHTS AND ENTERTAINMENT

Piazza Roma is dominated by the 13th-century **Tower of St. Mariano II,** once a fortified entrance to the ancient city. On summer evenings, young *oristanesi* rock and ramble through this *piazza* and the adjoining **Corso Umberto.** The pastel **Church of San Francesco** stands at the end of Via de Castro, at Piazza E. d'Arborea. Heavily reconstructed in Neoclassical fashion during the 19th century, the church's interior retains little of its original appearance. A notable remnant is the sublime wooden crucifix on which the emaciated and tortured body of Christ is draped. The townspeople originally attributed the cross to Nicodemus because they felt that such a vivid image could only have been captured by an actual eyewitness to the Crucifixion. (The artist was actually a 16th-century teacher of Catalán culture.) The sacristy houses a 16th-century polyptych of *St. Francis Receiving the Stigmata* and Nino Pisano's marble statuette of San Basilio, sculpted in the 14th century.

Down Via E. d'Arborea from P. E. d'Arborea is the magnificent **duomo.** Originally constructed by Lombard artists in the 13th century, it was completely renovated in the 18th. In addition to the Gothic windows and medieval multi-colored bell tower, the cathedral also holds Baroque paintings, some Neoclassical architecture, and an animated sculpture of St. Michael. The **Antiquarium Arborense,** Via Parpaglia, 37, near P. Eleonora, shelters a small but fascinating collection of artifacts from the Nuraghic, Punic, and Roman eras unearthed at Tharros. (Open Tues.-Sun. 9:30am-1pm and 4:30-7pm. Admission L4000.) Three km out of town on the road to Cagliari is the 12th-century **Basilica of Santa Giusta,** typically Sardinian in its synthesis of Lombard and Pisan influences. Far from inspiring pious tranquility, the sculpted façade depicts two lions dismembering and devouring a deer. Set against this macabre backdrop is a tremendous square cross composed of dark blocks.

On the last Sunday of *Carnevale* and the following Tuesday (usually in March), inhabitants of Oristano don their best traditional finery and celebrate the **Sartiglia.** Townspeople ride on horseback through the streets, sporting white masks and androgynous dress. Later, a team of *falegnami* (wood-workers) competes with a team of *contadini* (farmers) in a sort of joust: participants gallop down the street, trying to pierce 6-inch metal stars with their swords. The winning squad is thought to garner *buon auspicio* (good fortune) for its fellow workers. Dating back to the days of Eleonora d'Arborea, Oristano's beloved heroine, this festival stands as an important part of the town's heritage.

Away from the stampedes, the **Malu Entu Adventure Team** offers scuba-diving classes and expeditions, rents canoes and sailing boats, and leads guided hikes and mountain bike tours. It's based in the town of **Cuglieri,** 45km from Oristano (tel. (0785) 38 352).

Sinis Peninsula and the Costa Verde

The coastal areas surrounding Oristano offer everything that the better-known resorts do—except the concrete and the crowds.

On the southernmost tip of the peninsula, 17km west of Oristano, lie the ruins of the ancient Phoenician port of **Tharros.** Much of the city remains submerged, but excavations have revealed Punic fortifications, a Roman temple dedicated to Demeter, an adapted Christian baptistry, and a Punic shrine. A medieval watchtower crowns the hill. Nearby lie serene beaches, where crystal-clear water kisses the shore. A long, flat bike ride or an easy drive from Oristano will make up for the patchy ARST bus service (only in July and Aug., 4 buses daily, 40min., L5300 roundtrip). On the way to Tharros you'll pass two pagan shrines-turned-churches. **San Salvatore,** near

Cabras, was built above a pagan temple whose Roman deities (Venus, Cupid, and Hercules) are still visible on an underground wall. (Ask the curate to show you. No fixed hours, but don't come at lunchtime.) With a rustic stone interior and a wooden altar that is plainer than most kitchen tables, **San Giovanni in Sinis** is the oldest church in Sardinia.

If you're tired of sight-seeing, sprawl on the beaches or check out the village of **San Giovanni di Sinis.** Two beaches, **Putzu Idu** and **Cala Saline,** lie 15km north of San Giovanni on the peninsula. Beautiful, white-sanded, and uncrowded, they're worth a few quiet days of lolling. To get to Putzu Idu from Oristano, take the ARST bus marked "Cala Saline" right to the beach. Bus schedules change seasonally, but plan to get up early. Walk a few kilometers south along the coast to see the stunning cliffs at **Capo sa Starraggia.** Approximately 7km south, the lovely cliffs and silky white beach of **Is Arustas** reward the hardy hiker; the less ambitious can take an ARST bus directly to Is Arutas (same line as San Giovanni, L2800).

About 35km south of Oristano, the **Costa Verde** stretches for nearly 40km, a pleasant mingling of sandy coves and scintillating ocean. Yet apart from the two coastal towns of Porto Palma and Marina di Arbus (where there is a rudimentary campsite), there are few locals to speak of, and even fewer travelers. Six ARST buses per day take you part of the way to Arbus, though *not* to Marina di Arbus or Diane (1½hr., L6100)—you'll have to fend for yourself the rest of the way.

The only affordable accommodation in the area is **Hotel "Su Pallosu,"** Via Sa Margosa, 2 (tel. (0783) 580 21), in Marina di S. Vero Milis. Singles L40,000-50,000. Doubles L70,000-90,000. The local fishing community frequents the hotel bar. You can find cheap food, live music, and a friendly gathering every night at **Club Tomoka;** ask at the hotel for directions.

NORTHWEST SARDINIA

Alghero

The smell of burning wood, the soft echo of footsteps on cobblestone streets, and the caress of a cool sea breeze are bound to induce romantic nostalgia in Alghero. Don't be surprised to find yourself strolling by the sea at sunset, thinking of former romances and lovers lost. As might be surmised from a single glance at the ancient city walls, Alghero is a city steeped in history, and local residents have never quite freed themselves from the past. Conquered and subjugated by Pere I of Aragon in the 14th century, *algheresi* today still speak a melodious Catalán dialect. In fact, the town has earned the nickname "Little Barcelona of Sardinia."

ORIENTATION AND PRACTICAL INFORMATION

Arriving by ARST or FS bus, you will be dropped off at the corner of Via Catalogna and Via Cagliari, one block from the port. The tourist office, located in **Piazza Porta Terra,** lies diagonally across the small park, toward the towers of the *centro storico.* From the train station, follow **Via Don Minzoni** until it turns into **Via Garibaldi** along the waterfront. The old city will be on your left. City buses AF and AP run from the train station to the port.

Tourist Office: P. Porta Terra, 9 (tel. 97 90 54; fax 97 48 81), on your right as you walk from the bus stop and the park toward the old city. The most organized office in Sardinia, if not Italy. Cheerful, helpful staff speaks English, French, and German and offers an indexed street map, tours of the city, and daytrips to local villages. Open May-Sept. Mon.-Sat. 8am-8pm; May-Aug. also open Sun. 9am-noon; Oct.-April Mon.-Sat. 8am-2pm.

Telephones: Mellino, Via La Marmora, 5 (tel. 97 55 68) and **Pittalis,** Via Manzoni, 109 (tel. 97 72 73).

Currency Exchange: Banca Nazionale del Lavoro, across from the tourist office. Has a 24-hr. automatic exchange machine (bills only, no traveler's checks). Also changes money inside. Open Mon.-Fri. 8:20am-1:20pm and 3-4:30pm. The central **post office** at Via XX Settembre, 112, changes money Mon.-Fri. 8:15am-5pm and Sat. 8:15am-1pm.

Trains: At Via Don Minzoni (tel. 95 07 85), in the northern part of the city. Take the AP or AF city bus from the stop 1 block north of the tourist office (every 20min.), or stroll 1km along the port. Open daily 5:30am-9:30pm. If you buy your ticket at the **FS booth** at the port, you can ride the city bus to the station for free. To Sassari (10 per day, 40min., L3200). **Luggage Storage:** L1500.

Buses: ARST (information tel. 263 92 20) and **FS** (tel. 95 01 79) buses depart from Via Catalogna. Buy tickets for either line at the stand in the park. To Sassari (18 per day, 1hr., L4500-5000), Bosa (4 per day, 1½hr., L5600-7300), and Porto Torres (4 per day, 1hr., L5000).

Public Transportation: Orange city buses begin their routes every 20min. or so and cost L1100 per trip. (Book of 12 tickets L11,000.) Line AF travels between Fertilia and the port (every hr., 7:10am-9:40pm), line AP goes to the train station (every 20min., 5:40am-9:40pm), line AO runs to the *lido* (beach) and the hospital (every 30min., 7:15am-8:45pm), line AC goes to Carmine (every 30min., 7:30am-8pm), and *linea mercato* travels between both ends of the city passing the market (Wed. 9am-noon).

Taxis: P. Porta Terra (tel. 97 53 96), across from the tourist office.

Car Rental: Budget (tel. 93 51 67), at the airport in Fertilia; **Avis** (tel. 93 50 64), at the airport; **Autonolotaxi Farris Carlo,** Via Mazzini, 44 (tel. 97 85 51). Rates start at L130,000. Minimum age 25. V, MC, AmEx.

Bike/Moped Rental: Cycloexpress di Tomaso Tilocca (tel. 98 69 50), on Via Garibaldi at the harbor. Bikes L12,000 per day, mountain bikes L18,000 per day, tandem bikes L20,000 per day. Mopeds L25,000 per day. Scooters L50,000 per day. Insurance included. Ask for their English-language brochure with a complete listing of prices and restrictions. Another location on Banchine Porto. Open Mon.-Sat. 9am-1pm and 4-8:30pm.

Horse Rental: Club Ippico Capuano (tel. 97 81 98). 3km from Alghero. L25,000 per hr. to rent a horse (often more reliable than Italian cars). Special guided excursions for an afternoon—reservations recommended 2-3 days in advance. They will pick you up in Alghero for a charge of L5000 per car load.

Public Toilets: Stalls at the port, next to the train office. Toilets L500.

Pharmacy: All pharmacies open Mon.-Sat. 9am-1pm and 4:30-7:50pm, including **Farmacia Mugoni,** Via Sassari, 8, across from the market.

Emergencies: tel. 113. **First Aid:** tel. 99 62 33. **Ambulance:** tel. 97 66 34 or 98 05 87. **Hospital: Ospedale Civile,** Regione la Pietraia (tel. 99 62 00), a few blocks north of the train station on V. Don Minzoni.

Police: P. della Mercede, 4 (tel. 113).

Post Office: Via XX Settembre (tel. 97 93 09). Open Mon.-Sat. 8:15am-7:10pm. *Fermo posta* open Mon.-Sat. 9:30am-1pm and 2:30-6pm (L300). **Postal Code:** 07041.

Telephone Code: 079.

ACCOMMODATIONS AND CAMPING

Prices escalate and rooms vanish in July and August. Unless you've made a reservation far in advance or are willing to pay for half-pension, which doesn't come cheap, consider redirecting your search from the center of town to the hotels on the beach on the way to Fertilia. Or inquire at the tourist office for *agriturismo* opportunities.

Ostello dei Giuliani (HI), Via Zara, 3 (tel./fax 93 03 53), 7km from Alghero in Fertilia. Take the orange AF city bus from Via La Marmora next to the train station (every hr., 15min., L1100). ARST buses depart from around the corner for Fertilia. Walk through the small rose garden and into the loving arms of Mamma Margherita. Rooms tidy and pleasant. Clothes washed for free. Close to the beach. Midnight curfew is not strictly enforced. L14,000 per person. Hot showers L1500; cold showers free. Breakfast L2500. Scrumptious lunches and dinners L14,000. *Always* reserved to capacity in July and August, so call ahead and secure a place. Other times, just show up—Mamma will do her best to accommodate.

Hotel San Francesco, Via Machin, 2 (tel./fax 98 03 30). With your back to the tourist office, walk straight and take the 2nd right. Simple but comfortable rooms in the church cloister, all with swell bathrooms, colorful floral bedspreads, and prayers by Saint Francis over the beds to ensure sweet dreams. Breakfast included—enjoy it on the lovely sandstone patio. Occasional concerts. Reserve ahead in summer. Singles L40,000-50,000. Doubles L70,000-90,000. V, MC.

Pensione Normandie, Via Mattei, 6 (tel. 97 53 02), a 15-min. walk from the port. From Via Cagliari (which turns into Via Papa Giovanni XXIII), turn right on Via Mattei. Decent, nondescript rooms with closets that may well predate the *nuraghi*. Singles L30,000. Doubles L60,000-65,000.

Hotel San Guian, Via G.M. Angioy, 2 (tel. 95 12 22). One block down from the beach. Firm beds and immaculate bathrooms. Each room decorated with its own psychedelic color scheme. Singles L55,000-65,000. Doubles L90,000-110,000. Breakfast included. V, MC, AmEx.

Camping: Calik (tel. 93 01 11), 6km away, before the bridge into Fertilia. Large and crowded, 50m from the beach. L11,000-16,000 per person. Open June-Sept. **La Mariposa** (tel. 95 03 60), Via Lido, 3km away on the Alghero-Fertilia road and near the beach. Packed in summer. L14,000-20,000 per person, L7000 per car, L4500-5500 per small tent, L70,000-105,000 per bungalow. Open March-Oct.

FOOD

Two blocks up from the tourist office, at the corner of Via Cagliari and Via Mazzini, a **market** offers the freshest in Sardinian produce (but may be closed for renovation in the winter months of 1997). Every Wednesday, crowds engulf the open air market on Via de Gasperi. Take the special bus, marked "Linea Mercato," from Via Cagliari. Cheese-lovers should not miss the pungent **Casa de Formaggio,** at Via Mazzini, 43, which makes and ages a delicious *pecorino.* Open Tues.-Sun. 7:30am-1pm and 4-8pm. Specialty stores in **Piazza Civica** sell traditional Sardinian fare, including eucalyptus honey and a marmalade-filled pastry called a *tilicus.* Some of these stores also carry soy-based products for vegetarians. Beware of the *algherese menù;* most cost L25,000 and consist of little more than spaghetti with tomato sauce and the unavoidable fried calamari.

Ristorante La Muraglia, Bastioni Marco Polo, 7 (tel. 97 50 02). Offers a stunning view of the sea. Try their homemade *spaghetti botarga* (L13,000). Pizzas L7000-12,000. Open daily 11:30am-3:30pm and 6:30pm-2am. V, MC, AmEx.

Ristorante La Piconia, Via Principe Umberto, 27 (tel. 987 001). A cozy tunnel of a restaurant, with a wood-burning fire at one end and heavy wood tables at the other. Enjoy their *spaghetti al nero* (L10,000) or crispy pizzas (L6000-12,000). Cover L2000. Open Tues.-Sun. noon-3pm and 7pm-midnight. V, AmEx.

Jamaica Inn, Via Principe Umberto, 57 (tel. 97 41 10). A pub/restaurant that draws locals for the beer selection (including Guinness) and tasty *panini* (L5000-6000). Also serves up burgers (L5000) and fries (L4000). Pasta L9000-10,000. Open Tues.-Sun. 7pm-3am.

SIGHTS AND ENTERTAINMENT

A leisurely walk through the *centro storico* reveals tiny alleyways, half-hidden churches, and the ancient town walls. Don't miss the fantastic views of the sea along Bastioni Marco Polo. From P. Sulis, Via Carlo Alberto takes you to the **Church of San Francesco,** whose heavy Neoclassical façade conceals a graceful Gothic presbytery. Although built in the 14th century, the church was partially rebuilt in the 16th; the different colored stones show where the original left off and the reconstruction began. Nearby is the medieval **Via Principe Umberto,** whose sand-colored buildings are nicely complemented by brown-and-green shutters. Just down the street at #7 you'll find the beautiful 16th-century **Casa Doria,** built by the powerful Doria clan of Genoa who transformed the fishing village of Alghero into a well fortified stronghold in the 11th century. From here you can get the most interesting view of the **cathedral**—the back. Begun in 1552, the cathedral took 178 years to build, resulting in a motley Gothic-Catalán-Renaissance façade. Rebuilt in the 19th century, the church retains its striking Gothic choirs and *campanile*.

To this day, three strategically located medieval **towers** continue to stand guard over the city. **Torre del Portal,** on Piazza Porta Terra, was once one of two access routes to the fortified Catalàn city, complete with a drawbridge and an artificial moat. **Torre de l'Espero Reial** in P. Sulis, used as a prison in the 18th century, is a circular fortification with a grand view of the ocean. The **Torre de Sant Jaume** is commonly known as the **Torre dels Cutxos** (Dog's Tower) since it served as a 15th-century dog pound.

Those who prefer to see fish in water rather than on their plate can check out the **Mare Nostrum Aquarium,** Via XX Settembre, 1 (tel. 97 83 33), across from the old city. (Open daily May 5-10pm, June 10am-1pm and 5-10pm, July and Sept. 10am-1pm and 5-11pm, Aug. 10am-1:30pm and 5pm-12:30am, Oct. 4-10pm, Nov. open only weekends and holidays 4-9pm. Admission L8000, students L4000.)

In addition to the Jamaica Inn (see above), the **Zebra Bar,** Via Barcelonetta, 15 (tel. 97 76 33) attracts cool young *algherese* for cocktails and conversation. Open Thurs.-Tues. 7:30pm-3am. **Bar de Trò,** on Lungomare Valencia at a picturesque bend in the bay, offers live music nightly. Open 8pm-1am. **Rhapsody in Blues,** Via Garibaldi, 53 (tel. 98 45 22) serves up delectable crepes on the waterfront. Open 8pm until dawn.

■ Near Alghero

Dubbed "the miracle of the gods" by the Duke of Buckingham, the **Grotte di Nettuno** (tel. 94 65 40) is a vast natural wonder—an eerie cavern-complex of dagger-like stalactites and stalagmites. The caves delve into Capo Caccia, a steep promontory which juts out from Porto Conte (25km by land from Alghero, 15km by sea). The FS bus combs the beautiful coast (leaving at 9:15am, 2:50, and 5:15pm, returning at noon, 3:45, and 6pm; 1hr.; one way L3400, roundtrip L5700). Once there, descend the memorable 654 steps that plunge between massive white cliffs all the way to the sea. Grottoes open Nov.-March 9am-2pm, April-Sept. 9am-7pm, Oct. 10am-5pm. Groups admitted hourly. Admission L10,000; under 12 L6000. Boats leave Alghero's Bastione della Maddalena hourly on the hour at **Navisarda** (tel. 97 55 99; roundtrip 2½hr., L15,000, under 12 L8000). If you're on moped, ride to the *grotte* in about 30min., stopping at the exquisite **beaches of Capo Caccia** and **Porto Conte,** as well as the **Nuraghe of Palmavera** (10km out of Alghero), where an intriguing central tower dates from 1500BC. Open daily April-Oct. 9am-1pm and 3-6:30pm, Nov.-March 9am-5pm. Admission L4000. Price includes a guided tour; call ahead for a language other than Italian (tel. 98 07 50). Ten km down the road to Porto Torres lies the extensive **Necropolis of Anghelu Ruju,** a group of 38 tombs built around 3000BC by the local fishing tribes. You can also take the ARST bus marked "San Marco" from Alghero (departures at 7:05am, 1:45, and 4:35pm; L1700).

BOSA

Clinging to the hills above the mouth of the Temo, Sardinia's only navigable river, Bosa maintains the quiet charm of a small town. The *centro storico* along the river and the beach of Bosa Marina have managed to remain pristine. While tour buses have recently begun to encroach on the town, its narrow passageways, wildflowers, and old pastel buildings persist in their traditional splendor.

FS buses connect Bosa to Alghero (6:35am and 12:05pm, L5000), Nuoro (8 per day, L8000), and Macomer (8 per day, L3500). **ARST** buses travel to Oristano (6 per day, L9000), Sassari (6:25, 7, and 11am, L9000), and Olbia (19 per day, L18,500). Buses stop either in Bosa's *centro storico* or across the river in Bosa Marina where the beaches lie. (It's a 20-min. walk between the two.)

Pro Loco, an independent **tourist office** (tel. 37 61 07), sits at the tip of **Corso Vittorio Emmanuele**—the main artery of the historic district. The **post office** hides at the dead end of Via G. Pischedda (tel. 37 31 39); traveler's checks can be exchanged here (L2000 fee for all amounts up to L100,000; L5000 fee for any higher amounts). Open Mon.-Fri. 8:30am-6:15pm and Sat. 8:15am-12:45pm. The town's **telephone code** is 0785.

A hostel is presently being built in Bosa Marina on Via Sardegna. In the interim, budget accommodations are available at **Albergo Miramare,** Viale Colombo, 30, on the waterfront (tel. 37 32 00). All rooms with soft beds and small bathrooms with showers. Singles L30,000-45,000. Doubles L60,000. Not far from the shore is **Hotel Bassu,** Via G. Deledda, 15 (tel./fax 37 34 56). Ask for a room with a terrace. Singles L30,000-40,000, with bath L35,000-45,000. Doubles L50,000-60,000, with bath L65,000-70,000. Half-pension L49,000-61,000, with bath L58,000-79,000. Breakfast included. Near the *centro storico* is **Albergo Perry Clan,** Viale Alghero, 3 (tel. 37 30 74; fax 37 52 63). Pink and brown rooms are all complete with bath, A/C, and TV. Singles L30,000. Doubles L60,000. Two km away from Bosa is a campground near the beach, **Campeggio Turas** (tel. 35 92 70).

Market Melas has two locations in the old town—Via Martiri della Libertà and Via Marconi, 16 (tel. 37 33 63). Open Mon.-Sat. 7:30am-1pm and 5-8:30pm, Sun. 8:30am-1pm. **Ristorante La Pulce Rossa,** Via Lungo Temo (tel. 37 56 57), lies beside the river. Admire their colorful mural as you munch on *seadas al miele,* a tasty Sardinian dessert. Pastas L6000-11,000. Pizzas L6000-13,500. Open Tues.-Sun. 12:15-2pm and 7:30-11pm. Or enjoy a pizza in the handsomely decorated and air-conditioned **Ristorante Margherita,** Via Parpaglia (tel. 37 37 23). When your sweet tooth acts up, head to **Caffè Chelo,** Corso Vittorio Emmanuele, 62 (tel. 37 30 92) for ice cream (starting at L2500) or snacks (from L4000). Open Tues.-Sun. 7am-midnight.

At the far end of town is the **Castello Malespina,** built in the 12th century by the family of the same name. From the top, admire the throng of pastel rooftops against a backdrop of rolling hills. The view is absolutely breathtaking (and you'll already be gasping for air after the 327-step climb). Ask the curator to show you the **Chapel della Regina,** whose frescoes date back to 1112. The façade of Bosa's *duomo,* **Church of Santa Maria Immacolata,** is an amalgam of 13th- and 14th-century styles, but the interior is pure Baroque. Its ornate fixtures and beautiful frescoes are definitely worth seeing. After a long day of sightseeing, soothe your spirits with a leisurely stroll beside the tree-lined Temos or along the quiet **beach of Bosa Marina.**

Sassari

Sardinia's second-largest city sits atop a limestone plateau, where its founders sought refuge from the foreign invaders and malaria epidemics common to coastal territory. Today Sassari is an important petrochemical center, with modern suburbs surrounding its compact medieval core. Here in the capital of Italy's largest province, Sassarians enjoy the highest standard of living in Sardinia. The grandiose 18th-century Piazza d'Italia and the many expensive boutiques which line the city's wide boulevards lend Sassari an air of modernity and pretension. But the pleasant, old-fashioned character of the medieval city manifests itself in the evening gathering of Sassarians, young and old, in Piazza d'Italia.

ORIENTATION AND PRACTICAL INFORMATION

At the heart of the city is the newly restored **Piazza d'Italia.** As you stand facing the Banco di Napoli in the *piazza,* **Via Roma** and the **PANI station** are on your left. **Emiciclo Garibaldi** and the **ARST station** are straight ahead, with the leafy **Piazza Castello** beyond. The main shopping street, **Corso Vittorio Emanuele,** and the **train station** (down a little further) are on your right.

Tourist Office: Viale Umberto, 72 (tel. 23 35 34). One block up and 2 blocks to the right of P. d'Italia, on the ground floor of a nondescript office building. Free maps and a personable, English-speaking staff. Open Mon.-Fri. 8-11:30am and 4-6pm.

Budget Travel: CTS, Via Costa, 48 (tel. 23 45 85), off Viale B. Sassari. Open Mon.-Fri. 9:30am-1pm and 4:30-7pm, Sat. 9:30am-noon.

Currency Exchange: Available at any bank or a branch of the post office (Via Alghero, 102). Open Mon.-Fri. 8:10am-6:20pm and Sat. 8:10am-12:45pm.

Telephones: In the train station and at Via Cavour, 1 (tel. 25 70 00). Open Mon.-Fri. 8:30am-12:15pm and 3:30-6:30pm.

Airport: Near Alghera Fertilia, 35km to the south. ARST buses leave for the airport from the station 1¼hr. before departures. Both domestic and international flights. **Airport Information:** tel. 93 50 33.

Trains: P. Stazione (tel. 26 03 62), 1 block from P. Sant'Antonio. To: Olbia (9 per day, 2hr., L9800); Oristano (5 per day, 2¾hr., L13,600); Cagliari (4 per day, 3½hr., L20,000); Alghero (10 per day, 40min., L3200). Take the #8 bus from the station to avoid the long uphill trek to P. d'Italia. Buy tickets in the newsstand at the station (L1100). **Luggage Storage:** Open 6:30am-8:30pm; L5000 for 12hr.

Buses: PANI, Via Bellieni, 25 (tel. 23 69 83 or 23 47 82), 1 block from P. d'Italia. To: Cagliari (6:36, 9:36am, 2, and 7:15pm, 4hr., L24,400; nonstop at 6am, 2:15, and 6pm, 3¼hr., L26,000); Nuoro (6 per day, 2½hr., L13,100); Oristano (5 per day, 2¼hr., L13,900). Open Mon.-Fri. 5:30-6:35am, 8:30am-2:15pm, and 5-7:15pm; Sat.-Sun. 5:30-6:35am, 9-9:30am, noon-2:15pm, and 5-7:15pm. **ARST,** Emiciclo Garibaldi, 23 (tel. 26 00 06). To: Porto Torres (about every 30min., 5:20am-9:15pm, L2300); Castelsardo (12 per day, L3900); and Torralba (8 per day, L4500). **FS** (tel. 24 13 01), also at Emiciclo Garibaldi. Tickets in the bar next door at #26. Runs 13 buses per day to Alghero (1½hr., L4500 or L5000, depending on the time). Both counters open 5am-8:30pm.

Taxis: (tel. 234 630) at Emiciclo Garibaldi. 24-hr. taxi services are **Pinna Gianuario** (tel. 27 08 52) and **Radiotaxi Ruzzeddu** (tel. 29 92 42).

Car Rental: Avis, Via Mazzini, 2 (tel. 23 55 47). From L165,000 per day. Minimum age 24.

All-Night Pharmacy: Simon, Via Brigata Sassari, 2 (tel. 23 32 38). Open Mon.-Fri. 9am-1pm and 5pm-9am. Posts a weekly list of pharmacies open Sunday.

Emergencies: tel. 113. **First Aid: Ospedale Civile,** emergency ward on Viale Italia (tel. 22 06 21).

Police: Via Coppino, 1 (tel. 22 56 00).

Post Office: Via Brigata Sassari, 13 (tel. 23 21 78), off P. Castello. Open Mon.-Fri. 8:15am-7:40pm. Money and some other services not available after 1pm. *Fermo posta* available Mon.-Fri. 8:30am-12:30pm and 3:30-6:20pm. **Postal Code:** 07100.

Telephone Code: 079.

ACCOMMODATIONS

Unless you want to stay near chemical plants or pay big bucks, rooms in Sassari are few and far between. For information on camping, see **Platamona,** page 571.

Hotel Giusy, P. Sant'Angelo, 21 (tel. 23 33 27; fax 23 94 90), near the train station. Spotless, modern, and professional, though some rooms are noisy due to the busy streets. All rooms with private bath. Singles L50,000. Doubles L60,000. Breakfast included.

Pensione Famiglia, Viale Umberto, 65 (tel. 23 95 43). A large establishment offering massive rooms and equally massive furniture. Decor of a European hospital, though not quite as sterile—bring a flyswatter. Singles L25,000. Doubles L35,000.

FOOD

A wide selection of *pizzerie* lines **Corso Emanuele.** Any college ID allows you to eat at the **University Mensa,** Via dei Mille (tel. 258 20 14). Tickets must be bought in packs of 10 for L35,000, though you might be able to get a student standing outside to sell you a ticket for L1000. Meals include *primo, secondo, contorno,* and fruit. Open Mon.-Sat. 12:15-2:30pm and 7:30-9pm. Closed during August.

The large, enclosed **market** occupies P. Mercato, down Via Rosello from Via Vittorio Emanuele. Open Mon.-Fri. 8am-1pm and 5-8pm, Sat. 8am-1pm. The **STANDA** supermarket is on Viale Italia at Via Sardegna. Open Sun.-Fri. 9am-1pm and 4-8pm,

Sat. 9am-1pm. Or try the well-stocked **minimarket** (tel. 26 02 13), to the left as you exit the station. Open Mon.-Fri. 8am-1pm and 5-8pm, Sat. 8am-1pm.

Trattoria Da Peppina, Vicolo Pigozzi, 1 (tel. 23 61 46), off Corso Emanuele. Cozy and filled with locals. Reservations recommended. *Primi* L5000-8000, *secondi* L8000-15,000. Open Mon.-Sat. 12:30-2:30pm and 7:30-11pm.

Pizzeria Al Corso, Corso Emanuele, 148 (tel. 23 42 10). Perhaps the island's best pizza, loaded with cheese and toasted to perfection in a wood-burning oven (L4000-12,000). Even the plain mozzarella *margherita* will send your tastebuds into orbit. Pasta, dessert, and meat dishes (everything from horse to tripe) served as well. Cover for pizza L1500, otherwise L2500. Open Tues.-Sun. 7pm-1am.

Bar-Trattoria Gennargenta, Via Università, 53. Popular with local students. Friendly staff. Dark interior, but the food is filling. The student *menù* includes *primo, secondo, contorno,* fruit, wine, and coffee for L18,000. The tourist *menù* includes *primo, secondo,* and *contorno* for L15,000. Open daily 8am-11pm.

SIGHTS AND SEASONAL EVENTS

The **Museo Giovanni Antonio Sanna,** Via Roma, 64 (tel. 27 22 03), houses reconstructed *nuraghi,* Sardinian paintings, traditional costumes, and a pleasant garden. The graceful Roman statues and mosaics are a treat. (Open Mon.-Sat. 9am-1:30pm, Sun. and holidays 9:30am-1pm, 2nd Wed. of each month 4:30-7:30pm. Admission L4000.) Sassari's *duomo,* the **Cathedral of San Nicolò,** is a 13th-century Romanesque structure with a 17th-century Spanish colonial baroque façade (dubbed "an immense flower of stone" by Elio Vittorini). Currently closed for renovation. The **Church of Santa Maria di Betlem,** near the train station, is another hybrid. In addition to the church's Islamic features, its 14th-century Gothic vaults shelter elegant Baroque altars, and the adjacent cloister preserves a bronze-spigoted medieval fountain. (Open 7am-noon and 5-8:30pm.)

The lavish **Sardinian Cavalcade,** held on the second-to-last weekend in May, is Sardinia's most notable folk festival. The celebrations include a procession of costumed emissaries from dozens of villages all over Sardinia, a *Palio* (horse race), and a song-and-dance show. **I Candelieri,** the festival of the candlesticks, takes place on Assumption Day (August 14). The *Gremi,* or farmers' guilds, parade great wooden columns in the shape of enormous tapers through the streets in traditional Spanish dress. The festival dates back to the 17th century, when people reasoned that a lack of candle offerings to the Virgin had caused the latest plague.

■ Near Sassari

Castelsardo's striking location atop a lofty crest and its proximity to sandy beaches make it a popular stop along Costa Paradiso. Renowned across the island for its enchanting beauty, the town was once described by a Sardinian poet as a "flower of light that smiles from the top of a sharp promontory upon the glimmering sea." It offers a few cultural sights, including a museum and a late-Gothic **cathedral** (shamelessly replastered in drab stucco), which contains an impressive 15th-century painting of the *Madonna con Angeli.* A large castle made of lavender rock crowns the village and offers a breathtaking view of the sea. Only 34km northwest of Sassari, Castelsardo can be visited as a convenient daytrip (12 ARST buses per day, L3900). Watch for the elephant-shaped *nuraghe* just outside the town. If parting is too difficult and you prefer to find lodging in Castelsardo, try **Pensione Pinna,** Lungomare Anglona, 7 (tel. 47 01 68), across the street from the harbor. Ask for a room on the second floor with a view of the sea. Singles L27,000-47,000. Doubles L50,000-70,000, with bath L70,000-85,000.

Some easily accessible *nuraghi* await you 30km south of Sassari—most notably **Nuraghi Santu Antine** at **Torralba.** Some of the most interesting prehistoric architecture in the western Mediterranean can be found here. The central tower dates from the 9th century BC and the fortifications surrounding it from the 7th. The must-see **Museo della Valle dei Nuraghi** (Museum of the Valley of the *Nuraghi*) at Via Carlo

Felice, 97 (tel. 84 72 98) in Torralba, provides information on the *nuraghi* and other excavated relics. The staff also organizes tours of the actual site. (Admission L5000, student groups of any size can pay L70,000.) Both the museum and the site are open daily 8am-8pm. The Torralba **train station** (on the Cagliari-Sassari line) lies 1km from the monument, and PANI and ARST buses also run to the town (4km from the site, L4500).

The most convenient **beach** from Sassari is found at **Platamona,** a long white expanse of sand where the locals go on weekends. Take the orange city bus labeled "Via Budi Budi" (chant it on the ride for added fun) from Via Torre Tonda in the middle of the public gardens (every 40min., 30min., L4000 roundtrip). This bus also goes to the best camping spot near Sassari: the **International Cristina Camping Village,** Platamona (tel. 31 02 30). Get off the bus when you see the large sign on your right. It's a decent campground, perhaps a bit crowded with trailers, but featuring its own beautiful beach that makes it a worthy stopover. Camping L12,100 per person in June and September, L14,200 in July, and L16,800 in August.

NORTHERN COAST

The northern shore of Sardinia is its most crowded, and the one most likely to be confused with Miami Beach. The Emerald Coast (Costa Smeralda), Gallura, and the Gulf of Asinara are perhaps the three greatest casualties of the Eurotourist deluge. Still, the scenery here is stunning, with dazzling white cliffs that jut into truly turquoise water and intricate rock formations carved by the sinewy winds. Timing is everything: come in high-season only if you're prepared to pay top *lira* for a room.

Porto Torres

Porto Torres, believe it or not, is known primarily for its port. With few cultural attractions and beaches that pale in comparison to others on the northern coast, the city has eluded the encroachment of tourism with relative ease. Still, its serene shores and lively squares make it a pleasant stopover for those on their way to more inviting locales.

ORIENTATION AND PRACTICAL INFORMATION

Corso Vittoria Emmanuele, the city's main thoroughfare, runs from the port to the heart of the city. In a nondescript building on the port end lies the **tourist office,** P. XX Settembre, 2 (tel. 51 50 00). The smiling staff waits for tourists Mon.-Sat. 8am-2pm and 4-8pm, Sun. 8am-2pm. **Trains** connect the city to: Sassari (4 per day, L2000); Olbia (2 per day, 2½hr., change either at Chilivani or at Sassari and Ozieri, L12,000); Macomer, Oristano, and Cagliari (direct at 9am, 3 others per day require connecting trains at Sassari, L11,800, L15,600, and L22,800 respectively). **Luggage Storage** is at the station, L5000 for 12hr. **ARST buses** stop at the port and in P. Umberto off Corso V. Emanuele and run to Stintino (4 per day, L3900), Alighero (4 per day, L5000), and Sassari (about every 30min., 6am-10pm, L2300). Tickets can be purchased at Bar Acciaro, Corso V. Emanuele, 38, or at the newsstand in P. Umberto. Tirennia runs **ferries** to and from Genoa (7:30pm both ways, 12hr., *poltrone* L38,000-70,000); buy tickets at the Tirrenia office across from the port, Via Mare, 38 (open Mon.-Fri. 8:30am-noon and 3:15-7:30pm, Sat.-Sun. hours vary with season), or look for Tirrenia signs in front of travel agencies along Corso V. Emanuele. In summer Grimaldi Group runs luxurious—and expensive—ferries to and from Genoa (from Porto Torres June 29-Aug. 15 10am, Aug. 16-Sept. 16 10pm; leaving Genoa June 20-Aug. 15 10pm, Aug. 16-Sept. 16 10am; L70,000-118,000). **Taxis** (tel. 51 04 39) loiter at Corso V. Emanuele, 76. **Emergencies,** tel. 113. **First aid** or **fire emergency**, tel. 115. The **post office,** Via Ponte Romana, 77 (tel. 51 49 05), three blocks from Corso V. Emanuele, is open Mon.-Fri. 8:15am-6pm, and Sat. 8:15am-1pm, and **exchanges** foreign **currency** and

American Express Traveler's Cheques (L5000 fee) Mon.-Fri. 8:15am-5:05pm and Sat. 8:15am-12:45pm. The **telephone code** is 079.

ACCOMMODATIONS AND FOOD

The only budget hotel in town is **Hotel Roya,** Via Satta, 8 (tel. 50 22 78); with your back to the port, turn left off Corso V. Emanuele onto Via Petronia and then right after 5 blocks. Neat rooms with tile floors but unfinished walls. All rooms boast TVs, and some have balconies with obstructed views of the water. Singles L35,000, with bath L55,000, low-season L40,000. Doubles L75,000, low-season 65,000, with bath L90,000-110,000, low-season L75,000. Groceries and picnic provisions can be found at any of the markets on and around Via Balai; **Market Cossu,** Via Balai, 46, is open daily 8am-1pm and 4:45-8pm. You can also sit down and help yourself to the L18,000 *menù* at **Elisa's,** across from the port.

SIGHTS AND ENTERTAINMENT

Three pleasant **beaches** grace the shore of Porto Torres: **Scogliolungo, Acqua Dolci,** and **Balai.** All are within walking distance, and ATP buses #1 and 2 stop at each (L1100). If you are more motivated, the 30-min. bus ride to Stintino's spectacular **Spaggia di Pelosa** offers a bountiful reward. Built on the site of the ancient Roman city Turris Lybissonis, Porto Torres possesses a history worth exploring. Sadly, the local authorities seem to have done little in the way of preservation: the cobblestone streets lie under a thick cloak of asphalt, and the **Aragonese tower** by the port has been thoughtlessly plastered with cement. A trip to the otherwise fascinating **Roman ruins,** open daily 9am-7:30pm, requires stomping through knee-high weeds and waiting for tiny lizards to scurry by before you cross the wobbly planks. At the far end of Corso V. Emanuele stands the majestic **Basilica of San Gavino,** whose altar, pulpit, and 22 motley columns are all made of materials lifted from the ruins. The limestone interior of this 12th-century cathedral skillfully blends rustic simplicity with stately elegance. It thus serves as a fitting monument to its gallant namesake, a Roman soldier who staunchly refused to behead his Christian captives, Saints Pratto and Gianvario, and soon came to share both their faith and their fate. (The relics of all three martyrs are today stored in the church.) Ask the amicable curate to show you the Roman necropolis and early Christian coemiterium that lie underground. Any late-night excitement that the city can muster will be found at the outdoor **caffè** along (of course) Corso V. Emanuele.

Stintino

Stintino, 24km northwest of Porto Torres on the Capo del Falcone, was once a legitimate fishing village but has recently been swallowed up in the ever-spreading tourist trade. The winter population of fewer than 1000 swells to almost 20,000 in summer. Much of Stintino's transformation can be attributed to the captivating beauty of **Spiaggia di Pelosa,** a beach 4km outside town whose sparkling waters glisten against the bone-dry **Isola Asinara,** an island penal colony. An easy 500-m wade through thigh-deep water takes you to a tiny islet and its marooned 18th-century **Aragonese tower**—a great daytrip to the best beach near Sassari and Porto Torres. Four buses run to and from both cities: Sassari (1hr., L5400) and Porto Torres (20min., L3900). Don't miss the last bus, as impromptu camping is nearly impossible and hotels cater to European tourists with flexible budgets. If you're stranded, try **Albergo Silvestrino** at Via Sassari, 12 (tel. 52 30 07); its modern, elegant rooms might cheer you up. Singles L50,000-75,000. Doubles L75,000-135,000. Half-pension L80,000-140,000. Full-pension L95,000-160,000. All rooms with bath.

Santa Teresa di Gallura

Perched on Sardinia's northeastern tip, Santa Teresa di Gallura is a perky, pastel, beach town. The gentle sound of the waves lapping at the cliffs and beaches can be nearly hypnotic. The main scene here is the family vacation, making Santa Teresa a bit sleepy in the evening. From the small, immaculate **Rena Bianca** beach you can actually see Corsica across the hazy waters. This beach also has some of the biggest waves in Sardinia, perfect for riding to the shore.

ORIENTATION

Turn right from where the ARST bus stops and walk uphill toward the church. There, at **Piazza San Vittorio,** turn right to arrive at **Piazza Vittorio Emanuele.** To get to the beach, walk down the opposite side of the *piazza*. A dirt path leads away from the beach up the hill. At the fork, the lower path leads to **Isola Municca,** a stadium-like islet with high rocks that encircle a field of grass. The higher trail twists between magnificent granite formations and offers an excellent view of Corsica and Capo Testa, especially in the morning. Follow the hill to reach the isthmus connecting **Capo Testa** with the mainland. Otherwise, go back into town and take Via Capo Testa (3km) or the ARST bus from the post office mornings and afternoons. There are beaches on both sides of the isthmus. From Capo Testa's lighthouse, you can walk down to a secluded series of scenic coves. Paths lead south through the spectacular granite quarries of the **Valle della Luna.**

PRACTICAL INFORMATION

Tourist Office: P. Vittorio Emanuele, 24 (tel. 75 41 27). Assists with accommodations and has dozens of pamphlets advertising such local services as boat, moped, and horse rentals. Open Mon.-Sat. 8:30am-1pm and 4-7pm. The **Consorzio Operatori Turistici,** Via Maria Teresa, 9 (tel. 75 61 11/12; fax 75 61 12), at the top of the hill leading to the church, is a tourist's dream: it makes hotel reservations and offers information on all types of accommodations, boat tours, sporting activities, travel options, and local restaurants. Open Mon.-Sat. 9am-12:30pm and 5-8:30pm; during winter, morning hours only.

Telephones: Bar dello Sport, Via Mazzini, 7 (tel. 75 41 21).

Buses: ARST buses travel to: Olbia (7 per day, 1½hr., L7300); Sassari (5 per day, 3hr., L12,200); and Palau (7 per day, 40min., L3400) from Via Eleonora d'Arborea, adjacent to the post office off Via Nazionale. Tickets can be purchased at the Black and White Bar across from the station on Via Nazionale.

Ferries: Saremar (tel. 75 41 56) and **Moby Lines** (tel. 279 27) connect Santa Teresa to Bonifacio in Corsica (L11,500-14,500 and L14,000-18,000 respectively); tickets can be purchased at the port offices. You will also have to pay a L4000 port tax for entrance into Corsica. French visa required.

24-Hour Taxi: Call 75 47 41 or 75 40 07.

Car Rental: AVIS, Via Maria Teresa, 41 (tel. 75 49 06). Min. age 21. Open Mon.-Fri. 9am-12:30pm and 4:30-7pm, Sat. 9am-12:30pm; rent by phone 24hr.

Bike/Moped Rentals: GULP, Via Nazionale, 58 (tel. 75 56 89), offers mountain bikes (L20,000-25,000 per day), tandem bikes (L24,000-40,000 per day), and mopeds (L32,000-40,000 per day).

Horseback Riding: Scuola di Turismo Equestre, in nearby Marazzino (tel. 75 16 40), conducts guided excursions (L35,000 per hr.).

Boat Excursions: Consorzio delle Bocche, P. V. Emanuele (tel. 75 41 58 or 75 47 73), tours the archipelago islands (9:15am-5:30pm, L45,000-50,000 per person; alternative itineraries can be requested).

Scuba Diving: Tubarao Diving Center (Happy Fish), on Via Tubula (tel. 75 60 73) or at Via XX Settembre, 26 (tel. 75 51 80), offers a 7-day course for P.A.D.I. and S.S.I. certification (L400,000), guided excursions (L50,000-80,000), and package deals (accommodations, half-pension, and a dive for L90,000).

Public Baths: Clean booths await near the ARST bus stop and on the scenic path behind P. V. Emanuele.

Pharmacy: P. S. Vittorio, 2 (tel. 75 43 65). Open daily 9am-1pm and 5-8pm.
Emergency: tel. 113. **First Aid: Guardia Medica,** Via Carloforte (tel. 75 40 79), is open 24hr.
Post Office: Via Eleonora D'Arborea (tel. 73 53 24), across from the bus stop. Open Mon.-Fri. 10am-6:15pm and Sat. 8:05am-12:45pm. **American Express Traveler's Cheques** and foreign **currencies exchanged,** but only until 1:15pm on weekdays. **Postal code:** 07028.
Telephone code: 0789.

ACCOMMODATIONS AND CAMPING

Pensione Scano, Via Lazio, 4 (tel. 75 44 47), near the center of town on the way to Capo Testa. Blond wood furniture and ceramic tiles grace attractive rooms on a quiet street. Half-pension L50,000-79,000, with bath L58,000-90,000. Full-pension L60,000-92,000, with bath L68,000-105,000.

Hotel Bellavista, Via Sonnino, 8 (tel./fax 75 41 62), 2 blocks past P. V. Emanuele. Bright, airy rooms, all with balconies and elegant baths; some have incredible views of the sea (and cost more). Singles L40,000-45,000. Doubles L65,000-75,000. Half-pension L60,000-88,000. Full-pension L70,000-98,000.

Hotel del Porto, Via del Porto, 20 (tel. 75 41 54). Get off at the ARST port stop or turn from Via Nazionale onto Via del Porto and follow it to the port. Large rooms with views of the water and the Sardinian countryside. Friendly manager willing to answer questions about walks and beaches. Singles L30,000-52,000, with bath L40,000-55,000. Doubles with bath L55,000-80,000. V, MC, AmEx.

Camping: Arcobaleno (tel. 75 20 40), 10km from Porto Pozzo; you can take the ARST bus for Palau/Olbia and ask the driver to let you off at the site. L15,000 per person, including tent and car. Open June-Sept. Also **Gallura** (tel. 75 55 80), Loc. Li-Lucianeddi, 1½km from town. Near the beach, but big and likely to have openings. L12,000-17,500 per person, depending on season. Open May 15-Sept. 30.

FOOD

Most local restaurants are astronomically expensive. The delis and *alimentari,* fruit and vegetable markets, scattered along Via Aniscara off P. Vittorio Emanuele sell hearty, low-cost basics (open during regular business hours). There is also an **open-air market** by the bus station on Thursday mornings.

Papé Satan, Via La Marmora, 20/22. No phone. Look for the sign off Via Nazionale. Wacky white stucco booths on the back patio. Wood-burning ovens. Try the sinfully rich *pizza alla Papé Satan* (L11,500) or the *risotto "gamberi e limone"* (L15,000). Open daily noon-2:30pm and 7pm-midnight.

Gastronomia Artigiane del Corso, Via XX Settembre, 15 (tel. 75 57 25). *Menù* includes tasty *primo, secondo,* and *contorno* for L15,000. Or for a picnic pick up fresh and creative pre-prepared food like salmon lasagna or ravioli with clams.

Palau

Palau's most famous attraction is a rock. Sculpted by the wind into the shape of a bear, it appears in nearly every brochure on Sardinia. If that doesn't draw you, the nearby beaches will. Palau is a comparatively sleepy beach town whose main industry seems to be shuttling passengers across the bay to the island of La Maddalena. More beaches await there, as do a nature preserve and the American military.

ORIENTATION AND PRACTICAL INFORMATION

Palau is basically a one-street town. ARST buses drop you at the port end of Via Nazionale. The **tourist office** at Via Nazionale, 94 (tel. 70 95 70), lies uphill at the other end and can give you information on how to get to several nearby beaches. Open in summer Mon.-Sat. 8am-1pm and 4-8pm; in winter 8am-1pm and 3-6pm. **Ferries** for La Maddalena depart almost every 15 min., 5am-12:15am; buy tickets (L4000 adults, L2000 children under 12, L7500-15,500 cars, L3000-7500 *moto,* L1500 anyone whose tan is rich enough and swagger cocky enough to be mistaken for a local resident). Eight **buses** per day travel to Santa Teresa (L3400) and 15 per day go to Olbia (L4500). **Trains** also connect Palau to Olbia (15 per day, L4500 for the *centro*, L5000 for the port) and Santa Teresa di Gallura (8 per day, L3400). If you're too tired to walk to the beach, **rent a car** from Hertz at the Agenzia Viaggi Aquarius (open 9am-12:30pm and 4-7pm) or from Centro Servizio Autonoleggio, P. Chiesa, 2 (tel. 70 85 65). For a **taxi**, call 70 92 18.

ACCOMMODATIONS AND FOOD

The cost of accommodations in Palau may be prohibitively high for budget travelers, and multistar hotels scare most parsimonious tourists off. **Hotel La Roccia,** Via dei Mille, 15 (tel./fax 70 95 28), affords at least partial refuge. Azure linens, tile floors, and dark wood furniture adorn every room. Singles L55,000-65,000. Doubles L80,000-95,000. All rooms with bath. There are also several **campgrounds** near Palau. The closest is **Acapulco,** Loc. Punta Palau (tel. 70 94 97), L15,000-22,000 per adult, L12,000-18,000 per child. Some bungalows available for L28,000-40,000 per person. Caravans L55,000-95,000 for 3 people, L65,000-105,000 for 4. Open June 1-Oct. 15. **La Uva Fragola,** P. V. Emanuele, 2 (tel. 70 87 65), serves delectable pizzas, all named after boats docked at the port and topped with fresh vegetables and savory cheeses (L8000-12,000), and a variety of salads (including octopus). Cover L2000. Open daily 10am-2am for those late-night tentacle cravings. **Ristorante Robertino** dishes out flavorful spaghetti with scallops or *zuppa marinara* for L13,000. Cover L3000. Open Tues.-Sun. 12:30-2:30pm and 7:45-10:30pm. V, MC, DC.

■ Olbia

Most visitors only stop in Olbia on their way to other Sardinian destinations. With a single, unremarkable medieval church and nary a beach in sight, the city's main draw is its convenient ferry system connecting Sardinia to Corsica and the rest of Italy. Still, as port towns go, it's actually rather pleasant. Lounge for a while in one of the convivial outdoor *caffè* that line Olbia's leafy Piazza Margherita—there are many worse ways to spend an evening.

ORIENTATION AND PRACTICAL INFORMATION

Ferries arriving at the port are greeted by blue intercity **ARST** buses and a train timed to meet incoming passengers. The cluster of buildings to the right as you disembark houses a bar, a newsstand, and televisions to entertain stranded travelers. To reach Olbia's *centro,* take the waiting train to the first stop. (Those who are ready for more travel may continue on to Sassari.) To get to the tourist office, walk directly from the train station up **Via Pala** until it intersects with **Corso Umberto;** the **ARST station** will be about 200m to your right. Turn left and continue past **Piazza Margherita** on your right until you reach **Via Catello Piro** (also on your right), where you will find the tourist office. It's likely that your boat will arrive long before business hours, but don't despair—relax and revive yourself at one of several caffè along Corso Umberto. Gulp espresso and enjoy cream-filled pastries with other weary travelers as you wait for Olbia to come to life.

Tourist Office: Via Catello Piro, 1 (tel. 214 53), off Corso Umberto—look for the mod white building. Ask for *Alberghi & Campeggi* (a brochure of prices for almost every hotel and campsite in the Sassari province) or one of the numerous guides in Italian or English highlighting beaches, archaeological sites, and "trekking adventures." Open Mon.-Fri. 8am-2pm and 3:30-6:30pm, Sat.-Sun. 9am-noon. Summer Mon.-Sat. 8am-7pm, Sun. 8am-noon. Hours vary with staff availability.

Currency Exchange: Banco di Sardegna, Corso Umberto, across from P. Margherita. Open Mon.-Fri. 8:20am-1:20pm and 2:35-3:35pm. Or try **Immobiliare Saturn International** at Via Genova, 73 (tel. 256 24).

American Express: Avitur, Corso Umberto, 139 (tel. 243 27). Check cashing and mail service for cardholders on weekday mornings. Those without cards cannot cash personal checks or buy traveler's checks here. Friendly English-speaking staff. Open Mon.-Fri. 9am-1pm and 4-7:30pm, Sat. 9am-12:30pm.

Telephones: Bar Mabidue di Manghina Ottavio at Via De Filippi, 28, or in the lobby of **Hotel Minerva** at Via Nazzini, 6.

Trains: Via Pala (tel. 224 77), off Corso Umberto by the bus station. Trains run from the station to the port to meet departing ferries. To: Cagliari (5 per day, L22,600); Sassari (7 per day, L9800); and Golfo Aranci (7 per day, L2700). **Luggage Storage:** L5000 for 12hr. Open 6:10am-1:10pm and 1:30-7:10pm.

Buses: ARST, Corso Umberto, 168 (tel. 211 97), at the far end away from the water (actually just a place for the buses to pull in). Buy tickets at the Snack Bar Papagallo to the right of the station. Open Mon.-Sat. 6am-10pm. To: Nuoro (7 per day, L12,200); Arzachena (12 per day, L3400); Santa Teresa di Gallura (7 per day, L7200); and Palau (12 per day, L4500). Fewer buses on Sun., but frequency increases during the academic year. Schedule posted in the station and at the snack bar. Waiting room open daily 7am-7:30pm.

Ferries: Tirrenia, Corso Umberto, 17/19 (tel. 285 33 or 286 33). To: Civitavecchia (6pm, 11½hr., *poltrone* L33,900); La Spezia (4:30pm or midnight depending on the season, 5½hr., deck seat L82,500); and Genoa (departure times vary, 13½hr., *poltrone* L38,000-70,000 depending on the season). Open Mon.-Sat. 8:30am-1:30pm and 4:30-6pm. **Port office** (tel. 246 91) open when ferries are running—check 1½hr. in advance for schedule changes. **Linea dei Golfi** (tel. 221 26), in the port office, runs lines to Piombino, the port for Elba, and Livorno in Tuscany. **Moby Lines** also services Livorno (10am, deck seat L42,000-85,000; 10pm, deck seat L55,000-85,000). **Meridiana** sends ferries to destinations around Europe.

Taxis: (tel. 691 50), 24hr. service.

Car Rental: Budget (tel. 694 57); **Avis** at the airport or in town at Via Genova, 67 (tel. 224 20); **Hertz** (tel. 660 24). In town there's also **Gallura** (tel. 515 18 or 275 70) on Viale Aldo Moro. Rates start around L90,000 per day plus VAT and optional insurance. Mopeds starting at L55,000.

Pharmacy: Farmacia Lupacciolu, Corso Umberto, 134 (tel. 213 10), at the corner of Via Porto Romano. Open Mon.-Sat. 9am-1pm and 4:30-10pm. Check a local paper, *La Nuova Sardegna* or *L'Unione Sarda,* to find out which pharmacy in town is open on Sunday.

Emergencies: tel. 113. **First Aid: Guardia Medica,** Via Fausto Nocce, 4 (tel. 224 91), near the Church of San Simplicio. Evening and weekend assistance. Open Tues.-Fri. 8pm-8am, Sat. 2pm-Mon. 8am. **Hospital: Ospedale Civile,** Via Aldo Moro (tel. 522 00 or 522 01). Some English spoken.

Post Office: Via Acquedotto (tel. 222 51), 2 blocks off P. Matteotti. Open Mon.-Sat. 8:30am-7pm. **Postal Code:** 07026.

Telephone Code: 0789.

ACCOMMODATIONS

All of the hotels at the center of town are clustered around Corso Umberto. Sadly, the city has very little to offer the budget traveler, especially during the high-season.

Albergo Terranova, Via Garibaldi, 3 (tel. 223 95; fax 272 55), off P. Margherita. The hotel is divided into old and new sections. The older rooms, all without bath, are starkly furnished, though the geranium-bedecked balconies add some Sardinian warmth. Singles L25,000. Doubles L50,000. Half-pension L45,000. Full-pension L70,000. The newly renovated rooms, all complete with bath, are cheery and attractive. Singles L60,000. Doubles L95,000. Half-pension L70,000. Full-pension L90,000. Breakfast L8000. Prices increase by L10,000-20,000 in high-season.

Hotel Minerva, Via Mazzini, 6 (tel. 211 90), first right off Corso Umberto as you head from P. Margherita toward the water. The management is friendly, the rooms bright and airy, and the lobby amusingly eclectic. Singles L40,000, with bath L45,000. Doubles L60,000, with bath L65,000. Half-pension L70,000. Full-pension L90,000. Prices increase by L5000 in high-season. Breakfast a pricey L12,000 (just coffee). The management's plans to renovate in 1997 may mean limited availability, different rates, and (perhaps) even nicer rooms.

FOOD

For self-service bargains, shop at the **Mercato Civico** on Via Acquedotto (open Mon.-Sat. 7:30am-1pm and 4:30-8pm), or at the **STANDA** supermarket at Corso Umberto, 156 (open Mon.-Sat. 9am-1:30pm and 4:30-8:30pm). Vegetarians can stock up on soy milk and other supplies here.

Pizzeria il Portico, Via Olbia, 5 (first left as you enter the Piazza Margherita). This tiny pizzeria serves up large, delicious slices of the traditional pizza, as well as *focaccia* with chicken cutlets, meats, and your choice of topping. Cheese slice L2000, sandwiches starting at L3000. Open daily 11am-1am.

Ristorante Terranova, in the hotel of the same name. Though some of the seafood dishes are expensive, good-sized pizzas start at L7000. Other entrees range from L7000 to L18,000. Open daily noon-2:30pm and 7-11pm.

Ristorante da Paolo, Via Garibaldi, 18 (tel. 216 75). The combination of rugged brown stone and soft pastel tablecloths makes for a handsome decor. Try the house specialty, *porcetta* (L12,000). Entrees range from L9000 to L18,000. Open daily noon-2:30pm and 7-10:30pm.

SIGHTS IN AND NEAR OLBIA

A walk along the water in Olbia affords a hazy blue vision of Sardinian peaks and blue coasts, a welcome invitation or a fond farewell. Nearly all traces of Olbia's Greek, Roman, and medieval past have disappeared; the one exception is the 12th-century **Church of San Simplicio** behind the train station. Built in the Pisan-Romanesque style, the structure features an imposing façade of off-white granite.

Excursions from Olbia include trips to **S'Abe,** an archaeological site 6km away and to the "Giant's Tombs" (prehistoric burial grounds with megaliths) of **Su Monte,** on the road to **Castello Pedrese,** a 14th-century fortress. If you're on the bus to Nuoro, not far out of Olbia you'll pass surreal **Isola Tavolara,** an immense prism of rock protruding 450m out of the sea. Eight buses per day run to **San Teodoro,** 30km from Olbia (L3400), where a long, luxurious beach eases into ultramarine water. In July and August you'll be walking on a carpet of tourists, but go anyway—it's worth it. The only budget accommodations available can be found at **Hotel La Palma,** Via del Tirreno (tel. (0784) 86 59 62). Prices vary from low to high-season. Singles L35,000/75,000. Doubles L70,000/100,000. All rooms with bath. In August, half-pension L100,000. Full-pension L150,000. Up the road is the Cala d'Ambra **campground** (tel. (0784) 86 56 50) with satisfactory facilities (L11,000/13,000 per person, tent included). Reservations strongly recommended in summer.

TUNISIA

TUNISIA

Tunisia's appeal to visitors is, quite literally, legendary. Odysseus's crew preferred to remain here and eat lotuses, and Aeneas was so enamored with Carthage and Queen Dido that without some divine prodding, he never would have left to found Rome. Mythology has given the country a ringing endorsement, and the heroes never even got past the coast. Likewise, most visitors today are package tourists that fly into Cap Bon or Jerba, frolic in the surf for two weeks, and then leave without venturing farther. While they are surely missing out, the good news for solo travelers is that there will be few crowds to fight in Tunisia's interior.

Despite its small size, Tunisia offers an enormously varied cultural landscape. Tunis, the physical manifestation of Tunisia's industrialization and secularization, is only three hours from Kairouan, one of Islam's holy cities and witness to the country's profound faith. The green fields of the Tell, which once filled the granaries of ancient Rome, shelter the archaeological sites of Dougga and Bulla Regia. Just 200km away, Bedouin tribes live in oases within the inhospitable Sahara Desert.

Although Tunisia's national character is diverse to the point of schizophrenia, it remains a stable and prosperous state—particularly in contrast to its neighbors. With friendly people, affordable prices, and an infrastructure just rough enough to make for a good story back home, Tunisia will amply reward any tourist from Italy willing to hop on a ferry to this easily accessible Arab state.

Amnesty International and the Lawyers Committee for Human Rights have published reports implicating the Tunisian government in the violation of numerous human rights, including the right to a fair trial and freedom from arbitrary arrest. Tunisians under closest watch include persons accused of disseminating minority political ideas or aiding an unauthorized political organization.

ESSENTIALS

Planning Your Trip

Most of the information contained in the **Italy Essentials** section also applies to Tunisia. The following addenda should supplement what you already know.

The **Tunisian National Tourist Office (ONTT)** is a good source of information about the country and its regions. Its central office is at 1, av. Mohammed V, 1002 Tunis (tel. (01) 341 077; fax 350 997). Another good source of assistance is the **Agence Tunisienne de Communication Extérieure,** Av. Jean Jaurès, 1001 Tunis (tel. (01) 345 866; fax 353 445). In the U.S., contact the **Embassy of Tunisia,** 1515 Massachusetts Ave. NW, Washington, D.C. 20005 (tel. (202) 862-1850). The ONTT in the U.K. is at 77a, Wigmore St., London W1H 9LJ (tel. (0171) 224 55 98; fax 224 40 53). Rome's ONTT office is at Via Sardegna, 17 (tel. 482 36 65; fax 482 19 34). Major Tunisian cities also operate a local tourist office called the **Syndicat d'Initiative,** referred to in listings as the "Syndicat."

American and Canadian citizens do not need visas to enter Tunisia for up to four months, and U.K. citizens are exempt for up to three months. Australians, New Zealanders, and South Africans should obtain a visa from the nearest Tunisian consulate a few weeks before leaving home.

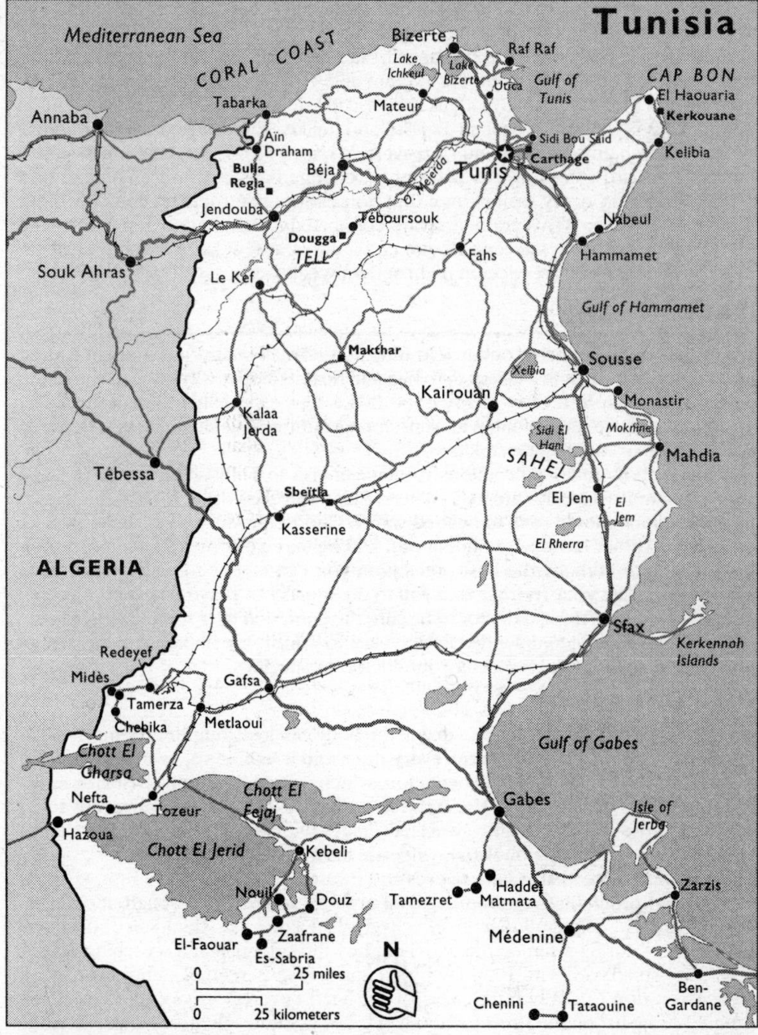

MONEY MATTERS

US$1 = 0.957D (dinar)	**1D = US$1.04**
CDN$1 = 0.70D	**1D = CDN$1.43**
UK£1 = 1.47D	**1D = UK£0.68**
IR£1 = 1.49D	**1D = IR£0.67**
AUS$1 = 0.76D	**1D = AUS$1.31**
NZ$1 = 0.65D	**1D = NZ$1.54**
SAR = 0.22D	**1D = SAR4.55**
IT L1000 = 0.63D	**1D = IT L1587**

The dinar (D) consists of 1000 millimes (ml). Sums are generally written with periods: 14.300 means 14 dinars, 300 millimes. Amounts under 5D are frequently expressed in thousands of millimes. **Save your exchange receipts:** 30% of what you exchange can be reconverted (up to US$100), but only if you have this documentation. It is illegal to export large amounts of Tunisian currency.

Banks are generally open for exchange in summer Mon.-Fri. 8-11am and in winter Mon.-Thurs. 8-11am and 2-4pm, Fri. 8-11am and 1:30-3pm. During **Ramadan** (see **Festivals and Holidays,** p. 587), banks are usually open Mon.-Fri. 8-11:30am and 1-2:30pm. **STB** is the largest bank in Tunisia, and unlike others, which are more selective, it will cash any major brand of **traveler's check** (300-500ml commission per check is standard). **Post offices** will only exchange hard currency. You can find **ATMs** at banks in every major town, but you cannot use their receipts for dinar reconversion. These ATMs are not always connected to international networks and will therefore not always accept foreign credit cards. A few large hotels and all airports provide exchange services at night and on weekends.

HEALTH

Two of the health concerns outlined in **Italy Essentials: Health** (p. 20) merit special attention by the tourist in Tunisia: **diarrhea** and **heatstroke.** Always wear a sun hat to prevent heatstroke and carry plenty of bottled water, especially in the desert. Most importantly, be sure that, along with sunscreen, your medical kit includes , chewable Pepto Bismol, or Kaopectate tablets.

No matter how many precautions you take, a visit to Tunisia is a gastrointestinal gamble; unfamiliar **cooties** are everywhere. Many travelers drink local water safely, but the cautious should stick to **bottled water.** Choose produce that can be peeled, don't eat food that has been standing out, and be sure your meals have been thoroughly cooked. Perhaps the best precaution you can take is to **wash your hands before eating, like your mother told you** to do. If diarrhea persists beyond a couple of days, seek out a Tunisian doctor to be sure the condition isn't something serious.

The **vaccinations** recommended for travelers to Tunisia are hepatitis, gamma globulin, tetanus, and typhoid—consult your doctor for specifics.

Desert Survival

Summer temperatures soar in the Sahara. The body can lose four liters or more of liquid per day—**drink a liter of water every hour and a half or so,** even if you're not thirsty. Thirst is the first sign of dehydration, which comes on rapidly. **Drinking enormous quantities of water after the fact is not effective—in fact, it's dangerous to do so in high temperatures.** Dilute sweet beverages with water to avoid a reaction to the high sugar content. Alcohol and coffee are intrinsically dehydrating.

Light-colored, breathable long sleeves and trousers reflect the sun's heat, keeping you cool and protecting you from harmful rays. A sweaty shirt, though uncomfortable, will prevent dehydration more effectively than a dry one. Thick-soled shoes will save your feet during a summer hike, when the sand can register a scorching 200°F/93°C. Carry sunglasses with 100% UV protection and sunscreen of sufficient strength (even if you don't usually burn). Keep your head covered—you can buy a wide-brimmed straw hat on the street for about 5D. Temperatures fluctuate unpredictably, so consider bringing a sweater or jacket as well. In winter, temperatures in the Sahara approach freezing point, and it occasionally snows.

SAFETY AND SECURITY

Tunisia's nationwide **emergency phone number** is 197.

You should encounter few problems in Tunisia if you remain sensitive to your surroundings. For general information on safety while traveling, see the **Italy Essentials: Safety and Security** section (p. 18). The brochure *Tips for Travelers to the Middle East and North Africa* is available from the Superintendent of Documents, U.S. Government Printing Office, Washington, D.C. 20402 (tel. (202) 783-3288). The U.S.

Department of State (tel. (202) 647-5225; fax service 647-3000) issues consular information sheets with updated travel safety bulletins for all foreign countries.

Violent crime in Tunisia is rare by Western standards, but thefts and scams are quite common. Urban areas which may be unsafe are the **souks** (market streets) and the **medinas** (old cities) in which they are located. Don't rely solely on tourist office maps to guide you through the maze-like medinas; stay oriented to main streets. Exercise particular caution at night or when traveling alone.

Some tourists have had problems with **con artists who claim to be guides.** If overly friendly people offer to show you around a city or give you directions, they may later turn around and demand compensation for being your "guide." In general, if there's something you don't want and won't pay for, make this absolutely clear right up front. Always negotiate a price for services *beforehand*.

Security forces are ubiquitous in Tunisia. The **police** (in blue) work in the cities and handle petty crimes, while the **garde national** (in khaki) patrol the roads, frequently stopping vehicles. Members of both forces are generally polite and nonconfrontational. **Carry your passport with you at all times.** Make sure your visa is updated and be prepared to explain your presence if you are not in a tourist town. Although national security is tight in Tunisia, the U.S. State Department has issued travel warnings about terrorism in neighboring **Algeria and Libya.** You can register with your country's embassy in Tunis to be enrolled in an emergency alert network.

In contrast to much of North Africa, Tunisia has harsh laws, fines, and jail terms for the possession or use of drugs. **Do not attempt to bring drugs in, take them out, buy them, or use them.** Don't even talk to dealers—some may be narcs. Even if they're not, remember that Tunisian law allows for guilt by association.

WOMEN TRAVELERS

Unlike residents of more conservative Muslim countries, women in Tunisia enjoy a good deal of personal freedom. In 1956, President Bourguiba presented his Code of Personal Status for Women, making Tunisia the first Arab nation to outlaw polygamy and to advance women's rights significantly. Nonetheless, women travelers from Western countries have encountered verbal harassment due to the belief that all Western women are "easy." Women touring Tunisia should make an effort to dress modestly and to travel in a group which includes men. These warnings are especially important when traveling in the south or in the interior, although men in Tunis and the north have been known to give unwanted attention as well.

LANGUAGE

As in most countries, attempts at the native language evoke an enthusiastic response from locals and discourage merchants looking for tourists to sucker. Here are a few handy **Arabic phrases:** *salaam aleikum,* or just *salaam* ("hello"), *ayee/aa* ("yes"), *la* ("no"), *shokran* ("thank you"), *samahanee* ("excuse me"), *min fadlak* to a man/*fadlik* to a woman ("please"), *la bes* ("how are you?"), *la bes hamdullah* (reply to *la bes*), *bi' as-salaama* ("good-bye"), *shwaya* ("a little"—a response to the inevitable "Do you speak Arabic?"), *kif kif* ("it's all the same"), *ka-desh* ("how much?"), *feen* ("where?"), *akhallim ingeleezee* ("Do you speak English?"), *may* ("water"), and two effective rebuffs for hustlers: *imshee* ("go away"), and *shooma!* ("for shame!"). Older people (50+) are particularly impressed if you address them as *"El Hadj,"* a courtesy title that politely assumes they've made the pilgrimage to Mecca.

Tunisians communicate with their hands, and two **hand gestures** in particular are good to know. Waving an open hand with the palm facing down seems dismissive to Westerners (as if someone is shooing you away), but in Tunisia it means "come here" or "follow me." Holding the tips of all five fingers together pointing skyward means "wait" or "be patient." Shaking this gesture means, um, just about anything.

Although Arabic is the official language of Tunisia, all Tunisian secondary school students study **French,** and most people who commonly deal with tourists speak a smattering of English and German as well. Some useful French words and phrases are: *bonjour* (bohn-ZHOOR; "hello"), *excusez-moi* (ess-KOO-zay MWAH; "excuse me"), *parlez-vous anglais, Madame/Monsieur* (PAHR-lay voo an-GLAY, mah-DAHM/muh-SYUR; "do you speak English, ma'am/sir?"), *combien* (kohm-BYEN; "how much?"), *je voudrais* (ZHUH voo-DRAY; "I would like"), *ça y'est* (SA YEH; "enough"), *où est/sont* (OO AY/SOHN; "where is/are?"), and *je ne comprends pas* (ZHUH nuh kohm-prahn PAH; "I don't understand").

GETTING THERE

There are no direct **flights** between North America and Tunisia. **Tunis Air** flies to most major European and North African cities, however, and offers a confusing array of roundtrip deals. Flights between Tunis and Marseille, France cost around 230D for students, 300D for other adults.

Visitors have been traveling by **boat** from Italy to Tunisia since 204BC, and it's still one of the best ways to get there. Try calling **Tirrenia** (tel. (0923) 218 96 in Trapani; tel. (01) 242 801 in Tunis) for ferry information:

Trapani-Tunis: June-Sept. and holidays deck chair L92,000; off-season L77,000. 7½hr. without stops. Departure from Trapani Mon. 9am; from Tunis Mon. 8pm.

Cagliari-Tunis: June-Sept. and holidays deck chair L107,000; off-season L91,000. 21½hr. Departure from Cagliari Sun. 7pm; from Tunis Mon. 8pm.

During the last two weeks of August, book tickets well in advance—all boats from Tunisia are packed with Europe-bound migrant workers. To buy a ferry ticket, you must show your bank receipt for the purchase of dinars and obtain a *Bons de Passage* from the bank itself—a minor but requisite bureaucratic hassle. You can buy tickets from all major travel agents. For departure info, see **Tunis: Ferries,** p. 590. All boat lines are supervised by the **Compagnie Tunisienne de Navigation (CTN),** which runs ticket offices at the ports in Tunis, Genoa, and Naples.

Upon arrival, you must fill out a detailed **customs** declaration, although it is unlikely that you will have any of the items asked about.

Once There

GETTING AROUND

To purchase ferry or plane tickets to destinations abroad, you must use *dinars* that have been purchased with hard currency, so keep a copy of your exchange receipt until you have cleared customs. The money exchanged for this reason does *not* count toward the 30% of the dinars you can re-exchange.

By Train

A major **train** line runs south from Tunis to Sousse, and then splits into an east line to Sfax and Gabes and a west line to Tozeur and Gafsa. Another line runs west through Jendouba to the Algerian border and splits into northwest branches ending in Bizerte and Tabarka. Although trains are infrequent, they're comfortable and have A/C. Second-class prices compete with the cost of other modes of transportation. For info, contact **Société Nationale de Chemins de Fer Tunisienne (SNCFT)** at the train station in pl. de Barcelone, Tunis, between rue de Hollande and av. de Carthage at 67 av. Farhat Hached (tel. (01) 24 99 99). Get a train schedule for all of Tunisia at the info booth in the Tunis station. The **Société du Métro-Léger du Tunis (SMLT),** on av. Mohammed V (tel. (01) 78 44 33), operates Tunis's light rail system.

By Bus

Buses are inexpensive and convenient, but crowded. Schedules change frequently and service can be painfully slow, especially in rural areas. Try to board at the point of origin—this strategy increases your chance of finding a seat and may get you onto an express, air-conditioned coach *(confort)*. In any given city there are at least two bus companies, generally occupying the same terminal. Sfax, Tabarka, and Tunis, however, have more than one station. The national **Société de Transports Rural et Interurbain (SNTRI)** runs intercity and international routes; their service is fast and comfortable. All large towns also have a **regional bus company** (with the acronym **"SRT"** in the title) that runs throughout the locale and to nearby cities. Each company has its own ticket window, and schedules are always in Arabic. Within Tunis, the **Société National des Transports** (tel. (01) 492 456) operates local buses.

By Louage

Tunisia has a well developed network of intercity taxis, or **louages.** These vehicles are without a doubt the most convenient form of transportation, as they are faster and more comfortable than buses and much more frequent than trains. *Louages* are usually white Peugeot station wagons with a red or blue stripe around the side. Most towns have at least one, if not two, *louage* "stations," usually vacant lots near the bus station where you can find them. The small placard displayed on the roof does not necessarily indicate where the *louage* is headed, just where it has been registered. Drivers often try to wait for 5 passengers before heading out. For most routes this means a 5-10-min. wait. If your destination is not a popular one, the driver may charge you extra for the unfilled seats; don't agree to this unless you're sure that there is no one else headed that way. Most *louages* have regular routes with fixed prices (although these are only displayed in Arabic). Use the rate of **3D per person per hour** as a general rule for determining the correct fare. If you feel you're being overcharged, though, use your fellow passengers as a reference; don't ever pay more than what another rider has paid for the same trip.

In rural regions, **camionettes** pick up where *louages* leave off, providing the same service in trucks that charge a pittance for a ride in the back. They are neither comfortable nor very safe, but some say they offer a certain adventurous appeal.

By Car

A **private car** is convenient for touring the Sahara, although bus and *louage* service is sporadically available. You must be at least 21 and have a valid international driver's license to rent or drive a car in Tunisia (see **International Driver's Permit,** p. 13). See **Tunis: Car Rental,** p. 590, for more information.

Before undertaking any desert expeditions with your own vehicle, **make sure that your car has been recently serviced and is in good running condition.** Carry water for drinking and for the radiator, and make sure your car is equipped with a spare tire and necessary tools. **Stay with your vehicle if it breaks down:** it's easier to spot than a person. Should the overheating warning light come on, stop and wait about 30min. for the car to cool. Never pour water over the engine to cool it; you could crack the engine block. Leave in the early morning or after midday to avoid the most oppressive heat.

By Thumb

> *Let's Go* does not recommend hitchhiking as a means of transportation.

Foreigners may find it fairly easy to **hitchhike** in Tunisia. Keep in mind that many Tunisians consider hitching tantamount to freeloading and may request a contribution. Therefore, since public transportation is so cheap, hitching will probably not save you much money. If you get stranded (quite possible), it might be your only hope. **Women should never hitch alone in Tunisia.**

ACCOMMODATIONS

Two groups administer Tunisia's **hostels.** The government's Ministry of Culture runs about 30 **Maisons des Jeunes,** originally designed to house traveling soccer teams. They tend to be large, functional, and clean, with all the charm of a locker room, charging a flat 4D per night. While convenient to the local stadium, they are often far from the center of town. **Not all of them are safe for women.** The 30 **Auberges de Jeunesse (HI)** are less institutional in character. Most have either just completed or are in the midst of undergoing renovations to conform to HI standards. These hostels are some of the best budget accommodations in Tunisia. The HI affiliate in Tunisia is the **Association Tunisienne des Auberges de Jeunesse,** 10, rue Ali Bach Hamba, BP 320-1015 Tunis RP (tel. (01) 352 277; fax 352 172).

The ONTT tourist board classifies and registers **hotels** on a zero- to four-star scale. Budget travelers should stick with the unrated (3-14D per person), one-star (12-20D per person), and two-star (14-29D per person) establishments. Prices plummet during the off season (September through June), particularly along the coast. The cheapest hotels lurk in the medinas, but women may not feel safe there. Proprietors often cram many beds into one room and then try to force tourists to pay for all of them, occupied or not. Plumbing in Tunisia can be primitive, and budget hotels generally have communal bathrooms. Even classified hotels rarely have hot water during the summer. Remember to **BYOTP** (toilet paper, that is).

Only a handful of official **campgrounds** exist in Tunisia, but they may be your only options in the south. As for unofficial camping, you can sleep on beaches and in parks only after obtaining permission from the property owner or from the nearest Police or National Guard station. It can be hard to get such permission, however, or even to find the right people to ask. In a pinch, most youth hostels will allow camping on their grounds for 500ml-2D per person, including use of their facilities. Public beaches are the most popular places for pitching a tent. Freelance camping leaves you vulnerable to muggings, though—**never camp alone.**

The **electric current** in Tunisian establishments is 220v AC.

FOOD

It is easy to eat very well and very cheaply in Tunisia. Be prepared for a lot of **couscous,** the North African staple of steamed semolina served with whatever else the cook feels like including: perhaps potatoes, veggies, fish, or meat. *Pommes de terre* **(potatoes)** and *haricots* **(beans)** are the other common starches, generally served in a spicy tomato sauce. **Lamb, beef,** and **liver** are usually grilled and served as *brochettes* or *mechoui* with fries and salad. *Rotisseries* serve inexpensive portions of chicken roasted on a spit. The coast offers excellent **fish,** although the cheaper places fry rather than grill. *Calamar* (squid) and *poulpe* (octopus) are seafood specialties. *Kamounia* combines meat, beef, or a falafel-meatball substance with cumin sauce. *Merguez* is a spicy sausage often included in *ojja,* a tomato and pepper stew with scrambled egg. *Tajine,* a Tunisian specialty, can be a meat stew with pot-luck ingredients, but more often it's a *quiche*-like concoction with or without meat.

The Tunisian national appetizer **brik** is nothing more than a fried egg wrapped in a wonton. A messy, greasy, and delicious snack, you should try it once. *Salade tunisien* is made with finely chopped cucumbers, tomatoes, onions, and sometimes tuna, but for a more genuine Tunisian **salad,** sample some *mechouia,* a spicy mass of mashed roasted peppers served in a lake of olive oil. Tunisian **soup,** *chorba,* varies considerably but generally consists of a spicy tomato base and meat stock. Satisfy your sweet tooth with *kab el ghazal* (almond-filled pastries shaped like "gazelles' hooves") or *makroudh* (date-stuffed biscuits soaked in honey, a specialty of Kairouan). No Tunisian dessert is sweeter than **fruit;** the enormous variety produced here includes figs, melons, strawberries, oranges, and plums. The cactus's prickly pear is one specialty,

First You Take a Blindfolded Camel...

How *do* Berbers make olives into oil? The olives are first pressed by a stone wheel turned by a blindfolded camel. The resulting mush is then placed in a flat palm container and thoroughly squashed by a heavy oak trunk. The oil is then stored until it ferments. What goes around comes around, and the chunky remainder becomes camel food. For info on touring olive presses, see p. 614.

sold at stands for 50ml a bud (great for sick tummies). Dates from the southern oases are another tasty choice.

Vegetarians have it tough in Tunisia, an unabashedly carnivorous nation. The very concept confuses most Tunisians, who view meat as essential to nearly every dish. *Couscous aux legumes* can be a lifesaver, but bear in mind that the cook may have simply picked (most of) the chunks of meat out of the sauce. The same goes for any other dish that you order *sans viande.* However, every town has a **produce market,** and all but the smallest villages have **supermarkets** ("Monoprix" or "Magasin General") which sell pasta and yogurt.

Tunisian restaurants can be divided into two categories: those that are holes in the wall and those that try not to be. Both types serve nearly identical menus, but the former are cheaper and quicker, while the latter pay more attention to aesthetics and hygiene. Tunisian cooking involves a great deal of preparation—restaurants fix food in advance and may therefore run out of certain dishes toward the end of the day. Arrive early for lunch or dinner to ensure the best selection.

There are other **drink options** in Tunisia besides the heavily-chlorinated water. *Citronade,* a concoction of lemons, sugar, and tap water, can kill the meanest thirst. Fresh orange juice is common, but *pâtisseries* often serve more exotic fruit juices. *Thé verit* is an acidic version of tea, steeped with mint, heavily sugared, and often served with almonds or pine nuts. Coffee in any form is excellent. Despite Islam's prohibition, **alcohol** is consumed in abundance. *Celtia,* the local brew, makes even Budweiser look strong (1.300D per bottle). Tunisia produces its own wine as well; reds tend to be on the heavy side, but *gris de Tunisie* and *Koudiat,* both rosés, receive favorable reviews. Tunisian liquor deserves some mention (and caution). *Thibarine* is a sweet date liqueur, while *boukha* is a skull-popping fig distillation. **Bars,** except for those in resort hotels, are generally seedy, all-male, and dedicated to serious heavy drinking. Male tourists may find them intimidating, and females may find them frightening.

KEEPING IN TOUCH

The phone code for Tunisia is 216. Each city also has its own code; dial the first zero only if you are calling from one region to another (not including international calls). You can insert up to 2D of coins into Tunisian telephones at once, which is coincidentally the cost of about a minute call to the U.S. Certain rural areas can be reached only with the operator's assistance (tel. 15; information in French tel. 12).

Although **post offices (PTT,** for *Poste, Téléphone, & Télégraphe*) usually have telephones, their hours are not always convenient, especially for calls to North America. **Taxiphones,** pay-phone banks with an attendant dispensing change, generally have later hours. You cannot access international phone companies from Tunisia, so **calling cards** are useless here. To make matters worse, the government has suspended **collect calls.** You'll have to suck up the cost of calling abroad yourself, or arrange for someone at home to call you at a local address. For international calls, dial direct (00—country code—area/city code—phone number). See the **Telephone Codes** chart in the **appendix,** p. 642.

Letters to the U.S. and Canada weighing up to 20g cost 550ml; postcards are 450ml. Letters to Europe are 500ml; postcards are 390ml. PTT offices are generally open in summer Mon.-Fri. 8am-noon and 3-6pm, Sat. 8am-noon; in winter Mon.-Sat. 7:30am-1:30pm. Ramadan hours (in early January) are usually 8am-3pm. Allow at least three weeks for mail sent from Tunis to arrive in the U.S., two weeks for European addresses. You can buy **stamps** at newsstands or tobacconists. Allow 10 days for U.S. mail to reach Tunisia, five days for European mail. To have a post office receive mail for you, the mailing address should include your name, the words *"poste restante,"* and the post office address (200ml per piece when you retrieve your mail). Send **telegrams** and **faxes** from telephone offices or post offices.

BARGAINING

If you come to Tunisia, be prepared to bargain; asking prices are about ten times the actual value. If you really intend to buy, avoid mingling with tour groups and shop late in the day when salespeople are anxious to unload their wares. Never appear interested when examining potential purchases: declare that you've done your shopping already and walk away; the price will decrease substantially. Above all, **never allow a price to escape your lips, unless you intend to pay it.** Never go shopping with a guide, who will collect at least 30% in commission. It is often possible to **barter** using American cigarettes, cheap digital watches, jeans, and t-shirts with English printing—consider bringing Western paraphernalia to trade for souvenirs.

HOSPITALITY

If a Tunisian family invites you home for dinner (a common practice in rural areas), here are some etiquette tips. Remove your shoes and socks before entering. Scoop food from the communal dish using bread held in your right hand. Eat only what's directly in front of you, although the host may also push a particularly "good" morsel in your direction. Bear in mind that the "best" cuts of meat in Tunisia are the ones with the most fat, but refusing it may insult your host. You're expected by tradition to **bring a gift.** Think of it as a thank-you gesture. Tea is a traditional offering, but kids also love chewing gum or pens. Residents of poor rural areas will appreciate a package of Band-Aids or aspirin. If there are English speakers in the household, surrender an old paperback. If you have a camera, your hosts will probably want to pose for a picture. Send them a copy as an expression of gratitude; the ritual of exchanging addresses takes place with even passing acquaintances.

Life and Times

HISTORY AND POLITICS

Tunisia has long treasured its ideological openness, although there is less tolerance today under dictator Ben Ali. Centuries of immigration and foreign influence have left their mark on this small nation, which today belongs as much to the Mediterranean community as to North Africa.

The earliest archaeological evidence of settlement in Tunisia dates from about 750BC, but legend attributes the founding of **Carthage** to the Phoenician Queen Dido in 814BC. By the 6th century BC, the city had become a major power in the Mediterranean through coastal and North African trade. Then Carthage and Rome went to war, initially over Sicily, in a series of conflicts known as the **Punic Wars,** comparable in relative size and scope to the World Wars of our century. Of the three wars, the second was the most significant. **Hannibal** of Carthage led an army and 370 elephants over the Alps in order to surprise the Romans from the north, trouncing them at Lake Trasimeno and Cannae. Nevertheless, the Romans prevailed in the end, permanently settling the conflict in 146BC.

Although the Romans sowed Carthage with salt to prevent its resurgence, the town soon flourished as a provincial capital. Tunisia was Rome's primary African granary; archaeological remains attest to the colony's wealth. Like much of the Roman Empire, it was sacked by the Vandals and then reconquered by the **Byzantine Empire** in AD533. Arab invasions began in 647, and Tunisia was incorporated into Baghdad's **Abassid Empire** in the 8th century. The Arab dynasties established the Islamic faith in Tunisia and built the medina sections of the present-day cities.

In the late 16th century, the **Ottoman Turks** seized Tunisia but soon yielded to their own powerful bureaucrats, the **Beys.** These rulers supervised the adoption of the 1861 constitution and pushed Tunisia toward Westernization, generally resulting in European "management" of its economy.

After invading Tunisia in 1881, the **French** organized and developed the country, seizing the best land for their own settlers. A nationalist consciousness soon developed among the intelligentsia, who founded the reformist **Destour Party** in 1920. A new generation of young agitators led by lawyer **Habib Bourguiba,** however, split off to form the more radical **Neo-Destour Party.** Bourguiba, jailed by the French, eventually escaped into exile and returned triumphantly to negotiate Tunisia's relatively painless transition to independence on March 20, 1956. A year later he deposed the last Bey, then the titular head of state, and became president-for-life.

Bourguiba introduced **social reforms** including equal rights for women and more equitable educational opportunities. By the last decade of Bourguiba's reign, however, Tunisia was in financial turmoil and a state of civil unrest. After 31 years in office, the elderly Bourguiba was deposed in a bloodless coup on November 7, 1987. He is now 91 years old and retired from politics, but his influence is still strong and his face continues to adorn the currency. He was replaced by **General Ben Ali,** who has attempted to reverse Tunisia's economic decline. Ben Ali's regime has gradually become a dictatorship, however; he reportedly won the 1994 elections with a suspicious 99.9% of the vote.

FESTIVALS AND HOLIDAYS

Islam is the primary force molding Tunisian cultural life. The major religious holiday is **Ramadan,** the Muslim month of fasting determined by the Islamic lunar year (Dec. 31, 1996 to Jan. 16, 1997 on the Gregorian calender). Observance of Ramadan affects all aspects of daily life. Shops and services close in the afternoons, and Muslims are forbidden to eat, drink, or smoke between sunrise and sunset. After sunset, streets swell with people, shops and businesses re-open, and festivities continue well past midnight. The end of Ramadan is marked by **Id al-Fitr,** a three-day celebration during which nearly all commercial activity comes to a standstill. In rural areas and smaller towns, restaurants and cafés close for at least a day.

Public holidays include: **January 1** (New Year's Day); **March 20-21** (Independence Days); **April 9** (Martyr's Day); **May 1** (Labor Day); **July 25** (Republic Day); and **November 7** (Anniversary of Ben Ali's coup). National festivals in southern Tunisia invariably include camel fights, folkloric presentations, and parades.

GULF OF TUNIS

Tunis

After the destruction of nearby Carthage, Tunis became a prominent military outpost for the Roman and Byzantine empires. The Moslems who swept through North Africa resided there, and under the Hafsid Dynasty Tunis replaced Kairouan as Tunisia's capital. The Ottomans took over the city in the 16th century, and France occupied it as part of a Protectorate in 1881. Tunis has nonetheless remained the dynamo of Tunisia and was named the capital of the independent nation in 1956. Islam's first "university town," the city's reputation for liberalism is still deserved.

While the travel brochures take visitors elsewhere to see the "real" Tunisia, Tunis embodies the nation's desire for acceptance as a member of the developed world. A new light rail system shuttles businesspeople to work, and female policemen oversee the hordes traveling along Avenue Habib Bourguiba. Men and women sip *café au lait* at the Café de Paris, while slick new taxis hurtle to the modern airport.

Tunis may be cosmopolitan, but the trappings of its past remain for those willing to seek them out. The most notable vestiges are the large medina, nearby Carthage, and the enchanting Bardo Museum. In addition, the large mosque Jemaq Zitouna, the traditional *chicha* cafés, and the souks still bustle with life and energy.

ORIENTATION AND PRACTICAL INFORMATION

It is a straight shot on the **Rue de la Kasbah** from the center of the **ville nouvelle** to the heart of the **medina.** This main street runs east to the **place de la Victoire,** home of the freestanding Bab Bhar in the *ville nouvelle.* Continuing east, **avenue de France,** with rue Charles de Gaulle running off to the right, leads to the post office. At the **place de l'Independence, avenue de France** becomes **avenue Habib Bourguiba,** the wide, tree-lined Tunisian version of the Champs Elysée. Two blocks down from pl. de l'Independence is the intersection of **avenue de Paris** to the left and the **avenue de Carthage,** which leads to the **train station,** to the right. Five blocks farther down av. Bourguiba is **place de 7 Novembre** (formerly place d'Afrique), a traffic circle with a four-sided clock tower. Get a free, detailed map of Tunis at the tourist office across the street to the left. Five blocks still farther is the **TGM Commuter Rail Station,** with trains to the 'burbs of Tunis (Carthage, Sidi Bou Said, and La Goulette).

The **SNCFT Gare de Tunis,** with service to most of Tunisia, is located two blocks down from av. Habib Bourguiba and to the right (follow the tracks of the Métro) in **place de la Barcelone.** This is also the site of a convenient Métro stop, with access to the **Bardo Museum,** the TGM Station, and the **Bab Soukka** national bus station.

Tourist Office: ONTT Reception Office (tel. 341 077), on pl. du 7 Novembre at av. Bourguiba and av. Mohammed V, the intersection with the huge clock. Look for the big green "i" outside the office. There are many brochures and free, detailed maps of Tunis. Staff speaks little English. Open Mon.-Sat. 8am-6pm, Sun. 9am-noon. There is another branch at the **TGM Gare de Tunis,** beside the main entrance, which has train and bus schedules and the same maps and brochures.

Budget Travel: Shop around at the agencies off av. Bourguiba and av. de Carthage.

Embassies and Consulates: U.S., 144, av. de la Liberté (tel. 782 566). **Canada,** rue du Sénégal (tel. 798 004). **U.K.,** 5, pl. de la Victoire (tel. 341 444), at the medina entrance, with service for citizens of **Australia** and **New Zealand. Italy,** 37, rue G. Abdennasser (tel. 341 811). Visas are required of U.S. and Canadian citizens staying longer than 3 months, and all Australian citizens. U.S., Canadian, and English citizens can get their visas renewed at the **British Consulate** Visa Section, 140/143, av. de la Liberté (tel. 793 322), across from the U.S. Embassy. Australians are not allowed to enter without getting a visa at the airport or ferry dock.

Currency Exchange: All **banks** along av. Bourguiba change cash, and most change traveler's checks. The **STB** beside the Hotel Africa is convenient for cash, traveler's checks, and V/MC transactions. Banks are open Mon.-Fri. 8am-noon. Some close and re-open later (from 4:30-6:30pm) while others remain open until 4pm. Some airport kiosks operate 24hr. International V/MC **ATMs** are located at the airport, beside Hotel Africa, and at pl. de la Victoire.

American Express: Carthage Tours, 59, av. Habib Bourguiba (tel. 354 993; fax 352 740). Emergency check cashing for cardholders only; others can only report lost or stolen traveler's checks here. Traveler's cheques (in dinars) sold. Open Mon.-Fri. 8am-noon and 2-6pm, Sat. 8am-noon.

Telephones: Two telecard phones exist in the **PTT,** rue Gamal Abdel Nasser, which also sells cards. More convenient are the ubiquitous taxiphones that only take change, but will also cash bills. 24hr. taxiphones are located on av. de Carthage, just off av. Bourguiba, and at the underpass by the intersection of av. de Paris and av. du Ghana.

Flights: Tunis-Carthage International Airport (tel. 236 000 or 235 000). Take bus #35 from av. Bourguiba near Hotel Africa to the airport *(aérodrome)* and back for 490ml, or take a taxi—the only option at night—for 3.500D. Note that the TGM "Aéroport" stop is actually a beach named Aéroport, not the airport. Tunis Air office is at 48, av. Habib Bourguiba (tel. 770 100; fax 288 100).

Trains: SNCFT Gare de Tunis, pl. de Barcelone (tel. 244 440), between rue de Hollande and av. de Carthage, 3 blocks off av. Bourguiba. To: Hammamet and Nabeul (2.300D), Sousse (4.850D), Sfax (7.950D), Gabes (11.550D), and Bizerte (2.550D). **Commuter Trains: TGM,** at the eastern end of av. Bourguiba, away from the medina and past the huge clock. To Sidi Bou Said (35min., 530ml) via

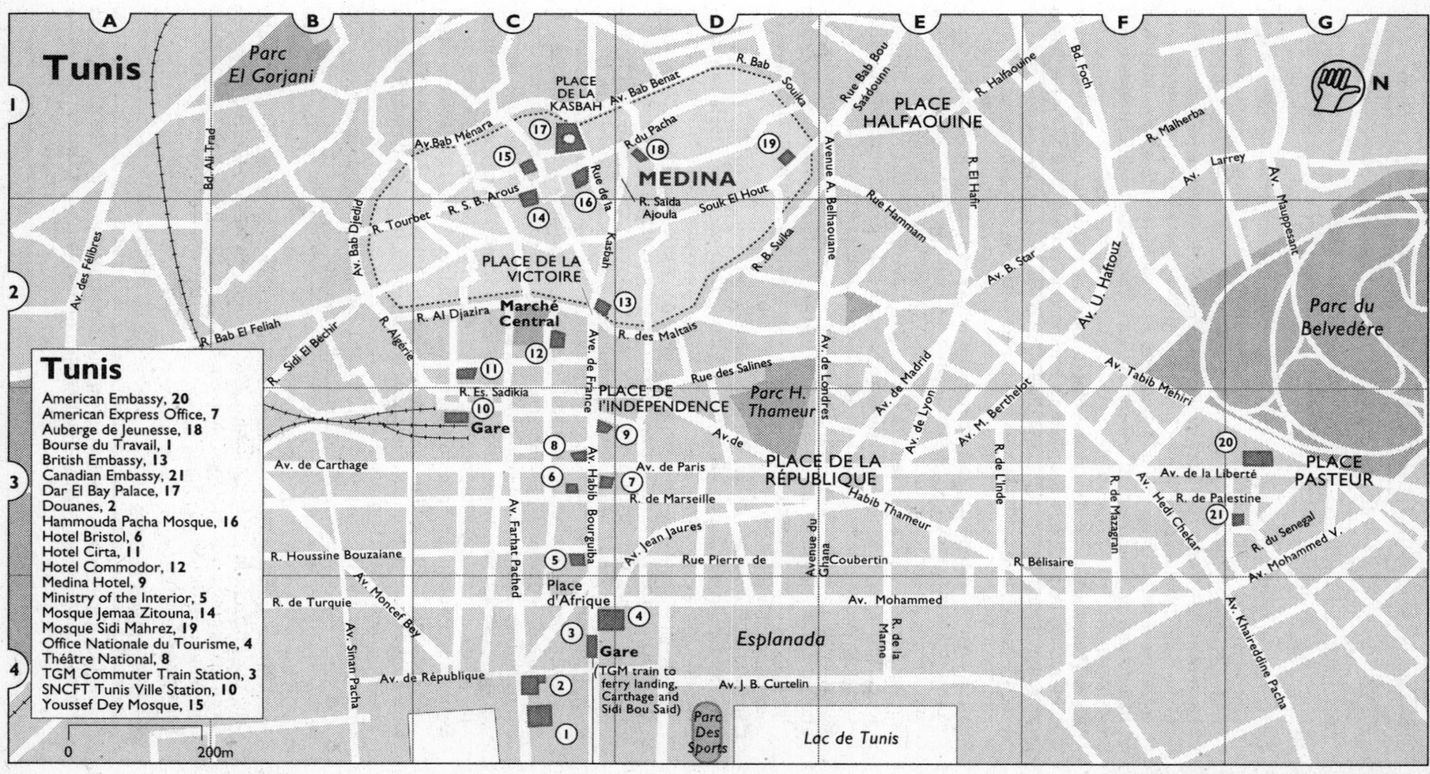
Tunis
Tunis
American Embassy, 20
American Express Office, 7
Auberge de Jeunesse, 18
Bourse du Travail, 1
British Embassy, 13
Canadian Embassy, 21
Dar El Bay Palace, 17
Douanes, 2
Hammouda Pacha Mosque, 16
Hotel Bristol, 6
Hotel Cirta, 11
Hotel Commodor, 12
Medina Hotel, 9
Ministry of the Interior, 5
Mosque Jemaa Zitouna, 14
Mosque Sidi Mahrez, 19
Office Nationale du Tourisme, 4
Théâtre National, 8
TGM Commuter Train Station, 3
SNCFT Tunis Ville Station, 10
Youssef Dey Mosque, 15
0
200m
N
A
B
C
D
E
F
G
1
2
3
4
Parc El Gorjani
PLACE DE LA KASBAH
MEDINA
PLACE HALFAOUINE
PLACE DE LA VICTOIRE
Marché Central
PLACE DE l'INDEPENDENCE
Parc H. Thameur
PLACE DE LA RÉPUBLIQUE
Parc du Belvedére
PLACE PASTEUR
Place d'Afrique
Gare
Gare
(TGM train to ferry landing, Carthage and Sidi Bou Said)
Esplanada
Parc Des Sports
Lac de Tunis
Bd. Ali Trad
Av. des Félibres
Av. Bab Ménara
Av. Bab Benat
R. Bab Souika
Rue Bab Bou Saâdounn
R. Halfaouine
Bd. Foch
R. Malherba
Av. Larrey
Av. Mauppesant
R. du Pacha
R. S. B. Arous
R. Tourbet
Av. Bab Djedid
Rue de la Kasbah
R. Saida Ajoula
Souk El Hout
Avenue A. Belhaouane
Rue Hammam
R. El Hafir
R. B. Suika
Av. B. Star
Av. U. Haftouz
R. Bab El Feliah
R. Sidi El Béchir
R. Algérie
R. Al Djazira
R. des Maltais
Ave. de France
Rue des Salines
Av. de Londres
Av. de Madrid
Av. de Lyon
Av. M. Berthelot
Av. Tabib Mehiri
R. Es. Sadikia
Av. de
Av. de Carthage
Av. de Paris
R. de Marseille
Av. Habib Bourguiba
Habib Thameur
R. de L'Inde
R. de Mazagran
Av. Hedi Chekar
Av. de la Liberté
R. de Palestine
R. du Senegal
Av. Mohammed V.
Av. Farhat Pached
Av. Jean Jaures
R. Houssine Bouzaiane
Rue Pierre de Coubertin
Avenue du Ghana
R. Bélisaire
Av. Moncef Bey
R. de Turquie
Av. Mohammed
R. de la Marne
Av. Khaireddine Pacha
Av. Sinan Pacha
Av. de République
Av. J. B. Curtelin

Carthage-La Marsa (30min., 530ml) and La Goulette. Mon.-Fri. every 15min., 5am-midnight. Fewer trains on weekends. **Luggage Storage:** Small lockers 2D for 24hr., large lockers 3D. Open 24hr.

National Buses and Louages: Bab el-Fellah (tel. 495 255), 1km from the train station, away from av. Bourguiba. On the opposite side of the overpass to the left at the end of av. de la Gare. Bus #50 goes here, but it is easier to take a taxi (500ml). To: Nabeul (2.380D), Kelibia (3.910D), Kairouan (6.500D), Sousse (6D), Gabes (13.400D), and Sfax (10.200D). **Bab Saadoun** (tel. 562 299) is a distant bus station with national service to Bizerte (2.930D), Tabarka (6.300D), and Le Kef (6.020D). From pl. de la Victoire take rue Mongi Slim to pl. Bab Souka, then rue Bal Saadoun in the same direction (30min.). Or hop on Métro #4 at pl. de Barcelone and get out at the Bab Saadoun stop (370ml). **Louages** are located outside both national bus stations and provide the most convenient access to Kelibia and El Haouria (both 4.500D).

Public Transportation: The central **Métro** hub is at pl. de Barcelone by the train station. Take Métro #4 to Bab Saadoun national bus station (370ml) or the Bardo Museum (500ml). Also stops near the Bab el-Fellah national bus station and the TGM Commuter rail, although taxi access is easier and nearly as cheap (500ml). The major **city bus** stops are near the TGM commuter rail, by the hotel Africa on av. Bourguiba and the national train station. Bus #35 leaves from near the Hotel Africa and goes to the airport (490ml). Buses are generally inconvenient, crowded, and, except for service to the airport, virtually the same price as taxis.

Ferries: Depart from **La Goulette** (tel. 275 000). Take the TGM train to Vieille Goulette. Tickets available at most of the travel agencies along av. Bourguiba and av. de Carthage. Arrive at least 2hr. before departure. Tickets to Italy 44D and up.

Taxis: 6, rue Ahmad Amine (tel. 783 311 or 282 211). Legally required to be metered, although some drivers will try to "bargain"—always make sure the meter is turned on. Three passengers is the usual maximum. 50% surcharge after 9pm. To airport for about 3.500D.

Car Rental: Europcar, 17, av. Habib Bourguiba (tel. 340 303 or 282 211), is the cheapest. A Renault Super 5 is 260D for 3 days, 520D per week. Open daily 8am-12:30pm and 2-7pm. **Avis,** in the lobby of the Hotel Africa (tel. 780 593), rents a Renault Super 5 at 260D for 3 days and 520D per week. **Hertz** is at 29 av. Bourguiba (tel. 248 559) and the airport. It is illegal for a rental car to carry more than 5 people including the driver. Always have passports ready for security checks. You must be 21 and have had a license for more than one year to rent and drive.

English Library: (tel. 341 444) on pl. de la Victoire. Use the door to the right before the entrance onto the rue de la Kasbah. A service of the British consulate. Periodicals, novels, and maps. Open Tues.-Fri. 10am-1pm; extended winter hours.

Laundromat: There are no coin-operated laundromats in Tunisia, but some dry cleaners take laundry by the kilo. Try **Laverie,** 15, rue d'Allemagne, across from the produce market. 5.500D per 5kg. basket. Open Mon.-Sat. 7am-6:30pm.

Swimming Pool: In the **Parc du Belvédère,** at the end of av. de la Liberté. Open July-Sept. 10am-5pm. 500ml. Take bus #5 from av. Bourguiba, near Hotel Africa.

Late-Night Pharmacy: 43, av. Bourguiba (tel. 252 507), or 20, av. de la Liberté (tel. 243 520). Open daily 9pm-10am.

Emergencies: tel. 190. **First Aid:** tel. 341 250. **Hospital: Hôpital Charles Nicolle** (tel. 663 010), bd. du IX Avril 1938 at rue Paul Bourde.

Police: tel. 197. Police brandishing assault rifles swarm along av. Bourguiba. Their chief barracks are off pl. du 7 Novembre.

Post Office: 30, av. Charles de Gaulle (tel. 650 121), 3 blocks off av. de France. Take the third right from pl. de la Victoire. *Poste restante* at window #7 (200ml per letter). Faxes at window #1. Open Mon.-Fri. 8am-6pm, Sun. 9-11am; during Ramadan open Mon.-Sat. 8:15am-3:45pm.

Telephone Code: 01.

ACCOMMODATIONS

Many budget hotels lurk in the medina off rue de la Kasbah and around the train station. Women should think twice about staying in the cheapest hotels, especially in the medina. Except for the hostel, most dirt-cheap hotels are also dirt-filled. The best option is the slightly more expensive Hotel Commodor.

Auberge de Jeunesse (HI), 25, rue Saida Ajoula (tel. 567 850). From pl. de la Kasbah (the plaza on the opposite side of the medina from pl. de la Victoire), head down rue de la Kasbah and take the second major left (there is a faded sign for the hostel). The hostel is 100m down the road on the right. Modern toilets, hot showers, plenty of travelers mingling in the pleasant courtyard, and an English-speaking warden. 4.500D per person. Breakfast 1D. Laundry on Tues. and Fri. (500ml per piece). Bike rental 8D per day. Reception open 6:30-10am and 4-11pm. Curfew 8:30pm, but the warden allows exceptions. HI members only.

Hotel Commodor, 17, rue d'Allemagne (tel. 244 941), 2nd right off av. Charles de Gaulle from av. de France. A cut above the rest, and not much more expensive. Polished wood lobby, pleasant tea salon, and spotless rooms. Singles 9.500D, with bath 13.600D. Doubles 18D, with bath 21D. The showers down the corridor cost 1.700D, so spring for the bath.

Medina Hotel, pl. de la Victoire (tel. 255 056), to the right of the square. Convenient and easy to find above the Restaurant Medina. Clean barracks-style medina hotel. Doubles 10D. Triples 13D. Quads 16D. Hot shower 1D (wear flip-flops).

Hotel Hammami, 1, pl. Bab Carthagène (tel. 260 451). From av. de France hang a right along rue Mongi Slim, which skirts the medina walls. Bear left through the square facing the Anglican Church (10min.). El cheapo. A classic, grungy medina hotel in a former law-school dorm. Single communal bathroom and remote location may prompt women traveling alone to stay elsewhere. Singles 2.500D, doubles 4.500D, triples 6D. Clean up in the nearby *hammam* instead of the shower.

Hotel Cirta, 42, rue Charles de Gaulle (tel. 241 582), across from the Hotel Agriculture. Adequately clean, relatively large rooms. Friendly manager may let you store luggage and accept incoming calls. Singles 8D. Doubles 12D. Triples 15D. Skanky showers 1.500D.

Hotel Bristol, 30, rue Mohammed el Aziz Taj, (tel. 244 836), down the small alley off av. de Carthage behind Café de Paris. Clean, cheap, centrally located cubbyholes. Singles 5D. Doubles 7D. Triples 11D. Quads 11D. Breakfast 1D.

FOOD

Non-Tunisian fare tends toward the mediocre here, with the unsurprising exception of French food. Don't even touch the Italian. Inexpensive Tunisian food *(tajines,* couscous, and *tripes)* can be found in and around the medina. Look for cheap pizza, sandwiches, and meat pies off av. de Carthage; they become more expensive as you approach av. Bourguiba. Don't miss the Café de Paris, on av. Bourguiba, the most popular place to go for tea or *café* in Tunis. The extensive **central market** on rue Charles de Gaulle sells produce and meat products. Open daily 3-8pm. **Monoprix,** a large supermarket chain with stores off av. Bourguiba on rue Charles de Gaulle and on rue de la Liberté at rue du Koweit, also stocks a selection of inexpensive edibles and useful toiletries. Open Mon.-Sat. 8:30am-1pm and 4-7:30pm.

Restaurant Carcassonne, 8, av. de Carthage (tel. 256 768). *Brasserie*-type place popular with tourists and locals. Vegetarians should try the quiche-like *tagine* (2D). Solid, 4-course *menu* a super-bargain at 3.200D. Open daily 8am-10pm.

M'Rabet (tel. 261 729), at the center of the medina in Souk el-Trouk. From pl. de la Kasbah, take a right off of rue de la Kasbah onto rue Sidi Ben Arons. Take the next right onto Souk el-Trouk, and the restaurant will be on the right. This 300-year old building contains the sarcophagi of an Ottoman sheik, his servant, and his daughter, M'Rabet. The traditional café downstairs is the coolest eatery in Tunis. Sit on a mat and indulge in *chicha* (about 2D) or Turkish coffee (700ml). Upstairs is a restaurant with a reputation for the best Tunisian food around. Entrees 7-9D. "Oriental shows" with belly dancers for 5D extra Sept.-June. Open Mon.-Sat. noon-3pm and 8pm-midnight.

Restaurant du Peuple, rue Mongi Slim, at pl. de la Victoire. A local hangout with inexpensive, delicious Tunisian cuisine. Heaping servings of *couscous à l'agneau* 1.900D. Spicy soup 600ml. Great for the budget traveler.

Pâtisserie Le Prince, 5, rue Ibn Khaldoun, off av. Bourguiba to the right from the medina. Look for the obnoxious green "Fast Food" sign. One of the few reasonable stand-up sandwich shops. Massive, greasy *chaourma* sandwich and fries 1.300D. Open Mon.-Sat. 6am-10:30pm.

Restaurant Des Palmiers, 11, rue d'Egypte (tel. 285 407), off av. de la Liberté. A 15-min. walk from av. Bourguiba, 7 blocks past rue du Ghana to the left. Tunisian dishes are fresh and served quickly. Try the *meloukya,* a delicious meat dish that looks deceptively unappetizing (1.750D). The lamb couscous is also excellent (1.900D). Open Mon.-Sat. noon-10:30pm. Closed mornings during Ramadan.

SIGHTS

The New City (Nouvelle Ville)

French-built modern Tunis is best seen as you stroll up the 70m-wide **av. Habib Bourguiba.** Along the way, you can stock up on flowers and such Tunisian souvenirs as Levi's 501 T-shirts and Michael Jackson bootlegs. The **place d'Afrique,** at the intersection of av. Mohammed V, was once adorned with an equestrian statue of Bourguiba that now resides in front of La Goulette. In its original place stands a four-legged clock tower. The site has been officially renamed **place du 7 Novembre 1987,** commemorating the recent *coup d'état* of President Ben Ali, whose likeness is plastered everywhere in somewhat Orwellian fashion.

Perhaps the most distinctive (and least attractive) aspect of the new city is the **French Colonial architecture.** Public buildings were designed in this style in an attempt to convey European culture to North Africa. (The virginal-white structures have aptly been described as "wedding cakes.") The **National Theater,** two blocks from pl. de l'Indépendance and now under renovation, appears condescending and formal with its classical motifs. The theater, however, pales in comparison to the **cathedral** which faces the square. This 1882 structure is a hybrid of Romanesque and Islamic styles. Its rounded edges and unsubtle statues are practically burlesque. The **French Embassy,** located across from the cathedral, is understated in comparison, though it once served as the executive seat of the Protectorate.

Medina

Before European colonization, Tunis was contained within the medina's fortified walls, which protected a self-sufficient network of commercial, domestic, and religious institutions and a maze of streets. At its best, the medina of Tunis is an evocative remnant of this exquisitely organized society. At its worst, it is a dispensary of oriental kitsch. Regardless, the medina is a lively commercial area integral to modern Tunis—a flea market-*cum*-shopping mall where residents bargain for jeans, deodorant, and Ace of Base albums. Whatever your motivations, the medina is a great place to wander. Turn down any small alley and you'll find yourself on a side street where the signs are only in Arabic. **Remember that exploring the medina can be unsafe, especially at night and especially for women.** On av. Bourguiba and around the mosque, young men claiming to be students may offer either to guide you around the sights (they will expect payment) or to accompany you to the grossly over-priced artisan shops (they will receive a commission). Also, beware of merchants who drag you upstairs to see their "terraces" and then request an outrageous fee for the privilege of having entered their shop.

Maps of the medina are available at the ONTT office (on the back of the Tunis map) and are posted at the Great Mosque and pl. de la Kasbah. From pl. de la Victoire, two main streets lead to the Great Mosque and the heart of the medina. Tour groups barge through **rue Jemaa ez Zitouna** (on the left), the place to go for stuffed toy camels and chintzy brass plates. **Rue de la Kasbah** (on the right) is equally congested with locals shopping for everything *but* souvenirs (clothes, watches, glasses, and the kitchen sink).

Rue de la Kasbah passes two masterpieces of Ottoman-influenced architecture. The first is the **Hammouda Pacha Mosque,** whose octagonal minaret is a distinctively Turkish feature that was popular in the 17th century. Strangely, the façade's ornamentation is actually derived from the European Renaissance style, since the mosque's patron was an Italian Muslim in the Ottoman civil service. This mosque's predecessor is a bit further down the street. The **Youssef Dey Mosque** was built in 1616, an early attempt by the Turkish to spruce up Tunis.

Souk el Bey is the name of the street heading left by the Youssef Dey Mosque. Another quick left leads to **Souk des Chechias,** named for the traditional crimson skullcaps still worn by some older Tunisian men. Crafted from luxuriously heavy felt, they were once Tunis's primary industry. (Unfortunately, the craft is now almost extinct.) The **Dar el-Bey,** straight ahead on Souk el-Bey, houses the Ministry of Foreign Affairs. A left here places you on **Souk el-Trouk,** where vendors sell just about everything: cheap sandals, dried fruit, circumcision outfits....

The **Jemaa Zitouna (Great Mosque)** presides at the end of this *souk,* the center of the medina. The **minaret** is a dignified, classically proportioned tower—the product of the Moroccan-based Almohad Empire of the 13th century—much in contrast with the ornate Ottoman style. For a price, you can have a look at the courtyard, whose columns were recycled from various Roman sites. Each teacher at the university here had his own column from which he would regularly instruct. The prayer hall is off-limits to non-Muslims; take this into consideration before paying admission. (Open daily 8am-noon. Admission 1.500D.)

The covered market along the Great Mosque's walls is the **Souk el-Attarine** (Perfume Souk), where aggressive vendors tout inexpensive Chanel knock-offs. **Souk el-Blag-Djia,** a market for factory and handmade shoes, becomes tiny rue el-Jelloud. When you see the sign "el-Jelloud," take a left into a cul-de-sac (Impasse Echemmahra). At the far end, ring the doorbell at #9 and ask to visit the small, elegant 17th-century **Tomb of Princess Aziza,** now a private residence. The princess had a charitable reputation, having established a dowry fund to enable poor girls to marry.

Walking back up Souk el-Attarine and turning left at the Great Mosque's minaret puts you on Souk des Femmes. Take the first right onto Souk el-Lefta, where charismatic dealers roll out beautiful carpets. (If you're reading this book, you probably can't afford one.) Many of the larger emporiums have intricately tiled terraces from which you can see the rooftops of the *souks* and the surrounding medina. The most famous is that of the **Palais d'Orient,** the large bazaar at 58, Souk el-Leffa. This enameled terrace dates to the 15th century, and its view is featured on hundreds of postcards. (Free.) Souk des Femmes becomes Rue Tourbet el-Bey, which predictably leads toward the **Tourbet el-Bey.** Built in the 18th century, this structure houses the tombs of several members of the Husaynid dynasty amidst rather excessive stucco detailing. The sacrophagi may seem narrow to non-Muslims because the Islamic dead are traditionally buried on their side facing Mecca to await Judgement Day. (Open daily 8:30am-6:30pm. Admission 1.500D.) From here follow the green tourist signs to the **Dar Ben Abdallah** (Museum of Arts and Traditions). This museum, housed in a fine old palace, depicts traditional Tunisian domestic life using rather frightening mannequins. The displays of household goods are excellent, illustrating how any sort of object can be imbued with the Islamic sense of style. A **museum annex** is devoted to traditional industries, most importantly *chechia*-making. Unfortunately, exhibit descriptions are only in French and Arabic. (Open Tues.-Sun. 9:30am-4:30pm. Admission 1.500D, 1D to take photos.)

Just down the street from the museum you'll find the **Mosquée des Teinturiers,** or dyer's mosque, built in 1716. Although closed to non-believers, the façade is worth seeing for its unusual red, green, and yellow eaves. Every neighborhood in the medina has its own mosque, generally organized around a specific craft. Each community also had its own *hammam,* bakery, and well. Worshipers go to the local mosque for daily prayers, and the Grande Mosque (Jemaa Zitouna) on Fridays. The dyer's stalls, **Souk des Teinturiers,** run past the mosque along rue des Teinturiers. Continue toward rue Jemaa Zitouna to complete the circuit of the medina.

The Bardo Museum

While a trip to North Africa generally means an escape from the endless "must-see" museums of Europe, Tunis offers no better diversion than the **Bardo Museum,** contained in the bey's old palace, and home to one of the world's finest collections of ancient art. The Bardo is most renowned for its Roman mosaics, transported here from various archaeological sites throughout the country. The size of the collection (and of the visiting tour groups) may overwhelm the spectator. Keep in mind that the labels are only in French and Arabic. To get to the museum, take Métro #4 from the train station at pl. de Barcelone to the Bardo stop (500ml). From the exit, walk down the street to the left and follow the road signs. A taxi will cost 2D.

The ground floor tour starts with a cross-shaped baptistery in the **Paleochristian Room,** to the left of the entrance, featuring brightly colored mosaic tombstones with sour-faced icons and Latin admonitions. Continuing forward, room VI displays artifacts from **Bulla Regia,** highlighted by twice-life-size statues of Roman gods and a mosaic of Perseus and Andromeda. On the opposite side of the ground floor lies the **Room of Baal Hammon,** one of the **Salles de la Civilisations Puniques,** with ritual slabs showing the Carthaginians sacrificing children to the dark goddess Tanit.

The palace's second floor displays the major attractions. The mosaics are not only important as works of art but as documents depicting the daily life of their epoch. They are grouped in rooms based on their places of origin. Room IX **(Carthage)** is the central exhibition hall, a courtyard with a Turkish twist housing sculpture and mosaics excavated at Carthage. The floor of the **Hadrumetum Room** is decorated with the immense *Triumph of Neptune* mosaic from Sousse, while the walls above are a backdrop for three semi-circular works depicting rural houses and a 4th-century piece entitled *Mosaïque du Seigneur Julius.* The adjacent Room XI contains a superbly preserved *Neptune in his Chariot*. Across from this room is the **Virgilius Room,** the former home of the bey's harem, devoted almost entirely to the exhibition of a single, small mosaic of Virgil surrounded by Muses. High school Latin scholars can have some fun (finally) by trying to guess which verse of the *Aeneid* Virgil is holding in his lap. Room XXVII displays relics from **Dougga,** including a celebrated mosaic of *Ulysses and the Sirens,* the latter quite homely but the former frightened nonetheless. Complete your odyssey at the **Uthina Room,** where a wall-mounted mosaic depicts the lovelorn Orpheus soothing the beasts with his music. Orpheus's disfigured face was probably the work of 5th-century vandals, who also had a field day on the statuary downstairs. (Open Tues.-Sun., 9am-8pm; Ramadan 9am-4pm. Admission 3.150D, 1D extra to take photos.)

■ Near Tunis: Carthage and Sidi Bou Said

Efficient TGM commuter trains at 15-min. intervals make **Carthage** (30min., 530ml) and **Sidi Bou Said** (35min., 530ml) easy daytrips from Tunis, though the trains may be crowded on weekends. Popular beaches include the spectacular 30-km stretch of **Raouad,** which begins just past **Gammarth,** and those of **La Marsa.** Be warned—the sand may be hard to find in the summer under a layer of pale German bodies.

CARTHAGE

Any visitor expecting to see magnificent reminders of Carthage's legendary history here will be disappointed. The few remains are mediocre at best, and there is little trace of the Punic Empire that once rivaled Rome for Mediterranean supremacy. Still, anyone with the barest sense of history and a little imagination cannot help but be impressed by the momentous aura of the site where Aeneas and Dido trysted and Hannibal plotted his campaign across the Alps.

The city's origins are attributed to the Phoenician Queen Dido, whose affair with the founder of Rome is described in Virgil's *Aeneid.* Little historical information is known about the first Carthaginian citizens except that they were phenomenal traders and had a habit of pissing off everyone whom they met. The Romans finally defeated them in 146BC; contemporary Roman accounts describe the immolation of the city in loving detail. As Rome's power in Africa grew, Carthage was refounded as the provincial capital, rising and falling along with the Roman Empire until a final defeat by the Vandals in 429.

Modern Carthage is essentially an overpriced suburb of Tunis, with only scattered remains of its former glory—some magnificent, others banal. The TGM Commuter Rail has stops near the major sights, which cover a distance of 2.5km. If you're short on stamina or time, get off at the **Carthage-Byrsa** station, visit the Tophet and the Punic Ports, then get back on the TGM to **Carthage-Hannibal** and visit the Roman baths. The nearby **beaches** of the Bay of Tunis are gorgeous and refreshing. Buy a ticket for all Carthage sites at either the Carthage Museum, the Roman baths, or the Amphitheater and Tophet Roman baths. (Admission 4.200D, photos 2D. Fend off guides or give them some loose change.) You can buy a map of Carthage in town, but it's better to get one in Tunis for free.

Carthage-Byrsa

Though most of the uncovered ruins in Carthage date to the Roman era, traces of the original Punic settlement remain at the cemetery **Tophet** (also called the **Sanctuary of Tanit**). Here, bushes conceal stones shaped like the planks of picket fences, each engraved with a circle atop a rectangle that balances on a triangle. This pictogram represents the figure of the bloodthirsty goddess Tanit, who demanded the sacrifice of first-born 12- and 14-year-olds in times of hardship. Each stone mourns one of the 1200 children who were sacrificed here. (Open daily 7am-6pm.) To reach the Tophet from the station, cross av. Bourguiba and head straight down av. Farhat, then take a left on rue Hannibal.

From Tophet, head down rue Hannibal with the sea to your right, following the signs to the **Punic Ports.** Almost nothing remains of what was once the world's greatest harbor, but determined archaeologists have reconstructed its contours. Inside the "Antiquarium" (the custodian will unlock it for you) are detailed models of the military port in the Punic and Roman periods. (Site open daily 7am-6pm.)

Carthage-Hannibal

The **National Museum of Carthage** occupies the site where an immense Roman temple once stood, and marble fragments still saturate the surrounding gardens. Inside are some Punic funerary steles (upright gravestones) and two expressive 4th-century sarcophagi in Italian Carrara marble. (Open daily 8am-7pm.) To reach the museum from the station, follow the palm-lined av. de l'Amphithéâtre up to its crest and take a left up the narrow dirt path just as the road is about to slope down again.

The most substantial remains of Carthage lie in the village of Hannibal. From the station, walk toward the water and turn left on rue Septime Sévère to find the 2nd-century Roman **Baths of Antoninus**—the single most impressive ruin in Carthage. Once rivaling Rome's Baths of Caracalla in size, the structure was gradually dismantled by villagers who used the site as a quarry. Unfortunately, you can't enter this forest of humpbacked pediments and fallen pillars. Near the entrance to the complex, you'll discover a tiny underground Christian chapel, whose floor is patterned with an ornithological mosaic. (Open daily 8:30am-7pm; off-season 8:30am-5pm.)

Next head away from the sea, up av. Des Thermes d'Antonin and under the railway tracks, following the signs to the **Roman Villas** and **Archaeological Gardens.** Here you will find two Byzantine churches and a Punic necropolis. The guides will likely tell you that the elegant villa was Hannibal's Palace (although Hannibal died 400 years before the villa was built). Over the hill lies the well preserved 3rd-century **Odeon.** (Open daily 8am-7pm.) Uphill from the station are the remnants of the Roman **amphitheater.** Another 2km ahead, the scrupulously restored **Theater of Carthage** provides the backdrop for the **Festival of Carthage** from July to mid-August. For info, contact the tourist office in Tunis or check the schedule in *La Presse.* The **American Cemetery** lies north of the Odeon, off rue Roosevelt (quite a trek from the station).

The immaculately groomed grass and stone stars may seem out of place in Tunisia, but their presence is most appropriate. The cemetery holds the remains of 2,840 servicemen, while a wall bears the names of the 3,724 men whose bodies were never recovered. A large mural depicts the North African campaign; the caretaker can provide details. (Open Mon.-Sat. 8am-6pm, Sun. 9am-6pm.)

SIDI BOU SAID

After getting sweaty and sandy in Carthage, the village of Sidi Bou Said (10min. farther down the TGM line, with return service to Tunis until midnight) is the perfect spot to rejuvenate. The streets are smooth cobblestone, the houses sport fresh blue and white paint, and purple flowers spill out of wall-top gardens. The attention to decorative detail in Sidi Bou Said is particularly charming. Look for carved doorknockers, brightly painted metal window grilles, and wooden window boxes thick with flowers. For natural beauty, admire the cliffs, the sea, or the beautiful Tunisian women—here you'll find the best pickup scene in the Tunis region. The town is packed with tourists, but generally calms down in the evenings.

From the TGM station, proceed to the right and turn left at the police station. Walk up the hill to the tiny **town square** (10min.). Follow rue Sidi Bou-Fares from there, then turn left and hike up the hill. A small tip will persuade the guardian to let you climb the **minaret.** For an even better view, hike up to the **lighthouse** that peers down from the hill's summit. (Tip 1D. Open whenever the caretaker is there.)

Heading right at the main square from the TGM station, you will come to a steep flight of 254 stairs that descends to a small, beautiful, but crowded beach. Before 10am or after 9pm, travelers can volunteer at the port to work on one of the tiny fishing boats that roam the sea all night and return at dawn. If you can spare several days, you may even get paid. Choose your fishing boat with discretion and go only with someone you trust.

The only budget accommodation is the truly excellent **Hotel Sidi Bou-Fares,** up the hill from the main square at #15 (tel. 740 091). The rooms are neat with thick walls, and the courtyard has an immense apricot tree to ensure midday shade. There are only eight rooms, and the hotel is extremely popular, so call ahead. Singles 12.500D. Doubles 22D. Triples with bath 30D. Breakfast included. If you're lucky enough to have a room at the Boufares, take advantage of the excellent lunches and dinners served in July and August for 7D, the best deal in town. **Restaurant Chergui,** off the main square (tel. 740 987), is also an attractive dining option. Try the *couscous poulet* for 4D, or the *tagine de fromage* (a meatless quiche) for 4D. Food is served in a beautiful, breezy courtyard with a nice view. V, MC. For dessert try the *bambolini,* fried dough saturated with sugar (250ml), sold at stands near the beach. In the cool evenings, the cafés quickly fill up with people. The **Café des Nattes,** off the central plaza, with steep stairs leading up to its front door, has a good pedigree; Cervantes, de Beauvoir, and Klee all sipped and quipped here. Those who partake say it's also a good place to smoke *chicha* in a traditional setting. Another excellent establishment is the nearby **Café Sidi Chabane.**

CAP BON PENINSULA

Stretching northeast toward Sicily, Cap Bon rests between the Gulf of Tunis and the Gulf of Hammamet. The cape's breezy hillsides, shady olive groves, and shimmering sea provide welcome relief from both the scorching heat of the south and the wearying bustle of Tunis. Cap Bon was ancient Carthage's supplier of limestone, but now its major boon is tourism. Vacationing Europeans crowd the peninsula's fine beaches and fill its azure waters at the beach towns of Nabeul, Kelibia, and Hammamet. Frequent buses link the villages of the peninsula with Tunis and each other. Inexpensive hotels are rare, but hostels are available.

Nabeul

Instead of the carpet of sunbathing tourists on the beaches of Hammamet, in Nabeul you'll have to compete only with the algae. Hammamet's sister city does possess its share of resort hotels and daytrippers looking to buy the famous local ceramics, but you'll have no trouble finding a few idyllic and unpopulated stretches of beach. The number of tourists peaks on Fridays for the town's **camel market** (although how visitors plan to get their dromedary friends through customs is somewhat unclear).

ORIENTATION AND PRACTICAL INFORMATION

The main street, **avenue Habib Thameur,** runs parallel to the beach, 1km away. It intersects **avenue Habib Bourguiba,** which runs past the train station to the beach. **Trains** from Tunis (7 per day, 1½hr., 2.800D), arrive in pl. du 7 Novembre, a traffic circle centered around a tree growing out of a massive ceramic vase. Across the street and to the right is a small **museum** of Carthaginian and Roman artifacts. Open Tues.-Sun. 8am-1pm and 4-7pm. Admission 1.100D. Also across from the station is a **Syndicat,** with an excellent free map of Nabeul and Hammamet. Open Tues.-Sun. 9am-1pm and 3-7pm. At **ONTT** (tel. 286 800), av. Taïeb Mehiri, the other large street leading to the beach, one block away and parallel to av. Bourguiba, the workers speak English and have the same useful maps. Head one block forward from the exit of the train station to reach av. Taïeb Mehiri, and take a right. The office is on the right, almost at the beach. Open July-Aug. 7:30am-1:30pm; Sept.-June 8:30am-1pm and 3-5:45pm. The **bus and louage station** (excepting Cap Bon *louages*) is located on av. Habib Thameur, four blocks toward Hammamet. Buses leave every 30min. for Tunis (1hr., 2.380D) and every hr. for Kelibia (45min., 2.200D). Both services stop at 6pm. *Louages* to Tunis (3D) leave from the bus station, while Kelibia *louages* (2.200D) leave from the station on av. Hached. Follow av. Thameur 500m after it becomes av. Farhat Hached, past av. Bourguiba, to reach the **Cap Bon louage station** on the right. Head away from the beach on av. Bourguiba for the **post office,** located two blocks after the intersection with av. Habib Thameur. Open Mon.-Sat. 8am-6pm. The **police station** (tel. 285 474) is located on av. Bourguiba between the train station and av. Habib Thameur. **Telephone code:** 02.

ACCOMMODATIONS AND FOOD

They could have filmed *Full Metal Jacket* in the barracks-like dormitories of the **HI Youth hostel** (tel. 285 547), but it's a good place to meet independent travelers and the location on the beach is marvelous. 3.7D per person. Breakfast included. Don't let the warden pressure you into full-pension—it's not worth the 6D. HI membership required. Back in town, the **Pension Les Roses,** rue Sidi Abdel Kader (tel. 285 570) off a. Hached and beside Restaurant du Bonheur, has cheery, clean rooms with hot water, towels, and soap. The hotel is small and popular, so call ahead. Singles 9D. Doubles 16D. Hot shower 500ml. The touristed **Hotel les Jasmins** (tel. 285 343), the only **campsite** in town, is 2km from the bus station down the Hammamet Road. 2D per person, 1.500D per car. Shower 2D. Cheap restaurants lie off av. Farhat Hached and beside the youth hostel on the beach. **Restaurant de la Jeunesse,** 76, av. Farhat Hached, by Pension Les Roses, serves decent *brochettes* or couscous for 3D. Open daily 9am-9pm. **Chez Papa,** also nearby on av. Farhat Hached, will stuff you with macaroni and mystery meat for 2.500D. Open 10am-10pm. **Azel Fast Food,** despite its off-putting name, actually has good tuna pizzas for 3D and chicken subs for 1.100D, and it's the only place open late: daily 10am-11:30pm. A picnic on the beach is always attractive; pick up the supplies at the **central market** behind the bus station.

Kelibia

Although most visitors to Kelibia are students at the Tunisian School of Fishery, the 6th-century Byzantine fortress overlooking the port recalls a time when the town was much more coveted by foreigners. The breeze that greets you as you arrive will lure you to the pristine sands of **El Mansourah** (2km north), perhaps Cap Bon's finest beach. The few hotels here will stretch your budget, but the tranquil location is certainly worth it. Kelibia and its environs are an easy daytrip from Tunis, Hammamet, or Nabeul, but a find like this deserves a longer stay.

ORIENTATION AND PRACTICAL INFORMATION

Buses and *louages* will deposit you in **Kelibia town,** a dusty, dull place noted solely for its 10 mosques, all with varied minarets. To get to **Kelibia Plage,** the more attractive area where the hotels and cafés are located (2.5km away), head left from the bus station waiting room. You'll arrive at a traffic circle with a monument in the center. Take a left, pass the **police station** (tel. 197) and the **PTT,** and you will eventually spot a sign for Kelibia Plage. Follow the sign to the fork in the road and bear left onto **avenue des Martyrs** (also known as **rue de la Plage**) for the most direct path to the beach. To avoid the hike, take a cab from the train station to the beach for 500ml. **Buses** run to Kelibia from Tunis's Bab el-Fellah (14 per day, 3.910D), with return service ending at 4pm. However, the simplest way to get to Kelibia from Tunis or Nabeul is by **louage** (4.500D from Tunis).

ACCOMMODATIONS AND FOOD

The best value is the **Hotel Florida** (tel. 296 248), next to the touristy Hotel Palmarina off av. des Martyrs. It's a bit pricey, but it's right on the sand and has a great view of the adjacent Borj. The best values are the motel-like bungalows with toilets and showers; otherwise, you will share a communal shower for the same price. Singles 15.500D. Doubles 24D. Breakfast included. The hotel also has an excellent **restaurant** with a 5D *menu*. Food is served on a terrace overlooking the sea. Open daily 12:30-3:30pm and 7pm-midnight. The Florida also runs a relaxed **bar** where seafarers swap yarns over cold Celtia (1.250D). Back toward town off av. des Martyrs, **Pension Anis,** av. Erriadii (tel./fax 273 128), is spotless and well managed. From the fork in the road coming from the train station, take a left onto av. des Martyrs and then a quick right onto av. Erriadii. Singles 13-15D. Doubles 20-24D. Breakfast and hot showers included. The **restaurant** at the Anis is good and inexpensive, with Tunisian staples running from 2D to 4D. Free-lance **camping** is often tolerated along Mansourah beach and the longer stretches of deserted beach farther north. Check with the police or any possible owner of the site, and be sure to consider safety. Around 500ml. Restaurant **El Borj** (tel. 296 164), on av. des Martyrs between Hotel Florida and the Borj, serves a good seafood omelet for 1.500D and cheap *poulet roti* (1.700D). The adventurous can try half a lamb's head for 2.200D. Away from Kelibia town, farther down av. des Martyrs (don't cut left to El-Mansourah), is the **Café Sidi el-Bahri.** On a terrace overlooking the sea, sample some of the most marvelous *chocolat chaud* anywhere (500ml).

SIGHTS

The remarkably intact **Borj** (fortress) looks down from the hill between Kelibia and Mansourah. Together with the fort at Hammamet, it controlled the eastern portion of the Cap Bon peninsula. Little remains of the original 4th-century BC walls. Most of the present battlements were added later by the Romans and Byzantines. In the 16th and 17th centuries, Spain controlled the fort and built the crenellations atop the walls. Borj was later occupied by the Turks and then the French. The anti-aircraft guns were made when the fort's Axis occupants came under attack by Allied aircraft. The fort is generally open all day during the summer, depending on the whim of the guardian. The road that winds around the base of the fort leads to **El Mansourah** and its ivory

beaches 2km away. No signs point you there, so just follow a sandy path, or hop in a taxi traveling back and forth to the beach (500ml).

■ Near Kelibia

EL HAOUARIA

El Haouaria is home to one of the most unusual sites in all of Tunisia: the **Grottoes Romaines** (Roman Caves), a labyrinth of underground pyramids carved out of the limestone rock along the shore. The caves were created by Punic and Roman limestone quarries and were inhabited by the slaves that worked the mines. You can explore the grottoes yourself, since the path between them is simple. A local guide (no matter what he tells you) just won't be necessary. The oddly shaped rock formation in the second large cave down the path from the ticket booth is called "Le Dromadaire," although it resembles an enormous Barney more than a camel. A series of other man-made grottoes is linked to this one, most of which are pyramidal with holes at the top to admit sunlight. (Grottoes open daily 8am-7pm. Admission 1.100D.) When you've finished exploring, consider joining the throngs of local boys who use the rock formations as diving boards into the Mediterranean.

To reach the caves, take a right from the bus station and walk straight along av. Bourguiba. Walk through the center of town, and 1.5km later, you will reach the shore and the ticket booth. The caves extend 1km in both directions, and, of course, the most interesting ones are those you have to pay for. If you decide to stay the night in El Haouaria, consider the **Pension Dar Toubib** (tel. 297 163), to the right off av. Bourguiba on the way to the caves, situated at the edge of town. Each spotless room has a shower and overlooks a charming garden. Singles 12D. Doubles 18D. The **Restaurant La Daurade,** at the entrance to the caves, is expensive, but a good place for *café* (600ml) and has an impressive view of the Mediterranean.

Buses to El Haouaria depart daily from Tunis's Gare Routière du Nord near the Bab Saadoun (4.300D), but bus service ends for the region at 4pm. A better bet is to take a **louage** from Kelibia (1.100D) or from Tunis itself (5D).

SAHEL

The **Sahel** (seashore) curves along eastern Tunisia from the Cap Bon peninsula to Sfax. This region was the base of the independence movement in the 1930s and has been the country's wealthiest area since independence was declared in 1956. Its residents have long benefitted from the region's prime soil and relatively high levels of rainfall, which have made Sahel a leading exporter of olives. While the northern city of Sousse swells its massive medina with package-tour visitors, Sfax in the south has industrialized with nary a tourist in mind. Monastir, the birthplace of former president Bourguiba, offers only the inflated trappings of a personality cult. Down the coast, the ancient port of Mahdia is the point of origin of the Fatimid dynasty. Inland, Tunisia's most sacred mosque resides in Kairouan, while at sleepy El Jem a Roman amphitheater bears witness to a great and cruel civilization.

■ Sousse

Sousse handles its status as a tourist attraction gracefully, remaining clean, inexpensive, and generally agreeable. Its central location on the Sahel made it an important site long before anyone invented the tour bus. Starting in the 3rd century BC, bloody battles were fought for control of it, each conquering people giving the town a new name: Hadrumetum under the Romans, Hunsericopolis under the Vandals, Justinopolis under the Byzantines, and Sousse under the Aghlabid Arabs. In recent years the city has grown and prospered, not at all hurt by the fact that President Ben Ali is the local boy who made good.

ORIENTATION AND PRACTICAL INFORMATION

Pedestrians, buses, cars, and a ridiculous miniature "Noddy Train" compete for space in the extended plaza, composed of the overlapping **place Farhat Hached, place Sidi Yahia,** and **place des Martyrs.** At pl. Farhat Hached, the road with the train tracks in the middle splits into **avenue Bourguiba** to the right and **avenue de la République** to the left. Going straight on av. Bourguiba will take you to the beaches of Sousse with their multi-starred hotels. The main pedestrian entrance to the medina lies at the far end of the plazas from av. Bourguiba, on the way to the port.

Tourist Office: ONTT Office de Tourisme, 1, av. Bourguiba (tel. 225 157), at the origin of av. Bourguiba by pl. Farhat Ached. Across the traffic circle by the medina walls is a **Syndicat.** Both tourist offices have maps, cultural event schedules, and fares and times for trains and buses, but the ONTT has the best stock. Both open Mon.-Sat. 7:30am-1:30pm and 3-6pm, Sun. 9am-noon and 3-6pm.

Currency Exchange: Banks line av. Bourguiba. Most are open Mon.-Fri. 8-11:30am and 2-5pm, Sat.-Sun. 9am-noon.

Telephones: To the left of the main pedestrian entrance to the medina, across from the bust of Farhat Hached.

Trains: The tracks at the fork in the road between the tourist offices lead to the **central train station.** To Tunis (11 per day, 2½hr., 4.850D) and Nabeul (8 per day, 2½hr., 3.550D, change at Bir Bou Regba). Trains to Mahdia and Monastir use the **Sousse Bab Jedid** station located near the port, 200m past pl. Farhat Hached. To Monastir (18 per day, 30min., 780ml) and Mahdia (11 per day, 1hr., 2D). Fewer trains run on Sundays.

Buses and Louages: Beside the Syndicat. Buses to: Tunis (6 per day, 5.500D); Kairouan (11 per day, 2.800D); Sfax (5 per day, 6D); El Jem (5 per day, 3.300D); and Mahdia (every hr., 2.500D).

Police Station On av. Bourguiba (tel. 225 566).

Night pharmacy: Off av. de la République (tel. 224 795).

Telephone Code: 03.

ACCOMMODATIONS AND FOOD

As you enter the medina through the main pedestrian entrance (by the "Soula Centre"), take a right after the Café Riadh El Medina, then a left when you hit the medina's walls. You'll find yourself at **Hotel de Paris,** 15, rue Rempart Nord (tel. 220 564). Rooms are spotless but basic, with only beds and a sink. Singles 10-11D. Doubles 15D. You can sleep on the terrace for 4D, but you'll have to pay an extra 500ml for the shower. To meet some Germans, head to the luxurious, modern **Hotel Medina** (tel. 221 722). From the main medina entrance, follow the walls of the Great Mosque to its rear. Each room has a shower and a toilet, and the bar downstairs is a mellow place to chat with both tourists and locals. Prices vary according to season. Singles 11-13D. Doubles 16-24D. Breakfast included. No singles are available in July or August. **Hotel Gabes** (tel. 226 977) on rue de Paris is a cheaper option. Facing the entrance to the Hotel Medina, walk 10m up the street to its right. Rooms have only beds and desks, and the shower down the corridor precludes privacy, but the price is right. Singles 6D. Doubles 10D. Cold, voyeurism-inducing shower 500ml. Eating out in Sousse is generally expensive. As a rule, avoid any place on av. Bourguiba or pl. Farhat Hached. An exception to this rule is the **Restaurant Sidi-Yahia,** on the right by the medina's entrance from the square with Farhat Hached's bust. Look for the beige and black awning with Arabic writing. It may seem touristy, but the clientele is strictly Tunisian. (Others are perhaps scared away by the none-too-clean floor.) Most entrees here are *spicy* and under 2D. A decent snack option is the random **juice stand,** just off av. Bourguiba, the second right from the pl. Farhat Hached. The stand sells fresh fruit juice, which is essentially whole strawberries and melons puréed in an industrial blender (600ml), and Middle Eastern pastries (400ml). Buy groceries at the **Monoprix** supermarket on av. Bourguiba. Open daily 8:30am-12:30pm and 3:30-7:30pm.

SIGHTS

The Aghlabids were a possessive bunch, and they built a citadel that has withstood time, European armies, and the rural Berber population. Access to the medina was made easier in 1943, when the Allies bombed a big hole in the walls near the place des Martyrs. Note the remarkably preserved outer walls, which protected a social and commercial system designed to be self-sufficient in times of siege. The medina's **Ribat,** an 8th-century fortress-within-a-fortress, commemorates war as an act of piety as much as a political tool. Like the other coastal *ribats,* it served as a "fighting sanctuary," where a special class of warrior-priests called *murabatin* divided their time between praying and smiting Christians. You can climb the **Khalaf Al Fata signal tower** for a good view of the area. The tower served as a link in the chain of beacons (*manar*) that could send messages from Egypt to Morocco overnight. (Open Tues.-Sun. 8am-7pm. Admission 2D.) Even the **Grand Mosque,** which is from the same era, has a military feel to it. The absence of minarets further emphasizes the building's low lines. As always, the prayer hall is closed to non-Muslims, but the simple, elegant courtyard is open to all visitors. (Open daily 9am-1pm. Admission 1.100D.) Outside the medina walls is a small but worthwhile **Museum of Antiquities,** with one of the best collections of mosaics outside of the Bardo Museum in Tunis. To get there, head uphill from the main entrance to the medina and walk about a kilometer along blvd. Maréchal Tito. The museum is just beyond the point where the army and police barracks confront each other from opposite sides of the street. (Open Tues.-Sun. 8am-noon and 3-7pm. Admission 2D, photo permit 1D.) Visitors with plenty of time might consider visiting the distant Roman catacombs, with 240 funeral galleries extending over 5km. Your best bet for transportation is to take a taxi (2D) to the main entrance, "Bon Pasteur." (Open daily 8am-noon and 3-7pm. Admission 2D.)

■ Near Sousse

MAHDIA

Mahdia's peninsula attracted little attention until the 10th century, when Obeidallah Said, claiming descent from Mohammed through Fatima, made it his capital and led a Shi'ite faction here in order to establish a new stronghold. Though he called himself "the Mahdi" (the final prophet of Islam), Obeidallah failed to conquer the Arab world as planned, and Mahdia declined in importance until Spain took over in 1550. When they abandoned the city, the Spanish destroyed the city's fortifications. The **Skifa Bab Zouila** ("Dark Entrance"), the only gateway to the medina, is a replica of the sole opening in a wall which sealed the peninsula off from the rest of the country. The 44m passageway was once protected by a complex series of gates designed to pen attackers into easily dispatched groups. The **Obeidite Mosque,** toward the port from pl. du Caire, is the world's oldest Fatimid mosque. Obeidallah erected the structure in 921, but cyclic deterioration and restoration have altered it—luckily without destroying the simple linearity of the original Fatimid design. Visitors are restricted to the main courtyard; extremely modest attire is required. (Inquire at the Syndicat for entrance hours, or try the mosque Sat.-Thurs. in late afternoon.)

Just inside the Skifa, the **Syndicat Tamarind** occupies the first building on the street (tel. 681 098). The English-speaking official will give you a brochure with a basic map of the peninsula. Open Mon.-Sat. 7:30am-1pm and 3-6pm. **Avenue Habib Bourguiba,** the new city's main artery, is home to a **police station** (at #71; tel. 681 099) and the **Magasin General** supermarket. Open Tues.-Sat. 8am-12:30pm and 2:45-7pm, Sun. 8am-12:30pm. Down the road there's a **post office** (tel. 681 714) on the left. Open Sept.-June Mon.-Sat. 8am-6pm, Sun. 9-11am; July-Aug. Mon.-Sat. 7:30am-2pm; Sun. 9-11am. **Buses** depart from the port area for: Monastir (10 per day, 1hr., 2.200D), Sousse (14 per day, 1¾hr., 2.300D), and El Jem (6 per day, 1hr., 1.700D). **Louages** are a more convenient option to and from Mahdia. Service is frequent and competitively priced to Sousse (2.250D) and El Jem (1.700D). *Louages* leave from the Esso station next to the port, two blocks from the Skifa and across from the **train station.** Eleven metro trains per day leave for Monastir (1hr., 1.470D), and continue to Sousse's Bab Jedid station (1½hr., 2D). **Telephones** are located at the train station. The **telephone code** is 03.

One of the best bargains in Tunisia is the cozy **Hotel Jazira,** 36, rue Ibn Fourat (tel. 681 629). To get there from rue el-Mahdi, turn left at pl. du Caire and follow the sign. This family-run establishment boasts new mattresses, crisp white linen, and a sublime ocean view. 7D per person. Hot showers included. Reserve in advance. If you have little money or the Jazira has no rooms, head for the **Maison des Jeunes** (tel. 681 559). With your back to the water, go up the street heading away from the Esso station next to the train station. It's clean, has warm showers, and the staff can probably provide you with your own room. 4D with HI card, 5D without. Mahdia's handful of restaurants is clustered in the port area. Evenings in the medina revolve around cozy **place du Caire,** where outdoor café tables brim with locals. The cheapest place to eat in Mahdia is **Restaurant El Moez.** Bear right on the street entering the medina to the Skifa's right, and bear right again when the road forks. The menu changes daily, but there's usually a filling dish of spicy macaroni (1.700ml) or a huge bowl of couscous and lamb (2D). The **market** near the bus stop and behind the Banque de Tunisie sells fresh produce and freshly killed chickens.

EL JEM

The tiny village of El Jem possesses one hotel, a handful of cafés, and a whole lotta **Roman amphitheater**—the sixth largest in the world. Thousands of tourists from Sousse and Manadir are bused in daily to see the coliseum, although none spend the night. As a result, this monument seems to be all that's saving modern-day El Jem from being swallowed up by the hot Tunisian sands. In its day the arena was not the source, but rather a result, of the region's prosperity. The original Roman city of Thydrus grew so rich on the olive oil trade that the residents rebelled against Roman taxes and crowned an old man named Gordian emperor in 238. In true imperial fashion, Gordian commissioned the amphitheater to keep his subjects docile. At its prime, the structure held 30,000 spectators and hosted games of all sorts—you can still see the pits in its sandy floor where beasts and gladiators prepared for competition. The rebellion soon petered out and, consequently, so did the construction. The damage you see today has little to do with time, however. In 1695, an overzealous government official ordered artillery to be fired at the amphitheater in an attempt to flush out a band of tax evaders. The coliseum is now packed with tourists during the day and hosts a series of mediocre Western art and music performances called the **Festival International de Musique Symphonique.** If anything, go just to see the amphitheater lit by hundreds of braziers. (Tickets 10D, but students may be able to finagle a last-minute discount.)

As you exit the train station, the road to the left leads to Sfax, the **Archaeological Museum** (a 10-min. walk from the coliseum) and another, smaller amphitheater. The mosaics found here provide evidence that the olive oil trade was lucrative. (All sights open daily 7am-7pm. Combined admission 4.200D, photo permit 1D.)

The drab main avenue of El Jem bears the predictable name of Bourguiba and runs from the arena to the **train station.** Next to the station you will find El Jem's best (and only) hotel. **Hotel Julius** (tel. 690 044) is actually a plush bargain. Singles 8.500D. Doubles 15D. Breakfast, private toilets, and showers included. Fast food joints surround the amphitheater, but better food and better prices await at **Restaurant de Bonheur** (tel. 690 421), one block from the hotel down the road to Sfax. In addition to the standard *poulet rôti* (3D), it also serves a delicious omelette with salad and fries (2D). Ask for it if it's not on the menu. Open daily 8am-10pm.

Facing the coliseum from the train station, you'll see a **police station** (tel. 690 700) and a **late-night pharmacy** up the road to the right. To the left, you'll find Restaurant de Bonheur, a **post office** (tel. 690 139; open Jul.-Aug. Mon.-Sat. 8am-1:30pm, Sept.-June 8am-noon and 3-6pm), **telephones** (open daily 8am-10pm), and **banks**. El Jem is served by seven trains a day to Sousse and Sfax (both

2.800D). **Bus service** is infrequent, but there are at least two each afternoon to Sousse and Sfax (2.800D), and to Mahdia (1.700D). **Louages** to Sousse, Sfax, and Mahdia are also available and are priced about the same as the buses. Both buses and *louages* depart from the square in front of the Hotel Julius, across from the train station. The **telephone code** is 03.

Kairouan

For centuries the faithful have made their way across the desert to the fourth-most-sacred mosque in the world—the **Mosque of Sidi Oqba** in Kairouan, dedicated to the saint who spread Islam across North Africa. The mosque was built soon after the town's founding in AD670, but Kairouan constructed most of its major buildings during the golden age of the Aghlabid dynasty (800-1057) and attained the religious and cultural preeminence that it retains today. In prestige, Kairouan ranks behind only the Islamic triad of Mecca, Medina, and Jerusalem; popular custom deems seven trips to Kairouan a fulfillment of the **Haj,** the pilgrimage to Mecca required of every Muslim. The city's devout nature has at times conflicted with the secularizing government. Citizens fiercely resisted both the outlawing of polygamy and Bourguiba's attempt to dispense with the Ramadan fast.

ORIENTATION AND PRACTICAL INFORMATION

Kairouan's organization is as legendary as the tale of its founding: historical sights are spread haphazardly around the large medina, and services remain scattered outside the walls of the old city. Street names are very rarely marked (even by Tunisian standards) and change often. Perhaps the spring led the planners to construct the bus and *louage* station 1½km away from the center of town.

Kairouan's transportation center is far away and difficult to reach from the heart of the city; it's advisable to grab a taxi instead—go anywhere in the city for under 1D. If you insist on walking from the **bus and louage stations** (next to each other), head left and follow the signs pointing toward "Sousse." Continue for about 15min. until you reach **rue de Gafsa,** turn left and walk along the medina walls until you hit the square in front of **Bab ech Chouhada,** the medina's principal south entrance. Av. 7 Novembre (formerly av. Bourguiba) starts at Bab ech Chouhuda, crosses the medina, and leads to **Bab Tounes,** the medina's principal northern gate. The city lies within **av. de la République,** which runs along Kairouan's north and east perimeter, and **rue Farhat Hached** in the south, which joins av. de la République at **pl. de la Victoire** (marked by a giant pedestal that once supported a statue of Habib Bourguiba and now supports a metal statue of a... what is it, anyway?).

Tourist Office: The **Syndicat** (tel. 220 452), **Tourist Information,** and a mysterious **Agence National de Patrimonie (ANP),** share the same building near the intersection of av. de la République and rue des Aghlabites. From Bab et Tounes, walk past the *louage* station and then down the wide rue des Aghlabites; the offices are 1km down at the end of the road to the right (across from the hospital). Better yet, pay 1D for a cab. You can buy the admission ticket to Kairouan's sites

Yes, But Are There RV Hookups?

Sidi Oqba Ibn Nafi, the warrior-saint who spread Islam across North Africa, established his capital here in AD670 when a precious gold chalice that had mysteriously disappeared from Mecca was discovered. A spring unexpectedly sprouted at the warrior's feet, and those in the know surmised that it connected to Mecca's well of Zem Zem. Evidently inspired by his miraculous discoveries, Oqba proceeded to banish all scorpions, snakes, and reptiles from the region. People soon acknowledged the sanctity of the spot, and the city founded by the saint acquired its present unassuming name—"camping place for camels."

from the Syndicat here (admission 4D, photo permit 1D) or at the sights themselves. Guides of Kairouan give a 1-1½-hr. tour starting at the Syndicat for 10D. Offices open Sat.-Thurs. 8am-6pm, Fri. 8am-1pm. You may have to sign a bureaucratic "Petition to the Mayor of Kairouan to see the sites of the city," more amusing than annoying.

Currency Exchange: Banks are spread throughout the city, particularly on the streets that lead from Bab ech Chouhada to av. de la République. **BNA,** across the street from the Bab ech Chouhada by Hotel Sabra, will cash traveler's checks or make Visa transactions. Open 7:30am-noon; Sept.-June 7:30am-noon and 2-5pm.

Telephones: Look for one of the omnipresent **Taxiphones** 2 blocks from the PTT on the road to Tunis, on the right, or at the booth at the bus station. Open daily 6:30am-1am.

Louages: With your back to Bab Tounes, turn left outside the medina and right onto av. de la République. Continue to the intersection with signs for various cities. Turn left and continue for about 5min. Continuous service to Sousse (3D), Tunis (7D), and smaller regional towns until about 8pm.

Buses: Gare Routière, a block past the *louages,* behind a small shopping complex with a large pharmacy. The **SNTRI** counter is inside and to the left; it serves Tunis (16 per day, 3hr., 7D), among other towns. The **regional** companies have schedules in Arabic and French and serve Sousse (10 per day, 1½hr., 2.390D); Sfax (3 per day, 2hr., 4.020D); Sbeïtla (4 per day, 2hr., 4.100D); and Le Kef via Makthar (4 per day at 5, 8am, 1, and 4pm, 2hr., 3.700D to Makthar; 2hr, 2.500D more to Le Kef).

Taxis: In front of the post office, at Bab ech Chouhada, and at Bab Tounes.

Late-Night Pharmacy: Pharmacie de Nuit, outside the medina walls. With Bab ech Chouhada behind you, take a right along the walls and then another right at the first 4-way intersection. Open daily 8pm-8am.

Hospital: (tel. 198 or 220 036), across from the tourist office.

Police: (tel. 197 or 220 452). Offices in the middle of the medina on av. 7 Novembre and off av. de la République near Hotel Splendid.

Post Office: (tel. 222 555) on pl. de la Victoire. From Bab ech Chouhada, head down av. 7 Novembre and turn right on av. Hached. Open in summer Mon.-Fri. 7:30am-1pm and 5-7pm, Sun. 9-11am; in winter Mon.-Sat. 8am-6pm, Sun. 9-11am. *Poste restante* is inconveniently located on the opposite side of town near the Grande Mosque (taxi 1D).

Telephone Code: 07.

ACCOMMODATIONS

Muslim pilgrims tend to stay in hostels attached to mosques, hence the dearth of budget hotels. Those that do exist are, like the sights, scattered throughout town.

Hotel Marhala (tel. 220 736), Souk el Bey. From Bab ech Chouhada, head onto av. 7 Novembre and turn right into the covered street with the multilingual "Old Market." A converted *medersa* (Koranic school) that approaches adorable. Animated rooms and a lovely, extended terrace. 5.500D per person. Showers included. Breakfast 1.500D. V, MC.

Hotel Sabra (tel. 220 260), just outside the medina at Bab ech Chouhada. Thirty rooms plus 2 lounges and a panoramic rooftop terrace (a good place to do laundry). Rooms are well lit, and the clean showers have *hot* water year-round. Very popular with independent travelers. Singles 8D. Doubles 14D. Breakfast included.

Hotel des Aglabides (tel. 220 880), pl. Port de Tunis. The best accommodation at this price. Built in a converted *fondouk,* the hotel has a pleasant courtyard and proper rooms. Mainly a locals-only affair, it is an inexpensive gem. 2.500D per person. Room with cold shower 5D per person. Free communal shower.

FOOD

Due to the intense heat and greedy vendors, beverages go for a whopping 600-900ml. (Café Sabra next to the tourist office sells soda for 300ml.) Always inquire about prices before ordering. Your cheapest options are the roast chicken dives along av. de la République. The **Magasin General** (1 block past the pedestrian mall opposite Bab ech Chouhada) is bigger than most Tunisian supermarkets and will fulfill your picnic needs. Open Tues.-Sat. 8am-12:30pm and 3:45-7:45pm, Sun. 8am-1pm. Do not fail to make a pilgrimage to Kairouan's sweet shops for the divine *makroudh* (Tunisian Fig Newtons), small biscuits stuffed with dates and smothered in honey (800ml per kilo).

Restaurant Barrouta, behind the Barrouta well in the medina. The best *menu* around, with salad, couscous, dessert, bottled water, and tea (4D). Walk through the kitchen to get to the tables, or eat outside. A wonderful, spicy sauce blankets omelettes (2D). Open daily noon-3pm and 6-9pm.

Restaurant des Arcades. Exit the medina and turn right at Bab Tounes, to the right of the large café with a balcony 20m away. Spicy *harissa* liberally coats all dishes. A locals-only affair, with the obligatory grimy floor and rough-and-tumble clientele. *Salade mechoui* and *haricots blanches à la viande* 2.500D.

Restaurant La Lanterne (tel. 224 886), on pl. de Tunis. Head straight out from Bab Tounes toward the arch, and look for the large "restaurant" sign on the left. A higher grade of greasy spoon than usual that caters to tourists. Couscous at tourist prices (4.500D), but safe for upset stomachs. Open daily 11am-3pm and 5-9pm.

Restaurant Sabra (tel. 225 095), next to Hotel Tunisia on rue Farhat Hached. Go right from av. 7 Novembre. Friendly, spotless, and refreshingly cool. Standard Tunisian couscous and *poulet roti* fare. *Menu* 4.500D. Open 10am-11pm.

SIGHTS

A **comprehensive ticket** for all the sights listed below is available at the tourist office or at the sights themselves. All sights are open daily from 8am to 6pm, except for the Grande Mosque, which closes at 1pm.

The **Aghlabite Pools,** just next door to the tourist office, once acted as cisterns for the city, a rather unpalatable thought given the shallow basins' rancid condition in the summer. At night the café by the pools is the principal hangout for local youths, and bumper cars light up for anyone over three years old. Head right along av. de la République to the **Zaouia de Sidi Sahab,** a venerable destination for pilgrims. The mosque houses the Mausoleum of Abou Zama, a companion of Mohammed who carried three hairs of the Prophet's beard with him (earning him the nickname "the Barber"). A green metal lattice protects his wooden tomb in the upstairs courtyard, to the left after entering. Flowery blue tiles cover the walls to eye level, and minutely filigreed gypsum takes it from there. Similar decoration lines a colonnaded corridor and a second, domed foyer. The ability to squeeze through the narrow gap between the corner columns in the final courtyard reputedly signifies *baruka,* good luck/saintly blessing.

From the *zaouia,* it's quite a hike to av. 7 Novembre. The curious and intrepid can work their way through the labyrinthine neighborhoods of the medina. To avoid getting lost, however, skirt around the old city by way of av. de la République. From Bab ech Chouhada, take the first right (by the taxiphones) to the **Zaouia of Sidi Abid el Ghariani,** where the 14th-century **marabout** (saint's tomb) rests serenely within another excellent example of the Andalusian decorative style that originated in Moorish Spain. A star attraction for pilgrims and tourists alike is **Bir Barrouta,** a holy well farther along av. 7 Novembre and slightly to the right. Within its narrow confines a blindfolded camel circles endlessly, delivering water from the mystical Meccan source. Legend says that a taste of this water will bring you back to Kairouan one day. Take a left onto a side street after exiting Bir Barrouta and walk 5min. to come to the **Mosque of Thletha Bibane** (The Three Doors), one of the oldest monuments in Kairouan. Though visitors cannot enter, the façade alone, with all its 9th-century calligraphy and floral relief, is worth the detour.

Despite its unusual peripheral location, the **Great Mosque** functions as the spiritual center of Kairouan and indeed of the entire Maghreb. The oldest Islamic monument in the Western world, the mosque was erected in 688 and rebuilt in 695. Most of what you see today is 9th-century Aghlabite work renovated and altered over the centuries. As the walls suggest, the mosque is a place of refuge; the call to prayer invites the faithful to "come to security" from the invading forces, a spirit kept alive today with the rather incongruous fans and water coolers in the prayer hall. As usual, non-Muslims can enter the courtyard but not the main prayer room. (Zebra-striped robes are provided for those not in proper attire, i.e. knees and shoulders covered.) The fortified walls and impressive gates warrant a tour themselves. Their defensive solidity contrasts starkly with the tranquil courtyard. Peer through the carved banana wood door on the right to catch a glimpse of the **mihrab** (prayer niche) and **minbar** (pulpit) brought from Baghdad in 862, two of the oldest examples of luster tile decoration in the world. Roman, Greek, and Punic capitals collected from all over Tunisia top the 296 columns throughout the prayer hall. The odd apparatus in the courtyard's center purifies trapped rainwater before sending it into a 12m-deep cistern below the mosque. Opposite the sanctuary stands **the oldest minaret in the world,** built in 836, 8½m wide and 38m high. Its ponderous appearance hints at a secondary, defensive purpose—note the decorative arrow-slits in the crenellations near the top.

Monuments aside, one of the most delightful aspects of visiting an Arab city as traditional as Kairouan is the potential for endless **wandering through the medina.** *Souks* line the alleys off av. 7 Novembre. On afternoons in the covered **Souk des Tapis,** past Bir Barrouta to the right of av. 7 Novembre, women auction their famous carpets to merchants from around the country eager to mark them up a few hundred percent. If you can't afford a Kairouan carpet (i.e. if your camel has not just laid a golden egg), you can purchase a *kessa* (a friction glove used in bathing), for which the city, for some reason, is also famous.

■ Near Kairouan: Archaeological Sights

SBEITLA

Sbeïtla's ruins, especially the Capitoline temple, are a mainstay of the tourist office's "Tunisie" posters. The origins of Sufetula remain uncertain, but the Romans appear to have built the town from scratch at the end of the first century AD. The place never attained real prominence, except possibly for a short time in the 7th century when the Patriarch Gregory elected to challenge the Byzantine authorities in Constantinople, proclaiming himself Emperor and making Sbeïtla his capital. He chose poorly—the following year 20,000 Arabs under Abdullah ibn Saad came by and beat the daylights out of Sbeïtla. The Arabs stayed for 14 months, pillaged the town, then retreated back to Egypt with Gregory's daughter. Sbeïtla never really recovered.

On arrival at the bus station, turn right with the train tracks behind you. Walk two blocks and turn left onto av. Belhaouane. Walk 1km until you come to the ruins, nicely heralded by the **Triumphal Arch** (AD195) that formerly marked the entrance to the city. Bear left 200m to find the small but well-kept **museum** on the left side of the street and the site entrance on the right. Ruins and museum open daily July-Aug. 6:30am-7:30pm; Sept.-June 8am-sunset. Museum closed Mon. Combined admission 3D, photo permit 1D. Enter opposite the museum and disregard anyone attempting to sell you "authentic" Roman coins and statues. A map with the major ruins and important sights labeled is to the left of the entrance, and farther down on the same path are the 7th-century **Byzantine Forts.** Enough walls and foundations survive to give an impression of an imperial town's grid-like structure. Climb inside and explore the **baths,** a staple of Roman colonial life, and stroll through the classical equivalent of a shopping mall. Sbeïtla's citizens could apparently buy all sorts of things; the stone with the **large carved phallus** near the forum was an unsubtle advertisement for a brothel. Step through the **Arch of Antoninus Pius** into the **Forum,** one of the best-preserved in the world. The enclosing walls and **Temples to the Capitoline Trinity** architecturally express both civic pride and imperial dominance. Though the three deities normally shared a temple, Jupiter, Juno, and Minerva each have separate, adjacent temples. Exit between the temples and head off for some early (3rd- to 7th-century) **Christian basilicas.** There is a miraculously preserved mosaic baptistery in the **Basilica of Vitalis.**

Three **buses** per day go from the Kairouan bus station to Sbeïtla (1:30-4:30pm, 2hr., 4.300D). Sbeïtla is also connected to the Roman ruins at Makthar (4 buses daily, 8am-2:30pm, 1½hr., 3.800D), where you can connect to Tunis and Le Kef. If you miss the last bus back to Kairouan at 2pm, take a **louage** for 4.800D. *Louages* also head to Kasserine (1.800D), with connections to Kairouan and the South.

MAKTHAR

Although one of the least-visited archaeological sites in the country, Makthar features a surprisingly extensive spread of ruins 110km west of Kairouan. Once the Carthaginian and (later) Roman city of **Mactaris,** it's not worth a special trip but makes an excellent stop if you're traveling between Le Kef and Kairouan. The Roman **Bab el Ain arch** divides modern Makthar, a small, unremarkable, impoverished town, from ancient Mactaris. Just beyond, a three-room **museum** serves as the entrance to the site; inside are a few well crafted funerary *stelae* and a rare example of **Latin carved in elegant cursive script.** Open April-Sept. daily 8am-6pm; Oct.-March 9am-noon and 2-5:30pm. Admission 3D, photo permit 1D. In the center, presiding over the site is the 2nd-century **Arch of Trajan.** From a distance the arch appears to stand alone, but as you approach you'll catch glimpses of the forum that lies behind it, strewn with fallen columns and broken rock. The **Roman baths,** 200m from the arch, are Makthar's largest ruins, and traces of mosaic remain upon the floor. Makthar possesses the identifiable remnants of another imperial cornerstone, the *schola,* Rome's version of a school for Hitler Youth (privileged young men who studied and socialized together and acted as an imperial paramilitary group). The *schola*'s basilica is along a path to the right of the Forum. The remnants of other buildings and temples lie scattered around the site, which you can inspect virtually undisturbed. Four **buses** leave daily from Kairouan to Makhtar (5, 8am, 1, and 4pm, 2hr., 3.700D) and continue to Le Kef (7, 10am, 3, and 6pm, 2hr., 2.500D). Buses depart opposite the Hotel Restaurant Mactaris. **Louages,** as always, are more flexible and more difficult to catch, but they exist to Kairouan or Le Kef. The station is on the road parallel to the street with Hotel Mactaris, one block up the hill.

Sfax

Although it is Tunisia's second-largest city, Sfax has little to offer as a cultural or tourist center. The reason, as any Tunisian will tell you, is that Sfaxians are too busy making money to be bothered with such things—even Sfax's tourist brochure acknowledges the city's reputation for commercial success. The massive wall surrounding the medina is the only reminder that Sfax is over 1000 years old, its history hidden under its bountiful banks, businesses, and buildings. Sfax's main street is (gasp!) **avenue Habib Bourguiba,** which leads straight from the exit of the train station. About 250m down av. Bourguiba is a large traffic circle, with **blvd. de la République** heading to the right. Following blvd. de la République, you will come to **Bab Diwan,** the medina's main entrance with four portals. The main street of the medina, **rue Mongi Slim,** starts just inside the right entrance of Bab Diwan and continues in the direction of blvd. de la République.

Seven **trains** run daily from Sfax to Tunis (4hr., 8.350D) via Sousse (2hr., 4.600D), and three run daily to Gabes (3hr., 5.100D). **Buses** leave much more frequently from the SNTRI depot just in front of the train station to Gabes (2½hr., 5.510D) and Jerba (3¼hr., 9.330D). The rival SORETRAS bus station is at the other end of av. Bourguiba (1km away) and offers service to local cities. **Louages** congregate outside Bab Diwan and have similar prices but later service as the buses.

The husk of a former Syndicat kiosk lies hidden on av. Bourguiba. The only currently functioning **tourist office** is in the Immeuble Carthago building on the third floor (tel. 211 040), two blocks behind Hotel Sfax Centre from av. Bourguiba. The office has the standard "touristic guide," with a decent map of both Sfax and Kerkannan and a list of local hotels. Open daily 8:30am-1:30pm. A **police station** (tel. 229 700) lies 100m back from the Hotel Sfax Centre toward the train station on av. Bourguiba. The **post office** (tel. 224 722) is across from the train station to the right. Open July-Aug. Mon.-Fri. 7:30am-1pm and 5-7pm, Sat. 7:30am-1pm, Sun. 9-11am; Sept.-June Mon.-Sat. 8am-6pm, Sun. 9-11am. There are **telephones** at the train station and at various central locations. Open daily 7am-11pm. **Telephone Code:** 04.

One of Sfax's virtues is its large number of cheap hotels, particularly in the medina. **Hotel de la Medina,** 53, rue Mongi Slim (tel. 220 354), about 100m along rue Mongi Slim on the left, offers clean rooms with sinks and towels for 4D per person. Hot showers 500ml. A number of options line rue Borj Ennar, just off to the right inside the far right entrance to Bab Diawan. If you are uncomfortable in the medina, try the generic **Hotel de la Paix,** 17, rue Alexandre Dumas (tel. 221 436). From the train station, head down av. Bourguiba and turn left just before the French Consulate. Unlike those at the medina hotels, these rooms have furniture and the bathrooms have toilet paper. Singles 7D, with shower 10D. Doubles 10D, with shower 15D. Lukewarm corridor showers 1D.

There are few budget restaurants aside from the fast food dives lining bd. de la République. A notable exception is the **Restaurant Tunisien,** just inside Bab Diwan at the far right portal, which serves a fine *couscous aux legumes* for 1.700D. (Look for the black and white Arabic sign.) The sandwich shop **Chez Sandra** (tel. 222 403), on av. Bourguiba one block past Hotel Sfax Centre from the train station, serves a delicious *sandwich au thon* for 800ml. Open 7am-midnight. Get fresh produce at the **market** on the opposite side of the medina from Bab Diwan, at the end of rue Mongi Slim. **Monoprix** sells the usual canned goods, pasta, and yogurt down the street to the left after Hotel Sfax Centre. Open daily 9am-1pm and 3:30-7:30pm.

Sfax is not a powerhouse of sights; even the **Great Mosque** on rue des Teinturiers, the road parallel and to the left of rue Mongi Slim from Bab Diwan, leaves something to be desired. The **gardens** to the left of the medina's entryway, shaded by the huge walls of the old city, are a pleasant place to pass time. Cap off the day with some Turkish coffee (with rosewater) at the cool **Café Diwan** (800ml). Head left after entering the medina and take the second left after 100m; the café stands within the medina walls. The **Archaeological Museum** (tel. 229 744), despite its small size, has a fine collection of everything from Caspian stone tools to Roman wall paintings, as well as mosaics for those who didn't overdose at the Bardo. The museum awaits in the domed building that also serves as the town hall on av. Bourguiba, 500m from the train station. Museum open Mon.-Sat. 8am-1pm and 3-6pm. Admission 1.100D, photo permit 1D.

■ Near Sfax: Kerkennah Islands

Though quite close (21km) to bustling Sfax, the Kerkennah Islands remain the city's antithesis. In mythology, the lovelorn nymph Circe imprisoned Odysseus here. Later, the Arabs disposed of adulterous women on the islands, and the French imprisoned Habib Bourguiba here until he escaped in 1945. These days, the islands' visitors are tourists who can't tolerate or afford the more developed island of Jerba. Voluntary exile here is so relaxing that it leaves you with nothing more pressing to do than daydream, but remember that the water is too shallow for a real beach vacation. If you have the right attitude, however, Kerkennah is an ideal location to watch the sunset and shun the rest of the world.

To get to the islands, catch a **ferry** from the terminal at Sfax at the stagnant body of water known as the "Corniche." Ferries (tel. 222 216) run five times per day in each direction from September through mid-June (1¼hr., 580ml; from Sfax at 4, 7:30, 11:30am, 3, and 6pm, from the islands at 5:30, 9am, 1, 4:30, and 8pm). From mid-June to the end of August, the number of ferries doubles. You will arrive at the westernmost point in the archipelago, **Gharbi,** connected to **Chergui** by the main road. On Chergui, four hotels cluster together in **Sidi Frej,** the *zone touristique* of Kerkennah. The islands' largest town is **Remla,** 7km away from the hotels. When you arrive at the ferry terminal at Kerkennah, you will find two types of **buses.** The mini-bus (tel. 281 234) goes directly to the hotels in **Sidi Frej** (1D). The larger buses stop near the hotels (780ml; ask for the *zone touristique*) and continue on to Remla (890ml from ferry, 350ml from Sid Frej). **Taxi** service is also available but costs around 4D from the ferry terminal to Remla.

The **Hotel Cercina** (tel. 281 228; fax 281 262) is the cheapest and most charming of the three beach hotels. The friendly, multilingual management will show you to a simple whitewashed room with shower. Singles 15D. Doubles 30D. Breakfast included. Prices dip to 10D and 20D respectively in winter. Bungalows, essentially huts with beds (singles 12D and doubles 24D, including breakfast and shower), and camping (3-4D per person) are also available. An extra 7D gets you full-pension (a tasty lunch and dinner) at the hotel's **restaurant.** Of the pricey two-star hotels down the beach, the Anglocentric **Grand Hotel** (tel. 281 265) is bloody good, beating the socks off of the other options and just a short walk down the beach from Hotel Cercina. Unfortunately, it doesn't fit the definition of "budget accommodation." Singles 30D. Doubles 60D. The best **restaurant** (and bar), particularly for seafood, is the **Cercina.** If it's available, sample the Kerkennah specialty of *tchich* (octopus soup, 2D). Dinner runs about 5D. Those on the cheap can head down Remla's main street and follow the signs on the right to reach its **Maison des Jeunes** (or "Centre de Stages et des Vacances"; tel. 281 148), which has spartan doubles and triples for 4D a head. Breakfast 1D. Hot shower 700ml, cold free. The hostel is near a pathetic rocky beach and rents windsurfing equipment (5D per hr.) and bicycles (1D per hr., 4D per day). The town has a rather meager **supermarket** (open daily 8am-1:30pm and 4-8pm), as well as the islands' **post office, pharmacy** (tel. 281 074), and **police station** (tel. 281 053). U.I.B. bank will **change money,** as will the hotels in Sidi Frej.

SOUTHERN TUNISIA

Berbers still dwell in caves, Bedouins still herd camels and harvest dates, and 20th-century civilization is still a mirage in the vast ocean of sand that is southern Tunisia. The great Saharan wasteland has only a few villages, all huddled close together. The diversity of the landscape is nevertheless surprising: sand dunes in the Great Eastern Erg, marshy salt flats at Chott el Jerid, green foliage of the oases, the jagged Ksour mountains, and the lunar landscape of Matmata. See **Desert Survival,** p. 580, for safety precautions to remember when traveling in this 45°C (113°F) region.

Gabes

Gabes's role as a transportation hub ensures that you will pass through it on the way to Jerba or the Sahara. Those who have a few hours to kill can explore the trails in the oasis of 300,000 palms behind the bus station. Otherwise, Gabes offers little—mediocre beaches, decent *souks,* and a few hotels. Pick up a straw hat (2.500-6D) in the *souk* at the end of av. Bourguiba before braving the desert. The **Foire de Gabes** in late July and early August showcases Arab music and local industrial products.

ORIENTATION AND PRACTICAL INFORMATION

The city's two major streets, **avenue Farhat Hached** and **avenue Habib Bourguiba,** intersect to become **avenue Habib Thameur,** which veers left to the beach. From the train station, walk two streets straight ahead to av. Farhat Hached, which leads left to the bus station and right to the intersection with Bourguiba. If you are coming from the *louage* and bus station, av. Farhat Hached is the street past the traffic circle, to the right at the fork in the road. **Rue Mongi Slim** runs from the train station to the bus station. The **tourist office** (tel. (05) 270 254) is on av. H. Thameur, 300m down from the intersection of avenues Bourguiba and Hached. Open Mon.-Sat. 8am-2pm.

Unless you're going to the beach anyway, it's not worth the walk, as the staffers are apt to close up shop and take off for a few days without any advance notice. You can view the available literature—a brochure with an extremely vague map and some info on Matmata—at the Hotel Néjib (the large hotel at the av. Bourguiba-Hached intersection). The **post office,** a 5-min. walk up av. Bourguiba from the intersection, doubles as a **currency exchange** but accepts only cash. Open July-Aug. Mon.-Fri. 7:30am-1pm and 5-7pm, Sat. 1:30-5:30pm, Sun. 9-11am; Sept.-June Mon.-Sat. 8am-1pm and 3-6pm. For traveler's check exchange, try one of the **banks** on av. Bourguiba. Gabes has **international taxiphones** on nearly every block of av. Bourguiba and av. Farhat Hached. Open daily 8am-9:30pm. Gabes is a good place to rent a car for the desert. **Hertz** (tel. 270 525) is located just up from the Bourguiba-Hached intersection, and **Avis** (tel. 270 210) is off av. Bourguiba, one block up from the post office on rue du 9 avril. Consult with the English-speaking staff about what sort of vehicle is appropriate for the destinations you wish to explore. A block and a half past the pharmacy, **Magasin General** sells all the pasta and canned goods you'll ever need. Open daily 8am-12:30pm and 3-7pm.

The **train station** is on av. Monji Slim, one block from av. Farhat Hached. Three air-conditioned trains per day (9am, 3:10, and 10:55pm) zoom to Tunis (6½hr., 11.550D), Sousse (4½hr., 7.950D), and Sfax (3hr., 4.850D). The **bus station** sits on the outskirts of town, where av. Hached merges with the road to Sfax, a 15-min. walk up av. Hached from the intersection. The destinations and schedules are in Arabic; you'll have to inquire at the counters of the three companies about the next bus to your destination. Buses run to Jerba (6 per day 7am-3pm, 4hr., 4.400D), Matmata (11 per day 5am-6:30pm, 1hr., 1.800D to *ancien Matmata*), Kebili (4 per day 9am-3:30pm, 2hr., 4.250D), Douz (1 per day at noon, 3hr., 5.300D), and Tatouine (2 per day, 2½hr., 5.420D). **Louages,** always more flexible and similarly priced, pitch up dust at the foot of the bus station. *Louages* go only to *Matmata nouvelle,* where you can take a bus to *Matmata ancien.*

ACCOMMODATIONS AND FOOD

The Gabes **youth hostel,** or **Centre de Stages et de Vacances (HI)** (tel. 270 271), is a bit hard to find, but it's a great deal. From av. Farhat Hached, to the left of the train station, turn onto rue Sadok Lassoued at Hotel Salama. Continue to the end of the street, turn right on av. Bourguiba, and take an immediate left, plunging straight through the *souk.* The hostel is 200m ahead on the left. Clean doubles and triples go for 4D per person. Curfew 10pm. Well shaded **camping** is available for 3D per person, 1D per tent. Egg included with the 1D breakfast. HI membership is required only if the hostel is nearly full. The hotels located between the bus and train stations are generally cheaper and nicer than those by the Hached-Bourguiba intersection. The best deal is **Hotel Medina,** rue Jilani Lahbib (tel. 274 271). Leaving the bus station, take a right at the traffic circle, then a left on rue Jilani Lahbib, one block up. The rooms and toilets are clean, and the hotel provides towels for the free cold showers. 6D per person. The easiest lodging to reach from the train station is at **Hotel Ben Nejima,** 66, rue Ali Jemel (tel. 282 276). Take the first left on rue Mongi Slim from the train station and walk a few blocks. Ben Nejima puts on a more upscale veneer and charges accordingly. Berber-style blankets are a nice touch, but toilet paper is neglected. Singles 8.500D. Doubles 12D. Showers 1D. The hotel's **restaurant** is decent and convenient, with *couscous au viande* for 2D. Only Tunisian fare is available in Gabes, served at the numerous restaurants off av. Bourguiba. **Restaurant Baghdad,** 177, av. Bourguiba, three blocks up from the PTT, is as good as it gets. They serve *brochette* (3D) and couscous (1.700D) on clean tablecloths. Open daily 8am-3pm and 6-10:30pm. The **produce market** sits with the other *souks* at the end of av. Bourguiba.

Jerba

The island of Jerba (sometimes spelled "Djerba") claims to be the legendary Land of the Lotus Eaters described in Homer's Odyssey. Its friendly residents supposedly offered Odysseus's crew a taste of their addictive lotus fruit, causing the Greeks to completely forget about their journey home. Roughly three millennia later, the 20km-long island still bills itself as a traveler's haven, despite the fact that the rise of Islam has made the famous local product a lot harder to come by. Jerbans today retain a fiercely independent streak, despite their link to the mainland in the form of a 7km causeway built in the days of Carthaginian dominance. The island's history cycles between foreign invasions and subsequent rebellions against new overlords. More recently, Jerba has become increasingly accommodating to invaders; daily direct flights from most European capitals keep Jerba's 27 luxury hotels and beaches full. Though the island is no longer the mythical paradise it once was, you'd be missing out if you were in southern Tunisia and didn't stop off for a day or two in breezy, leafy Jerba. It's wisest to avoid the string of expensive coastal towns and instead stay in **Houmt Souk,** the island's largest city and transportation hub—explore the beaches and interior from there. All *louages* and national buses stop at Houmt Souk. **The following listings are for Houmt Souk unless otherwise indicated.**

ORIENTATION AND PRACTICAL INFORMATION

Buses run to Gabes (6 per day, 4hr., 4.100D) and depart via Gabes for Sfax (3 per day, 5hr., 8.150D), Tatouine (2 per day, 3hr., 5.800D), and Tunis (2 per day, 10hr., 17.750D). **Louages** run slightly more often, cost a few hundred millimes more, and gather in front of the bus station. **Tunis Air** also flies once daily to Jerba's city **Mellila** from Tunis (50.500D). Tunis Air tickets are available at the large Tunis Air office on av. Bourguiba, toward the PTT from the bus station.

Av. Bourguiba leads straight from the bus station, past the *louages*, into Houmt Souk's *centre ville.* The cafés are almost always full, and, if you speak French, you may find an audience thrilled to hear tales of adventure (or your views on Saddam Hussein). The **Syndicat** (200m down the avenue on your left) is in a nice pavilion; on your right will be the confusing tangle of streets and *souks* where most of the hotels stand. The Syndicat can give you a handout with a map and answer any questions in English. Open July-Aug. Mon.-Sat. 7:30am-1:30pm; Sept.-June Mon.-Thurs. 8:30am-1pm and 3-5:45pm, Fri.-Sat. 8:30am-1pm. **Banks** line the avenue, and the **American Express** representative awaits at **Carthage Tours** (tel. 650 308). Car rental agencies include **Budget,** av. Abdelamid el Kadhi (tel. 653 444), and **Avis,** av. Med. Badra (tel. 650 151). There is a **late-night pharmacy** (tel. 650 707) behind the bus station, 100m past the ESSO station. Open 8pm-8am. The **police** (tel. 650 528) are on call at the top of av. Bourguiba, 50m down from the bus station. The **post office** lies just past the Syndicat. Open in summer Mon.-Fri. 7:30am-1pm and 2-5pm, Sat. 7:30am-1pm; in winter Mon.-Thurs. 8am-noon and 3-6pm, Fri.-Sat. 8am-12:30pm. **Taxiphones** are across the street from the post office and at the bus station. Both open daily 8am-9pm. **Telephone Code:** 05.

ACCOMMODATIONS AND FOOD

The beautiful **Auberge de la Jeunesse (HI)** (tel. 650 697) on rue Moncef Bey is situated in a *fondouk,* a centuries-old inn for traveling merchants. To find this excellent deal, follow av. Bourguiba to the PTT from the bus station. Cross the street from the PTT and enter place Sidi Abdelkader. Walk to the far left corner, by Bijouterie Ben Said. You will see a street branching off with a concrete drainage ditch in the middle. Follow the drainage ditch the 200m to its end, and turn left. The hostel is ahead on the right. A bed in one of the old cubbyholes surrounding the courtyard costs 4.500D. Breakfast, cold showers, and kitchen use included. The hostel is ostensibly for members only. Next door, the **Hotel Marhala** (tel. 650 146) is also a converted *fondouk.* The tiled rooms (which can be locked from the outside with enormous antique keys) have low beds and straw matting. All rooms are the same price, although only a few possess a private toilet and shower. Singles 10.500D. Doubles 16D. Breakfast included. From the hostel, making a left and then another left after the Marhala brings you to the **Hotel Sables d'Or** (tel. 650 423). It's not a *fondouk,* but it does have old-fashioned charm with its white stucco, wood ceilings, and Moroccan knick-knacks. All the rooms have showers, and the toilets positively shine. Singles 11D. Doubles 20D.

While all the restaurants in Houmt Souk gear themselves to tourists, some are much cheaper than others. The cheapest is **Restaurant Rihane,** 8, pl. Denad Haffouz, a left from pl. Sidi Abdelkader (on the left off pl. Mongi Bali across from the PTT). Their tasty *kamounias* (1.700D) taste a bit like falafel in a cumin sauce. Open daily 7am-10pm. Other cheap yet decent places are **Restaurant du Palmiers,** 45, rue de Bizerte (open daily 11am-4pm and 6pm-midnight), down the street from Hotel Sables d'Or; and **Restaurant du Sportif** (tel. 651 852) on av. Bourguiba across from the Tunis Air office (open 11am-4:30pm and 6:30-10pm). A filling meal at either place costs about 4D. **Marché Central** contains many souvenir stalls and a tiny **produce market.** Head under the sign off av. Bourguiba and take the first left.

SIGHTS

Near town, the 13th-century **Borj Ghazi Mustapha** is worth the walk. Once used by the pirate Dragut, Houmt Souk's fortress sits on the coast, looking out to sea. Facing Restaurant du Palmiers, turn squarely to your left and walk straight down the road in front of you, through the large intersection, and on to the Borj. (Open daily July-Sept. 8am-7pm; Oct.-June 9:30am-4:30pm. Admission 1.100D, photo permit 1D. Often inexplicably closed, but a walk around the perimeter is still worth the trip.) A small **museum** displays local costumes (with diagrams detailing the complex process of putting them on) and a pottery factory. Walk to the end of av. Abdel Hamid el Kadhi, the main road on the other side of the *souks* from av. Bourguiba, after it lurches sharply to the right. (Open Sat.-Thurs. in summer 8am-noon and 3-6pm; in winter 9:30am-6:30pm. Admission 2D, photo permit 1D.)

The best way to see the island is by **bike** or **moped.** Those from hotels are not cheap, so try either of the two "Location de Vélos" shacks on av. Abdelamid el Kadhi or the stand at the first bus stop for the *zone touristique* beaches. (Bikes 8D for 6hr., mopeds 20D for 6hr.) Bargain hard, and be assertive about which vehicle you get; once you've paid, it's tough to get a refund even if the bike self-destructs.

The **beaches** of Jerba are easy to reach by bicycle or bus. The best beaches are along **Sidi Mahares,** the location of many resort hotels and the *zone touristique* (bus #11 from the station, 500-800ml, depending where you stop; taxi, 3-4D). **Flamingo Point (Ras el R'mel)** is a sandy peninsula 5km east of Houmt Souk. The birds that give the beach its name flock here during the winter. The least accessible and thus the most peaceful beaches lie on the **west coast.** The 11km stretch of road (head past Mellita and the airport) is easy enough by bike or moped, but remember that there are no taxis returning to Houmt Souk. On a bike ride into the **interior,** you will come across traditional *houch,* fortress-residences with a single window in the *ghorfa* (tower). The historic **El Ghriba Synagogue** lies in Erriadh, 6km south of Houmt Souk. Jerba's small but enduring Jewish community claims to be descended from a group that fled Jerusalem in 584BC, after the fall of Jerusalem to Nebuchadnezzar. The present **synagogue** dates from the 1920s, built on the spot where a stone supposedly fell from heaven in the early 6th century BC. The temple is open for viewing during the week and conducts services on the Sabbath.

Matmata

Berbers have developed a remarkable way to beat the heat, a mode of habitation in which they carve a large central pit in the ground (about 10m deep and 10m wide) with tunnels connecting a network of adjoining chambers. The earth naturally insulates these homes against the day's heat and the night's cold. No less impressive are the *jessours*, agricultural terraces that line the hillsides. Their construction requires an immense amount of labor and demonstrates the Berbers' willingness to brave an inhospitable environment in order to preserve their identity and autonomy. While several "homes" along the Gabes-Matmata road are open to visitors, most are private residences. Bear in mind that **peering uninvited into a central courtyard is tantamount to peeping through someone's living room window.** Children will inevitably approach you and offer to show you their homes for a few hundred *millemes*. Those uncomfortable with this admittedly exploitative form of tourism can check out the **underground hotels** or visit the small **museum** of local crafts behind the PTT. (Open daily 9am-noon and 1:30-5pm. Be sure to tip the caretaker.)

ORIENTATION AND PRACTICAL INFORMATION

You can easily see Matmata as a daytrip from Gabes, but consider an overnight stay: although daylight scorches an endless parade of tourists, sunset introduces a cool, quiet nightfall. And there is certainly novelty in Matmata's unique hotels (converted pit dwellings), one of which claims that "Luke Skywalker slept here."

From Gabes, be sure to take the bus to *Matmata ancien*. If you end up in the dull *Matmata nouvelle*, you'll have to find a *louage* to *Matmata ancien* (600ml). The open hours of Matmata's **Syndicat** (tel. 230 114), 100m up the hill from the main bus stop, are haphazard even for a Tunisian tourist office. The posted hours are daily 8am-1pm and 3-6pm. If no one's there, try the **Café Ouled** across the street. There are few brochures and no maps here, but Matmata, with one main road, is simple to navigate. Next door to the Syndicat, Matmata's **post office, telephone office,** and **currency exchange** are all in the same building. The telephones are direct-dial; pay after you talk. The currency exchange will only change cash but is uneasy about taking U.S. money because "the dollar is easy to counterfeit." Try anyway. All three are open July-Aug. Mon.-Fri. 7:30am-1:30pm; Sept.-June Mon.-Thurs. 8am-noon and 3-6pm, Fri. 8am-12:30pm. There are **no banks,** so change traveler's checks in Gabes. **Taxiphones** are across the street by the café. The Syndicat posts a **bus** schedule on its door after hours. Nine buses per day run between Matmata and Gabes (1.700D), leaving Matmata from the pl. 7 Novembre, about 50m farther downhill from the Syndicat. If you are catching a bus, show up at least 45min. before the scheduled time, as drivers tend to be casual about departures. You can **hire a camel** at the Syndicat for 6D for 30min. (bargain hard). **Telephone Code:** 05.

ACCOMMODATIONS AND FOOD

Three of Matmata's hotels are literally holes in the ground. Due to the natural insulation, they'd be excellent places to sleep through the midday if it weren't for the busloads of gawking tourists. The **Marhala: Touring Club de Tunisie** (tel. 230 015) is the most expensive, but it has hot showers and the cool rooms, literally and figuratively. Singles 7.300D, full-pension 15.600D. Doubles 14.600D, full-pension 31.200D. From

Tinseltown in Tunisia

When the makers of *Star Wars* were searching for a set for their desert planet, they chose the otherworldly scenery surrounding Matmata, where the scorched terrain of twisted mountains and sprawling craters stretches to the horizon. (George Lucas returned with Steven Spielberg to take advantage of this surreal expanse for *Raiders of the Lost Arc.*) Nature adds special effects at sunset, when the ominous landscape assumes an eerie red glow. At any given time during the day no fewer than a dozen tour buses occupy the small village, and the Hollywood-style, multi-lingual "Welcome to Matmata" sign on the side of a nearby mountain is an incredible eyesore. With the moonrise, however, all becomes peaceful. Walk just a kilometer or so along either the Tamezret or the Gabes road to savor some memorable views.

the bus station, head away from the Syndicat. When you get to the fork in the road with a sign pointing right to Hotel Matmata, take a left. The Marhala is off the road, up ahead on the right. **Hotel les Berberes** (tel. 230 024) is cheap and has the best food of the three. The rooms contain a couple of beds and a lightbulb. Singles 6.800D, full-pension 11.500D. Doubles 13.600D, full-pension 23D. From the Syndicat, walk down the street with the large clock (to the right of the Café Ouled) and bear left. The hotel **Sidi Driss** (tel. 230 005) was the set for the **Skywalker farm** and **cantina** in *Star Wars.* This one-time "wretched hive of scum and villainy" bears no traces of the film, but you can stay here overnight. Singles 6.200D, full-pension 12D. Doubles 12.400D, full-pension 24D. Hot showers included. Sit down for a beer, and later you can tell your friends that you had a drink in the same bar where Han Solo whacked Greedo. Sorry, no droids allowed.

Matmata has a handful of restaurant-cafés, but the hotel pension-plans are decent bargains as well. All of them serve a *menu* of *brik,* couscous, and dessert. Bring your own drink, since the hotels' prices are inflated (1.600D for a bottle of water). The downside to eating lunch at the hotels is that hordes of package tourists also dine there. For picnic fare, there are several small grocery shops that sell bread, yogurt, canned goods, and juice; the most central one is located beside the bus station.

■ Near Matmata

The sleepy subterranean village of **Haddej** remains untouched by mass tourism and George Lucas. Chances are your welcome will be a band of local children shouting whatever French they know: "Bonjour! Bonjour! Un stylo!" A few *millimes* or a Bic ballpoint will earn you tour guides for the day. Ask to see an **olive press** (*pressoir d'olive*); the children will explain the multi-stage process in broken French and may offer you a sample of the oil from a storage well. (Be advised that a Berber's idea of good olive oil tastes spoiled to Western palates.)

Your young guides will dutifully bring you to the **Marriage Cave,** formerly the underground venue for the ceremony. The many-chambered cave contains kitchens, a room for the bride's preparation, and one for signing the marriage contract. The poor couple would spend the first days of their conjugal bliss in a tiny, windowless chamber while the rest of the village partied outside. The primary reason to go to Haddej is the 3-km **mountain pass** that connects it to Matmata and meanders through the most magnificently desolate landscape you could ever hope to find. Head up the road from the bus stop toward Gabes until you find the lookout (near the café marked "40 Gabes"). The trail is wide and easy to follow; by the time it gets complicated you'll be able to see Haddej's white buildings. Alternatively, take one of the Gabes-Matmata buses and get off at Tijma, 5km outside of Matmata. From there, a sign points out the 3-km paved road leading east to Haddej. Getting back is a problem; you must either hitch or wait for another Gabes-Matmata bus.

Tamezret, 13km to the west of Matmata, is a well preserved Berber village carved into the cliffs along the side of a mountain. Its stone houses huddle tightly together in defensive Berber style best seen from above. At the top of the town by the steepled building, enjoy a cup of mint tea with almonds at Café Benjelnaa (400ml), or clamber onto the roof for a look at the village below. One bus per day runs at noon from Matmata to Tamezret (800ml), supplemented very sporadically by *louages* (1D). Even if you don't make it to the village, a hike on the bumpy road is worthwhile for the dramatic landscape. Twenty-three km farther **Toujane** perches on the edge of a cliff split in two by a deep gorge. There are no restaurants or cafés here, but children tote small buckets with bottles of lukewarm soft drinks for 400ml. No public transportation is available to Toujane. Arrange to hire a *camionette* and driver for the day (a fair price would be around 50-60D).

Tataouine and Chenini

Venturing south from Gabes, you'll find multiple **Berber towns** hovering on the fringes of inhabited Tunisia. These villages, or *ksour*, possess names and lifestyles noticeably different from those in the Arab cities to the north. As often as not, these settlements stand in astoundingly harsh settings, a function of the Berbers' desire to maintain a separate culture. The town defenses, which have fended off Romans, Arabs, and Turks, are now open wide for the latest invaders and the much-needed money they bring with them.

TATAOUINE

The most convenient base from which to explore these Berber homelands is **Tataouine,** sometimes called **Foum Tataouine.** Apart from the **movie theater** on av. Bourguiba, which shows such classics as last year's Jean-Claude Van Damme flick (500ml), Tataouine does not have much to see or do. Since most visitors consequently blow through town or stay in an air-conditioned resort hotel, foreigners are a welcome novelty in the cafés—a good reason to spend the night. Everything from Islam to Michael Jordan is fair game over *chicha* and tea (albeit mostly in French).

The 125-km journey from Gabes south to Tataouine proceeds by way of **Medenine,** which was itself a Berber city of some interest until the 1960s, when the government bulldozed the entire place. Don't stay in the new, improved Medenine longer than it takes to change **buses** (almost every hr. from Gabes starting at 7am, 1½hr., 2.800D) or **louages** (3D). From Medenine take a connecting bus or *louage* to Tataouine (1hr., 1.850D). Buses leaving Tataouine include five to Medenine, one direct to Gabes (5:30am, 2½hr., 4.500D), and two to Jerba (6:30 and 10am, 3½hr., 5.500D). From the Tataouine bus station, take a right onto rue 1 Juin. Two blocks down is a large **monument,** an enormous concrete block whitewashed on one side and covered with Berber graphics on the other. Beside this unmistakable landmark sit the *louages.* The first right from the monument is **av. Farhat Hached,** the second **av. Bourguiba.** Tataouine's **post office** sits under a mountain at the end of av. Bourguiba and will **exchange cash.** Open Mon.-Sat. July-Aug. 7am-1:30pm, Sept.-June 8am-6pm. One block back toward the center of town and to the right, the **police** are on call (tel. 197). The **Syndicat,** with friendly, English-speaking staff but no maps, is 300m in the opposite direction on av. Bourguiba, past numerous **banks.** Office open daily 8am-4pm. Near the Syndicat on av. Bourguiba is the **late-night pharmacy.** Open daily 8pm-8am. **Taxiphones** are located beside the PTT. **Telephone Code:** 05.

Accommodations and food in Tataouine are affordable at the inelegant and inexpensive **Hotel Ennour** (tel. 860 131), on av. Bourguiba, unmistakable as you enter town on the road from Medenine. Dusty rooms run 3D per person, with showers upon request. Meals in the restaurant downstairs cost 1.500-2.500D. The **Hotel Medina** (tel. 860 999) on rue Habib Mestaoui is considerably more pleasant and centrally located. Rooms go for 5D per person, showers included. Restaurant prices are the same as those at Ennor. To get there, head right on av. Bourguiba from the monument, make a quick left and then another left. *Rotisseries* and sandwich shops abound on the side streets off av. Bourguiba. A decent, welcoming *rotisserie* is **Restaurant El Kaïma,** which is one block before the post office.

CHENINI

The Berber village of **Chenini** is the most spectacular and accessible of the South's *chorfa* (fortified granary) villages. The town perches precariously on a mountain ridge, originally positioned for easy defense from Arab invaders. The *ghar* (residences) are carved out of the mountain's soft clay, and their steep progression up the mountainside is a formidable sight. Make your way carefully up the paths through the nearly deserted town. The doors to many of the abandoned homes are open; if you climb inside, you will find baskets and large vases for storing seminola grain, which the departing Berbers left behind decades ago. If you climb the narrow paths to the top of the hill, you may be able to find houses with intact terraces. In some cases, stairs lead to these terraces, which offer spectacular views of the town and its desolate surroundings. **Be careful—the ruins are crumbling and potentially dangerous.** Navigate the path from the white mosque down the other side of the peak and onward to the abandoned **Mosque of the Seven Sleepers** (about 1km). The mosque's informal name refers to seven Christians whom the Romans supposedly buried alive here. According to local legend, when Muslim settlers uncovered the site centuries later, the seven woke up as if from a deep sleep, with enormous bodies that had grown while they slept; they then died after converting to Islam. Their gigantic tombs, which number more than seven, remain by the mosque. Since it is no longer in use, even tourists can enter the rather spooky site.

The cheapest and easiest way to make the 8-km trip to Chenini is to grab a seat in one of the *camionettes* that leave from in front of the Café du Sud on rue 2 Mars in Tataouine, near the post office (800ml each way). *Camionettes* leave about every 30min. from 9am to 4pm. The only other alternative is to charter a *louage.* The driver may try to hit you up for 25D, but never pay anything more than 15D roundtrip. The ride out to Chenini features some spectacular desert landscape, and for once there's not a telephone wire, souvenir stand, or TV antenna to be seen. The driver will drop you off at the **Relais Chenini,** which serves a standard, fixed-price meal for 5D. Below are the **post office** and the town's lone **telephone. Telephone Code:** 05. Be prepared to wait a loooong time for a ride back. The workers at the Relais Chenini drive back to Tataouine around 7pm and have been known to offer rides.

Keep in mind that while Chenini is the most impressive of the Berber villages near Tataouine, it is also the most touristed. Groups usually schedule their visits for Mondays and Thursdays (market days), but don't let the crowds daunt you—the steep, rocky hills and the endless views make Chenini worth it. Less-frequented villages include **Guermessa, Ghomrassen,** and **Ksar Hadada.** Getting there (and more importantly, getting back) can be problematic. If you don't have your own wheels, see what you can arrange at the Tataouine *louage* station. Much farther south (78km) lies the town of **Remada.** Beyond Remada, you must have a military pass for trans-Saharan expeditions toward Libya or Algeria. **Be warned that Americans are not welcome in Libya or Algeria. Be extremely cautious near the borders, as there is a great deal of tension in these areas.**

Douz

Douz will probably fit your description of a desert oasis: a haven of lush, green palms surrounded by endless sand dunes. Yet Douz is far more than a piddly pond flanked by a few trees and guarded by Omar Sherif; it is an enormous oasis and the gateway to the Sahara, where the only things that grow are the wind-crafted dunes. To Douz's south is the lifeless Great Eastern Erf; to the northwest lies the Chott Jerid, a perfectly flat expanse marking the location of a once-enormous salt lake, now dry except after heavy rains. Legend has it that Douz got its name when the French army's 12th battalion set up camp here in the 19th century—*douze* means "twelve" in French. Modern Douz still has army barracks (don't try to take photos—it's *not* appreciated), but the tourists continue to encroach. Package travelers tend to remain in the luxury hotels of the oasis, however, so the town proper remains relaxed, friendly, and inexpensive. The sleepy environs wake up considerably in the late fall due to an influx of migrant laborers for the date harvest.

ORIENTATION AND PRACTICAL INFORMATION

Public transportation places Douz within easy reach. Direct **buses** to larger cities are infrequent—there's only one per day to Tozeur (8am, 4D) and Gabes (6:45am, 5.100D), but eight buses run daily to nearby Kebili (1.070D), where you can make the necessary connections. Buses depart from pl. 7 Novembre beside the large clock. **Louages** line up under a canopy 25m down the street and speed off frequently to

Kebili (1.350D). From there, Gabes is easily accessible by *louage* (5D), as is Tozeur (4D). **Camionettes** wait across the street from the *louage* station, beside the entrance to the cemetery.

The first thing you'll see in Douz is **place du 7 Novembre,** marked by a statue of a camel and its Bedouin rider. To the rider's left is av. du 7 Novembre, which runs along one side of Douz's **market square.** If the camel weren't metal, it would be trotting straight down **av. Taieb Mehiri,** which eventually merges with **av. des Martyrs** and doubles back to the market square in one direction while continuing to the desert in the other. A 10-min. walk down av. Taieb Mehiri in the direction of the camel's gait leads to Douz's **ONTT Tourist Office** (tel. 470 351) and the **Syndicat.** The ONTT is open daily 8:30am-1pm and 3-6pm, and the Syndicat is open whenever the manager is not off leading camel rides. The worker at the ONTT speaks good English, has the standard mapless "Southen Tunisia" brochure, and will insult the unclassified hotels for no good reason. Those with **traveler's checks** can choose between Banque du Sud, one block to the camel driver's right, and an STB bank across from the clock. The banks are closed on weekends, when you should try the large hotels 2km down av. des Martyrs in the *zone touristique.* **Taxiphones** are next to the clock beside pl. 7 Novembre. Open 8am-10pm. Two **pharmacies,** one near the post office and the other on av. du 7 Novembre, trade off late-night responsibilities. Open daily 8am-1pm and 4-8pm. The **police station** (tel. 495 333) is next to the bank. The **post office,** with cash-only **currency exchange,** is on av. Taieb Mehiri. Open July-Aug. Mon.-Thurs. 7:30am-1pm; Sept.-June Mon.-Thurs. 8am-noon and 3-6pm, Fri.-Sat. 8am-12:30pm. **Telephone Code:** 05.

ACCOMMODATIONS AND FOOD

Regardless of price or location, all the hotels in Douz lie under by a thin film of sand. The budget hotels serve as unofficial contact points to meet other travelers heading into the desert. The most popular with backpackers, and the hotel with the most pleasant ambiance, is **Hotel Essaada** (tel. 470 824) on rue 1er Juin, one block from the clock. Women, for once, will not be hit on here, and the rooms are tight and proper. Downstairs is a Bedouin tent to snooze under, and the terrace is a congenial place to chat into the wee hours. 5D per adult, 3D per student. Cold showers. Breakfast 1D. The **Hotel Bel Habib** (tel. 495 115) on av. 7 Novembre is also a safe bet. Some rooms have balconies overlooking the market square. Take your mattress out on the terrace to rest in the fresh air. Singles 6D. Doubles 10D. Cold showers in summer. Three accommodating and lovable brothers run the **Hotel 20 (Vingt) Mars** (tel. 470 269). Take a left from av. Taieb Mehiri after the bus station and follow the signs. 6D per person. Showers included. Breakfast 1.500D. The best deal in the *zone touristique* is the posh **Hotel Roses des Sables** (tel. 495 484; fax 470 290), which offers perks like A/C, rooms with bath, and a swimming pool—but it's not a true budget accommodation. Singles 15D. Doubles 22D. Breakfast included. Camping is an option in Douz only if you have your own tent and can find some trees for shade. **Desert Club Camping,** on rue des Affections off av. des Martyrs, isn't much more than an empty lot with an overpriced Italian restaurant attached. The 3D-per-person price (5D per person in a big tent) is as expensive as a hotel. Douz possesses a number of cheap restaurants geared toward tourists but frequented by locals. **Restaurant Ali Baba** (tel. 470 269), one block up the Kebili road to the camel's right, could never seat all forty thieves but serves couscous (2D), of which the owner is justifiably proud. Open daily 6am-11pm. **Restaurant Caravan** (tel. 470 415), to the right of the SNTRI office by the clock, is rather oddly decorated, but the owner is friendly and the *ojja merguez* (1.200D) is a reliable stomach-filler. Open daily 7am-10pm. One block to the camel's left if the popular **Restaurant La Rosa** (tel. 495 465) on rue 7 Novembre. Not especially good or cheap, it caters to tourists with 2.500D hamburgers or *couscous à l'agneau.* The restaurant, however, is a good venue to meet fellow travelers.

SIGHTS

Douz is generally the staging post for desert adventure, but it does offer a little to the daytripper not planning on heading further south. You can tread through the sands of the highly photogenic **Great Dune,** marred only by the presence of tacky five-star neo-kasbahs, 2km past the tourist office in the *zone touristique*. You don't need a camel to hike up the highest dune; continue just a kilometer or two farther to get away from the hordes of *bernous*-clad tourists. An excellent **oasis hike** begins near the entrance to the market on av. des Martyrs. Following the signs for "Desert Club Camping" will bring you to the edge of the oasis. Take a right down the sandy road and into the thick of the palms. This track continues (bear right at the fork) through 1km of green vegetation before intersecting with a small paved road. A left here will take you through more oasis, past the Hotel Saharien and the abandoned Hotel Marhala, through a small village, and finally out of the oasis. The hike is about 3km and ends with a fantastic desert view at the stadium in the Place du Festival. Vacant 51 weeks of the year, the stadium comes to life in late December for Douz's **Festival International du Sahara,** when you can watch Berber tribes play sand hockey with a bran-filled ball or cheer on fighting camels. Hundreds of tourists saturate the town during this week, and most hotels tack extra *dinars* onto their prices.

The least expensive way to venture into the desert is to make arrangements at Hotel Essaada, Hotel 20 Mars, or Hotel Bel Habib. The going rate is 30D per day, including meals and tents, for multi-day excursions on camels. Several agencies also compete to send you into the desert. **Douz Voyages** (tel. 652 738) organizes camel rides into the Grand Erg; you will cook bread and meat in the sand and sleep under the stars in a Bedouin-style tent. It's all pretty contrived, but the experience is unforgettable. Longer excursions (at least six days) actually follow the annual migratory route of specific tribes. **Abdelmouda Voyages** (tel. 470 282), next to the Hotel Roses des Sables, is flexible in arranging tours, with no minimum group size and trips ranging from one day to two weeks. At both agencies, camel excursions cost 40D per day, while 4x4 expeditions that penetrate much farther into the Sahara cost 50D per day. If you're broke and *really* want to ride a camel, go to the Great Dune and bargain with one of the locals (try for 5D for a 1-hr. ride).

■ Near Douz

The smaller oases to the west of Douz attract fewer tourists and offer better views of the Erg. Seven buses a day (6:45am-2:30pm, 500ml) run to **Zaafrane,** 12km away along a (somewhat) paved road. You can also hire one of the frequent *camionettes* to Zaafrane (500ml). Arrange **desert camel rides** (5D per hr.) with the **Syndicat** (which does little else) by the Douz road. The **Hotel Zaafrane** (tel. 491 720), farther down and across the road, has decent rooms with A/C, as well as a bar, pool, and communal cable TV, but it's none too cheap. Singles 14D. Doubles 28D. Breakfast included. The hotel arranges **desert excursions** for 30D a day. For the same price as a regular night at the hotel, the staff will also let you stay at their new campground, with furnished Bedouin tents and a swimming pool, 8km into the desert. Arrange a 4x4 ride at the hotel. Buses continue across the wasteland to **Es-Sabria** and finally **El-Faouar** (both 1.500D). *Camionette* service to these towns is much harder to come by than for Zaafrane, but it exists at the same price as the bus. Es-Sabria, a tiny village 3km off the main road, is particularly attractive; tourists remain a novelty there, and the huge dunes and fine views are ideal for playing Lawrence of Arabia. If there's no bus heading back, walk through the oasis to the main road to hitch a ride. El-Faouar itself has little to offer besides its location fairly deep in the desert, making for a fabulous bus ride. Four **buses** per day (6:30am-3:30pm) return from El-Faouar and Es-Sabria via Zaafrane. **Hitchhiking** from the main road is also a fairly easy option, though *Let's Go* does not recommend it. *Camionettes* are the only way to get to **Nouil** (700ml), a nearby desert village with a small oasis. **Nouil Campement** (tel. 470 584) has an office on av. Taieb Mehri in Douz and offers "hotel-style" accommodations in large Bedouin tents. 8D per person. Half-pension 2.500D extra.

Tozeur

Despite its precarious location on the southwest edge of inhabited Tunisia between Chott Jerid and Chott Charsa near the Algerian border, Tozeur has done its best to stay in the middle of things. The ascetic Abu Himara ("the man on the donkey") led the forces of the Kharjite sect across the country from Tozeur to lay an unsuccessful siege on Mahdia, then Tunisia's capital. Later Tozeur switched gears and became a terminus for the trans-Saharan caravans dealing in wool, dates, and slaves. What with the slave market dwindling and all, Tozeur is now making a play to become the Hammamet tourist trap of the South. The oasis features a dozen resort hotels lining a *route touristique* and fleets of 4x4s and carpet merchants hungrily awaiting tourists. Don't write off Tozeur, however; the brickwork in the medina is unique and interesting, excursions to nearby Mides, Chebika, Tamerza, and Nefta reward travelers with some of Tunisia's most spectacular scenery, and the ride to Tozeur from Douz, through miles of barren *chott,* is a sight in itself.

ORIENTATION AND PRACTICAL INFORMATION

Tozeur's main street is the imaginatively named **avenue Farhat Hached,** heading west to Nefta and east to Kebili. **Avenue Habib Bourguiba,** the main north-south drag, connects with av. Hached at a square featuring a Tunisian independence monument that resembles a double-helical hunk of DNA. Heading 300m away from av. Hached on av. Bourguiba, past the plethora of souvenir shops, you will come to a large road heading to your right. This street is **avenue Abou El Kacem Ech Chabbi,** a.k.a. the *route touristique.*

National buses stop in front of the **SNTRI** office (tel. 451 557), on av. Farhat Hached near the double-helix statue, and serve Douz via Kebili (1 per day, 2½hr., 5D) and Tunis via Kairouan (5 per day, 4hr., 10.500D to Kairouan). **Louages** for the same price give or take a few hundred millimes are more convenient and frequent. To reach the station, located off av. de la Liberté, take a left onto Farhat Hached from av. Bourguiba. After passing a Mobil station, take a right onto the road with large walls on both sides, just past the Chiraz Restaurant and Bar on your left. The *louage* parking lot is ahead on the left. The **regional bus company** is across from the *louages* and runs six buses daily to Nefta (30min., 900ml). The **Syndicat** (tel. 450 034) resides in a brick-decorated building at the Bourguiba-Hached intersection. The helpful staff speaks English and distributes a very basic Tozeur map. Open Mon.-Sat. 8am-1pm and 3-6pm. The **ONTT tourist office** (tel. 454 503) is a hike down the *route touristique* but provides encyclopedic info on the entire region. Open July-Aug. Mon.-Sat. 8:30am-1:30pm; Sept.-June Mon.-Thurs. and Sat. 8:30am-1pm and 3-5:45pm, Fri. and Sun. 8:30am-1pm. **Currency exchanges** line both av. Hached and av. Bourguiba. Exchange traveler's checks at the **STB** at the end of av. Habib Bourguiba. After banking hours try the hotels on the *route touristique,* including the Warda (open 8pm-8am). A **taxiphone** station is next to the Syndicat on the *route touristique* two blocks toward Bourguiba from the Pension Warda. Both open daily 8am-10pm. From the Syndicat head left on av. Hached for 200m to find the **night pharmacy** (tel. 454 400), open daily 8pm-8am. In **medical emergencies,** call 198 for help. The **hospital** (tel. 450 400) is in town. **Police** (tel. 452 343) are 1km away in the opposite direction from the *louages* on Farhat Ached, by the entrance to the Gafsa road. The **post office** (tel. 450 130) is just off av. Bourguiba at pl. du Marché. Open July-Aug. Mon.-Sat. 7:30am-1pm; Sept.-June Mon.-Fri. 8am-noon and 3-6pm, Sat. 8am-12:30pm. **Telephone code:** 06.

ACCOMMODATIONS AND FOOD

Hotels in Tozeur are slightly pricier than their counterparts in other Tunisian cities, but they're good places to meet other travelers looking for partners for 4x4 excursions. The laid-back, palm-shaded campground should be your first housing choice. **Campement Beaux Rêves,** on the *route touristique* (tel. 453 331; fax 454 208), 1km past the ONTT office, features a café with *chicha* and reggae music. You don't need a sleeping bag or camping gear to stay here—everything, including fresh sheets, is provided. 3.500D per person whether you sleep in the open, the palm frond huts, the "Bedouin tent," or your own tent; cold showers included. To get to Tozeur's hostel, **Maison de Jeunes,** G.P. no. 3 (tel. 450 235), turn right onto av. Hached from av. Bourguiba and bear left (toward Gafsa) at the roundabout. Expect large, loud groups of Tunisians. One of the more decrepit of the country's hostels, with an unpleasant toilet/shower room, but the price is a low 3D per person. Right on the *route touristique* lies **Résidence Warda,** av. Abou El Kacem Ech Chabbi (tel. 452 547). A locus for independent travelers, Warda has clean, attractive rooms. The sinks even have plugs! Exchanges currency for 350ml per check. Singles 9.500D, with *en suite* shower 10.500D. Doubles 14D, with shower 16D. A/C 3D extra. Breakfast included. Try to get a room downstairs, since only the showers on the ground floor are warm.

On the right, as you head down av. Bourguiba past the statue that looks like an upside-down travel cup, waits the greasy, delicious food of the **Restaurant de la Medina,** higher in quality and lower in price than its neighbors. The *chorba* soup (500ml) is spicy and delicious (though not vegetarian-friendly), and they prepare their *ojja* (1.200D) with tuna instead of sausage. Open 10am-midnight. **Restaurant le Soleil,** av. Abou El Kacem Ach Chabbi (tel. 450 220), and **Restaurant Diamanta** (tel. 453 867), both across from the Warda, are so similar you'll forget which one you are in. Both are popular with tourists and offer outdoor dining and complimentary mint tea. Both serve *brochettes* (3D), *couscous à l'agneau* (2.500D), and *briks* (1D). Both are open noon-3pm and 6-11pm. The difference? Restaurant Diamanta is open daily, while Restaurant le Soleil is closed Sunday.

SIGHTS

Tozeur's medina, the **Ouled el-Hadef,** extends to the left as you walk down av. Bourguiba past the Syndicat. Lacking any major monuments, it is nonetheless a nice place to stroll. The patterns worked into the surrounding buildings' bricks derive from local Berber symbols; the building design originated in 8th-century Mesopotamia and cannot be found outside Iran except in Tozeur and nearby Nefta. This method of construction serves both a practical and ornamental purpose: the yellowish bricks, handmade from local clay and sand, insulate against the heat much better than other inexpensive building materials. The medina contains a **Museum of Archaeology and Traditional Arts** (tel. 450 034) that isn't worth the time; three small rooms present more dust than exhibits. (Open 8am-noon and 3:30-6:30pm; Sept.-June 8am-1pm and 3-5pm. Admission 1.100D.) Local flora and fauna fill the **Zoo Le Paradis,** the better of Tozeur's two zoos, located by the park of the same name. (Admission 1.100D.) Rent rickety **bikes** at a "Location de Vélo," on the same road as Le Paradis. (Bikes 1D per hr., 5D per day.)

Past the tourist office is the **Dar Cherait cultural center.** The pastel-colored pseudo-palace incorporates a tea salon, hotel, museum, and "mini-*souk*" into a hyperreal Tunisialand. The centerpiece of this fantasy, and the final insult to Tunisia's cultural identity, is the "1001 Medina Nights," a pre-fabricated, sized-down representation of an "oriental" city with costumed workers mugging for the cameras. In fairness, the museum, for all its sugar coating and bright colors, does give a sound introduction to Tunisian crafts and the life of the *pasha* (with predictable emphasis on the harem), and the explanations, unlike other Tunisian museums, are in English. (Open 8am-midnight. Admission 5D, photo permit 1D.)

A sandy path leads from the left of the cultural center, past a mosque and into the oasis. The track winds its way along a small stream for another kilometer before it finishes at the **Belvedere,** an impressive collection of rocks and gorges from which you can survey all 2500 acres of palm trees, plus part of the Chott. Men and boys come here to bathe; female loungers should expect unpleasant commentary.

■ West of Tozeur: Nefta and Vicinity

Nefta lies 23km west of Tozeur. A bastion for the charismatic Sufi brotherhoods since the 9th century, the town remains a place of pilgrimage. Nefta is noteworthy today for the **Corbeille de Nefta,** a natural bowl-shaped slope filled with palms. The site is eye-catching, but the Sahara Palace Hotel mars the view. More architecturally intriguing are the several mosques along the bowl's edge that comprise the **Ridge of Domes.** While the Corbeille is attractive, it's not quite as fabulous as the tourist offices might claim—especially if you've already seen the oases at Douz and Tozeur.

To get to Nefta and the Corbeille, take the bus or a *louage* from Tozeur (both 1D); you'll pass the **Syndicat** (tel. (06) 457 184) on your way in. The personable, English-speaking staff will answer questions. To reach the rim of the Corbeille, take av. Bourguiba until it splits just past the post office, then the unpaved right fork to the first street to the right, and keep heading in that direction for about 250m. To enter the Corbeille itself, take the dirt track down. The Corbeille features **open-air baths** with both hot and cold springs, which, unfortunately, are usually dry in summer. Women generally go in the morning, men in the afternoon. Intruding on the opposite sex is of course most impolite. It's important to remember that while this area is Nefta's big tourist attraction, it is (like most oases) just farmland, and as such, private property owned by locals. Don't be surprised by the scrappy guard-puppies that patrol the area—their bark is a lot worse than their bite.

The **Sahara** begins in earnest 10km down the road past Nefta. Except for a small shack or two, the scraggly bushes by the side of the road are the only signs of life. One shack, the **Marché des Roses des Sables,** an outdoor market for "sand roses," those gypsum rock formations found in *souks* all over Tunisia, serves as a convenient landmark. The desolate terrain abridges the "Tunisian Desert Experience," with the Chott salt flats on one side of the road and rolling dunes on the other. Moving past the market, you can walk out onto the Chott, a particularly good location for seeing mirages. Cross the road and walk 1km into the desert (make sure you can find your way back!), and you'll see the vegetation gradually decrease until there's nothing but fine sand and large dunes. (As always, **be sure to bring at least one liter of water per person per hour.**) The dunes are not as spectacular as those around Douz, but for first-time duners they are worth a look.

Buses, louages, and **camionettes** all pass the Marché on their way to the Algerian border and will be more than happy to leave you stranded for around 1.500D. Since traffic back to Nefta is extremely light, hitchhiking is very difficult. The few cars that do pass are either reluctant to stop or stuffed to the brim with immigrating Algerians. The safest way to see the Marché is to charter a roundtrip *louage* in Nefta (15-20D). Another 24km along the same road is the Algerian frontier; **Hazoua** provides one of the few points of entry. **Be warned that a great deal of tension exists between Tunisia and Algeria, and that Americans are not welcomed across the border; be extremely cautious in this area.**

■ Northwest of Tozeur

Perhaps the rawest, most gorgeous scenery in Tunisia awaits on the way to the oases **Chebika, Tamerza,** and **Mides.** Each of the small towns possesses spectacular scenery and photogenically ruined Berber villages to explore. Getting to these towns is difficult by public transportation and expensive by 4x4 or *louage,* but it's well worth the hassle. The circuitous routes themselves reward the intrepid (and patient) traveler with magnificent views.

Chebika is the least spectacular, least accessible by public transportation, and ironically the most touristed of the three oases. The old, abandoned village (there is a modern inhabited town nearby) sits on a rock platform beside two touristy cafés. Guides may offer to lead you to the small cascade, but they are unnecessary. From the cafés follow the new path, which leads directly to the falls. Feel free to take a shower with the locals under the cooling waters. If you continue up the path, you will come to the three sources of the stream. Climb the steep hill to the right, circle to the left, and continue up the mountain for 2km to reach another stream, littered with snail fossils and seashells from an era with a vastly different climate. To the left of the three sources is a path that leads to the top of the ruined village and offers an excellent view of Chebika's brilliant green swath slicing through a vast lifeless desert. Cut through the village back to the cafés to complete the loop.

Tamerza, connected by a rough, paved road to Chebika, reveals two waterfalls belonging to hot and cold springs, connected by a 1½km ravine. The pools below are popular swimming holes for (male) Tunisians but often dwindle in the heat of summer. The most spectacular fall is by **Hotel Cascades** (tel. 453 732), a good place to consider spending the night. The antiseptic rooms are pleasant, and there's even a pool in case you tire of the falls. Singles 9D. Doubles 18D. Breakfast included. The Berber village ruins are on the opposite side of town from the fall but are worth an exploration. Look for the white-domed *marabout* of a local Muslim saint.

In **Mides,** three lone palm trees cluster at the splendid gorge, which fills with up to 3m of water in winter. On the outcrop looking over the gorge is the deserted Berber village, and the hills 2km to the west mark Tunisia's border with Algeria. If you arrive here by 4x4 or *louage,* don't be content with peering into the canyon from the top. Double back about 25m and descend the easy slope to reach the canyon floor. The intrepid can walk the 6km through the canyon to Tamerza (some parts of the canyon are filled with water; you'll have to scale rocks to avoid these patches). Be sure to ask locals if the canyon is dry enough to reach Tamerza.

The best way to reach the towns is by *louage,* which must be rented for the day. Four people should be able to go to the three towns for 60D (15D per person) from Tozeur. A more expensive option, but one that will also let you drive on the salt flats themselves, is to hire a 4x4 vehicle and a guide for the day. Get a group together and pile as many people as you can into the 4x4s—they seat up to eight. **Hafsi Voyages,** av. Farhat Hached (tel. 452 611), offers the best deal, charging flat rates for a Land Rover and driver (80D per half-day, 120D per day). Other agencies charge 30D per person for a day-long excursion with a four-person minimum. **Mahari Voyages,** av. Farhat Hached (tel. 420 387), handles large tour groups, has a couple of English-speaking guides and the largest Land Rover fleet, and usually has extra spots to fill (11th-hour bargaining may pay off). Try to convince the driver to do the towns in the opposite order (Mides, Tamerza, then Chebika) to avoid the masses.

The stubbornly independent, the extremely cheap, and the slightly masochistic can get to Tamerza using **public transportation,** but it takes about 3hr. to get there and even more time (and luck) to return. Start with a *louage* from Tozeur to the mining center of **Metlaoui** (2.100D), and take another to nondescript **Redeyef** (2D). In Redeyef, ask to be let off near the *camionettes*. In front of the park, small pick-up trucks and the occasional bus make the trip to Tamerza and sometimes to Mides (1D; no buses to Mides). Even if you're lucky enough to get out there, finding a way back is hell. You might try to persuade a *camionette* driver to take you on a quick tour of both towns for around 10D. From Tamerza, you can hire a **donkey and guide** to negotiate a trail to Mides and walk back through the gorge, a 4-5-hr. excursion. The midday heat is brain-scrambling, and transport out of Tamerza dries up by 3:30pm, so you'll probably have to stay at Hotel Cascades (see above).

THE NORTHERN (CORAL) COAST

The north coast of Tunisia is the green part of the country. Thick fields and high forests run along the white beach that makes up the stunning coastline from Tunis to the Algerian border. The Coral Coast (named for the large reefs found offshore) has a lot more in common with neighboring Sicily (about 200 miles away) than it does with the rest of Tunisia: the climate is mild and breezy, people fill the streets until late at night, and the locals exude a *joie de vivre* uncommon in Tunisia. Come here to escape the hordes of Hammamet and Jerba, and as Tunisians say, "FEE-sah!"—"come quickly" before the *zone touristiques* of the north are firmly entrenched.

Bizerte

Jules Ferry, former prime minister of France and imperialist/colonist pioneer, said, "If I have taken Tunisia, it is to have Bizerte!" While M. Ferry may simply have been a fan of Bizerte's white beaches and pulchritudinous old quarters, more likely than not he was referring to its enormous natural harbor, strategically commanding the Mediterranean bottleneck between Africa and Sicily. People have exploited the site since the time of Carthage, when they dug the canal between the sea and the inland Lake Bizerte. Upon Tunisian independence in 1956, the French navy loved Bizerte so much that it decided to hold onto it. Bourguiba and company were peeved, and the situation came to a head in 1961 when Tunisian forces blockaded the base. Fighting ensued and resulted in 1000 Tunisian casualties and France's withdrawal. Bizerte's economy continues to revolve around the port, with its shipping and fishing activities; tourism plays second fiddle, despite the charm of the Old Port and the nearby beaches, including Raf Raf, one of the country's best.

ORIENTATION AND PRACTICAL INFORMATION

The town center can be perplexing because many roads run diagonally. **Av. Habib Bourguiba** runs the length of the city and separates the *nouvelle ville* from the medina. **Av. de l'Algérie,** which begins at the main **bus station,** cuts through the main square (**pl. 7 Novembre 1987,** with the fountain), crosses **av. Bourguiba,** and ends in **pl. Slah-Edine Bouchoucha,** beside the **Old Port,** the most beautiful and interesting part of town.

Blue-and-orange **buses** depart from the main station for nearby beach towns Ras Jebel (8 per day, 1.410D) and Ghar el-Melh (3 per day, 1.800D), both about an hour's ride. Buses run to Tunis's Bab Saadoun station (every hr., 1hr., last bus 6:30pm, 2.880D). One bus per day goes to Le Kef (7D) but leaves from in front of the **train station,** 500m further along the canal (away from the drawbridge; follow the signs for the "free zone"). *Louages* to Le Kef leave from the train station more frequently (8D). Four slow trains crawl daily to Tunis (5 on Sun., 1½hr., 2.650D). For the same price, *louages* make the same trip in two-thirds the time; *louages* to Tunis congregate in the shadow of the drawbridge just up from the bus station.

Tourist Office: ONTT, 1, rue de Istamboul (tel. 432 897). From the bus station, walk along the water past the bridge and the *louages* and make a left at the sign. Friendly, English-speaking staff distributes mediocre copies of a mediocre map. Open July-Aug. Mon.-Sat. 7:30am-1:30pm and 4-6pm, Sun. 10am-noon; Sept.-June Mon.-Thurs. 8:30am-1pm and 3-5:45pm, Fri.-Sat. 8:30am-1:30pm. A **Syndicat,** off av. Bourguiba (follow the signs near the Tunis Air office shaped like a paper airplane), is less helpful and has no map. Open daily 8:30am-1:30pm.

Currency Exchange: Cash only at the post office. If the **banks** on pl. 7 Novembre are closed, you'll have to trek to the **hotels on the Corniche.**

Telephones: Taxiphones litter av. de Bourguiba and the area around the Old Port. Try 2 blocks down av. de l'Algérie toward the Old Port from pl. 7 Novembre 1987. Open daily 8am-10pm.

Late-Night Pharmacy: rue Ali Belhaouane, off av. Bourguiba facing the Old Port. Open nightly 7:30pm-7:30am.

Hospital: (tel. 431 470) on rue Saussier.

Police: (tel. 197 or 431 500) on rue du 20 Mars 1956.

Post Office: (tel. 431 585). Half a block toward the Old Port from pl. 7 Novembre on av. de l'Algérie. Open Mon.-Sat. 8am-6pm, Sun. 9-11am; July-Aug. Mon.-Sat. 7:30am-1:30pm and 5-6pm, Sun. 9-11am.

Telephone Code: 02.

ACCOMMODATIONS

Tour groups pack the expensive resort hotels along the beach, and most cheap hotels in town fill in July and August, so arrive early. Though it's 4km south of town (on the road to Tunis) and usually packed in summer, the **Remel Youth Hostel (HI)** (tel. 440 804) is a great place if all you want to do is hit the beach. Take "Menzel Jemil" bus #8A or a "Ras Jebel" bus (both 250ml) and ask to get off at Remel Plage (taxi 1.5D). The hostel itself is nothing spectacular, but a fine stretch of beach is 100m away. HI members only. 4D per person. Shower and breakfast included. Cooking facilities available. A safe bet is the centrally located **Hotel Continental,** 9, rue du 2 Mars 1934 (tel. 431 436). Walk away from the main square on av. de l'Algérie and take the second right after the post office beside some taxiphones; the sign is broken, so keep your eyes peeled. Communal sinks are upstairs (a nuisance), and the rooms are bare but wholesome. Random tiles cover every inch for a colorful, if aesthetically appalling, effect. Singles 7.500D. Doubles 13D. Cold showers included. For peace and quiet head to the somewhat removed **Hotel Saadi** (tel. 437 528) on rue Salah Ben Ali. Walk away from the Old Port on av. Bourguiba and take the second right after the postmodern, airplane-shaped Tunis Air office. Saadi has large windows and is clean and cheap. Singles 6.500D. Doubles 10D. Cold showers in the corridor. Closer to the Old Port is **Hotel Africain,** 59, rue Sassi el Bahri (tel. 234 412), beside the Great Mosque. The hotel is conveniently located, with small, proper rooms for the price of a bowl of couscous (3D per person). Free cold showers.

FOOD

A lively covered **market** flourishes near the base of the Old Port. There's a **Monoprix Supermarket** on rue 2 mars 1934. From pl. 7 Novembre, walk diagonally on av. Taleb Mahri past the Office National des Pêches in the upper-left corner of the square. Open daily 8:30am-12:30pm and 3:30-7:30pm, Sun. 9am-12:30pm and 3:30-7:30pm. A number of touristy but reasonable restaurants cluster at the end of av. Bourguiba farthest from the port, including the popular **Restaurant du Bonheur,** 31, av. Thaâlbi (tel. 432 572). The 8.500D *menù* is good and the furniture is plush, but the price is high for this typical Tunisian fare. If you're broke, head next door to **Restaurant L'Aviation,** where you can savor the daily special (usually couscous or *spaghetti au poulet*) for 2.500D. Open daily 11am-10pm. More interesting is **Restaurant Edhalia** (tel. 436 490), one block farther up av. Bourguiba on the right, a pleasant Italian restaurant with ravioli or cannelloni for 2.500D. The large pizzas *au thon* (with tuna) are a bargain at 2.500D. Open daily noon-3pm and 6-10pm. On rue 2 Mars 1934, just past Hotel Continental, sits **Restaurant Cuisine Tunisienne,** a greasy spoon. Come for a quick *brik* (350ml) or spicy *ojjo merguez* (1.300D). If you're lucky, they'll have couscous (1.600D). Open daily noon-11pm.

SIGHTS

The collective aroma of coffee and rotten fish wafts through the air around the **Old Port.** By twilight, the normally quiet quay fills with tables of male café patrons sipping tea, admiring their surroundings and each other. Fruit and vegetable stalls ring the nearby **place Slah-Edine Bouchoucha,** above which rise the minarets of the Debaa Mosque and the 17th-century Grand Mosque. Two fortresses guard the port's entrance. The larger **kasbah** is a medina within a medina. Built in the 18th century, its crenellated battlements contain an entire residential quarter replete with its own mosque and shops. An extended café, lined with cannons, sits on the top level and offers a broad view of the port, the coast, and the medina. Enter at the end of the Old Port, 100m from the sea. (Open daily 9am-noon and 3-7pm. Admission to café 400ml. *Chicha* runs 2D.) The **Andalusian Quarter,** with its ancient archways, winding alleys, and nail-studded doors, lies just to the north, past the *kasbah* from the Old Port. The Old Town is most magical at dusk, when the half light gives its shabbiness a certain romantic aesthetic. Sheep wander the streets chewing hay, and caged parakeets twitter gaily from the shops. On the neighboring hilltop, the 16th-century **Spanish Fort** is now an open-air theater. The Turks actually built the fort, which received its name when the Arabs captured it from Don Juan (of Austria).

Cap Blanc, Africa's northernmost point, is perhaps the most spectacular sight near Bizerte. To get there, follow av. de la Corniche along the beach and up the coast to the *Radiophare du Cap Blanc* sign, then turn right. The rough road struggles to the top of **Jebel Nador** (288m), the perfect perch from which to view the glorious sunset. Below, chalky Cap Blanc protrudes into the sea. To reach its tip, descend the mountain and follow the trail leading off the road. The bike ride is scenic and challenging; count on 3hr. roundtrip. It's even longer to **Lake Ichkenl** but well worth the effort, especially if you like birds. The lake, one of only two Wetlands World Heritage sites (the other is the Everglades in Florida), is a rest stop for many rare birds migrating between Africa and Europe. Follow their lead and enjoy the beautiful surroundings.

Many bike- and moped-repair shops line av. Bourguiba near the Old Port. Although they're not technically rental shops, if you haggle a little they will rent you a mediocre bike (don't pay more than 10D per day). Two "luxury" beach hotels (4km out along the Corniche), the **Jalta** and the **Nadhour,** monopolize sports and entertainment. Both rent **horses** and **bikes.** The Nadhour also offers **windsurfing** and **tennis.** If you like **water-skiing,** ask at the Jalta's reception desk. Neither complex is within walking distance from the town. Bike out or take the "La Corniche" #1 bus (260ml), which departs regularly from av. Bourguiba near the Old Port.

■ Near Bizerte: Raf Raf

Along the coast of Bizerte, the mountains at **Raf Raf** plunge into the sea to form a crescent-shaped beach. The shore immediately in front of the cafés and vacation villas suffocates under a thick covering of Tunisian vacationers and their refuse, but a 1km walk along the shore (facing the sea, head right) brings you to relatively secluded, fantastic stretches of white sand. The rocky island of Pilar juts out of the crystal waters, and dark pine forests climb the mountains 50m away. Shallow water and strong surf make for good bodysurfing and boogieboarding.

In July and August, there are four **buses** each day direct from Bizerte to "Raf Raf Plage" (last one at 4:30pm, 1hr., 1.950D). During the rest of the year, you can take "Ras Jebel" buses to Ras Jebel (10 per day, 1hr., 1.400D) and hop in a *louage* (500ml) to Raf Raf town. The beach is a short walk downhill. You're unlikely to make it back to Bizerte or Tunis after 6:30pm, and staying overnight can be an expensive prospect, especially during the summer. The big towels that come with the **Hotel Dalia's** (tel. 441 630) rooms, however, serve admirably on the adjacent beach. Singles 22D. Doubles 32D. Breakfast included.

■ Tabarka

Ten km from the Algerian border, Tabarka teeters precariously on the fine line between mellow beach town and tourist-saturated resort. Although several luxury hotels and an international airport have recently appeared, the *zone touristique* keeps its distance from the town. A Genoese fortress perches dramatically over Tabarka, and the pleasant beaches beneath it lead to rocky cliffs. Mellower than the beach towns to the east, Tabarka offers an agreeable venue for sun and (a little) surf.

ORIENTATION AND PRACTICAL INFORMATION

Tabarka's main streets form a cross. A slender park runs from the mountains to the mini-amusement park and the beach along **rue de la Constitution.** 150m up from the amusement park stands a statue of Bourguiba and his pet dog, gazing serenely toward the beach (and the new condos that obscure it). At the statue, the main road, **av. Bourguiba,** intersects with **rue de la Constitution.** The helpful offices of the **ONTT** (tel. 444 491) are off av. 7 Novembre (parallel to av. Bourguiba) one block toward the beach. From rue de la Constitution, walk with the water to your left down rue 7 Novembre until you see the "Tourisme" sign a few blocks down. They'll give you a brochure-*cum*-map with the important points highlighted. Open July-Aug. Mon.-Sat. 7:30am-1:30pm; Sept.-June 8:30am-1pm and 3-5:45pm. **Taxiphones** and two **banks** are on av. Bourguiba, back toward the center of town. A small **change office** is also on av. Bourguiba, a block to the statue's left. Open Mon.-Fri. 5-7pm and Sat.-Sun. 9am-noon. The town has two main **bus** companies. The first, on av. Bourguiba 500m to the statue's right, is **regional** and runs one morning bus per day to Bizerte, Le Kef, and Jendouba; service is more frequent to nearby Aïn Draham. **SNTRI,** the **national** company, has seven buses per day to and from Tunis (last bus leaves Tabarka at 3:45pm; *confort* 7.140D, regular 6.150D). Tunis buses depart from rue du Peuple, parallel to av. Bourguiba and close to the Hotel Corail. A rather random bus to Bizerte leaves the empty lot beside the amusement park at 12:30pm (3hr., 6.100D). **Louages** (serving Tunis, Ain Draham, and Jendouba), originate near the regional bus station. The **late-night pharmacy** on rue Alzouaoui (off av. Bourguiba, one block to the statue's right and across from the Hotel Novelly), is on call 8pm-7:30am. **Police** (tel. 197) are at the end of the park closest to the mountains. There's a **post office** at the end of av. Bourguiba, away from *louages*. Open Mon.-Fri. 8am-noon and 3-6pm, Sat. 8am-12:30pm; July-Aug. Mon.-Sat. 7:30am-1:30pm. **Telephone code:** 08.

ACCOMMODATIONS AND FOOD

There are only a few hotels in Tabarka, and most of these are pricey and geared toward couples. If you arrive by yourself in high-season (July-Aug.), expect to pay the cost of a double room. Call in advance of your arrival, as the cheapest hotels are often booked solid. Only two hotels approach budget standards. The better, **Hotel de la Plage** (tel. 644 039) on av. 7 Novembre near the beach by the Port de Plaisance, has a terrace, wooden furniture, and gleaming showers and toilets. Singles 15D. Doubles 20D. The other option is the **Hotel Corail,** at 1, rue Tazerka (tel. 644 544), off av. Bourguiba, a few blocks to the Bourguiba statue's left. A fairly clean and spacious hotel, its rooftop terrace is one of the highest in the city. Singles with twin beds 12D. Cold showers included. The best part of town for low-priced, filling meals is rue Farhat Hached, off av. Bourguiba to the statue's left. **Restaurant El Hana** is a benign establishment on Hached that offers a savory, sizable bowl of couscous for 1.400D. Open daily 10am-10pm. For seafood, try the **Hotel de France** (tel. 644 577) on av. Bourguiba, which cooks up a *menu* for a fairly hefty 8D. Open noon-4pm and 6pm-midnight. **Restaurant La Sirène,** beside the park near the statue, has pleasurable outdoor dining and the standard Tunisian fare. *Poulet roti* 2D. Open 10am-10pm. You can get picnic supplies at the **supermarket** (Magasin General) across from the Bourguiba statue. Open Tues.-Sat. 8am-1pm and 4-8pm, Sun. 8am-12:30pm.

SIGHTS

The Lomellini family built Tabarka's most captivating sight, the **Genoese Fort,** an integral part of the city's history. The family received the Isle of Tabarka as ransom for the release of the Turkish pirate Dragut (who spent four years rowing a Genoese galley after being captured). Dragut proceeded to prove himself worthy of such a price: after his release, he captured Tripoli, destroyed a Spanish fleet, and conquered Jerba. Meanwhile, Tabarka remained in the hands of the Lomellinis for over 200 years. A road leads up to the fort, and although tourists cannot go inside the edifice, the view of the coastline from its base is sublime. Tabarka's other notable sight is the cluster of rocks at the end of town, **Les Aiguilles** (The Needles), a mainstay of Tabarka postcards. These huge (20m) natural spires shooting out of the water are striking, particularly at sunset. To get to Les Aiguilles, follow av. Bourguiba to its end (heading to the statue's left), and continue straight on the walkway with the sea to your right. Once there, pass through a natural arch in the rock to get to a charming, secluded rocky beach. If you somehow missed the plethora of mosaics in northern Tunisia, take a peek at the museum at **La Basilique,** the site of a French basilica (tel. 644 548). If you've been to the Bardo, don't bother. (Open Tues.-Sun. 9:30am-4:30pm. Admission 1.100D.)

TELL

"Tell" is an Arabic word for mountain, but don't expect the Alps. The mild climate and fertile fields of this northern interior region have made it a preferred spot throughout history for farming, not skiing. Passing through, you'll see sweeping countryside and a range of agriculture including wheat, olives, and hay. Bulla Regia and Dougga, the finest archaeological sites in Tunisia, testify to Tell's five centuries as Rome's primary granary, while the walled city of Le Kef has attracted worshipping Romans, Christians, Muslims, and legions of plundering mercenaries through the centuries.

Le Kef

Le Kef (also "El Kef") means "The Rock," an appropriate name for a fortress town built atop a craggy mountain strategically looking over the Tell. While the city considers itself the capital of the western region, it may be resting on its historical laurels; the large town is generally sleepy. The Carthaginians settled Le Kef in prehistoric times and dubbed it "Sicca." When the Romans took over they added the title "Veneria" to the name ("Sicca Veneria"), referring to the city's cult of the love goddess—not to the consequences of recklessly pursuing her impulses. The Romans perpetuated the belief that every year Venus flew between Rome and Le Kef accompanied by a flock of doves, and today's Islamic pilgrimages to Kairouan and to Mecca traditionally pass through Le Kef to solicit the doves' blessing.

Arab refugees from the Christian *Reconquista* of Spain later settled the town. Le Kef played an aggressive role in the history of Arab nationalism in the late 50s, when the FLN (a guerilla group fighting for Algerian independence) made the city their headquarters. Le Kef remains a fine place for launching campaigns—explore the Roman ruins of Dougga and Bulla Regia during the day, and return to wander the old town and admire its panoramas in the early evening.

ORIENTATION AND PRACTICAL INFORMATION

With hills reminiscent of San Francisco and views that stretch on forever, the medina, under the towering *kasbah,* feels like the *centro storico* of an Italian hill-town. The bus and *louage* station lies in the new city, 5min. downhill from the medina. Take a right out of the bus lot and up to the top of the steep hill, turn right again, then take the second left onto rue Ali Belhaouane. This street ends at **place de l'Indépendence;** the medina is up high. **Av. Habib Bourguiba** (the main road to Tunis) begins in pl. de l'Indépendence and heads uphill and to the right out of town.

Le Kef's **tourist office** (tel. 221 148) is located next to Café du Dinar in pl. de l'Indépendence. Comfortable couches and wooden tables make this unusual office a good place to unwind; friendly and knowledgeable volunteers run this establishment when it suits their whim. Opening times here are irrelevant; try your luck from 9am to 8pm. Also in pl. de l'Indépendence is a **bank** where you can exchange traveler's checks. You'll find telephones at **Taxiphones** on the way to the medina from pl. de l'Indépendence (open daily 7am-10pm) and if you bear right at the fork downhill from the tourist office (open daily 6am-midnight). Frequent **louages** supplement **bus** service to Jendouba (4 per day, 1hr., 2.200D), Tunis (16 per day, 4hr., 6D), Bizerte (1 per day at 7am, 4½hr., 6.650D), Kairouan (2 per day, 3½hr., 5.850D), Tabarka (6:15am, 3hr., 5.500D), and Gafsa (5:30am and 12:15pm, 4½hr., 8.900D). The **late-night pharmacy** (tel. 222 880) sits on the small street that winds upwards from pl. de l'Indépendence, 50m from the Café du Dinar (open daily 8pm-8am); the **police** (tel. 197) are in a large building up the hill from the bus station. For other **currency**

exchange and the **post office,** head to PTT, on the corner of rue Hedi Chaker and rue d'Algérie. Bear left at the fork downhill from the tourist office and walk 2 blocks. Open Mon.-Sat. 8am-6pm, Sun. 9-11am; July-Aug. Mon.-Sat. 7:30am-2pm. **Telephone code:** 08.

ACCOMMODATIONS AND FOOD

Finding a decent room in Le Kef is difficult. The **Hotel de la Source** (tel. 224 224), uphill from the tourist office and left on av. Bourguiba, has a magnificent exception: an elaborately tiled and stuccoed chamber fit for a *pasha* (20D, fits up to 4). The other rooms are anticlimactic, with ragged beds and cement-floored showers (5-10D for 1 or 2 people). Unfortunately, the hotel is not well marked—only a sign saying "Hotel" (that looks like "motel"), painted in black on the ochre exterior, distinguishes the building. The **Hotel El Medina,** 18, rue Farhat Hached (tel. 223 214), is as bare as any other hotel with this name, but the rooms are clean and painted in tasteful blue and gray. 6D per person. Frigid showers are free. Walk toward the medina from the tourist office and you'll see the signs pointing the way. If these choices aren't sufficiently posh (or expensive) for you, try the **Residence Venus** (tel. 224 695), on rue Mouldi Khamessi. The rooms are lovely and cool, some decorated with prayer rugs and Mickey Mouse lamps, some with a nice view of the *kasbah,* and each with a heated private bath. Singles 14-20D. Doubles 24-28D. Breakfast is included. From the tourist office, head right and follow the signs uphill.

In general, dining options in Le Kef are scarcer than Ben Ali's visible political opponents. **Restaurant les Ruines** (tel. 222 719) distinguishes itself with a large menu and cleanliness. Couscous 2D, *mechoui* 3D. Open daily 8am-10pm. An Arabic sign in red and blue marks **Restaurant de l'Afrique** (tel. 222 079), on rue Heidi Chaker just below pl. de l'Indépendance, across the street from the butcher. They serve tasty *mloukia* and *chakchouka* along with the main course, generally limited to *brochettes* or *poulet rôti* for 2D. Open daily noon-3pm and 6-10pm. Twice as expensive but three times as fancy, the **Restaurant Venus** (tel. 220 355) serves Tunisian cuisine and wine to a packed house. A/C. Entrees 4-5D. Confusingly far from its hotel namesake, the restaurant is up the hill from pl. de l'Indépendence on the way to Hotel Medina, and its hours are unpredictable.

SIGHTS

Sightseeing in Le Kef is an informal, slow-paced pleasure. With the exception of the regional museum, none of the sights charge admission, have a regular staff, or keep strict opening hours (although they try to stick to an 8am-noon and 3-7pm schedule). Most places of interest have an old guardian or caretaker; *inshah Allah* (Allah willing) he's around. Caretakers are invariably friendly and enthusiastic and will often give you a history lesson along with a tour.

Climb up through the medina from the steps starting to the right of the Hotel de la Source to reach the foot of the **kasbah** (1601), at the peak of Le Kef's massive rock, with a fine view of irrigated plains and the new town. The restored fortifications look like they could still put up a good fight, but the Turkish gateway generally stands open during the day. Beneath the *kasbah,* the well preserved 4th-century **Christian basilica** surrounds an open-air court with massive columns. The 8th century saw the basilica's conversion into a mosque, making it one of the oldest in the country. Restoration crews have recently removed the structure's minaret in an effort to re-Romanize the building. The basilica now houses an assortment of ancient artifacts, including *stelae* featuring the stylized, highly unclassical figures common to Neo-Punic art. The fluted domes and slender minaret of the **Mosque of Sidi Bov Makhlouf,** a treasure of Andalusian tiling, carving, and stained glass, clash with the rocky mass of its imposing neighbors, the *kasbah* and the basilica. Inside are the brightly ornamented coffins of several saints. If the caretaker is around, ask him to let you climb the minaret; the view is worth the uncomfortably compact stairway and the plethora of pigeons. (Don't forget to tip 500ml-1D.)

From the street running alongside the *kasbah*, take the second-to-last right to reach the **regional museum**, built inside an 18th-century mosque and primarily devoted to the customs of the nomads who migrate annually to the Tell. Many of the items displayed as artifacts are still in use today. For a dinar, the cordial caretaker will explain how the bike-lock for camels worked and point out where the *marabout* lies buried in the wall. (Open July-Aug. Tues.-Sun. 9am-1pm and 4-7pm, Sept.-June Tues.-Sun. 9:30am-4:30pm. Admission 1.100D, photo permit 1D). Turn right out of the museum and take the first left uphill to the **Bab Ghedive**, one of the few gateways in Le Kef's extensive set of walls and fortifications. Le Kefians call it **Bab-Ghdar**, or the Gate of Treachery, because of the popular belief that Governor Ghedive opened the gates for the French in 1881. The tourist office historians don't believe a word of it; they point out that the French attacked from Algeria, in the opposite direction. Beyond the *bab*, you abruptly step from the city out into a meadow where local herds graze. Children play soccer in the remains of the **Roman cisterns** straight ahead. The rectangular structures that look like wells are ventilation ducts for a complex sewage- and water-processing network that ran from the cisterns underground to the rest of the city. Later, in times of war, cowards used these tunnels to flee the enemy. This plateau may have supported the ancient **Temple of Venus**, although it has not yet been uncovered. If you explore the hills to the right, you'll find Christians, Arabs, and Jews together in harmony—three sets of graves and the remains of the **Basilica de Koor de Ghoula** have lain here for centuries. If you want to go inside the cisterns, ask at the tourist office; they'll take you down into another set of cisterns right next to the Hotel de la Source. Across from these lower cisterns, smack in the middle of the medina, are the ruins of some interesting fourth-century **Roman baths.**

On the street behind Hotel Medina, the **Eglise de Saint Pierre** (also known as Dar el-Kous) predates both the French and the Arabs. This 4th-century Roman basilica stands empty now, with few columns standing. Two blocks on the left past the Hotel Medina, an unmarked **synagogue** recalls the small Jewish community that the Turks quarantined to this street. Knock on the blue door on rue Markat Karama to see if the caretaker will let you peep inside. For an unusual outdoor excursion, hike up the **Jugurtha's Table,** a huge slab of stone that offers an orgasmic panorama. To get there, take a *louage* from Le Kef to the village of **Kalaat Senan** (2.300D). A 4km path leads to a 1500-year-old staircase cut into the mountain; from the top, you can look out over Algeria and the fields of the Tell.

■ Near Le Kef: Archaeological Sites

BULLA REGIA

While the extensive ruins at Dougga have gained more prestige, the site at Bulla Regia should be on even the most monument-weary tourist's itinerary. At first glance, the trip to remote Bulla Regia hardly seems worth the trouble. But look deeper (literally) and you'll see that Bulla Regia's treasures remain buried, in a series of **underground mansions** and sites. Bulla Regia was the capital of Numidia, a Punic kingdom that stretched throughout northern Tunisia and Algeria, until the Romans defeated Juba, the last of the Numidian heirs. Having achieved colony status during the reign of Hadrian (AD117-138), the town grew in prestige and wealth throughout the 2nd and 3rd centuries through the cultivation of olives. Like the Berbers in Matmata, the Romans of Bulla Regia decided that building underground villas would beat the heat. A 7th-century earthquake destroyed most of the above-ground sections of the city, but the underground chambers and museum-quality **mosaics** survive, recalling a way of life unique to the empire.

Orientation and Practical Information

To reach Bulla Regia, catch one of the four morning **buses** from Le Kef to **Jendouba** (1½hr., 2D); **louages** cost slightly more (2.500D). In Jendouba, all buses and *louages* stop in or near **place 7 Novembre 1987.** There are three bus companies in town, serving a variety of destinations, including Aïn Draham (1hr., 1.700D) and Tabarka (2hr., 2.500D). The last bus to Le Kef is at 3pm; *louages* (2.500D) make the run until mid-afternoon. **Buses** run every hr. or so to and from Tunis, stopping at the **SNTRI** office (3hr., 3D). Walk toward the center of the square and head left onto the Aïn Draham road, which heads in the right direction. If you're lucky, you may catch the blue-and-white **minibus** that runs to and from the site three times a day. It leaves from the Fina gas station in the morning (about 8-9am), midday, and evening (6-8pm). Yellow cabs are the only other option. Drivers will demand 2-3D to take you there. To get back, flag a cab on its way to Jendouba for only 500ml per place.

Sights

Purchase your entrance ticket at the **museum** across the road from the site. (Open Tues.-Sun. 8am-7pm; Sept.-March 8am-5:30pm. Admission 2D; photo permit 1D.) Here you can refresh your Bulla Regia history (assuming you read French or Arabic). Check out the statues of the somber-faced Bulla Regians, examine *stelae* with stick-figure representations of the Carthaginian goddess Tanit, and scope the map of the ruins. The main entrance to the site stands by the extensive 2nd-century **Baths of Julia Memma,** dominated by a massive arch. Head along the path to the right, which leads to the **theater.** The galleries off the theater remain intact, guarding the mosaic of a bear pawing the space in front of the stage. Toward the entrance of the site, beside the theater, is the large **Temple of Isis.** To the north of the theater (away from the road) are the ancient **market** and **forum,** containing a decimated capitol and temple of Apollo. Take the path leading away from the capitol until it passes a small pumping station, which continues to exploit the spring that supplied the Roman and Numidian settlements. On the left stands the cavernous **Maison de la Pêche** (Fishing Villa), whose subterranean chambers shelter a clam-shaped fountain and a mosaic of fishermen and assorted undersea life: squid, octopi, eels, and catfish. The house served as a tribunal and prison; the judge sat by the underground fountain and sent miscreants into cells behind him. The most elaborate underground construction lies farther along the path in the **Nouvelle Maison de la Chasse** (New Villa of the Hunt). Five entire rooms survive below, surrounding the most beautiful courtyard in Bulla Regia. Eight graceful Corinthian columns support the underground ceiling, while the blue sky looks down upon the central patio. In the adjacent above-ground rooms to the north, mosaics artfully depict gazelles, birds, and Romans coming back from the hunt. Continue down the path past the Maison de la Chasse to another yellow sign that points the way to the **Maison d'Amphitrite;** inside is an exquisite mosaic of Venus flanked by Poseidon and other mer-creatures—it's Botticelli's *Birth of Venus* minus the big clam. Heading back toward the baths, you'll run into the **Maison de Tresor** and its smaller subterranean dwellings. From here, walk away from the theater to reach the remains of a **Byzantine fort** and a **Christian basilica.** Peer down the wells you pass by—Bulla Regia may be deserted, but some of the wells harbor meter-long snakes.

DOUGGA

The Roman metropolis of Dougga, the largest and best-preserved ancient site in Tunisia, is everything you expected from Carthage but failed to find. From its temple to its toilets, the ancient city remains almost completely intact; it was inhabited up to a century ago, when locals were relocated down the hill to boost tourism. On a high bluff framed by pastures, olive trees, and grain fields, Dougga is the most scenic of Tunisia's ruined Roman cities. The site's extended area requires the better part of a day for a complete tour, although you can complete a cursory tour by surveying the small area around the ancient forum.

Orientation and Practical Information

You can get to Dougga on the Le Kef-Tunis **bus** line. Take any of the 16 daily buses from Le Kef to Tunis and ask to be let off at Dougga (1hr., 2.170D). There are nearly as many buses coming from Tunis (2hr., 4.100D). In Dougga town, the paved, steep road to the ruins begins at the Mobil station. It's a 3km walk to the site, although you might get lucky and hitch a ride. (250m before the ticket office, a track leads across the field into the ruins; the only thing stopping you from taking it is your conscience.) At the entrance to the ruins, a guide will tell you that your visit will be immeasurably poorer without his services. Unless you can agree in advance on a reasonable price (2-3D), shrug him off. To get home, flag down a bus on the main road headed for Tunis (every hr.) or Le Kef (every 1½-2hr.). The buses are green and white and run late into the evening. You can also reach the ruins at Dougga by way of **Teboursouk,** a neighboring village on the Le Kef-Tunis line. The roads are better on that side of the hill, but if you can't find a *camionette* (600ml to the turnoff to the sight, still 2km away), the walk is twice as long (6km). You'll have better luck getting to Le Kef or Tunis by *louage* from Teboursouk.

Sights

Dougga's main entrance (by the theater) opens onto the Teboursouk road. The Nouvelle Dougga road leads to the "back" of the site. (Open daily 8am-7pm; Sept. 16-March 3 daily 8:30am-5:30pm. Admission 2D, photo permit 1D). From here, a path leads to a ruined bath complex; take a left and walk up the hill to the romantically disheveled **Temple of Caelestis.** (Caelestis was the Latin version of the Carthaginian goddess Tanit.) An aqueduct stretches to the east and the **Arch of Alexander Severus** (the last of the "African" emperors). The path running from the arch to the right (west) leads to the ancient city center and the enormous **Capitol of Dougga.** This 2nd-century building deserves its reputation as one of the finest examples of Roman construction in Tunisia. Six slender, fluted columns crowned with a full triangular portico recall the grandeur of Rome. Inside there's half of a marble head of Jupiter, surrounded by a jumbled mass of fragmented Latin inscriptions (the cellar of this temple is a storehouse for the extra inscriptions found at the site). Adjacent to the capitol are the **Forum** and the **Plaza of the Twelve Winds,** where the careful eye will discern a circular compass rose carved into the marble pavement. Around the compass's border are the carved names of the winds. Two **temples,** one to Mercury and the other to "Augustan Piety," border the plaza, and the **market** extends to the south (downhill). With your back to the capitol, the path leading to the left ends at a set of stairs that descend into the large **Lycinian baths.** Many of the massive walls and interior colonnades of the baths still stand. Below, you can step down into the dark service tunnels. If you grope to the end of the tunnels you'll end up among the residences, more or less in front of the remarkably intact **House of Ulysses.** The place takes its name from a particularly well preserved mosaic, since moved to the Bardo Museum. Across the street, stairs lead down to the **House of Trifolium,** another relatively intact mansion. Dougga's largest building was not a temple or government structure, but a bordello. Archaeologists love to speculate about the function of the numerous small rooms that branch off the central courtyard. Next door are the **Cyclops Baths,** replete with ancient toilet seats—a useful place to wash up after a trip to the brothel.

One of the few major artifacts in the world still standing from the Punic Empire survives among the monuments of its conquerors. The pagoda-like tower visible down the hill is the **Lybico Mausoleum,** built in the 2nd century BC in honor of a Numidian prince. No one knows why the Romans left this monument standing once they had taken over Carthaginian territory. The tower displays a distinct artistic style yet does not vary greatly from the Roman structures. The mausoleum's columns, pediments, and charioteer miniatures show the cultural dominance wielded by Rome even before it gained political dominance over the Punic Empire.

APPENDIX

Language

Knowing a few basic words and phrases will make your trip much easier, and you'll find that even poor attempts at Italian will be appreciated. Take a phrase book (the *Barron's* book is fairly useful, and *Berlitz* has some handy phrases, though the vocabulary is geared toward business travelers) and practice before you leave. If you can learn only three complete sentences, learn *Parla inglese?* (PAHR-lah een-GLAY-zay: Do you speak English?), *Non parlo italiano* (nohn PAHR-loh ee-tal-YAHN-o: I don't speak Italian), and the always appropriate *Va bene* (vah BEH-neh: It's ok, it's cool).

In this section we include a rudimentary introduction to pronunciation, and some useful phrases and vocabulary. There are sections on general information and vocabulary, numbers, time, reservations by phone, transportation and directions, restaurant basics, and emergency and self-defense phrases. For more information on the Italian language, see page 78.

Pronunciation

VOWELS

There are seven vowel sounds in standard Italian. **A, I,** and **U** each have only one pronunciation. **E** and **O** each have two possible pronunciations, one tense and one lax, depending on where the vowel appears in the word, whether or not it's stressed, and regional accent (some accents don't even incorporate this distinction). It's difficult for non-native speakers to predict the quality of vowels, but you may be able to hear the difference, especially with **E.** We illustrate below the *approximate* pronunciation of the vowels, but don't worry too much about **E** and **O.**

a:	*a* as in f*a*ther *(casa)*
e: tense	*ay* as in b*ay* *(sete)*
e: lax	*eh* as in set *(bella)*
i:	*ee* as in cheese *(vino)*
o: tense	*o* as in bone *(sono)*
o: lax	between *o* of bone and *au* of c*au*ght *(zona)*
u:	*oo* as in droop (gusto)

CONSONANTS

Italian consonants won't give you many problems, except for the few quirks noted here. **H** is always silent and **R** is always rolled.

C and G: before **a, o,** or **u, c** and **g** are hard, as in *cat* and *goose* or as in the Italian word *colore* (koh-LOHR-eh), "color," or *gatto* (GAHT-toh), "cat." They soften into **ch** and **j** sounds, respectively, when followed by **i** or **e,** as in English *cheese* and *jeep* or Italian *ciao* (CHOW), "goodbye," and *gelato* (jeh-LAH-toh), "ice cream."

CH and GH: h returns **c** and **g** to their "hard" sounds in front of **i** or **e** (see above); making words like, *chianti* (kyahn-tee), the Tuscan wine, and *spaghetti* (spah-GEHT-tee), the pasta.

GN and GLI: pronounce **gn** like the **ni** in *onion*, thus *bagno* ("bath") is "BAHN-yoh." **Gli** is like the **lli** in *million*, so *sbagliato* ("wrong") is said "zbal-YAH-toh."

S and Z: An **s** found between two vowels or followed by the letters **b, d, g, l, m, n r,** and **v** is pronounced as the English **z**; thus *casa* ("house") sounds like "KAH-zah" and *smarrito* ("lost") like "zmahr-REE-toh." A double **s,** an initial **s,** or an **s** followed by any other consonant has the same sound as an English initial **s,** so *sacco* ("bag") is SAHK-koh. **Z** has a **ts** or **dz** sound; thus *stazione* ("station") is pronounced "staht-SYOH-nay," while *zoo* ("zoo") is pronounced "dzoh" and *mezzo* ("half") is "MEHD-zoh."

SC and SCH: when followed by **a, o,** or **u, sc** is pronounced as **sk,** so *scusi* ("excuse me") yields "SKOO-zee." When followed by an **e** or **i,** the combination is pronounced **sh** as in *sciopero* (SHOH-pair-oh), "strike." **H** returns **c** to its hard sound (**sk**) in front of **i** or **e,** as in *pesche* (PEHS-keh), "peaches," not to be confused with *pesce* (PEH-sheh), "fish."

Double consonants: The difference between double and single consonants in Italian is likely to cause problems for English speakers. When you see a double consonant, think about actually pronouncing it twice or holding it for a long time. English phrases like "dumb man" or "bad dog" approximate the sound of a double consonant. Failing to make the distinction can lead to some confusion; for example, *penne all'arrabbiata* is "short pasta in a spicy red sauce," whereas *pene all'arrabbiata* means "penis in a spicy red sauce."

APPENDIX

STRESS

In many Italian words, stress falls on the next-to-last syllable. When stress falls on the last syllable, an accent indicates where stress should fall: *città* (cheet-**TAH**) or *perché* (pair-**KAY**). Stress can fall on the third-to-last syllable as well. It's not easy to predict stress, so you'll have to pick this up by listening to Italian speech.

PLURALS

Italians words form their plurals by changing the last vowel. Words that end in an **a** in the singular (usually feminine), end with an **e** in the plural; thus *mela* (MAY-lah), "apple," becomes *mele* (MAY-lay). Words that end with **o** or **e** in the singular take an **i** in the plural: *conto* (KOHN-toh), "bill," is *conti* (KOHN-tee) and *cane* (KAH-neh), "dog," becomes *cani* (KAH-nee). There are several exceptions to these rules; for example, *braccio* becomes *braccia* in the plural. (But don't worry too much about irregular plurals.) Words with final accent, like *città* and *caffè,* and words that end in consonants like *bar* and *sport* do not change in the plural.

Useful Phrases and Vocabulary

GENERAL

Hi/So long (informal)	*Ciao*	chow
Good day/Hello	*Buongiorno*	bwohn JOHR-noh
Good evening	*Buona sera*	BWOH-nah SEH-rah
Good night	*Buona notte*	BWOH-nah NOHT-tay
Goodbye	*Arrivederci/arrivederLa*	ah-ree-veh-DAIR-chee/ ah-ree-veh-DAIR-lah
Please	*Per favore/per cortesia/ per piacere*	pair fah-VOH-ray/ pair kohr-teh-ZEE-ah/ pair pyah-CHEH-reh
Thank you	*Grazie*	GRAHT-see-yeh
You're welcome/May I help you/Go right ahead	*Prego*	PRAY-goh
Pardon me.	*Scusi*	SKOO-zee
May I get by?	*Permesso*	pair-MEHS-soh
I'm sorry.	*Mi dispiace.*	mee dees-PYAH-cheh
Yes/No/Maybe	*Sì/No/Forse*	see/no/FOHR-say

I don't know	*Non lo so*	nohn loh soh
I don't speak Italian.	*Non parlo italiano.*	nohn PAR-loh ee-tahl-YAH-noh
I don't understand	*Non capisco*	nohn kah-PEES-koh
What does this mean?	*Che vuol dire questo?*	kay vwohl DEE-reh KWEH-stoh
Is there someone who speaks English?	*C'è qualcuno che parla inglese?*	cheh kwahl-KOO-noh kay PAR-lah een-GLAY-zay
Could you help me?	*Potrebbe aiutarmi?*	poh-TREHB-beh ah-yoo-TAHR-mee
Could you repeat that?	*Può ripetere?*	pwo ri-PEH-teh-reh
Okay/I understand.	*Ho capito.*	oh kah-PEE-toh
What do I know?	*Che ne so io?*	keh neh soh EE-oh
I have *no* idea	*Boh.*	boh
this/that	*questo/quello*	KWEH-sto/KWEHL-loh
who	*chi*	kee
where	*dove*	DOH-vay
which	*quale*	KWAH-lay
when	*quando*	KWAN-doh
what	*che/cosa/che cosa*	kay/KOH-za/kay KOH-za
why/because	*perché*	pair-KEH
more/less	*più/meno*	pyoo/MEH-noh
How do you say...?	*Come si dice...?*	KOH-may see DEE-chay
What do you call this in Italian?	*Come si chiama questo in italiano?*	KOH-may see key-YAH-mah KWEH-stoh een ee-tahl-YAH-no
Wow! Holy Cow!	*Accidenti!*	ah-chee-DEHN-tee
I would like...	*Vorrei...*	vohr-RAY
Where is...?	*Dov'è...?*	doh-VAY
How much does it cost?	*Quanto costa?*	KWAN-toh CO-stah
reduced (price)	*ridotto*	ree-DOHT-toh
a student discount	*uno sconto studentesco*	OO-noh SKOHN-toh stoo-dehn-TEHS-koh
the consulate	*il consolato*	eel kohn-soh-LAH-toh
the station	*la stazione*	lah staht-see-YO-nay
the bank	*il banco* or *la banca*	eel BAHN-coh
the grocery store	*il negozio di alimentari*	eel neh-GOT-syoh di ah-lee-mehn-TAH-ree
the hostel	*l'ostello*	lo-STEHL-lo
the hotel	*l'albergo/la pensione*	lahl-BAIR-goh/ lah pehn-see-OH-neh
the street address	*l'indirizzo*	leen-dee-REET-soh
the building	*l'edificio/il palazzo*	leh-dee-FEE-choh/ eel pah-LAHT-soh
the church	*la chiesa*	lah kee-AY-zah
the synagogue	*la sinagoga*	lah see-nah-GOH-gah
the telephone	*il telefono*	eel teh-LAY-foh-noh
the sea	*il mare*	eel MAH-ray
the beach	*la spiaggia*	la spee-AHJ-jah
the hospital	*l'ospedale*	los-peh-DAH-leh
open/closed	*aperto/chiuso*	ah-PAIR-toh/KYOO-zoh
the post office	*l'ufficio postale*	loo-FEE-choh poh-STAH-lay

the entrance/the exit	*l'ingresso/l'uscita*	leen-GREHS-soh/ loo-SHEE-tah
the reservation	*la prenotazione*	lah pray-noh-taht-SYOH-neh
with bath/shower	*con bagno/doccia*	cohn BAHN-yo/DOHT-cha
bathroom	*il gabinetto/il bagno/ la toletta*	eel gah-bee-NEHT-toh/ eel BAHN-yo/ lah toh-LEHT-tah
the towel	*l'asciugamano*	lah-shoo-gah-MAH-noh
the sheets	*le lenzuola*	lay lehnt-SWOH-lah
the blanket	*la coperta*	lah koh-PAIR-tah
heating	*il riscaldamento*	eel ree-skahl-dah-MAIN-toh
How much does it cost?	*Quanto costa?*	KWAN-toh CO-stah
Where is...?	*Dov'è...?*	doh-VAY
May I buy you a drink?	*Posso offrirle qualcosa da bere?*	POHS-soh ohf-FREER-lay kwahl-COH-zah dah BAY-ray
Would you buy me a drink?	*Può offrirmi qualcosa da bere?*	pwoh ohf-FREER-mi kwahl-COH-zah dah BAY-ray
I'm drunk.	*Sono ubriaco.*	SOH-noh oo-BRYAH-coh
Are you drunk?	*È lei ubriaco?*	ay LAY-ee oo-BRYAH-coh
You're cute.	*Lei è bello.*	LAY-ee ay BEHL-loh
Your friend is cute.	*Il suo amico è bello.*	eel SOO-oh ah-MEE-cah ay BEHL-loh
I have a boyfriend/ a girlfriend.	*Ho un ragazzo/una ragazza*	oh oon rah-GAHT-soh/ oo-nah rah-GAHT-sah
I love you, I swear.	*Ti amo, ti giuro.*	tee AH-moh, tee JOO-roh

NUMBERS

1	uno	**20**	venti
2	due	**21**	ventuno
3	tre	**22**	ventidue
4	quattro	**30**	trenta
5	cinque	**40**	quaranta
6	sei	**50**	cinquanta
7	sette	**60**	sessanta
8	otto	**70**	settanta
9	nove	**80**	ottanta
10	dieci	**90**	novanta
11	undici	**100**	cento
12	dodici	**101**	centuno
13	tredici	**102**	centodue
14	quattordici	**200**	duecento
15	quindici	**813**	ottocento tredici
16	sedici	**1000**	mille
17	diciassette	**2000**	due mila
18	diciotto	**million**	un millione
19	diciannove	**billion**	un milliardo

APPENDIX

APPENDIX

TIME

At what time...?	*A che ora...?*	Ah kay OH-rah
What time is it?	*Che ore sono?*	kay OH-ray SOH-noh
It's 2:30.	*Sono le due e mezzo.*	SOH-noh lay DOO-ay eh MEHD-zoh
It's noon.	*È mezzogiorno.*	eh mehd-zoh-JOR-noh
It's midnight.	*È mezzanotte.*	eh mehd-zah-NOT-teh
tomorrow	*domani*	doh-MAH-nee
today	*oggi*	OHJ-jee
yesterday	*ieri*	YEH-ree
this evening/ tonight	*stasera*	stah-SEH-rah
week	*settimana*	seht-tee-MAH-nah
morning	*mattina*	maht-TEE-nah
afternoon	*pomeriggio*	poh-meh-REEJ-joh
day	*giorno*	JOHR-noh
night	*notte*	NOHT-teh
evening	*sera*	SAIR-ah
soon	*fra poco*	frah POH-koh
right away	*subito*	SOO-bee-toh
now	*adesso/ora*	ah-DEHS-doh/OH-rah
already	*già*	JAH
early (before scheduled arrival time)	*in anticipo*	een ahn-TEE-chee-poh
late (after scheduled arrival time)	*in ritardo*	een ree-TAHR-doh
early (in the day)	*presto*	PREH-stoh
late (in the day)	*tardi*	TAHR-dee
weekdays	*i giorni feriali*	ee JOHR-nee feh-ree-AH-lee
Sundays and holidays	*i giorni festivi*	ee JOHR-nee fehs-TEE-vee

Months (*i mesi*) aren't capitalized: *gennaio* (jehn-NAH-yoh), *febbraio* (feb-BRAH-yoh), *marzo* (MART-soh), *aprile* (ah-PREE-lay), *maggio* (MAHJ-joh), *giugno* (JOON-yoh), *luglio* (LOOL-yoh), *agosto* (ah-GOHS-toh), *settembre* (seht-TEHM-bray), *ottobre* (oht-TOH-bray), *novembre* (noh-VEHM-bray), *dicembre* (dee-CHEHM-bray). **Days of the week** are not capitalized either: *lunedì* (Monday, loo-neh-DEE), *martedì* (mahr-teh-DEE), *mercoledì* (mayr-coh-leh-DEE), *giovedì* (joh-veh-DEE), *venerdì* (veh-nair-DEE), *sabato* (SAH-bah-toh), *domenica* (doh-MEHN-ee-cah).

RESERVATIONS BY PHONE

Mastery of the following phrases should allow you to get through the process of reserving a room on the telephone.

Hello? (phone greeting).	*Pronto!*	PROHN-toh
Do you speak English?	*Parla inglese?*	PAR-lah een-GLAY-zay
Could I reserve a single/ double room with/ without bath for the second of August?	*Potrei prenotare una camera singola/doppia con/senza bagno per il due agosto?*	poh-TRAY pray-no-TAH-ray OO-nah KAH-meh-rah-SEEN-goh-lah/ DOHP-pyah KOHN/ SENT-sah BAHN-yo pair eel DOO-ay ah-GOHS-toh?
I will arrive at 14:30 (Remember, Italians use the 24-hour clock.)	*Arriverò alle quattordici e mezzo*	ahr-ree-veh-ROH ahl-lay kwaht-TOHR-dee-chee eh MEHD-zoh

How much is the room?	*Quanto costa la camera?*	KWAHN-toh KOHS-ta lah KAM-eh-rah
Okay, I'll take it.	*Va bene. La prendo.*	vah BEHN-eh. lah PREHN-doh

Some replies you might hear are:

Certainly!	*Certo!*	CHAIR-toh
I'm sorry, but...	*Mi dispiace, ma...*	mee dees-PYAH-chay, mah...
Nope, we're full.	*No, siamo al completo.*	noh, see-YA-moh ahl cohm-PLEH-toh
We don't take telephone reservations.	*Non si fanno prenotazioni per telefono.*	nohn see FAHN-noh pray-noh-tat-SYO-nee pair tay-LAY-foh-noh
You must arrive before 2pm.	*Deve arrivare primo delle quattordici.*	DAY-vay ahr-ree-VAH-ray PREE-moh deh-leh kwaht-TOHR-dee-chee
You'll have to send a deposit/check.	*Bisogna mandare un acconto/un anticipo/un assegno.*	bee-ZOHN-yah mahn-DAH-reh oon ahk-KOHN-toh/ oon ahn-TEE-chee-poh/ oon ahs-SAY-nyoh

TRANSPORTATION AND DIRECTIONS

a ticket	*un biglietto*	oon beel-YEHT-toh
a pass (bus)	*una tessera*	OO-nah TEHS-seh-rah
one way	*solo andata*	SOH-loh ahn-DAH-tah
round-trip	*andata e ritorno*	ahn-DAh-tah eh ree-TOR-noh
reduced (price)	*ridotto*	ree-DOHT-toh
a student discount	*uno sconto studentesco*	OO-noh SKOHN-toh stoo-dehn-TEHS-koh
the station	*la stazione*	lah staht-SYO-nay
the train	*il treno*	eel TRAY-noh
the airport	*l'aeroporto*	lah-ay-roh-PORT-oh
the plane	*l'aereo*	lah-AY-reh-oh
the (city) bus	*l'autobus*	LAU-toh-boos
the (intercity) bus	*il pullman*	eel POOL-mahn
the car	*la macchina*	lah MAHK-kee-nah
the ferry	*il traghetto*	eel tra-GHEHT-toh
the flight	*il volo*	eel VOH-loh
the arrival	*l'arrivo*	lahr-REE-voh
the departure	*la partenza*	lah par-TEN-dzah
the track	*il binario*	eel bee-NAH-ree-oh
the terminus (of a bus)	*il capolinea*	eel kah-poh-LEE-neh-ah
the train	*il treno*	eel TRAY-noh
Do you stop at...?	*Ferma a...?*	FAIR-mah ah
What time does the train for ... leave?	*A che ora parte il treno per...?*	ah kay OH-rah PAHR-tay eel TRAY-noh pair
What platform for...?	*Che binario per...?*	kay bee-NAH-ree-oh pair
Is the train late?	*È in ritardo il treno?*	eh een ree-TAHR-doh eel TRAY-no

My hovercraft is full of eels.	*Il mio hovercraft è pieno di anguille.*	eel MEE-oh OH-vehr-krahft ay PYAY-noh dee ahn-GWEEL-lay
Where does the bus leave for ...?	*Da dove parte l'autobus per...?*	dah DOH-vay PAHR-tay LAU-toh-boos pair
What time does the... open (close)?	*A che ora si apre (chiude)...?*	a kay OH-rah see AH-pray (KYOO-day)
I'd like a ticket for...	*Vorrei un biglietto per...*	vohr-RAY oon beel-YET-toh pair
near/far	*vicino/lontano*	vee-CHEE-noh/ lohn-TAH-noh
Turn left/right.	*Gira a sinistra/destra*	JEE-rah ah see-NEE-strah/ DEH-strah
straight ahead	*sempre diritto*	SEHM-pray dee-REET-toh
up/down	*su/giù*	soo/joo
here	*qui/qua*	kwee/kwah
there	*lì/là*	lee/lah
down there at the end	*giù in fondo*	joo een FOHN-doh
strike	*sciopero*	SHOHP-eh-roh

RESTAURANT BASICS

For more Italian food terms, see Essentials: Food, page 64.

knife	*il coltello*	eel kohl-TEHL-loh
fork	*la forchetta*	lah fohr-KAYT-tah
spoon	*il cucchiaio*	eel koo-kee-EYE-oh
napkin	*il tovagliolo*	eel toh-vahl-YOH-loh
plate	*il piatto*	eel PYAT-toh
drinking glass	*il bicchiere*	eel bee-KYAIR-eh
drink	*la bevanda*	lah beh-VAHN-dah
appetizer	*l'antipasto*	lahn-tee-PAHS-toh
first course	*il primo (piatto)*	eel PREE-moh PYAHT-toh
second course	*il secondo (piatto)*	eel seh-KOHN-doh PYAHT-toh
dish	*il contorno*	eel kohn-TOHR-noh
dessert	*il dolce*	eel DOHL-chay
cheese, cheese course	*il formaggio*	eel fohr-MAHJ-joh
breakfast	*(prima) colazione*	PREE-mah koh-laht-SYO-nay
lunch	*il pranzo*	eel PRAHND-zoh
dinner	*la cena*	lah CHAY-nah
meat	*carne*	KAHR-nay
vegetarian	*vegetariano*	veh-djeh-tahr-YAH-no
mineral water (without bubbles)	*acqua minerale (non gassata)*	AHkwah mih-nehr-AH-lay nohn gahs-SAH-tah
waiter/waitress	*cameriere/a*	kah-meh-ree-AIR-ray/rah
cover charge	*il coperto*	eel koh-PAIR-toh
service charge	*il servizio*	eel sehr-VEET-syoh
the tip	*la mancia*	lah MAHN-chah
Is the service included?	*È compreso il servizio?*	eh kohm-PREH-zoh eel sehr-VEET-syoh?
bill	*il conto*	eel KOHN-toh
May I have...	*Posso avere...*	POHS-soh ah-VAY-reh

May I pay by credit card?	*Posso pagare con una carta di credito?*	POHS-soh pah-GAH-reh kohn OO-na KAR-ta dee KREH-dee-toh

EMERGENCY AND DEFENSE PHRASES

Wait!	*Aspetta!*	ah-SPEHT-tah
Stop!	*Ferma!*	FAIR-mah
Help!	*Aiuto!*	ah-YOO-toh
Go away!	*Va via! Vattene!*	va VEE-ah/VAHT-teh-neh
Leave me alone	*Lasciami in pace!*	LAH-shah-mee een PAH-cheh
Don't touch me!	*Non mi toccare!*	NOHN mee tohk-KAH-reh
Piss off!	*Vaffanculo!*	vahf-fahn-KOO-loh
I'll call the police!	*Chiamo la polizia!*	KYAH-moh lah poh-leetSEE-ah
Could you help me find...?	*Mi potrebbe aiutare a trovare...?*	mee poh-TREHB-beh ah-yoo-TAR-eh ah troh-VAH-reh
I've lost my passport (my money)	*Ho perso il mio passaporto (i miei soldi)*	oh PEHR-soh eel MEE-oh pahs-sah-PORT-oh (ee mee-AY-ee SOHL-dee)
I've been robbed.	*Sono stato derubato.*	SOH-noh STAH-toh deh-roo-BAH-toh

APPENDIX

Glossary

The following is a partial glossary of Italian, English, and Arabic terms used in this book. Many are artistic, architectural, and historical, but some commonly used terms are included as well.

Abbazia Also Badia, an abbey.

Affitta camere A private home which rents rooms to tourists

Agriturismo A program which allows tourists to stay in farmhouses. Depending on the region, the cost of the stay may be offset by laboring on the farm.

Amphora Large two-handled vessel, used in ancient Greece to hold oil or wine.

Apse A semicircular, domed niche projecting from the altar end of a church.

Atrium An open central court, usually in an ancient Roman house or a Byzantine church.

Bab Gate (Arabic).

Baldacchino A stone or bronze canopy supported by columns over the altar of a church.

Basilica In ancient Rome, a building used for public administration. Early Christians adopted the architectural form, a rectangular building with an aisle and an apse, for their churches.

Battistero A baptistery; usually a separate, octagonal building near the town's *duomo* where the city's baptisms were performed.

Borgo A suburb, or a street leading into a suburb from the center of town. (Now these suburbs are often city neighborhoods.)

Campanile A bell tower, usually free-standing.

Camposanto A cemetery.

Cartoon A full-sized drawing used to transfer a preparatory design to the final work, especially to a wall for a fresco.

Caryatid A column in the shape of a female figure.

Castrum Ancient Roman military camp. Many Italian cities were originally built on this rectilinear plan with straight streets, the most important of which were the perpendicular *decumanus maximus* and *cardo*.

Cenacolo A "Last Supper" (often found in the refectory of an abbey or convent).

Chancel The space around the altar reserved for clergy and choir; the area was usually enclosed by a screen in medieval churches, but most are now open.

Chicha Arabic flavored tobacco (honey, cherry, etc.), often smoked in a hookah ("bong").

Chott A salt lake (Arabic).

Cipollino Onion marble; marble with veins of green or white.

Cloister A quadrangle with covered walkways along its edges, often with a central garden, forming part of a church or monastery.

Comune The government of a free city of the Middle Ages.

Condottiere The captain of a mercenary band hired by Italian cities to fight their medieval and Renaissance wars.

Contorno Vegetable served with a main dish

Corso Principal street.

Crenellations Notched parapets along the top of a fortified building (battlements).

Cupola A dome.

Diptych A panel painting with two leaves, often joined by a hinge.

Duomo A cathedral which serves as the the official seat of a bishop, and usually the central church of an Italian town.

Fermo posta Mail which is sent to a post office and held for a traveler

Ferragosto The Ides of August (Aug. 15), a national holiday and, in many locales, a time for riotous partying.

Fiume A river.

Forum In an ancient Roman town, a square containing municipal buildings and/or market space. Smaller towns usually have only one central forum, while large cities, such as Rome, can have several.

Fresco *Affresco,* a painting made on wet plaster. When it dries, the painting becomes part of the wall.

Frieze A band of decoration, either in sculpture or architecture.

Funicolare Funicular, a cable railway ascending a mountain.

Ghibelline One of the two great medieval Florentine political factions. The Ghibellines supported the Holy Roman Emperor (Frederick II when the troubles began) in his struggles against the papacy. Later, distinctions became blurred and being a Ghibelline merely meant that the rival town down the road or the rival family up the street was Guelph. See Guelph.

Giardino Garden.

Greek Cross A cross whose arms are of equal length.

Grotesque 1) Ugly. 2) Painted, carved, or stucco decorations of fantastic, distorted human or animal figures.

Guelph One of two great medieval Florentine political factions. The Guelphs supported the Pope in his struggles against the Holy Roman Emperor (Frederick II when the troubles began). Later, distinctions became blurred and being a Guelph merely meant that the rival town down the road or the rival family up the street was Ghibelline. See Ghibelline.

Hammam Turkish-style bath house common in Tunisia (Arabic).

Jemaa A mosque (Arabic).

Kasbah A citadel or fort, often used for civic purposes (Arabic).

Latin Cross A cross whose vertical arm is longer than its horizontal arm.

Loggia A covered passageway or balcony with an open arcade of columns on at least one side.

Lungo, Lung- Literally "along," so that a lungomare is a boardwalk or promenade alongside the ocean, and a lungarno in Florence is a street running alongside the river Arno.

Lunette A semi-circular frame in the ceiling or vault of a building that holds a painting or sculpture.

Maestà The Madonna and Child enthroned in majesty, always accompanied by angels and, in later medieval and Renaissance art, saints.

Marabout An Islamic saint, or the tomb in which a saint is buried

Mausoleum A large tomb or stone building with places to entomb the dead above ground.

Medina The fortified medieval part of an Arabic town.

Mensa A cafeteria, often at a university.

Mezzogiorno A nickname for the southern part of Italy.

Nave The large central space of a church's interior.

Nuraghi Cone-shaped fortified towers built of stone blocks with no mortar (most commonly found in Sardinia)

Offerta A fee for entrance to sights, usually churches and crypts. Although always "optional", it's never really optional.

Palazzo An important building of any type. Most were originally built as town houses for wealthy families.

Palio A banner. In modern times, has come to mean a horse race in which the neighborhoods of a city compete for a banner.

Panino A sandwich.

Piazza A city square. In Venice, the term *campo* (literally field) is usually used instead.

Pietà A scene of the Virgin mourning the dead Christ.

Pietra serena A soft, gray sandstone, easily carved.

Piscina A pool, or a wash-basin used by a priest before Mass.

Polenta Cornmeal porridge that defies description (much better than it sounds).

Polyptych A painting made up of several panels or sections.

Predella The base of an alterpiece, made up of small panel paintings.

Pulchritudinous The longest one-word synonym in this book for beautiful.

Putto (pl. *putti*) The little nude babies that flit around Renaissance art occasionally, and Baroque art incessantly.

Quatrefoil A four-lobed diamond pattern common in Gothic framing.

Rifugio (pl. *rifugi*) Type of refuge (alpine huts) scattered all over the Alps and Dolomites which offer beds and meals for hikers.

Salutation Hi, Mom!

Sciopero A strike, usually related to public transportation.

Scuola Modern word for "school," originally the Venetian name for a confraternity.

Settimana Bianca Literally "white week," special package for a week of skiing which offers a set price for room and board (sometimes the rate includes ski passes—check before making reservations).

Sinopia drawing A red pigment sketch made on a wall as a preliminary study for a fresco.

Souk Itinerant weekly market (Arabic).

Stigmata Miraculous body pains or bleeding that resemble the wounds of the crucified Christ.

Strada Street.

Tessera 1) One of the small (often square) component pieces of a mosaic 2) a bus pass, membership card, or phone card.

Thermae Ancient Roman baths and, consequently, social centers.

Transept The short arm of a cross-plan church.

Travertine A type of limestone, the chief building material in Rome, ancient and modern. Always light-colored, but sometimes with black speckles.

Triptych A painting in three panels or parts.

Trompe l'oeil (French for "deceives the eye".) A painting or other piece or art that creates an illusion for the viewer, as in a flat ceiling painted so as to appear domed.

Tufa Along with travertine (see above), the other major inexpensive building material of ancient Rome. A soft stone composed of volcanic ash. *Tufo* in Italian.

Villa A country house, usually a large estate with a formal garden.

General Information

Climate

Temp in °C Rain in cm	January		April		July		October	
	Temp	Rain	Temp	Rain	Temp	Rain	Temp	Rain
Brindisi	12/06	7.7	18/11	4.7	29/21	1.4	22/15	7.9
Cagliari	14/07	5.0	19/11	3.1	30/21	0.1	23/15	5.4
Milan	05/00	4.4	18/10	9.4	29/20	6.4	17/11	12.5
Naples	12/04	11.6	18/9	6.2	29/18	1.9	22/12	10.7
Palermo	16/08	7.1	20/11	4.9	30/21	0.2	25/16	7.7
Rome	11/05	7.1	19/10	5.1	30/20	1.5	22/13	9.9
Venice	06/01	3.7	17/10	7.8	27/19	5.2	19/11	7.7

Telephone Codes

The country code for **Italy** is **39.** The country code for **Tunisia** is **216.** To place a call to another city within Italy (or within Tunisia), dial the complete city code and then the phone number. From outside the country, dial the country code and then the city code, leaving off the first 0 of the city code. To call internationally from either Italy or Tunisia, dial 00 and then the country code.

COUNTRY CODES

Australia	61	**France**	33	**Spain**	34
Austria	43	**Germany**	49	**UK**	44
Canada	1	**Greece**	30	**USA**	1

CITY CODES

Brindisi	0831	**Milan**	02	**Rome**	06
Cagliari	070	**Naples**	081	**Venice**	041
Florence	055	**Palermo**	091	**Tunis**	01

Festivals and Holidays

Check the index under "festivals" for a list of town festivals. Among the more bizarre is Coculla's May celebration of *Festi di San Domenico Abate,* when people march through the city carrying a likeness of the saint draped with live snakes.

Less reptilian, though perhaps equally stomach-wrenching, is Italy's glut of jousting festivals—check out Arezzo, Ascoli Piceno, Barletta, and Oristano (among others) during the late summer. Another medieval legacy, the Sienese *Palio* features a bareback horse race in the town square, once in July and once in August. Other towns feature similar, less famous *Palii* (see index for page listings). On the third Sunday in July, Venetians commemorate the end of the plague epidemic of 1575 with a gondola procession and celebrate *Carnevale* in February with masks and some discreet street revelry. *Carnevale* action is much better in Ivrea, where anyone not wearing a red hat is likely to get dyed orange in the *Battle of Oranges.* Every June, Florence stages a soccer match with its players in 16th-century costume to commemorate Charles V's siege of the city.

Italy also hosts plenty of equally delicious food and art festivals. While food festivals and religious celebrations often end at nightfall, art festivals may span weeks or months. The month-long *Festival dei Due Mondi* (Festival of Two Worlds) in Spoleto, a delightful hodge-podge of classical art and cultural events, follows this trend. For a list of festivals, write to the **Italian Government Travel Office** (see page 5).

Take into account holidays, both legal and religious, when planning your itinerary. Banks, shops, and almost everything else shut down, but merriment abounds. Italy officially closes on the following dates: **January 1** (New Year's Day); **January 6** (Epiphany); **Easter Monday; April 25** (Liberation Day); **May 1** (Labor Day); **August 15** (Assumption of the Virgin); **November 1** (All Saints' Day); **December 8** (Immaculate Conception); **December 25** (Christmas Day); and **December 26** (Santo Stefano). Offices and shops in the following cities also shut down for feast days in honor of their respective patron saints: Venice (April 25, St. Mark); Florence, Genoa, and Turin (June 24, St. John the Baptist); Rome (June 29, SS. Peter and Paul); Palermo (July 15, Santa Rosalia); Naples (Sept. 19, St. Gennaro); Bologna (Oct. 4, St. Petronio); Cagliari (Oct. 30, St. Saturnino); Trieste (Nov. 3, San Giusto); Bari (Dec. 6, St. Nicola); and Milan (Dec. 7, St. Ambrose). Be prepared for other surprises as well.

Weights and Measures

1 centimeter (cm) = 0.39 inches	1 inch = 2.54cm
1 meter (m) = 3.28 feet	1 foot = 0.31m
1 kilometer (km) = 0.62 miles	1 mile = 1.61km
1 gram (g) = 0.04 ounces	1 ounce = 28g
1 kilogram (kg) = 2.2 pounds	1 pound = 0.45kg
1 liter (L) = 0.26 gallons	1 gallon = 3.76L
1 Imperial Gallon (U.K.) = 1.2 gallons	1 gallon = 0.83 Imperial Gallons
°F = (°C x 1.8) + 32	°C = (°F - 32) x .56

Index

INDEX

INDEX

INDEX

INDEX

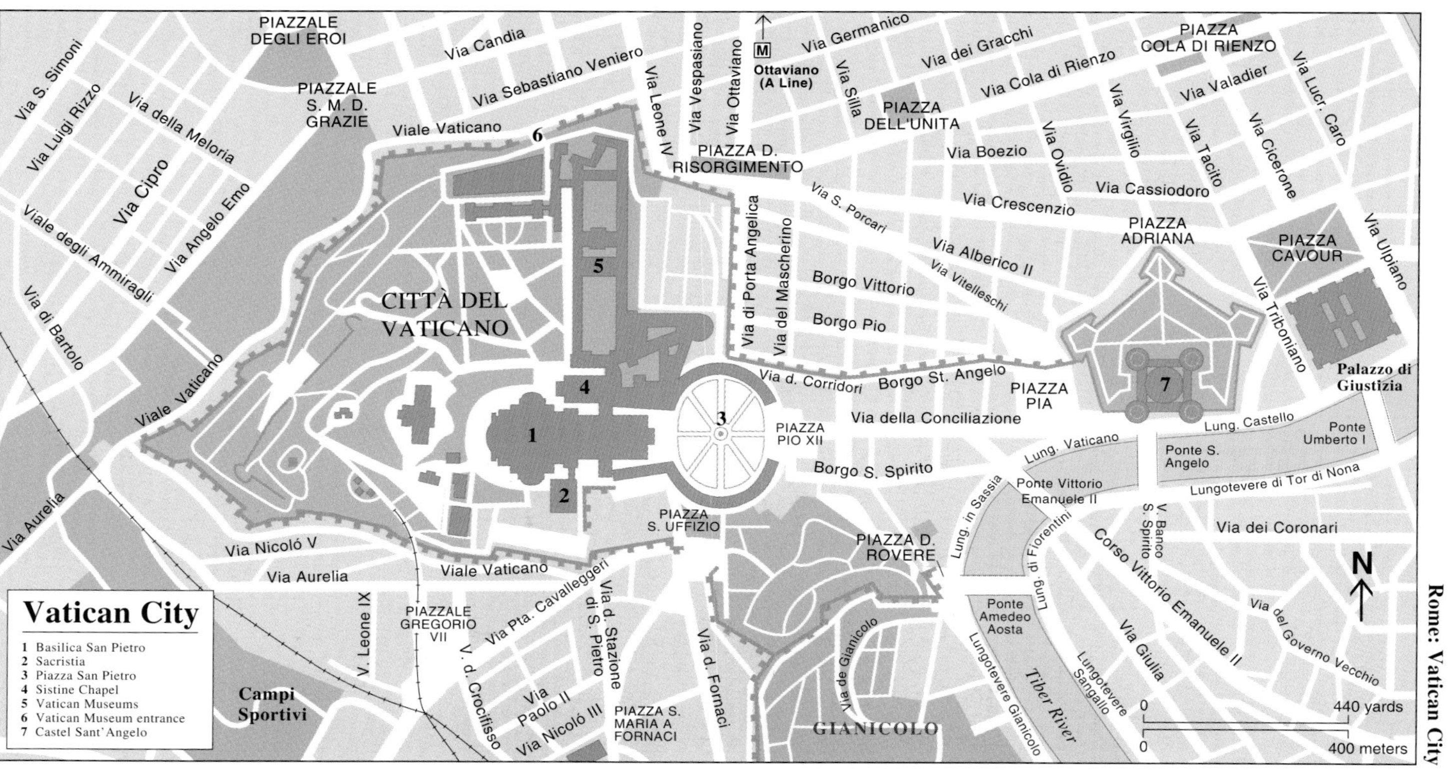
Vatican City
1 Basilica San Pietro
2 Sacristia
3 Piazza San Pietro
4 Sistine Chapel
5 Vatican Museums
6 Vatican Museum entrance
7 Castel Sant'Angelo
N
0
440 yards
0
400 meters
CITTÀ DEL VATICANO
GIANICOLO
Tiber River
Campi Sportivi
Palazzo di Giustizia
PIAZZALE DEGLI EROI
PIAZZALE S. M. D. GRAZIE
PIAZZA COLA DI RIENZO
PIAZZA DELL'UNITÀ
PIAZZA D. RISORGIMENTO
PIAZZA ADRIANA
PIAZZA CAVOUR
PIAZZA PIA
PIAZZA PIO XII
PIAZZA S. UFFIZIO
PIAZZA D. ROVERE
PIAZZALE GREGORIO VII
PIAZZA S. MARIA A FORNACI
Ottaviano (A Line)
M
Via S. Simoni
Via Luigi Rizzo
Via della Meloria
Via Cipro
Via Angelo Emo
Viale degli Ammiragli
Via di Bartolo
Viale Vaticano
Via Aurelia
Via Candia
Via Sebastiano Veniero
Viale Vaticano
Via Leone IV
Via Vespasiano
Via Ottaviano
Via Germanico
Via Silla
Via dei Gracchi
Via Cola di Rienzo
Via Valadier
Via Lucr. Caro
Via Boezio
Via Ovidio
Via Virgilio
Via Tacito
Via Cicerone
Via Cassiodoro
Via Crescenzio
Via Ulpiano
Via S. Porcari
Via Alberico II
Via Vitelleschi
Via Triboniano
Via di Porta Angelica
Via del Mascherino
Borgo Vittorio
Borgo Pio
Via d. Corridori
Borgo St. Angelo
Via della Conciliazione
Borgo S. Spirito
Lung. Castello
Ponte Umberto I
Ponte S. Angelo
Lung. Vaticano
Lungotevere di Tor di Nona
Ponte Vittorio Emanuele II
Lung. in Sassia
Lung. di Fiorentini
V. Banco S. Spirito
Via dei Coronari
Corso Vittorio Emanuele II
Via del Governo Vecchio
Via Giulia
Ponte Amedeo Aosta
Lungotevere Gianicolo
Lungotevere Sangallo
Via de Gianicolo
Via d. Fornaci
Via d. Stazione di S. Pietro
Via Pta. Cavalleggeri
V. d. Crocifisso
Via Paolo II
Via Nicolò III
V. Leone IX
Via Nicoló V
Via Aurelia
Viale Vaticano

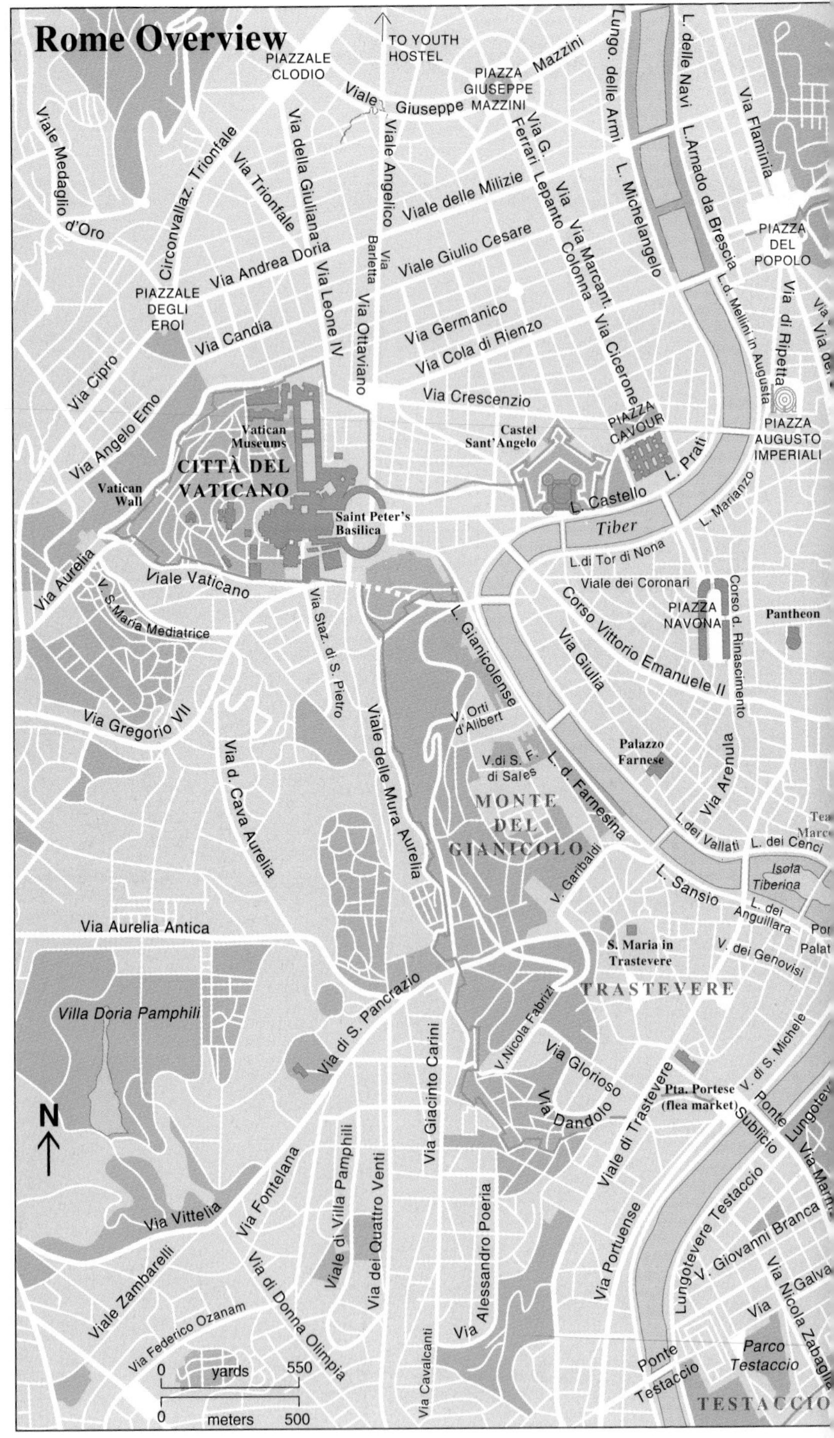

Rome Overview
TO YOUTH HOSTEL
PIAZZALE CLODIO
PIAZZA GIUSEPPE MAZZINI
Viale Giuseppe Mazzini
Viale Medaglio d'Oro
Circonvallaz. Trionfale
Via Trionfale
Via della Giuliana
Viale Angelico
Via G. Ferrari
Lepanto
Lungo. delle Armi
L. delle Navi
L. Arnado da Brescia
Via Flaminia
PIAZZA DEL POPOLO
Viale delle Milizie
Via Marcant. Colonna
L. Michelangelo
Via Barletta
Viale Giulio Cesare
Via Andrea Doria
Via Leone IV
Via Ottaviano
PIAZZALE DEGLI EROI
Via Candia
Via Germanico
Via Cola di Rienzo
Via Cicerone
L.d. Mellini in Augusta
Via di Ripetta
Via Cipro
Via Crescenzio
Via Angelo Emo
Vatican Museums
CITTÀ DEL VATICANO
Vatican Wall
Castel Sant'Angelo
PIAZZA CAVOUR
PIAZZA AUGUSTO IMPERIALI
L. Prati
L. Castello
Saint Peter's Basilica
Tiber
L. Marianzo
L.di Tor di Nona
Via Aurelia
Viale Vaticano
V. S.Maria Mediatrice
Via Staz. di S. Pietro
L. Gianicolense
Viale dei Coronari
PIAZZA NAVONA
Corso d. Rinascimento
Pantheon
Corso Vittorio Emanuele II
Via Giulia
Via Gregorio VII
V. Orti d'Alibert
Viale delle Mura Aurelia
Via d. Cava Aurelia
Palazzo Farnese
V.di S. F. di Sales
L. d. Farnesina
Via Arenula
MONTE DEL GIANICOLO
L.dei Vallati
L. dei Cenci
Isola Tiberina
V. Garibaldi
L. Sansio
L. dei Anguillara
Via Aurelia Antica
S. Maria in Trastevere
V. dei Genovisi
TRASTEVERE
Villa Doria Pamphili
Via di S. Pancrazio
Via Giacinto Carini
V.Nicola Fabrizi
Via Glorioso
Via Dandolo
Viale di Trastevere
Pta. Portese (flea market)
V. di S. Michele
Ponte Sublicio
N
Via Fontelana
Viale di Villa Pamphili
Via dei Quattro Venti
Via Alessandro Poeria
Via Portuense
Lungotevere Testaccio
V. Giovanni Branca
Via Nicola Zabaglia
Via Vittelia
Viale Zambarelli
Via di Donna Olimpia
Via Federico Ozanam
Via Cavalcanti
Ponte Testaccio
Parco Testaccio
TESTACCIO
0 yards 550
0 meters 500

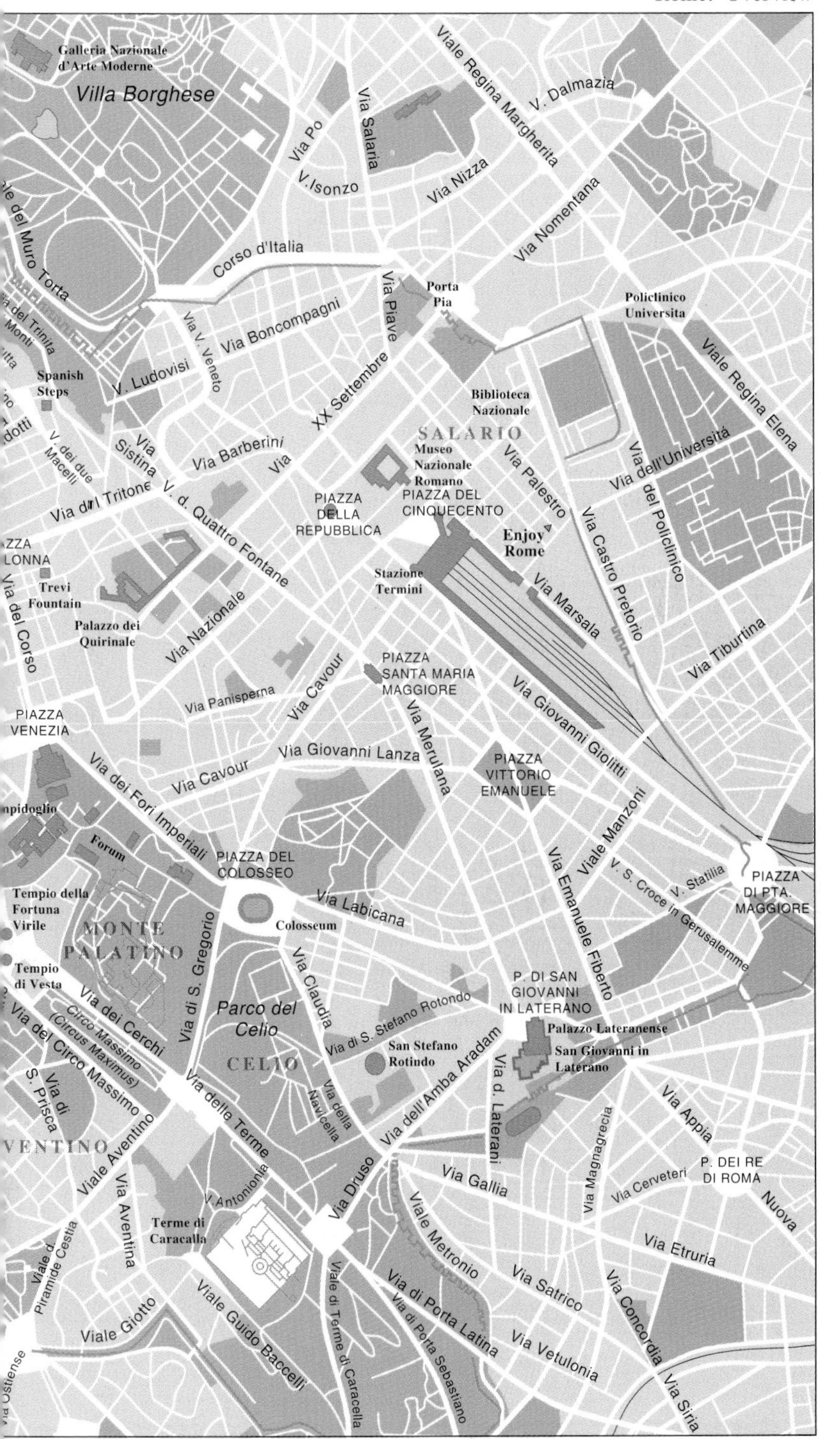
Galleria Nazionale
d'Arte Moderne
Villa Borghese
Viale Regina Margherita
V. Dalmazia
Via Salaria
Via Po
V.Isonzo
Via Nizza
Via Nomentana
Corso d'Italia
Via Piave
Porta
Pia
Policlinico
Universita
Via V. Veneto
Via Boncompagni
Spanish
Steps
V. Ludovisi
XX Settembre
Biblioteca
Nazionale
Viale Regina Elena
SALARIO
Museo
Nazionale
Romano
Via Palestro
Via dell'Università
Via del Policlinico
V. dei due
Macelli
Via Sistina
Via Barberini
Via
PIAZZA
DELLA
REPUBBLICA
PIAZZA DEL
CINQUECENTO
Via dell Tritone
V. d. Quattro Fontane
Enjoy
Rome
Via Castro Pretorio
Trevi
Fountain
Stazione
Termini
Via Marsala
Palazzo dei
Quirinale
Via Nazionale
Via del Corso
Via Tiburtina
PIAZZA
SANTA MARIA
MAGGIORE
Via Panisperna
Via Cavour
Via Giovanni Giolitti
PIAZZA
VENEZIA
Via Merulana
Via Giovanni Lanza
PIAZZA
VITTORIO
EMANUELE
Via Cavour
Via dei Fori Imperiali
Forum
Viale Manzoni
PIAZZA DEL
COLOSSEO
Via Emanuele Fiberto
V. Statilia
V. S. Croce in Gerusalemme
PIAZZA
DI PTA.
MAGGIORE
Tempio della
Fortuna
Virile
MONTE
PALATINO
Via di S. Gregorio
Colosseum
Via Labicana
Tempio
di Vesta
Via Claudia
P. DI SAN
GIOVANNI
IN LATERANO
Parco del
Celio
Via dei Cerchi
Circo Massimo
(Circus Maximus)
Via del Circo Massimo
Via di S. Stefano Rotondo
Palazzo Lateranense
San Stefano
Rotindo
San Giovanni in
Laterano
CELIO
Via dell'Amba Aradam
Via d. Laterani
Via di S. Prisca
Via della Navicella
Via delle Terme
Via Appia
Viale Aventino
Via Magnagrecia
P. DEI RE
DI ROMA
Via Druso
Via Gallia
Via Cerveteri
Nuova
V. Antoniona
Via Aventina
Terme di
Caracalla
Viale Metronio
Via Etruria
Viale d. Piramide Cestia
Viale di Terme di Caracella
Via di Porta Latina
Via Satrico
Via Concordia
Viale Guido Baccelli
Via di Porta Sebastiano
Viale Giotto
Via Vetulonia
Via Siria

Rome Transport

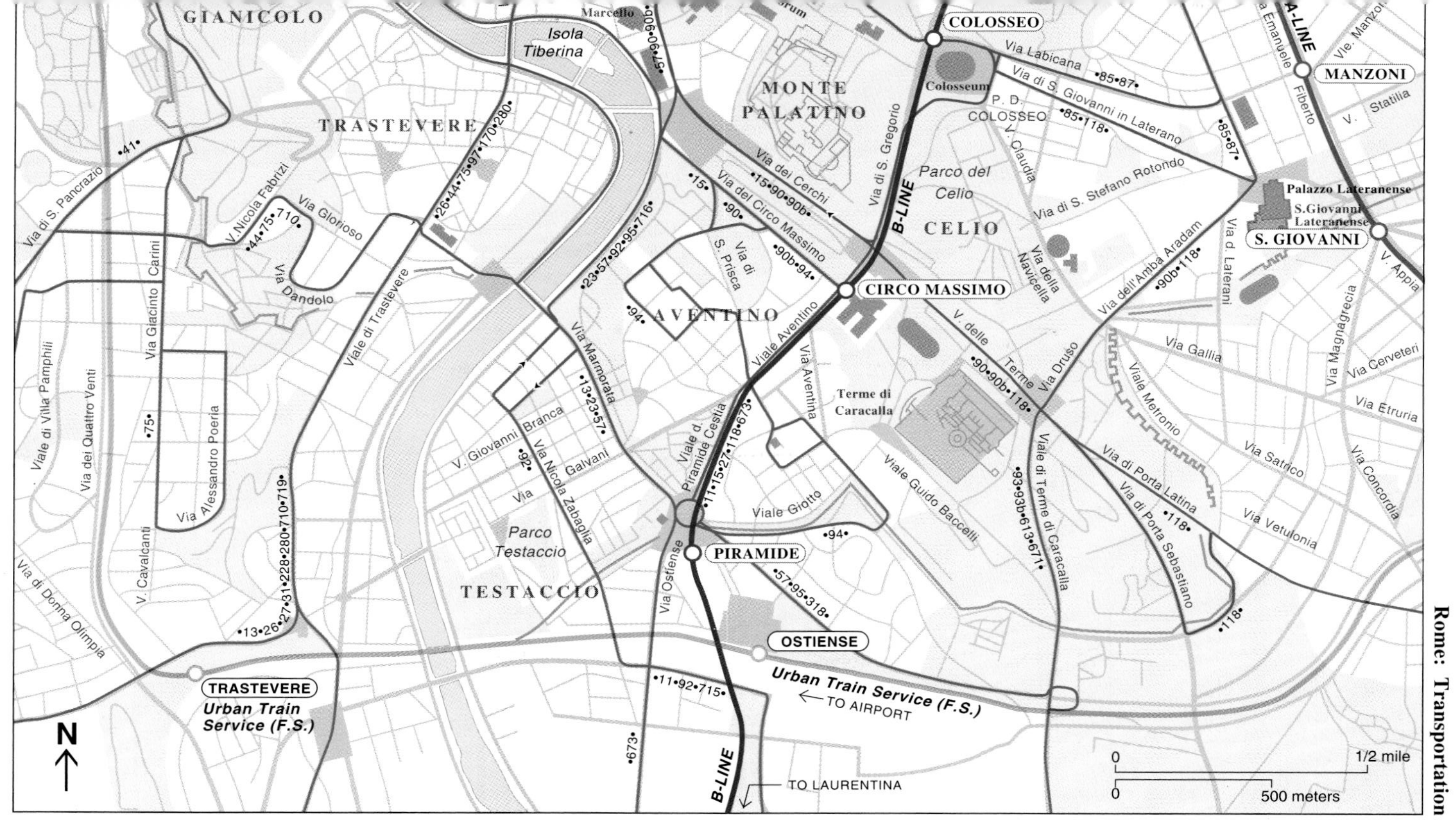
GIANICOLO
Marcello
Isola Tiberina
•57•90•90b•
MONTE PALATINO
COLOSSEO
Colosseum
Via Labicana
•85•87•
A-LINE
MANZONI
Via Emanuele
Fiberto
Vle. Manzoni
V. Statilia
TRASTEVERE
•41•
Via di S. Pancrazio
•26•44•75•97•170•280•
P. D. COLOSSEO
•85•118•
Via di S. Giovanni in Laterano
•85•87•
Via S. Gregorio
Parco del Celio
V. Claudia
Via di S. Stefano Rotondo
Palazzo Lateranense
S.Giovanni Lateranense
S. GIOVANNI
V. Appia
Via d. Laterani
V. Nicola Fabrizi
•44•75•710•
Via Glorioso
Via Dandolo
•15•
Via dei Cerchi
•15•90•90b•
Via del Circo Massimo
•90•
B-LINE
CELIO
•23•57•92•95•716•
Via di S. Prisca
•90b•94•
CIRCO MASSIMO
Via della Navicella
Via dell'Amba Aradam
•90b•118•
Via Giacinto Carini
Viale di Trastevere
•94•
AVENTINO
Viale Aventino
V. delle Terme
Via Druso
Via Gallia
Via Magnagrecia
Via Cerveteri
Viale di Villa Pamphili
Via dei Quattro Venti
•75•
Via Alessandro Poerio
Via Marmorata
•13•23•57•
Via Aventina
•90•90b•118•
Terme di Caracalla
Viale Metronio
Via Etruria
V. Giovanni Branca
•92•
Via Nicola Zabaglia
Via Galvani
Viale d. Piramide Cestia
•11•15•27•118•673•
Viale Guido Baccelli
•93•93b•613•671•
Viale di Terme di Caracalla
Via di Porta Latina
Via Satrico
Via Concordia
V. Cavalcanti
•27•31•228•280•710•719•
Parco Testaccio
Viale Giotto
•94•
Via di Porta Sebastiano
•118•
Via Vetulonia
Via di Donna Olimpia
TESTACCIO
Via Ostiense
PIRAMIDE
•57•95•318•
•118•
•13•26•
OSTIENSE
TRASTEVERE
Urban Train Service (F.S.)
•11•92•715•
Urban Train Service (F.S.)
TO AIRPORT
N
•673•
B-LINE
TO LAURENTINA
0 1/2 mile
0 500 meters

Walks

1 Piazza del Popolo
2 Ara Pacis
3 Mausoleum of Augustus
4 Palazzo Borghese
5 Spanish Steps
6 Trevi Fountain
7 Vittorio Emanuele Monument
8 Campidoglio
9 Teatro Marcello
10 Isola Tiberina
11 Palazzo Doria Pamphili
12 Church of Santi Apostoli
13 Church of San Marcello
14 Piazza di S. Ignazio
15 Piazza di Pietra
16 Piazza Colonna/ Column of Marcus Aurelius
17 Palazzo Chigi
18 Pantheon
19 Giolitti
20 Piazza Minerva
21 Church of Santa Maria Sopra Minerva
22 Church of San Luigi dei Francesi
23 Piazza Navona
24 Church of Sant'Antonio dei Portoghesi
25 Museo Napoleonico
26 Il Gesù
27 Largo Argentina
28 Church of Sant'Andrea delle Valle
29 Palazzo del Cancelleria
30 Chiesa Nuova
31 Piazza Sforza Cesarini
32 Campo dei Fiori
33 Piazza Farnese
34 Piazza della Quercia
35 Monte di Pieta
36 Church of Santissima Trinità dei Pellegrini

VILLA BORGHESE
V. del Muro Torto
VILLA MEDICI
Via Belvedere
Via Trinità del Monti
Spagna
M
PIAZZA DEL POPOLO
Via F. di Savoia
Via Orsini
PIAZZA D. LIBERTA
Ponte Margherita
Via Brunati
Via di Ripetta
Via del Vantaggio
Via del Babuino
Via Cola di Rienzo
Via Feder. Cesi
Tiber River
Via E. Q. Visconti
Via G. Bellí
Via Canova
Lung. in Augusta
Lung. dei Mellini
LARGO D. SCHIAVONI
Via Vittorio
Via P. Cossa
Via Lucr. Caro
Via Cicerone
Via Boezio
Via Ovidio
Via Cassiodoro
Via Tacito
Via Crescenzio
Via della Croce
Via della Carozze
PIAZZA DI SPAGNA
PIAZZA TRINITÀ D. MONTE
Via del Corso
PIAZZA AUGUSTO IMPERATORE
PIAZZA CAVOUR
Via V. Colonna
Ponte Cavour
PIAZZA D. PORTO DI RIPETTA
Via d. Condotti
Via Mario de Fiori
Via Propaganda
Via d. Due Macelli
Via Alberico II
Via Vitelleschi
PIAZZA ADRIANA
Castel Sant' Angelo
Via Tribioniano
Via Ulpiano
Lung. Prati
Via Tomacelli
Via Borgogna
Via Borghese
Via Frattina
Via Campo Marzo
Via delle Vite
PIAZZA DEI TRIBUNALI
Lungotevere Marzio
Via della Scrofa
Via Clementino
Via della Mercede
PIAZZA PIA
Via della Conciliazione
Lungotevere Castello
Ponte Umberto I
Via Prefetti
PIAZZA S. SILVESTRO
Via del Tritone
Lung. Vaticano
S. Angelo
Ponte
PIAZZA DEL PARLIAMENTO
Ponte Vittorio Emanu...
PIAZZA
Lungotevere di Tor di Nona
Via dell'Orso
LARGO CHIGI

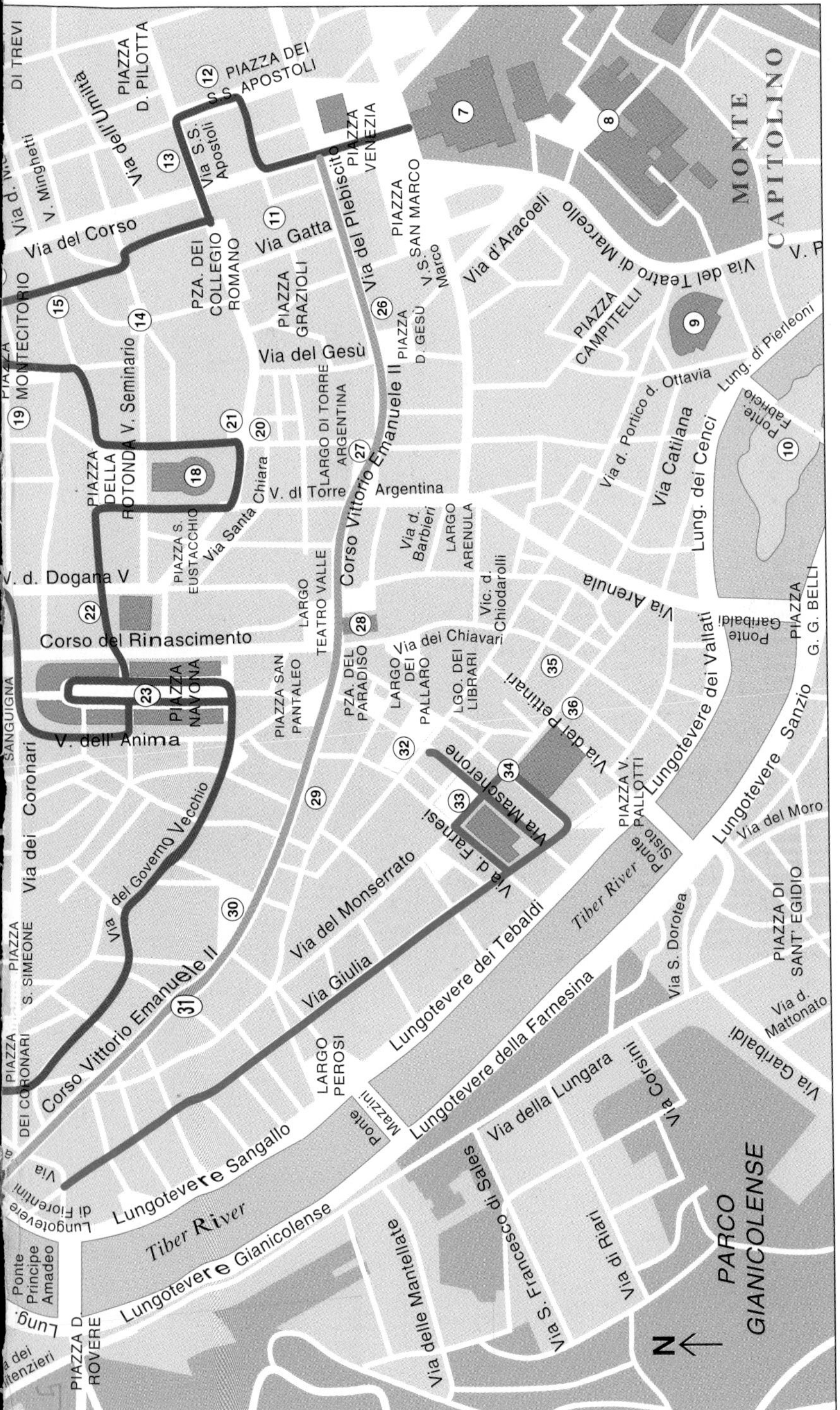

DI TREVI
PIAZZA D. PILOTTA
PIAZZA DEI S.S. APOSTOLI
Via dell'Umiltà
V. Minghetti
Via S.S. Apostoli
PIAZZA VENEZIA
MONTE CAPITOLINO
Via del Corso
Via Gatta
Via del Plebiscito
PIAZZA SAN MARCO
V. S. Marco
Via d'Aracoeli
Via del Teatro di Marcello
PIAZZA MONTECITORIO
PZA. DEI COLLEGIO ROMANO
PIAZZA GRAZIOLI
PIAZZA D. GESÙ
PIAZZA CAMPITELLI
Via del Gesù
V. Seminario
PIAZZA DELLA ROTONDA
LARGO DI TORRE ARGENTINA
Corso Vittorio Emanuele II
Via d. Portico d. Ottavia
Lung. di Pierleoni
Ponte Fabricio
Via Catilana
Lung. dei Cenci
V. dl Torre Argentina
Via Santa Chiara
PIAZZA S. EUSTACCHIO
Via d. Barbieri
LARGO ARENULA
V. d. Dogana V
LARGO TEATRO VALLE
Vic. d. Chiodarolli
Via Arenula
Corso del Rinascimento
PIAZZA NAVONA
PIAZZA SAN PANTALEO
PZA. DEL PARADISO
LARGO DEI PALLARO
LGO. DEI LIBRARI
Via dei Chiavari
Via dei Pettinari
Ponte Garibaldi
PIAZZA G. G. BELLI
Lungotevere dei Vallati
SANGUIGNA
V. dell' Anima
Via dei Coronari
Via del Governo Vecchio
Via Maschelone
Via d. Farnesi
PIAZZA V. PALLOTTI
Ponte Sisto
Lungotevere Sanzio
Via del Moro
Via del Monserrato
Via Giulia
Lungotevere dei Tebaldi
Tiber River
PIAZZA S. SIMEONE
PIAZZA DI SANT' EGIDIO
Via S. Dorotea
Lungotevere della Farnesina
Via d. Mattonato
Via Garibaldi
PIAZZA DEI CORONARI
LARGO PEROSI
Ponte Mazzini
Via della Lungara
Via Corsini
Via di Fiorentini
Lungotevere Sangallo
Tiber River
Lungotevere Gianicolense
Via S. Francesco di Sales
Via di Riari
Via delle Mantellate
PARCO GIANICOLENSE
Ponte Principe Amadeo
PIAZZA D. ROVERE
Lung.
N

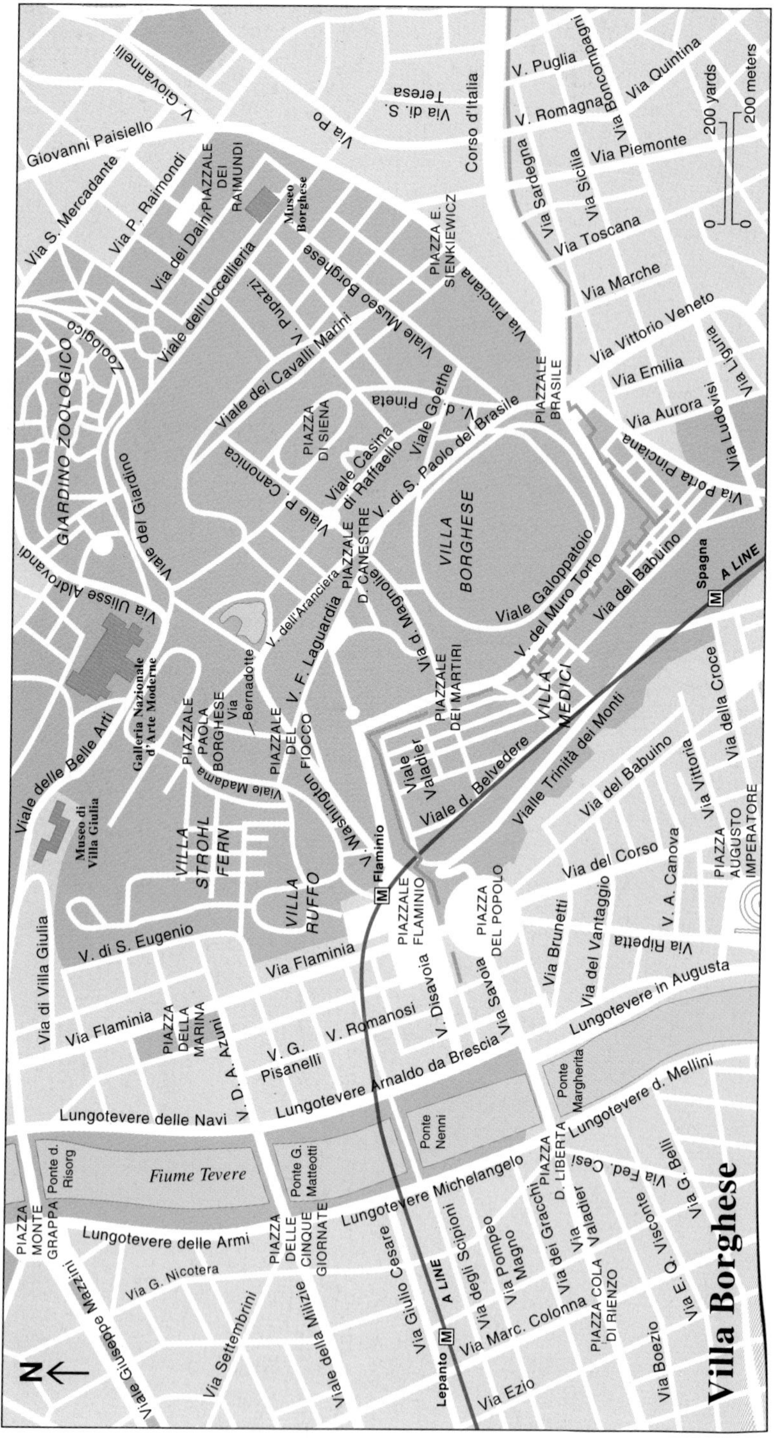

Villa Borghese

N
0 200 yards
0 200 meters

Giovanni Paisiello
V. Giovannelli
Via Po
Via di S. Teresa
Corso d'Italia
V. Puglia
V. Romagna
Via Boncompagni
Via Quintina
Via Piemonte
Via Sardegna
Via Sicilia
Via Toscana
Via Marche
Via Vittorio Veneto
Via Emilia
Via Aurora
Via Liguria
Via Ludovisi
Via Porta Pinciana
Via Pinciana
PIAZZALE BRASILE
PIAZZA E. SIENKIEWICZ
Museo Borghese
PIAZZALE DEI RAIMUNDI
Via S. Mercadante
Via P. Raimondi
Via dei Daini
Viale dell'Uccelliera
Viale Museo Borghese
V. Pupazzi
Viale dei Cavalli Marini
V. d. Pineta
Viale Goethe
PIAZZA DI SIENA
Viale P. Canonica
Viale Casina di Raffaello
V. di S. Paolo del Brasile
PIAZZALE D. CANESTRE
VILLA BORGHESE
Viale Galopatoio
V. del Muro Torto
Via del Babuino
Spagna
A LINE
GIARDINO ZOOLOGICO
Zoologico
Viale del Giardino
Via Ulisse Aldrovandi
Galleria Nazionale d'Arte Moderne
Viale delle Belle Arti
Museo di Villa Giulia
V. dell'Aranciera
V. F. Laguardia
V. d. Magnolie
Via Bernadotte
PIAZZALE PAOLA BORGHESE
PIAZZALE DEL FIOCCO
PIAZZALE DEI MARTIRI
VILLA MEDICI
Viale Madama
Viale Valadier
Viale d. Belvedere
Vialle Trinità dei Monti
Via della Croce
Via del Babuino
Via Vittoria
PIAZZA AUGUSTO IMPERATORE
VILLA STROHL FERN
V. Washington
VILLA RUFFO
Flaminio
PIAZZALE FLAMINIO
PIAZZA DEL POPOLO
Via del Corso
Via del Vantaggio
V. A. Canova
Via Ripetta
Via Brunetti
V. di S. Eugenio
Via di Villa Giulia
Via Flaminia
PIAZZA DELLA MARINA
V. D. A. Azuni
V. G. Pisanelli
V. Romanosi
V. Disavoia
Via Savoia
Lungotevere in Augusta
Lungotevere Arnaldo da Brescia
Lungotevere delle Navi
Ponte Margherita
Ponte Nenni
Lungotevere d. Mellini
Ponte d. Risorg
Fiume Tevere
Ponte G. Matteotti
PIAZZA MONTE GRAPPA
PIAZZA DELLE CINQUE GIORNATE
Lungotevere Michelangelo
PIAZZA D. LIBERTA
Via Fed. Cesi
Lungotevere delle Armi
Via G. Nicotera
Viale Giuseppe Mazzini
Via Settembrini
Viale della Milizie
Via Giulio Cesare
A LINE
Lepanto
Via degli Scipioni
Via Pompeo Magno
Via dei Gracchi
Via Valadier
Via Marc. Colonna
PIAZZA COLA DI RIENZO
Via E. Q. Visconte
Via G. Belli
Via Boezio
Via Ezio